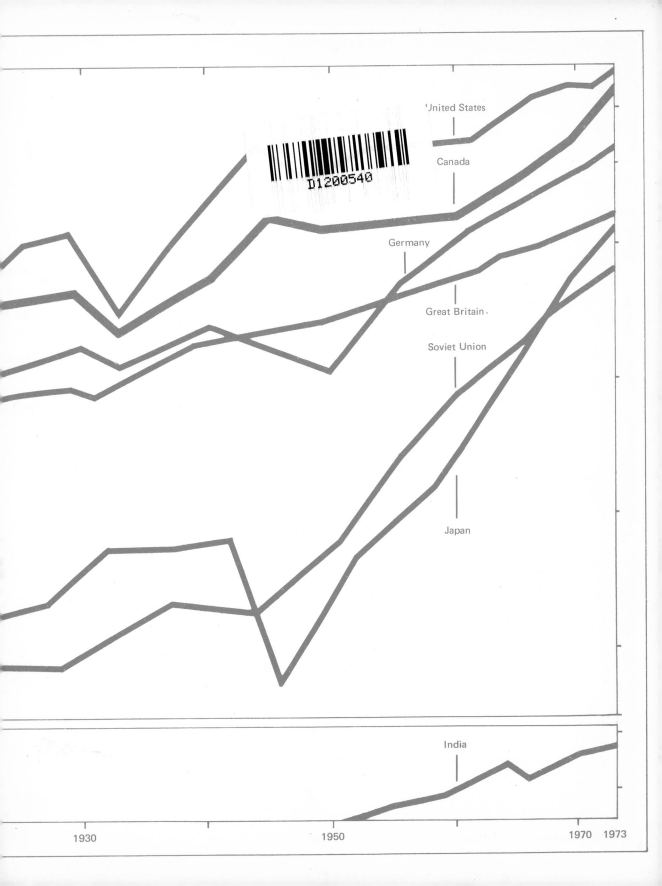

United States

Canada

Germany

Great Britain

Soviet Union

Japan

India

1930   1950   1970   1973

ECONOMICS

ECONOMICS

Fourth Canadian Edition

PAUL A. SAMUELSON
Institute Professor
Massachusetts Institute of Technology

ANTHONY SCOTT
Professor of Economics
University of British Columbia

McGRAW-HILL RYERSON LIMITED

Toronto   Montreal   New York   London   Sydney
Johannesburg   Mexico   Panama   Düsseldorf
Singapore   São Paulo   Kuala Lumpur   New Delhi

ECONOMICS
Fourth Canadian Edition
Copyright ©1966, 1968, 1971, 1975 by McGraw-
Hill Ryerson Limited. All Rights Reserved.

Adapted from   ECONOMICS   written by Paul A.
Samuelson. Copyright ©1955, 1958, 1961, 1964,
1967, 1970, 1973 by McGraw-Hill, Inc. All Rights
Reserved.

Library of Congress Catalog Card Number

ISBN 0-07-0 8 2 2 0 5-0

       4 5 6 7 8 9 10 BP 4 3 2 1 0 9

Printed and bound in Canada

PREFACE

This is an introduction to economics. It is written for a half-year or full-year course in economics. The book is directed primarily toward readers who, for the most part, will never be going on to further formal study in economics. This present edition is the most thoroughgoing revision of the last dozen years—a suitable commemoration, we would hope, for the twenty-fifth birthday of the book.

Why study political economy?

Economics is an important subject. Economics can also be an exciting subject. How could it be otherwise, when it deals with the great issues of unemployment and inflation, poverty and wealth, mere material growth and life-enhancing advancement? Dry-as-dust principles take on a new luster under the touch of relevance. For we have in political economy not a finished, embalmed corpus of conventional wisdom—but rather materials for the great debate on revolution, liberty, efficiency, and the endless quest for the good society.

Political economy is not an easy subject, not hammock reading for a lazy summer afternoon. But millions of readers—literally millions—have proved that they could learn the fundamentals of economics from this book. Some have studied it in English; many have read it in one of the numerous translations into other languages. A surprising number have learned economics by reading the book on their own.

How to study economics

This textbook has been carefully designed so that it can be used both in the stiffest honors courses for elite scholars and as well for freshmen taken from a cross section of the undergraduate population. The text is carefully—nay, even cunningly—prepared so that each reader can go as far with it as he cares to go.

Experience shows that an economics text has to be read with care. Each chapter is carefully planned. Each has a comprehensive summary. The diagrams and tables are defined so that each also tells its own story. With every new edition there has come new knowledge on how to utilize color most functionally—with key concepts set out boldly at each chapter's end, with basic principles flagged in red and with the diagrams' crucial points made to stand out for emphasis.

This functional design is one reason why a modern text can teach, in the same time, far more than we dared cover in the past. And economies of large-scale production make possible this lavish use of types and color. (Although the type is set by the modern computer, the pages of the book are as intricately laid out as in an illuminated medieval manuscript—and with the authors having to work with four distinct layers of film.)

No author can tell you how best to read a textbook. Obviously, this is not like a novel or detective story, not something designed for hit-and-run reading. The first time you read a chapter, turn its pages for perspective. Then read and underline, not stopping to overcome every difficulty. You will be pleasantly surprised to find that the final summaries and checklists of key concepts will help synthesize your understanding. And on review and rereading—giving independent attention to the self-contained story of the figures and tables—your understanding will deepen.

Divide and conquer

I should call to your attention the *Study Guide,* which Professors Romney Robinson and Gordon Munro have prepared to go along with this edition and which is cited later. Even if your instructor does not assign it, you may find it a great time-saver in the end. (Or for self-instruction in the analytical core of macroeconomics and microeconomics, you might want to get hold of *Economics: An Introductory Program,* which has been prepared by Professor Edward Foster.)

Study Guide

Programmed instruction

You will discover that harder or less important material—they are not always the same!—have been put in appendixes, or often in footnotes. And in this edition we have carried forward the experiment of giving some final "Questions for Discussion" that are marked as "extra-credit problems," which enable the more highly trained student to pursue on his own some of the fascinating further developments of the subject. If you are in a fast, brief course, don't be put off by this carefully planned layering of more difficult material: Experience has proved that this gives the more intensive course meat to bite into, without really inconveniencing those who work with the severest time limitations. And to the bright honors student, may we say: Don't be put off by the use of color and the attempt to state matters plainly. This book is as challenging as you may care to make it. (Several who are now prominent economists have written to say that they used parts of it in their final review for their Ph.D. oral exams.)

Optional matter

Aside from the usual updating and polishing of rough spots, this new edition rearranges chapters into a more coherent pattern: Thus, Chapter 6, on business organization, now follows the chapter on income distribution and inequality, forming with the chapters on labor and government a rounded introduction to the economic institutions of modern life. Other groups of chapters are extensively rearranged. Only the instructor who makes out course assignments will realize how pervasive these improvements in organization have become in the new edition.

Updating

Revised orderings

Most exciting to us has been the new *Weltanschauung* that permeates the new edition. Complacency with mainstream economics makes for dull—and essentially inaccurate—economics. The brand new chapter "Winds of Change: Evolution of Economic Doctrines" brings into the elementary course—at long last—a view of where political economy fits into the history of ideas and the intellectual

Critiques of mainstream economics and schools of thought

history of our times. For economics is after all much more than mere geometry.

It is a scandal that, until recently, even majors in economics were taught nothing of Karl Marx except that he was an unsound fellow. This was not out of intimidation by the plutocratic interests, but rather reflection of the fact that such independent and impassioned teachers of the last generation as John Maynard Keynes thought Marx sterile and dull. In this edition we have tried to treat Karl Marx as neither God nor Devil—but as a secular scholar whom half the world's population deem important. The rudiments of mature Marxism, as well as the insights of the resurrected Young Marx, are newly discussed in this revision.

Marxian economics

By the same token, this new edition pits the paradigms of mainstream economics against the critiques of conservative libertarianism—Hayek and Milton Friedman. And also against the iconoclasm of John Kenneth Galbraith.

Laissez faire libertarianism and Galbraithian iconoclasm

In this edition, we have particularly emphasized unsolved problems in modern economics: cost-push inflation; the quality of life versus mere GNP growth—Net Economic Welfare (NEW) versus Gross National Product (GNP); Zero Population Growth (ZPG), Zero Economic Growth (ZEG), and ecological doomsday; racial discrimination and the recognition (belated!) of sexual discrimination; "externalities," public goods, and interpersonal-equity considerations; and the principal criticisms of mainstream economics.

New winds

Since almost half the classes using this book are one-semester courses, I append to the Table of Contents a suggested one-semester outline. And in the *Instructor's Manual,* newly revised in co-authorship with Professor Harry Baumann, suggestions are given for flexible adaptation.

Forty per cent of the teachers using this book prefer to teach microeconomics before macroeconomics. A good case can be made for either ordering, and experimental programs show each to have advantages. This text has been carefully designed for either program. The instructor who wishes to deal first with microeconomics can skip from Part One to Part Three, knowing that the exposition and cross references have been tailored with his needs in mind. Because college courses in economics are taught both by large-lecture and small-section methods, we have used classrooms as laboratories, one year trying out lecturing to a large group and another year confining classes to 25 students. A good text must be prepared with both needs in mind.

Which order?

We have not hesitated to segregate some of the material into appendixes. Often this involves slightly more difficult topics, with which briefer courses can easily dispense. Sometimes, as in the case of the discussion of the stock market in Chapter 4's Appendix or the presentation of cases on supply and demand in Chapter 20's Appendix, the material is not more difficult, but is such as can be conveniently skipped. Occasionally a teacher has written me questioning the advisability of this use of the appendixes. My answer is a pragmatic one based on experimentation: Because courses differ in their time span and emphasis, it is incumbent upon an author to give signals as to which sections are organically necessary and which are dispensable. (For example, in this edition I have added a brief treatment of classical Marxism—variable capital, surplus value, and all that. The fact that it is put at the end of Chapter 41's Appendix will not inconvenience the reader eager for a terse account of this important subject; but this arrangement will be deemed a blessing by those instructors who lack the time for such a topic.)

To go with this edition, a completely revised *Study Guide* has been prepared by Professors Romney Robinson and Gordon Munro. Both as assigned by instructors and bought independently by students for self-study, the *Study Guide* has proved to be an impressive success.

Auxiliary teaching aids

Robinson and Munro Study Guide

Readings in Economics has been revised by Paul Samuelson to go with the present edition. In its seventh incarnation, generous selection from the great names of the past—Smith, Keynes, Ricardo, Marx—and the titans of the present age—Galbraith, Tobin, Friedman, Hayek, Sweezy, Solow, Burns, Kindleberger, Nader, Heilbroner—a broad spectrum of opinions is put before the student in a format convenient for assignment along with the text.

Readings in Economics

Our envy goes out to the reader, setting out to explore the exciting world of economics for the first time. That is a thrill which, alas, no one can experience twice.

Skoal!

To you who are about to begin, may I only say, *bon appetit!*

Paul A. Samuelson

PREFACE TO THE FOURTH CANADIAN EDITION

The demands of students, different from those of teachers, have been widely consulted in making this new revision of Paul Samuelson's textbook. In the first revision the task was broad but simple: to analyze economic events and policies against a background of Canadian data and institutional practices. To this was added some revision of the balance of the book, to reflect the Canadian economist's special concerns: international trade and foreign economic policy, regionalism and federalism, and raw-material production. These revisions did satisfactorily guide several successive groups of readers to the application of non-national principles of analysis to "our" economy, and they did save them from uncertainty about whether statements made in other works about the United States, or Great Britain, applied with equal force in Canada.

Although my revisions have been extensive, a majority of the topics and the purely analytical sections still remain much as they are in Professor Samuelson's ninth edition. For these, he is overwhelmingly the senior author. I have tried to make available to Canadian readers an up-to-date, readable introduction to the methods of economics, firmly embedded in our domestic context. Accordingly, I have had to describe a number of Canadian institutions, not always discussing how their functions are performed in other places. In addition, I have changed the emphasis in many chapters by frequent references to the open nature of the Canadian economy, which makes Canada particularly susceptible to the influence of goods and factors moving from abroad; and I have indicated the impact of this openness on our economic structure and policy.

I was prepared to make many alterations to stress the regional nature of our economy, as opposed to what I had always assumed to be an American emphasis on geographical unity. On close reading, this "difference" turned out to be very much a matter of degree: the American economist is in fact aware of regional differences and the problems they create for national policy. And so, although I added considerable material on this subject, I avoided overemphasizing "regionalism."

Other differences between the two economies (for example, Canada has two official languages, and there is more public ownership, and a higher rate of immigration in Canada than in the United States) were pointed out where relevant to understanding economics. But the original perception in the revision was paramount: the Canadian economy is part of a worldwide economy, and the Canadian economy works much as others do in this system of linkages and flows.

In this fourth edition, however, it has become possible to cater much more to the interests of students in their own country's problems. Both supply and demand are responsible. We now stand amidst a veritable landslide of sophisticated Canadian studies of the working and performance of our economy, on which revisions of this text can be directly or indirectly based. Contrasted with the shortage of information he faced ten or fifteen years ago, the Canadian economist has, at last, ample material at his disposal which enables him to speak with some authority on a wide spectrum of Canadian issues.

Demand is also responsible. Perhaps because analysis seems much more relevant to Canadian questions, students today show an increased interest not only in the economics of taxation, banking, and the tariff, but also in the economic analyses applicable to separatism, urban issues, foreign ownership, and rural poverty. Canadian readers also are interested in China, socialism, and racial prejudice, but for different reasons than those which apply elsewhere.

These considerations have led to the wholesale revision of chapters or appendices on the Eastern European economy, regionalism, the city, foreign ownership, racial prejudice and language discrimination, and resource policy that should take the interested reader some steps further in his own inquiry into these current questions.

This edition presents the most recent data available and refers to events and studies of current importance. For assistance with this attempt to present a completely accurate picture of the Canadian economic structure, I am greatly indebted to many people. Among my helpers, I should mention Elayne Van Snellenberg, Clive Southey, Mrs. Helen Moore, Mrs. E. V. New, Mrs. Sandy Pearce, Darcy McDowall, Jim Phelps, Peter Victor, and especially Floyd Sully. To the names of those who worked with me on earlier editions I must mention, first of all, a number of Canadian academics who responded generously to a request from me and McGraw-Hill Ryerson to make comments and suggestions about a new edition. Their help has been valuable and I have consulted their answers frequently. As was to be expected, there was little consensus among them about what was needed, but individual ideas took root in many different parts of the book, opening my ideas to fertile possibilities that I have tried to exploit. I must also mention comments that were received from my colleagues John Boyd, Russell Uhler, Peter Pearse, Gordon Munro, Spencer Star, John Young and especially John Helliwell; working with them and with Harry Campbell helped in many places.

Second, I must mention the members of the team who worked with me more directly. First among these was Jim Brander, who devoted many patient hours to the punctilious updating of data and policies, and to pioneering searches for new material. I relied heavily on the experience and good taste of Elizabeth Paterson for assistance on editorial matters. All of us are indebted to Estelle K. Murray for combining editorial and secretarial work to produce beautiful manuscripts. The editors and artists of McGraw-Hill Ryerson have made important contributions in redesigning the book and seeing it through the press expeditiously, in the face of storms and strikes. The index was prepared by Elizabeth Paterson.

For the student who would like to have additional assistance, a *Study Guide and Workbook* is available. Written by Professor Romney Robinson of the University of Toronto and rewritten for Canadian readers by Professor Gordon Munro of the University of British Columbia, this book has been carefully designed to provide the serious student with a ready means of testing his comprehension of the subject matter.

My greatest debt is to Professor Paul Samuelson who has turned me loose on this project; I must accept all responsibility for the alterations and additions to his earlier editions. My respect and admiration for his work is most clearly demonstrated by my increasing unwillingness to tamper with the analytical portions of his text, which have already served so many Canadian students. The need, in preparing these Canadian editions, to closely scrutinize the structure and wording of his book has impressed me with its breadth and unity. Hence, the disclaimer made at the outset in this Preface: my aim has not been to produce a new work but to bring to Canadians the advantages long afforded American readers by the availability of this book.

Anthony Scott
Vancouver, British Columbia.
June, 1975.

CONTENTS

PART 4   DISTRIBUTION OF INCOME: THE PRICING OF THE PRODUCTIVE FACTORS

PART 6   CURRENT ECONOMIC PROBLEMS

1

Basic Economic Concepts and National Income

1
INTRODUCTION

"The Age of Chivalry is gone; that of sophisters, economists, and calculators has succeeded."
EDMUND BURKE

As a scholarly discipline, economics is just two centuries old. Adam Smith wrote his pathbreaking book, *The Wealth of Nations* in 1776, less than 16 years before the new regimes in America and France had taken hold. And the nearness of timing was no coincidence: freedom from political tyranny was related to release of markets from ancient state interferences.

Adam Smith, of course, represented only a beginning. In more than the century and a half that elapsed from the publication of *The Wealth of Nations* to the publication of John Maynard Keynes' *The General Theory of Employment, Interest and Money* (1936), economics—or political economy, as it used to be called—went through many stages of development. At almost the halfway point, there appeared the massive critique of capitalism by Karl Marx: *Das Kapital* (1867), followed by two posthumous volumes. A billion people, some third of the world's population, view *Das Kapital* as economic truth.

And yet, without disciplined study, how can anyone form a reasoned opinion about the merits or lack of merits in the classical, traditional economics? Or about the achievements of the "New Economics" that has evolved since 1929? Or about the problems unsolved by radical mainstream economics?

FOR WHOM THE BELL TOLLS

Few study economics merely to judge these grand debates concerning historic capitalism, modern collectivist systems, or our mixed economy. We study in search of answers to many, and changing, questions. Here are some common ones:

What about "poverty midst plenty," as in the post-1929 Great Depression when factories lay idle and people couldn't find jobs? Has this given way to the modern pockets of poverty in various parts of Canada? Do these stem from sheer natural scarcity?

POVERTY, DEVELOPMENT, AND AFFLUENCE We grow more prosperous each year. Our present affluence is an outgrowth from our lower productivity prevailing in past generations. All over the world, men have become preoccupied with understanding this process.

How can preindustrial economies, teeming with masses of people and poorly endowed with natural resources, break through the vicious circle of poverty and backwardness? How can programs be formulated that will speed *economic growth and development*?

However, today in the affluent West, "Zero Population Growth" is a new goal, set by concerned people who are alarmed at the exhaustion of the globe's irreplaceable resources and at deterioration of environmental ecological balance.

How can a modern economy manage—if it should want to —to raise the *quality* of its economic life and forgo mere *quantitative* growth, and do so without bringing on itself a great depression with mass unemployment?

Look at the front flyleaf: Contrast the Western world's affluence with the poverty of India, whose growth curve barely shows on the chart; and note the success story of Japan within its century of contact with the modern world.

Undoubtedly this new interest in development and growth has made economics an exciting subject in the capitals of the world and a vital one for each separate region.

PERSONAL ROLE IN THE ECONOMY A more personal reason for studying economics is that it deals with many of the matters that will most concern each one of us:

What kinds of jobs are available? What do they pay? How much in goods will a dollar buy now, and how much later, in a time of galloping inflation? What are the chances of "bad times" when no one can find work? Will there always be buyers for the crops of farmers and the yields of fishermen? Are the black days of the depressed 1930s likely to return? Will technology make man obsolete? When should one work, run a business, or make a killing in land or in the stock market? Or shall one live on welfare?

ECONOMICS FOR THE CITIZEN   Beyond personal matters, economics also deals with political decisions in which each citizen must participate. Here are a dozen vital policy problems:

Ought the government to add to my taxes to help the jobless, or are there other things it can do to mitigate the problem of unemployment? Should I vote to build a new school and road now, or vote to put this aside until business slackens and cement prices come down and jobs are needed? Should I vote to keep married women out of public employment, so there will be more jobs for singles?

What about legislation to fight price-fixing and monopolies?

If you are a humanitarian, deeply concerned to improve the lot of the poor, the exploited immigrant, and the aged, will legislating a stiff, high minimum wage help or hinder the good cause for which you fight?

Why not "fair-share" rationing of food, housing, or energy?

Is it true that the prosperity of the Western world is dependent on military expenditures? Need peace, or the "threat of peace," cause unemployment? Should our government wash its hands of this problem, relying on individual entrepreneurship and private demand to replace spontaneously our exports to warring nations? Need our governments balance their budgets?

NATIONALISM TODAY   Many people are more interested in collective than individual welfare. They focus on the nation, its survival and its independence.

How much should be spent, or sacrificed, to assure its separateness? Should Canada trade with others, or avoid entangling itself? Should we invest in independent military strength? Is military security worth its cost? Can economics cast light on these questions?

A more recent concern is the decision about the selling of our energy and resource products. Should we hoard our scarce minerals, aiming for permanent self-sufficiency? If we sell, at what price? What region, and class, in Canada should get the profits?

WHAT ECONOMICS IS

Beginners used to want a short definition of economics; and in response to this demand, there was no shortage of supply. Here are a few such definitions:

1. Economics is the study of those activities which, with or without money, involve exchange transactions among people.
2. Economics is the study of how men choose to use scarce or limited productive resources (land, labor, capital goods such as machinery, technical knowledge) to produce various commodities (such as wheat, beef, overcoats, concerts, roads, bombers, yachts) and to distribute them to various members of society for their consumption.
3. Economics is the study of men in their ordinary business of life, earning and enjoying a living.
4. Economics is the study of how mankind goes about the business of organizing its consumption and production activities.
5. Economics is the study of wealth.
6. Economics is the study of how to improve society.

The list is a good one. Yet a scholar can extend it many times over. It is always hard to compress into a few lines an exact description of a subject, one that will differentiate its boundaries from those of other disciplines and convey to the beginner all the things it is. Economics certainly does involve all the elements stressed in these various definitions—and all those implied in the larger list that could be compiled.

Economists today agree on a general definition something like the following:

Economics is the study of how men and society end up choosing, with or without the use of money, to employ scarce productive resources, which could have alternative uses, to produce various commodities. It studies how the commodities are distributed for consumption, now and in the future, among various people and groups in society. It analyzes the costs and benefits of improving patterns of resource allocation.

QUALITY OF ECONOMIC LIFE

An introduction can serve as a preview. Even before studying economics, everyone will have heard of the

Gross National Product. This, as Chapter 10 will discuss, purports to measure the total of all goods and services produced each year in a nation. Although measured in money, it can tell us much about real goods and services—food, clothing, penicillin, and so forth.

But these days many critics of political economy have come forth. They deplore materialistic concentration on the *quantity* of economic goods. In the striking words of one concerned member of the New Left: "Don't speak to me of Gross National Product, GNP. To me GNP stands for Gross National Pollution."

What are we to think? Must modern economics make a fetish of *quantity* at the expense of *quality* of life? Or can we correct the official statistician's measure of Gross National Product so that it becomes more of a measure of Net Economic Welfare? That is, can we supplement GNP by a more meaningful measure NEW?

Figure 1-1 shows as the black curve the traditional measure of GNP per capita. From 1930 to 1970 this more than doubled. But during that same period in which we were getting more necessities and gadgets, we were also having to commute to work over more crowded roads and having to spend more to offset the growing pollution in the air.

Therefore, various economists (Kuznets, Nordhaus, Tobin, and Usher), believing that economic welfare is too important to leave to either statisticians or noneconomists, have tried to correct traditional GNP numbers to allow for disamenities of modern urban living, for enhanced leisure now enjoyed by the citizenry, for household work by wives that is ignored by the GNP statistician, and for various other adjustments.

The red curve in Fig. 1-1 shows that the resulting measure of per capita Net Economic Welfare, NEW for short, has grown since 1929. But it has clearly not grown as much as GNP itself has grown.

TRADING OFF QUANTITY TO GET BETTER QUALITY   There is something more shown by the figure. Economics cannot stand content to *describe* the truths of life. Political economy finds itself called on to help public opinion do something toward improving manifest evils. Look therefore at the dotted black and dotted red curves of growth from the mid-1970s to the end of the century. These show

how the electorate, if it really wishes to, can hope to *improve* the quality of economic life.

As conservative people love to repeat, "There is no such thing as a free lunch in this vale of tears." To get the *benefit* of higher NEW, what *cost* must we pay? Higher taxes and dearer electricity will be necessary if we are to fight pollution and urban blight. Hence, we'll all have to make the sacrifice of registering *slower* growth in ordinary GNP. (Raising the dotted red NEW line means lowering the dotted black GNP line. So it is not a case of pretending to be getting something for nothing.) Thus, *political economy shows people how, if they really wish to, they can trade off quantity of goods for quality of life.*

There is no need to explain these matters in this preview. It will be the task of Part Six to ensure that modern political economy responds to the new age's concern for ecology and the quality of human living.

LIGHT AND FRUIT

This discussion has illustrated an important truth: Every national issue mentioned requires economic understanding. A person who has never made a systematic study of economics is handicapped in even thinking about issues; he is like a deaf man trying to appreciate a symphony: give him a hearing aid, and he may still lack talent, but at least he has a fighting chance of sensing what music really is. The head of state[1] must be constantly making vital decisions that involve economics. But of course he need not *himself* be a professional student of economics; he need only be an intelligent "consumer" of the (often conflicting) economic information given him.

Of course most students do not expect to *specialize* in economics. Most will study it for only a term or two, and this book is intended to give an overview of the whole subject. One's view of the world can never be quite the same after even a single semester of economics.

---

[1] As an example, Winston Churchill was a great man—a leader without peer, an orator, a gifted writer, and a shrewd judge of the Hitlerian threat while most around him slept. Yet all his life, Churchill was a babe in the woods when it came to economics. In 1925, as Chancellor of the Exchequer, he put England back on the gold standard at the pre-1914 parity of U.S. $4.87 for the British pound. (Chapter 33 will explain what this means.) Experts at the time warned against such folly, and history has recorded that England never quite recovered from her stagnation of the 1920s.

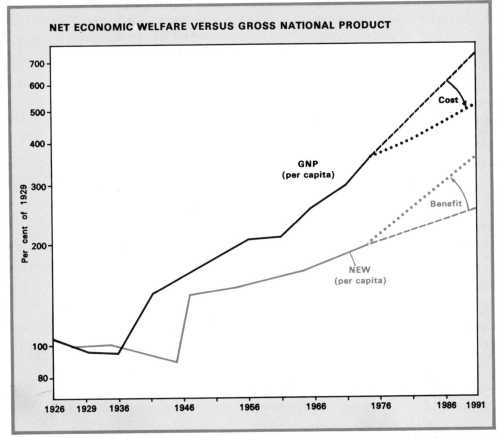

FIG. 1-1 We must compute "Net Economic Welfare" to gauge quality of economic life.
The upper black curve represents real GNP per capita (i.e., the value of output of Canadian goods and services in each year corrected for inflationary decreases in the purchasing power of a dollar and for changes in population). The lower red curve shows Net Economic Welfare (NEW for short). This further corrects the conventional measure of GNP to allow for pollution costs, disamenities of modern urban living, leisure, etc. (Source: Fig. 10-4).

C. P. Snow, scientist and novelist, once called for an end to the separation of "the two cultures." Economics is part of both these cultures, a subject that can combine the attractive features of both the humanities and the sciences. For two centuries, educated men have found in political economy the human interest of life itself, while at the same time economic principles display some of the logical beauty of Euclid's geometry. To appreciate the charms of quantum physics, sophisticated mathematical techniques must first be mastered; but to sense the aesthetic structure of economic analysis requires only a feeling for logic and a capacity for wonderment that

such mental constructs really do have a life-and-death significance for billions of men all over the world. Of course, mere beauty is not enough.

We do not study economics for its own sake, but for the light it sheds.

THE QUEEN OF THE SOCIAL SCIENCES

Economics borders on other important academic disciplines. *Political science, sociology, psychology,* and *anthropology* are all social sciences whose studies overlap those of economics. Some universities still have joint departments of "political economy" in recognition of this lack of clear limits between the subjects. Here is just one example of how they complement one another.

In impoverished India, cows are sacred animals and, numbering millions, are allowed to walk through the streets foraging for food. While a naïve economist might regard these herds as a prime source for protein supplement to an already inadequate diet, the more profound scholar will take the psychology of custom into account when analyzing Indian economic development.

Economics also draws heavily on the study of *history*.

Was it a coincidence that prices rose for centuries in Spain and Europe after Columbus discovered America with all its gold? Why did the age of the steamship and railroad help the prairie farmer, hurt the farmers of Vermont and Oxfordshire, and help the slum dwellers of London?

The interpretation of recorded history must be approached with *analytical* tools for facts will never "tell their own story"; yet this need for theorizing does not deny the old Chinese proverb "One peek is worth a thousand finesses." Facts count.

Among the numerous other subjects relating to economics, the study of *statistical methods* is of special importance. Governments and businesses issue vast amounts of numerical information. Most of what we know about the actual shapes of the various curves to be seen in turning over the pages of this book has to come from a careful statistical analysis of recorded information. The mathematical methods of probability and statistics find many of their most important applications in the realm of economics.

Although every introductory textbook must contain geometrical diagrams, knowledge of *mathematics* itself is needed only for the higher reaches of economic theory. Logical reasoning is the key to success in the mastery of basic economic principles, and shrewd weighing of empirical evidence is the key to success in mastery of economic applications.

NOBEL PRIZE IN ECONOMICS   Since the turn of the century Nobel prizes have been given annually in physics, chemistry, medicine and physiology, literature, and peace. As if to commemorate the coming of age of economics as a science, a new Nobel prize in economics was instituted in 1969.

The first award went jointly to Professors Ragnar Frisch of Norway and Jan Tinbergen of the Netherlands. Both men have been pioneers in the statistical, theoretical, and mathematical advances of the modern generation. Yet each has also been passionately concerned with economic policy, both within his own country and for the world at large. The recognition of these men symbolizes the recognition of the many-sided nature of economic scholarship.[2]

ECONOMIC DESCRIPTION AND ANALYSIS

It is the first task of modern economic science to *describe*, to *analyze*, to *explain*, and to *correlate* the behavior of production, unemployment, prices, and similar phenomena. To be significant, descriptions must be more than a series of disconnected narratives. They must be fitted into a systematic pattern —i.e., constitute true analysis.

Because of the complexity of human and social behavior, we cannot hope to attain the precision of the physical sciences. Economists cannot perform the controlled experiments of the chemist or biologist. Like the astronomer, we must be content largely to "observe." But economic events and statistical data observed are, alas, not as well behaved and orderly as the paths of heavenly satellites. Fortunately, our answers need not be accurate to several decimal places; on the contrary, if the right general *direction* of cause and effect can be determined, we shall have made a tremendous step forward.

ECONOMIC POLICY AND REFORM

This brings us to the important problems of economic policy. Ultimately, understanding should aid in *control and improvement*. How can the vagaries of the business cycle be diminished? How can economic progress and efficiency be furthered? How can adequate standards of living be made more widely

---

[2] Subsequent winners have been: Paul Samuelson (senior author of this book) for scientific analysis in theory, 1970; Simon Kuznets, for empirical description of economic growth, 1971; Sir John Hicks and Kenneth Arrow, for equilibrium and welfare theory, 1972; and Wassily Leontief for input-output methods, 1973; all are cited in this book.

available? How can the world avoid ecological disaster?

At every point of our analysis we shall seek to shed light on these policy problems. To succeed in this, we must all try to cultivate an objective and detached ability to see things as they *are*, regardless of our likes or dislikes. The fact must be faced that economic issues are close to everybody emotionally. Blood pressures rise and voices become shrill whenever deep-seated beliefs and prejudices are involved, and some of these prejudices are thinly veiled rationalizations of special economic interests.

WISHFUL THINKING VERSUS REASONED OPINION DIFFERENCES   We know that a doctor passionately interested in stamping out disease must first train himself to observe things as they are. His bacteriology cannot be different from that of a mad scientist out to destroy mankind. "Where it is a duty to worship the sun, the laws of heat will be poorly understood." (Wishful thinking is bad thinking and leads to little wish fulfillment.)

"Beauty is in the eye of the beholder" is an aphorism reminding us that judgments of better or worse involve *subjective* valuations. But this does not deny that one person's nose may be *objectively* shorter than another's. Similarly, there are elements of valid reality in a given economic situation, however hard it may be to recognize and isolate them. There is not one theory of economics for the Right Wing and one for the Left Wing, one for workers and one for employers, one for the Russians and one for the Chinese. On the basic economic principles concerning prices and employment, most—not all!—economists are in fairly close agreement.

This statement does not mean that economists always agree in the *policy* field. Economist A may be for full employment at any cost. Economist B may consider it less important than price stability. Basic questions concerning right and wrong goals to be pursued cannot be settled by science as such. They belong in the realm of ethics and "value judgments". The citizenry must ultimately decide such issues. What the expert can do is point out the feasible alternatives and the true costs that may be involved in the different decisions. But still the mind must render to the heart that which is the heart's domain. For, as Pascal said, the heart has reasons that reason will never know.

And peculiarly in the social sciences, we must realize that we are subjects—even victims—of our preconceptions, prejudices, sentiments, and sordid interests.[3]

THE ULTIMATE PAYOFF   The quotation that appears at the beginning of the book's last chapter, you will find, reads as follows:

Up 'til now philosophers have only interpreted the world in various ways. The point, though, is to *change* it!

These words of the twenty-six-year-old Karl Marx were chosen for his gravestone in London's Highgate cemetery. But they could serve as the motto on the shields of all the great masters of political economy. For, out of the scores of greatest economists in world history, at most two (and with them, it was something of a pose) were not primarily concerned with "doing good."

METHODOLOGY OF ECONOMICS: BRIEF PREVIEW

No one can understand a complicated subject such as chemistry without long and careful study. This is an advantage and a disadvantage. The man on the street or behind a newspaper desk cannot possibly consider himself a final authority on such a subject—which is all to the good. On the other hand, the new student of chemistry must become familiar with all the basic concepts for the first time, which takes a good deal of effort.

From childhood days on, everyone knows *something* about economics. This acquaintance is both helpful and deceptive: helpful, because much knowledge can be taken for granted; deceptive, because it is natural and human to accept superficially plausible views. A little knowledge may be dangerous. On close examination common sense may prove to be really nonsense.

A union leader who has successfully negotiated several labor contracts may feel that he is an expert on the economics of wages. A businessman who has "met a payroll" may feel that his views on price control are final. A banker who can balance his books may conclude that he knows all there is to know about the creation of money.

---

[3] Which questions we ask, and from what perspective we photograph the "objective reality"—these are themselves at bottom subjective in nature.

Each individual naturally tends to judge an economic event only by its immediate effects upon himself. A worker thrown out of employment in the buggy industry cannot be expected to reflect that new jobs may have been created in the automobile industry; but we must be prepared to investigate whether this is so.

In an introductory survey, the economist is interested in the workings of the economy *as a whole* rather than in the viewpoint of any one group. Social and national policies rather than individual policy are his goals. Too often, "everybody's business is nobody's business." It is just as well, therefore, to reiterate at the beginning that an elementary course in economics does not pretend to teach one how to run a business or bank, how to spend money wisely, or how to get rich quick from the stock market. Yet this is not to deny that general economics will provide a useful background for many such activities.

Certainly, the economist must know a good deal about how businessmen, consumers, and investors behave and think. This does not mean that those individuals must use the *same language and methods* in approaching their decisions as economists find useful in describing their behavior—any more than the planets need know that they are following the elliptical paths traced by the astronomer. Just as many of us have been "speaking prose" all our lives without knowing it, so too would many businessmen be surprised to learn that their behavior is capable of systematic economic analysis. This lack of awareness is not necessarily to be deprecated. It does not help a baseball pitcher to know the laws of aerodynamics; and if we become self-conscious about how to button our shirts, we may find it harder to do.

THEORY VERSUS PRACTICE   The economic world is extremely complicated. As we noted, it is usually not possible to make economic observations under the controlled experimental conditions characteristic of scientific laboratories. A physiologist who wishes to determine the effects of penicillin on pneumonia may be able to "hold other things equal" by using two test groups that differ only in the fact that they do and do not get penicillin injections. The economist is less fortunately situated. If he wishes to determine the effect of a gasoline tax on fuel consumption, he may be vexed by the fact that, in the same year when the tax was imposed, pipelines were

first introduced. Nevertheless, he must try—if only mentally—to isolate the effects of the tax, "other things being equal". Otherwise, he will understand the economic effects *neither of taxation nor of transportation improvements, nor of both together.*

THE POST HOC FALLACY   The difficulty of analyzing causes when controlled experimentation is impossible is well illustrated by the confusion of the savage medicine man who thinks that both witchcraft and a little arsenic are necessary to kill his enemy, or that only after he has put on a green robe in spring will the trees do the same.[4] As a result of this limitation and many others, our quantitative economic knowledge is far from complete. This doesn't mean that we do not have great amounts of accurate statistical knowledge available. We do. Reams of census data, market information, and financial statistics have been collected by governments, trade associations, and business concerns.

Even if we had more and better data, it would still be necessary—as in every science—to *simplify*, to *abstract* from the infinite mass of detail. No mind can apprehend a bundle of unrelated facts. All analysis involves abstraction. It is always necessary to *idealize*, to omit detail, to set up simple hypotheses and patterns by which the facts can be related, to set up the right questions before going out to look at the world as it is. Every theory, whether in the physical or biological or social sciences, distorts reality in that it oversimplifies. But if it is good theory, what is omitted is outweighed by the beam of illumination and understanding that is known over the diverse empirical data.

Properly understood, therefore, theory and observation, deduction and induction, cannot be in conflict. The test of a theory's validity is its usefulness in illuminating observed reality. Its logical elegance and finespun beauty are irrelevant. Consequently, when a student says, "That's all right in theory but not in practice," he really means, "That's not right in the relevant theory," or else he is talking nonsense.

THE TYRANNY OF WORDS   Particularly in the social sciences, we must watch out for the "tyranny of words." The world is complicated

---

[4] In logic this is sometimes called the *post hoc, ergo propter hoc* fallacy (after this, therefore necessarily because of this).

enough without introducing further confusions and ambiguities as (a) two different names are unknowingly being used for the same thing or (b) the same one word is being applied to two quite different phenomena.

Jones may call Robinson a liar for holding that the cause of depression is oversaving, saying, "Underconsumption is really the cause." Schwartz may enter the argument, asserting, "You are both wrong. The real trouble is underinvestment." They may go on arguing; but, if they really stopped to analyze their language, they might find that there were no differences in their opinions about the facts and that only a verbal confusion was involved.

Similarly, words may be treacherous because we do not react in a neutral manner to them. Thus a man who approves of a government program to speed growth will call it a program of "sensible planning," while an unsympathetic opponent will describe the same activity as "totalitarian bureaucratic regimentation." Who can object to the former, and who would condone the latter? Yet they may refer to the same thing. One does not have to be an expert in *semantics*— the study of language and its meaning— to realize that scientific discussion requires us to avoid such emotional terminology wherever possible.

SOCIAL VERSUS PHYSICAL SCIENCE?

Some distortions of thinking that result from emotion and prejudice are so blatant as to be clearly recognizable. But at a deeper level, one can ask:

Since economics deals with man and not with inanimate objects, and since the scientist is himself necessarily a man, can there be any hope of an *objective* science of economics? Can the methods of the physical sciences—observation and quantitative measurements, mathematical model building —ever work in the study of human affairs?

No simple answer can be given to this profound question. In a sense, precisely because we are ourselves men, we have an advantage over the natural scientist. He cannot usefully say, "Suppose I were an H_2O molecule; what might I do in such a situation?" The social scientist often, knowingly or unknowingly, employs such introspective acts of *empathy*.

Still a problem remains. Perhaps most experienced scholars would put it this way:

Slavish imitation of the physical sciences is a mistake in the study of humans and society. Yet there is no substitute for patient *attendance to the empirical facts* of life, and no substitute for *systematic reasoning* about them. As in the case of modern biology, great advances have resulted from mathematical scientific methods, despite the earlier warnings against imitating the physical sciences. Let experience tell the final story, and let no one be impressed by mere elegance of technique.

EXACTITUDE AND SUBJECTIVITY

But note this important point. Even in the so-called exact physical sciences, how we *perceive* the observed facts depends on the theoretical spectacles we wear. The light that hits a newborn baby's eyes forms no pattern: the baby sees but it does not perceive. Modern historians of science have learned the same lesson from gestalt psychology: post-Newtonians perceived the "same facts" differently from pre-Newtonians. To a degree we are all prisoners of our theoretical preconceptions. It is not so much discordant fact that kills off an old false theory as the final emergence of a new theory.

That is why science belongs to the young. The old know too many things that are just not so. To illustrate this we do not have to consider a soft science like economics, in which it is taken for granted that your uncles will believe that what was good enough for Arthur Meighen ought to be good enough for you. Let us listen to Nobel laureate Max Planck, the physicist renowned for his discovery of the revolutionary quantum theory. In his *Scientific Autobiography*, Planck reports what he observed in the development of physics:

This experience gave me also an opportunity to learn a fact —a remarkable one in my opinion: A new scientific truth does not triumph by convincing its opponents and making them see the light, but rather because its opponents eventually die, and a new generation grows up that is familiar with it.

Just as Galileo, Newton, and Einstein revolutionized perceptions in physics, so did Smith, Marshall, Keynes—indeed all the names that appear on the family tree of economics shown on the back flyleaf of this book—transform economic understanding. Figure 1-2, taken from a philosophic study of physics, illustrates the irreducible subjective element in *any* science. Does the picture show a bird

Fig 1-2. Facts tell different story to scientists wearing different theoretical spectacles:

If you look at problems of depression unemployment through pre-Keynesian glasses, you may think little of it is due to forces that government tax and expenditure policies can change. In (a) is this a picture of a leftward-looking bird? Or is it a rightward-looking antelope (or rabbit)? In the presence of (b)'s field of birds, most people think it a bird. But next to the footnote's field of antelopes, most will see it as an antelope. (Source: N. R. Hanson, *Patterns of Discovery*, London: Cambridge University Press, 1961.)

looking to the left? Or an antelope (or rabbit) looking to the right? It is not an optical illusion to say it is one rather than the other. Each is admissible.[5]

So it is with many scientific facts and theories. When you adopt a new systematic model of economic principles, you comprehend reality in a new and different way. We do not have to be students of physics or gestalt psychology to realize how literally these words apply to the contrasts between new and old economics, or between free-world and iron-curtain economics. So let us be forewarned.

PROBABILITY OF ERRORS: NORMAL OR NOT
There is another important difference between an exact science like physics and a less exact science like economics. Our laws may hold only "on the average," with considerable dispersion of exceptions around that average. Figure 1-3 gives a preview

[5] Contrast your gestalt perception of Fig. 1-2's image with its appearance when placed next to this field of antelopes. The bird-antelope ambiguity cannot be dismissed as an optical "illusion"; it is unlike the accompanying two lines, which are really the same length even though most people wrongly infer the lower line to be the longer. What Fig. 1-2 portrays is an objectively reproducible shape that looks subjectively different depending on the context in which it appears. But once we see the forelegs of the beast, we are right to perceive it as an antelope.

of a vital statistical relationship whereby consumption spending by families can be related to the dollar incomes people have. Note that the observation points do not fall exactly on the line, as they might in chemistry or astronomy. Still, we do see a pattern that is stable in a probability sense—the same sense in which a life-insurance company can *count on* a stable proportion of deaths in a sample of 100,000 policy holders of a given age (even though any one man's living or dying cannot be foretold).

And note a further important point: the chance deviations around the expected values will form an especially simple frequency pattern called the "normal curve of error." The normal curve is symmetric and bell-shaped; this is because the addition of *many independent* errors tends to give a resultant error which (through probable cancellation) is more likely to be small than large. When this normal distribution appears in economics, it resembles distributions from gambling dice, genetics, or surveying instruments.[6]

In economics, "normality" may not always prevail. Figure 1-4 here reproduces a later diagram, Fig. 5-4, depicting how abnormally spread out people's incomes are in comparison with the allegedly "normal"

[6] Gambling houses in Nevada and Monte Carlo know very well from experience that repeated coin tossing (or dice throwing) will generate a sequence with the following two properties: (a) If we write down 1 for heads and 0 for tails, a random series of tossing will give sequences—such as 0, 1, 0, 1, 1, 0, 1, 0, 0, 0, 1, 0—which eventually average out close to ½ by the famous "law of large numbers." (b) For a long enough sequence of random tosses of a symmetric coin, the fraction of heads appearing will approach a normal-error dispersion around the expected value of ½. This "central limit law" (of approach to a normal distribution) enabled mathematicians like de Moivre, Laplace, and Gauss to predict with great accuracy how often deviations will tend to occur, the expected size of the absolute errors halving when the sequence quadruples in length. Economic distributions, like that of income, may have tails too dispersed to be subject to this normal distribution.

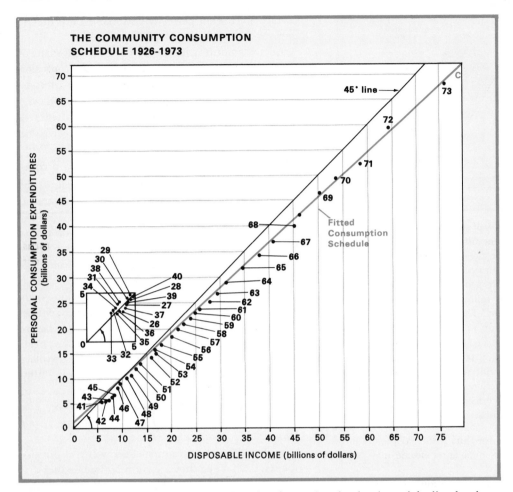

Fig. 1-3. A statistical consumption schedule fits data quite closely. A straight line has been passed through the scatter of black data points. Note the bad fit in World War II years. Can you verify that the slope of the fitted line is about .92? (Sources: M. C. Urquhart and K. A. H. Buckley, *Historical Statistics of Canada*, Cambridge University Press, Toronto, 1965; and Statistics Canada.)

distribution of their abilities (IQ's, verbal or mathematical aptitudes, etc.). The curve of distribution of incomes is asymmetric: unlike the symmetric normal curve, it has a long tail skewed to the right. This reflects the fact that while there are a few multimillionaires with incomes equal to hundreds of times the average income, no one can be that many dollars below the average. Such asymmetric super-extended distributions, alas, appear often in economics. One says "alas" because such abnormal probability laws do not lead to the same *precision of average behavior* that the natural sciences can often count on.

Despite the approximate character of economic laws, it is a field blessed with many important regularities and valid principles.

THE WHOLE AND THE PART: THE "FALLACY OF COMPOSITION"

A good final warning in economics is this: things are often not what at first they seem to be. The following true statements provide examples:

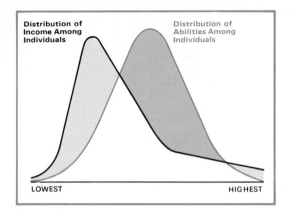

Fig 1-4. Abnormal as well as normal probability patterns of errors occur in economics:
Although behavior on the average is predictable in economics, there are exceptions and deviations around the average. The red curve depicts the well-behaved case in which the deviations follow the symmetric bell-shaped "normal curve of error." The black curve of abnormal error, which is skewed off to the right, has relatively more extreme deviations than does the normal curve. Where this occurs in the social sciences, we cannot guarantee laws of average behavior with quite so much accuracy. (Source: Fig. 5-4, where normal distribution of abilities is contrasted with asymmetric distribution of dollar incomes and great spread among them.)

1. If all farmers work hard and nature cooperates in producing a bumper crop, total farm income may *fall*, and probably will.
2. *One* man may solve his own unemployment problem by great ingenuity in hunting a job or by a willingness to work for less; but *all* cannot necessarily solve their problems in this way.
3. Higher prices *for one industry* may benefit its firms; but if the prices of *everything* bought and sold increased in the same proportion, no one would be better off.
4. It may pay Canada to reduce tariffs charged on goods imported, even if *other* countries refuse to do likewise.
5. It may pay a firm to take on some business at much *less than full costs.*
6. *Attempts* of individuals to save more in depression *may lessen the total* of the community's savings.
7. What is prudent behavior for an *individual* may at times be folly for a *nation* or a *province.*

Note this: Each of the above statements is true; but each is outwardly paradoxical. In the course of this book, the seeming paradoxes will be resolved. There are no magic formulas or hidden tricks. It is typical of economics that anything which is really

correct must seem perfectly reasonable once the argument is carefully developed.

At this point it is just as well to note that many of the above paradoxes hinge upon a single confusion or fallacy, called by logicians the "fallacy of composition." In books on logic, this is defined as follows: *Fallacy of composition:* a fallacy in which what is true of a part is, on that account alone, alleged to be also necessarily true of the whole.

Very definitely, in the field of economics, it turns out that what seems to be true for individuals is not always true for society as a whole; and conversely, what seems to be true for all may be quite false for any one individual. For everybody to stand on tiptoe to watch a parade does no good, even though a single person may gain a better view in so doing. Countless similar examples can be given in the field of economics. You might amuse yourself by checking over the previous seven examples to see which are probably related to the fallacy of composition. Or better still, find some new ones.

We have come to the end of our introductory survey. Perhaps the best answer to the question, "Why study economics?" is the famous one given by Lord Keynes in the final lines of his 1936 classic, *The General Theory of Employment, Interest and Money:*
". . . the ideas of economists and political philosophers, both when they are right and when they are wrong, are more powerful than is commonly understood. Indeed the world is ruled by little else. Practical men, who believe themselves to be quite exempt from any intellectual influences, are usually the slaves of some defunct economist. Madmen in authority, who hear voices in the air, are distilling their frenzy from some academic scribbler of a few years back. I am sure that the power of vested interests is vastly exaggerated compared with the gradual encroachment of ideas. Not, indeed, immediately, but after a certain interval; for in the field of economic and political philosophy there are not many who are influenced by new theories after they are twenty-five or thirty years of age, so that the ideas which civil servants and politicians and even agitators apply to current events are not likely to be the newest. But, soon or late, it is ideas, not vested interests, which are dangerous for good or evil."

SUMMARY

1. Economics, both a science and an art, is studied for a variety of reasons: to understand problems facing the citizen and family; to help governments in both underdeveloped and advanced nations promote mankind-fulfilling growth, while avoiding depression and inflation; to analyze fascinating patterns of social behavior; to alter the inequalities in the distribution of income and opportunity.

2. Among many definitions, the leading one today defines economics thus: How we choose to use scarce productive sources with alternative uses, to meet prescribed ends—what goods to produce, how, and for whom, now or later.

3. Overlapping with other social or behavioral sciences—psychology, sociology, history—economics uses the deductive methods of logic and geometry, and inductive methods of statistical and empirical inference. Because it cannot employ the controlled experiments of the physicist, it raises basic problems of methodology: subjective elements of introspection and value judgment; semantic issues of ambiguous and emotional meanings; probability laws of large numbers, both of normal-error-distribution and abnormally skewed type; fallacies of reasoning and fallacies of inference.

CONCEPTS FOR REVIEW

political economy as distinct
       from other disciplines
analysis and policy
practice and theory
wishful thinking, semantics
exactitude and probabilty
normal and skewed errors

subjectivity and theorizing
valuation and so-called "facts"
tyranny of words
controlled experiment
fallacy of composition
post hoc fallacy
definition of political economy

QUESTIONS FOR DISCUSSION

1. Would a major depression like that of the 1930s, or a peacetime inflation, affect you (a) seriously, (b) moderately, or (c) not at all?

2. Discuss the emotional content of the following words: regimentation, planning, usury, New Left, socialist, monopolist, gambling, speculation, "made in Canada," foreign ownership, free enterprise, cartels, thrift, hoarding.

3. Give examples of the fallacy of composition and of the *post hoc, ergo propter hoc* fallacy. Is the former involved in the debate over cigarettes and longevity? (Why not?) Is the latter involved in this debate? (Why so?)

4. Can you fit into the brief definition of economics many of this chapter's problems?

5. In Fig. 1-3, is income the cause and consumption the effect? Or vice versa? To answer this, economic study is needed. Similarly, does the fact that smoking and cancer are related prove that smoking causes cancer? Is low IQ among the poor genetically caused? How could you form a reasoned judgment?

6. "GNP should be corrected for the fact that city smog sends up my dry-cleaning bills and asthma-prescription charges. Also, when affluence cuts our work week from 45 hours per week to 40 hours per week, that may cut down GNP but surely it should raise Net Economic Welfare (NEW). Also, NEW excludes the defense expenditure that occurs in GNP, since citizens of a country are not improved in welfare when these go up—

however necessary or unnecessary they may be in this vale of tears. Same goes for expenditure on burglar alarms and watchdogs." Which corrections do you agree with?

7. "If society could get an extra 1 per cent annual growth in NEW by the sacrifice of half our ordinary GNP growth rate—say, by our spending more money on conservation and taxing refineries and smelters and the users of electric power for atmospheric pollution they create—this would be a great bargain." Evaluate.

8. Could a scientist believe in "changing the world," and yet not necessarily agree with a Marxian program for thoroughgoing revolution by force? How would different people draw the line? How would you, *before* your first course in economics?

A PREVIEW

Here in Part One we deal with the fundamental tools needed to analyze the basic facts and institutions of modern economic life, culminating this survey in the unifying concept of national income.

In Part Two we analyze the causes of prosperity and depression: how the processes of saving and investment interact to determine the level of prices, income, and employment; and how public monetary and fiscal policies can stabilize business activity at a healthy level of progressive growth.

Part Three is concerned with the forces of competition and monopoly, which act through supply and demand to help determine—efficiently or inefficiently—the composition of the national income, in terms of both goods and services produced and their prices. (Unlike Part Two's "macroeconomics," this is "microeconomics.")

Part Four treats distribution of income: wages, rent, interest, and profits.

Part Five discusses international trade in both its monetary and real aspects.

Part Six deals with some of our most vital current economic problems: growth analysis and development of backward countries; stabilization of employment and control of inflation; poverty, inequality, and the quality of economic life; economics of racial and sexual discrimination and problems of environmental blight.

2
CENTRAL PROBLEMS OF EVERY ECONOMIC SOCIETY

To get land's fruit in quantity
Takes jolts of labor ever more,
Hence food will grow like one, two, three . . .
While numbers grow like one, two, four . . .
Song of Malthus: A Ballad on Diminishing Returns   ANONYMOUS

At the foundations of any community there will always be found a few universal economic conditions. Certain background problems are as crucial today as they were in the days of Homer and Caesar, and they will continue to be relevant in the brave new world of the future.

In Section A of this chapter we see that every society must meet a certain trio of *basic problems of economic organization*. Section B shows that technological *knowledge*, together with limited amounts of *land, labor,* and *capital,* defines the available choices between goods and services open to a community and that these *production possibilities* are subject to change and to the law of diminishing returns. Section C develops the point that the basis of any economy is its *population*, or *human element*.

We shall leave to Chapter 3 those important special economic features characteristic of our own mixed economy—a system of private and public enterprise intertwined.

A. PROBLEMS OF ECONOMIC ORGANIZATION

Any society, whether it consists of a totally collectivized communistic state, a tribe of South Sea Islanders, a capitalistic industrial nation, a Swiss Family Robinson, a Robinson Crusoe—or, one might almost add, a colony of bees—must somehow confront three fundamental and interdependent economic problems.

1. WHAT commodities shall be produced and in what quantities? That is, how much and which of alternative goods and services shall be produced? Food or clothing? Much food and little clothing, or vice versa? Bread and butter today, or bread and grape plantings today with bread, butter, and jam next year?

2. HOW shall goods be produced? That is, by whom and with what resources and in what technological manner are they to be produced? Who hunts, who fishes? Electricity from steam or from waterfall or from atoms? Large- or small-scale production?

3. FOR WHOM shall goods be produced? That is, who is to enjoy and get the benefit of the goods and services provided? Or, to put the same thing in another way, how is the total of national product to be *distributed*[1] among different individuals and families? A few rich and many poor? Or most people in modest comfort?

These three questions are fundamental and common to all economies, but different economic systems try to solve them differently.

[1] WARNING: Usually, when an economist is talking about "distribution," he means the distribution of incomes—the principles which determine labor's wage, land's rent, capital's interest, and the whole FOR WHOM process. The man on the street usually means, by distribution, wholesaling and retailing—how *goods*, once produced, get distributed into the hands of the consumer. Avoid this last confusing usage.

CUSTOM, INSTINCT, COMMAND, OR THE MARKET In a primitive civilization, custom may rule every facet of behavior. WHAT, HOW, and FOR WHOM may be decided by reference to traditional ways of doing things. To members of another culture, the practices followed may seem bizarre and unreasonable; the members of the tribe or clan may themselves be so familiar with existing practices as to be surprised, and perhaps offended, if asked the reason for their behavior. Thus Kwakiutl Indians of high rank considered it meritorious to accumulate wealth and then give it away in the *potlatch*—a roisterous celebration. Such deviations from our own modes of distributing wealth toward taking turns at favor giving will not surprise anthropologists; from their studies they know what is correct behavior in one culture is often the greatest crime in another.

In the bee colony, all such problems, even those involving an elaborate cooperative division of labor, are solved automatically by means of so-called "biological instincts." (Fair enough as a description, but not much of an "explanation.")

At the other extreme we can imagine an omnipotent benevolent or malevolent dictator who, by arbitrary decree, decides WHAT, HOW, and FOR WHOM. Or we might imagine economic organization by decree, but with decrees drawn up by democratic vote or by selected legislative authorities.

As Chapter 3 develops at length, the WHAT, HOW, and FOR WHOM questions in a "capitalist free enterprise economy" are solved primarily[2] by a system of prices (of markets, or profits and losses).

THE LAW OF SCARCITY WHAT to produce, HOW, and FOR WHOM would not be problems if resources were *un*limited: if an *infinite* amount of every good could be produced, or if human wants were fully satisfied, it would not then matter if too much of any particular good were produced. Nor would it then matter if labor and materials were combined unwisely. Since everyone could have as much as he pleased, it would not matter how goods and incomes were distributed among different individuals and families.

There would then be no *economic goods;* i.e., no goods that are relatively *scarce;* and there would hardly be any need for a study of economics or "economizing." All goods would be *free goods,* the way pure air used to be.

In the world as it is, even children learn in growing up that "both" is not an admissible answer to a choice of "Which one?" Compared with backward nations or previous centuries, modern industrial societies seem very wealthy indeed. But higher production levels seem to bring in their train higher consumption standards. People feel that they want and "need" central heating, indoor plumbing, refrigerators, penicillin, education, movies, radios, television, green lawns, books, autos, travel, sports and concerts, music, chic clothes, and so forth. The biological scientist may tell them that they can be well nourished on a thin porridge for a few cents a day,[3] but that possibility leaves them as cold as the information that the chemicals in their bodies are worth only a couple of dollars. Anyone who has kept a family budget knows that the necessities of life—the absolute musts—have little to do with the minimum *physiological* needs of food, clothing, and shelter.

In *The Affluent Society,* J. Kenneth Galbraith[4] has eloquently pointed out that Americans today have for the most part gone beyond the level of physiological necessity; that often the consumer flits from one purchase to another in response to pressures of fashion and advertising. Without challenging Galbraith's thesis that the time has come to spend more on public needs and less on private needs, one may properly point out that our total product would have to become many times higher than its present level if everyone were to become able to live at the level of a moderately well-off doctor, lawyer, professor, or advertising man—to say nothing of the living standards of the really well-to-do.

---

[2] There has never been a 100 per cent purely automatic enterprise system, although Victorian England came close. Certainly in our system, the government has an important role in modifying the workings of the price system. We live in what may be called a "mixed economy."

[3] A study suggests that in North America modern standards of adult nutrition could be bought (in 1973) for about $95 per year. But what a diet this implies: kidneys, cabbage, beans, wheat flour, and not much else! Cf. George J. Stigler, "The Cost of Subsistence," *Journal of Farm Economics,* May, 1945, pp. 303-314. This paper achieved fame as a forerunner of an important mathematical technique of economics and national defense called "linear planning." Victor E. Smith of Michigan State University in the same journal (May, 1959, pp. 272-283) reported that a family of three could get a "palatable diet" for about 50 cents per person per day, perhaps 90 cents in the 1970s.

[4] John Kenneth Galbraith, *The Affluent Society* (Houghton Mifflin, Boston, 1958).

Whether or not people would be "genuinely" happier spending twice as much as now, observation suggests that people in the suburbs now act *as if* they want more income to spend: they take on extra work; they resist tax increases; they end up saving much the same fraction of their incomes as in 1900;

and middle-class mothers seem to work harder than their mothers did.

Therefore, while it recognizes the important germ of truth in the notion that ours has become an affluent society, economics must still contend with *scarcity* as a basic fact of life.

B. THE TECHNOLOGICAL CHOICES OPEN TO ANY SOCIETY

SOCIETY'S PRODUCTION-POSSIBILITY CURVE

We have discussed the basic economic fact that *limitation* of the total resources capable of producing different commodities necessitates a choice between relatively scarce commodities. This can be illustrated quantitatively by simple arithmetic examples and geometrical diagrams. Diagrams and graphs are indispensable visual aids in many aspects of economics. A little care at the beginning in understanding them will be rewarded manyfold later on.

Consider an economy with only so many people, only so much technical knowledge, only so many factories and tools, and only so much land, water power, and natural resources. In deciding WHAT shall be produced and HOW, the economy must really decide just how these resources are to be allocated among the thousands of different possible commodities. How much land should go into wheat growing? Or into pasturage? How many factories are to produce knives? How much skilled labor should go into machine shops?

These problems are complicated even to discuss, much less solve. Therefore we must simplify. So let us assume there are to be produced only two economic goods (or classes of economic goods). For dramatic purposes, we can choose the pair Adolf Hitler ranted about—guns and butter. These two commodities are commonly used to illustrate the problem of choosing between civilian and war goods, but the same analysis applies to *any* choice of goods. Thus the more resources the government uses to build *public* roads, the less will be left to produce *private* houses; the more the public chooses to consume of *food*, the less it can consume of *clothing*; the more society decides to *consume today*, the less can be its production of *machines and capital goods* to

turn out more consumption goods for the *next year or decade.*

NUMERICAL EXAMPLE But let us stick to the example of guns and butter. Now, suppose that *all* resources are thrown into the production of civilian goods (butter). There will still be a *maximum* amount of butter that can be produced per year. (The exact amount depends upon the quantitative and qualitative resources of the economy in question and the technological efficiency with which they are used.) Suppose 5 million pounds of butter is the maximum amount that can be produced with the existing technology and resources.

At the other extreme, imagine that 100 per cent of society's resources had been devoted instead to the production of guns. Only some maximum number of guns could then be produced: 15 thousand guns of a certain description can perhaps be produced if we are really willing to produce no butter.

These are two extreme possibilities; in between there are still others. If we are willing to give up *some* butter, we can have *some* guns; if we are willing to give up still more butter, we can have still more guns. A schedule of a number of possibilities is given in Table 2-1, *F* being the extreme where all butter and no guns are produced, and *A* being the opposite extreme where all resources go into guns. In between, at *E, D, C,* and *B,* butter is being given up increasingly in return for more guns. Butter is "transformed" into guns, not physically, but by diverting resources from one use to the other.

GRAPHICAL PRODUCTION - POSSIBILITY FRONTIER It is even more illuminating to represent this same "production-possibility schedule" graphically in Fig. 2-1, by measuring butter along the horizontal axis and guns along the vertical.

	ALTERNATE PRODUCTION POSSIBILITIES	
POSSI-BILITIES	**BUTTER** (millions of pounds)	**GUNS** (thousands)
A	0	15
B	1	14
C	2	12
D	3	9
E	4	5
F	5	0

TABLE 2-1. Economic resources can be shifted from butter production to gun production, in effect enabling us to transform butter into guns. The cost of getting extra guns can be reckoned as the extra butter we are forced to sacrifice.

The reader should now be able to go directly from the numerical table to the diagram: for *F*, by counting over 5 butter units to the right and going up 0 gun units; for *E*, by going 4 butter units to the right and going up 5 gun units; and finally, for *A*, by going over 0 butter units and up 15 gun units.

We may fill in all intermediate positions with dots, even those involving fractions of a million pounds or of a thousand guns, as in the so-called "production-possibility frontier" shown in Fig. 2-2.

The curve that we now have represents this fundamental fact:

A full-employment economy must always, in producing more of one good, be giving up something of another. This assumes, of course, that at least some resources can be transferred from one good to another; e.g., steel is used for guns and also for butter via farm machinery.

Substitution is the law of life in a full-employment economy. The *production-possibility frontier* depicts society's menu of choices.

UNEMPLOYMENT AND INEFFICIENCY

But what if there had been widespread unemployment of resources: idle men, idle land, idle factories? We have already warned that our eco-

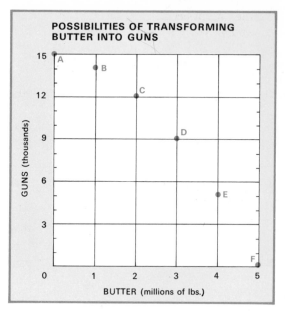

FIG. 2-1. Full employment of scarce resources implies guns-butter tradeoff.

As we go from *A* to *B* . . . to *F*, we are transferring resources from the gun industry to the butter industry. The cost of getting extra butter can be reckoned (along the tradeoff relation) as the extra guns we are forced to sacrifice.

On the diagram, the red point *A* is plotted by going up 15 and over 0. Similarly each red point is a careful plot of the table's pair of numbers. (Can you guess where the number midway between *B* and *C* might approximately fall? Read off *its* butter-guns numbers.)

nomic laws may then be quite different. This is one such instance.

With unemployment, we are not on the production-possibility frontier at all, but rather somewhere *inside* it. Thus *U* in Fig. 2-2 represents a point *inside* the *p-p frontier* where society is producing only 2 million pounds of butter and 6 thousand guns. If resources are idle, by putting them to work we can have more butter *and* more guns. We can move from *U* to *D* and *E* and thereby get *more* butter *and more* guns.

This throws important light on the different experiences in World War II of three countries: Canada, Germany, and Russia. After 1939, how was Canada able to arm for war and to enjoy civilian living standards higher than ever before? Largely by taking up the slack of unemployment and

FIG. 2-2. A smooth curve fills in the plotted points of the numerical production possibilities.
This frontier shows the menu of choice along which society can choose to substitute guns for butter, assuming a given state of technology and a given total of resources. Any point *inside* the curve, such as *U*, indicates that resources are not being fully employed in the best-known way. (Source: Fig. 2-1's numerical data.)

creating a sizeable war material industry. On the other hand, Hitler's war effort began in 1933, long before any formal declaration. It stemmed from a period of unemployment acute enough to win him the votes to get into power peacefully. Almost all the extra output made possible by utilizing previously unemployed workers and plants was siphoned into German war goods rather than into higher civilian consumption. Still a third case is that of the Soviet Union in World War II. The Russians had little unemployment before the war and were already on their rather low production-possibility curve. They had no choice but to substitute war for civilian goods—with consequent privation.

Business-cycle unemployment is not the only way of being inside the *p-p frontier*. If an economy is inefficiently organized, it may also be well short of the frontier—as in the defeated Germany of 1947 when the whole price system had broken down or in China of 1960, when the ideological drive for a "great leap

forward" resulted in ousting of experts and an abortive attempt to make steel in backyard furnaces, or as in an economy riddled with monopoly and subject to arbitrary decrees by corrupt and incompetent bureaucrats. (We shall analyze monopoly in Part Three. For China, see the Appendix to this chapter and Chapter 3.)

SOME USES OF THE PRODUCTION-POSSIBILITY CONCEPT

This concept, represented as a simple curve, can help introduce many of the most basic concepts in economics. For example, Fig. 2-2 illustrates the basic definition of economics given in Chapter 1, namely, the problem of *choosing* among *scarce* or limited resources ("means" capable of *alternative* uses), in order to achieve best *goals* ("ends"). Land, labor, and capital can be used to produce guns or butter along the frontier curve in Fig. 2-2. Where does the society choose to end up? Southeastward in the diagram, with much of civilian goods? Or northwestward, with much of defense goods? Economics is a *quantitative* subject: choice is not a qualitative matter of "either-or," but rather of how many of each good and just where we draw the line of final decision.

The production-possibility frontier also permits us to give a rigorous definition of scarcity.

Definition: "Economic scarcity" refers to the basic fact of life that there exists only a finite amount of human and nonhuman resources, which the best technical knowledge is capable of using to produce only a *limited* maximum amount of each and every good, as shown by the *p-p frontier*. And thus far, nowhere on the globe is the supply of goods so plentiful or the tastes so limited that the *average family* can have more than enough of everything it might fancy.

The production-possibility schedule can also help make clear the three basic problems of economic life: WHAT, HOW, and FOR WHOM.

WHAT goods are produced and consumed can be depicted by the point which we choose on the *p-p frontier*.

HOW goods are to be produced involves an efficient choice of methods and proper assignment of different amounts and kinds of limited resources to the various industries.

What would happen if the men well fitted for machine-tooling of guns ended up on the farms? We should be *inside* the *p-p frontier*, not on it. Or what if government regulations made the land most suitable for corn be used for wheat production, and the land most suitable for wheat be used for corn? We should end up with less of both corn and wheat, inside the production-possibility frontier on a diagram whose axes were labeled *C* and *W*. Being inside the frontier is a crime of *economic* inefficiency; but it need not involve any *engineering* inefficiency, since, on the wrongly allocated land, production might still be following the latest methods known to science.[5]

FOR WHOM goods are to be produced cannot be discerned from the *p-p* diagram alone. Sometimes, though, you can make a guess from it: if you find a society on its *p-p* curve with many yachts and few compact cars, you are justified in suspecting that it enjoys considerable inequality of income and wealth among persons.

PICTURES IN AN EXHIBITION

The graphs of Figures 2-3 to 2-7, on the following pages, are meant to be self-explanatory. They show that the production-possibility curve can illustrate many familiar, but basic, economic processes. Later chapters will deal with each of these in depth, and it is necessary here only to comprehend the common-sense ideas involved.

Figure 2-3 illustrates how a society consumes much food when it is poor but shifts toward comforts and luxuries as it develops, a topic to be met in Chapter 11.

Figure 2-4 illustrates how the electorate must choose between private goods bought at a price and public goods paid for largely by taxes, a topic to be met in Chapter 8.

---

[5] More difficult is the notion that the economy should often prefer scientifically *less* efficient methods over methods that are allegedly technically more efficient. EXAMPLE: Physics texts teach that converting heat to motion at 2,500°F is intrinsically more efficient than converting it at 1,200°F. Yet if metals that can stand the higher temperature are scarce and dear, it is *economically* better for the engineer and businessman to use the thermodynamically less efficient method!

Figure 2-5 illustrates how an economy chooses between (1) current consumption goods and (2) capital goods (machines, etc.), which makes possible more of *both* goods (consumption and capital) in the future. Much of Parts Two, Four, and Six will deal with this basic investment problem.

Figure 2-6 shows how Economy B, blessed by unusual scientific and engineering discoveries, might surpass A which was undergoing more thrift and investing for the future, but with less progressive technology. Part Six on growth will develop this theme.

Finally, Fig. 2-7 prepares us for the next topic, the law of diminishing returns.

THE LAW OF DIMINISHING RETURNS

The fixity of land in Figure 2-7 will alert us to a famous economic relationship, the so-called "law of diminishing returns." This law states the relation, *not* between two goods (such as guns and butter), but rather between an *input* of a factor of production (such as labor) and the output that it helps produce (such as butter or, in the traditional examples, corn).

More specifically, the law of diminishing returns refers to the amount of *extra output* that we get when we successively add *extra* units of a *varying factor input* to a *fixed* amount of some *other factor input*. (Note the emphasized words.)

Here is an example to illustrate the law of diminishing returns. We make the following controlled experiment: Given a fixed amount of land, say, 100 acres, we shall first add no labor at all. We note that there is then no corn output. So, in Table 2-2, we record zero product when labor is zero.

Now we make a second related experiment. We add 1 extra unit of labor to the same fixed amount of land. How much output do we now get? Pure reason cannot tell us: we must look to the facts of the experiment. When we do, let's say we observe that we now have produced positive output of corn exactly equal to 2,000 units (bushels or whatever units you choose to measure corn in). We now summarize the result of this second experiment: Adding 1 extra unit of labor to fixed land gives us extra output of 2,000 units.

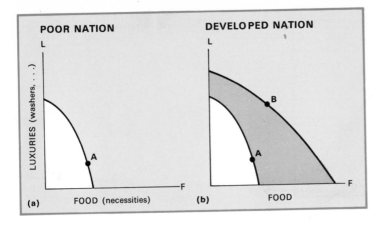

FIG. 2-3. Economic development and progress shifts *p-p frontier* outward.

(a). Before development, the nation is so poor it must devote almost all its resources to food, enjoying few comforts.

(b). After development, it goes from *A* to *B*, expanding its food consumption very little compared with its increased consumption of nonnecessities.

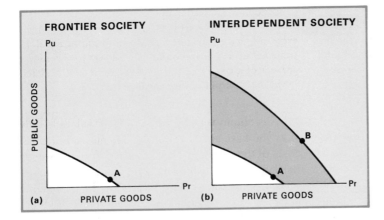

FIG. 2-4. With prosperity comes greater emphasis on public rather than private goods.

(a). The economy is poor and dispersed as in pre-Confederation days: the proportion of resources going to government is low.

(b). The economy is more prosperous and chooses to spend more of its higher income on governmental services (roads, defense, research, education); in dense urban life, it has no choice but to spend on traffic lights, police, and city planning.

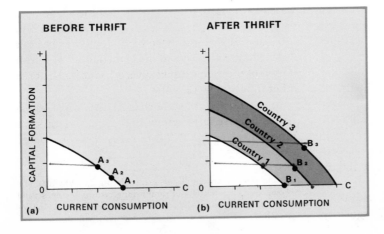

FIG. 2-5. Capital formation for future consumption forces sacrifice of current consumption.

(a). Three countries start out even, but Country 1 does no saving for the future at A_1 (merely replacing machines). Country 2 abstains modestly from consumption at A_2. Country 3, by democratic vote or private sacrifice, is at A_3, investing much in new machines and sacrificing much of current consumption.

(b). In the next years, Country 3 has forged ahead of Country 2, which has moved ahead of 1. Possessing more machines for labor to work with, Country 3 now has more of *both* goods.

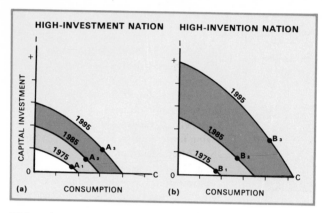

FIG. 2-6. Technical invention can more than match productivity gain from thrift.
(a). Country **A**, on the left, is thrifty and advances by accumulating capital goods.
(b). Country **B** advances even more from 1975 to 1985 because it spends more on science and technical research. From 1985 to 1995 it grows faster still by using both methods: technical progress and much capital formation.

MAN-YEARS OF LABOR	TOTAL PRODUCT, (BUSHELS)	EXTRA OUTPUT ADDED BY ADDITIONAL UNIT OF LABOR
0	0	
		2,000
1	2,000	
		1,000
2	3,000	
		500
3	3,500	
		300
4	3,800	
		100
5	3,900	

LAW OF DIMINISHING RETURNS

TABLE 2-2. Diminishing returns is a fundamental law of economics and technology.
Law of diminishing returns refers to successively lower extra outputs (e.g. of corn) gained from adding equal increments of a variable input (e.g. labor) to a constant amount of a fixed input (e.g. 100 acres of land). (Pencil in the extra output of the fourth laborer).

To observe the law of diminishing returns, we must make a third controlled experiment. We still hold land fixed. Once more we vary the labor input and make sure to add *again exactly the same extra unit of labor as before*; i.e., we now go from 1 unit of labor to 2 units of labor to match our earlier going from 0 labor to 1 labor. We breathlessly await the outcome of the experiment in terms of extra corn produced.

Shall we now have a total of 4,000 units of corn, which would, as before, represent exactly 2,000 extra units of output produced by the extra unit of the varying labor? Or shall we find *diminishing* returns, with the new extra unit of factor input adding less than the 2,000 extra units of output which was previously added?

If the law of diminishing returns does in fact hold, our experiment can have but one result. The second extra labor unit will add *less extra output* than did the first. Adding a third extra unit of labor will, if diminishing returns holds, result in *still lower* extra output. And so forth. Table 2-2 gives numerical values to illustrate exactly what diminishing returns means.

The law of diminishing returns is an important, often-observed, economic and technical regularity;

but it is not universally valid. Often it will hold only *after* you have added a considerable number of equal doses of the varying factor. Beyond that point, we say the law of diminishing returns has set in. (Before such a point the varying factors might be yielding *increasing* extra returns, since until then we find that adding extra varying factor inputs to a fixed factor input leads to increasing rather than diminishing extra outputs.[6]

Why is the law of diminishing returns plausible? Frequently we feel that by adding land and labor together—no factor input being fixed and all being varied in the same proportion so that the whole *scale* of operations is getting larger—output should also increase proportionately and extra outputs need not diminish. For why should the extra outputs diminish if each of the factor inputs always has as much of the other inputs to work with?

In short, *balanced* scale changes may often be expected to leave factor inputs and outputs in the same ratios. (Look at Fig. 2-7(a) to verify this.)

---

[6] If one were to change Table 2-2, replacing 2,000 by 900, one would find that the law of diminishing returns becomes valid only after the second row; at first there would actually be increasing extra returns to each equal additional unit of labor.

FIG. 2-7. Diminishing returns means outputs on fixed land cannot keep pace with population.
(a). We begin initially at the lower curve *A* on the left. But population now doubles and is able to spread over double the previous land, leaving each country and state in the same land-labor balance as before. Hence the new curve *B* permits exactly twice the scale of food and clothing production.

Finally, let labor and land both rise again by the same extra amount as between *A* and *B*. We end up a *C*, gaining fully as much of extra products as we did before from the same balanced *additions* of labor and land. Note that the arrows 1, 2, and 3 on each axis show no diminishing length.

(b). We begin at the same lower curve *A* repeated on the right. Now *Land is held constant* while population doubles. Each laborer has *less* land to work with than under balanced growth. Hence, the *B'* curve is below the *B* curve of Fig. 2-7(a).

Finally, add another equal increment of labor, still holding land constant. The new *extra* product is even lower, as shown by the diminishing lengths of the arrows 1, 2, and 3, which depict extra outputs. We'll soon understand the reasons for all this, after the "law of diminishing returns" is mastered.

On the other hand, when we do hold one factor input or group of factor inputs constant and vary the remaining factor inputs, we see that the varying factor inputs have *less and less of the fixed factor inputs to work with.* Consequently, we are not too surprised that such extra varying factor inputs begin to add less and less extra product.

In effect, the fixed factor of production (land) is decreasing in proportion to the variable factor input (labor). As we crowd the land more and more, we may still get some extra corn by intensive cultivation of the soil; but the amount of extra corn per unit of extra labor will become less and less. We shall see in Part Four that the real wage paid to workers depends upon the extra output a last man adds for his employer. Diminishing returns reveals that living standards in crowded China or India are low because of this basic technical truth, and not *merely* because land happens to be owned by the state or by private landlords.

In conclusion, we may summarize as follows:

The law of diminishing returns: An increase in some factor inputs relative to other fixed factor inputs will, in a given state of technology, cause total output to increase; *but after a point the extra output resulting from the same additions of extra factor inputs is likely to become less and less.* This falling off of extra returns is a consequence of the fact that the new "doses" of the varying factor inputs have less and less of the fixed resources or factors to work with.

ECONOMIES OF SCALE AND MASS PRODUCTION: A DIGRESSION

Before leaving this section we ought to take note of a phenomenon that is different from our controlled variation of one thing at a time.

Suppose we merely increase *"scale* of operations," i.e., increase all the factors at the same time in the same degree. In many industrial processes, when you double *all* factor inputs, you may find that your output is more than doubled; this phenomenon is called *"increasing* returns to *scale."*

Our previous law of diminishing returns always refers to cases where *some* factors were varied while some remained fixed. Hence, this case of increasing returns to scale is not a direct refutation of the law of diminishing returns.

Increasing returns to scale, or so-called "economies of mass production," are often associated with one of the following advances: (1) the use of nonhuman and nonanimal power sources (water and wind power, steam, electricity, turbines and internal-combustion engines, internal nuclear energy); (2) the use of automatic self-adjusting mechanisms (lathes, jigs, servomechanisms); (3) the use of standardized interchangeable parts; (4) the breakdown of complex processes into simple repetitive operations; (5) the specialization of function and division of labor; and many other technological factors as well. The automobile-production assembly line and the historical development of modern textile spinning and weaving are examples typifying these diverse factors.

Upon thought, it will be evident that *each of these economies or savings comes into full play only if a large enough number of units is being produced to make it worth while to set up a fairly elaborate productive organization.* If only a few guns are to be produced, they might just as well be produced by hand; but if resources are available to produce many thousands, it will pay to make certain elaborate initial preparations that need not be repeated when still more units are to be produced. In such cases, where mere scale matters much, the tendency for land fixity to force diminishing extra returns to labor could be thwarted for a long time by an increase in the total labor scale involved[7].

[7] Accordingly, it might come about that, unlike our earlier simplified picture, we should have to pay two butter units for our first gun unit; but to get still another gun unit we should have to pay only one butter unit because of the efficiency of mass production. This would be a case of decreasing rather than increasing extra-costs-for-one-good-in-terms-of-another. When strong increasing returns to scale predominate, advanced treatises show that you have to redraw Fig. 2-2 to be "bowed in" (convex from below) rather than "bowed out" (concave from below), at least near each axis.

Economies of scale are very important in explaining why so many of the goods we buy are produced by large companies, as Karl Marx emphasized a century ago. We shall see that they are important in helping explain "the division of labor" and pattern of "specialization." They raise questions to which we shall return again and again in later chapters—as, for example, monopoly.

LAW OF INCREASING (RELATIVE) COSTS

We are now in a position to explain why the *production-possibility frontier* has been drawn in a bowed-out (concave from above) curve in all our diagrams. If the *p-p frontier* were a straight line, the relative costs of getting some extra guns in terms of sacrificed butter would always be the same. Economists would term this a case of "constant (relative) costs." But actually it is more common in life to meet the law of increasing (relative) costs.

Definition: The "law of increasing (relative) costs" prevails when in order to get *equal* extra amounts of one good, society must sacrifice ever-increasing amounts of the other good.

A bowed-out or concave curvature of the *production-possibility frontier* depicts the law of increasing (relative) costs—as shown by the fact that when we want more farm goods (e.g. butter), their (relative) cost rises in terms of sacrificed manufactures (e.g. guns), as seen in Fig. 2-8, by the steeper absolute slope at C than at B.

Why is this reasonable? We shall see that the law of increasing (relative) costs is related to, but definitely not the same thing as, the law of diminishing returns. We'll see that, along with the law of diminishing returns, economists must be able to assume that manufactures and food use the factors of production, such as labor and land, *in different proportions or intensities* to deduce this law of increasing (relative) costs.

To derive the law of increasing (relative) costs, let us use an oversimplified example. In Fig. 2-8, suppose that Manufactures (clothing) require *labor alone* and negligible land. But suppose that Agricultural Food (butter) requires, along with labor, fertile

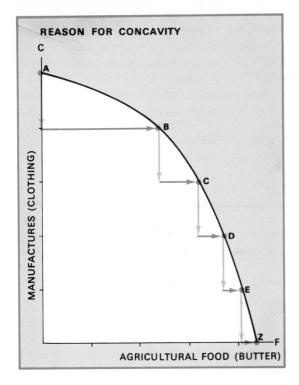

REASON FOR CONCAVITY

MANUFACTURES (CLOTHING)

AGRICULTURAL FOOD (BUTTER)

FIG. 2-8. Land scarcity for food, plus diminishing returns, entails increasing (relative) costs.
In going from *A* to *B, B* to *C, C* to *D, D* to *E,* and *E* to *Z,* we have to give up equal amounts of Manufactures as we transfer equal labor amounts out of the manufacturing industry. Note the equal vertical arrows below *A,* below *B,...,* etc. But, as equal units of varying labor are added to fixed agricultural land, diminishing returns yield less and less of extra food—as measured by the shorter and shorter horizontal arrows. This accounts for the curve's bending, or for the law of increasing relative costs.

land that has grown scarce enough to have become private property. Now we have the two ingredients needed to explain the law of increasing (relative) costs shown in the *p-p frontier:* The two industries use land and labor in different proportions; so transferring varying amounts of labor onto fixed Agricultural land will turn out to bring into play the law of diminishing returns. Let us see exactly how.

Begin by using all labor to produce Manufactures, at *A* in Fig. 2-8. Now sacrifice equal amounts of Manufactures to get more Agriculture, going to *B* and *C.* How is this transformation accomplished? By transferring *equal amounts of labor* away from Manufactures (since no land is used there at all). But note that these equal amounts of transferred labor are applied to a fixed total of Agricultural land. As equal amounts of varying labor are applied to a fixed land factor, each has less and less acres to work with and hence adds less and less of extra Agriculture product. We see then why each new Agriculture is procured at higher and higher costs in terms of Manufactures.[8]

---

[8] The common sense of this law of increasing (relative) costs does not depend upon one of the goods using labor alone. It depends only on having the two goods—call them clothing and butter—differing in the proportions of factors they require. Thus, note that the first few clothes can be produced in part with the kind of resources that are no good for butter anyway. If more clothing is wanted, we must use resources that are valuable for butter production; and if we insist upon having all clothing, we must be prepared to take farmers and farmlands, which are very efficient in the production of butter, and transform them to the production of clothing even though they can produce only very little in this sphere. Thus, increasing (relative) costs are to be expected in such a case. (Even if resources could be divided into two uniform classes, such as homogeneous land and homogeneous labor, increasing costs would still result from the fact that clothing and butter do not require the same proportion of these resources—butter taking more land, and clothing requiring relatively more labor. An extra-credit problem, for geometry-inclined students, returns to this problem at the end of Chapter 27.)

C. THE UNDERLYING POPULATION BASIS OF ANY ECONOMY: PAST AND FUTURE POPULATION TRENDS

Now that we have studied the law of diminishing returns, let us put it to work in this last part of the chapter to underline the crucial importance of population growth to fixed resources.

THE MALTHUSIAN THEORY OF POPULATION

The law of diminishing returns has an application in the field of population. Around 1800, Thomas

Robert Malthus, a young English clergyman, used to argue at breakfast against his father's perfectionist view that the human race was getting ever better. Finally the younger Malthus became so agitated that he wrote a book. His *Essay on the Principle of Population* (1798) was an instantaneous best-seller. It went through several editions and for a century influenced the thinking of people all over the world (including Charles Darwin, the expositor of the famous doctrine of biological evolution). It is still a living influence today. Malthus' views depend directly on the law of diminishing returns, and continue to have relevance.

Malthus first took the observation of Benjamin Franklin that, in the American colonies where resources were abundant, population tended to double every 25 years or so. Malthus postulated, therefore, *a universal tendency for population—unless checked by food supply—to grow at a geometric progression.* Now, anyone with imagination knows how fast geometric progressions grow—how soon 1, 2, 4, 8, 16, 32, 64, 128, 256, 512, 1,024, . . . , becomes so large that there is no space in the world for all the people to stand.[9]

All this left members of the perfectionist school, such as the elder Malthus and William Godwin, unimpressed. So at this point Malthus in effect unleashed the devil of the law of diminishing returns. Refer back to Fig. 2-7(b).

As population doubles and redoubles, it is exactly as if the globe were halving in size, until finally it has shrunk so much that food and subsistence fall below that necessary for life. Because of the law of diminishing returns, food tends *not* to keep up with the geometric-progression rate of growth of population.

Mind you, Malthus did not say that population *would* increase at these rates. This was only its *tendency* if unchecked. He considered it an important part of his argument to show that, in all places in all times, checks do operate to hold population down. In his first edition he put emphasis on *positive* checks that act to increase the death rate: pestilence, famine, and war. Later he backed down from this gloomy doctrine and held out hope for the human race through *preventive* checks operating on the birth rate. Although the birth-control movement is called neo-Malthusianism, clergyman Malthus advocated only *moral restraint* with prudential postponement of early marriages until a family could be

supported. In fact, he preached that the struggle for existence was an illustration of the wisdom of Nature, keeping poor people from getting soft and lazy.

This important application of diminishing returns illustrates the profound effects a simple theory can have. Malthus' ideas had widespread repercussions. His book was used to support a stern revision of the English poor laws, whereby destitution was considered a result of laziness and unemployment a state to be made as uncomfortable as possible. His opinions also bolstered the argument that trade-unions could not improve the welfare of workers, since any increase in their wages would only cause them to reproduce until there was again barely subsistence enough for all. Even in the 1970s, the computer makes headlines when it spells out the "limits of growth" by a more elaborate simulation of Malthus' geometric and arithmetic progressions.[10]

FALSE PROPHECIES OF MALTHUS Despite the statistics covering many countries incorporated in his later editions, it is today recognized that his views were oversimplifications. What has happened to his forecasts?

In the first place, in his discussion of diminishing returns, Malthus never fully anticipated the miracles of the Industrial Revolution. In the next century, technological innovation *shifted* production-possibility frontiers rapidly *outward* as in Figure 2-6(b). This made possible better standards of living for more people.

In the second place, however, his gloomy predictions were reinforced by medical advances, which were prolonging human life and further lessening the positive checks to population growth.

Nor — in the third place — did he anticipate that after 1870, in most Western nations, female *fertility*, as measured by the actual size of families, would begin to fall far short of family *fecundity* or biological reproductive capacity.

Nevertheless, the germs of truth in his *Essay* are still important; for the falling death rate has eclipsed the falling fertility rate in India, Haiti and China, and

---

[9] In modern terminology, Franklin was saying that the *rate of natural increase* was about 3 percent (or 30 per thousand) per year. At 3 percent compound interest, money doubles in 25 years; at 6 percent, in about 12 years. (A handy rule of thumb is that doubling time is approximately equal to 70 divided by the growth rate.) The rate of natural increase in a year is: [(total births)—(total deaths)] ÷ (population). The rate for Canada in 1973 was 0.83 percent, i.e., a doubling of population about every 84 years (apart from the extra effect of immigration).

[10] See the study, *The Limits to Growth* (Universe Books, New York, 1972), prepared at MIT for the Club of Rome by Dennis Meadows and other disciples of Jay Forrester, the inventor of the computer's ceramic memory device and philosopher of industrial, urban, and world dynamics. Excerpts from this study appear in Paul A. Samuelson, *Readings in Economics* (McGraw-Hill, New York, 1973, 7th ed.).

POPULATION OF THE WORLD (in millions)				
	1800	1940	1970	1985 (estimate)
Europe (including all of U.S.S.R.)	188	572	705	802
North, South, and Central America	29	277	511	715
Asia, Africa, and Oceania	702	1,396	2,416	3,416
World	919	2,245	3,632	4,933

TABLE 2-3. World population quadrupled since 1800. Even with birth rates falling generally, population of the less developed world will grow relative to the developed world: instead of having twice the population of the developed regions as now, a century from now the presently undeveloped countries will have six times as many people! (Source: UNESCO.)

the net numerical effect has been much as Malthus foretold, in these countries where the balance of numbers and food supply is vital.

Table 2-3 shows how much world population has increased.[11] This increase was made possible mainly through the declining death rate, resulting from scientific advances in medicine and from the improved living standards made possible by the Industrial Revolution. Life expectancy of a Western baby has doubled since 1800 to over 70 years at present, and standards of living far exceed those of any previous century.

Even more dramatic has been the reduction in death rates in low-income regions. Ceylon offers the dramatic case where control of mosquitoes by DDT greatly reduced malaria, cutting the death rate by 34 per cent in a single year.[12] In India alone, one of the fruits of modern science has been a great increase in average life expectancy. In the last 20 years India's population grew by at least 120 million, an amount greater than the combined populations of France and England. Professor Kingsley Davis of California, an expert on population, has warned against the facile

[11] An official estimate places 1974 population of the People's Republic of China at about 800,000,000.

[12] The side-effects or long-run repercussions of DDT usage are now being felt. However, it *did* reduce Ceylon's death rate by substantially eliminating malaria.

belief that it is primarily hunger (or even malnutrition) which makes life so short in poor societies. Disease is important as an independent factor: if science greatly lengthens life without greatly increasing productivity and greatly changing preindustrial attitudes, the fears of Malthus take on a new relevance.

CONTROLLING POPULATION GROWTH

As we shall see in Part Six, much of the world is in a state of underdevelopment and poverty. If the birth rate were to continue at the high levels typical of the past—when you had to have six or more children in order to ensure that there would be a surviving child to feed you in your old age and to carry on your line —population numbers would explode, and the law of diminishing returns would wipe out the gains from technical progress. Little wonder then that, wherever religious and ethical attitudes permit, there is beginning to be an active birth-control movement.

As fewer children die before adulthood, people all over the world seem eager to limit unwanted births. Slowly but surely there has been increased use of the loop, the Pill, and other chemical and mechanical devices; there have been changes in mental attitudes, particularly where women are able to control fertility, so that even methods based on rhythm are applied more effectively; sterilization—male vasectomy, tube tying, etc.—often follows on attainment of desired family size. The older practices of infanticide and infant exposure, relied on in the past by so many cultures, have given way to legal and illegal abortions. Ethical debate accelerates over celibacy and chastity, the right to life of the embryo and foetus, women's liberation and the cult of masculinity ("machismo"). Yet it remains the sober truth that *the globe's population is growing more rapidly right now than ever before in the history of the world!*

DECLINE AND RISE OF BIRTH RATES

At the end of World War I, people still feared the Malthusian curse of overpopulation. However, within a generation, the pendulum had swung to the other extreme; for Western Europe and most of North America were undergoing a profound revolution in population, and best sellers carried such flashy titles as *The Twilight of Parenthood* and *England Without People.*

After 1870—earlier in France—birth rates began to drop in most countries of Western European civilization. After World War I, and especially after the Great Depression of the 1930s, the drop became precipitous.

This trend was reflected in the Canadian fertility rate, shown in Table 2-4. (This rate is found by summing the number of thousand children born in a year per thousand women in each of the childbearing years, 15 to 49. This is equivalent to the average number of live children a woman would bear if she passed through her years of potential motherhood with the fertility of women for each age current in the given year.)

Thus before World War II, there was reason for the population expert to despair for the future of the population of Western nations. Indeed, in 1943 one member of parliament remarked that the case for the new family allowances rested on the fact "that we already are within sight of the beginning of a decline in our population." The following year, the Family Allowance Act was passed granting to mothers a monthly average allowance of $6.04 per child.

WAR AND POSTWAR UPSWING IN FERTILITY Just then a remarkable reversal occurred. The full explanation has not yet been found. During and after World War II the pattern of fertility began steadily to climb.

Some of the reasons are, of course, obvious. With the war came prosperity, and the backlog of depression-deferred marriages began to melt. The desire to avoid wartime conscription, and postwar arrival of

COMPONENTS OF CANADIAN POPULATION GROWTH RATES[1] 1870—1973

Year	(1)[2] Population as of June 1	(2) Birth Rate	(3) Death Rate	(4) Natural Increase	(5) Immigration Rate	(6) Emigration Rate	(7) Net Rate of Increase	(8)[3] Total Fertility Rate
1870	3,625	33.7	17.4	16.3	6.8	6.0	17.1	n.a.
1880	4,255	32.5	16.9	15.6	8.8	7.9	14.7	n.a.
1890	4,779	28.6	17.0	11.6	15.6	16.0	11.2	n.a.
1900	5,301	27.2	16.2	11.0	7.8	5.6	13.2	n.a.
1910	6,988	30.4	13.1	17.3	40.3	28.6	29.0	n.a.
1920	8,556	29.2	13.3	15.9	16.0	4.6	27.3	n.a.
1931	10,377	23.0	10.1	12.9	2.3	2.3	12.8	3.20
1941	11,506	22.7	10.0	12.7	0.8	0.7	12.8	2.82
1946	12,292	28.8	9.4	19.4	4.9	3.3	21.1	3.36
1951	14,009	27.8	8.8	19.0	15.4	2.3	32.1	3.48
1956	16,081	28.6	8.2	20.4	15.8	3.4	32.9	3.85
1961	18,238	25.9	7.8	18.1	3.8	3.0	18.9	3.86
1966	20,015	19.0	7.4	11.6	10.7	4.2	18.1	2.83
1969	21,001	17.6	7.4	10.2	7.7	3.9	14.1	2.39
1970	21,297	17.2	7.4	9.8	6.5	3.6	12.7	2.31
1971	21,568	16.8	7.3	9.5	5.7	3.4	11.7	2.19
1972	21,820	16.6	7.4	9.2	5.6	1.9	12.9	2.14
1973	22,095	15.9	7.4	8.5	8.3	n.a.	n.a.	n.a.

[1] Growth rates are number per 1,000 of population per year
[2] Population for 1901 and before are as of April 1
[3] Fertility rate is the sum of age—specific fertility rates
n.a. = not available at time of publication—Fertility rates for 1870—1925 do not exist.

TABLE 2-4

(Sources: O. J. Firestone, *Canada's Economic Development 1867-1953* (London, 1958); M. C. Urquhart and K. A. H. Buckley, *Historical Statistics of Canada,* (Toronto, 1965); A. Romaniuc, "Potentials for Population Growth in Canada: A Long-term Projection", *A Population Policy for Canada,* by the Conservation Council of Ontario and The Family Planning Federation of Canada (Toronto, 1973); *Bank of Canada Review, May 1974* (Ottawa, 1974); Statistics Canada 91-514, *Population Projections for Canada and the Provinces 1972-2001.*

NET REPRODUCTION RATES FOR VARIOUS COUNTRIES

Canada	1.28	1930-35	Germany		
	1.16	1935-39	Total	0.71	1933
	1.03	1971	West	1.18	1966
United States			Belgium	0.90	1939
Total	0.98	1930-40		1.13	1967
	1.72	1960	Netherlands	1.15	1935-39
	1.07	1971		1.28	1968
White	0.96	1935-40	Australia	0.98	1935-39
	1.66	1960		1.35	1966
	1.16	1967	Palestine		
Nonwhite	1.14	1935-40	Moslems	2.17	1940
	2.04	1960	Jews	1.61	1945
	1.56	1967	Israel		
United Kingdom	0.78	1935-39	Jews	1.73	1966
	1.29	1966	Japan	1.49	1935-39
France	0.87	1935-37		0.74	1966
	1.25	1967	India	1.25	1931
Sweden	0.78	1935-39		1.31	1941
	1.09	1967	Soviet Union	1.72	1926
				1.54	1938
				1.14	1965

TABLE 2-5. Net reproduction rates make correction for changing age distribution: A NRR (net reproduction rate) permanently greater than 1 means ultimate population growth. A NRR less than 1 means ultimate population decline. The NRR for Canada is now barely above 1. (Source: Office of Population Research, Princeton University; authors.)

unmarried immigrants, also had something to do with the increase in marriages. The number of bachelors and spinsters shrank; and the age of (first) marriage fell sharply, so that more than half the girls were married by the time they were twenty-one, and half the men by the age of twenty-two!

With many more recent marriages, it was only natural to expect the fertility rate to leap upward. But more than that, couples stepped up the rate at which they had children. In the 1950s third and fourth children became fashionable among all classes, a dramatic reversal from the prewar situation. (See Figure 2-9)

FERTILITY RATES, BIRTH RATES, AND NET REPRODUCTION RATES

The crude birth rate, the ratio of total births per year to total population (*not* the ratio of births to potential mothers as is often thought) can be very mis-

leading. For example, when fertility was falling in the 1930's, and some American and European populations (not Canada's) had really begun to fail to reproduce themselves, crude birth rates fell only slowly and disguised this fact. Why? For the reason that, in those years, there were so many women of childbearing age in consequence of the large families of *their* mothers' fertile 1900 generation.

How can we correct for these temporary ups and downs in the age structure of the population? Demographers do so by concentrating on "age-specific fertility." That is, they ask: How many births occur to 1,000 women of age 15-19, age 20-24, ... age 45-49. They are then in a position to construct more useful measurements of fertility such as the total fertility rate, defined on page 28 and presented in Table 2-4.

Another measurement, which also takes account of death rates, is the net reproduction rate (NRR). Demographers ask how many total births will 1,000 newly born female babies give rise to throughout their lives? Only if this generation's 1,000 women leave behind them more than 1,000 girl babies (who in turn do the same, . . .) will the population hold its own in the long run.[13]

Table 2-5 shows that the richer countries of Western Europe had pre-World War II net reproduction rates (NRR) far below unity. Then, from 1940 to 1960, they had rates *far above* the critical level of unity. Since 1960, NRRs have fallen everywhere.

ANOTHER TURN OF THE TIDE

Throughout North America, fertility rates at all ages of mothers began to fall sharply in 1959-60, pulling the NRR down with it. The *total* number of children born in Canada peaked in 1958 and is now one-third lower, even though the female population is one-third higher. The fertility rate has plummeted toward the crucial 2.13 figure at which a mother and father just replace themselves. A fertility rate of about 2.13, in Canada, currently yields a NRR of 1.00.[14]

In 1969, the rise in the number of new families did reverse the decline in the total number of births, but only for two or three years.

---

[13] The total fertility rate, already defined as the average number of live children a woman would bear, if she passed through her years of potential motherhood maintaining the current fertility of women at each age, is computed as follows:

Total Fertility Rate (for a given year) = [(live births in year to mothers of age 15) ÷ (no. of 15-year-old women)] + [(no. of live births in year to mothers of age 16) ÷ (no. of 16-year-old women)] + . . . + [(no. of live births in year to mothers of age 25) ÷ (no. of 25-year-old women)] + . . . + [(no. of live births to mothers of age 49) ÷ (no. of 49-year-old women)]

Demographers define the net reproduction rate (NRR) as the average number of *girl* babies that will be born to a representative newly born girl in her lifetime." Thus, if 1,000 girls born in 1970 will, by 2015 A.D., have produced 1,600 girl babies, the NRR = 1,600/1,000 = 1.6; and were such a rate to be maintained indefinitely, population would ultimately be growing at the rate of 60 per cent per "generation", i.e., about every 25 years, the average age of a mother when giving birth. (Explain exactly what NRR = 0.7 or = 1.0 means, showing why 1.0 is the watershed between decay and positive growth.)

[14] The current world fertility rate has been estimated at 4.7, made up of 2.7 in developed countries and 5.7 in underdeveloped nations. For a world forecast that uses these concepts, see Tomas Frejka, "The Prospects for a Stationary Population", *Scientific American*, March 1973.

There are two reasons why the critical fertility rate is significantly higher than 2.0. First, there are more males born than females (recall that the NRR depends only on female births while the fertility rate considers *all* live births); and second, some females die before reaching or completing their childbearing years.

ECONOMICS AND SOCIOLOGY No doubt economic factors are involved here. Professor Richard Easterlin of the University of Pennsylvania has put forward an interesting hypothesis. He speculates that a young married couple will be less eager to have many children if their current income is falling far below that which their own families had a few years earlier. He points out that in the 1950s, when young people were scarce and their incomes relatively high, they hastened to have many children. In the early 1970s, when the vast crop of war babies has been coming into the labor market and bidding down incomes, the comparison is less favorable. In Easterlin's view, this helps to explain the decline in NRR.[15]

Women's liberation and new patterns of social psychology reinforce these economic factors. Mothers with infants are beginning to stay in the labor market. Demands for day-care centers will undoubtedly accelerate. The Census reports a clear pattern: In those regions where income opportunities for women are most favorable, the birth rate has dropped most. Thus, economics and sociology are mutually reinforcing.

Whatever the explanation of the turn of the tide in North America, let us be clear on four things: (a) the Canadian birth rate, until the 1970s a little higher than the American but about the same in the 1970s, tends to rise and fall at the same times; (b) both rates have been high compared to those in other advanced nations; (c) even if fertility rates continue to fall, total Canadian births should rise in this decade because of family formation among members of the post-war baby boom; (d) birth rates in North America and Europe are as little as one-half of those in Africa and Latin America; and there is considerable variation among the less developed countries' birth rates.

When birth rates fall, migration becomes a strong force shaping national populations.

MIGRATION

Canada's is an open economy—immigrants and their families add to the population and emigrants reduce it. Three great periods of immigration (1880-1890,

---

[15] Data limitations have made it difficult for Canadian demographers to either confirm or reject this hypothesis.

1900-1930, and 1950-1960) brought almost two-thirds of the nine million settlers and workers who have come to Canada. Most of these new arrivals have been between 20 and 44 years of age, and have tended to distort the age-structure pattern. In some decades, however, emigration from Canada (mostly to the United States) has exceeded the inflow (mostly from Europe); and, over the past 120 years, emigration is believed to have offset more than three-quarters of immigration. (See Table 2-4.) This musical chairs game was formerly regarded as a "displacement" of resident Canadians by foreigners, and gave support to the political theory that Canada was not able to absorb large numbers of new workers and dependents. But recent data suggest that it is largely the new immigrants themselves who move on to the United States or back to their country of birth, a certain percentage remaining permanently in Canada.

Thus as Fig. 2-9 shows, the net migration rate [(immigration) − (emigration)] ÷ (population) has generally been positive since World War I.

PREDICTING CANADA'S POPULATION

We can see how these ideas and concepts are applied by examining Fig. 2-9.[16] The heavy line shows the total population of Canada since 1900. Throughout the period, death rates have fallen steadily but fertility rates have bounced up and down as shown in Fig. 2-9. Interestingly, the cycles of net immigration rate and fertility have been parallel, suggesting that young families faced with the socio-economic forces mentioned above, have decided to migrate on the same motives as they have decided on having children.

The dashed lines show how population experts have attempted to forecast Canadian population. Number 1 was made in 1936, and, reflecting the current perspectives about fertility and immigration, disastrously undershot after 1950.

Number 2, made in 1956, had been misled by the high fertility rates of those years into overestimating the population of the 1970's.

Number 3 is a mechanical projection based on the rate of natural increase of the early 1970's, plus net immigration of 100,000 per year.

Number 4, by Dr. A. Romaniuc, reflects a courageous attempt to forcast Canadian fertility rates. In the variant shown, these are assumed to fall from 2.19 in 1971 to 1.90 (less than replacement!) by 1985, and to remain constant thereafter. (Net immigration is assumed to be 100,000 per year.)

On these bases, the total population should be in the neighbourhood of 40 million in 2030 A.D. However, should the fertility rate *rise* to 2.82 by 1985, population by 2030 would soar to 60 million!

Lesser assumed migration flows, of course, lower these forecasts, but the larger the country, the smaller is the quantative importance of new arrivals. Thus everything turns on family size. Will the tide turn again? [17]

ECONOMIC EFFECTS OF POPULATION GROWTH

The economic impact of large population changes is easily observable. The sprawling suburbs and numerous new schools of the 1960s reflected the post-war population upsurge. And the unused elementary and secondary classrooms of the 1970s show how that boom has dwindled. People of university age will be twice as numerous in 1981 as they were in 1961 (and may well decide to double the post-secondary enrollment of 1974).

[16] (1) Highest of two 1936 projections by M. C. McClean and W. Burton Hurd assumes no net migration and a fertility rate of about 2.9.
(2) Hood-Scott forecast assuming net immigration of 75,000 annually, initial (1955) fertility rate of 3.74 and 1985 fertility rate of .3.51.
(3) Crude 1973 projection assuming 100,000 net immigration and net rate of natural increase of 0.85 percent.
(4) A. Romaniuc 1972 forecast assuming net immigration of 100,000, computed on the basis of a declining fertility rate to 1985, and a constant fertility rate of 1.90 thereafter. (Published in *A Population Policy for Canada*, Toronto, 1973.)

[17] Since this Figure was prepared, Statistics Canada's population estimates and projections division has prepared further projections. See for example *Population Projections for Canada and the Provinces 1972-2001*, Catalogue No. 91-514, Information Canada, June 1974. This group's "low" projection for fertility for 1985 was 1.80; and its "medium" projection was 2.20. See also various papers by W. M. Illing, for example, CANDIDE, Project No. 9, Economic Council of Canada, Ottawa.

FIG. 2-9. Population forecasts are usually wrong.
Canadian population is shown here on a "ratio" scale, with equal percentage changes being represented by equal distances. This technique tends to flatten out the exponential percentage growth rates shown. (Source: See footnote 15)

Today about 37 percent of the Canadian population is under 20 years of age. With the low forecast mentioned above, the population will "age" remarkably, only 22 percent being under 20 by 2031. Almost one-quarter of Canada's population will be over 65, dependent on the labor force for its income. However, if the population soars to 60 million, with high immigration, the age structure will be much more youthful, with only 14 percent of the population over 65.

ZERO POPULATION GROWTH   As we shall see repeatedly, in Part Six and elsewhere, there is now a strong movement for Zero Population Growth (ZPG). Even if, for the advanced countries like the United States, there is little likelihood of famine and lagging food supplies in the next half-century, what about the long, long run? What about the amenities of life—elbow room and open spaces? What about pollution and ecology? What about the ethics of those in the advanced world, who, just because they reached affluence first, have been getting more than their fair share of the depletable natural resources of the world—rich copper, iron, and oil deposits?

Slowdown in growth of numbers could not alone alleviate the crisis in ecology. *At least two-thirds of the problem stems from our burgeoning per capita standard of life.* Just so that more people can have more fast cars and more comfortable home environments summer and winter, the globe is ravaged by strip mining, oil spills into the ocean, and threats of nuclear radioactivity from power generation.

Moreover, to stop population growth in its tracks now, it would not suffice to bring the NRR down to 1. To accomplish no growth in numbers, the current generation would have to drop its average family size down to one child per family, not merely reduce it from three to two. So the problem will long remain: How can we improve the quality of life for our still growing (albeit more slowly growing) population?

ECONOMIC ISSUES IN POPULATION TRENDS   We have seen that limited growth in population is vital for the underdeveloped world because of the ancient curse of Malthusian diminishing returns. We shall see in later chapters that for the advanced nations, there may be an optimum population size, not too large and not too small, but where scale is just large enough to permit an optimal division of labor.

Can a nation afford *not* to grow? If living in and having large families are deemed pleasures, stabilizing the population will involve some inevitable psychic costs. But what if the alternative is eventually standing room only?

Consider another problem. It was not so long ago that people said, "Babies are good for the diaper and baby-food industry. Young people are needed if we are to have jobs in the beer, record, and ice cream industries. In a growing population, the need to provide durable goods for the population creates a favorable balance of investment in relation to saving and avoids mass unemployment. In short, a capitalistic society cannot afford not to have GNP growth, lest grass grow in the streets."

We shall see, when we come to master Part Two's analysis of the post-Keynesian mixed economy, that society today—perhaps for the first time!—*can afford not to grow* in numbers if that is what most pleases the people. Just as there is no need to dig holes and fill them up just to make jobs, so there is no longer need to go through the motions of filling up the countryside with people just in order to keep the wheels of industry humming nicely.

ESTIMATED FUTURE POPULATION OF DIFFERENT COUNTRIES IN 1985 (in millions)

	ANNUAL GROWTH (% per year)	1970	1980	1985
United States	1.3	205	235	253
United Kingdom	0.6	55.7	59.5	61.8
France	0.8	50.8	55.3	57.6
Soviet Union	1.0	243	271	287
Sweden	0.7	8.0	8.6	8.8
Italy	0.8	53.7	57.9	60.0
Japan	1.2	103	116	121

TABLE 2-6. Nation sizes will look different in the future.
Any differences in growth rate accumulate into significant changes. Note how the United States and the Soviet Union grow relative to Western Europe. (Source: United Nations.)

SUMMARY

A. PROBLEMS OF ECONOMIC ORGANIZATION

1 Every economy must somehow solve three fundamental economic problems: WHAT kinds and quantities shall be produced of all possible goods and services; HOW economic resources shall be used in producing these goods; and FOR WHOM the goods shall be produced, i.e., the distribution of income among different individuals and classes.

2 Societies meet these problems in different ways—by custom, instinct, command and in our mixed economy, largely by a system of price and markets.

3 The basic problems are important because of the fundamental fact of all economic life: with limited resources and technology, standards of living are limited. Economic goods are *scarce* rather than free: society must choose among them, because not all needs and desires can be fulfilled.

B. TECHNOLOGICAL CHOICES OPEN TO ANY SOCIETY

4 With given resources and technology, the production choices open to a nation between two such goods as butter and guns can be summarized in the *production-possibility curve*, or *frontier*. This indicates the way in which one good can be transformed into another by transferring resources from its production to that of the other.

5 Production-possibility curves can illustrate many basic economic processes: how we use relatively *less* of our resources for food *necessities* as we develop; how we choose between *private* market goods and *public* governmental goods; choose between *current consumption* and *capital goods* that enhance *future* capacity to produce. The *p-p frontier* can illustrate *technical progress* and pave the way for diminishing returns.

6 *The law of diminishing returns* asserts that, after a point, as we add more and more of a variable factor input (such as labor) to a fixed factor input (such as land), the amount of extra product will fall off. This law is really a matter of proportions: the varying factor input has less and less of the fixed factor input to work with.

7 *Economies of mass production or of scale* are often described as "increasing returns *to scale.*" The word "scale" is a warning that *all* factor inputs are being varied simultaneously, with none held fixed as in the law of diminishing returns. Many processes do pass through an initial stage of increasing returns to scale.

8 In accordance with the *law of increasing-relative costs,* to get equal extra amounts of one good you must incur the sacrifice of ever larger amounts of other goods. This is shown by a bowed-out (concave from below) *p-p frontier.* Only if the two industries used all productive factors in the same proportion would you be able to avoid encountering the law of diminishing returns as you transfer relatively more of a varying factor onto another relatively fixed factor.

C. UNDERLYING POPULATION BASIS OF ANY ECONOMY: PAST AND FUTURE POPULATION TRENDS

9 Malthus' theory of population rests on the law of diminishing returns. He thought that a population, if unchecked, would tend to grow in geometric rate, doubling every generation or so. But each member of the growing population would have less natural resources and land to work with. Therefore, because of diminishing returns, income

would have a tendency to fall so low as to lead to a stable population at a level of starvation and pestilence.

10 For a century and a half after Malthus, populations grew by leaps and bounds everywhere. Numbers grew primarily because death rates fell sharply as a result of improved medical and public health technology; yet technological progress in industry more than offset the law of diminishing returns.

11 After 1870 fertility rates began to fall. Prior to World War II, advanced nations had net reproduction rates below 1 and faced depopulation. After 1939, the middle classes temporarily swung back toward a larger-family pattern. But in recent years, there has been a general swing of the tide back toward much lower fertility rates. Zero Population Growth (ZPG) is a movement that the modern economy can afford if it wants to.

12 Immigration is an important but declining influence on Canadian population. Emigration, and fertility, now attract more attention than the immigration of workers and their families.

CONCEPTS FOR REVIEW

economic and free goods
distribution
substitution and law of scarcity
production-possibility frontier
law of diminishing returns
total versus extra product
productive factors or inputs

increasing returns to scale
law of increasing (relative) costs
    of one good for another
Malthusian population theory
age distribution of population
net reproduction rate (NRR), ZPG
idle resources and unemployment

QUESTIONS FOR DISCUSSION

1. Without looking at the next chapter, can you anticipate how a price system through supply and demand solves the three problems of economic organization?

2. Explain what economists mean by "*scarcity*," by *free goods*, by *inefficiency*.

3. Draw society's *p-p frontier* if scientific inventions increased the productivity of given resources in butter production only, and not in guns.

4. If land were increased in a number of steps and labor were held constant, would the law of diminishing returns hold? Illustrate and tell why this would indeed happen.

5. Describe and contrast (a) the law of diminishing returns; (b) the law of increasing (relative) costs; (c) the phenomenon of increasing returns to scale.

6. How many children were there in your great-grandparents' family? In your parents' family? How many do you think there will be in your own family?

7. "Population pressure doesn't cause war, as is commonly believed. Careful study suggests cause and effect are just the reverse. Nations that want to expand try to persuade their citizens to grow in numbers so the nation will be militarily strong and will have a pretext for expansion." Discuss.

8. "A *geometric progression* is a sequence of terms $[g_1, g_2, \ldots, g_t, g_{t+1}, \ldots]$ in which each term is *the same multiple* of its predecessor, $g_2/g_1 = g_3/g_2 = \cdots = g_{t+1}/g_t = \beta$. If $\beta = 1 + i > 1$, the terms grow like compound interest. An *arithmetic progression* is a sequence $[a_1, a_2, a_3, \ldots, a_t, a_{t+1}, \ldots]$ in which the *difference* between each term and its predecessor is the same constant: $a_2 - a_1 = a_3 - a_2 = \cdots = a_{t+1} - a_t = \alpha$." (Malthus

gratuitously assumed food to grow in an arithmetic progression.) Give examples of each. Satisfy yourself that any geometric progression must *eventually* surpass any arithmetic progression.

9. *Extra-credit problem* for those mathematically inclined: We can illustrate the "linear programming" technique referred to in footnote 3 on Stigler's least-cost-diet problem. Suppose each unit of milk, beans, and meat has respectively (1, 8, 2) calories and (4, 2, 1) vitamins. Suppose each unit of the 3 goods costs ($1, $2, $3) respectively. Suppose you must buy at least 120 calorie units per month and 180 vitamin units. Can you show by experiment that the least monthly cost is $60 per month, with meat not being bought at all, and with milk at 40 and beans at 10 units? Mathematically the linear programmer writes this as

$$\text{Minimize } Z = \$1X_1 + \$2X_2 + \$3X_3, \text{ subject to}$$
$$1X_1 + 8X_2 + 2X_3 \geq 120$$
$$4X_1 + 2X_2 + 1X_3 \geq 180$$
$$X_1 \geq 0, X_2 \geq 0, X_3 \geq 0$$

A similar linear programming problem will define a *p-p frontier* like that shown here. Suppose food (such as butter) and manufactures (such as clothing) each take 1 unit of labor. But food, being land intensive, takes 4 acres of land, while manufactures take only 1 acre. If society has 1 (million) men and 2 (million) acres, the frontier is defined by

$$1X_1 + 1X_2 \leq 1$$
$$4X_1 + 1X_2 \leq 2$$

the first giving the heavy dark red part and the second the heavy light red part.

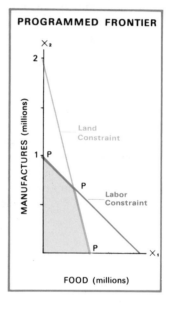

PROGRAMMED FRONTIER

Appendix: Alternative Economic Organizations

THE CHOICE

Surprisingly many ways of organizing the economy are in use: tribal custom, feudalism, religious sanctions, and so forth. In the more developed societies, however, the range of choice among types of organization is narrowed. The requirements become demanding. A workable industrialized system must be able to answer the WHAT, HOW, and FOR WHOM questions satisfactorily to a large sophisticated population, while adapting to changing tastes for new products and the advancing techniques for making them. Indeed most people would say that the choice had, after the last 100 years, narrowed to two: capitalism versus the various forms of collectivism. This Appendix is concerned mainly about the forms that socialist and communist, economic organization may take.

Of course, historians will rightly object to the idea of "choice" of economic system. Few peoples have had the opportunity to pick their next system from a menu; and revolution has, like indigestion, often been required to correct their choices. Rather, most societies have, while developing, simply adapted the systems used by their neighbors or imposed by their conquerors. Thus in 1867 the Fathers of Confederation felt neither the desire nor the power to devise a new scheme for organizing the Canadian division of labor, trade, specialization. Instead they carried on the individualist system then in use in Britain and the United States, already familiar to farmers and businessmen in Quebec and the other provinces.

This Appendix is also designed to correct the impression that the alternative systems are definite and uniform. Our own system, for example, is a changing compromise. It is often called "capitalist" in that most productive capital goods are the private property of persons and firms, who thus tend to steer our economy's production differently from how it would be steered if capital were collective, or state, property. But in this book we see again and again that decisions about the use and price of capital are to some degree influenced or even made by the state. The state also influences choices and decisions about work, families, saving, and so forth. So "capitalism," like the "enterprise system," "price system," and "market system," is simply a description of part of what is called hereafter the *mixed economy*.

Pure capitalism, undiluted *laissez-faire*, died before Queen Victoria did. The rest of this book will be about the mixed economy. So let us turn briefly to the systems.

THE CRISIS OF CAPITALISM

Marx wrote *Das Kapital*, subtitled "an analysis of capitalist production," in 1867. He dwelt mainly on the historical development and stability of the European economy's stages, culminating in the industrialization of the 19th century, as perceived alike by him, his utopian-socialist contemporaries, and the classical political economists Adam Smith and David Ricardo. Arguing that the capitalist system could no longer perform the complicated tasks assigned to it, he foretold repeated and deepening "crises" of shortage, hunger, unemployment, and revolt until a new power appeared capable of sweeping away the old and creating the new system.

World War I appeared to many to be this final crisis of the old system, and in Russia a Marxist revolt did sweep away much of the old. But elsewhere new governments of new states were established on non-revolutionary lines, and the future of the capitalist way of life seemed, for a decade, serene.

Then it was assailed by the rise of the dictatorships, the Great Depression, and the next war. By 1950 the war-weakened world economy was divided into great blocs. The great communist powers, the Soviet Union and China, and the other socialist countries of Eastern Europe formed one such bloc. On the other side was "the West," a non-homogeneous collection of mixed economies ranging from right-wing Switzerland and America to left-wing Norway and New Zealand. And a little aside stood a third bloc, the watchful new nations and the old less-developed nations, committed to neither economic system represented by the other two blocs.

Little wonder, then, that profound social philosophers, like Harvard's Joseph Schumpeter, thought in 1945 that they could foresee the end of capitalism in the next few years. Rejecting the Marxist predictions, they nevertheless feared that the staggering problems of development and post-war recurring cycles of inflation and unemployment would lead the West to massive state interventions that would, in themselves, amount to the end of capitalism.

In this they were apparently wrong. The modern mixed economy, using the "new economics" of monetary and fiscal policy,[1] has been able to perform well against cyclical instability. The war-destroyed European nations recovered by a mixture of private initiative and state planning. Japan, Israel, and other less-developed societies all sprinted ahead. Rates of productivity growth increased everywhere. The Marxian historical timetable—savagery to feudalism, feudalism to capitalism, capitalism to socialism and on to communism—has for the moment been shown not to be inevitable. Is it a fairy tale?

This question, of the inevitability of final capitalist crisis and the resurgence of peoples in new economic systems, is itself a sufficient reason to survey the alternative systems, not all of which are Marxist.[2] The systems are also of interest as part of the intellectual history of the human

[1]As outlined in Chapters 13 to 16 later in this book.
[2]See the Appendix to the next chapter, page 57.

race, and of the social history of protest. But most of all, they are of interest in disabusing our minds of the tyranny of certain facile generalizations which, like most facile generalizations, simply will not stand up to the hard facts of actual experience.

Thus, is it true that without free markets for goods and services, democratic freedoms and political civil rights cannot prevail? Many economic libertarians argue that *personal liberties* and *property* liberties are one and are inseparable. But are they right? At the other extreme, many advocates of socialism argue that "political democracy" is but a sham if the state does not get rid of "production for profit" and replace it by "production for use" and guarantee "fair shares" all around. But are they right?

And in particular, is the argument correct in the learned and persuasive book, *The Road to Serfdom* (1945), by Friedrich Hayek (of Austria, Britain, the United States, and Germany), that each step away from the market system and toward the social reforms of the welfare state, is *inevitably* a journey that must end in a totalitarian state with neither efficiency nor liberty? The opposing view is that gradual evolutionary reforms are the only way to prevent a cataclysmic descent through revolution into communist dictatorship. If the evolutionists are right, Hayek is quite wrong. Let us review the troops.

A BOUQUET OF ISMS

Men have always had visions of a more perfect society: Plato's Republic, Sir Thomas More's Utopia, Marx's Dictatorship of the Proletariat, and so on without number. It is only too easy to look at concrete present-day imperfections and then to contrast them with the ideal features of a vaguely defined utopia. Beyond agreeing that the present order has faults, different schools of reform have little in common.

At the one extreme are the anarchists, who believe in no government at all; at the other, the apologists for an all-powerful collectivized, totalitarian, communistic social order, where the first person singular is all but replaced by the first person plural. Within the field of socialism itself, we find subdivisions: Christian socialism, state and Marxian socialism, guild socialism, Fabian (evolutionary) socialism, and many others.

In the minds of some Canadians, socialists are still bearded characters who meet in a candle-lit cellar to plot sabotage and bloody revolution. Worse, such people use the term "socialist" as a disparaging stereotype to discredit anyone who believes in pensions, medical services, progressive taxation, monopoly regulation, a tax on capital gains, free love, or even the encouragement of student protest.

Some are so suspicious that they support some welfare and socialization policies in order to "forestall the socialists." At the other extreme are people who have brought with them various brands of socialism or Marxism from their European birthplaces, agrarian radicals, home-made revolutionaries, and a very large group whose ideas stem from their trade union affiliations, ranging from Gompers-type laborism and Catholic socialism to west-coast syndicalism and communism. (The reader should turn to Chapter 7 for a description of these threads in our labor organization.) Many persons at the "left" of this wide and disparate spectrum of theories adhere to the New Democratic Party (NDP, based on the former CCF) or to Bolshevik, Maoist, Trotskyite or other communist parties. But political loyalties aside, some "socialist" ideas will be found in the platforms or the minds and members of all parties: Quebec Liberals and separatists, prairie Conservatives, and British Columbian Social Crediters.

Looking abroad, we see that while the United States has managed to sustain two huge parties both of which are free to advocate the free-enterprise system while experimenting with elements from other "isms," elsewhere politics are generally divided among anywhere from three to twelve or more parties. Almost all have the words "liberal," "radical," "progressive," or "socialist" in their titles, and we must be careful in interpreting their viewpoints. First, bear in mind that European parties often represent a *class* of persons: farmers, pensioners, small retail traders, landholders, industrialists, workers, or other distinct groups. The name matters less than the representation. Second, "liberalism" in Europe was a nineteenth-century revulsion from church, nobility, and government toward individual self-determination; "radicalism" was an extreme form of this individualism. Thus radicals often oppose what we now think of as left-wing objectives. Third, "progressives" stand for different things in different places. In Canada and the United States in the 1920s and 1930s they were western-farm-based and stood for easy money in financial policy and for a mixture of individualism and collectivism in other economic matters. But elsewhere the word is associated with socialist aims. Fourth, "socialism" does not mean much in a European party title: France has a party paradoxically called Radical Socialist, which is radical (individualist) and conservative. Even Hitler's party was called "national socialist" (Nazi).

One important distinction most "socialist" parties do wish to maintain is the difference between the *means* each advocates on the route to socialism. Some espouse violence, revolution, and the seizure of property and the reins of power. Others, like Britain's Labour Party and the ruling parties in most of Scandinavia pursue a gradual, non-revolutionary extension of socialism by peaceful and democratic means. Although they differ from the European social democrats in important details, Canada's socialists in the NDP party would wish to be classified with them when a broad survey of all the "isms" is being made.

It is clear, therefore, that we do not have to master all the thousand and one different "isms" in order to understand the world today. It is enough to understand something of (a) relative *laissez-faire*, or mixed-economy private enterprise, (b) socialism, (c) communism, and (d) fascism. There is no hard and fast boundary between these; it is a matter of degree. Moreover, we cannot even range these along a line, with fascism at the extreme right

wing and communism at the extreme left wing. In some ways—although neither would admit it—communism and fascism have much in common.

FASCISM

This is easier to characterize politically than economically. Be it in Hitler's Germany, Mussolini's Italy, Franco's Spain, Salazar's Portugal, or Perón's Argentina, fascism is usually characterized by a one-man dictatorship, by one political party with all others abolished, by the disappearance of civil liberties of the type granted in our Bill of Rights. Fascistic movements are always highly nationalistic, often with emphasis placed on a vaguely defined "master race" which exploits minority groups. In the words of Mussolini, fascists are urged to "live dangerously"—to value war and national power as ends in themselves. The individual is to be secondary to the state.

On the economic side, Mussolini's fascism happened to toy with the notion of a "syndicalist," or "corporate," state; each industry and group of workers was organized in a syndicate, and these were to meet and bargain and plan how the economy should be run. However, this syndicalism has never come to much and has not been especially characteristic of other fascist regimes. Almost all of them are against free and militant trade-unionism; almost all give the central government great regulatory power over every sphere of economic life. Some work hand in glove with religious authorities; others are anti-church. Often capitalists and the lower middle classes contribute to the initial strength of fascist movements; but later, when the fascist movement begins to take on—as they sometimes do—revolutionary aspects, the capitalists may regret the Frankenstein's monster that they helped to create.

Their only consolation lies in the fact that one of the earmarks of a fascist regime is opposition to communism; often it sails into power by exaggerating the immediate likelihood of a Bolshevik revolution, and after it has come into power, the threat of communism is used as an excuse for the suppression of democratic processes.

Fascism is the great spoiler. It thrives on the breakdown of markets and democratic processes. Often its leaders are revolutionaries turned reactionary. Its followers are military officers, dispossessed farmers and small merchants, groups who are losing economic and social status or who resent newly rising groups—big business, blacks, foreigners, the poor living on governmental welfare assistance, etc. Big business itself chimes in, both to hedge its bets and in token of its fear of a communist takeover.

ORDER AND ECONOMIC EFFICIENCY? We have seen that many economies may be subject to the disorder of creeping inflation. Full employment and price stability are then apparently incompatible goals. Undoubtedly, the struggle by union workers to raise their hourly wage rate has for its goal improving labor's share of the total pie of GNP. But, in fact, higher hourly wages lead to higher

prices as corporations fight back to preserve their share of property in the pie of GNP. Real wages are seen not to be capable of being raised much, if at all, by the bootstrap operation of militant collective bargaining, slowdowns, strikes, sitdown strikes, general strikes, and so forth.

Lenin is often quoted (by Keynes, for one) as having once said: "We shall contrive the death of capitalism by debauching its currency." There is no evidence he ever wrote this; at least no one has been able to locate the quotation. But his alleged aphorism can be improved on, in the following form.

"The best way to ruin a mixed economy—to kill off its full-employment progress and exacerbate its class struggles—is to contrive (as was done in Peron's Argentina) a 40 per cent overnight increase in wage rates. The result will be structural inflation, lockouts, strikes, breakdowns, bankruptcies, and public unrest."

When a mixed economy is running badly, experiencing both inflation and unemployment at the same time, will there then emerge a demand for a fascist takeover—to restore "orderly conditions and promote economic growth"? Alas, the answer too often is, Yes.

It is even sadder to have to witness an occasional economic success of such dictatorial regimes—in the short run. Thus, in the 1970s, the Brazilian military regime may be hard on professors, intellectuals, and a free press. But, as people used to say in Mussolini's time, "At least the trains run on time. . . ." And, when one looks in the U.N. *Statistical Year Book*, one finds that Brazil has in recent years been the veritable Japan of Latin America, averaging annual rates of real GNP growth of 10 per cent per year.

Benevolent despotisms, history demonstrates, rarely remain benevolent, and almost never even stay efficient. Mussolini failed to deliver what his speeches promised. Hitler's Germany, we now know from captured records, was a poorly run economy. If one Pakistani dictator seems for a time to make the agricultural sector grow, the next dictator plunges the country into dismembering warfare!

The blueprint of fascism, in blunt fact, rarely works out well in real life even in its own terms.

SOCIALISM

In defining fascism we were able to point to Nazi Germany or fascist Italy. Socialism cannot be so easily described. Of course, we can describe the Swedish socialist government or the British Labour Party's program, but these do not present dramatic contrasts with our system. In many ways they are very similar to the mixed systems produced by our own provincial NDP governments and even by the eclectic governments in Ontario and Quebec. They certainly fall far short of the central direction of Eastern Europe, Russia, or China.

A few common elements seem to characterize socialist philosophy:

1. *Government ownership of productive resources.* The role of private property is gradually to be lessened as key industries such as railroads, coal, and even steel are gradually nationalized. Unearned profits from increases in

land value are also limited. (In West Germany and the United Kingdom, enthusiasm for nationalization seems to be ebbing.)

2. *Planning.* Instead of permitting the free play of profit motives in a *laissez-faire* market economy, coordinated planning is to be introduced. Sometimes the program of "production for use rather than profit" is advocated; advertising expenditure on gadgets is to be reduced; workers and professional people are to develop instincts of craftsmanship and social service so that they will be guided by other motives than those of our "acquisitive society."

3. *Redistribution of income.* Through government taxing powers, inherited wealth and swollen incomes are to be reduced. Social security benefits and cradle-to-grave welfare services provided by the collective purse are to increase the well-being of the less privileged classes.

4. *Peaceful and democratic revolution.* As distinct from communism, socialism often advocates the peaceful and gradual extension of government controls—revolution by ballot rather than by bullet. This strategy is more than a means; rather, it is a deep philosophical tenet of faith.

BRITISH SOCIALISM   A brief look at British socialism will point out the modern issues. Just when Adam Smith's classical "liberal" economics had won the day from its mercantilistic and feudal predecessors, English intellectual opinion began to move beyond *laissez-faire* and toward socialism. A key example is John Stuart Mill, who was brought up by an eighteenth-century exponent of utilitarian individualism, but who had by the last half of the nineteenth century turned to a kind of socialism. And in the twentieth century, university and night-school intellectuals were won to the Fabian doctrines of the inevitability of *gradualism*; and the socialist views of Bernard Shaw and Beatrice and Sidney Webb had also become the views of the trade-union movement.

All this was hidden until World War I. After that war, the Liberal party was ground away between the millstones of the Conservative and Labour parties. And after World War II, Labour really came into power. Its early goals included (a) vast extension of welfare services by the state—in which Conservative governments in large degree have acquiesced; (b) heavy redistributive income and estates taxation—in which to a degree the Conservatives also acquiesce; (c) extensive centralized planning, including stringent regulation of industrial location and of local land use and zoning; and finally (d) initially a fairly sweeping program of nationalization, beginning with coal, power, and railroads and, in the doctrines of the left wing of the party, reaching beyond steel to many branches of wholesaling and distribution, engineering, and ordnance.

Today, the Labour Party finds itself quite divided on how far to carry traditional socialism. This shows itself in debates over the extent to which nationalization should be pressed and the degree to which reliance should be placed on market mechanisms. At the intellectual level, now that so many of the goals set up years ago in *Fabian*

Essays have been realized, there is much soul searching going on; and challenging new Fabian essays are hard to write. Is "redistribution of income and wealth among individuals and welfarism designed to make capitalism work well" adequate? And can the mixed economy command the idealistic enthusiasms that more sweeping reforms are able to fire? Has the improvement of living standards pushed the militant poor up into the contented middle classes? Has making society more fluid tended to drain off the bright son of poor parents to Oxford and the Establishment, alienating him from the radical trade-union tradition?

Nor is this quandary unique to Britain. In Sweden, Norway, Denmark, Australia, and New Zealand, the so-called "middle way" of moderate labor socialism has now been in, or knocking at the door of, power for a third of a century. Yet every one of these economies begins to look more and more like what we ourselves have become since the institution of Ontario Hydro, workmen's compensation, family allowances, hospital insurance, and Quebec steel.

FRENCH "INDICATIVE PLANNING"   Ideologically rather removed from traditional socialism is the remarkable development in France of planning by the state. Even before De Gaulle, many important industries were owned and run by the French government: railroads, electricity, and mines, for example. The tools of economics—marginal-cost pricing of power, benefit-cost analysis of the worthwhile program of investments in these state industries—deserve much of the credit for the remarkable rate of real growth in France during the last two decades. But that is not all.

Even private industry is brought into a comprehensive national plan. There is, however, one important difference from the traditional planning of socialist societies. In the French mixed economy, participation in *Le Plan* is mostly voluntary. (But, as everywhere these days, what business firm dares get the authorities too angry at it—particularly when permission to go to the capital markets is controlled by government?)

Representatives of different industries sit down together in committees, presided over by the civil servants who serve the plan. Businessmen are given quantitative information on national goals for the years just ahead; and they respond with information on what these goals will mean for their own industries. In turn, these replies are made the basis for a recalculation of the aggregates and the details of the plan.

In the end, each industry learns that it can count on an expanding market. And as business firms in those industries proceed to meet these indicated goals, they do generate the production, income, and demand called for by the plan.

How has it all worked out? Apparently, remarkably well if we can judge by results. Almost too well to be credible, when one considers the informality of the arrangements and their quasi-voluntary nature. In the late 1960s, many an English reformer would have traded some of the "pie in the sky" of traditional socialism for some pragmatic fruits of indicative planning.

Similarity must not conceal diversity. In Egypt and many countries recently released from colonialism, there has been widespread nationalization of industry; but, as yet, there have been few cases where the result has been a rapid rate of real economic growth. Similarly, the economy of Argentina, despite resources and technology that many a poor country would envy, stagnated under state controls introduced by Dictator Perón. What has been the relation between the particular brand of socialism of Sukarno's Indonesia, Castro's Cuba, and Nkrumah's Ghana and their respective GNPs?

MARXIAN COMMUNISM AND SOVIET RUSSIA: HISTORY

Marxian communism represents a departure both from earlier utopian socialist movements and also from evolutionistic socialist movements of the last century. Karl Marx (1818-1883), who began as a student of Hegelian philosophy but ended up as the messiah of a new doctrine of "scientific socialism," worked in exile with his friend and financial sponsor Friedrich Engels to establish a whole new theory of economics and history. For three-quarters of a century after Karl Marx and Friedrich Engels issued their 1848 *Communist Manifesto*, numerous international socialist conferences were held; yet outside the British Museum, not much seemed to be accomplished.

In 1917, the big moment came. Czarist Russia was knocked out of the war by the Germans. Lenin, a follower of Marx, was transported in a sealed railroad car across Germany and into Russia. Aided by Trotsky, Lenin's Bolsheviks snatched power from the moderate Kerenski regime that had overthrown the monarchy. Preaching peace and promising land for the peasants and a dictatorship of the proletariat, the followers of the Red hammer and sickle gained adherents in the navy and army and forcibly took power.

There followed the "ten days that shook the world." The meeting of the democratic Constituent Assembly, only few of whose elected representatives were pro-Bolshevik, was forbidden. An army was organized and trained by Trotsky, and successive towns were won over to the revolutionary forces—often by strategic capture of the water and power supply alone. Then followed a great civil war between the Red and White armies, the latter aided by Poland and Western powers. In the end, the officers of the White army ended up chiefly in Paris, driving taxicabs and drinking vodka to the memory of Czar Nicholas.

THE REVOLUTION ACHIEVED The world expected a Russian collapse; but the communist regime persisted—not without experiencing horrible famines, in which literally millions perished. Aristocrats and bourgeoisie were ruthlessly "purged" and "liquidated"—new words for age-old processes brought to a new perfection. The Commu-

nist party was the only political party permitted; only a few per cent of the population could belong to this elite group; it elected the members of local "soviets" of factories and farms. These elected representatives to still higher soviets, until, at the very top, over all the federated Union Republics, stood the Council of People's Commissars of the Supreme Soviet of the U.S.S.R. (Union of Soviet Socialist Republics).

The Soviet leaders had no blueprints to guide them. Marx had confined himself largely to the faults of capitalism and had revealed very little about what the promised land was to be like. It was not even on the timetable that backward Russia, which had hardly emerged from feudalism into capitalism, should experience its revolution before the downfall of the top-heavy industrialized nations like Germany. During the 1920s, Lenin compromised with capitalistic enterprise in the NEP (New Economic Policy). But in 1928-1929, the first Five-Year Plan for industrialization of manufacturing and collectivization of agriculture was introduced. This was followed by later Five-Year Plans.

Because of the rapid pace of capital formation, war preparedness, and the state of Russian technology, consumption was severely rationed throughout these years. Workers had ration cards that were honored at specific stores, but money continued to be used. Excess money income could be spent only upon special goods at higher prices than the basic ration. Real and money wages differed among occupations, with piece rates and incentive pay for high productivity becoming ever more dominant.

STALINISM Stalin, one of Lenin's many lieutenants, finally won out in the struggle for power after Lenin's death in the early 1920s. Trotsky and other old-line revolutionaries were accused of plotting with foreign powers against the Soviet Union, and in the middle 1930s a tremendous purge of generals and officials culminated in the sensational Moscow trials—sensational because all the defendants vied with each other in avowing their own guilt. After the Chamberlain-Hitler appeasement pact, Nazi Germany and Soviet Russia in 1939 signed a non-aggression pact, which lasted until Hitler—flushed with his victory over Poland and France and lusting for the farmlands of the Ukraine—attacked Russia.

With fanatical patriotism and aided by the Western allies, the Russians traded their blood for the Germans' until few Germans were left in the Russian homeland. After the defeat of the Axis, the short-lived comradeship with the West flickered out, and the world stood in the shadow of the hydrogen bomb, with Russia trying to spread her influence over Europe and Asia and with the Atlantic nations, the United States, and ourselves bent on stopping her on the one hand, and China threatening her on the other.

In the postwar period, Stalin's one-man rule became more and more paranoid, and his death in 1953 brought in the inevitable revulsion toward his regime. What seemed to be a thaw set in under the committee rule of Khrushchev, and sprigs of criticism began to push up their sprouts. But the Poles, Hungarians, and Leningrad students learned that winter was not quite over. Peaceful coexistence became the new official line, and was continued after Khrushchev's replacement by the committee rule of Brezhnev. Faced by the rivalry of China, Russia was in no mood to tolerate a free press and electorate in Czech-oslovakia, much less dissident intellectuals at home.

The actual operation of the Soviet Union's economy will be reviewed in the Appendix to Chapter 3 following. There is found the answer to the question of how the Soviet Union decided the three basic problems: WHAT is to be produced, HOW, and FOR WHOM?

SUMMARY TO APPENDIX

1 A variety of economic systems have evolved which seek to answer the WHAT, HOW, and FOR WHOM questions of the population and economy. In the course of evolution, the systems themselves are ever changing. The stereotype *laissez-faire* system no longer exists. Nevertheless different systems have certain identifiable economic features.

2 Marx wrote of the imminent demise of the capitalist system due to inherent weaknesses of capitalism itself. The modern mixed economy has replaced capitalism in many countries and has on the whole performed well, but the rise of the modern mixed economy did not follow the Marxian timetable. A principal reason for surveying alternative systems is to gain some measure of insight into various systems and to rid ourselves of facile generalizations about various systems.

3 Fascism is more a political than an economic entity, usually involving strong nationalism, a dictatorship, and the disappearance of civil liberties. The government is given strong regulatory power over the economy.

4 Socialism, despite the widespread use of the label, is a difficult system to describe and define. Common elements in a socialist system are: (1) Government ownership of productive resources; (2) Centralized or governmental planning; (3) Redistribution of income; and (4) Introduction of socialism by peaceful and democratic "revolution."

5 British Socialism has its roots in intellectual history, but it became functional after World War II when the Labour Party came into power. Its original goals were extension of state welfare services, heavy redistributive income and estate taxes, extensive centralized planning, and large-scale nationalization. Today many of the original goals have been realized, and the British Labour Party finds itself divided on how far to carry traditional socialism and the means of implementation.

6 French "indicative planning" provides an interesting example of state economic planning wherein private planning participates "voluntarily" in the plan.

7 Marxian Communism was implemented in Soviet Russia after the 1917 revolution—not without setbacks and both economic and human cost. Moreover, because Marx had never provided a blueprint for the communist society, the government had to feel its way through a variety of policies and five-year plans. Consumption was sacrificed to investment in industrial and military capital formation. Stalin's regime became increasingly repressive, while Khrushchev and his successors have chosen peaceful coexistence.

CONCEPTS FOR REVIEW

laissez-faire, mixed economy
anarchism; fascism, socialism, communism
nationalization of industry
indicative planning, French style

QUESTIONS FOR DISCUSSION

1. Make a list of a number of "isms," describing each and its history.
2. Describe your own vision of Utopia. Does it differ from the present?
3. Compare and contrast fascism and communism. What is the relation of socialism and capitalism to each other? To *laissez-faire* and the mixed economy?
4. "The Russians claim that they have 'industrial democracy.' This is clearly a different commodity from political democracy as we know it. Even defenders of the Soviet Union will admit that expressions of opinion against the government or the Communist party will not be tolerated. Free press—in our sense—is forbidden. Even if a majority of the Russian people were to prefer their form of government, no one should blind himself to its great differences from our own concepts of democracy and freedom." Discuss this as objectively as you can.

3
PRICE FUNCTIONING
OF A "MIXED ECONOMY"

Every individual endeavours to employ his capital so that its produce may be of greatest value. He generally neither intends to promote the public interest, nor knows how much he is promoting it. He intends only his own security, only his own gain. And he is in this led by an invisible hand *to promote an end which was no part of his intention. By pursuing his own interest he frequently promotes that of society more effectually than when he really intends to promote it.*

ADAM SMITH, The Wealth of Nations (1776)

THE MIXED ECONOMY

Most of our attention will be devoted to the special features of economic life found in twentieth-century industrial nations (with the exception of the Communist nations surveyed in the Appendix to this chapter). In most of these countries there was a trend in the past few centuries toward less and less direct governmental control of economic activity; gradually feudal and preindustrial conditions were replaced by greater emphasis on what is loosely called "free private enterprise," or "competitive private-property capitalism".

Long before this trend had approached a condition of *laissez-faire* (i.e., of complete governmental non-

interference with business), the tide began to turn the other way. Since late in the nineteenth century, in almost all the countries under consideration, there has been a steady increase in the economic functions of government.

Ours is a "mixed economy" in which both public and private institutions exercise economic control.

Section A of this chapter shows how our mixed economy tackles the three problems of economic organization that must be met by any society. Section B describes some fundamental characteristics of the present economic order.

A. HOW A FREE ENTERPRISE SYSTEM SOLVES THE BASIC ECONOMIC PROBLEMS

In a system of free private enterprise, no individual or organization is *consciously* concerned with the triad of economic problems set forth in Chapter 2: WHAT, HOW, and FOR WHOM. This fact is really remarkable.

To paraphrase a famous economic example, let us consider such a city as Toronto, or Montreal. Without a constant flow of goods in and out of the city, it would be on the verge of starvation within a week. A variety of kinds and amounts of food is required. From the surrounding counties, from the ten provinces, and from the far corners of the world, goods

have been traveling for days and months with Central Canada as their destination.

How is it that more than 2 million people are able to sleep easily at night without living in mortal terror of a breakdown in the elaborate economic processes upon which the city's existence depends? For all this is undertaken *without coercion or centralized direction* by any conscious body!

Everyone notices how much the government does to control economic activity—tariff legislation, pure-food laws, utility and railroad regulations, minimum-wage regulations, fair-labor-practice acts, social security, price ceilings and floors, price and incomes policies, public works, national defense, national and local taxation, police protection and judicial redress, zoning ordinances, municipal water or gas works, and so forth. What goes unnoted is how much of economic life proceeds *without* government intervention.

Hundreds of thousands of commodities are produced by millions of people more or less of their own volition and without central direction or master plan.

NOT CHAOS BUT ECONOMIC ORDER

This functioning alone is convincing proof that a competitive system of markets and prices—whatever else it may be, however imperfectly it may function —is not a system of chaos and anarchy. There is in it a certain order and orderliness. It works.

A competitive system is an elaborate mechanism for unconscious coordination through a system of prices and markets, a communication device for pooling the knowledge and actions of millions of diverse individuals. Without a central intelligence it solves one of the most complex problems imaginable, involving thousands of unknown variables and relations. Nobody designed it. It just evolved, and like human nature, it is changing; but it does meet the first test of any social organization—it can survive.

A dramatic example of the importance of a pricing system is Germany after World War II. In 1946-1947 production and consumption had dropped to a low level. Neither bombing damage nor postwar reparation payments could account for this breakdown. *Paralysis of the price mechanism* was clearly to blame: Money was worthless; factories closed down for lack of materials; trains could not run for lack of coal; coal could not be mined because miners were hungry; miners were hungry because peasants would not sell food for money and no industrial goods were available to give them in return. Prices were legally fixed, but little could be bought at such prices; a black market characterized by barter or fantastically high prices existed. Then in 1948 a "miracle" happened. A thoroughgoing currency reform set the price mechanism back into effective operation. Immediately production and consumption soared; again the

WHAT, HOW, and FOR WHOM were being resolved by markets and prices.

The fact to emphasize is that such so-called miracles are going on all around us all the time—if only we look around and alert ourselves to the everyday functioning of the market. A revolutionist out to destroy the capitalist system could ask nothing better than a great inflation or deflation that would paralyze the price mechanism.[1]

THE INVISIBLE HAND AND "PERFECT COMPETITION"

Students of economics have to avoid the error of thinking that a price mechanism must work chaotically if it is not controlled by somebody. Having learned this lesson, they must not go to the other extreme and become enamored of the beauty of a pricing mechanism, regarding it as perfection itself, the essence of providential harmony and beyond the touch of human hands.

Adam Smith, whose *Wealth of Nations* (1776) is the germinal book of modern economics or political economy, was thrilled by the recognition of an order in the economic system. Smith proclaimed the principle of the "Invisible Hand": every individual, pursuing only his own selfish good, was led as if by an invisible hand to achieve the best good for all, so that any interference with free competition by government was almost certain to be injurious. (See this chapter's initial quotation.)

Undoubtedly this was a valuable insight. But, on reflection and after two centuries of experience, we must recognize some of the realistic limitations on this doctrine.

The virtues claimed for free enterprise are fully realized only when the complete checks and balances of "perfect competition" are present.

Perfect competition is defined by the economist as a technical term: "Perfect competition" exists only in the case where no farmer, businessman, or laborer is a big enough part of a large total market to have any personal influence on market price. On the other hand, when his grain, merchandise, or la-

---

[1] In the 1970s governments in the Soviet Union and Eastern European countries are rediscovering some virtues of a pricing system.

bor is large enough in size to produce required depressing or elevating effects on market prices, some degree of monopolistic *imperfect competition* has set in, and the virtues of the Invisible Hand must be that much discounted.

Actually, some of the praise of perfect competition is beside the point. As discussed earlier, ours is a mixed system of government and private enterprise; as will be discussed later, it is also *a mixed system of monopoly and competition.* A cynic might say of perfect competition what Bernard Shaw is said to have said of Christianity: The only trouble with it is that it has never been tried.

Historians quarrel over whether there ever was a golden age of free competition. And certainly, competition is not now perfect in the economist's sense. We do not even know whether, because of the fundamental nature of large scale production and technology, consumers' tastes, and business organization, effective competition is becoming less or more intense. (More on this in Chapter 6.)

In any case, society need not accept as inevitable any trend toward big business, mergers, trusts, and cartels such as began to swell in the 1890s. The challenge is to work out laws and customs that help to improve the working of our less-than-perfect competitive system. The polar cases—*laissez-faire* and totalitarian dictatorship of production—dramatize economic principles. Yet the relevant choice for policy is not a decision between these extremes, but rather the degree to which public policy should do *less* or *more* in modifying the operation of particular private economic activities.

THE PRICE SYSTEM

Just how does the unconscious automatic price rationing mechanism operate? The bare outlines of a *competitive* profit-and-loss system are simple to describe.

Everything has a price—each commodity and each service. Even the different kinds of human labor have prices, usually called "wage rates." Everybody receives money for what he sells, and uses this money to buy what he wishes.

If more is wanted of any one good—say, shoes—a flood of new orders will be given for it. This will cause its price to rise and more to be produced.

On the other hand, what if more of a commodity —such as tea—becomes available than people want to buy at the last-quoted market price? Then its price will be marked down by competition. At the lower price people will drink more tea, and producers will no longer produce quite so much. Thus equilibruim of supply and demand will be restored (as the next chapter and Part Three will show).

What is true of the markets for consumers' goods is also true of markets for *factors of production* such as labor, land, and capital inputs. If welders rather than glass blowers are needed, job opportunities will be more favorable in the welding field. The price of welders, their hourly wage, will tend to rise, while that of glass blowers will tend to fall. Other things being equal, this will cause a shift into the desired occupation. Likewise, an acre of land will go into sugar cultivation if sugar producers bid the most for its use. In the same way, machine-tool production will be determined by supply and demand.

THE GENERAL-EQUILIBRIUM SYSTEM   In other words, we have a vast system of trial and error, of successive approximation to an *equilibrium system of prices and production.* We shall see later that the matching of supply and demand and of prices and costs helps solve our three problems simultaneously. Here are the bare outlines of competitive equilibrium:

1. WHAT things will be produced is determined by the *dollar votes* of consumers—not periodically at the polls, but every day in their decisions to purchase this item and not that. Of course, the money that they pay into business cash-registers ultimately provides the payrolls, rents, and dividends that consumers receive in weekly income. Thus the circle is a complete one.

2. HOW things are produced is determined by the competition among different producers. The method that is cheapest at any one time, because of both physical efficiency and cost efficiency, will displace a more costly method.

The only way for producers to meet price competition and maximize profits is to keep costs at a minimum by adopting the most efficient methods. For example, synthetic rubber will be made from oil rather than alcohol if the price of the one is in a certain relation to the price of the other; or electric power will be generated by steam rather than nuclear power if the price of coal is below some critical level. The large tractor-operated farm will displace the family-size farm if this leads to lower costs of production.

International example: Bob Jones farms *extensively*, with much Canadian land relative to each hour of labor; Pierre Reny farms *intensively*, using much labor to each hectare of French land. Who orders these sensible HOW decisions, which properly adjust to the fact that France is more densely populated than Canada? Parliament? The Chamber of Deputies? The UN? Of course not. The price system is society's signaling device. Like a master who gives carrots and kicks to coax his donkey forward, the pricing system deals out profits and losses, to get WHAT, HOW, and FOR WHOM decided.

3. FOR WHOM things are produced is determined by supply and demand in the markets for productive services: by wage rates, land rents, interest rates, and profits, all of which go to make up everybody's income—relative to everyone else and relative to the whole. (Of course, the character of the resulting distribution of income is highly dependent upon the *initial* distribution of property ownership, upon acquired or inherited abilities, educational opportunities and presence or absence of discriminations against women or particular races.)

Note this: Consumer votes do not by themselves determine WHAT goods are produced. Demand has to meet a supply of goods; so business cost and supply decisions, along with consumer demand, help to determine WHAT. Just as a broker may help arrange a match between buyer and seller, the auctioneer in the commodity market acts as the go-between who reconciles the consumer votes and business decisions that meet in the market. He helps to *ration* the supplies. (The next chapter explains how.) The profit seeker is society's agent to determine HOW, seeking least factor-costs for producing each good and being punished by ruthless competition if he fails to use best methods.

A PICTURE OF PRICES AND MARKETS

To amplify this highly simplified explanation, turn to Fig. 3-1. It gives a bird's-eye view of the way market pricing reconciles public demand and supply with business supply and demand. Note that markets serve as the connecting device between the public and business. Twenty minutes of poring over this diagram may be worth hours of disconnected musing about economic pricing. (In Chapters 10 and 32, similar circular-flow diagrams will appear.)

A competitive system is impersonal but not completely so. The consuming families face business enterprises on two fronts, with only prices in between. One front is the widely dispersed one, the retail market on which consumers buy thousands of small items from a score of different retail establishments; grocery, drug, and department stores; movie theaters; gasoline stations; and from electric-power companies, government post offices, landlords, railroad lines, and insurance companies.

On the other front—the market for labor and other productive services—relations are not always so peaceful. To the family breadwinner his wage is not simply another price; it is the difference between luxury and comfort, between comfort and privation. The laborer may feel inferior to the large corporation in bargaining power, and he may turn to collective bargaining by means of trade-unions. By doing this, he may at times be helping to restore competition, while at other times he may be causing conditions to deviate still further from perfect competition.

ETHICAL ASPECTS OF INCOME DISTRIBUTION

The above picture of competition tending toward efficiency, toward being on the production-possibility frontier and not inside it, is a highly over-simplified one. But even if the system worked as perfectly as described above—which everybody knows not to be the case—many would not consider its determinations ideal. In the first place, goods go where there are the most votes or dollars. A rich man's dog may receive the milk that a poor child needs. Why? Because supply and demand are working badly? No. Because auction markets are doing what they are designed to do —putting goods in the hands of those who can pay the most, who have the most money votes. Defenders and critics of the price mechanism should

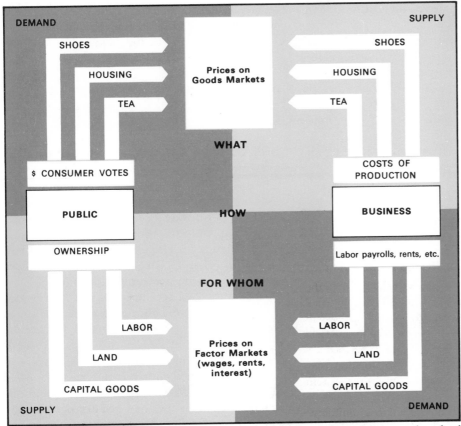

FIG. 3-1. The competitive price system uses supply-demand markets to solve the basic economic problems—WHAT, HOW and FOR WHOM:

All demand relations are shown in the dark brown areas; all the supply relations in the light-red areas. See how consumer dollar votes of demand interact in the upper goods markets with business cost-supply decisions, thus helping determine WHAT is produced. And HOW business demand for inputs or productive factors meets the public's supply of labor and other inputs in the lower factor markets to help determine wage, rent, and interest income—i.e., FOR WHOM goods are produced. Business competition to buy factor inputs and sell goods most cheaply determines HOW goods are to be produced. (Warning: All parts of the diagram interact together. WHAT depends on the lower part, just as FOR WHOM depends on the upper part—carpenter wages depend on housing demand, and demand for yachts depends on oil-land royalties.)

recognize this fact.[2] And when a democratic society does not like the distribution of dollar votes under

laissez-faire, it uses redistributive taxation and transfers to rectify the situation.

Consider another tendency of an efficient market system. Suppose the invention of automatic machines should cause the competitive price of labor to fall, thereby reducing incomes of the poor. Would all ethical observers regard that as necessarily right or ideal?

Should the fact that a man inherited 500 square miles of range land, for which oil companies offer a

---

[2] Cecil Woodham-Smith, *The Great Hunger: Ireland 1845-9* (Hamish Hamilton, London, 1962), relates the unbelievable details of how a *laissez-faire* Victorian government let millions of Irish children, women, and men literally starve when a fungus destroyed the potato crop. Gilbert Tucker, *The Canadian Commercial Revolution, 1845-51* (Carleton Library, Toronto, 1964) recounts the same government's cold attitude to the attempts of Canadian organizations to relieve cholera-ridden Irish immigrants.

million dollars per year, necessarily justify so large an income?

These questions are discussed widely and repeatedly. Whether incomes should be completely determined by a competitive struggle—the survival of the survivors—is an ethical question that goes beyond the mechanics of economics. In the modern mixed economy, the electorate insists on providing minimum standards when the market fails to do so. Economics teaches how interventions can be accomplished at least costs in terms of inefficiency.

IMPERFECTIONS OF COMPETITION

As we said earlier, one drawback to the picture of the price system as described above is the fact that, in the real world, competition is nowhere near "perfect." Firms do not know when consumer tastes will change; therefore they may *overproduce* in one field and *underproduce* in another. By the time they are ready to learn from experience, the situation may have changed again. Also, in a competitive system many producers simply do not know the methods of other producers, and costs do not fall to a minimum. In the competitive struggle one can sometimes succeed as much by *keeping knowledge scarce* as by keeping production high.

The most serious deviation from perfect competition comes from *monopoly elements*. These—as we shall see later on—may result in wrong pricing, creation of distorted patterns of demand by repetitive advertising, incorrect and wasteful resource allocation, and monopoly profits. We shall be reminded again and again how strict is the economist's definition of a "perfect competitor"; the mere presence of vigorous rivalry is not enough for perfect competition.

MONOPOLY ELEMENTS The economic definition of "imperfect competitor" is *anyone who buys or sells a good in large enough quantities to be able to affect the price of that good.* To some degree that means almost all businessmen, except possibly the millions of farmers who each produce a negligible fraction of the total crop. All economic life is a blend of competitive and monopoly elements. Imperfect

(monopolistic) competition is the prevailing mode, not perfect competition. An approximation to perfect competition may be the most society can strive for.

Of course, as we shall later see, a businessman cannot set his prices completely as he pleases and still make profits. He must take into account the prices of goods that are substitutes for his own. Even if he produces a trademarked coal with unique properties, he must reckon with the prices charged for other coals, for oil and gas, and for house insulation.

Businessmen, farmers, and workers both like and dislike competition. We all like it when it enables us to expand our market, but we label it as "chiseling," "unfair," or "ruinous" when the knife cuts the other way. The worker whose livelihood depends on how the market prices his labor may be the first to howl when competition threatens to depress wages. Farm groups, aware of what competition can do to agricultural prices, constantly bring pressure to bear on the government to restrict production and thereby raise prices.

In the idealized model of an efficiently acting competitive market mechanism, consumers are supposed to be well informed. They recognize low quality and avoid it; they never buy drugs that turn out to be poisonous or ineffective. Most important, their "desires" are supposed to represent genuine "wants" and "needs" and "tastes." But in actual life, as critics like Galbraith never tire of pointing out—business firms spend much money on advertising to *shape* — and, some insist, *distort* —consumer demands. We are terrorized into buying deodorants; from childhood on, we are conditioned to desire what business wants to sell.

The sequence "consumer demand → corporate price and production" is often inverted to become "corporate advertising → consumer demand → high price and profit."

Some of the basic factors responsible for monopoly-creating bigness in business may be *inherent in the economies of large-scale production.* This is especially true in a dynamic world of technological change. Competition by numerous producers would simply not be efficient in many fields and could not last. Trademarks, patents, and advertising are often responsible for still other market imperfections. It would be humanly impossible, therefore, to attempt to create *perfect* competition by law. The problem is one of achieving reasonably effective "workable competition."

We shall proceed later to a more microscopic examination of supply and demand. After that discussion we shall be in a position to appraise the workings of the price system more judiciously. A competitive price system is one way of organizing an economy, *but not the only way*. Admiration should not inhibit reform. Still it is of interest that socialist nations are making increasing use of the price mechanism in their "command" societies. (See Appendix.) A price system is not perfect, but neither are its alternatives.

ECONOMIC ROLES OF GOVERNMENT

It was said earlier that ours is not a pure price economy but a *mixed economy* in which elements of government control are intermingled with *market elements* in organizing production and consumption. The economic roles of government are now so important that two chapters in Part One are devoted to them. Their activities can be briefly indicated here. Democracies are not satisfied with the answers to WHAT, HOW, and FOR WHOM given by a perfectly unrestrained market system.

WELFARE MINIMA Such a system might dictate that certain people starve from lack of income while others receive inadequate or excessive incomes. Therefore the citizenry through their government step in with transfers to supplement the real or money incomes of some individuals. Thus, governments many provide hospital beds for citizens or may present the needy with monthly allowances in times of unemployment or old age. Minimum standards of life are widespread modern goals.

PUBLIC SERVICES AND TAXES More than this, government provides certain indispensable "public goods" without which private and community life would be unthinkable but which by their nature cannot appropriately be left to private enterprise. Government came into existence once people realized, "Everybody's business is nobody's business."

Obvious examples of public goods are the maintenance of national defense and of internal law and order, and the administration of justice and of contracts.[3]

By and large, in its expenditure of money, government is behaving exactly like any other large spender. By casting sufficient votes in the form of dollar bids in certain directions, it causes resources to flow there. The price system then takes over and performs much as if these were private rather than public needs.

Actually, most government expenditure is paid for out of taxes collected. It is here that an important element of *coercion* enters. It is true that the citizenry as a whole imposes the tax burden upon itself; also, each citizen is sharing in the collective benefits of government. But there is not the same close connection between a benefit and a tax payment as holds when the individual citizen puts a dime into a gum machine or makes an ordinary purchase. I need not smoke Buckinghams or buy nylon stockings or choose fried eggs, but I must pay my share of the taxes used to finance the various activities of government.

Moreover, a second important form of coercion is involved in the universal custom of passing governmental laws: thou shalt not sell false weight, thou shalt not employ child labor, thou shalt not burn houses, thou shalt not pour out smoke from thy factory chimney, thou shalt not sell or smoke opium, thou shalt not charge more than the ceiling price for food, and so forth. This set of rules gives the framework within which private enterprise functions; it also modifies the direction of that functioning. Together with government welfare minima expenditure and taxation, the *commands of government* supplement the price system in determining *what, how and for whom* goods will be produced.

It would be fruitless to debate whether public activity or private enterprise is the more important.

---

[3] Here is a later example of a government service: lighthouses. These "public goods" save lives and cargoes; but lighthouse keepers cannot reach out to collect fees from skippers. So we have here a divergence between *private* and *social* advantage. Philosophers and statesmen have always recognized the necessary role of government in such cases of "external-economy divergence between private and social advantage." Much more on public goods will come later in Chapters 8, and 23, and elsewhere.

Without either, our economic world would be an entirely different one.

STABILIZATION Finally, as we shall see in Parts Two and Six, it is part of the government's function to help *stabilize* acute and chronic cycles of unemployment and inflation and to help achieve and maintain healthy economic growth.

B. CAPITAL, DIVISION OF LABOR, AND MONEY

There are three further important features of modern economic society:

1. Modern advanced industrial technology rests upon the use of vast amounts of *capital*: elaborate machinery, large-scale factories and plants, and stores and stocks of finished and unfinished materials. "Capitalism" got its name because in this system capital, or "wealth," is primarily the private property of somebody—the capitalist.

2. The present-day economic system is characterized by an almost incredibly elaborate degree of *specialization* and intricate *division of labor*.

3. Ours is a system that makes extensive use of *money*. The flow of money is the lifeblood of our system. It also provides the measuring rod of values.

All these features are interrelated, each with the other, and all with the price mechanism described in Section A of this chapter.

Thus we shall see that, without the great facility for exchange which money provides, an elaborate division of labor would be impossible. Money and capital become related through credit activities of the banking system and through the organized financial markets upon which securities can be transformed into money by sale or vice versa. Of course, the link between the price mechanism and money is immediate and obvious.

CAPITAL AND TIME

No one has trouble seeing that production of economic goods can result from use of such inputs as labor and land (including in the latter term natural resources). These are often called "*primary* factors of production," for the reason that neither land nor (these days) labor is regarded as a result of the economic process, but instead exists by virtue of physical and biological rather than economic factors.[4]

Capital, which is the word often used to refer to capital goods generally, is a different kind of production factor. A capital good differs from the primary factors in that it is *an input which is itself the output of the economy.*

Capital goods, then, represent *produced* goods that can be used as factor inputs for further production, whereas labor and land are primary factor inputs not usefully thought of as being themselves produced by the economic system.

Part Four will show that, just as wages and rent are the factor-prices of primary labor and land, the 6 or 10 or 15 per cent interest rate per annum can in a more subtle way be regarded by the apologists for capitalism, as the factor-price that rewards and rations society's scarce supply of various capital goods and investment projects.

Because an interest rate is a percentage per unit of time (per month or year or decade), it calls our attention to another way of looking at capital—a way that stresses its special relationship with time. Let us survey this important economic role of capital. If men

---

[4] Some qualifications will be evident. Land can sometimes be made by drainage or filling in; this has been accomplished with much of the Tantramar marshes and with Toronto's lake shore. Natural resources such as minerals are laid down by nature, but it may take much economic effort to locate, use, and process them. Therefore they come to have some of the properties of capital goods. Even if one abandons in the Western world a Malthusian theory of population, whereby people seem to be given a cost of production not unlike that of machines, one realizes that the process of education consists of investing in people, thereby making them more productive factors of production. When you see a medical-school graduate, you are in a certain sense looking at an expensive chunk of capital or at an economic production factor that is partially capital.

had to work with their hands on barren soil, productivity and consumption would be very low indeed. Thus, when an anthropologist asked of mourning tribesmen, "Who died?" they replied, "What is death? We have lost the needle!" Over a long time our own economy has amassed a vast stock of equipment, factories and housing, inventories, and drained land.

Men learned very early that the simple, direct methods of production can be improved upon by using *time-consuming indirect methods.*

We who are inside the economic system are not conscious of *how roundabout* productive processes have become. An outside observer would be struck with the fact that almost no one in our system seems to be producing *finished goods.* Almost everyone is seen to do work of a preparatory nature; with final consumption a distant future goal. The farmer spends his time in fattening hogs, the truck driver in carrying them toward market, and the packer in advancing them further toward the last stage of consumption. A steel worker prepares pig iron, part of which will become a hammer to build a house; another bit will become part of a pig-iron furnace; which in turn will prepare pig iron to be used in making further hammers and more pig-iron furnaces; and so forth.

THE NEED TO FORGO PRESENT CONSUMPTION

The fact that it takes time to get things started and synchronized is important. It explains why society does not automatically replace all direct processes by more productive indirect ones, and all indirect processes by still more indirect processes. The advantage in doing so is balanced by the initial disadvantage of having to *forego present consumption goods* by diverting resources from current production to uses that will bear fruit only after some time.

To the extent that people are willing to save—to abstain from present consumption and wait for further consumption—to that extent society can devote resources to new capital formation.[5] And to the extent that people are unconcerned about the future, they may at any time try to "dissave"—to snatch

---

[5] We shall later see that, *sometimes* in our modern monetary economy, the more people try to save, the less capital goods are produced; and paradoxically, that the more people spend on consumption, the greater the incentive for businessmen to build new factories and equipment.

present pleasures at the expense of the future. How? By diverting resources away from the endless task of *replacing and maintaining* capital and to the job of producing extra present-day consumption goods. (Turn back to Fig. 2-5 of Chapter 2, to review the process of forgoing current consumption in favor of capital formation which adds to future production possibilities.) We may summarize as follows:

Economic activity is future-oriented. By the same token, current economic consumption is largely the consequence of past efforts. In progressive societies some fraction of potential current consumption is sacrificed to new production of capital goods which will increase future production.

CAPITAL AND PRIVATE PROPERTY RIGHTS

Physical capital goods are important in any economy because they help to increase productivity. This is as true in the Russian economy as it is of our own system. But there is one important difference. By and large, it is private individuals who own the tools of production in a mixed economy.

What is the exception in our system—government ownership of the means of production—is the rule in a socialized state where productive property is collectively owned. The returns from such real capital goods accrue to the government, not to individuals directly. The government then decides for whom such income is to be distributed. The communist government also decides how rapidly resources are to be invested in new capital formation: the government decides by how much *present* consumption should be curtailed in order to add to the total of factories, equipment, and productive stocks of goods that are necessary if *future* output is to rise.

Individual capitalists earn interest, dividends and profits, rentals and royalties on the capital goods that they supply. Every bit of equipment has a deed, or "title of ownership" that is supposed to belong to somebody directly—or if it belongs to a corporation, then indirectly it belongs to the individual stockholders who own the corporation. Moreover, each kind of capital good has a money market value; hence each claim or title to ownership of a capital good also has a market value. A share of common stock of Canadian Pacific is quoted at a certain price; a Massey-Ferguson bond at its price; a mortgage on a house is valued at some amount; the deed to a house and lot is appraised by the real-estate market at some price; and so forth.

It should be pointed out that our mixed-economy governments and their offshoots do own a good deal of the national real capital, e.g., Canadian National Railways as well as provincial hydro and gas companies. But none is large enough to permit government to control, through it, the *total* rate of capital formation.

Also, we note that the *legal property rights of an individual are relative and limited.* Society determines how much of his property a man may bequeath to his heirs and how much must go in inheritance and estate taxes to the government. Society determines how much the owners of public-utility companies—such as electric and gas firms or telephone companies—can earn and how much independence they may exert in running their business.

Even a man's home is not his castle. He must obey zoning laws and, if necessary, make way for a highway or slum-clearance project. Interestingly enough, most of society's economic income *cannot* be capitalized into private property. Since slavery was abolished, human earning power is forbidden by law to be capitalized. A man is not even free to sell himself: he must *rent* himself at a wage.

SPECIALIZATION, EXCHANGE, AND DIVISION OF LABOR

Turn now to the second characteristic feature of the present-day economy. The economies of mass production upon which modern standards of living are based would not be possible if production took place in self-sufficient farm households or regions. *Specialization* of function permits each person and region to use to best advantage any peculiar differences in skill and resources. Even in a primitive economy men learn that, rather than have everyone do everything in a mediocre way, it is better to institute a *division of labor*—better for fat men to do the fishing, lean men to do the hunting, and smart men to make the medicine, with each exchanging his products for the goods he needs.

Besides resting upon any interpersonal differences in ability, specialization accentuates and creates differences. Hunting makes a man thin and good at stalking prey; a region with no resources especially adapted to weaving may nevertheless develop skills which give it advantages in this. Specialization usually pays even with no natural or acquired differences in skills: often in this way alone can a large enough volume of activity be reached to realize all the economies of large-scale production mentioned in Chapter 2. Two *identical* Indian twins might find it better for one to make all bows and the other all arrows because only in this way could each be making enough of each item to warrant introducing improved techniques.

To illustrate the increased productivity of specialization, Adam Smith provided the classical example of pinmaking. One man could at best make a few dozen imperfect pins per day. But when a small group of men are subdivided with respect to function so that each performs simple repetitive operations, they can turn out hundreds of thousands of perfect pins per day.[6]

---

[6] Smith recognized that specialization and division of labor were limited by the extent of the market, i.e., by the volume of goods that can be sold. Smith would have approved of the European Common Market, which aims to lower the internal tariff barriers to trade and create a market big enough to support fruitful mass production and specialization.

The following passage describing the extent of specialization in meat slaughtering is often quoted: "It would be difficult to find another industry where division of labor has been so ingeniously and microscopically worked out. The animal has been surveyed and laid off like a map; and the men have been classified in over thirty specialties and twenty rates of pay, from 16 cents to 50 cents an hour. The 50-cent man is restricted to using the knife on the most delicate parts of the hide (floorman) or to using the ax in splitting the backbone (splitter); and wherever a less skilled man can be slipped in at 18 cents, 18½ cents, 20 cents, 21 cents, 22½ cents, 24 cents, and so on, a place is made for him, and an occupation mapped out. In working on the hide alone there are nine positions, at eight different rates of pay. A 20-cent man pulls off the tail, a 22½-cent man pounds off another part where good leather is not found, and the knife of the 40-cent man cuts a different texture and has a different 'feel' from that of the 50-cent man. Skill has become specialized to fit the anatomy. . . .

"The division of labor grew with the industry, following the introduction of the refrigerator car and the marketing of dressed beef. . . . Before the market was widened by these revolutionizing inventions, the killing gangs were small, since only the local demands were supplied. But when the number of cattle to be killed each day increased to a thousand or more, an increasing gang or crew of men was put together; and the best men were kept at the most exacting work." From J. R. Commons, *Quarterly Journal of Economics,* vol. XIX, 1904, pp. 3,6.

Moreover, the simplification of function made possible by specialization lends itself to mechanization and the use of labor-saving capital. At the same time it avoids the wasteful duplication of tools that would be necessary if every man had to be a jack-of-all-trades; and it also saves time lost in going from one job to another. The modern conveyor system of automobile assembly illustrates the efficiency of specialization. Today automation is the watchword.

SPECIALIZATION AND ALIENATION

Despite the efficiency of specialization, it may also have the effect of making work tedious and without purpose. Extreme specialization means that a worker does but one single thing: Charlie Chaplin's classic movie *Modern Times,* in which the worker spends his whole lifetime accomplishing nothing more than the turning of bolt 999 on the remorseless assembly line, points up the problem. Specialization, too often, breeds half men—anemic clerks, brutish stokers. No wonder that men and women, as their real incomes rise in modern society, so often find themselves at the same time becoming socially "alienated."

The young Karl Marx, while still in his neo-Hegelian stage and before he had studied political economy, prophetically discerned the inhumane (and inhuman!) alienation involved in modern industry. Although his emphasis changed in maturity, Marx never completely lost sight of alienation. In his culminating *magnum opus, Das Kapital (Capital),* he wrote that in the better society of the future, industry in modern society is compelled

. . . under penalty of death, to replace the detail-worker of today, crippled by the life-long repetition of one and the same trivial operation, and thus reduced to the mere fragment of a man, by the fully developed individual, fit for a variety of labours, ready to face any change in production, and to whom the different social functions he performs, are but so many modes of giving free scope to his own natural and acquired powers.

Out of self-interest, personnel officers in large corporations are learning that a loosening up of the elaborate division of labor may be profitable. It apparently is not good for GM to run itself like an antheap. Nor, for that matter, is the best way to run an army necessarily the best way to run an industry.

Volvo and Saab in Sweden are experimenting with work teams who follow the job rather than stand at one point in the assembly line like machines. Secretarial pools give way to personal assistantships because you can't keep people happy working in an impersonal pool. If the boss, like a superior officer in the army, is always right and must never be talked back to, he may find he will never be told that the corporate ship is springing leaks and sinking. Participatory democracy may be a luxury that only an affluent society can afford; but where the old patterns of subordination and domination in an inflexible hierarchy no longer wash, the canny corporation may find that it cannot afford the luxury of unyielding refusals of alienated workers' demands for greater responsibility, variety and relevance.

SPECIALIZATION AND INTERDEPENDENCE

Specialization and division of labor involve one further serious problem—*interdependence.* A single-celled low form of life such as the paramecium may not be particularly good at doing anything complicated, but it can live alone and like it. In higher animals such as man, every cell will die if the heart cells fail. When all goes well, the extreme specialization of cells is very efficient—but at the cost of extreme interdependence.

In modern economic society this process is carried to the *n*th degree. In medieval times the artisan made one article and exchanged it for many others. But today a worker produces only a fraction of a single good, or he may simply turn bolt 999 on the assembly line. Such may be his whole life. In exchange he will receive an income adequate to buy goods from all over the world.

Thus, specialization involves complete mutual dependence. A bank in Austria fails, and the natives of Fiji, who carry water in empty Standard Oil cans lose their livelihood—yes, and may even starve. In the backwash of a strike or war, a breakdown in transportation and the economic fabric of exchange reveals how perilously modern economic life depends upon exchange. Would we, if we could, turn the clock back to a simpler and poorer life? Or can we keep the advantages of division of labor by finding policies that will prevent breakdown?

THE USE OF MONEY

Along with capital and specialization, money is a third aspect of modern economic life. Without the use of money our present division of labor and exchange would be impossible. To be sure, as we'll see in Chapter 15's full-fledged discussion of money, we could imagine a state of *barter*, where one kind of merchandise is traded directly for another. In primitive cultures it is not uncommon for food to be traded for weapons, or aid in the building of a house exchanged for aid in clearing a field. Even in the most advanced industrial economies, if we strip exchange down to its barest essentials and peel off the obscuring layer of money, we find that trade between individuals or nations largely boils down to barter—transforming one good into another by exchange rather than by physical transmutation.

Money is a means, not an end in itself. But the King Midas fable reminds us that means may themselves become perverted into ends. And it is no fairy tale that, once a society has become dependent on the mechanism of money, there can be a breakdown of exchange.

Under barter, if I am hungry and you are naked, I can always sew your clothes while you bake my bread. But after 1929, in the richest capitalistic country in all history, the banks failed; money was hoarded; people went hungry while other people went in rags.

The whole of Part Two of this book will deal with the problems of macroeconomics that are rooted in society's dependence on a money economy.

Barter represents a great improvement over a state of affairs in which every man had to be a jack-of-all trades and master of none. A great debt of gratitude is owed to the first two ape men who suddenly perceived that each could be made better off by giving up some of one good in exchange for some of another. Nevertheless, simple barter operates under grave disadvantages. An elaborate division of labor would be unthinkable without the introduction of a great new improvement—the use of money.

In all but the most primitive cultures men do not directly exchange one good for another. Instead they sell one good for money, and then use money to buy the goods they wish.

SUMMARY

A. PRICING AND MIXED ENTERPRISE.

1. In our mixed private enterprise system, the price mechanism, working through supply and demand in competitive markets, operates to answer the three fundamental problems of economic organization. The system is not perfect, but it works to solve the WHAT, HOW, and FOR WHOM.

2. The dollar votes of people affect prices of goods; these prices serve as guides for the amounts of the different goods to be produced. When people demand more of a good, a competitive businessman can make a profit by expanding production of that good. Under perfect competition, he must find the cheapest method of production, using labor, land, and other factors that are relatively cheap and economizing on the use of relatively expensive factors; otherwise, he will incur losses and be eliminated.

   At the same time that the WHAT and HOW problems are being resolved by prices, so is the problem of FOR WHOM. The distribution of income is determined by competitive bidding up or down of factor-prices—wages of each kind of labor, rents of land, royalties of books, and various returns to capital. Anyone possessing fertile well-located land or widely admired crooning ability will be supplied with many dollar votes for his use in the markets for consumer goods. Anyone without property or education and with skills or sex that the market cares little about will receive a low annual income; the price system doesn't try for equality.

3. Our economy is mixed in two senses: Governments modify private initiative and participate alongside it; monopolistic elements impair the working of perfect competition.

B. CAPITAL, DIVISION OF LABOR, AND MONEY

4. Capital goods—produced inputs such as machinery, housing, and inventories of goods in process—add tremendously to a nation's output. *Roundabout,* time-consuming methods take time to get started: hence, adding to the stock of capital goods requires a temporary sacrifice of present consumption. The interest rate serves to ration and to coax.

5. Under the mixed economy, capital goods are largely owned as private property; the incomes they produce go to their owners and to taxes. Under communism, the state owns capital goods. In no system are private-property rights unlimited.

6. Specialization and division of labor characterize modern economies. This raises productivity, but at the cost of interdependence and alienation.

7. Elaborate systems of present-day exchange go beyond barter to the use of money. But now money, which is only a means toward the end of acquiring goods, can become a fetish of its own. And later chapters will show how, at the macroeconomic level, in the absence of modern fiscal and monetary policy, the world could be plunged into deep depression—"poverty midst plenty"—or, at other times, into galloping inflation.

CONCEPTS FOR REVIEW

mixed economy
factors of production
demand-and-supply markets for
    goods and for factors
profit seeking, cost minimizing
capital goods
four roles of government
public goods

coercion
price "rationing"
perfect and imperfect competition
roundaboutness of production
abstinence and waiting, forgoing
dissaving by failure to maintain

QUESTIONS FOR DISCUSSION

1. During World War II did we let consumers' dollar demand determine their sugar consumption? Why not? Why recourse to rationing? Should we ration scarce petroleum products?

2. Could supply and demand for labor work out to give salesmen with a "gift of gab" five times the income of skilled surgeons? At other times could it operate to give surgeons twice the income of accountants?

3. Do you think that an "instinct of craftsmanship" and a "sense of social responsibility" could ever replace the "profit motive"? Read the chapter head's Invisible Hand quotation aloud. What do you think Smith is trying to say there? And here: "I have never known much good done by those who affected to trade for the public good."

4. List a number of cases where the government modifies the working of an automatic price system. For example: pure food and drug laws; minimum wages; interest ceilings.

5. List cases where monopoly elements intervene. How can business by advertising shape, as well as respond to, consumer demands and wants?

6. If it should not be able to borrow abroad, what must China do if it wishes to become an efficient industrialized nation in the next few generations?

7. "Lincoln freed the slaves. With one pen stroke he destroyed much of the capital the Southern United States had been able accumulate over the years." Comment.

8. Marx pointed out that, under barter, the natural sequence is "clothing-food-clothing-food . . ."; more generally, "commodity-commodity-commodity. . . ," or "C-C-C." In a natural money economy, the sequence becomes "commodity-money-commodity- . . ." or "C-M-C . . . ."(Explanation: I sell my cloth for the money I'll use to buy your bread.) But, Marx points out, when capitalism becomes perverted, people want to pile up money for its own sake and not for the commodities it can buy; money's sole purpose then is to use commodities to beget more money in the perverse sequence: "M-C-M . . . ." Discuss.

Appendix: What, How and For Whom in the Soviet Union, Yugoslavia, and Maoist China

How does the Soviet Union today get the three basic problems decided: WHAT shall be produced, HOW, and FOR WHOM?

In broad outline,[1] the picture is this: The state owns almost all factors of production: factories, mines, and land. Workers generally earn their living by wages; they do have considerable choice of occupation, but a Soviet citizen does not have unlimited right to seek employment in any region and industry that happens to capture his fancy.

WHAT A political decision is made that defense and capital formation are to be pushed hard; what is left over is permitted to go to consumers' goods. While a Russian can indicate his preferences among different goods by the way he spends his income, any resulting shortages or gluts have only recently been permitted to result in the bidding up or down of consumer-goods prices, thereby automatically producing the positive or negative returns that serve to rechannel resources. So long as goods were very scarce, central planners could decide that people would want so much of food, so much of shoes, and so much of various other necessities of life. Any and all of these were eagerly bought as they became available: if the local store or commissary had shoes not exactly your size, you were glad to take them a little large rather than do without.

Now that some of the comforts—and even luxuries—of life are beginning to become available, it is no longer enough to think of giving people what they need. Centralized planning has become a little more difficult. These days, certain goods will not get bought at all, and the planners have come to learn that they must cut back on them. Even advertising and selling have reared their heads in Russia! It is harder to learn what people do want than what they do not want, and marketing surveys are still in their infancy. The Soviet commissars are not so skilled in determining what people would want most if they had the choice; but they do find it useful to watch what other Europeans like to consume and then belatedly introduce such products. Experts tell us this imitative pattern, which is not at all irrational (since it assumes that what one human being will like, so will another), is becoming more common.

With respect to capital goods and military expenditure, *direct state decisions* are made. Industrialization is pushed hard: electrification, transportation, mining devel-

opment, a big push in chemicals and fertilizers, collectivization of agriculture and crop patterns—*such matters are broadly determined by conscious political decision.*

HOW Private enterprise is negligible in importance. Instead, the typical Soviet factory will be a state-owned *enterprise*:

just as the president of General Motors owns little of its total stock, the manager or head of this state-owned enterprise has no ownership of its capital; but he does get better-than-average pay for his work, plus various travel expenses, auto transport, and other special privileges. He may even get bonuses, and his chance of promotion to a bigger enterprise will depend upon how well his enterprise meets its "quota".

It used to be true that the managerial bonus was tied to total output alone, disregarding the quality of the goods or the efficiency with which they were produced. This system resulted in the hoarding of production materials which might have been well used by other enterprises, or in devious schemes to have the manager's quota set unrealistically low so that, on paper, the manager would appear highly productive. Stories have even been told of a transport enterprise which moved carloads of water back and forth in order to claim it had met a target of so many ton-miles. Similarly sewing machines and tractors were manufactured "efficiently" without a model change long after the demand for them had been saturated.

In recent years, however, such meaningless physical quotas are beginning to be replaced by "profitability" criteria of performance that do involve *economic valuations* (in terms of the scarcity of resources) of diverse goods.

Today, the success of many enterprises producing consumer goods, as well as the success of a few other enterprises, is judged on the basis of a profit rate that includes a charge on capital used by the enterprise. In order to make a profit at all, the goods or services of the enterprise must be sold, and that means they must be of acceptable quality. In this way, particularly in the field of consumer goods, a higher degree of efficiency is encouraged. Although the enterprise still operates on the plan handed to it from above, the profitability criterion is a step in the direction of rational pricing methods. (But it is worth noting that under this new decentralization of management, Russia has the same grave difficulty as the West in persuading industries to stop polluting rivers and the air! In both economies, no price is set on the exploitation of the environment.)

The decision of how to combine various productive factors—land and labor, degree of mechanization—appears to depend on a mixture of purely technical considerations and adaptations to the scarcities of various economic resources. A continual process of trial and error goes on.

---

[1] Marshall I. Goldman's *Comparative Economic Systems* (New York: Random House, 1971, 2nd ed.), is an excellent reference. See also, in P.A. Samuelson's *Readings in Economics* (New York: McGraw-Hill, 1973, 7th ed.), articles by Harvard's expert Abram Bergson.

The observer finds operations curiously uneven: on the one hand, he may see a military ballistic plant which has achieved a precision of ball bearings and gyroscopes rivaling the best in the world; on the other hand, he may find things being done in an almost unbelievably primitive way, with the quality of output practically worthless. (EXAMPLE: A Soviet farmwoman may be assigned one cow to take care of; on an Ontario dairy farm, a man and wife may take care of 50 cows, in addition to performing countless other daily chores.)

All Soviet economic life is a pyramid tapering upward. Above the individual enterprises in an industry and region will be a regional economic council. Above the regional councils will be a council of ministers; alongside the ministries will be the planners of the Gosplan. Experts tell us it is quite misleading to concentrate on the organizational charts of the process, for *there is a constantly changing mixture of centralization and decentralization*; commands delegated responsibility, and initiative; carrots of reward and kicks or imprisonments as penalties.

Some things are very much the same everywhere. The head of an enterprise will, almost certainly, be a member of the Communist party. A successful bureaucrat there is something like a successful "organization man" here: he must be obedient but resourceful, both obsequious and arrogant, energetic and nonsentimental. The point is not that the worst types get ahead. Rather the point is that ability does count on the average; but mere technical ability without the skill of getting along with people will not usually be enough either in Hamilton or in Volgograd. Padding of expense accounts and contriving to hold business meetings near popular Black Sea resorts or spas in the Caucasus Mountains are complained of regularly in the Soviet press.

Experts also tell us that it is quite naive to think that there is an elaborate formalized structure of planning, so that one could write a treatise on pure communistic economics that would equal in length a treatise on the general equilibrium of purely competitive market systems, which is long indeed.

FOR WHOM   To a considerable degree the Russian economy works for the security of the state and for the future. How much the present generation of Russians consume of private goods is not primarily determined by their day-to-day spending and working decisions. True, they do earn wages (and a small amount of interest or lottery winnings on government bonds is also permitted). Moreover, wages are by no means equal, and certainly not higher for the needy and handicapped than for the energetic and skilled. Skilled workers get much more than unskilled. Free trade-unions as we know them do not exist, but woe to the manager who gets all the workers against him. Piece rates and incentive systems are frequently used, and there is much exhortation toward working hard for the fatherland and for the "brotherhood of man." (Soviet novels often had for their plots the tale of how a good boy and girl foil the malingering of antisocial culprits and by use of a virtuous tractor overcome the recalcitrance of the stub-

born soil. Boy meets girl here as everywhere, but the durable goods are much in evidence.)

Social classes as Marx and Engels knew them in 1848 may not exist in the Soviet Union. But there is a definite pattern of social and political stratification. A poor boy who is bright may become a physicist and live well. It is important for him to rank high in the exams that select the few who can go to college. (His way at the university is completely paid for, just as the comrade who puts the shot in the Olympics is paid to pursue that occupation.) After graduation he hopes to score well enough to be able to pursue the study of physics in Moscow, rather than be sent out as a technician and engineer to the Ural Mountains or some other distant post. As a well-paid professor he can look down on all but the top bureaucrats: he may have a car, a cottage in the country, and finely equipped laboratories. Of course, he cannot take it with him, but he can at least hope to give his son a good start in the stiff educational competition.

There are various economic devices by which the system ensures that it gets the FOR WHOM it desires—heavy emphasis on *industrialization* and *military security*.

For one thing, goods at every stage of production are subject to heavy taxation (the so-called "turnover tax," which is assessed on the *total* value of an item at each successive stage of production rather than on the true value *added*). The resulting elevation of prices in relation to wages paid out ensures that the public will be able to consume only a part of all that they can produce, in quite the same way as our economy uses taxes to siphon resources away from private and into public channels. Overall anti-inflationary policy is needed there as here!

Another device is to set a much higher mark-up over production costs for consumers' goods, ensuring that they generally are priced much higher (and hence their consumption is discouraged) than are military and capital goods. As a third device, certain consumers' goods, such as comfortable housing, are just not purchasable at any price for any but the few lucky persons of peculiar economic and political advantage.

By all such methods the Soviet authorities fight the battle against the price inflation that would burst out as workers try to spend their incomes on the limited supply of consumers' goods. To one who has studied modern economics, it is evident that these are devices by which their society determines FOR WHOM goods will be produced in accordance with *social* decision making.

NEW TRENDS IN EASTERN EUROPEAN ECONOMICS?

Communist economics is in a state of flux. In recent years intense debates have broken out in Poland, Hungary, Czechoslovakia, and within Russia itself concerning the use of some kind of supply-and-demand pricing, coupled with profitability criteria that look a little like the analytical tools of Western economics. Nineteenth century Marxian concepts seem to be reserved for training of the young, especially for alleged explanation and denouncement of capitalistic economies. Among the high-level planners themselves, few words are squandered on Marxist interpretation. Instead, as in the much-debated writings of E. Liberman, there are attempts to get away from setting of crude quantitative goals expressed in physical units. There is to be emphasis on quality and on weighting items by their importance, setting for the plant manager the goal of maximizing something very like a *profitability* magnitude. The hope is to get him to try new products and methods and economize on input requirements, rather than concentrate on establishing a low output quota for his plant. Since 1967, the Soviet Union, and the satellites, notably Czechoslovakia, have experimented with various partially-free markets.

Mathematical methods, such as the input-output analysis associated with W. W. Leontief of Harvard, have been released from Stalin's ban, and are debated as a possible tool for helping the planners allocate their available resources. More advanced methods, known in the West as linear and more general mathematical programming, have been developed by eminent Soviet mathematicians (Kantorowich, Pontryagin, . . .); rates of discount, rather like the interest rates used in mixed economies to screen out less important capital or investment projects, have been proposed in considerable variety. Although it cannot yet be said that planners anywhere in the world rely primarily on the socialist game of a pricing system as will be described in the Appendix of Chapter 32, there seems increasingly to be a pragmatic mixture of physical accounting, and economic planning. And the pendulum oscillates between epochs of decentralization and of centralization.[2]

All in all, it is a vulgar mistake to think that most people are miserable in the Marxist countries. Although it is undoubtedly true that few citizens of the West would trade their degree of economic comfort and political freedom for life in the Soviet Union, it is also true that a Soviet citizen thinks that he is living in a paradise in comparison with life in China or in earlier times. Remember that life under the czars was no bed of roses for most classes; and to the eye of the traveler from impoverished Asia and Africa, the rising degree of Russian affluence must seem impressive.

Figure 3-2 shows recent growth *per capita* rates for the U.S.S.R., China and the western economies. Obviously,

---

[2]Agricultural performance, still seems to be remarkably bad on the Russian collective and state farms. These appear to be much too large for efficiency, averaging 7,000 and 22,000 acres of sown land, in contrast to the 400-acre average of our efficient commercial farms. Private farming is permitted in only minute degree, but the product of these private efforts seems to be many times higher per unit of input than on the collective and state farms. Uniform rules, ill informed and subject to swings of fad and fashion, get imposed on everybody in a region. Supplies of tractor equipment, spare parts, fertilizers, and fungicides are quite limited, and optimal use is not made of them by the rural populace, who have little incentive to be efficient. Despite unfavorable weather, much improved efficiency would seem technically feasible and is being sought after in each of the communist bloc economies by different methods, each closer to the price mechanism of the capitalist or free market economy.

Russia and the West are adopting new technologies at about the same rate.

DIVERSITY ON THE LEFT: YUGOSLAVIA

YUGOSLAV DECENTRALIZATION The communist resistance-movement came to power under Tito after World War II. From 1945 to 1950 a program of planned development along conventional Stalinist lines worked out badly—both in terms of planning goals and in comparison with post-World War I similar years. Following the political break with the eastern European socialist economies in 1948, Yugoslavia undertook a new "separate path to socialism" involving "decentralization and popular participation." The experiment has excited much interest abroad, both for its own sake and as a successful retreat from Soviet dominance.

In essence, Titoism involves a return to greater dependence on market pricing, on profitability criteria and incentives. It does not mean abandonment of socialism and one-party control, nor of central planning of macroeconomic goals. But it does mean that a factory may be run by its own workers in many sectors of the economy. Here is a sample case.

Twenty to one hundred workers in a factory form a workers' council. Nominally they elect their own managers. (They may even advertise for a trained executive!) They "borrow" their capital from the central pool. (Sometimes capital is "auctioned" off to the highest bidder.) *The firm can decide to produce what it thinks will sell.* It may import raw materials from abroad, sometimes even on foreign credit. It can cut costs in the hope that, after it has paid its income and land taxes, what is left over can go to the workers as bonus income or be plowed back into the enterprise.

How have things worked out? From 1950 to 1975 progress has been uneven, and there have been oscillations between centralization and decentralization. But the system has been viable, and growth under it has surpassed that of the earlier Stanlinist period. Even if the cynicism expressed by insiders concerning the amount of power the workers themselves exercise is justified, this system of syndicalist structure presumably offers some countervailing influence to the power of the bureaucrats, those whom Milovan Djilas has called "the new class." The test to come will be when Tito dies.

MAOIST CHINA China is as far to the left of the U.S.S.R. as Yugoslavia is to the right. But by any common-sense definition, China is under-developed: a huge population wresting a living from limited resources. For centuries, population pressure and uncertain crops have kept millions of her people on the brink of starvation.

By the calculations of Western economists—such as Alexander Eckstein of the University of Michigan—China's real growth rate of national output from 1963 to 1970, about 6½ per cent per year, was better than in the preceding Nationalist regime, in the 'twenties and 'thirties. It was achieved while Mao's strategy was to put all his eggs in one basket: he put all his investment funds into manu-

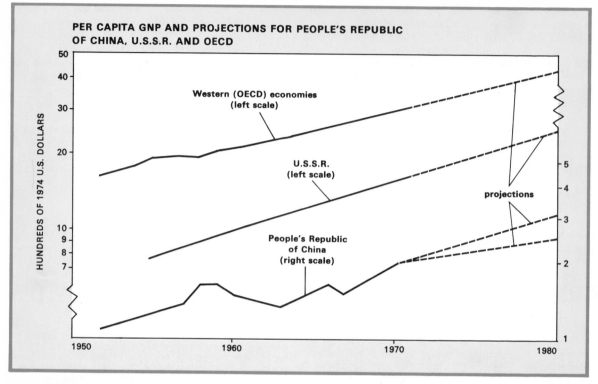

FIG. 3-2. Will China's productivity catch up to the West?
These curves show a comparison of *per capita* GNP figures,
which ignores differing population growth rates and stresses
growth of individual consumption and output possibilities.
The OECD (Organization for Economic Cooperation and Development) consists of 22 European, North American, and Asian market-system economies; its growth rate is dominated by
the U.S.A., Japan and Germany. The U.S.S.R. and China data
were drawn from a number of sources, especially measurements by the World Bank, Ellen Mickiewicz and Alexander Eckstein. All projections are geometric extensions of
past data; China's extend the last five, and the last ten years.
Note that the curves are plotted on a "ratio", not on an "arithmetic" vertical scale.

facturing. In this strategy he relied on the "collectivization" of peasant farming to make up for his de-
priving agriculture of investment funds.

This collectivization process, in 1958, was transformed
into Mao's "Great Leap Forward." Enterprises as large as
whole counties, "communes," took over from the family
and the village as a way of life and from the farm and the
collective as the unit for economic planning and production. Furthermore, industry itself was in large part to be
decentralized and meshed with the rural commune.

The excesses of this frenzied reorganization (e.g., the
attempts to make iron and steel in backyard furnaces),
and set-backs in farm output led to a strong political reaction, and Mao lost much of his nominal power. The Liu
Shao-ch'i group reinstated but modified the old priorities,
finding some funds for investment in agriculture and light
industry. But some of the economic costs of the Great
Leap had still to be paid: in the communes the peasant incentives were impaired, and in industry the help received
from Russia was abruptly terminated.

These problems were aggravated by several years of
bad crop weather, beginning in 1959. During this period

much food was imported, especially grain from Canada.

Yet, although the policies of the Great Leap clearly
failed, it is not so clear that they were all irrational. Thus,
although the backyard steel furnaces produced little steel,
the quest for an "intermediate technology" (that is, production processes suited to countries that are rich in labor
but poor in capital) does make sense. And the agricultural
communes, for all their problems, were intended to increase agricultural output, not merely to increase the
state's share of a fixed level of crops. (In fact, Mao has
written sharply of Stalin's agricultural procurement as
"draining the pond to catch the fish.")

Since 1959 there has been an almost complete blackout
of economic data, in the domestic Chinese press as well
as in Peking's foreign-language publications. Yet we do
have a few bits and snatches of information. For example,
a delegation of Pakistani officials visiting China in 1965
asked for and received a set of official figures for grain
output. According to these figures, the 1957 level of grain
output was restored by 1961. Of course, population had
grown in the meantime, so that the 1957 *per capita* figure
was not reached again until about 1963. (The Chinese

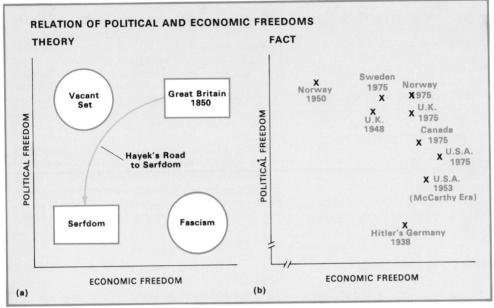

FIG. 3-3. History and current experience deny that economic reform must lead to serfdom.
The libertarian thesis of Hayek alleges—as in (a) on the left—that government modification of market *laissez faire* **must lead inevitably to political serfdom. But confronting this hypothesis with the facts—as marshaled in (b) on the right—we do not find it validated.**

have launched vigorous birth-control campaigns, but population growth remains nearly 2 per cent a year.) If these Chinese grain statistics are reliable, they indicate a substantially more rapid recovery from the "bad years" after the Great Leap than outside observers had previously guessed.

Beginning in 1966, Chairman Mao (or those around him) began to reassert control over economic policies, through the mechanism of the Great Proletarian Cultural Revolution. Published attacks on economic reforms of the Yugoslav type, on Western technical knowledge, and on Liu Shao-ch'i himself became very strident. (Liu was called a "renegade, hidden traitor, and scab.") But what effect this has had on the organizing or the functioning of the economy is still a matter for conjecture. In 1969, Professors Liu and Galenson of Cornell argued as follows:

"The national product fell by roughly 15 per cent from 1958 to 1961. . . . Only by 1965 did the economy finally regain the 1958 level. . . . The Great Proletarian Cultural Revolution . . . led to a loss of 400,000 specialists who would have completed their training during 1967-68 had the schools not been closed. . . . Economism—i.e., efficiency, became one of the worst epithets. . . . Revolutionary mass enthusiasm replaced trained management. . . . Essentially, there has been no significant economic growth for the decade 1958-68."[3]

But recent reports show much higher growth rates. Since the late 1960's, rapid increases in industrial produc-

tion, and particularly in farm production, have testified not only to the better harvests, but also to improved organization and morale. The two projections in Figure 3-2 show the difference between the last five years and the last ten years of *per capita* output.

A NONECONOMIC VIEW

There is a temptation for those living in the most prosperous part of the world to succumb to complacency, both about themselves and about their mixed economy. And indeed the Western world has made tremendous progress since even so recent a date as 1929.

But at the same time, we find that many features of economic life, which we are about to study in detail, are ethically troublesome, especially to the younger generation. We see economic change and improvement over the last century, yet we are still faced with many seemingly unanswerable questions. For example, how fast must a mixed economy ideally change over time? You cannot expect a hungry mother in Nova Scotia to give the same answer as a debutante from Havergal.

Thus we are faced with value judgments above and beyond the scope of the "neutral science" of economics. We must remember that these same value-judgment questions lie in the background of our purely economic discussions of the remaining text. Beyond the internal questions of technical economics, there emerge basic political questions concerning the possible combinations of (1) *individual* freedom—civil liberties and personal rights—

[3]Letter to *New York Times*, 17 June, 1969, by Professors Walter Galenson and Ta-Chung Liu.

(2) *economic* freedoms—not only in WHAT and HOW to produce (by personal choice versus central control and plan), but also FOR WHOM to produce (decisions by private resource owners versus the state). The possible combinations are usually unheeded. At one extreme, almost always those who wish to reform the workings of the system wish to turn to government for new programs and measures. But those concerned to conserve what they regard as valuable in our society counter them with the arguments: "In seeking *a better division* of the pie, you will *reduce the size* of the pie by creating distorting inefficiencies. But more important, *personal and property freedoms are one and inseparable.* Only in the Herbert Spencer *laissez-faire* society, that you find so repellent, will men be free to speak their minds and choose their rulers."

Let us momentarily and cautiously relax the rigor of analysis and speculate about what has not yet been capable of scientific agreement.

What are the presumed relationships, suggested by experience and plausible reflection, between the state of individual freedoms and the interventions by government in the mixed economy?

Figure 3-3 suggests an eclectic alternative to the despairing extreme of a Hayek who says, Economic reform is the road to serfdom; and to the extreme of those who, like Sidney and Beatrice Webb, argued: Political democracy is nothing without the economic democracy that comes only with collective ownership of the means of production.

Then perhaps one may read in the face of history the more optimistic message: One can have the best of both worlds—programmed improvement of the workings of the market economy along with those best things of life that aren't measured in monetary terms—freedom to do one's own thing, freedom to criticize, and freedom to change.

SUMMARY TO APPENDIX

1 State ownership of the factors of production is basic to the Soviet system. Workers earn wages and have a degree of choice of occupation.

2 The WHAT question in the Soviet Union is largely answered by state planners. The division between defense and capital formation and consumer goods is purely a state decision, although the consumer exerts some influence over the assortment of consumer goods to be produced.

3 The HOW decision is made partly by the central planners and partly by the manager of a state enterprise in response to bonus criteria. Economic valuations in terms of resource scarcity are becoming more prevalent in determining HOW than they were in earlier years.

4 The FOR WHOM decision is largely made by the state, although income will determine which individuals receive consumer goods—provided the goods are available. The state turnover tax and a much higher mark-up over production costs for consumer goods assure that monetary command over resources is diverted to the state so that the emphasis on industrialization and military security may continue—at the expense of consumption.

5 New trends behind the Iron Curtain include the adoption and adaptation of certain Western tools such as profitability criteria and the use of discount rates which resemble interest rates. Similarly, experiments with partially free markets have occurred in several Soviet bloc countries as the pendulum oscillates between centralization and decentralization. In satellite countries the issues of pricing and/or planning are being debated.

6 Yugoslavia has experimented with decentralization and with popular participation which involves greater dependence on market pricing, profitability criteria, and cooperative organization; though central planning of macroeconomic goals remains an important part of the system.

7 Maoist China is at the other extreme of the communist spectrum. After uneven spurts and changes in policies. China may be moving ahead economically, although the data available after 1959 is sketchy at best.

8 One must be careful in comparing the "success" of different systems because the starting conditions, the goals, and the means of measurement vary among systems. Value judgements which are beyond the scope of the "neutral science" of economics are involved.

CONCEPTS FOR REVIEW

centralized planning, Soviet style
Yugoslavian hybrid
Chinese pattern
centralization and decentralization of planning   new U.S.S.R. pricing and profitability trends
economic freedoms, individual freedoms,

QUESTIONS FOR DISCUSSION

1 Outline WHAT, HOW and FOR WHOM in the Soviet Union.
2 What economic aspects of the Western world have predisposed developing countries like Ghana, Egypt, and Indonesia to experiment with the Soviet path to development?
3 Consider the place of Canada, China, the U.K. and the U.S.S.R. in Figure 3-3, in the light of events since 1974.

4
SUPPLY AND DEMAND: THE BARE ELEMENTS

You can make even a parrot into a learned political economist—all he must learn are the two words "supply" and "demand." ANONYMOUS

Every short statement about economics is misleading (with the possible exception of my present one). ALFRED MARSHALL

Chapters 2 and 3 and their Appendices introduced the three basic problems every economy must face.

1 WHAT shall be produced of the great variety of possible goods and services, and in precisely what quantities?

2 HOW shall society combine its different productive factors—land, labor, and so forth—to produce each good?

3 FOR WHOM shall goods be produced—which is the problem of how the national product is to be distributed among the different members of the populace with their different labor skills and ownerships of land and capital goods?

Chapter 2 showed that a variety of systems could be thought of to solve these three problems. WHAT, HOW, and FOR WHOM might be determined by custom, instinct, or central command. But Chapter 3 indicated that our mixed economy relies primarily on none of these to solve its basic problems. Instead it relies on a system of markets and prices.

The consumer, so it is said, is the king. Or rather, with every man a king, each is a voter who uses his money as votes to get the thing done that he wants done. His votes must compete with other men's votes; and the people with the most votes end up with the most influence on what gets produced and on where those goods go.

Now our task is to see just how this spending of money votes—this system of "consumer sovereignty"—takes place under the checks and balances of economic competition.

THE MARKET MECHANISM

Let us take an example. You wake up this morning with an urge for a new pair of shoes. You would not think of saying, "I'll go down to the city hall and vote for the mayor most likely to give me a new pair of shoes. Of course, I mean a new pair of size 9, soft-leather, dark-brown shoes."

Or, to take an actual case from history, suppose men begin to get prosperous enough to afford meat every day and do not have to fill up on potatoes. How does their desire to substitute meat for potatoes get translated into action? What politician do they tell? What orders does he in turn give to farmers to move from New Brunswick to Alberta? How much extra rent does he decide will be needed to bribe landlords to transfer land from potato production to cattle grazing? And how does he make sure that people get what they want of pork and lamb as well as of beef? And who is to get the choice cuts?

Why belabor the obvious? Everyone knows it never worked itself out that way at all. What happened was this. Consumers began to buy fewer potatoes and more meat. *That raised the price of meat and cut the price of potatoes.* So there resulted losses to the potato growers and gains to the ranchers. Ranch labor found it could hold out for higher wages, and many a potato digger quit his job for a better-paying job elsewhere. In time, the higher meat prices brought larger productions of beef, pork, and lamb. And the different parts of the cow—its horn, hide, liver, kidneys, choice tenderloin, and tough ribs—got auctioned off for what each part would bring.

To show that it is not some important government official or businessman who sets relative prices, see what actually happened when science discovered that liver was good for anemia. Kidneys, mysteriously, were previously dearer than liver. In fact, according to the records, you could hardly give liver away before this discovery. Now go to the butcher shop: price liver; and, if you can find any, also price kidneys. A veritable revolution has taken place; the price of liver has risen greatly relative to the price of kidneys, so as to *ration* the limited supply of liver among the eager demanders for it—all through the *impersonal* workings of supply and demand.

A system of prices Similar revolutions are taking place in the economic market place all the time. As people's desires and needs change, as engineering methods change, as supplies of energy resources and other productive factors change, the market place registers changes in the prices and the quantities sold of commodities and productive services—of tea, sugar, and beef; of land, labor, and machines. There exists a *system of prices*, a concept that is far from obvious.

The purpose of this chapter is to show how supply and demand work themselves out in the competitive market *for one particular good*. We shall define a demand curve and then a supply curve. Finally, we shall see how the market price reaches its competitive equilibrium, where these two curves intersect— where the forces of demand and supply are just in balance.

THE DEMAND SCHEDULE

Let us start with demand. It is commonly observed: The quantity of a good that people will buy at any one time depends on price; the *higher* the price charged for an article, the *less* the quantity of it people will be willing to buy; and, other things being equal, the lower its market price, the more units of it will be demanded.

Thus there exists at any one time a definite relation between the market price of a good (such as wheat) and the quantity demanded of that good. The relationship between price and quantity bought is called the "demand schedule," or "demand curve."

The table of Fig. 4-1 gives an example of a hypothetical demand schedule. At any price, such as $5 per pushel, there is a definite quantity of wheat that will be demanded by all the consumers in the market —in this case 9 (million) bushels per month. At a lower price, such as $4, the quantity bought is even greater, being 10 (million) units. From Fig. 4-1's table we can read the *quantity demanded at any price*, by comparing Column (2) with Column (1).

THE DEMAND CURVE

The numerical data can be given a graphic interpretation also. The vertical scale in Fig. 4-1 represents the various alternative prices of wheat, measured in dollars per bushel. The horizontal scale measures the quantity of wheat (in terms of bushels) that will be demanded per month.

A city corner is located as soon as we know its street and avenue; a ship's position is located as soon as we know its latitude and longitude. Similarly, to plot a point on this diagram, we must have two coordinate numbers: a price and a quantity. For our first point *A*, corresponding to $5 and 9 million bushels, we move upward 5 units and then over to the right 9 units. A dot marks the spot *A*. To get the next dot, at *B*, we go up only 4 units and over to the right 10 units. The last dot is shown by *E*. Through the dots we draw a smooth dark brown curve, marked *dd*.

This picturization of the demand schedule is called the "demand curve." Note that quantity and price are inversely related, *Q* going up when *P* goes down. The curve slopes downward, going from northwest to southeast. This important property is given a name: the *law of downward-sloping demand*. This law is true of practically all commodities: wheat, electric razors, cotton, ethyl gasoline, cornflakes, and theater tickets.

The law of downward-sloping demand: When the price of a good is raised (at the same time that all other things are held constant), less of it will be demanded. Or, what is the same thing: If a greater quantity of a good is thrown on the market, then— other things being equal—it can be sold only at a lower price.

DEMAND SCHEDULE FOR WHEAT		
(1)	(2)	(3)
PRICE ($ per bu.) *P*	QUANTITY DEMANDED (million bu. per month) *Q*	
A $5	9	
B 4	10	
C 3	12	
D 2	15	
E 1	20	

FIG. 4-1. A downward-sloping demand curve relates quantity to price.

At each market price, there will be at any time a definite quantity of wheat that people will want to demand. At a lower price, the quantity demanded will go up—as more people substitute it for other goods and feel they can afford to gratify their less important wants for wheat. Compare table's *Q* and *P* at *A, B, C, D, E*.

In the figure, prices are measured on the vertical axis and quantities demanded on the horizontal axis. Each pair of *Q, P* numbers from the table is plotted here as a point, and a smooth curve passed through the points gives us the demand curve.

The fact that *dd* goes downward and to the right illustrates the very important "law of downward-sloping demand."

Ignore column (3). It will be explained on page 67

REASONS FOR LAW OF DOWNWARD-SLOPING DEMAND

This law is in accordance with common sense and has been known in at least a vague way since the beginning of recorded history. The reasons for it are not hard to identify. When the price of wheat is sky high, only rich men will be able to afford it; the poor will have to make do with rye bread, just as they still must do in poorer lands. When the price is still high but not quite so high as before, persons of moderate means who also happen to have an especially great liking for white bread will be coaxed into buying some wheat.

Thus a first reason for the validity of the law of downward-sloping demand comes from the fact that *lowering prices brings in new buyers*.

Not quite so obvious is a second, equally important, reason for the law's validity; namely, each

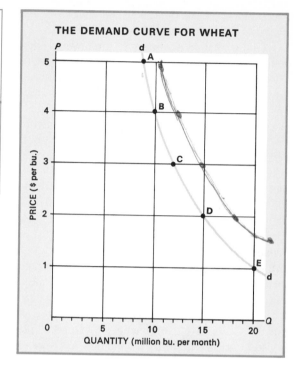

THE DEMAND CURVE FOR WHEAT

reduction of price may coax out some *extra purchases by each of the good's consumers*; and—what is the same thing—a rise in price may cause any one of us to buy less. Why does my quantity demanded tend to fall as price rises? For two main reasons. When the price of a good rises, I naturally try to *substitute* other goods for it (rye for wheat or tea for coffee, for example). Also, when a price goes up, I find myself really poorer than I was; and I will naturally cut down on my consumption of most normal goods when I feel poorer and have less real *income*.

Here are further examples of cases where I buy more of a good as it becomes more plentiful and its price drops. When water is very dear, I demand only enough of it to drink. Then when its price drops, I buy some to wash with. At still lower prices, I resort to still other uses; finally, when it is really very cheap, I water flowers and use it lavishly for any possible purpose. (Note once again that someone poorer than I will probably begin to use water to wash his car only at a lower price than at which I buy water for that purpose. Since market demand is the sum of all different people's demands, what does this mean? It means that even after *my* quantity demanded stops expanding very much with price decreases, the *total*

SUPPLY SCHEDULE FOR WHEAT		
(1)	(2)	(3)
POSSIBLE PRICES ($ per bu.) P	QUANTITY SELLERS WILL SUPPLY (million bu. per month) Q	
A	$5	18
B	4	16
C	3	12
D	2	7
E	1	0

FIG. 4-2 The supply curve relates price to the quantity produced.

The table lists, for each price, the quantity that producers will want to bring to market. The diagram plots the *(P, Q)* pair of numbers taken from the table as the indicated black points. A smooth curve passed through these points gives the black upward-sloping supply curve, *ss*.

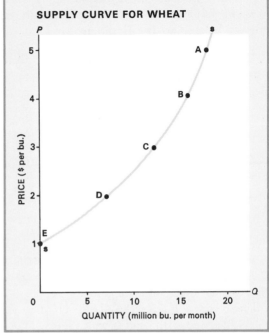

bought in the market may still expand as new uses for *new people* come into effect.)

To confirm your understanding of the demand concept, imagine there is an increase in demand for wheat brought about by a boom in people's incomes or by a great rise in the market price of the competing corn or simply by a change in people's tastes in favour of wheat. Show that this *shifts* the whole demand curve in Fig. 4-1 rightward, and hence upward; pencil in such a new curve and label it *d'd'* to distinguish if from the old *dd* curve. Note that such an increase in demand means that more will now be bought at each price—as can be verified by carefully reading off points from the new curve and filling in a new *Q* column for Fig. 4-1's table.

THE SUPPLY SCHEDULE

Let us now turn from demand to supply. The demand schedule related market prices and the amounts *consumers* wish to buy. How is the supply schedule defined?

By the *supply schedule, or curve,* is meant the relation between market prices and the amounts of the good that *producers* are willing to supply.

The table of Fig. 4-2 illustrates the supply schedule for wheat, and Fig. 4-2 plots it as a supply curve. Unlike the demand curve, the supply curve for wheat normally rises upward and to the right, from southwest to northeast.

At a higher price of wheat, farmers will take acres out of corn cultivation and put them into wheat. In addition, each can now afford the cost of more fertilizer, more labor, more machinery, and can even afford to grow extra wheat on poorer land. All this tends to increase output at the higher prices offered.

As will be seen in Part Three, our old friend the law of diminishing returns provides one strong reason why the supply curve would slope upward. If society wants more wine, more and more labor will have to be added to the same limited hill sites suitable for producing wine grapes. Even if this industry is too small to affect the general wage rate for labor, each new man will—according to the law of diminishing returns—be adding less and less extra product; and hence the necessary cost to coax out additional product will have to rise. (Cost and returns are opposite sides of the same coin, as will be shown later.[1])

[1] While the exceptions to the law of the downward-sloping demand are few enough to be unimportant in practice, we shall encounter in Part Three some interesting exceptions to the upward-sloping supply curve. Thus, suppose that a family farmer produces wheat and its price rises so much as to give him a much higher income. With wheat so lucrative, he is at first tempted to *substitute* some of his leisure time to produce more of it. But won't there reasonably come a time when he feels comfortable enough at his higher *income* to be able to afford to take things easier and supply less *Q*?

How shall we depict an increase in supply? An increase in supply means an increase in the amounts that will be supplied at each different price. Now if you pencil the new supply curve into Fig. 4-2, you will see that it has shifted *rightward*; but for an upward-sloping supply curve, this change means the new *s's'* curve will have been shifted rightward and *downward* (not rightward and upward as in the case of a shifted downward-sloping demand curve). To verify that *s's'* does depict an increase in supply, fill in a new column in the table of Fig. 4-2 by reading off points from the new diagram carefully.

EQUILIBRIUM OF SUPPLY AND DEMAND

Let us now combine our analysis of demand and supply to see how competitive market price is determined. This combining is done in Fig. 4-3's table. Thus far, we have been considering all prices as possible. We have said, "If price is so and so, sales *(Q)* will be so and so; if *P* is such and such, *Q* will be such and such; and so forth." But to which level will price *actually* go? And how much will then be produced and consumed? The supply schedule alone cannot tell us. Neither can the demand schedule alone.

Let us do what an auctioneer would do, i.e., proceed by trial and error. Can situation *A* in Table 4-3, with wheat selling for $5 per bushel, prevail for any period of time? The answer is a clear No. At $5, the producers will be supplying 18 (million) bushels to the market every month [Column (3)]. But the amount demanded by consumers will be only 9 (million) bushels per month [Column (2)]. *As stocks of wheat pile up, competitive sellers will cut the price a little*. Thus, as Column (4) shows, price will tend to fall; but it will not fall indefinitely to zero.

To understand this better, let us try the point *E* with price equal to only $1 per bushel. Can that price persist? Again, obviously not, for a comparison of Columns (2) and (3) shows that desired consumption will exceed production *at that price*. Storehouses will begin to be emptied; *disappointed demanders who cannot get wheat will tend to bid up the too-low price*. This upward pressure on price is shown by Column (4)'s rising arrow.

We could go on to try other prices, but by now the answer is obvious.

The equilibrium price, i.e., the only price that can last, is that at which the amount *willingly* supplied and the amount *willingly* demanded are equal. Competitive equilibrium must be at the intersection point of supply and demand curves.

Only at *C*, with a price of $3, will amount demanded by consumers, 12 (million) bushels per month, exactly equal the amount supplied by producers, 12 (million). Price is at equilibrium, just as an olive at the bottom of a cocktail glass is at equilibrium, because there is no tendency for it to rise or fall. (Of course, this stationary price may not be reached at once. There may have to be an initial period of trial and error, of oscillation around the right level, before price finally settles down and the amount supplied balances the amount demanded.

Fig. 4-3's diagram shows the same equilibrium in pictorial form. The supply and demand curves, superimposed on the same diagram, cross at only one intersection point. This point *C* represents the equilibrium price and quantity.

At a higher price, the black bar shows the *excess* of amount supplied over amount demanded. The arrows point downward to show the direction in which price will move because of the competition of *sellers*. At a price lower than the $3 equilibrium price, the black bar shows that the amount demanded exceeds the amount supplied. Consequently, the eager bidding of *buyers* requires us to point the arrow indicators upward to show the pressure that they are exerting on price. Only at the point *C* will there be a balancing of forces and a stationary maintainable price.

Such is the essence of the doctrine of supply and demand.

EFFECT OF A SHIFT IN SUPPLY AND DEMAND

Now we can put the supply and demand apparatus to work. Gregory King, an English writer of the seventeenth century, noticed that when the harvest was bad, food rose in price; and when in was plentiful, farmers got a lower price. Let us try to explain what happens by our diagrams.

Fig. 4-4(a) shows how a spell of bad weather *reduces* the amount that farmers will supply at each and every market price and thereby displaces the equilibrium point *E*. The *ss* curve has shifted to the left and has become *s's'*. The demand curve has not changed. Where does the new supply curve *s's'* intersect *dd*? Plainly at *E'*, the new equilibrium price

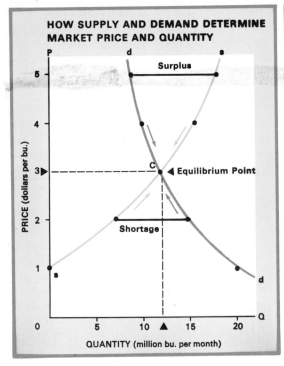

HOW SUPPLY AND DEMAND DETERMINE MARKET PRICE AND QUANTITY

SUPPLY AND DEMAND SCHEDULES FOR WHEAT

	(1) POSSIBLE PRICES ($ per bu.)	(2) QUANTITY DEMANDED (million bu. per month)	(3) QUANTITY SUPPLIED (million bu. per month)	(4) PRESSURE ON PRICE
A	$5	9	18	Downward
B	4	10	16	Downward
C	3	12	12	Neutral
D	2	15	7	Upward
E	1	20	0	Upward

FIG. 4-3. Equilibrium price is at the intersection point where supply and demand match.

Only at the equilibrium price of $3, shown in the third row, will the amount supplied just match the amount demanded.

In the diagram, at the *C* equilibrium intersection the amount supplied just matches the amount demanded. At any lower *P*, the excess amount demanded will force *P* back up; and at any *P* higher than the equilibrium, *P* will be forced back down to it.

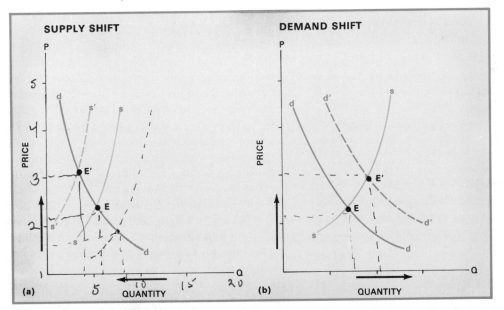

FIG. 4-4. When either the supply or the demand curve shifts, equilibrium price changes.
(a). If supply shifts leftward for any reason, the equilibrium-price intersection will travel up the demand curve, giving higher *P* and lower *Q*.
(b). If demand shifts rightward, the equilibrium will travel up the supply curve.

where the amount demanded and the new reduced amount supplied have again come into balance. Naturally, P has risen. And because of the law of downward-sloping demand, Q has gone down.

Suppose the supply curve, because of good weather and cheaper fertilizers, had *increased* instead. Draw in a new equilibrium E'' with lower P and higher Q.

Our apparatus will also help us analyze the effect of an increase in demand. Suppose that rising family incomes make everyone want more wheat. Then at each unchanged P, greater Q will now be demanded. The demand curve will shift rightward to $d'd'$. Figure 4-4(b) shows the resulting travel up the supply curve as enhanced demand competitively rasies equilibrium price (to the E' intersection).

TWO STUMBLING BLOCKS: "METHODOLOGY"

It is well to pause here to consider two minor sources of possible confusion concerning supply and demand. These have puzzled students of economics in all generations. The first point deals with the important fact that in drawing up a demand schedule or curve, one always insists that "other things must be equal." The second deals with the exact sense in which demand and supply are equal in equilibrium.

"OTHER THINGS EQUAL" To draw up a demand schedule for wheat, we vary the price of wheat and observe what would happen to its quantity bought *at any one period of time in which no other factors are allowed to change so as to becloud our experiment.*

Specifically, this means that, as we change wheat's P, we must not at the same time change family income or the price of a competing product such as rye or anything else that would tend to *shift* the demand schedule for wheat. Why? Because, like any scientist who wants to isolate the effects of one causal factor, we must try to vary only *one* thing at a time. True enough, in economics we cannot perform controlled experiments in a laboratory, and we can rarely hold other things constant in making statistical observations of economic magnitudes. This limitation on our ability to experiment empirically in economics makes it all the more important *to be clear in our logical thinking*, so that we may hope to recognize and evaluate important tendencies—such as the effect of P on Q demanded—when *other* tendencies

are likely to be impinging on the situation at the same time.

The case of demand shift in Fig. 4-4(b), can illustrate this common fallacy based upon a failure to respect the rule that other things must be held equal in defining a demand curve. Suppose that the supply curve shifts little or not at all. But suppose the demand curve shifts up to $d'd'$ in good times when jobs are plentiful and people have the incomes to buy more wheat; and suppose in the more depressed phase of the business cycle demand always shifts down to dd. Now take a piece of graph paper and plot what would actually be recorded in the statistics of the wheat market.

In boom times you would record the equilibrium point E', and in bad times the equilibrium point E. Take a ruler and join the points E and E'. The fallacy to be avoided like the plague is expressed as follows: "I have disproved the law of downward-sloping demand; for note that when P was high, so too was Q—as shown by E'. And when P was lowered, instead of that change increasing Q, it actually lowered Q—as shown by E. My straight line joining E and E' represents an upward-sloping, not a downward-sloping, demand curve; so I have refuted a basic economic law."

Being alerted beforehand, one detects the fallacy of this argument. For at the same time that P went up, other things were *not* held constant; rather, income was also raised. The tendency for a rise in P to choke off purchases was more than masked by the countertendency of rising income to raise purchases. Instead of testing our economic law by moving *along* the demand curve, the beginner has measured changes that result from the *shift* of the demand curve.

Why is this bad scientific method? Because it leads to absurd results such as the following: "On the basis of my revolutionary refutation of the law of downward-sloping demand, I confidently predict that, in the years when the harvest is especially large, wheat will sell for a higher rather than a lower price." Not only will such reasoning lead to absurd predictions that would lose fortunes for a speculator or a miller, but it also leads to a failure to recognize other important economic relationships, such as the fact that, when family incomes go up, demand curves for goods such as wheat tend to shift rightward.

MEANING OF EQUILIBRIUM The second stumbling block is a more subtle one, less likely to arise but not so easy to dispel. It is suggested by the following:

"HOW can you say that the equality of supply and demand determines a particular equilibrium price? For, after all, *the amount one man sells is precisely what another man buys.* The quantity bought must always equal the quantity sold, no matter what the price; for that matter, whether or not the market is in equilibrium, a statistician who records the Q bought and the Q sold will always find these necessarily identical, each being a different aspect of exactly the same transaction."

The answer to this must be phrased something like this:

You are quite right that measured Q bought and measured Q sold must be identical as recorded by a statistician. But the important question is this: At which P will the amount that consumers are *willing to go on buying* be just matched by the amount that producers are *willing to go on selling?* At such a price, where there is equality between the *scheduled* amounts that suppliers and demanders want to go on buying and selling, and only at such an equilibrium P, will there be no tendency for price to rise or fall.

At any other price, such as the case where P is above the intersection of supply and demand, it is a trivial fact that whatever goods change hands will show a statistical identity of measured amount bought and sold. But this measured identity does not in the least deny that suppliers are eager at so high a price to sell more than demanders will continue to buy; and that this excess of *scheduled supply* over *scheduled demand* will put downward pressure on price until it has finally reached the equilibrium level where the two curves intersect.

At this equilibrium intersection, and there alone, will everybody be happy: the auctioneer, the suppliers, the demanders—as well as the patient statistician, who always reports an identity between the measured amounts bought and sold.[2]

WHAT SUPPLY AND DEMAND ACCOMPLISHED: GENERAL EQUILIBRIUM

Having seen how supply and demand work, let us take stock. The economic system has adjusted itself following the increase in demand for wheat. The scarce goods of society have been rationed out. Who did rationing: a board? a committee? No. The auc-

tioneering mechanism of competitive price did the rationing. It was a case of "rationing by the purse."

FOR WHOM goods are destined was *partially* determined by who was willing to pay for them. If you had the money votes, you got the wheat. If you did not, you went without. Or if you had the money votes, but preferred not to spend them on wheat, you did without. The most important needs or desires for goods—if backed by cash!—got fulfilled.

The WHAT question was being *partially* answered at the same time. The rise in market price was the signal to coax out a higher Q of wheat. It was the signal for other scarce resources to move into the wheat-production industry from alternative uses.

Even the HOW question was being *partially* decided in the background. For with wheat prices now high, farmers could afford to use more expensive tractors and fertilizers and less fertile soils.

Why the word "partially" in this description of how the competitive market helped solve the three problems? Because this wheat market is but one market of many. What is happening in the corn and rye markets also counts; and what is happening in the market for fertilizer, men, and tractors obviously matters much.

We must note that the pricing problem is one that involves *interdependent markets*, not just the "partial equilibrium" of a single market.[3]

There are, so to speak, auctioneers operating simultaneously in the many different markets—wheat, corn, fertilizer, and land; labor, wool, cotton, mutton, and rayon; bonds, stocks, and personal loans, and foreign exchange in the form of English pounds or Ger-

---

[2] A similar question of "measured identity" versus "scheduled intersection" could arise in the discussion of income determination in Chapter 12.

[3] The alert reader will not have to be reminded that the competitive market gives goods to those with money votes and does so efficiently. But the distribution of the money votes depends on for how much you can sell your labor and property in competitive and imperfectly competitive factor markets, and it is affected in an important way by (1) how lucky you are, (2) how lucky your parents and in-laws were, and (3) the advantages and disadvantages of your genetic and acquired skills and aptitudes. If a student writes on a final exam, "FOR WHOM is decided (in part) by how people decide to use their money votes," he is not wrong. Indeed, he gets possibly 50 per cent credit. However, he will not get the other 50 per cent unless he adds, "The basic problem of FOR WHOM is the process by which the money votes *themselves* get assigned to particular persons. This is primarily not by the supply and demand equilibrium of a single good's market but the equilibrium of the labor, land, and other interdependent factor markets of Part Four. And factor supplies depend much on distribution of ownership, and hence on the inheritance of wealth."

man marks. Each ends up at the equilibrium intersection point of his supply and demand schedules—wheat, corn, fertilizer prices, and land rent; labor wage, wool, cotton, mutton, and rayon prices; bond price and its interest yield, stock prices and dividend yield, interest charges on personal loans, an exchange rate of $2.43 per pound or 3 1/8 marks to the dollar.

No market is an island unto itself: when wool *P* rises (because, say, of sheep disease abroad), it pulls up the *P's* of domestic labor, fertilizer, and land needed for expanded wool output; and it raises the *P's* of rival goods like cotton that some demanders will now turn to; it might well lower the *P* of wool spinners and of suit-company stock shares, since the latter must now pay more for their raw materials and may bid less eagerly for spinning labor.

The new "general-equilibrium set of interdependent prices" adjusts to the new situation. The price system meets the problem posed by the basic definition of economics: the study of (1) how *scarce means with alternative uses*—limited land and labor that can be switched from one industry to another—are allocated, and (2) how to *achieve ends or goals*—as prescribed by the tastes for wool, nylon, food, and housing of sovereign consumers, possessed of factors of production that give them money-income votes for the market place. Each separate market, with its supply and demand curves, is doing its bit toward creating the general-equilibrium set of prices, which in our society resolves the basic economic problems of WHAT, HOW, and FOR WHOM.

PERFECTION AND IMPERFECTIONS OF COMPETITION

Our curves of supply and demand strictly apply only to a *perfectly competitive* market where some kind of *standardized* commodity such as wheat is being auctioned by an organized exchange that registers transactions of *numerous* buyers and sellers. The metal exchange in London and the grain exchange in Winnipeg are two such. Stock Exchanges, such as those in New York, London, Toronto, and Montreal, do not auction goods and commodities or productive services rendered by factors of production; but they do provide a market where shares of common stocks such as those of General Motors and Imperial Oil are

auctioned at each moment of the working day. Many corporate bonds are also bought and sold in the bond division of these exchanges.

The economists' curves of supply and demand are important ways of idealizing the behavior of such markets. They do not pretend to give an accurate microscopic description of what is going on during each changing moment in such a market place, as men from the various brokerage houses are milling around on the trading floor while frantically giving hand and voice signals to the specialist who serves as auctioneer for each grain or company stock. Nonetheless, the tools of supply and demand do summarize the important average relationships resulting over a period of time from such organized trading.

As far as these fundamental tools of supply and demand are concerned, it matters little what kind of exchange the goods are traded on: whether hand signals, slips of paper or modern computers are used; whether the auction is of the familiar kind, where the auctioneer calls out a *minimum* starting price and accepts higher and higher bids until only one high bid is left to get the Renoir painting in question; whether there is a "Dutch auction," where the price starts high instead of low and moves downward at stated time intervals until an eager buyer, fearing that someone else will get in the bid first, finally gives the first bid and gets the merchandise; or whether the auctioneer asks for written bids and offers in order to be able to make up a table or chart like those of Fig. 4-3 and find the equilibrium intersection at one fell swoop in effect by solving two simultaneous equations.

Indeed, the market need not have a single auctioneer: all the bidding may well take place by telephone calls and personal contact as in the case of the market for Canadian government bonds, which is a much more perfect one than the corporate bond market on the floor of the Toronto or Montreal Stock Exchange. The same can be true of stocks listed on the so-called "over-the-counter market," a market which is conducted throughout the country completely by telephone and by daily mailing of price-quotation lists by different brokers. (As an example, an important stock such as Pine Point, which was listed originally on this market, may actually behave more nearly like our competitive model than does some stock *inactively* traded on the floor of the Toronto Stock Exchange.)

Fig. 4-5. Supply-and-demand tools have many applications: to goods, acres of land, laborers, exchange rates.

Economists often use straight-lined *dd* or *ss* schedules purely for simplicity. Can you interpret the four cases?

PERFECTION OF COMPETITION AS A LIMITING POLE. Needless to say, the requirements for absolutely perfect competition are as hard to meet as the requirements for a perfectly frictionless pendulum in physics. We can approach closer and closer to perfection but never quite reach it. Yet, this fact need not do serious damage to the usefulness of our empolying the idealized concept. Actually, it matters little to the economic scientist that different grades of wheat will call for slight variations from the quoted market prices. Nor does it matter in the case of standardized cotton goods, so-called "gray goods," that they are sold and bought in an informal way by many competing firms: so long as there are *numerous* buyers and sellers on each side, *well-informed* about quality and about each others' prices and having no reason to discriminate in favor of one merchant rather than another and no reason to expect that variations in their *own* bids and offers will have an *appreciable effect* upon the prevailing market price—so long as all this is true, the behavior of price and quantity can be expected to be much like that predicted by the curves of supply and demand.

The various diagrams in Fig. 4-5 illustrate how the tools of supply and demand might be used to give a good approximate description of various economic situations other than that of a staple commodity such as wheat: there is pictured a competitive market for cotton gray goods (unbleached cotton bolts); for a factor of production such as newly graduating electrical engineers, whose price is represented by a wage per month; for a capital asset such as a corner lot of land or a bond; and finally, as will be explained later in the discussion of international trade in Part Five, a foreign exchange market in which the price in Canadian dollars of a single unit of any foreign currency is determined by the bids of those who need foreign currency and by the offers of those who want to sell such currencies to get Canadian dollars.[4]

To be sure, not all today's markets are anywhere near to being perfectly competitive in the economist's sense. We shall see later, in Part Three, that elements of market power or imperfection may enter in, and these will require us to modify the competitive model. After we have learned how to handle such cases, we shall recognize that the market mechanism is a blend of competition and imperfections—for which the competitive analysis, properly qualified, is still an indispensable tool for interpreting the modern mixed economy.

[4] Question 11 at the end of this chapter reproduces from a newspaper its financial reports for a single day, showing what might have been the market price quotations for grains, bonds, gold, common stocks, and foreign exchange. After studying economics, one is in a better position to understand the basic forces underlying these price quotations; but only experience and study can make one reasonably expert at the hazardous game of forecasting. The stock market is discussed in this Appendix; Chapter 21's Appendix discusses the economics of speculation in organized commodity markets.

SUMMARY

1 A basic problem of economics is how the mechanism of market pricing grapples with the triad of problems WHAT, HOW, and FOR WHOM.

2 By the *demand schedule* we mean a table showing the different quantities of a good that people will—at any time and with other things held equal—want to buy at each different price. This relationship, when plotted on a diagram, is the *demand curve.*

3 With negligible exceptions, the higher the price the lower will be the quantity demanded, and vice versa. Almost all commodities are subject to this "law of *downward*-sloping demand."

4 The *supply curve or schedule* gives the relations between the prices and the quantities of a good that producers will—other things equal—be willing to sell. Usually supply curves *rise upward* and to the *right:* diminishing returns implies that higher P is needed to coax out higher-cost extra Q.

5 Market equilibrium can take place only at a price where the quantities supplied and demanded are *equal.* At any price higher than the equilibrium intersection of the supply and demand curves, the quantity producers will want to go on supplying will exceed the quantity consumers will go on demanding; downward pressure on price will result as some sellers undermine the going price. Similarly, the reader can show why a price lower than the equilibrium price will meet irresistible upward pressure from bids of excess buyers.

6 Competitive pricing *rations* out the limited supply of goods to those with desire or need backed by money votes. Along with helping to decide FOR WHOM, it signals changes in WHAT shall be produced and in HOW goods shall be produced. But any one market only "partially" helps solve the WHAT, HOW, and FOR WHOM because of its interdependence with other commodity and factor markets in setting "the general-equilibrium system of prices."

7 Organized trading markets exist for a number of staple commodities such as wheat; they may also exist for some common stocks, bonds, and other financial items. There are still other markets that behave much like an auction market, even if there is no formal auctioneering procedure: so long as there are numerous well-informed suppliers and demanders, each *too unimportant to have by himself an appreciable effect upon the price* of the standardized good in question—so long as such conditions prevail, the tools of supply and demand will give an adequate approximation of the behavior of such markets. Yet, as will be seen later, a good deal of modern economic reality departs from the strict competitive model of the economist, and he must find tools applicable to monopoly and imperfect competition.

CONCEPTS FOR REVIEW

demand schedule or curve
law of downward-sloping demand
supply schedule or curve
diminishing returns
equilibrium intersection
shifts of curves

movements along a curve
how supply and demand in one market
   "partially" solve WHAT, HOW, and
   FOR WHOM
general equilibrium prices
imperfectly competitive situations

QUESTIONS FOR DISCUSSION

1. Although we'd all like to escape the hardship implied by higher price, show that rising market prices may perform some useful functions in time of scarcity. Show how such hardships might work themselves out in some different kind of economy.

2. Define carefully what is meant by a demand schedule or curve. State the law of downward-sloping demand—that there is some kind of *inverse* relation between *P* and *Q*, the latter going down when the former goes up.

3. Define the concept of a supply schedule or curve. Show that an increase in supply means a rightward and downward *shift* of the supply curve. Contrast this with the rightward and upward shift implied by an increase in demand. Why the difference? Treat the cases of decreased supply and demand.

Industrial stocks

Range 1974 High $	Low $	Company	Indic. Div. Rate $	High $	Low $	Latest $	Net Chge. $	Sales 100s	Yld. %	P/E ratio Ind. latest 12 Mos.	1973 or latest interim		1972 or latest fiscal year	
6.50	5.00	A-1 Steel and Iron A	ʀ0.60	6.25	6.00	6.25	+0.37	3ᴠ	9.6	7.6	'73 Feb	ᴀ.82	'72 Feb	ᴀ1.03
5.50	4.60	Do. B	ᴘ0.15	ʟMay24,1974		4.75	....	nil	3.2	5.8	'73 Feb	ᴀ.82	'72 Feb	ᴀ1.03
3.45	2.00	A.G.F. Mgt. B pfd.	ᴘ0.31	2.02	2.02	2.02	—0.03	5ᴛ	15.3	5.9	Feb 3m	.07	'73 Nov	.39
6.50	3.50	Abbey Glen Property	...	3.75	3.50	3.50	—0.25	138ᴛ	..	6.0	'73 Dec	.58	'72 Dec	.46
2.20	1.00	Do. warr.	...	1.05	1.00	1.00	unch.	41ᴛ	..	..	....	....	......	....
14.75	10.37	Abitibi Paper	0.40	11.37	10.50	10.87	unch.	442ᴛ	3.7	5.3	Mar 3m	.65	'73 Dec	1.62
51.00	46.50	Do. 7½% ser. A pf.	3.75	47.00	46.50	46.50	—0.75	3ᴛ	8.1	..	'73 Dec	x40.93	'72 Dec	x11.65
13.50	11.00	Acklands Ltd.	0.96	12.25	11.37	11.75	+0.25	42ᴛ	3.4	6.5	Feb 3m	.55	'73 Nov	2.87
14.75	12.00	Do. 2nd pf. ser. A 6% cv	*0.40	13.00	12.87	12.87	+0.12	20ᴛ	7.5	..	'73 Nov	x26.06	'72 Nov	x9.59
11.75	6.75	Acres Ltd.	0.20	7.25	6.87	7.00	—0.12	80ᴛ	2.9	3.5	Mar 3m	.53	'73 Dec	2.94
44.00	39.25	Do. 7.20 pfd.	3.60	39.25	39.25	39.25	—0.25	3ᴛ	9.2	..	'73 Dec	x5.83	'72 Dec	x3.61
1.60	0.33	Do. warr.	...	0.39	0.35	0.38	+0.04	96ᴛ	..	..	......	......	......	....

Government of Canada bonds

May 31, 1974

			Bid	Ask	Yld.
7	Canada	... Jun 74	99.86	99.90	8.50
6	Canada	... Jun 74	99.83	99.87	8.60
8	Canada‡	.. Oct 74	99.60	99.70	8.82
4¼	Canada	.. Dec 74	97.70	97.80	8.92
5¼	Canada	.. Dec 74	98.25	98.35	9.00
7¼	Canada	.. Apr 75	98.55	98.65	8.96
6¼	Canada	.. Apr 75	97.95	98.05	8.98
7¼	Canada	.. Jul 75	98.15	98.25	8.98
5¼	Canada*	.. Oct 75	95.75	95.85	8.88
7¼	Canada♦	.. Dec 75	97.50	97.70	8.89
5¼	Canada	... Apr 76	94.05	94.15	9.04
3¼	Canada	... Jun 76	90.15	90.25	8.69
5¼	Canada	... Jun 76	94.30	94.50	8.82
6¼	Canada♦	... Aug 76	94.70	94.90	8.89
5¼	Canada	... Oct 76	92.70	92.90	8.94
7	Canada	.. Dec 76	95.60	95.80	8.92
6¼	Canada	∴. Apr 77	93.90	94.00	8.94
7	Canada♦	... Jul 77	95⅛	95⅜	8.74
7	Canada	... Sep 77	94⅞	95⅛	8.75
3¾	Canada	... Jan 75/78	84.25	84.75	8.74
8	Canada	... Jul 78	97.25	97.75	8.66
7¾	Canada♦	.. Oct 78	97.00	97.50	8.75
7	Canada‡	.. Apr 79	93.00	93.25	8.74
6¼	Canada	... Jun 79	90.75	91.25	8.69
3¼	Canada	... Oct 79	76.50	77.00	8.73
5¼	Canada	... Dec 79	86.75	87.25	8.70
6¼	Canada	... Apr 80	88.25	88.75	8.75
5¼	Canada*	.. Aug 80	84.25	84.75	8.75
7¼	Canada*	.. Dec 80	93⅝	93⅞	8.76
4¼	Canada	... Sep 83	73⅝	73⅞	8.67
5	Canada*.	... Jun 88	67.00	69.00	8.92
6¾	Canada	... Feb 89	80.00	82.00	8.95
5¼	Canada*	.. May 90	67.00	69.00	8.94
5¾	Canada	∴. Sep 92	69.50	71.50	8.95

			Bid	Ask	Yld.
6¼	Canada	... Oct 95	75.00	77.00	8.93
3¾	Canada	... Mar 98	53.00	55.00	8.01
3	Canada	... Sep. perp.	34.00	36.00	8.33

Winnipeg cash

—Cash Price—
May 31, 1974   Prev. week
Close

			$ per bushel		
Oats—					
3 Cw.	......	1.81	1.78	1.78	1.78
Barley—					
1 Feed	....	2.20	2.13	2.17	2.13
2 Feed	....	2.18½	2.11¼	2.15½	2.11¼
1 Cw.	......	2.60	2.50	2.60	2.50
Flax—					
1 Cw.	......	9.82½	9.46½	9.65	9.46½
2 Cw.	......	9.77½	9.41½	9.55	9.41½
3 Cw.	......	9.32½	8.96½	9.24	8.96½
Rye—					
1 & 2 Cw.	..	2.57	2.39½	2.43½	2.40
3 Cw.	......	2.52	2.34½	2.38½	2.25
Rapeseed—Vancouver					
#1 Cdn.	...	6.97	6.67	6.67	6.97
#2 Cdn.	...	6.82	6.50½	6.50½	6.82

Gold bars quoted

Closing Rate on London Market
June 3, 1974

Latest price .... U.S.$155.50

Previous price .... U.S.$162.00

Daily US$-UK£ rates

June 3, 1974

	U.S.$	U.K.£
Mon.	.9624	2.3083
Fri.	.9620	2.3054
Thurs.	.9624	2.3025
Wed.	.9628	2.3025
Tues.	.9616	2.3011
Ave.	.96224	2.30396

U.S. rate reported by Bank of Canada. U.K. bid rate reported by Toronto Dominion Bank.

Gold bars quoted

Rate Reported by Toronto Stock Exchange
Feb. 26, 1971

Canadian kilo bars of gold approximately 32 oz. each.

	Bid	Asked
	—per oz.—	
Latest price	$38.85	$39.85
Previous week	$38.65	$39.65

Reprinted from the *Financial Post*, June 8, 1974 and March 6, 1971

4. What factors might increase the demand for wheat? The supply? What would cheap mechanical pickers do to cotton or blueberry prices? To farm wages?

5. Spell out arguments to show that competitive price must settle down at the equilibrium intersection of supply and demand. Use too-high or too-low P.

6. "An increase (or decrease) in supply will lower (or raise) price. An increase (decrease) in demand will generally raise (lower) price. While we can predict that an increase in demand accompanied by a decrease in supply will be followed by a rise in price, we cannot guess without further information what will happen if we *simultaneously increase* demand and *increase* supply." Verify. Puzzle out this use of parentheses, common in economics, for alternative cases.

7. "A simultaneous increase of demand and decrease of supply, as in question 6, is statistically impossible. Demand and supply are identically the same thing." Comment in terms of the section "Two Stumbling Blocks."

8. Depict and analyse voluntary blood donations contrasted with paid blood suppliers. (*Hint:* adapt Fig. 4-3, with $P = 0$ as the voluntary price.) What are the pros and cons of voluntarism? See Richard Titmuss' fine book, *The Gift Relationship* (Pantheon Books, New York, 1971).

9. "If there is only one seller or only a few very large sellers, monopoly and imperfect competition theory will need to be considered rather than the tools of competitive supply and demand. If products are far from being standardized, then each brand-name seller may well have *a degree of control over his price* not enjoyed by the perfect competitor as defined by the economist." Verify.

10. *Extra-credit problem* (only for those who know some mathematics): The demand curve is a functional relation between Q and P, namely, $Q = f(P)$. Downward-sloping demand means Q falls as P rises, or in terms of calculus, that $df(P)/dP < 0$. Other variables, such as income (X_1) or price of rye (X_2), are being held constant, etc.; hence $f(P)$ is short for $f(P; X_1, X_2, \ldots)$, and a change in any X_i shifts the demand curve. Similarly, denote the supply functional relationship between Q and P by $Q = s(P)$, with $ds(P)/dP > 0$. Then, equilibrium intersection price, P^*, is the root of the equation $f(P) = s(P)$. (For $f(P) = 9 - P$ and $s(P) = 2P$, verify that $P^* = 3$ and $Q^* = 6$. Graph these intersecting straight line schedules.)

11. Try to puzzle out what the newspaper reports on the opposite page mean. Note the difference between the gold prices in 1971 and 1974.

Appendix: Stock Market Fluctuations

Wall Street means the New York Stock Exchange and the brokers' houses and financial firms that go with it. It dominates the world's exchanges. Every second, supply and demand bid up and bid down the prices of common stocks (equity shares). One year a man makes a fortune; another year he is ruined.

The New York Stock Exchange lists more than a thousand securities, as do the Paris *Bourse* and the London Stock Exchange (and many other "exchanges" for the trading of inter-bank obligations, foreign currencies, metals, and farm products). Its origins were like a club's, with rules for membership. Rights to trade are still *memberships* dictated not by the government but by the other members. In order to trade directly on the New York Stock Exchange you must buy a seat. Some other exchanges, like New York's American Exchange, or Montreal's Canadian Exchange, began as "curb" exchanges: brokers literally met on the street curb to buy and sell, giving hand signals to clerks hanging out the windows to record transactions. The price of seats is lower than on the main exchanges.

Nowadays every advanced country where shares are widely held has its exchange. Canada has Toronto and Montreal. In addition, there are important regional exchanges in Chicago, Boston, Vancouver, and Winnipeg, that deal in local or smaller industries' stocks not listed in New York or Toronto.[1] In fact the regional exchanges might cease to exist if the market for all "local" stocks broadened and if the larger exchanges were to permit trading by more than the limited number of select "seat-holders.[2]

PEOPLE'S CAPITALISM

The stock exchanges for many years tried to sell the notion of "people's capitalism," in which everyone owns stocks and therefore will vote to take account of the interests of property. Few would oppose the notion of a wider and more equal distribution of wealth, but it is a bit of a confidence trick to entice a union worker—or his wife—into owning a few shares so that at the polls they will go easy on corporate tax rates—when, in fact, their own well-being is trivially affected by what happens to the few

shares they own compared to even a 1 per cent change in wage rates or pension benefits.[3]

In any case, less than a million of over 22 million Canadians (and about 35 million of over 210 million U.S. citizens) own any appreciable amount of stocks, and that is a generous estimate. Now that private and public pension funds are beginning to invest in common stocks, low-income people indirectly are beginning to acquire some protection of their savings against inflation, a privilege that until recently was enjoyed primarily by the affluent (apart from those poor who held "the widow's friend," a little real estate.

THE GREAT CRASH

One traumatic event long kept the general populace fearful to venture into stock ownership—the memory of the 1929 panic and crash on Wall Street, which ushered in the long and painful Depression of the 1930s.

During the fabulous stock market boom of the "roaring twenties", Pullman porters, housewives, college students between classes—all bought and sold stocks. Most purchases in this wild "bull" market were "on margin"; i.e., the buyer of $10,000 worth of stocks had to put up only $2,500 or less in cash and borrowed the difference, pledging his newly bought stocks. What matter that he had to pay his broker 6, 10 or 15 per cent per year on his borrowing when in one day Massey-Harris or Abitibi might jump 10 per cent in value!

The most wonderful thing about a bull market is that it fulfills its own hopes. If people buy because they think stocks will rise, their act of buying sends up the price of stocks. This causes them to buy still further, and sends the dizzy dance off on another round. And unlike a game of cards or dice, no one loses what the winners gain. Everybody gets a prize! Of course, the prizes are all on paper and would disappear if everyone tried to cash them in. But why should anyone wish to see such lucrative securities?

When the whole world is mad, 'tis folly to be sane. Suppose one had been so wise or so naive as to believe that the public-utilities holding companies were paper pyramids on cardboard foundations; or that certain dream real-estate developments were midway between pine thicket and swamp? What could such a social misfit have done?

He would soon learn the first rule of property values: "A thing is worth what people *think* it is worth." Unfortunately, to be successful, this has to be applied in connection with the second rule, which is as hard to follow in practice as belling the cat or catching birds by putting salt on their tails: "Don't be the sucker left holding the bag."

---

[1]Trading, valuing, and speculating in some shares of some industries, like mining and petroleum, are very specialised. Some "regional" exchanges are actually providing a location for specialists.

[2]In the 1965 *Windfall Report*, Mr. Justice Arthur Kelly said of the Toronto Stock Exchange members: "The view that the Exchange was a private gaming club seemed to have motivated them (i.e. the broker owners) in turning to their own advantage special privileges which were not available to the public." Since that time, stricter regulations on inside information and trading have been imposed by most exchanges and their governments.

[3]Note that many of these people are not directly concerned because "their" shares are either locked in a safety deposit box and rarely considered for disposal or managed by a pension or mutual fund.

When the black October crash of 1929 came, everyone was caught, the big-league professionals and the piddling amateurs—John D. Rockefeller, Sir James Dunn, Sir Harry Oakes, and the economics professor in Alberta. The bottom fell out of the market. Brokers had to sell out the "margin" accounts of investors who could no longer pony up extra funds to cover the depleted value of their collateral,[4] sending the market down still further. Even those who did not buy on margin lost one-third of their capital by the end of the year, and five-sixths by 1932!

The bull market was over. The bear market had taken its place. And as the former had lived on its dreams, so the latter was consumed by its own nightmares. Billions of dollars of security values were wiped out every month, taking with them not only the capital of gamblers out for speculative gains, but also the widow's mite supposedly invested for steady income. A "blue chip" stock like United States Steel fell from a 1929 high of 261 to a 1932 low of 21, while less respectable securities dropped off the board completely, becoming worthless. Even though U.S. President Hoover and his administration were friendly toward business, in vain did they try to restore confidence by predicting "prosperity is just around the corner" and "Stocks are excellent buys at their present levels."

Finally, the stock market began to follow general business recovery. Figure 4-6, shows the movements of stock market values over the whole period. Although stocks were bullish in 1936-1937 and again during World War II, it was not until the mid-fifties that they returned to anything like the peak levels of 1929. The boom in glamor growth stocks, which ended in the mid-1962, mid-1966, and 1969 collapses, confirmed the fact that human nature never changes much.

In Figure 4-6, the index of Canadian share prices (on an annual, not daily basis) is superimposed over the Dow-Jones, New York, average. The day-to-day fluctuations (important to the speculator) are not shown. But it is clear that the two markets have moved together, as would be expected when investors in both countries can choose which market to invest in.

FAVORABLE ODDS

Actual historical experience has shown that, even in the face of the great crash, over a lifetime one would have done better in risky common stocks than in safe gilt-edged bonds or savings accounts.

It was shown in the 1930s that equity holders did better than bondholders for most of the years between 1870 and World War I. A study at the University of Chicago in the 1960s found that this had become even more true in the 1925-1960 years.

In an age of inflationary price creep and growth of the mixed economy, you can throw a dart at the financial page to select your portfolio of stocks at random and, on the average, come out substantially ahead of your "prudent" brother who stays invested in government bonds and savings deposits!

Again, Fig. 4-6's charts of the 30 Dow-Jones "blue chip" industrial stocks and Statistics Canada's Index of Canadian common stock prices illustrate these facts.

THE CULT OF EQUITIES

People, of course, go from one extreme to another. After shunning the stock market for many years, by the 1970s they began to think that you couldn't lose in it. As a result, they bid up common-stock prices to the point where their dividend yields are scarcely 3 per cent, whereas good bonds in Canada yield 7 or more per cent. Why this inverted structure when bonds are allegedly safer yet yield more?

Obviously, investors—most of whom are in fairly high tax brackets—are shooting for low-tax capital gains rather than heavily taxed dividends. Capital gains, too may help more than bonds to keep investors' purchasing power ahead of inflationary erosion.

Experience with markets abroad shows that all good things eventually come to an end. Once Canadian or U.S. stock prices get bid high enough, there is plenty of room for steep declines, and investing in common stock has ceased to be as much of a one-way street as it seemed to be between 1945 and 1970.[5]

OUTGUESSING THE MARKET?

To the age-old question, "Does the market follow business activity or business activity follow the market?" no simple answer can be given.

It is reasonably clear that business activity, national income, and corporate earnings determine stock prices and not vice versa; and also that the psychological effects of market movements no longer have primary importance. But still the market can occasionally anticipate changes in national income and total purchasing power. It then appears to be leading them when really it is following what it thinks they will be doing later.

HOW TO INVEST There are no simply stated foolproof rules for making money out of the stock market. Anyone who can accurately predict the future course of business activity will prosper; but there is no such person. At least four main classes of investors and speculators can be distinguished.

1. The group who simply buy and hold. Because the national economy has a long-term upward trend, they fare reasonably well over the long run. They might do a little better if they followed the statistical advice of investment

---

[4]Frederick Lewis Allen's amusing and interesting chronicle of the 1920s, Only Yesterday, gives a detailed account of the role of the stock-market boom in American life. J. K. Galbraith's The Great Crash, 1929 (Boston: Houghton Mifflin, 1955) is more recent and recounts vividly the events of 1928-1931.

[5]How high is high enough? No sorcerer can tell for sure. But economic science warns: "Once 'the percentage ratio of share earnings to price plus reasonable estimate of annual percentage growth in earnings that is maintainable comes to exceed the safe interest rate on bonds. Fasten your seat belt and hold on to your hat!'"

FIG. 4-6. The only sure thing about stock prices is that they will fluctuate.
The upper line represents the Dow-Jones Average; the lower line traces the similar Statistics Canada Investors Index (1961 = 100) (Sources: Dow Jones and Co. Inc.; Canadian Statistical Review, *Historical Summary*; and Financial Post)

services as to how to switch to companies of more favorable growth prospects. Surprisingly, though, repeated academic studies show that neither the best mutual funds nor investment counselors often do better over the long run than the Dow-Jones average of 30 industrial stocks or of the similar Statistics Canada Investors Index of Canadian traded stocks.

The effect of this holding group is neither to stabilize nor to destabilize prices; to the extent that they freeze shares off the market and limit the number of tradings, they tend to make the market "thinner." In a thin market there are so few transactions that the attempt to buy a few hundred shares of a stock may send its price up a few points because of the absence of ready sellers around the ruling market price. A simultaneous attempt to sell may depress the price a few points.

2. At the other extreme are the hour-to-hour, day-to-day ticker watchers, to be seen in every brokerage office. Generally speaking, they buy and sell, sell and buy. Usually, they make money only for their brokers.

The existence of this group has the effect of making the market less thin. Because of this group, any investor can expect to be able to liquidate his market holdings at any time at some price, although not at a price predictable in advance nor that he would like. Still, even this restricted "liquidity" enhances the attractiveness of securities traded on organized exchanges over and above the unlisted issues of smaller companies bought and sold by brokers over the counter. So it is argued.

3. In between are those speculators who play intermediate swings of many months or years. The least successful of these are the amateurs whose entrance into the market at the top when it is too late is supposed to be the signal for the "smart money" to leave. The most successful speculators are those who are able to avoid the extremes of enthusiasm of the mob and to discern underlying company, industry, and GNP conditions. This does not mean that they simply buy because a stock looks low and sell when it looks high. On the contrary, they buy when stocks look as if they will continue to rise. When a drop seems imminent, they sell short or, more conservatively, they simply go into cash or high-grade bonds. (It takes cool nerves to sell short, because on the whole the market is overoptimistic; and, also, your potential loss is unlimited. But if a single individual does it cleverly, he may achieve success in avoiding the losses of a bear market.

The behavior of such speculators is often destabilizing to prices. They "pile on" to a price rise and send it farther; they similarly *accentuate* a decline.

Thus, in the mid-1960s certain so-called "performance" or "venture" mutual investment funds became prominent. The funds would buy electronic or airline glamor stocks just before the latter stocks became glamorous. Then as people saw the funds buying, the public would be attracted to the same stocks. After the prices of the glamor stocks and hence of the funds' shares had been bid up, the performance funds would sell out to the public at a nice profit, moving on to new fields ripe for conquest. The evident perils in this are well illustrated by a modern Wall Street story.

A broker phones me, telling me to buy XYZ at $2.00 a share. I buy 100 shares. He phones me to say: "XYZ has risen to $3.00; better buy a couple of hundred more." I do. He calls again: "Better buy 300 XYZ at $5.00." Again I do, but when next he calls I finally refuse to buy and ask to sell. "What, sell XYZ," he says, "sell it *to whom*?" (*In joco veritas*.)

Despite these possible dangers, the popularity of venture mutual fund stocks have been growing rapidly in Canada. A report on Canadian Mutual Funds, published in 1969, stated ". . . competition between mutual funds has tended to accord more emphasis to comparisons of rate or return (performance) than is warranted even by the undoubted importance of that information."[6] The report went on to warn that many Canadian investors seemed to be forgetting that a high return carried with it a high degree of risk of loss. Any judgment based upon performance over a matter of months or a year is subject to doubt—5 years would be a minimum time period for adequate assessment. Nevertheless investors moved rapidly into these performance funds.

[6]Canada: Committee on Mutual Funds and Investment Contracts, *Report* (Queen's Printer, Ottawa, 1969), p. 62.

4. Finally, there are individuals who study special situations. From public or inside sources, they learn in advance of changes in the fortunes of particular companies: of rumored bankruptcies; of special stock dividends, split-ups, or mergers; of likely earnings and dividend announcements. When combined with the successful characteristics of the third group, members of this group—such as the elder statesman of two wars, Bernard Baruch—make the largest profit from the market. Since World War II some alert operators have been able to run $1,000 up to $10,000,000 or more—at the same time keeping profits in the form of less heavily taxed capital gains.

But the would-be investor must take to heart Baruch's caution:

If you are ready to give up everything else—to study the whole history and background of the market and all the principal companies whose stocks are on the board as carefully as a medical student studies anatomy—if you can do all that, and, in addition, you have the cool nerves of a great gambler, the sixth sense of a kind of clairvoyant, and the courage of a lion, you have a ghost of a chance.

SCIENCE OF STOCKS

Buying common stocks is an art, not a science. No one can draw the line between risky speculation and safe investment. But an art or craft, being science in a still-primitive state, has its general rules of behavior. Here are a few gleaned from scientific study of this unscientific field.

1. You can't compile a good track record by *consulting the stars*. Don't laugh. Financial services have gotten rich —their clients haven't though—by selling astrological advice, and one man made a fortune purporting to interpret the signals being given in the comic strips!

2. Hunches work out to nothing in the long run.

3. *The best brains in Wall Street scarcely do as well as the averages* (Standard & Poor's, Dow Jones, Statistics Canada stock price index etc.) At first this seems surprising. They have all the money needed for any kind of research and digging. But remember, they are all competing with each other; and if there is a bargain for one man to see, it is also there for another; and hence it will already have been wiped out of existence by competitive bids.

4. Chartists claim to see in plots of stock prices "resistance levels," "gaps," "head-and-shoulder formations," "flags," "pennants," "channels"—all of which are supposed to improve your odds of guessing right. Experienced investors say: "The chartists generally end up with holes in their shoes. So forget it."

5. Are there then no good tricks? Alas, few indeed. Because inflation and growth push the country ahead, a random investment will probably show capital gains in the long run. Not much more can be said.

Statisticians have demonstrated that the day-to-day changes in stock prices are very much like a "random-walk"—like the brownian motion you see in a microscope due to the chance impacts of invisible and unpredictable atoms on just-visible huge molecules or colloidal particles. Wall Street doesn't believe this random-walk theory, but the Ph.D.'s in the business schools laugh at their disbelief. Describing this "greater fool theory" in which you hope to unload on some other sucker is easier, than for all to practice it successfully.)

6. To have unusual performance, you must be able to predict increases in the per share earnings of companies *before* the market place in general is aware of them. *Afterward* is too late. For each stock tends to sell at a certain "price-earnings ratios,"—e.g., stagnant and cyclical C.P.R. at 12/1, glamorous IBM at 40/1. And if you are correct in foretelling an unanticipated rise in earnings, the market will probably mark up the stock price once those earnings become visible. (As a kicker, if you are early in recognizing an area of glamorous earnings growth, you may find the market multiplying your holdings by higher and higher price-earnings ratios—and after that has happened, it is a good time to get out. Computer calculations show that the "gun-slinging performers" do better than the averager in rising bull markets; they pay for this by doing worse in falling bear markets. Why? Because the performance-happy money managers tend to buy stocks that are volatile in both direction.)

7. The above strategy of anticipating changes in earnings is easy to state but practically impossible to put into practice even if you have a vast research staff and inside management contacts. Hence, unless you like the fun of investing your own money—and are willing to pay something for that fun in the form of bad performance—most amateurs would be well advised to buy shares in some mutual fund. A mutual fund buys 30 to 100 stocks deemed best by professional money managers and gives you your prorated share in them. If the market goes up, your mutual fund shares will probably go up; but it works both ways. (WARNING: Most mutual funds are sold by salesmen who get a fat commission for doing so—usually an 8 per cent "load" skimmed off your principal. Through the mail or from some banks and trust companies you can buy no-load funds involving no sales commission at all, which experience shows do about the same on the average as the heavy-load funds. How do the no-load funds manage this? Simply by paying the same management fees to money managers but cutting out the selling expenses—the equivalent in finance of the "discount retail store" that quotes low prices for cash-and-carry. (You can recognize no-loads on the financial pages by *equality* of "bid" and "asked")).

CONCEPTS FOR REVIEW

New York, Toronto, Montreal, and other exchanges
common stocks or equities
great crash
dividend versus bond yield
equities and inflation protection
price-earnings multiple
random-walk versus chartism
mutual funds: load and no-load
performance or venture funds

5
AFFLUENCE AND POVERTY: INDIVIDUAL AND FAMILY INCOME

Such poverty as we have today in our great cities degrades the poor, and infects with its degradation the whole neighbourhood in which they live. And whatever can degrade a neighbourhood, can degrade a country and a continent and finally the whole civilized world, which is only a large neighbourhood.

GEORGE BERNARD SHAW

Everyone realizes the importance of income. If you can know but one fact about a man, knowledge of his income will probably reveal most about him. Then you can roughly guess his political opinions, his tastes and education, his age, and even his life expectancy.

Furthermore, unless a family has a steady stream of money coming in every week, month, and year—even though it has saintly endurance—that family is ill. Not only its materialistic activities, but its non-materialistic activities—the things that convert existence into living—must suffer.   It is commonplace to state that our standard of living and level of family income is the highest in all the world. But few people realize how small the *average* Canadian or American income really is, or how great the range between the highest and the lowest incomes.

This chapter gives some basic facts about incomes and wealth, here and abroad. North America has been described by Harvard's J. Kenneth Galbraith as The Affluent Society. And the mixed economies of Western Europe are following hot on our heels.

Yet the Affluent skyscraper remains based on a foundation of poverty; and as we shall see, this kind of poverty is new in history and different from that found in most other parts of the earth.

THE DECLINE OF POVERTY

It is now well over a century since Karl Marx and Friedrich Engels in 1848 issued the *Communist Manifesto* containing the lines: "Workers of the world unite! You have nothing to lose but your chains." While some of Marx's predictions about the

future of industrial capitalism were proved correct in the intervening years,[1] one prediction about the laws of motion of capitalist development, entertained by many Marxists, has proved to be quite wrong. Their assertion that *the rich will become richer and the poor will become poorer*[1] cannot be sustained by careful historical and statistical research. In Europe and in North America, there has definitely been a steady, secular improvement in minimum standards of living, whether measured by food, clothing, housing, or length of life. This fact is clear from statistics to be presented shortly.

FROM BAD TO LESS BAD It used to be fashionable for economic historians to dwell on the evils of the Industrial Revolution and the poverty-ridden condition of the masses in the disease-producing cities. In point of fact, no Dickens novel did full jus-

---

[1] "The modern labourer, on the contrary, instead of rising with the progress of industry, sinks deeper and deeper below the condition of his own class. He becomes a pauper, and pauperism develops more rapidly than population and wealth." K. Marx and Freidrich Engels, *The Communist Manifesto* (1818), widely reprinted in economic anthologies, as for example, P. A. Samuelson, *Readings in Economics* (McGraw-Hill, New York, 1973), 7th ed. Also "[along with the centralization of capitalists, technological change, and capital accumulation] grows the mass of misery, oppression, slavery, degradation, exploitation . . . the revolt of the working class . . . The monopoly of capital becomes a fetter upon the mode of production. . . . Centralisation of the means of production and socialisation of labour at last reach a point where they become incompatible with their capitalist integument. This integument is burst asunder. The knell of capitalist private property sounds. The expropriators are expropriated." Karl Marx *Capital*, vol. I (1867), chap. XXXIII. Marxologists still dispute whether the immiserization and pauperization of the labor classes was meant literally, or only in terms of relative shares of labor and property, or even only in terms of growing worker discontent and alienation.

tice to the dismal conditions of child labor, length of the working day, and conditions of safety and sanitation in early nineteenth-century factories. A work week of 84 hours was the prevailing rule, with time out at the bench for breakfast and sometimes supper. A good deal of work could be got out of a six-year-old child; and if a man lost two fingers in a machine, he still had eight left.

However true their lurid picture of industrial factory towns, the earlier historians erred in thinking that conditions were clearly worse than in the preindustrial era. The earlier "putting-out," or domestic system, in which wool or yarn was provided to workers for them to spin or weave in their homes, brought the worst conditions of the sweatshop into the home. The whole family was, figuratively, forced to run on the treadmill to keep alive.

Furthermore, poverty is never so obvious in the country as in the industrial cities, where it forces itself on the observer. The idyllic picture of the healthful, happy countryside peopled by stout yeomen and happy peasantry is a mirage in most parts of the world. Even the best known slum areas of Montreal or Halifax, not to mention Harlem and Chicago's black belt, present to their residents better conditions than the rural slums they have escaped: north-central New Brunswick and Newfoundland (where about 60 per cent of the "farms" produced for sale crops worth less than $2,500 in 1971); beautiful Gaspé (where three or four times as many children die in their first year as in Toronto or Montreal). Farther west people live in misery and squalor in Indian settlements, ghost mining towns, and isolated farming communities.

Modern historians therefore emphasize that the living standards of the industrial present, inadequate as they may seem, are nevertheless great improvements over previous periods of commercial enterprise and agrarian feudalism.[2]

TWO WORLDS?

Most of Asia and Africa are even today at lower levels of living than were the Western countries before the Industrial Revolution. Figure 5-1 shows how fortunate Canada's growth in output has been.

A great economic statistician, Simon Kuznets of Harvard, has recently shown that the leading Western nations have for decades been averaging rapid rates of growth of output per head. Examine the front leaf chart to see how fast countries have grown.

What about the progress of the poorer countries? We lack data to give firm answers. Professor Kuznets has made shrewd guesses and inclines to the view that their productivity growth has been lagging behind. He makes the important observation:[3]

". . . the presently developed countries were already in advance of the 'rest of the world' when modern industrialization began—and the latter only increased the disparity."

Table 5-1 indicates the wide international gap between per capita incomes. However, such figures should be cited with great caution. For one thing, they are only national *averages,* and conceal local disparities that may be as wide as the international spread. Newfoundland, for example, only recently attained the per capita income enjoyed in Ontario years earlier. The economist would expect that mobility of labor and capital would help the slowest regions to catch up as the lowest-paid factors attracted canny employers from high-wage areas. But, in fact, for years at a time the gap does not narrow; Newfoundland jogs on with half the personal income of Ontario. Another defect of the international comparison stems from the concept of *standard of living.* Putting all per capita incomes into U.S. dollars ignores variation in national ways of enjoying goods and services and differences in leisure, environment, public health and other elements in Chapter 1's N E W concept. In particular, dif-

---

[2] "The bourgeoisie, during its rule of scarce one hundred years, has created more massive and more colossal productive forces than have all preceding generations together. Subjection of nature's forces to man, machinery, application of chemistry to industry and agriculture, steam-navigation, railways, electric telegraphs, clearing of whole continents for cultivation, canalisation of rivers, whole populations conjured out of the ground—what earlier century had even a presentiment that such productive forces slumbered in the lap of social labour?" K. Marx and F. Engels, *The Communist Manifesto* (1848).

[3] Simon Kuznets, "Quantitative Aspects of the Economic Growth of Nations: 1," *Economic Development and Cultural Change,* Vol. V (1956), p. 25. From 1956 to 1975 there have been some success stories: Thailand, Taiwan, Korea, and Mexico, for example, have made some remarkable progress.

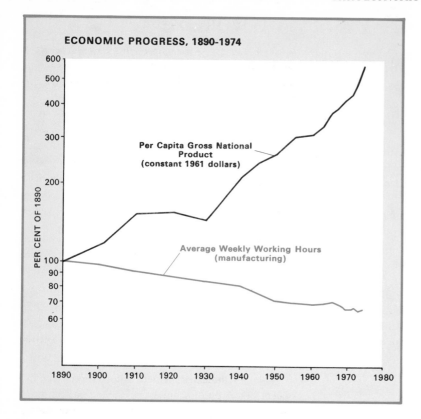

ECONOMIC PROGRESS, 1890-1974

Per Capita Gross National Product (constant 1961 dollars)

Average Weekly Working Hours (manufacturing)

PER CENT OF 1890

FIG. 5-1. Higher productivity has given us more product and more leisure.

Technological improvements, better capital goods, and more highly skilled labor have raised production faster than the growth of population. Note: This is a "ratio," or "semilog," chart; the vertical scale is arranged so that equal vertical distances depict equal percentage rather than equal absolute changes. Example: 400 is as far above 200 as 200 is above 100. (Source: Urquhart & Buckley, *Historical Statistics of Canada,* Cambridge University Press, 1965; and O.J. Firestone, *Canada's Economic Development 1867-1953,* London: Bowes & Bowes, Ltd., 1956; *Canadian Statistical Review, May 1974,* Ottawa: Information Canada, 1974.)

ferences in climate and taste and in the goods available render comparisons of private spending of per capita income deceptive. Glancing again at Table 5-1, who is to say who has the greater well-being, an Italian or a Japanese? Has such a question any economic, or philosophical, meaning?

DISTRIBUTION OF INCOME IN CANADA

A poll of students will show that they are not very sure what their own family incomes really are. Usually it turns out they have a slightly exaggerated notion of their father's earnings. In addition, there are some people so inept at keeping records and with such variable earnings that they do not themselves know how much they make. Even where income is known within the family, there is a quite natural reticence to reveal it to outsiders; thus investigators who made a 1939 survey of the birth-control habits of native white Protestants of Indianapolis often found it

Per Capita GNPs, 1973			
United States	$5,980	Israel	$2,080
Canada	4,920	Czechoslovakia	1,920
Sweden	4,910	Soviet Union	1,800
Denmark	3,860	Portugal	830
West Germany	3,830	Brazil	530
France	3,750	China (Taiwan)	520
Norway	3,720	Turkey	370
United Kingdom	2,670	Korea (South)	310
Japan	2,610	U.A.R. (Egypt)	230
Italy	2,110	India	

TABLE 5-1. Spread of real income is wide.
All estimates have been converted into 1973 U.S. dollars at exchange rates designed to reflect actual purchasing powers: but all estimates should be regarded as rough approximations, particularly in countries at drastically different stages of development. (Sources: Agency for International Development; Center for International Studies, MIT; updating by authors.)

harder to get financial data than intimate personal information.

In the absence of statistical knowledge, it is understandable that one should form an impression of the North American standard of living from the full-page magazine advertisements portraying a jolly family in an air-conditioned mansion, with a Mercedes, a station wagon, a motor launch, and all the other good things that go to make up comfortable living. Actually, of course, this sort of life is still beyond the grasp of 90 per cent of the public and even beyond most families from which the select group of college students comes.

THE SOBER TRUTH   In the middle 1970s, after 15 years of prosperity, the average Canadian family gets about $265 per week. Such an average is derived by pretending that all families, and unattached persons, divide the total income equally. Of course, in real life, income is distributed far from equally; and there is no guarantee that an attempt to divide it equally would leave the total unchanged.

If the members of a classroom, or of the whole country, write down their family incomes on cards, these cards may be sorted into different classes; i.e., some cards will go into the $0-to-$999 class, some into the $1,000-to-$1,999 class, and so forth. In this way we get the *statistical frequency distribution* of income. At one extreme will be the very poor, who have drawn a blank in life; at the other, the very rich. In between fall the vast majority.

Table 5-2 summarizes recent statistics on this subject. Columns (1) and (2) give the *income class interval*. Column (3) shows the percentage of families and individuals in each income class. Column (4) shows the percentage of the total of all income that goes to the people in the given income class. In Column (5) the data are divided into five quintiles of equal numbers of people, as shown in Column (6). Column (7) is computed from (4), showing what percentage of total income goes to the people who belong in the given quintile *or have still lower incomes*.

This table shows it would be a great mistake to think that the poor and the rich are equally distributed around the middle. A glance at the income distribution in Canada shows how pointed is the income pyramid and how broad its base. "There's always room at the top" is certainly true; this is so because it is hard to get there, not because it is easy. If we made

an income pyramid out of a child's blocks, with each layer portraying $1,000 of income, the peak would be far higher than the Eiffel Tower, but almost all of us would be within a yard of the ground.

The middle, or "median," income class (which divides the upper from the lower half of the families and lies halfway through the people in the middle quintile) corresponds to a modest income—only about $11,700 in 1975-76 values in the *1965* table. The median income falls short of the average (or "arithmetic mean") income of $13,267. This is primarily because the distribution of incomes is always a skewed one, with a long tail of incomes stretching out *above* the mean.

POVERTY IN AN AFFLUENT CANADA

In the 1960s, inspired perhaps by President Kennedy's War on Poverty, Canadian governments dropped their complacent acceptance of widespread poverty amidst affluence. Both Canada and the United States, and their provinces or states, and municipalities, launched or accelerated gigantic social programs. Prior to Chapter 40's extended discussion, here is a brief outline of the forces organized against poverty.

Aid was traditionally given by the provinces (and the municipalities) to those in need. Beginning in 1927, Ottawa began to offer social welfare directly or by sharing provincial assistance expenses 50-50. Nowadays the two levels of government spend almost 6 billion dollars on welfare, not to mention vast sums for old-age retirement and hospital and medical care. More constructively, the federal welfare program includes about 500 million dollars for manpower centers and placement; for relocation and mobility of workers; and for training programs. For depressed communities, especially backward rural areas, the Agricultural Rehabilitation and Development Act (ARDA) and other Regional Development schemes have studied, experimented, and innovated in the betterment of whole communities.

DEFINITION OF POVERTY   Economists have tried to come at the measurement of the low-income problem in two ways. The first is to postulate a minimum-decency (or minimum-subsistence) income,

Frequency Distribution of Income of Canadian Families and Unattached Individuals, 1971

Estimated 1975-76 Income Class ($ thousands) (1)	Actual 1971 Income Class ($ thousands) (2)	Per cent of People in this Class (%) (3)	Per cent of Total Income (%) (4)	Boundary of fifth (quintile) ($) (5)	Cumulative Percentage of People (%) (6)	Cumulative Percentage of Income (%) (7)	Theoretical Absolute Equality (%) (8)	Theoretical Absolute Inequality (%) (9)
	0-1	5		0				
0-4.4	1-1.9	8	1	Lowest fifth	20	4	20	0
	2-2.9	6	2					
				3,100 (4,700)				
	3-3.9	7	3					
4.5-8.9	4-4.9	6	3	Second fifth	40	14	40	0
	5-5.9	6	4					
				6,300 (9,200)				
	6-6.9	6	5					
9.0-13.4	7-7.9	6	5	Middle fifth	60	32	60	0
	8-8.9	7	7					
				9,300 (14,000)				
	9-9.9	6	7					
13.4-17.9	10-11.9	11	14	Fourth fifth	80	57	80	0
				12,900 (19,000)				
	12-14.9	11	17					
18 and up	15-24.9	11	22	Top fifth	100	100	100	100
	25 and up	2	10					

TABLE 5-2. Income pyramid shows inequality of incomes.
Much information is compressed here. The incomes were measured back in 1971, so the estimated 1975-76 equivalents are shown in brackets. The income classes are separated approximately to show fifths (quintiles) of the whole Canadian population of families and unattached individuals; the actual boundaries between these fifths are written in Column (5) for 1971 and 1975-76. (Source: Statistics Canada publication no. 13-207, 1973.)

and investigate who are below it. This is the "poverty-line" approach. The second, on page 88, is to measure the spread of incomes between the rich and the poor: the degree of inequality.

Let us see how large the group is that is stuck below some adequate income level. Economists have two techniques for this. First, from social-service workers they have taken over carefully calculated budgets purporting to measure the cost of a barely-adequate living standard. To check and supplement such data, the Economic Council of Canada has used a second method. It is based on the finding[4] that poor families generally must and do spend most of their income on essentials, having little left over for drugs, medical care, education, recreation, travel, or savings. Conservatively, the ECC decided to classify as "low-income families" those that spend 70 per cent of their income entirely for food, clothing, and shelter. They then found which income levels showed this kind of spending. They found for example, that in 1971 a family of five, living on $5,400 per year or $105 per week, would on the average have to spend more than three-quarters of its income on essentials. The 1975 equivalent is about $8,100, or about $5,000 for two persons. They were classified as just falling below the poverty line.

Judged by these standards, tables such as Table 5-2, for the late 1960s showed at least 800,000 families below the minimum-decency line! And this was down from 1961—the ten years of prosperity have lifted 2 or 3 per cent of Canada's families above the poverty level.

Not surprisingly, such a decline in poverty always accompanies a period of prosperity; cycles in unemployment and poverty move together. If we ignore these cyclical swings, and look at the long trend, a gradual poverty decline shows up in the figures. This can be explained by the fact that the rise in the cost of living over the years has been slower than the rise in family money incomes. (In Canada, for instance, a typical wage now will buy more than *twice* as much as in the period following World War I. But the *minimum*-decency notion, of how much a wage-earner *ought* to have, has also gone up; for *as the nation as a whole gets more prosperous, the definition of minimum standards is raised.*)

4 From "Engel curves"—see Chapter 11, footnote 2.

The decline is certainly visible. Goldberg and Podoluk[5] found that the lowest one-fifth of wage-and-salary earners received only 2 per cent of all such incomes in 1931, but almost 4 per cent by 1951.[6] But at the same time, the *number* of impoverished persons is not decreasing rapidly even though their proportion of the total population may be decreasing. Canada's anti-poverty policy has been aimed heavily at rural squalor and low incomes. There is much justification for this rural emphasis. For example, the Senate Committee found that in 1967 the average earnings of rural families were $7,500 while the average income of similar families in metropolitan areas was $9,600, or 30 per cent greater. Both of these statistics included some families in very serious poverty, but the rural situation was by far the worse.[7]

Table 5-2, Column (4), shows that 19 per cent of all families were below the $3,000 line in 1971. To raise them all above this low line would not, in fact, be expensive; it is easy to calculate that the sum required is about 3 per cent of personal income.

Take a sample of 1,000 families. Their mean income is $8,800 and their total income therefore is 8.8 million dollars. The poorest 19 per cent of the families would require 0.57 million dollars in order to receive $3,000 each (190 families multiplied by $3,000). This is about 6 per cent of total income; but these families already earn about 3 per cent. Thus, a further transfer of about 3 per cent of total income is needed to raise the income of these families to $3,000. (This calculation can easily be adapted to show the expense of other anti-poverty goals.) Moving from this sample of 1,000 families to the whole population, the required 3 per cent of total family income is less than 2 per cent of GNP.

One trouble with such a transfer program to deal with poverty is that a minimum of one million would be literally dependent on government relief of various kinds. Of course, many are wholly dependent

5 Simon Goldberg and Jenny Podoluk, "Income Size Distribution Statistics in Canada—A Survey and Some Analysis," *Income and Wealth Series VI* (London: Bowes and Bowes, 1957), p. 159. They found that family wage incomes were more evenly distributed than individual incomes.

6 The Special Senate Committee report, *Poverty in Canada,* reports a similar trend up to 1967, as does the Statistics Canada report of 1971. See also Adams, *et al., The Real Poverty Report,* (Edmonton: Hurtig, 1971). Both these books choose higher standards than the Economic Council of Canada or Statcan.

7 Less than ten per cent of metropolitan families were in poverty, compared with almost 40 per cent of rural families.

now: they include a disproportionate fraction of women (especially widows with children), old persons, young workers with children, unemployed persons of all ages, and members of such groups as Indians, Negroes, new immigrants, and (as we have seen) rural people.

However, most people believe that transfers, or a "guaranteed income," like the dole of the 19th century, are *not* the single answer to this problem. To the extent that aid is needed, anti-poverty programs must distinguish between the situations of each kind of family in poverty in order to arrive at a permanent solution. Remember too that low and high incomes allocate factors of production, including labor. To increase lower incomes without thought of the cause may simply perpetuate a poverty problem.

HOW TO MEASURE INEQUALITY

Measuring inequality among income classes is the alternative to measuring the number in poverty. How great is the spread of incomes, and how shall we find a measure of the degree of inequality of income distributions? From Table 5-2 we can see that in 1971 one-fifth of Canadians had incomes below $3,100, and one-fifth lay above $12,900. Of course the fact that there are the same numbers of families and unattached individuals in the bottom and top quintiles does not mean that they each receive the same percentage of total income. Actually, the lowest fifth received less than one-tenth of the income received by the top fifth, as Column (4), or (7) can confirm. The irregularity in these percentages has suggested a measure of inequality. First, we can ask what per cent of total income goes to each successive or 20 (or any) per cent of the population. These are seen in comparing the cumulative totals in Columns (6) and (7). Notice that the most affluent, top, fifth gets more than 43 per cent (100—57) of the income—much more than the bottom three-fifths! But, if incomes were absolutely uniformly distributed, the lowest 20 per cent of the population (which in this case would mean *any* 20 per cent) would receive exactly 20 per cent of the total income; the lowest 80 per cent would receive 80 per cent of the income; and the highest 20 per cent would also get only 20 per cent of the income.

In order to plot the degree of inequality on a so-called Lorenz curve, examine coloured columns of Figure 5-2's table, whose cumulative percentages contrast the patterns of (8) absolute equality, (9) absolute inequality, and (7) actual 1971 Canadian inequality.

Absolute equality is depicted by the Column (8) numbers. When plotted, these become the red equality diagonal of Figure 5-2's Lorenz diagram.

At the other extreme, we have the equally hypothetical case of absolute *inequality*, where everybody (say, 99 out of 100 people) has no income, except for one person who has *all* the income. This is shown in Column (9) of the table. The lowest, 0, 20, 80, and 99 people have no income at all. But the lowest 100 do include the last man; and all the people, of course, have all the income. The lowest curve on the Lorenz diagram—the dark, almost right-angled line represents this limiting case of absolute inequality.

Any actual income distribution must fall between these extremes. Its Lorenz curve is given in Figure 5-2 by the indicated intermediate curve, with the *shaded area* indicating the deviation from absolute equality, and hence giving us a measure of the degree of *inequality* of income distribution. (Since we shall meet Lorenz curves often, this figure deserves careful study.)[8]

TRENDS IN EQUALITY

What is happening to the degree of inequality of incomes in modern nations? Is it getting greater, as pessimists feared? By calculating Lorenz and other curves, scholars find that inequality is definitely less in Canada than it was in 1931, but slightly *more* than

[8] M. O. Lorenz was a German statistician of the 1900s. Another way to measure income-inequality deserves mention here. The Italian-born Swiss professor of economics Vilfredo Pareto was often called, with somewhat questionable accuracy, the ideological precursor of fascism. By using a certain logarithmic chart called the "Pareto chart," he found that the "upper tail" of the income data of many different countries and many different times fell along straight lines of almost the same slopes. He came to believe this to be a fundamental natural law. According to Pareto's Law, there is an *inevitable tendency for income to be distributed in the same way—regardless of social and political institutions and regardless of taxation.* In the past 65 years, more careful studies have refuted the universality of Pareto's Law, as well as its inevitability. Thus, in Great Britain, in the period just following World War II, income taxation had gone so far as to leave only 70 people with incomes of more than $24,000 after taxes were paid! More on this in Chapter 38's discussion of inequality.

DISTRIBUTION OF FAMILY AND UNATTACHED INDIVIDUAL INCOME IN CANADA, 1971

Curve of Absolute Equality

Actual Distribution, Canada, 1971

Deviation from Absolute Equality

Curve of Absolute Inequality

PER CENT OF INCOME RECEIVED

PER CENT OF FAMILIES AND UNATTACHED INDIVIDUALS

Fig. 5-2. Lorenz curve measures degree of inequality between opposite limits.

By plotting from Table 5-2 we can see that the actual distribution-of-income curve lies between the two extremes of absolute equality and absolute inequality. The shaded area of this Lorenz chart (as a percentage of half the square's area) measures relative inequality of income.

it was at the end of World War II. A glance at Fig. 5-3(b) will show that the United Kingdom and North America have rather similar degrees of inequality of incomes, the major difference apparently not being attributable so much to differences in social philosophy as to the fact that there is a larger fraction of subsistence farmers and low-paid urban and nonwhite workers in the North American economy.

Which country today has the greatest equality? No one knows how to compare the inequality in the Soviet Union [9] or China with that in mixed economies. If we confine ourselves to the noncommunist world,

it has been suggested that Israel may lead the list. Sweden and other mixed economies have low inequality, as the comparison in Fig. 5-3(a) shows.

Before industrialization, was there a golden age of greater equality of distribution? Fragmentary historical data suggest otherwise. Have developed societies generally greater inequality than underdeveloped nations? Casual tourist observation often suggests the reverse; the extremes of poverty and wealth *appear* greater in poor countries than in industrialized ones. The limited statistics available do confirm this view; thus, the Lorenz curve for a country like Ceylon in Fig. 5-3(a) will show greater inequality than will such a curve for Western countries, like Sweden or the United States. In general, as development proceeds, incomes within a nation are believed to become more equal. (The Lorenz curve for Black Americans shows slightly *more* inequality than does the curve for whites.)

DISTRIBUTION OF WEALTH

A Lorenz curve of distribution of *wealth* ownership shows considerably more inequality than does a

[9] A very careful study of wage inequalities in Russia's communistic economy, done by Abram Bergson, in *The Structure of Soviet Wages* (Cambridge, Mass.: Harvard University Press, 1944), showed inequalities and dispersions between the best-paid and the poorest-paid workers surprisingly like those of our own society. Shostakovich, other top Soviet musicians, and top scientists probably make more there than do similar persons in the West. The inequality of political privilege among Soviet bureaucrats, military officers, Communist party members, and the Soviet public at large is not susceptible to precise numerical measurement. *Employment* incomes in mixed economies like Australia and Sweden were found in a 1965 study to be slightly more equal than in Poland.

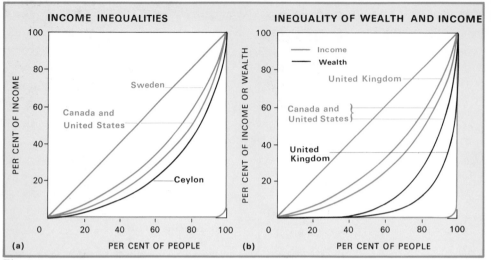

Fig. 5-3
(a). Advanced economies show less inequality of income distribution than do preindustrial economies.
(b) Inequality differs among nations and is different for income than for wealth.

curve of *income* distribution. Figure 5-3(b) shows how great is the difference between the wealth and income curves. Whereas the United Kingdom, and Canada and the United States have similar inequality of *incomes*, note that the United Kingdom has much greater inequality of *wealth* than do Canada and the United States. In part this is because certain peers and tycoons in Britain own tremendous concentrations of land and other property. But study of the data shows that much of the difference comes from the fact that many North Americans of quite modest incomes do have positive net worth (i.e., assets minus liabilities), whereas this is less common among lower-income Britons.[10]

Turn back to Fig. 3-1. It shows that the FOR WHOM problem is determined by (1) the price that people can get for the factors they supply—land, labor, machinery, and general capital goods, and (2) the amounts of these factors that they start out with. If labor could be ignored, then the distribution of incomes would be about that determined by the distribution of wealth: at the same interest return, twice

the wealth will yield twice the income. Hence, property incomes show great Lorenz inequality.

The earnings from work—wages, salaries, earnings of unincorporated entrepreneurs—are evidently less unequally distributed. But of course they are not uniform, as the following sections show.

INCOME DIFFERENCES AMONG OCCUPATIONS

What single profession seems to make the most money? In recent years it has without question been the doctors. They have forged well ahead of lawyers. Medical doctors and surgeons have been estimated to have mean earnings close to $45,000 in 1973, and lawyers $10,000 less. Why the difference? Primarily because the costs of training doctors are so high and the capacities of our medical schools are so low. Although the demand has increased, North America as a whole does not train many more doctors than it did in 1910. Canadian training has expanded from a low pre-war level, but we depend surprisingly on immigrant doctors to keep ahead. This slowness of supply keeps incomes (the price of medical consultation) high; and medical societies are accused of helping to keep the doctors' incomes up by various devices, including the insistence on high standards of training.

[10] Canadian data on the distribution of wealth are just now being developed. But data derived from a consumer-survey of net worths in seven Canadian cities suggest that the Canadian distribution of wealth is not unlike the American. (J. V. Poapst, *Consumer Survey*, Study for the Porter Commission, Appendix A, Table 90.)

Lawyers and notaries, dentists, architects and engineers, and accountants are estimated to have 1973 mean incomes of about $32,000, $30,000, $25,000 and $22,000 respectively. Teachers and professors as a class have a mean salary of about $11,000. Full professors at the largest universities get over $25,000; older professors and professors of physics and engineering average higher incomes than do younger professors and professors of Greek and botany. Teachers' salaries have been improving recently, and now nurses are the lowest-paid of all professionals. Their median salary is still not much above $8,000. And even with special perquisites, the final figure is unbelievably low.

Do incomes increase with age? Not in the lowest-paid manual jobs. For such work, a man is at his best in his early twenties; after that he goes downhill. In the professions and in business executive jobs, earnings do increase with age. Professors at age 50 have salaries twice those of new lecturers; and some outside income too. Doctors and lawyers reach their prime around fifty; many can hope to work beyond the normal retirement ages. A junior executive with a good M.B.A. degree will begin training at over $1,000 a month; if he is very successful, he may retire as chairman of the board, earning, say $150,000 a year and with stock bonuses and retirement provisions.[11]

On the other hand, many corporations and institutions have been fixing inflexible retirement ages of sixty-five. With improvements in life expectancies, this poses a problem of long years of wasteful and unhappy retirement. The ultimate solution seems to be along these lines: Let each man taper off slowly rather than abruptly, other factors besides chronological age being decisive.

IS COLLEGE WORTH WHILE?

How do education and training affect lifetime income? Are they worth their cost? The evidence answers, Yes. Family heads who attended only 8 years of school had an average income of only about $4,500

in 1971. Those who completed college did two and a half times as well. Unemployment among high-school dropouts exceeds that of graduates by a growing margin.

Even if you have to borrow, put off years of gainful employment, live away from home, and pay for food and books, your lifetime earnings in the professions that are open only to college graduates will probably turn out to be more than compensatory. (Good grades help: "grinds" end up with slightly higher pay than do "big men on campus"; both outearn the anonymous face in the college crowd.) In recent studies it appears that those who graduate from college in 1975 will earn, between ages 18 and 64, about $650,000, while those of their generation who only graduate from high school will earn about $400,000. Those who only finish elementary school will earn but $300,000. Going on to do graduate work will add less than 8 per cent to the 4-year graduate's lifetime earnings. (But full-time female workers with the B.A., until recently at least, do no better than male high school graduates!) But, in general, the case seems established that investment in "human capital" has a high lifetime return.[12]

Skills, learning ability, and general knowledge are the chief reason. Another may be that college acts as a screen or filter for employers, helping them to catch future employees with the highest abilities.[13]

---

[11] Salaries of top officers do increase with the size of the firm, but by no means in strict proportion. U.S. statistics suggest that the head of Corporation A, twice the size of Company B, will *not* get twice the salary that the head of B gets, but only about 30 per cent more.

[12] Money is not everything—better to be uneducated, poor and happy than to be well-off and miserable? A 1960 study on mental health reported a survey of how people with different education compared mentally. Were college graduates worried and depressed in comparison with those of little schooling? Surprisingly, the answer was, Definitely not. College graduates reported greater happiness and less mental illness. True, they were more introspective; but coupled with this went a greater sense of well-being and satisfaction. Their perspectives were broader and aspiration levels higher; and when they worried, their worries tended to be over genuine rather than imagined troubles. Only 38 per cent of high school graduates say they are "very happy" in their marriage, as against 60 per cent for college graduates. Only 70 per cent of high school graduates say their job is "enjoyable" as against no less than 89 per cent for college graduates.

[13] Pennsylvania's P.J. Taubman and U.B.C.'s T.J. Wales found that as much as half the private yield on a B.A. in 1946 reflected "the use of education as a relatively inexpensive screening device by employers". *Journal of Political Economy*, 81, Jan. 1973. The private yield—actually about 8 per cent—is the annual percentage return to an individual on the tuition and personal foregone wages sustained in spending four years obtaining a B.A. degree instead of entering the labor force; it is analogous to the yield on bonds shown in Question 11 of Chapter 4 and the Appendix to Chapter 4.

Indeed the yield on investments in human capital, in many societies, may be higher than that on tools and buildings. But the problem for both planners and students is to distinguish between training and ability.

DIFFERENCES IN ABILITY AND INCOMES

In Part Four we shall study in detail the economic principles underlying the distribution of income. Our common sense enables us to anticipate part of its analysis and suggests that one factor helping to explain differences in income must be *differences in people's abilities.*

Differences in people may be physical, mental, temperamental, or even moral. They may be associated with biological inheritance; or with social and economic environment.

These differences are easy to exaggerate and provide us with only part of the answer to the puzzle of income distribution. Physical traits (such as height or hip girth) and measured mental traits (such as intelligence quotient or tone perception) appear to be *not* so different among people as are the differences in income distribution. Often the scientist who measures individual traits finds that they are "normally" distributed, with most people in the middle and fewer people at each end, as represented by the bell-shaped curve of Fig. 5-4 (If their IQ scores depart from the normal distribution, psychologists often *rescale* them so as to force agreement!) Incomes— even those from work, but especially those from property ownership—are distributed *skewly,* as shown by the other curve with a very long tail off in the direction of the highest-paid individuals.

Actually, there is nothing particularly sacred about the so-called "normal curve." If *heights* of cubes (not people) are normally distributed, then their *volumes* will be skewed off to the right. Moreover, careful examination of census data on incomes suggests that *each kind of wage* income may tend to approximate roughly a bell-shaped distribution curve of modest asymmetry. But when we add together the distributions of earnings for women as well as men, for property owners as well as workers, for lucky speculators, and other diverse groups, the great "skewness" of the whole distribution does emerge. Moreover, if we follow each wage earner over a period of

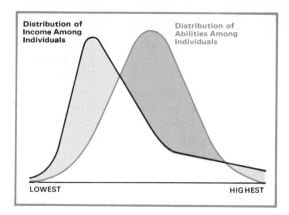

Fig. 5-4. Are abilities more normally distributed than market incomes?

Heights, intelligence quotients, and many measured human traits seem to follow a so-called "normal" bell-shaped statistical distribution. Market incomes seem to be more skewed, highest incomes being more than a hundred times the lowest (as in the black curve).

years, a pattern of dispersion will emerge, one of the important factors causing differences among individuals being the different degrees of unemployment they suffer.

Perhaps a warning is in order at this point against jumping to the conclusion that there is something *necessary* and *inevitable* about this dispersion of income. Within the framework of the mixed economy, fundamental changes in education have already made changes in inequality. Moreover, as no one knows better than the man at the top, our system of progressive income taxation has already greatly changed the relative take-home and—what is more important —the "keep-at-home" pay of the high- and low-paid. Simon Kuznets has verified that lifetime incomes are less unequal than those of any one year. Thus, many with low incomes for a year like 1975 are retired people who did not always have such low incomes, or those with recent bad luck. Further, the modern system of welfare transfers is recognized as an improvement by observers who remember the bad old days of *laissez-faire* when countless people literally starved while no one even noticed.

In particular, we must remember that the chief victims of our tolerance of inequality are members of minority groups, and "segregated" labor forces such as that of Quebec. The disabilities of these segments of our society are dealt with in Chapter 40.

Class Origins of 611 Canadian-Born Members of the Economic Elite	NUMBER	PER CENT
Father in economic elite	135	
Father in other elite groups (government, clergy, military, etc.)	13	
Wife from an elite family	41	50
Father in substantial business	42	
Attended private school	75	
Attended university and/or father in middle-class occupation	197	32
Probably lower than middle-class origins	108	18

TABLE 5-3. Anyone can climb the ladder of success, but it helps to start high.

In Porter's sample, another 150 members of the elite were foreign-born. Many of them had scientific and engineering backgrounds; otherwise, their orgins appeared to be much like those of the Canadian-born elite. (Source: John Porter, *The Vertical Mosaic*, Toronto: University of Toronto Press, 1965; and the *Canadian Journal of Economics and Political Science*, 1957, p. 390.)

ECONOMIC STRATIFICATION AND OPPORTUNITY

The New World has always been considered the land of opportunity, where anyone with ability might get ahead in the world. The success legend of Horatio Alger, Jr.'s, "poor but proud" hero who worked his way to the top and married the boss's daughter—has no doubt been overdrawn. But it did have elements of truth as compared with the former situation in European countries, where an aristocratic tradition lingered and where free schooling beyond the primary grades was established late in history.

For example, the "old school tie" and the correct accent were until recently almost indispensable to political and social advancement in Britain; even with the free scholarship system, few members of the lower or middle class could jump this hurdle. In this country, few people even recognize a "prep school" accent, and variations in speech are geographical rather than social.

Moreover, ours has been a rather more materialistic civilization in which success is interpreted in business terms. Because "money talks," it is easier for outsiders to break into the upper crust than it would

be in a culture that puts greater emphasis upon tradition. The *nouveaux riches* of one generation may become the social arbiters of the next.

RECRUITMENT OF THE ELITE Nevertheless, careful investigations of the social origins of the "business elite" have turned up some surprising facts. The *economic* elite of Canada was defined by John Porter to consist, in 1955, of nearly 1,000 businessmen who shared 1,300 of the 1,600 directorships of the 900 largest or most powerful corporations, and were, for the most part, managers or presidents themselves of one or more of the corporations. Typically, the member of this elite was not a poor immigrant or a farm boy, nor was he born in a slum; more likely his father was also in the elite of *his* day, was able to buy his son a good education and often to insert him directly into the family enterprise. Table 5-3, on this page, summarizes one part of Porter's findings.

Do such studies of the "power elite" indicate that North American economic society is hardening along caste lines? Two diametrically opposite explanations of the statistics are possible:

(1) In the past there was high social mobility in Canada and the United States: all the cream rose to the top, leaving naturally less gifted people at the bottom.

(2) There are strong, perhaps growing, barriers to circulation between the economic classes.

Some economists incline to the first view, feeling that "you can't keep a good man down." Many sociologists would disagree, particularly if one is crass enough to enquire about the absence of women, Asians, blacks, Indians, or even southern Europeans among these elites. They would emphasize the thousand and one subtle psychological, social, economic, and educational disadvantages of the children of less fortunate families; that equal ability is not always able to give rise to equal achievement.[14]

[14] When the first edition of this book was written, the senior author inclined toward the view that it was becoming increasingly difficult to go from the bottom to the top. Now he is not sure. Recent careful studies of the origins of business leaders back before 1900 suggest that the present may compare favorably with the good old days, which may not have been so good after all. Increasingly, as organizations become bigger, the elements of nepotism and personal favoritism seem to become less important, and the increasing emphasis upon civil-servant-like quasi-objective tests of performance suggests greater mobility among the elite. Perhaps we are becoming a "meritocracy." *(Continued on page 94.)*

Whichever view is right, the implications for policy are the same. Human beings are a nation's most important form of social capital—high-yielding form, moreover, in which we have invested too little in the past. Talent, wherever it may be, is worth seeking out and nurturing. And, as it will be discussed in later chapters, equality of opportunity has not always been a feature of Canadian society. The position of minority groups in our country gives us particular cause for concern.

SUMMARY

1   Incomes of the poorest today are higher than in earlier times. The belief that the poor are becoming poorer in modern industrial nations will not stand up under careful factual examination. Since the Industrial Revolution incomes and standards have been showing a definite rise.

2   Incomes and standards of life in Western Europe and in North America are not only higher than in other continents, but are rising faster annually than in the underdeveloped nations.

3   The median income, revealed in factual studies of the distribution of Canadian incomes, is lower than popularly believed. The differences in living standards are very great between professions and between regions.

4   The Lorenz diagram is a convenient device for measuring the spreads or inequalities of income distribution. It shows what percentage of total income goes to the poorest 1 per cent of the population, to the poorest 10 per cent, to the poorest 95 per cent, and so forth. The modern distribution of Canadian income appears to be less unequal than in 1931 or than that in underdeveloped countries, but it still shows a considerable measure of inequality with little change in recent decades.

5   An interesting question is to try to relate the skew distributions of income to education and human capital formation on the one hand and to the more "normal" differences in human mental and physical abilities on the other.

6   There is strong positive correlation between income and social status of a person's parents and grandparents and his own, but the exact direction of causation is hard to establish.

7. Within the affluent society the public war against poverty goes unceasingly on. As each rampart is conquered, higher standards of performance are set by society for itself. The vicious circle by which poverty is environmentally inherited has to be broken if the anti-poverty war is to be won. The problems of poverty and disadvantaged minority groups will be discussed later in Chapter 40.

The arithmetic of "transition probabilities" can be made to yield the following results. Divide society into two classes, so that I am either a U in the Upper class or a *non-U* in the Lower. If a child's chance to move out of his parents' class is as great as to stay in, then 1/2 the children, grandchildren, great-grandchildren, and descendants generally of a U parent will be U's. But if there is social stratification so that a child has only 1/4 chance of moving into a class different from his parents, 3/4 (= 1/2 + 1/4) of the children of U's will be U's. However, it can be deduced that only 5/8 (= 1/2 + 1/8) of grandchildren of U's will be U's; and only 9/16 (= 1/2 + 1/16) of their great-grandchildren. Evidently, the chance of remote descendants of U's being also U's goes ultimately down to 1/2, with 50 per cent of the excess above the 1/2 equality level wiped out at each new generation. Hope for the *non-U's* means despair for the U's only if a fair race is deemed a tragedy. For more on the arithmetic of transition probabilities, see W. Feller, *An Introduction to Probability* (New York: Wiley, 1957).

CONCEPTS FOR REVIEW

income distribution
mean and median
per capita incomes
minimum budget

Lorenz curve of income and wealth
normal and skew distributions
human capital
social stratification
war against poverty

QUESTIONS FOR DISCUSSION

1. Let each member of the class write down on a slip of paper an estimate of his own family's income. From these, draw up a frequency table showing the distribution of incomes. What is the median income? The mean or average income?

2. How much do you think it takes for a childless married couple to live comfortably in your community? How would the money be spent?

3. Were your parents better off than their parents? What does this suggest with respect to the advantages and disadvantages of capitalism and the modern mixed economy?

4. Formulate some of your own ethical beliefs concerning how unequal incomes should be for people of different abilities and needs. How do you justify these beliefs? Would a nineteenth-century Canadian agree? A Russian today? A Chinese? A South Sea Islander? What would be the relevance of the U.S. Bureau of Labor Statistics report that those in the under-$3,000 income class give 4 per cent of their income to church and charity while those in the over-$10,000 class give 3 per cent?

5. How does the fact that different cities and regions have different costs of living affect comparisons of *real* incomes?

   Thus in Charlottetown living is about 10 per cent more expensive than in the average city. Vancouver and Halifax are also expensive places. Winnipeg and Regina run below average. Small towns run nearly 10 per cent below big cities. Although a teacher, secretary, or mechanic in Amsterdam earns less than half the comparable Toronto salaries, most living costs (other than services and rents!) run only about 25 per cent less.

6
BUSINESS ORGANIZATION
AND INCOME

*The able businessman generally finds that in the long run the capital at his command grows in
proportion to his ability.*
ALFRED MARSHALL

Business, labor, and government form the chief institutions of an economy. The Chapters that immediately follow deal with the last two institutions; this chapter focuses on the first, business.

To understand our mixed economy, we must first understand the organization and functioning of business enterprise. The first part of this chapter leads up to the analysis of the modern corporation, primarily by an extensive case study; the last half deals with the financial structure of corporations, particularly the modern large-scale or "giant" corporation. The Appendix presents a brief introduction to the fundamentals of accounting. Without some comprehension of accounting, there can be no deep understanding of the economics of enterprise. The "new industrial state"—to use the name John Kenneth Galbraith has coined for our large corporate bureaucracy—is something new in history.[1] If the corporate structure is not to control man, society must see that it stays subject to control.

BIG, SMALL, AND INFINITESIMAL BUSINESS

There are more than 600,000 business units in Canada. The majority of these enterprises are very small-scale units, owned by a single person. Most are here today and gone tomorrow, the average life expectancy of a business being only six years. Some will terminate in bankruptcy; many more will be voluntarily brought to a close with sighs of regret for dashed hopes and an expensive lesson learned; still

others will come to a joyous end when their "self-employed" owners finally land good, steady jobs.

Faster than old businesses die, new ones are born. The present population of business concerns grew up as a result of the cumulative excess of business births over business deaths during previous years. As an economy grows, we can expect a continued excess.

By number the tiny, transient, self-owned "individual proprietorship" is the overwhelmingly dominant form of business. But in terms of dollar value, political and economic power, payrolls, and employment, only slightly more than one-hundred "giant corporations" occupy a strategically dominant position.

TINY BUSINESS Let us glance briefly at the role in our economy of "infinitesimal businesses." There are more than 275,000 farmers in Canada; 120,000 retail and grocery store owners, many of them over 65 years of age and earning less than the minimum taxable income; about 20,000 service stations, or one for every 250 cars; and so it goes.

Some of these ventures are highly successful; but it is still true to say that most do not earn for their owners much more than they could get with less effort and risk by working for somebody else. Thus, chain stores do about half of all the grocery business, the rest being divided among the independents. Most of these independents consist of the so-called "Ma and Pa" stores, doing less than $200 of business every day. These are often started by people who have only a few thousand dollars of initial capital—less than half the amount necessary for an adequate grocery store to do the volume of business necessary if the owner is to earn even minimum wages for his ef-

[1] John Kenneth Galbraith, *The New Industrial State* (Boston: Houghton Mifflin, 1967), p. 320.

fort. Such small-scale efforts are doomed; when the owner's initial capital is used up, they are finished. They illustrate why one-third to one-half of all North American retail businesses are discontinued within 3 years.

Of course, business fields differ in the amount of capital required. To build a modern service station in Ontario recently cost between $100,000 and $150,000 (land included), but the average cost of renting a station is only $6,000-$8,000 per year. Occupations with a high "rate of turnover of inventory"—such as vegetable stores—obviously require less initial capital than drugstores, hardware stores, or jewelry stores, where some items of stock stay on the shelves for 3 to 5 years and where the average "turnover ratio" of annual sales to stock of inventory may be a great deal less than one.

Aside from the capital necessary to open a business, there is the tremendous amount of personal effort required. Self-employed farmers usually work from 55 to 60 hours per week during the peak summer months. Similarly, it has been estimated that the people who are their own bosses put in more hours per week than wage earners. Who, on holiday, has not pitied some self-employed proprietor and all his family whose weekend drudgery barely bring them $5,000 per year?

Still, people want to start out on their own. *Theirs* may be the successful venture. Even if they never do succeed in earning more than a few thousand a year, many are attracted by being able to make their own plans and escaping much of the monotony of wage employment.

THE SINGLE PROPRIETORSHIP

We gain insight into the principal forms of business organization—(a) the single proprietorship, (b) partnership, and (c) corporation—by following the history or a particular business venture as it grows from a small beginning into a good-sized corporation. In the last part of this chapter, we shall turn to the subject of the giant corporation and its modern economic role.

Let us suppose you decide to start a business to produce toothpaste. Perhaps you simply looked up an old formula in the *Encyclopaedia Britannica*. You need no permission; you simply wake up one morning and say, "Today, I am in business!" And you are.

You can hire as few or as many men as you wish, borrow whatever capital you can. At the end of the month whatever is left over as profits—after all costs have been met!—is yours to do with as you like. And, apart from personal income tax, there is nothing to stop you going to the cash-register at any time, taking out $800 if you find it there, and spending it as you wish.

The costs and losses of the business are all yours, too. If your sales fail to cover your costs, your creditors can ask you to dig deep into your own pocket. In legal terms, an individual proprietor has *unlimited liability* for all debts contracted by his business. Almost all his property is legally attachable to meet those debts.

BUSINESS GROWTH AND THE NEED FOR SHORT-TERM CAPITAL

Suppose your low price induces a supermarket chain to place a large order for tubes of paste to be marketed under its name. Though you are now making more money, you find yourself harder pressed for cash than before. Why? Because you are not *paid in advance* for your sales, whereas you must pay your workers and suppliers promptly. To start, you must put out money and get nothing back, i.e., nothing except the certainty of future payment on the sales orders which you have booked, nothing but a miscellaneous batch of "goods in process"—unfinished toothpaste and so forth.

To some extent, the stringency of cash can be relieved by your not paying for supplies until the end of the month or even longer. However, there is a limit to how far your suppliers will let you run up bills. Also, letting your so-called "accounts payable liabilities" pile up has an expense, because goods are often billed at 2 per cent discount if paid within 30 days. When you do not take advantage of such discounts, you are, in effect, paying a very high interest rate—up to 24 per cent per year.

Where is such a single proprietor to borrow? A consumer loan company would probably charge you 3 per cent per month or 40 per year for the $40,000 you need; and even it will prefer to lend to a man with a steady wage that can be "attached" or "garnisheed" in case of non-payment. If you own a home without a mortgage, a loan at 13 or 14 per cent might be raised upon it. To do so appears to risk your family's future well-being; but your personal wealth is in jeopardy whatever you do. So you may go ahead and mortgage.

Why can't you call on your bank for a commercial loan at 12 per cent? Ordinarily, a chartered bank will not provide "venture capital" for an unproven enterprise. The local manager looks at your chequing balance and finds it has always been near the vanishing point; this is natural, since as fast as payments have come in, you have had to write cheques for your creditors. Ordinarily, the bank likes to establish "lines of credit", idle part of the year, and fully-loaned during the busy season. Such loans are cancelled when the cash comes in. It is futile to pretend that 3 months from now your growing business will be more flooded with cash than now. The more you grow, the more cash you'll need; you know it, and your banker knows it.

Sometimes bank managers are allowed to extend "term loans" of some years' duration. But even if allowed, the manager could not conscientiously provide capital for a business like yours. No matter how glorious the future of the business appears, to the banker you are only one of numerous would-be entrepreneurs; and most, he knows, are destined for failure even in the best of times, and almost all would be wiped out if a serious recession should come along. At the best, he would have to charge you an extra risk premium of perhaps 10 per cent more, in addition to, say, 12 per cent interest. Otherwise, his gains would not offset his losses.

There are a few other possibilities. Your bank might give you a Small Business Loan at 12 per cent for several years, for which you would have to offer collateral and undertake to spend the loan on property and equipment. (The government, under the Small Business Loans Act, in effect insures the bank against your being wiped out.) Or you might turn to the Federal Industrial Development Bank which has power to lend at longer term, perhaps on a ten-year mortgage at about 14 per cent. But it, too, would be helpful chiefly if you needed more building or machinery, not cash. Finally, in some cities and provinces there are local lenders, sometimes publicly supported, who have limited funds to help bring a business to town or keep it there.

With these uncertain sources of capital, your business will still suffer from growing pains. You will soon exhaust all possibilities of raising loan capital. Perhaps the time has come to look for a partner.

THE PARTNERSHIP

Any two or more people can get together and form a partnership. Each agrees to provide some fraction of the work and capital, to share some percentage of the profits, and of course to share the losses or debts. A purely oral agreement will do; but it makes for less misunderstanding if you draw up a formal partnership agreement.

In the case of the toothpaste business, suppose your brother-in-law takes a part ownership in the business in return for putting up $40,000 capital. Like you, he is to work for the company for, say, $12,000 per year as compared with your $18,000. You are to receive two-thirds of all profits or losses, computed after the stipulated wage-like withdrawals are treated as costs; he gets one-third.

Your partner has put up $40,000 in cash. What have you brought into the venture? You contribute, of course, some unfinished barrels of toothpaste and some receivables for goods already delivered. Are these all?

Actually, what you bring to the partnership is an intangible but valuable asset: the profitable sales orders and the know-how, or what are called "good will." In short, you are bringing with you a *potential profit-earning power* over all costs and drawings, of, say, $21,000 a year. You are letting your partner have a $12,000-a-year job—which we shall assume is perhaps equal to what he can get elsewhere—and, in addition, for $40,000 he is purchasing a one-third slice of $21,000 every year.

To get this much per year from bond investments would cost him much more than $40,000. He would have to buy $78,000 worth of 9 per cent government bonds to get such a return, or $70,000 worth of 10 per cent private bonds. Aside from the risk he is assuming, your partner is getting a good buy for his $40,000, since he will annually collect some 17½ per cent on his investment. So your two-thirds share is justified by the good will that you supply.[2]

---

[2] Good will and capitalized earning power are discussed in the accounting Appendix to this chapter.

THIS IS THE WAY WE GROW

And your business continues to prosper and grow. Each year, both partners agree to take out of the business only their drawings and about a fifth of their share of profits, plowing the rest of the profits back into the business.[3] Why does a business like this grow? Here are some possible reasons:

(1) toothpaste sales have risen as a result of your adopting a trade name, advertising, and sending out salesmen.

(2) economies of large-scale production enable you to cut your price.

(3) "vertical integration": you decide to produce your own chemical raw materials, and you also become your own wholesaler, thus operating three rather than only one "stage of production."

(4) "horizontal integration": you take advantage of a profitable opportunity to buy out a competitor who produces similar toothpaste.

(5) "complementary products" such as soap and lipstick are added, because the new lines will help to spread the overhead expenses, and your salesmen might just as well get more orders when making each call.[4]

(6) Finally, you may grow just because you are producing a better toothpaste.

NEW NEEDS AND SOURCES FOR CAPITAL

The enterprise finds itself in the same paradox: the more successful it is and the faster it grows, the harder up it is for capital. The $40,000 of new "equity capital" did not stay long in the form of cash. It was quickly transformed into circulating assets such as goods in process and supplies. In part it went to pay off the most pressing liabilities.

The remainder was used as a down payment on a factory building and equipment. The difference between the down payment and the purchase price of

the factory was secured by a mortgage loan on the property. The mortgage money was advanced by a life-insurance company and was to be amortized or paid off in installments over a period of 20 years, along with 12 per cent interest per year on the actual principal still unpaid at any time. In case the loan should not be paid, the holder of the mortgage of course has the right to foreclose the mortgage, i.e., to take over the ownership of the building and sell it for what it will bring. Since the down payment on the factory came to about one-third of its price, since this price was a bargain price to begin with, and since each year the insurance company will be getting back part of its principal, the risk taken by the company is not very great.

Despite the continuous plowing of profits back into the business, growth still causes you to need more capital. But now, having established your reputation, so to speak, new avenues of borrowing are open. Your banker will be glad to lend you money over the busy periods. An industrial finance company, such as the Traders' Finance Company, will advance you safe, but as yet uncollected, "accounts receivable".

Suppose, when all is said and done, you need still more capital than you can raise by any kind of borrowing. The painful necessity arises of getting more "equity" capital by letting some new people share in the profits (and losses) of the business. (As a matter of fact, even if you could still find some institutions to borrow from, it would be unwise to do so. You have already superimposed too many liabilities and fixed charges on a narrow equity base. As long as things go well, it would be nice to earn 16 per cent profit on capital that costs you only 12 per cent. But if losses should occur, they will fall all the more heavily on you, the two partners, who are the residual owners and debtors.)

DISADVANTAGES OF THE PARTNERSHIP FORM

One possibility of getting more ownership capital is to admit new partners. There is no limit to the number of partners that you can admit; there have been partnerships in the brokerage and banking fields involving more than 100 people. However, every time

---

[3] Why do you decide to take any profits from the business at all? Because you need the cash to pay your personal income taxes, which are levied not only on your salaries but also *upon your respective shares of the partnership's earnings.*

[4] You might even become an infant "conglomerate", growing by adding *unrelated* activities to your business (e.g., machine tools, car repairs, horoscopes).

a new partner is admitted, or one dies or resigns, a whole new partnership must be formed.[5]

As the number of partners increases, there emerges a feature that has been soft-pedalled in our discussion up to now. While a single proprietor is liable without limit to the full extent of his private fortune for all the debts he contracts, in a partnership each partner is similarly liable for all debts contracted *by the partnership*. If he owns 1 per cent of the partnership and the business fails, then he will normally be called upon to foot 1 per cent of the bills and the other partners will be assessed their 99 per cent. But if they are broke, the 1 per cent partner will be called upon to pay *for all*.   This feature of *unlimited liability* reveals why both single proprietorships and partnerships tend to be confined to small, personal enterprises (even apart from the difficulties of raising capital). No less than the single owner, the partner draws back from putting his personal capital into complex ventures promoted and guided by his partners, over whom he can exercise little control.[6]

Undoubtedly, unlimited liability and the red tape needed to ensure continuity are the main drawbacks to the partnership form.

THE CORPORATION

Therefore, unless you are in one of a small number of professions, you will probably decide to form a cor-

---

[5] More weighty is the real disadvantage stemming from the fact that a partnership can be dissolved whenever any party finds the existing arrangement unsatisfactory and wishes to withdraw. The law of partnerships also makes it impossible for any partner to sell his share to a new party without the consent of his partners; if agreement cannot be secured, a costly liquidation of the assets of the partnership may be inevitable.

The reader may recall that the novelist William Dean Howells has his famous title character Silas Lapham, a rising self-made paint tycoon, present his partner with the ultimatum: "You buy me out or I'll buy you out." Silas' two excuses, that his were the real brains and energy responsible for the success of the business and that the proffered price exceeded his partner's original investment, were cleverly seen through by Mrs. Lapham. She pointed out that, without the partner's money at the critical time, the business could never have succeeded and that Silas' offer to sell was premised upon the knowledge that his partner was not in a position to buy the whole of the business.

[6] Most provinces have enacted provisions for "limited partnerships," a compromise between the partnership and the corporation. The general partners usually control operations, as above. But a group of limited partners may contribute capital to a specified amount and have their liability limited to that amount.

poration rather than a partnership; you will incorporate in the province in which you operate.

Centuries ago, corporation charters were awarded by governments very rarely and only by special acts of the king and legislature. In the seventeenth century, several joint stock companies were chartered for trade, such as the East India Company. Another, the Hudson's Bay Company, was very active. Incorporation at this time was expensive and complicated; either a charter had to be obtained from the Crown or a special bill had to be passed. The early railroads here and abroad often had to spend as much money in getting a charter through the legislature as in preparing their roadbeds. Gradually, corporation laws were modified, and in the mid-nineteenth century it became possible to obtain a general charter without applying for an act of Parliament. Under the present system, a limited company may be incorporated under the federal Companies Act or under a provincial Companies or Corporation Act (although some corporations, such as railroads, banks, and insurance companies, can still obtain charters only by special acts of Parliament or the provincial legislature). Ordinary business corporations, however, are created by the following procedure: an application for a charter is made to the Secretary of State by a minimum of three persons intending to incorporate; a memorandum of agreement between the applicants is drawn up by a lawyer, wherein the proposed by-laws of the company are set out; a charter (known as letters patent) is then issued and the corporation is established.

Let us see how the incorporating procedure works in the case of your toothpaste company. You decide to issue 20,000 shares of common stock in the corporation: 6,700 going to you and your spouse; 3,300 to your partner; and the other 10,000 to be sold to outside interests. Although each share is to have an initial stated value of $10, your lawyer has advised you, for convenience, to make them no-par shares.

The 10,000 shares to be sold to the public are to be marketed through the local office of an *investment dealer*. These firms are simply merchandisers of securities; and as with any merchant, their profit comes from the difference between their buying and selling prices. They must drive a hard bargain, since the costs of selling the securities of such a small business are high. Thus they may offer you $10 and plan to resell at a price of $12.50 per share. Had you been a large company, you might have held out for as much as $12.25 out of the $12.50 selling price, because of the threat that you might take your offering to another dealer.

For a large company the investment dealer would probably also have agreed to *underwrite* the new issue of 10,000 shares; he would have guaranteed the purchase of the full 10,000 shares at a set price. If the market then refused to buy all these shares from the investment dealer at his announced price, he, not you, would have to absorb the loss. But he probably regards your business as too small and untried to justify his assuming the risk of underwriting. So if he cannot sell all the shares, you end up raising less capital. (Also as a *"sweetener",* he may insist upon being given warrants—which are options to buy stock later at a specified price.)

CORPORATION STRUCTURE. Fortunately, all goes well, and he hands over $100,000 for the securities sold. Unlike the partnership, you need not concern yourself with the people to whom he has sold the shares or with the fact that they may resell. Their names are registered with the company or its bank agent so that you will know where to send dividends or the announcements of stockholders' meetings.

Ordinarily, each share gives its owner one vote. Those with 100 shares get 100/20,000 of both the votes and the dividends.

The outside owners of 10,000 shares have paid in $100,000 to the company. What have you and your partner paid in? Obviously not cash, but rather a sizable amount of earning assets: plant, equipment, goods in process, and perhaps good will, which is, as we have already seen, the capitalized value of the presumed "excess earning power" of the business, resulting from its trademarks, patents, know-how, and so forth.

Back in the old days before 1929, you and your investment dealer might have evaluated the good will as liberally as you wished, possibly giving yourself 20,000 rather than 10,000 shares. This practice has been called "watering the stock." Today, you would have to submit any public issue to the scrutiny of government officers and the Stock Exchange. They would have to satisfy themselves that there were no misleading claims in your prospectus. However, *Caveat emptor*—let the buyer beware—still prevails as a doctrine!

PRIVATE ADVANTAGE The corporation has solved most of the problems that bothered you about the partnership. It is an almost perfect device for the raising of large sums of capital.

Of first importance, every stockholder now has *limited liability,* indicated to the world by the addi-

tion of the word "Limited" (Ltd.) to the company name. After paying $12.50, no investor can be assessed further if the company becomes bankrupt.

Of secondary importance are advantages that stem from the fact that the corporation is a (fictitious) "legal person" created by the state. It can sue in court, and be sued, distinct from its owners. The power of an owner or employee to commit his associates financially is strictly limited. The corporation may have "perpetual succession" or existence; it does not have to be reconstituted each time an owner sells his shares, or dies. Thus ownership is not only divisible but inexpensively transferable. No group of shareholders can force any other group to sell or retain their holdings, and only a majority vote rather than unanimity is needed to reach day-to-day business decisions. Normally, the stockholders prefer to elect directors (a dozen or so members) to represent them between annual meetings, in much the same way that democratic electorates select legislative representatives to act for them. As we shall see, however, the analogy with "democracy" is frequently misleading.

You will face one disadvantage to incorporation that has beome increasingly serious in recent years. *The government taxes corporate income;* most sizable corporations must pay almost half of each extra dollar of income. (This is *in addition* to the personal income tax that owners pay on dividends they get.)

But loopholes in tax law tend to mitigate this disadvantages of the corporate form. *Undistributed* corporate profits tend to escape *personal* income taxes; only paid-out dividends are fully taxed. A rich man who is taxed about 70 cents of every dollar of personal income can say, "Why pay such rates on partnership earnings? Let's incorporate, pay the lower corporate tax, keep dividends low, and reduce our taxes".[7]

---

[7] To some extent he is only putting off the evil day, for his dividends later will be taxable when he receives them. But against their certainty must be weighed these factors: (a) the delay in paying tax is itself worth money to him; (b) tax rates may change favourably; (c) for certain cases the government allows the distribution of past profits at what amounts to a flat 25 per cent personal tax; (d) for some years Canada has reduced "double taxation" of profits by allowing personal taxpayers some credit for taxes paid "on their behalf" through the corporation tax; and (e) lawyers may be able to work out a way of having the accumulation of past profits come to the shareholder as a "capital gain" rather than as dividends—and tax collectors may be able to prevent them.

Another loophole is used to avoid double taxation when the owners of a closely held corporation vote most of its earnings to themselves and their relatives in the form of high salaries, pensions, and perquisites. The National Revenue Department tries to check up on such padding of expenses; but it is always hard to know whether a given in-law is worth $40,000 a year and whether a trip to a Bermuda convention is truly a business rather than a personal expense.

SOCIAL ADVANTAGE When Prime Minister Gladstone was shown electricity on a visit to Michael Faraday's laboratory, he asked, "What is the use of electricity?" Faraday gave the amusing reply, "I suppose some day, Sir, you may come to put a tax on it." Surely the advantage of the corporate force to society is not merely that the state can tax it.

Large-scale production is technically efficient, and a large corporation is an advantageous way for investors to pool the *irreducible risks* of business life. Without limited liability and the corporation, the mixed economy simply could not reap the benefit that comes when large supplies of capital can be attracted to competing corporations that produce a variety of complementary products, that pool risks, and that best utilize the economies of sizable research units and managerial know-how. That is why the privilege of the corporate form is legalized.

HOW A CORPORATION CAN RAISE CAPITAL

Let us suppose your corporation continues to grow. What *new* forms of financing are available to you?

BONDS You may now issue bonds. In Canada, a typical bond is a "debenture," which is simply a promissory note, nicely printed on gilt paper, issued in $1,000 or other denominations so as to be readily marketable for resale. A bond is a security promising to pay a certain number of dollars in interest every 6 months or so for a number of years until it matures. At that time the borrowing company promises to pay off the principal of the bond at its face value. (Often the company has the right to call in the bond before its maturity date by paying the bondholders

some previously agreed-upon price.) The dollars paid every six months are usually called the "coupon" payments.[8]   Ordinarily, payments for coupons and principal must be made on time, regardless of the company's earnings. Otherwise the company is in default and can be taken to court like any debtor.[9] Of course, there is no particular reason why a partnership could not borrow by the use of bonds; but ordinarily it would not be well enough known to succeed in interesting a lender. For that matter, a small corporation can rarely raise capital by issuing bonds.

COMMON STOCKS Issuing bonds and issuing common stocks are opposite methods of financing. The common stockholder is providing "equity" capital. He shares in profits and in control of business decisions, but he must also share in losses. His is a more risky venture, because he can never receive any dividends until the fixed charges owed to the bondholder are paid off. The bondholder gets a limited but steadier income. Unless the corporation is bankrupt or in danger of being so, the bondholder ordinarily has no legal control over the decisions of the business; but a wise management will take care to stay on good terms with all sources of future capital.

PREFERRED SHARES Between bonds and common stocks are so-called "preferred shares." These pay *at most* a stated dividend—say, a stipulated 6 per cent of the face value per share—no matter how profitable the business becomes. The preferred shareholder is more likely to get his dividend even when profit is small than is the common stockholder, because legally he stands next in line after the bondholder and before the common stockholder. The latter gets no dividends if the preferred share fails to receive its full dividend.

---

[8] A hybrid form of bond called a parity bond has been successfully used by the British Columbia Hydro Authority. These bonds, guaranteed by the provincial government, pay a specified rate of interest (7 per cent on a 1973 issue) but have an additional feature whereby the holder may, at any time, cash in the bond for the full purchase price. Normally the principal of a bond is not repaid until maturity.

[9] Such bonds are general claims against all the assets of a corporation. Mortgage bonds, secured by all or some pieces of property are not uncommon. Convertible bonds, which can be exchanged for a stated number of common shares, are a popular hybrid. There are even income bonds, whose interest is payable only if there are large enough earnings; but Canada's 20 per cent dividend tax credit (see footnote 7) makes these rare.

ADVANTAGES OF DIFFERENT SECURITIES: RISK AND SAFETY

From the standpoint of the investor, bonds, preferred shares, and common stock form a sequence of increasing risk and decreasing security—balanced by an increasing chance of making high earnings or capital gains. Thus a risky, unsecured mining share will yield double or triple the percentage on a bond—if the mine pays at all! But a number of tax influences spoil this neat sequence. Because common stocks may rise in value and give untaxed capital gains, they now often have a spread of dividend yields that begins even lower than bonds: some "growth stocks" yield less than the safest government bond. (To test his understanding of these three forms of securities, the reader should make sure that he understands why common stocks tend to be better investments in time of sudden inflation than the other two.) Another tax aspect is the attractiveness given to preferred and common stocks by the Canadian dividend tax credit —to reduce their personal income tax, holders are willing to buy stock even when its yield is out of the sequence suggested above.

In any case, bonds are far from being a perfectly safe investment. During the depression, many companies went bankrupt and defaulted on their bonds, paying off only a few cents on the dollar. The basic risk in all corporate investment is a possible loss of earning power, which will greatly reduce the value of its assets. Often a company will undergo reorganization in which the original stockholders may be squeezed out (this is why many Canadian mining companies have the word "Consolidated" inserted into their titles). The courts may appoint a "receiver" or trustee to run the business, and the bondholders may be given bonds (or even stocks!) equal only to some fraction of their original investment. And of course, certain bondholders have prior claims over holders of other types of bonds.

Bonds are also more vulnerable than stocks and shares to changes in general credit conditions. The less easy it is to get credit, the higher are all rates of interest, including bond yields. And (as will be explained in detail in Chapter 30) this tends to push bond prices down. Thus the holders of bonds may suddenly find, when market rates of interest rise, that the value of their bonds has dropped without any change in the basic soundness of the corporation, or the coupon payments that it makes every 6 months. Common stock is least prone to this effect; preferred shares tend to react like bonds.

From the corporation's view, the safety of the three types of security has an ordering which is the reverse of the private investor's. Bond debt creates low but inflexible fixed charges. These may be embarrassing in bad times. (In the Great Depression, the bondholders of many of the largest Canadian firms were in the United States or Europe. This meant that Canada as a whole had to find a fixed amount of foreign currency to pay abroad every year, even when Canadian exports were bringing in only a fraction of their previous foreign-currency earnings. Economists then likened this to the plight of the corporations, calling it the "fixed overhead burden of the staple economy.") Preferred stock is slightly better with respect to flexibility; and equity capital is most flexible of all.

COOPERATION

Few people who wanted to make toothpaste would think of starting a co-op. But cooperative societies are an alternative to the corporation, and they do sell a lot of toothpaste, not to mention apples, fish, maple syrup, and Eskimo carvings. Furthermore, they have played a major role in the development of the western provinces' economy and politics. They are on the whole more important in Canada than in the U.S., but are insignificant in both countries alongside the huge European organizations.

The movement is scarcely growing in Canada, but it is far from static in newly-developed countries.

In a *marketing* co-op, farmers, fishermen, or other producers form a society to act as a collector, processor, and distributor of their goods. In place of a corporation's shareholders, each co-op member contributes some capital and is entitled to just one vote.[10] Thus, the democratic nature of cooperation is stressed. Each year between seasons the "profit" after all costs (including a price paid to each member for the produce he has delivered) is distributed in proportion to patronage: a farmer who has delivered 4 per

---

[10] Usually, following the famous Rochdale (England) principles laid down by pioneer cooperatives in 1844, members receive a fixed rate of interest on their capital share.

cent of the wheat to a pool will get, in addition to his price, 4 per cent of whatever amount the directors choose to distribute to the members. Such co-ops sell about one billion dollars worth of produce every year in Canada.

Often these same people, and city dwellers in Europe too, will form *consumers'* cooperatives, organizing wholesale buying units and running their own retail stores, service stations, medical clinics, and funeral centers. The same Rochdale principles apply. Usually the co-ops do not engage in keen price competition with other retailers, but instead sell at stable prices to their membership and distribute the equivalent of "bargains" in the patronage dividend every year. Consumer co-ops have been one of the most important outlets for grocery products in Britain. But it appears that the very democratic structure of co-ops makes it hard for them to hire and to work with aggressive managers and staff without becoming a commercial business, which of course they wish to avoid.

Cooperatives usually hold evangelical attitudes toward this type of business organization, and work hard to bring about its growth.[11] But in Canada their recent success has been greatest in the credit union. This is a type of savings bank, organized internally on similar lines to producers' co-ops; members often have a common bond, such as belonging to the same parish or co-op, or trade union. Their members deposit savings, and the problem of lending these savings safely (mostly to other members) is simplified by the common bond and the directors' personal knowledge of all their members. About 10 per cent of all consumer credit flows through credit unions.

PUBLIC OWNERSHIP

In a mixed economy, the lines between private and public business become blurred. Served as Canadians are by the CBC, CNR, Air Canada, and Atomic Energy of Canada Ltd., provincial hydro and telephone utilities, and liquor stores, and municipal theaters, garbage collection, libraries, and water utilities, it is clear that the role of government discussed earlier on page 49 has been extended and varied.

The minimum necessary role for government is surveyed in Chapter 8. Sometimes, as in the case of the CNR, the government has taken over ownership after the collapse of the previous private corporations. Sometimes, as in the case of the liquor board and the utilities, provincial governments have wished to get different pricing, availability of services, or investment policies than profit-seeking owners would provide. In particular, many Crown corporations have had as their purpose the *development* of a region, product, industry, or service, rather than profit in the direct sense. Usually they monopolize most of their market.

The displacement of private by public enterprise (often said to be an NDP goal) has actually closely paralleled the growth of private corporate firms in Canada. Political parties of all complexions have encouraged public ownership.[12] Consequently, debate about public ownership tends to center either on personalities or on claims for its efficiency in particular cases, rather than on its generic advantages.

THE GIANT CORPORATION

While we should not infer that all corporations go through three stages, we have now carried our toothpaste enterprise far enough. The next sections will be devoted to the economic position and power of the very large modern corporation and the problems that it creates for the economy. It is these factors which play the dominant role in today's economy.

A 1973 list of the largest corporations reads like an honor roll of Canadian business, almost every name being familiar household words. Alcan Aluminum Ltd., Imperial Oil (Esso), George Weston Ltd., Massey-Ferguson, Canadian Pacific (CPR), Bell Canada, Canada Packers (York meats), Distillers Corporation-Seagrams, and T. Eaton Co. and the big three auto manufacturers all have assets or sales in the top ten. But even the largest of these is a pygmy compared to the huge American corporations (with which many large Canadian firms are connected). In automobiles, General Motors, Ford, and Chrysler; in trade, A & P, Sears, and F. W. Woolworth; in food, Kraft, Borden, and Swifts; in soaps and oils, Lever Brothers and Procter and Gamble—all

---

[11] The tax laws appear to favour co-ops over corporations: co-ops get special tax treatment for patronage dividends. This gesture may account for their survival and growth. In any case, it does lead to complaints that the cooperator is unfairly undertaxed compared to the shareholder in competing firms. See R.C. McIvor's "Canadian Cooperatives and Credit Unions: The Tax Scene Revisited" in the *Canadian Tax Journal* Vol. 20 (Jan.—Feb. 1972).

[12] In 1969, Britain changed its Post Office from government department to a public business corporation. A similar conversion of Canada's postal department to a Crown corporation is contemplated.

dominate the scene in both countries. One of the largest of all is A. T. & T. to which the Canadian Bell system is linked.

The size of financial organizations can hardly be measured by sales or assets. But, judged by the funds that they manage or control, such chartered banks as the Bank of Montreal, The Royal Bank, and the Canadian Imperial Bank of Commerce, and insurance companies like the Sun Life and Manufacturers Life must be classed with the large industrial companies and compared to such giants abroad as the Bank of America, the Chase Manhattan Bank, National City Bank, Metropolitan Life and Prudential Life in the United States, or Barclay's Bank and the Prudential Assurance Co. of England.

Altogether there are now over 300 U.S. companies with assets above the billion-dollar mark, and a dozen or so in other countries! (Outside the United States, many of the largest business are publicly owned, like the CNR and Ontario Hydro. But few of these, anywhere, would make the top 300).

The tremendous concentration of economic power involved in giant corporations may be gauged from the following facts: The top 100 industrial firms now account for two-thirds of the earnings of all Canadian industrial corporations. In the grocery trade, four chains accounted for 60 per cent of sales in 1973. The field of transportation and communication is highly concentrated. The Canadian National Railways and the Canadian Pacific Railway together with Air Canada and Canadian Pacific Airways dominate rail and air transport. The telephone industry is dominated by the privately owned Bell Telephone Company which accounts for 60 per cent of the operating revenue of the industry. Branch banking insures that the financial sector of the economy is highly concentrated. Furthermore, the Canadian assets of nine leading insurance companies constitute three-quarters of all Canadian life insurance assets. In the light of the evidence, it appears that about three-fifths of Canada's output (excluding government administration and defense) originates in sectors dominated by large corporations.[13]

[13] Gideon Rosenbluth, "Concentration and Monopoly in the Canadian Economy," in *Social Purpose for Canada*, edited by M. Oliver (Toronto: University of Toronto Press, 1961). Much of the above information is collected annually by the *Financial Post*.

Their power did not grow overnight, but since World War II, the largest corporations have, if anything, grown faster than the economy.

Most corporate growth involved continual plowing-back of profits and new stock and bond issues. But there is another way. Since World War II, more and more existing firms have been acquired in "horizontal" (potential competitors) or "vertical" (suppliers and customers) mergers. Even more recently there was a wave of "conglomerate mergers," bringing together scores of companies belonging to quite unrelated industries. The giants meet repeatedly on diverse battle-fields: Bell, Molsons, Noranda, CPR, Southams, Imperial Oil, and CIL compete in the sale of dozens of products. Foreigners, however, have usually taken over Canadian firms in the same industry as the parent's; American, Japanese, and European firms tend to concentrate on acquiring subsidiaries in vertical and horizontal, not conglomerate, mergers.

Whether by their own financing or by merger, corporate growth breeds success—and success breeds further success.[14] But there are economic and political barriers to largeness, and firms do not grow indefinitely. The statistical evidence on profits suggests that profits increase with the size but that the very biggest firms in an industry sometimes seem to show a slight dropping off of *percentage* profits compared with the next to the largest.

So, just as a hotel may be always full—but with different people—so do we find the list of biggest corporations to be a changing one; nevertheless the list changes at a very slow rate.

DIVORCE OF OWNERSHIP IN THE LARGE CORPORATION

Let us examine the internal workings of one of these giant corporations. *The most striking feature is the diversification of ownership among thousands and thousands of small stockholders.* In 1970 more than 34,000 people had preferred shares, and more than 244,000 had common shares in Bell Telephone of Canada, although most holdings were very small indeed (10 shares or less). The stock exchange has a

[14] A larger percentage of small firms than of large firms falls in the class of firms making losses.

goal of "people's capitalism," in which the masses have appreciable ownership of society's capital. Now over 18 per cent of urban households do own some publicly traded stock; and others own untraded securities. Yet it is highly probable that as few as 10 per cent receive an appreciable return.

In a path-breaking study,[15] Berle and Means pointed out that this wide diversification of stockholding has resulted in a *separation of ownership and control*. Recent studies show that in the typical giant corporation in the United States, all management together—officers and directors—hold only about 3 per cent of the outstanding common stock. The largest single minority ownership groups typically hold only about a fifth of all voting stock. Such a small fraction has been deemed more than enough to maintain "working control".

LEADERSHIP AND CONTROL OF THE LARGE CORPORATION

The goal of keeping a large corporation's management either efficient or democratic is a difficult one. Until recent years, only a dozen stockholders would turn up for the annual meeting, where decisions are really settled by use of "proxies". Each stockholder is asked to mail in a proxy permitting the management to exercise his votes. Some do not reply; but enough usually do to establish a quorum and a comfortable plurality for management. Stock exchange and security authorities are trying to improve the democratic structure of corporations by insisting that motions to be decided at the annual meeting be indicated on the proxy statement; also, rival groups must be permitted mailing access to the stockholders, and so forth. Such reforms remove protection from idle, incompetent, or unscrupulous managements.

Nevertheless, most corporation managements could be said to be self-perpetuating. Whether the

corporation runs well or poorly, whether the managers work efficiently or not, the typical small stockholder can do little about it. He can rubber-stamp approval or relieve his feelings by not voting. In either case management goes undisturbed.

Recently, there has been some change. Managements are becoming less free to do whatever they can get away with. Government rules now ease the task of minority groups wresting control from the ingroup, after courting support from individual shareholders and investment funds. Even more constraining is the latent threat of a takeover by a hungry conglomerate. If the old management sits sluggishly on an under-used clump of liquid assets, disappointing earning expectations, its shareholders may eagerly support a takeover by a ruthless outsider. Neither of these devices, however, do much more than ensure efficiency: control may pass from one small minority to another.

But, is undemocratic minority control an evil? The dissatisfied stockholder, unlike the unhappy citizen in a dictatorship, can always sell out, and buy into another company whose policies he prefers. Democracy is thus not an end in itself. Though stockholders in a badly managed corporation must accept a low price when selling their shares, the market-price decline will also hurt both the corporation's chances of raising more capital and the purses of individual company officers. These consequences give shareholders more power to control the corporation than any individual realizes. In any case this power, not democracy is the issue; the goal for the mixed economy should be consumer, not shareholder, sovereignty.

A MANAGERIAL REVOLUTION IN THE NEW INDUSTRIAL STATE

Who makes corporate decisions? Primarily, the increasingly important class of *professional managers* —what Galbraith calls the "technostructure." The old-time captain of industry, for all his creativeness and ability to calculate the risks necessary to build up a great enterprise, often had something of the buccaneer in his make-up and an irresponsible "the-public-be-damned" attitude. In company after company, the original founder has been replaced

---

[15] A. A. Berle, Jr., and Gardner C. Means, *The Modern Corporation and Private Property* (New York: Commerce Clearing House, 1932). See R. A. Gordon, *Business Leadership in the Large Corporation* (Washington: Brookings Institution, 1945), Chapter II. R. J. Larner in a 1966 *American Economic Review* study has shown that the Berle-Means Thesis on separation of ownership and control was even truer in the 1960s than in 1929: whereas 6 of the 200 largest U.S. corporations were privately owned (80 per cent or more of the stock) in 1929, in 1963 there were none; and 84.5 per cent of the firms had no group of stockholders owning as much as 10 per cent!

by a new type of executive, usually having a different surname. He is less likely to be a self-made man than a graduate of a well-known business school: he will probably have acquired special training and management skills. The new professional executive is more adept at public relations and in the handling of people. He is necessarily more the "bureaucrat," often interested as much in preserving the *status quo* as in taking extreme risks.

Typically, the dominant man will be the president of the corporation. As he begins to feel his years, he may be made chairman of the board of directors. The chairman of the board, together with a small executive or steering committee of the board of directors, advises and approves the actions of the president and his many vice-presidents.

The exact role of the board of directors varies from company to company and from group to group. Some "outside" directors are simply well-known men selected to give prestige. Others are insiders with special knowledge who take an active part in determining policy; they may be vice-presidents or employees of the corporation. So long as management possesses the confidence of such directors, they will not actively intervene to dictate specific policies. This administrative procedure is also familiar in the boards of governors of a university or charity. It is not too unlike the parliamentary system of ministerial responsibility.

CONFLICTS OF INTEREST Generally speaking, because both will have the same interest—to maximize the growth in earnings and the market price per share—there need be no fundamental cleft between the goals of management and the ordinary stockholder. But in two important instances they may be in conflict. First, insiders may vote themselves and their friends large salaries, expense accounts, bonuses, retirement pensions, and stock options at the stockholders' expense.[16] Second, the

managers have an understandable tendency not to distribute profits, but to try to make the organization grow and perpetuate itself. The psychological reasons are subtle and by no means always selfish. But when profits are plowed back into a company, there is reason to suspect that the same capital could be better invested by the stockholders elsewhere or be spent upon consumption. Indeed, the case occasionally arises when a company would be well advised to wind itself up and pay back its capital. But a cynic might doubt that management is likely to vote itself out of work.

Thorstein Veblen, at the turn of the century, looked forward to a time when engineers would run the price system. John Kenneth Galbraith has in our time become the philosopher of the new industrial state. In his words:

". . . the influence of the technostructure of the mature firm extends to *shaping the demand* for its particular product or range of products. . . . [emphasis added]

"Paralleling these changes, partly as a result and partly as a cause, has been a profound shift in the locus of economic and political power. The financier and the union leader are dwindling influences in the society. They are honored more for their past eminence than for their present power. The technostructure exercises much less direct political power than did the antecedent entrepreneur. But that is because it has far more influence as an arm of the bureaucracy and in its influence on the larger climate of belief. The scientific, technical, organizational and planning needs of the technostructure have brought into being a large educational and scientific estate."[17]

THE MULTINATIONAL CORPORATION

The new role of the "technostructure" of modern management is seen most clearly when it goes international. Then the firm becomes a "legal person," apparently different from its founders and, even, from its native land.

As a first step, a firm may take over, or set up, a subsidiary. It will choose a country with markets made too expensive by transport or tariff barriers to serve from the home plants.

Some such subsidiaries have been found to be less immediately profitable than branch plants back

---

[16] Other conflicts can involve outright cheating; executives may take bribes, throw business to their own companies, or violate securities rules by using inside knowledge and spreading false rumors to make market profits on the company's stock. The management of Texas Gulf Sulfur and the Windfall mine came under fire in 1965 for just this behavior in connection with Northern Ontario mining discoveries. A recent president of Chrysler had to resign when it was discovered he had secret ownership in a supplying firm. Such cases are rare, but not rare enough.

[17] John Kenneth Galbraith, *The New Industrial State* (Boston: Houghton Mifflin, 1967), p. 320.

home. Then why were they set up? Seemingly, they were symptomatic of the main management's own determination to expand, even if shareholders could find better investments on their own. And once set up, their management makes the interests of the owners even more remote. Market and legal differences, of course, mean that foreign subsidiaries must be given more local discretion than would be given to a simple branch plant. Often, then, it becomes difficult to determine in whose interest it is being run. Sometimes little profit is being remitted; managers at home must delegate powers to managers abroad whose chief interest is survival—not even personal promotion, if the manager is a national of the new country.[18]

But competition with other multinationals and home-grown rivals often requires a complex mixture of flexibility in some departments and firm centralized direction in others. Financing is usually chosen as the centralizing control, while local officers are allowed most discretion in labor policy, product variation, and marketing. The free worldwide movement of funds—to wherever money can serve the corporation best—is the bloodstream of the corporation. This free movement is achieved by dividend and royalty payments, by judicious "transfer pricing" of goods and materials traded between national subsidiaries; loans, and remittances. But generalizations are difficult. While none can ignore finance, some corporations stress central technological change, the obtaining of raw materials, or global image as the instrument of parental control.

Their freedom to experiment with control methods is being much reduced by their increasingly hostile reception in "host" countries. In the former colonial countries, especially those on guard against Western "imperialism", distrust of foreign owners may be so great as to lead to their expropriation or to compromise forms of joint ownership. Even in more industrialized societies, like Canada and Australia, not to mention western Europe, there is much expressed alarm at le défi américain—the penetration of markets by American technology and managerial attitudes. While few hosts can yet bring themselves

to exclude a new corporate taxpayer from the U.S. or Europe, some, like Canada, are now refusing them permission to buy out or buy into an existing local company, and all are making special rules about foreign ownership, the number of local directors, etc. As we have already seen, directors have limited power over management even in their own country, so it is not to be expected that such rules will clip the wings of multinational growth substantially, although they may induce some firms to go for joint enterprises rather than direct investment.

Another reason for expansion abroad is to obtain control over raw materials: petroleum, minerals, timber and chemicals. This motive explains why extractive and agricultural firms like Standard Oil of New Jersey, Royal Dutch Shell and Unilever are close behind General Motors and IBM in the 1971 rankings of global corporations with sales over $1 billion.

There are at least 210 such corporations today, according to a recent U.N. count. The value-added (payroll, taxes, interest and profits) by each of the top ten multinationals was in excess of $3 billion. Thus their value-added was greater than the GNP of any of 80 countries. If we add the other two hundred multinationals, the total value-added runs to over $500 billions: about 20 per cent of gross national product of western mixed economies![19]

Eighty per cent of their total activity is undertaken by American, British, French and German corporations.

Canadian attitudes to U.S. (and European and Japanese) investment are, as Prime Minister Trudeau put it, those of one who must sleep with an elephant. The fear of being rolled on cannot be quieted by assurances of industrial growth, or employment. Even the majority that does not believe in a conspiracy or a takeover, worries about so many economic decisions being made outside the country. Will Safarian's finding that such managements have been statistically indistinguishable from those of domestic firms continue to be valid?

---

[18] A good recent study of management and behavior is A. E. Safarian's *Performance of Foreign Owned Firms* (Montreal: Canadian American Committee, 1969).

[19] i.e., excluding centrally-planned economies like China, Russia and those of eastern Europe. These *value-added* statistics are smaller than the more usually cited *sales* statistics, which by including all the purchases of goods and materials by multinationals, could exaggerate their share up to one-third of western GNP. For discussion and data, see *Multinational Corporations in World Development*, UN-1973, Code No. ST/ECA/190.

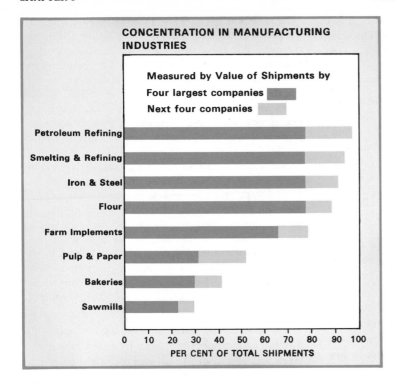

FIG. 6-1. Some industries have few sellers: "oligopolies". Others have many.

These concentration percentages tend to remain constant over decades. (Source: Statistics Canada, 1968, 31-514.)

We can return to foreign ownership later (in Chapter 26 and the Appendix to Chapter 35). Here we ask further where the central decisions are taken. Is local autonomy, reported a few paragraphs above to be inevitable, on the increase? No, say reporters. Sometimes it is not clear what the "nationality," if any, of such huge firms is. Some subsidiaries have flourished faster than the parents, and head offices may be moved where taxes are low or restrictions fewest. Their senior management may then become not only separated from ownership, but also from national allegiance. It is likely that in the next decade, quicker overseas communications will reduce the independence of subsidiaries. If so, much economic power may be wielded neither by local officers, nor by owners of shares and property, nor by governments in parent countries, but by the managerial structure of the multinational firm itself, in some respects *independent* of national connections or any responsibilities.[20]

[20] "The relation between ownership and control in the large corporation is different when the corporation is a subsidiary. Ownership is not widely diffused among many stockholders, but rather concentrated, often to the point of the parent being the

OLIGOPOLY

In view of all the above facts, it is not surprising that most industries are dominated by a very few, large, corporations. Their share of output (measured by "shipments") is often vastly greater than their numerical importance would suggest. In Figure 6-1 the relative importance of the top four and eight firms, in eight large industries, are shown. When there are only a few firms selling, economists identify the group as an "oligopoly".[21]

sole stockholder. In effect, ownership rights are exercised by the management of the parent corporation. The management of a subsidiary, wishing to exercise effective control over decisions, faces not a multitude of relatively powerless shareholders but the managers of its parent." *Foreign Ownership and the Structure of Canadian Industry*, Report of the Task Force on the Structure of Canadian Industry, M. E. Watkins (Ottawa: Queen's Printer, 1968), pp 32, 33. Reproduced with the permission of Information Canada.

[21] Does the multinational corporation encourage oligopoly? Economist G. Rosenbluth showed in 1970, for Canadian corporations, that while in a given industry foreign-controlled firms tended to be larger than domestic-controlled firms, there is no evidence of a foreign tendency to seek out concentrated industries for investment. (*CJE*. 1970, p. 15).

Oligopoly (and monopoly) prevent the determination of price by competitive markets. This subject, and the concern of governments to encourage competitive production and exchange, is discussed in Part Three. There it is shown that when oligopoly prevails, each producer attempts to set his own price, rather than simply to accept it. In general, the price so determined tends to be too high, and to be accompanied by higher profits and misallocated resources.

BIG BUSINESS AND MULTINATIONALS IN THE DOGHOUSE

The public these days does not act as if it has a favourable opinion of large-scale business enterprise. Although an increasing number of technically-trained and scientific students obtain MBA degrees, business-recruiters report a reluctance of top students in other fields to soil themselves on the executive ladder. Public opinion polls in 1972 showed that 60 per cent of the population held business in low approval.

Only part of the reason is in oligopolistic price-setting; after all, this is a part of economic theory that most voters and politicians seem not to understand. Part of the antipathy stems from a dislike of bigness itself. In recent years, even the courts have tended to condemn large corporations for their sheer bigness, even if the corporations in question charged *lower* prices than their rivals. Large firms recognize this attitude, and General Motors or Stelco would be most reluctant to swallow up competitors until they alone accounted for, say, 90 per cent of their industry.

But this antagonism runs into a strong defense of business. It is said that it alone can undertake the research and development that lead to a rising standard of living. Time and again even government has handed its research problems over to the firms competent to see the project through, as with the development of a commercial atomic power plant by the Canadian General Electric Company for the federal Atomic Energy of Canada Ltd. In the words of Schumpeter, a world-famous economist who died in 1950: [22]

"The modern standard of life of the masses evolved during the period of relatively unfettered 'big business.' If we list the items that enter the modern workman's budget and from 1899 on observe the course of their prices not in terms of money but in terms of the hours of labor that will buy them—i.e., each year's money prices divided by each year's hourly wage rates, we cannot fail to be struck by the rate of the advance which, considering the spectacular improvement in qualities, seems to have been greater and not smaller than it ever was before. . . .

Nor is this all. As soon as we go into details and inquire into the individual items in which progress was most conspicuous, the trail leads not to the doors of those firms that work under conditions of comparatively free competition but precisely to the doors of the large concerns—which, as in the case of agricultural machinery, also account for much of the progress in the competitive sector—and a shocking suspicion dawns upon us that big business may have had more to do with creating that standard of life than keeping it down."

The case for the *multinational* big business (not, however, for monopoly) is said by Harry Johnson to stem basically from the advantages of the corporate form itself:

What does the corporation do that is economically beneficial by comparison with previous forms of economic organization? Essentially, it applies organized rationality to the production and distribution of goods and services. In so doing it achieves economy and greater efficiency in a multitude of directions: selection of managerial and other personnel by capacity for efficiency rather than by social status; exploitation of economies of scale both in production and in market research...and research in the acquisition of and application of relevant economic knowledge; and the organized development of superior technological and managerial methods...

Johnson goes on to argue that the multinational corporation brings to the host country a "package" of capital, tested technology, managerial ability and knowledge of foreign markets. This "package" has

[22] J. A. Schumpeter, *Capitalism, Socialism, and Democracy* (New York: Harper, 1942). Whatever the merits of the Schumpeter thesis, it is still true that there have been great productivity changes in competitive agriculture; that many basic inventions come from independent persons or small companies; and that there is no evidence of an upswing in inventiveness during the 1890s, a decade of monopoly concentration.

Reference should be made to J. Kenneth Galbraith's doctrine of "countervailing power" in *American Capitalism* (Boston: Houghton Mifflin, 1952). It is there argued that big units do characterize American life, but that "big labor" checks big business, and vice versa; that big Sears and A & P check their big suppliers, and so a kind of tolerable equilibrium is achieved, albeit not one of a competitive type.

two advantages for the host country: it breaks down the barriers to efficiency, mobility and trade that the modern nation-state tends to erect.

The second reason is that the development of new productive knowledge, both technical and managerial, is an expensive business. It is a great human fallacy to believe that because I have the same number of arms, legs and heads as you, and enjoy a reputable position in my own society, I should be able to do anything you can do, without putting in the work of learning that you have done . . .

. . . productive knowledge has a peculiar economic character: once it has been acquired, it costs little to extend its application over more territory.[23]

But these contentions are not widely accepted. Studies do not always show that big business is needed to develop and introduce technical change. For one thing, new inventions have come from single persons or very small firms. For another, governments are arguing that they can, and must, take a major responsibility for research and development. A third point is that competitive little business, like agriculture, is also capable of big technological changes (see Chapter 21); the 1890 boom in business concentration did *not* produce a boom in inventions.

The case against *multinationals* depends upon complex arguments about the transferability of technology, and the suitability of the technology itself to new countries. But of course it goes further; it is based both on economic nationalism as an end in itself, and as a means to legal, administrative and political self-determination free of the imperialistic taint of the new global corporations. To friends, the multinational is good because it clips the wings of the idiosyncratic, nonconforming nation-state. To its enemies, these are its evils. It propels the national corporation to taking political power away from independent peoples, imposing homogeneity on diversity and "extraterritoriality" on sovereignty.

If these authors *are* correct about the necessity of our reliance on business for technical progress, and the international transmission of ideas, the future problem may not be one of choosing between large monopolistic corporations and small-scale competitors, but rather that of devising ways to improve the social and economic performance of large corporate aggregates. To keep the tremendously creative abilities of the modern large-scale international corporation working toward the public good—that may have to be the goal for the years ahead. But if Schumpeter's belief is wrong, we may find ourselves turning to public policies to provide centralized research and development, to support the lonely inventor, and to develop both the crown corporation and the small firm.

Neither the "military-industrial complex" nor the multinational can be allowed to call the tune. In mixed economies with true voter and consumer sovereignty, they must dance to the music the people (through governments and markets) prescribe.

SUMMARY

1 The present population of businesses has grown up as a result of a cumulative excess of business births over business deaths. The great majority of businesses consist of infinitesimal single proprietorships, largely in retail and service establishments. Their turnover is rapid.

2 One should understand how an enterprise grows, its needs and avenues for short-term or long-term capital, and the advantages and disadvantages of the corporate form over the single proprietorship and partnership.

3 One should also be acquainted with the fundamental legal rights involved in the corporation and with the general features of bonds and of preferred and common stocks.

[23] Harry G. Johnson, "Economic Benefits", in Hahlo, Smith and Wright, eds., *Nationalism and the Multinational Enterprise,* Sijthoff, Leiden, 1973, pp. 168-9. The same volume has interesting counter-arguments by Eric Kierans and Abraham Rotstein, and useful references to other Canadian and foreign writers. The best-known work by an economist is Kari Levitt, *Silent Surrender,* MacMillan, Toronto, 1970. A more balanced discussion of multinational firms can be found in a book of readings edited by Giles Paquet, *The Multinational Firm and the Nation State,* Collier-Macmillan Canada, Don Mills, Ontario, 1972. The study by the Trudeau government, the "Gray Report" is officially entitled *Foreign Direct Investment in Canada,* Ottawa, 1970.

4 Compared to the United States, Canadians are major users of government enterprise and cooperatives as effective alternatives to the modern corporation.

5 The problems created by the separation of ownership and control and by the concentration of economic wealth and oligarchy power in the giant corporation deserves serious study.

6 The modern corporation may be the chief instrument for the organization, and innovation, of technology, and its transmission between countries. But its bigness and multinationalism has attracted much criticism.

CONCEPTS FOR REVIEW

single proprietorship

turnover ratio

partnership

limited and unlimited liability

investment banking

securities commissions

cooperatives, Crown corporations

corporate, personal income tax

retained earnings

bonds; common, preferred stock

equity capital

good-will earning power

minority control, proxy

director, executive, technostructure

oligopoly, concentration

conglomerate, merger

Galbraithian new industrial state

bigness, innovation, research

multinational corporation

transferability of know-how, technology

QUESTIONS FOR DISCUSSION

1. Imagine you are starting a business of your own. Write its case history.
2. Compare the advantages and disadvantages of (*a*) the single proprietorship, (*b*) the partnership, and (*c*) the corporate form of business organization.
3. List ways of raising capital for small, medium, and large businesses.
4. What are the advantages and disadvantages of different securities?
5. Discuss the structure of the large modern corporation.
6. What is meant by calling ours the age of the "Managerial or Bureaucratic Revolution?", of the "Multinational Corporation?" Does this apply inside government?
7. Give examples of conflict of interest between stockholders and management. Of coincident interests. Of problems of democratic control.
8. Defend "bigness as such." Attack it. What evils might accompany it?
9. What are the economic disadvantages of public ownership? Why is it so prevalent in Canada? Give examples of how local public enterprises obtain capital.
10. The cooperative, owned by its consumers, suppliers or workers, is also particularly important in Yugoslavia, where workers' firms have great autonomy from the government. Guild socialism, an alternative to social democracy, is also based on this approach. Evaluate as an alternative to private business in a mixed economy.
11. "Galbraith thinks of the giant corporations as *absolute* monarchs. Actually, they are constitutional monarchs who reign only so long as they don't rule. Ford could not force Edsel on the market, RCA lost hundreds of millions in computers, banks failed to get acceptance for their own credit cards, and Swan, Ajax and Dial show that soap companies can't predict their own acceptability." Appraise.
12. "Foreign ownership leads to Canadian subsidiaries being "truncated" so that many important activities are carried out by the parent or by other foreign subsidiaries." Give examples. Is this an evil or an advantage?

Appendix: Elements of Accounting

In this "age of accounts" a little literacy in accounting has become a prime necessity.

THE BALANCE SHEET

We begin with the two fundamental accounting statements: the Balance Sheet and the Statement of Profit and Loss (or the so-called "Income Statement").

The Balance Sheet is presented in a report, usually annually. It represents an instantaneous "still picture" of the condition of the enterprise on some particular day, usually the last day of the year. (Unlike a movie camera that records the "flow" over time of water in and out of the bathtub, the Balance Sheet gives a picture of the "Stock" of water now in the tub.)

Corresponding to the dollar value of every *asset*—tangible or intangible—there must necessarily be an exactly equal total amount of *claims* or *ownership*. The value of a $40,000 house is exactly matched by somebody's claim to its ownership, say, of $25,000 owed to a creditor and $15,000 owned by its owner.

This is the fundamental identity underlying every Balance Sheet:

Value of Assets = **value of total claims or ownership**
            = **value of liabilities (owed)**
                + value of proprietorship (owed)
that is,   **Assets = Liabilities + Net Worth**

Or, what is the same thing, by definition of owner's equity,
Net Worth (owner's equity) = Assets – Liabilities

Let us illustrate this by considering a simple Balance Sheet, as shown in Table 6-1; on the left, this lists Assets, and on the right, Liabilities and Net Worth for a new com-

pany—say, the Apex Toothpaste firm—whose operations have just begun.

A blank space has been deliberately left next to the Common Stock Net Worth item because you should realize that the only correct entry compatible with our fundamental Balance-Sheet truism is $200,000. A Balance Sheet must always balance—because Net Worth, i.e., ownership of the "residual claimants," always adjusts itself to make a balance.

To illustrate this, suppose a thief steals all the cash, and a fire burns up one-half the inventory. The accountant will learn of this sad news without turning a hair. "Total Assets are down $60,000 all told; Liabilities remain unchanged. This means that total Net Worth has decreased by 60,000, and I have no choice but to write its total down from the previous 250,000 to only 190,000."

Such is his way of keeping score.

A number of interesting facts are revealed by even this simple Balance Sheet. First, it is customary to divide up Assets according to whether they will be convertible into cash by normal operations within a year or the normal accounting cycle, the first category being called Current Assets, and the second, Fixed Assets. The Liabilities can also be subdivided into Current and Long-term Liabilities, depending upon whether they come due in less than a year.

Here is something to be emphasized about a Balance Sheet: Although its two sides must balance *in total*, no single item on one side is matched by an item on the other side. Thus, Bonds do not correspond in value to the Equipment or Buildings, nor do Capital items correspond to Cash. The only correct statement about a Balance Sheet is that creditors have a general claim of a definite value against the enterprise, and owners have a residual claim against the rest.

BALANCE SHEET OF APEX TOOTHPASTE, INC.,
AS OF DECEMBER 31, 1975.

ASSETS		LIABILITIES AND NET WORTH	
		Liabilities	
Current Assets:		**Current Liabilities:**	
Cash	$ 20,000	Accounts payable	$ 20,000
Inventory	80,000	Notes payable	30,000
		Long-term Liabilities:	
Fixed Assets:		SBL note	50,000
Equipment	130,000	Bonds payable	50,000
Buildings	170,000	*Net Worth*	
		Capital:	
		Preferred stock	50,000
		Common stock	. . . .
Total	$400,000	Total	$400,000

TABLE 6-1

Most of the specific items listed are more or less self-explanatory. Cash consists of coins, currency, and money on deposit in the bank. Cash is the only asset whose value is exact rather than an estimate. All other valuations involve some arbitrary assumptions, albeit careful assumptions. Moreover, all accounting valuations must be made relative to the actual intended purpose or use of the asset in question. If a business is a going concern and not in the process of liquidation, the accountant will be careful not to value doubtful assets at the low figure they would bring at a forced sale; he, rather, will value them at their cost to the company in its normal operation.

Inventory, consisting, in the case of our toothpaste company, of sugar, chemicals, tubing, raw materials, and other goods in process, can be valued in many different ways. Some conservative companies use original cost of the inventories or present market value, whichever is lower. Especially difficult problems arise when the prices of materials vary from month to month. Should we figure the chemical cost of the toothpaste at the original price of the ingredients actually used, which of course were bought some time ago when prices were different? Or should we figure, as our cost, the price that must *now* be paid for the chemicals to replace those being used up? An elementary discussion cannot go into these two possible methods of inventory valuation.[1] Obviously, the choice of one of the two methods will make a great difference in stated profits during a time of inflation or deflation. It will also make a difference in income taxes. Therefore the government is compelled to say, "Use whichever method you wish, but having made up your mind, stick to it on this item." So much for inventories.

If we assume that the Equipment and Buildings items were bought just at the end of 1975, then their Balance-Sheet values will be listed equal to their purchase price. This follows a fundamental accounting rule or convention: "At time of purchase a thing is presumed worth what the enterprise pays for it." However, as we shall see in connection with the Income Statement and the next year's Balance Sheet, hard problems are involved in deciding how exactly to evaluate equipment and buildings that have depreciated through use and age.

On the Liabilities side, Accounts Payable are, as their name implies, the sums owed for goods bought and charged. Notes Payable are promissory notes owed to the banks or to a finance company. The SBL Note listed under the Long-term Liabilities is a 5-year loan guaranteed by the federal Small Business Loans Act. The Bonds Payable are a long-term loan, floated at a 7 per cent coupon rate, and not due for 15 years. (NOTE: What appears as a Liability to this company may show up as an Asset to someone else; thus the creditors who own these bonds will carry them as left-hand-side Assets, "Bonds Receivable.")

Turning now to Net Worth items, we find that 500 shares of $100, 4 per cent, cumulative (non-participating) pre-

[1]Accounting texts refer to them as "First-in-first-out" (FIFO) and "Last-in-first-out" (LIFO) and analyze them in detail.

ferred stock have been issued; and 20,000 shares of no-par common stock were issued at $10 each. (Fill this in under correct heading in Table 6-1.)

This completes our first glance at a simple Balance Sheet.

THE STATEMENT OF PROFIT AND LOSS, OR INCOME STATEMENT

Now let time march on. During the following months, the firm is profitably engaged in producing and selling toothpaste. To show its *flow* of income over the 12 months of the year, we must turn to its Income Statement, or—as many companies prefer—the Statement of Profit and Loss, Table 6-2.

This is a statement which reports the following: (1) Apex's revenues from sales in 1976, (2) the expenses to be charged against those sales, and (3) the profit remaining after expenses have been deducted. That is,

Total Profit = Total Revenue − Total Costs.

(the fundamental identity of the Income Statement).

You will understand it better if at first you disregard the figures in the Manufacturing Cost of Goods Sold section (the indented figures) and look only at those in the right-hand column. Sales were $240,000; and the total Manufacturing Cost of Goods Sold came to $170,000. After deducting another $14,000 for Selling and Administrative Costs, $56,000 remained in Net Operating Profit. Out of this, a total of $6,000 + $17,500 in interest and taxes had to be paid, leaving $32,500 in Net Earnings after Taxes (or Profit). Dividends of $2,000 on the preferred and $10,500 on the common were paid, leaving $20,000 of Addition to Earnings retained in the Business.

Now turn to the indented Manufacturing Cost of Goods Sold section, which lists the costs incurred in this part of the business. The firm's outlays for materials, labor, and miscellaneous expenses are listed, together with an item for Depreciation. (Depreciation is worth a section to itself, and we shall consider it soon.) The sum of these four items ($175,000) is the Total Manufacturing Cost. Then follows what may seem a puzzling adjustment. The value of the inventory on January 1 is added, and that of the year-end inventory is deducted. The result, which differs from Manufacturing Cost by $5,000, is the Manufacturing Cost *of Goods Sold*. What is the difference between these terms, and why this inventory adjustment?

Apex began the year with inventory of $80,000 in raw materials and finished goods. During the year, it built up inventories by an extra $5,000. In this case, it would be false to attribute all the manufacturing cost to *the goods actually sold*. Some of these costs are really attributable to goods to be sold *in the future*. To neglect this fact would be to overstate the Manufacturing Cost of Goods Sold in this year; it would be subtracting too much from this year's Net Sales and understating this year's Profits.

If there had been no change in the amount of inventory, then all would be simple: Manufacturing Cost and Manufacturing Cost of Goods Sold would be identical.

INCOME STATEMENT OF APEX TOOTHPASTE, INC.,
FROM JANUARY 1, 1976, TO DECEMBER 31, 1976.

Net Sales (after all discounts and rebates)		$240,000
Less: Manufacturing Cost of Goods Sold:		
Materials	$ 50,000	
Labor Cost	100,000	
Depreciation Charges	20,000	
Miscellaneous Operating Cost	5,000	
Total Manufacturing Cost	$175,000	
Add: Beginning Inventory	80,000	
	$255,000	
Deduct: Closing Inventory	85,000	
Equals:		
Manufacturing Cost of Goods Sold	$170,000	170,000
Gross Profit (or Gross Margin)		$ 70,000
Less: Selling and Administrative Costs		14,000
Net Operating Profit		$ 56,000
Less: Fixed Charges and Local Taxes		6,000
Net Earnings before Income Taxes		$ 50,000
Less: Corporation Income Taxes		17,500
Net Earnings after Taxes		$ 32,500
Less: Dividends on Preferred Stocks		2,000
Net Profits of Common Stockholders		$ 30,500
Less: Dividends Paid on Common Stock		10,500
Addition to Surplus		$ 20,000

TABLE 6-2

On the other hand, what if we had had less inventory on hand at the year's end than at the beginning? Clearly, we would be fooling ourselves if we did not recognize that the cost of the goods we have sold this year ought really to be *greater* than the money we have paid out to labor and to other firms. We would have neglected the cost element of used-up and unreplaced inventory.

Summary: To reach a valid figure for Manufacturing Cost of Goods Sold, we must adjust the Manufacturing Cost figure thus:

If the Closing Inventory shows an increase over the Beginning Inventory, deduct that increase; if the Closing Inventory has decreased, add that decrease.

Instead of subtracting $5,000 directly from the $175,000 total manufacturing expense, the accountant does it in two steps. Rather than working with the difference between the two, he first adds the total Beginning Inventory, then subtracts the Closing Inventory. This procedure has the advantage of being standardized; it is the same whether inventory is up or down, whereas a single change-in-inventory figure would in some cases be a subtraction, in others an addition. And the accountant's method also reveals the change in inventory relative to the size of the total inventory.

Note that the items in Table 6-2 differ from Table 6-1's Balance-Sheet items. Income items refer to *flows* over time: moving-picture action. Balance-Sheet items refer to *stocks* at an instant of time: still pictures.

DEPRECIATION (CAPITAL COST ALLOWANCE)

At first, one may wonder why any Depreciation Charges have been made for 1976. The buildings and equipment were newly bought at the beginning of the year, and surely they will not have been worn out already. (It will, of course, be necessary to spend money on men to maintain the equipment and keep the factories painted; but their wages are already included in Labor Cost or Miscellaneous Operating Cost and are not included in Depreciation Charges.)

Here is where the farseeing wisdom of the accountant comes to the fore. He points out that not a cent may have to be spent upon replacement of equipment for 10 years, at which time all the machines may *suddenly* have to be bought anew. It would be nonsense to charge nothing to depreciation for 9 years and fool yourself into thinking you are making a nice profit and then suddenly in the tenth year you have to charge off all the value of the machines at once and think you have incurred a great loss in that year.

Actually, he points out, the equipment is *being used up all the time.* A truer, undistorted picture of net income or profit will be reached if the costs of the capital equipment are spread more evenly over its lifetime. The value of equipment declines as a result of age and use; it depreciates from its price as new to its final scrap value. In recognition of this, the accountant depreciates the value of fixed capital items by some *gradual* formula. Of the various proposed methods, here are two widely used ones.

The first is called "straight-line depreciation." Suppose that you have a truck whose cost new is $10,100 and whose economic life is 10 years; after this its physical life may continue but its economic life will be over, because of its unreliability and maintenance costs. Suppose that its scrap value at the end of 10 years is $100. According to the straight-line method, you will each year charge off to depreciation one-tenth of the lifetime decline in its total value, $10,000 (new price minus scrap value). Thus, $1,000 will be entered in Depreciation Charges every year.

A second method of more rapid early depreciation has become popular. In Canada, income tax regulations *require* all taxpayers (except farmers and fishermen) to use this method for tax purposes. Instead of writing off a new asset steadily by the straight-line method, firms must use the "declining-balance" method.

Disregarding scrap value as negligible, consider the 10-year $10,000 truck. Instead of taking one-tenth its value for depreciation in the first year, the tax law lets you charge off, under the declining-balance method, twice that amount, or 2 X 10 per cent = 20 per cent in its first year. So you get a much larger deduction for tax purposes. Evidently you cannot go on charging off that amount for each year of life, since that would leave you with zero value by the halfway point, at the end of 5 years. What the declining-balance method does is to let you take off 20 per cent of *remaining* value or balance each year. In the second year, then, you take off 20 per cent of the $8,000 of remaining value, or $1,600. In the third year you take off 20 per cent of what is left, namely, of $6,400. So the process goes. It can be calculated that by the time the asset has reached half the length of its useful life, you have been permitted to write off for tax purposes almost two-thirds its value—rather than one-half, as under the straight-line method. It is later in life that the declining-balance method begins to be less generous in order to compensate for its early generosity.[2]

DEPRECIATION AND PROFITS Although depreciation is usually figured by some apparently exact formula, every accountant knows that the allowances are really very rough, being subject to large and unpredictable errors and involving arbitrary corrections and assumptions. He comforts himself with two thoughts: (1) A rough method of depreciation, like an imperfect watch, is often better than none at all. (2) Mistakes in depreciation will ultimately "come out in the wash" anyway.

Let us see why a mistake in depreciation ultimately tends to correct itself. Suppose that the truck lasts 15

years rather than the predicted 10. We have then been overstating our depreciation *expenses* during the first 10 years. But in the eleventh and later years there will be no depreciation charged on the truck at all, since it has already been written down to its scrap value by the end of the tenth year. Our profits in these later years tend, therefore, to be overstated by about as much as they were understated in the earlier years. After 15 years, everything is pretty much the same after all. That is, except for taxes. Different methods of depreciation result in a different apparent distribution of earnings over time, and therefore in a different pattern over time of corporation income taxes. Naturally, a businessman prefers a method of depreciation that will make his income average out more steadily over time, so as to keep his effective tax rate as low as possible and permit him to cancel off losses against profits; and he also likes a fast method (such as the declining balance) that enables him to put off the evil day of taxes as far as possible.

Governments often allow accelerated depreciation to encourage investment, especially if the new property is to be in a region the government is trying to build up. This may vary from 100 per cent write off in one year (i.e., taxable income reduced by the whole amount of new investment) to various straight-line depreciation rates over 3, 4, or 5 years. This approach reduces the harmful effect of taxation on "venture capital" by cutting actual taxes paid. The Kennedy administration, following a policy adopted by Sweden some years ago, introduced in the 1960s an "investment tax credit" that actually gave a subsidy to firms investing in new equipment. This tax credit could be turned off and on to stabilize investment.

THE RELATION BETWEEN THE INCOME STATEMENT AND THE BALANCE SHEET

Now we must relate the description by the Income Statement of what has happened during the year to the Balance Sheets at the beginning and end of the year. Table 6-3 shows the Balance Sheet of our toothpaste corporation at the end of its first year of operation. It has prospered.

Net Worth, the difference between Total Assets and Total Liabilities, has increased between the beginning and end of the accounting period by $20,000—from $250,000 to $270,000. The amount of this increase, as seen by comparing Balance Sheets, just equals the earnings or profits *available* to the common stockholders but not paid out to them in dividends, or as we saw at the bottom of the Income Statement, just equal to $30,500 minus $10,500, or $20,000 of undistributed profits.

Some Net Worth item has recognizably risen by $20,000. It would clearly never do to increase the Preferred Stock Capital Account, because such stockholders are not the residual claimants to the profits of the corporation and no new stock has been sold. Conceivably, one could add the $20,000 to the Common Stock Capital Account. However, this is not done. Instead, the Common Stock Capital Account is left at its original par or issued value.

---

[2]Still a third method, called the "service-unit method," or "unit-of-production method," can be mentioned only briefly here. According to this we should estimate the number of miles, loads, or service units that the truck will perform in its life. Thus, if the truck goes a million miles in 10 years and its loss of value during that time is $10,000, then each mile used up represents about 1 cent.

BALANCE SHEET OF APEX TOOTHPASTE, INC., AS OF DECEMBER 31, 1976

ASSETS			LIABILITIES AND NET WORTH	
			Liabilities	
Current Assets:			**Current Liabilities:**	
Cash		$ 17,000	Accounts payable	$ 10,000
Inventory		85,000	Notes Payable	17,000
Sinking Fund to Retire Debt		5,000	Taxes Payable	21,000
(Government bonds)				
Fixed Assets:			**Long-term Liabilities:**	
Equipment	$130,000		SBL Note	50,000
Less: Allowance (or Reserve)			Bonds Payable	50,000
for Depreciation	15,000			
		115,000	*Net Worth*	
Buildings	$170,000			
Less: Allowance (or Reserve)			**Capital Stock:**	
for Depreciation	5,000		Preferred Stock	50,000
		165,000	Common Stock	200,000
Intangible Assets:			Earnings Retained	
Patents		10,000	in the Business:	20,000
Good Will		21,000		
Total		$418,000	Total	$418,000

TABLE 6-3

RETAINED EARNINGS It is more informative to create a new account called Earnings Retained in the Business or Retained Earnings[3]—to show how much of the increase in "book value" or Net Worth has resulted from accumulated undistributed earnings plowed back through the years.

In many ways, Earnings Retained in the Business can be misleading. It sounds like something extra or unnecessary, or too often like a nice spare chunk of cash which the company's workers or stockholders might hope to stage a raid against. Actually, Earnings Retained in the Business is decidedly not an Assets account, much less a pool of liquid cash. It simply indicates a part of the ownership—over and above Liabilities to creditors and original subscribed capital ownership—in the polyglot Assets of the corporation. A glance at Table 6-3 will convince us that the $20,000 of Surplus is not matched by an equivalent amount of cash on the Assets side.

We must again warn against trying to link *specific* items on the two sides of the Balance Sheet. Only the final *totals* correspond. It is not even possible to say exactly how the $20,000 plowed back into the business as Retained Earnings, was used. An addition to Surplus must be associated with an increase in Assets and/or a decrease in Liabilities —that is all we can say.

It would be an equal mistake to think that the profits of a corporation accrue in the form of cash, so that on the last day of the year, just before the board of directors decided upon its dividend rate, there was some $30,500 of cash on

[3]Sometimes this is called "Surplus" or "Earned Surplus" but the terms are increasingly frowned on as being misleading.

hand, available either for the stockholders or to be reinvested in the business. In the case of our Apex Toothpaste company, the very handsome profit earned was largely embodied in the form of new, non-cash Assets and lowered Liabilities; not very much more than $10,500 could have been paid out as cash dividends without forcing serious changes in the financial decisions of the company—decisions such as to borrow more, to grow more slowly, to sell off some of the equipment and inventory at a loss, or to operate with a ludicrously low cash balance.

SUMMARY OF ELEMENTARY ACCOUNTING RELATIONS

Before taking a last look at the new complexities introduced in the 1976 Balance Sheet over that of the 1975, we may briefly summarize the relationship between Balance Sheets and Income Statements:

1. The Balance Sheet indicates an instantaneous financial picture: it is like a measure of the stock of water in a lake.

2. The Income Statement shows the flow of sales, cost, and revenue over the year or other accounting period: it measures the flow of water in and out of the lake, measures the progress of the firm over the year.

3. The change in total Net Worth between the beginning and the end of the period—as shown by comparing the new and old Balance Sheets—is also to be understood from an examination of the changes in Retained Earnings as appended at the end of Table 6-2's Income Statement: the change in the lake's level over the year we can relate to the flows during the year. (If new common stock is sold,

that will be revealed by comparing the two Balance Sheets.)

There do remain, however, certain changes in the Balance-Sheet items from their previous levels in the earlier period to which the intervening Income Statement gives no clue. A closer look at the December 31, 1976, Balance Sheet will therefore prove instructive, although enough has been said already to introduce the reader to the fundamentals of accounting.

DEPRECIATION ALLOWANCES AND FUNDS

The new Balance Sheet looks much like the old for the most part; but some new items are present for the first time. The last of these new items, Earnings Retained in the Business, we have already explained. Among the Liabilities there is a new item, called Taxes Payable of $21,000. It is not hard to understand. The taxes that the corporation will have to pay the government are as much short-term Liabilities as the Accounts Payable or Notes Payable.

Let us turn to the Assets side for new items.[4] The first stranger, entitled "Sinking Fund to Retire Debt," is listed midway between the Current and Fixed Assets. It is an asset consisting of, say, 6 per cent government bonds which are to be held for the purpose of ultimately paying off the bonds you issued to raise the money to buy your machines. The nature of this Sinking Fund is very understandable; it is simply a pool of liquid Assets set aside for a specific future purpose.

ALLOWANCE FOR DEPRECIATION Turning to the Fixed Assets, we find ourselves in for a surprise. From our previous discussion of the Depreciation Charges of the Income Statement, we should have expected the Buildings and Equipment items to total $280,000. Why? Because at the beginning of the year they added up to $300,000, because no new equipment was bought during the year, and because the Income Statement told us that $20,000 of depreciation accrued during the period as part of the necessary costs of production.

Why, then, are these Fixed Assets carried on the new Balance Sheet at the old $130,000 and $170,000 figures? Looking more closely, we see that they really are not. From the $130,000 nominal Equipment valuation, there is subtracted a $15,000 Allowance for Depreciation, so that really only $115,000 is carried for Equipment. Similarly, from the $170,000 original value of the Buildings, there is subtracted a $5,000 Allowance for Depreciation. Our faith in the accountant's wisdom is restored; but we may still wonder why he goes through this roundabout procedure of stating "two" as "four minus two" instead of simply as "two."

Actually, he has his good reasons. An honest accountant knows his Depreciation estimate is only the roughest

of estimates. Were he simply to guess and put down the final figure of $115,000 for Equipment, the public would not know how much reliance to place upon the figure. So he puts down $130,000 of original value, which is firmly rooted in the solid fact of original cost; and he then carefully isolates his own calculated Allowance for Depreciation. Then the public is in a better position to evaluate the reliability of the final $115,000 figure. The roundabout procedure does no harm, and may do good.

Now we know the precise meaning of Allowances for Depreciation. They are not sums of money; they are not sinking funds of liquid Assets that can be spent on replacement. They are simply *subtractions from overstated Assets figures*. Thus, the Allowance for Depreciation of Buildings of $5,000 is simply an explicit correction of the original value of the Buildings, which would be an overstatement of their value. This correction must be made to keep Assets and Net Worth from both being artificially inflated.

It must be made regardless of whether at the same time any money is or is not being set aside into Sinking Funds. Note that there is no Sinking Fund to retire debt incurred to acquire buildings, and that the Sinking Fund is here only one-third as large as the estimated Allowance for Depreciation of Equipment. As a matter of fact, businesses rarely set aside any considerable sums of money in replacement sinking funds. This is because liquid gilt-edge bonds earn at most only a few per cent interest, whereas capital invested in the firm's own activities usually brings in much more.

INTANGIBLE ASSETS

Only one further new category of Assets can still be found on the December 31, 1976, Balance Sheet. To illustrate that an asset need not be a tangible commodity, a piece of equipment, or a sum of money, a patent has been introduced into the picture. Let us suppose that it is a patent on a profitable new chemical process, which gives us exclusive production rights for 17 years.

Such a patent is obviously worth money. Of course, as 5, 10, 12, and 16 years pass, the patent will be coming near to the end of its 17-year life and will be declining in value. Therefore, some amortization formula will be applied to it much as if it were a truck.

GOOD WILL AND MONOPOLY EARNING POWER So much for Patents as an illustration of an intangible asset. Let us suppose that, at the same time we bought the patent, we also took over a rival toothpaste company. This horizontal combination will presumably add to our monopoly position and earning power. Therefore we were willing to buy the company for more than its trifling Assets —which happened to consist solely of a little inventory— were worth. Perhaps part of the purchase price went as profits to those who promoted this little monopolistic merger.

An example of the capitalization of earning power is J. P. Morgan's formation of the giant United States Steel

---

[4]Neither this Balance Sheet nor the previous one contains a frequently met Current Assets item called Prepaid Expenses. Often an enterprise will pay its rent or buy some of its supplies a number of months in advance. Properly, the enterprise is regarded as possessing on its Balance Sheet an equivalent asset.

Corporation at the turn of the century. He bought out the Andrew Carnegie steel plants and combined them with half-a-dozen other holdings. But in economics, as in atomic physics, the whole is equal to more than the sum of its parts.

After Morgan had put the pieces together, he found himself with some 130 million dollars of extra capital value!

Who was hurt by this transaction? Certainly not Carnegie or Morgan. Even the people who bought the stock had no right to complain that it had been "watered," since for many years they got more than a fair return on their investments. To have sold them the stock for its actual cost (without water) would be (1) to make them a free gift of the enlarged profits of the concern, and (2) to give them the privilege of reselling the stock at the higher price that its earning power could earn for it in a competitive stock market. (Of course the consumer was not given the full benefit in lower steel prices of the efficiencies achieved by the merger; but in terms of standards of the time, the merger wasn't illegal or necessarily unethical. Accounting conventions, however, are not concerned with such matters of public policy and political economy as whether the consumer will or will not now pay higher prices. The careful accountant will tell our toothpaste company or J. P. Morgan the same thing: "If you paid a certain sum of money for a concern, it must presumably be worth that much to you. If its Net Worth and book value don't show this worth, we must recognize it by "Good Will."

The intangible asset Good Will is thus the difference between what a company pays in buying out another company and what it gets in identifiable Assets.

ACCOUNTING ABUSES

In economics and finance nothing can be measured with the great accuracy of the physical sciences. But approximate measurement will suffice, so long as the method of measurement remains roughly the same over time.

Nowhere is this better illustrated than in accounting. When auditors certify that a company has prepared its accounting reports properly, they are not really able to swear that all measurements are 100 per cent accurate. But *it is valuable for anyone who is contemplating buying the stock of the company to know that the usual methods of accounting have been adhered to.* For example, when the company reports a rise of 10 per cent in earnings per share over the previous year, then, even though there may be some uncertainty in the exact figures for each year, the direction of the improvement should be not at all in doubt.

Unfortunately, in the 1960s and 1970s certain abuses crept into the accounting used by some of the "conglomerates." Here are a few examples that the accounting profession is belatedly engaged in correcting.

1. Manipulation of the way the assets taken over by the conglomerate are treated—good will adjustments and selling off low-book-value assets at a claimed profit—have

been used to permit the conglomerate *to report rising per share earnings every year even though actual operating earnings have fallen.*

2. Conglomerates will issue many securities that are *convertible* into common stock—convertible bonds, convertible preferred stock, warrant options to buy new common stock at low prices, stock options for executives and underwriters. These really are potential common stock which, in many cases, are sure to become actual common stock. Hence, accounting committees insist that we restate the earnings per share to allow for this *dilution*—and then what looks like a rising profile of earnings per share may actually be a dismally falling one.

3. Sometimes a small conglomerate will take over a larger corporation that is cash-rich, using in the end the money of the company swallowed to do so. Even where this is not illegal or unethical, it may be possible only because the old accounting book values of the absorbed firm carried its assets *concealed by under valuations.*

4. Sometimes conglomerates give the appearance of becoming more profitably efficient in their operations than their predecessor companies, when actually all the improvements in per share earnings have resulted merely from taking advantage of tax loopholes—such as changing convertible preferred stocks into convertible bonds so that their dividend return will now appear in the form of interest, which is deductible under the law from corporation income subject to taxes. There may be nothing illegal or even unethical about this razzle-dazzle, but the alert investor will have to learn how to discern that this is all that is taking place and that further improvement is not possible.

The accounting profession and government agencies are working to reform some of these abuses. But, alas, the old adage *caveat emptor*—let the buyer beware—must still prevail.

CONCLUSION

Finally, some interesting relations between economics and accounting can be briefly mentioned. (1) All Balance Sheets depend on valuation of Assets, which is one of the basic questions of the capital and interest theory discussed in Part Four. (2) National-income statistics depend on the accounting data of sales, cost, and so forth, as Chapter 10 shows. (3) As we shall see in a later discussion of how firms set price, accounting cost data play an important role in price determination.

Business accounts deal with *money* magnitudes; the economist tries to probe deeper to the underlying *real* magnitudes. Especially in periods of great inflation or deflation, the conventions of ordinary accounting may give strange results.

One example is the problem of changing price levels and depreciation. Suppose prices are rising sharply. If I sell my goods for enough to cover labor and other costs and also to cover depreciation, you might think I am breaking even. What would the tax collector say who figures my depreciation on the basis of the past low prices originally paid for my machines and building? He, too, would say I am breaking even. But in fact I can be said to have been selling my goods at a *real* loss; for when my machines and buildings have worn out, I shall not have enough money to *reproduce them* at the new higher price

level. The same is true of a merchant who sells off his inventory at less than replacement cost.

So we must beware of fictitious money overstatements of real profits during rising prices and of fictitious understatements of profits during falling prices. (Later, in national-income statistics, you will note that profits are "adjusted" for inventory revaluations.)

SUMMARY TO APPENDIX

Instead of a lengthy recapitulation, here is a check list of accounting concepts that you should understand:

1 The fundamental Balance-Sheet relationship between Assets, Liabilities, and Net Worth and the breakdown of each of these categories into Current and Fixed Assets, Current and Long-term Liabilities, Capital and Earnings Retained in the Business.
2 The character of the Income Statement (or Profit-and-Loss Statement) and the relationship between undistributed profit and Retained Earnings changes on the new Balance Sheet.
3 The whole problem of Depreciation, both in its income-statement aspect as a necessary expense, which need not be an expenditure, and in its balance-sheet treatment as a deduction from a purposely overstated asset; also the logic of principal depreciation methods. Although any errors in calculating depreciation tend to cancel out eventually, recent tax concessions that allow rapid depreciation do improve the cash position of corporations.
4 Intangible assets like patents and good will, sinking funds, and other general items.

CONCEPTS FOR REVIEW

Balance-Sheet identity	Manufacturing Cost, inventory change
Income-Statement identity	Depreciation (as expense and allowance)
Assets, Liabilities, and Net Worth	straight-line or faster depreciation
Current versus Fixed Assets	Intangible Assets—Patents, Good Will
Dividends, Retained Earnings	Accounting conventions and
Manufacturing Cost of Goods Sold	price levels

QUESTIONS FOR DISCUSSION

1. Describe the Balance Sheet's right-hand side. Its left-hand side. What items must match from the "fundamental identity"?
2. You are a banker deciding whether to lend money to the toothpaste company. Why be especially interested in current items?
3. Write out a list of many different Assets, describing the nature of each in a few lines. Do the same for Liabilities.
4. Is an Income Statement a "still picture" at an instant of time? Why not?
5. A company has 10 million dollars of net sales and 9 million dollars of costs of all kinds (including taxes, etc.). It rents its equipment, its inventory does not change in the year, and it has no preferred stock. It pays no dividends. Draw up its simplified 1976 Income Statement.
6. The same company as in question 5 owes no money, having been completely equity-financed years ago. Fill in the year-end Balance Sheets below.

ASSETS			LIABILITIES AND NET WORTH		
	1975	1976		1975	1976
			Liabilities	0	0
			Net Worth	$50 million	....
Total	$50 million	....	Total	....	....

7. Redo problems 5 and 6, making the following changes: In addition to the other expenses, its buildings depreciate by 2 million dollars; also its inventory has fallen off by 3 million dollars.

Draw up an Income Statement showing its loss for the year, and adjust its 1976 Balance Sheet accordingly.

8. Describe two methods of calculating Depreciation, and explain tax advantages.

9. Guess how much you would pay for a business that is sure of yielding a net profit of $15,000 per year with little risk of principal. Suppose its Total Assets exclusive of Good Will were valued at $100,000. What would you guess for Good Will?

10. Why would use of the word "Surplus" rather than "Retained Earnings" encourage the fallacy of thinking that this represents a hunk of cash that the shareowners or union negotiators might hope to tap?

7
LABOR UNIONS AND INDUSTRIAL RELATIONS

"It is always possible to bind together a considerable number of people in love, so long as there are other people left over to receive the manifestations of their aggressiveness."

SIGMUND FREUD

The preceding chapters have dealt with important elements of the mixed economy: consumers and producers. Supply and demand obviously link them in the marketplace. But most consumers are also members of the labor force, at some time. Half of our hours awake are spent on the job, so that four-fifths of the national income stems from wages and salaries.

This chapter deals with the links between employers and workers. The working of supply and demand is not so obvious. Instead, collective bargaining between unions and management suggests that wages and salaries get determined in other ways. This chapter surveys the unions that carry out collective bargaining on behalf of their members, and the laws that control them. Because unions play an important part in Canadian social life and politics, as well as setting the price of labor, this descriptive chapter is separated from Chapter 29 on wage determination.[1]

Who Belongs to Unions?

More than 2 million Canadians, about one-third of the nonfarm working force, belong to unions. Half of

[1] This chapter is shorter than in previous editions, because much historical material has been deleted or summarized. The interested reader can now turn to two excellent and readable treatments.

On trade unions, see especially S. Jamieson, *Industrial Relations in Canada,* Macmillan, Toronto, 1973, 2nd edition. On collective bargaining laws and institutions, see H. D. Woods, *Labour Policy in Canada,* Macmillan, Toronto, 1973. 2nd ed. (Volume I of *Labour Policy and Labour Economics in Canada* by H. D. Woods, Sylvia Ostry and M. A. Zaidi, Macmillan, Toronto, 1973, 2nd ed.)

The whole field has been strengthened by the publication of the report of the federal Task Force on Labour Relations, 1968, and its many accompanying studies.

them work in manufacturing, where their unions blanket the largest industries.

This is not a stable situation. The growing population makes more potential members available. Furthermore, unions are still being organized in many industries. Figure 7-1 shows that these two processes have been proceeding at an accelerating rate since 1911. It shows the steady advance up to World War I, the spurt and decline of the war and post-war years, the slow growth up to 1929, the relapse into the Great Depression, the steady growth into and through World War II, the stagnation of the early sixties, and the steady growth since then.

To what unions do workers belong? Here are the six largest, with size of membership: the United Steelworkers of America (U.S.A.), 165,055; the Canadian Union of Public Employees (CUPE), 157,919; Public Service Alliance of Canada (PSAC), 129,652; the United Automobile, Aerospace and Agricultural Implement Workers of America (UAW), 102,933; the United Brotherhood of Carpenters and Joiners of America (CJA), 74,362; and the Quebec Teachers' Corporation (CEO), 70,000.[2]

Most international unions belong to the merged American Federation of Labor and Congress of Industrial Organizations (AFL-CIO) in the United States and to the Canadian Labour Congress (CLC) in Canada. However, several of the largest, including the Public Employees are Canadian national groups (they have no American affiliation but belong only to the CLC federation); and another union, the Teamsters, following a row about corruption, became for a while independent of both AFL-CIO and the CLC.

[2] Canada Department of Labour, *Labour Organizations in Canada, 1972* (Ottawa: Information Canada, 1973).

MEMBERSHIP IN LABOR UNIONS

FIG. 7-1. Union membership still grows, but slower than labor force. Of nonagricultural paid workers, approximately 34 per cent belong to unions, as against 15 per cent in 1931. The recent trend has shown rapid increase in periods of high employment, in spite of forecasts of slow decline. "Automation" may retard future growth as difficult-to-organize white-collar workers supplant production workers. (Source: Department of Labour, *Labour Organizations in Canada, 1972.*)

An additional 218,621 workers belong to the largely French-speaking Confederation of National Trade Unions (CNTU) which has a structure unlike that of the AFL-CIO group of unions.

Statistics of memberships understate the influence of unions. Many nonunion people are covered by union agreements on wages, hours, and working conditions. If you took a solemn oath never to join a union or work under a union agreement, you would have to give up all hope of being a worker in many sectors of manufacturing. You would have to give up a career in mining; in construction and in transportation. Where could you go? You could avoid unions on the farm, in domestic service, and in many finance, trade, and service occupations.

Within government itself is the new frontier of unionization: policemen, postal workers, and clerks. Besides outright trade unions, there are many organizations of professional people—like the Canadian Medical Association (CMA), to which 30,000 doctors belong, and the Canadian Association of University Teachers—which in fact are important forces lobbying for higher incomes and specified working conditions. You would be naïve to think that the CMA and similar associations are not important influences on the interplay of supply and demand, even though economic betterment is not primary in their official constitutions.

NATIONAL AND LOCAL UNIONS

There are three layers in the structure of North American unions: (1) the *local* union, (2) the *national* union (American unions with Canadian chapters are called *international* unions), and (3) the *federation* of national unions.

To a member, the *local* is the front line of unionism. He joins the local in his plant or town. He pays his dues to it. Usually, the local union signs the collective bargaining agreement determining his wages and work conditions.

But the local is only a single chapter or lodge of the national union. Thus, a linotypist in Toronto belongs to the local union located there, but this is one of hundreds of local chapters of the International Typographical Union, whose headquarters is in Colorado Springs. Part of the local dues—one-half or less, usually—goes to the national or international union; the bylaws and practice of the local cannot transcend the broad policies laid down at the top. The local president and other officers are probably workers; but the important business agent has a full-time job, his salary often paid by the national union. National unions often join their locals in collective bargaining.

Altogether there are about 160 national and international unions in Canada. We have seen that six of these have more than 70,000 members. The average national or international union has about 14,000 members; but, if we exclude the 20 largest, the average size is about 7,200.

The number of local union chapters or lodges is no less than 10,462. Some have as few as a dozen men.

The vast majority of locals number from 50 to 1,000 workers, with an average membership of 225.

NATIONAL UNIONS AND THE FEDERATION

The AFL-CIO and the CLC are federations dependent on member national and international unions for financial support. But the national unions have insisted upon their "sovereignty" and their right to "exclusive jurisdiction" over workers in their area. Most of the headaches and fights stem from jurisdictional disputes.

The public thinks of the federation as being the most important part of the labor movement; but it is not. It acts more as a spokesman for labor attitudes than as the boss of the leaders of the various unions.

Figure 7-2 gives the CLC and AFL-CIO organization chart. Members belong to a local, which (a) belongs to a national or international union, or is a single entity directly chartered by the CLC; and (b) usually belongs to a city labor council and a provincial federation which support locals in difficult negotiations and act in labor's interest in city and provincial politics. Every international union belongs to the CLC and the AFL-CIO; Canadian na-

tional unions belong only to the CLC. These grand federations have contact with local membership largely through the nationals and internationals. (A bigger diagram would show some other boxes, especially departments of the CLC that coordinate trades and crafts in the building industry.)

THE URGE TO UNIONIZE

What are the general functions of unions? They differ from the medieval guilds, which accommodated masters, craftsmen, and apprentices. Why were men tempted to form and join the new organizations?

WAGES AND WORKING CONDITIONS In past centuries wages were low everywhere. Productivity was then low, so that no way of dividing the social pie could have given the average man an adequate slice. But workers often felt that they were at the particular mercy of the boss. They felt poor, uninformed, and helpless to hold out economically against the employer, with his greater staying power in any conflict. Shops were organized on dictatorial principles, and orders were passed down from on high; the worker was but a cog in the machine, a dehumanized robot. Such was the worker's image of the situation as revealed in historical records.

Men gradually discovered that in numbers there is strength. One hundred men acting in concert seemed to have more bargaining power than all had by acting separately. Workers began to meet in chapels and taverns. They formed fraternal societies for mutual contacts, entertainment, and discussion. Gradu-

FIG. 7-2. The international structure of federated unions. Internationals and locals are the important units in the federations. Internationals belong to both the **AFL-CIO** and the **CLC**, and provide an essential link between them. Quebec members of the **CNTU** have no international links, and have a less decentralized structure.

ally such early unions began to offer mutual death benefits and various other forms of insurance, and promoted self-education. They also began to propose *standard wage rates* that members were to insist on getting paid.

Naturally, employers fought back. Their smaller number had always enabled them to act in concert in setting wages and working conditions, to the despair of the workers. Now they learned that strength came from formal cooperation. Each employer backed up the other and refused to hire men on the "blacklist" of known labor agitators. Singly and in concert they invoked the powers of the law against labor "conspiracies."[3]

We can use the supply and demand apparatus of Chapter 4 to illustrate this history. Figure 7-3, while oversimplified, shows that workers who participate in concerted action to set standard wages must accept the consequences in changed numbers of jobs.[4] Imagine the curves to refer to the supply and demand conditions in a particular local labor "market."

A strong bosses' association might refuse to pay more than $2 per hour, and a competitive supply of only 7 thousand workers would accept this wage. Had the market been freer, competition among masters for men and among men for jobs would have led to movement along the arrows to the equilibrium wage C, and work for 12 thousand. If instead a new union imposes a standard wage rate of $5 on unorganized employers, there would be a competitive demand for only 9 thousand members; another 9 thousand workers in excess supply at this wage would have to take jobs elsewhere, or remain unemployed.[5]

But organized workers or employers are bucking eager market forces. At $5 the excess supply of workers may lead to wage cutting back down toward C.

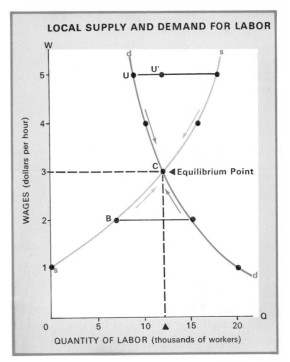

FIG. 7-3 Workers and bosses set non-competitive wages: At the C equilibrium wage, the amount of labor supplied just matches the amount demanded (jobs offered). At a lower wage B, organized bosses find only 7,000 willing workers. Alternatively, a strong union may hold the wage at $5 as long as excess unemployed workers don't offer to work for less. If they do, the union wage will collapse back to C. (A really tough union may even battle its way to U', if monopolistic bosses wish to avoid costly strikes.) (Source: Figure 4-3, with minor modifications, and Table 4-3.)

Even if the local labor force is limited, the supply curve reveals that new arrivals will be attracted by the high wage. Symmetrically, the bosses (without the union) would have difficulty holding the wage down to $2. An *excess demand* for 7 thousand men exists among employers at this bargain price, and they will each tend to shade their wage offers upward toward equilibrium C, in spite of their resolve to bargain together.

Most North American unions exist for *economic* betterment: to try to get not only higher wages, but also shorter hours, more vacations, fringe benefits such as pensions, and better working conditions. Such direct economic goals can, as in the diagram, be

---

[3] The chief weapons used by employers to fight unions were (1) discriminatory discharge of union members, (2) the blacklist, (3) the lockout, (4) the "yellow-dog" contract, (5) the labor spy, (6) the strikebreaker and armed guards, and (7) the "company union." More recently, employers have used the courts to fight against unions.

[4] Chapter 28, page 000, shows that this is only the second of four ways by which unions can attempt to raise wages.

[5] A very tough union might even impose on a monopolistic group of employers an all-or-nothing bargain at U': 12 thousand jobs at $5, or shut down forever. This would probably put some weak employers out of business.

thought of as a form of wage, having a money cost to the employer and a money value to the worker. The formal analysis here, stemming from Chapter 4 and developed fully in Chapter 29, indicates how industrial relations can be visualized. At least in part, the union attempts to operate on the employers' demand curve; the employers' association tries to work on the supply curve.

OTHER GOALS While economic goals are the major preoccupation and reason for the existence of unions today, unions do also still perform purely social functions. Unions may back blood drives and charities, start cooperative stores, credit unions, and scholarship funds. Indeed unions may fill the lives of some members just as churches, lodges, and junior leagues occupy others. (This is not to deny that a co-worker down the line may never do more than pay his union dues; or that still another non-union worker, whose wage is nevertheless determined by collective bargaining, may detest the whole idea of organized labor.)

POLITICS Canadian unions, like many European and unlike most American unions, have from earlier days carried this habit of group action beyond the quest for direct benefits and self-help into politics. For example, instead of merely a neutral and dutiful interest in "civic betterment," a frequent committee activity of American unions, Canadian unions have often nominated "Labor" candidates in municipal and school-board elections. And in wider political arenas, some groupings of Canadian unions have backed various parties.

At an earlier stage, the unions were divided between support for the Liberal party and the radical parties.

Since the 1930s, however, there has been a trend toward increasing collective support for the participation in the Co-operative Commonwealth Federation (CCF) and its successor the New Democratic Party (NDP). But, unlike the British Trades Union Congress, the Canadian unions are unable to "deliver" their members' votes effectively; the political tendencies of Canadian unionists, while stronger than those of their American brothers, have not shown the unanimity and devotion that carried the British Labour party and the European Social-Democratic parties into power.

ORIGIN AND GROWTH OF THE CANADIAN LABOR MOVEMENT

EARLY CRAFT UNIONS Before Confederation, Canadian labor was organized only in a few highly skilled trades such as type-setting. The form of organization was brought with them by British immigrant workers. Sometimes, especially in boom periods, other tradesmen (often in building—carpenters and masons—and in shoemaking) either formed similar groups or joined together in local all-trades unions.

In the 1870s this tendency was magnified by contacts with new American trade (skilled workers) unions, and permanent affiliations were made with American "National" unions of iron molders, printers, and railway workers, and with one or two British building and iron-workers' societies. At the same time, the locals formed interunion local committees, later known as "Trades and Labour Councils," in Toronto, Montreal, and other cities. The steady development of these *craft* unions continued for decades, with increasing help from and affiliation with American bodies.

THE TLC Fighting off the rival "Noble Order of the Knights of Labor", (a general union of all workers originating in the U.S. which tended to avoid hard-headed bargaining and serious politics), the craft unions began to seek forms for joint action among unions. In 1886, they formed what was to become the Trades and Labour Congress of Canada (TLC), just as the Americans were forming the American Federation of Labor (AFL). Both stuck to the line established by Samuel Gompers, who helped to found and dominated the AFL from 1886 till 1924:

1. *"Business unionism,"* aiming at day-to-day higher wages and better working conditions, not engaging in the class struggle to alter the form of society. Labor was to get more and still more by evolution, not by violent revolution.

2. *Federalism,* each national union having exclusive jurisdiction over its own trade. "Dual unionism," where more than one group claimed the right to organize a region, shop or trade, was out.

3. *Voluntarism,* rejecting the interference, or the aid, of government in organization and collective bargaining.

4. *Political neutrality,* supporting candidates who helped labor, whatever their ideology.

Eventually these four principles turned out to be the dominant philosophy of the American labor movement, and so of the international unions to which the Canadian locals were attached.

INDUSTRIALISM AND RADICALISM

Gompers' principles of business unionism drew in new tradesmen from the booming industries of the 1900s. But they spawned much opposition too, along four lines:

1. *Industrial unionism* Rival organizers argued that industrial unions, uniting all the trades and jobs in one plant, were more effective than craft unions, uniting all workers of a particular skill.

2. *Catholic social philosophy* In Quebec the clergy organized workers into *syndicats,* similar to units being organized in France, Holland and Belgium. These were to embody the anti-individualist sentiments in Pope Leo XIII's encyclical *Rerum Novarum.* The *syndicats* organized mostly French-speaking, unskilled urban workers in Montreal and Quebec, and rural resource-industry workers. They thus conflicted with the TLC's older craft unions. Preferring cooperation to strikes, they formed no central federation till the 1920s, and were widely regarded by the English-speaking, Protestant unions they challenged as company unions and strikebreakers.

3. *Marxism and syndicalism* In many parts of Canada, isolated groups set up rival industrial and region-wide groups with anti-capitalist and anti-governmental aims to spice their wage objectives. Two of them, the I.W.W. (Industrial Workers of the World, or Wobblies) and the O.B.U. (One Big Union) were very successful in western Canada, and organized Winnipeg's unprecedented *General Strike* of 1919.

4. *Canadian nationalism* From time to time efforts were made to start business-like unions in opposition to the internationals. The most successful were the railway non-operating workers on the C.N.R.

Seen from 1975, what has become of these four issues?

The battle for industrial unionism is over. For twenty-five years two continent-wide congresses fought the craft-versus-industrial union battle. But by the mid-fifties, the two giant groups were willing to amalgamate, joining international unions organized on either (and some on both) principles. The CLC represents this amalgamation in Canada.

Quebec is still a battle ground. The international unions in the CLC (and its provincial Quebec Federation of Labor) are fighting for survival against the reactivated *syndicats.* Federated as the Canadian National Trade Union (CNTU), these have worked more closely together than the QFL locals, veering from year to year among a triad of ideologies: strong business unionism, political syndicalism, and French-language nationalism and even separatism. On some wage issues they have joined forces with the QFL against the provincial government. But the two are essentially rivals, and the CLC is today granting increased independence to its QFL to enable it to meet the CNTU challenge for Quebec union dominance.

Outside of Quebec, left-wing radicalism seems to have vanished from labor unions. In late-Depression and war days, the Communist Party in Canada threw enormous energy into organizing industrial unions. Many of labor's spokesmen were avowed communists, and others were fellow travellers. But middle-of-the-road unionists, and socialists, had driven them (or their unions) out of the congresses by 1957. In any case, the younger members were not interested; recruitment to the party fell off; and the newly-organized white-collar and civil service workers had other fish to fry. In the 1970s the inter-union splits have largely healed.

On the other hand, CLC membership had acquiesced in a weak affiliation with the NDP, which commits neither the separate international unions nor the individual members. It has produced some useful organizing and financial support for the NDP, although political scientists say that the union movement has not been able to deliver much more voting power to the NDP. (The situation is a little different in provincial politics.) Within the NDP, the unionist members tend to concentrate on labor-union objectives, leaving more socialist and nationalist aims to the rival "waffle" group.

Nationalism has remained a divisive issue. In the last decade, newly-formed all-Canadian unions have showed more staying power than in earlier decades, and have succeeded in winning some locals away from powerful internationals like the steelworkers and the pulp and paper union. These have responded in two ways. Some have fought back vigorously, probably reflecting the views among their Canadian leadership. Others are compromising, giving more independent status to their Canadian locals and executives. The latter decision looks like the pattern of the future.

The large new white-collar unions and civil service federations, mostly unattached to American parents, are also helping to change the tone within the CLC.

The discussion of "foreign domination" obscures an urgent internal economic question. By having the scattered 2.4 million Canadian organized labor force grouped into 4,900 locals, most of them duplicates of locals in the United States, plus some 5,500 locals of Canadian groups, Canadian labor, like Canadian business, finds itself overorganized. There are not enough members (at an average of less than 300 members per local) to undertake the leadership, bargaining, research, and political action required for the movement to flourish. Instead, hundreds of small meetings every month monopolize the time and funds of local leaders. Probably larger groups covering greater portions of industry and larger regions are indicated, but there are few signs that such regrouping is coming about. In the meantime the conservative bias of most unions, the vested interest of local officials in their positions, and the inability of the unions to adapt advantageously to technical change and automation are the result.

After a long history of strife, the union movement seems to have settled down, with only a few industrial sectors to be organized. Success may be measured by the extent to which a new breed of man moves to the top. Back in the days when unions were being born and fighting for their lives, colorful men or radical parties offered leadership. The new men who are replacing them are often educated men with gifts as *administrators*. With millions of members and literally hundreds of millions of dollars in their welfare funds, North American unions are in need of men who can administer, who can deal persuasively with politicians, management, and the public, and who can understand some of the larger issues involved. For the traditional union organizer, an important function still exists. The postal workers of Montreal bear witness to the demand for organizing

unions among restless unskilled workers and among civil servants and teachers.

HOW DEMOCRATIC ARE UNIONS?

Earlier we discussed the problems involved in democratic control by stockholders of corporation management. Similar problems arise in connection with unions. It is true that union officials are elected to office and all union members are given equal votes. But officers once elected often stay in power for a considerable time, and between annual conventions the union is usually run by a small executive group. Well-known leaders like Jean Marchand, Louis Laberge or Joe Morris have on the whole been popular with members; but a member who disagreed with the general policies they laid down would not get very far.

The average member does not participate very actively in policy formation, especially young unskilled and mobile members of large industrial locals. But the rank and file still have influence, largely negative. The professional leader, whatever his feelings about wage rates, inflation, politics, Canadianism or socialism, cannot commit members who will not follow him. In wage and working-condition matters, just as in churches, student councils, and other organizations, the leadership is continuously pressed by a more active minority. The stiffer demands they favour are backed by their threat to nominate another slate of leaders while the majority of the membership (less enthusiastic about the necessary strikes to back up such demands) are usually absent when decisions are made. As a result, the leaders tend toward the dictates of the minority, or, as frequently happens, lose their jobs.

HOW COLLECTIVE BARGAINING WORKS[6]

Let us examine how collective bargaining is carried on. Consider a production-line worker in a factory that has just been organized. A CLC union has petitioned its provincial[7] Labour Relations Board for an

[6] Chapter 29 includes a more analytical discussion of the collective bargaining process.
[7] Actually less than one million workers come under federal, rather than provincial, arrangements.

election to determine the exclusive bargaining agent in this plant. The worker marks a secret ballot in favor of the union, and it wins more votes than an existing "company union" which has no outside affiliations and which management prefers to deal with. The board then certifies the new union as the collective bargaining agent for the plant, limiting any other union from negotiating directly with management.

A day is set for the new union representatives to meet representatives of management at the bargaining table. Seated at the table may be a vice-president in charge of industrial relations, and perhaps with him a lawyer who specializes in the labor field. On the union side will be the local business agent of the union and a small committee of union officers; and, sometimes, handling the negotiations will be an expert from international union headquarters. He may be neither a lawyer nor a professional economist, but the economic research staff of the union helps him prepare an extensive brief backing up the local's demands.

Hourly wage rates are not the only issue in bargaining. In addition, the union may ask for a dues *checkoff* (whereby union dues are automatically deducted from the payroll of union members). The union may bargain for a *union shop* requiring all employees to become union members within 30 days after employment. Pension and health-insurance demands may be discussed at the bargaining table. In many industries where piece rates prevail, the structure of rates is an important subject for negotiation; the exact work load—how many looms each man will attend, and similar matters—may be discussed, and the general problem of how rapidly technological improvements shall be adopted will enter into the final contract. The seniority rights of workers and a grievance procedure for handling cases of discharge—these and many other problems will come into collective bargaining.

Indeed, management has become worried over the inroads that organized labor has been trying to make into what it regards as its prerogatives. Many employers claim they find it hard to hire whom they will, fire for just cause, determine work methods, and decide on the order in which people will be laid off. They feel that every new decision occasions a meeting of a new committee; and time that could better be spent on production must be devoted to labor relations. They claim the worker acts as if he has a right to any job he has held for some time. Such critics complain that many unions oppose incentive wage schemes, insist upon rigid seniority, discourage efficient work methods, and seriously limit the autonomy of management. Recent casebooks on collective bargaining devote more space to issues arising from the workers' and the unions' rights in jobs than to any other single subject.

But at last the agreement, covering many pages of fine print, is signed. Everything is set down including provisions for grievances that arise during the life of the contract; usually, too, there are provisions for the *arbitration* of issues that arise under it, each side agreeing in advance to accept the decision of an impartial outside arbitrator. The usual life of an agreement is one or more years, no strikes being allowed, with provisions made for reopening negotiations for a new agreement under specified conditions.

Collective bargaining is a complicated business—a matter of give and take. And of course, all may not go well. If employer resistance hardens, the management side may attempt to discredit the union or prevent its continued existence. The union may tighten up its organization, in order to make good its latent threat to strike. Union headquarters, and other employers, may intervene to keep down the heat, or to add to it. Restlessness, conflict, frustration, and even violence may flare up. The government may provide rules to channel the negotiations, and to prevent excesses, for eventually, everyone must conform to a single agreement. This in itself may be a source of restlessness. Wherever workers must perform according to decisions made elsewhere, in narrow conditions of work which they cannot understand or choose, the results are wild-cat strikes and bad relations with the employer and within the union itself. In discussing this alienation and discontent of individual workers, the recent Task Force on Industrial Relations commented:

" ... The collective bargaining process may be compounding the situation by subjecting workers to a new but equally frustrating type of subordination. While improving the worker's status *vis-a-vis* his employer, collective bargaining has trapped him in a collective set of rules and regulations which can contain him even more. Individualism can be sacrificed as easily in a bilateral system of industrial government as in a unilateral one. Workers may thus come to rebel not only against their employer and their work, but also against the very agent and process which have been introduced to protect their interests."[8]

Role of Government in Collective Bargaining

Although unions are relatively free from controls, government has played an important role in their historic development. Two hundred years ago when labor first tried to organize in England and America, the common-law doctrines against conspiracy in restraint of trade were used against their members. Well into this century, unions and their members have been convicted by courts, assessed for damages, and harassed by various injunctive procedures.

The problem for unions was to obtain recognition from employers, so that they might bargain, without at the same time becoming either a "conspiracy in restraint of trade," vulnerable to criminal proceedings, or a legal entity like a corporation open to injunctions and civil suits for damages by outraged employers. In 1892 Canadian criminal law finally removed the obstacles to employees combining and making agreements (with employers) "in restraint of trade." The civil recognition of unions appeared slowly, and is still in the process of development. A maze of "labor law" exists providing for union and management conduct at every stage of industrial relations, further complicated in Canada by the relatively minor role of the federal government (as compared with the provincial governments) in labor matters.[9]

CHANGING NOTIONS OF THE PUBLIC INTEREST Government intervention in collective bargaining is based on the theory that the general public has an interest, as well as labor and management. The first specifically Canadian formulation of this theory was embodied in the "IDI Act", the In-

dustrial Disputes Investigation Act, brought in by young William Lyon Mackenzie King in 1907.[10] Although in the next sixty years, Ottawa and the provinces were to make many experiments with labor law, the IDI principles were everywhere clearly visible. In brief, this Act replaced voluntary or non-existent labor relations with a *compulsory* sequence of meetings between union and management, before a board. Until this sequence of investigation was completed, the right to strike was suspended. Compared with the previous situation, and the legal routes being followed by other countries, the Act was unique in implying *recognition* of the union and in relying on *investigation and publicity* to help remedy any wrong or dispute. The IDI Act was a Dominion measure, and it applied only to industries (like railroads and shipping) not under provincial jurisdiction. But between its passage in 1907 and 1925, it broadened in coverage until most of the organized workers in Canada came directly under it. Following an adverse Ontario court decision in 1925, till 1939 most union negotiations were governed by a kaleidoscopic variety of provincial laws, all basically variants of the old Dominion 1907 IDI Act.

THE INFLUENCE OF THE WAGNER ACT The IDI Act and its provincial relations embodied the principle that strikes and lockouts were against the public interest. Hence the government should intervene *in disputes*. This outlook changed in response to the ideas in the (American) Wagner Act, passed in 1935. Increasingly, Canadian legislation introduced the idea that labor *organization* was in the public interest. Hence the government should intervene earlier, to assure that no workers were unrepresented by unions of their own choosing. During World War II the federal government worked out a blend of the IDI and Wagner principles, to which, after the war, most provinces on regaining labor jurisdiction added their own ingredients. Some Canadian acts make unions liable to suits, forbid secondary boycotts and sympathetic strikes, and ban the "closed shop"—an arrangement where the employer must take new employees from among union members.

---

[8] *Canadian Industrial Relations*, Report of the Task Force on Industrial Relations (Ottawa: Queen's Printer, 1969), p.98. Reproduced with the permission of Information Canada.

[9] The following paragraphs are about *collective bargaining* law. Do not forget that governments also make many laws about hours of work, safety, child labor, workmen's compensation and holidays. These laws affect the environment in which collective bargaining proceeds.

[10] King had examples from which to work, of course. The provinces had attempted to set up *voluntary* conciliation machinery earlier. King and others had applied similar machinery to railway disputes in 1900. The whole idea, including elements of compulsion, stemmed from an early New South Wales statute.

Most provinces and the Dominion now have labor relation boards, whose chief job is to certify groups as the union with whom an employer or group of employers must bargain. Thus they have to decide on sticky questions: should machinists at a mine be represented by a machinists' union, or by the industrial union that claims jurisdiction over the whole mine, including muckers, cooks, and truck drivers? Such boards also often take votes to ascertain the workers' wishes on a bargaining unit, and also to define their attitude to striking during bargaining. Provinces also have compulsory *conciliation*, sometimes superintended by the labor relations board. In nearly all provinces, striking is forbidden (1) during the life of an agreement,[11] and (2) until some mediation or conciliation procedure has been followed. Now, though, IDI-type formal conciliation boards are no longer compulsory, and the parties can proceed to a strike vote or lockout.

In Quebec a rather different system is followed. Briefly, it provides that wages and hours of work agreed upon by workers and employers in a region's industry are "extended." That is, the government "decrees" that these conditions shall be obligatory for similar firms in that district. In operation since 1934, this is actually a non-Parliamentary way of setting labor standards, since the decreed wage now amounts to a minimum wage, at least for that industry.

An unresolved problem for Canadians is the organization of civil servants and other public employees. These workers and the public long believed that it was against the public interest to allow strikes to interfere with the conduct of essential Crown functions, ranging from fighting in a war (where a strike is called mutiny) to putting out fires. But the extension of Crown functions to running railroads led to the organizing of some government employees, and the growth of urban functions led to the organizing

of municipal workers. (So that the CUPE and the PSAC are composed chiefly of public employees.) Now teachers, postmen, and white-collar workers are organized, and the civil service commissions are beginning to act like management in collective bargaining. Indeed, *de facto* collective bargaining is proceeding everywhere among public workers, and only the legal form and the right to strike are in doubt. In this respect, Canada is like most European countries, but quite unlike the United States.

CURRENT BARGAINING PROBLEMS

The key labor policy issues facing Canada in the 1970s are these:

1. Organized labor tries to improve its money wage rates, in the vain hope that this will not induce a commensurate rise in prices; hence this leaves *real wages* little or no better off. Because the strike is labor's ultimate bargaining weapon, and the right to refuse a wage increase even though this brings on a strike is the employer's ultimate weapon, work stoppages provide the headlines in labor relations.

2. In an age of rapid technical change and much talk of "automation," union men are often more concerned about pension "fringe benefits" and *job security* than about mere money wage gains. What good is a raise in pay for a job that no longer exists?

3. Modern mixed economies seem to be subject to a new disease—a tendency for anything like an approach to full employment to lead to "creeping inflation."

STRIKES   The power to strike is central to present-day collective bargaining. This power is exercised sparingly. The "per cent" curve in Figure 7-4 shows that the loss of labor-days in strikes and lockouts is growing at about the same rate as the labor force. Indeed the common cold causes more lost work than strikes do.

In Chapter 29 we shall see that, without the right to strike, a union's power to bargain would, for better or worse, be substantially altered. Although striking workers suffer heavy losses and demoralization, the strike or the power to call a strike can wring concessions from very tough employers. Yet many employers have been willing to risk the financial and trade

[11] This no-strike feature has long been a distinct part of Canadian labor law. Disagreements during the life of a contract are usually about the interpretation of the contract: seniority rules for promotion, firing and re-hiring after a close-down; unfair dismissal; whether a worker comes into one pay class or a higher one. They are invariably settled by an *arbitrator*, a mixture of investigator and judge, appointed jointly by the union and management, or sometimes by the government. In a few industries, arbitrators also take the place of conciliators, if the parties cannot agree on a new contract. But the essence of arbitration is that, unlike conciliation, both parties agree in advance to accept the arbitrator's ruling.

FIG. 7-4. Time lost from work stoppages is relatively small.
While time lost from strikes and lockouts is measured in thousands of labor-days, as a percentage of total labor-days worked, it never reached one-half of one per cent in the period 1955-1971, and it averaged 20% over this period. (Source: Canadian Department of Labour, Economics and Research Branch, *Strikes and Lockouts in Canada, 1971*.)

losses of a shutdown, and have thus resisted union demands without a strike.

When strikes involve key industries (such as steel or oil), key functions (such as communications), or are spread out across the whole country, the losses to bystanders and the general public may be much greater than to the main parties. Then it seems the rights of private property, and of "free collective bargaining" must both be subject to limitations, in the public interest; and wages must be determined by political means or arbitration.

These are not academic questions, as the police and postal strikes evidence. In fact, the government, while stating a preference for private settlement, will not let a crippling strike persist beyond the point of public safety.

The unionization of public and quasi-public workers—teachers, air controllers, firefighters, police, and defense employees—accentuates the problem of avoiding pivotal work stoppages.

PRODUCTIVITY RESTRAINTS Unions become especially concerned when new techniques or processes threaten the job security of their members. The word "sabotage" arose when laborers threw their wooden shoes (sabots) into the works of the new machines brought in by the Industrial Revolution to replace workers. "Featherbedding" refers to any rules imposed on employers merely for the purpose of keeping up the demand for workers: use of small shovels, limitation on number of bricks laid per day, requirement that use of music recordings be accompanied by a stand-by orchestra that does nothing but draw pay, requirement of a fireman (i.e., coal shoveler) on a diesel engine under the pretense that he is needed for safety reasons. Entrenched unions have power to enforce uneconomical makeshifts. The railroads have been a flagrant example. As Chapter 29 will show, there are limits on how much unions can raise wages, but their powers are particularly great in connection with dying industries.

WAGE-COST CREEPS Repeatedly we shall be discussing the problems involved in inflation. Few modern countries have been able for long to enjoy simultaneously (1) reasonably full employment and (2) reasonably stable price levels. Part of the difficulty will be found to arise in the realm of monetary and fiscal policy. Part may come from a tendency for wage rates to be sticky against downward adjustments, but only too prone to rise in excess of productivity improvements even before full employment is approached. In the words of the 1969 Report of the Task Force on Industrial Relations:

"Collective bargaining is meant to serve the economic and related interests of those who choose to make use of it, and not necessarily those of society as a whole. Although these two sets of interests may at times coincide, they may also conflict. Unrealistic expectations about the relationship between collective bargaining and the attainment of society's economic objectives should be avoided."[12]

SUMMARY

1 Labor unions occupy an important but not expanding role in our economy, in terms both of membership and of influence. Their present structure is in three layers: (*a*) local unions, (*b*) national and international unions, and (*c*) federations of unions (CLC and CNTU), the first two being the most important.

2 By the 1880s, the typical pattern of federated, gradualistic business unionism had been established. Since 1933 this pattern has been modified in the direction of *industrial* unionization of whole mass-production industries rather than relying solely upon *craft unionization* of skilled workers. Political activity has fluctuated.

3 Union *economic goals* can be represented and analyzed in supply-and-demand terms.

4 After a union has been recognized by a Labour Board as the exclusive bargaining agent, management and labor representatives meet together to negotiate a contract fixing wage rates, work conditions, productivity standards, degree of union recognition, seniority rights, and grievance procedures.

5 In 1907 the IDI Act established the system of compulsory conciliation before the right to strike.

6 Right up until the middle 1930s there was bitter opposition to unions. But finally, government swung to support collective bargaining, and since the principles of the Wagner Act (1935) were woven into federal and provincial laws, most primary and manufacturing industries have become partly unionized. The result has been easier organization but still vigorous collective bargaining between the opposing groups. After 1947 the provinces felt the laws had become one-sided in favor of labor and gradually changed the balance. Strike threats in crucial industries always invoke governmental action.

7 Aside from strikes and featherbedding, a major post-World War II problem has been the relation of wage increases to the price level. If patterns of "successive rounds of general wage increases" are established that go far beyond the 2 or 3 per cent yearly increase in productivity, then the price level is almost sure to rise in an inflationary manner and "cost-push" inflation will become a serious problem—as we shall see in Chapter 19.

---

[12] *Canadian Industrial Relations*, Report of the Task Force on Industrial Relations Ottawa: Queen's Printer, 1969), p. 112. Reproduced with the permission of Information Canada.

CONCEPTS FOR REVIEW

national and local union	strike, lockout, work stoppage
CLC and CNTU federations	labor relations boards, recognition,
UAW, USA, CBRT	conciliation, arbitration
collective bargaining	IDI, Wagner Acts
business versus revolutionary unionism	featherbedding
craft versus industrial unions	wage-cost push on prices
excess supply and excess demand	automation and occupational trends

QUESTIONS FOR DISCUSSION

1. Describe the structure of organized labor. Describe the layers of the union movement. Which are the largest unions in your locality?
2. Until the middle 1930s, American and Canadian unions followed the "craft" principles associated with Samuel Gompers. What are these? How have they been modified since the 1930s? What factors explain why Canadian labor has been more active in politics than American labor, but less active than European labor?

8
THE ECONOMIC ROLE
OF GOVERNMENT EXPENDITURE
AND REGULATION

Democracy is the recurrent suspicion that more than half the people are right more than half the time.
E. B. WHITE

Government plays an increasing role in the modern mixed economy. This is reflected in (*a*) the quantitative growth of government expenditure, (*b*) redistribution of income by the state, and (*c*) direct regulation of economic life. We survey these in this chapter. In the next chapter we survey government taxation and provincial and local finance. Part Two will study how government fiscal (tax and expenditure) policy helps achieve full employment and fights inflation. In Part Six we analyze government's role in the fights against discrimination, inequality and environmental blight.

THE GROWTH OF GOVERNMENT EXPENDITURE

Before World War I, federal, provincial, and municipal government expenditure amounted to little more than one-tenth of our whole national income. During World War II, it became necessary for the government to consume about half of the nation's greatly expanded total output. In this century, the outlay on all government activities in Canada rose from half a billion dollars spent in 1913 to about 50 billion dollars per year in the mid-1970s.

For more than a century, Canadian income and production have been rising. Over the same long period, in almost all countries and cultures, the trend of government spending has risen even faster. Each period of emergency—each war, each depression, each epoch of enhanced concern over poverty or discrimi-

nation has shifted government activity to a higher trend line; for as U.K. economists Peacock and Wiseman have argued, spending seems never to return to previous trends after such "displacements". (But Toronto's Richard Bird, in 1970, denied that these displacement shifts were observable for Canada; he perceived only slow steady trends.)[1]

Is the end in sight? While many observers complain of the growth of government, the rate of growth has certainly faltered, if it is compared to the gross national product (as it should be, to allow for changes in size of the economy and increases in the price level). Figure 8-1 shows the historical trend of total government expenditure in the mid-20th century, relative to GNP. That rich countries do tend in one period, to spend more on government than do poor countries is shown by Figure 8-1. That Canada spends more than her poorer self in the Confederation period a century ago is shown by the fact that in Figure 8-2 today's top line of 35 per cent was, back then, about 7; like Nigeria today!

These facts about public finance make clear the increasingly important economic role of government. Note that mixed economies, such as Sweden, France, and (supposedly *laissez-faire*) Germany spend relatively more on government. And these happen to be the kinds of nations which have shown the greatest growth and progress in recent decades. Contrary to the "law" enunciated by Australia's Colin Clark— that taxing more than 25 per cent of GNP is a guar-

[1] Richard M. Bird, *The Growth of Government Spending in Canada*, Canadian Tax Foundation, Toronto, 1970.

antee of quick disaster—the modern welfare state has been both humane and solvent.[2]

THE GROWTH OF GOVERNMENT INTERVENTION AND REGULATION

The increase in collective expenditure is only part of the story. Besides larger direct participation by government in national production, there has been a vast expansion in its laws, regulations, and executive fiats governing economic affairs.

Perhaps the North American frontier in the nineteenth century came as close as any economy ever has to that state of *laissez-faire* which Carlyle called "anarchy plus the constable." The result was a century of rapid material progress and an environment of individual freedom. There were also periodic business crises, wasteful exhaustion of irreplaceable natural resources, racial and sexual discrimination, extremes of poverty and wealth, corruption of government by vested interest groups, and at times the supplanting of self-regulating competition by monopoly.

No longer does modern man seem to act as if he believed "That government governs best which governs least." Gradually, and in the face of continuing opposition, the powers of government were interpreted broadly and used to "secure the public interest" and to regulate the economic system.

POLITICAL EVOLUTION With the passage of time, the radical doctrines of one era became the accepted and even reactionary beliefs of a later era. Legislation was expanded to include minimum-wage laws; Workmen's Compensation laws (1910); unemployment insurance, old-age pensions, public subsidy for medical care; maximum-hour laws for children, women, and men; regulation of factory conditions, compulsory collective bargaining, and

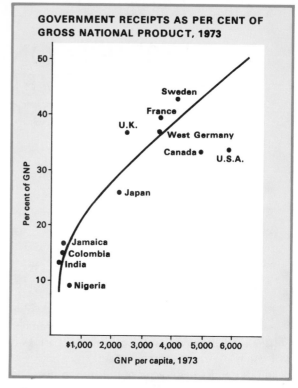

FIG. 8-1. Government's share of national product is greatest in wealthy, developed lands.
Governments of poor, less developed countries show a tendency to tax and spend less, relative to GNP, than advanced countries. (Sources: IMF; UN; Richard Musgrave, *Fiscal Systems*, 1969. Table 5-1; curve fitting and updating by authors.)

fair-labor-relations acts. And, as the authority of government expanded, so did the activities of its own departments (and Crown corporations). Not only the army and the post office, but also the CNR, a short-lived merchant fleet, the CBC, Air Canada, the Wheat Board, and Polymer Rubber were founded by the federal government; a large number of provincial and municipal undertakings were started, and new ones are initiated every year. Private property is never wholly private, individual enterprise rarely individual, and free enterprise not completely free.

To understand this trend toward all-pervasive government, one must acquire a certain historical perspective. Each new step generated strong political feelings on both sides. Thus much of the 1937 CCF (NDP) platform, which would today cause no flut-

---

[2] When account is taken of high Canadian per capita incomes, our government share is a modest one. Still we raise a larger fraction from personal income taxes than does a country like France. Studying the pattern among scores of countries reveals that the share of government tends to be least at low income per capita and where foreign trade—which is an easy object to tax in poor nations—is relatively unimportant. Exceptions remain, e.g., the low portion for the Caribbean countries compared with those of South America.

tering of pulses, was once considered dangerously radical. Canada cannot, and would not if it could, return to the conditions of the nineteenth century, as recalled by reconstructed pioneer villages and the old Ontario school reader. Still, it would be wrong to think these historical processes inevitable. The role of government is never stable.[3]

The next decade may see a decline in government control of those services in which people now feel the state must intervene. Society may, as with the post office, even reverse its preferences for public ownership.

FEDERAL, PROVINCIAL, AND MUNICIPAL FUNCTIONS

Although in 1867 it was expected that the provinces and municipalities would do most of the government spending, by 1870 Ottawa already did more than half. By the turn of the century, however, the municipalities and the provinces had developed more duties and more sources of revenue, and the federal share fell to 38 per cent. The federal government did little more than pay for national defense, meet pensions and interest on past wars, finance a few public works, and pay the salaries of judges, legislators, and other government officials. Almost all its tax collections came from liquor and tobacco excises and particularly from tariff duties levied on imports. Life was simple. Municipal governments performed many functions and depended primarily on property taxes for their finance.

Interrupted by World War I, the relative decline of federal spending continued till at least 1933. Figure 8-2 shows that in the late Depression the federal government began to spend more on goods and services. Transfer payments[4] (mostly welfare, plus interest on the public debt) bulged. The war costs of 1939-41 kept Ottawa ahead of the provinces and deflated transfers. But at the same time, the provinces began to grow in needs and power; so that today pro-

vincial and municipal spending on goods and services exceeds federal spending. (In most years since the 1920s, the municipalities have spent slightly more than the provinces, but the proportions have been close. Good data are not available for the period before the 1920s.)

FEDERAL, PROVINCIAL AND LOCAL EXPENDITURES The Canadian federal government is by far the biggest business in the country. It buys more typewriters and more steel, meets a bigger payroll, and handles more money than any other organization. The numbers involved are so large that they convey no meaning to the human mind. (When the detailed spending of the departments he controlled in the King and St. Laurent governments were queried in Parliament, C. D. Howe snapped, "What's a million?" His answer outraged MPs and the press, but they would be calmer today. The mere translation of such Parliamentary proceedings now costs well over a million a year.)

We all know what it means to be a mile from home, but the assertion that the sun is 93 million miles from the earth or that there are enough molecules in a glass of water to make a string of pearls from here to kingdom come always leaves us unimpressed. Perhaps public expenditure will have more meaning if we remember that each billion dollars amounts to about $45 per Canadian man, woman, and child. A current federal annual budget of about 14 billion dollars would be equivalent, then, to about $600 per capita—just over one month's income for the average Canadian family. In the main, the cost of past and future wars accounted for the greatest percentage of expenditure in the past: in the 1950s, when today's students were children, defense, veterans' services, and debt together amounted to *half* of all spending. Today, however, they have fallen to about one-third of federal outlays, slightly less than health, welfare and pensions. General payments to *other* levels of government have gone down because the provinces now collect their own direct taxes through the federal tax collector, instead of depending on their former grants, handed out by Ottawa. Other important items include aid to farmers and to transportation; and all additional costs of a central government: civil servants, diplomats, courts, clerks, Parliament itself.

---

[3] For a discussion on the proper scope of government, see a Swarthmore College debate between George J. Stigler and P. A. Samuelson in P. A. Samuelson, *Readings in Economics* (McGraw-Hill, New York, 1973), 7th ed.

[4] Transfer payments are defined as those government expenditures or payments made outright to the recipient and not in return for current production of goods and services. They are discussed on pages 139-141 of this chapter.

PROVINCIAL AND MUNICIPAL But it is in the provincial and municipal budgets that the real growth is taking place. As Fig. 8-2 showed, provincial and municipal expenditure on goods and services are nowadays together equal to *twice* federal expenditure. This is not surprising when you remember that all the problems of urban growth, roads, hospitals, schools, (and the payment of interest on debt on these subjects from past capital projects) are provincial and local responsibilities. No rule is permanent, but Canadian experience, since the 1890s, seems to have been as follows: in periods of population growth and land development, the financial onus is on the provinces and the cities; but in periods of war and high unemployment, the federal government becomes the chief spender.[5]

THE FIVE CHANGING ACTIVITIES OF GOVERNMENT

The last quarter of a century has witnessed great political changes. How great have been the economic changes? How great have been the departures from the traditional capitalistic system? We can tackle these questions by considering government activity under five headings:

DIRECT CONTROLS First, as noted, there has been an increase in the amount of government *control.* Much of this regulation can hardly be dignified by the title of "planning", and market prices still run most activities. Economic analysis of government intervention in the marketplace deserves detailed discussion and will be met in later chapters.

SOCIAL CONSUMPTION OF PUBLIC GOODS Second, as we have also seen, the increase in government expenditure means that as a nation we are consuming more of our national product *socially* rather than individually through private money purchases. Rather than pay to ride on the public roads as we do to ride on railroads, we pay for such valuable services by taxes.

Note that socially-consumed goods and services are largely *produced* by private enterprise. The government pays for a hospital or typewriter, but these are produced by a business firm. And so it is with most government expenditure on productive goods. This is not what the original socialists meant by socialism—government ownership and operation of factories and land.[6]

STABILIZING FISCAL AND MONETARY POLICY As will be seen in Parts Two and Six, a third important function performed by modern governments involves the control of runaway price inflation and the prevention of chronic unemployment and stagnant growth. Two principal weapons are used: monetary and fiscal policy.

A central bank—which is a bank for bankers and which is given the power to issue currency—either is directly in the executive branch of government or, more commonly, is set up as a public nonprofit organization ultimately responsible to the legislature. We shall study how our version of it, the Bank of Canada, exercises *money and credit policies* in the interest of high production and price stability.

Since the beginning of recorded history, governments have had constitutional authority over money. But only in the last 40 years has it become widely recognized that *fiscal policy* of government—*variations* in expenditure and tax totals, which create a surplus or deficit rather than a balanced budget—has profound effects on unemployment, total production, money and real incomes, and on the level of prices. Bad fiscal policy can make the business cycle worse. Stabilizing fiscal policy can moderate the ups and downs of business. Now that governments are large, claiming to have *no* fiscal policy is like claiming to be dead: left to themselves, budgets will definitely not balance; a policy of trying to balance the budget in every month, year, decade, or over the whole business cycle involves deliberate (and rash!) social choice.

Chapters 13, 14, 17 and 18 will study monetary and fiscal policy in depth.

GOVERNMENT PRODUCTION There has been continued expansion in this fourth direction in recent decades. Historically, our government has performed certain direct productive operations, and not others. The post office has long been a function

---

[5] This is an important subject. For more information, see the *Canada Year Book*, or obtain *The National Finances*, published annually by the Canadian Tax Foundation.

[6] See the discussion of socialism, communism, and fascism in the Appendix to Chapter 2.

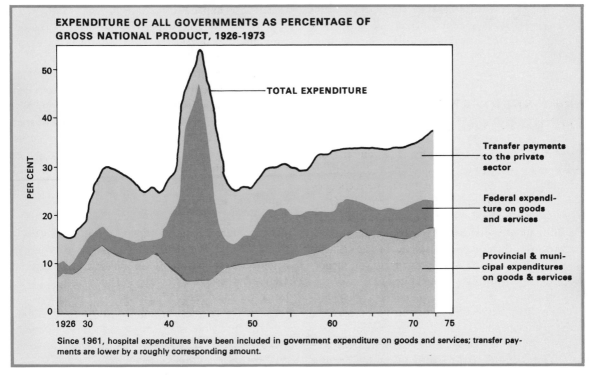

EXPENDITURE OF ALL GOVERNMENTS AS PERCENTAGE OF GROSS NATIONAL PRODUCT, 1926-1973

TOTAL EXPENDITURE

Transfer payments to the private sector

Federal expenditure on goods and services

Provincial & municipal expenditures on goods & services

Since 1961, hospital expenditures have been included in government expenditure on goods and services; transfer payments are lower by a roughly corresponding amount.

FIG. 8-2. Transfer payments and municipal and provincial expenditures are the most rapidly growing expenditures.

Federal expenditure began to rise in the Great Depression, and increased even more during the war. Defense spending has contracted during recent years and development and welfare spending of provinces, urbanization problems, and the increased decentralization of the whole federation have combined to make Ottawa's share less than half of total government expenditures. (Source: *The National Finances* and Economic Council of Canada, *Sixth Annual Review.)*

of government, while we have (since World War I) divided the management of railroads, telegraphs, airlines, and even pipelines between public and private corporations. Airports are usually publicly owned but bus terminals are private. The federal government provides most wharfs and harbors; provincial governments own many hydro and telephone systems; and municipalities run water utilities and street transport systems.

The reasons for drawing the line at one place rather than another are partly historical and are to some degree changing; but, economically, the distinction is not completely arbitrary, as we saw in connection with developmental enterprises. Again, the legislatures have decided that, in the special case of "public utilities affected with public interest," there is limited possibility of effective competition among

many independent producers, and so they must be publicly regulated or owned; but one would not expect the production of soap to be a natural candidate for governmental operation.

In connection with this fourth category, which involves the use of human and other resources directly by the government, we should recognize that there has been a substantial rise of the federal payroll and in the number of government employees.

WELFARE AND TRANSFERS Fifth and finally, we turn to an activity of government that has expanded tremendously since 1929 and that will continue to loom large in the decades ahead, namely, government *welfare payments*, which transfer purchasing power to the needy or worthy without regard to their providing a service in return. This category of transfer expenditures deserves further discussion (just below). Because of their magnitude, our whole mixed economy is sometimes called the "welfare state".

TRANSFERS AND TAXES IN THE WELFARE STATE

Transfer payments are mostly made to veterans, old people, the handicapped, and unemployed people. It is important to understand that government cheques received by such people differ economically from those received by civil servants or government suppliers. In our later discussions of national-income accounting, the difference will show up again: the former are not counted as national income or output, but simply as "transfers." The latter are part of national income.

Government expenditures (a) do cover services rendered; (b) do use up resources and national production; and (c) do provide direct or indirect collective consumption to the Canadian community as a whole. However financed (by taxes, sale of postage stamps, or otherwise) the dollars are spent to provide services for public use. In this they are like dollars used by a large railroad to provide passenger services. Both flows of dollars are part of national income.

Transfer payments are something else again. Socially, they may be some of our most desirable expenditures, but nevertheless they are not part of national output or national income. Why? As an example, let us consider a blind widow's pension. (a) The widow does not render any concurrent services to the government or its citizens in exchange for the pension. (b) She does not provide any labor, land, or capital, or current national production in exchange for the pension. (c) Her pension is for her own enjoyment and not for the collective consumption of the public. It is true that the pension does increase her purchasing power, does permit her to live more adequately and to buy goods and services from other individuals. These goods and services *that she buys* are part of the national income and output; but they are *attributable* to (and have already been counted as the output of) the people and private factories that have produced them, not to her or the government.

Transfer expenditures have grown greatly in recent years. They grew partly as a result of the Depression, which made relief expenditures necessary, but they grew mostly because new minimum standards of health, nutrition, and security have been set up by the collective conscience of the Canadian people. Society now rules that children shall not have rickets because of the bad luck or weakness of their parents; that poor people shall not die young because of insufficient money for operations and needed care; that the old shall live out their years with some minimum of income. Current discussion of "guaranteed annual income" or a "negative income tax" reflects this view.

Do welfare payments expand the public sector of the economy? We shall later see that, "on the first round," these payments do not directly consume goods and services; but by swelling the purchasing power of their recipients, they do create orders and jobs for the business sector "on the second round." The thing to note is that *the production induced by this respending is probably both privately produced and privately consumed*.

Unless these payments are financed by new money creation or by bond borrowing, larger taxes will have to be levied on the public, and it is in recognition of this link between taxpayers and welfare recipients that they are called "transfer payments."

In connection with welfare programs of the government, mention should be made of the fact that various *redistributions* of income among citizens are also accomplished *by the form in which the government allocates the burden of the taxes it levies* on different groups and classes. The next chapter shows that there is a tendency in modern states for the well-to-do to be taxed absolutely and relatively more heavily than those below the median income level.

Thus, suppose there were no program of direct governmental transfers. But suppose the government made the very rich pay all the taxes for national defense and most of the taxes for civilian programs. Is it not evident, then, that it would be altering the distribution of the after-tax disposable incomes that different classes have to spend on bread, cars, and anything else?

One must include in the activities of the modern welfare state both programs of *transfer payments* to be spent by pensioners and those on assistance and *redistributions of income* brought about by arranging that the higher income classes will bear the bulk of the tax burden.

For the rest of this chapter we shall try to use the tools of economic analysis developed earlier to understand the nature of the various governmental programs already surveyed.

GRAPHICAL ANALYSIS OF GOVERNMENT ACTIVITY[7]

The production-possibility concept of Chapter 2, particularly Fig. 2-4 gives insight into the nature of government activity. Fig. 8-3(a) indicates further how society can choose between (*a*) *private goods* (bread, shoes, haircuts), which families buy voluntarily out of their after-tax incomes at prices set by markets, and (*b*) *public goods* (destroyers, services of policemen and civil servants, weather forecasts, cleanup of Lake Erie), which we consume collectively and which involve government expenditure (financed by taxes, deficit borrowing, printing of money).

What determines the actual E_1' position, which represents about one-quarter of the toal product devoted to *public goods* and three-quarters to *private?* It is legislative decision that puts E_1' where it is and also determines the exact composition of the social expenditure as divided between the three levels of government.

What about the composition of the private sector at the point E_1'? On reflection, one realizes that it does indeed depend on governmental decision making, but only in the following respects: (1) Welfare transfers by government help to determine the distribution of spending incomes of people in the private community, money which they can spend voluntarily for different goods in the market. (2) Tax legislation by our representatives decides how to allocate the tax burden among different individuals

and classes; such decisions impinge in a similar way on the allocation, in the background, of E_1''s *private goods* among persons.

Aside from transfer and tax influence, the private consumption of goods is determined by voluntary market decisions of individuals—as they decide to buy white rather than rye bread, beef rather than pork, boats rather than autos, and Scotties rather than Kleenex.

Suppose international tension ended, thereby permitting us to cut down greatly on government expenditure and on taxes so as to leave people with more money to spend individually. Provided the economic system were made to run smoothly without temporary or permanent unemployment, you should be able to show that the point E_1' would then move down the *p-p frontier* curve toward more private and less social spending.

Suppose the electorate agrees with Galbraith's *The Affluent Society*, and decides it would prefer to enjoy less private consumption of cars and other things and enjoy more social consumption of public goods like roads and hospitals. You should be able to show the upward and leftward movement of E_1' as it climbs the production-possibility frontier.

WASTE IN GOVERNMENT AND SCOPE

Our diagram helps to disentangle a common confusion. Government expenditure can be reduced in two quite different ways: First, the people can succeed in making their public activities more *efficient*. They can abolish graft and waste and insist on better planning of programs and on more efficient administration. This is sometimes called "cutting out fat without cutting muscle."

Second, they can change the *scope* of government, reducing public expenditure by having the government drop many of the functions it performs. The government can build fewer roads, provide less weather information, cease to do research, abandon conservation activities, and so forth. Fig. 8-3(b) helps keep the problem of efficiency in government distinct from the problem of scope of government. Its move from E_1 out to E_2 on the *p-p frontier* shows the result of a successful program of increasing the *efficiency* of government activity: we can now get the same quantity of government goods and services for

---

[7] The next two sections are separable from the rest of the chapter. A complete distinction between the economist's narrow category of public (social) goods, that are *collectively consumed*, and the mixture of social and private goods that are actually provided in the public sector, is postponed until later in this chapter.

Cutting out waste is not the same as cutting scope of government.

FIG. 8-3(a). Along society's production-possibility frontier giving choices between private and public expenditure on goods and services, we begin at a point such as E_1'.

FIG. 8-3(b). Cutting out waste and increasing governmental efficiency take society from E_1, inside the *p-p frontier*, out to it. This permits the previous level of government to be reached at E_2 with less sacrifice of private goods. (Cutting down on scope without change in efficiency would mean, however, moving inside the frontier down to E_3.) At E_4 the populace has decided to allocate the new affluence that efficiency has brought among new extra goods of both private and governmental type.

less sacrifice of resources from the private economy. If the electorate wants to leave the scope of government unchanged, E_2 the new point will be due right of old point E_1, with same G_1 level of social consumption but with private goods now increased as shown.[8]

As an alternative to the above case, suppose people succeed in reducing government expenditure solely by cutting down on the *scope* of government activity. Then there will have been no change in efficiency. Inside the frontier, the nation moves down and to the right of E_3.

Consider still another alternative. Suppose everyone favors efficiency and we do succeed in getting out to the *p-p frontier*. But now the electorate decides it will use its greater affluence for *both* private and additional social wants. If it decides to spend its extra income on something from both categories, then it

[8] This might have come about in the background in something like the following way: the savings in efficiency resulted in tax reductions large enough to give people the extra income sufficient to use up all the resources released by the government.

will move up and to the right to the point marked E_4.[9]

SOCIAL AND PRIVATE WANTS: EXTREME *LAISSEZ-FAIRE*

Let us return from graphs to the basic issues. *Why is governmental use of goods and services ever required at all?* What light can economic analysis

[9] Recall the alleged law that no government can tax and spend more than 25 per cent of the national income without creating disaster; or that the increase of the public sector for defense, public works, education, and free hospital services has gone as far as our country can stand economically. If there were an absolute real limit, the transformation curves would have a corner at about E_1 and would move off horizontally to the left. There appears to be no evidence of any such discontinuity. The possibility that inflation might be the consequence of going northwest of some critical E point is a quite different argument; after study of Part Two, one can appraise such an allegation. Fig. 38-2 will discuss the fact that as society taxes to transfer from private to social consumption, some distortions of incentives and efficiency are likely to result; in changing the division of the pie, you may *alter its size*. This constitutes one of the genuine costs of government, and sensible electorates will want to give it due weight in deciding whether this should lower or expand government's proper scope.

throw on the need for the five activities of government ennumerated on pages 138-139?

In the first place, suppose all goods could be produced efficiently by perfectly competitive enterprise at any scale of operations. And suppose that all goods were like loaves of bread, the total of which can be definitely divided up into separate consumptions of different individuals, so that the more I consume out of the total, the less you consume. And suppose that there were neither altruism toward other people nor envy of them. And suppose that each person had equal initial access to human and natural resources, had equal opportunity in every sense, and could carry on his activities independently of others, much as in pioneer days.

If *all* these idealized conditions were met, would there be any need whatsoever for a mixed economy or any government functions at all? Indeed, why speak of "a society" at all, since the world could then be regarded as an array of independent atoms with absolutely no organic connections among them? Clearly, such a case of zero government is at one extreme pole.

Yet even in this minimal case, if there were to be a division of labor between people and regions, and if a pricing system such as that described in Chapters 3 and 4 and in Part Three were to work, the need would soon grow for government courts and policemen to ensure honesty, fulfillment of contract, nonfraudulent and nonviolent behavior, freedom from theft and from external aggression, and guarantee of the legislated rights of property. This would be *laissez-faire* with minimal government—and a very good system it might be if the ideal conditions presupposed for it could ever exist.

SOCIAL WANTS IN REAL LIFE

Each and every one of the idealized conditions enumerated above is lacking in some degree in real life as mankind has always known it. Abilities, opportunities, and ownership of property exhibit disparities, depending on biological and social history. Further, it is a fact that many kinds of production can take place most efficiently only in units too large for "perfect competition" as defined exactly by the economist; and many other imperfections mar the simplicity of the supposition.

All this forms the subject of analysis throughout this book—analysis designed to provide perspective for the important compromises that a free society must make. But here, in a chapter on public expenditure, we shall concentrate on the factors that call for governmental activity.

MERIT WANTS Why do we let people generally decide what shoes they will buy with their own money, but not what heroin or LSD? Evidently, just as we believe that children of six years of age are to be second-guessed in their buying decisions, we also *paternalistically* overrule some private adult decisions. Usually, this is done sparingly and only with great hesitation: an adult in good mental health is generally assumed to be free to make the best decision on *his* own wants, needs, and desires.

Before Rousseau, children were treated as if they were little adults (as old paintings will reveal). Since Freud, we realize that as adults we are still only grown-up children—still imperfect beings subject to error, regret, and myopia.

Thus, children's allowances are given in Canada to the mother rather than the father, in the hope that more of it will be spent on milk rather than beer. Again, why do we give the needy below-cost or free hospital services, rather than give them cash to spend either on operations or on TV sets, as they wish?

Clearly, all economies—free, mixed, or controlled —have some sector of what Harvard's Richard Musgrave calls "merit wants." To promote merit wants, government does in a degree exercise paternalism (or, for that matter, maternalism)—taxing cigarettes, forbidding dangerous drugs, subsidizing health care and old-age retirement provision.

Milton Friedman and Beatrice Webb will naturally differ on the optimal degree of such activities—the former advocating freedom of an addict to (quietly!) commit slow suicide, the latter telling families how they should allocate their basic consumption. But there never has been an economy in which merit wants are either completely absent or completely dominant.

PUBLIC GOODS. Let us consider national defense as an example *par excellence* of public goods. Nothing is more vital to a threatened society than its security. But national defense, regarded as a commodity, differs completely from the case of a private commodity like bread. Ten loaves of bread can be divided up in many ways among individuals in a group. But national defense has to be provided more or less automatically in the same amount for all. Most individuals will appreciate it, much as they appreciate quantities of bread; but even among them some would be more willing to give up more bread, if necessary, for a given level of defense than others would. Some, who are pacifists, will aver that defense expenditure does not interest them particularly; while still others may sincerely experience pain from this social good and would require much bread to bribe them into voluntarily voting for national defense.

Could market *laissez-faire*, with no political voting and coercion, give the group the national defense desired by the majority? Evidently not. If I knew that I was going to be protected anyway by the defense you had paid for, why should I come into the market place and exercise a dollar demand for it? Patriotism would of course motivate me; but it would show itself in the way that I and my neighbors *voted in elections* and in the way we acquiesced to the coercive fiats legislated by our responsive government, rather than *in our day-to-day private purchasing*.

To be sure, the example of national defense is a dramatic and extreme case. But when you think of the night policeman, the presiding judge, the appropriation for a park concert, or the damming of a river upstream to prevent floods downstream—indeed, when you think of government activities in general—you find the same common element:

The benefits from a public or social good, unlike those from a purely private good, are seen to involve *external consumption effects on more than one individual*. By contrast, if a good can be subdivided so that each part can be *competitively* sold separately to a different individual with no external effects on others in the group, it isn't a likely candidate for governmental activity.

In Parts Three and Six, much more will be said about external effects: so-called "external *diseconomies*," such as the smoke from my factory chimney which contaminates the air for all; and "external economies," such as the advantage your fruit trees get from the straying bees I raise to help pollinate my own fruit trees. It is enough here to give examples of government activities justifiable because of external effects.

Take our earlier case of a lighthouse to warn against rocks.[10] Its beam helps everyone in sight. A businessman could not build it for a profit, since he cannot claim a price from each user. This certainly is the kind of activity that government would naturally undertake. It would meet Abraham Lincoln's test: "The legitimate object of government is 'to do for the people what needs to be done, but which they can not, by individual effort, do at all, or do so well, for themselves.'"

Or take the case of government provision of research on wheat farming. No one competitve farmer is large enough; and he also knows he cannot retain the monetary advantage of the research financed by him. Nevertheless, there is a great benefit to the group and to society from learning about and adopting any improvements that might be uncovered by research on farming. As a result of these considerations, because of a clear *externality* in the use of knowledge, no prudent private firm can be expected to invest its scarce dollars up to the point of best advantage to the group as a whole.[11] Therefore governmental activity in this area, whether in its own laboratories or by commissioning of private university research, may well be a desirable act of representative democracy. (Where a government project, like an atomic pile, involves external *dis*economies, policy makers will have to take them into account.)

This concludes our brief economic analysis of the essential reasons for government activities, and of

---

[10] The analysis of this section owes much to the nineteenth-century analysis of the Scandinavian Knut Wicksell and other economists and to the important treatise by Richard A. Musgrave, *The Theory of Public Finance* (McGraw-Hill, New York, 1959). In the lighthouse example, one thing should be noticed: the fact that the lighthouse operators cannot appropriate a fee, in the form of a purchase price from those it benefits, certainly helps to make it a suitable social or public good. But even if the operator were able —say, by radar reconnaissance—to claim a toll from every nearby user, that fact would not necessarily make it socially optimal for this service to be provided like a private good at a market-determined individual price. Why not? Because it costs society zero extra cost to let one extra ship use the service; hence any ships discouraged from those waters by the requirement to pay a positive price will represent a social economic loss—even if the price charged to all is no more than enough to pay the long-run expenses of the lighthouse. If the lighthouse is socially worth building and operating—and it need not be—a more advanced treatise can show how this social good is worth being made optimally available to all, (particularly in Fig. 31-2).

[11] Unless it can *patent*, and keep to itself, the rights to produce and sell a new seed or machine.

the forms these activities take. In Part Three the discussion will go beyond the questions of government finance and will develop the economic principles that determine when a government might prudently intervene in *laissez-faire* to restrain monopoly, regulate it where it is inevitable, and use tax or subsidies to offset distorting external diseconomies and economies. The next chapter will discuss public finance as it relates to the tax systems of the federal, provincial, and local governments and will discuss expenditures of the provinces and localities and their coordination with the federal government.

SUMMARY

1 The economic role of government has been a generally expanding one. More and more activities in our complex, interdependent society have been coming under direct regulation and control. Five types of activity are stressed.

2 A larger fraction of the total output here and abroad has been going to collective consumption of *public* rather than *private* goods.

3 An increasing part of the national income is being *transferred* by taxation and government welfare expenditure from the relatively rich to the relatively poor.

4 There has been in Canada a trend towards state ownership of industry and society's means of production. Yet there has been little detailed "planning".

5 After World War I, federal expenditure increased more rapidly than provincial and municipal expenditure. During the Depression of the 1930s, expenditures on relief, public works, and similar matters expanded the federal budget. But the postwar budget remained many times the size of the prewar levels because of increased defense and development outlays, interest on the public debt, and welfare payments.

6 Provincial and municipal expenditures have been rising since the Second World War: the principal items are education, health, highways, public welfare, and the ordinary police and safety functions of government. These budgets now *exceed* that of the federal government.

7 The production-possibility frontier of Chapter 2 can help distinguish between reducing government expenditure (*a*) by reducing government waste or (*b*) by reducing governmental scope of activity.

8 Economic analysis of private goods consumable solely by individuals points up the contrast with social *public* goods which involve "external consumption effects" on more than one individual in the group. National defense, research, law enforcement, conservation, lighthouse operation, hospital and school operation, and similar activities must pass the test of involving such "external effects" if they are to be easily justifiable as government activities or they must be defended in terms of paternalistic "merit wants".

CONCEPTS FOR REVIEW

GNP level and government spending
public debt and budget
laissez-faire versus controls
fiscal policy

welfare state, socialism
transfer expenditures
private versus public goods
paternalistic "merit wants"
efficiency and scope

QUESTIONS FOR DISCUSSION

1. Name things which government does now that it did not do in the past.
2. Between now and 1990 how would you expect the government's share in the national income to develop? Why? What factors affect your answer?
3. How much does the increasing economic cost of government reflect decreasing efficiency? How would you go about making a scientific study of this?
4. Government expenditure on goods and services represents public goods, many of which are *produced* by market-operated private enterprise." Appraise.
5. Define, giving examples, transfer payments, redistributive taxes, and welfare programs. Are hospital insurance and medical insurance, respectively, transfers?
6. Does the expansion of government functions reflect radicalism? Does conservatism logically associate itself with fewer government functions and smaller governments?
7. Prove to your own satisfaction that the very existence of "a society" indicates that some roles exist for government. What are they?

9
FINANCING GOVERNMENTS

The division of responsibilities and taxing powers is the essence of a federal state.
ROYAL COMMISSION ON TAXATION, 1966.

The previous chapter was about the five activities of government in a mixed economy, and their essential explanation. This chapter's discussion of government finance stresses taxation at the federal, provincial and local levels. Finally comes the problem of tax incidence—upon whom does the burden of each tax ultimately fall? How does the tax burden on rich and poor compare with their respective benefits from government expenditures?

ECONOMIC NATURE OF TAXATION

FINANCING REAL EXPENDITURE The state (i.e., the government) needs money to pay its bills. It gets the dollars to pay for its expenditures primarily from taxes. However, what the state really needs to build a bridge or run a lighthouse is not so much money as *real economic resources*: steel and watchmen—in short, the use of society's scarce supplies of labor, land, and capital goods.

In deciding how to tax themselves, therefore, the people are really deciding how resources needed for social wants shall be taken from all the various families and from the enterprises they own and be made available for public goods and services.

ALTERING DISTRIBUTION OF INCOMES The State also spends on *welfare transfers*, which go to particular individuals in the community for them to spend on their private needs and wants. Again, money is a veil that cloaks the *redistribution* of command over real goods and services which results from action by the state to tax some and give to others.

However, people are rarely so nearly identical. To tax unlike people we must modify the dictum of horizontal equity as follows:

If equals are to be taxed equally, there is a presumption that unequals are to be taxed unequally.

This corollary, dealing with *un*like taxpayers, raises questions about how to achieve *vertical*, instead of *horizontal*, equity. It brings back the old problems. Neither the benefit principle nor the optimal-sacrifice principle, used with this corollary, can by itself resolve society's tax-policy issues.

Imagine that Man *A* and Man *B* are alike in every respect, except that *B* is ten times richer in income and property. What does the benefit principle require? Should *B* pay the same *absolute* tax dollars for police protection as *A*? Or should he pay the same *percentage* of his income as tax to defray police expense? Or should he, his wealth requiring more police protection than *A*'s poverty, achieve fairness by paying a *larger percentage* of his income in taxes?

The general philosophy of optimal-sacrifice or redistributive taxation similarly leaves unanswered the question of the best tax formula. It is one thing to say that the rich have greater "ability" to pay taxes than the poor, that their "sacrifice" is less when they pay a dollar of taxes than when the poor pay a dollar. This still leaves open the question: *How much* differently should unequals in income be taxed? What do we mean by "vertical equity"?

The coordination of the two aims has exercised many philosophers of public finance.

PRAGMATIC COMPROMISES IN TAXATION

How many modern mixed societies tended to resolve these difficult philosophical questions? Democracies have generally adopted pragmatic solutions that will please neither the zealots in favor of benefit notions nor the zealots in favor of thoroughgoing redistributional-sacrifice notions. Modern tax systems are, in fact, an uneasy compromise.

Where various public services at the local and national levels are peculiarly for the benefit of recognizable groups, and where those groups have no special claim for favorable or unfavorable treatment by virtue of their average incomes or other characteristics, modern governments generally rely on taxes of the benefit type. Thus, local roads are usually paid for by local residents; taxes collected on gasoline may on the whole be devoted more specifically to road construction than to schools or libraries.

PROGRESSIVE AND REGRESSIVE TAXATION
On the other hand, extensive reliance has been placed on *graduated income taxes*. A man with $20,000 of income is taxed more than a man with $10,000 of income—even if the former claims to benefit very little from government expenditures. Not only does the higher-income man pay larger income tax, but he in fact pays a progressively *higher fraction* of his income. This "progressive graduation" of the rate of tax is in contrast to a strictly "proportional tax" that makes each man always pay exactly the *same proportion* of his income, and in even greater contrast to a so-called "regressive" tax, which takes a larger fraction from low incomes than it does from high.

Definition: A tax is called *proportional, progressive,* or *regressive* depending upon whether it takes from high-income people the *same* fraction of income, a *larger* fraction of income, or a *smaller* fraction of income than it takes from low-income people.

The words "progressive" and "regressive" can be misleading. They are technical terms relating to proportions that taxes bear to different incomes. They have to be appraised on their merits, and it would be wrong to read into the word "progressive" emotional overtones of being up-to-date or particularly right-minded.

A personal income tax that is graduated to take more and more out of each extra dollar of income is progressive. While many taxes on sales of goods will be seen to be regressive, the reader should know that a tax on fine wine, which only the rich can afford, might well be progressive. Even a tax that is strictly proportional on estates left at death could be pro-

gressive, since the man with twice the income tends on the average to have and bequeath more than twice the wealth.

DIRECT AND INDIRECT TAXES
Aside from their degree of progressivity, taxes can also be classified under the headings *direct* or *indirect*.

"Indirect taxes" are usually defined as taxes that are levied *against goods and services* and thus only indirectly on people. Examples: excises or sales taxes; cigarette taxes; tariff duties on imports; turnover taxes, which, in contrast to retail excises, are levied every time a farmer sells wheat to a miller and a miller sells flour to a baker and on all transactions at any stage of production; value-added taxes, which tax only the costs added at each stage of production.

"Direct taxes" are levied directly on people (e.g., income, inheritance, real property, and poll taxes).

There are, of course, many borderline cases that do not fall neatly into one category or the other. We generally associate direct and progressive taxes together; indirect and regressive (or proportional) taxes together. But there are many exceptions to such a rule: a poll tax of $2 per head is a direct tax, but a highly regressive tax in that it takes a larger fraction of income from the poor than from the rich; as mentioned, an indirect tax on cameras or rare brandy might well be more progressive than many income taxes.[1]

Modern tax systems are, to repeat, a compromise. They give some weight to benefit notions; some weight to sacrifice and redistribution notions; and, one may add, some weight to expediency and politics —and to the economic fact of life that increasing certain taxes, however favorable it looks to an ardent re-

---

[1] Throughout the world, economists today do not often use this indirect-direct distinction for analytical purposes. It was inherited from theorists of the Classical School, especially David Ricardo and John Stuart Mill (the influential nineteenth-century economist). But a clearer distinction (between income and sales tax, for example) will not do for today's political, legal, and constitutional discussions, because in some federations, nineteenth-century legal draftsmen (such as the Fathers of Confederation) assigned taxing rights between the central government and the provinces or states simply by stating that "the provinces may levy only direct taxes." Since 1867, finance ministers and judges have often debated John Stuart Mill's definition of "direct taxation." According to Mill, a direct tax is "one which is demanded from the very persons who, it is intended or desired, should pay it. Indirect taxes are those which are demanded from one person in the expectation and intention that he shall indemnify himself at the expense of another: such as the excise or customs."

distributionist, would at the same time be expected to harm people's incentives and the efficiency of society's use of resources.

FEDERAL TAXATION

The wide variety of present federal taxes[2] is indicated by Table 9-1. Of these, the first two, personal income taxes and estate taxes, bear down "progressively" more on people with higher incomes.

Sales taxes are relatively "regressive" in that they take a larger fraction of the poor man's income than they do of the rich man's.

The corporation tax is intermediate in its effects. In one way, it is progressive, since most dividend dollars do go to people of more than median income. (Although it is true that many poor widows and orphans own some shares of stock, still the total that they own is not a large fraction of all stock shares.) But to the extent that corporations can pass the tax on to the consumer in higher prices, a tax on business profits may end up being regressive or proportional.

A brief glance at the various taxes will be helpful.

SALES AND CUSTOMS TAXES

In order of regressiveness, these would probably come first, and there has long been controversy over them. Most federal regressive taxes are truly "indirect"; they are hidden among the costs of production and marketing and are completely unknown to consumers. Almost half of this revenue is raised by a general sales tax of 12 per cent at the manufacturers' level; but about one-quarter is levied as customs (import) duties and at least another quarter in special taxes on liquor, tobacco, and other "luxury" items. Prior to World War I Canada depended on the customs duty for its national revenue; even now it relies on it and other indirect taxes more than do the United States or the United Kingdom. However, economists believe this type of tax is very regressive, because many foods and fuels (which make up much of the budget of low-income families) are not exempt from it.

[2] The "progressiveness" of each of these taxes is classified according to the *Report of the Royal Commission on Taxation 1966-67* (chaired by Kenneth LeM. Carter), Vol. 2 (Ottawa, Queen's Printer).

REVENUE RECEIPTS OF FEDERAL GOVERNMENT, FISCAL/1974		
	Millions	Percent
Progressive		
Personal income tax	$ 9,000	40
Intermediate		
Corporation tax	3,100	14
Pension and Unemployment Insurance (U.I.) levies	1,700	8
Other taxes, investments, etc.	3,100	14
Regressive		
Sales and excise taxes	4,100	18
Customs levies	1,400	6
Total Revenue	$ 22,400	100

TABLE 9-1. Canada's federal government depends on income, sales and corporation taxes. (The various sources of old age security, Unemployment Insurance Commission (U.I.C.) and pension plan revenues have been assigned here to income, sales and corporate taxes. Sources: Canadian Tax Foundation, Public Accounts, *Budget Speech*, authors' forecasts.)

VALUE-ADDED TAXES

Mention should also be made of a new tax that has been widely used by the Common Market countries of Europe. The value-added tax, or VAT, as it is called for short, *collects at each stage of production:* thus, for a loaf of bread, VAT is collected at the farmer's wheat stage of production; also at the miller's flour stage of production; at the baker's dough stage; and finally, at the grocer's delivered-loaf stage.

How, then, does it differ from a so-called "turnover tax," widely used in the U.S.S.R. and by Common Market countries before VAT? A turnover tax simply taxes *every* "net sales" transaction made: wheat, flour, dough, bread. (See Appendix to Chapter 6.)

The Canadian provincial sales taxes hit sales only at the consumer level; the federal manufacturers, customs and excise taxes only the wholesale level. VAT *is* like a turnover tax in being applied at every stage, but it differs in that "materials" and other purchases from taxable firms are subtracted first. The miller is taxed on his flour minus whatever he paid for his wheat. Thus he pays only on the wage and salary cost of milling, and on the interest, rent, royalty, and profit cost of this milling stage of production. (Table 10-2 in the later chapter on national income will explain all this.)

PENSION AND UNEMPLOYMENT INSURANCE CONTRIBUTIONS

Virtually everyone must make payments or contributions for two kinds of federal income-security and retirement benefits.

1. OLD AGE AND RETIREMENT The Canada Pension Plan obtains payroll taxes of 1.8 per cent from both employers and workers, up to about $110 per year. The funds are building up from the starting year, 1966. People retiring in the mid-1970s receive up to $140 per month. (In addition to the CPP, most married pensioners can receive a basic and "escalated" supplement of about $350.[3]

The Quebec Pension Plan is similar to the CPP. Taken by itself, the CPP financing falls between the intermediate and regressive categories. Because the contributions have an upper limit, its chief impact is on low-wage earners, but the benefits are progressive.

2. UNEMPLOYMENT INSURANCE This system of contributions and benefits is very complicated to explain but is well understood by many students. Workers pay about 1.4 per cent of their wages and employers about 2.0 per cent, up to about $5.00 per week altogether. Persons laid off and unemployed can receive about $115 per week in benefits, for varying periods, after a waiting period.

CORPORATION INCOME TAXES After a corporation has paid all its expenses and reckoned its annual income, it must pay part of this "profit" to the federal and provincial governments. In 1974 a typical manufacturer must pay about 30 per cent to the federal government and about 11 per cent to his provincial government. (If his business is very small, or if he is not a manufacturer, the rates are different.)[4]

Many people think the peacetime tax rate is too high, that corporations are discouraged from venturing on worthwhile (but risky!) job-making investment projects. They argue that a small corporation would be able to grow more rapidly if it could plow back into the business what the government takes in taxes. Proponents of these views also say it is unfair "double taxation" for the government to tax corporate earnings and also to make the stockholders pay personal income taxes on the dividends received from corporations. To meet this criticism, Canada has since 1949 toned down the "double taxation" of corporate income by permitting individual taxpayers to deduct from their personal income tax 20 per cent of their Canadian dividends. This "dividend tax credit"[5] has the effect, at least on paper, of assuring that owners of the shares of small corporations pay taxes on profits only once, and pay only about 30 per cent extra tax on the earnings of large corporations.

There are some who argue that corporations should be taxed heavily, with the bigger corporations taxed at progressively heavier rates. They believe that, if government must collect large sums of money and if further increases in the personal income tax are not feasible, then a tax on corporations is better than a sales or payroll tax. Moreover, they point out that corporations do not distribute all their earnings to stockholders but retain some to be plowed back into the business. The stockholder may avoid personal income tax on these corporate savings by capital-gains loopholes, as we shall see. According to these critics, a corporation tax will at least partially remedy the situation. The problem is too complex for a final evaluation here.

THE PROGRESSIVE PERSONAL INCOME TAX

Spring used to be an unhappy season, for people had to make a lump-sum payment for taxes on the previous year's income, which had often already been spent. Now April is no longer quite so cruel a month. All through the year employers automatically withhold from each paycheque most of what we shall have to pay to the government. This puts us on a

---

[3] "Escalated" amounts are sums of money that rise annually at the same rate as the consumer price index (CPI). Other terminology: the sum may have a "cost-of-living" adjustment; it may be "indexed" to the CPI; its "real" amount may be kept constant in "1972 dollars."

[4] In wars, this and other countries have had an "excess-profits tax" on corporations and other firms in addition to the above ordinary income tax. Thus, during World War II, on all their profit they paid up to 70 per cent in taxes, some corporations being taxed 80 cents of extra dollars earned and keeping only 20 cents.

[5] A tax credit is a sum subtracted directly from one's tax bill whereas a tax exemption or deduction is a subtraction made to arrive at taxable income, on which the tax is then figured.

pay-as-you-go basis: by the end of the year our taxes are more or less all paid up.

For some two million families, with low earnings and no appreciable property income, that is all there is to it. They simply fill in a short form showing what has been earned and what has already been deducted. The government refunds any excess they have paid.

Those with sizable incomes must fill out a complex form.

How much does a typical person have to pay at each income level? As an example, a married couple with two small children may have been taxed as follows in the spring of 1974. See Figure 9-1. First he subtracted a minimum $3,600 plus standard exemptions to cover contributions to charity, medical costs, union dues, etc.; total $4,000. The remainder was "taxable income." Total tax to Ottawa and his province, is shown by the two curves on the right, which show how progressive the tax really is. If this family has only $9,000 altogether, its tax would be about $121 or 1 per cent. But if it has $50,000, its tax is about $20,000 or 40 per cent; the rate on its last income dollar is about 60 per cent.[6]

Each of the points on the horizontal axis corresponds to a "tax bracket". Note that it always pays to earn more income. This 60 per cent of the marginal $1,000 income is called the "marginal tax rate" —it finally reaches about 67 per cent on a taxable income of $100,000. No matter how much tax must be paid, some part of every extra layer of income can be kept by the taxpayer: it is never worthwhile to earn less income to save income taxes. The provincial income tax amounts to about 29 per cent of the federal tax collections. Thus it too is progressive, especially if the wife works.

Taxpayers who have some dependents, or a disability, pay less tax than do single people without disabilities. This results from exempting part of their income before taxable income is determined. While such allowances do reduce tax rates on the poor (and put many persons below the income tax level altogether), they also reduce the taxes of the rich. Indeed, the current $3,600 exemption for a wife

FIG. 9-1. The income tax schedule climbs progressively as income grows. The provincial tax is about 29 per cent of the total. This family is assumed to have $4,000 of deductions and exemptions before income "assessed" for tax begins. Note horizontal axis is on logarithmic or ratio scale. (Sources: National Revenue Dept. and Canadian Tax Foundation.)

and two children means a saving of about $2,000 in taxes for a $50,000-a-year executive, but does nothing for a family in poverty with about $5,000 in income. Those who would help the taxable poor should urge a lower tax curve for the lower income brackets (a tax credit), not income deductions and exemptions. Those who would help the really poor should urge that the curve be depressed below the axis and continued to the left to pay a *negative* income tax.

FISCAL DRAG AND INDEXATION   The proportion of Canadian tax revenue that comes from personal income tax has risen from 8 per cent in 1939-40 to 30 per cent today. This is not just because rates have gone up.

It is because the average family is now so much better off that, even at *unchanged* rates, the total collections would have more than doubled. This is best illustrated by the fact that while in 1939 7 per cent of the labor force paid taxes, today 85 per cent do.

At the same time, of course, rates have gone up (especially on the lowest incomes), and the popu-

---

[6] That is why magnates attempt not only to get much of their income in the form of dividends (which will bring in a "dividend tax credit"), but also to realize their gains as "capital gains," which may bear lower tax, or which may even go untaxed.

lation and number of earners have almost doubled. Thus, even with the same over-all structure of federal taxes, we may expect the proportion of revenue coming from personal income tax to increase steadily. This phenomenon of a large change in revenue, because of taxpayers moving into different tax brackets, is one aspect of *built-in-flexibility* in the total tax system, and will be referred to again later (sometimes as "fiscal drag").

Some of this change in revenue is not due to higher real incomes, but to inflation. Earners are rushing up the pay ladder not only with higher prices but also to higher tax rates. To aid them, the whole system has been "indexed". The tax *brackets* are raised annually at about the same rate as the consumer price index. Thus higher money wages need not mean a higher *rate* of tax.

TAXATION AND INEQUALITY The progressiveness of income tax tends somewhat to reduce the inequality of disposable income. Note how the area of the inequality on the Lorenz diagram on Fig. 9-2

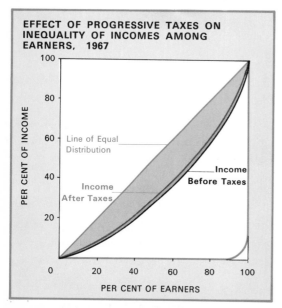

FIG. 9-2. Progressive taxes tend to reduce inequality of the distribution of after-tax incomes. The black line represents the unequal distribution of income before taxes. The curved red line to the left of it shows how progressive (or "graduated") taxes result in a more equal distribution of "disposable" income after taxes. (Source: *Taxation Statistics*, 1969.)

has been reduced; progressive taxation has shifted the curve a little nearer to the 45° line of equality. But most readers will not find the shift impressive.

LOOPHOLES AND EROSION OF THE TAX BASE On paper our tax rates look progressive. But many items in the total income base escape taxation. First, there are exemptions of $1,600 per person. Second, real income in the form of owner-occupied homes avoids taxation. Third, there is also some illegal tax evasion—cheating by farmers, doctors, waiters, or salesmen with fake expense accounts, but this is said to be surprisingly small. Fourth, more important than evasion is legal tax *avoidance*, which is possible because Parliament has permitted so many tax "loopholes" that allow large amounts of income to go untaxed or to be taxed at lower levels. For example, certain industries, especially mining and petroleum, are given handsome tax exemptions. The single largest tax loophole is the fact that any capital gains I realize on the sale of an asset above its original cost is more lightly taxed than is ordinary income.

If loopholes were closed and the erosion of the tax base corrected, rates on all income levels could be reduced without revenue loss.

Here are a few facts. Less than two-thirds of all true income is included in the tax base. Those with incomes of over 1 million dollars do not in fact pay an over-all rate of 70 or even 50 per cent. In 1973, 55 per cent of all Canadian income taxes came from the low-bracket rates of 13 per cent or less: It is not the rich who pay for the bulk of government; they are too few. It is the median income group, who, by their numbers, predominate. Critics often say, "The tax collector digs deep into high incomes, but with a sieve."

By the mid 1970s, after voters learned that 204 Canadians with tax-sheltered incomes over $25,000, including 8 with incomes over $100,000, paid not a cent of tax in 1971, a taxpayers' revolt threatened. But so far, Parliament has only begun to make token moves against depletion allowances for oil, capital gains, tax losses claimed by gentlemen farmers, and other forms of tax-sheltered income.

PROGRESSIVE TAXES, INVESTMENT, AND SPENDING

Do high income taxes discourage effort and risk-taking. So far as effort is concerned, this is not an easy question to answer. For we shall later see that taxation will cause some people to work harder in order to make their million. Many doctors, scientists, artists, and businessmen who enjoy their jobs and the sense of power or accomplishment that they bring will work as hard for $30,000 as for $100,000; still others may prefer more leisure to more work as a result of progressive taxes. The net result is hard to evaluate. We shall return to this problem in Parts Four and Six.

The effects of progressive tax rates on risky investment could be quite adverse. In part, the government says to the taxpayer, "Heads I win, tails you lose." But recent important reforms have improved the taxpayer's ability to carry forward or carry backward his losses, and also to spread out an extraordinarily high income by averaging it with the previous four years' income, thereby moderating greatly the penalty for erratic earnings from venturesome investment.

Careful studies at the Harvard Business School, cited in Part Four, confirm what has just been said—that there are in fact sufficient perfectly respectable "loopholes" open to wealthy people so that they may typically pay but 50 per cent tax rates, not the 70 per cent shown in tax tables. They take risks and try for less heavily taxed capital gains;[7] they invest in shares with tax credits; they drill for oil, grow trees, or feed beef cattle—all more lightly taxed.

Opposing any unfavorable effect of progressive taxes on investment, jobs, and national growth, there is an offsetting effect. To the extent that dollars are taken from frugal wealthy people who spend small fractions of their extra dollars rather than from poor ready spenders, progressive taxes may tend to keep spending power at a high level—at too high a level if inflation is threatening. But statistics on how people

spend extra dollars, as we shall later see, suggest that this effect on total spending may not be so great.

Economic science can point out these various crosscurrents of progressive taxation. The disincentive effects are worrying. Has the voter enough information to judge such costs, and the progressivity gains, to decide which combination of equality, fairness, and incentive to initiative he favors in our society?

PROVINCIAL AND MUNICIPAL REVENUES

No table is needed to convey the essential information about provincial and local finance. Remember five sources and you've remembered everything: the provinces place heavy reliance on (a) *consumer sales taxes,* (b) *income taxes,* and (c) *rentals* and fees from provincial natural resources, while the municipalities depend almost exclusively on (d) real-estate *property taxes.* In addition both provinces and municipalities get vast sums (up to one-third of their annual revenues) in (e) *grants* from federal and provincial governments. Of the traditional sources, the local property tax and the provincial sales tax are "regressive" in the terms used in the previous discussion. But more and more the provinces depend on their income and corporation taxes, and the municipalities, particularly the school boards, on the provinces. Therefore, the degree of progressiveness is increasing.

PROPERTY TAX The property tax still accounts for over twenty-five per cent of total revenues of provinces and municipalities. It is levied primarily on real estate, land, and buildings. Each locality sets an annual tax rate. In a large city $55 on each $1,000 of assessed valuation (5.5 per cent, or 55 mills) might be the rate. If my house has been assessed at $20,000, my tax is $1,100. However, in many places assessed valuations tend to be but a faction of true market value. Houses like mine may have a market value of $40,000, but be assessed at half that. My true tax rate is less than 5.5 per cent.

In colonial times, a man's total income and wealth may have all been connected with real estate; if so, then the effect of a tax on such property would have been roughly the same as a proportional tax on income, and hence its classification as a direct tax. To-

---

[7] When we remember the loopholes discussed in this study, which show how the well-to-do can hope to convert heavily taxed income into untaxed or less heavily taxed capital gains from risky ventures, we find that *high tax rates may encourage risk-taking by those who seek capital gains* and who know that the government finances up to 70 per cent of their deductible costs.

day, when so much of wealth and income is divorced from real estate, the property tax may be regressive relative to income—especially since small properties tend to be assessed relatively higher than large.

The property tax is rather inflexible. Assessments and rates change slowly. In bad times, when real-estate values fall, the property tax is burdensome, giving rise to bankruptcy, mortgage foreclosures, and forced sales. In the zooming postwar economy, valuations and rates have been edging up. Metropolitanization is likely to create a crisis for the property tax: affluent districts may have to help equalize school expenditures for poor districts; pressure for province-wide property tax assessment and collection therefore mounts, along with pleas for revenue from other (federal and provincial) taxes.

HIGHWAY-USER TAXES As the name suggests, these revenues come from two primary sources: from a tax on gasoline and from use fees on trucks, autos, and drivers. In Canada, they have been shown by M. Q. Dalvi to be less than the cost of roads, (*Canadian Journal of Economics,* Nov. 1969). Most revenues are assigned to the "Consolidated General Fund" for schools or welfare, just as some colleges use profits from football games to buy fencing foils or even Greek manuscripts.

Nevertheless, highway taxes are usually justified on the ground that the taxpayer is simply paying for the *benefit* of using the roads in much the same way as he pays for a railroad ticket or for his use of water and electricity.

SALES TAXES Provinces exploit this consumer-spending tax base. Each purchase at the department, drug, and grocery store pays a percentage tax. (Usually, food and medicines are exempt.) Also, provinces usually add their own liquor and tobacco excises to the federal excises. Most people—including many cigarette smokers and moderate drinkers—feel vaguely that there is something immoral about tobacco and alcohol.[8] They somehow think two birds are being killed with one stone when these articles are taxed: the province gets revenue, and vice is

made more expensive. (Note the element of self-contradiction here.)

The same moral attitude would hardly apply to a 5 per cent tax on everything a consumer buys: shoes, soap, a church candle. Rich and poor are taxed alike on each dollar spent: since the poor are forced to spend a larger portion of their total dollars, one sees that a sales tax on nonluxuries is a regressive tax, taking a larger fraction of low than high incomes.

PROVINCIAL INDIVIDUAL INCOME TAXES
The provinces have had the right to all "direct" taxes since 1867, and since 1962 have all returned to exercising this right on personal incomes. In general, Ottawa makes "tax room" for provincial income taxes equal to about thirty percent of the basic federal tax. The provincial treasury may collect this itself, but customarily Ottawa collects for all the provinces. Thus the *provincial* income tax tends to be just as progressive as the national.

BUSINESS TAXES Provinces and localities often charge license fees for the privilege of acting as a corporation, being an auctioneer, and so forth. Some provinces tax the net income of a corporation as well and collect miscellaneous other fees from business enterprises.

RESOURCE REVENUES In addition, all provinces but Prince Edward Island collect special natural resource revenues. Some of these are actually landlord's income from the sale or rent of Crown land: Alberta gets royalties and bonuses from oil rights, and most provinces get a royalty or Crown due from miners' and loggers' privileges and licenses to exploit public lands. But other revenues are true specific taxes on the business exploitation of privately owned natural resources; there are various levies like property taxes, producing relatively little revenue, and important business income taxes on logging and mining, collected in Ontario and British Columbia. These fatter taxes apply to the harvest of public and private lands alike. The precise legal or political theory behind the imposition and acceptance of this patchwork of rents and taxes is obscure, but they produce considerable provincial revenue for six of the provinces.

---

[8] In a hearing of the 1969 British Columbia Royal Commission, a former head of the Provincial Liquor Commission testified that the Liquor Board's view was that consumption of alcohol was evil!

DEATH TAXES Death taxes in Canada have been changed in the last few years and are in a tangle. As in other countries, there are alternative basic concepts: succession or inheritance taxes on individuals who succeed to wealth upon the death of a relative or friend; and estate taxes, levied upon the dead giver's estate as a whole.

Up to 1958, most Canadian estates were liable to *"succession duties"*, a legal hybrid in which a certain rate was levied progressively on the estate as a whole, and another (inheritance tax) rate to each beneficiary, the rate depending on the amount of the bequest and the relationship of the recipient to the dead giver. For example, widows paid the lowest inheritance rate. Quebec, Ontario, and British Columbia presently use this hybrid principle. Ottawa, once committed to the estate-tax approach, has now withdrawn from all death taxes. The remaining provinces tend to levy straight estate taxes, allowing large exemptions for dependents.: the rate of tax for the estate (from 15 to 50 percent) is applied to each inheritor's share, less exemptions appropriate to his relationship. A "gift tax" may also be levied, to discourage tax avoidance by dispersing estates *before* death.

Death Taxes are progressive and can be heavily redistributive. Social reformers attach great importance to death taxes for the purpose of preventing the development of a permanent moneyed caste, living not on its effort and intelligence, but on its property bequeathed from one generation to the next. Yet, as of the late 1960s, the right to "split income," to make gifts, and to set up complex "trusts" all these have reduced death-tax collections to a low level.

FEDERAL FINANCE AND INTERGOVERNMENTAL PAYMENTS

The federal government has access to more revenue sources (tax bases) than the other two levels of government: it *may* levy all the direct and all the indirect taxes. Furthermore, the progressiveness and built-in-flexibility of its pattern of taxes allows it to keep up with rising costs without having to legislate frequent new tax rates. Yet the spending responsibilities of provinces and municipalities are just as important, and have grown as fast as, or faster than, federal needs.

To overcome this deficit, Ottawa has made increasingly larger payments to the provinces, the legal and political nature of which varies widely. Indeed, the political history of federation is implied by the history of these payments. But only three kinds of payment belong in a quick survey of the period from 1960 to 1970.

CONDITIONAL GRANTS Ottawa decides on the need for some social service, and provides the funds. But the provinces administer the service and put up some funds too. (EXAMPLE: In 1973 Ottawa granted over 1 billion dollars to the provinces on the condition that (*a*) the money was used for hospital insurance and (*b*) the provinces matched this amount, roughly, dollar-for-dollar.)

UNCONDITIONAL GRANTS Sometimes called block grants, these funds have no strings attached. Uncommon in the United States, they were until about 1962 the mainstay of our grant system. They were designed to help each province plug the gap between its needs and its revenue sources. Since 1963, however, they are limited to the poorer provinces, as their self-explanatory name suggests—Equalization Grants. Unconditional grants remedy a traditional objection to conditional grants: Ottawa's dictating the policies and activities of the provinces. But an unconditional grant runs into another objection: Ottawa has no control over vast sums it raises from its taxpayers, the spending of which is handed over to the provincial legislatures.

Total unconditional grants are equal only to about one-third of total conditional grants. (In other federations the ratio is even less.) Most federal grants work toward narrowing the great regional differences between the eastern provinces and the rest. They also strengthen minimum standards within each province. But from east to west and from city to backwoods, there remain sizable differences. It still matters where one is born.

SHARED TAXES Taking the place of older federal unconditional grants is the provincial personal income tax, which the federal government collects at rates set in the provinces. It amounts to about 30 per cent of federal income tax, depending on the province: the lower the personal incomes in the province, the higher the rate it sets. This tax is just as progressive as the federal income tax.[9]

Similarly, *within* the provinces there are both conditional and unconditional grants from the provincial treasuries to the municipalities, school boards, etc. The former are primarily for schools and welfare. The latter prevent a too-heavy dependence on the property tax, the only other important source open to most municipalities. Both help maintain, throughout each province, certain minimum standards of schooling and other public services. In this way, well-to-do suburbanites who have fled the city are made to share the burden, and richer regions can help backward areas.

DOUBLE TAXATION OF PROVINCIAL INCOMES

Both in provincial corporation and personal income taxes, there are serious legal problems about the "residence," "domicile," or "locus" of taxpayers or of taxable incomes, especially when a person has several homes, or a business has branches and handles transactions in many provinces. Though this threat of double taxation is annoying, and the rulings are usually arbitrary, the present situation at its worst involves filling out two or more income tax returns and hiring lawyers to make sure that the highest taxes are avoided (whenever the taxpayer can, by his conduct, affect the jurisdiction in which he is taxable). It is a far better situation than that in the late 1930s. Today the income and corporation taxes are more or less coordinated.

Thus, as Fig. 9-2 shows, neither the average nor the marginal total tax paid to all governments approaches more than about 70 per cent. But in the 1930s, a tangle of separate income taxes, levied independently by Ottawa and the provinces, sometimes resulted in marginal rates, from two or more levels of taxes, greater than 100 per cent! After a certain income, it did *not* pay to earn any more. (Actually, it paid to leave certain provinces, or in the case of certain millionaires, to leave Canada altogether.[10]

Tax coordination also is increasing in other ways. One recent development is property-tax crediting: in Alberta, Manitoba and Ontario, provincial income taxes payable are reduced by municipal property taxes paid. Ontario also plans to follow U.S. practice in crediting sales tax paid.

PROVINCIAL AND LOCAL DEBT

Even when these extra "senior-government sources" are counted in, it is still not true that the total of provincial and municipal expenditures equals the total of their revenues. The difference represents new borrowing or debt repayment. The war prosperity swelled provincial tax revenues. At the same time it became impossible to build new schools and highways. As a result, most provinces were then able to run a surplus and retire a part of their previously accumulated debt.

But since the war, provinces and municipalities have again been increasing their debts. Their costs have risen as new school and highway projects have been undertaken. In the 1970s it is provinces and municipalities that are subjected to the greatest financial strains.

Currently economists are giving thought to ways of coordinating the timing of municipal and provincial spending (and borrowing) so that along with federal spending they will counterbalance private spending spurts and stops over the business cycle. The new tax independence of the provinces makes such coordination administratively more difficult than it would have been over twenty years ago. But schemes are being devised to give provinces (and perhaps municipalities) financial incentives to delay capital borrowing and spending in boom periods, while making it easier for them to borrow during slumps. To do this, it will be necessary somehow to bring them, with the federal government, into closer contact with the money-creating Bank of Canada.

---

[9] In the U.S. there is a much-disputed proposal for "tax sharing", to aid the states. Under it, part of the federal income tax would be routed to the states on an origin, or per capita, basis.

[10] The famous Rowell-Sirois Report on Dominion-Provincial relations recommended methods of overcoming this type of double taxation (1940). During World War II the problem was solved by the provinces *renting* their rights to levy income taxes to Ottawa. Since then the system has gradually returned to the freedom of

the provinces to levy whatever taxes they choose; but the federal government "abates" a proportion of its direct taxes and most provinces choose to levy this share of federal tax (in 1967: 28 per cent of personal income tax; 10 per cent of corporate tax; and 75 per cent of federal estate tax).

Note that "double taxation" may have two meanings: (a) corporate profits may be taxed by corporation and personal taxes; (b) any income may be taxed by two jurisdictions. In its second meaning, double taxation between countries is prevented by a series of tax treaties between Canada and her neighbors.

CONCLUSION: THE THORNY PROBLEM OF TAX INCIDENCE

In ending this survey of taxes and other revenues, let us note a few warnings. Even if the electorate has made up its mind about how the tax burden shall be borne by individuals, the following difficult problems remain:

Who ultimately pays a particular tax? Does its burden stay on the person against whom it is first levied? One cannot just assume that the person a legislature says a tax is levied on will end up paying that tax. He may be able to *shift* the tax: shift it "forward" on his customers, by raising his price as much as the tax; or shift it "backward" on his suppliers, who end up charging him less than they would have done had there been no tax.

Economists therefore say: We must study the final incidence of the tax—the way its burden ultimately gets borne, the totality of its effect on commodity prices, factor prices, resource allocations, efforts, composition of production and consumption, and the quantities of each commodity produced and each factor supplied. To locate a tax's final incidence therefore is so broad a problem as to require all the advanced tools of economics for its detection.

EXAMPLE: Does a tax on wheat raise the price to the consumer by as much as itself, so that the incidence is on the consumer? Or does the tax raise the price by half itself or not at all, so that the incidence is partially on the producers? Does it change oat prices? And does the tax kill off all or much of wheat production, so that it is having incidence effects beyond those which show up in money prices and wages and even beyond the burdens that you can allocate among the different citizens?

However, we can get the feel of the problem by asking about the effects which are felt by either the buyer or the seller of a taxed commodity. Imagine, for example, that the government levies a tax of 10 cents a yard on the cotton gray goods mentioned earlier in Chapter 4, page 73, no matter what the price. In Fig. 9-3, the demand curve *dd* shows the quantity *Q* bought at each price *P*. And, before the tax, *ss* shows the amounts sellers will be willing to offer at each *P*. *E* shows equilibrium price and quantity.

Now, the effect of a tax is to *shift ss*. In order to get sellers to offer a particular *Q*, it is now necessary

FIG. 9-3. A tax falls on both buyers and sellers: A ten-cent tax shifts the price upward by less than 10¢. Thus the incidence is partly on buyers and partly on sellers.

to pay them the old *P* plus the government's 10 cents. Hence, the supply curve shifts upward 10 cents, to the parallel position *s's'*. The amount consumers must pay rises, consequently, from *E* to *E'*. But have consumers paid the full tax? No. Because the distance from *E'* to *E''* is equal to 10 cents, the rise in price must be less, only about 7 cents, while sellers take a 3-cent cut in the amount they receive. Their net amount—available for their own income, or for the wages of their workers—falls from *E* to *E''*. Unless *dd* is vertical, or *ss* horizontal, the incidence will always be divided between buyers and sellers. It is rarely on one party only. And because *Q* also falls, land and labor must be reallocated to other markets, where prices and wages will change, causing changes in demand for still other commodities ... until the "burden" of the tax is seen to extend far beyond the two parties to the cotton-goods market.

In Part Three, Chapter 20, this thorny problem is tackled further, with the help of the "elasticity" concept (see Fig. 20-6); and it is raised again in Part Four. The question of tax incidence is both relevant and current, although economists are not yet agreed on final results. Some think the corporate income tax falls mostly on the consumer; some argue it falls mostly on stockholders and capitalists.

Figure 9-4, on the next page, is a valiant attempt to determine statistically how progressive or re-

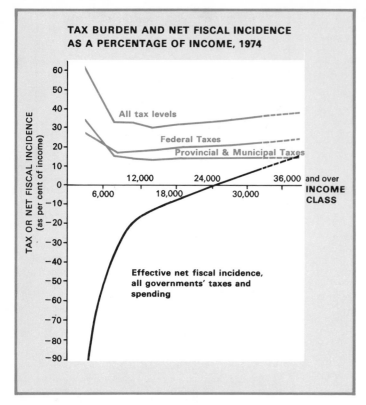

FIG. 9-4. Who pays the taxes and who gets the benefits?—a revision of an expert's estimate.

(Sources: *The Incidence of Taxes and Public Expenditures in the Canadian Economy,* by **W. I. Gillespie,** Study Number 2, Royal Commission on Taxation, 1966, updated by authors; "The Taxes We Pay (1968)" by **R. A. Herriot** and **H. P. Miller,** in the *Conference Board Review: 1972 Ontario Budget.*)

gressive our over-all tax and expenditure structure was in 1961. Experts agree that the results of such a study can be only approximate, since no one knows just how a corporate tax or other tax gets shifted. Even an expert is not a magician capable of making a controlled experiment in which he (*a*) measures things without taxes, then (*b*) measures things with taxes, and finally (*c*) determines tax incidence as the difference between these situations.[11] Furthermore, the horizontal axis has been for this edition drastically adjusted to make allowance for the two hundred per cent rise in money personal incomes in the 15 years since 1961. Thus the precise income at

which tax incidence begins to rise, and "net fiscal incidence" becomes positive, is in mid-1970, very much open to argument.

Note the slow progression of *tax* around the median income level. The very affluent do get taxed to help the poor, but the man in the middle is something of a forgotten man when it comes to tax burden. But, as the lower curve in Fig. 9-4 shows, when we attempt to determine which classes benefit from government expenditure, the needy show a much more favorable "net incidence" (i.e. negative burden or positive fiscal benefit) than the affluent.

SUMMARY

1 Taxes enable the government to pay for the *real* resources it needs for its public activities. Taxes also finance welfare transfer expenditures that change the distribution of income; and the over-all way taxes are levied affects the final distribution of incomes among people.

[11]For an in-depth study of tax incidence in Canada, see Allan M. Maslove, *The Pattern of Taxation in Canada* (a study prepared for the Economic Council of Canada), Ottawa, 1973.

2 Notions of "benefit" and of "proper sacrifice or redistribution" are the two principal theories of taxation. Justice implies taxing equals equally, unequals unequally. Direct and progressively graduated taxes on incomes are in contrast to indirect and regressive excises.

3 Almost half of federal revenue comes from personal and corporation income taxes. The rest comes from "regressive taxes" on sales and imports. The personal income tax, except for loopholes and erosion of the tax base, is steeply progressive, tending to redistribute income from rich to poor.

4 The property tax is the most important source of municipal revenue. Sales taxes and resource revenue are important for the province. In the postwar period, provinces and municipalities have been spending more than they tax, thereby increasing their debts.

5 The federal government makes large tax payments to the provinces, as well as conditional and unconditional grants for highways and social welfare. The provinces help the municipalities in education, highways, and public assistance.

6 The incidence of a tax is its ultimate division of burden, its total effect on prices and other economic magnitudes. Those upon whom a tax is levied may succeed in shifting part of its burden forward or backward. The tools of Parts Three and Four will help in tackling this difficult problem. Progression in the benefits of public expenditure offsets in part the regressive curves of taxation.

CONCEPTS FOR REVIEW

tax revenues and real resources
benefit and sacrifice notions
direct and indirect taxes
progressive, proportional,
   regressive taxes
provincial and municipal expenditures

provincial and municipal taxes
exemptions versus credits
horizontal and vertical equity.
conditional and unconditional grants
budget surpluses and deficits
tax incidence and shifting

QUESTIONS FOR DISCUSSION

1. Make a list of different taxes in order of their progressiveness. What is the importance of each at the federal, provincial, and municipal levels?
2. How do you think different government functions should be allocated among the three levels of government? How about revenues and grants?
3. Should a citizen in Ontario be taxed to help a citizen in Newfoundland? To help a citizen in Quebec? In Ontario? In Mexico or India?
4. "Since people don't change their smoking habits as a result of taxation, and since the poor smoke, a tax on cigarettes is really no different from a tax on bread." Do you agree? If so, what ought to be done?
5. Who pays for education in Canada? Try to trace back the incidence, and suggest improvements.
6. "More kids and cars mean municipal expenditure and debt." Evaluate.
7. Is the property tax on a house a direct or an indirect tax? The tax on a developer building new houses for sale or rent? How does the Canadian constitution define property taxes?

10
NATIONAL PRODUCT
AND INCOME

The time has come, the walrus said, To speak of many things. Of shoes, and ships, and sealing wax, Of cabbages—and kings

LEWIS CARROLL

One of the most important concepts in all economics is the national income—or, technically, the gross national product (GNP). This measures the economic performance of the whole economy. Of course, man does not live by bread alone. Nor does our society live by GNP alone. But on our way to the state of affluence where material well-being will fall to the second level of significance, we do need a summary measure of aggregate economic performance.

This chapter's discussion of national income can serve as the unifying summary of Part One's introduction to the *basic economic processes and institutions* of modern mixed societies. Alternately, this analysis of national income, its anatomy and accounting structure, can be regarded as the introduction to the treatment of macroeconomics of Part Two—the study of the physiological forces that determine total employment, production, real income, and the price level. The concept of national income is indispensable preparation for tackling the great issues of unemployment, inflation, and growth. In these days, however, there is concern lest mere material growth be at the expense of the quality of life and the ecological environment. Hence, we must break new ground to devise ways of correcting and converting the GNP concept into a better measure of NEW—net economic welfare.

THE YARDSTICK OF AN ECONOMY'S PERFORMANCE

What is national income? It is the loose name we give to the money measure of the over-all annual flow of goods and services in an economy. Often, in-stead of it, we use the almost equivalent, precise term "national product" or "net national product" (NNP);[1] or perhaps more often the slightly different concept of "gross national product" (GNP).

If you asked an economic historian just what the Great Depression really meant, his best brief answer would be: "From a 1929 NNP of 5.5 billion dollars there was a drop to a 1933 NNP of 3.0 billion dollars. This halving of the money value of the flow of goods and services in the Canadian economy caused hardship, bankruptcy, riots, and political turmoil."

In brief, national income or product is the final figure you arrive at when you apply the measuring rod of money to the flows of diverse apples, grain, and machines that any society produces with its land, labor, and capital resources.

TWO MEASURES OF NATIONAL PRODUCT: AS GOODS-FLOW OR AS EARNINGS-FLOW

How do we measure the net national product, NNP? The general idea is simple. Fig. 10-1 shows the circular flow of dollar spending in an economy with no government and no accumulation of capital or net saving going on.

FLOW-OF-PRODUCT APPROACH Each year the public consumes goods and services: goods such as apples, oranges, and bread; services such as haircuts. The public spends dollars for these consumer

[1] We shall have occasion below to note the special and narrow use of the term "national income" by Statistics Canada.

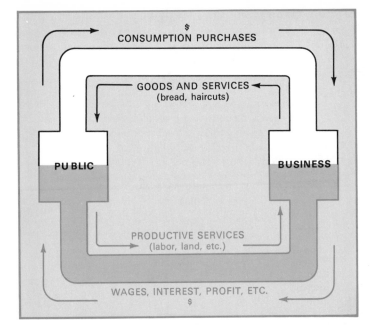

FIG. 10-1. Net national product is measured as flow of output or as equal flow of costs.

In the upper loop, people spend their money on final goods; the total dollar flow of these per year is one measure of net national product, NNP.

The lower loop measures the annual flow of costs of output: the earnings that business pays out in wages, rent, interest, dividends, and accrued profits. With profit properly reckoned as a residual, the two measures of NNP must always be identical. (Same will be true of GNP.)

goods, as in the upper loop of Fig. 10-1. We add together all the consumption dollars spent for these final goods to arrive at the total of NNP.

Thus, in our simple economy, one can easily calculate national income or product as the sum of the annual flow of final goods and services: (price of bread × number of loaves) + (price of apples × number of apples) + . . .

Why use market prices as weights in evaluating and summing diverse physical commodities and services? Because, as we shall see in Part Three, market prices are reflectors of the relative desirability of diverse goods and services.

The *net national product*, or "national income evaluated at market prices," as it is technically named, is definable as the total money value of the flow of final products of the community over a given period of time—usually a year.[2]

EARNINGS OR INCOME APPROACH There is a second, equivalent way to calculate NNP in so simple an economy. Go to the lower loop in Fig. 10-1: What is the total cost of output which business is

paying out to the public? It is paying out wages, interest, rents, and profit. Why? Because these factor earnings of land, labor, and capital are the *costs* of production of the flow of product. (NOTE: Here the economist, unlike the accountant, does count profit as a cost or earning item.)

The statistician can measure the annual flow of such factor earnings or income in the lower loop.[3] In this way, he will *again* arrive at the NNP.

Net national product is also definable, from a second viewpoint, as the total of factor earnings (wages, interest, rents, and accruing profits) that are the costs of production of society's final goods.

Now we have calculated NNP by the upper-loop flow-of-product approach and by the lower-loop earnings-flow approach. Which is bigger? Answer: They must be *exactly* the same.

Here is the reason for this identity. Recall that we have included "profit" in the lower loop—along with wages, interest, and rents. What exactly is profit? Profit is what you have left over from the sale of product (your apples, bread, oranges, and manicures) *after* you have paid the other factor costs. *So profit*

[2] In our first, simplest model, the only final product is private consumption expenditures. But in a moment we shall see that government expenditures on goods and services, private net investment, and net exports are also to be included.

[3] When we leave our simple model, taxes will have to be included here properly.

automatically is the residual that takes on the size needed to make the lower-loop approach via earnings exactly *match the upper-loop approach via flow of goods.*

All this reflects the useful device of double-entry which accountants use to keep the two sides of their books in perfect balance.

To sum up: NNP, or net national product, is measurable as the flow of product; but it is also con-

venient for the statistician to measure it via the earnings approach in the lower loop. With the proper definition of profit and its inclusion as an economic earning and cost, each approach will yield exactly the same NNP.

An example will show how to go from business accounts to national accounts in the simplest case, without government and investment, and where all final products are produced from land, labor, and capital in 10 million identical one-stage firms or farms.

INCOME STATEMENT OF TYPICAL FARM				
OUTPUT ATTRIBUTABLE TO FARMING		EARNINGS		
Sales of goods (wheat, apples, etc.)	$1,000	Costs of production		
		Wages	$ 800	
		Rents	100	
		Interest	25	
		Profit (residual)	75	
Total	$1,000	Total	$1,000	

Adding all the 10 million farms gives the NNP account easily in this trivial case.

NATIONAL PRODUCT ACCOUNT (in millions!)			
UPPER-LOOP FLOW OF PRODUCT		LOWER-LOOP EARNINGS OR INCOMES	
Final output (10 × 1,000)	$10,000	Wages (10 × 800)	$ 8,000
		Rents (10 × 100)	1,000
		Interest (10 × 25)	250
		Profit (10 × 75)	750
NNP total	$10,000	NNP total	$10,000

Note that the definition of profit makes the firm's two sides balance; hence the two NNP approaches must still match after summation.

AVOIDING "DOUBLE COUNTING" OF INTERMEDIATE GOODS

Returning to current money figures, we can now show how to handle "intermediate" goods (which are not truly *final* goods) and thus avoid counting anything two, three, or more times.

IGNORING INTERMEDIATE GOODS We do want to count bread in NNP, but we must *avoid also*

counting in the dough that goes to make the bread. That would indeed be double counting, since the only reason we want the dough is for the final bread. Turn back to the two-loop diagram in Fig. 10-1. You can see bread (and haircuts) there; but you do not see any dough, flour, or wheat. Where are they? These are so-called "intermediate products" that are produced during all the stages leading up to the final bread product, and they are hidden in the block marked "business." That is as it should be. We do not want such intermediate products to be double-counted along with the final product.

USING "VALUE ADDED" TO AVOID DOUBLE COUNTING A new statistician who is being

BREAD RECEIPTS, COSTS, AND VALUE ADDED

(in cents per loaf)

STAGE OF PRODUCTION	(1) SALES RECEIPTS	(2) COST OF INTERMEDIATE MATERIAL OR GOODS		(3) VALUE ADDED (WAGES, PROFIT, ETC.) (3) = (1) — (2)	
Wheat	8	— 0	=	8	
Flour	11	— 8	=	3	
Baked dough	20	— 11	=	9	
Delivered bread	30	— 20	=	10	
	69	— 39	=	30	(sum of value added)

TABLE 10-1. NNP is the summation of "value-added" of all the separate production stages. To avoid double counting, we carefully calculate value added at each stage, subtracting all the costs of materials and intermediate products not produced in that stage but bought from other business firms. Note that every intermediate product appears both in Column (1) and with opposite sign in Column (2); hence it is canceled out.

trained to make NNP measurements might well be puzzled, saying:

I can see that, if you are careful, your upper-loop approach to NNP will avoid including intermediate products. But I'm a little uncertain whether or not you might find yourself in some difficulty when you use the lower-loop approach. After all, doesn't Statistics Canada gather income statements from the accounts of business firms? Won't it then be picking up what millers pay to farmers, what bakers pay to millers, and what grocers pay to bakers? Won't this result in double counting or even triple and quadruple counting of some items that go through several stages of production?

This is a legitimate question. Fortunately, we can give it a satisfactory answer. The statistician making lower-loop earnings or factor-cost measurements is always very careful to use what he calls the "value added" approach.[4]

The value-added approach refuses to include *all* the expenses shown on each firm's business income statement in the lower-loop factor earnings. Which expenses are excluded? All purchases of materials and services from *other* business firms are excluded, because those dollars will get properly counted in NNP from the reports of such *other* firms.

EXAMPLE: Apex Co. buys electric power from the Ontario Hydro. This expense on the Apex income statement is *not* included in value added. Why should it be? It is not a wage, interest, rent, or profit payment. In fact, it is not a payment to any Apex productive factor; hence it never shows up in the lower loop at all. It stays inside the business block, where it and all other such expenditures by a firm on intermediate goods are carefully subtracted from Apex's receipts. What is left? Apex's true value added—which is exactly the sum of *its* wages, interest, rent, and profit costs.

Mind you, the electric power was produced by the Hydro workers—and by the Hydro interest, rent, and profit receivers. So do not fear that this electrical activity will get overlooked by the NNP statistician. It will not. He will pick it up as the value added of the Ontario Hydro. This is as it should be: we want to count each thing once, not twice or three times.

Table 10-1 illustrates by means of the several stages of a loaf of bread how careful adherence to the value-added approach will enable us to subtract the intermediate expenses that show up in the income statements of farmers, millers, bakers, and grocers— ending up with the desired equality between (a) net value of final bread and (b) the lower-loop factor-

[4] Perhaps recall at this point VAT, the value-added tax of Chapter 9's page 149. Unlike a turnover tax that hits all intermediate goods as many times as they are in exchanged goods—wheat in flour, wheat in dough, wheat in bread (along, of course, with wheat in wheat!)—VAT taxes only each stage's own wage, profit, and other costs (its value added). To accomplish this, it lets firms subtract out the costs they pay from earlier production stages.

costs embodying the sum of the value-added data of all stages. All this can be summarized as follows:

Value-added approach. To avoid double counting, we take care to include in net national product only final goods, and not the intermediate goods that go to make the final goods. By resolutely sticking to the *value added* at each stage, taking care to subtract expenditures on the intermediate goods bought from other firms, the lower-loop earnings

approach properly avoids all double counting and records wages, interest, rent, and profit exactly on time.

Our earlier example with 10 million farmers can now have added to it 10 million second-stage manufacturers, who buy wheat and farm goods and add value to them by processing them into bread and other final products by the use of labor, land, and capital. Alongside the farmer's income statement we now have the manufacturer's income statement.

INCOME STATEMENT OF TYPICAL MANUFACTURER			
OUTPUT ATTRIBUTABLE TO MANUFACTURING		**EARNINGS**	
Sales of goods	$5,000	Costs or "value added"	
Minus goods bought from		Wages	$3,500
other firms	—1,000	Rent	100
		Interest	100
		Profit (residual)	300
Total	$4,000	Total	$4,000

To get total NNP for society, we can add the left-hand sides of the 10 million farmers *and* 10 million bakers; or to

get lower- rather than upper-loop NNP, we add the right-hand items for *all* these 20 million firms.

NATIONAL PRODUCT ACCOUNT (in millions)			
UPPER-LOOP FLOW OF PRODUCT		**LOWER-LOOP EARNINGS OR INCOMES**	
Final output (finished bread, etc.)		Wages (8,000 + 35,000	$43,000
[50,000 = 10,000 (on farms)		Rent (1,000 + 1,000)	2,000
+ (50,000 — 10,000) (in		Interest (250 + 1,000)	1,250
manufacturing)]	$50,000	Profit (750 + 3,000)	3,750
NNP total	$50,000	NNP total	$50,000

NET INVESTMENT, CAPITAL FORMATION

So far, we have banished all capital growth from our discussion. We talked of people as wanting to currently consume bread, apples, oranges, and haircuts.[5] In real life, however, people often want to devote

part of their income to saving and investment. Instead of eating bread *now*, they may want to build new machines to help produce more bread for *future* consumption, or they may want to add to the inventory of bread in their deep-freeze compartments. In short, we must recognize that the final goals of people do include net investment or capital formation, not simple current consumption.

If people are using part of society's production possibilities for capital formation rather than consumption, the economic statistician recognizes that he must include such output in his upper-loop flow of NNP. So really, we must modify our original definition to read:

[5] Indeed, the economic statistician counts in the NNP all consumption items that people want to spend *their* incomes on. He draws the line at illegal expenditures, e.g., opium consumption or prostitution (but not at alcohol, cigarettes, bubble gum, or legal vices some moralists deplore). When black-market operations were important, he found it necessary to supplement his statistics with estimates of black-market money transactions.

Net national product is the sum of *all* final products, such as consumption goods and services, and including also *net* investment.

This net investment (or net capital formation) will include the net additions to our stock of (1) buildings, (2) equipment, and (3) inventories.

WARNING: To economists, "investment" always means real capital formation—production of added goods in inventories, of new plants, houses, and tools. To the layman, investment means merely using money to buy an outstanding share of GM stock, to buy a corner lot, to open a savings account. It is important not to confuse these meanings: If I take $1,000 from my safe and now put it in the bank or buy common stock from a broker, the economist says that neither investment nor saving has gone up from this act alone. Only if some physical capital formation takes place is there investment; only if society consumes less than its income, devoting resources to capital formation, is there saving.

Now the time has come to go from NNP to GNP —to take into account depreciation of capital goods.

NET INVESTMENT EQUALS GROSS INVESTMENT MINUS DEPRECIATION

How does the economist get accurate figures on net investment?

First he has to make estimates of inventories and of their changes. Harder still is his task of estimating net investment in buildings and equipment.

Why can't he just jot down *all* the buildings built and *all* the machines produced, add them in with his calculated net inventory change, and let it go at that? He does indeed make such a calculation. But the resulting figure is too large—*too gross*. Recognizing this he gives a new name to the result, namely, "gross investment" rather than "net investment."

Why the word "gross"? The statistician uses this word to emphasize that he has not yet made any *allowances for the using up of capital*, i.e., no allowance for capital *depreciation*. (Recall the accounting appendix of Chapter 6.)

One would not think much of a statistician who estimated the change in human population by ignoring deaths. If he just added up gross births, without subtracting a good estimate for deaths, he would get an exaggerated notion of the net change in population. The same holds for economic equipment and buildings: net change is always gross births (of capital) minus deaths (or capital depreciation).

Definition: Net investment always equals gross investment minus depreciation.

Table 10-2 gives typical figures relating *business* net and gross investment. They differ only by depre-

BUSINESS GROSS AND NET INVESTMENT (millions of dollars)		
	1932	1973
New construction—Residential	$ 76	$ 6,500
—Non-residential	123	7,000
Machinery and equipment	108	8,300
Change in business inventories	—100	700
Business Gross Investment	$207	$22,500
Allowance for capital consumption or depreciation (also = difference between GNP and NNP)	—508	—12,700
Business Net Investment	$—301	$ 9,800

TABLE 10-2. To go from gross to net investment, we subtract depreciation of capital.
After subtracting capital depreciation from business *gross* investment, we get business *net* investment. Note that the final figure was negative in 1932, as can be seen also in Fig. 10-3. Can you explain this? Notice that this table like Table 10-4 presents *business* investment alone. For data including *government* capital formation in investment, see Table 10-5. (Source: Statistics Canada, *Canadian Statistical Review*, 11-003.)

ciation; and fortunately, this is a sluggish item that grows slowly over a period of a few years.

GROSS NATIONAL PRODUCT VERSUS NET NATIONAL PRODUCT

Gross investment can be estimated fairly accurately, requiring no difficult depreciation estimate. For this reason governments and the United Nations sensibly decided to calculate a gross national product figure *first* rather than a net national product figure.

Gross national product (GNP) is equal to the sum of final products such as consumption and *gross* investment (which is the sum of the increase in inventories plus *gross* births or production of buildings and equipment). GNP = NNP + Depreciation.

This is important to know, for official statisticians at Statistics Canada do not present NNP data. They concentrate on GNP for the very good reason that depreciation figures cannot be quickly and accurately measured each quarter. Table 10-2 suggests it will be easy enough to go from GNP to NNP, or vice versa, once we know the total depreciation figure that is to be subtracted or added. The economist is quite content to work with GNP figures, knowing that the two concepts do move in parallel fashion.[6]

We have seen that NNP calculated by the upper-loop purchases approach must be identical to the lower-loop earnings-flow NNP. Obviously, if depreciation is added to both, the totals will still be identical. To distinguish the *concepts* from each other, Statistics Canada has given a special name to each: if the national total is calculated by the flow-of-product approach, it is called gross national expenditure (GNE); if it is reached by the earnings-flow approach, it is called GNP.

Gross national expenditure (GNE) is identical in amount to gross national product (GNP). GNE is the sum of all final outputs. GNP is the sum of all factor earnings.[7]

[6] Here is a convenient rule of thumb: NNP is usually about 88 per cent of GNP, depreciation since 1962 having been very close to 12 per cent of GNP.

[7] To be consistent, GNE minus depreciation ought to be named net national expenditure (NNE). But although this term has been used by some economists, NNP is commonly used for the net figure calculated by either method.

These are the basic concepts of national-product accounting. But now we must include two real-world sectors we have ignored: the government and international trade. Both produce final outputs and factor earnings.

GOVERNMENT EXPENDITURE ON GOODS AND SERVICES

GNE must somehow take into account the billions of dollars of product that a nation collectively consumes. But how do we measure government consumption?

After some debate,[8] the income statisticians of Canada, the United States, and the United Nations decided to use the simplest method of all. To the flow of (1) consumption product and (2) investment product, they simply add (3) *all* government expenditure on goods and services. (Repeatedly in the next few chapters, you will see $C + I + G$, which stands for these three components.)

Here are examples. Along with bread consumption and gross investment, we introduce into GNE government expenditures on jet fighters. We include government expenditure on the services of jet pilots, judges, policemen, national-income statisticians, firemen, and agricultural chemists.

In short, all the government payroll expenditures on its employees plus the goods (typewriters, guns, and airplanes) it buys from private industry are included in this third great category of flow of product, labeled G and called "government expenditure on goods and services."[9]

Fig. 10-2 pictures GNE and its major components.

EXCLUSION OF TRANSFER PAYMENTS

Does this mean that every dollar the government pays out is included in GNP and GNE? Definitely

[8] Why is the valuation of government output a problem? Simply because so little of the goods and services which the government produces ever reach the market. They have no market price to serve as a value guide.

[9] Although these government expenditures can be broken down between current collective consumption and collective investment, this is not easy to do; and in many official statistics, no breakdown is given. Statistics Canada's recent estimates of "government gross fixed capital formation" run at about 16 per cent of total government expenditure.

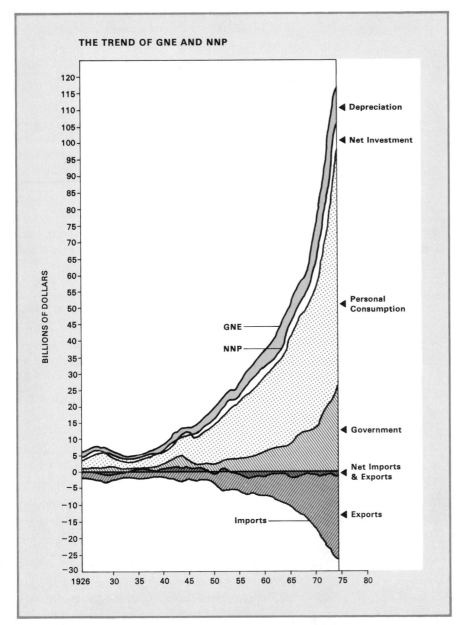

THE TREND OF GNE AND NNP

FIG. 10-2. The large mass in the middle is consumption, which dominates GNE. But note the World War II and postwar growth of government, near the bottom axis. NNP is the second line from the top; it has grown at the same rate as GNE. Net imports entered the GNE total *negatively* in the 1960s; and, as net exports, positively in World War II. [Imports are plotted downward from the zero axis, and exports are then plotted upward from imports, leaving a narrow band of net imports (minus) or net exports (plus). Government spending is measured upward from the wiggly net import line, minus or plus; and all other spending bands are added upward from government.] (Source: Urquhart and Buckley, *Historical Statistics of Canada,* Cambridge University Press, 1965; and Statistics Canada.)

not. If you get an old age pension from the government, we call that a "transfer payment" and do not treat it as part of GNE. Why not? Because it is not a government expenditure on final goods and services of this year. Or if your aunt receives a widow's assistance payment, that welfare expenditure is also considered a transfer item. The same goes for pensions to the blind, veterans, and other welfare recipients. These transfers are not payments for *current* productive services.

Many other government transfer items[10] could be mentioned, but we can conclude with one large item: interest on the public debt. The interest paid on federal bonds was included years ago in GNP, but the fairly universal custom now is for countries to treat this as a transfer item. It is not now included in G, on the argument that it is not a payment for current goods and services.[11]

Do not think that the Minister of Finance's budget fails to take account of all government transfer payments. The budget back on page 138 did include these: the government surplus does equal taxes minus the sum of G *and* transfers. The official budget also includes some purely bookkeeping expenses. But do not confuse these budget accounts with national-income accounts, which are related but distinct.

TREATMENT OF TAXES In using the flow-of-product approach to compute GNE as $C + I + G$, we need never worry about taxes or how government finances itself. Whether the government taxes, issues interest-bearing IOUs, or prints new non-interest IOU banknotes, the statistician computes G as the value of government expenditure on goods and services (evaluating these items at their actual costs to the government, wherever the money came from) and the private $C + I$ at actual market prices.

It is all very well to ignore taxes in the upper-loop flow-of-product approach. But what about in the lower-loop earnings or cost approach to GNP? In this lower loop, we do indeed have to take account of all taxes.

Consider wages, for example. Part of what my employer pays me in wages I have to give to the government in the form of personal income taxes. So these direct taxes do definitely get included in the wage component of the lower loop, and the same holds for direct taxes (personal or corporate) on interest, rent, and profit.

Or take the sales and other indirect taxes that manufacturers and retailers have to pay on a loaf of bread (or on the wheat, flour and dough stages). Suppose these indirect taxes total 5 cents; and suppose wages, profit, and other value-added items add up to 30 cents in cost to the bread industry. (We do not care how much of this 30 cents later goes to direct taxes.) What will the bread sell for in the upper loop? For 30 cents? Of course not. The bread will sell for 35 cents, equal to 30 cents of factor-costs plus 5 cents of indirect taxes.[12]

Hence we always find taxes included in the lower-loop cost approach to GNP and NNP.

NET EXPORTS

Countries with "open" economies, like Canada, the United Kingdom, and Japan, cannot afford to ignore data on their exports and imports. In the United States, where exports and imports are a relatively small part of GNE, this sector is often buried in some other part of GNP; but by contrast, almost one quarter of Canada's output of goods and services goes abroad. How is it to be taken into account when it is clearly not shown in the closed circuit of loops in Figure 10-1?

---

[10] The name "transfer payment," as used in Chapter 8 and here, is a little misleading. If you tax me to give a relief dole to my unemployed neighbor, that does sound like a "transfer." But suppose you print a new 20-dollar bill to give him, or borrow by selling bonds to make relief payments. He gets money that is *not* transferred from anybody else. Economists still call the relief payments transfers, regardless of how they are financed.

[11] How to treat government items in GNE is still somewhat controversial. Some experts say that part of G is really "intermediate" rather than "final" product—much like dough rather than bread—in that it merely contributes to final product already counted in (e.g., weather information for farmers who help give us our daily bread). But few nations make estimates of how much such double counting may be involved in the G figures.

[12] This is plainly so by definition of our residual profit and from the fact that residual profit is treated as a cost; but this result definitely says *nothing at all* about whether the tax is passed forward to the consumer or backward to the factors, whose wages and other returns might have been higher had there been no taxes. Chapter 19 analyzes such a "tax incidence" problem of the sort described in Chapter 9.

First, Canadian GNP is understood to mean the income or product accruing to all "permanent residents" of Canada. Residents are not necesarily citizens and may live temporarily abroad. If Lord Thompson owns a newspaper in Canada and is permanently resident in Britain, his income therefrom is added into the *British* GNP, rather than the Canadian. Similarly, if a Canadian earns dividends from a British mine, this is part of the Canadian income and not the British, being treated as payment for a property service that we have exported.

It is obviously not easy to calculate international flows of income and expenditure. Fortunately, economists have been measuring the balance of payments for each country far longer than they have been calculating the national income. Details of the method will be discussed in Part Five. The bare logic, however, is as follows. Exports (*E*) are all goods and services for which residents of other countries pay Canada: items such as wheat, and services such as shipping, insurance, accommodation for American tourists, dividends and interest payments on Canadian capital abroad, and fees for Canadian engineers working in foreign countries. Imports (*M*) are similar goods and services bought by Canadians from foreign sellers and include interest and dividends paid for the use of foreign capital in Canada.

Although our exports such as wheat and ore are primary products, they are final output from the Canadian point of view as no further value will be added to them here. Hence, exports must be included with *C*, gross *I*, and *G* to comprise GNE. But the flow of imports shows that much of the final expenditure by Canadians must include foreign goods and services. Therefore imports must be subtracted from GNE. The usual method is to calculate "net exports" (*E − M*), the surplus of exports over imports. In fact, this "surplus" may be a deficit, as has often been the case for Canada in recent years: the whole term (*E − M*) can be positive or negative. (*E − M*) is shown by the thin wiggle along the bottom axis of Figure 10-2.

Now that the government and foreign trade have been brought into the picture, a final comprehensive definition can be given.

GNE is definable as the sum of the four major components in the upper-loop flow of product: personal *consumption*, plus *government* expenditure on goods and services, plus *gross investment* in new machines and structures, plus *net exports* of goods and services. In defining NNP we simply adapt the above definition by altering gross investment to net investment.

GNP and NNP are each definable as a lower-loop total of costs: to factor-costs such as wages, interest, rents, and profit (always carefully excluding double counting of intermediate goods brought from other firms), there will have to be added all the indirect business taxes that do show up as an expense of producing the flow of products; and in the case of gross national product there will also be included depreciation expense, whereas the net national product will be less by the amount of this estimated expense.

The two loops yield identical magnitudes by definition (i.e., by careful adherence to the procedures of "double-entry" bookkeeping).[13]

REAL VERSUS MONEY GNE: USING A PRICE INDEX TO "DEFLATE"

We saw that GNE uses the measuring rod of money prices in the market to combine diverse apples, bread loaves, and other goods to a single total figure. But one would hardly choose to measure things with a rubber than a wooden yardstick—one that stretched in your hands from day to day.

This is one of the problems economists have to solve when they use money as their measuring rod. Everyone knows that inflations and deflations can send most prices up or down. Or, as the economist puts it, "The value of money does change between years like 1929 and 1933, or 1939 and 1975 or 1976.

What can be done about this? Economists can repair most of the damage due to the changeability of our measuring rod by using an *index number of*

---

[13] Statisticians must always work with incomplete reports and must fill in some gaps by estimation. As will be seen in a moment, approximate guesses can differ somewhat from GNP by what is officially reported as the "residual error of estimate."

GROSS NATIONAL EXPENDITURE, GROSS NATIONAL PRODUCT, AND NET NATIONAL PRODUCT, 1973—(billions of dollars)

(GNE, or Flow-of-Product Approach)			(GNP, or Earnings and Cost Approach)	
C: Personal consumption expenditure on goods and services		$ 69	Wages, salaries, and supplements	$ 64
			Military pay and allowances	1
I: "Gross" investment (Inventory accumulation and *business* capital spending)		23	Corporation profits before taxes	15
G: Government spending:		27	Deduct: Dividends paid to non-residents	− 1
Goods and services	23		Depreciation	13
Fixed capital	4		Interest and miscellaneous investment income	5
E-M: Current account balance		− 1	Accrued net income of farm operators	3
Exports of goods and services	30		Net income of non-farm unincorporated firms, including rent	7
Imports of goods and services	− 31		Inventory valuation adjustment	− 2
			Indirect taxes less subsidies	15
Residual error of estimate		(0)	Residual error of estimate	(0)
GNE: Gross National Expenditure		$119	GNP: Gross National Product	$119
Depreciation or consumption allowance		− 13	Depreciation or consumption allowance	− 13
NNP: Net National Product		$106	NNP: Net National Product	$106

TABLE 10-3. Here are two ways of arriving at GNP in actual numbers. The left side measures flow of product at market prices. The right side measures flow of costs (factor earnings and indirect taxes). NNP, which excludes depreciation, is also shown. The columns don't add due to rounding. (Source: Statistics Canada, 11-003.)

prices.[14] A 1929-1933 comparison will illustrate the process by which one uses a price index number to "deflate" a "current *money* GNE", converting it into a "*real* GNE in terms of dollars of unchanged 1929 purchasing power".

[14]Computing a price index would be easy if all prices were to change by the same percentage. When all *P's* triple, the index rises from 100 to 300; when all halve, it drops to 50. If *P's* increase in different degrees, but all end up between double and triple their base, the index is certainly between 200 and 300. Just where? Evidently we need some kind of an *average* of the price changes, each being *weighted* in accordance with its approximate economic *importance*. The official indexes are good approximations, but some basic problems remain: getting an accurate sample of prices; allowing for quality improvements; deciding which average to use (arithmetic or geometric mean, median, etc.); defining relative-economic-importance weights, in a static and in a changing world. Note that the average price change of the goods a poor man buys might be different from the index appropriate for a rich man—because necessities and luxuries may show different rates of inflation.

Table 10-4 gives the actual 1929 and 1933 GNE figures to the close approximations of 5.5 and 3.0 billion dollars. It shows a fall of money GNE to 55 per cent of its old level. But the government estimates that prices of goods and services dropped on the average about 25 per cent in the Depression. Using 1929 as a base of 100, this means the 1933 price index was about 75. So our 3.0 billion-dollar 1933 GNE was really worth more than 55 per cent of the 5.5 billion-dollar GNE of 1929.

How much more? Table 10-4 divides through by the price index number to "deflate" and shows that *real GNE fell only to three-quarters the 1929 level:* thus in terms of dollars of 1929 purchasing power, it fell down to 4.0 billion dollars. Hence, part of the fall shown by the money GNE was due to the optical illusion of the changing price yardstick.

Figure 10-3 shows the history of *money* (or "nom-

SAMPLE CALCULATION OF REAL GNE

DATE	(1) MONEY GNE, BILLIONS OF CURRENT DOLLARS	(2) INDEX NUMBER OF PRICES	(3) REAL GNE, IN BILLIONS OF 1929 DOLLARS $(3) = \frac{(1)}{(2)} \times 100$
1929	5.5	100	$\frac{5.5}{100} \times 100 = 5.5$
1933	3.0	75	$\frac{3.0}{75} \times 100 = 4.0$

TABLE 10-4. To convert money GNE into real GNE we deflate by dividing by price index.

Using price index of Column (2), we deflate Column (1) to get real GNE Column (3). (Riddle: Can you show that 1929's real GNE was 4.1 billion dollars in terms of 1933 prices? Hint: With 1933 as a base, 1929's price index is 133 1/3.)

inal") GNE, expressed in the actual dollars and prices that were current in each historical year). Then, for comparison, the *real* GNE (expressed in 1969 dollars) is shown.[15] Note that part of the increase in money GNE is spurious, being due merely to inflation of our money yardstick's price units in the last 30 years.

CANADA'S GNE, GNP, AND NNP

Armed with an understanding of the concepts involved, we can turn to the actual data in the important Table 10-3, a table which merits lengthy study.

FLOW-OF-PRODUCT APPROACH Look first at the left side of Table 10-3. This gives the upper-loop flow-of-product approach to GNE. We have four components. Of these, C and G and their obvious classifications require little comment.

[15] Readers should be warned that the deflated GNE series is revised from time to time rendering comparisons between widely-separated years and between countries very risky. Two of the chief difficulties are obtaining reliable price indexes for investment goods, and allowing for productivity increases in construction. The last major revision by Statistics Canada was in 1972. Naturally, the more severe the inflation, the more controversial become the decisions about specific deflating techniques.

FIG. 10-3. Money GNE has illusory rate of growth because of price inflation.

The steepness of the money GNE exaggerates the rise of real Canadian production. A price index has been used to deflate GNE to produce the colored "1961-dollar" curve. The third dashed curve is further "deflated" to allow for the growth of population. Note the ratio scale. (Source: Statistics Canada.)

The final net-export item will be discussed further in Chapter 13. Remember that it may be positive *or* negative: in 1973 we had a deficit on current account, so that net exports were minus one billion dollars. (In some GNE accounts net exports (being the extra exports not paid for by imports) are shown as our "net foreign investment" (exports we lend to foreigners at our expense), so that 1969 negative net exports would be negative net foreign investment. Net foreign investment could then be added to domestic business net investment to get total investment. But in Canada we usually keep them separate.) In any case, along with C, G, and domestic I, net exports do represent a fourth component of the flow of product.

Adding up the four components on the left gives the important total GNP of 119 billion dollars. This is the harvest we have been working for: the money measure of the Canadian economy's over-all performance for 1973. (Finally, note that if we subtract depreciation from the GNE figure, we get NNP of 106 billion dollars, which is smaller because it contains net rather than gross investment in its measure of product.)

LOWER-LOOP FLOW-OF-COST APPROACH

Now turn to the right-hand side of the table. Here we have all the value-added items plus taxes and depreciation.

A few explanations are in order. Wages,[16] salaries, and supplementary incomes include all take-home pay and fringe benefits, and they also have in them the income tax deductions and other taxes that wage earners have to pay.

Interest is a similar item. (Note again, interest on government bonds is not included as part of G or GNP, being treated as a transfer.)

Rent income of persons requires only one explanation. It of course includes rents received by landlords. In addition, if you own your own home, you are treated as paying rent to yourself. This is a so-called "imputed" item and makes sense if we really want to measure the housing services the Canadian people are enjoying and do not want the estimate to be changed every time a tenant buys the house he has been renting. Admittedly, this imputed item has to be estimated, since no one reports rental receipts on his own home.

Depreciation on capital goods that were used up, 13 billion dollars, must appear as an expense in GNP, much like other expenses.

Lastly, turn to profit. This should be the last kind of income dealt with because it is residual—determined as what is left after all the other items have been taken into account. There are two kinds of profits: those of corporations and those of unincorporated business. Corporate profits of 15 billion dollars are shown, but we must deduct one billion

dollars in dividends paid to foreigners; for remember that we are deriving the gross *national* product. The remainder will be divided between: corporate taxes, undistributed corporate profits "plowed back" into the company, and dividends. But this disposition is not shown here.

Unincorporated-enterprise profits arise on farms and from such proprietorships and partnerships as are found in running retail stores, law offices and those few manufacturers that remain unincorporated. The table calls these profits "incomes", because they really comprise a mixture of returns on labor, land, and capital put into the business by their owners.

At the end, we tack on not only the residual error of estimate and inventory valuation adjustment,[17] but also business *indirect* taxes. The latter have to be included if the lower loop is to match the upper loop. Recall that business and personal direct taxes are already part wages, rents, interest, or profits.

Again, on the right side, the flow-of-cost approach gives us the same 119 billion dollars of GNP and the same NNP figure of 106 billion dollars (after subtracting depreciation).

FOUR RELATED CONCEPTS: DISPOSABLE, PERSONAL, AND NATIONAL INCOMES, AND GROSS DOMESTIC PRODUCT

Table 10-3 summarized the fundamentals of national-income accounting. For purposes of broad economic description, our task is over. But a businessman, citizen, or statesman who wants to follow carefully just what is happening from month to month and quarter to quarter in the Canadian economy or abroad will benefit from a brief digression to define four other concepts that are measured and reported on by Statistics Canada and similar official units elsewhere.

---

[16] The late Sir Arthur Bowley of the London School of Economics noted how remarkably constant over almost a century is wages' share of national income. No one is sure why this should be so. (The wages' share does rise at the expense of profit during recession; in recent decades the wage share has perhaps shown a slight upward creep, as seen in Chapter 37.)

[17] The statistician must trace the "inventory-valuation adjustment" throughout both accounts. On the GNE side, he shows investment in inventories as their physical change times the average price ruling *within* the year. Thus the profits of unincorporated and incorporated firms (especially farms holding stocks of grain) as shown above contain a markup (or markdown, if prices of grain, etc., fell within the year). To make the totals in the two loops match (i.e. to make GNP equal to GNE) he then subtracts this markup from the GNP side, as is reported in "inventory-valuation adjustment."

Disposable income, personal income, (narrowly defined) national income, and gross domestic product (GDP) are useful rearrangements of the above data.

Disposable income (DI). How many dollars per year do private individuals and families have available to *them* to spend? The concept of disposable income tries to answer this question. Broadly speaking, to get disposable income, one subtracts depreciation and all taxes (direct or indirect) from GNP, subtracts all corporate earnings that were not paid out in dividends (i.e. were retained as corporate savings), and adds in transfer payments of welfare or interest-on-federal debt type. The result is, so to speak, *what actually gets into our hands and is left there for us to dispose of as we please.*[18]

Disposable income is an important series of data because, as will be seen in Part Two, it is this sum (suitably adjusted to take account of interest on loans that the consumer must pay) that people divide between (a) consumption spending and (b) net personal saving. Thus, in recent years people have been spending about 94 per cent of disposable income on consumption and interest and about 6 per cent on net personal saving. It is this series that will be watched eagerly by a department-store head and a policy maker apprehensive over inflationary pressure or too little consumption spending.

Personal income (PI). Unlike disposable income, personal income measures what persons receive, before they pay direct taxes. So disposable income plus personal direct taxes = personal income. This total can be calculated more quickly than disposable income. DI and PI tend to move closely together over time.

National income (NNI), *narrowly defined.* We have followed the common practice and used the term "national income" to refer generally to all the concepts of this chapter—GNE, GNP, NNP, and so forth. But mention should be made of a narrower sense in which Statistics Canada defines the term. Indeed, for technical reasons, it prefers this total to NNP. Its full name is Net National Income at Factor Cost (NNI), and, it stands mid-way between NNP and DI. It is simply NNP without the indirect business taxes (hence the term "at factor cost" in its full name.)[19] All direct taxes, personal and corporate, are left in, as are the

undistributed earnings of corporations. All transfers are left out. Thus it might be called the full factor earnings of *productive* activity.

Thus we have two bits of national-accounts terminology: "factor cost" means that indirect taxes have been subtracted from the "market prices"; and "net" means that depreciation has been subtracted from "gross".

Gross domestic product (GDP). While GNP measures Canadians' income from production, wherever it is, GDP measures Canadian production, whoever gets paid for it. How many dollars' worth of products are made by factors of production *used* in Canada? The GNP does not answer this question; for Canadian work done by a commuting American autoworker or Swiss engineer is left out: the GNP regards their incomes as payments for "imports of work." The GNP also leaves out interest and dividends paid to foreign lenders and owners; but adds in interest, wages, and dividends paid to Canadians out of production abroad. GDP adjusts for these characteristics. It includes every factor payment made in Canada (even to foreigners, for imported factors) and excludes incomes of Canadians earned for factor services abroad. (Consequently, the GNP can be divided down totally by kinds of income, wages, interest, etc.; whereas the GDP can be divided down to show *all* total factor rewards in *each* industry. Not surprisingly, then, the GNP is often used for Canadian income studies, while the GDP is a background for industry studies. The Appendix to this chapter says something more about the GDP.)

These four important national-income concepts, GDP, NNP, NNI, and DI, are alike in their movements. That is why most people are content to watch NNP (or GNP) alone, occasionally supplementing it with data on disposable income.

BEYOND GNP TO NET ECONOMIC WELFARE (NEW)

In the very first chapter, we saw that, these days, there is considerable disenchantment with mere material goods and services, and hence disenchantment with the GNP as a measure of economic welfare. Fortunately, as we saw back in Fig. 1-1 on page 5, modern economists can begin to adjust the GNP numbers in order to get a more meaningful measure of growth in "net economic welfare" (NEW):

PLUSES: EXAMPLE OF LEISURE First, in the briefest way, let's see what is wrong with GNP as now measured. Suppose you decide, as you become

---

[18] The spread on pages 178-179 of the Appendix containing Table 10-5 and Fig. 10-5 could be useful to help you follow these interrelations.

[19] Recall that GNP is a measure of the total values of all final goods and services sold. As Table 10-3 shows, each of these values contains, basically, two things: the cost of hiring factors (including a profit payment), and indirect taxes such as sales tax and excise. Thus GNP is the value of output "at market prices" —what people have to pay. But NNI is this value "at factor costs"—what people are paid. Indirect taxes are a wedge between factor costs and market prices.

more affluent, to work fewer hours, to get your psychic satisfactions from *leisure* as well as from goods and services. Then the measured GNP goes down even though welfare goes up. Or, as the Appendix will explain, consider the work women do in the home not for formal pay. The value-added that a master cook imparts to a gourmet family dinner never enters into the goods and services of the GNP —not in the upper-loop nor in the lower-loop.

MINUSES: HIDDEN POLLUTION AND ECOLOGICAL COSTS
The above understatements and inadequacies of the GNP are easy to understand. More difficult are some overstatements contained in conventional GNP measures. Along with adding in "goods" (e.g., pleasurable air conditioning), GNP should be adjusted so that it subtracts out "bads" (e.g., the pollution of air and water that is involved in generating the power for the air conditioning). Clearly we must adjust for any such "bads" that escape the GNP statistician whenever society is both failing to prevent pollution and failing to make power users pay the full costs of the damage they do.

EXAMPLE: I enjoy 10,000 kilowatt hours of power for air conditioning, paying the hydro company 1 cent per kilowatt hour. That 1 cent goes for its labor, plant costs, oil-coal-nuclear-hydroelectric fuels. But suppose the company incurs no money costs at all for the damage it does the environment: sulphur from its coal and oil, coal dust, heating of rivers, oil slicks in waters, etc. Did I say "incurs no costs?" I mean, suppose it (and I, the ultimate consumer) gets off scot-free: the costs go on, but they are not faced up to. Suppose they are ½ cent per kilowatt hour. (That is, to restore the environment, which people really think ought just to be done, makes true power cost 1½ cents per kilowatt hour.) Then the GNP flow of "goods" must somehow have subtacted from it $50 of pollution "bads" to show the true NEW.

Warning: NEW differs from GNP when pollution costs go unmet or unnoticed. If society made the hydro company (and me!) pay $150 for factors, fuels and restoration expenses to provide me with "air-cooling plus restoration of ecological balance", real GNP would need no correction. Why not? Because $150 of money GNP, deflated by 1-1/2 cents of price, would yield real GNP of exactly 10,000 kilowatt hours plus an undamaged environment—the correct result when no "bads" are allowed to be created along with the "goods".

Query: Does this mean, as some noneconomists claim, that "GNP is so stupid a measure that it actually is raised by the fact of pollution—when industry spends more on pollution prevention and control, this raises GNP". No, neither real GNP nor NEW will, when correctly measured, be *enhanced* by the curse of pollution or other regrettable costs (such as for police against criminals, locks against burglars, defensive fighter planes against offensive bombers and missiles). The reason is economic, not statistical. It is obvious that if science invented a costless way of producing power *without* pollution, less resources would be needed to provide my 10,000 kilowatts of clean power—

FIG. 10-4. Does NEW (net economic welfare) grow slower than GNP? Both NEW curves are actually index numbers showing how a $1,000 per capita income in 1926-1930 has grown, when leisure and pollution are taken into account. More production means more pollution, less leisure. Low valuation of increased leisure gives curve NEW (a); growing congestion and pollution slow growth below GNE. Higher valuation of new leisure gives variant (b) of NEW. Now look at the projections of GNP and NEW into the future, shown by the dotted straight lines. They show what may happen if we don't take action about congestion and pollution. But if people really wish to improve the quality of life—and not just talk about doing so—we must pay the cost. That is, we must adopt some public and private policies that sacrifice some ordinary GNP growth to get more NEW growth. Note that the stepped-up line of NEW brings a less steep GNP line. (Source: see footnote 20.)

and hence *more resources* would be available for other good things of life (books, paintings, ...). Hence, properly reckoned, NEW and real GNP would be larger, not smaller, if pollution were nonexistent—and the same money GNP could be deflated by lower prices, to give a higher real GNP.

In summary, when concerned economists (like Nordhaus and Tobin) calculate net economic welfare, they attempt to adjust GNE numbers downwards for the disamenities, congestion and pollution that have escaped costing, and adjust it upward for increased leisure, and length of life. We shall not here ennumerate all the various adjustments made in going from real per capita GNE to NEW.[20]

Figure 10-4 tells the main story. It's an historical report on what we've already seen in Fig. 1-1. As there, we see that NEW probably grows more slowly than GNP, as one expects in a densely populated, congested world. And if you leaf back to page 4, you will recall the point which was made there and which will be developed in Part Six.

Public policies can choose to improve economic welfare, NEW—if necessary, at the deliberate sacrifice of mere GNP growth. Political economy must serve mankind's wishes. There is no need for men to be chained to mere material growth unless they wish to be.

This chapter has now given us the tools to chart the progress and health of an economy. It is a culmination of the introductory survey that is the task of Part One. It is a prelude to the subject of Part Two, analysis of *macro*economic forces determining the level, trend, and fluctuations of GNP and of the general level of prices.

SUMMARY

1. Gross national product, GNP, is definable as a dollar flow of total product for a nation; the sum of consumption plus investment (domestic and foreign) plus government expenditure on goods and services. GNP = $C + I + G$. (NNP is definable in the same way, but investment, I, now being interpreted as net, rather than gross, investment.)

2. By use of a price index, we can "deflate" money NNP or GNP (in current dollars) to arrive at a more accurate measure of "real NNP or GNP, expressed in dollars of one base-year's purchasing power". Use of such an average price index (of consumer-goods, investment-goods, and government-goods prices) is an approximate way of allowing for the rubber yardstick implied by changing levels of prices.

3. Because of the way we define residual profit, we can match the flow-of-product measurement of GNP (or NNP) by the lower-loop flow-of-cost measurement. This uses factor earnings, carefully computing *values added* to eliminate double counting of intermediate products. And after adding all (before-tax) wage, interest, rent, depreciation, and profit income, it adds to this total all *indirect* tax costs to business. (GNP definitely does *not* include transfer items such as receipt of interest on government bonds, or receipt of welfare pensions, or consumer-loan interest).

---

[20] There have been a number of valuations of leisure. See Simon Kuznets, *Income and Wealth of the United States,* Cambridge, 1952, W. C. Hood and A. D. Scott, *Output, Labour and Capital,* Ottawa 1956. For a very recent study with some proposed "social indicators", see Economic Council of Canada, *Eleventh Annual Review: Economic Targets and Social Indicators.* Information Canada, Ottawa, 1974, pp. 12 – 14 and 73 – 107.

In Fig. 10-4, the valuation of leisure, survival and consumer capital underlying NEW (b) is based on forthcoming work by Queen's University's Dan Usher.

In variant (a) the authors have subtracted from the Canadian GNE per capita of Figure 10-3 the disamenity valuation of W. Nordhaus and J. Tobin in "Is Growth Obsolete?" in *Economic Growth,* N.B.E.R., New York, 1972. The NEW (b) curve is based on a combination of Usher with Nordhaus and Tobin.

The NEW curves are actually index numbers with base $1,000 in 1926 – 29.

4. An "open" economy is one which relies heavily on trade with other nations, so that exports are largely relative to GNP. Net exports = exports – imports, and may be positive (surplus) or negative (deficit). Positive net exports may be viewed as a loan to, or investment in, other nations.

5. Net investment is positive when people are devoting part of society's resources to creating more buildings, equipment, and inventory than is currently being used up in the form of depreciation. Net investment equals gross investment minus depreciation. As depreciation is hard to estimate, the statisticians have more confidence in their measures of gross than of net investment.

6. For the foregoing reason, the official statistics put greatest stress on gross national product rather than net. GNE = GNP = NNP + Depreciation, always. Since depreciation is sluggish, and rarely varies much from twelve per cent of GNP (or fourteen per cent of NNP), we can generally use GNP and NNP interchangeably.

7. Disposable, personal, (narrowly defined) national income, and GDP are four additional official measurements. GDP is GNP plus wages, interest, and profits paid to foreigners less foreign factor incomes paid to Canadian residents. NNI is simply NNP with indirect business taxes (gasoline, sales, and other nonincome taxes) removed. Personal income (PI) is what factors are paid for productive activity. Disposable income (DI) is what people actually have left to spend on consumption or to save after all taxes, corporate saving of undistributed profits, and transfer adjustments have been made.

8. Gross national product needs to be modified if we are to approximate to a better measure of Net Economic Welfare (NEW). The Nordhaus-Tobin calculation of NEW adds to GNP certain items—such as value of leisure and housewives' services. It also subtracts from GNP unmet costs of pollution, other disamenities of modern urbanization, and still other adjustments. The result still shows a positive growth in NEW, but at a different rate than GNP, probably slower.

More information about national-income accounting is given in the Appendix to this chapter. Also given are some selected figures on the nation's recent economic history: the Statistics Canada important production index; and data on employment and unemployment. These vital aggregates chart a nation's economic health.

CONCEPTS FOR REVIEW

GNP in two equivalent views:
    upper-loop product flow
    lower-loop costs
    price index

1975 money NNP (or GNP) in current dollars, and 1975 real NNP (or GNP) in 1958 dollars

intermediate goods, double counting, value added

gross investment – depreciation = net investment

NNP + depreciation = GNP = GNE

$GNP = C + I + G + (E - M)$
government transfers
indirect and direct taxes

net exports of goods and services

dividends, undistributed profits

income of unincorporated enterprise

valuation adjustment

GDP, NNI, PI and DI

NEW: leisure, intermediate costs, unmet disamenities (pollution)

RECONCILIATION OF NATIONAL INCOME CONCEPTS (billions of dollars)

	1926	1936	1946	1956	1966	1973
Gross National Product (GNP)	5	5	12	31	61	119
Less:						
Depreciation (Capital consumption allowance)	1	1	1	4	7	13
Indirect taxes minus subsidies	1	1	1	4	8	15
Residual error of estimate	-	-	-	-	-	-
Equals:						
Net National Income (NNI)	4	4	9	23	46	91
Less:						
Undistributed corporate profits	-	-	1	1	3	6
Corporate taxes	-	-	1	1	2	3
Plus:						
Net transfers (and adjustments)	-	-	2	2	5	11
Equals:						
Personal Income (PI)	4	4	10	23	46	93
Less:						
Personal Taxes*	-	-	1	2	6	17
Equals:						
Personal Disposable Income (DI)	4	3	9	21	40	76
Less:						
Personal net saving	-	(-)	1	1	3	7
Equals:						
Consumption (C)	4	3	8	20	36	69
Plus:						
Government (G)	-	1	2	4	10	23
Net investment (Net I)						
(business and government)	-	(-)	1	5	9	14
Exports–Imports (E-M)	-	-	-	-1	-1	-1
Equals:						
Net National Product (NNP)	4	4	11	28	54	106
Plus:						
Depreciation	1	1	1	4	7	13
Residual Error of estimate	-	-	-	-	-	-
Equals:						
Gross National Expenditure (GNE)	5	5	12	31	61	119

*Income taxes, succession duties, estate taxes, employer and employee contributions to social insurance and government pension funds, and other.

TABLE 10-5. How the official statistics of national income are interrelated. Each total corresponds to a block in Fig. 10-5—the reader should examine them together. Note that the NNP figure is not shown explicitly in the national accounts. Detail may not add to the totals shown because of rounding. Also, note that Government (G) is, here, government *current* expenditure on goods and services only. (Source: Statistics Canada.)

Each of these items can raise an argument. Each has an element of intermediate business expense in it, and each an element of consumption. The tax collector and the national-income statistician do not always agree on the treatment of these, and we can raise questions about each one's decisions. (EXAMPLE: The tax collector will not let anyone deduct his commuting costs to work *in town*; but out of town he may be able to. The sandpaper is clearly deductible from taxable income and from GNP; but the overalls are not if it can be shown that wearing them saved an ordinary suit's wearing out. So it goes. Close decisions and arbitrary ones.)

3. *Gifts* that are not disguised payments for work done or for goods and services are not included in GNP. They are like government transfers that we have already discussed. The same goes for the allowance a father gives his son. But what about the fee he pays the son for mowing the lawn? In logic it should be in GNP, but it rarely is.

4. If I buy an old painting, a corner lot, or a used car from someone else, that transaction is not a final trans-

PRINCIPAL ECONOMIC AGGREGATES (all income data in millions of current dollars)

(1) Year	(2) Gross National Product $ Million	(3) Net National Income (at Factor Cost) $ Million	(4) Personal Disposable Income $ Million	(5) Net Saving as Percentage of Disposable Income	(6) Government Expenditure on Goods and Services as Percentage of GNE	(7) Index of Gross (Real) Domestic Product (1949= 100)	(8) Civilian Labor Force (Thousands)	(9) Unemployment as Percentage of Civilian Labor Force	(10) Consumer Price Index (1961= 100)
1926	5,146	4,086	3,961	10.6	7.6	–	3,658	3.0	59
1930	5,720	4,343	4,267	-2.4	8.8	–	4,060	9.1	53
1936	4,634	3,314	3,452	-2.8	9.7	52	4,466	12.8	47
1946	11,885	9,363	8,923	10.0	13.9	90	4,862	3.4	60
1947	13,169	10,206	9,584	5.5	10.2	94	4,954	2.2	66
1948	15,127	11,834	11,079	9.8	9.6	97	5,035	2.3	75
1949	16,300	12,708	11,849	7.8	10.6	100	5,092	2.8	77
1950	17,955	13,888	12,688	5.6	10.7	106	5,198	3.6	80
1951	21,060	16,294	14,794	9.7	13.4	115	5,230	2.4	88
1952	24,042	18,504	16,072	9.8	15.1	123	5,344	2.9	90
1953	25,327	19,270	16,904	8.0	15.1	127	5,386	3.0	89
1954	25,233	18,979	16,984	4.5	15.2	124	5,476	4.6	90
1955	27,895	20,948	18,239	4.1	14.5	136	5,585	4.4	90
1956	31,374	23,432	20,153	4.9	14.1	148	5,738	3.4	91
1957	32,907	24,522	21,107	4.6	13.9	147	5,970	4.6	94
1958	34,094	25,458	22,646	5.3	14.2	149	6,120	7.1	97
1959	36,266	27,105	23,948	3.3	13.7	156	6,186	6.0	98
1960	37,775	28,147	25,075	3.3	14.0	158	6,391	7.0	99
1961	39,080	29,062	26,011	2.8	16.2	161	6,518	7.2	100
1962	42,353	31,649	28,243	5.6	16.0	171	6,608	6.0	101
1963	45,465	34,100	30,018	5.4	15.7	180	6,748	5.5	103
1964	49,783	37,198	31,725	4.2	15.4	193	6,933	4.7	105
1965	54,897	40,969	35,149	5.5	15.1	206	7,100	3.9	107
1966	61,421	46,032	38,579	6.7	16.0	219	7,420	3.6	111
1967	65,608	49,306	41,709	6.3	16.6	224	7,631	3.9	115
1968	71,454	53,871	44,964	5.6	16.9	235	7,919	4.8	120
1969	78,537	59,868	50,557	5.4	17.6	246	8,162	4.7	126
1970	84,468	64,211	54,071	5.9	19.4	252	8,374	5.9	130
1971	93,402	70,449	59,288	7.6	19.8	267	8,631	6.4	133
1972	103,407	78,704	66,284	7.7	19.9	281	8,891	6.3	140
1973	118,678	90,700	75,667	7.4	19.4	301	9,279	5.6	150
1974 (est)	145,000	115,000	–	–	20.0	310	9,600	5.0	165

TABLE 10-6. These aggregates chart the nation's economic health. Forecasters like to use the GDP index because it moves sensitively. Statesmen worry about the unemployment figures. (Source: Statistics Canada.)

action to be put into GNP. He and I have just *exchanged assets*: money for picture. Nothing has been produced.[1]

So this is more in the nature of a special kind of transfer.[2] It illustrates an important fact: the total dollar volume of all intermediate transactions greatly exceeds the volume of

[1]If a broker earns a fee for arranging the deal, that fee is counted as part of GNP. Just as some men produce satisfactions in the form of bread, brokers and salesmen produce satisfactions in the form of bringing transactors together.

[2]Do not confuse this kind of transfer with the government transfers we have talked about.

the final transactions that we call national income or product. The loops of Fig. 10-1 include only a minority of the transactions that are taking place within the business and public blocks of that diagram.

Note, too, that we try not to let *capital gains due to mere price changes* enter into GNP. If Wall Street bids up my Ford stocks, I may feel rich and spend more of my DI. But that windfall gain is not attributable to current economic activity, and the statistician tries to keep it out. For similar reasons he makes the inventory valuation adjustment in corporate profits.

5. One could go on giving borderline cases, but we conclude with only one more. In measuring GNE, we are not interested in consumption and investment goods merely for their money value: *money is the measuring rod used to give some approximate figure to the underlying "satisfactions" or "benefits" or "psychic income" that comes from goods.* Strictly speaking, then, each time I play a phonograph record, shouldn't that act get into the GNE at its fair market value? Yes. And if I have put a dime in a juke box, it may in fact get directly into the GNE; but playing it at home will not get it directly into the GNE.

Indirectly, this enjoyment of a psychic pleasure does tend to get in the GNE to the extent that I wear out the record by playing it. Hence, as I replace my records, my consumption purchases at the store give a rough money measure of my enjoyments—but only a rough measure.

The statistician admits this, defending his practice by saying that a man's house is his castle and no accountant can enter his abode to measure his actual current consumptions; instead, he settles for treating a thing as consumed when it enters his abode. This all works well enough, except in one case.

More and more these days we spend our consumption dollar on durable consumers' goods. Actually, then, in the years that we are building up our home inventories of such durable goods, our true psychic consumption is being overstated by our retail purchases; and vice versa in the years when we run them down. (NEW takes some account of this.)

Some purists say, "In GNE, let's try to estimate actual home consumption of services or durables and put that in C, not in the mere retail purchases of the year." Statistics Canada thinks this too hard a job to do, but for special purposes economists have tried to make (from gas and mileage records, for example) more accurate estimates of auto consumption than is provided by new car sales.[3]

Fortunately, in the long run, the two methods tend to come to the same thing, particularly if society is not growing too fast or too unsteadily.

---

[3]It is interesting that in the case of a house, the most durable consumers' good of all, the officials do actually follow this principle: they do not take expenditures on a house as its C, but estimate the house use separately.

A THIRD APPROACH TO NATIONAL PRODUCT: GDP

In developing the flow-of-product approach, we eventually subtracted all payments for productive activity except "factor costs" and "indirect taxes." We wound up with estimates of expenditure on *final output*, that are classified as C, G, gross I, or (E – M). This tells us nothing about the value added in each *industry* (such as agriculture, printing, baking, railways, etc.), because the output of most industries is the input of others, therefore it doesn't make up a part of *final* output, and it isn't reported in GNE or NNP accounts.

It is possible, however, for statisticians to find out how much value is added in each industry, and to add these amounts together. This has been done for years in such well-known, though partial, indexes as the Index of Industrial Production (and the U.S. Federal Reserve Board Index). The final index is an average of the indexes for each of the industries, each one measuring the growth or decline of value added ("deflated," as on page 169) in that industry. These indexes are extremely useful as a third, industry-by-industry, value-added measure of aggregate product.

Statistics Canada has expanded the coverage of its total index from manufacturing and mining industries only to the whole economy. This expanded index is called the Gross Domestic Product at factor cost (GDP). It is called "Domestic" rather than "National" product because it concentrates on the *production or output* generated within Canada rather than the income of Canadian residents. Thus the chief difference in definition between GDP and GNP or GNE (apart from indirect taxes) is that if earnings arising from production go to a foreigner, they are left out of the GNP but remain in the GDP. For example, the wages of a Detroit resident working in Sarnia are included in GDP but not in GNP. Conversely if a Canadian gets dividends from foreign production, the dividends enter GNP but not GDP. In other countries, and sometimes in Canada, the GDP is called the real domestic product. It is useful because it tells us about the Canadian final output or production *per se* and because of its fine breakdown into industries. Furthermore the GDP measure provides a fairly independent check on the trends, long-run and quarterly, of the "deflated" GNP and GNE. Table 10-6 gives indexes since 1936.

THE IDENTITY OF MEASURED SAVING AND INVESTMENT

To pave the way for the discussion of intersecting saving and investment schedules in Chapter 12, we can here show that the national-income statistician defines the saving he measures as exactly the same thing as the investment he measures. This equality of measured saving and measured investment is an identity of double-entry bookkeeping and holds by definition.

What is the measure of investment? Forgetting government and foreign trade, we know I is the output in the upper-loop that is not C. What is the measure of saving S? Again forgetting government and corporate saving, we know that S is that part of the lower-loop disposable income, or GNP, that is not spent on C. To summarize:

$$I = \text{upper-loop GNP minus } C$$
$$S = \text{lower-loop GNP minus } C$$

But the two loops must give the same measure of GNE or GNP. So $I = S$; the identity between measured saving and investment.

Our task will be done once we bring the corporation and the government into the picture. Investment is just as before. But now gross saving S must be split into three different terms: (1) net personal saving, which people do out of their disposable incomes; (2) gross corporate, more accurately, business saving, that part of corporate incomes which they fail to pay out as dividends plus depreciation; finally (3) net government surplus (or "saving"), which represents the algebraic excess of its tax revenues over its expenditure on goods and services and on transfers.

Our identity of measured S and I now has to be written in terms of the three components of total S.[4]

$$I \equiv NPS + GCS + NGS$$

---

[4]The eager reader can test his grasp of this fundamental identity (which must hold at all times whether or not an economy is in equilibrium or is galloping to or from an equilibrium) by going back to the discussion (page 173) of how disposable income is defined in terms of GNP – taxes – GCS + transfers, and how $NPS = DI - C$. These relations combined with the $C + I + G$ breakdown of NNP can be used to give an algebraic demonstration of our identity, (ignoring $E - M$).

Thus, from the definition of DI,

$$GNP = DI + GCS + T_x - T_r$$

Adding and subtracting G and splitting up DI gives

$$GNP = C + [NPS + GCS + (T_x - T_r - G)] + G$$
$$= C + [NPS + GCS + (NGS)] + G$$

But recall the upper-loop definition

$$GNP = C + [I] + G$$

So we do indeed verify

$$[I] = [NPS + GCS + NGS]$$

2

Determination of National Income and its Fluctuations

11
SAVINGS, CONSUMPTION, AND INVESTMENT

We are all Keynesians now.   MILTON FRIEDMAN

In Part One the groundwork was laid for an understanding of the concept of national income. Now we can go beyond the anatomy of the problem to its physiology. What causes national income to rise? To fall? Why is GNP what it is at any time, rather than something larger or smaller? What causes too little total spending—recession and depression? What causes too much total spending—inflationary rises in the index of prices? Part Two analyzes these basic problems of 'macroeconomics', which is defined as the study of the aggregate performance of the whole GNP and of the general price level.

This chapter provides an introduction to what is called the "modern theory of income analysis." The principal stress is upon the *level of total spending as determined by the interplay of the monetary forces of saving and investment.*

Although much of this analysis is due to an English economist, John Maynard Keynes (later made Lord Keynes, before his death in 1946), today the broad fundamentals of the "new economics" are increasingly accepted by economists of all schools of thought, including, it is important to notice, many who do not share Keynes' particular policy views and who differ on technical details of analysis.[1] Because

political economy is a dynamic science, post-Keynesian analysis represents an evolution and development beyond the breakthroughs of 40 years ago.

In recent years 90 per cent of North American economists have stopped being "Keynesian economists" or "anti-Keynesian economists." Modern economists are "post-Keynesians," keen to render obsolete any theories that cannot meet the test of experience or applicability. Thus, in the 1970s post-Keynesians accord an importance to the role of money in the process of income determination that would have surprised the first disciples of Keynes (but which would not at all have surprised that brilliant virtuoso of finance). Even Marxian economists, who at first resented Keynesian economics literally as a "mere palliative" to the ills of capitalism, have come to recognize its explanatory powers.

THE CLEAVAGE BETWEEN SAVING AND INVESTMENT MOTIVATIONS

The most important single fact about saving and investment activities is that in our industrial society they are generally done *by different people* and done *for different reasons.*

This was not always so. And even today, when a farmer devotes his time to draining a field instead of to planting and harvesting a crop, he is saving and at the same time investing. He is "saving" because he is abstaining from *present* consumption in order to provide for larger consumption in the *future*—the amount of his saving being measured by the difference between his net real income and his consumption. But he is also "investing"; i.e., he is under-

---

[1] Keynes himself was a many-sided genius who won eminence in the fields of mathematics, philosophy, and literature. In addition, he found time to run a large insurance company, to advise the British Treasury, to help govern the Bank of England, to edit a world-famous economic journal, and to sponsor ballet and drama. He was also an economist who knew how to make money by shrewd speculation, both for himself and for King's College, Cambridge. His 1936 book, *The General Theory of Employment, Interest and Money,* created the greatest stir in economic thinking of the century and will live as a classic. Readers today will also enjoy his own *Essays in Persuasion and Biography,* and Robert Lekachman's *The Age of Keynes.*

taking net capital formation, improving the productive capacity of his farm. Not only are saving and investment the same things for a self-sufficient farmer, but his reasons for undertaking them are the same. He abstains from present consumption (saves) only because he wants to drain the field (to invest). If there were no investment opportunity whatsoever, it would never occur to him to save; nor would there be any way to save for the future, should he be so foolish as to wish to.

In our modern economy, net capital formation or investment is largely carried on by business enterprises, especially corporations. When a corporation or a small business has great investment opportunities, its owners will be tempted to plow back much of its earnings into the business. To an important degree, therefore, some business saving does still get motivated directly by business investment.

Nevertheless, saving is *primarily* done by an entirely different group: by individuals, by families, by households. An individual may wish to save for a great variety of reasons: to provide for his old age or for a future expenditure (a vacation or an automobile). Or he may feel insecure and wish to guard against a rainy day. Or he may wish to leave an estate to his children or to his children's children. Or he may be an eighty-year-old miser with no heirs who enjoys the act of accumulating for its own sake. Or he may already have signed himself up to a savings program because an insurance salesman was persuasive. Or he may desire the power that greater wealth brings. Or thrift may simply be a habit, almost a conditioned reflex, whose origin he does not himself know.

Whatever the individual's motivation to save, it often has little to do with the investment opportunities of society and business.

This truth is obscured by the fact that in everyday language "investment" does not always have the same meaning as in economics. We have defined "net investment," or capital formation, to be the net increase in the community's real capital (equipment, building, inventories). But the plain man speaks of "investing" when he buys a piece of land, an old security, or any title to property; for economists these are clearly *transfer* items. What one man is buying, someone else is selling. There is net investment only when *additional real capital* is created.

In short, even if there are no *real* investment opportunities that seem profitable, an individual may still *wish* to nonconsume—to save. He can always buy an existing security asset; he can accumulate, or *try* to accumulate, cash.

THE VARIABILITY OF INVESTMENT

Thus, we are left with our proposition: Saving and investing are often desired by different individuals and for independent reasons. While it is families who primarily decide to save, net capital formation takes place largely in business enterprise.

The amount of investment itself is *highly variable* from year to year and decade to decade. This capricious, volatile behavior is understandable when we come to realize that profitable investment opportunities depend on *new* discoveries, *new* products, *new* territories and frontiers, *new* resources, *new* population, *higher* production and income. Note the emphasis on "new" and on "higher."

Investment depends largely on the *dynamic* and relatively unpredictable elements of *growth* in the system, and importantly on elements outside the economic system itself: technology, politics, optimistic and pessimistic expectations, "confidence," governmental tax and expenditure, changes in the supply of money, legislative policies, and much else.

The extreme variability of investment is the next important fact to be emphasized.

The independence of forces operating on saving and on investment is like the independence of forces operating on Chapter 4's supply and demand schedules. While recognizing this independence, we should also recognize two qualifications.

(*a*) Often at the corporate level, decisions to invest are closely related to the funds that corporations are able to save out of their earnings and that need not be paid out in dividends; (*b*) at all times, but particularly in times of tight money and high interest rates, how much entrepreneurs can indulge their desire to invest in new, profitable opportunities will depend on how much finance is made available to them by people's saving.

Just as the independent forces operating on supply and demand are resolved by what happens to market prices, we shall see that saving and investment decisions, in their turn, are resolved by what happens to the level of income and employment and to interest rates.

We shall see that an industrial system such as ours can do many wonderful things. It can mobilize men, tools, and know-how to respond to any given demand for goods. Over time it can improve upon its own response. But there is one thing it can't do.

Unless proper macroeconomic policies are pursued, a *laissez-faire* economy cannot guarantee that there will be exactly the required amount of investment to ensure full employment: not too little so as to cause unemployment, nor too much so as to cause inflation. As far as total investment or money-spending power is concerned, *the laissez-faire* system is without a good thermostat.

For decades there might tend to be too little investment, leading to deflation, losses, excess capacity, unemployment, and destitution. For other years or decades, there might tend to be too much investment, leading to periods of chronic inflation—unless proper public policies in the fiscal (i.e., tax and expenditure) and monetary (i.e. central bank) fields are followed.

Nor is there an Invisible Hand guaranteeing that the good years will by themselves equal the bad; nor guaranteeing that scientists will discover just in the nick of time precisely enough new products and processes to keep the system on an even keel. From 1855 to 1875 railroads were built all over the world. In the next two decades nothing quite took the place of this activity. The automobile and public utilities produced a similar revolution in the 1920s. In the 1930s plastics and radio had no comparable effect on total net investment. In the years immediately following World War II, much of the time we were plagued by too much investment spending relative to the resources released by those acts of renouncing consumption which economists call "saving." Then in the Diefenbaker years of the 1950s, Canada experienced sluggish growth, with increasing unemployment. The years of the 1960s were years of unusual growth. As the 1970s developed, the Vietnam era and world shortages left their inflationary heritage.

Thus we see that the instabilities are not all on the downward side. Economic history is, alas, a history of inflations. Anyone who comes of age today has seen prices almost double in his own brief lifetime. Unless proper policies are followed, he can look forward to gyrating prices for the rest of his life.

While a realist must recognize that an economy like ours of 1929 or of the 1970s will not *by itself* maintain stability of prices and full employment, critics should still recognize that there are certain elements in a pricing economy that can work toward stability if given a chance to operate and if helped by vigorous public stabilizing actions. The money supply cannot be left to chance. As we shall see later, *the structure of interest rates*—which determines how costly and hard it is to get credit for investing activities—can be helped by Bank of Canada monetary policy to play a *stabilizing* role in moderating investment fluctuations. Also, to a considerable extent the frictions that keep various prices inflexible and sticky in a modern mixed economy can be offset by public fiscal actions.

This, then, is one of our most important economic lessons.

Where the stimulus to investment is concerned, the system is somewhat in the lap of the gods. We may be lucky or unlucky; and one of the few things you can say about luck is, "It's going to change." Fortunately, things need not be left to luck. We shall see that sensible monetary and fiscal policies can be followed that greatly enhance the stability and productive growth of the mixed economy. We shall also encounter some stubborn unsolved problems in our struggle to reconcile full employment and reasonable price-level stability.

The next chapters will show how investment and saving determine the equilibrium level of national income. First, we must understand the important budgetary patterns, reflecting how people consume and save at different income levels.

BUDGETARY EXPENDITURE PATTERNS

No two families spend their money in exactly the same way. Yet statistics do show that there is a predictable regularity—on the average—in the way peo-

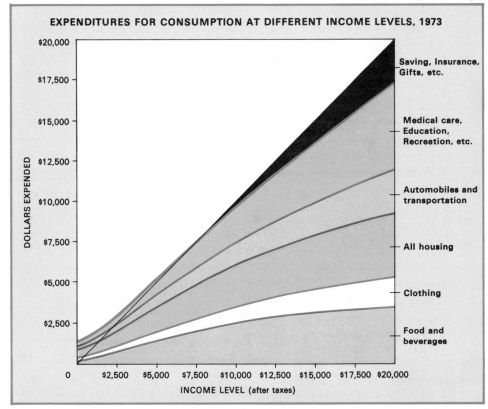

EXPENDITURES FOR CONSUMPTION AT DIFFERENT INCOME LEVELS, 1973

FIG. 11-1. Family budget expenditures show regular income patterns.
Careful sampling of urban families verifies the importance of income as a determinant of consumption expenditure. Notice the drop in food as a percentage of higher incomes. Note also the rise in saving, from below zero at low incomes to substantial positive levels. (Source: Derived by authors from family budget studies of various years by Statistics Canada and U.S. Departments of Labor and Agriculture; updated to mid-1970s incomes.)

ple allocate their expenditures on food, clothing, and other major items. Literally thousands of budgetary investigations have been made of the ways that people at different levels of income spend their money; and there is remarkable agreement on the general, qualitative patterns of behavior.[2] What are they? Figure 11-1 tells the story.

Poor families must, of course, spend their incomes largely on the necessities of life: food, shelter, and, in lesser degree, clothing. As income increases, ex-

[2] Figure 11-1's behavior patterns are called "Engel's Laws," after the nineteenth-century Prussian statistician Ernst Engel (not to be confused with Karl Marx's friend Friedrich Engels). The average behavior of consumption expenditure does change fairly regularly with income; but averages do not tell the whole story. Within each income class, there is considerable spread around the average.

penditure on many food items goes up. People eat more and eat better. They shift away from cheap, bulky carbohydrates to more expensive meats and proteins—and to milk, fruit, vegetables, and labor-saving processed foods.

There are, however, limits to the amount of extra money that people will spend on food when their incomes rise. Consequently, *the percentage importance of food expenditure declines as income increases.* (Actually, there are a few cheap, but filling, items such as potatoes or sausage whose consumption decreases absolutely with income increase. These are called "inferior goods" in Part Three.)

After you get out of the very poorest income class, your proportion of income spent on shelter is pretty constant for a wide range. This is expressed in a familiar rule of thumb: One week's salary should cover one month's expenditure on rent and house utilities. The other rule of thumb—that you should pay about 2 years' income for a house—has a hollow ring these days.

Expenditure on clothing, recreation, and automobiles increases *more than proportionately to after-tax income*, until high incomes are reached. Of course, luxury items, by definition, increase in greater proportion than income; and in many ways, as we shall soon see, saving is the greatest luxury of all, especially at very high incomes.

THE PROPENSITY TO SAVE AND THE PROPENSITY TO CONSUME

An important use of after-tax income is saving for the future rather than consuming now. This saving facet is what interests us most. It is a matter of common observation that rich men save more than poor men, not only in absolute amounts but also in percentage amounts. The very poor are unable to save at all. Instead they "dissave," i.e., spend more every year than they earn, the difference being covered by going into debt or using up previously accumulated savings. Thus, income is a prime determinant of saving, as shown in Table 11-1.[3]

This table gives data on saving and consumption indicative of *family patterns* in the early 1970s, the so-called "propensity to consume" and "propensity to save." Column (2) shows the net saving that accompanies each level of disposable income. The "break-even point," where the family neither saves nor dissaves, instead consuming all its income, falls at $8,000. Below this, as at $7,000 or $6,000, it actually consumes more than its income; it dissaves (see the − $110 and − $170 items). Above $8,000 it begins to do positive saving (see the +$150 item).

Column (3) shows the consumption pattern of each income level—the so-called "propensity to consume." Since each dollar of income is divided between the part consumed and the remaining part saved, Columns (3) and (2) are not independent: they must always exactly add up to Column (1). (Check that they do.)

Economic analysis is interested not simply in the total figures of saving and consumption, but in the *extra* saving and consumption that each *extra* dollar of income brings. Thus, as income goes from $8,000 to $9,000, the extra $1,000 of income is divided between $850 of extra consumption and $150 of extra saving—split up 85 and 15 per cent, so to speak. (Where did these numbers come from? You get them from $8,850 minus $8,000 and from $150 minus $0. And verify that the division between consumption and saving of extra dollars beyond $9,000 is, respectively, 75 and 25 per cent, then 64 and 36 per cent. ... Does it seem reasonable to you that richer people will consume a little less of each extra income dollar than will poorer?[4])

Family propensity-to-save and propensity-to-consume patterns have been rather stable. (Workers, however, have generally seemed to save less than the self-employed.)

To understand how saving and investment determine the level of national income and employment, we must continue to study in detail (1) the propensity-to-save schedule, relating saving and income, and its twin brother (2) the propensity-to-consume schedule, relating consumption and income.

THE PROPENSITY-TO-CONSUME SCHEDULE IN DETAIL

Table 11-2 rearranges these same data in more convenient form. First, verify its similarity to Table 11-1. Then, disregard its Columns (3) to (5) and concen-

---

[3] These cross-section data do not depict long-run behavior of each family when its income moves from a *permanent* low level to a *permanent* high level. Transitorily, saving rises much; but as people get accustomed to higher "permanent income," consumption rises and saving becomes moderate. Surprising as it may seem, statistics show that people with $15,000 of *permanent* income save about the same fraction of their income as do people with $10,000 of *permanent* income. (NOTE: In this and later chapters, consumer interest, mentioned in Chapter 10's Appendix, is ignored.)

[4] Students at first find it hard to understand that even when family income is below the break-even point and saving is negative, nonetheless each *extra* income dollar goes partly into positive extra saving and partly into positive extra consumption. To convince yourself, compare row 2 of Table 11-1 with row 1. Adding $1,000 to $6,000 of income gives $7,000. This extra income makes consumption go from $6,170 to $7,110, a gain of $940, with $60 of extra saving.

PROPENSITY OF FAMILIES TO SAVE AND CONSUME

(1) DISPOSABLE INCOME AFTER TAXES	(2) NET SAVING (+) OR DISSAVING (−)	(3) CONSUMPTION
$ 6,000	$ −170	$ 6,170
7,000	−110	7,110
8,000	0	8,000
9,000	+150	8,850
10,000	+400	9,600
11,000	+760	10,240
12,000	+1,170	10,830
13,000	+1,640	11,360

TABLE 11-1 Most saving is done by families with incomes considerably above the average.

The break-even point at which people cease to dissave and begin to do positive saving is here shown at $8,000. How much of each extra dollar do people around this income level devote to extra consumption? How much to extra saving? (Answer: About 85 cents and 15 cents, respectively.)

trate on how consumption expenditure goes up at each higher level of income.

This same consumption-income relation can be shown even more vividly in diagrammatic form. If Fig. 11-2, the total of consumption expenditure in Column (2) is plotted against family disposable income of Column (1); through the resulting circles *A, B, C, D, E, F,* and *G,* a smooth curve has been drawn.

This relation between consumption and income is called the *consumption schedule,* or *propensity-to-consume schedule,* or often simply the *propensity to consume.* It is a basic, important concept whose general properties we must study.

It will help you to understand its properties if, first, you look at the 45° line also shown in Fig. 11-2. Inasmuch as the vertical axis of consumption has been drawn to the same scale as the horizontal axis of income, any point lying on the 45° helping line has the following simple property: Its indicated consumption expenditure—measured by the vertical distance of the point from the horizontal axis—is *exactly equal to 100 per cent* of its indicated level of disposable income—measured by the horizontal distance of the point from the vertical axis. (Use your

PROPENSITY TO CONSUME AND TO SAVE

	(1) Disposable Income (after taxes)	(2) Consumption Expenditure	(3) Marginal Propensity to Consume (MPC)	(4) Net Savings (4) = (1) − (2)	(5) Marginal Propensity to Save (MPS)
A	$ 7,000	$ 7,110		$ −110	
			$\frac{890}{1,000}=0.89$		$\frac{110}{1,000}=0.11$
B	8,000	8,000		0	
			$\frac{850}{1,000}=0.85$		$\frac{150}{1,000}=0.15$
C	9,000	8,850		+150	
			$\frac{750}{1,000}=0.75$		$\frac{250}{1,000}=0.25$
D	10,000	9,600		+400	
			$\frac{640}{1,000}=0.64$		$\frac{360}{1,000}=0.36$
E	11,000	10,240		+760	
			$\frac{590}{1,000}=0.59$		$\frac{410}{1,000}=0.41$
F	12,000	10,830		+1,170	
			$\frac{530}{1,000}=0.53$		$\frac{470}{1,000}=0.47$
G	13,000	11,360		+1,640	

TABLE 11-2. Numerical table shows consumption and saving schedules and marginal propensities.

Each dollar of income that is not consumed is saved. And each dollar of income goes into extra consumption or extra saving—giving important concepts we need: marginal propensity to consume and to save, MPC and MPS. (Note: $890 = $8,000 − $7,110. How about $850?)

eye to verify that any point *not* on the 45° line cannot possibly be equidistant from the two axes.)

THE "BREAK-EVEN" POINT The 45° line will tell us right away, therefore, whether consumption spending is equal to, greater than, or less than the level of income. The point on the consumption schedule where it intersects the 45° line shows us the level of disposable income at which families just break even. This break-even point is at *B*; here, consumption expenditure is exactly equal to disposable income; the family is borrowing nothing and on balance saving nothing.

Similarly, *anywhere else* on the propensity-to-consume curve, the family cannot be just breaking even. To the right of point *B,* the curve lies below the 45°

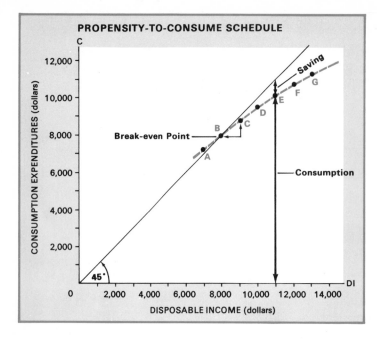

FIG. 11-2. A curve plots the consumption schedule.

The curve through *A, B, C,* ... is the consumption schedule, or the propensity to consume. Its slope at any point, measured by forming a little triangle and relating altitude to base, is the MPC, the marginal propensity to consume. The 45° line helps locate the break-even point and helps our eye measure net saving. Can you see how? (Source: Table 11-2 and extrapolation beyond *G.*)

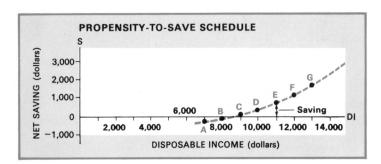

FIG. 11-3. The saving schedule is the mirror twin of the consumption schedule.

This saving schedule comes from subtracting consumption from income. (Graphically, we vertically subtracted the consumption schedule from the 45° helping line.) Note that the break-even point *B* is at the same $8,000 level as in Fig. 11-2.

line; the long arrow in Fig. 11-2 shows that the vertical distance (consumption expenditure) is less than the horizontal distance (disposable income). If the family is not spending all its income, then it must be saving the remainder. The 45° line tells us more than that; it enables us to find *how much* the family is saving. Net saving is measured by the distance from the propensity-to-consume curve up to the 45° line, as shown by the appropriate saving arrow in black

Similarly, to the left of point *B,* our 45° helping line tells us that the family is for the moment somehow spending more than the income it receives. The excess of consumption over income is its "net dis-

saving" and is measured by the vertical distance between the two curves. To review:

When the propensity-to-consume schedule lies above the 45° line, the family is dissaving. Where the two curves meet, the family is just breaking even. Where the propensity to consume lies below the 45° line, the family is performing net positive saving. And the amount of dissaving or saving is always measured by the distance between the the two curves.

THE "PROPENSITY-TO-SAVE SCHEDULE"

This means that we can easily derive from the consumption schedule in Fig. 11-2 a new schedule: the propensity to save, or as it is sometimes called, the "saving schedule."

Graphically, this is shown in Fig. 11-3. Again we show disposable income on the horizontal axis; vertically, we now show what the family *does not* spend; i.e., we show its net saving, whether negative or positive in amount.

This propensity-to-save curve comes directly from Fig. 11-2. It is simply the distance between the 45° line and the propensity-to-consume schedule. At a point such as *A* in Fig. 11-2, the fact that the family's savings were negative was indicated by the propensity-to-consume schedule lying above the helping line. Figure 11-3 shows this fact of negative saving directly, and similarly for the positive saving that begins when family income pushes past point *B*.

THE MARGINAL PROPENSITY TO CONSUME

In the next chapter, we shall be attaching much importance to the *extra* amount that people will want to spend on consumption if given an *extra* dollar of income. Economists are so interested in this concept that they have given it a special name, the "marginal propensity to consume," or MPC. (The word "marginal" is used by the economist to mean "extra"; thus, marginal cost will later be defined as extra cost of producing an extra unit of product; marginal utility as extra utility; marginal revenue as extra revenue; and so forth.)

Column (3) back in Table 11-2 shows how we compute the marginal propensity to consume. From *B* to *C*, income rises by $1,000, going from $8,000 to $9,000. By how much does consumption rise? Consumption grows from $8,000 to $8,850, or by $850. The extra consumption is therefore .85 of the extra

income, as we saw earlier. Out of each extra dollar of income, 85 cents goes to consumption and 15 cents goes to saving. We therefore can say that the marginal propensity to consume, or MPC, is .85 between *B* and *C*, which agrees with Column (3) of Table 11-2.

You can easily compute MPC between other income levels. In Table 11-2, MPC begins at .89 for poor people and finally falls to .53 at higher incomes.

MARGINAL PROPENSITY TO CONSUME AS GEOMETRICAL SLOPE   Now we know how to compute MPC numerically. What is its geometric meaning? It is a numerical measure of the steepness of slope of the consumption schedule.[5] Look again at Fig. 11-2. Near points *B* and *C* a little triangle is drawn. As we move to the right from *B* by $1,000, in order to stay on the schedule, we must go up by $850; this gives a numerical slope of $850/$1,000, or .85.

NOTE: If higher incomes have a lower MPC, the family consumption schedule will look slightly bowed (convex from above, concave from below.)

THE MARGINAL PROPENSITY TO SAVE

Along with the marginal propensity to consume goes a mirror-twin concept, the "marginal propensity to save," or MPS. This is defined as *the fraction of each extra dollar that goes to saving instead of to consumption.*

Why are MPC and MPS related like mirror twins? Since each extra dollar of income must be divided between extra consumption and extra saving, it is obvious that if MPC is .85, then MPS must be .15. (What would MPS be if MPC were .6? Or .99?) A comparison of Columns (3) and (5) of Table 11-2 confirms our common-sense feeling that at any income

[5] By the numerical slope of the line *XY*, we always mean the numerical ratio of the length *ZY* to the length *XZ*.

See the accompanying drawing. If *XY* were a curve, we could find the slope at any point on it (1) by placing a ruler tangent to it, and (2) by applying the procedure for this triangle to that tangential line.

If the line is the consumption schedule, its slope is the MPC, i.e., is the *marginal* propensity to consume. We'll see that if the line is the saving schedule, its slope will be defined as the MPS, i.e., is the *marginal* propensity to save.

level, MPC and MPS must always add up to exactly 1, no more and no less.[6]

BRIEF REVIEW OF DEFINITIONS

For the record, let us jot down the main definitions now learned:

1. The propensity-to-consume schedule (or consumption schedule) relates in a table or a curve the level of consumption to the level of income.

2. The propensity-to-save schedule (or saving schedule) relates saving to income. Since what is saved is the same thing as what is nonconsumed, saving and consumption schedules are mirror twins in the sense that

> Saving + consumption = disposable income

3. The "break-even point" is the income level where net saving is zero. Below it, there is dissaving, or negative saving; above it, positive net saving. Graphically, the break-even point is where the 45° helping line intersects the consumption schedule, or where the saving schedule intersects the horizontal axis.

4. The marginal propensity to consume (MPC) is the amount of *extra* consumption generated by an *extra* dollar of income. Graphically, it is given by the slope of the consumption schedule—a steep slope meaning a high MPC and a flat one meaning a low MPC.

5. The marginal propensity to save (MPS) is the *extra* saving generated by an *extra* dollar of income, or the slope of the saving schedule. Because the part of each dollar that is not consumed is nec-

essarily saved, MPS = 1 — MPC always. Hence, higher income that lowers MPC must raise MPS, implying a concave (from below) consumption schedule and a convex saving schedule.

THE COMMUNITY'S OVERALL CONSUMPTION SCHEDULE

So far we have been talking about the budget consumption patterns shown by typical families at vary-

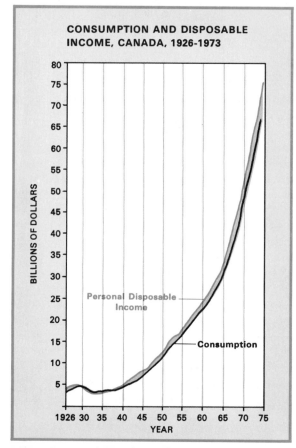

FIG. 11-4. National Consumption spending has moved with national income.

An important determinant of fluctuations in consumption expenditure has been fluctuations in income to spend. Good forecasts of consumption come from income data. Can you see how great saving became during World War II's goods shortage and rationing? (Source: **Urquhart and Buckley,** *Historical Statistics of Canada,* **and Statistics Canada.**)

---

[6] You can also verify from Fig. 11-3 that the numerical steepness of slope of the propensity-to-save schedule is the geometric expression of MPS. This schedule will always have the opposite curvature to that of the consumption schedule; as MPC falls, MPS must rise. And since every extra dollar divides up between positive extra consumption and extra saving, it follows that neither the consumption nor the saving schedule *anywhere* has a slope as steep as the 45° line, which by definition has a slope of 1. Remember, we are here discussing *marginal* propensities. Thus, at point *A*, the family is spending more than its income; but that does not alter the fact that, at *A*, its *marginal* propensity to consume out of *extra* income is less than 1. (These family data show more exaggerated curvature that would seem realistic in the 1970s for *permanent* income levels.)

ing income levels. To study what determines *a nation's* income, we are interested in a propensity-to-consume schedule slightly different from the family-budget schedule. We want the "community propensity-to-consume schedule," relating total consumption to total "disposable (after tax) income." This is because we are interested in how the total of *all* consumption spending in Canada changes as the total of our spendable income rises.

While aggregate income is not the only factor determining aggregate consumption, common sense and statistical experience tell us that it is one of the most important factors. Look at Fig. 11-4 to see how closely consumption seems to follow yearly disposable income; the only exceptional period is that of World War II, when goods were scarce and rationed and people were urged to save.

Figure 11-5 shows this relationship between consumption and disposable income in the form of a "scatter diagram" for the years 1929 up until 1972. Each dot marks the magnitude for each year. The resulting scatter of points shows no particular curvature; so a straight-line consumption schedule was drawn in. The actual data fall near, but not exactly

FIG. 11-5. A statistical consumption schedule fits data quite closely.
A straight line has been passed through the scatter of black data points. Note the bad fit in World War II years. Can you verify that the MPC slope of the fitted line is about .92? (Sources: Urquhart and Buckley, *Historical Statistics of Canada*; and Statistics Canada.)

on, the "fitted" consumption schedule,[7] reminding us that economics is not, like physics, an exact science. A good rule of thumb is this: Out of each dollar of disposable income, just over 90 cents goes for consumption; most of the remaining 10 cents goes for saving (except for about 2 cents for consumer interest).

QUALIFICATIONS

We are now prepared for the theory of income determination. We have introduced the crucially important concepts of consumption and saving schedules that will be used in the next chapter. But warnings are in order.

The community consumption schedule must be in some sense an aggregation of the family schedules. Yet even if we knew that the family schedules were perfectly reliable, we should still have to know something about the *distribution of incomes* before we could get the new points of total consumption of the national schedule. Thus, when a national-income rise is associated with the distribution of extra income that is *typical* for such a rise, we shall be moving upward on our unshifted community consumption schedule CC.

Aside from the distribution of income, there is a second factor that must be taken into account in any attempt to relate the family and national patterns. Suppose my income were to go from $15,000 to $50,000 a year. Would I spend and save my money in the same way that the budget studies showed $50,000-a-year people spend their money? Not necessarily. Especially at the beginning, I would be a *nouveau riche* and have different patterns of behavior.[8]

A third reason why it is difficult to go from the family to the national consumption schedule is suggested by the expression "keeping up with the Joneses." Back in 1920, if your family had $2,000 worth of purchasing power, you would have been quite well-off and above the break-even point of zero saving. But today many people have incomes above that level. Because man is a social animal, what he regards as "necessary comforts of life" depends on what he sees others consuming. So today, with $2,000 of income, you would be desperately poor and unable to make ends meet. This fact that one man's consumption depends upon the incomes and consumption of others means that we cannot expect the final community pattern to be the simple sum of the separate family patterns. It also means that we must expect the consumption schedule to be shifting upward each decade as living standards rise. Hence, in Fig. 11-5, one would be foolish to push the line back to the income of 1900 or forward to 1999. It is a succinct description of history, rather than a strict law of nature.[9]

Chapter 10 showed that the national-income accounts *always measure* an identity between saving and investment. The present chapter showed that the *motives* and *desires* behind saving and investment are generally quite distinct—which certainly raises the suspicion that the total flow of dollar spending is not guaranteed to proceed at exactly the same rate year in and year out. The hard facts of history confirm this suspicion: at times the economy experienced overexuberant demand and inflation; at times—and they used to be of considerable duration —it experienced considerable unemployment and excess capacity; in the absence of determined public programs of fiscal and monetary controls, only at rare times have economies enjoyed full employment and steady price levels.

The next two chapters investigate how the forces of saving and investment interact to produce an equilibrium level of national income, which can be at high or low employment and which can be conducive to price stability or to price inflation.

---

[7] So that no reader may think there is great accuracy in this line, let it be mentioned that it was fitted by stretching a black thread from the lower corner through all the data (excepting those for World War II) at what appeared a reasonable position. As in the case of supply and demand curves in Chapter 4 and Part Three, it will be convenient to go back and forth between drawing propensity-to-consume schedules as curved lines or more simply as straight lines when doing so does no gross violence to the actual facts.

[8] Modern theoretical and statistical researches by Professors Merrit Brown, James S. Duesenberry, Milton Friedman, and Franco Modigliani suggest strongly that if people were generally to get a prescribed percentage increase in their incomes that was permanent, they would probably add more to their long-run consumption expenditure than would be indicated by budget studies recorded for a single year such as 1950 or 1975. This warning, which appeared earlier in footnote 3, is worth repeating.

[9] The community consumption schedule will shift as prices change and total population grows. So, instead of working with simple, total dollar C, statisticians may correct it for Price and Population, by working with doubly deflated C/(Price × Population); likewise, they may replace DI by its doubly deflated DI/(Price × Population), to get *per capita real* income.

SUMMARY

1 Motivations making people want to engage in saving and to engage in investing are different. History shows there is no automatic tendency for the same number of dollars to get spent always at the same rate. Hence, our modern mixed economy would be subject to inflationary and depression swings if proper public fiscal and monetary policies did not act to help stabilize the economy and reinforce its spontaneous internal mechanisms that strive to achieve stability.

2 Income is one of the most important determinants of consumption (food, clothing, all items together) and of saving. The propensity to consume is the schedule relating total consumption to total income. Because any dollar of income is either saved or consumed, the propensity-to-save schedule is the other side or mirror twin of the propensity-to-consume picture. The characteristics of the consumption and saving schedules are summarized on page 190.

3 We could aggregate the family consumption schedules to get the community propensity-to-consume schedule, (a) if we knew the distribution of income for each level of disposable income; (b) if families always stuck to the same consumption-income patterns in the short run and the long; (c) if we could forget the fact that one man's consumption is influenced by the income levels of his neighbors; and (d) if price levels, population, corporate saving, and taxes could be neglected. So we must allow for these qualifications.

CONCEPTS FOR REVIEW

family motives for saving
business motives for investing
volatile investment decisions
consumption and saving
    schedules
propensity to consume or to
    save
MPC and MPS
MPC + MPS = 1

break-even point and 45° line
after-tax, or disposable, income
permanent versus transitory
    income
community consumption schedule
    versus family schedule
shifts of CC with price, time,
    income distribution, etc.

QUESTIONS FOR DISCUSSION

1 Summarize familiar budget patterns: food, clothing, luxuries, saving.

2 What are some of the reasons why people save? What are some of the forms in which they keep their assets?

3 Exactly how were the MPC and MPS in Table 11-2 computed? Illustrate between A and B. Explain why it must always be true that MPC + MPS = 1.

4 I consume *all* my income. Draw my consumption and saving schedules.

5 Do you think the break-even point is the same in Toronto as in Newfoundland? What do you think is the current break-even point in your community? List a number of ways a person can incur negative net saving for a while.

6 "Along the consumption schedule, income changes more (absolutely) than consumption does." Why? Show that this is even more true on the saving schedule.

7 Contrast the meaning of this chapter's opening quotation with the following 1966 letter to the editor of *Time Magazine* by Professor Milton Friedman of the University of Chicago.

Sir: You quote me (Dec. 31) as saying: "We are all Keynesians now." The quotation is correct, but taken out of context. As best I can recall it, the context was: "In one sense, we are all Keynesians now; in another, nobody is any longer a Keynesian."

8 *Extra-credit problem*: Suppose this equation for *CC* holds: $C = 200 + 2/3DI$. Now calculate the MPC as $dC/d(DI) = 2/3$. From the identity $S + C \equiv DI$, verify the formula for the *SS* schedule: $S = -200 + 1/3DI$. From this calculate *MPS* as $dS/d(DI)$ and verify that it does equal $1 - \text{MPC} = 1 - 2/3 = 1/3$.

12

INCOME DETERMINATION: THE SIMPLE THEORY AND THE MULTIPLIER

Given the propensity to consume and the rate of new investment, there will be only one level of employment consistent with equilibrium.

J. M. KEYNES (1936)

Economists are agreed that an important factor in causing income and employment to fluctuate is fluctuations in investment. Whether we are to face a situation of inflationary bidding up of prices or shall live in a frigid state of mass unemployment depends, as will be seen upon the level of investment.

From 1953 to 1963, the Canadian economy suffered from a growth in unemployment and some insufficiency of total demand. Memories are short, and there is danger that we shall forget the tremendous costs that were associated with the mass unemployment of the prewar Great Depression. It is scarcely an exaggeration to say that the economic costs of that depression were of the same general magnitude as the costs of all the economic resources which had to be used up in World War II itself. Figure 12-1 reminds us that in past years the Canadian economy, because of failure to maintain full employment growth, lost billions of dollars' worth of goods and services.

By the late 1960s, concern shifted to "overheating" of the economy or excessively high levels of demand in relation to the productive capacity of the nation, a situation which was accompanied by inflation with its own myriad problems. For a while we encountered the rare and costly combination of continued high levels of price increase along with rising unemployment. But in the early 1970s full employment ruled with all prices soaring.

POVERTY Figure 12-1 might also serve to remind us that nations are actually subject to three kinds of poverty:

(1) Ancient poverty due to famine and inadequate production potential;

(2) Unnecessary poverty due only to bad purchasing-power behavior of the system;

(3) Poverty due only to uneven and undesirable distribution of an opulent total GNP.

Long ago, for our advanced Western nations, overt poverty of the first type was conquered in the triumph of technology. This is illustrated by Fig. 2-3 (*a*) and (*b*). But only with the development of modern income analysis has Type (2), "poverty midst plenty" —like that of 1929-39—been rendered obsolete. Here in Part Two we learn how and why. Then in Part Six we can grapple with the third kind of poverty, which does still remain to challenge us.

This chapter and the next two outline the modern theory of income determination. Because the problems are so important and because the analysis is so useful, Section A of the present chapter stresses the fundamentals—how saving and investment, or what is the same thing, how consumption and investment interact to determine the equilibrium level of national income (or GNP) at full employment, below full employment, or with over full employment inflationary conditions. Then, in Section B, we turn to the interesting "multiplier" principle that shows how each dollar change in investment leads to more than a dollar—i.e. to a "multiplier"—change in GNP, and to an analysis of deflationary gaps and of price inflation.

Once the tools of this chapter are mastered, we are ready to understand the next chapter's analysis of how government expenditure and government tax policy can alter the income equilibrium, and of the change in the analysis that is necessary when we formally admit exports and imports to our income theory.

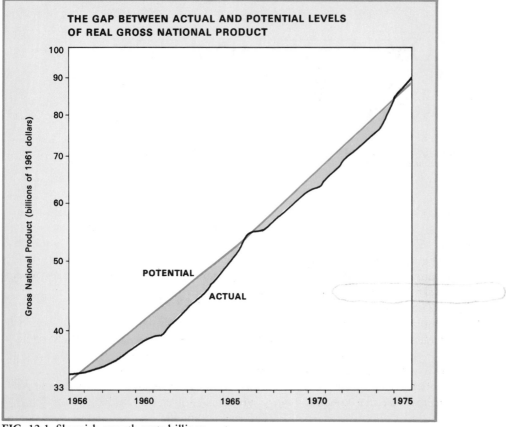

FIG. 12-1. Sluggish growth costs billions.
The shaded area shows the gap between what we actually produced in recent years and what our economic system was capable of producing at reasonably high employment and capacity utilization. On a few occasions, such as in 1965 and 1974, the economy overshoots "reasonable" achievements. (Source: Based on data from Statistics Canada and estimates by the Economic Council of Canada. Extended to 1974 by authors.)

A. USING THE CONSUMPTION AND SAVING SCHEDULES TO DETERMINE INCOME

The last chapter gave a simplified picture of the propensity-to-consume and the propensity-to-save schedules for the community. As we've already discussed, the consumption and saving schedules are drawn up on the basis of our knowledge of the thriftiness of different families, the distribution of incomes between families, and so forth.

Initially we shall make the further simplifying assumptions that there are no taxes, undistributed corporate profits, depreciation, transfers, government expenditure, or foreign trade of any kind to worry about; hence, we do not have to concern ourselves for the moment with any distinction between gross national product and disposable income, and we can use the word "income" to refer to either. Also, we shall initially neglect any changes in the price level.

Figure 12-2 shows the nation's propensities to consume and to save. Each point on its consumption schedule shows how much the nation will *want to continue to consume* at that level of disposable income. Each point on the saving schedule shows how much it will want to continue to save at that income level. Recall that the two schedules are clearly related: since $C + S$ = income always, the CC and SS curves are Siamese twins that would add up always to the 45° line.

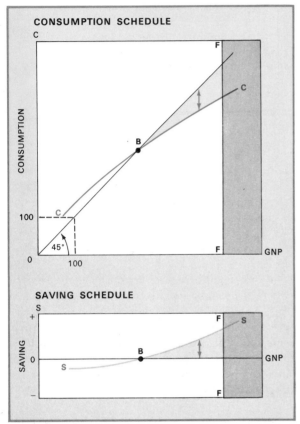

FIG. 12-2. Society's national income determines its consumption and saving.

CC is the propensity-to-consume and SS is the propensity-to-save schedule for the community.

Recall that these are closely related: the break-even point B is shown on the upper diagram where CC intersects the 45° line and on the lower diagram where SS intersects the horizontal axis. Can you explain why the vertically aligned arrows *must* be equal? (The curvature is slightly exaggerated here to help identify the two schedules. The two points marked 100 should help emphasize the important property of the 45° line: it depicts a vertical distance equal to exactly 100 per cent of the horizontal distance.)

The vertical black line FF depicts the full-employment GNP. Above this critical level *real* product cannot increase (and beyond it we could no longer adhere to our simplifying assumption of ignoring price-level changes).

HOW INCOME IS DETERMINED AT THE LEVEL WHERE SAVING AND INVESTMENT SCHEDULES INTERSECT

We have seen that saving and investment are dependent on quite different factors: Saving tends to depend in a "passive" way upon income, while volatile investment often depends upon various non-income factors (dynamic growth, technical invention, interest rates, money supply, and so forth).

For simplicity, first suppose investment opportunities are such that investment would be exactly 6 billion dollars per year regardless of the level of GNP. This means that, if we now draw a schedule of investment against GNP, it will have to be a *horizontal* line—always the same distance above the horizontal axis. Turn to Fig. 12-3, where this investment schedule is labelled II to distinguish it from the SS savings schedule. (II does *not* mean Roman numeral two.)

The saving and investment schedules intersect at E, which corresponds to a level of GNP equal to the distance from O to M.

This intersection of the saving and investment schedules is the equilibrium toward which national income will gravitate. Under our assumed conditions, no other level of income can perpetuate itself.

The remaining pages of this chapter are devoted to the single task of explaining this important truth.

STABILITY OF THE EQUILIBRIUM. Let us see why the equilibrium income must eventually be at E, the point of intersection between the investment and saving schedules. We consider three cases.

The first case is that in which the system is *at E* itself, where the II schedule of what business firms *want* to invest and keep investing just intersects the SS schedule of what families *want* to save. Consequently, everyone will be content to go on doing just what he has been doing. Firms will not find inventories piling up on their shelves, nor will they find sales so brisk as to force them to produce more goods. So production, employment, and income spending will remain the same. GNP in the first case

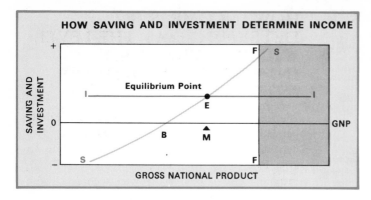

HOW SAVING AND INVESTMENT DETERMINE INCOME

FIG. 12-3. Equilibrium determination of national income is shown by intersection of saving and investment schedules.

E marks the spot where investment and saving curves intersect. Equilibrium is at the intersection of SS and II curves because at no other level of GNP could the desired saving of families continually match the desired investment of business.

does truly stay at the point E; and we can rightly call that "equilibrium."

The second case is where the system is *first* at a GNP *higher* than at E, so that it begins east of E, at an income level where the SS schedule is higher than the II schedule. Why can't the system stay there indefinitely? Because at such an income level, families are saving—are refraining from spending on consumption—*more* than business firms will be *willing to go on investing.* Firms will thus find they have too few customers and that their inventories are piling up against their wishes, and they will not want to go on being forced into such undesired inventory investment. What can they do about it? They can certainly cut back production and lay off workers. This moves GNP gradually downward, which means westward in Fig. 12-3. Where does the system stop being in such disequilibrium? Only when it gets back to E, the equilibrium intersection point. There the longer-run tendency to change has disappeared.

The third case should be mastered by the reader. Show that if GNP were *below* its equilibrium level, strong forces would be set up to move it eastward back to E. (HINT: At any GNP level where families' *intended* saving falls short of business firms' *intended* investment, the result is consumption of more goods than are being currently produced. What does this mean? It means that business will find itself having to sell inventory off its shelves faster than its production line is producing such goods. Once businessmen notice that they are being forced into less investment, i.e., into more *involuntary* investment, than the II curve shows they

want, what will they do? They will then expand production and hire new men. This will complete the demonstration that the system does move back eastward until it gets to E.)

All three cases then lead to the same summary:

The only equilibrium of national income is at E, where the saving and investment schedules intersect. At any other point, the *desired* saving of families will not match the *desired* investment of business, and this discrepancy will cause businessmen to change their production and employment levels in such a way as to return the system to the equilibrium intersection.

Before we go on, a warning is in order. An equilibrium level like E is a point where the system tends to stay. But there is nothing necessarily optimal about every equilibrium point. Note the vertical black line FF and the gray shaded area to the right of it in Fig. 12-3 that depict full-employment income. Note the fact that the E equilibrium shown is at a level of GNP lower that that corresponding to F's full employment.

During a great depression, a capitalistic system may be firmly stuck at a point of very great unemployment. It is then at the E given by its low II schedule. No one would make the mistake of thinking that such a deep-unemployment equilibrium point is in any sense a good thing. Instead, the government would intervene in the economic system to try to shift the curves until a new equilibrium point E' was attained at a desirable level (as in Fig. 12-7).

INCOME DETERMINATION BY CONSUMPTION AND INVESTMENT

There is a second way of showing how income is determined, other than by the intersection of the saving and investment schedules. The final result is exactly the same, but our understanding and confidence in the theory of income determination will be increased if we work through this second approach.

This second approach is called the consumption-plus-investment rather than the saving-investment approach. The $C + I$ approach[1] takes advantage of the Siamese-twins property of the saving and consumption schedules. Thus it must always lead to exactly the same equilibrium income as does the saving-and-investment approach. This is shown by the fact that when you line up Fig. 12-4 vertically under Fig. 12-3, you always find that in both charts E marks exactly the same GNP equilibrium.

The $C + I$ approach has the advantage of concentrating on *total spending*: spending for consumption goods plus spending for investment goods. The $C + I$ approach vertically adds the II schedule of business' *desired* investment to the CC consumption schedule of families' *desired* consumption spending.

Only where the two *desired* amounts of spending add up to equality with the value of GNP being produced will there be equilibrium.

With what must the combined $C + I$ schedule intersect to depict this equilibrium? Figure 12-4 introduces a 45° line to provide our looked-for intersection point. The 45° line, we have seen, has the useful property that it lays out in the vertical direction a distance always exactly equal to the income shown on the horizontal axis. So the 45° line is admirably designed to depict the expense that firms are incurring for the productive factors required to produce national output, and which they must be getting back if they are to feel safe to continue hiring the same number of men and producing the same level of GNP.[2]

[1] When government is brought into the picture, $C + I$ will become $C + I + G$. Adding foreign trade will make it $C + I + G + (E - M)$.

[2] As the intermediate texts would put it: If the system is not at this intersection, there will be *unintended* inventory investment or disinvestment and/or *unforeseen windfall* profits or losses. As a result, there cannot be equilibrium; but rather a chain of new

HOW CONSUMPTION AND INVESTMENT DETERMINE INCOME

FIG. 12-4. Alternatively, equilibrium GNP level can be shown by intersection of $C + I$ schedule with 45° line. Adding II to CC gives the $C + I$ curve of total spending. At E, where it intersects the 45° line, we get the same equilibrium as in the saving-and-investment diagram. (Note the similarities between this figure and Fig. 12-3; the investment added to CC is the same as II of Fig. 12-3; B and F each come at the same place on the two diagrams, *and so must the E intersection*.)

We can summarize the $C + I$ method of income determination thus:

The equilibrium level of national income is at the intersection of the $C + I$ schedule of desired total spending with the 45° line depicting value of total output.[3] This equilibrium E corresponds exactly to

decisions will be set up to expand or contract output, and possibly to raise or lower prices. So the system will move in disequilibrium until it ends up at the intersection point of equilibrium. Those same intermediate texts point out that *measured S* and *measured I* stay identical even during the worst disequilibrium, by virtue of some people's experiencing unintended losses or gains and/or experiencing unintended investment or saving. (Remember, too, that economists include profit in total business expense.)

[3] Some writers like to call the $C + I$ curve an aggregate *demand* curve, and the 45°-line curve an aggregate *supply* curve. Then, using Chapter 4's language, they say: The equilibrium level of income is where the aggregate demand and supply curves intersect.

the saving-and-investment equilibrium because of the Siamese-twins relation between the consumption and the saving schedules.

We shall see in the next chapter that the $C + I$ approach has great advantages in helping to analyze government expenditure and fiscal policy. It easily turns itself into an exactly similar $C + I + G$ approach.

ARITHMETIC DEMONSTRATION OF INCOME DETERMINATION: A DIGRESSION FOR A THIRD RESTATEMENT

A thoughtful reader may still want to know more about *why* the equilibrium level of income will have to be at the intersection of the saving and investment schedules. What forces will push income to that level and no other?

An arithmetic example may help verify this important matter. Table 12-1 shows an especially simple pattern of the propensity to save against income. The break-even level of income where the nation is too poor to do any net saving on balance is assumed to be $1,000 billion. Each change of income of $300 billion is assumed to lead to a $100-billion change in saving and a $200-billion change in consumption; in other words, MPC is for simplicity here assumed to be constant and exactly equal to 2/3, with MPS = 1/3. For this reason, the saving propensity schedule SS in Fig. 12-5 takes on the especially simple form of a perfectly straight line.

What shall we assume about investment? For simplicity, let us suppose again that the only level of investment that can be voluntarily maintained indefinitely is exactly $200 billion, as shown in Column (4) of Table 12-1.

Now, Columns (5) and (6) are the crucial ones. Column (5) shows how much total expense business firms undergo at each level of national production for wages, interest, rent, *and* profit. This is the GNP of Column (1) copied once again into Column (5), because our repeated discussions in Chapter 10 showed that upper- and lower-loop measurements must be the same.

Column (6), on the other hand, shows what business firms would in fact be *getting back* in the long

INCOME DETERMINATION BY SAVING AND INVESTMENT
(in billions of dollars)

(1) Levels of GNP and *DI*	(2) Scheduled con-sumption	(3) Sched-uled, Planned, or Main-tainable Saving (3)=(1)-(2)	(4) Sched-uled, Planned, or Main-tainable Invest-ment	(5) Expense Incur-rable by Business to Produce GNP (5) = (1)	(6) Scheduled Spending That Would Perman-ently Come Back To Busi-nesses (6) = (2)+(4)	(7) Resulting Tendency of Income
$2,200	$1,800	$400	$200	$2,200 >	$2,000	Contrac-tion
1,900	1,600	300	200	1,900 >	1,800	Contrac-tion
1,600	1,400	200	200	1,600 =	1,600	Equilib-rium
1,300	1,200	100	200	1,300 <	1,400	Expansion
1,000	1,000	0	200	1,000 <	1,200	Expansion
700	800	-100	200	700 <	1,000	Expansion

TABLE 12-1. The tendency for income to go to its equilibrium level is shown by arithmetic table.
The red row depicts the equilibrium GNP level, where the $200 billion that businessmen will be *willing* to continue to invest is just matched by families' *intended* and *maintainable* saving. (In higher rows, firms will be forced into unintended inventory investment and will respond by cutting production and GNP back to equilibrium. Interpret the lower rows' tendency toward expansion of GNP toward equilibrium.)

run in the form of scheduled or voluntary consumption spending plus scheduled or voluntary investment. (It's really Fig. 12-4's red $C + I$ schedule.)

When business firms as a whole are temporarily producing a high total product, higher than the sum of what consumers will buy and what business as a whole wants to be investing in equipment and inventory accumulation, businesses will find themselves forced involuntarily to pile up inventory of unsalable goods. At the same time, their total sales revenue will be so low as to be putting disagreeable downward pressure on their profit position. With scheduled SS above II, therefore, they will want to contract their operations, and GNP will tend to fall. (Contrariwise, when $II > SS$ and inventories are being involuntarily depleted and profit margins improving, they will increase their employment, and production and GNP will rise.)

When business firms as a whole are temporarily producing at an expense greater than what they can recover, they will want to contract their operations, and GNP tends to fall. When they are getting back more than their current expense for production, they increase their production and GNP rises.

Only when level of scheduled saving in Column (3) exactly equals scheduled investment in Column (4) will business firms stay continually in aggregative equilibrium. Their sales will there be just enough to justify continuing their current level of aggregate output. GNP will neither expand nor contract.

This same story is shown in Fig. 12-5. GNP can be read in either of two ways: on the horizontal axis or (from the nature of a 45° line) as the equivalent vertical distance from that axis up to the helping 45° line. The line *SS* represents the saving schedule; the line *II* represents the scheduled level of investment that can be maintained over time. Consumption can also be seen in the figure. Since income not saved is consumed, consumption is always the vertical distance from the saving schedule to the 45° line.

Now we can use Fig. 12-5 to confirm what has just been shown by the arithmetic of Table 12-1. No level of income can *long persist* if it is higher than the equilibrium level given by the *scheduled* saving and investment intersection at $1,600 billion. To the right of the intersection point *E*, the expense incurred by businesses would exceed the *amount received back* by businesses in the form of maintainable consumption plus maintainable investment.

Graphically, this is shown by the following: The amount continuously paid out by business is the whole distance up to the 45° line, i.e., from *Q* to *R*; but the amount that would continuously be received back by business would be only the sum of voluntary investment *QK* and consumption *JR*. There is a gap of *JK*.

Businesses face a real dilemma. For a while they could keep their prices high and let unsold goods pile up on their shelves, but that would not represent an equilibrium situation and could not persist. Or for a while they could lower prices on their goods and sell below needed cost with less profits; but that, too, could not last.

FIG. 12-5. Graph reinforces table's story of tendencies restoring equilibrium.

Only at *E* is there no gap between *scheduled* saving and investment. A gap like that shown at *JK* will soon cause firms to cut their production, which explains the westward arrow pushing GNP back to *E*'s equilibrium level.

Show that the opposite gap at *J'K'* will mean that firms find their sales so great as to deplete their inventories; interpret the eastward arrows showing that firms expand production to push GNP back to *E*.

Thus, it is completely clear that income cannot *permanently* be maintained higher than the equilibrium level—*the level where the amount of saving that people want to do is matched by the amount of investment businessmen are willing to maintain.* A persistent gap of the *JK* type must, through attempts to cut down losses and excessive inventories, result in a contraction of employment and gross national product back toward the equilibrium point, where there is no gap. Therefore the arrow near *Q* points leftward back toward the equilibrium level.

A similar argument shows why income will tend to raise from any place to the left of the equilibrium-intersection level. Indicate on the diagram the relation between business expense and what business can permanently receive back. Show that there will be a favorable gap (as at *J'K'*): Businesses either will be selling so much as to be depleting inventories on their shelves or will be temporarily raising their prices.

A similar argument shows why income will tend to rise from any place to the left of the equilibrium-intersection level. Indicate on the diagram the relation between business expense and what business can permanently receive back. Show that there will be a favorable gap (as at *J'K'*): Business either will be selling so much as to be depleting inventories on their shelves or will be temporarily raising their prices and earning extra profits. In either case, they will be tempted to expand their employment and production. And when they do, the result will be a rise in income back toward the equilibrium-intersection level.[4] Thus ends our digression.

[4] The recorded income statistics never show the gap depicted in *JK* and by Column (6) minus Column (5). Why not? Because these are gaps in people's *scheduled* quantities. They show levels that cannot continue to persist. On the other hand, the *measurable* statistics of saving and investment are definitionally equal no matter what income is doing: thus, when inventory is *involuntarily* piling up, the Statistics Canada statistician cares not that its identity of investment and saving is the result of *unintended investment.* Why should it? It need never go beyond the anatomy of the problem. But we—interested in dynamic physiology of income determination—are vitally interested in schedules. (NOTE: In the last few pages, words such as "voluntary," "scheduled," and "maintainable" were repeated and stressed to call attention to the difference between a magnitude permanently persisting as a schedule and the actual amounts measured after the fact in any disturbed short run. In the supply and demand schedules of Part Three, the same problem will recur; Chapter 4 showed that the wheat bought is always numerically identical with the wheat sold; but only at equilibrium market price do the *scheduled* amounts intersect.)

THE SIMPLIFIED THEORY OF INCOME DETERMINATION RESTATED

Figure 12-6 pulls together in a simplified way the main elements of income determination. Without saving and investment, there would be a circular flow of income between business and the public; above, business pays out wages, interest, rents, and profits to the public in return for the services of labor and property; and below, the public pays consumption funds to business in return for goods and services.

Realistically, we must recognize that the public will wish to save some of its income, as shown at the spigot *Z*. Hence, businesses cannot expect their consumption sales to be as large as the total of wages, interest, rents, and profits. Why not? Because dollars saved do not come back *as consumption sales.*

Some monetary cranks think that this saving necessarily means unemployment and depression. Such a view is simply incorrect. If there happen to be sufficiently profitable investment opportunities, business firms will be paying out wages, interest, and other costs *in part for new-investment goods* rather than 100 per cent for consumption goods. Hence, to continue to be happy, business needs to receive back in consumption sales only *part* of the total income paid out to the public—only that part which involves the cost of current consumption goods. The saving that the public wants to make will do no harm to national income so long as it is not greater than what business can profitably continue to invest.

In Fig. 12-6, investment is shown being pumped into the income stream at *A*. The handle of the pump is being moved by (1) technological invention, (2) population growth, and (3) other dynamic factors that affect the profitability of investment (such as the opening of new regions to development).

When the investment pump is going at a rapid, steady pace, NNP is high and is at its maintainable equilibrium rate where scheduled saving at *Z* just balances scheduled investment at *A*.

This demonstrates that the pessimistic monetary cranks who thought that saving was always disastrous were plain wrong. Early members of the Social Credit Party, too, were obsessed with the leak in the system at *Z*; they stood for a steady inflow of new

FIG. 12-6. Dynamic investment pumps national income up and down:

Technological change, population growth, and other dynamic factors keep the investment pump handle going. Income rises and falls with changes in investment, its maintainable equilibrium level being realized only when intended saving at Z continues to match intended investment at A.

money at A to keep the circular flow from running dry, regardless of how strongly the pump handle was going anyway. But there is also a second misconception: some go to the opposite extreme and insist that saving and investment can never, in our modern mixed economy with all its frictions and rigidities, cause income to be too high or too low. They make the fatal error of automatically, and without regard to banking policy and fiscal policy, connecting the pipe at Z with the inflow at A.

Many books have been written on this subject of equilibrium income determination, and it is only in the last few decades that economists have learned how to separate the truth and falsity of both extremes. The next one-hundred or so pages will deal with this important question, in its relation to income, "inflationary or deflationary gaps," exports and imports, banking, and business-cycle policy. An essential step in the exposition is the next section's "multiplier" analysis.

B. THE "MULTIPLIER"

Now that we have seen how the intersection of saving and investment determines the level of national income, we realize that an increase in investment will increase the level of income and employment. Thus, an investment boom may bring a nation out of a deep or mild depression—by having a higher II schedule cut the SS schedule at a higher equilibrium level for NNP.

An increase in private investment will cause income to expand; a decrease in investment will cause it to contract.

This is not a very surprising result. After all, we have learned that investment is one part of net national product; when one of the parts increases in value, we should naturally expect the whole to in-

crease in value. That is only part of the story. Our theory of income determination gives us a much more striking result.

Modern income analysis shows that an increase in net investment will increase national income by a *multiplied* amount—by an amount greater than itself! Investment spending—like any independent shifts in governmental, foreign, or family spending—is high-powered, double-duty spending, so to speak.

This amplified effect of investment[5] on income is called the "multiplier" doctrine; the word multi-

[5] Our later analysis will show that the multiplier can apply also to government and other shifts in spending; but first we stick to the simplifying assumption of shifts up and down of a horizontal investment schedule.

plier itself is used for the *numerical coefficient showing how great an increase in income results from each increase in such investment spending.*

Some examples will make this terminology clear. Let there be an increase of investment of 5 billion dollars. If this causes an increase of income of 15 billion dollars, then the multiplier is 3. If instead the resulting increase in income were 20 billion dollars, then the multiplier would be 4.

Definition: The multiplier is the number by which the change in investment must be multiplied in order to present us with the resulting change in income.

No proof has yet been presented to show that the multiplier will be greater than 1. But using ordinary common sense one can see why, when I hire unemployed resources to build a $1,000 garage, there will be a *secondary* expansion of national income and production, over and above my primary investment. Here is why.

My carpenters and lumber producers will get an extra $1,000 in income. But that is not the end of the story. If they all have a marginal propensity to consume of 2/3, they will now spend $666.67 on new consumption goods. The producers of these goods will now have an extra income of $666.67. If their MPC is also 2/3, they in turn will spend $444.44 or 2/3 of $666.67 (or 2/3 of 2/3 of $1,000). So the process will go on, with each new round of spending being 2/3 of the previous round.

Thus a whole endless chain of secondary consumption respending is set up by my primary $1,000 of investment spending. But it is a dwindling chain, and it all adds up to a finite amount. By either grade-school arithmetic or high-school geometric progression,[6] we get

$$
\left.
\begin{array}{c}
\$1,000.00 \\
+ \\
666.67 \\
+ \\
444.44 \\
+ \\
296.30 \\
+ \\
197.53 \\
+ \\
\cdots
\end{array}
\right\}
=
\left\{
\begin{array}{c}
1 \times \$1,000 \\
+ \\
\frac{2}{3} \times \$1,000 \\
+ \\
(\frac{2}{3})^2 \times \$1,000 \\
+ \\
(\frac{2}{3})^3 \times \$1,000 \\
+ \\
(\frac{2}{3})^4 \times \$1,000 \\
+ \\
\cdots
\end{array}
\right.
$$

$$
\begin{array}{c}
\$2,999.999 \\
\text{or} \\
\$3,000
\end{array}
\qquad
\frac{1}{1-\frac{2}{3}} \times \$1,000, \text{or } 3 \times \$1,000
$$

This shows that, with an MPC of 2/3, the multiplier is 3, consisting of the 1 of primary investment plus 2 extra of secondary consumption respending.

The same arithmetic would give a multiplier of 4 if the MPC were 3/4, for the reason that $1 + 3/4 + (3/4)^2 + (3/4)^3 + \ldots$ finally adds up to 4. If the MPC were 1/2, the multiplier would be 2. The size of the multiplier thus depends upon how large the MPC is; or it can be expressed in terms of the twin concept, the MPS. If the MPS were 1/4, the MPC would be 3/4, and the multiplier would be 4. If the MPS were 1/3, the multiplier would be 3. If the MPS were 1/X, the multiplier would be X.

By this time it is plain that the simple multiplier is always the upside-down or "reciprocal," of the marginal propensity to save. Our general multiplier formula (taxation and corporation saving being negligible) is always

$$
\text{Change in income} = \frac{1}{\text{MPS}} \times \text{change in investment}
$$

$$
= \frac{1}{1 - \text{MPC}} \times \text{change in investment}
$$

In other words, the greater the extra consumption respending, the greater the multiplier. The greater the MPS "leakage" into extra saving at each round of spending, the smaller the final multiplier.

GRAPHICAL PICTURE OF THE MULTIPLIER

Up to this point, we have discussed the multiplier in terms of common sense and arithmetic. Will our saving-investment analysis of income give us the same result? The answer must of course be, Yes.

---

[6] High-school algebra says the formula for an infinite geometric progression is $1 + r + r^2 + r^3 + \ldots r^n + \ldots = \frac{1}{1-r}$ as long as r is less than 1 absolute value. This progression is central to the various "multipliers" in these two chapters and to Chapter 15's deposit-expansion process.

In this case, MPC = r. If the MPC were changing along a curved schedule, in the multiplier progression we should have to use an MPC at an income level somewhere between the original and the final level. Footnote 7 in the next chapter handles a non-horizontal *II* case.

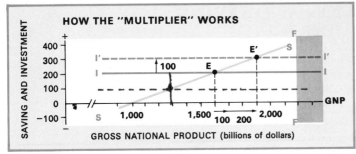

FIG. 12-7. Each dollar of investment is shown as "multiplied" into 3 dollars of income.

New investment shifts *II* to *I'I'. E'* gives the new equilibrium income, with income increasing 3 for each 1 increase in investment. (NOTE: The broken horizontal black arrow is 3 times the length of the vertical black arrow of investment shift, and is broken to show 2 *secondary* consumption respending for each 1 *primary* investment.)

Suppose, as back in Table 12-1 the MPS is 1/3 and a new series of inventions comes along and gives rise to an extra $100 billion of continuing investment opportunities, over and above our previous $200 billion. Then the increase in investment should raise equilibrium GNP from $1,600 billion to what? To $1,900 billion if the multiplier is indeed correctly given as 3 by our previous analysis.

A look at Fig. 12-7 can confirm this. Our old investment schedule *II* is shifted upward by $100 billion to the new level *I'I'*. The new intersection point is *E'*. And lo, the increase in income is exactly 3 times as much as the increase in investment. This is be-

cause an MPS of only 1/3 means a relatively flat *SS* saving schedule. As the black arrows show, the horizontal income distance is 3 times as great as the "primary" vertical saving-investment distance, the excess being the secondary "consumption respending."

In short, income must rise enough to bring out a volume of voluntary saving equal to the new investment. With an MPS of 1/3, income has to rise by how much in order to bring out $100 billion of new saving to match exactly the new investment? Only one answer is possible. By exactly $300 billion,[7] verifying our multiplier arithmetic.

---

[7] Alter Table 12-1 to verify this answer. In Column (4), we now put in $300 billion instead of $200 billion of investment. The new equilibrium level of income now shifts one row up from the red equilibrium row. The multiplier can also work downward; thus a decline of $1 billion in investment spending will induce an endless chain of negative items, leading ultimately to a $3-billion *reduction* in equilibrium income. (Check by cutting *I* from 200 to 100 in Table 12-1.)

We can also derive algebraically the simple investment multiplier formula used in the example above.

We know that in equilibrium of this simple economy

$$(1)\ GNP = Y = C + \overline{I}$$

(Bar over symbol means that it is constant.)

Now suppose scheduled consumption is given by the following simple linear equation:

$$(2)\ C = \overline{C} + bY$$

where $\overline{C}$ is a constant amount of consumption, even when $Y = 0$. This consumption equation is also called a *consumption function* because it says that consumption depends upon, or *is a function of*, GNP. *b* the marginal propensity to consume MPC, is represented here and in Fig. 11-2 as the steepness of the slope of *CC*. Footnote 5 of Chapter 11 showed that the steepness is the amount by which consumption increases, ΔC, for any increase in income, ΔY. That is,

$$MPC = b = \Delta C\ /\ \Delta Y$$

Where *CC* is curved, *b*, is not a constant, but becomes smaller with higher incomes.

Scheduled investment is assumed to remain constant at some given level, written as $\overline{I}$:

$$(3)\ I = \overline{I}$$

Now we simply substitute (2) and (3) into the NNP equation, so that

$$Y = C + bY + \overline{I}$$

or

$$Y - bY = Y(1 - b) = \overline{C} + \overline{I}$$

Hence

$$(4)\ Y = \frac{1}{1 - b}\ (\overline{C} + \overline{I})$$

Here, then, the multiplier is $1/(1 - b)$, or, in the terminology of the text, $1/(1 - MPC)$.

As shown in Chapter 11, Fig. 11-3, $1/(1 - b)$ is also equal to $1/MPS$. The multiplier expression $1/(1 - b)$ applies not only to unchanged total $\overline{I}$ but also to *changes* in investment ΔI. It will be shown below that this multiplier can be applied to autonomous schedule shifts in consumption ΔC (Fig. 13-2); and, in the next chapter, to changes in government purchases ΔG, or in exports ΔE.

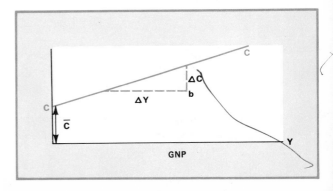

SUMMARY

A. USING THE CONSUMPTION AND SAVING SCHEDULES TO DETERMINE INCOME

1 Unlike the ancient poverty due to famine in a pre-industrial society, and unlike modern poverty due to uneven and bad income distribution, "poverty midst plenty" was due to "production gaps" between what full employment operations could produce and what actual *laissez-faire* saving-investment intersections caused to get produced. Here we study the appearance of this gap, and in the next chapter we shall study how fiscal policy can do something about improving the acceptability of macroeconomic equilibrium.

2 The motives that make people want to save are often different from those that make businesses want to invest. Net investment tends to depend on such autonomous elements as new population, new territory, new inventions, new tastes, and other growth elements; consumption and saving tend to behave in accordance with passive schedules plotted against national income.

3 People's wishes to save and the willingness of businesses to invest are brought into line with each other primarily by means of changes in income. The equilibrium level of national income must be at the *intersection* of the saving and investment schedules, SS and II, or what is exactly the same thing, at the *intersection* of the consumption-plus-investment schedule C + I with the 45° line.

4. If incomes were temporarily above the equilibrium level, business would find itself unable to sell all it was producing at prices that fully covered expected costs of production. For a short time inventories might pile up involuntarily, and sales at a loss or untenable profit margin might take place, but eventually employment and production would be cut back toward the equilibrium level. The only equilibrium path of income that can be maintained is at the income level where families will voluntarily continue to save exactly as much as business will voluntarily continue to invest.

B. THE "MULTIPLIER"

5 Investment (and any autonomous schedule shift) has a *multiplier* effect on income. When investment changes, there is an equal *primary* change in national income. But as these primary income receivers in the capital-goods industries get more earned income, they set into motion a whole chain of additional *secondary* consumption spending and employment.

   If people always spend about 2/3 of each extra dollar of income upon consumption, the total of the multiplier chain will be

$$1 + 2/3 + (2/3)^2 + \ldots = \frac{1}{1 - 2/3} = 3$$

The multiplier works forward or backward, amplifying either increases or decreases in investment. The simplest multiplier is numerically equal to the reciprocal of the MPS; this is because it always takes more than a dollar's change in income to bring forth a dollar's change in saving.

6 To sum up for the simplified case of this chapter: Investment calls the tune; investment causes income to rise or fall until *voluntary, scheduled* saving has adjusted itself to the level of *maintainable* investment.

CONCEPTS FOR REVIEW

consumption schedule *CC*
saving schedule *SS*
45° helping line
break-even point
C + I schedule
equivalent intersection of *SS*
  and *II*, or *C + I* and
  45° line
equilibrium intersection and
  forces moving GNP

intended maintainable saving and
  investment versus measurable
  identity of saving and
  investment
multiplier impact of primary *I*
  and secondary *C* spending

$$\text{multiplier} = \frac{1}{1-\text{MPC}} = \frac{1}{\text{MPS}}$$

$$= 1 + (\text{MPC}) + (\text{MPC})^2 + \ldots$$

QUESTIONS FOR DISCUSSION

1 Can you recall from the last chapter how the *CC* and *SS* schedules are in a mirror-twins relationship, with MPC + MPS = 1 always? Why does the break-even point come at the same level of income (which will be on the horizontal axis in the lower part of Fig. 12-2 and on the 45° line in the upper part)?

2 If investment were always zero, show that equilibrium would take place at the break-even point. (HINT: Income must fall to the low permanent level at which the amount that people would want to go on saving was zero—namely the break-even point.)

3 The saving-and-investment and the 45° line (or *C + I*) diagram are two different ways of showing how national income is determined. Describe each. Show their equivalence.

4 Reconstruct Table 12-1 assuming that net investment is equal to (*a*) $300 billion (*b*) $400 billion. What is the resulting difference in national income? Is this greater or smaller than the change in *I*? Why? When *I* drops 100 (or by 1) below $200, how much must GNP drop?

5 Describe briefly (*a*) the common sense, (*b*) arithmetic, and (*c*) geometry of the multiplier. What are the multipliers when MPC = .9? .8? .5? When MPS = .1? .8?

6 Work out the explosive chain of spending and respending when MPC = 2. Explain the economics of the arithmetic of the divergent infinite geometric series.

7 Let *Y* be GNP in billions of dollars. If $C = a + bY = 300 + \frac{2}{3}Y$ and $I = \bar{I} = 200$, solve $Y = C + I = (300 + \frac{2}{3}Y) + 200$ to get $Y^* = 500/(1 - \frac{2}{3}) = 1,500$. Increase $\bar{I}$ by 1 and verify that Y^* goes up by 3. What is the multiplier? Why?

13
INCOME DETERMINATION: FISCAL POLICY, INFLATION, AND THRIFTINESS

The only good budget is a balanced budget. ADAM SMITH OF GLASGOW (1776)

The only good rule is that the budget should never be balanced—except for an instant when a surplus to curb inflation is being altered to a deficit to fight deflation.
WARREN SMITH OF ANN ARBOR, (UNIVERSITY OF MICHIGAN, 1965)

Short-term instabilities ... call for tactical departures from long-term fiscal policy stability.
ARTHUR SMITH OF OTTAWA (FORMER CHAIRMAN, ECONOMIC COUNCIL OF CANADA, 1969)

Chapter 12 set forth the essentials of the modern theory of income determination. Here we must go on to discuss a number of important applications and qualifications.

How do changes in thriftiness—rises in the propensity to save and falls in the propensity to consume—affect the level of national income? What paradoxes lurk there?

How does the theory of income determination analyze inflation and deflation—the so-called "inflationary" or "deflationary gaps"?

Finally, and most important for human welfare, what are the effects on output, employment, and price stability of government fiscal policy—of public expenditure, of public taxation, of budget deficits and surpluses?

HOW SHIFTS IN THE CONSUMPTION SCHEDULE OR THRIFTINESS AFFECT INCOME

We have seen that investment affects incomes. Let us now consider *shifts* in scheduled *saving* (changes in "thriftiness") and *consumption*. Won't the new *S'S'* schedule intersect an unchanged *II* schedule in a new equilibrium *E'*? At a lower GNP?

Yes, and yes. Figure 13-1 shows that an upward shift in saving—and, what is the same thing, a downward shift in the consumption schedule—will tend in the absence of any change in the investment schedule to *lower* equilibrium GNP.

Common sense tells us why. If people consume

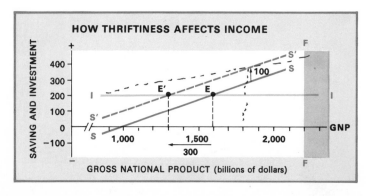

FIG. 13-1. Saving-and-investment diagram shows how thriftiness can kill off income.

A desire to consume less at every income level will shift the saving schedule upward. With *II* unchanged, equilibrium drops to the *E'* intersection. Why? Because income has to fall—and fall, note, in a *multiplier* way—until people feel poor enough to again want to save what the system can invest.

less out of their incomes and if business will not willingly invest more, sales will fall and production must soon be cut. Cut how far? Until so much national income has been destroyed as to make people feel poor enough so that they will finally end up not trying to save more than business will go on investing.

Perhaps this point seems obvious. But Fig. 13-1 tells us something more surprising. It shows that a $1 upward shift in the saving schedule will kill off $3 of income. Contrariwise, a $1 downward shift in the saving schedule, which means a $1 upward shift in the consumption schedule, will produce a similar multiplier $3 increase in income. (Note in Fig. 13-1 that the horizontal arrow is 3 times the vertical arrow.)

In short, just as investment spending is "high-powered spending," with multiplier effects on income, consumption spending that represents a genuine shift in the propensity to consume and save will also be "high-powered"!

We shall meet many examples of this. Thus, the next chapter shows how reducing taxes can increase consumption—and thereby expand income by more than that consumption shift. Or, for a second example, take the spending prophets of the Great Depression. A famous Harvard economist, Frank Taussig, went on the radio to urge everyone to save less: to spend more on consumption. What had he in mind? He spoke before the modern theory of income determination was known; but he presumably meant that such spending would on the first round give jobs and incomes to people; that their respending on consumption would create second-round jobs and income; and that it would continue thus in a multiplier chain. (Major Douglas, the inventor of Social Credit,

also sometimes argued that saving was excessive. More consumption was needed, he urged, in promoting his monetary schemes for bringing this about. But his intuitive analysis lacked the multiplier.)

A last example will arise in connection with the next sections' "paradox of thrift." The following summary paves the way for it.

If scheduled investment holds constant, an upward shift in the saving schedule—which means an equal downward shift in the consumption schedule—will kill off national income in a multiplier way until income falls low enough to bring people's new desired saving again into equality with investment opportunities. Thus an *attempt* to save may not lead to more saving in some situations, but instead may then simply reduce national income.

INDUCED INVESTMENT

Until now we have always treated net investment as an autonomous element, absolutely independent of national income. All our investment schedules have been drawn as horizontal lines, their level being always the same regardless of GNP. This simplification can now be relaxed.

Any practical businessman will tell you that he is more likely to add to his plant or equipment if his sales are high relative to his plant capacity. In the short run (before businessmen have had time to adjust their capital stock to a changed plateau of income), it is reasonable for us to draw the *II* schedule in Fig. 13-2 as a rising curve. An increase in employment and national product may *induce* a higher level of net investment.

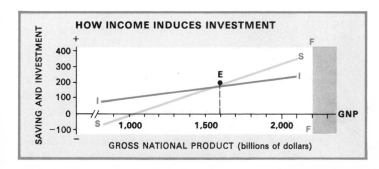

FIG. 13-2. Higher income induces more investment.

Now we drop the assumption of a horizontal *II* schedule. Now *II* slopes upward, showing intended investment less than $200 billion at low GNP and more than $200 billion at high GNP. Equilibrium is still at *E*, where *SS* intersects *II* from below.

As before, the equilibrium level of (maintainable) national income is given by the intersection of the investment and saving schedules, or by E in Fig. 13-2 So long as the SS curve always cuts the II curve from below, businessmen's action must finally bring the economy back to the equilibrium level.[1]

Induced investment means that anything which increases national income is likely to be good for the capital-goods industries; anything hurting national income is likely to be bad for them.[2]

THE PARADOX OF THRIFT

This throws new light on the age-old question of thrift versus consumption.

An increased desire to consume—which is another way of looking at a decreased desire to save—is likely to boost business sales and thus increase investment. On the other hand, a decreased desire to consume—i.e., an increase in thriftiness—is likely to reduce inflationary pressure in times of booming incomes; but in time of depression, it could make the depression worse and reduce the actual amount of net capital formation in the community. *High consumption and high investment are then hand in hand rather than opposed to each other.*

[1] If the two curves crossed in the opposite way, the little arrows in Fig. 12-5 would point out instead of in and we should have unstable equilibrium; then the economy would rush away—in either direction—from the intersection neighborhood. A physical analogy may help: An egg on its side is in "stable equilibrium"; given a slight disturbance, it returns to equilibrium. An egg on its tip is in "unstable equilibrium," a light touch topples it.

[2] Here is the algebra for an induced-investment multiplier. As before,
(1) $Y = C + I$
Because I is not fixed, but a simple function of Y, we write:
(2) $Y = (\overline{C} + b\,Y) + (\overline{I} + d\,Y)$
(3) $Y = \dfrac{1}{1 - b - d}\,(\overline{C} + \overline{I})$
The fraction $1/(1 - b - d)$ is the multiplier in a situation where $\$1/d$ new investment is induced by every $\$1$ of new income. Is this more elaborate multiplier bigger or smaller than the simple multiplier? Compare the two: $1/(1 - b)$ differs from $1/(1 - b - d)$ in that (when b and d are less than 1) the denominator of the latter is smaller. Therefore the new induced-investment multiplier, for a shift in CC, SS, or II, is larger than the simple multiplier.
Another way of thinking about this is in the $r + r^2 + \ldots r^n + \ldots$ secondary-consumption series. An additional secondary chain of *induced investment* spending $s + s^2 + s^3 + \ldots s^n + \ldots$ will reinforce the original. (r = MPC and s = marginal propensity to invest.)

This surprising result is sometimes called the "paradox of thrift." It is a paradox because most of us were taught that thrift is *always* a good thing. Ben Franklin's *Poor Richard's Almanac* never tired of preaching the doctrine of saving. And now along comes a new generation of financial experts who seem to say that the old virtues may be modern sins in depressed times.

PARADOX RESOLVED   Let us for the moment leave our cherished beliefs aside and try to disentangle the paradox in a dispassionate, scientific manner. Two considerations will help to clarify the whole matter.

The first is this. In economics, we must always be on guard against the logical fallacy of composition. That is to say, what is good for each person separately need not always be good for all; under some circumstances, private prudence may be social folly. Specifically, this means that the *attempt* of each and every person to increase his saving may—under the conditions to be described—result in a reduction in *actual* saving by all the people in the community. Note the italicized words "attempt" and "actual"; between them, in our imperfect mixed economy, there may be a world of difference when people find themselves thrown out of jobs and with lowered incomes.

The second clue to the paradox of thrift lies in the question of whether or not national income is at a depressed level. If we were at full employment, then obviously the more of our national product we devoted to current consumption, the less would be available for capital formation. If output could be assumed to be always at its maximum, then the old-fashioned doctrine of thrift would be absolutely correct—correct, be it noted, from both the individual and the social standpoints. In primitive agricultural communities, just as in the Ontario Scottish settlements of John Kenneth Galbraith's boyhood, there was truth in Franklin's prescription. The same was true during World Wars I and II, and it is true during periods of boom and inflation: if people will become more thrifty, then less consumption will mean more investment.

But according to statistical records, full employment and inflationary demand conditions have occurred only at intervals in our nation's history. Much of the time there were some wasting of resources, some unemployment, and some insufficiency of demand, investment, and purchasing power. When this is the case, everything can go into reverse. What once was a social virtue may then become a social vice. What is true for the individual—that extra thriftiness means increased saving and wealth—may then become completely untrue for the community as a whole.

Under conditions of unemployment, the *attempt to save* may result in *less,* not more, saving. The individual who saves cuts down on his consumption. He passes on less purchasing power than before; therefore someone else's income is reduced, for one man's outgo is another man's income. If one man succeeds in saving more, maybe it is because someone else is forced to dissave. If one man succeeds in hoarding more money, someone else must do without.

HIGH *C* INDUCING HIGH *I* Thus, when there is stubborn unemployment, consumption and investment can be complementary, not competitive. What helps one helps the other. The attempt to cut down on consumption (to save) then only results in a reduction of income until everyone feels poor enough no longer to try to save more than can be invested. Moreover, at lower levels of income, less, and not more, capital goods will be needed. Therefore *investment will actually be less.* (As will be seen again and again, with prudent public and private policies, our system will be restored to proper operation, so that the paradox of thrift can be robbed of its applicability.)

Let us clinch our common-sense understanding of this paradox by combining Figs. 13-1 and 13-2 into Fig. 13-3. An increase in thriftiness or the desire to save will shift the SS curve upward to S'S'. Note that the new intersection E' is now at a lower level of income. Because of induced *disinvestment,* the drop in income will also mean lower investment. Thus both income and investment have actually decreased. The attempt to save more in depression times has resulted in less actual saving.

If true, this is an important lesson. It will never again be a satisfactory measure to urge men in time of depression to tighten their belts, to save more in order to restore prosperity. The result will all too likely be the reverse—a worsening of the vicious deflationary spiral. At such a time, many of the usual arguments go into reverse. An economic lobbyist of the capital-goods industries would, if he has their selfish interests at heart, advocate less thriftiness in depressed times, so that the consumption schedule will be pushed upward, and so that attempts to save —which then really lead only to decreases in income —will be discouraged. For only then will investment and sales of heavy capital goods flourish.[3]

Later, we shall see how fiscal and monetary policies can rid the paradox of thrift of its terrors.

THE DEFLATIONARY GAP

The multiplier is a two-edged sword. It will cut for you or against you. It will amplify new investment, as we have seen. But it will also amplify negatively any *decrease* in investment. Thus, if investment opportunities drop by 3 billion dollars in our earlier examples, then national income will have to fall by three times as much—by 9 billion dollars. If net investment drops away to zero, income will have to fall to the break-even point where the community is made poor enough to stop all net saving.

This reminds us once again that there may be nothing particularly good about what we have called the equilibrium level of national income. If investment is low, the equilibrium level of income will involve much unemployment and waste of national resources. The only level of national income that we are entitled to regard as a desirable goal is that near to full employment; but we shall end up at such a level of high employment only if investment opportunities happen to be as large as full-employment saving.

Unless this full-employment saving is "offset" by private investment (or by public policies), the nation cannot continue to enjoy full employment. There is then said to be a "deflationary gap," its size being measured by the deficiency of investment compared with full-employment saving.

We can picture the deflationary gap in Fig. 12-5 as the vertical distance between the saving and in-

---

[3] We have seen that this line of argument does not apply in conditions of full employment. It also requires some slight modifications to allow for the fact that thriftiness, by lowering income, may also lower interest rates and promote investment, or it may depress wages and prices and thereby increase the real purchasing power of people's money holdings enough to destroy their initial thriftiness. These qualifications are discussed later; in our imperfect mixed economy they seem rather unimportant considerations during deep depression.

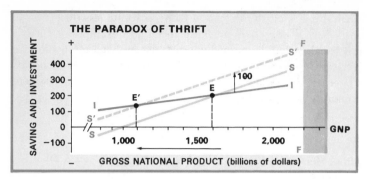

FIG. 13-3. An attempt to save more can well result in less actual saving and investment.

The shift of *SS* upward to *S'S'* depresses income; and the drop of income kills off some investment, moving us southwest along the sloping *II* schedule. (If the system were straining at the full-employment level of *F*, the effect of increased thriftiness would be beneficial to *I* as against *C*.)

vestment schedules at the full-employment level of income indicated by the vertical line *FF*. Or, as in Fig. 13-4, we can picture the deflationary gap on a consumption-plus-investment graph. Suppose that 2,200 billion dollars represents the full-employment income. Suppose that, at this income level *G*, the scheduled total of *C + I* adds up to only 2,000 billion dollars, as shown at *H*. *This leaves a 200-billion dollar deflationary gap between H and G.* Since obviously we cannot then remain at full employment, what will happen? Will income drop by only 200 billion dollars? Clearly not. It must drop by some greater multiple of the original deflationary gap. If each dollar of reduced income results in a cut of $2/3 in consumption spending, income will have to fall until it has dropped three times as much as the original deflationary gap (see point *E* in Fig. 13-4.)[4]

THE PROCESS OF PRICE INFLATION

Instead of a deflationary gap, we may have an inflationary gap. If scheduled investment tends to be greater than full-employment saving, then more goods will be demanded of business than it can pro-

[4] What can be done about this? If we continue to leave the government and foreign trade out of the picture, we must have either an increase in investment or an increase in consumption. By how much must the level of investment or of consumption shift upward if full employment is to be restored? If we include government spending, and exports, how great must they be to remove unemployment? By the full 12 billion dollars of lost income? Surely not. Because of the multiplier, to wipe out a deflationary gap, the *C + I + G + E* schedule need shift upward only by the amount of the gap itself, not by any multiple of the gap. (In a saving-investment diagram like Fig. 13-3 you measure the deflationary gap by the vertical distance between the *SS* and *II* schedules at the full-employment income *FF* .)

duce, and prices will begin to rise. Figure 13-5 shows how we measure the inflationary gap as a vertical distance: The new *C' + I'* curve lies *above* the 45° line at the full-employment level by the distance *GH'*, giving us an inflationary gap of 3 billion dollars.

If full-employment saving falls short of scheduled investment at full-employment, there is said to be an "inflationary gap," its size being measured by the excess of the *C + I* schedule above the 45° line's full-employment level (which is the same thing as the excess of full-employment scheduled *II* over *SS*).

Now what will result from the 200 billion-dollar gap? Can production rise by 600 billion dollars to give us a new equilibrium at *E'* ? Plainly not. Everyone is already fully employed, and factories are producing at their practical capacity points. The region to the right of the vertical full-employment line through *F* is a never-never land. It shows us what we should like to be able to produce, but not what we are actually able to produce. Although an inflationary gap is the opposite of a deflationary gap, its effects upon employment and production are of a slightly different qualitative nature. A deflationary gap can move production leftward, down to three-quarters or even one-half of a full-employment level; but an inflationary gap cannot possibly move employment rightward to 150 per cent of full or maximum employment. The economic system cannot move in *real terms* very far to the right of the black full-employment line.

DEMAND-PULL INFLATION The excess in purchasing power can result only in price increases and an inflationary spiral; *money* national income will rise because of "paper" price-tag changes, but

FIG. 13-4. Spending Deficiency.
The deflationary gap is always measured at the full-employment GNE level. It is the vertical distance there between the 45° line and the $C + I$ schedule, that is, GH. Such a deflationary gap will depress income in a multiplied way. (Later, after government is introduced, we'll relabel $C + I$ as $C + I + G$.)

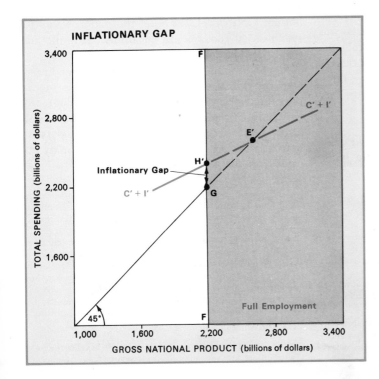

FIG. 13-5. Spending Excess.
GH' measures the inflationary gap. People are trying to buy more than can be produced, and thereby they are inflating the price level. (With all prices changing and no longer ignorable, the EE point and the spending schedules are likely to shift upward, so it would be a mistake to regard E' as an actually attainable equilibrium point of *real* income.)

real national product cannot go above its maximum full-employment level. Unfortunately, the upward movement of prices will continue for as long as there is an inflationary gap,[5] i.e., until we are lucky enough for investment or consumption demand to fall off or smart enough as a nation to adopt corrective policies that will wipe out the inflationary gap.

Far from being "depression economics," modern income analysis has many of its most important applications in connection with the process of inflation and what can be done about it. During and after World War II, the concept of the inflationary gap was indispensable in indicating the quantitative magnitude of taxation needed to keep decontrolled prices from rising; and without understanding the rudiments of income analysis, we cannot follow the important economic issues discussed in Parliament and the public press.[6]

FISCAL POLICY IN INCOME DETERMINATION

When there is a large inflationary or deflationary gap, the government is called upon to do something about the price rise or the widespread unemployment. Tax and government expenditure policies—the general name for which is "fiscal policy"—will change the equilibrium level of income. So we must now explicitly introduce government fiscal policy into the picture to see exactly how income determination is affected. As you might guess, we now consider a $C + I + G$ spending schedule to show the equilibrium that results when government is in the picture.

It will simplify our task if in the beginning we analyze the effects of government expenditure with taxes held constant. With taxes in the picture, we can no longer ignore the distinction between disposable income and net national product. But with the tax revenue first held constant, they will differ always by the same amount; and taking account of such taxes, we can still plot the CC consumption schedule against GNP rather than against DI.

In Chapter 10 we learned that national product consists of three rather than two parts; namely,

GNP = Consumption expenditure + private investment + Government expenditure on goods and services
$$= C + I + G$$

Therefore, on our 45°-line diagram in Fig. 13-6, we must superimpose upon the consumption schedule not only private investment but also government expenditure G. This is because public road building is economically no different from private railroad building, and collective consumption expenditure involved in maintaining a free public library has the same effect upon jobs as private consumption expenditure for movies or rental libraries.

We end up with the three-layered $C + I + G$ schedule showing the amount of total spending forthcoming at each level of GNP. We now must go to the intersection with the 45° line to read off the equilibrium level of national product. At this equilibrium GNP level, the total the nation wants to spend on all goods is just equal in value to the full costs of production of these goods.

Figure 13-6 shows that government expenditure, taken by itself and disregarding taxes, has a multiplier effect upon income just like that of private investment. The reason is, of course, that a chain of *respending* is set into motion by the road builders, librarians, and other people who receive primary income from the government.[7]

---

[5] The process does not end with higher prices. The new higher price level will not equilibrate total supply and demand once and for all. On the contrary, since the higher prices received by businesses become in turn somebody's income—that of worker or property owner—demand again shifts upward and prices will continue to rise. Attempts of labor to secure higher wages as compensation for the soaring cost of living may only cause the inflationary spiral to zoom at a dizzier speed. (Lord Keynes formulated this theory of inflation in 1939.)

[6] See Chapter 19 for further discussion of inflation, which includes along with the present kind of "excess-demand", or "demand-pull", inflation the possibility of "creeping cost-push inflationary tendencies".

[7] Our saving-investment diagram will give the same answer as the 45°-line diagram. The increase in government expenditure means an equivalent increase in the government deficit if taxes have not been increased. Net saving must always equal private investment + government deficit. Therefore we add the deficit on top of the II curve and get our new greater equilibrium level of national income at the intersection with the SS curve. Following Chapter 12's footnote 7, we could employ Fig. 13-6 to show how induced investment or government expenditure (i.e., induced by a changed level of income) will enter into the multiplier. The final change in income resulting from a unit upward shift in the $C + I + G$ schedule will always turn out to be $\frac{1/(1-k)}{k}$ where k is the slope of the $C + I + G$ schedule and might be called the "marginal propensity to spend (inclusive of induced $C, I,$ and G effects)."

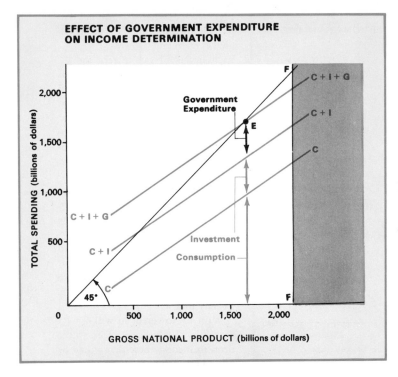

FIG. 13-6. Government expenditure adds on just like investment in determining the equilibrium GNP.

On top of consumption spending and investment spending, we now add government spending on goods and services. This gives us the $C + I + G$ schedule. At E, where this intersects the 45° line, we find equilibrium. (What if G increases or decreases? Can you show the multiplied changes in income?)

To show the effects of an extra 100 billion dollars of G, shift $C + I + G$ in Fig. 13-6 up to $C + I + G'$ and show that the new E' will record a multiplier response of GNP to the government spending.

TAXATION AND DOWNWARD SHIFT OF CONSUMPTION SCHEDULE

Now let us turn to the depressing effects of taxes on the equilibrium GNP level. Without graphs, our common sense tells us what must happen when the government *(1)* takes away more from us in taxes while *(2)* at the same time holding its expenditure constant. Extra taxes mean lower real disposable incomes, and lower disposable incomes mean lower consumption spending. Obviously, if investment and government expenditures remain the same, a reduction in consumption spending will then reduce national product and employment; or if we already are having an inflationary gap, the new taxes will help close the gap and wipe out excessive inflationary price increases.

Our graphs can confirm this reasoning: the increase in taxes does *not* lower consumption directly,

but reduces disposable income. $I + G$ is unchanged, but now with lower disposable income, the consumption schedule CC can remain accurate only by *shifting downward*. So in all, the $C + I + G$ schedule must also shift downward. Pencil a new $C' + I + G$ schedule into Fig. 13-6 confirm that its new intersection with the crucial 45° line must definitely be to the left—at a *lower* equilibrium level of GNP.

THE TAX MULTIPLIER A change in T will have a multiplier effect, like shifts in I, C, or G, but the per-dollar effect of change is weaker. In both Figs. 13-6 and 13-7, a rise of 300 billion dollars in G shifts the $C + I + G$ schedule vertically upward by the same amount, but an increase of 300 billion dollars in taxes *lowers* $C + I + G$ vertically by less than 300 billion dollars.

Why? In Fig. 13-7 CC *is* shifted to the right by exactly the amount of the tax. This *rightward* shift measures the increase in the GNP necessary for consumption to remain at its former no-tax level. Fig. 13-7 shows that the CC schedule also shifts downward when it is moved to the right. The extent of the *downward* shift depends on the MPC. By experimentation, you can confirm that when MPC = 0, T

EFFECT OF TAXES ON CONSUMPTION SCHEDULE

FIG. 13-7. **Higher tax will cut disposable income and shift** *CC* **schedule (to right and) down.**

Each dollar of tax lowers the *CC* schedule. Why? Because *CC* is shifted to the right by the amount of the tax. (**EXAMPLE:** First, GNP = $1,300 at *U* with zero tax; *DI* = $1,300 also, *CC* shows consumption at *U* of $1,100. Now introduce tax of $300; GNP must equal $1,300 + 300 = $1,600 if *DI* is to remain $1,300 and consumption $1,100 there. So *UV* arrow shows *C'C'* is shifted rightward by exact amount of the tax.) A rightward *CC* shift means a downward *CC* shift. But the downward shift is only two-thirds of the rightward shift if *CC's* slope of MPC = 2/3. (Verify that *WV* = 2/3 *UV*.)

With *CC* lowered, so will *C + I + G* in Fig. 13-6 be lowered. Show the drop in income there that would be caused by such a tax increase.

does not shift *CC* downward at all, whereas when MPC = 1, the downward shift equals the rightward shift. For an intermediate MPC, 2/3, if *T* = 300 billion dollars, any point on *CC* shifts right by 300 billion dollars, and down by only 200 billion dollars.

In common-sense terms, a change in taxation (and hence in disposable income) elicits not only a change in spending, but also a change in saving. The greater is MPC, the greater is the tax impact on spending relative to saving, and so the greater is the downward shift in *CC*.

The "tax multiplier" measures the total (net) primary and secondary effects on total spending of a change in taxation. For example, an individual may find that a tax increase of $1,000 has reduced his disposable income by the same amount. If his MPC is 2/3, this means that he will spend $666.67 less on consumption goods, and that, as a result, the producers of those goods will suffer a decrease of $666.67 in income. If their MPC is also 2/3, they in turn will reduce their expenditures on consumption goods by 2/3 of $666.67, or $444.44. Thus the primary effect on consumption, plus the secondary effect on the next person's consumption, and so on, will be *minus* ($666.67 + $444.44 +

$296.30 + ...), or –$2,000. This chain is identical to the series described in Chapter 12, on page 206, except that it starts out with $666.67 instead of $1,000. Thus it can also be expressed by the same geometrical progression used on page 208, 1 + 2/3 + (2/3)² + (2/3)³ + ..., that finally added up to 3. Three, multiplied by the initial drop in consumption of (2/3 × –$1,000) gives you –$2,000.

The final formula for the *I* or *G* multiplied was: change in Investment × $\frac{1}{1-\text{MPC}}$. For a change in tax the multiplier formula is nearly identical; the change in tax is first multiplied by MPC, then the old multiplier is applied:

$$\text{Change in income} = \frac{1}{1-MPC} \times MPC \times \text{change in tax}$$

$$= \frac{MPC}{1-MPC} \times \text{change in tax}^8$$

---

[8] More formally, the ordinary multiplier progression is
$$1 + r + r^2 + r^3 + r^4 \dots r^n = 1/(1-r).$$
The taxation multiplier discussed above simply subtracts one from each side of the equation:
$$r + r^2 + r^3 \dots r^n = 1/(1-r) - 1.$$
The tax multiplier can be left in this form as $1/(1 - \text{MPC}) - 1$; or it can be converted to
$$1/(1-MPC) - (1-MPC)/(1-MPC) = MPC/(1-MPC),$$
as in the text.

Now we know something that common sense did not immediately tell us. When extra G is added to an already-balanced budget in a full-employment economy, then *if* we are determined to avoid an inflationary gap, we must raise tax collections by more than the extra G. We must "over-balance" the budget.[9]

We can easily reverse the above analysis to explain why tax reductions help to fight a sluggish recession. Each dollar of tax reduction leads, through an upward and leftward shift in CC, to an increase in people's disposable income by a dollar and to almost a dollar increase in initial consumption spending.

Hence the power of dollars of tax reduction as a weapon against mass unemployment is less than increases in dollars of government expenditure.

Because tax potency is slightly less than expenditure potency, such a program may involve a larger deficit than an expenditure program would; but it also means that there is expansion of the private rather than of the government sector of the economic system. The United States, Japan, and the

United Kingdom all used this tax-cut mechanism in the mid-sixties to increase their employment and income levels, a remarkable example of modern fiscal policy at work. The tax-change mechanism has also been used in Canada and the U.S., in the form of surcharges and tax-reductions.

QUALIFICATIONS TO SAVING AND INVESTMENT ANALYSIS

The theory of income determination sketched in the last two chapters is a powerful tool.[10] It helps us to understand the ups and downs of the business cycle. It helps us to understand how foreign spending and buying affect domestic employment and income. It helps us to understand how governmental fiscal policy can be used to fight inflation and unemployment. All these topics are developed in later chapters.

But it would be a mistake to think that an economist can be made out of a parrot simply by teaching him the magic words "saving" and "investment." Behind the scenes of these schedules a great deal is taking place.

It should be noted that an increase in the public's holding of government bonds and other wealth may shift the consumption schedule upward. Increases in the community's supply of money and other liquid assets will shift the CC and other schedules. Or rising living standards (resulting from advertising and the invention of new products) may shift the consumption schedule up, just as it has in the past.

In short, it is an oversimplification to regard investment as *always* an autonomous factor, and consumption as *always* a passive factor depending upon income. True, this is a fruitful oversimplification. But, as we have already seen, some of net investment may be "induced" by income changes in the short run; and we shall soon see that changes in interest costs, availability of credit, and stock of money can alter the swings in investment and total spending. Furthermore, consumption also will sometimes shift autonomously even though income has remained constant. And the reader can verify, by experimenting with the saving-investment and the 45°-line diagrams, the truth of our earlier assertion that such shifts in the CC or SS schedules do have multi-

---

[9] Advanced treatises call this phenomenon the "balanced budget multiplier theorem". New public works of G dollars raise GNP by $G \times 1/(1 - \text{MPC})$; while new balancing taxes of I dollars cause GNP to drop by $T \times \text{MPC}/(1 - \text{MPC})$. If $T = G$, the final effect on GNP is therefore $T \times (1 - \text{MPC})/(1 - \text{MPC})$, or T dollars. Hence a balanced fall or rise in G and I will move GNP by just the amount of the fall or rise. Note, contrary to footnote 1, that it is not merely the deficit or surplus $(G - T)$ that has GNP effects. Here is a fuller demonstration: Let

$$(1) \quad \text{GNP} = Y = C + I + G$$

and following footnote 7 in the last chapter, let:

$$(2) \quad DI = Y_d = Y - T$$
$$(3) \quad C = \overline{C} + bY_d$$
$$(4) \quad I = \overline{I},$$
and
$$(5) \quad G = \overline{G}$$
$$(6) \quad T = \overline{T}$$

Then, substituting in (1),

$$(7) \quad \text{GNP} = Y = \overline{C} + b(Y - \overline{T}) + \overline{I} + \overline{G}$$
$$= \frac{1}{1 - b} [\overline{C} - b\overline{T} + \overline{I} + \overline{G}]$$

This is the simple multiplier expanded to a world of government G and T. However, if $T = G$ in a balanced budget, then

$$(8) \quad \text{GNP} = Y = \frac{1}{1 - b} [\overline{C} + \overline{G}(1 - b) + \overline{I}]$$
$$= \frac{1}{1 - b} [\overline{C} + \overline{I}] + \overline{G}$$

Notice that the multiplier for $\overline{C}$ and $\overline{T}$ is still $1/(1 - b)$, but the multiplier for $\overline{G}$ is now 1. The absolute size of the budget (not the deficit alone) matters for the size of Y, even when taxes match $G!$

These multipliers, as shown in equations (7) and (8), apply as well to *changes* in $C, I, G,$ or T.

[10] Advanced discussions show that corporate saving can be handled graphically much like taxes.

plier effects upon national income—*exactly* like the multiplier effects of changes in *I* and *G*.

After the survey of foreign trade effects and business cycles in the next chapter, the succeeding chapters will discuss money and banking, to show how changes in the supply of money, credit, and interest rates cause spending schedules and their intersections to shift.

SUMMARY

1 The *attempt* to save more is quite different from the achievement of increased saving for society as a whole. The "paradox of thrift" shows that an increase in thriftiness may reduce already depressed income and, *through induced effects on investment*, may actually result in *less* investment. Only when employment remains full or unchanged are consumption and investment necessarily competing. Only then are private virtues always social virtues.

  The moral is not for each individual to squander his money during a depression, trying to be patriotic. Instead, by proper national policies, we must re-create a high-employment environment in which private virtues are no longer social follies.

2 In short, we must avoid both *inflationary and deflationary gaps,* so that full-employment saving and investment just match without demand-pull inflation. We measure the size of the deflationary or inflationary gap as *(a)* the vertical discrepancy at full-employment income between the saving and investment schedules, or what is exactly the same thing, as *(b)* the vertical distance between the *C + I* (or *C + I + G* when government is in the picture) schedule and the 45° line.

3 An increase in government expenditure—taken by itself with taxes and investment unchanged—has expansionary effects on national product much like those of investment. The schedule of *C + I + G* shifts upward to a higher equilibrium intersection with the 45° line.

4 An increase in taxes—taken by itself with investment and government expenditure unchanged—depresses the equilibrium level of national product. The schedule of consumption plotted against GNP is shifted downward and rightward by taxes; but since extra dollars go partly into saving, the dollar drop in consumption will not be quite so great as the dollars of new taxes. Therefore, to combat a given inflationary or deflationary gap, we may require an even larger change in taxation.

5 The art of economics consists in recognizing both the core of truth in the simple theory of income determination and also its needed qualifications. In later chapters, we shall see how the money supply and interest rates may also cause shifts in the schedules that determine levels of national income.

  We leave to the final chapters of Part Two the analysis of government monetary and fiscal policy. In the intervening chapters we turn to an analysis of the wild dance of the business cycle, to the analysis of money, banking, and interest policy.

CONCEPTS FOR REVIEW

"production gap"
poverty midst plenty
multiplier effects on income of
  consumption or saving shifts
induced investment
paradox of thrift
inflationary, deflationary gaps

cumulative demand-pull inflation
underemployment equilibrium
C + I + G schedule
fiscal policy (expenditure and taxes)
G effect on equilibrium
tax effect on *CC* and equilibrium
qualifications to the analysis

QUESTIONS FOR DISCUSSION

1 "Even if the government spends billions on 'wasteful' cold-war armaments, during a depression this action helps create jobs and several billions of new useful production." Discuss critically.

2 Give arguments for and against thriftiness. Contrast carefully (*a*) the individual and the community viewpoint, and (*b*) conditions of boom and depression.

3 Describe effects upon income of (*a*) government expenditure and (*b*) taxes.

4 "The purpose of fiscal policy is to wipe out inflationary or deflationary gaps. If $C + I + G$ is too high, we have an inflationary gap; and we raise taxes to shift the new $C' + I' + G'$ schedule downward, thereby wiping out the inflationary gap." Explain. Show how (*a*) an increase in tax rates or/and (*b*) new government expenditures fight a *deflationary* gap.

5 Analyze the economics of the 1975–76 debates on a needed change in taxes: increase or decrease?

6 If family formation and family size decline further, housing demand in North America will evaporate. How might we nevertheless preserve full employment? Explain your program in terms of shifts of the $C + I + G$ schedule.

7 Let GNP = Y, DI = Y_d = $Y - \overline{T}$. Let T = 100, and C = 200 + 2/3 Y_d. When $\overline{G}$ = 0 = $\overline{T}, \overline{I}$ = 100, we use formula Y = 200 + 2/3 $(Y - \overline{T})$ + $\overline{I}$ + $\overline{G}$ to solve for Y^* = 900. Likewise, verify the values in the following quadruplets of values for $(\overline{I}; \overline{G}; \overline{T}: Y^*)$: (101;0;0: 903), (100;1;0: 903), (100;0;1: 898), (100;1;1: 901).

8 *Extra-credit problem:* If II rises with income instead of being horizontal, we must amplify the multiplier formula, $1/\text{MPS} = 1/(1 - \text{MPC})$, to the form $1/(\text{MPS} - \text{MPI})$. In Figs. 13-2 and 13-3, MPI = 2/15. Show that the old multiplier of $3 = 1/(1/3)$ now becomes $5 = 1/(1/3 - 2/15) = 1/(3/15) = 1(1/5)$. Solve $Y = C + I = (A + 2/3 Y) + (B + 2/15 Y)$ for $Y^* = 5(A + B)$, where a shift in the CC schedule is a shift in A, and a shift in II is a shift in B.

14

THE OPEN-ECONOMY MULTIPLIER, AND THE ACCELERATOR

The fault, dear Brutus, is not in our stars—but in ourselves ...   WILLIAM SHAKESPEARE

We have examined the economic forces operating to determine the level of national income—the balance of saving and investment. In Section A, we explore the workings of the same process in an "open economy" that also exports, and imports. This not only adds to the realism and urgency of fiscal-policy discussions, but acts as a curtain-raiser for a fuller discussion of international trade in later chapters.

Then in Section B, we look at the existence of business cycles and consider one of the best-known theoretical explanations of cycles, the acceleration principle, which explains changes in all-important investment.

A. FOREIGN TRADE AND INCOME DETERMINATION

In an "open" economy like Canada's, changes in national income can often be traced back to changes in exports or imports. The theory of income determination shows how foreigners buying more of our goods, or Canadians trying to buy more foreign-made goods, can change the Canadian GNP. Although one end of these transactions is outside the country, our end can be influenced and controlled by government action. For example, by setting high customs duties, the government dissuades Canadians from buying foreign-made wines, TV sets, and breakfast cereals. And, by reducing taxes on petroleum, it encourages foreigners to buy Canadian oil, which thus becomes cheaper measured in foreign moneys.

So we must first find where foreign transactions fit into our theory, and then survey the results of some typical policies. In a very complete treatment, we would stretch out our basic equations to read GNP = $C + I + G + (E - M)$ and show how changes in each of the parts of the equation would affect each other part, and so, finally affect the GNP as a whole. But to keep our task simple, we initially omit government taxing and spending, and later bring them in only insofar as they influence the "foreign sector" of the economy.

In order to take the parts of the foreign sector one by one, we begin with exports, supposing that imports are zero. This allows us to delay tracing through the economy the desires of those exporters whose sales abroad have gone up or down to raise or lower the amount of imported goods that they and their suppliers want to buy.

Except in indirect ways we can safely neglect, national income does not influence exports. Sales to foreign customers are among those "autonomous" factors in a country's economic equilibrium. We may suppose, then, that export opportunities are such that foreigners would buy exactly $20 billion-worth every year, *regardless* of our GNP. This means that, if we now draw a schedule of exports against GNP, it will have to be a *horizontal* line—always the same distance above the axis. Look at Fig. 14.1, where this schedule is labeled *EE* to distinguish it from *II*, the investment schedule. *Both* are autonomous amounts of spending. (Indeed, most of the above paragraph is identical to the discussion of *II* on page 199.) So we add exports and investments to get the horizontal *I + E* schedule.

Suppose the economy is in equilibrium at *e*, with savings equal to domestic investment opportunities.

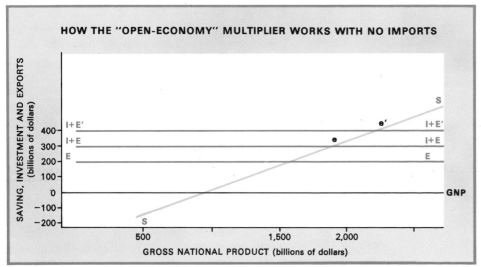

FIG. 14-1. Each dollar of exports can be multiplied into three dollars of income.
New exports shift the "autonomous" spending schedule up from $I + E$ to $I + E'$. e' gives
the new equilibrium GNP, with income increasing 3 for every 1 in exports. Notice that
this diagram is almost the same as Fig. 13-1. Imports are zero.

Now the economy gets a chance to sell an extra 100 billion dollars' worth of goods annually abroad. The old circular flow of consumption and investment is now joined by the output of restarted mills and factories, and the putting to work of unemployed loggers and factory hands. If these workers all have a marginal propensity to consume of 2/3, they will now spend this fraction of 100 billion dollars on new consumption goods. The makers of these foods, clothes, and so forth will get extra sales and will spend 2/3 of 2/3 of 100 billion dollars extra. So the process goes on.

Just as on page 206, the final change in Canadian income can be worked out by the multiplier arithmetic:

$$\text{Change in income} = \frac{1}{MPS} \times \text{change in exports}$$

In this case, the change in Canada's GNP would be: $\frac{1}{1-2/3} \times 100$ billion dollars, or 3×100 billion or 300 billion dollars. The multiplier, as on page 206, is 3. It follows from all that was said earlier about the multiplier, that if our exports had been previously 300 billion dollars and *fell* to 200 billion dollars, the

Canadian income would fall by a multiplied amount. Here it is:

$$\text{Change in income} = \frac{1}{1-2/3} \times (300 - 200 \text{ billion}) = 3 \times (- \$1 \text{ billion})$$
$$= - \$3 \text{ billion}$$

The upward working of this can be seen in Fig. 14-1. Before the export boom, GNP is in equilibrium at 1900 billion dollars, with exports of 200 and investment of 100 matched by savings of 300. After the boom has begun, investment is joined by added exports of 100 making total "autonomous" spending of 400. (But the increase in such spending is only the 100 billion dollars in exports.) Thus the new equilibrium will be found where $(I + E)$ cuts the SS schedule at e'. Here the GNP has increased to 2200. An increase in exports of 100 billion dollars has yielded an additional increase in GNP of 200 billion dollars.

This is the main importance of exports in income-determination theory. They act *exactly* like government spending on goods and services, or investment, or any other "autonomous injection" of spending, in having a multiplied effect on GNP. If imports remain at zero, the effect of a change in exports (a shift in the *EE* schedule) is the same as the effect of a change in investment.

The thoughtful reader will say, "But how are these exports paid for? You have held imports unchanged, so the foreigners are not sending extra goods in return." The question points to a matter that can be clarified in Fig.14-1. With imports at zero, foreigners can pay for these extra exports in one of two ways: they can in effect borrow from Canadians to pay the loggers and factory hands who produce the exports; or they can send money (not imports) to pay for the goods.

The first way of paying, borrowing from Canadians, is like using Canadian savings. This is seen in Fig. 14-1, where total savings at *e'* covers both investment and exports. So the GNP has expanded, with the export growth, until *the amount of saving that people want to do is matched by the amount of investment that businessmen are willing to maintain plus the amount of exports that foreigners want to take.* Clearly, by this way of paying, foreigners are going to go farther into debt to Canadian lenders every year. But this need not concern us here; all we need note here is that increased exports will raise GNP until they are matched by increased savings.

The second way of paying is sending money to Canada. Briefly, it amounts to adding foreigners' funds to Canadian assets. These funds must be matched by Canadian saving, until again $S = I + E$. When these are equal, GNP again comes into equilibrium.[1]

We need not worry about the details of these two ways of paying, except to notice what surprises most students; if there is no change in imports, exports are just like investment, and must be matched, in final equilibrium at *e'*, by intended saving.

IMPORTS ENTER THE PICTURE[2]

The simplicity of this addition of exports to our income-determination theory is due to our purposeful

omission of imports. Including imports, however, is necessary, for we know that imports do not remain constant. Look at the lowest curve, below the axis, in Fig. 10-3. When Canadian incomes rise, Canadians buy more of all goods, including foreign-made goods. Thus the lumber-workers, and their suppliers who are now exporting more, will have higher incomes to buy not only more food and clothing but also more cars and TV sets, with their imported parts, more insurance from a foreign seller of actuarial services, and more gasoline from foreign service stations on the extra holidays they are now able to take outside Canada.

We know too that GNP = $C + I + G + (E - M)$, and we have learned how income determination works when each of these items changes, except the *M* at the end.

First we must examine what our symbols, *C*, *I*, and *G* mean. A review of Chapter 10 shows that they refer to Canadian spending on kinds of goods: consumer goods, government goods, and investment goods. But what happens when these three categories include both home-made and foreign-made goods? The propensity-to-consume schedule becomes, in part, a propensity-to-import schedule; and the government and investment spending schedules also reveal a demand for imports. Thus our theoretical tools are too dull to cut into the economic system to show what is happening to imports.

This difficulty, however, can be simply overcome by a once-for-all re-defining of our terms. Let C^D be the consumption of goods of domestic origin, so that $C^D C^D$ is the propensity-to-consume home-made items of food, clothing, services, and so forth. Similarly, we redefine *II* to become $I^D I^D$, where I^D is investment expenditures on goods of domestic origin. Assume, however, as in Fig. 12-7 and Fig. 13-1, that all investment is constant, not induced. (From here on, we again ignore government, though similar modifications would have to be made for its purchases.) Then upper-loop GNP includes the sum of all goods and services *made in Canada*, including consumption, investment, and export goods, but not imported goods or services to be used in making, or used directly as, consumption, investment, and export goods. In symbols:

$$GNP = C^D + I^D + E$$

---

[1] Just how a foreign capital inflow can be added to Canadian saving is a question of how to "transfer" income or wealth from one country to another. It can be done most simply by moving gold, or some other good; that is, by importing something from abroad. But we have ruled out imports so far. The question now becomes one for advanced theory, where it is referred to as the "transfer problem."

[2] This section is more difficult and rigorous than the rest of this chapter. Bringing in *M* is a bit trickier than bringing in *E*. In Canada, imports amount to between 20 and 25 per cent of GNE. This is too big an item to slide over by merely looking at "net exports," $(E - M)$, as a single number.

With these definitions, imports do not appear at all in the value-added or purchases loop of the circular flow of the economy.

But of course they must be taken into account in the income or production loop. In the *disposing* of GNP, people can buy consumer goods made in Canada, save, or buy imports.[3] In symbols:

$$GNP = C^D + S + M$$

This means that when persons' incomes rise, their spending and their suppliers' respending will not only go to consumption goods made by other Canadians (who can respend the income), but also may "leak" through *two* channels: saving or imports from abroad. Through the combination of these "leakages," our chain of induced domestic purchasing power will peter out faster than if domestic disposable income were saved or entirely spent on home-made goods. For there is no reason to believe that people's saving *intentions* will be different when they can buy both home-produced and foreign goods: the propensity-to-save will be as it was in a "closed" economy, and the import leakage will be added to it.

Our propensity to save, therefore, remains at $(1 - 2/3)$, or $1/3$. But let us say that for every 1 billion dollars of *extra* spending, Canada imports $1/6$ billion dollars of foreign-made goods.[4] This means that the marginal propensity to import (MPM) is $1/6$. With these two propensities, we can estimate the propensity to consume domestic products; arithmetically

it must be the residual after saving and imports. If, out of every additional billion dollars in income $1/3$ goes to saving and $1/6$ to imports, then only $1/2$ goes to buy home-made consumption goods.

$$\text{MPC}^D = 1 - (\text{MPS} + \text{MPM})$$
$$= 1 - (1/3 + 1/6)$$
$$= 1/2$$

Now we can trace the effect of any additional outlays in the GNP, such as exports or investment. Suppose exports rise by 1 billion dollars. The workers and owners of export plants (and their suppliers) will respend half of this on home-made goods, the other half being divided between their purchases of imported goods and their saving. And so it will go at every stage. The whole multiplier will now add up to only $1 + 1/2 + (1/2)^2 + \ldots$ or only $2 = \frac{1}{1-\frac{1}{2}}$, instead of 3, as was the case when there were no imports. (The reader now should go back to the paragraph above where exports rose by 2 billion dollars. With imports taking $1/6$ of each autonomous increase in spending, what would be the final GNP?)[5]

---

[3] We must be precise about M, imports. Recall that consumption spending is now divided between C^D and imported consumption goods, C^M; and similarly I now consists of I^D and I^M, imported machinery and other capital goods. Similarly, G consists of G^D and G^M. Then total M is defined as $C^M + I^M + G^M$. In the text, G^M is neglected for simplicity's sake.

[4] These pages on the foreign-trade multiplier avoid complexities which may occur to perceptive readers. Because little restriction has been placed on the marginal propensity to import (MPM), it might, therefore, cause consumption imports to increase with increasing GNP so fast that I and G, even though fixed in amount, must be spent on changing combinations of domestic and foreign goods (I^D and I^M, G^D and G^M). If so, the perceptive reader might well complain about the unlikelihood of government spending a larger fraction (of its fixed $G = G^D + G^M$) on imports G^M simply because GNP is higher. A more complete foreign-trade multiplier discussion which would show changing total G and I, each having changing import percentages, is quite possible but is algebraically complex. More advanced works do this. Here we wrap up increasing purchases of all types of foreign goods into one aggregative MPM, showing simply the ratio of the change in all imports to the change in GNP.

[5] We can follow footnote 7 (page 207) of Chapter 12 to derive an algebraic formula for the multiplier in an open economy. We know: The equilibrium equation is

$$(1)\quad GNP = Y = C^D + I^D + X + G$$

Then continue to distinguish between C^D and C^M and between I^D and I^M, so that $M = C^M + I^M$. We will continue to assume scheduled I is not induced, so that both I^D and I^M are constant (shown by a bar over the symbol) so that $\bar{I} = \bar{I}^D + \bar{I}^M$, and

$$(2)\quad \bar{I}^D = \bar{I} - \bar{I}^M$$

Let the scheduled consumption of home-produced goods and services be

$$(3)\quad C^D = \bar{C}^D + cY$$

where c is the domestic marginal propensity to consume, MPC^D. Taxes are neglected, for simplicity, and X and G are given and are independent of imports:

$$(4)\quad X = \bar{X}^D$$

and

$$(5)\quad G = \bar{G}^D$$

Substituting these expressions in the GNP equation given at the beginning of this footnote, we obtain

$$GNP = Y = \bar{C}^D + cY + \bar{I}^D + \bar{X}^D + \bar{G}^D$$

whence

$$GNP = Y = \frac{1}{1 - c}[\bar{C}^D + \bar{I}^D + \bar{X}^D + \bar{G}^D]$$

Here the multiplier derived, $1/(1 - c)$, is, in the text above, $1/(1 - \text{MPC}^D)$. The items in the square bracket are constant amounts of spending on home-produced goods; the multiplier would also apply to *changes* in C, I, X, or G: $\triangle C$, $\triangle I$, $\triangle X$, or $\triangle G$.

If we look at our multiplier formulas, we find that this is a general rule:

So long as some fraction of income at every stage is leaking into domestic saving, a new dollar of exports will raise income, but can never lift it by enough to call forth a full dollar of new imports. That is, if the propensity-to-consume, -save, and -import add up to 1, the existence of a positive MPS means that MPM must be less than 1.

Figure 14.2 shows the whole process diagrammatically. SS is the same propensity-to-save schedule as earlier: 1/3 of every additional dollar of income is saved. Thus it has the same slope as before, rising one dollar for every three dollars it moves to the right.

To it is *added* the propensity-to-import consumption goods schedule, so that the vertical distance between SS and $S + M$ shows the imports for every level of GNP. The total vertical distance from the horizontal axis up to $S + M$ shows the total consumption "leakage" for every GNP on that axis.

When the GNP is in equilibrium at 750 billion dollars, it turns out that saving is less than investment and imports more than exports. However, $S + M = I^D + E$. This shows that *it is not necessary*

for GNP equilibrium that $S = I^D$ or $E = M$. Only the sums need be equal.

See what happens when E increases by 100 billion dollars. $I^D + E$ moves up to $I^D + E'$, from 300 billion dollars to 400 billion dollars cutting the $S + M$ schedule at f. Along the horizontal axis, GNP moves from 750 billion dollars to 950 billion dollars. Notice that saving is now closer to investment. But the failure of exports to equal imports, or of investment to equal savings is unimportant. What really matters is that the extra saving-and-importing is equal to the extra exports; and that again $S + M = I^D + E$. The GNP is again in equilibrium. The multiplier is obviously at work.

$$\frac{\text{Change in}}{\text{income}} = \frac{1}{\text{MPS} + \text{MPM}} \times \text{change in exports}$$

$$= \frac{1}{1 - \text{MPC}^D} \times \text{change in exports}$$

In this case, the effect on GNP is $\dfrac{1}{1/3 + 1/6} = \dfrac{1}{1/2}$ = 2 × change in exports, or 200 billion dollars. This change can be read along the bottom axis between 750 and 950 billion dollars.

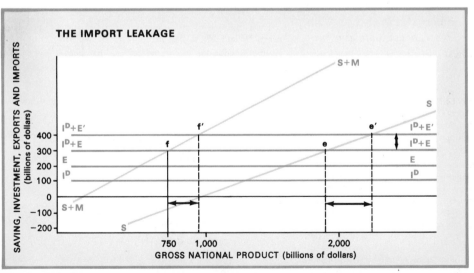

FIG. 14-2. With both savings and import leakages, the multiplier falls from 3 to 2. When an increase in exports raises $I^D + E$ to $I^D + E'$, GNP is also raised. But the extra import leakage reduces the multiplier from 3 to 2, as shown by the colored arrows. (Source: this is based on Fig. 14-1. All imports M are assumed to be consumption goods; i.e. $C^M = M$, and $I^M = G^M = E^M = 0$.)

THE OPEN-ECONOMY MULTIPLIER

The point of all this is that when the economy is "open" to foreign trade, a rise in income and employment may be hindered by a rise in imports. Extra spending, autonomous schedule shifts of C, I, or G, may be largely (but not completely) siphoned off through two leakages: savings and imports.

Note that the import leakage is *always* with us. It is an error to associate the "foreign-trade multiplier" and the "import leakage" solely with changes in exports, arising abroad. The process of responding *any* injection of private capital formation, increased personal consumption outlays, public projects, etc., will, like a responding of export proceeds, lead to a diversion into the buying of imported goods and services.[6]

This explains why fiscal policy in Canada must be weaker, dollar for dollar, than it would be if the economy were closed. It is weaker than in the United States, even though both countries have the same MPC; for the U.S. MPM is small.

Thus the simple multiplier of the last chapter, which applies only in an economy with no trade abroad, must give way to a more general formula:

$$
\begin{aligned}
\text{Change in} \\
\text{income} &= \frac{1}{\text{MPS} + \text{MPM}} \times \begin{array}{l} \text{change in } I,\, E, \\ \text{and/or } G \end{array} \\
&= \frac{1}{1 - \text{MPC}^D} \times \begin{array}{l} \text{change in } I,\, E, \\ \text{and/or } G \end{array}
\end{aligned}
$$

TRADE POLICY AND NATIONAL INCOME

We see now why economists try hard to calculate a country's MPM. In an open economy, a jump in exports can raise the NNP dramatically, and so increase employment. Indeed, the multiplied effects of exports and the dampening effect of imports tempt policy makers to manipulate them to close both inflationary and deflationary gaps.

In inflation, lowering the domestic price of foreign currency makes imports potentially cheaper. And bringing in more imports will reduce total domestic spending and thus cool the inflationary gap. The same policy, exchange-rate upward revaluation, will make some exports too costly for foreigners to buy, cut E, and again cool the inflationary fires. Short-run reduction of tariff barriers will have the same effect.

In a slump what can be done? First, imports are often cut, by raising tariffs, by imposing quotas, and through exchange-rate devaluation. Exports, too, can be promoted, though final action depends on foreign governments.

We shall see in Part Five that such policies, especially those used in recessions, are dangerous when rigidly followed. They are like cutting off our nose to spite our face in that they invite retaliation from abroad in the form of higher tariff walls against *our* exports. They also have wasteful long-run effects because they encourage each nation toward self-sufficiency instead of the more efficient international specialization and division of labor in production. But, looking at trade from the standpoint of domestic full employment alone, it must be admitted that exports do have a multiplier effect on GNP, and it must be agreed that imports are a serious leakage which dampen the effect of domestic attempts to achieve stability.[7] You can see this for yourself by showing on Fig. 14-2 the effect of an increase in tariffs. (HINT: At every income level, imports will now be lower. Thus the vertical distance between S and S + M must become narrower. What is the effect on GNP?)

To summarize, the simple multiplier $\frac{1}{\text{MPS}}$ applies only to a simple economy, having only C and I spending. With the addition of government and foreign sectors, "the" multiplier becomes more complicated, containing not only MPS but also MPC^D and the "propensity to invest." The effects of "injections" also increase in complexity, including not only I, but also *shifts* in C, I, G, and E.

---

[6] More advanced treatments of the general multiplier will take account of the fact that there is a different MPM for each of I, G, and E. If I is induced, and has import content, then the total schedule $(I^D + E^D + G^D)$ *may* increase with GNP. If so, and if the schedule is cut from below by the $(S + M)$ schedule, the intersection will indicate a stable GNP, as discussed in Chapter 12.

Note that another "leakage," taxation, has been omitted from the text above. Assiduous footnote readers may see a rough synthesis of all three leakages in Chapter 19, footnote 5.

[7] There are many policies that have the "right" kind of effect. For example, depreciating the Canadian dollar will help to raise exports (how?) and, by putting up the prices of foreign-made goods, cut down the propensity-to-import. Boosting the level of customs tariffs will also cut down imports. Such policies, used to raise income and employment, have been called by Cambridge economist Joan Robinson "beggar-my-neighbor" policies; for they tend, in reducing the import of goods from other countries, to export unemployment to those countries instead.

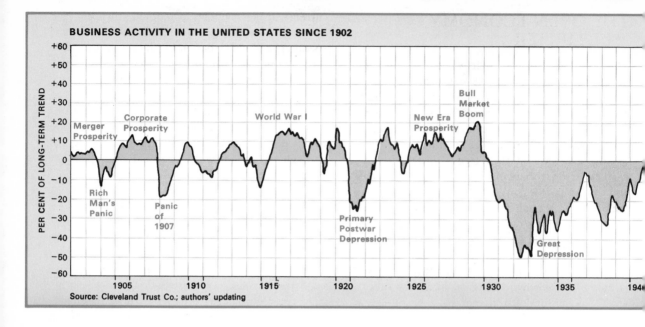

BUSINESS ACTIVITY IN THE UNITED STATES SINCE 1902

Source: Cleveland Trust Co.; authors' updating

B. FLUCTUATIONS IN NATIONAL INCOME AND THE ACCELERATION PRINCIPLE

We have examined the economic forces operating to determine the level of national income—the balance of saving and investment. We now turn to the problem of how the level of national income has fluctuated, and to an explanation of the period-by-period processes which propagate these fluctuations. Any serious science should try to test bold theoretical formulation against a careful description of the empirical facts of life.[8]

PROSPERITY AND DEPRESSION

Business conditions rarely stand still. Prosperity may be followed by a panic or a crash. National income, employment, and production fall. Prices and profits decline, and men are thrown out of work. Eventually the bottom is reached, and revival begins. The recovery may be slow or fast. It may be incomplete, or it

may be so strong as to lead to a new boom. The new prosperity may represent a long, sustained plateau of brisk demand, plentiful jobs, buoyant prices, and increased living standards. Or it may represent a quick, inflationary flaring up of prices and speculation, to be followed by another disastrous slump.

Such, in brief, was the so-called "business cycle" that used to characterize the industrialized nations of the world for the last century and a half at least, ever since an elaborate, interdependent *money economy* began to replace a relatively self-sufficient pre-commercial society. Is the business cycle a thing of the past, a museum piece? This we must study.

No two business cycles are quite the same. Yet they have much in common. They are not identical twins, but they are recognizable as belonging to the same family. No exact formula, such as might apply to the motions of the moon or of a simple pendulum, can be used to predict the timing of future (or past) business cycles. Rather, in their rough appearance and irregularities, business cycles more closely resemble the fluctuations of disease epidemics, the vagaries of the weather, or the variations in a child's temperature.

---

[8] The first (1969) Nobel laureates in economics, Ragnar Frisch of Norway and Jan Tinbergen of Holland, made important contributions to both the theory and the measurement of the elements of business fluctuations. The accelerator-multiplier interaction has been analyzed particularly by Nobel laureate Paul A. Samuelson. (A.D.S.)

FIG. 14-3. Are business cycles calming down?
For 25 years now North America has had no significant depressions. But it was not always so. (Source: Cleveland Trust Co.)

From these introductory remarks, it will be clear that business fluctuations are simply one further aspect of the economic problem of achieving and maintaing high levels of jobs, production, and progressive growth.

MEASURING AND FORECASTING THE BUSINESS CYCLE

Figure 14-3 shows how the American economy has been plagued by the uncertainties of the business cycle since 1900. The compilers of this remarkable, well-known, chart have carried it back to the 1860s, and the same sequence of peaks and troughs is to be seen, although with slightly greater regularity in the nineteenth century. Nothing can match the sustained and costly slump of the post-1929 Great Depression. Turning points in the Canadian economy are similar, and the same pattern is reflected in England, Germany, and other foreign nations, with surprisingly few variations.

But it is a strange fact that the North American countries, although they have grown faster since their establishment than most other countries, have always tended to have greater average amounts of unemployment and greater variation in unemployment than these other countries. Not only was this true in 1933, when our percentage of unemployment rivaled even that of Germany, but it appears to have been the case for almost as far back as we have any records or indications. Only in the last 30 years have we avoided deep unemployment, but still our rates exceed those suffered in other western economies.

Figure 14-4 on the following page, shows a number of diverse post-World War II economic "time series," presented for comparison. Note the all-pervasive common pulse of the business cycle: the recessions of 1953-1954, 1957-1958, 1960-61, and 1970. These fluctuations show up in production, unemployment, incomes, and even in such particular series as stock-market prices and building. Moreover, if data had been included on such noneconomic matters as marriages, births, and malnutrition, we should also have been able to see in them the heavy hand of the business cycle. Even political elections follow the business cycle: in slumps, the ins go out.

Here we stick to the facts and statistics. Later, in the Appendix to this chapter, we will go into the history of cycles in more detail and attempt to devise hypotheses and explanatory theories to account for the complex facts.

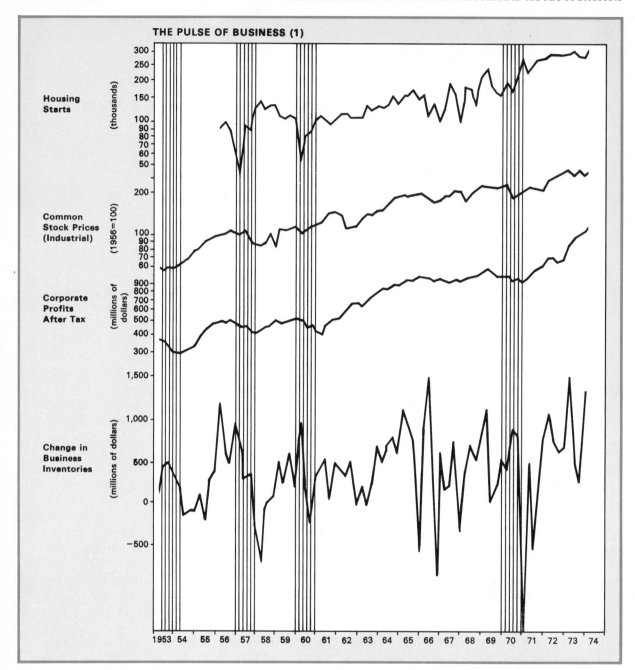

FIG. 14-4. Most economic activities show a common cyclical pulse.

The stretches composed of vertical black lines show recession contraction periods; the unshaded stretches show expansions. Whether 1970 should be counted as a contraction in Canada is controversial. The upper curves are series that tend to turn before the others; but this tendency is variable. (Sources: *Bank of Canada Review*, Statistics Canada 11-003 and 61-003, *Canadian Business Trends,* by the Conference Board in Canada, *Monthly Business Analysis*, by W. A. Beckett Associates Ltd.)

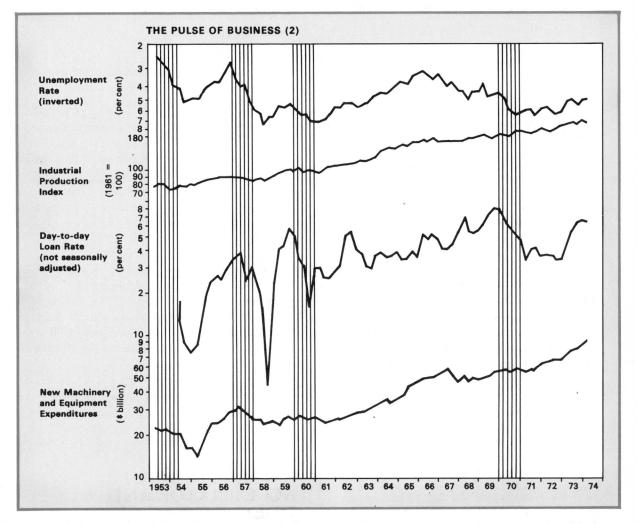

THE PULSE OF BUSINESS (2)

THE ACCELERATOR PRINCIPLE

A theoretical process, showing how investment demand may be induced by *growth* of sales and income, has been given a rather high-sounding name—the "acceleration principle." Almost all writers bring it in as one strand in their final business-cycle theories. Let us examine how this internal cyclical mechanism works itself out and interacts with our earlier multiplier analysis and other factors.

According to this law, society's needed stock of capital, whether inventory or equipment, depends primarily upon the level of income or production. Additions to the stock of capital, or what we customarily call *net* investment, will take place only when

income is growing. As a result, a prosperity period may come to an end, not simply because consumption sales have gone down, but merely because sales have *leveled off* at a high level (or have continued to grow, but at a lower rate than previously).

A simplified arithmetical example will make this clear. Imagine a typical textile-manufacturing firm whose stock of capital equipment is always kept equal to about 2 times the value of its yearly sales of cloth.[9] Thus, when its sales have remained at $30 million per year for some time, its balance sheet will show $60 million of capital equipment, consisting of

---

[9] To keep the discussion simple, we use the exaggerated ratio 2/1 and ignore changes in interest rates or degree of utilization of capacity. The reader can include inventory change and plant change along with equipment change in the analysis.

perhaps 20 machines of different ages, with 1 wearing out each year and being replaced. Because replacement just balances depreciation, there is no *net* investment or saving being done by the corporation. *Gross* investment takes place at the rate of $3 million per year, representing the yearly replacement of 1 machine. (The other $27 million of sales may be assumed to be wages and dividends.) The first phase of Table 14-1 shows this.

Now let us suppose that, in the fourth year, sales rise 50 per cent—from $30 to $45 million. Then the number of machines must also rise 50 per cent, or from 20 to 30 machines. In that fourth year, instead of 1 machine, 11 machines must be bought—10 new ones in addition to the replacement of the worn-out one.

Sales rose 50 per cent. How much has machine production gone up? From 1 machine to 11; or by 1,000 per cent! This *accelerated* effect of a change in consumption or other final items on investment levels gives the acceleration principle its name.

If sales continue to rise in both the fifth and the sixth year by the same $15 million, then we shall continue to have 11 machines (10 + 1) ordered every year.

So far, the acceleration principle has given us no trouble. On the contrary, it has given us a tremendous increase in investment spending as a result of a moderate increase in consumption sales. But now we are riding a tiger.

According to the acceleration principle, consumption has to continue to keep increasing in order for investment to stand still!

If consumption should stop growing at so rapid a rate—if it should level off in the seventh year even at the high level of $75 million per year—then net investment will fall away to zero, and gross investment will, for many years, fall back to only 1 machine (see Table 14-1). In other words, a drop of zero per cent in sales has resulted in a 90 per cent drop in gross investment and a 100 per cent drop in net investment! (See the third phase of Table 14-1.)

The acceleration principle can work in both directions. Should sales now drop below $75 million, gross investment would drop away to nothing for a long time; in fact, the firm might want to disinvest by selling off some of its used machinery. (Fill in the fourth phase with the needed zeros—to signify that nothing is now being replaced.)

It is clear that a recession can set in just because sales have stopped growing so rapidly, even if not dropping absolutely but only leveling off at a high rate.

INTERACTIONS OF ACCELERATOR AND MULTIPLIER

Needless to say, the curtailment of production in the machine-producing industries will curtail income and spending on food and clothing and will lead to still further "multiplier" changes in spending. This itself might ultimately cause textile sales to stop growing altogether, or even to decline. This in turn will cause a further accelerated drop in net investment.

Thus, we may be in a vicious circle where the acceleration principle and the multiplier interact to produce a cumulative deflationary (or inflationary) spiral.

Our example used machines. Does that mean the acceleration principle is not involved in the inven-

THE ACCELERATION PRINCIPLE (in millions of dollars)				
Time	Yearly Sales	Stock of Capital	Net Investment NI	Gross Investment (NI + depreciation)
First phase				
First year	$30	$ 60	$ 0	1 machine at $3 = $3
Second year	30	60	0	1 machine at $3 = $3
Third year	30	60	0	1 machine at $3 = $3
Second phase				
Fourth year	$45	$ 90	$30	(10 + 1) machines at $3 = $33
Fifth year	60	120	30	(10 + 1) machines at $3 = $33
Sixth year	75	150	30	(10 + 1) machines at $3 = $33
Third phase				
Seventh year	$75	$150	$ 0	1 machine at $3 = $3
Fourth phase (to be filled in by reader)				
Eighth year	$73½	$147	−$ 3	___ machines at $3 = $___

TABLE 14-1. Acceleration principle links GNP growth rate to level of investment.
Investment fluctuates more than sales: to keep the level of investment from falling, sales must not even falter in their rate of growth.

tory "recessions" (such as 1920-1921, 1937-1938, 1948-1949, 1953-1954, 1957-1958, 1960-1961)? Not at all. The same principle—that stocks of capital goods tend to be held in some proportion to sales per unit time—is valuable to help explain short inventory cycles.

This analysis can also explain how a downturn can result from the previous expansion itself. Suppose, in a situation of unemployment, we get income growing again. The rising income induces, via the accelerator, new investment. The new investment induces, via the multiplier, further rises in income. Hence, the rate of growth of output may be "self-warranting."

But how can a system grow forever at 6 or 7 per cent if its labor force grows only at 1 or 2 percent and if workers' productivity grows at 2 or 3 per cent? It can't. The self-warranting expansion, even if we are lucky enough to get and keep it, must ultimately bump into the full-employment ceiling. Like a tennis ball (and unlike a wad of gum), it is likely to bounce back from the full-employment ceiling into a recession. Why? Because the minute the system stops its fast growth, the accelerator dictates the end of the high investment supporting the boom. Like an airplane that falls once it loses its motion, the economic system plummets downward.

Similar accelerator-multiplier analysis may explain the ultimate end of a recession and an upturn. When output plummets downward rapidly, the acceleration principle calls for negative investment (or disinvestment) greater than the rate at which machines can wear out. This wear-out rate puts a floor on how far it (the SS-II intersection) can push the economy below its break-even point.

Bumping along such a basement floor means that eventually firms will work down their capital stock to the level called for by that low level of income; and now the acceleration principle calls for a termination of disinvestment! Our image must shift from gum, ball, and airplane to that of an Olympic diver: once he stops moving downward under the water, he is buoyed up again. A new cycle can begin and repeat itself.

It is easy to see that, in the acceleration principle, we have a powerful factor making for economic instability. If business sales go up and down, the acceleration principle can intensify their fluctuation. It induces net investment on the upswing, but causes about the same amount of net *disinvestment* on the downswing.

In the long run, if the system is growing because of population increase and technical progress, then the acceleration principle works primarily as a stimulating factor: growing national income causes extensive growth of capital, which in turn means brisk investment demand and relatively low unemployment![10]

We have seen that an economic system may well fluctuate and yet grow over the long run. The interested reader may wish to see the Appendix to this chapter, which discusses business cycle theory and the methods by which economists forecast the future. The following chapters will go on to discuss money and banking to show how the changes in credit, interest rates, and the supply of money may cause the spending schedules and their intersections to shift.

SUMMARY

A. FOREIGN TRADE AND INCOME DETERMINATION

1 An increase in exports—with imports unchanged—has the same impact on GNP as an increase in investment (leaving government and taxes out of the picture entirely). The *II* schedule in the saving-investment diagram shifts up to become *I* + *E*, and its intersection with the saving curve shows the new GNP.

---

[10] The Appendix of Chapter 36 discusses warranted growth further, in connection with so-called "Harrod-Domar models of growth."

2 Imports are a leakage, much like savings. The greater the GNP, the greater are imports. The tendency of extra income to be spent on extra imports is called MPM. This may be large, but never large enough to convert all extra domestic spending into extra imports, so long as the marginal propensity to save is above zero.

3 In the final equilibrium, total investment and exports must be equal to total savings and imports. But exports need not be precisely equal to imports. Any difference is made up by foreign lending or borrowing, the NNP remaining in equilibrium.

4 The multiplier that recognizes all leakages in the continued respending of consumption dollars from initial I, G, or E must include import leakage, MPM. In an open economy with imports and exports, this is "the" multiplier.

$$\text{Change in GNP} = \frac{1}{\text{MPS} + \text{MPM}} \times \text{change in } I, E, \text{ and/or } G$$

$$= \frac{1}{1 - \text{MPC}^D} \times \text{change in } I, E, \text{ and/or } G$$

5 In the absence of foreign retaliation, policies that assist exports and inhibit imports tend to raise GNP and employment—and price levels. Correspondingly, policies that raise imports and reduce exports are deflationary, and may be helpful or harmful to stability. Such manipulation of foreign trade may have harmful long-run effects, however, which are discussed in Part Five.

B. FLUCTUATIONS IN NATIONAL INCOME AND THE ACCELERATION PRINCIPLE

6 Fluctuations in national income are often called business cycles because they tend to take on a definite cyclical pattern. The West has known business cycles since before 1900. The Appendix to this chapter contains further discussion.

7 One often-heard explanation of the business cycle is that changes in investment are linked to changes in final sales. The acceleration principle states that net investment depends upon *changes* in the level of income or consumption. The multiplier and the accelerator interact, bringing in dynamic rates of change, influencing levels of income and investment, and causing economic instability.

The art of economics consists in recognizing both the core of truth in the simple theory of income determination and also its needed qualifications. In later chapters we shall see how interest rates, exchange rates, and other factors may cause shifts in the I, G, and E schedules that determine levels of national income.

We leave to the final chapter of Part Two the analysis of government monetary and fiscal policy, and to Part Five the exploration of other aspects of international policy. In the next few chapters we turn to an analysis of money, banking policy, and interest policy.

CONCEPTS FOR REVIEW

multiplier effect of
   an increase in exports
leakages
the open-economy multiplier
MPM and MPC^D
$I^D + E$ and $S + M$ schedules

regularity of business cycles
accelerator response to
   consumption change
ceiling
accelerator-multiplier
interaction

QUESTIONS FOR DISCUSSION

1 Redraw Fig. 14-2 so that at an equilibrium point like e' exports are greater than imports. Now Canadians in effect lend to foreigners. Would you recommend a policy of increased foreign aid (giving, not lending) to raise Canadian employment? Can you construct a diagram in which the rise of exports from E to E' results in imports rising to exceed the new exports? Why not?

2 Write an explanation of the acceleration principle. Combine it with the multiplier.

3 Consider the impact of a "buy-Ontario" policy. Will Ontario's campaign, if successful, have a larger multiplier effect than a "buy-Canadian" policy?

4 Consider the effect of a tariff on Fig. 14-1. If the foreign countries retaliate and raise their tariffs, how will this be shown on the Figure?

5 *Extra-credit problem* on accelerator-multiplier cyclical oscillations: Let consumption today, C_t, depend by the multiplier principle on yesterday's disposable income, Y_{t-1}, according to the formula $C_t = 100 + \frac{1}{2}Y_{t-1}$, Let investment today, I_t, be the growth in the stock of machines since last period: $I_t = K_t - K_{t-1}$. Suppose, by the acceleration principle, K_t is always $\beta = 2$ times consumption sales, $K_t = \beta C_t$. Then, from the identity $Y_t = C_t + I_t$, after some substitutions we get $Y_t = C_t + 2(C_t - C_{t-1}) = 3C_t - 2C_{t-1} = 3(100 + \frac{1}{2}Y_{t-1}) - 2(100 + \frac{1}{2}Y_{t-2}) = 100 + \frac{3}{2}Y_{t-1} - Y_{t-2}$. (*a*) Show that if we start the system at equilibrium with $Y_0 = Y_1 = 200$, $(Y_2, Y_3, \ldots)$ will stay at 200. But show that, if the system is given an upward push from equilibrium so that $Y_1 = Y_0 + 64 = 264$, we get the perpetually oscillating "business cycle" (200, 264, 296, 280, 224, 156, 110, 109, $153\frac{1}{2}$, $221\frac{1}{4}$, $278\frac{3}{8}$, ...). (*b*) If either of the numbers, $\frac{1}{2}$, or 2, is lowered a little, show that the oscillations of the new "second-order difference equation with constant coefficients" will dampen down and the system will eventually return to the 200 equilibrium. If either is raised a little, say, $\frac{1}{2}$ to $\frac{3}{4}$ and 2 to 3, the system's oscillations become bigger and bigger.

Appendix: Business Cycles and Forecasting

Economists, businessmen, investors, and the housewife glancing at the morning paper, all are concerned with business cycles and the future trend of the economy. Economists therefore have attempted to formulate a theoretical foundation against which empirical facts or statistics may be tested. We have, of course, not one but many theories of the business cycle. Similarly, we have many series of statistics. When these statistics are inserted into a theoretical framework, they will give us information about the present state of the economy and its possible future trends.

STATISTICAL CORRECTION FOR SEASONAL VARIATION AND FOR TRENDS

First, of course, we must remove from our statistical data irrelevant, disturbing factors, such as *seasonal* patterns, and also certain so-called long-term "trends." If Eaton's sales went up from November to December, 1960, we cannot conclude from this that the 1960 recession shown in Fig. 14-4 did not exist. Retail trade goes up every Christmas, just as Niagara Falls hotels tend to be crowded in summer. The statistician attempts to remove the "seasonal influence" by carefully studying previous yearly patterns. If he finds that every December tends to involve about 150 per cent as much business as the average month of the year, and every January only 90 per cent, then he will take the actual raw monthly data and divide all the December figures by 1.5, all the January figures by 0.9, and so forth for each month. After this has been done, the statistician will end up with a time series of monthly department-store sales which have been "seasonally adjusted." These will show what we expected all along, that business was really still declining throughout all the last months of 1960, because December's improvement was less than the seasonal norm.

Another kind of problem arises when we examine the fluctuations through time of such a rapidly growing time series as electric-power production or, in Fig. 14-4 industrial production. Such a growing series did not decline in any recession. But the recession is evident there, nevertheless. It rears its ugly head in the form of a *slowing down of the rate of growth* of the time series as compared with its normal or long-term "secular trend."

If we draw a smooth trend line or curve, either by eye or by some statistical formula, through the strongly growing components of NNP, we discover the business cycle in the twistings of the data above and below the trend line. If we measure the vertical deviations from the trend line and plot them on a separate diagram, we get a reasonably clear picture of the business cycle.[1] Let us take a look at it.

THE FOUR PHASES OF THE TRADITIONAL CYCLE

Early writers on the business cycle, possessing little quantitative information, tended to attach disproportionate attention to *panics* and *crises* such as the collapse of the South Sea Bubble in 1720, the severe credit panic of 1837 (which aggravated the political causes of the Canadian rebellions of that year), the world-wide slump of 1873 (which stopped the new Confederation, literally, in its railroad tracks), the brief downturn of 1893, the postwar crash of 1921, and, of course, the cataclysmic "Black Tuesday" on Wall Street, on October 29, 1929. Later writers soon began to speak of two phases of business: prosperity and depression, or boom and slump, with peaks and troughs marking the turning points in between.

Today, it is recognized that not every period of improving business need take us all the way to full employment. For example, throughout the decade of the 1930s there was a measure of recovery from the 1932-1933 trough levels, but we could by no means speak of the period as one of true prosperity. And from 1957 to 1965, unemployment never dropped even to a 4 per cent level.

The cycle used to be broken up by many economists into four phases, the two most important ones being called the periods of "expansion" and "contraction," or "recession." The expansion phase comes to an end and goes into the recession phase at the upper turning point, or so-called "peak." Similarly, the recession phase gives way to that of expansion at the lower turning point, or so-called "trough," or "revival." Thus, the four phases are supposed to keep repeating themselves in the over-simplified picture as shown in Fig. 14-5. Note that the emphasis here is not so much on *high* or *low* business activity as on the dynamic aspects of *rising* or *falling* business activity. (But do not forget the unemployment gap and the importance of growth trends.)

Each phase of the cycle passes into the next. Each is characterized by different economic conditions[2] and requires special explanatory principles. But let us continue with more facts before attempting analysis and theorizing.

LENGTH OF CYCLE How long have the traditional economic cycles been? This depends upon how many minor cycles you wish to count. Most observers have no trouble in agreeing on the major cycles, which were about 8 to 10 years in length. Everyone agrees that the late 1920s represents a period of prosperity and the early 1930s one of depression, and similarly with other past major business

---

[1] The reader may be referred to any standard textbook on statistics for these technical procedures. However, cautious judgment must be exercised in using the mechanical tools of statistics. A

beginner, carelessly "eliminating a trend," may throw out the baby along with the bath water if not careful, or at least distort the true appearance of the infant.

[2] For example, during expansion we find that unemployment, production, prices, money, wages, interest rates, and profits are usually rising, with the reverse true in recession.

FIG. 14-5. The business cycle, like the year, has its seasons.
Cyclical expansions follow contractions, with turning points in between. Following the leadership of the National Bureau of Economic Research of the United States, statisticians have dated these phases for the economic story of many countries. Not every peak reaches "prosperity" in the sense of low unemployment. Nor does every threatened recession materialize.

cycles. Not all economists, however, attach importance to the shorter minor cycles that are to be seen in economic charts. In 1924 and 1927, there were small dips in business activity. Shall we call the 1920s, therefore, three different (minor) cycles or one major prosperity period? In 1948-1949, 1953-1954, 1957-1958, and again in 1960-1961, we suffered mild recessions. Should these count as cycles? And if so, why not the 'pauses' in 1951, 1962, and probably 1969-1970?

In an elementary introduction of this type, it is perhaps best to stick primarily to major business cycles. For our purposes we may accept the summary that Harvard's Alvin Hansen gave to pre-World War II economic history:[3]

The American experience indicates that the major business cycle has had an average duration of a little over eight years. Thus, from 1795 to 1937 there were seventeen cycles of an average duration of 8.35 years. . . .

Since one to two minor peaks regularly occur between the major peaks, it is clear that the minor cycle is something less than half the duration of the major cycle. In the one hundred and thirty-year period 1807 to 1937 there were thirty-seven minor cycles with an average duration of 3.51 years.

. . . It appears that the building cycle averages somewhere between seventeen and eighteen years in length, or almost twice the length of the major business cycle. . . .

. . . American experience indicates that with a high degree of regularity every other major business boom coincides roughly with a boom in building construction, while the succeeding major cycle recovery is forced to buck up against a building slump . . . the depressions which have fallen in the interval of the construction downswing are typically deep and long. And the succeeding recovery is held back and retarded by the unfavorable depressional influence from the slump in the building industry.

The long swings in building construction and other series, which average anywhere between 15 and 25 years in length, are often called Kuznets cycles, being named for

[3]Alvin H. Hansen, *Fiscal Policy and Business Cycles* (Norton, New York, 1941), pp. 18-24.

the scholar who first noticed them in 1930.[4] Work by A. F. Burns, S. Kuznets, and other U.S. National Bureau scholars suggests that these pervasive swings have been associated with fluctuations in immigration and natural rates of population growth, in railroad building and capital imports, and in the rate of growth of the money supply. Federal economist D. J. Daly has noted them for Canada too. They are of interest because they seem to involve three factors: variations in the supply trends of labor and other resources available to the economy; variations in productivity trends relating to the efficiency with which those supplies can be used; and, what is still provisional but important, variations in the average intensity with which resources get used—in other words, variations in rates of unemployment.

Was the notable sluggishness of the Canadian economy in the last part of the 1950s and early 1960s a reflection of our passing into a less favorable phase of the Kuznets cycle? Or, as some then thought, was it a forerunner of some more ominous trend? Or merely the natural relaxation after a post-war sprint?

In any case, remember that fiscal and monetary policies can compensate for adverse phases of the Kuznets cycle —which man does not regard as one of those disasters, like earthquakes and volcanoes, which science can do nothing about.

[4]Kuznets cycles should not be confused with *alleged very long waves*, whose complete cycle length is about half a century. Thus, from the end of the Napoleonic Wars in 1815 to the middle of the nineteenth century, prices tended to fall and times tended to be unusually hard, on the average. After the Californian and Australian gold discoveries following 1850, and as a partial result of the Crimean War and the American Civil War, prices tended to rise. A new long cycle of falling prices followed the 1873 depression and lasted until the 1890s, when there was a great increase in gold production following the African and Klondike gold discoveries. Whether these long waves are simply historical accidents due to chance gold discoveries, inventions, and political wars, it is still too soon to say. The interested reader may be referred to J. A. Schumpeter, *Business Cycles* (McGraw-Hill, New York, 1939), Chaps. 6 and 7, where long cycles are called "Kondratieffs."

A FIRST CLUE TO BUSINESS FLUCTUATIONS: CAPITAL FORMATION

Hansen's emphasis on *construction* gives us our first clue to the causation of the business cycle. Certain economic variables always show greater fluctuations than others in the business cycle. Thus, if we plot pig-iron production and cigarette consumption side by side, we hardly notice the business cycle in the latter. But in the pig-iron series there is little else to see but the business cycle. Why? Because cigarettes are nondurable consumers' goods, and in both good and bad times people are going to smoke the same amount. Pig iron, on the other hand, is one of the principal ingredients of capital and durable goods of all kinds: of plant equipment and durable machinery, of industrial and residential construction, and of automobiles, washing machines, and other durable consumers' goods.

Check this by reexamining Fig. 14-4. Note how volatile is the housing starts series. Note that production and profit fluctuations coincide with investment fluctuations.

By their nature, durable goods are subject to violently erratic patterns of demand. In bad times their new purchase can be indefinitely postponed; in a good year, everyone may suddenly decide to stock up on a 10-year supply of the services of durable goods.

Our first clue to the nature of the business cycle lies, then, in the fact that it is the durable- or capital-goods sector of the economy which shows by the far the greatest cyclical fluctuations.

Their swings are wide compared with those of the economic time series which represent primarily consumption of services, of nondurables, and the *services* of durable goods. Except for a few short, choppy surface disturbances in such series, the latter tend to follow the general flow of income in a rather passive fashion. Ordinarily, consumption movements seem the effect rather than cause of the business cycle; however, there is good reason to believe that the movements of *durable* goods represent key causes in a more fundamental sense.

HOW SAVING AND INVESTMENT SCHEDULES APPLY

It is comforting to find that statistical analysis supports the emphasis in previous chapters on the crucial importance of the capital investment process. The income-determination theories of the last chapter do indeed help in understanding economic history. Here are but a few reminders:

1. *Wars* have always been great disrupters of an economy. How do they transmit their economic effects? Plainly, they lead to great swings in the G component of the C + I + G schedule, and this causes even greater swings in the over-all level of production and incomes. Inflationary gaps appear at full-employment NNP, leading to price inflation.

2. In minor cycles of the postwar type, it is common for considerable fluctuations in the rate of *inventory investment* to occur. In the years of expansion, inventory accumulation is at a positive rate as merchants seek to rebuild their stocks and accommodate them to the growing level of sales. When merchants veer from a positive rate of inventory accumulation to a negative rate, the I component in the C + I + G schedule goes down: then the production line is cut back, men are put on fewer average hours per week or are laid off, wages and profits fall, and all this gets registered in a multiplied drop in NNP or in its failure to grow along a normal trend.

3. When there are longer waves in construction and equipment, the I component in the C + I + G schedule causes the whole schedule and its equilibrium to go through slow swings of considerable amplitude.

4. While it is an oversimplification to say that the consumption schedule never shifts over time, U.S. economists S. Kuznets and R. Goldsmith have made National Bureau of Economic Research studies indicating the overall stability of saving behavior relative to income over a long period. Their general finding is that, aside from short-term cycles, the percentage saved out of income has been remarkably the same over the last century.

The one situation in which we cannot regard consumption purely as a passive and predictable force comes in those times when consumer demand for autos and other durable goods fluctuates. (E.g., the fact that Canadians and Americans liked the new 1962 and 1963 cars helped much to accelerate the recovery from the 1960-1961 recession.) Such *shifts* in the CC schedule also contribute to movements in the C + I + G intersections, which, like any other shifts in autonomous factors, involve double-duty multiplier reactions.

A FEW THEORIES OF THE BUSINESS CYCLE

When it comes to explanations of why the income schedules shift, an industrious student could easily compile a list of separate theories of the business cycle that would run into the dozens.[5] Each theory seems to be quite different; but when we examine them closely and throw out

---

[5] We may mention just a few of the better-known theories: (1) the *monetary* theory—attributes the cycle to the expansion and contraction of bank credit, (Hawtrey, Friedman, et al.); (2) the *innovation* theory—attributes the cycle to the clustering of important inventions such as the railroad (Schumpeter, Hansen, et al.); (3) the *psychological* theory—treats the cycle as a case of people's infecting each other with pessimistic and optimistic expectations (Pigou, Bagehot, et al.); (4) the *underconsumption* theory—claims too much income goes to wealthy or thrifty people compared with what can be invested (Hobson, Sweezy, Foster and Catchings, et al.); (5) the *overinvestment* theory—claims too much rather than too little investment causes recessions (Hayek, Mises, et al.); (6) the *sunspot-weather-crop theories* (Jevons, H. L. Moore). The interested reader should consult G. Haberler, *Prosperity and Depression* (Harvard University Press, Cambridge, Mass., 1958, 4th ed.), or other business-cycle texts for further information.

those which obviously contradict the facts or the rules of logic, or which just appear to be conveying an explanation when really they are not saying anything at all—when we do all this, we are left with relatively few different explanations. Most of them differ from each other only in emphasis.

One man believes the cycle to be primarily the result of fluctuations in total net investment, while another prefers to attribute the cycle to fluctuations in the rate of technological inventions and innovations, which act on business *through* net investment. A third man says that the root of the cycle is to be found in the fact that the creation of deposit money by our banking system causes investment spending to expand and contract so as to create boom and bust.

These sound like three different theories, and in most advanced textbooks they might be given the names of three different writers, but from our standpoint they are but three different aspects of the same saving-investment process. As we shall see, this does not mean there is perfect agreement among all theories of the cycle or that there are not some important differences in emphasis among different writers.

EXTERNAL AND INTERNAL FACTORS

To classify the different theories, we may first divide them into the two categories of primarily *external* and primarily *internal* theories.

The external theories find the root of the business cycle in the fluctuations of something outside the economic system—in sunspot cycles, in wars, revolutions, and political events, in gold discoveries, in rates of growth of population and migrations, in discoveries of new lands and resources, and finally in scientific and technological discoveries and innovations.

The internal theories look for mechanisms within the economic system itself which will give rise to self-generating business cycles, so that every expansion will breed recession and contraction, and every contraction will in turn breed revival and expansion, in a quasi-regular, repeating, never-ending chain.

If you believe in the sunspot theory of the business cycle—and no respectable economists today do—then the distinction between external and internal is rather easy to draw; although even here, when you come to explain how and why disturbances on the surface of the sun give rise to the business cycle, you begin to get involved in the internal nature of the economic system. But at least no one can seriously argue that the direction of causation is in doubt, or that the economic system causes the sunspots to fluctuate, instead of vice versa. However, when it comes to such other external factors as wars and politics, or even births and gold discoveries, there is always some doubt as to whether the economic system does not at least react on the so-called "external" factors, thereby making the distinction between external and internal not such a hard and fast one. Still, no one will deny that any such "feedback" effects take us outside the traditional boundaries of economics, and this is our justification for distinguishing between external and internal theories.

THE BUSINESS CYCLE IN EACH ECONOMY

Another branch of business-cycle research is concerned with the transmission of fluctuations from one economy to another. The data indicate that each of the main recent contraction periods and expansion periods (shown in Fig. 14-4) is duplicated, almost to the day, in Canada and the United States. With some explainable lags, similarly parallel curves are found in Europe and elsewhere in the Western economy. Yet this was not always so: D. J. Daly has pointed out that while the U.S. GNP began to increase its rate of growth in 1911, the Canadian rate fell steadily from 1909 to 1919. But such divergences, which can be accounted for in part by Canada's previous immigration boom and her involvement in the war after 1914, are fairly rare. Most national statistical series are so coincident with one another that it is worth the time of researchers to try to explain the divergences that do occur.

This parallelism can be regarded in two ways, which overlap each other considerably. One group of economists says:

The Western group of nations is really all one economy. This entire system is experiencing the same external shocks (sunspots, innovations, wars, and changes in population growth) and is carrying out a single internal process of saving and investing. Thus there is no more reason to expect cycles to differ between countries than there is to expect England and Scotland to have different cyclical data.

The second group of economists says the first group claims too much:

You do not *know* that one Western economy actually exists. We propose to study the "transmission" of cycles from country to country, and then we shall understand better whether the United States and France are as strongly linked as England and Scotland.

Their research has used both theory and statistics.

The theorists have been studying how a drop in U.S. GNP will be accompanied (through the foreign-trade multiplier mechanism) by a drop in imports. This is the same as a drop in other countries' exports, and *their* multiplier mechanisms will result in a drop in their GNPs. But which will come first? In the example, the *cause* of the other countries' drop was the U.S. contraction. But all three contractions (the U.S. GNP, trade, and the other GNPs) may be simultaneous, or in any order. Thus, merely looking at the crude data will neither prove nor disprove the hypothesis that cycles start in the United States and are diffused to supplying countries.

The statisticians have given most attention to trying to find which series contract first in each country. One of their most interesting studies has been the relation between the Canadian and the U.S. economies. Gideon

Rosenbluth, for example, has suggested that export trade cannot explain the marked correspondence between the two countries: instead we must look to the vast network of foreign ownership, capital movements, cultural ties, inventions, and advertising to explain the coincidence. To a certain extent, therefore, his work (and that of other Canadian economists) tends to support the England-and-Scotland approach.

Much work remains to be done on the international transmission of cycles. But it is clear that the following discussion is applicable: for *either* business cycles originate in one country (with the mechanisms described below) and are communicated to other smaller countries; *or* the West is one big economy, in which case our discussion will apply to the entire area. In Chapter 34 we will return to some other aspects of the links between national economies. But here we consider the West as one big unspecified economic unit.[6]

PURELY INTERNAL THEORIES

As against the crude external sunspot theory, we may describe some simple examples of possible, crude internal theories.

"ECHO" WAVES OF REPLACEMENT If machinery and other durable goods all had the same length of life (say, 8 or 10 years), then we might try to explain a business cycle of the same length by this fact. If a boom got started—never mind how—then there would be a bunching of new capital goods all of the same age. A few years later, before these goods had worn out, there would be little need for replacement. This would cause a depression. But after 8 or 10 years all the capital equipment would suddenly wear out and would all have to be replaced, giving rise to an inflationary boom. This in turn would give rise to another complete cycle, with new echoing cycles of depression and boom every decade. Thus, self-generating "replacement waves" provide a purely internal business-cycle theory.

Actually, not all equipment has the same length of life; and identical automobiles produced on the same day will certainly not all be replaced at the same time. Consequently, any bunching of equipment expenditures will tend over time to spread itself out, at most giving rise to weaker and weaker replacement peaks. Twenty-five years after World War I one might have noted a deficit of births because of that conflict; another generation later, the dip would be hardly noticeable; and today it is just as if there had never been that particular violent disturbance of population. Replacement waves, therefore, are like the vibrations of a plucked violin string; they tend to dampen down and die away, unless there is a new disturbance.

PSYCHOLOGICAL SELF-GENERATING CYCLES The laws of physics guarantee that friction will lessen any purely autonomous physical fluctuations. In social science, there is no law like the conservation of energy to prevent the creation of purchasing power. Therefore a much better example of a self-generating cycle than replacement waves would be the case where people become alternately optimistic and pessimistic, each stage leading as inevitably to the next as the manic stage of some people leads to the depressive stage. We cannot rule out such an internal theory. Nor can we be satisfied with it as it stands, for it says and explains little.

COMBINING EXTERNAL AND INTERNAL ELEMENTS INTO A SYNTHESIS

Everyone has observed how a window or a tuning fork may be activated into pronounced vibration when a certain note is sounded. Is this vibration externally or internally caused? The answer is, Both. The sounded note is certainly an external cause; but the window or tuning fork responds according to its own internal nature, coming into strong resonance, not with *any* sounded note, but only with one of a certain *definite* pitch. It takes the right kind of trumpets to bring down the walls of Jericho.

Similarly, we may look upon business cycles as not unlike a toy rocking horse that is subjected to occasional outside pushes. The pushes need not be regular; great technical innovations never are. But just as the wooden horse rocks with a frequency and amplitude that depend partly upon its internal nature (its size and weight), so too will the economic system respond to fluctuations in external factors according to its *internal* nature. Both external and internal factors are important, then, in explaining the business cycle.

SYNTHESIS Most economists today believe in a synthesis or combination of external and internal theories. In explaining the major cycles, they place crucial emphasis on fluctuations in *investment* or *capital* goods. Primary causes of these capricious and volatile investment fluctuations are to be found in such external factors as (1) technological innovation and (2) dynamic growth of population and of territory. With these external factors, we must combine the internal factors that cause any initial change in investment to be *amplified* in a cumulative, multiplied fashion—as people who are given work in the capital-goods industries respend part of their new income on consumption goods and as an air of optimism begins to pervade the business community, causing firms to go to the banks and the securities market for new credit accommodation.[7]

---

[6]When we examine "long" cycles, such as the building cycle of 17 to 25 years, we note the research findings of Brinley Thomas and Simon Kuznets: that European and North American cycles have sometimes been directly out of phase with each other. When business and investment opportunities were up in North America, those in Europe were down, and migrants and capital tended to flow westward.

[7]With two dice you can manufacture something that looks a little like a business cycle. Record the results of successive tosses—as in the number sequence: 7, 4, 10, 3, 7, 11, 7, 2, . . . Then take 5-period moving averages—such as the successive numbers $(7 + 4 + 10 + 3 + 7)/5 \equiv 6\ 1/5$, $(4 + 10 + 3 + 7 + 11)/5 = 7, \ldots$ etc. A plot of these will look not too different from GNP or price fluctuations! Explanation: the random numbers are like exogenous investment shocks; the moving average is like the economic system's (or the wooden horse's) internal smoothing reactions of $C + I + G$ type.

Also, it is necessary to point out that the general business situation definitely reacts in turn on investment. If high consumption sales make businessmen optimistic, they are more likely to embark upon venturesome investment programs. Inventions or scientific discoveries may occur independently of the business cycle, but their appreciable economic introduction will most certainly depend on business conditions. When GNP moved up in the 1960s year after year it was reasonable to expect that a considerable volume of capital formation (new machines, added inventories, construction) would be induced. Therefore, especially in the short run, investment movements are in part an *effect* as well as a cause of income movements.

In the longer run, no matter how high a plateau of income is maintained, the stock of capital goods will become adjusted at a higher level and new net investment will drop off to zero unless there is (1) a growth of income, (2) a continuing improvement of technology, or (3) a never-ending reduction in interest rates.

The first of these processes, showing how investment demand may be induced by growth of sales and income, has been given a rather high-sounding name—the "acceleration principle," which we met on page 231 of this chapter. Most writers bring it in as one strand in their final business-cycle theories.

FORECASTING THE FUTURE OF BUSINESS ACTIVITY

Businessmen have to form guesses about the future in making their investment and production decisions. If they thought next year would bring a depression, they might want to reduce inventory now. If, on the contrary, they expected prices to rise greatly several months from now, they might hasten today to buy goods in advance and to add to equipment and plant. Similarly, speculators would like to know the future in order to be able to buy or sell common stock and make a profit. And more important, policy makers in Ottawa would like to have a peek at next year's national-income accounts to be able to take remedial fiscal and monetary actions now.

Statisticians and economists cannot yet make accurate forecasts. Their guesses occasionally turn out to be quite wrong. Nonetheless, people insist that they do their best. Why? Because lack of any forecast usually itself involves an *implicit* forecast and noneconomists have an even worse long-run average score at making forecasts than do trained statistical economists.

FORECASTING THE ECONOMIC FUTURE What methods do the best forecasters use? No simple description can be given, but here are a few of the most common practices.

1. They follow the national-income accounts very closely: GNP every quarter; personal income every month; new construction; equipment spending; the important short-run behavior of inventory change; estimates of com-

ing government expenditures and taxes. They also watch monthly data: price indexes, the Statistics Canada index of production, exports, changes in the rate of growth of the money supply, and reports on unemployment and job totals. In addition, they watch many diverse statistics as they become available: department-store sales each week; chain-store sales and automobile dealer sales each month; new orders and inventory changes of manufacturing and trade each month.

2. In recent years, the forecaster can study various *surveys* of future events: the Statistics Canada Department of Trade and Commerce questionnaire of business intentions to invest and the Department of Labour forecast. The attitudes reported by purchasing agents are important for inventories. For consumers, random sampling by public and private survey groups gives information on whether or not the consumer is in a buying mood and what his spending intentions are. For businessmen generally, *The Financial Post* and *Fortune* take frequent polls of opinions about future and present intentions. In Europe the technique of polling heads of businesses has also made great progress.

3. Many forecasters then try to draw up "C + I + G + (E − M) – type models" to make *approximate guesses* about future changes. They try to come out with a range of probable answers, not with a single answer accurate to two decimals.

4. Some reinforce these guesses by considering whether most diverse time series—such as those in Fig. 14-4—are going up or down. Are certain so-called "leading-indicator series," such as average hours worked per week, stock prices, construction awards, and new orders, predominantly signaling a turn now?

Men long looked for a statistical series (or group of series) that would manifest a turn a *fixed* number of months before business turned generally. Such a "leading indicator" would be invaluable for forecasting purposes; however, no such perfect guide has been discovered. Geoffrey Moore and Arthur F. Burns at the U.S. National Bureau of Economic Research, and Julius Shiskin at the U.S. Census Bureau, have found that certain series, such as have already been mentioned, can give some help in identifying turning points in advance and in confirming that they have just occurred. Forecasters cannot yet rely on indicators alone, for the reason that (as in periods like 1951, 1962 and 1967) they may give misleading signals; in expansions, the indicators often turn down too many months before the true peak; in recessions, they turn up only a month or two before the upturn—by the time the data become available for smoothing, their main (important) purpose is to tell us we have indeed already turned the corner. The Canadian government and private forecaster W. A. Beckett have made use of similar information. Economists look forward with interest to further improvements in these techniques, and practical forecasters do supplement this kind of information. Found among the useful leaders are new orders for durables, housing starts, and inventory changes; stock prices, corporate profits, and industrial materials prices; average workweek hours; rate of growth of the money supply, etc.

5. This is the age of computer forecasting. Thanks to the pioneering work of the Netherland's Nobel laureate

Jan Tinbergen, today most computers have a good number of macroeconomic models of the GNP. The Bank of Canada, Statistics Canada, University of Toronto have all produced well-known econometric models (e.g. RDX-2; CANDIDE; TRACE); some of these trace their ancestry to work by Lawrence Klein or the Wharton School model and many banks, large firms and private consultants have their own.

How do computer models operate? Essentially, they try to build up consistent statistical estimates of the components of $C + I + G$, based upon past patterns of experience. Thus Fig. 11-5's fitted CC schedule provides an example—a primitive example—of the methodology involved. But nowadays dozens of multiple-correlation equations are typically involved. How successful are these computer models? According to careful audits by the National Bureau of Economic Research, they do better than naive guesses that merely estimate that tomorrow will be as much above today as today was above yesterday. If judgment is applied to the computer equations in order to alter their coefficients in accordance with the most up-to-date qualifying information, computer models do about as well at forecasting as do the most experienced and rarest economists of great judgment and flair. Even this remark does not do justice to the computer's contribution: The best practitioners of the art of judgmental forecasting gladly admit that these days their judgment has fed into it the *results* of computer analyses. What is to be hoped is that the elements of *art* in economic forecasting—which admittedly are still very important—will increasingly be reduced in importance in comparison with the elements of *science* in such forecasting. But it will be a long time before the millennium of accurate and noncontroversial forecasts finally arrives.

6. Aside from forecasting models of the general $C + I + G$ type, in recent years simpler monetarist models have been employed. These are sometimes referred to as black-box models in which changes in the U.S. money supply over earlier periods are fed in as the principal inputs; by a complicated process that monetarists say need not be investigated so long as the forecasting method works, one derives, as output from the black boxes, multiple-regression equations estimates of the money value of U.S. GNP.

Perhaps the most successful example of such a monetarist forecasting method has been the work of the Federal Reserve Bank of St. Louis, which has produced pretty fair estimates of quarterly changes in GNP on the basis of changes in the money supply over the previous five quarters (and, but with much reduced weight, changes in government expenditures over a similar interval). Future research must settle whether simple models that estimate totals rather than components will perform best, or whether eclectic combinations of $C + I + G$ and monetary models (like RDX-2) will be the most useful—useful not only in crude forecasting, but also estimating policy changes of an optimal type.

Experience shows that economic forecasts are indispensable for public and business decisions. Economists' forecasts, although not infallible, average out to be more accurate than those of readers of tea leaves, senatorial hunch players, computer robots, or simple extrapolaters of present levels and trends. Although not perfect, economists' GNP forecasts are the best science can produce.

REQUIEM FOR THE BUSINESS CYCLE?

Is the business cycle dead? Has the New Economics ended once and for all this curse of historic capitalism, in the same way that modern medicine has ended such scourges as polio and smallpox?

Many people do believe that the business cycle has finally been tamed. And indeed, study of Fig. 14-4 shows that the economy has reduced recessions in the post-World War II period to brief and infrequent punctuations in the progress of sustained growth. It used to be the case, under historic capitalism, that the charts showed the shadings of recession half the time.

Yet, to paraphrase Mark Twain's comment on the report of his demise, "It is *premature* to speak of the death of the business cycle." Back in 1929, just before the great stock-market crash, experts spoke of the country as being in a "new era" of perpetual prosperity. The gods take their revenge on those who are too proud.

What can be said scientifically about the outlook for business fluctuations? Most economists would pretty much agree with the following formulation:

Although nothing is impossible in an inexact science like economics, the probability of a great depression—a prolonged, cumulative, and chronic slump like that of the 1930s, the 1890s, or the 1870s—has been reduced to a negligible figure. No one should pay any appreciable insurance premium to be protected against the risk of a total breakdown in our banking system and of massive unemployment in which 25 per cent of the workers can find no jobs.

The reason for virtual disappearance of great depressions is the new attitude of the electorate. By the $C + I + G + (E - M)$ analysis of this and earlier chapters, economic science knows how to use monetary and fiscal policy to keep any recessions that break out from snowballing into lasting chronic slumps. The electorate in a mixed economy insists that any political party which is in power will take the expansionary actions that can prevent depressions.

Suppose we grant that great depressions are virtually a thing of the past. Does this mean that we must have perpetual prosperity—that recessions will never happen again, being replaced by what are euphemistically called "rolling readjustments" or mere "pauses"? Most scientists take a more cautious attitude, summarizing thus:

A mixed economy may still be subject to occasional *recessions:* inventory fluctuations can still occur; changes in cold-war spending can have initially destabilizing effects upon general business activity; attempts to bring inflation under control may sometimes result in downturns.

Nevertheless, now that the tools of income analysis are more widely understood and their use becoming mandatory, the probability of recession in any one year is less in the mixed economy than it used to be. Expansion periods tend to be frequent and longer.

Lest we close on an overoptimistic note, let us take warning that the forces of democracy are not so strongly balanced in the direction of controlling creeping inflation —as we shall see. And future scientists may have to redefine the phases of the business cycle, so that in economies like Germany or the United States we count as unsatisfactory those years in which the economy actually *grows less than its potential grows*, thereby wasting its true productivity in mounting "gaps."

SUMMARY TO APPENDIX

1 The business cycle is a pulse common to most sectors of economic life and to various countries. Movements in national income, unemployment, production, prices, and profits are not so regular and predictable as the orbits of the planets or the oscillations of a pendulum, and there is no magical method of forecasting the turns of business activity.

2 The four phases of expansion, peak, recession, and trough can be separated for analysis and can be distinguished from seasonal or long-term trends. The resulting pattern of 8- to 10-year major cycles, shorter minor cycles, and longer Kuznets construction cycles has been carefully described by economists, statisticians, and historians and found to be roughly coincident in Western economies.

3 To explain the cycle, our first clue is to be found in the greater amplitude of fluctuations of investment or durable-capital-goods formation. Although most economists agree on this fact, they differ in their emphasis upon *external* or *internal* factors. Increasingly, however, the experts are tending toward a *synthesis* of external and internal factors. On the one hand, importance is attached to fluctuations in inventions, in population and territorial growth, and in gold discoveries and political warfare. On the other hand, economists stress too the way that these external changes in investment opportunities are modified by the reactions of the economic system; the credit practices of banks and the monetary policies of the Bank of Canada; waves of optimism and pessimism; replacement cycles; the multiplier and the acceleration principle, which bring in dynamic rates of change as well as levels; and other feedback effects of growth on investment.

4 Forecasting is still inexact. Those with the best long-run batting averages follow national-income and related statistics very closely. They rely heavily on surveys of government, consumer, and business intentions. They reinforce their $C + I + G + (E - M)$ and money-supply guesses with the study of leading, coincident, and lagging indicators.

CONCEPTS FOR REVIEW

business cycle, turning point, phase
peak, trough, expansion, recession
seasonal and trend corrections
internal and external theories
international transmission

acceleration principle
replacement waves, sunspots
forecasting methods
leading, coincident, and
  lagging indicators

QUESTIONS FOR DISCUSSION

1. Describe the history of various cycles in this country. Would you include 1969-70 among the list of cyclical downturns?
2. Describe the different phases of the cycle. In what one are you now? How do you know?
3. Which theory or theories of the cycle do you like best? Why?
4. "The ups-and-downs of the traditional business cycle are less important objects of study today than the level of unemployment and the trends in real output growth and in the general price level." Explain and appraise.
5. Why is it important to be able to forecast the future of business activity? Give business and government examples. How would *you* forecast?

6. The concept of the business cycle needs to be redefined in modern times as follows: "Expansion should be defined as years when GNP grows faster than *trend*; recession defined as years when GNP grows slower than *trend*. Then we will again have recession half the time, on the average." Support the merits of this view.

7. Is forecasting a science? An art? How may the computer change the mix of qualitative judgment and quantitative formulas?

15
PRICES AND MONEY

Only one fellow in ten thousand understands the currency question, and we meet him every day.
KIN HUBBARD

Earlier chapters showed how the modern economist finds it convenient to analyze the forces making for expanding or contracting money income in terms of saving and investment schedules, or what is the same thing, in terms of the components of consumption, investment, and government spending. For the most part, except in the inflationary-gap section, it was assumed that price levels would not change much until an approach to high employment was reached. Or alternatively, it was tacitly assumed earlier that all the schedules were expressed in terms of dollars which had been corrected for changes in the measuring rod of the price level. Accordingly, until now, a shift in the schedule of consumption-plus-investment-plus-government spending could be thought of as expanding employment and production.

Now we want to focus on changes in the *price levels*. Why do prices rise swiftly in major wars? Why do prices increase millionsfold in galloping inflation when a disorganized nation is printing new currency by the bale? Why do prices begin to creep upward even *before* an expansion of $C + I + G$ spending re-stores the system to full or high employment? Why in a modern mixed economy might prices and wages rise even at a time of apparent excess plant capacity and slack labor markets?

These vital, and difficult, questions can be most fruitfully approached by the following program. This chapter will first give the facts about price-level changes and some of their effects. Then it will discuss the concept of barter, the nature of money and the basic facts about the supply of money, M. Finally, the important "quantity theory of money," in its crude and sophisticated forms, will provide an initial glimpse into the importance of banking and Bank of Canada monetary policies, as discussed in subsequent chapters.

We shall discover that changes in the money supply have an important effect in causing the $C + I + G + (E - M)$ spending schedule to shift upward or downward and we shall see that a new kind of inflation—"cost-push"—has reared its head alongside conventional "demand-pull" inflation.

A. PRICES AND MONEY

Figures 15-1 and 15-2 are a remarkable long series of price indexes, mostly wholesale, linked together. They show the historical ups and downs of price levels, as seen from the point of view of some clairvoyant persons now dead. The first shows the long sweep of British prices since the time of Oliver Cromwell. The second shows Canadian prices since 1848. At first glance there seem no general upward or downward trends. But, as the chart of consumer prices (cost-of-living) in Figure 15-4 will also show, the long upward grind since World War II is quite without parallel in detailed records. Today's college students have seen a sustained cut in the value of the dollar never experienced by their ancestors.

As an omen for the future, note one very significant fact: After World War II there was no decline in prices at all comparable with what had followed previous wars. Wages and prices seem to have become "sticky" as far as *downward* movements are concerned; also, government has become quick to stem

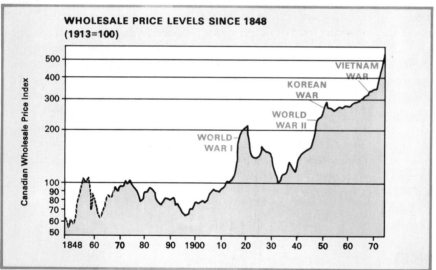

Figures 15-1 and 15-2. The prices increases since World War II are without precedent. Note the prices have usually spurted up during and after wars. (Sources: Canada: Urquhart and Buckley *Historical Statistics of Canada,* and Statistics Canada; U.K.: Mitchell and Deane, *Abstract of British Historical Statistics.*)

any depression of prices or output that threatens. Recent government targets for price stability have not been to reverse price increases—to restore former price levels—but simply to *slow* further increase. If prices rise in good times and scarcely fall at all in bad times, what is their indicated long-term direction? The answer is plain.

INFLATION, DEFLATION, AND REDISTRIBUTION OF INCOME AMONG GROUPS

First, some definitions will be useful.

By *inflation* we mean *a time of generally rising prices* for commodities and factors of production —rising prices for bread, cars, haircuts; rising wages, rents, etc.
By *deflation* we mean a time when most prices and costs are falling.[1]

Neither in inflation nor in deflation do prices all move in the same direction or in exactly the same proportion. As a result of changes in *relative* prices and in total spending, the two processes of inflation and deflation cause definite and characteristic changes in (1) the distribution of income among economic classes and in (2) total output.

Unforeseen inflation tends to favor debtors and profit receivers at the expense of creditors and fixed-income receivers. Deflation has the opposite effect.

Suppose you lend $1,000 today and are paid back one year from now. If in the meantime prices have doubled, then your debtor will be paying back only one-half as much real purchasing power as you gave him. If prices were to increase a trillionfold, as they did in the German inflation of 1920-1923, then the wealth of creditors would be completely wiped out. This actually happened to German university endowments and life-insurance assets.

Economists call the rate of return, adjusted for declining purchasing power in this way, the *real* rate of return (i.e., the market interest rate minus the annual rate of increase in the price level). A Canadian security bought for $75 in 1970 will pay off about $100 in 1975. But will the real rate of return be as high as zero per cent—will $100 in 1975 have as

much purchasing power as $75 had in 1970? A Canadian who bought a long-term Government of Canada bond in 1939 and who kept it while reinvesting the interest payments at the going yields would scarcely have held his own in terms of the real purchasing power of the dollar. Admittedly, after 1954 he would have made some progress: a hundred dollars invested then would become $140 a decade later (by compounding the interest payments), whereas the *real purchasing power* would have slipped only so far that an item sold for $100 in the mid-fifties would have cost $120 in 1964. That is, over the entire period 1939-1970, the depreciation of purchasing power roughly equalled the rate of return; only in the shorter sub-period 1954-1964 was it somewhat less.

On the other hand, one who invests his money in real estate, in common stocks, or in sacks of flour makes a great money profit during unforeseen inflation. The volume of business sales shoots up. Prices rise between the time that businessmen buy and sell their merchandise. Fixed or overhead costs remain the same; other costs rise, but not so rapidly as prices. For all these reasons profits increase— often faster than does the cost of living. In periods of great inflation, every reckless fool can—must—become a great financier.

In time of *deflation*, the shoe is on the other foot. Creditors and fixed-income receivers tend to gain at the expense of debtors and profit receivers. If prices fall between the time that a creditor lends money and is repaid, then he gets back more purchasing power than he lent. Between the time that a merchant buys and sells goods, he will have to take a loss.

The school teacher who keeps her job finds that her real income has increased. The widow who withstood the temptation to buy common stock during the boom and instead put all her money into gilt-edge government bonds finds herself better off. At the same time the government finds that the real burden of its public debt goes up relative to tax collections and national income. A hoarder who earns no money interest on his mattress cache nevertheless finds the real value of his wealth increasing every day as prices fall. If prices fall at the rate of 10 per cent rate of interest in rewarded for his antisocial act of hoarding at a 10 per cent rate of interest in real terms, while the businessman who is foolish enough to give someone a job may find that he cannot even

---

[1] "Deflation" sometimes has a secondary meaning too, namely a *drop in real output and an increase in unemployment* regardless of price behavior. And even our simple definition of inflation as rising prices will occasionally need modifying: thus in 1947 when wartime price controls were removed, prices shot upwards. Did stability of prices mean no inflation before 1947? Hardly. As scarcities of goods increased from 1939 to 1947, we were having "suppressed inflation." The 1947 price rise was primarily a "symptom" of the disease we were already experiencing.

get back his original outlay, much less earn a profit.

Modern research suggests that the greatest redistribution of income resulting from inflation is from older people to younger people. The dollars one puts aside at 25 for retirement at 70 often shrink in purchasing power: if prices rise at an average rate of about 3 per cent per year, the real purchasing power of a dollar held for 45 years will halve and halve again in that period.[2]

ANTICIPATED INFLATION. Once an inflation has gone on for a long time and is no longer "unforeseen", an allowance for a price rise will gradually get itself built into the market interest rate. Thus, once we all expect prices to rise at 4 percent per year, my pension funds invested in bonds and mortgages will tend to pay me 8 percent rather than 4 percent. This adjustment of interest rates to chronic inflation has been observed in Brazil, Chile, and indeed in almost all other countries with a long history of rising prices.

Chapter 19 will present a discussion of "indexing", a means by which wage-earners, pensioners and taxpayers can be protected from the effects of an inflation that is foreseen but at an unknown rate. Brazil has pioneered in enforcing this system on all private prices and public charges.

EFFECTS OF CHANGING PRICES ON OUTPUT AND EMPLOYMENT

Aside from redistributing incomes, inflation may affect the total real income and production of the community.

An increase in prices is usually associated with high employment. In mild inflation the wheels of industry are well lubricated, and output is near capacity. Private investment is brisk, and jobs are plentiful. Such has been the historical pattern.

Thus, many businessmen and union spokesmen, in appraising a little deflation and a little inflation, speak of the latter as the lesser of two evils. The losses to fixed-income groups are usually less than

the gains to the rest of the community. Even workers with relatively fixed wages are often better off because of improved employment opportunities and greater take-home pay; a rise in interest rates on new securities may partly make up any losses to creditors; and increases in pensions and transfers may partly make up losses to the retired. The ultimate sufferers are those who have least market power and least political power; conceivably, an inflationary, full-employment society could also arrange for their welfare by a transfer system.

In deflation, on the other hand, the growing decline in output causes the community's total well-being to be less; so the gainers get less than the losers lose. As a matter of fact, in deep depression, almost everyone—including the creditor who is left with uncollectible debts—suffers.

The above remarks show why an increase in consumption or investment spending is thought a good thing in times of unemployment, even if there is some upward pressure on prices. When the economic system is suffering from acute depression, few will criticize private or public spending on the ground that this might be inflationary. Actually, most of the increased spending will then go to increase production and create more jobs and more real income.

But the same reasoning shows that once full employment and full plant capacity have been reached, any further increases in spending are likely to be completely wasted in price-tag increases. (Recall Chapter 12's discussion of "inflationary gaps.")

GALLOPING INFLATION

Slow price increases are one thing. But when each increase in prices becomes the signal for an increase in wages and costs, which again sends prices up still further, we may be in the midst of a malignant, galloping hyperinflation. Nothing good can be said for a rapid rise of prices such as took place in Germany in 1920-1923 and more recently in China and Hungary. Production and even the social order are then disorganized. The total wealth of large groups of the population is wiped out as money becomes worthless. Debtors ruthlessly pursue creditors in order to pay off their obligations in valueless money. Speculators

---

[2] Even flexible "indexed" pension plans give less and less *real* income to pensioners who start their retirement with adequate income.

profiteer. Workers rush to spend their pay cheques before prices rise still further, but in doing so they only bid prices up even faster. As one Southerner said during the Confederate inflation of the American Civil War:

We used to go to the stores with money in our pockets and come back with food in our baskets. Now we go with money in baskets and return with food in our pockets. Everything is scarce except money. Prices are chaotic and production disorganized. A meal that used to cost the same amount as an opera ticket now costs twenty times as much. Business is often at a standstill because no one knows how much to charge. (We'll settle after the war, some say.) As a result, everybody tends to hoard "things" and to try to get rid of the "bad" paper money, which drives the "good" metal money out of circulation. A partial return to barter—with all its inconveniences—is the result.

Aside from hyperinflations of the German 1920-1923 type, we do see in countries like Chile and Brazil chronic inflation—say at the rate of 20 to 50 per cent per year—that goes on decade after decade. Somehow the people learn to live on such a merry-go-round. They hoard goods; buy homes; never, never lend money at ordinary interest rates; etc. Sometimes, as in Brazil, the economy manages to show real growth; too often, as in Argentina and Chile, growth suffers.

Fortunately, there are few cases of hyperinflation except during war or in the backwash of war and revolution. The primary fear today for our mixed economy is about our steady upward *creep* in prices. Will such a creep inevitably become a trot? A trot become a canter? A canter become a gallop? Few economic experts would regard such a development as inevitable. But they are still concerned with too fast and steady a creep of prices as we'll soon see.

THE CHOICE OF GOALS OF LONG-TERM PRICE BEHAVIOR

Ideally we all want a progressive full-employment economy in which the excesses of the business cycle are moderated. We want to control the "mad dance of the dollar" as the business cycle passes from boom to crisis and slump. But as far as the *long-run trend* of prices is concerned, there are three possible programs that different economists sponsor as the soundest modern compromise goal. All three assume that output (real GNE) is increasing every time because of population increase, capital formation, and technological progress.

1. *Prices—on the average—are to be stable.* Total dollar spending rises. Money wages, and real wages also, rise as a result of increases in productivity over time.

2. *Prices are to be gently rising.* Total dollar spending rises even faster than prices or output alone. Money wages also rise steadily; but the increase in real wages is not quite so great, because of the upward trend in the cost of living.

3. *Prices are to be falling steadily.* The total of money wages and property income remains almost constant. But the increase in output resulting from improved technological productivity is passed on to *all* consumers in lower prices. Real wages rise even though money wages may remain constant. Such a fall in prices need not depress business activity unduly, provided that it results from previous reductions in cost.

All three solutions are tolerable if unemployment can be kept at a low figure. And in some ideal frictionless system, it would not matter much which pattern were followed, as long as the trend in prices was foreseeable and all adjustments were made to it. However, economic history and analysis suggest that we do not live in an ideal frictionless system. In a modern mixed economy, high employment is *least* likely to be maintained under the third possibilty of falling price levels.

Most vigorous periods of healthy capitalist development without political unrest have come during periods of stable or gently rising prices. Capitalism itself developed during the centuries when Spanish New World gold flowed in—not because anyone planned it that way, but because the resultant general price increase eased the transition into the exchange economy with widespread use of coins and money.

BARTER VERSUS THE USE OF MONEY

When W. Stanley Jevons, over a century ago in the first textbook on money, wanted to illustrate the tremendous leap forward made by man when he turned from exchange by barter to the use of money, he could not do better than to quote experiences like the following.

Some years ago since, Mademoiselle Zélie, a singer of the Theatre Lyrique at Paris, . . . gave a concert in the Society Islands. In exchange for an air from *Norma* and a few other songs, she was to receive a third part of the receipts. When counted, her share was found to consist of three pigs, twenty-three turkeys, forty-four chickens, five thousand cocoa-nuts, besides considerable quantities of bananas, lemons, and oranges. . . [I]n Paris . . . this amount of live stock and vegetables might have brought four thousand francs, which would have been good remuneration for five songs. In the Society Islands, however, pieces of money were scarce; and as Mademoiselle could not consume any considerable portion of the receipts herself, it became necessary in the mean time to feed the pigs and poultry with the fruit.

As was noted in Chapter 3, inconvenient as barter obviously is, it represents a great step forward from a state of self-sufficiency in which every man had to be a jack-of-all-trades and master of none.

Nevertheless, simple barter operates under grave disadvantages. An elaborate division of labor would be unthinkable without the introduction of a great new improvement—the use of money. Men need not directly exchange one good for another. Instead they sell one good for money, and then use money to buy the goods they wish. At first glance this seems to complicate rather than simplify matters, to replace a single transaction by two transactions. Thus, if I have apples and want nuts, would it not be simpler to trade one for the other rather than to sell the apples for money and then use the money to buy nuts?

Actually, the reverse is the case: the two transactions are simpler than one. Ordinarily, there are always people ready to buy apples and always some willing to sell—at a price—nuts; but it would be an unusual *coincidence* to find a person with tastes exactly opposite my own, with an eagerness to sell nuts and buy apples. Such a coincidence would be as unlikely as the chance of flipping a dozen "tails" in a row. (Even if the unusual should happen—as occasionally it must—there is no guarantee that the desires of the two parties with respect to the exact *quantities* and terms of the exchange would coincide.)

To use a classical economic phrase: Instead of there being a double coincidence of wants, there is

likely to be a want of coincidence; so that, unless a hungry tailor happens to find an undraped farmer who has both food and a desire for a pair of pants, neither can make a trade.

Money does simplify economic life. But do not suppose that, for society as a whole, a mere increase in the total of money will enable people to consume more than the real products technically producible with existent totals of labor, land, and capital. And, as we've seen, money can misbehave and produce recession and inflation.

HISTORICAL STAGES OF MONEY

If we were to reconstruct history along hypothetical, logical lines, we should naturally follow the age of barter by the age of commodity money.

COMMODITY MONEY Historically, a great variety of commodities has served at one time or another as a medium of exchange: cattle (from which come the Latin stem of "pecuniary" and also the words "capital" and "chattel"), tobacco, leather and hides, furs, olive oil, beer or spirits, slaves or wives, copper, iron, gold, silver, rings, diamonds, playing cards, wampum beads or shells, huge rocks and landmarks, and cigarette butts.

Each of the above has some advantages and disadvantages. Cattle are not divisible into small change; but while it is being hoarded, such "money" is likely to increase by reproduction, giving the lie to the doctrine of Aristotle that "money is barren." Beer does not improve with keeping, although wine may. Olive oil provides a nice liquid currency that is as minutely divisible as one wishes. Iron will rust and is of so little value that one would need a cart instead of a pocketbook. The value of a diamond is not proportional to weight but varies with the square of its weight; if cut into pieces, it loses value.

The yearly additions to (by mining) or subtractions from (by use in teeth, jewelry, and electric relays) the accumulated stock of *precious metals* are small in percentage terms; so their total amounts and value do not fluctuate widely. Silver has luster but will tarnish in air. Gold keeps its attractive sheen but, unless mixed with an alloy, is soft. Gold's high specific gravity make detection of counterfeiting and admixture easy; but through most of historical time, gold's scarcity value has been so great per ounce as to require inordinately minute coins for ordinary purchases.

Most kinds of money tended once to be of some value or use for their own sake. Thus, even wampum had decorative uses, and paper money began as warehouse or mint receipts for so much metal. But the intrinsic usefulness of the money medium is now the least important thing about it.

PAPER MONEY The age of commodity money gives way to the age of paper money. The essence of money, its intrinsic nature, is typified by paper currency. *Money, as money rather than a commodity, is wanted not for its own sake but for the things it will buy!* We do not wish to use up money directly; but rather to use it by getting rid of it; even when we choose to use it by holding it, its value comes from the fact that we can spend it *later on*.

Money is an artificial, social convention. If for any reason a substance begins to be used as money, all people will begin to value it, even if they happen to be teetotalers or vegetarians or disbelievers in its intrinsic usefulness. As long as things can be bought and sold for a given substance, people will be content to sell and buy with it. Paradox: money is accepted because it is accepted!

The use of paper currency (dollar bills, fives, tens, . . .) has become widespread because it has many conveniences as a medium of exchange. Currency is easily carried and stored away. By the printing of more or fewer zeros on the face value of the bill, a great or small amount of value can be embodied in a light, transportable medium of little bulk. By the use of decimal points, it can be made as divisible as we wish. By careful engraving, the value of money can be made easily recognizable and protected from counterfeiting and adulteration. The fact that private individuals cannot create it at will in unlimited amounts keeps it scarce, i.e., an economic, and not a free, good.

Given this limitation in supply, modern currencies have value, i.e., can buy things, independently of any gold, silver, or government backing. The public neither knows nor cares—and need not know or care—whether its currency is in the form of certificates, or coin. So long as each form of money can be converted into any other at fixed terms, the best is as good as the worst.

BANK MONEY Finally, along with the age of paper money, there is the age of bank money, or bank chequing deposits. Today at least nine-tenths of all transactions, by value if not number, take place by cheques. A professor has his salary paid directly into his bank account, after income taxes have already been withheld by his employer. His rent or dentist bills are paid by cheque, his gasoline and hotel bills, by a credit card. Except for petty sums for lunches and carfare, he needs little cash.

A MONEYLESS ECONOMY IN THE FUTURE? In the age of the electronic computer, there is less and less need to carry currency or even to have to depend upon one's chequebook. A credit card serves increasingly for most transactions. We can perhaps envision a day when, by telephone or automatic insertion of a noncounterfeitable card into a computer terminal, central memory and data banks will record most transactions. Money as a unit of account will still serve its function; but anything so crude as a poker chip, coin, or bill will be largely dispensed with in favor of records that automatically balance out each person's inpayments and outpayments over a lifetime.

We may sum up the essence of money briefly: Money is the modern medium of exchange and the standard unit in which prices and debts are expressed. By controlling the behaviour of money and credit, the government and its central bank can hope to affect the balance of saving and investment expenditure—the level of real and money GNP, the rate of price-level fixation.

By quickening or moderating the growth in the money supply, the Bank of Canada can hope to raise or lower the $C + I + G$ intersections of earlier chapters. Here lies the vital importance of monetary theory.

THE THREE KINDS OF MONEY: COINS, CURRENCY, AND BANK DEPOSITS

Let us list the main kinds of money now in daily use: small coins, paper currency, and chequing-account bank-deposit money.

COINAGE First, there are the coins we use for small change: copper pennies, nickel five-cent pieces, and silvery dimes, quarters, half-dollars, and dollars. These constitute our small coins. Children think them important; but in total they do not add up to very much—in fact, to about one-seventh of the community's cash. Because the metal in all these coins is worth far *less* than their face value, they are termed "token money".[3] These coins are valued far beyond their metallic worth only because they can be readily converted into other money—20 nickels to the dollar, and so forth. Coins with negligible metallic value are not forced upon us; their quantity is limited by our demand for them to buy gum and newspapers, or to put in various vending machines.

CURRENCY Far more significant is the second kind of money: paper currency. Most of us know little more about a one-dollar or five-dollar bill than that each is inscribed with the picture of a Canadian statesman or the Queen, that each bears the signature of one or another Bank of Canada official, and—most important of all—that each has a number showing its face value.

Examine a dollar bill or some other paper bill. You will find it says "Bank of Canada / One dollar / This note is legal tender".

It was not always thus. Paper currency issued by the Crown or the government has at various times represented the willingness of the Treasury to exchange that note for silver or gold. For example, the British pound sterling has its name because it once stood for one pound of sterling silver. And the U.S. one dollar bill had printed on it "Silver Certificate" because Congress (until 1963) required that each bill be backed by an appropriate weight of silver. On demand, the government would give the bearer a silver dollar or silver metal! And in 1853, when the Canadian currency was established, its dollar was based on the British pound,

a gold coin, with $4.86 2/3 (Canadian) to the pound, or $10.00 to the eagle, the American gold coin. Small coins, including American decimal coins and British shillings and pennies, were then almost the only hand-to-hand currency. But when, decades later, "Dominion notes" were issued by the Department of Finance, they had this old relationship to the pound and eagle coins.

Until the 1930s, most bills in Canada were either these "Dominion notes" or true "bank notes." The latter were issued by the chartered banks, bore pictures of the banks' presidents or premises instead of the sovereign, and were fully accepted as a substitute for legal tender by everyone as long as the issuing bank was known to be able to exchange them, on demand, for legal tender. Since 1935 these private bank notes (of which a very few are still in existence) and Dominion bills have been replaced by today's Bank of Canada bills. All they will get you is more Bank of Canada bills!

Today, and for many decades, all Canadian currency and coinage has been essentially "fiat" money. It is money because it is decreed to be so, and because we all accept it. Metallic backing has no real meaning any more (except, as will be seen later, when it serves to limit the total supply of fiat money).

Many middle-aged people today can remember from their childhood receiving five- or ten-dollar gold pieces for their birthdays. Because most of these pieces have been called in, they are now valuable for their weight in gold, or for their scarcity as coinage, whichever is greater. The U.S. buying price for gold, which has dominated world values since World War I, jumped from $21 to $35 per ounce in 1933-4, as part of the Roosevelt anti-depression program. In many places (especially in the United States) the holding of gold coins became illegal, to support the calling-in of coins by the Treasury. Today many countries are following Canada's lead in permitting dealing in and owning of coins and bullion bars. But few people bother: a country's paper money is accepted in all its regions. Only when people fear that the *international* value of paper money is in peril, do they rush to trade it for gold or a preferred currency.

From the standpoint of understanding the nature of money, it is perhaps simpler that gold certificates and coins no longer exist. The modern student need not be misled, as were earlier generations of students, by some mystical belief that "gold backing" is what gives money its value. Certainly gold, as such, has little to do with the problem. In the late 1960s

---

[3] If a dictator insisted on supplementing the paper currency with coins whose metallic value equaled or came near their face values, he would show what an amateur he was at finance. Thus, as soon as platinum or silver rose enough in price on the auction markets of the world, the dictator would find his coins were being melted down for their metallic content for teeth, electronics, jewels, and photography. It is because coins and currency are made of cheap materials that they avoid this fate. Do facts bear out this theory? They do. When the price of silver rose in 1963 most governments had to stop using silver in coins; The Canadian mint stopped using silver in 1968. To keep new coins from being melted down and hoarded, they substituted cheaper cupronickel materials.

most experts ridiculed the claim that "money has more value if it can be exchanged into gold," asserting that without its monetary uses metallic gold would fall in price.[4] They argued that industrial gold, dental inlays, and wedding rings would be cheaper, and gold miners poorer, when the United States stopped guaranteeing the gold price. By 1970, however, experts were less sure: the 1968 runs on the London gold market, following some nervousness, did reveal a *precautionary* and a *non-monetary* gold demand strong enough to yank its price up from $35 (U.S.) per ounce, even when the U.S. guarantee to buy was revoked. This event did not refute any basic principle, but it does show how little economists knew about this key commodity's demand.

This precautionary demand for gold is not necessarily based on a view that gold will again be needed to back the world's currencies. Rather, it stems from knowledge that governments' actions strongly—and heedlessly—affect the value of money, and conservatives are convinced that governments cannot be trusted to refrain from abusing this power. Hence they publicly advocate reducing governments' powers that may further erode the value of a dollar, and privately hold their wealth in the form of titles to commodities (today including gold) that appear to be inflation-proof. Figure 15-3 shows how the free-market price of gold has departed from its previous anchor at $35 per ounce and floated up with all the other metals. Gold is now just a commodity. True, some buyers are gambling that it may regain its monetary status, but there is gambling in other metal markets too.

As we shall see in subsequent chapters and in the international discussions of Part Five, gold still does have a limited role to play in financial international transactions and in determining the world-wide trends of reserves held by the various central banks. Herein lies its true role in twentieth-century economics.

FIG. 15-3. Gold prices now parallel other metals.
The left-hand scale is that for the *Economist's* index of all metal prices, mostly those traded on the key London Metal Exchange. The right-hand scale shows the U.S. dollar prices of gold.
(Source: *Economist*, July 8, 1974.)

Limitation in the supply of money is the necessary condition if it is to have value. If currency is so unlimited in amount as to become practically a free good, people would have so much of it to spend as to bid up all prices, wages, and incomes sky-high. That is why constitutional powers over money and banking are never given to private groups but are always vested in government.

BANK DEPOSITS There is also a third category of what economists call money. This involves so-called "demand deposits"—made up of bank deposits subject to chequing on demand.

If I have $1,000 in my chequing account at the Bank of Montreal, that deposit can be regarded as money. Why? Because I can pay for purchases with

---

[4] That gold affects prices only through its ability to *limit or to expand the volume of paper money and total spending* was overlooked by foolish European chancellors of the exchequer who, after World War I, tried to stop inflation by *accumulating* new gold reserves through the purchase of gold on the open market with newly *printed* money! Of course, the effect was just the opposite. Only after they had reversed the process and used their gold to buy up and burn outstanding paper money did they enjoy any success.

cheques drawn on it. The deposit is like any other medium of exchange, and being payable on demand, it serves as a *"standard of value," or "unit of account,"* in the same sense at $1,000 worth of silver quarters; i.e. both the deposit and the quarters are convertible into standard money or cash at fixed terms, dollar for dollar and penny for penny.

Possessing the essential properties of money, bank demand deposits might just as well be counted as money. And they are.[5]

Actually, as noted, bank money is quantitatively more important than currency because most transactions are made by cheque. The convenience of cheques for mailing, for paying the exact sum of money due, for providing a receipt in the form of the canceled cheque voucher, for protecting against loss when stolen or misplaced (while unendorsed or, for that matter, endorsed)—all these advantages are obvious and explain the widespread use of bank money.

Table 15-1 illustrates the quantitative importance of the three kinds of money: coin, currency, and demand deposits. The total of these is called M_1, money as narrowly defined.

LIQUID ASSETS, OR "NEAR-MONEY"

Along with the total of money M_1, Table 15-1 also shows the total of money broadly defined, M_2. What is meant by this broader concept? Different economists define the term differently. Table 15-1 includes in money the total interest-bearing savings and time deposits which any person could quickly cash in, but excludes the total of government bonds which anyone could present for redemption or sell for cash in the open market.[6]

Suppose you have $10,000 on demand deposit and your brother has $5,000 on demand deposit plus $5,000 in a credit union; will your spending habits be very different? Probably not, and that is why M_2 is important. Time and savings deposits in chartered

MONEY SUPPLY OF CANADA, (end of 1973) (billions of dollars)	
Coins	0.6
Notes	4.6
Chequable deposits:	
Bank, demand	8.9
Bank, other	7.0
Near-bank	4.7
Total M_1	26.1
Non-chequable	
Savings deposits	14.3
Fixed-term deposits	31.3
Sub-total	45.6
Total M_2	71.6

TABLE 15-1. M_1 the supply of money—chequable deposits plus currency—is the key macroeconomic variable (Source: Bank of Canada.)

banks and "near banks" have gained mightily on demand deposits in recent decades providing all the more reason why we cannot be content with M_1 alone.

Because it is difficult to draw a hard-and-fast line at any point in the chain of things that do have a direct bearing on spending, the exact definition of M, the money supply, is partly a matter of taste rather than of scientific necessity. (Along with M_1 and M_2, economists have been able to define more than a dozen different money-supply concepts: M_3, $M_{1\frac{1}{2}}$ . . .!)

A century ago, demand deposits would not have been included in M. Today all economists would include demand deposits, since even the most stubborn adherent of the old narrow concept has to admit that the existence of chequing accounts does economize on the use of currency and thus acts much like an increase in the effective amount of currency. And most Canadian economists would argue along the same lines for inclusion of personal interest-bearing bank savings deposits in the measurement of the money supply.[7]

DEFINITIONAL PROBLEMS Economists are not all agreed on nomenclature in this field. Many would go so far as to append to M_1 and M_2 a further

---

[5] My balance on deposit in the bank is usually called money—not the cheques I write.

[6] Some Canadian chartered-bank personal-savings deposits (unlike those in the United States) are widely chequable and withdrawable although they are legally subject to notice. So most Canadian economists include them in M_1, rather than merely in M_2. Not every economist would include non-bank chequable deposits in M_1 (item 5 in Table 15-1)

[7] Some scholars, in attempting to include government bonds in money, prefer to give them some fractional weight and add them into a total called "effective" money supply, M_3.

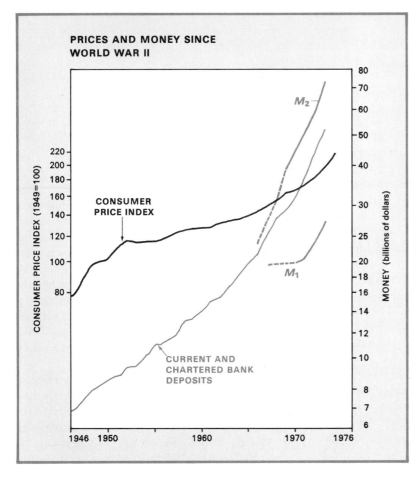

PRICES AND MONEY SINCE WORLD WAR II

CONSUMER PRICE INDEX (1949=100)

MONEY (billions of dollars)

M_2

M_1

CONSUMER PRICE INDEX

CURRENT AND CHARTERED BANK DEPOSITS

1946 1950   1960   1970 1976

FIG. 15-4. Money and prices wind upward.

Total money supply has risen faster than the consumer price level. But important turning points have similar timing.

(Sources: Price Index: Urquhart and Buckley, *Historical Statistics,* and Statistics Canada. Urquhart and Buckley, *Money Supply,* and *Bank of Canada Review,* March 1974, p. 19, and authors' estimates.)

category of "liquid" assets (those that are easy to trade or redeem at fixed or predictable prices) called "near-money."[8] In the total, they would now include government bonds that anyone can present for redemption or sell at some price (perhaps not predictable long in advance). These near-money items have many of the properties of money.

True, you don't pay your monthly expenses directly with bonds, and so we hesitate to call such items "money." Still, the fact that you have an asset so easy to cash means that your current spending habits are probably affected in much the same way as

they would be if you owned a larger bank deposit instead of government bonds.

For the most part, this book will follow the most common practice and define the total money supply thus:

M is the sum of coin and currency in circulation outside the banks, plus *chequable* demand and personal time and savings deposits in banks and near-banks (after various routine adjustments are made in this magnitude). Along with this narrow definition of M (which we may call M_1), it is sometimes useful to work with a broader definition (called M_2), which includes non-chequable deposits and certificates deposits in addition to M_1.

Figure 15-4 shows how the various concepts of money supply have been growing. Good data for M_1 and M_2 (i.e. for *chequable* bank and for near-bank

[8] It would not be illogical to subtract out from people's liquid assets their current liabilities (charge accounts, installment loans, etc.). Along with income, perhaps their resulting "net worth" would be the single most important determinant of their spending.

deposits) is available only for recent years. But the shape of all curves suggests that M_1 has doubled in 10 years. The figure also shows the recent rapid swelling of M_2. The long statistical series is the total of currency and *all* chequable bank deposits (this tends to include some savings deposits that were held like interest-bearing securities, not like current accounts).

B. THE DEMAND FOR MONEY TO HOLD

What are the functions of money? Here are some just discussed new ones:

1. Money is a *medium of exchange* enabling us to transact our national income and product without recourse to hopelessly inefficient barter.

2. Money is the *unit of account* in which we express prices for current transactions, and also for future or deferred transactions (such as when I borrow $1,000 today and agree to pay back $1,200 three years from now).

3. Money is a safe *way of holding* at least part of one's *wealth*—safe against the ups and downs inherent in stocks, land, homes, and bonds. When all these are going down in price, the canny hoarder of money is the most successful speculator in the community. (When prices rise, however, many holders suffer.)

4. Money holding is a necessary *precaution* against having a sudden expense occur or an unexpected delay in a receipt due from someone else. Similarly, the "liquidity" of money enables one to take advantage of a bargain in goods or in securities that might suddenly come up.

All these functions are worth paying for. And we each do incur a cost in holding a coin, a bill, or a demand deposit—namely, *the sacrificed interest and profit yield* that might be obtained from other assets.

Massey Ferguson works just as hard to keep down its unnecessary cash as it does to keep down its unnecessary steel inventory and wastage. The business manager of a famous cartoonist was aghast to find that he had kept $120,000 idle in a demand deposit, earning no interest for years, merely because he never read his mail!

It is clear from the above that there are two main motives for *holding* money (for remaining "liquid"): (1) for the convenience of ordinary *transactions* needed at each level of income, and (2) to fill a prudent *precautionary* need arising from the uncertainties of safety and return from other forms of wealth, and the uncertainties of timing of expense outpayments and receipt inpayments.

At the turn of the century Alfred Marshall of Cambridge University and Irving Fisher of Yale summarized the factors determining the amount of money emanded thus:

Transaction and Precautionary Demands: The higher our annual incomes, the more dollars of business we will want to transact; with various allowances for economies of scale, people hold M at any time about in proportion to their *income* rate per year or month. (This *transaction demand* for money will be shifted downward a little when the interest rates offered on good bonds, savings deposits, and other close money substitutes rise. At higher interest you will economize on your cash balance, making each dollar turn over more rapidly.)

People also hold M as a precautionary store of wealth, not wanting to put all their eggs in the basket of risky assets and wanting to be prepared for bargains or sudden expenses. This *precautionary* (or "asset") *demand* for money will be much affected by factors other than income: total wealth; level of sacrificed interest and profit yields; optimism, pessimism, and plain uncertainty about the future; expected changes in prices of goods and assets and expected changes in interest rates—all the speculative elements that any investments depend on.

The elements in the second paragraph of this summary are in Marshall and Fisher, but were not much emphasized until the 1930s, when Keynes and practical bankers noted that transaction demand could not account for massive changes in cash holdings. Keynes dealt with both types of asset demand as people's "liquidity preference." Keynesian liquidity preference will be encountered next in Chapter 18.

Another school of thought, both pre-1930 and much more recent, emphasizes the M-and-income link by using the concept of "velocity of circulation of money," and to this we now turn.

VELOCITY OF CIRCULATION OF MONEY

It is a historical fact that as dollar GNP has grown, so has M. With M today ten times as large as it was before World War II, dollar NNP is even more than ten times as large as its earlier figure. Nor is this merely history. If GNP grows from its 1974 level of almost 140 billion dollars to reach 280 billion dollars in ten years, the betting odds are that M will also be nearly double its present amount then—a fair bet even before we know whether changes in M will be the "cause" of changes in GNP or the "effect" of them.

Why should there be any connection? M is a stock magnitude, something you can measure at an instant of time like any other balance-sheet asset. GNP is a flow of dollar income *per year*, something that you can measure only from income statements that refer to the passage of time between two dates.

A new concept can be introduced to describe the Fisher-Marshall ratios between two such different magnitudes: it is called the "velocity of circulation of money" per year and is written as V.

Definition of velocity: The rate at which the stock of money is turning over per year to consummate income transactions is called the velocity of circulation of money (or more exactly, the *income velocity, V*).

If the stock of money is turning over very slowly, so that its rate of dollar income spending per year is low, V will be low. If people hold less money at each instant of time relative to the rate of NNP flow [(price of apples × apples) + (price of oranges × oranges) + . . .], then V will be high.

The size of V will tend to rise with interest rates. Also, V can change over time with changes in financial institutions, habits, attitudes, expectations, and relative distributions of M among different kinds of institutions and income classes; but these changes in V need not, however, be abrupt, volatile, or completely unpredictable.

In every case, this formal definition[9] of the velocity of circulation of money holds:

[9] More advanced discussions show that because GNE contains ($E - M$) net exports, it is a less appropriate numerator for the definition of V than $C + I + G + (M - E)$. But GNP will serve as a rough approximation.

$$V \equiv \frac{GNP}{M} \equiv \frac{p_1 q_1 + p_2 q_2 + \dots}{M} \equiv \frac{\text{sum } pq}{M} \equiv \frac{PQ}{M}$$

Here P stands for the average price level and goes up and down with an index of the price level, while Q stands for real (as distinct from current dollar) national product and has to be computed statistically by the previously mentioned process of "deflating" GNP with a price index.

Here is a helpful example. Table 15-1 shows that by late 1973 M_1 was about 26 billion dollars. GNP was then about 119 billion dollars per year. So 119 divided by 26 gives us an income velocity of about 4.5 per year. (This rough figure happens to be close to the U.S. figure of recent years, 4.9.) This expression means that each unit of money was used for GNP transactions 4 1/2 times a year; or putting this in an equivalent way, at any time during the year people were holding money that amounted to over 12 weeks' average income.[10]

THE QUANTITY EQUATION OF EXCHANGE: AN IDENTITY

After economists have invented the concept of velocity of circulation of money, they can rearrange its formal definition to get a new identity called the "quantity equation of exchange":

$$MV \equiv PQ$$

This comes merely from shifting M from the denominator of our last definition's right-hand side over the numerator of the other side. By definition of V, the left-hand side in this new equation is identically equal to GNP, the rate of current national income or product per year. But the right-hand side, by virtue of what we have just defined P and Q to be, also is definitionally the same thing as GNP.

EXAMPLE: If there were only a single good in the GNP, a billion baskets of bread selling at a price of $5 each, the

[10] In looking at the statements of particular banks, one does not know whether the "turnover" in chequable accounts is for GNP final transactions or for non-GNP transactions like transfers and intermediate goods. Such turnover figures tell us how often a dollar turns over in *all kinds* of transactions each year. They are much larger than income velocities. In 1963, current accounts in Canada turned over 68 times a year; savings accounts 1½ times. With its stock exchange, New York City turns its deposits over 205 times a year; but deposits in other U.S. cities turn over only 59 times.

NNP $\equiv PQ$ = 5 billion dollars per year; when there is more than one commodity, we sum all such $p \times q$ products; and if all the q's stayed unchanged and all their p's doubled, then the average price level as denoted by P would double, naturally giving us a 10- rather than 5-billion-dollar GNP.[11]

All the definitional equations have been written with the three-bar identity symbol rather than with the more common two-bar equality symbol. This is to drive home the fact that they are what logicians call a "tautology"—statements which by themselves tell us nothing about reality but which would hold true by definition even if Canada reverted to barter or if its M halved while its NNP grew tenfold. Although it is important to remember that the equation of exchange is such a tautology, *it is not legitimate to infer from this fact that it must thereby be useless.* It may, or may not, be a useful way of separating out for individual analysis the factors apt to lead to empirical relations which do best describe actual economic life. Subsequent chapters will show that careful description of income determination by $C + I + G$ schedules and how they are interrelated by changes in banking policy can also be expressed in terms of the magnitudes in the Equation of Exchange, and vice versa.

THE QUANTITY THEORY OF MONEY AND PRICES: A HYPOTHESIS

THE CRUDE QUANTITY THEORY   If 1970 M was four times 1939 M, then an adherent of what can be called the "crude quantity theory of money and prices" would have to predict that the 1970 price level P should be almost exactly four times 1939 P. The fact that prices only *doubled* in that period would be a refutation of this crude notion that the price level moves in direct proportion to the money supply.

Arithmetically, the crude Quantity Theory might be written $P = kM$, where k is a positive proportionality constant

that depends on units used; thus, if P and M are measured by index numbers which were 100 in the same base year, k could be replaced by 1.0 or omitted. Note that this is not intended to be an irrefutable definitional identity, but rather a useful empirical relationship about k's constancy.

The idea behind the crude Quantity Theory is simple. If the government effects a thousandfold increase in M, then one can predict that there will be a galloping inflation in which P rises a thousandfold. Or more cautiously, at least somewhere between five-hundredfold and two-thousandfold. Crude as this notion is, there is some usefulness to it. Thus when the head of the German central bank denied that its printing truckloads of currency had anything to do with the 1920-23 trillionfold increase in prices, his statement was nonsensical. If he had said, "I am just a civil servant, forced, by the clamor of the populace in a defeated nation with grave external and internal disorganization, to take part in an upward race between P and M"—if he had said this, we could feel sorry for him. But who can seriously deny the elementary theory that a vastly larger bidding of German marks for a limited supply of goods must have sent prices expressed in marks skyward?

Money differs basically from ordinary goods like wheat or steel. We want wheaten bread for its own sake, steel for hammers or knives. We want money *only for the work it does in buying us wheat or steel.* If in 1923, all German prices are a trillion times what they were in 1920, it is natural to want about a trillion times as much M as in 1920. Therein lies the valid case of the crude Quantity Theory. But we must be wary of extrapolating it to real-life cases where all P's have not changed in the same balanced proportions.

Rudimentary as it is, then, the crude Quantity Theory linking P directly to M is useful to describe periods of hyperinflation and various long-term trends in prices, such as those in Spain and Europe after New World gold was discovered.

Since galloping inflation can put an intolerable strain on a democratic society, it is well to preach the crude Quantity Theory in season and out of season — not because in its crudest form it is in season very often, but because it is so urgently needed in those disorganized times when its message is in season.

---

[11] Some find the following "explanation" of this necessary equality helpful. Every income transaction involves sale receipts equal to $p \times q$, which leads to the PQ totals on the right. But it is M that is used in such transactions. How much in a year? The stock M times its average velocity per year. Thus, value equals value, and the two sides must be the same.

A SOPHISTICATED QUANTITY THEORY

Few people still subscribe to the crude Quantity Theory. Yet we should not use its inadequacies to damn the whole idea that money can have important effects on macroeconomic magnitudes such as investment, employment, production, and prices.

The next few chapters will show how *monetary policy* does have an important influence on the *total of spending*—on the $C + I + G$ intersections of GNP. This analysis can be translated quite easily into the language of V and M, even though it was not fashionable to do so a couple of decades back. Since there has been something of a revival of interest in the Quantity Theory fostered in recent years by a number of competent economists, it is worth taking an eclectic approach here and reviewing the fundaments of a sophisticated Quantity Theory approach, leaving until later a more extensive reconciliation of the various approaches.

The proof of the pudding is in the eating, and the test of all theories is their correspondence with the facts. Fig. 15-3 shows that consumer prices and the supply of money have both generally grown, but by no means in perfect concordance.

Economists such as Chicago's Milton Friedman are not surprised to find M growing sixfold while P merely doubles; for they believe that only in time periods when real output remains roughly the same— say, at a high-employment level—can one expect M and P to be directly related. They expect M and GNP (or PQ) to be related. This belief is based upon the hypothesis that the velocity of circulation V can be predicted to be reasonably constant, or if not constant, at least subject to predictable changes.

While it is a fact that GNP has climbed somewhat faster than M since 1939, this rise in velocity has been a gradual one and perhaps one that might have been expected from the fact that 1939 was still a depressed year and still a time of very low interest rates and abnormally low V.

Historically, one observes that V has exhibited a downward trend since 1870, moving down somewhat as real income has grown. The short-run cyclical swings in V are quite the opposite: when production and real incomes have gone up, V has tended also to have a short-run rise; when output has fallen

in the short run, V has fallen too. During the recent decades of (*a*) creeping inflation, (*b*) high nominal interest rates, and (*c*) computers, credit cards, and better methods for scheduling inventories of money, V has been gradually rising.

A sophisticated quantity theorist cannot be accused of believing that V is a fundamental constant of nature. What he does believe is that controlling the behavior of M *will help much* to control GNP, for the reason that the resulting changes in V will either be so small or so predictable as to make one confident that dollar GNP will still move *in the same direction as* M. Qualitatively, this is in agreement with almost any modern theory of income determination, and the only possible argument concerns the confidence with which one can predict the quantitative potency of effects on GNP of changes in $M,$ in comparison with other stimuli, such as fiscal policy and external investment swings.[12]

So, from all of the points of view, the discussions in the ensuing chapters—how chartered banks can create demand-deposit M as the Bank of Canada authorities affect their reserve positions, how a central bank such as the Bank of Canada itself operates, how monetary policy fits with income determination and with stabilizing fiscal policies—are of tremendous importance. Chapter 18, in particular, deals further with the sophisticated quantity theory approach.

---

[12] It may be mentioned here that the *crude* Quantity Theory would be correct, if in the following rearrangement of the tautological equation of exchange $P \equiv (V/Q)M$, the expression in parentheses were a strict constant. Thus, if both V and Q changed little, or if their changes were always largely self-canceling, the crude theory would be correct. But once scholars agree that V may change appreciably when the economy goes from a 1929 high-interest prosperity to a 1939 low-interest depression, and that Q may fall from a full-employment 1929 level to a level that is far below full employment in some later year, they realize that a more sophisticated theory of money, production, interest rates, and prices must be studied. A rather crude form of rejection of the significance of M was provided by the Radcliffe Committee Report published in 1959 by the British government. After arguing (correctly) that PQ is affected by over-all "liquidity" and bears no *simple* proportionality to M, it incorrectly inferred that induced changes in V are as likely as not to offset fully any contrived changes in M. The presumption in *all* modern theories—Keynesian as well as pre-Keynesian!—is that a continued rise in M *will* definitely tend to expand PQ. Note the logical fallacy in Radcliffe's argument: "Money alone matters" is false; *ergo,* money doesn't matter."

FIG. 15-5. The central bank (the Bank of Canada) controls the M supply by fixing "reserves" total.

At left the central bank feeds the input of high-powered (reserves) money into the chartered banking system, regarded as a black box (to be examined in the next chapters). The chartered banks produce as amplified output on the right the public's supply of M. Hence, central responsibility for rate of growth of the money supply rests with government's central bank.

GOVERNMENTAL CONTROL OF THE SUPPLY OF MONEY

All schools of economics are today agreed that changes in the supply of money are important for macroeconomics. In earlier centuries, it was the happenstance of gold and silver mining discoveries that dictated the chaotic trend of the money supply. Today in all countries, that is a thing of the past.

As we shall see in the next few chapters, it is the government's own central bank—in Canada, the Bank of Canada, in the United States, the Federal Reserve System, abroad, the Bank of Japan, the Bank of England, the Bank of Italy, the Banque de France, the German Bundesbank—that determines the rate of growth of a nation's money supply. If it were merely a matter of paper currency, there being no other forms of money, we'd merely have to analyze how the government puts the printing press to work: to help pay for its expenditures or to lend out to private investors.

The next chapter will show that matters are a bit more complicated once we recognize the important role of the private commercial banks in providing the bank-deposit component of the money supply. Fig. 15-5 gives a simplified preview of what will be spelled out in Figs. 16-1 and 17-1: (*a*) how the government's central banks determine the supply of the "high-powered money that constitutes the reserves of the commercial banks"; and (*b*) how the *input* of these high-powered reserves into the "black-box" of the chartered banking system enables the chartered banks to produce as *amplified output* the community's supply of money (currency plus chequable deposits, namely M_1).

Hence, the modern mixed economy is no longer left at the mercy of the workings of the pump handle of investment as dependent on innovations, business confidence, and population growth. Modern government can modify, control, and offset the exogenous fluctuations in *II* and *CC* schedules by its control over the high-powered money reserves of the commercial banks and by control over its budget deficits and surpluses. The remaining chapters of Part Two show how all this works.

SUMMARY

A. PRICES AND THE MONEY SUPPLY

1 It is unrealistic to expect that expansions in investment and other spending will have effects solely on employment and output. Changes in price levels must be expected as well. The effects and causes of a general rise in prices and wages (i.e., inflation) and a general fall in prices (i.e., deflation) are vital.

2 Historically, prices have shown their greatest swings in times of war. But in this century the trend in prices seems to have been more of a one-way climb: the absence of a drop in prices after World War II is perhaps a sign that modern mixed economies are no longer likely to tolerate lengthy periods of unemployment, soft business conditions, and falling prices. Creeping "cost-push" inflation is a new disease distinguishable from conventional "demand-pull" inflation in which too much money spending (too much $C + I + G$ or, what is the same, too much MV) bids for the limited supply of goods and labor available at full employment and *pulls up* prices and wages.

3 Inflations and deflations are never of the balanced type in which all prices and wages are anticipated to move by the same percentage, with no one helped and no one hurt by the process. In the past, inflations have typically favored debtors, profit seekers, and risk-taking speculators. Unseen inflation has hurt creditors, fixed-income classes, pensioners, and conservative and timid investors. The old rather than the young are its prime victims.

4 Aside from redistributional effects of inflation out of a fixed level of production, mild inflations like those found throughout most of capitalism's history have been regarded as being a little more likely to keep employment high and business brisk than mild deflations do. But the cause of the inflation may make a difference, and the threat that a mild creep of prices could break into a trot or gallop shows that complacency about price rises could be harmful to those who cannot adjust.

If the processes were *foreseen* and steady, there would not be much difference among the three possible long-term patterns that various economists favor: (*a*) steady prices, with money and real wages rising with productivity; (*b*) gently rising prices, with money wages rising even faster than real wages and productivity; (*c*) slowly falling prices, with money wages constant and real wages rising as every consumer's dollar buys more and more goods—a pattern perhaps not feasible in rigid mixed economies. Without exchange, division of labor could not be highly developed. Simple barter is inefficient and tends to be superseded by the use of money. Commodity money is in turn superseded by paper money and bank money. Unlike other economic goods, money is valued because of social convention; *we value money indirectly for what it buys rather than for its direct utility.*

5 In addition to coins, currency, demand deposits and chequable personal savings deposits —whose sum is the money supply *M1*—there are also very important near-money or liquid-asset items: time or savings deposits (which pay interest and are *de facto* withdrawable at short notice, and which many economists include in a broad definition of money, M_2), "near-money" such as government bonds (which anyone can quickly liquidate into cash, at a price that depends on market forces at the time). However defined, *M* has increased mightily over the decades.

B. THE DEMAND FOR MONEY AND THE QUANTITY THEORY

6 The demand for money consists of a *transactions* demand primarily related to income, and a *precautionary* (or asset) demand much dependent on interest and profit rates, wealth, volatile expectations, risk aversion, and speculative price expectations. The sum of these two demands was called, by Keynes, "liquidity preference."

7 The (income) velocity of circulation of money is defined as the ratio of dollar GNP to M. While V is definitely not a constant, its movements are subject to some regularity and predictability; and from its *definition*

$$V \equiv \frac{\textbf{GNP}}{M} \equiv \frac{PQ}{M}$$
$$\textbf{MV} \equiv \textbf{PQ}$$

8 The crude *Quantity Theory* of money and prices regarded P as almost strictly proportional to M. Useful as this view is in hyperinflation and for certain long-term trends, few would today uphold it in this crude form. It is generally agreed that action by the government and banks to affect the supply of money, its availability to investor borrowers, and the interest cost of such borrowings can have important effects on the total of *consumption + investment + (net exports)* spending, and thus on prices and wage levels. So all schools can agree on the central importance of the next two chapters' analysis of just how the government through its central bank controls the input of "high-powered (reserves) money" that, after being fed into the amplifying black box of the commercial banking system, results in amplified outputs of the community's total supply of money, M. Chapter 18 resumes discussion of the sophisticated Quantity Theory.

CONCEPTS FOR REVIEW

fiat money	coin, token money, currency
sticky price levels	transactions demand
real rate of return	precautionary demand
inflation	liquidity preference
deflation and technological	demand versus time deposits
cost-price reduction	M_1, M_2, near-money
redistribution and employment	Quantity Equation of Exchange,
effects of price-level trends	$MV \equiv PQ$; V definition
hyperinflation; chronic and	Crude Quantity Theory,
creeping inflation	$P = kM$
barter, commodity M,	high-powered (reserves) money
metallic M, paper currency	"demand-pull" vs. "cost-push"
bank deposit M	
real versus money wage	

QUESTIONS FOR DISCUSSION

1. If sure of inflation ahead, what might you do to protect yourself? List some of the happenings that accompany galloping and mild inflation.
2. Explain what is meant by "near-money" and how it got its name.
3. If we printed and spent 10 billion dollars in new Bank of Canada notes, what do you think would happen to prices? Is there some truth, then, to the crude quantity theory? Differentiate between the crude and sophisticated quantity theorists in terms of who they regard $MV \equiv PQ$.
4. Show that the Marshall-Fisher-Keynes summary implies nonconstant V.

16
THE CHARTERED BANKS
AND DEPOSIT CREATION

"Is it deposited?" I asked in a hollow, vibrating voice.
"It is," said the accountant.
"Then I want to draw a cheque ..."

STEPHEN LEACOCK, My Financial Career

The importance of bank deposits as part of the community's money supply has been established. This chapter continues with two distinct topics. First, we examine briefly the important facts and functionings of the modern banking system, showing how the present-day commercial bank gradually began to keep only "fractional cash reserves" against its deposits. Second, we see just how the banking system "manufactures" banking deposits—the most important component of our money supply.

A. NATURE AND FUNCTIONING OF THE MODERN BANKING SYSTEM

THE PRESENT STATUS OF BANKING

Like most of the Western world, Canada has a *branch* banking system of large banks chartered by Parliament. (Since 1960, four new companies have gone through the process of applying to Parliament for Acts to become "chartered banks," and three have been successful.) They have among them 5,000 branches in Canada and 150 branches abroad, most of them in the West Indies.

This provides about one branch for every thousand families, a striking contrast to the United States where 13,000 independent *unit* banks, with their (relatively few) branches, provide one main office or branch for every three thousand U.S. families. The Canadian, British, and other banks are for all purposes under national government supervision, but about two-thirds the U.S. banks (the smaller banks) are for most purposes supervised by state governments. Canadians notice three results of their system in contrast to the American: (1) there are, obviously, many more offices giving full banking services; (2) the ten banks are more *concentrated*, offering almost identical services at almost identical prices, and

maintaining through their head offices personal contact with one another and with officers of the Bank of Canada; and (3) the rate of bank failure is very low.

A primary economic function of commercial banks is *to hold demand and personal savings deposits and honor cheques drawn upon them*—in short to provide the economy with the largest component of the money supply and the payments system itself.

A second important function is to lend money to merchants, homeowners, farmers, and industrialists.

Banks have a variety of competitors in the performance of these functions, such as trust and mortgage companies; all are able to make loans and to accept notice, or *savings*, deposits. In some countries, such as the United States, bank savings deposits cannot be withdrawn without notice, sometimes as long as 30 days. In Canada, the practice has been that personal savings deposits can be withdrawn immediately, upon presentation of a cheque. For all practical purposes, therefore, personal savings deposits function in the same way as *demand* deposits; both are chequable and hence "spendable," as explained in Chapter 15 footnote 6. Further, trust and mortgage company savings deposits, in Canada, are becoming increasingly chequable.

The chartered banks are by no means, therefore, our only "banking institutions." However, they do hold the vast bulk of both demand and personal savings deposits in Canada, thus providing most of the "bank money" that can be conveniently used as a medium of exchange. Therein lies their primary economic importance.

The second and related function of banks is their credit function: they help manufacture short-term credit for businesses and families; they make long-term mortgage loans; and (despite an older view that banks should only lend seasonally) they increasingly provide intermediate-term credit through "term loans" of more than a year's duration.

CANADA'S CENTRAL BANK: THE BANK OF CANADA

Unlike Britain whose Bank of England was founded in 1694, and the United States where the Federal Reserve system was set up in 1913, Canada got along until the mid-1930s without a central bank. The Department of Finance acted rather like a central bank in administering a series of "Finance Acts." These empowered the Department to buy government bonds from the banks with new Dominion Notes, under certain circumstances: in other words, to expand the money supply. This power was widely used in World War I.

But by 1934 the Great Depression's unemployment had convinced many persons that a discretionary (nonautomatic) mechanism was needed, to prevent the *contraction of bank deposits during deflationary periods*. The public was not sure what a central bank could do against a depression; many radicals overrated its potentialities to "reflate" the country out of low prices and incomes; but everyone felt that the near-automatic working of the banking system was not good enough.[1]

Following the advice of a Royal Commission under Lord Macmillan, the government set up a "private" central bank in 1934, with a government-appointed Governor and Deputy. This was partly a concession to the principle of private enterprise, but also partly a realization of the theory that in "preserving orderly conditions" in the money markets, and in attempting to control P by controlling M, central banks ought to have some independence from political pressures in Ottawa. This theory was not tested until the 1950s, for in 1938 the Bank of Canada was made a Crown corporation.

The structure of the Bank of Canada today is simple. At the top are twelve Directors, the Deputy Minister of Finance (without a vote), the Deputy Governor, and the Governor. The last two, who are appointed by the Directors, actually run the Bank, and hold office for eight years at a time.[2] The Board of Directors meets only eight times a year; but an Executive Council (the Governor, Deputy, Deputy Minister of Finance, and only one Director) acts for the Board and has all its powers. Even a superficial examination of the Bank's constitution, therefore, suggests that the Governor with his officers and the government will have to make most decisions without the help of the scattered Board members.

The Bank has a staff of about 800, of whom over 200 are in "regional agencies" in the main cities. The rest are in Ottawa, many of them performing fiscal and financial functions for the government and managing exchange-rate operations. But in the following paragraphs, we refer only to those functions which are *essentially* those of a central bank: not only to coordinate and control the chartered banks, but also to help *regulate the nation's money supply and credit conditions*.

To whom is the Bank responsible? In the long run, it must be the government: the government has a vote in the appointment of the Governor and Deputy Governor; the Deputy Minister of Finance sits (without vote) on both the Board and the Executive; and the Cabinet can veto any decision of the Executive. But most of these powers take time to exercise, and the veto power must obviously be used in moderation if the Governor and Executive Committee

---

[1] However, unlike critics in other countries, Canadian advocates of a central bank could not say that Canada was, in the 1920s, tied to the international gold standard. In some countries, the outflow of gold to other countries meant that the losing economies would have to reduce their money supply in an even greater proportion. The Finance Acts, however, allowed the Department of Finance to maintain the supply of Dominion Notes (the reserves for the structure of bank money) and even to expand this supply, in periods when gold was flowing out of the country. A contraction of the money supply did take place, but not because there was no official mechanism to allow the banks to maintain their customers' deposits.

[2] The first Governor, Graham Towers, had two terms. J. M. Coyne had one. The next Governor, Louis Rasminsky, held office from 1961 to 1973, when G. K. Bouey was appointed.

are to have any incentive to take independent responsibility for actions within their jurisdiction.

Most of Graham Towers' term was during the Depression and the war when there was obviously no scope for independent Bank behavior. But during James Coyne's term it was clear that the government did not disapprove of the measure of independence revealed by Bank actions, until a fairly direct contradiction of aims and of means was revealed in 1959 and 1960. An unpleasant public dispute then arose, and Mr. Coyne was replaced eventually by Louis Rasminsky. The latter, on assuming office in 1961, said:

I do not suggest a precise formula but have in mind two main principles to be established: (1) in the ordinary course of events, the Bank has the responsibility for monetary policy; and (2) if the Government disapproves of the monetary policy being carried out by the Bank, it has the right and the responsibility to direct the Bank as to the policy which the Bank is to carry out.

There the matter rests. No open disagreement between the Bank and the government has since been mentioned. Being in the last analysis subservient to the Cabinet, the Bank now takes its place alongside the formerly-independent Bank of England, which has a right to protest publicly but must coordinate its policies with those of the government. The present status of the Federal Reserve Board in the United States is less clear. Not only has it claimed stronger allegiance to Congress than to the Executive (president), but in the absence of clear directives from Congress, it has acted, occasionally, very much like an independent arm of government. Since the middle 1950s, however, cooperation has prevailed with the executive branch (the Treasury, White House, and Council of Economic Advisers) and conflict has been minor. With the American system of checks and balances among branches of government, such differences are perhaps inevitable and healthy; but it is widely felt today that Canada's and Britain's parliamentary system cannot tolerate a central bank if it is more than a "semi-detached" wing of the national government.

BANKING AS A BUSINESS

Banking is a business much like any other business. The chartered bank is a relatively simple business

concern. A bank provides certain services for its customers (depositors and borrowers) and in return receives payments from them in one form or another. It tries to earn a profit for its stock owners.

A chartered bank's balance sheet shows certain assets, certain liabilities, and certain capital ownership. Except for minor rearrangements, the bank's published balance sheet looks, on the whole, much like the balance sheet of any other business, and rather simpler than most.

A special feature of the balance sheet shown in Table 16-1 is that such a large portion of the banks' liabilities are subject to chequing: all demand and many personal savings deposits can be withdrawn "on demand." It is as well to repeat: Canadian banks *may* require warning (notice) before depositors withdraw savings. They rarely do. And their vital re-

Consolidated Balance Sheet of ALL CHARTERED BANKS, JANUARY 1974 (billions of dollars)			
ASSETS		**LIABILITIES**	
Reserves (cash and central bank deposits	3.0	Chequable deposits (demand and savings)	16.8
Government of Canada bills and bonds	7.2	All other deposits (term, etc.)	29.0
Other liquid assets	1.1		—
Sub-total: Canadian Liquid Assets	11.3	Sub-total: Canadian Deposit Liabilities	45.8
Loans	32.3	Government of Canada Deposits	2.2
Mortgages and Securities	6.9	Shareholders' Equity and other liabilities	2.1
Sub-total: Less Liquid Assets	39.2		
Foreign Currency Assets	—1.4		
Other	1.0		—
Total: Chartered Bank Assets	50.0	Total: Chartered Bank Liabilities	50.0

TABLE 16-1. Chequable deposits are key bank liabilities. Reserves and demand deposits will receive most attention in our analysis. Reserves and sub-totals are defined to meet legal requirements. Figures are rounded.
(Source: **Drawn from weekly and monthly statistics for early January, 1973,** in *Bank of Canada Review.*)

serves are, as we shall see, created and controlled by the central bank.

This fact is intriguing to the economist because he chooses to call such demand liabilities money; but to the banker it is a familiar condition which has long since been taken for granted. He knows well that, although it would be possible for every depositor suddenly to decide to withdraw all his money from the bank on the same day, the probability of this is quite remote. Each day, as some people withdraw their money, others normally make deposits tending to cancel the withdrawals. In a growing community new deposits more than offset the withdrawals from an average bank.

This, however, need not be strictly true at any one moment, in any one day, or in any one week. By chance alone the amount of withdrawals might exceed deposits for some period of time—just as a coin may land with heads rather than tails turned up for a consecutive number of tosses. For this reason, the banker would voluntarily keep a little cash handy in his vaults and perhaps a "reserve deposit" at the central bank. *Normally, the cash in the bank's own vaults and its deposits at the central bank*—as far as prudent protection from withdrawals is concerned and disregarding involuntary *legal requirements* to be mentioned soon—*need be only a small fraction of the bank's total deposits*; and the same mathematical law of large numbers that makes life insurance possible assures the banker that the larger his bank and more numerous his independent depositors, the smaller this fraction need be.

HOW BANKS DEVELOPED OUT OF GOLDSMITH ESTABLISHMENTS

All these facts are so much taken for granted by every modern banker that he is hardly aware of them; but it was not always so. According to superficial but useful history, commercial banking began with the ancient goldsmiths who developed the practice of storing people's gold and valuables for safekeeping. At first such establishments were simply like parcel checkrooms or warehouses. The depositor left his gold for safekeeping, was given a receipt, later presented that receipt, paid a small fee for safekeeping, and got back his gold.

Quite obviously, however, money is wanted only for what it will buy, not for its own sake. Money has an anonymous quality, so that one dollar is just as good as another, and one piece of pure gold as good as another. The goldsmiths soon found it more convenient *not* to have to tag the gold belonging to any one individual so as to be able to give to him upon request exactly the same piece of gold that he had left. Instead, the customer was quite willing to accept a receipt for an amount of gold or money *of a given value*, even though it was not the identical particle of matter that he actually left.

This "anonymity" is important. Therein lies a significant difference between today's bank and a checkroom or warehouse. If I check my bag at the airport and later see someone walking down the street with that same suitcase, I call my lawyer and sue the Department of Transport. If I mark my initials on a $10 bill, deposit it in my bank account, and later notice it in the hands of a stranger. I have no grievance against the bank management. They have only agreed to pay me on demand *any* $10 of legal tender.

But let us return to the goldsmith establishments, which are supposed to typify the first embryonic chartered banks. What would balance sheets of a typical establishment look like? Perhaps like Table 16-2.

We assume the company has long since dropped its activities as a smith and is principally occupied with storing people's money for safekeeping. Over past time, 1 million dollars has been deposited in its vaults, and this whole sum it holds as a cash asset. To balance this asset, there is a current deposit liability of the same amount. Actually, such a business need have no other assets (except the negligible value of its office space and vaults). But its owners could have —on the side, so to speak—subscribed $50,000 of capital to be lent out at interest or to buy securities such as stocks or bonds. On the asset side this amount is shown under the heading Loans and Investments; this is balanced on the right-hand side by a similar sum in the Capital and Retained Earnings account.

At this primitive stage, the bank would be of no particular interest to the economist. These investment and capital items have nothing to do with the bank's deposits; if all the bank's loans and investments should go sour and become worthless, the loss would fall completely on the stockholders who

BALANCE SHEET OF EARLY BANK			
ASSETS		**LIABILITIES AND NET WORTH**	
Cash	$1,000,000	Capital and retained	
Loans and		earnings	$ 50,000
investments	50,000	Demand deposit	
		liability	1,000,000
Total	$1,050,000	Total	$1,050,000

TABLE 16-2. The first goldsmith bank held 100 per cent cash against its demand deposits. Only 1-to-1 creation of deposits out of new reserves was possible at this primitive stage. There was nothing "high powered" about reserves in those days.

have agreed to take that risk in the hope of making a profit. Every depositor could still be paid off in full *out of the 100 per cent cash reserves* held by the bank. The bank would still cover its overhead and clerical expenses by making its customers pay storage charges. These would presumably vary with the length of time the customer left his money for safekeeping, the average amount of his money that required safekeeping, and the number of times the turnover of his account made a clerk wait on him and keep records.

Economists could ignore such a bank's operations. The bank money[3]—the demand deposits created jointly by the bank's willingness to accept a demand obligation and the customer's willingness to hold a deposit—would *just offset* the amount of ordinary money (currency or coin) placed in the bank's safe and withdrawn from active circulation. The process would be of no more interest than if the public decided to convert some dollar bills into an equivalent amount of dimes. One might then say that the banking system has a *neutral* effect on spending and prices—not adding or subtracting from *total M* or its velocity.

MODERN FRACTIONAL RESERVE BANKING

Let us return to our early goldsmith-banker to see how modern banks gradually evolved. If he were an

[3] The economist would consider the demand deposit as money as soon as the custom grew up for depositors to pay for the goods they bought by giving the storekeeper a little note to the bank saying, "Mr. Goldsmith, pay to the order of T. Eaton Co. $2.99, (signed) John Q. Doe." In other words, as soon as the use and acceptability of cheques became customary.

alert fellow, he would soon notice that, although his deposits are payable on demand, they are not all withdrawn together. He would soon learn that, although 100 per cent reserves are necessary if the bank is to be liquidated and all depositors are to be paid off in full, such reserves are not at all necessary if his bank is a "going concern." New deposits tend to balance withdrawals. Only a little till money, perhaps less than 2 per cent, normally seems needed in the form of vault cash.[4]

At first he probably thought this discovery too good to be true. Then perhaps he recalled the story of a rival bank whose dishonest clerk ran off with 95 per cent of its cash reserve—which was never discovered for 12 years. No one ever had occasion to go to the back rooms of the vault because all withdrawals were financed by recently deposited money held in the front vaults.

We can imagine our intelligent banker—at first cautiously—beginning to acquire bonds and other earning assets with some of the cash entrusted to his care. Everything works out all right: depositors are still paid off on demand, and the bank has made some extra earnings. Gradually, the banker no longer feels it necessary to conceal from his depositors what he is doing. If a depositor complains, the banker retorts, "Your money is safe. If you don't like my way of doing business, you are at liberty to withdraw your funds. Besides, haven't you noticed that the new method of fractional cash reserves has enabled me to *lower my service charges to you?* Also, it has enabled me to give a helping hand to our local businessmen who need more capital to buy new tools, buildings, and inventories. Such capital formation benefits consumers because they get better goods for lower prices. It also creates jobs for workers."

Little wonder, therefore, that banks should want to maximize their profits by putting most of the money deposited with them in earning assets and

[4] If the bank could pay off its depositors with one of its own cheques (or as in former times with one of its paper bank notes), it might not have to keep any till money at all. By judiciously limiting the rate at which it was making loans and investments, the bank could ensure that the cheques it received from other banks plus cash deposited were just matched by its outpayments. An occasional temporary outward drain of funds could be met by permitting the bank to pay by cheque what it owed to other banks for the few hours or days until some part of its asset portfolio could be liquidated or until it contracted its operations so as to get a surplus of inpayments over outpayments.

keeping only fractional cash reserves against deposits.

Indeed, as long as business confidence remains high and bank managers are judicious in their choice of loans and investments, there is no reason why the bank should keep much more than 2 per cent cash reserves against deposits.

DIVERSIFICATION AND LIQUIDITY OF EARNING INVESTMENTS   But what if the banker makes a mistake in his investments? Since nobody's judgment is perfect and all investments involve some element of speculative risk, this is certainly a possibility to reckon with. To lessen the chance of extreme losses, the banker can try to *diversify* his investments, not putting all his eggs in one basket. Besides, a conservative bank will have a considerable amount of capital put up by the stockholders. For example, capital stock may have been issued equal to 10 per cent of demand deposits. Then, even if all the bank's assets are in earning investments rather than in nonearning cash, depositors are protected against all capital losses that do not exceed 10 per cent of the bank's investment portfolio. Ordinarily, this will be sufficient, as long as it keeps to high-grade bonds, government-insured mortgages, and conservative business loans.

There is one last requirement the bank must meet if we are to give it an A+. The management must watch the general trend in the size of its deposits to make sure that its locality is not becoming a "ghost town" and that it is not losing deposits steadily over time. Were that the case, the bank's investment portfolio would have to be arranged to hold securities and loans that could be gradually liquidated and converted into cash to meet depositors' withdrawals. (Or, it might establish a branch in the town where deposits are moving.)

SECONDARY RESERVES   Even if the bank is not a declining business, prudent managers must still protect themselves against a temporary surge of withdrawals. To hold cash against such a contingency would be costly, since cash earns no yield. They will usually decide, therefore, to hold in their portfolios as "secondary reserves" some "liquid" securities that always have a ready market and can be easily sold without much loss before maturity.

Short-term government bonds serve this purpose admirably. Called "bills," "notes," or "certificates," they fluctuate little in value. Many can be liquidated simply by not buying new ones as the old ones come due every 90 days or 12 months. Even long-term government bonds, with 30 years of life before they mature, provide liquidity in the sense that in normal times they can always be transferred[5] to some other buyer at some quoted market price—albeit a varying price.

The important thing for liquidity is not the *date of maturity* of the bond or loan, but rather how "shiftable" it is to some other investment institution. A 90-day loan to a local merchant, which is nonshiftable, is in this sense less liquid than a 90-year gilt-edge bond traded on a securities exchange.

LEGAL RESERVE REQUIREMENTS

The above precepts of sound banking practice are quite simple and understandable. They are a little harder to carry out in practice than to state in principle; but the same is true of most prescriptions for wise living.

CASH RESERVES   If we compare a "going and growing" bank with any corporation, the surprising thing is not how little cash reserves the banks keep, but that they keep any at all (in excess of minimal till-money requirements). *As long as financial skies are sunny, the same profit-maximizing logic that compels the abandonment of a system of 100 per cent reserves argues in favor of negligible reserves!*

Yet, if we turn to the facts, we find that a prudent modern bank is expected—and required by law!—to keep a substantial portion of its assets in nonearning cash. About six per cent of all Canadian deposits must be kept as "cash reserves." Roughly two-thirds of these reserves are kept on deposit at the Bank of Canada, the other one-third in notes and coins.

Actually there are two cash reserve percentages: 12 per cent of demand deposits and 4 per cent of notice (savings) deposits. The *weighted* average of these two is about the 6 per cent given in the text above. Prior to 1967, one cash ratio, 8 per cent, applied to both demand and savings deposits. For simplicity, the following pages are based on the

---

[5] There is a saying, "You can sell governments bonds even on Sunday."

assumption of the continuation of this single 8 per cent cash ratio, which is half-way between the two legal figures. (United States' ratios are 16 1/2 per cent (in large cities) and 12 per cent (elsewhere) against demand deposits, and 6 per cent against time deposits (everywhere).)

It must be emphasized that these *cash ratios are required of chartered banks in order to control their behavior.* The many (though unimportant) American banks that are *not* members of the Federal Reserve system do not voluntarily keep such large amounts of nonearning cash as a precaution against withdrawals as the members are obliged to keep. The recent Report of Canada's Royal Commission on Banking and Finance (The Porter Report) showed that trust companies, many of which have deposit liabilities to customers that are chequable like the chartered banks' savings deposit accounts, maintain lower cash reserve ratios against deposits. Indeed many experts agree with the Porter Commission's recommendation that *all* institutions in competition with the banks for this kind of time-deposit business should be subject to similar cash-reserve ratios.

Other experts, and the banks themselves, argue that the legal ratios are too high. One line of argument is that, in Canada, the chartered banks are so few that a large proportion of the withdrawals from any one bank will very soon be redeposited *in the same bank* by other customers. This claim, of course, makes sense for the three largest banks—Royal, Montreal, and Commerce—but not for the other six smaller banks. A simpler argument is merely that money required as legal reserves doesn't earn the bank that owns it one red cent. Bankers think wistfully of the interest earnings they are missing:

Twelve per cent of our demand deposits is more than is needed for safety. After all, our withdrawals never bunch up much; the spreading of our customers across the country, in many industries and kinds of business activity, and the laws of probability take care of that. Besides, if we ever need more, we could sell off some government bonds or bills, or turn to the Bank of Canada or to a stronger chartered bank for help. Probably 5 per cent is all that prudence requires with so many ways out of temporary trouble.

There is much in what they say. American ratios have come down with the years, and since 1967 Canadian ratios have again been lowered a few points. One of their arguments doesn't hold much water though: spreading risks of heavy unexpected withdrawals across the country means that if one bank should suffer a "run on the bank," the others would be doing so too, for they frequently have branches in the same place.

But all this controversy is not very serious anyway. The banks know, and the Porter Commission's recent discussion shows, that the main purpose of legal cash ratios is *not* to make deposits safe and liquid, payable on demand. What is it, then?

The vital function of any legal reserve requirement is to enable the authorities in the Bank of Canada to be able to control the amounts of deposits—or bank money—that the chartered banks can create. By imposing fixed legal reserve requirements, Ottawa can limit the growth of bank deposits to its desired target.

SECONDARY RESERVES   Further indication that the purpose of legal reserves is to provide a keyboard in each bank on which the monetary authorities can play is given by the Canadian requirement that the chartered banks keep an *additional* percentage of their reserves against deposits, chiefly in the form of interest-earning assets. Chief among these is the 90-day Treasury Bill, but the banks may also count as part of this "secondary reserve" day-to-day loans to money-market dealers and additional cash. By setting up a total requirement of, 8 per cent cash and, say, 7 per cent in other liquid assets, or 15 per cent altogether (the rates assumed in our examples), the Bank of Canada is enabled to affect the makeup of the whole portfolio of earning assets held by the chartered banks (as in Table 16-1). And controlling the assets the banks may acquire means controlling their lending operations. To repeat, the main aim of setting up a legal secondary-reserve requirement is not to protect customers by making sure the banks hold a safe quantity of reserves. It is to force the banks to hold things (cash and treasury bills), the value or supply of which Ottawa can change.

Just how all this works, we shall soon learn.

THE GOVERNMENT STANDS BEHIND THE BANKS

Banks are much safer now than they were in the nineteenth century. If this safety doesn't stem from legal cash reserves, to what is it due?

Some Canadians will claim that Canadian bankers are the answer. The overwhelming number of bankers with Scottish names has given the public the idea that the Canadian branch system was brought here from Scotland, and is based on different principles than the failure-rife American system. But economic historians, beginning with the work of Adam Shortt of Queen's, have shown this is simply not true. The early Canadian banks picked up their charters (organization charts, in fact) from predecessors in New York State which in turn traced their ancestry to systems of banking pioneered in the early days of the United States. The early Scottish-Canadian bankers learned their banking arts in Canada. The branch system was popular with American bankers, but was prevented by state legislatures, largely for reasons irrelevant to banking theory. Canadian bankers (as opposed to their American colleagues) did not until recently make loans on uninsured mortgages, or loans depending heavily on collateral such as cars and other equipment; these were forbidden by Canadian banking law. No doubt there are national banking types: British, Swiss, and Chinese bankers all work in their distinctive ways. But differences between their opportunities, national economies, and banking laws are much better explanations of their different systems than are the men themselves.

Indeed, for many decades the small Canadian banks did have a poor nineteenth-century record, and many of their customers lost their deposits. The happier record of the twentieth century has two basic explanations. One of these we have already mentioned. The branch system means that risks of sudden withdrawal in one area, and the losses from them, are balanced by events in other areas.

Also, being large, they have more experienced managers and supervisors, who examine and approve the larger or riskier loan applications. Finally, being large, they are better able to prevent and absorb the occasional embezzlements that might shake small banks to their foundations.[6]

1. *Regulation of bank formation.* Since Confederation, Ottawa has had complete control over money and banking. Promoters wishing to start banks receive charters from Parliament, after their applications have been scrutinized by the Treasury Board (a committee of the Cabinet) and by Standing Committees of the House of Commons and of the Senate. These charters are granted under the Bank Act, a unique piece of legislation that must be reviewed, before its renewal, every ten years. All bank charters expire every ten years, and are renewed, phoenixlike, with, and on the terms of, every new Bank Act. The 1967 Bank Act aimed to keep control of banks among Canadian residents; but this revision has more to do with Canadian attitudes to foreign ownership than with the conduct of banking.

2. *Bank Regulation.* The Act, added to over the years, states what banks may and may not do. Until recently, it prohibited lending at rates above 6 per cent, thus confining the banks to dealing with customers whose credit was very good. But this upper limit has now been swept away. The Act also, over the decades, forced the bank to stick to "commercial banking"; that is, to the making of loans that make possible commercial transactions that promise to lead to the quick repayment of the loan. With several exceptions, it forbade the making of mortgage loans, loans against chattels, or for the acquisition of equipment.

These restrictions are now of historical importance, explaining the present characteristics of the chartered banks and their managers. Since 1966-1967, there has been almost no legal restriction on the type or term of a bank loan, or on the rate of interest that might be charged. Thus, in their *assets* (loans), the chartered banks are today in possession of the same freedom that they have long had in the creation of *liabilities*: they can invent new kinds of deposit accounts, or issue new kinds of cheques.

It follows that, while our chartered banks are, as we shall see, restrained or encouraged in their lending activities by the Bank of Canada, they are today relatively free to compete, to offer services, and to levy charges, as they wish.

---

[6] The last failure when customers lost some of their deposits was that of the Home Bank in 1923. On other occasions, before and since then, banks experiencing losses have been aided, by merger or otherwise by the stronger banks. U.S. banks frequently failed until the 1930s: 659 in prosperous 1929 alone! But the power of each of the relatively large Canadian banks to spread its risks and losses over large reserves is now duplicated by the insurance of most American depositors with the Federal Deposit Insurance Corporation (FDIC), which fully covers each deposit up to $10,000. In 1967 the Canadian Deposit Insurance Corporation was created to provide a similar service for Canadian banks *and* near-banks.

Readers should not assume that the many small U.S. banks are hopelessly vulnerable to these dangers. In addition to insuring their depositors against losses, privately or through the large FDIC, the U.S. federal government and many states have bank inspectors and auditors who guard against unskilled or dishonest accounting and lending practices.

3. *Formation of the Bank of Canada.* The third great step forward was the establishment of a central bank. In emergencies it is required to stand like a Rock of Gibraltar, ready not only to use the full monetary powers of the government to stem collapse of the banking system, but also to help particular banks whose weakening threatens the deposits of its customers. It can then truly act as a "lender of last resort." But in normal times, it controls money supply and credit conditions, and acts as a final lender or bankers' bank only as part of its general monetary role.

In these ways the government stands behind the supply of credit created by the banks. The fewness and largeness of Canada's ten banks does not call for anything more. If protection of depositors were the only problem, the banks could probably get along pretty well with no governmental supervision at all. As with legal reserve ratios, so with special government banking functions: their purpose is to provide a set of tools by which Ottawa can protect and control the money supply and credit conditions. We shall see in later chapters how this protection and control lead to stable prices and full employment.

B. THE CREATION OF BANK DEPOSITS

CAN BANKS REALLY CREATE MONEY?

We now turn to one of the most interesting aspects of money and credit, the process called "multiple expansion of bank deposits." Most people have heard that in some mysterious manner banks can create money out of thin air, but few really understand how the process works. Few understand that all our money arises out of debt and IOU operations.

Actually, there is nothing magical or incomprehensible about the creation of bank deposits. At every step of the way, one can follow what is happening to the banks' accounts. The true explanation of deposit creation is simple. What is hard to grasp is that false explanations still circulate.

According to these false explanations, the managers of an ordinary bank are able, by some use of their fountain pens, to lend several dollars for each dollar deposited with them. No wonder practical bankers see red when such power is attributed to them. They only wish they could do so. As every banker knows, he cannot invest money that he does not have; and money that he invests in buying a security or making a loan soon leaves his bank.

Bankers, therefore, often go to the opposite extreme. They sometimes argue that the banking system cannot (and does not) create money. "After all," they say, "we can invest only what is left with us. We don't create anything. We only put the community's savings to work." Bankers who argue in this way are quite wrong. They have become enmeshed in our

friend the fallacy of composition: what is true for each is not thereby true for all.

The banking system as a whole can do what a single bank cannot do: it *can* expand its loans and investments many times the new reserves of cash created for it, even though each small bank is lending out only a fraction of its deposits.

Our answer, then, to the basic question is in the affirmative: Yes, the banking system and the public do, between them, create about $12.50 of bank deposits for each new dollar of reserves that is created for the banks. Let us see how.

Figure 16-1 gives a preview of the process. The black box represents the banking system as a whole: Bank 1, which receives the initial new deposit, is at top; Bank 2, 3, . . . , and all other banks (not shown) are listed below. We shall study how $1 of new reserves, deposited at the left as input into the box, produces $12.50 of total deposit money, shown at the right. But Bank 1 cannot do this in one single step; as the black arrows between the banks show, all banks get involved in the lengthy secondary chain of money creation. Though the chain has many links, each is a dwindling fraction and the whole effect does add up to the 12.5:1 total.

HOW DEPOSITS ARE CREATED: THE FIRST-BANK STAGE

We begin with a brand-new input of $1,000 high-powered (reserves) money brought to a bank. Where

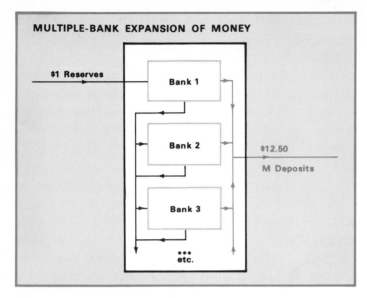

MULTIPLE-BANK EXPANSION OF MONEY

$1 Reserves

Bank 1

Bank 2

$12.50

M Deposits

Bank 3

•••
etc.

FIG. 16-1. All banks together do what one can't do alone!

For each dollar of new reserves deposited at left into a bank, the system as a whole creates at right about $12.50 of cheque money. The black arrows in the box show that Bank I cannot do it alone. As we'll see, second, third, and other banks will get their share of the expansion.

it came from is not important. It could have come from someone's having deposited the proceeds received from his selling a bond to the Bank of Canada (which may have paid for it by printing off twenty 50-dollar bills). We shall see that *in the end* the banking system is going to manufacture $12,500 of new demand deposits out of this, thus taking in $1,000 of one kind of *M* (currency) and converting it into $12,500 of another kind of *M* (chequable)—for a net gain of $11,500!

FIRST BANK STAGE Now if banks were to keep 100 percent cash-reserve balances, like the old goldsmiths, they could not create any extra money out of a new deposit of $1,000 left with them. The depositor's $1,000 chequing deposit would then just match the $1,000 of reserves.

The change in the bank's balance sheet, as far as the new demand deposit is concerned, would be as shown in Table 16-3(a).[7]

The bank has not created this deposit *alone*. The customer had to be willing to make the deposit. Once he took the initiative, the bank was also willing to accept his chequing account. Together the bank and the public "created" $1,000 of bank money, or deposit. But there is yet no multiple expansion, or 12.5 for 1,

[7] Important note: When bankers refer to their loans and investments as "investments" they mean their holdings of securities. They do not mean what we mean by *I* in *C + I + G*, namely, net capital formation for the community.

ORIGINAL BANK IN INITIAL POSITION			
ASSETS		**LIABILITIES**	
Reserves	+$1,000	Deposits	+$1,000
Total	+$1,000	Total	+$1,000

TABLE 16-3(a). Multiple-bank deposit creation is a story with many successive stages: 1st, newly created reserves get deposited in original first-generation bank.
We begin the process of money expansion by having the central bank—the Bank of Canada—provide some new high-powered reserves that constitute the initial deposit.

or anything else. So long as the banks keep 100 per cent reserves, the growth of bank *M* is just equal to the growth of new reserves created by the Bank of Canada.

Suppose, now, that the bank does not have to keep 100 per cent reserves. Suppose that the law requires it to keep only 8 per cent legal reserves. (Remember that the actual legal cash reserves in Canada are 12 and 4 per cent against demand and notice deposits, respectively. In the discussion it is assumed that these two types of deposits are equal, so that the average rate is 8 per cent or about one-twelfth. Of course, a bank may always keep larger reserves if it wishes to; but if there are many outstanding alternatives such as relatively safe, interest-yielding govern-

IMPOSSIBLE SITUATION FOR SINGLE SMALL BANK			
ASSETS		**LIABILITIES**	
Reserves	+$1,000	Deposits	+$12,500
Loans and investments	+11,500		
Total	$12,500	Total	$12,500

TABLE 16-3(b)
2nd, Bank can't lend out eleven times its new deposit . . .

ORIGINAL BANK IN FINAL POSITION			
ASSETS		**LIABILITIES**	
Reserves	+$ 80	Deposits	+$1,000
Loans and investments	+$ 920		
Total	+$1,000	Total	+$1,000

TABLE 16-3(c)
only eleven-twelfths of its deposit.

ment bonds or numerous profitable lending opportunities, the bank will not find it profitable to keep much more reserves than the law requires.)

What can the bank now do? Can it expand its loans and investments by $11,500 so that the change in its balance sheet looks as shown in Table 16-3(*b*). The answer is definitely, *No*. Why not? Total assets equal total liabilities. Cash reserves meet the legal requirement of being 8 per cent of total deposits.

True enough. But how did the bank pay for the investments or earning assets that it bought? Like everyone else, it had to write out a cheque to the person who sold the bond or signed the promissory note. If all such people would promise not to cash the bank's cheque—or what is the same thing, to hold all such money frozen on deposit in the bank—then, of course, the bank could buy all it wanted to without losing any cash.

But, in fact, no one will borrow money at 10 or 12 percent interest just to hold it all in the bank. The borrower spends the money on labor, on materials, or perhaps on an automobile. The money will *very soon*,[8] therefore, have to be paid out of the bank. And if—as is likely—the bank is but one of several banks serving that city, county, province, and country, only a fraction of the sums withdrawn will ever come back to the original bank in another customer's deposit.

This loss of cash by a bank expanding its investments is even more clearly seen if the bank buys

[8] If the bank made loans of $920 to its own customers, and they kept them on deposit, then for a brief period it would have deposits of $1,920. But as its borrowers spent their money, and unless the people who got that money were customers who put the money back on deposit in this original bank, it would soon find itself forced by the cash "drain" to other banks, toward the position of Table 16-3(*c*).

a bond rather than making a local loan. When my bank buys a government bond, what are the chances that the person who sells the bond will happen to have an account with it? The likelihood is as low as 1 in 9. Probably he lives in Montreal, or Vancouver, and deals with a rival bank. So my bank knows it will soon have to pay out *all* the money it placed in bonds. A bank cannot "eat its cake and have it, too." The bank cannot buy a bond and expect to keep its cash at the same time. Table 16-3(*b*) gives, therefore a completely false picture of what an individual bank can do.

Does this mean that Table 16-3(*a*) tells the end of the story? Must the bank, therefore, behave like the 100 per cent reserve goldsmith bankers?

Of course not. Although the bank cannot jack its deposits up to twelve and one half times its cash reserve, it certainly can *reduce its cash down* to 8 per cent of its deposits. Nothing is easier. For, as we have seen, all it has to do is acquire $920 worth of earning assets—bonds or loans. In a day or so it will lose practically all this·cash as its cheques come back for·payment. Now its balance sheet will be as shown in Table 16-3(*c*).

As far as this first bank is concerned, we are through. Its legal reserves are just enough to match its deposits. There is nothing more it can do until the public decides to bring in some more money for deposit.

Before leaving the single small bank, note this important fact: It has created money! How? Clearly *it* retains from the public only $80 of cash *M*; and it has added $1,000 of bank-deposit *M* to the public's total. Thus, its activity has created a net increase of $920 in money supply ($M_1$ to be precise).

REPERCUSSIONS ON THE OTHER BANKS

But the banking system as a whole cannot settle down yet. The people who sold the bonds or borrowed from the bank will presumably deposit the proceeds in some other bank or pay them to someone else who will make such a deposit. Our original bank has thus lost $920 *to some other banks* in the system.

SECOND-GENERATION BANKS

If we lump these other banks all together and call them "second-generation banks," their balance sheets now appear as shown in Table 16-3(*d*). (Our original bank might even constitute a part of the second generation as some of its cheques fell into the hands of its own depositors.) To these banks the dollars deposited are just like any other dollars, *just like our original deposit*; these banks do not know, and do not care, that they are second in a chain of deposits. They do know, and they do care, that they are now holding too much nonearning cash. Only 8 per cent of $920, or $73.60, is legally needed against $920 deposits. Therefore they can, and will, use the other 92 per cent to buy $846.40 worth of loans and investments, so that in a few days, their balance sheet will have reached equilibrium as shown in Table 16-3(*e*).

So much for the second-generation banks. They too have created money. Thus far, the original $1,000 taken out of hand-to-hand circulation and put into the banking system has given rise to $1,000 (first-generation deposits) plus $920 (second-generation deposits). The total of money has increased, and the end is not yet in sight. Here is the reason.

LATER-GENERATION BANKS

The $846.40 spent on the second-generation banks in acquiring loans and investments will go to a new set of banks called the "third-generation banks." The reader should by now be able to fill in their balance sheets as they look initially [see Table 16-3(*f*)]. Evidently, the third-generation banks will at first have *excess reserves* of an amount equal to 92 per cent of $846.40 or $778.69. After this has been spent on loans and investments—and only then—the third-generation banks will reach the equilibrium of Table 16-3(*g*).

The total of bank-deposit M is now $1,000 plus $920 plus $846.40, or almost $2,767. This is already

over 2.5:1 expansion of the original cash deposit. But a fourth generation of banks will clearly end up with 92 per cent of $846.40 in deposits, or $778.69; and the fifth generation will get 92 per cent of $778.69 or $716.39; and so on; until finally, we shall have all of the total sum of the infinitely many generations.

FINAL EQUILIBRIUM

What will the final sum: $1,000 + $920 + $846.40 + $778.69 + $716.39 + ...? If we patiently work out the sum by arithmetic, we shall find that it leads "finally" to $12,500. Table 16-3(*b*) shows the complete effect of the chain of deposit creation, and we can also get the same answer in two other ways, by common sense and by elementary algebra.[9]

Common sense tells us the process of deposit creation must come to an end only when no bank *anywhere in the system* has reserves in excess of the 8 per cent reserve ratio to deposits. In all our previous examples no cash reserves have ever leaked out of the banking system, but have simply gone from one set of banks to another set of banks. Everyone will be at equilibrium only when a consolidated balance sheet for all the banks together—for the first, second, and hundredth generation—looks as shown in Table 16-3(*i*). For if total new deposits were less than $12,500, the 8 per cent ratio would not yet be reached and equilibrium would not yet have been everywhere attained.

If the reader will compare Table 16-3(*i*) with Table 16-3(*b*) previously judged "impossible" on page 273, he will see this:

The whole banking system *can* do what no one bank can do by itself. It can expand its deposits to 12.5 times the *initial* new reserves deposit. *Bank money has been created 12.5 out of 1—and all the*

---

[9] This can be proved by algebra as follows:

$$\$1,000 + \$920 + \$846.40 + \ldots$$
$$= \$1,000 \left[1 + .92 + (.92)^2 + (.92)^3 + \ldots\right]$$
$$= \$1,000 \left[\frac{1}{1 - .92}\right] = \$1,000 \times \frac{1}{.08} = \$1,000 \times 12.5$$
$$= \$12,500$$

Just as the old multiplier (Chapter 12, page 206) made a flow of income rise threefold to generate the one-third of itself equal to the new dollar of I, here deposit M must rise twelve and one half-fold so that 8 per cent of it will match the new dollars of reserves that started the chain.

SECOND-GENERATION BANKS IN INITIAL POSITION			
ASSETS		LIABILITIES	
Reserves	+$920	Deposits	+$920
Total	+$920	Total	+$920

TABLE 16-3 (d)
3rd, The money lent out soon goes to new banks . . . .

FINAL POSITION OF SECOND-GENERATION BANKS			
ASSETS		LIABILITIES	
Reserves	+$ 73.60	Deposits	+$920
Loans and investments	+ 846.40		
Total	+$920	Total	+$920

TABLE 16-3(e)
which in turn lend out eleven-twelfths of it.

INITIAL POSITION OF THIRD-GENERATION BANKS			
ASSETS		LIABILITIES	
Reserves	+__	Deposits	+__
Loans and investments	0		
Total	+__	Total	+$846.40

TABLE 16-3(f)
4th, Eleven-twelfths of 11/12 of original reserves go to . .

FINAL EQUILIBRIUM OF THIRD-GENERATION BANKS			
ASSETS		LIABILITIES	
Reserves	+$67.71	Deposits	+$846.40
Loans and investments	+$778.69		
Total	+$846.40	Total	+$846.40

TABLE 16-3(g)
third generation banks, who lend 11/12 of it again.

while each bank has invested and lent only a fraction of what it has received as deposits![10]

Who creates the multiple expansion[11] of deposits? Three parties do so jointly: the public by always keeping its money in the bank on deposit; the banks by keeping only a fraction of their deposits in the form of cash; the public and private borrowers who make it possible for the banks to find loans and attractive earning assets to buy with their excess cash. There is also a fourth party, the central bank, which, by its activities, determines what quantity of new reserves come to the banking system.

[10] In effect, each small bank creates $1M$ out of $.08M$ but not $12.5M$ out of $1M$. (NOTE: Whenever $1 of new reserves produces $12.50 of new demand-deposit money, the *net* creation of M is only $12.50 − $1 = $11.50. So when one writes a 12.5:1 expansion expression, it means that there is associated with this an 11.5:1 *net*-creation-of-M expansion.)

[11] There is nothing paradoxical in the fact that total bank deposits are several times greater than the amount of paper cash in existence anywhere; the same is true of the total of government bonds and real-estate values. Deposits are something that banks *owe* their customers; cash is *left* at a bank, but it does not *remain* in that bank. Throughout its lifetime a dollar may have been *left* at many banks, just as it may be used over a long period of time to buy hundreds of dollars of merchandise. The one thing to keep firmly in mind is that bank deposits are one of the three forms of modern money and, quantitatively, the most important.

It is the government's central bank that is the originator of the money supply, M. It will be the task of the next chapters to survey and explain this process.

Before leaving this section, test your knowledge of credit creation by tracing in detail what happens when the Bank of Canada permanently kills off $1,000 of reserves by selling a government bond to a widow who withdraws cash from her demand-deposit account to pay for it: (1) Her local bank loses $1,000 of reserves and $1,000 of deposits. But it previously held only 8 per cent cash reserves or $80 against her deposit. Clearly, it must have given up to her some of its legally necessary cash reserves held against its other demand deposits. Show that its total reserves are now below the legal minimum. (2) Therefore it must sell $920 worth of investments or call in that many loans. The first-generation bank will be in equilibrium only when its balance sheet finally looks as shown in a newly constructed Table 16-4(a).

But in selling its securities, our original bank has drained $920 from a second generation of banks: and they in turn, by liquidating securities and loans, drain reserves from a third. And so it goes—until the widow and Bank of Canada's withdrawal of $1,000 of reserves from the banking system have produced a chain "killing off" $12,500 worth of deposits throughout the whole system and $11,500 of bank-earning assets. The student should follow through each stage: Table 16-4(b), Table 16-4(c), . . .

MULTIPLE EXPANSION OF BANK DEPOSITS THROUGH THE BANKING SYSTEM

POSITION OF BANK	NEW DEPOSITS	NEW LOANS AND INVESTMENTS	RESERVES
Original banks	$ 1,000.00	$ 920.00	$ 80.00
2nd-generation banks	920.00	846.40	73.60
3rd-generation banks	846.40	778.69	67.71
4th-generation banks	778.69	716.39	62.30
5th-generation banks	716.39	659.08	57.31
6th-generation banks	659.08	606.37	52.72
7th-generation banks	606.37	557.86	48.51
8th-generation banks	557.86	513.43	44.43
9th-generation banks	513.43	471.86	41.57
10th-generation banks	471.86	434.11	37.75
Sum of first 10 generation banks	$ 7,070.09	$ 6,504.19	$ 565.90
Sum of remaining generation banks	5,429.91	4,995.81	434.10
Total for banking system as a whole	$12,500.00	$11,500.00	$1,000.00

TABLE 16-3(h). 5th, Through this long chain, all banks finally create deposits twelve and one-half times reserves. All banks together do accomplish what no one small bank can—multiple expansion of reserves into M. The final equilibrium is reached when every dollar of original new reserves, whenever it comes to rest in the banking system, supports $12.50 of demand deposits.

(From the second generation on, the data have been rounded off to two decimal places.)

You should also be able to show how an initial deposit of $7,000 can result in $100,000 of bank deposits if banks keep only 7 per cent reserve ratios.

A "MONOPOLY" BANK AND CHAIN BANKING

In all the above processes, it was assumed that no cash "drained" out of the banking system into someone's mattress; or, what is more important numerically, into permanent hand-to-hand circulation. (The latter used to be called "increased pocket-money needs.") In the absence of such drains, the banking system was then in the enviable position of finding that withdrawal cheques were always redeposited somewhere within itself.

In this condition, it is easy to see that a hypothetical single "monopoly bank" with many branches, which served the whole economy and took the place of the consolidate banking system outlined above, would be able to do *at once* what we have said each

CONSOLIDATED BALANCE SHEET SHOWING FINAL POSITION OF ALL BANKS TOGETHER

ASSETS		LIABILITIES	
Reserves	+$ 1,000	Deposits	+$12,500
Loans and investments	+ 11,500		
Total	+$12,500	Total	+$12,500

TABLE 16-3(i). 6th, all together end up doing what single one couldn't. Contrast this with Table 16-4(b)'s impossible feat of one lone, small bank.

small bank cannot do. Its balance sheet could quickly go to the condition shown in Table 16-3(b) or 16-3(i). It could write cheques on itself freely to pay for securities or make loans, knowing that the people to whom they are paid would always redeposit their proceeds in the same one and only monopoly bank.

CHAIN BANKING   It is now obvious that the Canadian system of chain banking belongs somewhere between the examples' system of many unit banks and the "monopoly bank." The cash drain from one branch now moves out into the banking system, probably to be redeposited in some other town. But the chances are now not so small that the redeposit will be in another branch of the same bank.

In Canada there are only ten chartered banks, all with branches. If they were all the same size, each bank would have one chance in ten that its loans and security payments would flow back into one of its own branches. Such odds are obviously infinitely better than those for an American bank: if all U.S. banks were the same size, a banker there would have only one chance in thirteen *thousand* that he would be the second generation depository for one of his own out-payments. With these odds, Canadian banks can clearly afford to have lower reserve ratios than American banks; and this is probably why *legal* cash ratios in Canada have always been, in fact, set lower than in the United States. (The U.S. reserve ratio for demand deposits in the main financial centers is about 17 per cent; for demand deposits elsewhere it is 12 per cent.)

Actually, for some Canadian banking business, the odds are better than one in ten. For the banks are not the same size. Roughly speaking the three largest banks (Canadian Imperial Bank of Commerce, Bank of Montreal, and Royal Bank of Canada) together

EQUILIBRIUM POSITION OF ORIGINAL BANK LOSING A DEPOSIT			
ASSETS		**LIABILITIES**	
Reserves	−$ 80	Deposits	−$1,000
Loans and investments	− 920		
Total	−$1,000	Total	−$1,000

TABLE 16-4(a). When the Bank of Canada kills off reserves, a multiple contraction begins to take place . . . ending in 12 1/2 to 1 less *M*.

operate one-half of all the branches in Canada and more than two-thirds of all their deposit liabilities. For any one of these banks, the odds are about one in five that their payments will be redeposited in their own branches. What is more important, any one of them can rely on nearly one-fifth of all their payments flowing back to them. If the legal cash ratio of one-twelfth happened to be right for the average Canadian payment from any bank, then these banks could lend out *more* than their excess reserves over the legal amount, knowing that almost one-fifth would be "self-returning." This temptation, of course, exists but it is barred by law.[12]

SIMULTANEOUS EXPANSION OR CONTRACTION BY ALL BANKS

In the previous section we have seen how the banking system can reach the limits of its expansion through many successive rounds or generations. If we allow half a week for cheques to clear at each stage and for decisions to be made, then 5 to 8 weeks might be required for the process substantially to work itself out through more than a dozen rounds.

As a practical matter, it is not necessary to follow the route of each dollar deposited through its successive rounds. Here is why. A rise in reserves will usually affect almost all the banks at the same time. They all receive some new deposits at about the same time. They all have excess reserves in the first instance, and all together make loans or buy securities.

---

[12] The analytical reader should note that the real reason for the large self-returning flow is not the large number of branches but the small number of chartered banks. But of course he would have to admit that, in turn, the concentration in banking is probably caused by the branch system.

If a single bank, all by itself, writes cheques to acquire securities, these cheques go to other banks and it loses cash. But when all are writing cheques simultaneously and in balance, there will tend to be a cancellation of new cheques deposited in each bank against those paid out. No one bank need lose cash reserves. Hence, without going through the successive generations of the previous section, all banks together can simply and blithely expand their loans and investments—so long as each does not jeopardize its reserve position—until deposits are finally brought into a 12.5:1 relation to reserves. Then the banking system has reached the limit of its ability to create money.

One could follow through the similar process by which all banks *simultaneously* contract money 12.5:1 for each dollar of reserve withdrawn from the banking system, and one could also show how a monopoly bank would contract. Figure 16-2, similar to Fig. 16-1, retells the multiple expansion story for a monopoly bank and for simultaneous multiple expansion.

TWO QUALIFICATIONS TO DEPOSIT CREATION

Finally, two qualifications to the ideal condition must be made. We have shown that $1,000 of new reserves put into a bank can ultimately result in an increase of $12,500 of bank deposits. This assumed that all the new money remained somewhere in the banking system, in one bank or another at every stage, and that all banks could keep "loaned up" with no "excess reserves."

LEAKAGE INTO HAND-TO-HAND CIRCULATION   It is quite possible, however, and even likely, that somewhere along the chain of deposit expansion some individual who receives a cheque will not leave the proceeds in a bank but will withdraw it into circulation or into hoarding outside the banking system. As a matter of fact, in boom times when bank deposits are expanding, there is usually at the same time an increased need for pennies, dimes, and paper currency.

The effects of such withdrawals on our analysis are simple. When $1,000 stayed in the banking system, $12,500 of new deposits were created. If $100 were to leak into circulation outside the banks and only

FIG. 16-2. Other routes to multiple expansion.
In (a) there is no need for arrows within the box, because there is only one big bank. In (b), the arrows between the banks run in both directions and can be ignored.

$900 of new reserves were to remain in the banking system, then the deposits created would be $11,500 ($900 x 12.5). *The banking system can always amplify in a 12.5:1 ratio whatever amount of new reserves is permanently left with it,* given our assumed 8 per cent reserve ratio.

POSSIBLE EXCESS RESERVES Our description of multiple deposit creation has proceeded on the assumption that the banks stick fairly close to their legal reserve ratios. But there is no reason why a bank cannot choose to keep an *excess* over the required amount of reserves. Thus, suppose the original bank receiving a new $1,000 deposit had been satisfied to hold $920 of it in excess reserves. Then the whole process would have ended right there, with no multiple expansion of deposits. Or if banks were always to keep 17 per cent excess reserves, on top of the 8 per cent legal requirement, we would have a chain of expansion of deposits $[1 + \frac{3}{4} + (\frac{3}{4})^2 + \ldots]$, with only a 4:1 rather than a 12.5:1 expansion of deposits.

Back in the 1930s excess reserves—i.e., reserves over and above legally required reserves—were substantial, since bankers were then leery of loan opportunities and even of relatively safe government bills that were paying less than 1 per cent interest. Had the banking system then received $1,000 of new reserves, perhaps half might have gone into excess reserves. Nowadays excess reserves are less important,

since large banks find attractive uses even for one-day funds.[13]

The level of excess reserves depends more on the attitudes of banks toward the interest rates they can earn than on their fears that withdrawals will catch them unawares. When short-term interest rates become very low, and a banker finds that keeping an extra million dollars in idle reserves would not much change his earning position, he is not very anxious to get rid of all excess reserves. But as profit opportunities improve, he becomes more aggressive in putting his idle reserves to work earning a return for the stockholders.

The possibility that the excess reserves of banks can change over time is an important reminder that

---

[13] A rather complex mechanism also exists, and flourishes, whereby banks can "lend" reserves to each other for a day or so at a time. The banks make day-to-day loans of large amounts to dealers in treasury bills and other short-term paper. These loans can be called back by any bank before noon on any day. Dealers whose loans are thus called back can turn to other banks, and thus the other banks indirectly "lend" reserves to those calling their loans. If no other banks have cash to spare, the dealers can turn to the Bank of Canada which always stands ready to accommodate them (at rather high rates of interest). These highly liquid loan assets constitute much of the third item ("other") in Table 16-1. The system has been in operation only since the mid-1950s, and is a special version of a "discount" market which has existed for decades between the Bank of England and the commercial banks in London. The system, which has many technical advantages, is too complex to go into here.

there is nothing mechanical and completely accurate about using a 12.5:1 or any other *fixed* ratio for money creation.

Accordingly, there is nothing automatic about deposit creation. Four factors are necessary: the banks must somehow receive new reserves; they must be willing to make loans or buy securities rather than hold new excess reserves; someone must be willing to borrow or to sell securities; and the public must choose to leave its money on deposit with the banks, not depleting them of reserves.

SUMMARY

A. THE MODERN BANKING SYSTEM

1 The Canadian banking system consists of ten chain banks, chartered by the federal government. Three of them are quite large and have deposits equal to about 65 per cent of total deposits in Canadian banks.

2 The functions of chartered banks are numerous and overlap with those of such other financial institutions as trust and mortgage companies, credit unions, finance companies, and insurance companies. But in their function of providing demand-deposit M, the commercial banks perform a unique and important economic role. Their demand deposits constitute the single most important component of our money supply or medium of exchange. And they are important sources for credit.

3 The Bank of Canada is an arm of the government, run by a Governor, Deputy Governor, and Board of Directors. The government is represented at its meetings and participates in making appointments to it. Unlike the U.S. Federal Reserve System it is not in any sense a private enterprise.

Although it undertakes a variety of jobs for the government, connected with the currency, with the exchange rate and with the selling and retiring of government bonds, its wide powers are applied for the public interest, not for banking profit. It works with the Department of Finance and Treasury Board, though in day-to-day matters it sometimes adopts independent attitudes that have led it into real conflict with the national government. As opposed to the multitude of aims of government, the Bank of Canada's single main goal is to control the supply of money and credit conditions, in this way helping to achieve full employment with stable prices. A natural but minor adjunct of this continuous job is to backstop the chartered banks, and other parts of the financial system, in times of crisis.

4 Modern banks gradually evolved from the old goldsmith establishments in which money and valuables were stored. It finally became general practice to hold far less than 100 per cent reserves against deposits, the rest being put into securities and loans for an interest yield. Fractional-reserve banking had evolved.

5 If the government did not stand ready to use its emergency powers to protect the banking system, an attempt by all depositors at the same time to withdraw their money would ruin any fractional-reserve banking system; but knowing the government is ready to act, people will never put it to the test.

The chartered banks are required to keep legal cash reserves (on deposit with the Bank of Canada or in till money) in some proportion to their deposits, and they must also maintain secondary reserves. These legal reserve requirements are *not* primarily to protect deposits but to permit the Bank of Canada to control the total supply of M and keep credit conditions conducive to proper over-all spending—to proper $C + I + G$ and MV or PQ totals.

B. THE CREATION OF BANK DEPOSITS

6 If banks kept 100 per cent cash reserves against all deposits, there would be no net creation of money when new, high-powered reserves are fed by the central bank into the system. There would be only a 1:1 exchange of one kind of money for another kind of money.

7 Modern banks in Canada are required to keep legal reserves of only 12 per cent against demand deposits and 4 per cent against notice (savings) deposits. For analytical discussion, assume that 8 per cent, or $1/12.5$, represents the average of these two rates. Then the banking system as a whole—together with public or private borrowers and the depositing public—does create deposit money almost 12.5:1 for each new dollar taken out of circulation and left on deposit somewhere in the system.

8 Each bank is limited in its ability to expand its loans and investments. It cannot lend or invest more than it has received from depositors; it can lend only about 92 per cent as much. Its deposits are twelve and a half times its cash, only because its cash decreases, and not because its deposits increase; but it does create 1 unit of bank money for the 8 per cent of reserves it retains.

9 The system as a whole can expand at once, as each bank cannot. This can be seen if we examine a monopoly bank in a closed community. The cheques written by such a bank always come back to it; therefore the only restriction upon its ability to expand its investments and deposits (its assets *and* its liabilities in double-entry bookkeeping) is the requirement that it keep 8 per cent cash-reserve ratios against deposits. When deposits have expanded until they are twelve and a half times the new reserves, the monopoly bank is "loaned up" and can create no further deposits until given more reserves.

10 In present-day Canada, there is no monopoly bank. Nevertheless, the same 12.5:1 expansion of bank deposits takes place. The first chartered bank receiving a new $1,000 of deposits spends 92 per cent of its newly acquired cash on loans and investments. This gives a second group of banks 92 per cent of $1,000 in new deposits. They, in turn, keep 8 per cent in cash and spend the other 92 per cent for new earning assets; this causes them to lose cash to a third set of banks, whose deposits have gone up by 92 per cent of 92 per cent of $1,000. Obviously, if we follow through the successive groups of banks in the dwindling, never-ending chain, we find for the system as a whole new deposits of $1,000 + $920 + $846.40 + $778.69 + . . .

$$= \$1,000 \times [1 + .92 + (.92)^2 + (.92)^3 + \ldots]$$
$$= \$1,000 \left[\frac{1}{1 - .92}\right] = \$1,000 \left[\frac{1}{.08}\right] = \$12,500$$

Only when each dollar of the $1,000 of new reserves supports $12.50 of deposits somewhere in the system will the limits to deposit expansion be reached. Then the system is loaned up; it can create no further deposits until it is given more reserves.

11 In practice, it is not necessary to wait for the successive rounds on the route of $1,000, $920, $846.40, . . . , to work themselves out. Usually, many banks tend to get new reserves at about the same time. If they all expand their loans and investments approximately in balance, their outpayments will tend to cancel each other. Thus, each will not lose cash; and all together can rather quickly expand their earning assets and deposits to the 12.5:1 limit.

12 The Canadian system has only ten chartered banks, with many hundreds of branches. Thus each lending bank can expect that an appreciable proportion (as much as one-fifth) of its loans and security-purchase payments will flow back as deposits into its *own* branches. This places the actual Canadian (also British, Swedish, etc.) system between the many-small-banks system and the hypothetical monopoly or one-bank system of the examples. Large Canadian banks could safely keep less than the required legal cash reserve, but are forbidden to do so. The smaller Canadian banks are not in the same position of expecting to get a good share of their own cheques returning for deposits in their own branches; if there were no legal ratio, they would probably voluntarily keep about the same ratio anyway.

13 As a minor qualification to the above discussion, we must note that there will be some leakage of the new cash reserves of the banking system into circulation *outside* the banks. Therefore, instead of $12,500 of new deposits created, as in the previous examples, we may have something less than that—the difference being due to what is withdrawn from the system.

A second qualification results from the fact that a bank may keep *excess reserves* above legally required reserves. While big banks do not hold much excess in prosperous times, others may hold varying amounts of excessive reserves, depending upon interest rates and precautionary expectations. So there is nothing automatic about a 12.5:1 or other fixed-gear ratio.

In this chapter we have seen how bank deposits are kept at about twelve times the legal reserves of the banking system. In Chapter 17 we shall learn how the Bank of Canada makes bank reserves go up when an expansion of the total money supply is desired. When a contraction of the quantity of money is in order, the authorities pull the brakes. Instead of pumping new reserves into the banking system, they draw off some of the reserves. We shall see that in so doing they are able to reduce the quantity of money, not 1 for 1, but (as just shown) 12.5 for 1.

CONCEPTS FOR REVIEW

Bank of Canada, Governor,
  Board of Directors,
  Department of Finance
bank balance sheet
goldsmiths and fractional-
  reserve banking
legal cash reserve ratio
  requirements
original high-powered
  reserve
diversity and liquidity
  of earning assets

"generations" of banks
deposit creation for a monopoly
  bank versus a chain system
  of banks
excess reserves, leakage of
  reserves
qualifications to multiple
  deposit creation
ultimate Bank of Canada
  controls of M

QUESTIONS FOR DISCUSSION

1. Suppose that all banks kept 100 per cent reserves. How different would they be? What function do legal reserves perform? What are "excess reserves"?

2. Assume a 10 per cent reserve ratio. Trace the process of multiple bank expansion, duplicating Tables 16-3(a) to 16-3(i). Reverse the process.

3. Do bankers create deposits? Who does? If a banker receives a new deposit and new reserves, is he always able to find borrowers? Can he always expand his holdings of government securities? How does he go about it?

4. "My bank's books always balance. I merely *pass on* to investors the savings that money depositors bring to my bank. Who dares say a banker can create M or demand deposits?" Do you dare?

5. "The central bank should create new reserves indefinitely, as long as we bankers can find good productive loans to make, because then each new M will be balanced by new product Q and prices won't rise and the community will get a higher real NNP indefinitely". This view was widely supported by the founders of the U.S. Federal Reserve System in 1913. Can you see where the implied elasticity of M could be harmful in a world of fluctuating $C + I + G$ schedules? (HINT: Banks would expand M in booms and contract M in recessions.)

6. *Extra-credit problem:* Suppose the public always holds 1/21 of its M in currency and 20/21 in demand deposits. Then if banks always keep 1/5 of reserves against demand deposits, verify that each R of new new reserves gives rise to total M as follows:

$$M = \frac{1}{\frac{1}{21} + \frac{1}{5}\frac{20}{21}} R = \frac{21}{5} R = 4.2\ R;\ \text{deposits} = \frac{20}{21}\frac{21}{5} R = 4R;\ \text{currency} = .2R$$

17
THE CENTRAL BANK
AND MONETARY POLICY

There have been three great inventions since the beginning of time: fire, the wheel, and central banking.
WILL ROGERS

The Bank of Canada is our central bank, a bank for bankers and for the government. Every central bank has one prime function:

It operates to control the economy's supply of money and credit. If business is getting worse and jobs are getting scarce, the Bank of Canada will try to expand money and credit. But if spending threatens to become excessive, so that prices are rising and there are many job vacancies, then the Bank of Canada will do all that is possible to step on the brakes and contract money and credit.

The policy of the equivalent U.S. central bank, the Federal Reserve, has been aptly said to "lean against the wind" of prevailing deficient or excessive aggregate-demand spending, to promote optimal real growth and price-level stability. All mixed economies rely on such a central bank.

In a nutshell that is the function of central banking. In this chapter we shall survey the weapons that the Bank uses to expand or contract money and credit.

HOW MONETARY POLICY WORKS TO CONTROL SPENDING

What is the exact process by which the Bank affects general spending? The last chapter showed that chartered banks must have reserves to support their assets and deposits. (So important are these "reserves" that we shall capitalize the word for the rest of this chapter.) The law says that these Reserves must have at least a certain ratio to Canadian deposit liabilities. These are shown respectively as the first

item on the asset side and the first sub-total on the liability side of Table 16-1. The ratio is 3.0/45.8 or approximately 6.5 percent. This was the formula legal ratio at that time, which for simplicity and consistency we simply assume to be legally set at 8 percent, or 1/12.5. Here are five steps of the process:

1. *The first step of the Bank, therefore, when it wants to put on the monetary brakes, is to act to cut down on the Reserves available to the banks.*

2. *Each dollar contraction in bank Reserves forces about a $12.50 contraction in total bank money, i.e., in total demand deposits.* (Recall Chapter 16's analysis of multiple deposit creation in a fractional-reserve banking system.)

3. *The contraction in total money makes credit generally "tight", that is, both dearer and less available.* We shall see that less M will raise interest rates. As important, less M will make credit less *available* to people.

Interest rates will also rise for mortgage borrowers (builders and home buyers); for local governments that want to build schools and roads; and for businessmen anxious to build plants, buy new equipment, promote new ventures, or add to inventory; for public utilities needing new power stations or transmission lines.

Reinforcing higher interest cost will be an important *rationing effect* on investment and other components of total $C + I + G$ spending. This contractionary effect comes from the fact of credit's decreased availability. Thus, if you want to build a house, it matters to you that the interest rate has risen from 10 to 12 percent. If you are like most families, it matters even more that you may find it hard to get a mortgage with a low down payment. You may find your lender's manner a shade cooler; and he may discourage you from buying the $60,000 house that you really prefer to the $45,000 one you have been considering. When M is scarce, turndowns on loans become common.

4. *With credit expensive and hard to get, private and public investment will tend to fall.* Why this downward shift in the I and G schedules? This is because people's decisions as to whether it is profitable to build a new house or plant, order a new machine, and hold more inventory usually depend upon how they can finance such investment spending.[1] If they have to pay a high interest rate or find it very hard to get loans, they often scale down their investment plans. The same holds for provincial and municipal governments. The old road gets patched up and that new road postponed when the town finds it cannot float its bonds at any reasonable interest rate. The gymnasium and library are cut out of the new school plans when the citizens learn their tax rate is going up because it now costs more to borrow.

5. *Finally, the pressure on credit and on investment spending will, through the downward shift in the $I + G$ schedule, have downward effects on income spending, prices, and jobs.* The multiplier analysis of Chapters 12 and 13 showed how such a drop in investment will depress income spending sharply.

If the Bank of Canada has been right in its diagnosis of inflationary conditions the drop in money income will be just what the doctor ordered to help the situation. M contraction will have succeeded in reducing the inflationary gap—in eliminating demand-pull inflation.

RECAPITULATION

This five-step sequence—from the Bank of Canada's changing the chartered bank's Reserves, to 12.5:1 changes in total M, to changes in credit's interest cost and availability, to changes in private and public investment spending, and finally to multiplied changes in money income—is vital. By rereading the ital-

---

[1] Later chapters (particularly Chapter 30) show that higher interest rates tend to depress the market value of wealth items: land, bonds, buildings, equipment. With their total wealth less and installment credit hard to get, people's CC schedule may also drift down along with their II schedules and the GG schedule.

icized parts of the previous section, you can consolidate your understanding of it. (Better still, psychologists tell us we learn fastest by participating. The previous section was explained in terms of a time when the Bank wants to *contract* business activity. Tackle the problem of how things proceed when the Bank wants to *expand* business activity.)

Figure 17-1 drives home the five-step sequence by adding to the black box of the member banks (as already shown in Fig. 15-3), the capital markets in which interest rates and credit availability are determined. Then, in turn, from the capital market (shown as a circle) we get the familiar $C + I + G + (E - M)$ link of total spending (shown as the final diamond). Be sure you can follow the steps from the far left (where the Bank of Canada initiates changes in Reserves) to the far right (where the money level of GNP, the price level, and the rate of employment are affected by monetary policy).

BALANCE SHEET OF THE BANK OF CANADA

Now that we have surveyed the process of monetary policy with a telescope, let us study the mechanism in some detail. We shall not attempt to put Bank of Canada policy under a microscope, since that is the job of an intermediate course in money and banking; but we do want to get a general idea of exactly what weapons the Bank can use to affect bank Reserves.

Look at Table 17-1. This lists the balance sheet of the Bank of Canada. The Bank holds a negligible amount of gold. Canadian government securities make up most of the assets—the significance of this item will be explained soon. The foreign exchange assets are usually roughly balanced by foreign-exchange liabilities. Advances to chartered banks are very rare and usually zero. The interest rate the Bank of Canada charges banks for such loans is called the "Bank Rate," and it is varied by the Bank as part of its monetary policy.

The right-hand side lists the usual capital accounts: original capital subscribed plus "rest fund" or accumulated surplus. This would be much greater for so profitable a business were it not for the fact that the Bank gives back to the Treasury all its excess profits.

Notes in circulation are the Bank's principal liabilities. These are the one, two, five, and ten-dollar

HOW BANK OF CANADA MONETARY POLICY AFFECTS INCOME DETERMINATION

FIG. 17-1. Monetary policy integrates nicely with aggregate demand management and $C + I + G$ income determination.

Be sure you understand how the Bank of Canada raises high-powered Reserves at left; thereby raising total M; which, working through the capital and securities markets, lowers interest rates, i, and improves credit availability; leading to upward shifts of $C + I + G + (E - M)$; and ultimately increasing GNP, real output (Q), and price level (P). Q cannot grow above its full-employment level. (To warn against thinking monetary policy is the whole story in aggregate demand management, note that fiscal and exchange-rate policies also feed into $C + I + G + (E - M)$ diamond.)

bills, etc., we all carry in our wallets. These IOUs cost the Bank no interest, and it is highly privileged to have been granted by Parliament this monopoly power to issue all of our currency except coinage.

BALANCE SHEET OF BANK OF CANADA, JANUARY 1974

(billions of dollars)

ASSETS		LIABILITIES	
Gold and		Notes in circulation	
foreign exchange	0.8	outside banks	4.5
Advances to		Reserves of chartered banks	
chartered banks	0.1	(notes and deposits)	3.0
Government of Canada		Government of Canada	
bills and bonds	5.9	deposits	0.1
All other assets	1.0	Foreign deposits	—
		Other liabilities	
		and capital	0.3
Total Assets	7.9	Total Liabilities	7.9

TABLE 17-1. Central bank notes and deposits underlie the money system.

Chartered-bank Reserves, assets in Table 16-1, appear as liabilities here. The Bank of Canada controls them in order to control the economy's M. To do so, it controls its earning assets: government bonds and bills. (Figures are rounded. Source: *Bank of Canada Review*).

Little comment is needed on several of its deposit liabilities: government deposits, foreign central bank deposits, and miscellaneous.

Of vital importance, though, are the chartered bank's reserve balances kept by them on deposit at the Bank of Canada. Along with small amounts of vault cash, these are the Reserves we have been talking about, which provide the basis for multiple deposit creation by the banks.

We shall see that the Bank, *by altering its holding of government securities*, can create changes in the Reserves of the chartered banks—thereby starting off our earlier-mentioned five-step sequence. The total of the Government of Canada securities is watched carefully; its moves reflect the desires of the Bank of Canada to ease or restrain credit conditions. (Later, Fig. 17-2 will show how these important balance-sheet items have changed in recent years.)

DISCRETIONARY MONETARY POLICIES BY THE BANK OF CANADA: OPEN-MARKET OPERATIONS

To initiate the mentioned five-step stabilization sequence, the Bank of Canada has two main tools, which are listed in order of their present importance: (1) open-market operations, (2) bank-rate policy.

(We shall review its five minor tools later in this chapter.)

By selling or buying government bonds in the open market (mostly in Toronto and Montreal), the authorities can tighten chartered bank Reserves or loosen them. These so-called "open-market operations" are the Bank of Canada's most important stabilizing weapon.

At frequent intervals, even as you read this book, the officers of the Bank are meeting to decide whether to pump more Reserves into the banking system by buying treasury bills (i.e., short-term bonds) or longer bonds, or whether to tighten things up a little by selling government securities. It is a never-ending job.

To see how an open-market operation changes Reserves, let us suppose that the Bank of Canada thinks the economic winds are blowing up a little inflation. The Executive Committee holds its weekly meeting. The committee surveys the credit situation. This results in instructions to the securities department, one of which is to "sell 100 million dollars of government bonds from our portfolio to contract Reserves and over-all credit." To whom are the bonds sold? No one knows: to the open market. The dealers in government bonds—there are about half a dozen big ones—will not reveal the names of the buyers. But you can guess that they are primarily insurance companies, commercial banks, and big business firms.

The buyer will most likely pay for the Bank of Canada bonds by a cheque drawn on his bank ac-count. The Bank of Canada will present this cheque for payment to his bank. That bank will then lose an equivalent amount of its Reserve balances with the Bank of Canada. Table 17-2(a) shows the final effect on the central bank's balance sheet. The open-market sale has cut down on the Bank of Canada's assets and liabilities. (It has also initially cut down on bank Reserves and their demand deposits owed to the bond buyer.)

Actually, this shows only the *initial* potency of open-market sales. In all likelihood the 100 million-dollar sale of government bonds will result in a 1250 million-dollar cut in the community's money supply. We've seen why—in Chapter 16. Let us continue to assume that Reserves are kept at 8 per cent of demand and savings deposits.

Reserves go down by 100 million dollars, and that tends to set off a 1250 million-dollar contraction of deposits. Table 17-2 shows the banks' position after Reserves have been extinguished by the open-market operation. In the end, the Bank of Canada's open-market sale has put 12.5:1 downward pressure on bank deposit M.

To test your understanding of open-market operations, consider the reverse process. Suppose incomes and jobs are at too low a level. What will the Bank of Canada's Executive Committee want to do? Buy government bills on the open market and thereby create new Reserves for the chartered banks? Produce thereby a 12.5:1 expansion in M, thus making credit cheaper and more easily available to investors and consequently encouraging an upward shift in $C + I + G + (E - M)$ and a multiplier increase in GNP? (Locate in Fig. 17-1, the (color) point A at which open-market operations impinge.)

ASSETS OF BANK OF CANADA		LIABILITIES OF BANK OF CANADA	
U.S. securities	$100	Chartered bank deposits	$100
Total	$100	Total	$100

TABLE 17-2(a)

ASSETS OF CHARTERED BANKS		LIABILITIES OF CHARTERED BANKS	
Reserves	$100	Demand deposits	$1250
Loans and investments	1150		
Total	$1250	Total	$1250

TABLE 17-2(b)

Open-market sale cuts Reserves initially . . . . ultimately cuts deposits.
When an open-market sale kills off $100 million of Reserves, it induces a $1,250 million drop in total demand deposits. The member banks must call in loans and sell off their "investments" (i.e., their securities) up to $1,150 million.

BANK RATE POLICY: A SECOND WEAPON

The Bank of Canada also makes loans to the chartered banks. These we call "advances." They occur rarely and, when they do, are very small. Whenever the central bank is making advances, the banks are borrowing Reserves from the Bank of Canada. If advances are dropping or are made hard to get, the central bank is helping Reserves to contract.

Unfortunately, the Bank of Canada is not free to pursue an advance policy exactly the way it wants to. It cannot send salesmen out to drum up more loans to banks whenever it wants to expand them. All it can do is wait for banks to come to it. All it can do is name the "Bank Rate" which sets its interest charge for such advances.

In theory, the central bank could get more advances business by lowering Bank Rate, and could discourage banks from seeking this credit by raising it. But on the whole its role must be passive. It can sit and wait. It can say "No." It can set an attractive Bank Rate. But it certainly cannot *set* its amount of advances at any figure it wishes. Only in its open-market operations can it take an active role

Two points of detail about advances and Bank Rate: (1) The U.S. Federal Reserve central bank, at its foundation in 1913, planned to make loans to commercial banks by "rediscounting" the promissory notes they had received from their customers. In effect, they could sell these loans and IOUs to the Federal Reserve bank for their face value minus interest at the rather high Bank Rate. This would protect bank borrowers against their local bank's ever running out of the power to lend for worthy investments. This is still possible in the United States and thus advances are called "discounts." But in fact today most U.S. banks sell government bills and bonds, not promissory notes to the Fed when they want help.

The whole idea is unpopular anyway today because the Fed does not want commercial banks to have the power to automatically increase their credit to customers, when they are short of Reserves, by rediscounting. Such power leads to an *elastic* money supply and to the aggravating of inflationary or depression problems.

(2) The Bank of Canada, for technical reasons, discourages the chartered banks from applying directly to the central bank for advances. It prefers to develop a system adapted from the Bank of England and now more or less common with central banks everywhere: forcing the banks to try to get cash for their Reserves from the money market before, as a last resort, they apply to the central bank for advances.

It works this way. A chartered bank, short of Reserves, calls in some of its very short-term loans to bond dealers and traders. (These are made on a day-to-day basis.) These money-market dealers have used the loans to finance their business inventories of securities. What are they to do now? First they try another chartered bank. If it can make a replacement day-to-day loan, everyone is happy and the first bank has in effect turned some of its earning assets (loans) into Reserves (cash), which were *indirectly* obtained from the second bank. Second, if the dealers cannot find a bank to make the loans, they apply to the Bank of Canada for a loan, pledging some of their inventory of bills and bonds (government securities). Thus the Bank of Canada is practically "rediscounting" these bills. The dealer must pay Bank Rate for this advance. In this second case, the first chartered bank has indirectly obtained Reserves from the central bank. In the first case, the central bank was not involved at all.

CHANGING THE BANK RATE In every economy, people in business and finance listen carefully for announcements of change in the central bank's interest rate. When, in 1964, the Bank of England raised the British Rate from 5 to 7 per cent, it meant that loans and money-raising would be tighter and dearer to British borrowers. It also meant that North American lenders would find lending to British borrowers more profitable than to Canadian or U.S. business; so they began at once to sell their New York and Toronto securities and buy bonds in London. This "flight of capital" was stemmed the next day by raising the Federal Reserve discount rate and the Bank of Canada's Bank Rate. The example illustrates two things: (*a*) changes in the central bank's lending rate touch off many more events than mere changes in chartered bank advances—they often serve as an official signal of general policy intentions, visible to everyone concerned; (*b*) especially in the international economy, from which neither the large United States nor small Canada is insulated, Bank Rate changes often *follow* rather than lead market changes.

Even in a closed economy (one cut off from world capital flows), Bank Rate often follows the market. Even when the central bank doesn't have to protect the local money markets from winds of change blowing up elsewhere, they rarely rely on Bank Rate as their main monetary policy tool. Instead, they depend on open-market policy. What happens then? If the open-market policy is to tighten credit conditions, the chartered banks will find themselves steadily shorter of Reserves. The central bank wants them to reduce loans and investments—but they may attempt to obtain more Reserves instead, by seeking advances directly from the Bank of Canada or indirectly through the money market. If the profit on their investments is high, chartered banks will find it profitable to pay high Bank Rate for Reserves rather than cut down their investments (and loans). To prevent this (that is, to prevent the banks circumventing the aims of the original open-market operations), Bank Rate must now go up enough to make borrowing Reserves unprofitable.

For this reason, we usually find the Canadian Bank Rate fractionally higher than the rate banks can earn on short-term investments in the Toronto and Montreal money market. Indeed, for many years, Governor Coyne followed the policy of automatically, by formula, making Bank Rate depend on bill rates of the day; a policy fully understood by the money market. This particular formula procedure for setting Bank Rate has now been dropped. But as Fig. 16-2 shows, Bank Rate is still kept very close to the bill rate.

Because Bank Rate changes usually *reinforce* other policy measures, their chief role in all countries is to act as a *signal*. The mere announcement of a fall in official Bank Rate means that a high rate is no longer needed to reinforce open-market operations. That is, open-market operations must no longer be in effect to force monetary contraction. So the dealer, businessman, and borrower know at once that "credit is being eased"; and the local bank manager knows, even before his regional superintendent phones him, that he can be more helpful in meeting the loan requests of his customers. Further, other lenders outside the banking system know that they will have to cut their loan rates, or their customers will go to the banks instead. Thus, on the *signal* of the Bank Rate's cut, the whole money market begins to ease credit conditions. (The reader should check his understanding by rereading the effect of open-market operations, and working out what would happen if Bank Rate were not raised.[2])

---

[2] Note that both demand and supply come in here. A higher Bank Rate merely signals that supply is reduced. Lending interest rates go up, so that borrowers, together, want fewer or smaller loans.

AN ABANDONED WEAPON: CHANGING RESERVE REQUIREMENTS

The chartered banks must maintain a certain minimum cash ratio to deposits—8 per cent in our examples. If the Bank of Canada were to raise this cash ratio, say by one percentage point a month, it would very quickly make credit conditions tight. The banks' existing holdings of cash (and Reserves at the Bank of Canada) would be less and less adequate for their deposits. They would have to reduce deposits in an effort to conform with the new legal cash requirements. If, on the other hand, the Bank of Canada wished to ease credit conditions, it could help by cutting legal cash reserve ratios.

Until May, 1967, the Bank of Canada had such powers to alter the reserve ratio. But it never used the powers, and abandoned them in the 1967 revision of the Bank Act.

Changing reserve requirements is a powerful tool that is used, occasionally, by the U.S. Federal Reserve system. It is not used every day, as in the case of open-market operations, which produce about the same effect. If we look at the working of this weapon in the United States, we can see why the Bank of Canada never used it even when it could.

Exactly how does an increase in required reserve ratios operate to tighten credit? Suppose the U.S. commercial banks had built up deposits in a 5:1 fashion as a result of the required ratio having been 20 per cent, with excess reserves being negligible. Now suppose the Federal Reserve Board wants to tighten credit and raises the required ratio to 25 per cent. Even if it does nothing by the way of open-market operations or discount policy to change bank Reserves, the commercial banks now have to contract greatly their loans and investments—and their deposits.

Why? Because in effect some of their previous Reserves have been impounded. Now the bank deposits can only be in a 4:1, not a 5:1, ratio. So there will have to be a drop by one-fifth in all deposits.

If loanable funds move in from abroad, as in our 1964 British example, supply at the higher interest rates may actually fall very little. This is because British open-market operations cut the supply of Reserves for British banks only. Foreign lenders are now in a position to replace British banks and lenders in London markets. But only as long as rates in London are higher than those in the United States or elsewhere. So the rate of interest must stay up, and this will dictate that total loans asked for by London borrowers will be smaller. Try drawing supply and demand curves to show these events.

MEMBER BANK ASSETS		MEMBER BANK LIABILITIES	
Reserves	$ 20	Demand deposits	$100
Loans and			
investments	80		
Total	$100	Total	$100

TABLE 17-3(a)
Raising reserve ratio leads from 5-to-1 . . . .

MEMBER BANK ASSETS		MEMBER BANK LIABILITIES	
Reserves	$20	Demand deposits	$80
Loans and			
investments	60		
Total	$80	Total	$80

TABLE 17-3(b)
to final 4-to-1 deposit expansion.

Raising Reserve requirements forces U.S. commercial banks to contract. Note sale of bonds and investments.

This painful cut will start to take place quickly. For as soon as the Federal Reserve Board signs the new fiat raising requirements to 25 per cent, banks will find themselves deficient with respect to Reserves. They will have to sell some of their bonds and call in some loans. The bond buyers will use up their demand deposits, and the borrowers whose loans are called will have to use up their demand deposits to pay back such loans. The process ends only after banks have brought down their deposits to four rather than five times their Reserves.

Table 17-3 shows how their combined balance sheets might look after the change. You may be sure that so great a change in so short a time would result in *very high interest rates*, in unavailable credit, in great cuts in *I* (and possibly in local *G*), and in great reductions in national income and employment. Hence, this powerful weapon of changing reserve requirements is rarely used, even in the United States.

AN INCREASINGLY IMPORTANT WEAPON: SECONDARY RESERVES

Since 1955 the Bank of Canada has tended to play less on the chartered banks' Reserves and more on their Liquid Assets (as shown in the first sub-total of Table 16-1). These consist of Government of Canada bonds (many of them soon to reach their maturity date), treasury bills, day-to-day loans to dealers in government bonds and bills and a number of minor, easily-sellable, or soon-to-be-cashed items. Banks originally began to hold these assets for the interest they earn, not because of government requirements; they round out and liquefy their holdings of less liquid customer IOUs, mortgages and corporate securities.

The *secondary reserve requirement* compels the banks to keep (at least) a certain fraction of their earnings assets in one of three particular liquid forms: any cash that is not part of primary legal cash

reserve; treasury bills; and day-to-day money-market loans. This secondary reserve ratio requirement may be set by the Bank of Canada at any percentage between 0 and 12, of the banks' Canadian dollar deposit liabilities (see Table 16-1 again).

Hence, although it cannot now change the legal cash-reserve ratio, the Bank of Canada has a new power to alter the secondary-reserve ratio. (It is now set at 8 percent.)

What is the advantage of this weapon over the cash-reserve ratio? When the *cash-reserve ratio* is raised, the banks try to convert their holdings of government securities into cash to meet the increasing cash requirement. Such selling forces down the price of securities, raises their yield, and so raises the market rate of interest, even if the Bank of Canada does not want this interest-rate effect. (Incidentally, it would also reduce the earnings of banks for reasons that had nothing to do with their performance or their competitive effectiveness.)

But if instead the *secondary-reserve ratio* is raised, the banks need not all sell liquid assets such as treasury bills. The liquidity they have accumulated in slack times is simply immobilized and prevented from serving as the reserve basis of an expansion of bank lending or easing of credit conditions. Further, the banks do not lose the earnings from their liquid securities, as they would in responding to a rise in the cash reserve ratio.

It appears that the new power to change the secondary-reserve ratio is more delicate than the former power to change the cash ratio.

SWITCHING GOVERNMENT OF CANADA DEPOSITS

This technique makes use of the government's own business deposits, most of which can be kept either at the central bank, or in private banks. The Bank of Canada, as banker to the government is as free to switch these deposits back and forth, as it is to buy or sell government bonds for open-market operations. (See Table 16-1, on the liability side.)

When chartered banks lose these deposits, their Reserves fall, with a consequent induced contraction in loans and M. Contrariwise, when the central bank places government deposits in the private banks, the banks' Reserves rise and credit expands. Thus the general effect is similar to that of open-market operations, with a few interesting differences: (*a*) the Bank cannot switch more dollars than the government owns; (*b*) switching leaves little or no statistical trail behind it; and (*c*) because switching does not involve the sale of bonds and so has no immediate effect on security prices or the rate of return on them, it can (like altering the secondary reserve ratio) have a more gentle effect on credit conditions than open market operations have.

MORAL SUASION AND OTHER "QUALITATIVE" CONTROLS

The Bank of Canada and the monetary experts in the government are always concerned about the supply of credit and money. But they also take an interest in *who* is getting the credit available. This is partly because the credit availability to certain sectors of the economy (export industries, home builders, farmers) may be a special object of national social policy. It is also because changed credit conditions may have a magnified effect on national interest rates, prices, incomes, employment, and growth if they are allowed to concentrate on a particular sector.

Thus it wants to exert an influence on the distribution of credit, not its total amount. In technical jargon, it wants to use "qualitative," not "quantitative," controls. (The word quality in this use refers to the *kind* of bank customers to be favored or hindered rather than to their merit, the riskiness that they won't repay, or other aspects of their personal or financial "quality.") It is just the opposite of "quantity" of credit.

"MORAL SUASION" This phrase is now part of official banking and economic jargon. Moral suasion is the opposite of the impersonal, mechanical weapons such as open-market operations and the two others. It involves personal contact between the Bank of Canada and the chartered bankers. On being questioned about moral suasion (which, being conducted in private meetings, is never fully known about except by rumor), Governor Rasminsky answered in 1964:

The way moral suasion works in practice is that the Governor of the Bank of Canada meets with the executive officers of the chartered banks, expresses to them certain views regarding whatever it is he is trying morally to persuade them to, and asks for their cooperation in enforcing those views, which might relate on occasion to the distribution of credit. (That is, to the distribution of the banks' assets between extending loans to one kind of customer as against another, and between loans and securities.) . . .

The minimum liquid asset ratio agreement was of this type; it was in November and December of 1955 . . .

From what I know of the matter, such suggestions (from the Bank of Canada) give rise to a good deal of give and take in discussion, but suggestions of this sort are not made unless there is a clear public interest in them being followed, and since the central bank by and large is somewhat reluctant to use these techniques, . . . the general experience is that the public interest is recognized by the chartered banks and after the discussion the cooperation of the chartered banks is forthcoming.

There is no doubt that in Canada moral suasion can be a powerful weapon. There are only ten banks; they all know the total national banking situation well, and are probably in sympathy with the central bank's problems. Just as important, the central bank is by law directly and indirectly in a position to "induce" their agreement—any bank that refuses to go along can have its business harmed by Bank of Canada operations later. But there is no record that threats of such harm actually occur in discussion; the evidence for their powerfulness is tangential: the installment finance companies, which are *not* responsible to the Bank of Canada, refused to change their policies in 1956 when Governor Coyne held a moral-suasion session with them. The ten banks recognize the latent power exercised over them by the Bank of Canada in a way that other financial companies do not.

Other evidence can be found abroad. The Bank of England, the birthplace of moral suasion, has a similarly small group of bankers to deal with, over whom it exerts immense moral power if it chooses. The Federal Reserve Banks in the United States also frequently call in their members for heart-to-heart talks. But there are so many banks, many of them very small, that maverick bank officers, who refuse to go along with moral suasion, will be found in every region. They prefer to take the risks rather than submit to suggestions that they change lending policies which are presently much in their interest. Consequently, moral suasion plays a weaker role than rules and laws in the United States. It is a technique that works best when there are few banks.

As the examples mentioned suggest, the usual aim of moral suasion in all countries is to influence the banks' asset or lending policies. The central bank may want them to favor certain kinds of borrowers, or to reduce their "margin" lending to stockbrokers, their "term" lending for up to five years, their lending to particular industries, or, as with the 1972 "Winnipeg" agreement, their interest rate on very large, short-term deposits. These are restrictions on the *distribution* rather than on the *availability* of credit. When the latter is to be changed, open-market operations will be, even in the long run, the favoured weapon.

CONTROL OVER INSTALLMENT TERMS In

mid-1970, the federal government—*not* the Bank of Canada—claimed powers to set limits on installment contracts. Great Britain and the United States had done this, very effectively, for some years. Canada last did so during wartime emergency. Such powers may compel large down payments, large installment payments (short terms), and high charges—or the opposite, and thus shift the *CC* function. (In fact, the necessary legislation got lost in the events of May-June, 1970, and has not been proclaimed. But consumer finance control is likely to recur as a weapon of the central authorities).

MORTGAGES Again, the law restrained the banks

from going heartily into mortgage business. (There were also some ways around this.) The result was that the money market raised much of its mortgage money from specialized mortgage companies and from the government's Central Mortgage and Housing Corporation. (There are other examples in farm lending, consumer credit against chattels, and term lending.) First the removal of the 6 per cent maximum interest rate and then the removal of any top NHA mortgage rate in 1969 changed the situation

radically. The banks were permitted to enter the mortgage field, and they did so with gusto. Today, the federal and provincial governments as well as the Bank are active in mortgage control.

OTHER GOVERNMENT INFLUENCES Apart from central bank powers, the Ottawa government can make, and has made, laws about banking that affect the quality of bank credit. Sometimes the effect is negative or indirect.

CONSUMER LOANS Commercial banks could not until 1967 charge more than 6 per cent on loans, by law. (They did charge more, however, on consumer loans by asking 6 per cent per year on the *original* loan, while the amount already repaid by the borrower increased. Thus the interest payments were collected at a steadily higher rate on the unpaid balance of the loan. Mathematical tables show that the typical interest payment over the whole life of such bank consumer loans works out at about 10 per cent per annum.) The 6 per cent maximum meant that *commercial* borrowers whose projects were too risky to be given credit at this low price were forced to go elsewhere for credit. Royal commissions on banking gave attention to this matter, usually suggesting that there was no *economic* reason for holding commercial banks to business that is safe at 6 per cent. But members of Parliament were unwilling to change the law, which they believed protected voters against "usury". Actually, what it did was close the banks to many voters forcing them to have recourse to more usurious financial firms.

All these regulations and new institutions had their virtues. They gave protection to some borrowers. And they left the chartered banks as very solid institutions by protecting their depositors against the banks' engaging in types of lending that might ultimately endanger their deposits.

But there are unintended results too. As competitive theory would predict, bank regulations encourage "near-banks" and other institutions to flourish. If these were owned by the government, they often worked in direct contradiction to central-bank policy. If they were private, their Reserves and policies would be under no control at all, except indirectly through the chartered banks with whom they deal. For this reason, many experts argue that the banking powers of the chartered banks should be broadened, if only to keep credit conditions directly under central-bank control.[3]

FOREIGN EXCHANGE, GOLD AND THE MONEY SUPPLY

Until now we have been speaking as if all changes in total M originate in deliberate actions by the Bank of Canada, aimed at changing bank Reserves in a desired direction. In all countries, and particularly in Canada, there is, however, an external force that may affect our M, namely foreign exchange movements and gold flows. These are primarily transactions in U.S. dollars or pounds-sterling to or from abroad. But it should be realized that while these flows can affect our M, the standard weapons of monetary policy can *offset* any such changes if they are thought to be against the national interest.

Part Five will deal with international trade in detail; here we need touch only upon its banking aspects. When Canadian exporters are selling more goods abroad than importers are buying, foreigners balance their books by sending us foreign exchange. (Actually, they rarely mail foreign currency; instead their payments result in Canadians owning deposits in foreign banks.) This is like new cash to Canada. People connected with exporting will make new deposits of their export earnings. The reader now may well ask, "Won't these deposits be a source of new chartered bank Reserves? And won't they make possible the familiar 12.5:1 expansion process—just as in our earlier examples where a widow, or a seller of bonds in a Bank of Canada open-market operation, or anyone else brought new Reserves to deposit in a chartered bank?" The answer is, Yes—*if* the export earnings have a form legally suitable for becoming Reserves. For example, when gold was still both a domestic and an international currency, and new export earnings always became a net addition to Canadian banks' Reserves, permitting a 12.5:1 expansion. Today, the effect of new foreign earnings depends on how we handle them. They may force a change in domestic M; alternatively we can offset (or "Sterilize") them, or adjust our rate of exchange.

THE OLD GOLD STANDARD Canadian currency was, until the Great Depression, convertible or redeemable in gold. Canadian banking and money markets were not very well developed, but in theory Canadians, Americans, and most Europeans used gold coins, gold certificates (a warehouse receipt for gold), or paper currency redeemable in gold.

In those days, when "America" sold more exports than she bought imports, the difference was received in gold bars. Whoever got the bars (the exporter, or a bank serving a group of exporters and importers) took them to the government and received gold coin or redeemable paper money. The exporter would take them to his bank, or the bank would put them to the credit of its exporting customers. Then would begin one of our familiar multiple expansions of credit. (The amount of expansion would depend upon the legal or customary reserve ratio of the day. In the United States it was lower than today's; in Canada it was higher.) The opposite effect, a *contraction of M*, would result if "America" exported gold bars to Europe, to pay for a surplus of imports over exports. This tended to occur when Canada, for example between 1900 and 1913, was growing very fast and badly needed supplies from abroad even when she had nothing new to sell. Chapter 33 gives more details—all we need know is that under an international gold standard, foreign transactions *automatically* changed domestic M.

SINCE THE DEPRESSION Since 1934 neither the Bank of Canada, nor the United States government, nor the United Kingdom has been prepared to redeem its currency in gold. Canada's gold stock did "stand behind" central bank notes till World War II, but in 1939 the government took over the gold stock and has held it in its Exchange Fund Account ever since. Today, neither Canada, the U.S. nor the United Kingdom stand ready to deliver any set amount of gold for a unit of their currency.[4]

---

[3] Under the constitution, control over banking is clearly a federal power. But consumer protection, housing, stock exchanges, credit unions, mortgages, trust companies and insurance are under provincial jurisdiction. Hence the Bank of Canada cannot be given exclusive power over "near-banks".

[4] Official statistics suggest that in 1974 Canada held 900 tons of gold, worth about $925 million. Earlier editions of this book made a valiant attempt to summarize the monetary position of gold. Today the subject is for specialists and antiquarians only. As Figure 15-3 showed, gold is just a commodity, a handy export item, more owned by central banks than by individuals by the accident of history. In many countries free dealing in gold is allowed at a free world market price. The U.S. stands ready to buy or sell the U.S. dollar from or to other governments in exchange for gold at $42.22 per ounce, but not much business is done.

FOREIGN EXCHANGE AS A CONSTRAINT ON MONETARY POLICY

While our currency and Reserves are today independent of gold backing or the duty of gold redemption, our M is not yet independent of foreign transactions. Exports and imports still affect our credit conditions; and foreign considerations still influence our monetary policy. Much of this will come up again in Part Five, but the reader neglects it now at his peril. Today there is no country whose domestic economic health is free of balance of payment effects.

When an exporter gains foreign currency (or a deposit in a foreign bank) he sells it to his bank for Canadian dollars. He is then out of the transaction. If his bank has many such purchases, it sells them, through official brokers in Montreal and Toronto, to other banks who need them to supply foreign exchange to Canadian importers. Imagine now that exporters have more foreign money to sell than importers need. Their banks will still try to get rid of this foreign money, for they want Reserves in Canadian funds. Their efforts to dispose of it will drive down the price of foreign currency in Canadian terms; that is, tend to drive *up* the international value of Canadian money.

FREE EXCHANGE RATES If official policy is to allow the exchange rate to find its own level, no intervention will occur when the Canadian dollar rises. What are the consequences?

The foreign customers of our exporters, like foreign buyers of Canadian land and securities, now have to pay more, and may decide to trade elsewhere. Foreign shares and goods bought by Canadian investors and importers are now cheaper, and will be brought in. Our tourists abroad get a windfall—unless their foreign currency was bought at the old rate!—but foreign tourists to Canada stay away in droves. Those who gain tend to buy more, and those who lose buy less: these are the familiar adjustments to a change in any price, including foreign exchange. These reactions, and adjustments, change demand and supply and prevent the rate from drifting upward (or downward) forever.

Our interest here lies in the connection between the exchange rate's level and freedom to conduct internal monetary policy. What must the monetary authorities do when the rate moves up? Nothing, unless they wish to push it back again. Normally, any rate is as good as any other. A change in the exchange rate, when it is unimpeded, will alter foreign-trade and other flows, but not in a way that need make credit conditions tighter, or easier.

Of course, the rate of exchange and monetary conditions are not independent. Open-market operations and other monetary weapons *will* change the exchange rate predictably. For example, a policy of selling bonds will cut Reserves, reduce M, and tighten credit conditions. The five-step sequence presented on page 283 will then shift down $C + I + G + (E - M)$ schedules, including the *import content* of each of these types of spending. Such a fall in demand for imports will tend to reduce the Canadian demand for foreign currency, and produce a "strengthening"—an upward movement—in the value of our dollar. But this exchange-rate effect of the bank neither weakens nor strengthens the initial open-market operation, which can be continued until its domestic goal has been achieved.

CAPITAL MOVEMENT Monetary policy may also influence exchange rates indirectly through capital movements. Thus monetary policy conducted through open-market operations will tend not only to raise the rate of interest on Canadian bills and bonds (as discussed on page 283) but also to attract foreign bidders for such bonds. Their offers become a "capital movement" which tends to move the rate of exchange toward an appreciation of the Canadian dollar.

The Bank of Canada can have a very potent effect on exchange rates, and realizes it.

Similarly easy-money conditions and low yields on government securities may cause a short-run capital exodus that depresses the exchange rate. Either way, this exchange-rate effect is not undesirable in itself. But it may deter the Bank from vigorous monetary policy.

FIXED EXCHANGE RATES To allow such flexibility is frequently against government policy. We return to our export example, assuming now that exchange rates are to be fixed. The government to enforce a decision to keep the world value of Canadian dollars at a certain level, must now prevent export-earned foreign moneys from falling in price in Canadian terms. Since there is no money-market buyer who will take them *at the price the govern-*

ment wants to maintain, the government's Exchange Fund Account must buy the foreign currency itself.[5]

It is at this stage that domestic *M* is affected. For the Exchange Fund Account (EFA) must have a supply of Canadian dollars with which to make quick offers for any foreign currency that threatens to fall in price below the predetermined limit acceptable to government exchange-rate policy. This Canadian cash must be advanced from the government's own chartered bank deposits. To acquire a chartered bank's foreign exchange for the EFA, the government writes a cheque on its own deposits in another bank. Thus one bank gains a deposit in selling foreign exchange, and another loses Reserves as the government's deposit is drawn upon. In effect, therefore, Reserves are shunted from one chartered bank to another, total *M* is unchanged, and the government's own holdings of foreign currency have increased.

What if the government's deposits at chartered banks are insufficient to purchase all offered foreign exchange? Two alternatives present themselves. If the government borrows from the public or increases taxes to replenish its deposits, deposits are transferred from the public to government, but Reserves and therefore total *M* are unaffected. This transaction, in which the government raises money from the bond buyer or taxpayer to buy foreign exchange for the EFA, is similar to the government's raising money to buy an Old Master for the National Gallery: *M* does not change.

Alternatively, the government may borrow from the Bank of Canada. Then the proceeds of the bonds will be new deposits in the Bank of Canada which the banks selling foreign currency can add to their Reserves. It is this type of case that the familiar 12.5:1 expansion process will begin. It turns out that foreign transactions have "caused" Canadian *M* to expand, just as would have happened if gold were still

in use. Foreign currency has been allowed to become an addition to Reserves.

To test his understanding, the reader should work out what happens when Canadian imports exceed exports. The EFA will now gain Canadian dollars and lose some of its stock of foreign money, as a result of an attempt to keep Canadian dollars from selling at below the desired price in, say, U.S. dollars. These Canadian dollars will be returned to the government, which may buy back some of its bonds from the public or lower taxes. If it buys bonds from the Bank of Canada, this will, as described in the section on open-market operations, reduce chartered bank Reserves and so contract the Canadian *M*.

It must be stressed, however, that neither of these operations now *automatically* changes Canadian *M*. The expansion of Reserves depends on whether and to what extent the government decides to issue bonds to the Bank of Canada, or to run down its own funds instead. Even if it has no funds, the whole operation can be offset by a simultaneous Bank of Canada open-market operation to reduce chartered bank Reserves. In effect, it buys bonds from the government while selling bonds to the money market. Reserves and *M* will not change.

FREEDOM TO CONDUCT MONETARY POLICY But although the Bank of Canada may be able to offset or "sterilize" the flows of foreign currency, it is still unable to cut itself out of international financial influences. For the Bank must keep two goals in view; not only a nice control of Canadian *M*, but also a healthy rate of exchange (and balance of international payments). If the first goal calls for credit ease, in order to encourage domestic *I* and *G*, the result observable to foreigners will be that Canadian interest rates will fall. This means that both Canadians and foreigners will prefer to move their funds to other countries, where they can get relatively higher interest rates on their deposits and loans. There will be a resulting "drain" of foreign currency. For example, the EFA will find that it is having to supply more and more of its stock of U.S. dollars to Canadian banks whose customers want to buy them. The result may eventually be that either (*a*) the EFA runs out of foreign currency and has to let the value of the Canadian dollar fall, or (*b*) the government has to persuade the Bank of Canada to let Canadian interest rates rise again. If (*a*) is an unacceptable policy, then the efforts of monetary policy to encourage

[5] All this is based on the assumption that Canada has a fixed exchange rate. Before 1961-1962, and since June 1, 1970, there has been no official value of the Canadian dollar. Its price in U.S. dollars is determined, each day, by supply and demand. Under a pure flexible exchange-rate system, the government does not interfere in the exchange market. (The Canadian government may stabilize the exchange market when it is deemed necessary, but no attempt is made to maintain a set rate.) As discussed on page 293, the government and the central bank allow the flexible rate to bear the impact of changes in trade or in capital flows.

the growth of GNP through credit ease must be abandoned.

The example is familiar to many countries. It is difficult, with a fixed rate of exchange, to achieve a healthy economy at home and to maintain a balance of international payments. We shall see in a later chapter that this fear of exchange-rate collapse has constrained the use of monetary policy, and has led either to the use of flexible rates, or to the suggestion that reliance be put upon fiscal policy instead.

ARE CENTRAL BANKS DOING THE RIGHT THING?

About the performance of any central bank, two questions can be asked: What is it trying to do?, and, Is it succeeding?

THE AIMS OF CENTRAL BANKS TODAY

First, although we do not discuss them till later, let us always remember that most central banks must be chiefly concerned with the foreign value of the currency and the state of international monetary reserves. This role naturally influences much of their domestic action, and they must get A's or E's on their report card for decisions most citizens never hear about.

The other aim is to help control price levels and employment trends by manipulating the money supply, as outlined in this chapter and the next. In this the central banks to have the support of Keynesian and post-Keynesian economists who in their various ways believe that the supply of M, "credit conditions," "availability," or "liquidity" does matter, and should be used to augment fiscal policy and international policy in adjusting the pitch of domestic business activity.

But this support, from academics at least, has never been whole-hearted. For in the first place, in the essential Keynesian system, "money matters" *only* through its effect on borrowing terms, the interest rate, and so, on new $C + I + G$. Because this linkage is loose and insensitive, many economists are more interested in fiscal than in monetary policy. The great Crash of 1929 and the following Depression punctured the illusion that the Bank of England or the U.S. Federal Reserve could tame the business cycle. Ever since, the majority of the experts think

that monetary policy essentially *reinforces* stabilizing fiscal policies.

But, in the second place, the majority now is confronted by an important contending minority. A school we may call the "monetarists," led by the able economist Milton Friedman of the University of Chicago, and depending on a quasi-Keynesian tradition at Chicago and in Europe, is preaching that "only money matters." This group—the same group that has revived interest in the 1930-vintage Fisherian quantity theory (Chapter 15)—believes that essentially everything that can be done to control macroeconomic aggregates, i.e., inflationary gaps, epochs of depression, and slow growth, must be done by control of the money supply *alone*. Fiscal policy, Professor Friedman insists, should be confined only to helping to shape how much of the macroeconomic total is in the public sector as against the private sector, and in shaping the trend of interest rates and of the consumption share of GNE. On the basis of his superb studies of the history of money in the United States and of many other countries, he is convinced that fiscal policy in *itself* has no predictable effect on the prospects for inflation or deflation, for high employment or mass unemployment.[6]

Such negative, critical monetarism is extreme. But since it is proposed by economists with serious scientific interests, it should not be rejected just because it does not involve a mid-ground position. After all, scientific truth *could* turn out to be at one extreme rather than in the middle.

MONETARISTS VERSUS THE ECLECTIC MAJORITY Where does the difference lie? A study and weighing of the evidence in favor of monetarism finds it—as a guide to policy—not only extreme but also essentially wrong. Recall what are the elements of the majority, eclectic view. Their neoclassical, post-Keynesian synthesis holds (a) that

---

[6] For an interesting application of monetarist ideas to the Canadian problems of demand management in an open economy, see T. J. Courchene, "Stabilization Policy" in L. H. Officer and L. B. Smith, eds., *Issues in Canadian Economics* (McGraw-Hill Ryerson, Toronto, 1974). The standard references are M. Friedman and A. Schwartz, *A Monetary History of the United States* (Princeton University Press, for the National Bureau of Economic Research, Princeton. N.J., 1963), and articles pro and con monetarism by Friedman, Samuelson, and Walter Heller in P. A. Samuelson, ed., *Readings in Economics*, 7th Edition (McGraw-Hill, New York, 1973).

both fiscal and monetary policies and instruments matter much, (b) that the velocity of circulation is induced to increase systematically when interest rates rise, making it more economical for people to turn over their cash balances more rapidly (the "precautionary balances" of Chapter 15 are, as argued there, sensitive to the rate of interest), and (c) that open-market purchases which create new M for the community—and ease credit conditions—have their stimulating effects on I and other GNE spending dampened by the reduction in the liquid interest-bearing government bonds now held by the community, and the rise in the holding of essentially idle money.

Now examine some recent episodes. In both Canada and the United States, taxes were cut in 1964-1965. There was an increase in business spending thereafter. The Friedman view, for the United States, is that the stimulus was due to the extra M created to help finance the government deficit. In 1968-1970 taxes in both countries were raised, by a "surcharge." Friedman says that the only effect on inflation is that stemming from changes in the money supply in the period. Indeed, to a U.S. monetarist, the unprecedentedly long expansion of the 1960s would have taken place even if the budget had always been in balance at a low level—provided the Federal Reserve central bank had made M grow as it actually did during the decade.

The majority of U.S. experts do not believe this, arguing that interest rates early in the decade would have been much lower and GNE spending lower because of the difference in the velocity of circulation that would have been induced. That is, M changes would have been chiefly differences in precautionary balances (defined in Chapter 15, p.256) producing some fall in interest rates and rise in I, but not as much as the fiscal-policy-induced rises in GNE.

Economics is not an exact science. We cannot repeat the 1960s under controlled conditions to settle the debate. Therefore, an author should present in a textbook a framework of analysis that can be shaded in favor of either of these two scientifically proposed models. And this edition, particularly, has been written to make this possible.

For even if, in the end, monetarism should be deemed by the jury of science to have been one-sided, (1) it is based on evidence; (2) an increasing minority of important university economists embrace it, even outside Chicago; (3) it has an increasing following in government agencies (like the Joint Economic Committee) and even inside the central banks. More

important, Friedman's evidence has been used by eclectic post-Keynesians like Yale's Tobin and MIT's Modigliani in their own insistence that *money does matter much*, and their opposition to the view of other post-Keynesians (especially those who prevailed in Britain's famous Radcliffe Report on banking in 1959) that money does not matter much or at all.

In the United States, these debates consider domestic policy and results alone. Canada must also compare monetarism with eclectic policy when capital inflows and exchange rates may be affected.

For example, dedicated, closed-economy neo-Keynesian dogmatists may predict that a planned budget deficit will have most of its desired effect through its influence on $C + I + G + (E - M)$ spending. However, monetarists will predict that this action's effects, if any, will stem from the necessity to sell bonds to the central bank, and so increase M. Practical economists will find it difficult to observe a distinction between the two predictions. The change in $C + I + G + (E - M)$ will induce more imports, a net outward movement of Canadian payments, and so a fall in the rate of exchange. At the same time, the rise in M and the fall in the yield on all Canadian bonds will induce more financial investors to quit Canadian securities and, also via a net outward movement of Canadian payments, produce a fall in the value of the Canadian dollar.

Both *predictions* about the rate of exchange converge. What of the Keynesian-monetarist theoretical dispute? The Keynesian says that the observed exchange-rate decline stems mostly from trade changes, because the increase in M is more likely to change velocity than the rate of interest. The monetarist argues that the same observed effect is due to short-term capital movements, with every fiscal action changing the interest-rate differential between economics.

Psychologically, however, the two teams of economists will be found to be examining different effects. The Keynesian will be hoping and predicting that the fiscal policy will increase employment, but will worry about possible price increases along the Phillips curve, and about exchange rate side effects. The monetarist, regarding the fiscal policy as a disguised increase in M, will be pessimistically predicting price increases and exchange rate adjustments, positive that the lowest achievable or "natural" rate of employment (see Chapter 19) and output cannot be budged by monetary expansion.

Monetarists will claim that price and exchange-rate changes are inevitable. Eclectic Keynesians will argue that whether and how much prices rise depends on conditions being present to touch off demand-pull or cost-push inflation: the Phillips curve may indeed be horizontal at the time. And they will maintain further that international capital movements depend on how much M changes do change bond prices in Canada (the community may hold much of the extra M as idle balances rather than using it to bid up the price of bonds—bid down the rate of interest that would touch off both more I and more capital outflow).

SELF-ADJUSTMENT, FINE TUNING, AND LEANING AGAINST THE WIND These disputes are not academic or long-run. They shape day-to-day policy. You might think that a monetarist like Friedman, convinced that money matters exclusively or most, would want to use control over the money supply to fight against the ups and downs of business activity. But you would be wrong. Dr. Friedman insists that *no* "fine tuning" will work. Money does matter most, but *its* effects are not perfectly predictable, there being always uncertain lags and leads between cause and effect.

Reinforcing Dr. Friedman's skepticism about fine tuning is his philosophical position—really the "Chicago" position, echoing earlier individualist writers—that "rules" and not "discretionary authority by men or committees" should prevail. Hence his sole recommendation for monetary policy, his constructive advocacy, is elegantly simple.

Let the central bank stabilize the growth rate of the money supply every year and every month—at some agreed-upon constant rate say, between 5 and 6 percent per year. Then, abandoning active fiscal policy, and all fine tuning, let the free market take care of the rest, including a floating rate of exchange. Let no man, no Governor, no committee try to manage interest rates, unemployment, price levels, or foreign balances.

In logic, one could be a monetarist—i.e., a believer in the *sole* importance of M—without giving up a

"lean against the wind" philosophy. Such a monetarist would not want to set a constant-growth-rate-in-M goal; but rather a stabilizing, *counter*cyclical M policy. But mere logic cannot settle this issue. If the time lags between M and GNP are long and variable, a well-intentioned countercyclical policy might result in doing more harm than good: thus, the central bank zigs to counter the economy's present zag; but by the time this act takes effect, the economy is on its next zig. While such whipsawing cannot be ruled out, statistical analysis of "automatic control theory in the presence of errors" will show that neither is it inevitable. One must pragmatically relate optimal M policy to the pattern of experience.

RECENT FINANCIAL EVENTS

So much for the still, cross-sectional picture at a point of time. To see changes that have been taking place, refer to Figure 17-2 which depicts some of the variables presented every month in the *Bank of Canada Review*.

The period covered begins in 1970. Recall from earlier chapters that 1969-70 had some of the makings of a recession, with the unemployment rate rising. This is shown by the uppermost curve. But, prices were also increasing *at an increasing rate* (second curve). The rate of exchange was freed (or made flexible) in 1970. However, the government intervened, as explained on page 293, to protect Canadian exporters by preventing the Canadian dollar rising "too much". This was accomplished by the *EFA*'s purchase of U.S. dollars. The fund's need for Canadian dollars was financed not only by taxes but also by borrowing, as shown in the next curve of federal net financial requirement, most of which was a foreign-exchange purchasing requirement.[7] The result was an expansion in the holdings of the public debt by both the chartered banks (not shown), and, especially by the Bank of Canada.[8] This was the basis for an expansion of Reserves (not shown), which in turn permitted an increase in M, (next curve), and postponed an increase in interest rates, i, (next curve), which indeed fell for several years.

---

[7] The rest of the financial requirement stemmed from a small budgetary deficit. See also Fig. 19-2 (surplus and deficit).

[8] See Table 17-1.

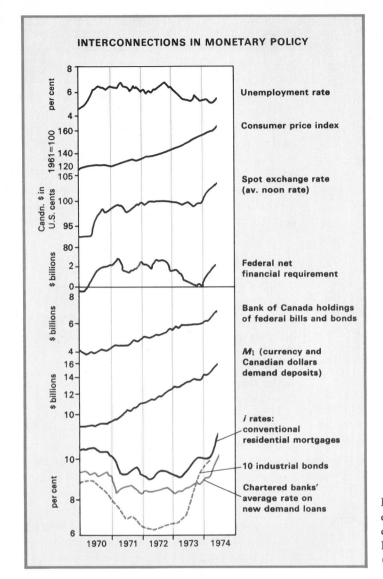

FIG. 17-2. Bond operations expanded money supply, gradually reduced unemployment.
Dollar amounts are on ratio scale.
(Source: *Bank of Canada Review.*)

These are simply a group of curves. No causation, from one to the other is proved. Nevertheless, it can be argued that the aims of monetary policy were not to restrain an increase in M or in P, but to restore full employment by monetary ease and to keep the exchange rate from cutting off export sales. In all this it succeeded. The exchange rate was kept from rising. Unemployment gradually drifted down (real GNP and Q drifted up).

All this was accomplished by letting M increase by at least 15 percent per year. Prices, the escape valve for all these pressures, rose from 8 to 15 percent per year.

THE FUTURE Economics is an exciting subject because there is always much to learn. Unquestionably the central banks in the future will give less weight than they did in the past to stabilizing interest rates even when that meant destabilizing the economy and the rate of growth of the monetary supply. Undoubtedly the control of "hot money" flows in search of higher interest rates must be better reconciled with monetarist closed-economy dogmas. The monetarists have made important contributions to economic knowledge. But turning over the steering of monetary policy to an autogyro-robot formula would represent, the authors believe, an inefficient retreat to coarse tuning that would jeopardize full employment, reasonable price stability, and desirable foreign balance.

SUMMARY

1 The Bank of Canada is a central bank, a bank for bankers. Its duty is to control the community's supply of money, and its credit conditions. Its five-step mode of action goes thus: (1) it contracts Reserves, which (2) causes multiple contractions in total deposits, which (3) makes credit conditions tight (involving high interest rates), which (4) depresses private and public investment spending, which (5) puts a multiplied damper on both money income and prices.

2 The powerful weapons the Bank uses are (a) open-market operations, (b) Bank-Rate policy, and (c) changes in secondary-reserve ratios. It depends heavily on (d) moral suasion. The government of Canada and the central banks of other countries (but not the Bank of Canada) can change legal cash ratios and exert selective controls over particular interest rates, margin borrowing, installment down payments, and mortgage finance terms.

3 Sales by the Bank of Canada of government securities to the open-market represent a positive act which reduces its assets and liabilities and which reduces the Reserves of the chartered banks, and hence their base for deposits. Powerful day-to-day open-market operations should be understood by every student of monetary policy.

4 Under a fixed exchange rate, foreign exchange outflows will reduce Reserves and M unless offset by other Bank of Canada open-market purchases of bonds. Under flexible exchanges, inflows don't affect M. Domestic macroeconomic goals are sometimes constrained by international considerations.

5 The main facts of finance, as show by the table of changing money and liquid assets, are to be understood in terms of this chapter's analysis. The view of monetarists—that the money supply dominates aggregate demand and that it should be set always at a fixed growth rate—clashes with the view of the majority's post-Keynesian synthesis—that, while M matters much, so also do tax, expenditure, and investment shifts in $C + I + G$, and that "leaning against the wind" will improve on automatic M rules. All agree, "Money matters".

CONCEPTS FOR REVIEW

the five-step sequence
Reserves
availability and cost of credit
liquid asset ratio requirements
Bank of Canada notes
open-market purchases and sales
Bank Rate, advances
changing secondary reserve ratio

legal reserve ratio requirements
moral suasion, interest ceiling
Exchange Fund Account
selective credit controls
offsets to foreign exchange flows
monetarism, leaning against the wind
fine tuning

QUESTIONS FOR DISCUSSION

1. Trace the effects of a 10-million-dollar open-market purchase. An open-market sale. In terms of Fig. 17-1, pencil in open-market operation and bank-rate borrowing at A on the red Reserves input branch. Pencil in the legal reserve ratio charges as the gearing at B on the light red output-of-M branch.

2. Trace the effects of a doubling of primary-reserve requirements; a halving. Which alters bank earnings more: open-market or primary-reserve-requirement action?

3. List the weapons of monetary control of the central bank. How powerful are they (*a*) to control M, (*b*) to control interest rates, (*c*) to control prices, and (*d*) to control employment and unemployment?

4. You patent a better mousetrap and sell the patent rights to a foreign manufacturer. Trace the resulting impact on Canadian M.

5. "In the heyday of the gold standard, gold movements affected prices only because our fathers used them as a barometer, signaling them to expand or contract the total of money supply. Of course, the gold standard was a stupid system; but they were wiser to tie themselves to such an imperfect system than to trust corrupt legislatures—whose tendency is always to print inflationary paper money." Discuss.

6. Discuss the following 1939 statement of the U.S. Reserve Board: "The Federal Reserve System can see to it that banks have enough reserves to make money available to commerce, industry, and agriculture at low rates; but it cannot make the people borrow, and it cannot make the public spend the deposits that result when the banks do make loans and investments.

7. Some people say, "Measure monetary tightness by heights and rises in interest rates." Some say, "Measure tightness by general credit conditions." Others say, "Measure tightness only by what is happening to the growth rate of M." Eclectics say, "Use all three measures and more." What do you say?

8. The Economic Council of Canada is often interpreted as agreeing with the Chicago position that the central bank's discretionary judgment should not be used on a month-to-month basis. Instead the Bank of Canada should only ensure that M grows at the right rate every year (e.g., 5 per cent). Give both sides of this debate between monetarists and the post-Keynesian mixed-economy majority. How have events since the revaluation of 1970 tilted the scientific issues?

18
SYNTHESIS OF MONETARY ANALYSIS AND INCOME ANALYSIS

About this time there was a cry ... for more paper-money ... I was on the side of an addition, being persuaded that the first small sum struck in 1723 had done much good, by increasing the trade, employment, and number of inhabitants in the province, since I now saw all the old houses inhabited, and many new ones building ... The utility of this currency became by time and experience so evident, as never afterwards to be much disputed ... Tho' ... there are limits beyond which the quantity may be hurtful.

BENJAMIN FRANKLIN

Chapters 12 and 13 showed how saving and investment schedules intersect to determine the level of national income. And the succeeding chapters have shown how changes in Bank of Canada policy affect the community's stock of money.

In this chapter, we relate these two analyses. Monetary analysis is seen to fit in well with the modern theory of income determination; thus the stage is set for stabilizing aggregate demand management—(1) central bank monetary policies, and (2) government fiscal policies (public expenditure and taxation, with the implied budget deficit or surplus).

It is these macroeconomic programs—fiscal policy and monetary policy—that have to be coordinated to achieve the goals of a progressive economy: one that enjoys reasonable price stability and lives up to its production potentialities.

This chapter shows how stabilization policies work and interact. We leave more detailed study of demand management and inflation issues for the remaining chapter of Part Two.

MONEY, LIQUIDITY PREFERENCE, MARGINAL EFFICIENCY, MULTIPLIER

In this section we deal with the effect of monetary policy (only) on GNP. The next section deals with fiscal policy (only). Then we synthesize them.

The last chapters showed that M expansion by the central and chartered banks can shift upward the $C + I + G + (E - M)$ intersection point of Chapter 12.

What is the same thing, an increase in M shifts upward the $SS — II$ intersection point of Chapter 12, as follows:

When the central bank increases M, it primarily affects investment, shifting II upward. Its expansion of M bids up bond prices and thus bids down interest rates and makes credit loans more easily available to investors. Therefore, it has become more profitable to undertake new investment projects. In the simplest case, the sequence is this:

$$M \text{ up} \rightarrow i \text{ down} \rightarrow I \text{ up} \rightarrow \text{GNP up, up}$$

New graphs can illuminate this; and they can also show the process by which a shift in $C + I + G$ schedules—as, e.g., shifts due to increased exports, or a technical investment boom—can increase the velocity of circulation (V), in the $MV = PQ$ relation of Chapter 15. The shift thereby increases GNP beyond any change originating in M itself.

Chapter 15 (page 256) showed that the demand for money, along with depending positively on the level of income transactions, also depends inversely on the interest and profit yields sacrificed in order to have the safety and convenience of holding M. To get more M held by the community, the Bank must, therefore, *bid down interest rates enough to make people find it advantageous to economize less on their cash balances and hold more M.* The so-called "liquidity-preference schedule" of Fig. 18-1(a) shows how an increase in M resulting from monetary policy (open-market purchases, etc.) leads initially to a re-

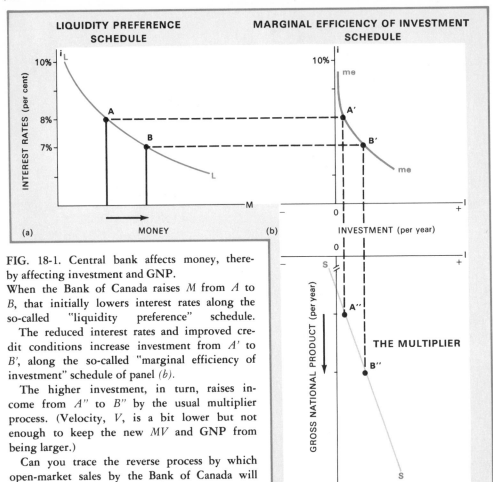

FIG. 18-1. Central bank affects money, thereby affecting investment and GNP.

When the Bank of Canada raises M from A to B, that initially lowers interest rates along the so-called "liquidity preference" schedule.

The reduced interest rates and improved credit conditions increase investment from A' to B', along the so-called "marginal efficiency of investment" schedule of panel (b).

The higher investment, in turn, raises income from A'' to B'' by the usual multiplier process. (Velocity, V, is a bit lower but not enough to keep the new MV and GNP from being larger.)

Can you trace the reverse process by which open-market sales by the Bank of Canada will contract M and GNP, and do this by raising interest rates enough to cut down on I?

duced interest rate—from A's 8 per cent to B's 7 per cent.[1]

[1] Advanced courses deal with this schedule; here the reader is asked to take its shape (and stability) largely on faith. The schedule is the aggregate of demand curves of persons and businesses showing how much of a particular asset—money—they wish to hold, rather than trade that M for bonds or securities. This amount depends, of course, on the precautionary and speculative advantages of being liquid (holding money) rather than holding bonds and securities, and therefore depends on the prices of bonds and securities. There is no single price for all bonds and securities, but there is one single market yield or return common to all of them: the rate of interest. For any security or asset, the relation is present discounted value of $ market price = future coupon or dividend

$$= \frac{N_1}{(1 + i)} + \frac{N_2}{(1 + i)^2} + \dots \frac{N_t}{(1 + i)^t} + \dots$$

receipts (N_t) as shown in the Appendix to Chapter 30.

Figure 18-1(b) picks up the story to show how reduced interest rates (and what does not show on the graph but is lurking in the background, namely, greater *availability* of credit) make more investment profitable. On Fig. 18-1(b)'s so-called "marginal efficiency of investment schedule," the drop in interest rate induces the rise in investment from A' to B'.

Figure 18-1(c) is merely Chapter 12's saving-investment diagram, page 200, turned on its side to line it up with Fig. 18-1(b)'s investment axis. Note

For each higher value of the prices of each of the total stock of securities in existence, i must fall. The negative slope of the liquidity-preference schedule shows that as the M stock rises, it will be held by everyone only after everyone has bid up the prices of the securities and so bid down the implied yield expressed as a ratio, or rate of interest.

that the interest drop from A to B led to the investment rise from A' to B', and this (through the multiplier) has led to the GNP rise from A'' to B''.

To clinch understanding of this vital sequence, consider the following *reverse* case where monetary policy is contracting to wipe out an inflationary gap:

Monetary contraction (open-market sales, increase cash- or secondary-reserve ratios, etc.) bids up interest rates [2] and decreases credit availability. This depresses investment spending, and via the multiplier depresses income even more. The basic sequence is now

M down $\rightarrow i$ up $\rightarrow I$ down $\rightarrow$ GNP down, down

Retrace the reverse BA, $B'A'$, and $B''A''$ sequence in Fig. 18-1 to see how money and income determination interact.

Depression model. This reconciliation of the theories of money and of income determination is, of course, oversimplified and needs some qualifications. For example, it does not emphasize what can happen in *severe depression* when the liquidity-preference curve is practically *horizontal* because interest rates are already so low that people are quite indifferent whether they hold M or the near-M government treasury bills that the Bank wants to swap for M. In such a rare, but possible, case, the potency of monetary policy is at least temporarily very low. This is summarized in the aphorism "The central bank can pull on a string (to curb booms), but it can't *push on a string* (to reverse deep slumps)." Indeed, in such depressed times the profit expectations of businessmen are likely to be so low that they would not employ men and machines on new investment projects even if you let them borrow temporarily at a zero interest rate. In this case, the marginal-efficiency schedule of Fig. 18-1(*b*) is practically vertical; and again the chain of monetary action loses potency. (It is these "depression models" which are often, but wrongly, associated with the name of Keynes; and if they were his sole cases, his ideas would only rarely be of great interest in modern times.)

Classical case. The opposite "classical" or "monetarist" case, equally extreme, occurs when the liquidity schedule is practically vertical, so that each unit of M is under a strong compulsion to circulate at a constant velocity (with V a hard constant). (It can also occur when the marginal-efficiency schedule is so horizontal that the slightest reduction in interest rate is enough to wipe out any deflationary gap and the slightest rise in interest is enough to wipe out any inflationary gap. Appendix readers will find more on these polar cases there.)

As most economists interpret the history of the last few centuries, this extreme case is not deemed realistic. They cannot agree with the extreme classical view known as "Say's Law of Conservation of Purchasing Power." The Appendix to this chapter discusses this matter further. It is enough here to characterize Say's Law as alleging:

"There cannot be any such thing as a saving-and-investment problem. What is not consumed is surely destined to be spent on investment goods, without the possibility of any snag."

QUALIFICATIONS Eschewing polar cases, we must notice a difficulty raised by experts in corporate finance about the relevance for monetary policy of the *me* schedule. They point out that many large firms finance their investments *out of retained earnings* and the cash flow generated by their own operations. Many avoid going to the banks or outside markets for borrowings or stock flotations. (Example: The great DuPont Company has not borrowed a cent for more than 50 years, yet has been an important source of progress in the chemical field.) As well, large firms simply borrow or lend in New York when the Bank of Canada makes the Canadian money market unattractive.

To the degree that investment does depend upon internal or foreign funds that are insulated from domestic market fluctuations in interest rate and credit availability, the potency of monetary policy is just that much less: it then takes greater action by the Bank to produce the same effect. One could go on to give other bits of evidence used to play down the importance of monetary policy (as, for example, the fact that when investors are uncertain about the future, small changes in safe-asset interest rates may have little effect upon the high profit rates investors require as inducement to undertake investment, and hence I may be insensitive to monetary policy).

Qualifications are not all in the direction of playing down the importance of M. We have noted in passing that credit policy does have some influence on G and C in $C + I + G$. Higher market evaluations

---

[2] Of course, if this monetary constriction is successful in ending rapid price inflation, interest rates in the longer run will not have to include a premium to cover depreciation of the dollar's real purchasing power. So the *initial* rise in interest rates from M restriction may well be reversed *in the end*. The real rate can converge on the market rate of interest.

(a)

(b)

FIG. 18-2. Fiscal policy means public expenditure and tax policy

(*a*). An increase of 10 in government expenditures on goods and services will shift *C + I + G* up to *C + I + G'*, raising income to *E'*. Moreover, there is involved the usual multiplier effect of induced consumption spending (and, for that matter, induced private investment spending).

(*b*). Lowering taxes by 10 has similar expansionary effects of income. Lower tax collection gives you more disposable income out of GNP, and hence shifts the consumption schedule upward. We go from *E* to *E'* as a result of the new *C' + I + G* schedule. (Dollar for dollar, tax reduction is a little weaker than *G* increase. Why? Because some tax rebate is saved rather than used to shift *CC* up. A cut in taxes of 10 shifts *CC leftward* that much, but *upward* only by 2/3 × 10 = 6 2/3 when the MPC is 2/3.)

CONTRAST WITH FISCAL POLICY AND INCOME DETERMINATION

Let us now survey the fiscal policy powers of government. Aside from the central bank, the government has another major way of affecting current spending (as seen in Chapter 13). As part of its *fiscal policy* the government can expand its expenditures: build useful public roads and schools, hire more civil servants, increase defense expenditure, do a hundred and one useful (or foolish) things to expand total spending. This could be shown in a saving-investment diagram like Fig. 18-1(*b*), by shifting the *me* curve to the right.

But better still, we can show it as an *upward shift in the G component* of the *C + I + G* schedule that was used as an alternative way to show income equi-

of land, plant, and equipment, and of securities generally, may shift *CC* up. In the long run, if the increase in *M* comes, let us say, from gold mining or Treasury printing (and not merely from a swap by the Bank of Canada of *M* for near-*M*), the new *M adds directly to people's net worth,* and this does lead them, other things equal, to spend more on *C*, on *I*, and on *G*.[3]

---

[3] There is another channel by which *M* gains in potency. New *M* and lower *i* should raise common stock prices. New corporations can float new issues of stock more easily and cheaply. So with the cost of capital down, corporations will be induced to expand their investment; again, up goes *C + I + G* and GNP.

Some economists used to hope that higher interest rates would stimulate saving and kill consumption; i.e., they hoped an interest increase would shift up the *SS* schedule in Fig. 18-1(*c*), thereby reinforcing the effect of a downward shift in *II*. Experience, and the analysis of Chapter 30, suggest that, outside the area of installment-financed consumer durables, these effects are probably weak and cannot be much counted on. (Warning: The *B* points in Fig. 18-1 are final equilibria only if the Bank of Canada now creates just enough further *M* to satisfy enhanced "active" or *income* needs; otherwise, we repeat the cycle with *LL* shifted by changed GNP level, finding final equilibria generally somewhere between the *A* and *B* points. See the Hicks-Hansen diagrams in the Appendix for a rigorous handling of this transactions-need feedback problem.)

librium. Figure 18-2(a) recapitulates the demonstration on page 000 of how an expansion of public expenditure G leads to an expansion of income.

The same type of chart[4] can show, in Fig. 18-2(b), the other side of fiscal policy—changes in tax collections. To raise GNP the fiscal authorities cut taxes: this gives people higher disposable income, and since they have a positive propensity to consume out of extra income, this means they will consume more.

How can we show the increased consumption on Fig. 18-2(b)? We can show the effect of reduced taxes as an *upward shift* of the CC schedule, which is plotted against GNP and is a major component of the pictured C + I + G schedule. With taxes lower, we subtract less from each level of GNP to get the corresponding level of disposable income. So, with higher disposable income corresponding to each GNP, we must show higher consumption—hence the higher CC and C + I + G curves.

We may summarize the effects of fiscal policy:

Increased G raises income by raising the GG component of C + I + G. Reduced taxes raise the CC component of the C + I + G schedule. Both together —which also means deficit financing or a reduction in the budgetary surplus—result in an ever greater upward shift of the C + I + G schedule and of equilibrium income. In the reverse case of contractionary fiscal policy, the final C + I + G schedule shifts downward.

Here is a good test of one's understanding of the mechanics of fiscal policy: try showing what the effects on GNP of Mitchell Sharp's 1968 increase in personal income tax rates could be presumed to be (1) with no change in government expenditures and (2) with a simultaneous rise in G, as was expected.

LESSENED POTENCY OF TEMPORARY TAX CHANGES An important qualification is in order. Suppose, that in 1976 the government introduces a tax rise to combat inflation. But suppose it says that the new tax surcharge is only going to be *temporary*. Then, definitely, the deflationary effects on total GNP spending will be lessened by the fact that everybody expects the tax to apply only for a temporary time.

Let's review why. Suppose a typical family earns $12,000 a year, pays $2,000 in normal taxes. Its permanent disposable income, what it can count on and plan for, is $10,000. So, for the next many years, it will become adjusted to a living standard appropriate to this presumed level of permanent income.

But now suppose a temporary tax surcharge of $1,000 is introduced by the government. Everyone knows it is to last only one or two years. Should our family now get adjusted to a living standard of only $9,000 of disposable income— cutting down on its consumption, CC, spending by the 10 per cent temporary cut in its this year's income? That would go against human nature—and ordinary prudence. Better, surely, for the family to dip a little into the rate at which it normally saves. UPSHOT: A tax change known to be temporary will have less than the usual impact on CC and C + I + G schedules and on GNP. *Temporary tax-rate changes have less potency than permanent tax-rate changes.*

BUDGET DEFICITS INTERACT WITH M CHANGES

So far, we've been treating monetary policy and fiscal policy as if they take place independently. On one occasion, the Bank of Canada acts to change M. On another occasion, the government legislates a budget deficit. How nice to be able to observe these separate controlled experiments and learn experimentally what is the separate potency of fiscal policy and of monetary policy.

But, of course, it doesn't happen that way in real life. Not only do these two separate things tend to happen simultaneously so as to frustrate the economic historian's chance to determine the separate effects of each. Worse than that, or actually better than that from the standpoint of policy, often an act of fiscal deficit spending will be *purposely* combined with an act of central bank money creation. Much more powerful will be the expansionary effect on GNP of a fiscal deficit that is financed by M creation than of one financed by government bond sales to the public.[5] It is no accident that mixed economies

---

[4] The treatment here recapitulates the treatment on page 217 of Chapter 13 and best handles the effects of personal income taxes. For more complicated analysis of sales and profit taxes, also taking account of tax effects on investment, see intermediate texts.

[5] Careful readers will realize that the financial requirements of the federal government, i.e. its deficit, were already shown in the monetary-policy survey of Fig. 17-2.

deliberately combine the two macroeconomic weapons.

To verify this, contrast the case (a) of a deficit or new G expenditure financed by M change, with (b) one financed by bond sales. In the last case, start with an initial increase in C + I + G and GNP. With M unchanged, what will happen to interest rates now that GNP has gone up? To get M for their new transactions, people will be selling off some of their bonds, thereby depressing bond prices and raising interest rates. But these higher interest rates will mean, other things being equal, that I now drops a bit. So our initial increase in C + I + G, due to new higher G, will be later reduced by an induced slight drop in I. By contrast, in (a) the Bank of Canada to match the deficit creates the new M needed to keep interest rates from rising and I from falling. So the new G is a complete add-on to the C + I + G schedule.

The same thing can be put in the monetarist language of MV = PQ. A fiscal deficit in the form of higher G will push up interest rates if the Bank of Canada holds M constant. People will cause V, the rate of turnover of their cash balance, to rise a bit now that the interest cost of holding their cash balances has gone up. The higher V with fixed M means higher GNP. But how much more expansionary the same fiscal policy will be if the Bank of Canada, aiming to keep interest rates from rising, acts to create new M in MV = PQ.[6]

THE SYNTHESIS AT WORK: FRONTIER RESOURCE PROJECTS

To appreciate how modern tools of macroeconomic analysis and aggregate demand management really work, let us apply them as a case study to one of the prevailing long-run problems of Canadian growth.

[6] In the polar case of an extreme monetarist, V is a hard constant that will not rise even with higher i. In such a pole, an increase in G has no effects on GNP, being offset by an equivalent reduction in C + I. But there seems no plausible reason to expect people in their inventory decisions on how much M to hold to take no account of the higher interest yields they must now forego. Only in the most extreme hyperinflation, when people are holding absolutely minimal cash balances and V cannot be speeded up further (even by a doubling of the rate of inflation and melting of the purchasing power of cash held), would we expect this extreme pole to be reached.

A notable feature of Canadian economic development is its dependence on large capital-intensive projects. These tend to be indivisible, or "lumpy": in contrast to residential or factory expansion, all or a large part of each project must be built at one time. The project has no usefulness until the whole thing is finished. Our history is filled with the social, regional and political ramifications of these huge ventures, which always need explicit government approval and usually have government financial and planning support as well. Examples: the opening of all-Canadian canal navigation from Montreal to Lake Superior; the Intercolonial Railway; the C.P.R.; the Beauharnois, Niagara, Columbia and St. Lawrence power projects; and looking to the future, the James Bay power project; and northern gas and oil pipelines. All of these provide "infrastructure" services to other industries. In addition there are enormous directly-profitable resource-exploitation complexes like the Shawinigan, Kitimat, Flin Flon, Sudbury, Elliot Lake, Pine Point and Quebec-Labrador.

Canada is today so large an economy that such vast projects can be started and finished with much less macroeconomic disturbance than fifty years ago. Nevertheless, the James Bay and Arctic pipeline projects promise to be nearly as potentially disturbing in their way as the C.P.R. one hundred years ago.

Are these mammoth undertakings blessings or curses? Given that they (eventually) become the well-built structures that deliver the services for which they were designed, may not their building confront the macroeconomy with widespread strains and stresses that cancel their advantages?

PREDICTION VS ADJUSTMENT There are two questions here. One is analytical: can we discover the impact on jobs, business, and cities, of new construction and of its completion? The other is, can we soften this impact, so that these projects need not be rejected or postponed because of their undesirable, economy-wide effects? The answers can be optimistic: today we can predict and we can moderate, much more than we could before the introduction of modern analytical tools.

As for prediction of economic impact, this is not the place to discuss this complex, inter-disciplinary procedure in detail. Mathematicians, environmentalists, lawyers, engineers, sociologists, architects and political scientists all have contributions to make. Suffice it to say that economists, helped by computer models such as RDX-2, CANDIDE and TRACE, can simulate the effects of future construction activity on the different labor markets (skilled worker shortages), finance markets (credit conditions), and individual supplying industries (factory expansion, delivery dates and capacity limitations) as they will be experienced by the *rest of the economy*. At a more aggregate level, they help to predict the effect of particular projects on such major macroeconomic variables as $(C + G + I)$; the balance of payments $(E - M)$; i; and the rate of exchange in each year or month during the construction build-up and completion.[7]

A quite different question, to which we may apply our monetary-fiscal analysis, is the role of aggregate demand policy in cushioning the effect of very large changes in G or I.

The very fact that we ask *this* question shows the pronounced change in our ability to control the economy. Fifty years ago such projects were promoted simply because they created jobs; because in their absence, prolonged and profound unemployment was feared. Today it is widely known that there are many monetary and fiscal means to generate jobs. A project must be worthwhile and we must be able easily to adjust to its completion and perhaps eventual removal and cleanup before we will agree to its starting. So we confine ourselves to the partial question; given that the project is socially profitable, how can we deal with the problem that people will be made jobless when the project's I is completed?

For example, during pipeline construction, various industries and sectors will expand: there will be not only extra-shift production in factories and mines but also induced investment (involving some accelerator-like reactions) in new capacity and by *their* suppliers. Much capital and labor will move from their previous uses to new products or new plants. Labor and capital will move in from Europe, Japan and the U.S. Transportation routes: railroads, roads and rivers will be expanded or used more intensively. Townsites, hospitals, schools, trailer camps, shopping plazas and red-light districts will come into being near the project sites. Just as all these are set-

tling down, their *raison d'etre* will come to an end with the completion of construction. The factories and mines must go down to one-shift production or switch to supplying inputs for some other project. The temporary townsites may be abandoned; the railways revert to their old schedules.

In some cases private enterprisers will think of new things to make or do with the facilities and work forces that are no longer needed: new products and services or export contracts will emerge and some construction equipment will be salvaged, to be sold at auction for use in other frontier projects.

THE FORWARD LOOK But by themselves these adjustments to the end of a project may not relieve but aggravate the problem of joblessness that is emerging for the thousands of workers; the conversion of swords into ploughshares may now create unexpected unemployment in the ploughshare industries. People will now look for desperate remedies. Some will advocate the forcible repatriation of workers who immigrated when the project was at its peak; others demand that the new facilities soak up extra workers for ordinary operating duties; and still others will advocate new projects of a leaf-raking nature to create jobs for those laid off.

Modern students of income determination and demand management take a more fruitful tack. They say:

Regardless of why these jobs came to an end, why aren't there enough *new* jobs being generated to absorb them? What fiscal and monetary policies are needed to create the new $C + I + G + (E - M)$ to hire them anew?

Don't look back; look forward to see what you have to do to restore high, useful, employment. Better still, this approach means you need not decide whether the pessimists are right who argue that the unemployment following big projects (like that following big wars) is so serious a problem as to justify avoiding resource development.[8] Why care? *We know that monetary and fiscal (and exchange-rate) demand management of the correct magnitude will be needed to avoid the twin perils of an underemployed, or an overheated, economy.*

---

[7] For an example, see the chapters by J. H. Helliwell and others in the *MacKenzie Gas Pipeline*, ed. P. H. Pearse (McClelland and Stewart, Toronto, 1974).

[8] Of course, there are other, quality-of-life and environmental reasons for avoiding huge, destructive, irreversible projects without assurance that the *NEW* gains are adequate.

GRAPHICAL RESTORATION OF HIGH EMPLOYMENT

To apply this fruitful approach, we can look for income equilibrium where the $C + I + G$ schedule just intersects the 45° line, as shown in Fig. 18-3.

Suppose that the end of pipeline construction has made 30 per cent of the labor force jobless. (A monstrous exaggeration!) Hence the underemployment deflationary-gap equilibrium at E' is now 30 percent to the left of the full-employment line of Fig. 18-3 at FF. Let us make quite unfavorable assumptions: (*a*) that government leaves its expenditure G as it was; (*b*) that new investment, now that the project is complete, has fallen to I'; and that (*c*) neither the new project nor its services give consumers a new appetite for services, so that the CC schedule (and propensity to save) will be unchanged. In short, of the components of GNE, only I has shifted.

Result: trouble. Many are out of work. Unions are disturbed, city councils are desperate, immigrant families are prohibited from bringing in their relatives, and the economy is not producing or consuming at potential.

DEMAND MANAGEMENT TO THE RESCUE

All this can be cured. Here is how. Let the central bank fight this slump by making credit much cheaper and much more freely available. (Recall open-market purchases, lowering of reserve requirements, and lowering the Bank Rate.) What will this do to the I schedule? Push it up. At the same time, let the government cut down on the heavy taxing it was doing in the previous full-employment situation. This will increase people's disposable incomes, increase their consumption spending, and thus shift upward the C part of the $C + I + G$ schedule. (Maybe I will get further shifted, too.) Without increasing government expenditure directly, we can thus shift the $C + I' + G$ schedule far enough upward until the new $C' + I'' + G$ schedule intersects the 45° line at the new full-employment level E''. Alternatively, since there are always pressing needs in the public sector and overseas, expansion of G and E could be used to help shift $C + I + G' + (E' - M)$ up to the target level. Fig. 18-3 shows how these upward shifts have restored a full-employment equilibrium. By proper policy we have adjusted from a slump to a boom. *People now enjoy 30 percent more output without being forced into*

FIG. 18-3. Demand management policies liberate mixed economy from unemployment due to "lumpiness" of construction.

bread lines. They are not made to work short hours and do not have to take Mondays off because the limited work has to be shared.

OTHER "PROBLEMS" Figure 18-3 illustrates the approach of demand management New Economics to many issues: electrification, mechanization, automation, regional decline, obsolescence of a city's main product, a new rage to buy imported products, and post-war demobilization and nation-wide or world-wide disarmament. Instead of being regarded as "problems", all these occurrences can now be hailed as opportunities to make use of the brains, skills, productive power of the labor force, factories, etc. released as a result of them.

You should be sure you know how to use Figure 18-3 to handle situations where the cause is a massive increase in I; an increase in C, G, or E; or a spontaneous decrease in any of C, I, G, or E. A change in M, either way, is also possible. You should be able to show how contractionary monetary and fiscal policy would be needed to wipe out the inflationary gaps created when C, I, G, or E had increased too far, as well as how expansionary policies could compensate for deflationary losses of employment suffered when these GNE components shrink.

As a final test, suppose that resource and raw-material imbalances threaten Canadian jobs. Perhaps energy is now so expensive that Canadian energy-consuming refineries and industries cannot meet the new prices offered by other energy consumers. Or perhaps German and Japanese exporters have such miraculous improvements in productivity as to kill off their Canadian manufacturing competitors. Can you bring macroeconomics to the rescue in these *long-run* problems?[9]

Of course, the higher dollar demand engineered by fiscal and monetary policy cannot be expected to provide the same kind of jobs using exactly the same skills and paying exactly the same wage rates. Inevitably there will still be important transitional problems for particular workers, firms, and regions.[10]

Programs of retraining and of increasing labor mobility and flexibility are vital (as Chapters 29 and 40 both discuss), along with aggregate demand policies to ensure proper aggregate dollar demand. Regions that produce one or few "staple" products (wheat, fur, coal, wooden ships), or depend on depleted mines and forests particularly need these special manpower policies. But they must be fitted into a growing full-employment GNP.

THE NEW MIXED ECONOMY

Critics used to regard the classical principles of economics as out of date. Looking out the window at the long bread lines and the men selling apples on street corners, they said:

Why speak of scarcity? Or efficiency? Or growth? Of fairness? Throw away your tools of supply and demand, your finespun theories of market pricing. Tear up the rule book. We live in a new era in which everything is upside down: attempts to save kill off investment: a hurricane or war is a blessing in that it creates jobs and gives food to the starving unemployed. Sanctions imposed by the United Nations on trade hasten a country's development. Capitalism is doomed to collapse in a crisis of underconsumption and overproduction.

What is the modern economist's answer to all this? He says:

You are right to question the classical principles. All principles should be subjected to the closest examination with respect to both their logic and their factual relevance. The classical arguments were oversimple, and they admittedly did not allow for the facts of nineteenth- and twentieth-

century life. But experience since 1932, and careful logical reasoning, suggest that money and aggregate $C + I + G + (E - M)$ spending *will not manage themselves.* A *laissez-faire* system is doomed to wasteful ups and downs of the business cycle and perhaps to long fits of stagnation.

Even among the economists of Eastern Europe there has developed a recognition of the new scientific knowledge about macroeconomic policy.

Simple capitalism has been replaced virtually everywhere by the mixed economy ("the managed economy"). Everywhere in the Western World[11] governments and central banks have shown they can win the battle of the slump if people want them to. They have the weapons of fiscal policy (expenditure and taxes) and of monetary policy (open-market operations, discount-rate policy, legal reserve ratio policy) to shift the various schedules that determine national income and employment. Just as we no longer meekly accept disease, we no longer need accept mass unemployment.

Under the managed macroeconomics of the mixed economy, many of the old classical principles of microeconomics will again apply; but now they apply because our macroeconomics has validated their premise of adequate demand—not because the world is lucky enough to have them apply *automatically* and at all times. This is a brave answer, and essentially—most careful economists would today say—an accurate answer. But let us not be too boastful of our modern conquest of instability. There is no warrant for smugness. Let us quietly add the following qualifications:

The worst consequences of the business cycle, which Chapter 14 showed plagued capitalism from its beginning, are probably a thing of the past; but that does not mean that the cycle is gone. "Fine tuning" is not yet here. We still have minor inventory fluctuations, still shall have transitions from war to peace and from one kind of boom to another. The difference will be this: the age-old tendencies for the system to fluctuate will still be there, but no longer will the world let them snow-

---

[9] Never forget that adjusting aggregate demand in Canada will involve changes in imports, exports, capital movements, immigration, foreign ownership, tariffs, the exchange rate and the tourist trade. See Figure 17-1 for some indication of the ramifications of deficit financing to deal with a short-run problem.

[10] Especially Indians, Eskimos and others who had been quickly trained for non-recurrent frontier jobs.

[11] This, of course includes Japan, India, and other Asian nations; Australia and New Zealand; Latin America; and the new African states.

ball into vast depressions or into galloping inflations—no longer will we let our banking system falter and our nation go through the most painful debt deflation and bankruptcy.

THREE QUALIFICATIONS

We should recognize that all Canadian political pressures do work to make a drastic slump unlikely. But can we be sure that the same pressures are strong enough to deal with three problems that are just as serious?

1. *International flow of unemployment.* Sceptics may smile at the thought of *Canadian* political pressures uniting to fight a slump: "Canadian employment and income determination obviously depend on exports and so on foreign (U.S. and Japanese) markets. Can Canadian monetary or fiscal policy hope to make up for crashes abroad?" For such doubters, the theory above is something for our customers abroad to use—it can never save us. They are right. Canada is only a small part of the Western economy. We can only hope that the modern mixed economies can, when a slump appears imminent, quickly focus the weapons of full employment on this crucial target.

At the same time, in milder crises, we must use the theory ourselves to resolve our "open-economy" problem of keeping a balance in international financial relations while dealing with domestic income and employment. This is the trick of keeping *both* internal and external balance.

For example, we have already seen that domestic monetary policies, changing interest rates, can attract or repel foreign capital. Capital-flow variations, in turn, can affect the value of our dollar. What then? *If* policy is to keep the exchange rate fixed, domestic policies will have to be altered to reverse the capital flow, or to arrange some compensating flow of other kinds of foreign money. On the other hand, *if* policy allows the dollar to float, exports and imports may have to adjust at the expense of important voting groups.

More on this in later chapters. The important contributions of Harry Johnson, Robert Mundell, Grant Reuber, and others have so far shown that certain combinations of domestic and foreign stabilization policy *are* compatible; but others rule each other out.

2. *Regional or "structural" unemployment.* In Canada's diverse economy, nation-wide "full employment" may actually represent over-full employment in Ontario and unemployment in Newfoundland. In such circumstances, monetary and fiscal policy may not be widely accepted by all parties, especially when the slump is not yet cataclysmic enough to alarm all regions or industries.

Our aggregate demand weapons can do little about this disparate "structure" of the Canadian labor employment market. It can attempt to spread capital and jobs more evenly; and it can try moving the men to the work. These policies now exist. Furthermore, it is at least conceivable that "aggregate" monetary and fiscal weapons can be applied selectively: heavily in some regions and lightly elsewhere. A start on this approach was made in 1968-1969 and widened in 1970 in the application of anti-inflation policies.

3. *Inflation.* Can we be so sure that the same pressures that may unite against a slump will operate against creeping inflation? What about "cost-push" inflation rather than "demand-pull" inflation?

Chapter 19 will show that the mixed economy is still far from knowing all the important answers to this new dread disease. The Appendix to the present chapter explores further the analysis of money and of income determination.

SUMMARY

1 Monetary policy by the central bank is an important way of shifting the saving and investment schedules, or of shifting the total schedule of $C + I + G + (E - M)$ spending.

2 Along the downward-sloping "liquidity-preference schedule," higher M induces a lower interest rate—enough lower to persuade people to hold all the new M. Along the downward-sloping "marginal efficiency of investment schedule," lower interest rate and

more available credit make it profitable for new investment projects to get done. Along the familiar saving-investment multiplier-type diagram, the induced increase in I leads to higher production and income.[12]

3 Fiscal policy means governmental tax and expenditure policy. It, too, affects income determination by shifting the spending schedules. Higher expenditure on goods and services directly raises the G component of $C + I + G$ schedule and thus raises its equilibrium intersection. Taxes work in reverse: *reduced* tax rates, by shifting the CC schedule leftward and upward, push *up* the $C + I + G$ schedule; increased tax rates have the opposite, contractionary effect; and in either case, tax changes are, dollar for dollar, a little less potent than government expenditure changes.

4 Monetary and fiscal policy interact. A budget deficit financed by new M will raise GNP more than one paid for by issue of government bonds. Historically, much of the M created by the Bank of Canada and other banks originated in deficit financing.

5 The important case of construction lumpiness shows how, by combination of fiscal and monetary policies, a modern economy can ensure the restoration of high-employment equilibrium even in the worst case where the end of a new project is reducing the need for men to do any given amount of work and is not bringing in its train any spontaneous expansion of dollar demand elsewhere.

6 Modern democracies have the fiscal and monetary tools, and the political will to use them, to end chronic slumps and galloping inflations. This makes obsolete the fear of overproduction and underconsumption, and obviates the need to bolster purchasing power by military or imperialistic programs. But it does not solve problems of income inequality or of monopolistic and other imperfections at the microeconomic level. Part Two's handling of unemployment merely sets up the stage for the again-relevant microeconomic problems of Parts Three and Four. But Chapter 19 shows that complacency over cost-push inflation is quite unjustified.

7 Regional and foreign constraints reduce our freedom to use these neoclassical weapons, and reduce their power.

CONCEPTS FOR REVIEW

M down $\rightarrow i$ up $\rightarrow I$ down $\quad\rightarrow$ GNP down = MV down	marginal-efficiency schedule
Shift of $C + I + G$: through monetary policy and through tax and expenditure changes	leftward CC shift from tax cut
	fiscal and monetary interaction
	automation and unemployment
expenditure versus tax potency	macroeconomics of mixed economy
liquidity-preference schedule	foreign-balance constraints

---

[12] The appendix shows that if there is a deep-depression inelasticity of investment response to interest and/or a deep-depression horizontality of LL representing indifference to money holding, the effect of new M will fall to nil. In quantity-theory language, then and *only* then will the contrived rise in M be completely negated by a compensating fall in V, leaving $MV = PQ$ = GNP quite unchanged. Usually the induced drop in interest rates will cause V to decrease, but not by enough to offset the new M in the now higher MV. Only in the other extreme case of monetarism will V be a hard constant, responding in no systematic way to i, CC, II, and GG changes. The great neoclassical writers—Marshall, Wicksell, Pigou, Irving Fisher—never believed in such monetarism.

QUESTIONS FOR DISCUSSION

1. Redo Fig. 18-1(a), (b), and (c) to show tight monetary policies. Trace the steps.
2. Wipe out a 1990 deflationary gap created by the finishing of massive frontier projects by (a) fiscal policy alone, (b) monetary policy alone, and (c) any blend of the two. Which path leads to full employment with slowest growth (i.e., least capital formation for the future)?
3. "Fiscal and monetary authority should be in one agency, or at least be coordinated. Otherwise they may conflict, one undoing what the other does." Discuss.
4. Use Fig. 18-2 to show that increasing G and taxes at the same time will tend to have canceling effects on income. Difficult question: Can you follow the intricate reasoning which has argued that, dollar for dollar, changes in G are a little more potent than changes in taxes—so that a balanced-budget decrease in G is likely to be a bit deflationary?
5. Consider automation, the replacement in industry of people by machines. Explain how the tools that stabilize the economy after a change in frontier resource development can handle an increase in automation-created unemployment.
6. Explain critically the new look in macroeconomics.
7. To offset underconsumption, capitalism *must* engage in cold-war spending and imperialism. Show how $C + I + G$ analysis now makes this view archaic.

APPENDIX: Mechanisms of Money and Income Determination

This is a brief discussion of how money, interest, investment, income, prices, and velocity of circulation are interrelated. Classical views that there can never be unemployment, and depression versions of the Keynesian system, will turn out to be alternative poles of such an analysis. And what most economists would consider to be the most realistic description of how our economy works and what are potencies of policy weapons will fall somewhere on the continuum between these extreme poles.

The topics will be covered in this order: velocity interrelations; classical and monetarist models; liquidity preference and income determination.

BEHAVIOR OF VELOCITY Instead of the chain $M{\rightarrow}i$ ${\rightarrow}I{\rightarrow}$GNP (or its even further elaboration to take account of wealth-capitalization effects and effects on G and C schedules), some proponents of monetarism prefer to short-circuit the process and use the concept of velocity. They write

$$M{\rightarrow}MV = \textbf{GNP}$$

This asserts that an increase in M, unless *offset fully* by an induced shift in V of the type that neither they nor the believers in the four-link chain consider likely, will serve to increase dollar GNP with all the applied effects of the product of $P \times Q$.[1]

These different modes of language can formally represent the same facts, just as an account in English or an account in French can be given of any sequence of events. In a sense, therefore, reasonable men will not argue about terminology and semantics.

At a deeper level, however, those who prefer one terminology usually think that certain hypotheses about the real world are more fruitful than others. Thus, those who like to use *MV* usually have more definite views about the probable behavior of *V*, and its invariance under a wide range of alternative conditions, than do those who like to use the $C + I + G$ and liquidity-preference approach explicitly. While the bulk of economists today incline toward the eclectic view, there is no need to be dogmatic about the matter. If the day ever arrives when the proponents of the velocity approach can prove by their researches that

theirs is the more convenient tool, pragmatic scholars will welcome all its help. In any case, post-Keynesians and monetarists both agree that "money matters much."

CLASSICAL PRICE FLEXIBILITY

More basic than the question of whether to use or not use the terminology of either school is the contrast between a *frictionless* system in which all market prices are *flexible* and the *realistic* world of a mixed economic system that exists here and elsewhere in the West. Many classical economists thought unemployment to be quite impossible because in their frictionless models whatever is not spent in one direction gets automatically spent in another.

SAY'S LAW This view, called Say's Law, since its statement in 1803 by French writer J. B. Say, has been much debated because of the ambiguous form in which it was expressed: thus, Say and other classical writers felt that overproduction was impossible by its very nature, since all value relations were relative—shoes being comparable with spoons at some proper relative price; they felt that what a worker saves gets spent as truly on employing men in the machinery trades as what the worker spends on giving work in the food or other consumers' industries; they had at least a vague notion that the interest rate in a flexible capital market would always find a level at which (full-employment) saving and investment schedules would intersect; they, or their more sophisticated followers, had the notion that, if only the money wage would fall flexibly far enough, it would always bring out job offers for every willing worker. So went their rather vague arguments.

In the years since 1800, there were often short periods of considerable unemployment, and on a few occasions there were longer periods of considerable unemployment or of *under*employment. So economists wanted to go beyond the simpler formulations of Say's Law: to deny some of its implicit presumptions about flexible prices and wages, or to abandon it and work from alternative hypotheses.

Today it is clear that the alternative approaches are fully capable of being reconciled, so that there is only a difference of a degree and of realism between them, not a difference of kind. A. C. Pigou of Cambridge University showed in 1943 how his older cherished beliefs could be related to what he had first thought were Keynesian heresies; his reconciliation goes thus.

PIGOU EFFECTS Let there be a certain M in the system that consists of coins or of imperishable paper currency. Suppose that initially there is unemployment because the SS and II schedules interesect to the left of the full-employment level. Suppose interest rates are in equilibrium

---

[1] Some proponents would think V will stay constant after a sizable change in open-market operations; others would not think this is a necessary assumption. Some, impressed by the empirical fact that in past short-term upswings, rises in M and V have tended to coincide, choose to extrapolate this *post hoc* experience; others set up more complicated hypotheses, depending upon the environment upon which the open-market operations impinged. Many agree with our later liquidity-preference theory, whose Hicks-Hansen diagrams can be thought of as a theory of velocity —i.e., a theory in which V is an increasing function of the interest rate i.

on every bond and security market, with auctioneers finding matching supply and demand bids. And just to complete the simplified discussion, suppose there is no central banker or fiscal authority to do anything about the situation.

A sophisticated follower of Say would now assert: "There is just one flaw in this equilibrium. Men who want to work at going wages are not employed. To be fair, whether or not this is realistic, you should also imagine an auctioneer for the labor market. He makes the wage rate expressed in money fall whenever there is excessive labor supply."

Pigou agrees. He lets the wage rate fall. Money wages being an important cost of production, for all the reasons discussed in Parts Three and Four, this drop will result in considerable lowering of all prices. When prices and wages are low enough, what will happen to the SS and II intersection? Suppose I am a typical man who previously owned an acre of land, a machine, and $100 in cash. (I also may have owed on a mortgage or may have held someone's IOU stated in terms of money; but for the community as a whole, such interpersonal money liabilities and assets have to *cancel* out. Recall also that there are no government bonds in the picture to worry about.)

For dramatic effect, suppose that wages fall to one-thousandth (0.001) of their previous level; suppose, although it is unnecessary except for simplicity of exposition to stick to the same number, that prices of all things also fall to 0.001 of their previous levels. This means that my acre of land and machine will fall to 0.001 of their previous value. Everything falls in value—except one item. My $100 bill is still a $100 bill. But now in terms of its real purchasing power, I own the equivalent of what was $100,000 before. I am rich!

Will I spend the same amount on consumption and on saving out of *income* levels that are the same as before either in money or in real terms? I will not. I am rich and can consume more before I die.

At some point, because of the enhanced *real wealth effect* of the increased purchasing power of the hard money in the economic system (induced by a large enough wage and price fall), CC schedules will shift up in real (not money) terms, and SS schedules shift equivalently downward. The new SS and II intersection can thus be moved to the right of the full-employment level. So, even if there were no favorable effects of the price-level or interest change on the II curves, *by getting money wages and prices far enough down, the condition of "full employment" could theoretically be achieved. QED.*

Pigou thus vindicated abstract classical principles by recourse to this "hard-money effect," which economists today call the "Pigou effect" in his honor.[2] But being a realistic observer of the difficulties of getting wages to move flexibly downward in a mixed capitalistic society, and having lived through eras in which the dynamic process of debt deflation led to bankruptcy, riots, slump, and even revolution, Pigou hastened to point out that he did not recommend such hyperdeflation to cure capitalism's unemployment. He much preferred to accomplish the same thing by increasing dollar M; and actually, he adhered to the general notions of Part Two of this book. The fact that he often liked to use the word "velocity" in his Keynes-like theory shows that mere semantic matters are indeed of limited importance.

CRUDE QUANTITY THEORY IN THE CLASSICAL MODEL Recall now the crude quantity theory, which held prices must always be proportional to the amount of money—so that doubling M must exactly double P. For many situations in the realistic world—with its sticky prices, boom, depression, and thousands of changes always going on to confound the experiment—we saw that the crude quantity theory was not a good predicting device. But if we confine our attention to the perfectly frictionless model of the classical type used by Pigou and others in the above discussion, we can find an important nucleus of truth in the crude quantity theory; and we can understand better the reasons why it has some degree of predictive value during galloping inflations and over certain long-enough time intervals.

Recall Pigou's fantastic but happy equilibrium which has made the representative man feel rich enough to save as little as society can invest at full employment. Now suppose his $100 bill had been a $10 bill. Do you see that merely by having all prices go down still another nine-tenths the equilibrium could be *exactly* restored, with every relative price and wage just the same as before and every physical commodity and input the same as before? *Cutting M to one-tenth has cut P to exactly one-tenth in this classical model.*

In this abstract model the crude quantity theory has come into its own. In the tautological equation of exchange $MV \equiv PQ$, there has not been the slightest reason for the Q or V to have changed (waiving all dynamic questions of how the system gets into the new equilibrium and "forgets" all its past price levels). So P does equal kM, where k is the ratio V/Q, whose numerator and denominator will have been constant in this abstract example, however much they may vary in reality.

This long-period full-employment frictionless classical model has the further property that *no* change in interest rates can come from the *balanced* change in M. As David Ricardo argued, if all prices and wages change in exactly the same proportion, so that what used to be called 4 pence is now 2 pence, then any asset that used to pay 5 per cent per annum in the form of 50 pence on 1,000

---

[2]Mention may be made here of a non-Pigou, non-Say, non-Keynes version of full employment originated by Professor Nicholas Kaldor of Cambridge. He is widely interpreted to believe that, within wide limits, any change of I will induce just enough shift of the share of income accruing to thrifty profit receivers to produce a long-run *full-employment* intersection of SS and II always. If only it were valid such a view would be important. If only. . . .

pence will now be paying 5 per cent in the form of 25 pence on 500 pence.

It should not be necessary to stress that the real world as we know it is a far cry from the abstract model. This is true especially in the short run; in the longer run, to the degree that all price adjustments get made and other disturbances are ruled out, the abstract model fits somewhat better. The art of economics is to know how to blend the elements of absurdity and of relevance of such a model in interpreting living events and policy.

PERMANENT PUBLIC DEBT Even in the extreme classical model, all P's would not be proportional to M alone! Interest-bearing public bonds, which correspond to no government capital formation and which no taxpayer rationally expects to have to help retire *in his lifetime,* have effects similar to those of the noninterest *IOUs* we call M. Thus the Pigou effect from hyperdeflation involves an increase in the real value of such bonds *along with* an increase in the real value of hard-money M. Since a rational taxpayer will reckon that he *will* have to help pay taxes to keep up the interest payments (during his life-time) on the public debt, $1 of such debt will not have the potency to produce as much spending as will $1 of M. Nevertheless, believers in a crude quantity theory in an extreme classical model *should* reformulate their theory to say:

Doubling M and permanent public debt will, other things equal, double all P's and leave all relative P's, physical quantities, and interest rates unchanged in the new long-term equilibrium. *Doubling M alone represents a nonneutral change* **whose substantive effects are the greater the shorter is taxpayer life expectancy and the higher is the interest rate.**[3]

LIQUIDITY PREFERENCE AND INCOME

We have seen that the amount of money people will hold depends upon the interest rate and is a declining function of interest in the sense that you must contrive lower yields on securities to coax people to be willing to hold more money. Fig. 18-1(a) showed this liquidity-preference link between the stock of M and interest.

We expand the theory behind this schedule by saying that there is not one but two reasons for holding money. The first reason, the *store-of-wealth, asset,* or *precautionary* motive is "passive": it depends on the interest rate on bonds. That is, the amount demanded rises as i falls. A new, second, reason is the *transactions* motive: money is needed to meet payrolls and pay for purchases. The part of the M-stock held for this motive can be said to depend upon the level of income: this so-called "active" component of M demand is a function of the level of GNP. The amount demanded rises as GNP rises. (Note that if velocity were a strict constant for *all* money and not just

for this idealized active-money component, there would be no room at all for a nonvertical liquidity-preference curve LL of Figure 18-1(a). Note too that the distinction between the two elements of money demand were explained more fully on page 256 of Part B of Chapter 15.) Actually, of course, we cannot separate dollars into two stocks held for different reasons; we must be satisfied to say that the demand to hold the total M stock is a function *both* of income and of interest, rising with GNP and falling with i.

Of these two influences on M demand, only i was represented in the text of this chapter and its Figure 18-1. Bringing in GNP does appear to complicate that simple model. For the level of GNP determined in part (c) of that figure must now feed back to determine amount of M demanded. But, if the amount of M to hold is fixed by central bankers, then the change in GNP must change i, I, S, and GNP, i, I, . . . and so on, until all variables are in general-equilibrium agreement.

We can treat this complication as an advantage, making use of this feedback to outline a less simplified diagrammatic presentation of this chapter's story. Nowadays we call it the Hicks-Hansen diagram, named for Sir John Hicks[4] of Oxford, who developed it, and Alvin Hansen of Harvard, who popularized it. It is better than Figure 18-1 because it is more versatile and because it avoids the illusion of one-way causation from the amount of M to the level of GNP.

IS CURVE The name of this curve, shown in Figure 18-4, reflects its derivation from the equality of S and I at various combinations of i and GNP. It tells the story told by Figure 18-1(b) and (c), independently of the story in (a). There we saw that when i changes, we do wind up with a changed GNP.

Back in Figure 18-1, this took place in two steps. First, the marginal-efficiency step of 18-1(b) in which a changing i changed I in the opposite direction; and second, the old multiplier relation, in which the change in I results in an amplified change in income (GNP) in the same direction. The compression of these two steps into one is the *IS* relation, each point of which stems from one correspondence or combination of I and S when their *schedules* are fixed and their scheduled values are equal. Each point on the *IS* curve represents a macroeconomic equilibrium in the *product* market of investment and consumption.

The new element in our model is the *LM* curve (for *L*iquidity-preference and *M*oney). Each point on this curve represents an equilibrium in the financial markets where cash is exchanged for bonds.

LM CURVE This relationship is also shown in Figure 18-4. It is drawn so that its shape takes into account the dependence of money-holding demand on *both* GNP and i.

---

[3]Warning: Doubling M and PD (Permanent Debt) does not mean you can add $M + PD$ and treat that magnitude as if P's were proportional to it. Rather it is the case that ($2M, 2PD$) implies $2P$.

[4]Nobel laureate in Economics for 1972, along with Kenneth J. Arrow of Stanford and Harvard.

That is, we have recognized not only the *transactions* motive for holding "active money", which depends primarily on income; but also the *precautionary* (or "asset") store-of-wealth motive for holding money, which depends upon the interest rates investors speculate will be earned on alternative stores of wealth (bonds, stocks, land, real capital goods—earning assets in general). Figure 18-1(*a*) showed the effect of such speculation on "asset" demand for *M*.

It is important to emphasize that the *LM* schedule is drawn up on the proviso that the total amount of *M* is *fixed*. Each point on *LM* shows that for people to be in equilibrium with higher GNP levels, at which steadily larger parts of the given *M* stock must be placed in transactions uses, they must be "coaxed" out of holding money for asset and precautionary motives and into holding securities. This the financial markets accomplish by offering higher interest rates. Thus LM slopes north-eastward. The *LM* curve shows all the combinations of *i* and GNP that yield equilibrium, with a given supply of *M*, in the markets for financial assets.

Now Figure 18-4 combines the marginal-efficiency-multiplier curve *IS* with the liquidity-preference curve *LM* to show that their interaction does determine the equilibrium level of income and of interest rate for each given total of *M*. *E* shows the equilibrium intersection. There and only there has the existing amount of money created just a low enough interest rate and just high enough investment to lead to a maintainable level of income: at this indicated GNP and *i* rate, the existing *M* supply just covers the transactions and holding demand for money. QED.

HICKS-HANSEN SYNTHESIS

INTEREST RATES

IS

LM

IS'

IS'
LM'

E

LM'

IS

GNP

LEVEL OF INCOME

MONETARY AND FISCAL POLICY

What if the central bank in applying monetary policy engineers an increase in *M*? What will that do to the *LM* curve? Now with more money to be held at each level of income, the interest rate will have to be bid down. Hence, the *LM* curve clearly shifts downward (and hence rightward, as shown by the dashed line *LM'*). What about the *IS* curve? It does not have the money supply in it anywhere; *IS* stays unshifted by an *M* change. The rightward shift of *LM* increases the equilibrium GNP and the equilibrium interest rate moves downward. Pencil *E'* in.

By contrast to monetary policy, which shifts the *LM* curve, *fiscal policy* shifts the *IS* curve. How? An increase in government expenditure *G* (just like an increase in any component of a *C* + *I* + *G* schedule) will shift the *IS* schedule *rightward*. Why? Because it leads to a higher income level at the same interest rate. Thus, you can show that expansionary fiscal policy leads to a new *E* higher on the unshifted *LM* curve, with equilibrium income and interest rate higher.[5] (Test yourself by penciling in on Fig. 18-4 a new *LM* curve for central bank contraction and a new *IS* curve for fiscal contraction. Contrast the new *E* intersections where the interest rate is concerned.)

CLASSICAL AND DEPRESSION MODELS

CLASSICAL POLE Fig. 18-5 shows at the extremities of the *LM* curve the extreme "classical" pole and the extreme "depression" (or so-called "liquidity-trap") pole.[6] Where *LM* turns almost vertical, no shift in the *IS* curve can increase GNP: that is because money's velocity has reached its limit. (Note the constancy of GNP at E_1 and E_2.) At this classical pole, then, fiscal policy would accomplish little unless accompanied by central banking change in the money supply. Few modern economists think present-day mixed economies operate in such an extreme region. (In any case they would probably combine fiscal policy with monetary policy where such a threat became serious.)

DEPRESSION POLE At the other extreme, at vanishingly low interest rates such as prevailed in the late 1930s, the *LM* curve might turn horizontal. If the central bank engineered an increase in *M* by open-market purchases which involved swapping a near-money treasury bill for *M* itself, the central bank would merely succeed in shifting the *LM* curve rightward, leaving its horizontal part virtually unchanged. In such a situation, and particularly where extreme inelasticity of the depression marginal-efficiency curve makes *IS* virtually a vertical line, monetary policy is

[5]Note that foreign-trade policy can easily be brought in. For example, a policy that increased net exports (*E* — *M*) by devaluation would be similar to the text's increasing of *G*, shifting *IS* rightward.

[6]Sometimes the "depression model" is called the "Keynesian model," but most authorities agree that this is bad terminology in that Keynes' *General Theory* covered all cases from the beginning and not merely that of the Great Depression.

FIG. 18-5

FIG. 18-6

practically impotent to affect GNP. (Note the virtual identity of GNP at the E_3 and E_4 intersections.)

INTERNAL AND EXTERNAL BALANCE[7]

We can extend the Hicks-Hansen diagram to illustrate the problem of attaining full-employment stability at home without losing financial respectability abroad. The extension requires a new curve, related this time to Chapter 17's discussion of the foreign-exchange market. Just as the *IS* curve shows combinations of *i* and GNP in which $S = I$; and just as the *LM* curve shows pairs of *i* and GNP at which a given *M* fully serves both transactions and assets motives for holding money; so the *FP* curve shows equality between Canada's sources of foreign currency (exports and capital inflows) and Canada's demand for foreign currency (imports and capital outflows). When these are equal, the foreign price of Canadian currency ($C) will tend neither to rise nor to fall.

If they stay on the *FP* curve, authorities maintaining a fixed exchange rate need not have recourse to the Exchange Fund Account, or EFA (see page 294, above). Alternatively, if the rate of exchange is free, speculators will find that it remains at one particular level; currency dealers can rely on an unchanged value of $C.

What can we say about the shape of *FP*? It slopes upward and rightward. To see why, take one point, where an-

nual inflows = outflows = 1 billion dollars. Moving northward from it, *i* rises and capital inflows increase total inflows to over 1 billion dollars and threaten to raise the value of the $C. This can be compensated, however, by a rise in money outflows, from imports. Imports rise, according to MPM (Chapter 14) only when GNP rises. So, to keep an international financial balance along the curve, when *i* rises, GNP must also rise. This gives the curve a slope to the north*east*.

Another property of *FP* is that it divides Fig. 18-6 into two areas. All points to its left have a GNP that is too low (or an *i* that is too high). Currency inflows exceed outflows; so there the $C tends to rise indefinitely. Similarly, to the right of *FP*, *i* is too low and GNP too high—the $C is over-valued and sinking. Only along *FP* is the *i*-GNP combination just right to keep our dollar at a constant level overseas.

POLICY Fig. 18-6 introduces the policy problem. At E_1 the economy is at under-employment equilibrium, where *IS* and *LM* intersect, and foreign payments are in balance, as shown by the fact that an *FP* equilibrium line also passes through E_1. Now let us assume that fiscal-policy is used to move *IS* out to *IS'*. The new equilibrium would be at full-employment E_3, in the absence of foreign-payments constraints. But nothing happens to shift *FP*. If the government wishes to keep *foreign* balance, then *i* and GNP can both rise to E_2, but with domestic employment and GNP well below the desired E_3. Alternatively, the economy can move to E_3, but the $C will decline indefinitely: GNP-induced imports are too high and *i* too low. An exchange-rate crisis proceeds steadily, while employment remains high.

[7]Most readers will wish to skim this section, and return to it after Part IV's chapters on the balance of payments. For a clear, but advanced, explanation of *IS, LM* and *FP* curves and their relationships under various kinds of policies, see D. E. Bond and R. A. Shearer, *The Economics of the Canadian Financial System* (Prentice-Hall of Canada, Toronto, 1972), Chapters 20 and 21.

In such predicaments we find, from time to time, the authorities of every open economy. *IS* and *LM* curves have shown that there are often two policy routes to vitalizing the internal economy; but how to reconcile the desired intersection with external balance? Most of the discussion of foreign economic policy is actually about how to do this by shifting *FP* to *FP'*. Part Five goes into this in depth. It is not difficult to see what must be done: either there must be fewer imports for each level of GNP (brought about by import controls, tariffs, and/or foreign-exchange regulations) or less capital outflow (brought about by tax concessions, loans from foreign governments and banks) at each domestic *i*.

Of course, a steady fall in the $C may eventually increase exports, and this might push *FP* (farther than *IS*) to the right. Then no action need be taken. Furthermore, both *IS* and *LM* may shift upward, thus attracting foreign capital into the country to the higher *i*.

THE FOREIGN CONSTRAINT That foreign balance can be a serious constraint on the choice of domestic policy is shown by Fig. 18-7. The economy is originally at E_1. This position is flawed by serious unemployment. One remedy is to increase *M*, thus shifting *LM* to *LM'*; intersecting *IS* at E_2. This position, however is not tenable; it is far from *FP* and hence suffers from steady currency depreciation. *Expansionary* monetary policy, therefore, will not work.

The correct mix is a *tight* monetary policy to raise *i*, offset internally by expansionary *fiscal* policy. Thus, *M* is reduced by open-market operations and *LM* shifts back to *LM''*, cutting *FP* at E_3. Now domestic equilibrium is far to the left at E_4 and unemployment is more serious than ever. This calls for fiscal policy. With reduced taxes or in-

FIG. 18-7

creased *G* and transfer payments, the government may shift *IS* up to *IS'*, where all three curves meet in E_3. Internal and external balance are attained.

In other words, monetary policy could *not* be used to deal with unemployment in this case. Fiscal policy was called for; for reasons quite different from those that governed the choice in the closed-economy classical and depression cases.

SUMMARY TO APPENDIX

1 The causal interrelations between *M, i, I,* and GNP could also be expressed in *MV* language. So long as one expects any induced changes to *V* to be such as not *fully* to offset the original change in *M*, then changing *M* can in one step be described as changing GNP. Semantics alone would be involved, were it not true that special hypotheses about the constancy of *V* may seem tenable to monetarists who use this concept.

2 In a perfect classical world without frictions and with an inflexible hard-money public-debt base, Pigou proved in the 1940s that a sophisticated version of Say's Law could be asserted. For policy and realistic description, he preferred not to rely on hyperdeflation to produce such "Pigou effects." Pushing such a full-employment model to its logical limits, however, does enable one to reaffirm the crudest quantity theory in which *P* becomes strictly proportionate to *M* and public debt (the degree of the proportion varying only when extraneous *real* changes take place).

3 Hicks-Hansen diagrams[8] succeed in synthesizing fiscal and monetary policy, the theory of income determination and the theory of money; in addition they help synthesize the monetarist and

[8]Much, but not all, of the wisdom of post-Keynesian macroeconomics can be neatly depicted on the Hicks-Hansen diagram, which doesn't really do justice to the Pigou effect. Thus, suppose there is a permanent increase in people's net worth from the creation of new money (so-called "outside" money). (Think of gold from mining discoveries; or think of currency printed by the government to fight a war; but don't think of new *M* just created by an open-market operation by the central bank, for the reason that largely offsetting the new *M* in people's net worth will be their loss

of near-money bonds sold to the central bank.) It is standard in the Hicks-Hansen diagram, Fig. 18-4, to let this new *M* shift the light red *LM* curve rightward. Agreed. But the Pigou effect says that this new liquid net worth will also raise people's propensity to consume, their *CC* and *C + I + G* schedules. So, to be correct, the change in *M* should also shift the red *IS* schedule rightward and upward, reinforcing the *LM* shift. (See extra-credit problem 4 for numerical *IS* and *LM* curves. There and in Fig. 18-4, the horizontal axis can be thought of as representing *money* GNP, with *P*

Keynesian theories of macroeconomics by providing a definite and general theory of the velocity of money.

4 The choice of policies depends on economic determinants shaping *IS, LM,* and *FP* curves. Chapter 19 will discuss another policy problem of the 1970s—various types of inflation, possible solutions, and the "incomes policy" dilemma.

CONCEPTS FOR REVIEW

Say's Law and
    classical models
Pigou effects
crude quantity theory
induced changes in *V*
public-debt effects

liquidity preference:
    M dependence on
      both GNP and *i*
    Hicks-Hansen *LM*
      and *IS* intersection
depression and
    classical models
internal and external
    balance

QUESTIONS FOR DISCUSSION

1. Is it reasonable for you to hold relatively less *M* and have a faster *V* when *i* is 9 rather than 1 per cent? When inflation is galloping? Use your answer to criticize simple monetarism.

2. Explain the Pigou-effect mechanism for restoring full employment when wages and prices are perfectly flexible. What is the role of public debt?

3. Show that a rise in *G* or a lowering of taxes will shift *IS* rightward in Fig. 18-4 and will raise GNP at new *E*. What will *M* contraction do?

4. *Extra-credit problem:* Intermediate texts can use mathematical symbols to summarize a simple version of this Appendix. Let real saving, *S*, depend on real income, $Q = $ GNP/P, namely: $S = S(Q) = 1Q$, say, much as in Fig. 18-1(*c*). Let real investment, *I*, depend inversely on the interest rate, as in Fig. 18-1(*b*)'s marginal-efficiency schedule, namely: $I = I(i) = 1/i$, for example. In the equation of exchange $MV = PQ$, let velocity, *V*, be an increasing function of the interest rate, namely: $V = V(i) = 4.4i/(1 + i)$, for example. Pick units so that full-employment output is $Q_F = 1$ (100 billion dollars, perhaps); and suppose that, prior to full employment, prices are constant (as determined by sticky wage-cost levels, etc.), so that by choice of units $P = 1$ until an inflationary gap lifts the price level. Finally, let the money supply, *M*, be set by the central bank at the level $\overline{M}$. Then to determine our two unknowns, *Q* and *i*, in Fig. 18-4 we have the two equations for the *IS* and *LM* schedules

$S(Q) = I(i)$ or $.1Q = 1/i$,
marginal efficiency and multiplier

$M = PQ/V(i)$ or $\overline{M} = Q/[4.4i/(1 + i)]$,
liquidity-preference theory of *V*

Solving (by simple substitution or otherwise), we get *Q* as an increasing function of $\overline{M}$, and *i* as a decreasing function. After $\overline{M}$ has become so large that full-employment Q_F has been reached, along with its corresponding i_F and V_F, we put Q_F in both equations and solve for the price level *P*, with *P* now simply proportional to $\overline{M}$ (in accordance with the classical quantity theory of money), namely: $P = (V_F/Q_F) M$.

NOTE: for the suggested special formulas above, substitution gives $i = 10/Q, V = 44/(Q + 10)$, $\overline{M} = Q(Q + 10)/44$, a quadratic equation for *Q* in terms of $\overline{M}$. To get full-employment $Q_F = 1$, evidently, $\overline{M} = 11/44 = 1/4$ (i.e., 25 billion dollars, with $V_F = 4$ per year, or once every 3 months on the average); and $i_F = 10/Q_F = 10$ per cent per year. For underemployment equilibrium, the quadratic's relevant root is given by $Q = -5 + \sqrt{25 + 44\overline{M}}$. Verify that $\overline{M} = 1/4$ does yield $Q = 1$; and, for $\overline{M} > 1/4$, $P = (4/1\overline{M} = 4\overline{M}$. If *P* has classical downward flexibility replace $P = 1$ by $Q = Q_F = 1$ and solve for $P = 4\overline{M}$ for any $\overline{M}$.

constant prior to full employment in an oversimplified Keynesian fashion. Or, suppose you are ultraclassical and think prices and wages are flexible downward whenever real GNP is below the full-employment level and out-of-work men bid down the *P* level. Then the axis in Fig. 18-4 can depict *real* GNP; and each drop in

the *P* level will shift *LM* rightward until the equilibrium *E* point slides south-eastward on *IS* to the level of full employment. Any further increase in *M* will raise *P* proportionately à la Quantity Theory, but leave all real points, axes, and curves on the diagram intact.)

19
DEMAND MANAGEMENT AND FULL EMPLOYMENT WITHOUT INFLATION

I believe that all parties in this parliament and most Canadians share the view that the national budget is no longer a matter of the government accounts that should be balanced every twelve months on some financial rule of thumb. We view the national budget now as an integral part of the nation's business, influenced by and having an influence upon the state of employment, income, and prices.

MINISTER OF FINANCE, BUDGET SPEECH, 1948

We have seen in earlier chapters that the behavior of saving and investment determines the level of national income and employment. We have seen that investment and other spending often fluctuate widely from year to year. History shows how painful and wasteful the business cycle has been in the past. Today everyone is in agreement that, unless we succeed in laying to rest the ghost of instability, chronic slump, and snowballing inflation, our mixed economic system itself will be in jeopardy.

What prescription follows from our economic diagnosis? No single answer can be given; there is no single cure-all for the economic ills of society. Business, labor, the provincial governments, and agriculture must of course attempt to pursue price and wage policies aimed at maintaining a stable, high-employment economy. The Bank of Canada can also do much, by way of interest and monetary policy, to moderate instability. While all these measures are being used, powerful help is still needed from the weapon of public *fiscal policy* (i.e., governmental tax and expenditure policies, budgetary deficits or surpluses). The sum of these two policies (reinforced by exchange-rate policy) is known as *demand management*. Neither fiscal policy nor monetary policy alone is a cure-all, but taken together they constitute a formidable armory of stabilization weapons.

As the chapter unfolds you will agree with the warning that much of its subject is still controversial. Even economics experts are divided. Some prefer re-liance on monetary policy alone. Some worry about fiscal policy's effects on increasing government debt. Some prefer direct intervention—to prevent inflation—rather than indirect reliance on demand management policies. And yet it is fair to say that the technical differences among economists on these issues pale into insignificance in comparison with the ideological battles on monetary, fiscal (and debt) and price-and-wage fixing proposals among politicans, businessmen, unionists and between left-wing and right-wing.

As will be seen in this chapter, experienced researchers into the facts and analytical principles have today, all over the world, quite different answers to these questions from those of the man in the street and of our forefathers. The problem for an introductory text is to explain the logic and experience underlying modern doctrines, not to indoctrinate the student into any one view of budgets, banks or controls.

SHORT-RUN AND LONG-RUN DEMAND MANAGEMENT

By monetary policy we mean the application of monetary and credit stimulus or braking; and by fiscal policy, we mean the process of shaping public *taxation* and *public expenditure* in order (*a*) to help dampen down the swings of the business cycle, and (*b*) to contribute toward the maintenance of a growing, high-employment economy free from excessive inflation or deflation.

Without fiscal and monetary policy, the economic system might in a particular year be threatened with a deflationary gap. Suppose private consumption and investment spending were too weak to provide adequate employment. What action then is called for?

The Bank of Canada would use expansionary monetary policy to try to stimulate private investment. To the degree[1] that its efforts were not fully successful, the fiscal authorities would still be faced by a deflationary gap. This would be the signal for the Ottawa government to introduce tax and public-expenditure policies designed to help reachieve stable full employment.

Monetary and fiscal action, but now in reverse, is called for in the case where private investment, net export and consumption decisions threaten the economy with an inflationary gap. With prices rising and employers vying desperately for nonexistent workers, the Bank of Canada would initiate contractionary credit programs aimed to reduce the inflationary gap. But if the saving-investment or $C + I + G + (E - M)$ intersections still threaten the economy with a sustained inflationary gap, it is then the clear duty of the Minister of Finance to initiate higher tax rates and/ or lower-public-expenditure programs in the attempt to restore a high-employment equilibrium without inflation.

In summary, fiscal policies dealing with taxes and public expenditure, in cooperation with stabilizing monetary policies, have for their goal a high-employment and growing economy—but one without demand-pull inflation. In demand management the fiscal and monetary authorities "lean against the prevailing economic winds", thereby helping provide a favourable economic environment within which the people can have the widest opportunity for achievement.

OUR IMPORTANT "BUILT-IN FISCAL STABILIZERS"

One might get the impression from the above remarks that fiscal policy helps stabilize the economy

only so long as government officials are carefully watching trends, are successfully anticipating future developments, and are meeting promptly to take decisive actions. Such "discretionary" fiscal policies, involving the making and changing of explicit decisions, are indeed important; they are, unfortunately, only part of the story.

The modern fiscal system has great inherent *automatic stabilizing* properties. All through the day and night, whether or not the government is in session, the fiscal system is helping to keep our economy stable. Whatever the Cabinet is doing, powerful automatic stabilizers go instantly into action to curb sudden upward or downward spurts.

What are these mysterious stabilizers? They are primarily the following:

1. *Automatic changes in tax receipts.* We saw in Chapters 8 and 9 that our federal tax system depends progressively on personal and corporate incomes. What does this mean for stability?

It means that as soon as income begins to fall off, and even before Ottawa makes any changes in tax rates, the tax receipts of the government also fall off. Now, reductions in tax receipts are just what the doctor prescribes in case of a dip in income. So our present tax system is a mighty and rapid built-in stabilizer.

Taxes stabilize against *upward* as well as downward movements. In times of demand-pull inflation this is a good thing. But if it impedes healthy real growth we call it "fiscal drag". And because it forces low-income taxpayers into higher tax brackets, we tend to "index" the personal income tax, thus modifying the stabilizing effect.

A century ago, writers thought that *stability* of tax revenue was a good thing, and they would have looked with disapproval on the present-day tendency for tax receipts to rise and fall with national income. Today, most economists believe just the reverse should be the goal. Thus, to dampen a boom, a budgetary surplus is desirable. There are two ways to produce such a surplus\ by a reduction in government expenditure, yes; but also by an increase in tax receipts. To fight a recession, there are likewise two ways open; raising expenditures, or lowering tax rates. Further, adjusting taxes interferes less with the private economy than altering the scale of public G. How lucky we are, therefore, that our present tax

---

[1] How much of the stabilizing load is carried by monetary and how much by fiscal policy depends on international-payments constraints. Also, the financing of deficits and surpluses itself helps shape the course of money-supply growth.

system has to some degree "automatic flexibility," with its receipts tending to rise in inflationary times and to fall in times of depression. This is a powerful factor stabilizing the economy and moderating the business cycle.[2]

2. *Unemployment compensation and other welfare transfers.* Since World War II, we have built up an elaborate system of unemployment compensation. Soon after men are laid off, they begin to receive benefits from the unemployment insurance fund. When they go back to work, the benefits cease; and their contributions to finance unemployment compensation rise when employment is high. During boom years, therefore, the unemployment reserves grow and exert stabilizing pressure against too great spending; conversely, during years of slack employment, the reserve funds are used to pay out income to sustain consumption and moderate the decline.

Other welfare programs—such as relief payments outside this social security system—also show an anticyclical automatic behavior of a stabilizing type.

3. *Price supports.* The various programs to aid agriculture and primary industries which we shall discuss later in Part Three, act like built-in stabilizers.[3]

4. *Federal finance.* Under tax-sharing formulas to pass tax collections from Ottawa to the provinces, the federal government has usually agreed to maintain payments even if GNP or local tax collections should go down. On the other hand, the provinces are among the most volatile and intemperate spenders when booms are on, thus destabilizing inflationary periods.

5. *Corporate savings and family savings.* Our private institutions also have built-in stabilizers. Thus, the custom of corporations maintaining their dividends, even though their incomes change in the short run, does cause their retained savings to act like a shock absorber or built-in stabilizer.[4] And to the extent that families try to maintain previous living standards and are slow to adjust upward their living standards—to this extent, they too help stabilize. (To the extent that they rush out to spend extra income on down payments or hysterically cut down on consumption when GNP drops, they hinder stability and reinforce cyclical fluctuations.)

6. *Imports.* If firms and families spent a constant percentage of disposable income on imports, the tendency of foreign goods to siphon off part of total spending would be the same in inflationary times as in recession. However, luckily, the import percentage is usually highest when the economy is overheated. What would otherwise be an inflationary gap is filled by foreign-produced goods.

Still other stabilizers are "built in" to the economy, but these are the main ones.

LIMITATIONS OF AUTOMATIC STABILIZERS

Before leaving the subject of automatic stabilizers, we should stress two things. First, the built-in stabilizers are our first line of defense, but are not by themselves sufficient to maintain full stability. Second, reliance on them in preference to discretionary programs raises some philosophical and ethical questions. Let us look at these points.

The automatic tendency for taxes to take away a fraction of each extra dollar of GNP means that the size of the "multiplier" is cut down. Each dollar swing in investment—whether caused by sunspots, inventions, or anything else—will now have its destabilizing effect on the system reduced *but not wiped out completely.* Instead of such disturbances having their effects on GNP multiplied three or more times, there will now—because of the auto-

---

[2] Some experts advocate increasing the stabilizers by having Parliament pass a law bringing in "formula flexibility," in which tax *rates* vary *automatically* with changes in various aggregative price and income indexes. But Parliament is traditionally unwilling to turn over to the Cabinet even discretionary power over taxes. In any case the Carter Commission *Report* (Volume 2, 1966) thought "formula flexibility" inadequate to deal with fluctuations and recommended discretionary policy.

[3] When dollar spending drops off and farm prices fall, the federal government pays out dollars to farmers and absorbs surpluses. When inflation brews and prices soar, the government warehouses put forth goods and absorb dollars, thus cushioning any movement. However, note that by pushing up the prices of raw materials, support formulas can also have an "escalating", or destabilizing effect; and to the extent that they simply limit supply at all times, they may redistribute and lower rather than stabilize income.

[4] To the extent that corporate investment is itself linked to corporate saving, this stabilizing influence is negated. A rise in the wages/profits ratio is a partial stabilizer on dips.

matic stabilizing effect of taxes—be a multiplier effect of only 1.5 or 2 times.[5]

In short, a built-in stabilizer acts to reduce *part* of any fluctuation in the economy, but it does not serve to wipe out 100 per cent of the disturbance. It leaves the rest of the disturbance as a task for fiscal and monetary discretionary action.

Philosophically, some reformers dislike the need to have human beings decide policy. They speak of a "government of laws and not of men." They advocate setting up automatic rules and mechanisms that would go into action without ever depending on human decisions.

At the present time an automatic gyropilot can keep an airplane pretty stable while the pilot catches a nap; but when something unusual comes up, the human pilot must take over. No one has yet found a gadget with all the flexibility of man. Similarly in the social field: we have not arrived at a stage where any nation is likely to create for itself a set of constitutional procedures that will displace the need for discretionary policy formation and responsible human intelligence.

DISCRETIONARY FISCAL POLICY

The principal weapons of discretionary fiscal policy —programs which involve explicit public decision

---

making—are *(1)* varying public works and other expenditure programs, *(2)* varying transfer expenditure programs, and *(3)* varying tax rates cyclically.

PUBLIC WORKS When governments first began to do something active about depressions, they tended to initiate work on public investment projects for the unemployed. Often these were hastily devised, and in that they aimed primarily to create work for people, they often were rather inefficient; e.g., road building using as little machinery as possible to make the work stretch, leaf raking during the depression by relief workers, trumped-up pork-barrel projects of low utility and lacking careful planning. The extreme case is the mythical program to dig holes and then refill them.

The day is long past when a modern nation will let its economy collapse to the point where its only rescue must come from hastily contrived and wasteful public-works spending. The modern emphasis has, rightly, shifted away from such "make work" projects. Indeed, where a disturbance is expected to be a short one, economists today rely much more on a temporary change in tax rates than on an abrupt change in public works.

Why this shift away from public works as a stabilizer? People now realize that it takes a long time to get a post office started or to put into effect programs for highway and airport construction, or for slum clearance. Plans must be made; blueprints drawn; land acquired by purchase and expropriation; existing buildings razed; and then new structures and roads constructed. All this may take five or more years; and, at the least, half of this time may elapse before any sizable amount of money will get spent on labor and materials. Suppose the recession turns out to last a year at most, followed by two years of steady advance. Then, just in the third year, when the economy may have gone all the way from too little demand to too much demand, there will suddenly come onto the market the government spending that was intended to help a recession. Municipal and provincial work also have a long leg. All such timing makes fiscal policy an aggravator of instability.

The above remarks obviously can be applied to an inflation; a cancelling of government spending on airports and schools, already half-completed, may fail to produce GNP efficiently; the suddenly-employed factors may have lower productivity in other jobs than in completing the public works. And the cancelling of completely new

---

[5] We know from Chapter 13's footnotes 2 and 9 that MPC = b as used in the simple multiplier formula must be cut down to allow for both imports and taxes. Here we evaluate this effect, on the rough assumptions that imports and taxes can both be identified with consumption.

First, imports: Let MPC = 0.666; MPS = 0.333; MPM = 0.166
Then $MPC^D \equiv c = (1 - 0.666 + 0.166) = 0.5$
Next, taxes that reduce disposable income below NNP:
Let $T = t\,Y = 0.35\,Y$
Because $Y = \bar{C}^D + c(Y - T) + \bar{I}^D + \dots,$
then $Y = c(Y - tY) + \bar{K}$
where $\bar{K}$ is the sum of constants $\bar{C}^D, \bar{I}^D, \bar{G}^D, \bar{E}$, etc.
Then
$$Y = \left\{ \frac{1}{1 - c(1 - t)} \right\} \bar{K}$$
where the fraction is the multiplier modified for imports and taxes.

What is the numerical effect of the modification? The simple multiplier was
$$\frac{1}{1 - MPC} = \frac{1}{0.333} = 3$$
The modified multiplier is $\dfrac{1}{1 - 0.5\,(1 - 0.35)} = 1.5$
approximately, much weaker. The Report of the Carter Commission (Vol. 2) estimated that the attenuated multiplier for Canada was less than 2.

projects may have an impact at the wrong time—years in the future.

Of course, it is still possible to gain a stabilization effect by slowing-down, or speeding-up, on going projects. This more refined approach to timing, is greatly helped by planning models of the economy as a whole. For example, the Bank of Canada's RDX-2 and other computer simulations have been used to study the best dates to commence, and complete, large energy projects such as the arctic gas pipeline.

WELFARE EXPENDITURES We saw that existing welfare programs, such as unemployment compensation and old-age retirement payments, do act as automatic stabilizers, rising automatically when incomes fall and needs increase.

In addition to such built-in stabilizers, it is possible for the federal or provincial government to institute various discretionary programs of transfer expenditures that will further stabilize. Thus, the government could refrain from giving some pending old-age bonus in inflationary times and push forward such disbursements in depressed times. If it intends to lower farm price support payments, the government might hope to time the change to coincide with boom times. Most important, in times of prolonged unemployment, the federal government has moderated the decline by prolonging the period for which the jobless can get paid unemployment compensation. It is precisely in times of *sustained* unemployment that the present system is most deficient, and it is in such times that there will be minimal harmful effects on job mobility and incentives from increasing unemployment disbursements.[6]

In inflationary periods, a major drawback in using welfare transfer programs for short-run stabilizing purposes is the political fact that it may not be easy to terminate such emergency programs after full employment has been reached and passed.

[6] Economists Cairns and Courchene have analyzed the expansionary and mobility-creating effects of the Canadian unemployment insurance. (See James P. Cairns, "Unemployment Insurance in Canada: The Problem of Conflicting Principles," *Canadian Journal of Economics and Political Science,* Vol. XXVIII, No. 2 (May, 1962), pp. 262-268; and J. J. Courchene, "Interprovincial Migration and Economic Adjustment," *Canadian Journal of Economics,* Vol. III, No. 4 (November, 1970), pp. 550-576. The 1970 *White Paper* proposals on unemployment insurance would make the scheme more expansionary, but might have perverse mobility effects, driving unemployed migrants back to regions where unemployment is worst.

VARIATION OF TAX RATES If there is good reason to think that a disturbance will be brief, a temporary rise or cut in income tax rates can be a very good way of keeping disposable incomes from changing and of preventing the disturbance from snowballing. Under our payment-at-the-source system, the moment the federal government decides the economy needs a brake or a push through tax change, employers can begin to change the amounts witheld from salary paycheques. Some provincial tax collections are linked to the federal system.

An obvious difficulty is that it takes Ottawa a long time to debate and act on tax changes, though the delay is probably less than in changing spending. A more psychological objection to temporary suspension of tax rates to counter disturbances comes from the political fact of life that in our democracy it may be hard to get tax rates back after the emergency is over. Political sentiment to fight unemployment is often easier to mobilize than sentiment to fight inflationary gaps and more-than-full employment. (In long slumps this may be good.) Furthermore, as we've seen in Chapter 18, if people know tax changes are temporary and will not be altering their permanent incomes much, they may not vary their consumption spending very much.

SURPLUS AND DEFICIT FINANCING: STAGNATION, EXHILARATION, AND CONTRIVED GROWTH

So far we have been talking only about ironing out the business cycle. If the business cycle were around some "normal" level, most people would not worry too much so long as the boom-time budgetary surplus were always matched by the depression budgetary deficit. With such regularity, *the budget would be balanced over the business cycle* even though not balanced in every single year or month. There would be no secular trend upward in the public debt, nor downward.

Suppose population is proliferating, new inventions are zooming, and investment is generally excessive relative to full-employment saving. If this threatens to go on most of the time, will not active fiscal policy require a budgetary surplus most of the time? Such a condition of "secular exhilaration" *will* lead to a secular decline in the public debt.

But how can one be sure that the cycle will be so regular? Contrariwise, what if our continental economy is in for what Harvard's Alvin Hansen called "secular stagnation" that is, a long period in which (1) slowing population increase, (2) passing of the frontier's free land, (3) high corporate saving, (4) the vast piling up of capital goods, and (5) a bias toward capital-saving inventions will imply depressed investment schedules relative to saving schedules? Will not an active fiscal policy designed to wipe out such deflationary gaps then result in running a deficit *most of the time*, leading to a secular growth in the public debt? The modern answer is "Under these conditions, yes; and over the decades the budget should not necessarily be balanced".

There is a third possibility. Suppose a nation is concerned to accelerate (or slow down) its own rate of growth. Suppose its government decides to in-

crease the fraction of full-employment income that gets devoted to capital formation rather than to consumption. If public policy succeeds in stepping up net investment by aggressively easy credit or other policies, how can consumption spending be cut down to prevent excessive dollar demands from precipitating inflation? Primarily by having the government pursue an austere fiscal policy: raising tax rates and cutting down on marginal expenditures, thereby contriving a *chronic* budget surplus to offset easy money.

Equally important these days, suppose the nation wants to increase public projects against pollution and poverty at the expense of private investment. The government will then run a deficit, and the Bank of Canada will offset any threatened inflation by tight money that cuts down on business capital formation. In brief, one cannot set in advance the optimal trend of surplus or deficit. A diagram can summarize long term budget alternatives. Figure 19-1 illustrates three variants of modern fiscal policy, all

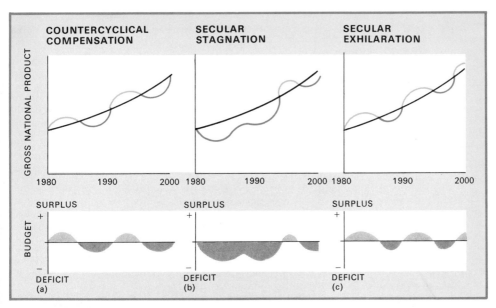

FIG. 19-1. Whether surpluses should balance deficits must depend on circumstances.
In every case the trend line of policy-achieved full-employment output is shown in black. How the GNP would grow in absence of active fiscal policy is shown in red. The indicated budget policy, of successful "leaning against the wind," is shown in gray below. In (a), the light areas of surplus cancel out the dark areas of deficit over the business cycle. In (b)'s case of secular stagnation, the dark deficits prevail over the surpluses and the debt trends upward. In (c), surpluses predominate on the average and debt declines.

in contrast to a budget balanced in every single year.

In Fig. 19-1(a) we see *simple compensatory finance* to iron out the business cycle, with boom surpluses canceling out depression deficits.

In Fig. 19-1(b), under secular stagnation, surplus periods are rarer and do not suffice to keep the public debt from having a tendency to grow chronically (along with the growing GNP). (In the Appendix to this chapter, we study the consequences and true burdens of public debt growth.)

In Fig. 19-1(c), with GNE spending either spontaneously strong or made strong by expansive Bank of Canada policy, the tendency for the system to run inflationary gaps much of the time is countered by budget surpluses most of the time, with the public debt tending to decline in the long run.

In the longer run, deficits may cancel out, or public debt may trend upward or downward.

REGIONAL INSTABILITY Canada's peculiar regional structure and external dependence create further questions to be answered. Suppose all the Canadian economy is zooming except a particular region. Should the whole economy be slowed down, or should special transfer payments be made to compensate or adapt that region? Suppose the problems of stagnation indicate that tax cuts are ineffective. How are the provinces to be induced *and* helped to step up the public works and welfare that are their own constitutional duties? Will political opinion support the economist who might then urge on Quebec or the prairies policies that the local people are opposed to?

Presumably time and statesmanship will settle these questions. But how are we to reconcile their solution with our *external* relationships? Public works nowadays have a high "import content" (refer back to Chapter 14. Thus expenditures to offset stagnation may "leak" out without having much or any multiplier effect on domestic employment. Conversely, in booms, decisions to delay federal public works may be nullified if private business and provinces borrow money in New York to speed up their own *I* and *G*. The impatient advocate of stabilization policies says, in effect, "Close the borders to these flows of money and goods." But if we do so, other nations will retaliate, cutting down our $E - M$ and driving us toward low-level self-sufficiency. We cannot escape easily from being a unit of the international economy.

DEMAND MANAGEMENT AT WORK Do tax changes work? Controlled experiments are not possible in economics, but the tax cut of 1965 will serve as an illustration. Unemployment was steadily over 5 percent in the early 1960s. In the Atlantic Provinces it sometimes rose to 10 or 12 percent. Statisticians calculated that real GNP was from 5 to 7 percent below its potential.

In 1965 the government decided to cut most personal income tax rates by 10 percent to provide a "stimulus to economic expansion". As there had already been a federal deficit, steadily since 1959, to cut taxes further was indeed "new economics".

Only after a long campaign of education did the man in the street generally become persuaded of the following precepts:

1. To the extent that a tax cut succeeds in stimulating business, our progressive tax system will collect extra revenues out of the higher income levels. Hence, a tax cut *may* in the long run imply little (or even no) loss in federal revenues, and hence no substantial increase in the long-run public debt.

2. There is no need to balance the budget, or try to balance it, in every year. In a growing economy prudent policy does not even require that the budget be balanced over a decade, or over a complete business cycle. So long as continuous deficits do not result in the public debt growing faster the GNP grows, good economic health can prevail. For the economy, "balance" means full employment and healthy growth with no wasteful gap between our potential and our actual real output, and also no inflationary gap.

At first the nonexpert public remained skeptical about these doctrines, though they have been central to recent monetary and fiscal surveys and reports. Recently, however, two influences have changed many people's thinking:

1. The American 10-billion-dollar tax cut of 1964 and to a lesser extent the Canadian tax cut of 1965 were able to change consumption. Of course they did not bring full employment overnight. Instead, they produced just about the gradual rise in consumer spending that the propensity-to-consume concept had predicted. They also stimulated investment. Finally, the multiplier doctrine worked much as

textbooks had predicted. Indeed the Canadian finance minister found it necessary to raise taxes again the next year, to withdraw the stimulus of 1965.

2. The general view taken in the Carter Commission's *Report* and special studies was that federal discretionary fiscal policy contributed without question to the stability of the Canadian economy in the period 1945-1963.[7] Viewed over the shorter period since 1954, the fiscal policy was found to be pressing in the right direction more than half the time, and really wrong ("perverse") only in three years. This is strong support against the contrary view that (because of ignorance and long lags) fiscal policy may work so inefficiently and slowly as to *de*stabilize.

EPILOGUE

In economics, to repeat, controlled experiments are not possible. Other things did not remain the same while taxes were being changed. At the very time that tax pressure was being relaxed and employment was rising, prices were also rising. It is now believed that the episode did prove that tax-cuts would work; but also showed how little we are able to understand and predict all the great economic forces at work at any time. Vietnam war spending was just rising to its crescendo; manufacturing excess-capacity was disappearing; and unemployment was chiefly the problem of the rural, unindustrialized, regions. The tax cut was encouraging an expansion of aggregate demand that in retrospect is seen to have been "too strong for too long". Indeed, the "normal" levels of unemployment have been surpassed by the economy by mid-1964. The tax cut helped aggregate $C + I + G (E - M)$ spending rise at more than 10 percent per year, but the labor force and productivity were growing at less than 8 percent.

But no one knew these facts, and they are still in contention today. What seems clear is that politicians and voters, advised by economists, were using the brave tax-cut policies of 1965 to solve the serious employment stagnation of the earlier 1960s, and so widening the inflationary gap of the late 1960s.

DISCRETIONARY STABILIZATION AGAIN

Some say this episode proves that information and performance lags are too long to justify discretionary management of aggregate demand. Just as in our discussion of public works a few pages back, so with tax, monetary and spending policies in general: a change in policy today may have its effect the day after to-

morrow, when today's problems have already been replaced by new, and opposite, problems. Critics say that the most that can be done is to promote steadiness: to reduce the instability of aggregate demand by (a) reducing the instability of government's own stop-start policies, including its control policies and (b) encouraging long-run growth. This means that government should abdicate from the short-run "balance-wheel" throne.

But this is easier said than done. For one thing, Canada's instability does not arise from the stop-start nature of its own governmental control actions, but from the booms and collapses triggered by international events and sharp changes in internal social attitudes and technologies. Among the international influences are the wars and crises in the countries with whom we trade and from whom we borrow; chiefly the United States, but also the U.K. and Japan. Additionally, we are beset by worldwide food, fuel and exchange-rate panics. To these must be added the surprisingly sudden domestic effects of changes in fertility rates, family formation and the new tastes for leisure and new discoveries about pollution dangers. These bring consequent strains in our construction, school, health and transport sectors. Non-discretionary, "steady" demand policies will not put out the fires that these events touch off; instead there is widespread agreement that the economy must adjust to these new events with new energy, education, welfare or pollution-abatement programs. In economic matters, voters are telling governments that they are elected to act in discretionary fashion.

RECOGNITION

Discretionary policy requires recognition of new trends before they are reversed, early enough to do something about them. The difficulty of recognition was illustrated in the late 1960s. Demand-pull inflation, added to the low-key creeping price rise of the whole post-war period, meant that prices had been rising for more than a decade. Many workers, employers and students had never even seen a fall in price levels. As a natural consequence, stubborn inflationary *expectations* played an increasing part in private wage demands and business offers.

But at the same time, there was still unemployment. It rose to 8 per cent in 1972. Even in the peak price year, the winter of 1973-4, unemployment seemed stuck at 6 per cent. Obviously,

---

[7] See the Royal Commission on Taxation (the Carter Commission) *Report*, Volume 2, 1966, Chapter 3; and Study Number 17, *Canadian Fiscal Policy 1945-1963*, by R. M. Will, 1966, Chapter 5.

this is not the old unemployment disease that called for more purchasing power; more money and more spending would simply add to the problem. "Demand management" is the wrong treatment for "stagflation"—unemployment and inflation at the same time. (Figure 19-2 shows that the symmetrical counterpoint of unemployment rate and price rate increase seemed destroyed around 1966; thereafter both unemployment *and* the annual increase of prices rose.)

THE OPEN QUESTION

This is the specter that haunts the mixed economy everywhere. Can a nation simultaneously enjoy the blessings of full employment and price stability? Or is there a fundamental dilemma of choice between high employment and reasonable price stability? Must full employment lead to creeping inflation? And to accelerating inflation? Is there no way to fight inflation in a modern mixed economy other than to engineer deliberate unemployment and a contrived slowdown to cool off the economy?

Put another way: Is there need for a new thing called an "incomes policy" to reinforce and back up macroeconomic fiscal and monetary policies? And if there is such a need, where is the ideal incomes policy to be found? In direct *price-wage controls* by government? In voluntary *wage-price guideposts* or guidelines in a freeze? Or is any goal of an incomes policy a snare and a delusion?

WHAT SCIENCE DOESN'T KNOW Questions, questions, questions. For the most part, the chapters of a modern economics textbook speak with crisp decisiveness: that thing is true; this thing is false; these matters are still subject to some dispute, etc. But the first duty of any discipline is to tell the truth. If, in the present state of medical knowledge, certain kinds of cancer cannot be cured or even checked, it is the duty of the good physician to face up to this fact, to profess the limits of scientific knowledge and therapy.

So it is the duty of modern political economy to record a simple truth. In the current state of knowledge about the modern mixed economy, no jury of competent economists can reach broad agreement on how to recommend a feasible and optimal incomes policy.

POLES OF THOUGHT A minority of the jury (primarily Chicago School Libertarians but including some left-wing radicals) will *deny that any incomes policy is needed*, deny that any problem exists; or will insist that if such a problem does perhaps truly exist, no incomes policy is going to do anything but make it worse.

Another minority (primarily admirers of John Kenneth Galbraith but including many Tory businessmen) have an equally simple position. "In time of war, we controlled prices and wages by imposed ceilings and commands. Peace is no different from war. The only solution for the creeping wage inflation and its concomitant inflation of oligopolistically administered prices is *permanent wage-price controls*."

Minorities on a jury do not make for an agreed decision. The bulk of economic experts, and this remark applies as well to Western Europe as to North America, admit to the complexity of the problem. They feel forced to recognize the existence of a *new* kind of inflation: "cost-push (or sellers') inflation" that differs in important degree from old-fashion "demand-pull (or demanders') inflation." New diseases require new remedies—if we can find them.

Whatever view wins out among informed juries of the future, analytical study of the patterns of experience is the first step.

DEMAND-PULL INFLATION

We saw earlier how monetary and fiscal policy can stimulate the economy to the point of full employment and beyond. If the total of·consumption-plus-investment-plus-government spending exceeds the value of what the economy can produce at full employment, demand dollars will beat against the limited supply of producible goods and services and will bid up their prices. Since labor is a service and since at such times the labor market has become very tight, the bidding up of wages is also part of the process.

But the direction of causation is clear-cut. It proceeds *from* demand *to* inflation.

Thus, if the 1922 German central bank prints off trillions and trillions of paper marks and these come into the market place in search of bread or housing, it is no wonder that the German price level rises trillionfold. This is demand-pull inflation with a vengeance. But the matter would not be essentially different if there were an 1849 gold discovery in California. Or if the central bank created new currency and bank deposits in large enough amounts to bring the system past the point of full-employment spending.

It is important to emphasize that monetarists, who think that M change in an $MV \equiv PQ$ Quantity Equation is the only good clue to explain macroeconomics, agree with post-Keynesians in their diagnosis of *what* demand-pull inflation is. Although the post-Keynesians prefer to use a $C + I + G$ approach, both models agree that it is "too much money spending beating against a limited supply of goods producible at full employment" that constitutes the essence of demand-pull inflation.

CURING DEMAND-PULL INFLATION   If only the world of the last part of the twentieth century were more like that of a century ago with its simple demand-pull inflation! Knowledge of modern macroeconomics would then make cure of inflation fairly simple. Brushing aside some short-run problems of forecasting changes in total demand, economists are agreed on the general direction in which macroeconomic policy has to work to wipe out an inflationary gap of the demand-pull type.

To recapitulate briefly, both $C + I + G$ or its equivalent MV, can be brought down by *demand management!* This includes (*a*) *monetary policy* (reducing the level or rate of growth of the money supply by central bank open-market sales, and by reinforcing reserve-requirement increases), and (*b*) *fiscal policy* (reducing government expenditure, increasing tax rates, increasing budget surpluses and reducing budget deficits). The art of dealing with demand-pull inflation is to apply the *proper dosage* of monetary and fiscal policy—fighting unemployment by enough expansion to lead the system to the lip of the cup of full employment, yet with enough moderation so that the flow of purchasing power does not spill over that lip in price inflation; fighting an inflationary gap by cutting back by just enough to bring the system back to a reasonably recognizable full-employment level, without causing an overshoot into recession and depression unemployment.

Admittedly, no one can read the future perfectly. Hence, macroeconomic dosage could not be expected to be exactly perfect in every short run. But *there would be no excuses for chronic slumps or chronic eras of inflation in the simple demand-pull world!* It

is time to leave that paradise for the cold real world of the present.

A NEW KIND OF INFLATION?

No country in the world has been simultaneously enjoying (*a*) full employment, (*b*) free markets, and (*c*) stable price levels. A glance at a chart of the price level changes will remind us that we live in a one-way era of creeping inflation. The same story is told in Germany and Japan, Sweden and Switzerland, Italy and France, in all the mixed economies of the world.[8]

What differentiates modern inflation from that of the past is this: Prices and wages begin to rise *before* any identifiable point of full employment; *before* tight labor markets and full-capacity utilization is reached.

Under modern cost-push (or sellers')inflation, a mixed economy may experience "stagflation"—stagnation of growth and employment at the same time that prices are rising!

Clearly, no sophisticated wielding of the tools of $C + I + G$ or of $(E - M)$ or of MV is going to be able to cure the new disease by administering the simple monetary-fiscal policy mix appropriate to demand-pull inflation.

For, *when we apply the monetary and fiscal brakes, at the same time we limit the rate of cost-push inflation we shall kill off the golden goose of prosperity.* Many will regard the remedy as worse than the disease.

STRUCTURAL ELEMENTS   Indeed, this throws a new light on the reasons that underlie "excessive expansion of monetary and fiscal policy." It is not that central bankers and parliaments have suddenly lost their senses, creating excess purchasing power like drunken sailors. Nor that they have less economic knowledge than their predecessors did. It is rather that the mixed economy, under the prodding of populist democracy, gets itself into a *structural bind!*

If demand management involving full-employment policy is not expansionist enough to match the

---

[8] A glance at Latin America shows that galloping inflation, with chronic price rises of 10, 20, 50, and 70 per cent per year, long prevailed in Chile, Argentina, Brazil, and elsewhere.

push of wages and costs, then the result will be slow growth and mass unemployment. The electorate will soon replace any central bankers or heads of state who practice the simple nineteenth-century virtues of fixed money supply with balanced budgets.

COST-PUSH, OR SELLERS', INFLATION

The growth of cost-push inflation has been a gradual evolution. At the end of World War II, Lord Beveridge, the father of the British social security system, foresaw the dilemma between full employment, stable prices, and free markets: adoption by the state of a price (control) policy is a natural and probably an inevitable consequence of a full employment policy.[9]

UNION PUSH ONLY? Businessmen naturally point to increases in wage costs as the reason for their having to raise prices. Often public opinion puts the blame on union leaders who force rises in money wage rates that exceed any rises in labor productivity. Inevitably, unless profit margins can be squeezed indefinitely, such wage costs must be accompanied by price rises. So it is argued.

This view of union leaders as the villains of the drama failed to fit the facts. First, experts on organized labor pointed out that the rank and file are usually even more militant than their leaders. When a leader runs behind his constituency, he gets thrown out of office—as with the head of the steelworkers. Second, the immediate post-1945 inflation was pretty much of the traditional demand-pull type, being attributable to the wartime buildup of liquidity and unsatisfied consumption and investment needs. A number of historical studies have shown that often it was nonunion wage rates that rose first and most, because of the lags involved in collective bargaining; it was as accurate to say that unions *slowed up* inflation as that they made it accelerate.

But most important was the fact that the large corporations who bargain with unions have been able to pass on the wage increases to the consumer and to pretty much maintain profit margins.

ADMINISTERED PRICE-WAGE PUSH. Even in periods of unemployment and industrial excess ca-

pacity, the price index continues to advance. Therefore some experts began to wonder whether this was not often a case of *price-push* as well as "wage-push". Nor did it seem to take many strikes to get wage increases along with the price increases. The wage-push happened *outside* the unionized industries, too. Observers said:

In pushing for higher wages, labor is pushing against an open door. The employers do not fight the increases the way they used to. They act as if they think the government will keep aggregate demand high enough to buy the higher-cost output; so they grant the wage increases, and this sends up costs of production, which sends up the prices that firms charge for their goods. The result is a new kind of inflation. When the government tries to handle it by demand-control weapons, it creates unemployment and a recession as in 1957-1958, 1960-1961 and 1970. From 1958 to 1963, prices were nearly stable, but it seemed to require unemployment of more than 5 per cent to make this so.

Thus explanatory emphasis has shifted away from exclusive reliance on wage-push. A series of studies of manufacturing industries in the United States and Canada, initiated in 1959, has shown that the response of that sector to increased consumer demand is better described as general cost-push. As demand expands, more wage-earners are first hired, as inflationary-gap analysis $C + I + G + (E - M)$ analysis would predict. But before anyone's notion of full employment has been reached, wage increases are touched off. They are apparently influenced by wages in the U.S. or in other sectors, and by the consumer price index.

Assume that at the same time prices of materials are rising for reasons that are external to the Canadian economy.

The reaction of employers seems to be as follows. First, an increase in demand is met by running down inventories or by taking orders for more remote future delivery. Prices quoted do not rise. Then more labor is hired, and more materials and energy are ordered. A rise in wage rates may be absorbed for a while in lower profits. However, a rise in material or energy prices is more quickly passed on to enable manufacturers to keep profits up. Then, with a lag, labor wage increases are also passed on to the consumer in higher prices. Eventually, the pricing be-

---

[9] W. H. Beveridge, *Full Employment in a Free Society*, London, Allen & Unwin, 1945.

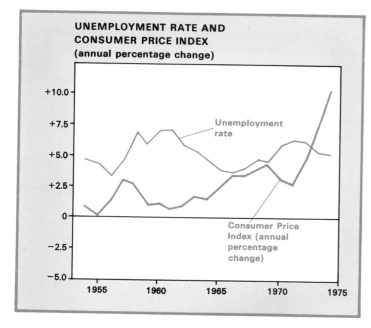

UNEMPLOYMENT RATE AND CONSUMER PRICE INDEX
(annual percentage change)

FIG. 19-2. A new kind of inflation: "cost-push (or sellers')."
Since 1965 the C.P.I. has tended to rise; its increase did not fall to zero even in years of contraction of unemployment such as 1970. The 1968-71 "stagflation" induced official recourse to income-tax "surtax" rates and budgetary surpluses. But these did not cool it off —so great was C.P.I. momentum that the demand pressure secured much unemployment but little inflation control.

haviour of business looks as through the businessman had a profit "target" to maintain.

Thus the *earnings* of workers and of employers may have risen more than the initial increase in consumers' demands for manufacturers at the original prices.

It follows that with their increased earnings they are now able to buy, at the old prices, more manufactures than are being produced.[10]

The whole process was generalized by A. P. Lerner. He called it *sellers' inflation.*

If all sellers, both of labor and goods, negotiate and determine the prices of their services so as to try to get among them all *more* than 100 percent of the total national product, the result cannot be other than a frustrating upward push of the price level—a case of sellers' inflation.

Figure 19-2 shows that low unemployment rates —as in the post 1965 boom when the average fell

close to the 3 per cent level—are associated with a quickening of price inflation. But it also shows the stagflation that characterized the next eight years. Soon after 1966, unemployment rose toward the 6-8 per cent levels that were to be a feature of workers' (and especially students') lives until mid-1973. But this easing of total demand did not mean that prices were steady, or falling. To the contrary. Both the wholesale and consumer price index began to rise. They faltered in 1970-1, but thereafter resumed a steady march up to the 10-15 per cent annual increase experienced in 1973.

This same incompatibility of full employment with price stability can be observed in mixed economies everywhere. Indeed, after 1967, there was a veritable wage explosion all over the world. This important phenomenon calls for new analytical tools of description, interpretation, understanding, and prediction.

THE PHILLIPS-CURVE TRADEOFF: FULL EMPLOYMENT OR PRICE STABILITY?

To understand conventional "demand-pull" inflation is easy in an idealized model where wages cannot rise so long as there is still one unemployed worker to

---

[10] For a discussion of this process see the study for the Canadian Prices and Incomes Commission by Taylor, Turnovsky and Wilson: *The Inflationary Process in North American Manufacturing,* (Ottawa, 1973). Do wage increases precede or lag behind an increase in the demand for the goods the workers make? For the view that they lag, see the final report of the Commission itself: *Inflation, Unemployment and Incomes Policy,* (Ottawa, 1972), Chapter 6. This report is in the nature of an expository inquiry into the causes and nature of price increases, especially between 1953 and 1972, and is well worth consulting as an accompaniment to this Chapter.

keep down the wage rate. And in the same idealized model of demand-pull where goods are all auctioned off in perfectly competitive markets, there could be no general price rises so long as there is spare capacity available to produce more output at (marginal) costs no higher than the ruling prices.

SIMPLE DEMAND-PULL In such a model, begin with full employment, where the macroeconomic managers have created just enough $C + I + G = MV$ spending to absorb all the full-employment output. If the managers now raise total spending by, say, 10 per cent, there will be more dollars of spending coming on the demand markets than can be supplied with goods at the previous equilibrium prices. We have engineered one of Chapter 13's so-called "inflationary gaps." Prices will then generally rise—ultimately by the 10 per cent needed to match the added $C + I + G$ spending. At the higher prices, employers will scramble to get more workers, bidding up wages ultimately also by 10 per cent (and thus leaving profits also higher by 10 per cent, but with all real or deflated wages being exactly the same as before).

Note that money wage rates have risen by 10 per cent more than productivity (which in our simple example has actually not changed at all) is rising. But that fact tells us nothing about the direction of causation (which we know in this case definitely *not* to have been from wages as cause to prices as effect). Whenever prices are rising and the relative sharing of profits-to-wages is constant, as a matter of mere arithmetic, money wage rates must be outstripping average labor productivity by the amount of the price rise, with real wages merely matching the productivity rise. But contrary to the confused arithmetic of conservative financial columnists, when real wages are thus advancing in line with average labor productivity, that does not mean that labor is "appropriating" or absorbing *all* the fruits of technological progress (which admittedly may have come from better machines and management methods as well as from greater worker effort or skill). It merely means that profit receivers and labor *share* in progress on same terms as before—say, at the usual (¼, ¾) fractions.

In this first simplified model, demand has *pulled up* prices and wages. Hence the repeated use of the name "demand-pull."

SIMPLE COST-PUSH Now drop the notion that labor gets auctioned off at a flexible wage rate. Go to the other extreme. Suppose that by union power and by the strong pressure of custom in the non-unionized areas, wage rates always rise by 8 per cent per year regardless of the amount of unemployment. And, since we are not trying to be entirely realistic, suppose that labor productivity always rises by exactly 3 per cent per year. Then, if the employers can always administer their prices so as to keep the share of profit (or property return) unchanged—say, near the conventional one-fourth level—how will prices all rise?

By arithmetic, we find that prices must rise by 5 per cent per year—which is the 8 per cent wage rise minus the 3 per cent productivity rise. The real wage rate also rises by only the 3 per cent productivity rise—since the 8 per cent money-wage rise has the 5 per cent of price rise deflated out of it. The total *real* return to property owners has also risen by the 3 per cent change in average labor productivity —because the relative wage share stays at three-fourths.

Note that nothing at all has been said thus far about demand, about $C + I + G$ or MV total spending. In this extreme cost-push model, demand has nothing to do with prices—which get set exclusively by wages and productivity. Prices rise at 5 per cent per year whether there is recession or prosperity, tight or loose Bank of Canada and fiscal policy, a Chapter 13 inflationary or deflationary gap. What, then, is the role of demand in this paradoxical extreme model of simple cost-push? In this extreme cost-push model demand has *no* effect on prices, P. It becomes completely a theory of output, Q, if P is determined elsewhere. Demand can still determine how total PQ = GNP behaves at all times; for these are simply other names for total $C + I + G$ or MV spending (as we saw in Chapter 15's tautological "equation of exchange"). With P in PQ given, demand has only real GNE or Q to determine.

POLICY DILEMMA Let us examine the problems now created for the macroeconomic managers of fiscal and monetary policy.

If we began at full employment and money wage rates go up by 8 per cent instead of the 3 per cent of productivity growth, unless the macro managers engineer an increase in aggregate demand of 8 per cent

—big enough to match the wage increase, which means big enough to finance the 5 per cent increase in P and the 3 per cent increase in Q—full employment will ebb away. (Perhaps the union leaders and oligopolists were counting on the managers to create the needed increase in demand.)

Thus, suppose the macro demand managers wrongly think they are facing old-fashioned demand-pull inflation when actually they are facing simple cost-push. Logically, they might decide to hold total GNP demand constant. What will happen? Output and employment will drop by 8 per cent a year! First 1 man out of 12 will be unemployed; then 2; . . . ; and if the irresistible force of cost-push meets the immovable object of macroeconomic policy, in the end the system will run down to literally nothing, with the last starving man losing his job and dying out. This is not a very likely outcome, for no doubt the macro managers will drop their stubborness and will create enough money spending to countenance the creeping inflation *indefinitely.*

Neither simple pole It is too bad that the simple demand-pull model is not realistic, for under it the job of the macro managers would be the easy one of turning on or off the faucets of fiscal and monetary policy to keep employment just full but never overfull. And it is indeed fortunate that the nightmare of *simple* cost-push is also not realistic, for in simple cost-push there is simply no control of inflation or influence on it that the macro managers can contrive.

The real world is somewhere between the two extremes. The amount of unemployment does in some degree hold down the excess of money wage increase over productivity increase. Budget surpluses and open-market sales—all the weapons in Part Two's macro arsenal to control $C + I + G$ or MV total spending—can now have some effect on price and wage inflation (but, alas, at the same time some effect on output).

Thus, when the Vietnam war reinforced a rise in spending that was not offset by determined tight-enough budgetary and central bank policy, there was a quickening in the rate of price inflation; from 1965 to 1968, we had mostly demand-pull inflation. But demand-pull for three years led inevitably to cost-push in subsequent years 1969 through 1971. See Fig. 19-2 for all this.

In some ways the macro managers are thrown into the most perplexing of all possible worlds. They are neither in the easy world of simple demand-pull nor the hopeless world of simple cost-push where they can do nothing about the rate of inflation. They are in the difficult world where the attempt to bring an 11 per cent rate of inflation down to 6 per cent may, at least in the short run, necessitate a retardation of real growth like that of early 1967 or 1969-1971, with rising unemployment, unrest, and all the wastes of a growing gap between our achieved and potential GNP. They must trade unemployment for price stability.

THE PHILLIPS CURVE Professor A. W. Phillips, formerly of the London School of Economics and the Australian National University, made a pioneering attempt to quantify this tradeoff relationship between unemployment and price-wage rises. Figure 19-3 pictures the typical downward-sloping Phillips curve, in which as you move leftward to reduce unemployment, then the rate of price and wage creep along the curves becomes higher. It fits best the

FIG. 19-3. The Phillips curve depicts the crucial tradeoff between degree of unemployment and wage-price creep. Red wage-change scale on right-hand vertical axis is higher than black left-hand price-change scale by assumed 3 per cent rate of average productivity growth. The greater is unemployment on the horizontal axis, the lower is rate of price inflation.

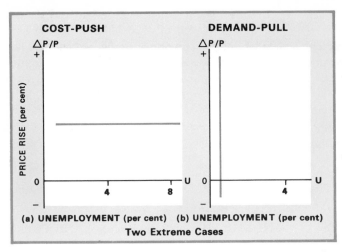

(a) UNEMPLOYMENT (per cent)   (b) UNEMPLOYMENT (per cent)
Two Extreme Cases

FIG. 19-4. In simple cost-push, Fig. 19-4(a) shows the curve to be completely horizontal with no tradeoff possible. Figure 19-4(b) shows the curve becoming completely vertical in simple demand-pull, with no tradeoff being necessary. (Some versions of demand-pull show the curve as L-shaped.)

1950-1960 period, some of which is shown in Figure 19-2.

On the diagram's horizontal axis is the percentage of unemployment. On the black left-hand vertical scale is the algebraic percentage change per annum in average prices; on the right-hand red scale is the accompanying percentage change in money wage rates per hour. These two scales differ only by the postulated amount of productivity increase per year (so that the price change of 5 per cent per year would correspond to a wage change of 8 per cent per year if productivity grew by 3 per cent per year and its fruits were shared in the same old proportions by labor and nonlabor).

(A higher rate of productivity growth will show itself in an equal downward shift of the curve and scale. Thus, with productivity growing at 6 per cent per year, an 8 per cent wage increase would correspond to only a 2 per cent annual price rise. A profit squeeze could be similarly shown.)

Be it noted that the MV and $C + I + G$ approaches to aggregate dollar spending are still applicable *offstage*, but one needs the information of the Phillips curve to translate the resulting product $P \times Q$ into its separate components. In a simple demand-pull model, the Phillips curve would be a vertical line at the minimal unemployment level: Q would then always correspond to full employment, and P would float in free labor markets to whatever level total money spending would determine. In simple cost-push the Phillips curve is a horizontal line, with no

level of unemployment leading to price stability.[11] By contrast, the real-life curve slopes downward somewhere in between.

The Phillips curve depicts the tradeoff between unemployment and price-wage inflation in each short run.

The Phillips curve is a dramatic way of describing the dilemma for macro policy, even though it does not go beyond description to give us "explanation." Thus, the problem is posed: How can a mixed economy supplement monetary and fiscal macro policy by an incomes policy *designed to give itself a better Phillips curve*? Better in what sense? Better in the sense that it will permit us to enjoy a lower minimum level of unemployment at which the system can avoid undue price inflation.

LONGER RUN. Before grappling with the hard problems of policy, we should reemphasize that economics is not an exact science. The data will not really fit any one Phillips curve perfectly. More important still is the fact that the illustrated Phillips

[11] Actually in Fig. 19-4(a), if the macro managers insisted on boosting demand faster than the indicated wage rise, they would push the system to such minimal unemployment as to cause a frantic bidding up by employers of the market wage rate *above* the wage administered by the unions; and this gives rise to what in Scandinavia has been called the "wage drift", in which wages always run ahead of the minima set by collective bargaining. This means the horizontal curve really ceases to be horizontal when you move near to the vertical axis.

curves represent *short-term* relationships that will definitely shift in the longer run.

Thus, if we run a slack economy for many years of the fifties, we may kill off inflationary expectations and slow down wage demands. In short, much unemployment, long maintained, may gradually *shift* the short-term Phillips curve leftward. Then we may be deluded in the 1960s into thinking that high $C + I + G$ can go on for long periods without bad price and wage misbehaviour. The 1970s disabused us. More than 100 months of uninterrupted price increase, with growing $C + I + G$ may shift the short-term Phillips curve rightward, making the policy problems of the 1970s that much harder. A vicious circle follows: As people fear and expect price inflation, they shift upward their effective Phillips curves and bring on stagflation—unemployment and inflation. And years of retardation may be needed before inflationary momentum is overcome.[12]

INCOMES POLICIES: FREEZE VERSUS SQUEEZE

We turn here from analysis of the tradeoff to the pressing problems of policy for our mixed economy. Not only have we not learned how to avoid compromises between price stability and full employment, but neither have the nations from whom we might borrow experience. Even aside from the complications of international transmission of inflation, the dilemma that demand policies must bring about unduly slack capacity, regional hardship and general unemployment in order to prevent overshooting potential GNP has inspired the search for more direct weapons to stop price increases.

Stop-go demand management policies were tried for more than ten years in the British economy. While they were not applied firmly enough to prevent creeping inflation, they did exact a cruel price in

terms of business growth, productivity and living standards. Later, Britain and many European countries, the U.S., Japan and Canada turned to direct government intervention or pressure to prevent rapid wage and/or price increases. These *wage-price,* or *incomes,* policies have taken various forms;

1. *Government controls* of wages or price increases (or as in the case of the short-run U.S. Nixon policies, *freezes* on prices and wages) constitute the toughest version of a wage-price policy. Some of these policies have been unexpectedly successful for short periods, in Finland, 1967-1971, and United States, 1971-3. Robert Stanfield promised his own Canadian variant of a freeze in 1974, but the voters rejected this proposal decisively.

Sometimes employers agree to price restraint if the government will "get tough with unions". Such talk is easy. But in practice, as Britain's Heath government learned before it was toppled, government confrontations with organized labor serve to breed resentment, widen class conflict, encourage nihilistic strikes and slowdowns, and demoralize workers, management and investors.

2. *Voluntary quasi-official "guideposts"* proved better than nothing in the Netherlands and a few other countries. Canada tried this approach when its Prices and Incomes Commission, set up in 1969, with UBC's John H. Young as chairman, attempted to persuade unions and businesses to accept price restraints. The unions would not agree. The Commission later recommended in a final report that voluntarism (attempts to apply an incomes policy without sanctions—teeth) should be avoided. But the Commission did imply that the stop-start effects of using demand policy against unforseen inflation could be moderated by controls of the type above.

3. *Collective bargaining between one vast association of employers and one vast association of unions?* J. K. Galbraith has referred to this technique as employing the "countervailing powers" of the great business and labor blocs to achieve success in wartime price controls. The government sits in as referee. Something like this has had a trial in Scandinavia and the Netherlands. But after some years of success, all restraint ended, and devastating rates of inflation followed. (This policy obviously depends both on the existence of the two blocs and of constitutional power in one government to act as concil-

---

[12] Once again, remember that controlled experiments are not possible. Two warnings about the Phillips curve approach arise from recent research and recent events. First, work by Vanderkamp, Kaliski and others on Canadian data detect such instability (volatility) in the position of the curves that statisticians may despair of isolating a stable behavioural relationship comparable to the consumption function. Second, other elements than wages and wage expectations entered the 1973-4 inflation: raw materials demands and prices, especially for energy, exploded all over the world, and influenced price formation directly.

iator and referee. It is not clear that Ottawa has the needed jurisdiction.)[13]

4. *Insulation from foreign price and wage influences.* This is the subject of Part Four.

However, it is obvious that to a Canadian businessman the effect on his profits and prices of a rise in the imports which he must buy, or compete with, is much like the effect of higher wages or higher prices of his Canadian rivals. It has also appeared that Canadian labor markets are much influenced by the course of wages in the U.S. Many experts advocate preventing these effects by letting a flexible exchange rate dampen them or screen them out.

Canada's three-person Commission, in 1969-1970, aimed for an *agreed* upper limit on wage, salary, rent and price increases, similar to a blend of No. 2 and 3 above. But discussions were broken off in early 1970, largely because of trade-union refusal to continue participation. (The Commission's role then became that of a study group reporting on causes and remedies for price instability in 1972.)

Canadians now seem agreed on three aspects of such programs. They can work if (*a*) the accompanying demand management policy is not expansionary, (*b*) the wage-price spiral is seen by the public as temporary, so that after the control period, the causes of the spiral will have abated and (*c*) the participating spokesmen are able to "speak for" their constituents: farmers, unionists, pensioners, provincial governments, manufacturers, etc. The first condition was not met in 1970. The second is the task of the Commission. What about the third? Who

in heterogeneous Canadian life can speak for all Canadian labor? Who can, in this land of wildcat strikes, palace revolutions and international unionism deliver worker agreement to a single wage formula? Not even in the centralized U.S. AFL-CIO can George Meany control his federated employers, the 20 million U.S. union members. No one can even begin to do so in Canada. On the employers', farmers' and provinces' side, the same differences exist. No one can commit all Canadian vegetable growers, or sawmills, or refiners, or real-estate brokers, or mayors. This is forgotten by those who advocate, with J. K. Galbraith, a return to the countervailing powers of the spokesmen for the great blocs of capitalism during World War II.

INDEXING WITH OPEN INFLATION? All the above cures for creeping inflation have been advocated, and in every combination. In despair, some economists ask:

What's so bad about inflation anyway? It is better than mass unemployment and excess industrial capacity. Moreover, by various sliding scales in wage contracts, indexed income tax brackets, government bonds with fixed *real* rates of return, and indexed pensions all of *guaranteed real purchasing power*, the human burdens of unanticipated inflation can be substantially reduced.

Undoubtedly such devices are better than a masochistic throttling down of the economy that puts the burden for fighting inflation on the marginal workers who can least afford to bear that burden—young workers, minority workers, female workers, unskilled workers.

But will the rate of inflation accelerate once you stop fighting it? Skeptics sound a warning:

The system does not really have a permanent choice between less-unemployment-cum-more-price-inflation and more-unemployment-cum-less-price-inflation. It has a choice only between less unemployment *now* at the cost of more unemployment *later*. It all comes out in the long-run wash! There is a law of conservation of unemployment in any economy.

Some try to define a long-run Phillips curve from the systematic shiftings of the short-run curves (in much the same way that Fig. 20-5 is able to depict

---

[13] Various comparisons of the policies have been published. David C. Smith, writing in 1966, surveyed foreign experiences and recommended persuasively against an incomes policy for Canada. The Economic Council of Canada came to the same decision. A later study from the Canadian perspective in Frank Anton has described them from a more recent point of view. Analytical studies, such as those by Queen's University's Richard G. Lipsey and by Lloyd Ulman of California have usually been pessimistic. In the mid-1970s, attention has turned in other directions: (a) the possibility of a worldwide recession; (b) the transmission of inflation among countries; and (c) the possibility of monetary inflation being generated internationally. See David C. Smith, *Incomes Policies*, special study No. 4 for Economic Council of Canada, 1966; Frank R. Anton, *Wages and Productivity* (Toronto, Copp Clark, 1969), and Lloyd Ulman and J. Flanagan, *Wage Restraint: A Study of Incomes Policies in Western Europe* (California, Berkeley, 1971).

long-run Marshallian supply curves from systematically shifting short-run supply curves). The long-run Phillips curve tends to be twisted clockwise, as in Fig. 19-5(a). There is even one strong theory, suggested by W. Fellner and H. Wallich of Yale, M. Friedman of Chicago, and E. Phelps of Columbia, which in effect says: "The Phillips tradeoff is based only on the *illusion* of *unanticipated* price-wage inflation. Once the system settles down to any constant rate of price-wage inflation, people will come to learn the fact and to expect it in the future. So you will then have just as much excess wage pressure over that constant rate as you had when prices were stable. There is really a 'natural rate of unemployment,' defined by a vertical long-run Phillips curve as shown in Fig. 19-5(b). If you temporarily bring unemployment below the natural rate, your short-term curves will twist upward indefinitely and your price rise will accelerate; if you temporarily bring unemployment above the natural rate, the short-term curves will there twist downward indefinitely and your price rise will decelerate. In order for people to be adjusted to the rate of price change so that it will not be accelerating or decelerating, you have to be *on the long-run vertical line.*" These writers conclude: "Since you will be stuck with the natural rate of unemployment in the long run anyway, the macro managers should keep demand growing at only the rate of real growth of the system—say, 4 to 5 per cent per year so that *Ps* will be steady. To reduce unemployment's natural rate, policies other than macro fiscal and monetary measures are needed—such as repealing minimum-wage laws or restrictive union practices." Critics of these writers say that by the time *their* proposed equilibrium is reached, the system may well have been torn apart by voter revolt, urban riots, and unemployment-induced hardships and dissatisfactions. And besides, the data of experience are not yet available to judge whether Fig. 19-5(a) or 19-5(b) is the more realistic.

No statistical evidence establishing so definite a view has yet been forthcoming. And, even if this pessimistic view were to have an element of truth, no doubt many would argue that, in an uncertain world, it is better to grasp the lower unemployment that can be had at hand than wait for the lower unemployment that, so to speak, can be found only in some future bush.

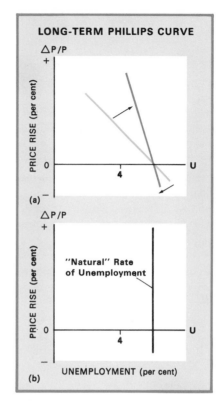

FIG. 19-5.

Still, extensive studies of the last decade, covering the experiences of all the mixed economies of the world, justify the following observation.

Keeping unemployment in a mixed economy down below some critical region does result in a *tendency* for the rate of creeping inflation to become a canter or even a gallop. To avoid accelerating inflation, one must find new tools of incomes policy to *shift* Phillips-curve tradeoffs, short-run and long-run, and not merely turn on the steam of fiscal and monetary policy to move the system along unchanged Phillips curves that look temporarily appealing.

REDUCING STRUCTURAL UNEMPLOYMENT FOR BETTER PHILLIPS CURVES

Wide agreement will be found among economic and labor-market experts over the following four programs to lower the sustainable rate of unemployment (i.e., to shift the Phillips curve leftward at least a little).[14]

1. *Manpower training programs* so that the unskilled will qualify for the jobs that are available, and those with obsolete skills can retread themselves.

2. *Improved labor-market mechanisms* with better communication concerning job vacancies and human availabilities can reduce the float of transitional unemployment.

3. *Regional relocation* programs and subsidies, both for workers and industries, could aid in reducing geographical pockets of unemployment and poverty.

4. *Reduction of discrimination* against particular classes in the labor force on the side of employers and coworkers, and *increased realism* on the side of would-be workers concerning the remunerations and qualifications relevant to viable employment opportunities. In particular, some flexibility in minimum wage rates for the young and handicapped, if such can be found without undermining competitive standard rates, would help improve the Phillips curve and bring down high unemployment rates among marginal workers.

5. Subject to more controversy, but still increasingly favored by many economists, is a program *to make the government the employer of last resort* for those who genuinely seek work that they cannot find and who can contribute more to society by being productive than by being unhappily idle.

In 1970-4 the problem of creeping inflation became the problem of sustained cost-push or sellers' inflation. It vies with secular stagnation for recognition as the most important problem faced by the economic scientists of the western mixed economies. Secular stagnation may be solvable by sustained fiscal policies and other demand-management tools. But

creeping inflation is not a problem that even if runaway inflation does slow itself down, will go away. Demand management seems ineffective, or even (with higher interest rates and taxes) to add to cost-push. And incomes policies have been abandoned by the experts and rejected by the voters. High on the agenda of political economy remain better cures for the general problems of stagflation and inflation in the modern mixed economies.

CONCLUSION TO PART TWO: MACROECONOMICS OF THE MIXED ECONOMY

As the quotation beginning this chapter shows, the Canadian government assumed responsibility for stable employment, income, and prices in 1948. This claim is now regarded as a duty. Even if there were not such parliamentary proclamations, it is a fact all over the world that the populace of modern mixed economies require that their representative governments pursue economic policies that attempt to keep employment high, growth strong, and prices stable.

Part Two has presented the economic *tools of macroeconomics*: how the various schedules determine levels and movements in incomes and prices; and how monetary and fiscal policies can shift those schedules so as to avoid deflationary and inflationary gaps and promote growth. In Part Six certain special problems connected with the modern era—growth, cost-push demand, inflation, and so forth—will be discussed in greater detail.

The finding of our macroeconomic analysis rejects both the classical faith that *laissez-faire* must by itself lead to utopian stability and the pre-World War II pessimism that classical microeconomic principles have become inapplicable to the modern world. Instead we end up with the reasoned prospect that appropriate monetary and fiscal policies can ensure an economic environment which will *validate* the verities of microeconomics—that society has to choose among its alternative high-employment production possibilities, that paradoxes of thrift and the fallacies of composition will not be permitted to create cleavages between private and social virtues or private and public vices.

By means of appropriately reinforcing monetary and fiscal policies, a mixed economy can avoid ex-

---

[14] It can be seen that these policies can be interpreted two ways. They are indeed "supply policies" which, taken in conjunction with demand policies can (by shifting the Phillips curve leftward) reduce the steady level of unemployment. But they can also be seen as shifting the "natural" rate of unemployment referred to in Figure 19-5.

In both connections attention should be paid to the contention of Simon Fraser University's Herbert Grubel and associates that new generous unemployment-insurance laws are increasing labor force participation but not employment. The Prices and Incomes Commission's report and its special studies refer to the unusually high unemployment rates in Canada compared to other countries, and are also consistent with a view that the "natural" rate in Canadian society is as high as 5 percent, due to demographic, regional and job-search peculiarities.

cesses of boom and slump. This being understood, the paradoxes that robbed the older classical principles dealing with small-scale "microeconomics" of much of their relevance and validity will now lose their sting. The broad cleavage between microeconomics and macroeconomics has been closed by active use of fiscal and monetary and exchange-rate policy,[15] (save for the unsolved dilemma of cost-push inflation in the mixed economy!)

With good conscience we can turn to the analysis in Part Three of how the great social aggregates of national income and employment *get determined in their detailed parts* and to Part Four's analysis of *income distribution.*

SUMMARY

1 When private investment and consumption spending create an inflationary (or deflationary) gap, it is the task of fiscal and monetary policy to offset the gap in the attempt to preserve price stability, high employment, and growth.

2 Fiscal weapons refer to taxation and expenditure policies. In this connection, the modern economy is blessed with important "built-in stabilizers." Requiring no discretionary action, tax receipts change *automatically* when income changes, thereby reducing the size of the multiplier and serving to wipe out part of any disturbance. (The same stabilizing effect is realized by unemployment compensation and other welfare transfers that automatically grow as income declines; by price supports for agriculture; by federal finance; by the propensity of corporations to pay out in dividends only part of their current earnings; and by variations in the percentage of income spent on imports.)

3 Because the automatic stabilizers never fully offset the instabilities of an economy, scope is left for discretionary programs. Public works and other expenditure on goods and services can involve such time lags in getting under way as to make their use to combat short recessions undesirable. Discretionary variations in transfer expenditures and in tax rates—politics aside—have greater short-run flexibility.

4 When men began to drop the notion that the government's budget had to be balanced in every year or month, they first thought that it would be in balance over the business cycle —with the boom-time surpluses just matching the depression deficits. It is today realized that only by coincidence would the prosperity years just balance in their intensity the depression years, especially with the desired mix of consumption and capital formation.

5 If, as a few believe, we are in for "secular stagnation," with private saving and investment schedules tending much of the time to produce deflationary gaps, fiscal policy will probably succeed in maintaining stable high employment only by having a long-term increase in the public debt. If, as others believe, we are in for "chronic exhilaration," with demand so brisk as to lead much of the time to inflationary gaps, then active fiscal policy will probably mean a bias toward surplus financing and a secular downward trend in the public debt. Perhaps the majority of economists feel there is no need to try to predict what the distant future has in store, being prepared to advocate programs that the developing situation calls for.

---

[15] Naturally, one can point out many needed qualifications to this optimistic formulation. But events of recent decades and the most painstaking economic research in universities, industry, and government justify our concentrating on the doughnut—not on its hole.

6   Every mixed economy has the effective knowledge and ability to utilize monetary and fiscal policies to create—by useful peacetime expenditures—a sufficiency of overall purchasing power. *M* creation and fiscal deficits have succeeded all over the globe in banishing fear of chronic depression. The problem remaining is of a new kind—cost-push inflation and stagflation.

7   The distinction between inflationary gap, or demand-pull inflation ("demanders' inflation") and recent cost-push inflation ("sellers' inflation") is crucial. Old-fashioned demand-pull inflation can be controlled by proper dosage of monetary and fiscal policy—central-bank policy and budgetary spending-taxing policies.

8   In modern cost-push inflation, prices and wages begin to creep upward *even before* employment is full and industrial capacity fully utilized. To clamp down on monetary and fiscal policy to fight such inflation will only result in unemployment and stagnation. But not to act is to accept creeping inflation that may accelerate into a canter or gallop.

9   The Phillips curve relates the tradeoff between price inflation and the degree of unemployment in the system—by its position in the short run, and also by its induced shiftings in the longer run. Thus, suppose that at unemployment levels below 5 per cent, money wage rates always rise 4 per cent faster than the 3 per cent productivity growth of the system; then the price level will creep forward at 4 per cent as corporations pass on the cost increases and maintain their profit margins. We have a case of sellers' inflation.

10 An "incomes policy" is needed to supplement fiscal and monetary policy—in order *to give the mixed economy a better Phillips curve*. But it remains an unsolved problem of modern economics to get experts to agree on an incomes policy: benign neglect, governmental guideposts (voluntary or quasi-voluntary), direct wage-price controls, centralized collective bargaining, stop-go driving of the economy to cool it down, manpower and retraining programs to lower the natural level and range of structural unemployment—all these continue to be debated and studied.

CONCEPTS FOR REVIEW

demand management	cost-push (sellers')inflation
monetary policy (*M* supply and credit conditions)	versus demand-pull inflation and inflationary gap
fiscal policy (taxes,*G*, in *C* + *I* + *G*)	stagflation (inflation-cum-stagnation)
discretionary and automatic stabilizers	Phillips-curve tradeoff dilemma incomes-policy debate
surplus and deficit financing	guideposts and price-wage controls
secular stagnation and exhilaration	improved labor-market structure

QUESTIONS FOR DISCUSSION

1. "No nation can avoid having a fiscal policy. With the government such an important part of the present-day economy, it is almost impossible even to define a 'neutral fiscal policy.' It is even harder to give rational reasons for preferring such a policy to an active program aimed at preventing inflation and deflation." Examine critically.

2. List various "built-in stabilizers." Show how they work in the 1970s.

3. What phase of the business cycle (if any) are you now in? What tax and expenditure policies would seem appropriate? Qualitatively, how would you vary the relative importance of different taxes (income-tax rates and exemptions, sales taxes, or property taxes) to fight unemployment or inflation?

4. From the early 1870s to the middle 1890s, depressions were deep and prolonged, booms were short-lived and relatively anemic, and the price level was declining. What long-run fiscal policy should have been followed in that quarter of a century?

5. "Canada in 1914-18 lacked taxing capacity. So our Great War (like the U.S.'s wars of 1776, 1812, and its civil war) had to tolerate an inflationary gap, and to be financed by demand-pull inflation". Explain what this means.

6. "Unemployment was high in the construction industries in 1973, but wage rates were rising in many regions by more than 10 per cent per year". Show that this is cost-push (sellers') inflation rather than demand-pull in a labor-auction market.

7. What is a Phillips curve? What is on its horizontal axis, or better, axes? Why is it good to get the curve shifted to the left and down?

8. Explain what is meant by "incomes policy." Debate the alternative proposals.

9. Can mere science in political economy provide the same answer on the degree to which we should compromise between the evils of unemployment and of inflation for (a) an M.P. representing the Atlantic provinces, and (b) a spokesman for the Vancouver Island retirement areas, full of elderly people retired on fixed pensions?

10. What do you expect will happen, during sellers' inflation, after direct price-and-wage controls are applied then lifted? Would this have been the economic aftermath of the controls proposed by Robert Stanfield in the July 1974 election? (Consult the price data before you answer.)

APPENDIX: THE PUBLIC DEBT AND MODERN FISCAL POLICY

In Canada—as in Britain, Germany, Japan and Holland—statesmen, editors and the citizenry never know what their current budgetary deficits (or surpluses) are. (Test yourself!) In this they are like most economists who, if asked to make a list of important economic issues, will usually put the debt near the bottom. But they are unlike a small group of well-informed Canadians who, like most Americans, would put the debt at the top of the list.

Our task is not to explain this difference of attitude, but to survey the *economic* effects of debts, as they arise from demand management. Monetary policy's "open market operations" in effect change the amount of federal debt in the hands of the public. But such changes are trivial compared to the growths in debt from federal, provincial and municipal deficits. The facts on deficits and the size of the debt are presented in figures and tables. But most of the Appendix surveys the analysis of the economics of public debt—not the volatile flow of annual deficits, but the slowly-changing stock of government bonds, debentures and short-term treasury bills.

No introduction can go into all the intricacies involved in a correct appraisal of the public debt. But modern economists give attention to the debt's true burden and diagnose its problems in a way significantly different from the approach the layman used to take.

BURDENS AND BENEFITS OF THE PUBLIC DEBT

As is argued below, the main way that one generation can put a burden on a later generation is by using up currently the nation's stock of capital goods, or by failing to add the usual investment increment to the stock of capital.

Thus much of our buildup of today's federal unmatured debt of 30 billion dollars occurred during World War II.[1]

[1]What is government debt? It consists of many types of I.O.U.'s of three levels of government. Here is one listing that gives orders of magnitude in 1972, in billions of dollars:

Federal Debt
Unmatured debt (direct and guaranteed securities):	30
Canada Savings Bonds, annuities, pensions, and other liabilities:	22
Less: Cash and other assets	−35
Equals: Net debt	17

Provincial Debt
Direct and guaranteed securities only	27

Municipal and Local Debt
Direct and guaranteed debentures only	8

The top item; federal unmatured security debt is often called the "national debt", but it greatly overstates the net debt of Ottawa to the rest of the economy, and neglects the debts of other government levels. Unmatured federal securities have about 4.25 years to run on the average, having been redeemed and reissued as they mature. This term is short: from 1938 to 1960 it varied between 6 and 11 years.

The primary burden of that war came from the need *then* to eat up capital goods without replacing them in order to maximize our war effectiveness and shorten the conflict. Notice that it was the prohibition of machine manufacture and building construction and repair that produced this real burden, and not the happenstance that Parliament decided to finance part of the war effort on a loan-deficit basis rather than on a full tax-as-you-go basis.

Looking to the future, we can say that *increases in public debt that are incurred in time of full employment* and involve no government capital formation, but *which do require that private investment be held down* (by monetary policy or by inflation itself), do represent a "burden." On the other hand, running a deficit and incurring debt when there is no other feasible way to move the $C + I + G + (E - M)$ equilibrium intersection up toward full employment actually represents a *negative* burden on the immediate future to the degree that it actually induces more current capital formation than would otherwise take place!

There is a second aspect of the public debt that needs stressing. An *external* debt (owed to foreigners) does involve a net subtraction from the goods and services available to the Canadian people to the extent that (a) we have to send goods abroad to pay interest on that debt, and (b) the incurring of the external debt was unproductive, failing to add to our capacity to turn out such goods and services.

An *internal* debt (owed by the government to its own citizens) is quite a different matter. Certainly one cannot blithely ignore an internal debt on the ground that "we owe it all to ourselves." There definitely are problems arising from the existence of an internal debt—but they do differ from those of an external debt.

The popular image is that the public debt, prorated over the population, is like a load on each man's back. According to this same image, when Ottawa adds a dollar to the debt by running a current deficit of a dollar, that is like just one more rock added to the load our children or grandchildren will already have to carry on their backs.

This image is misleading in two ways. First it exaggerates the burdens that are truly involved. Second, by giving a mistaken view of the debt burden, it lays itself open to refutation and thereby to the mistaken conclusion that there are, after all, *no* burdens connected with the public debt.

As a preview to a judicious appraisal, see how vulnerable the foregoing image is.

POLAR CASE OF ZERO BURDEN Suppose all debt came from World War II. The war is over. Suppose all Canadian families (1) share equally in ideal nondistorting taxes, (2) hold equal shares of public-debt bonds, (3) all live forever (as individuals or as a cohesive family). With no debt held abroad, (4) "we all owe it to ourselves."

"Then such bonds are not rocks on our shoulders, nor even paper weights. If we unanimously voted to abolish the bonds, there would be no real difference. If an enemy bombed our homes and factories, that would be a genuine personal and national burden. But if an enemy bombed our bond lock-boxes out of existence, that would merely save us the red tape of taxing ourselves to pay each of us back in bond interest just what the extra tax took away."

So goes the argument. Notice how simple the above refutation is. And how clever in taking the wind out of the sails of those who use the the the over-simplified rock-burden image. Moreover, the refutation is—granted its assumptions—logically rigorous.

Has the refutation proved the war involved no grievous burden? It has been cunningly silent on that matter. The Devil's Advocate who produced the refutation would, if pressed by a Tireless Truthseeker, have to concede much.

A DIALOGUE

DEVIL'S ADVOCATE Yes, the war involved a grievous economic burden at the time. We had to work hard and long hours. We had to cut wartime consumption to the bone: do with little meat, no cars, no travel—make do with few of the things that make life enjoyable rather than merely tolerable.

TIRELESS TRUTHSEEKER With severe rationing controls, the contemporaneous wartime burden of sacrificed consumption would, according to your view, be much the same even if the war had been financed by pay-as-you-go wartime taxes instead of deficit?

D.A. Precisely. Postwar canceled tax receipts, instead of bonds, would make no difference.

T.T. But surely, we used up capital goods during the war by not replacing them. The enemy had to be fought with current 1939-1945 goods and not with 1970 goods. By using up capital goods *then*, we could throw more resources into the war effort. And that did put a real burden *on us in the postwar period* since we inherited less capital goods at war's end. In the postwar period we've had to consume less in order to rebuild those capital goods; and we've had to consume less than we should have if 1939-1945 had given us the normal peacetime increase in capital.

D.A. True. But wartime rationing produced that result. If no wartime deficits and bond indebtedness had been created, that *genuine burden* on the postwar group due to the war would still have had to take place.

T.T. I feel there must be a catch somewhere. Your argument sounds too facile.

1. I can't help feeling that the existence of the public debt leads to (*a*) to tax distortions as we collect taxes to pay its interest, and (*b*) to a lower consumption schedule when poor people with higher MPC pay taxes for bond interest to wealthier people with a lower MPC.

2. Moreover, people don't live forever, and it is not irrational of them to feel wealthier because of the public debt (since they need count on paying taxes for debt interest *only through their remaining lifetime*). This increase in the CC propensity to consume could be at the expense of net capital formation in a full-employment postwar year, requiring contractionary M policy that hurts investment.

3. Besides, a fair part of our public debt is external and held abroad: sending them goods to cover the interest payments does constitute a definite subtraction from our GNP available for domestic consumption and investment.

4. While it may be true that transfers of purchasing power—between individuals living at one time, between individuals at different ages of their life spans, and between individuals alive today and yet unborn—can be engineered by the government without using the device of the public debt at all, yet I can't help believing that society is led by the presence of the debt to make some transfer decisions that it probably wouldn't otherwise have made.

5. If the decision to have a budget deficit in depression times (or in times when the international balance of payments made expansionary monetary policy infeasible) merely prevents unemployment, then I admit the implied deficit adds to, rather than subtracts from, the capital stock bequeathed to the postdepression times. But when a decision to have a deficit leads to a compensating cut in private capital formation through inducing more restrictive Bank of Canada monetary policy than would otherwise be the case, I say that such a way of increasing the public debt does *itself* put a real burden on the backs of later citizens.

6. Of course, I admit that floating a public debt to add to useful government capital is as legitimate as floating private debt to build useful private capital—because in each case the new paper assets are matched by real income-creating assets.

7. But in a well-run full-employment system, I have to regard loan finance for *current* public consumption as putting a kind of burden on the future through its effective cutting down on net capital formation at the time, and subsequently through its wealth stimulus on consumption that may be competitive with investment.

D.A. I've never denied anything you are saying. I merely assumed away most of your genuine burdens. If I may say so, you are now shifting over to the side of the angels and are beginning to analyze the true and false burdens of the public debt—and not merely using vivid analogies that obscure rather than illuminate the truth, the whole truth, and nothing but the truth.

SUMMARY OF DEBT BURDENS AND BENEFITS

1. *Capital-bequeathed burden.* The principal way one generation puts a burden on itself later or on a later generation is by bequeathing it less real capital than would otherwise have been the case. Any growth of public debt that has this effect—as in the case of full-employment borrow-

ing for current public consumption that has to be offset by contractionary monetary policy that will lower investment —most definitely does involve a genuine "burden."

2. *External-debt burden*. Any public debt that is externally held does involve a current burden on the citizens at home, since in the end they have to send goods abroad corresponding to the interest payments and debt service. (Of course, if the original borrowing from abroad resulted in equivalent fruitful capital goods here, their fruits will cover the external-debt service; so the net effect of such external borrowing, taken as a complete package, would be favorable to us.)

3. *Transfer effects*. Taxing Peter to pay Paul bond interest, even if they are the same person, is certain to cause some harmful distortions of personal and business decisions. (EXAMPLE: Paul is taxed 10 per cent of his income to pay himself $1,000 of bond interest. He is under the illusion, and properly so as an individual, that he can work less and cut down on his tax. But here is a fallacy of composition. If all taxpayers slack off, we simply have to increase the tax rate. Result: we all end up working less because taxes on each individual matched by exactly equal interest payments to him do not economically cancel out!)

Correlated with public-debt operations, but not always in an intrinsic way, are certain transfers that take place between different individuals, living at the same time, between the same individual at different periods of life, and between successive generations.[2]

4. *Wealth stimulus to consumption*. The existence of public debt, for reasons already seen, makes the average man feel wealthier. For good or evil, it raises his propensity-to-consume schedule: this may, in a poorly functioning system, be a great thing to reduce unemployment and increase both consumption and investment. Or in a system where employment can be counted on to remain full by virtue of price flexibility, luck, or monetary management, the increase in C may be at the expense of I and reinforce the capital-bequeathed burden (paragraph 1). (In extreme cases, a dollar of public debt might ultimately kill off a dollar of real capital goods.)

5. *Effects on interest and money policy*. A large debt gives the Bank of Canada great leverage for massive

open-market operations to achieve stabilization. Many experts believe that the existence of a broad market in government securities makes possible extensive open-market operations of a stabilizing type and tends to enhance the effectiveness of monetary policy. Debt management by the Bank by a proper policy of open-market operations in bonds of all maturities that was properly carried out could enhance the stability of a modern system.

6. *How to analyze true debt effects*. We must render unto intermediate and advanced texts what is theirs. Suffice it to say here that penetrating analysis requires a theoretical model of some complexity. At the least, it should involve the interplay of three kinds of assets: real capital goods (equipment, plant, etc.); government bonds; supply of money, M (which is the non-interest-bearing, never-maturing "debt" of government). Then we should not ask: "What is the absolute burden of the public debt?" Rather, we ask: "Given the choice of loan-financed deficit over M-financed or over *laissez-faire* unemployment, what will the differential effects be?"

The answers will be illuminating.[3]

THE QUANTITATIVE PROBLEM OF THE DEBT

To assess the importance of the present public debt, we must turn to the facts. Do interest payments on it swallow up most of the national income? How does the total of all interest payments, public and private, compare with past years and with the experience of other countries? What about the future?

To see how the present debt compares with the past and with some other countries, look at Table 19-1. It shows for selected times and places the size of national debts and their relationship to size of national income and interest payments. Thus, in 1973 our net national debt of about 18 billion dollars represented much less than one year of national income, and its interest payments represented only about 2.6 per cent of net national product. Note that Britain in 1818, 1923, and 1946 had an internal debt estimated at two or three times national income, and interest on the debt as a percentage of national income far exceeded anything that we need look forward to; yet the century before World War I was Britain's greatest century —greatest in power and material progress. Furthermore,

[2]EXAMPLES: Twin Jane Day worked hard in World War II; twin Rose did not. Because our government used deficit financing, Jane ended up in 1945 with bonds rather than tax receipts. (Jane may have been motivated to work harder by the bribe of postwar command over goods.) Since 1945 Jane has been receiving a larger share of consumption than Rose; Rose is being taxed more than would otherwise have been the case in order to help pay interest and principal to Jane: Moral: A public debt can definitely involve *internal transfer effects* between individuals of the same or different ages.

Even if Jane Day had died in 1965, she could have consumed more in 1945-1965 by selling off her bonds.

The burden of *this* extra consumption could be imposed on those born after 1965 (1) by causing a reduced capital stock after 1965 due to lowered investment in 1945-1965, but also (2) by having an intermediate generation of young postwar workers (employed in 1945-1965 and who have bought Jane's bonds out of their personal saving) supported in their old age by the 1980 workers who will pay taxes on the public debt.

[3]Two quite different diagnoses can both be valid depending upon assumptions!

Heretical case: Deep depression deficit spending was the *only* feasible way of reducing 1933-1935 unemployment; such debts added to consumption and to capital formation then and to the capital stock and GNP potential in 1980.

Classical case: Failing to tax to finance the war raised our debt and forced the central bank to tighten M and reduce capital formation spending; so war debt is a genuine burden in 1980 in the form of lower real capital then; but by 1990, paying it off by taxing enough to produce a budget surplus while at the same time unemployment is kept full by the central bank's loosening M and inducing extraordinary capital formation—that will remove the burden from post-1990 generations at the expense of having put it on the 1980-1990 generation, whose heavy taxes cut down on their consumption in those years.

FEDERAL DEBT AND INTEREST CHARGES RELATIVE TO NET NATIONAL INCOME		
(1)	(2)	(3)
Year	Size of Debt in Years of Net National Income	Interest Charges as a Percentage of Net National Income
Canada (millions of dollars):		
1973	0.19	2.6
1950	0.82	3.1
1940	0.65	2.5
1935	0.92	4.4
1930	0.49	2.8
1920	0.46	2.2
1910	0.18	0.7
1870	0.19	1.2
United States (billions):		
1973	0.41	1.7
1945	1.5	2.0
1939	0.7	1.3
1929	0.2	0.7
1920	0.3	1.3
1916	0.0+	0.0+
1868	0.4	1.9
Britain (millions):		
1970	1.0	3.4
1946	3.0	5.4
1923	1.9	8.2
1913	0.3	0.8
1818	2.1	7.7

TABLE 19-1. Growing debt holds little peril for a dynamically growing economy.
The countries' methods of measuring debt and income vary, but everywhere the burden is declining when the economy grows. (U.S., U.K: gross national debt; Canada: federal net debt.)

(Sources: *Economic Almanac,* **U.S. Department of Commerce; U.S. Treasury; United Nations;** *Colwyn Report; Statistical Abstract of United Kingdom; Canada Year Book, Public Accounts of Canada,* **1966;** *The National Finances,* **1966-67, Canadian Tax Foundation; Urquhart and Buckley,** *Historical Statistics of Canada,* **Cambridge University Press, 1965; and Bank of Canada** *Statistical Summary.***)**

as the table shows, her national debt was not substantially reduced; but with the steady growth of her national income, the debt and its charges shrank to almost nothing in relative magnitude!

GROWTH IN THE ECONOMY In dispassionately analyzing the growth of the debt, there is one error we must avoid: *We must not forget that the real national product of Canada is an ever-growing thing.*

Our population grows lustily. As to productivity, there is no indication that man-hour efficiency and new techniques have begun to slacken off. Upon this, "stagnationists" and "exhilarationists" both agree. What seemed like a big debt in 1867 would be nothing today. What our children will come to regard as a big debt, our great-grandchildren will deem relatively unimportant.

This explains why England and France, in the crucially formative years of the capitalistic system and the Industrial Revolution, were able to go on—not only decade after decade, but century after century—with their budgets in balance less than half the time. Figure 19-6 shows that growth since 1936 has drastically reduced the ratio of net national debt to net national income.

This fact of growth explains why, in Canada, where real national product grows at about 3 to 4 per cent per year, the public debt might increase by more than 100 per cent in 25 years without its relative percentage burden growing at all.

This would give the wildest believer in government spending an average deficit of over 1 billion dollars per year before he would have to turn to such even more unorthodox financial expedients as printing money or selling interest-free bonds to the central bank.

Could a nation fanatically addicted to deficit spending pursue such a policy for the rest of our lives and beyond? Study of the mechanics of banking and income determination suggests that the barrier to this would not be financial. The barrier would have to be political; and the effects of such a policy depend crucially upon whether it impinges on an economy that is already inflationary or deflationary. And if the electorate learn the half-truth that expenditure is expansionary, while forgetting the fact that unpleasant taxes may be necessary to curb undue expansion, then the long-term outlook may be in the direction of rising prices.

Now we have looked carefully at the facts about the public debt here and abroad and have given the economic principles that underlie the burdens of a public debt. We have seen that there are certain definite problems involved, but that laymen often have mixed-up notions as to what are and are not genuine burdens.

There are many major problems ahead for our economy: inflation, slump, pollution, conservation and congestion, adequate growth, international balance of payments, and many others. Prudent fiscal and monetary policies impinge on them all; but in a sober man's list of grave problems, the present magnitude of the public debt does not come near the top.

DEFICIT FINANCING AND GROWING DEBT

Undoubtedly the major reason for concern about the public debt does not involve sophisticated questions of whether or not it affects the stock of real capital goods. Our major concerns are our discomfort at the prospect of debt growing forever and our embarrassment at "going into the red".

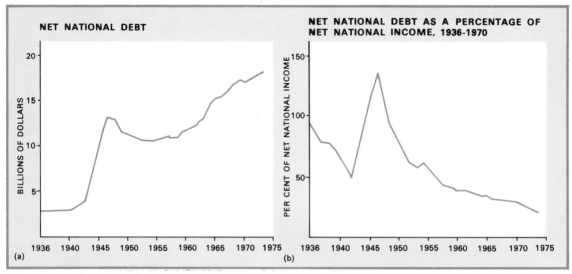

FIG. 19-6. While private debt outstripped natural income growth, public-debt ratio fell steadily in the postwar period. Most of the federal debt held by the public came from wars. In the last 20 years, its ratio to the growing NNI has declined steadily. (**Source:** *National Finances* **Table 19-1**)

ANALOGY "How can the government go on running up debt? If I or my wife lived beyond our means and ran a debt, we'd soon learn what trouble is." The person speaking has overlooked the fallacy of composition: what is true for each unit may not be at all true for the whole of society.

"Why do conservatives complain about the size of the public debt? Private debt has grown tremendously faster in the postwar period than public debt, and you don't hear complaints about that. All credit involves debt. The pyramid of credit could be called the pyramid of debt. If people are to have liquid assets, other people or institutions must have liabilities—d--t to the squeamish." The speaker here is also trying to use analogies with private finance, but this time to the advantage of a program for large deficits.

Both analogies are in principle suspect. Each contains some element of truth, but every strand of such arguments needs critical testing.

Thus, it is true that private debt is more than twice the public debt, and that it more than doubled in the last twenty years, while federal debt grew little at all. But it is also true that the private assets to back up that private debt have also gone up. And it is also true that one could imagine an economy—not ours!—where everything was financed by *equity* issues without fixed debt.

What does the federal government use to pay its debt interest and refundings? Obviously, *it is the taxable capacity of the country's national product that any government can rely on.*

So long as the money NNP (or GNP) grows at 4 or 5 per cent from now until kingdom come, the public debt of the federal government can grow at those rates, ultimately passing one, two, or any number of trillion dollars. No inflation need result if the process takes place in balance. And no bankruptcy or increase in relative tax burden. And no embarrassment to the Treasury. Like life itself, there is no end to the process.

The above analogy is given only for those who feel a psychological need for reassuring analogies and as an antidote to misleading pessimistic analogies.

BALANCING THE BUDGET The analogy says nothing about the great harm governments can do if they spend their funds rashly. Nor does it provide the needed guidance for the amount of deficit financing.

It would be a tragedy if people, in giving up their irrational fears of deficit financing, were thereby led to call the sky the limit. Unlimited spending can produce inflation, chaos, and waste. It is to be hoped that the discipline of rationality can replace superstition and misunderstanding. After the accounting shibboleth of a balanced-budget-every-year has lost its power to limit public spending, the modern mixed economy must replace it by another calculus. People in Parliament or Main Street do yearn for simplifying precepts.

Various rules have been suggested, and whole books written to explain the accounting and budgetary procedures implied for politicans and civil servants. All have advocated "balance" but over different periods or among selected financial items only. For example, one author argued that deficits or surpluses should be allowed to accumulate, and made to balance only "over the cycle". Another advocated that governments should distinguish more clearly between their capital and current budgets, just as business does. Only the latter need be balanced annually.

Perhaps the most helpful is one which was proposed in the 1940s by the Committee for Economic Development, a liberal business group, and has been used by Royal Commissions and the Economic Council of Canada. It says: "Don't balance the budget over each year, or even over each business cycle. Instead, set the budget so that it can be financed by the tax revenues that *would* be generated from a high-level full-employment economy." It will be helpful to see just what this "full-employment balanced-budget" notion implies.

When, as in 1961, we had over 7% unemployment and a large gap between our actual output and our full-employment potential, we were of course running a budget deficit.[4]

But modern economists make a new calculation, asking: "Suppose we were now at high or full employment, say with less than 4 percent of the labor force unemployed and with firms at their desired 95 percent of capacity. With all the higher tax revenues that such an increase in NNP would bring, what then would our budget deficit be?"

The answer to this question—for *all* governments, and not just Ottawa—is indicated in Fig. 19-7. It shows that many of the long years in which governments were running at a deficit and adding to the total government debt would, even with the same spending programs and tax rates, have been years of breaking even or of debt reduction if there had been high employment. There has really been a "full-employment surplus" in most years since 1963!

To summarize, the "full-employment budget surplus or deficit" measures what *would* be the budget position *if the economy were at full employment and the legislated tax and spending structures were in effect. What does this imply over the long run?*

FIG. 19-7. Government deficits are illusory.
The red line shows the actual surplus of deficit of all Canadian governments as a percentage of the actual GNP. The black line shows the *surpluses* as percentages of GNP that such taxes and spending could have created had there been full employment.
(Source: *Tenth Annual Review* of **Economic Council of Canada and Statistics Canada; Canada Pension Plan and Q.P.P. reserves are omitted.**)

In an era when growth would produce extra tax receipts that go beyond desired new programs, tax rates would have to be cut lest a growing full-employment surplus produce "fiscal drag" and keep us from keeping full employment. Or, as is more relevant in the mid-70s, an era of burgeoning public needs will necessitate rising and equitable increase in, taxation.

SUMMARY TO THE APPENDIX

1. Many of the most commonly heard arguments against the national debt are patently false. However some genuine burdens of national borrowing, and so of the national debt, do exist. To the degree that we now follow policies of reduced capital formation which will pass on to posterity less capital goods, we can directly affect the production possibilities open to them. To the degree that we now borrow *from abroad* for some transitory consumption purpose and pledge posterity to pay back the interest and principal on such *external debt*, we do place upon that posterity a net burden, which will be a subtraction from what they can later produce. To the degree that we now bequeath to posterity an *internal debt* but no change in capital stock beyond what would anyway have been given to them, there may be various internal transfer effects as one group in the community receives at the expense of another group a larger share of the goods then produced. At any one time there is no "net burden" of such internal transfers quite like the net subtraction involved in the external-debt payment, but there can be important transfer effects between people of different ages then living and certain effects within the lifetime of each generation on how

[4]This was true whether you used the official "administrative budget", or the so-called "cash budget", or the more informative "national accounts budget".

much its members will receive of such consumption at at what ages. And the process of taxing Peter to pay Paul, or taxing Peter to pay Peter, can have definite costs: these can involve various distortions of production and efficiency, but should not be confused with the actual sending of goods abroad.

2. The fact that Canada is a growing nation with ever increasing national income means that in real terms the burden of the debt has been decreasing over time and that the ratio of net national debt to net national income has fallen drastically since 1936.

3. The private and public analogy of the public debt contains only an element of the truth and needs critical testing. As long as the taxable capacity of the nation's national product grows over time, no serious threat is posed by a national debt that expands at a rate equal to or less than the rate of increase in national product.

4. Budgetary deficits should be seen in relation to GNP, and to potential GNP.

QUESTIONS FOR DISCUSSION

1. Show briefly why "burden of the debt" is a complicated economic issue.

2. Comment on the 1840 views of the historian Macaulay:

   At every stage in the growth of that debt the nation has set up the same cry of anguish and despair. At every stage in the growth of that debt it has been seriously asserted by wise men that bankruptcy and ruin were at hand. Yet still the debt went on growing; and still bankruptcy and ruin were as remote as ever. . . .

   The prophets of evil were under a double delusion. They erroneously imagined that there was an exact analogy between the case of an individual who is in debt to another individual and the case of a society which is in debt to a part of itself. . . . They made no allowance for the effect produced by the incessant progress of every experimental science, and by the incessant efforts of every man to get on in life. They saw that the debt grew; and they forgot that other things grew as well. . . .

3. "Inflation has lifted the burden of the debt from the shoulders of future taxpayers." Is this correct? Who has assumed the burden?

4. Much of Canada's debt is held abroad, as are the securities and shares of Canadian business. In what sense is this debt a "burden"? Is it decreasing?

3

The Composition and Pricing of National Output

20
DETERMINATION OF PRICE BY SUPPLY AND DEMAND

The end is easily foretold,
When every blessed thing you hold
Is made of silver, or of gold,
   You long for simple pewter.
When you have nothing else to wear
But cloth of gold and satins rare,
For cloth of gold you cease to care
   Up goes the price of shoddy.

GILBERT AND SULLIVAN, *The Gondoliers*

Part One of this book described the modern economic system and discussed the nature of national income. Part Two gave the modern theory of income determination: it showed why and how incomes, job opportunities, and levels of price fluctuate; it showed how money and banking fit in with income analysis; and most significantly, it showed how fiscal and monetary policy can keep the aggregate system working tolerably well. Today such analysis is called macroeconomics.

PREVIEW

Now Parts Three and Four analyze *micro*economics, which deals with the following important questions: What determines the relative prices of particular goods? What determines the quantitative breakdown of the national-income aggregates into various kinds of goods and services?

In order to understand the *system* of market prices which strikes an equilibrium among people's tastes for different goods and the scarcities of total resources that can produce them, Part Three studies in detail the tools of supply and demand that Chapter 4 introduced briefly.

Part Four follows with a closely related supply-and-demand analysis of what determines the prices of factors of production. Why are wages growing? Why does the share of land rent in the economy move in this way or that? What determines interest?

Why have unskilled wages been falling relative to white-collar wages? Such problems constitute the subject of "distribution of income" in Part Four.

We shall see that the concepts of supply and demand as they are developed further in this chapter are vital tools for mastering the analysis of varied branches of microeconomics. (As a matter of fact, the supply-and-demand tools are indispensable in explaining the international trade problems of Part Five and the current economic issues of Part Six.)

MICROECONOMICS VERSUS MACROECONOMICS?

Macroeconomics deals with the big picture—with the macroaggregates of income, employment, and price levels. But do not think that microeconomics deals with unimportant details. After all, the big picture is made up of its parts. Mere billions of dollars would be meaningless if they did not correspond to the thousand-and-one useful goods and services that people really need and want. And who would be impressed by a vast national income if its distribution among human beings was a matter of caprice and pointless inequality?

There is really no opposition between micro- and macroeconomics. Both are vital. You are less than half-educated if you understand one while being ignorant of the other. We cannot even say which comes first: some books begin with one; some with the other. And surveys show that even books like this one, which begin with macroeconomics, are used by about 40 per cent of the courses to teach microeconomics first.

Forty years ago our society had such poor mastery over its macroeconomics as to make people naturally give less emphasis to microeconomics. With millions starving because of a slump, who could get excited about whether mutton or pork was in a proper relative-price configuration? Or who thought much about white-collar wage trends relative to unskilled wages, when the unemployed tramped the streets in shirts so faded you could not tell their color?

Today we hope all that is changed. Now that man has gained considerable mastery over his macroeconomic problems, it is natural for the classical problems of microeconomics to move again to the forefront of his attention.

REVIEW OF FUNDAMENTALS OF SUPPLY AND DEMAND

Chapter 3 discussed how a system of pricing and of markets performs the task in any mixed economic system of determining WHAT shall be produced, HOW goods shall be produced, and FOR WHOM they are to be produced. Then Chapter 4 introduced the basic concepts of supply and demand: their description in terms of schedules of numbers and in terms of intersecting curves. It will be assumed that each reader has this material fresh in his mind, or has gone back to review what was learned earlier, or will stop and take time to master it now.

Our task here is to put the tools of supply and demand to work: to show how they help explain changes in price, in the short run and in the long run; to help predict what effect a tax will have on competitive price; to evaluate various policies that interfere with the laws of supply and demand.

We shall make repeated efforts to see what it is that market pricing is accomplishing in terms of the

efficiency with which the economy fulfills its basic functions.

All through Part Three new tools of economic analysis will be introduced and the old tools will be gradually developed. But it would be a mistake for any reader to become enamored of tools for their own sake. It is the application of the tools to the richness of modern economic life that makes them exciting. Experience shows that one cannot understand the economic world of the present and the future without having at his command a systematic method of analyzing it. And the testimony of generations of students is that, however far away they later move from formal schooling and examinations, their understanding of the basic economic processes is forever keener, once they have mastered the elementary tools of economic analysis.

REVIEW   Glancing back at the supply-and-demand diagram in Fig. 4-3 we see how equilibrium P comes at the intersection of competitive dd and ss curves. We note that any departure above equilibrium creates an "over-supply" condition leading back to equilibrium, and that any fall in P below equilibrium creates an "excess demand" that bids P back up to restore the equilibrium.

The succeeding diagram, Fig. 4-4(a) shows how a shift in supply, such as might be brought about by a bad harvest, will be likely to increase the equilibrium price P and decrease the equilibrium quantity Q. The new E' intersection point is found to be higher on the unshifted demand curve—just far enough up to cut consumption down to the depressed harvest level.

This illustrates well an important principle, the law of downward-sloping demand—the fact that the demand curve slopes down toward the southeast, in reflection of the observation that people will buy more at lower prices and buy less at higher ones. Likewise, Fig. 4-4(b) shows how an upward shift of the demand curve leads to a higher equilibrium price. So much for review.

A. ELASTICITY OF DEMAND AND SUPPLY

Second-graders, it is found, know that an increase in supply, whether because of an abundant harvest or for whatever reason, is likely to depress price. So it is

no surprise that Gregory King, the English writer of the seventeenth century mentioned earlier, should have remarked on this fact. But King also observed a fact perhaps less obvious: his studies convinced him that farmers as a whole received *less* total revenue when the harvest was good than when it was bad!

This fact, that high agricultural Q tends to be associated with low $P \times Q$, is one that every Minister of Agriculture has had to reckon with in facing the farm problem. To understand it and to lay the groundwork for the discussion of farm problems in Chapter 21, we must in this chapter consider and master a new and important economic concept, "elasticity of demand." Henry Ford, and any businessman tempted to cut his price in order to sell more goods and make more profit, is also interested in the concept of elasticity. And when the Canadian Transport Commission lets a railroad *raise* its prices in order to cut down on passenger-service losses, the elasticity concept is crucially involved.

ELASTICITY OF DEMAND

Various goods differ in the *degree* to which the Q bought will respond to changes in each respective P. Wheat Q may go up much less than 1 per cent for each 1 per cent cut in wheat P; Henry Ford's Q may rise far more than 1 per cent for each 1 per cent reduction in its P; in between is the borderline case of a good whose Q just halves whenever its P doubles, where the percentage changes are just in balance.

Elasticity of demand is a concept devised to distinguish these three cases. Thus, the first case of weak percentage response of wheat Q is put into the category of "inelastic demand." The second case of a great percentage response is put in the category of "elastic demand." The borderline case is called "unitary elasticity of demand."

Here is how the economist goes about defining the three cases:

The crucial thing to concentrate on is the *total dollar revenue* that buyers pay to sellers. If consumers buy 5 units at $3 each, what is total revenue? It is not given by the $3 P alone; nor by the 5-unit Q. Total revenue is always, by definition, price times quantity, or the $15 product $P \times Q$. By arithmetic multiplication, total revenue can always be calculated for each point in a demand schedule or diagram.

Elasticity of demand is important primarily as *an indicator of how total revenue changes* when a fall in P induces a rise in Q along the demand curve.

Definition of elasticity of demand: This is a concept devised to indicate the degree of responsiveness of Q demanded to changes in market P. It depends primarily upon *percentage* changes and is independent of the units used to measure Q and P. Elasticity ends up qualitatively in one of three alternative categories:

1. When a cut in P raises Q so much as to *increase* total revenue $P \times Q$, we speak of *elastic* demand—or of elasticity of demand *greater than unity*. The percentage change in Q exceeds the percentage change in P. $E_d > 1$.

2. When a percentage cut in P results in an exactly compensating percentage rise in Q so as to leave total revenue $P \times Q$ exactly *unchanged*, we speak of *unitary elasticity of demand*—or of elasticity of demand that is numerically *exactly equal to unity*. $E_d = 1$.

3. When a percentage cut in P evokes so small a percentage increase in Q as to make total revenue $P \times Q$ fall, we speak of *inelastic* demand—or of elasticity of demand that is *less than unity* (but not less than zero). $E_d < 1$.

Figure 20-1 gives a graphic example of the three cases. In each case, P is halved from A to B, but it would make no difference if the example used instead a much smaller percentage change in P. Perhaps at a first glance, it will be easiest to begin with the borderline case of unitary elasticity of demand.

In Fig. 20-1(b), the doubling of Q exactly matches the halving of P, with the result that the total revenue collected remains unchanged at $1,000. This can be shown graphically by comparing certain rectangular areas. How? Price and quantity can be easily read off the curve at any point; but how do we read off total revenue, which is their arithmetic product $P \times Q$? When we recall that the area of a rectangle is always equal to the product of its base times its altitude, the answer is easy:

Total revenue at any point is always as shown by the area of the rectangle which that point makes with the two axes. (Check that the shaded rectangle at A does have a base equal to Q and an altitude equal to P.) Hence, if our eye watches how the area of each point's rectangle changes as we cut price and move down the demand curve, we can know in which of the three categories of elasticity such a movement happens to fall.

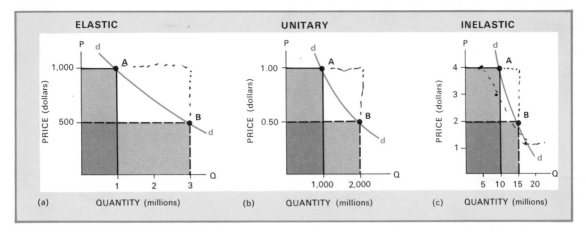

FIG. 20-1. Elasticity of demand comes in three cases, depending on how total revenue moves.
In cutting P from A to B, we raise, leave unchanged, or lower the rectangle of total revenue, depending on whether demand is elastic, unitary elastic, or inelastic. That is, elasticity depends on percentage response of Q to each percentage change in P.

Clearly, in the middle diagram, the areas are remaining exactly the same because of offsetting changes in their Q bases and P altitudes; consequently, this is the case neither of elastic nor of inelastic demand, but rather is the borderline case of unitary elasticity of demand.

The reader can now verify that Fig. 20-1(a) does correspond to *elastic* demand, with total revenue going up when P is cut and elasticity hence greater than unity. And Fig. 20-1(c) does correspond to the opposite case of *inelastic* demand, with total revenue falling off when P is cut and elasticity less than unity. [Which diagram best represents the Gregory King finding that smaller harvests meant higher total revenues for farmers? Which best represents the early belief of Henry Ford, that if only he could reduce his cars' P, he would encounter a tremendous increase in cars sold? Surely, 20-1(c) and 20-1(a), respectively.]

NUMERICAL MEASUREMENT OF ELASTICITY: A DIGRESSION[1]

The general notion of elastic, inelastic, and unitary elasticity as an indicator of the percentage responsiveness of quantity to price and as an indicator of how total revenue behaves is now clear. But some readers will be curious to know how these qualitative cases can be given exact numerical measurement by economists. What does it mean to say that the elasticity demand is 1.0? 2.3? 0.5? To answer this question, we give the following definition for a coefficient of elasticy E_d between two different price points on a demand curve:

$$\text{Elasticity coefficient } E_d = \frac{\text{per cent that } Q \text{ has risen}}{\text{per cent cut in } P}$$

Note that the movements along P and Q are in opposite directions because of the law of downward-sloping demand. Note, too, the use of *percentages*, which brings in the nice property that the units of a good or of money—bushels or pecks of wheat, dollars or pennies—do not affect elasticity.[2]

Do not get bogged down in numerical details of E_d calculation. Now that you have mastered the general idea of elastic, inelastic, and unitary demand, you can proceed to numerical examples.

Always there is a slight ambiguity about percentage changes. Suppose a grocer buys bread for 15 cents and sells

---

[1] In a short course the next two sections can be skipped.

[2] Units will affect the *slope* of the demand diagram, just as the draftsman can make a curve look steep or flat in slope by changing the scale of one of his axes. So the purpose of the next section is to help you avoid confusing *slope* and *elasticity*. As Fig. 20-1(b)'s curve with $E_d = 1$ shows, it is not a straight line with constant slope that corresponds to a curve of constant elasticity, but rather one whose slope varies in order to keep the percentage of changes in the same ratio. (Mathematicians call the unitary-elastic curve a ["rectangular"] hyperbola and know that it plots as a straight line on double-log paper.)

Numerical Calculation of Elasticity Coefficient

P	$-\triangle P$	Q	$\triangle Q$	$\dfrac{P_1 + P_2}{2}$	$\dfrac{Q_1 + Q_2}{2}$	$E_d = -\dfrac{\triangle Q}{(Q_1+Q_2)/2} \div \dfrac{\triangle P}{(P_1+P_2)/2}$
6		0				
	2		10	5	5	$10/5 \div 2/5 = 5 > 1$
4		10				
	2		10	3	15	$10/15 \div 2/3 = 1$
2		20				
	2		10	1	25	$10/25 \div 2/1 = .2 < 1$
0		30				

TABLE 20-1. Dividing percentage price cut into percentage quantity rise gives numerical elasticity.

Each P cut, $-\triangle P$, is related to the average P, $(P_1 + P_2)/2$; each Q rise, $\triangle Q$, to the average Q, $(Q_1 + Q_2)/2$; the resulting ratio gives numerical E_d, a measure expressed in percentage (dimensionless) units, not in absolute slope units.

for 25. Is that the 66 2/3 per cent markup that comes from relating the change of 10 to the lower base 15? Or is is the 40 per cent change that comes from relating 10 to the higher base 25? No one answer can be said to be right, and no one definitely wrong. Fortunately, when it comes to very small percentage changes, as from 100 to 99 or from 100 to 101, the difference between 1/100 and 1/99 becomes hardly worth talking about. For small changes, it does not matter much how you calculate the percentage changes; but for larger ones it may make quite a difference, and no single answer can be declared to be the right one.

What is a good rule to use? Long experience suggests this: As good a rule as any is to relate the price change to neither the higher nor the lower of the two P's, but to their average. Thus, is a cut from 101 to 99 a change of 2/99 or 2/101? By our convention, it is neither: we call it a change of 2/100, because the average of 99 and 101 is $(99 + 101)/2 = 200/2 = 100$.

Table 20-1 is self-explanatory: it shows how to calculate E_d for three movements along a dd curve. We shall be seeing that most dd curves start out elastic at high P and end up inelastic at low P, passing through unitary elasticity at an intermediate position where total revenue $P \times Q$ is at its maximum. Table 20-1 illustrates this.

GRAPHICAL MEASUREMENT OF ELASTICITY: A DIGRESSION

Students tend to make a simple mistake: They often confuse the slope of a curve with its elasticity; they think a steep slope of dd must mean inelastic demand, and a flat slope must mean elastic demand. This is not quite true. Why not? Because slope of dd depends upon *absolute* change in P and Q, whereas elasticity was seen to depend upon *percentage* changes.

The straight line dd in Fig. 20-2(a) illustrates the fallacy of confusing slope and elasticity. Everywhere it has the same absolute slope. But toward the top of the line, where (1) P is high and its percentage change low and (2) Q is very low and its percentage change therefore almost infinitely great, our numerical formula for E_d results in a very high elasticity.

Thus, above the midpoint M of any straight line, demand is elastic, with $E_d > 1$; at the midpoint, demand is of unitary elasticity, with $E_d = 1$; below the midpoint, demand is inelastic, with $E_d < 1$.[3]

---

[3] Intermediate books tell how to calculate E_d at any one point on a straight line: E_d equals the length of the line segment below the point divided by the length of line segment above it. Since M is halfway, the formula there gives $E_d = 1$, unitary elasticity. At B, it gives $3/1 = 3.0$; at R, $E_d = 1/3 = 0.33$.

Knowing how to calculate E_d for a straight line enables you to calculate it for any point along a curved dd. (1) Draw with a ruler the straight line tangent to the curve at your point (e.g., at B in Fig. 20-3); (2) calculate the E_d for the straight line at that point (e.g., E_d at $B = 3/1$); (3) identify your resulting E_d as the correct elasticity for the dd curve at your chosen point. Question 7, page 368 proves the truth of the geometrical rule for calculating E_d.

NOTE: E_d at a point can be shown to be mathematically equivalent to the following limit:

$$\frac{-\triangle Q}{Q} \div \frac{\triangle P}{P} = -\frac{P}{Q} \frac{\triangle Q}{\triangle P} \longrightarrow -\frac{P}{Q} \frac{dQ}{dP}$$

as $\triangle P$ goes to zero, taking $\triangle Q$ with it and making it immaterial

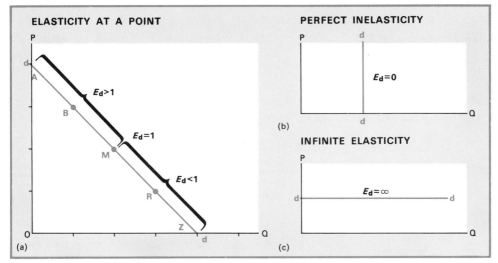

FIG. 20-2. Absolute slope and percentage elasticity are not the same.
All points on *dd*'s straight-line demand in (a) have same absolute slope; but above the mid-point price, demand is elastic; below it demand is inelastic; at it demand is unitary. Only in the case of perfectly vertical or horizontal curves, as in (b) and (c), can you infer elasticity and elasticity from slope alone.

When many people make the same mistake, there is usually a reason. The limiting cases of *completely vertical* and *completely horizontal* demand curves, shown in Fig. 20-2(b) and (c), do validly portray the limiting cases *completely inelastic* and *infinitely elastic* demands. But do not think that the in-between cases, where most of reality falls, can have their elasticities depicted by slope alone.

Now, we go back to the mainstream of demand and supply.

ELASTICITY OF SUPPLY

What we did for demand, we can also do for supply. Economists introduce the concept of "elasticity of supply" to give an indication of percentage increase in the amount of Q supplied in response to a given percentage rise in competitive P. (Note that in the case of a *rising* supply curve, we now speak of an *increase* in P, rather than of a *decrease* in P as was

which of the P's and Q's or their averages we use to compute percentage changes. Intermediate texts show that, when you plot *dd* on double-log paper, it becomes correct to identify slope with elasticity—because double-log paper does measure percentage changes. (See Footnote 15 page 368 for more on this.)

done in the case of a downward-sloping demand curve.)

If the amount supplied is perfectly fixed, as in the case of perishable fish brought to today's market for sale at whatever price they will fetch, we face the limiting case of *perfectly inelastic* or vertical supply. If we have a horizontal supply curve, so that the slightest cut in P will cause Q to become zero and the slightest rise in P will coax out an indefinitely large supply, we are at the extreme of *infinitely elastic*

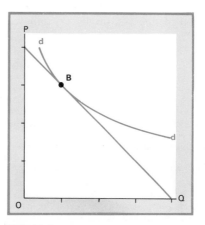

FIG. 20-3

supply. Between such extremes, we call supply elastic or inelastic depending upon whether the percentage rise in Q is respectively greater than or less than the percentage rise in P bringing it about.[4]

Supply elasticity is a useful concept but not quite so useful a concept as demand elasticity, for the reason that elasticity of demand has the major additional function of telling us what is happening to total revenue.

There is, however, an important fact that supply elasticity can help describe. A given change in price will tend to have greater and greater effects on amount supplied as we move from the momentary situation to a short-run period of time and on to the long-run period. This means:

Elasticity of supply tends to be greater in the long run, when all adjustments to the higher price have been made, than in shorter periods of time.

Let us see why.

MOMENTARY, SHORT-RUN, AND LONG-RUN EQUILIBRIUM

Alfred Marshall, Cambridge's great economist at the turn of the century, helped forge these tools of supply and demand. We can review our understanding of equilibrium and at the same time advance our knowledge if we survey Marshall's important emphasis on the *time element* of the problem.

He distinguishes at least three time periods: (1) *momentary* equilibrium, when the supply is fixed; (2) *short-run* equilibrium, when firms can produce more within given plants; and finally (3) *long-run* equilibrium (or "normal price"), when firms can

abandon old plants or build new ones and when new firms can enter the industry or old ones leave it.

Let us imagine that the demand for a perishable good, such as fish that cannot be preserved, increases from dd to $d'd'$. With the amount of fish supplied unchanged, the stronger demand will sharply bid up the momentary price of fish. This is shown in Fig. 20-5(a), where the fixed supply curve $s_m s_m$ runs up to the new demand curve $d'd'$ to determine the new sharply higher momentary equilibrium price shown at E'. The price has had to rise so much in order to *ration* the limited supply of fish among the now eager demanders.[5]

But with so high a price prevailing in the market, skippers of the fishing boats will be motivated to hire more men and to use more nets. Even if the period is so brief that they do not have the time to get new boats built, they will in the short run begin to bring to the market a greater supply of fish than they did at the old momentary equilibrium. Figure 20-5(b) shows the new $s_s s_s$ short-run supply schedule, and shows that it intersects the new demand curve at E'', the point of short-run equilibrium. Note that this equilibrium price is a little lower than the momentary E' price. Why? Because of the extra supply of fish induced in the short run by more intensive use of the same number of boats.

Figure 20-5(c) shows the final long-run equilibrium, or "normal," price. The higher prices that long prevailed have coaxed out more shipbuilding and attracted more trained sailors into the industry.

---

[4] A numerical coefficient of supply elasticity Es is defined thus: Es = (percentage change in Q)/(percentage change in P). Figure 20-4 shows three straight-line supply curves: at A the line going through the origin has elasticity of exactly 1.0; the steeper curve is inelastic, with elasticity coefficient less than 1; and the flatter curve is elastic, with elasticity coefficient greater than 1. (If—as we shall see can happen—the supply curve actually bends up backward, elasticity of supply as here defined could actually become negative.) Also, for a supply curve with curvature, one can reckon its elasticity at a point A' by drawing a straight line with a tangential ruler and seeing which curve of Fig. 20-4 it resembles; or plot it on double-log paper and study its slope at A', in comparison with that of a 45° line. (Verify that supply is elastic at A'.)

[5] If the short-run stock of goods could be carried over into the future without perishing, the $s_m s_m$ curve would not need to be perfectly vertical. Marshall points out that people might want to reserve some of their supply for the future at low present Ps, giving the $s_m s_m$ curve some positive slope.

FIG. 20-4

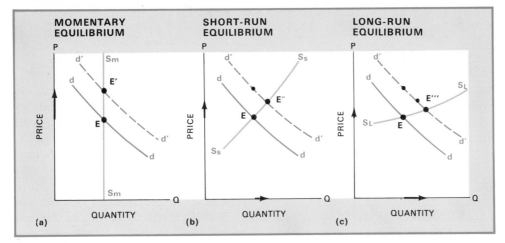

FIG. 20-5. Effect of demand increase on price varies in Marshall's three time periods.
Marshall distinguishes three different time periods, depending upon whether supply elements have time to make (a) no adjustments (momentary equilibrium), (b) some adjustments of labor and variable factors (short-run equilibrium), (c) full adjustment of all factors fixed as well as varying (long-run equilibrium). The longer the time for adjustment, the greater the elasticity of supply response and the less the rise in price.

Where the long-run supply curve, $s_L s_L$ intersects the demand curve $d'd'$ at E''' is the final equilibrium reached after *all* economic conditions (including number of ships and shipyards) have adjusted to the new level of demand.

Note that the long-run equilibrium price is not as high as the short-run equilibrium price, and not nearly as high as the momentary equilibrium price. Yet it is a little bit higher than the price that prevailed previously when demand was lower. Marshall would call this a case of "increasing cost" and would regard it as the normal one to be met in most sizable competitive industries. Why normal? For a variety of reasons. When a large industry (which has already achieved the economies of large-scale production) expands, it must coax men, ships, nets, and other productive factors away from other industries by bidding up their prices and thus its own cost. So the long-run supply curve $s_L s_L$ will usually be sloping gently upward as in Fig. 20-5(c). Only if the industry is small compared with the total of all other users of its factors will Marshall's $s_L s_L$ curve in Fig. 20-5(c) be horizontal—which is called the case of "constant cost."[6]

Another explanation for an upward sloping industry long-run supply curve and hence for increasing costs to the industry is found in the fact that all firms within the industry are not identical. Various firms have different degrees of technical and managerial know-how, different methods of production, different locations, etc. As greater and greater quantities of output are to be supplied, firms which are relatively less efficient are induced to enter the industry—to enter production. Thus this marginal firm enters at a higher cost per unit than do the "infra-marginal" firms already in production, although all firms supply the item only at the higher supply price of the marginal firm. At any lower price, the marginal firm would not be induced to enter production and hence the industry would not move to the right on its supply curve. So the long-run supply curve $s_L s_L$ will usually be gently sloping upward as in Fig. 20-5(c).

The reader can test his understanding of all the foregoing discussion by now assuming a downward shift in the demand curve back to dd. Show what happens in the new momentary run; in the short run; and in the long run. The Appendix to this chapter presents various cases of supply and demand. Chapter 23 will give in greater detail the factors underlying the various supply curves.

[6] See the cases in the Appendix.

B. APPLICATIONS AND QUALIFICATIONS OF SUPPLY AND DEMAND

Other things being equal, as economists are fond of saying, there is a unique schedule of supply or demand in any period of time. But other things will not remain equal. The demand for cotton is declining over the years because of reductions in the price of synthetics. The supply schedule of radios is shifting because technological progress permits more to be produced at the same cost. As costs and tastes change, as incomes vary, as the prices of rival products (coffee in relation to tea) or of cooperating products (sugar in relation to tea) change, our schedules will shift. What will be the effects on consumption, production, and price? That we must now study.

All beginners in the field of economics must beware of a common error. They must take care not to confuse an increase in *demand*—by which is meant a *shift* of the whole curve to the right and upward, as more is now bought at each same price—with an increase in the *quantity demanded* as a result of moving to a lower price *on the same demand curve*. By "demand" is meant the whole demand curve; by "supply" is meant the whole supply curve; by an "increase" in demand or supply is meant a *shift* of the whole curve in question to the right. To indicate a single point on a demand curve, we speak of the "quantity bought" or the "quantity demanded" *at a particular price*. A movement *along* the same curve is "a change in the quantity demanded as a result of a price change." It does not represent any change in the demand schedule. The need for this warning will appear in a moment.

INCIDENCE OF A TAX[7]

We can illustrate the case of a shift in the entire curve by referring to supply and demand schedules for a good like wheat. Fig. 20-6 shows an equilibrium price at *C* of $3 per bushel before a tax is imposed.

Let us now introduce a new factor, which will disturb this equilibrium. In particular, assume that the government imposes a sales tax on wheat. On each

and every sale, the producer is required to pay a tax of $1 per bushel of wheat.

What is the final effect, or what economists call the "incidence," of the tax? Is its burden shifted back completely onto the producer who must pay it in the first instance? Or may it be shifted forward in part to consumers? The answer can be derived only from our supply and demand curves.

There is no reason for the demand curve of the consumers to have changed at all. At $3, consumers will still be willing to buy only 12 (million) bushels;

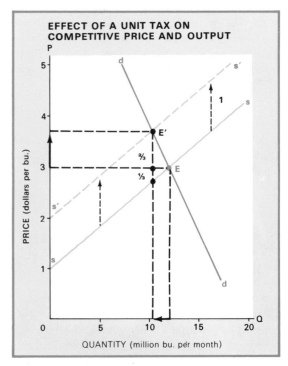

FIG. 20-6. Wheat tax falls both on consumer and producer.

A $1 tax shifts *ss* up $1 everywhere to give parallel *s's*', shown as a dashed line. This intersects *dd* in new equilibrium at *E'*, where price to consumer has risen $2/3 above old *E* equilibrium and where price to producer has fallen by $1/3. The black arrows show change in *P* and *Q*. (Had *dd* been very elastic and flat relative to *ss*, most of the $1 tax would have fallen on the producer. Had *ss* been completely horizontal, the whole $1 tax would have been shifted forward onto the consumer.)

---

[7] For a brief review of the problems of tax incidence reread the final section of Chapter 9, page 157.

they neither know nor care that the producers must pay a tax.

But the whole supply curve is shifted upward and leftward: leftward because at each market price the producers will now supply less as a result of the tax; upward because, to get the producers to bring any given quantity to market, say, 12 (million) units, we must give them a higher market price than before—$4 rather than $3, which is higher by the exact amount of the $1 tax the producer must pay.

The student should be able to fill in a new supply column, resembling Column (3) of the table with Fig. 4-3, but with each price raised by $1. Here in Fig. 20-6, the demand curve *dd* is unchanged, but the supply curve *ss* has been shifted up everywhere by $1 to a vertically *parallel* supply curve *s's'*.

Where will the new equilibrium price be? The answer is found at the intersection of the new demand and supply curves, or at *C'*, where *s's'* and *dd* meet. Because supply has decreased, the price is higher. Also, the amount bought and the amount sold are less. If we read the graph carefully, we find that the new equilibrium price has risen from $3 to about $3 2/3. The new equilibrium output, at which purchases and sales are in equilibrium, has fallen from 12 (million) per month to about 10.6 (million) bushels.

Who pays the tax? Well, the wheat farmers do in part, because now they receive only $2 2/3, ($3 2/3 – $1), rather than $3. But the consumer also shares in the burden, because the price received by the producer has *not* fallen by as much as the tax. To the consumer, the wheat now costs $2 2/3 plus the $1 tax, or $3 2/3 in all. Because consumers want wheat so badly, they pay 2/3 of the tax, and producers pay 1/3 of the tax.[8]

To check his understanding of the above reasoning, the student should consider the case of an opposite shift in supply. Let the government pay producers a subsidy of $1 per bushel of wheat instead of taxing them this amount. Shift *ss* down to the new curve *s"s"*. Where is *C"*, its intersection with *dd*?

What is the new price? The new quantity? How much of the benefit goes to the producer? How much to the consumer?

Summary. A sales tax on a good will raise its price most and reduce its quantity least when the demand curve is most *inelastic*. When the supply curve is most inelastic, *Q* and *P* to the consumer will change least, while *P* to the producer falls most.

The tax is shifted forward onto the consumer when *dd* is very inelastic. It is shifted backward onto the producer when *ss* is relatively the more inelastic.

Only with the apparatus of supply and demand can the economist analyze the incidence of various different taxes—import tariffs, cigarette and liquor excises, payroll and corporation taxes, etc.

A COMMON FALLACY

By now the student has mastered supply and demand. Or has he? He knows that a tax will have the

---

[8] There is another and equivalent way to handle this tax problem, which is shown in Fig. 20-7. If the consumer were thought of as paying the tax in the first instance, you could subtract $1 everywhere from his *dd* curve. The new *d'd'* will intersect *ss* at the same new *Q*, and the same $2 2/3 and $3 2/3 prices will prevail. It goes without saying that all these figures are hypothetical.

  This is the legalistic view of Canadian provincial sales taxes: They are levied "directly" on the consumer, not "indirectly" on farmers or producers.

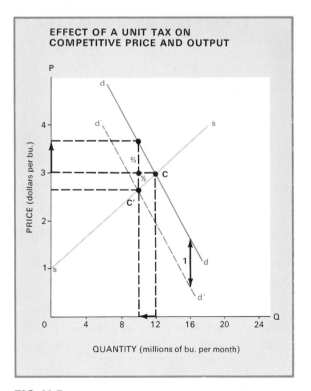

EFFECT OF A UNIT TAX ON COMPETITIVE PRICE AND OUTPUT

FIG. 20-7

effect of raising the price that the consumer will have to pay. Or does he know this? What about the following argument of a kind often seen in the press and heard from the platform:

The effect of a tax on a commodity might seem at first sight to be an advance in price to the consumer. But an advance in price will diminish the demand. And a reduced demand will send the price down again. Therefore it is not certain, after all, that the tax will really raise the price.

What about it? Will the tax raise the price or not? According to the editor's written word and the parliamentarian's oratory, the answer is, No. Evidently, we have here an example of the treachery of words. One of the four sentences in the quotation is false because the word "demand" is being used in the wrong sense. The student has already been warned against confusing a movement *along* an unchanged curve with a shift in the curve. Actually, the correct answer[9] would be more or less as follows:

A tax will raise the price to the consumer and will lower the price received by the producer, the difference going to the government. At the higher price a smaller quantity will be bought by consumers. This is as it should be, because producers are also supplying a smaller quantity at the lower price which they receive. Thus the amounts willingly bought and sold are in balance where the new *ss* and *dd* schedules intersect, and there will be no further change in price.

IS THE LAW OF SUPPLY AND DEMAND IMMUTABLE?

Competitive price and quantity are determined by supply and demand. But does not price depend on other factors, such as the amount of money created by the government or whether there is a war going on? Actually, price does depend on many such factors. However, they are not *in addition* to supply and demand, but are included in the numerous forces which determine or *act through* supply and demand. Thus, if government's printing of currency gives everyone higher incomes, it will shift demand curves and raise prices. But it is still true that competitive price is determined by supply and demand.

At this point a thoughtful reader should be moved to voice protest. Little has been said about price as

being determined by cost of production. Should not this be listed as a third factor in addition to supply and demand? Our answer is a stubborn "No."

Competitive price is affected by cost of production only to the extent that such cost affects supply.

If God sends nutritious manna from heaven without cost but in limited supply, then its price will not be zero but will be given by the intersection of the demand and supply curves. On the other hand, if it would cost $50,000 to print the national anthem on the head of a pin, but there is no demand for such a commodity, it simply will not be produced and would not command $50,000 if it were produced. (What the market price of something nonexistent should be called is left to the reader's pleasure.)

This does not mean that cost of production is unimportant for price determination. Under competition it is especially important. But its importance shows itself *through its effects upon supply*. Businessmen produce for profit. If they cannot get a price high enough to cover their past costs, then they will not like it. Nevertheless, once the crop is in, so to speak, there is not much they can do about it under competition. They have no choice but to minimize their short-term losses. But they will not continue *in the future* to supply goods at prices that fail to cover the *extra* costs incurred to produce these goods. Thus supply depends intimately on cost especially on what Chapter 23 and later chapters will call "extra" or "marginal" cost; and so too must price depend on this.

Moreover, to say that price equals cost does not in itself tell us which is the cause of which. In many cases where an industry uses a productive factor highly specialized to itself (e.g., baseball players, opera singers, vineyard land), *price determines cost rather than vice versa*. Grain land is dear because the price of grain is high. Apartment buildings sell for little because rents are low. This type of relationship was overlooked by the farmers who petitioned during World War II for a higher milk price "because the price of cows is high." If their request had been granted, they would soon have observed the price of cows chasing the milk price upward.[10]

---

[9] H. D. Henderson, *Supply and Demand* (Cambridge, London, 1922), p.27, explains this.

[10] Where a factor of production is inelastic in supply, as in all these cases, its cost is "price-determined" rather than "price-determining" and its return is called an "economic rent." See Case 3 in the Appendix and also footnote 1 of Chapter 28.

USEFUL CATEGORIES Thus, supply and demand are not ultimate explanations of price. They are simply useful catchall categories for analyzing and describing the multitude of forces, causes, and factors impinging on price. Rather than final answers, supply and demand simply represent initial questions. Our work is not over but just begun.

This should help to debunk the tendency of neophytes to utter sagely, "You can't repeal the law of supply and demand. King Canute knew he could not command the ocean tide to retreat from his throne on the seashore. Likewise, no government can get around, or interfere with, the workings of supply and demand."

It would be better not to have learned any economics than be left with this opinion. Of course the government can affect price. It can do so by affecting supply or demand, or both. In Chapter 21 we shall examine how government programs for restricting farm production can raise price and income by cutting down on supply. Similar programs by government cartels have been pursued all over the world: Brazil has burned coffee to raise its price; Britain during the 1920s tried artificially controlling the price of rubber; sugar and cocoa are still under international control.

These governments have not violated the law of supply and demand. They have worked (not always to good purpose) through the law of supply and demand. The state has no secret economic weapons or tricks. What is true for the state is also true for individuals. Anyone can affect the price of wheat as long as he has sufficient money to throw on the market or wheat to hold off it.

Trade-unions often influence wages, or try to, by directly or indirectly affecting the supply of labor. Anyone with a somewhat distinctive commodity may try by advertising to increase the demand for his product and, by restricting supply, to raise price above his extra costs of production. It should be emphasized, however, that as soon as individual producers grow in size and become important enough to affect the price of the things they sell, they then cease to be perfect competitors in the strict sense, and their behavior has to be analyzed in terms of a blend of monopoly and competition, i.e., in terms of imperfect competition as described in Chapters 25 and 26.

PRICES FIXED BY LAW

There is one genuine interference with supply and demand whose effects we must analyze. The government sometimes sets by law a maximum price or a minimum wage. In war or in peace, wage and price controls may be legislated by government—as, for example, in the Nixon Phase I and Phase II programs of the early 1970s.

Recently, a floor of $2.50 was put under hourly wages of many workers. These interferences by law are quite different from government actions, previously described, which work *through* supply and demand.

PRICE CEILINGS AND RATIONING Consider, say, the market for sugar, which has ordinary curves of supply and demand such as we have repeatedly met in this chapter. Suppose that the government through a Price Stabilization Board establishes an order prohibiting sugar from rising above 7 cents a pound (retail). Now, because of prosperity or bad crops, let demand be so high and supply so small that the equilibrium price would have been 20 cents a pound if the government had not intervened. This high price would have contributed to "profiteering" in that industry, it would have represented a rather heavy "tax" on the poor who could least afford it, and it would only have added fuel to an inflationary spiral in the cost of living, with all sorts of inflationary reactions on workers' wage demands. So go the arguments of price fixers.[11]

Therefore the government, through the Price Stabilization Board, decides to hold the line on prices. It passes a law putting a maximum price on sugar at the old level of 7 cents a pound. The line *JK* in Fig. 20-8 represents the legal price ceiling. Now what will happen?

At the legal ceiling price, supply and demand do not match. Consumers want thousands of pounds of sugar in excess of what producers are willing to supply. This is shown by the gap between *J* and *K*. This gap is so large that there will not long be enough sugar on grocers' shelves or in the warehouse to

---

[11] Most economists would, in normal peacetime, favor controlling inflation by the demand-management tools of macroeconomics —fiscal and monetary policies—rather than by simply legislating price ceilings that lead to chaotic rationing of the "shortages," and often to black markets and law evasion.

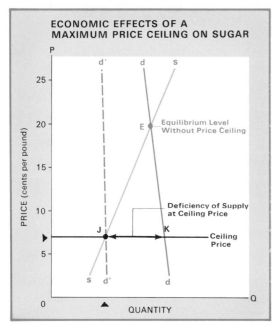

ECONOMIC EFFECTS OF A MAXIMUM PRICE CEILING ON SUGAR

FIG. 20-8. A legal maximum price, without rationing, leaves a gap between demand and supply.

Without a legal price ceiling, price would rise to *E*. At the artificial ceiling price, supply and demand do not balance and some method of rationing, formal or informal, is needed to allocate the short supply and bring the effective demand down to *d' d'*, shown as a dashed line.

body must be left at the end of the line when the sugar is gone.

The price mechanism is stymied and blocked. Nonmonetary considerations must determine who is the lucky buyer and who the unlucky one: the warmth of the smile that the customer flashes on the grocer, his or her previous standing at the store in question, the amount of other things the customer is willing to buy, or the accident of being in the store when the sugar is put on the shelves.

Nobody is happy, least of all the harassed grocer. Were it not for the community's elementary sense of fair play, the situation would soon become intolerable. Patriotism is more effective in motivating people to brief acts of intense heroism than to putting up day after day with an uncomfortable situation. It is no wonder that black markets occasionally develop; the really surprising thing is how infrequently they do occur.

If for political or social reasons market price is not to be permitted to rise high enough to bring quantity demanded down to the level of quantity supplied, the ultimate solution may require outright allocation or rationing.

make up the difference. Somebody will have to drink bitter coffee. If it were not for the maximum-price law, this somebody would gladly bid the price up to 8 or 9 cents or more, rather than do without sugar. As in our earlier discussion (Fig. 4-3) we could have shown this by putting an upward-pointing arrow perpendicular to *JK*. Such an arrow would not stop pointing upward until price had been bid up to the equilibrium level of 20 cents.

But it is against the law for the consumer to bid a higher price. Even if the consumer should be so unpatriotic, the seller could not legally take the higher price. There follows a period of frustration and shortage—a game of musical chairs in which somebody is left without a seat when the music stops playing. The inadequate supply of sugar must somehow be rationed. At first, this may be done by "first come, first served," with or without limited sales to each customer. Lines form, and much time has to be spent foraging for food. But this is no solution, since some-

Once rationing is adopted, and people are given tickets dependent on family size, most people heave a sigh of relief, because now sellers need not turn people away and buyers can count upon getting their fair quota of the limited supplies. Of course, there are always some cranky customers, longer on intuition than brains, who blame their troubles on the mechanism of rationing itself rather than on the shortage. "If only the government could print more ration tickets," they sigh. Such people are like the ignorant ancient kings who used to slay the messengers bringing them bad news. Their complaints need not be taken seriously; they only serve to add spice to the human comedy.

Just how do ration coupons work out in terms of supply and demand? Clearly, the Price Stabilization Board tries to issue just enough of them to lower the demand curve to *d'd'*, *where supply and the new demand balance at the ceiling price.* If too many coupons are issued, demand is still too far to the right and we encounter the old difficulties, but in lesser degree. If too few coupons are issued, stocks of sugar

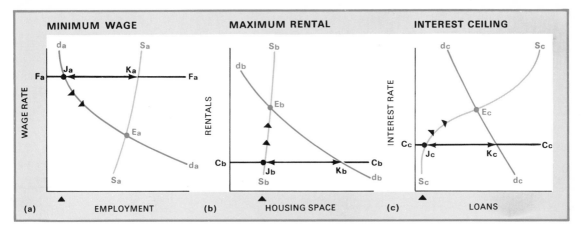

FIG. 20-9. When government by fiat sets maximum or minimum prices, troublesome gaps may arise.

Setting minimum-wage floor at $F_a F_a$, high above free-market equilibrium rate E_a, results in forced equilibrium at J_a. The too-high floor freezes workers into unemployment from J_a to K_a. Lowering the minimum wage will move us down along dd, as shown by black arrows, increasing employment. (If dd is elastic, total wage payrolls rise though hourly rate falls!)

(b). Setting maximum rental ceiling at $C_b C_b$, far below free-market equilibrium at E_b, causes fringe of unsatisfied renters between forced equilibrium at J_b and K_b. Raising the ceiling rate moves the system up $s_b s_b$, as shown by black arrows: new construction provides more living space, and old quarters are used more efficiently.

(c). Setting maximum interest rates at $C_c C_c$, far below free-market equilibrium rate E_c, results in drying up of available funds. Desperate borrowers at $J_c K_c$ turn to loan sharks. Raising interest ceiling moves system toward more loans, as shown by black arrows on $s_c s_c$.

will pile up and P will fall below the ceiling price. This is the signal for liberalizing the sugar ration.

One goes to an insane asylum to learn to appreciate normal human behavior. So, too, the breakdown of the price mechanism during war gives us a new understanding of its remarkable efficiency in normal times.

Goods are always scarce, in the sense that there is never enough to give everyone all he wishes. Price itself is always rationing scarce supplies: rising to choke off excessive consumption and in order to expand production; falling to encourage consumption, discourage production, and work off excessive inventories.

MINIMUM FLOORS AND MAXIMUM CEILINGS When there arises any kind of emergency or state of general shortage and inflation, political pressures for wage and price freezes develop. Experience has taught most economists, whether they be liberals or conservatives, that such emergency measures work very well in short emergencies but create more and more distortions the longer they are in effect. Economists therefore, in contrast to politicians, tend

to recommend that such direct fiats be reserved for emergency periods and not squandered on minor peacetime situations.

Nevertheless, as Adam Smith well knew when he protested against the devices of the mercantilist advisers to the earlier kings, most economic systems are plagued by inefficiencies and inequities stemming from inexpert interferences with the mechanisms of supply and demand. A few such interferences are shown in Fig. 20-9.

1. *Minimum wage rates.* These often hurt those they are designed to help. What good does it do a youth to know that an employer must pay him $2.50 per hour, if the fact that he must be paid that amount is what keeps him from getting a job?[12]

2. *Rent ceilings.* Everyone hates a landlord and loves a farmer. Even in peacetime maximum rentals are often fixed by law. These fiats may do short-run good; but they may also do long-run harm. Thus,

---

[12] See P. A. Samuelson, *Readings in Economics,* (McGraw-Hill, New York, 1973, 7th ed.), for arguments pro and con minimum-wage legislation. See also Chapter 22's Appendix for graphical analysis of economic inefficiency of controls and rationing.

France had practically no residential construction from 1914 to 1948 because of rent controls. If new construction had been subjected to such controls after World War II, the vigorous boom in French residential building since 1950 would never have taken place.

3. *Usury laws*. Interest rates have always been an object of suspicion. No longer is lending at interest a crime, but in many places a maximum rate is set by law.

Unfortunately, this ceiling is often far below what would be set by the competitive supply-and-demand market, after account is taken of riskiness and administrative expense connected with small loans. The result? Funds dry up completely. Cheap insured NHA housing mortgage loans were no use to those who could not get a loan in 1966-1968. And the "protection" of borrowers by Canada's 6 per cent ceiling on bank loans (till 1967) simply forced the public to borrow elsewhere at double this rate or more.

EFFICIENCY OF SUPPLY-DEMAND PRICING AND "EQUITY"

We do not study competitive pricing for the beauty of the subject. Nor for its realism alone, since often monopoly elements spoil the competitive picture. We study it for the light it throws on *efficient* organization of an economy's resources. The pathology of interference with supply and demand helps to bring out the remarkable efficiencies produced by perfect competition when it is able to operate.

Why then do politicians and the populace keep interfering with the mechanism? Because man does not live by efficiency alone. He is interested in the question: Efficiency *for what?* And *for whom?* Most of these floors and ceilings are set in the name of "equity"—to help some group deemed deserving at the expense of some other group deemed already affluent and amply well-off. Just as Robin Hood "robbed the rich to help the poor," these devices try to create or restore a distribution of real income considered more equitable. Their advocates are willing to pay some price in the form of lower efficiency and higher waste to bring about a "fairer" distribution of income. Economic science cannot pronounce that

they are necessarily wrong, provided that they face the cost.

MONOPOLY INTERFERENCES WITH SUPPLY AND DEMAND

Aside from governmental interferences, there are serious monopolistic interferences with supply and demand. Competitive supply and demand is one way of organizing an economy. It is one way of getting the job done, but of course it is not the only way relied on in actual modern society. Certainly, when one or a few producers get monopoly control of an industry, they can move the final outcome away from the competitive equilibrium point. As we shall see later, a monopolist can reduce output and make the consumers travel up their demand curves to higher prices.

Is such an interference with supply and demand a "good thing"? If the monopolist were a more worthy soul than the rest of us, or if he were much poorer and had greater need for money than the rest of us, some might rise to defend his act of raising price. Or if he took our money and devoted it to better causes (charity, scientific research) than we should do, some might still defend him as a modern-day Robin Hood.

Chances are, however, that anyone in a position to contrive a monopoly will be at least as well off as his customers, and there is not much reason to think he would be of finer clay than anyone else. And though Robin Hood may have been all right in his day, in our day we tend to think it is the government that ought to do any subsidizing of worthy causes, not self-appointed monopolists; and we hope government can be more efficient in financing its good causes out of tax revenues than any monopolist could ever be. So what probably needs emphasis is this:

Any *haphazard* interference with competitive supply and demand is likely—save in some exceptional circumstances—to be a bad rather than a good thing.

Thus, a monopolistic interference in Industry A reduces its output needlessly relative to Industry B. The fact that it produces such scarcity is reflected in the higher P_A/P_B ratio it creates, relative to the citizenry's desires for the goods and to their true relative costs as measured along the production-possibility frontier or by undistorted competitive costs. The monopoly may also lead to a bad distribution of income in that it may give extra income to one who already has as much income as he deserves.

At this point monopoly's *restriction in output* relative to that of competitive industries perhaps needs more stressing than its distortion of the income distribution. For what if we taxed away the monopolist's ill-gotten gains?[13] We should then have rectified the income-distribution distortion of monopoly. But the community would still be left enjoying less of the (monopolized) consumption goods that it really does want in terms of what it really can produce.

Like sin, monopoly is one of those things most people are against. Therefore one need not labor the point that monopoly interferences with supply and demand are probably a bad thing. Still, it is better to know analytically why.

GOVERNMENT INTERFERENCES WITH SUPPLY AND DEMAND EVALUATED

In conclusion let us appraise government interferences. Surely the government means well and its interferences are not to be as harshly judged as those of a monopolist?

Well, that all depends. If the government happens to know better than people what is really good and evil, its interferences may improve matters. An example might be opium. We do not treat the consumer as a sovereign who can decide how much opium he will spend his money votes on. Where opium is concerned we adopt a paternalistic attitude, treating the consumer a little the way we treat the insane, minors, and other "incompetents." Society is similarly beginning to move against cigarettes.

But where cerise-colored cars or bubblegum are concerned, we usually are content to let the consumer spend his own dollars in his own way. We recognize

that advertising has given us one set of tastes, which may not be intrinsically better than some other set, but in the interests of freedom we do treat the consumer as sovereign.

As we have seen, the matter becomes more complicated if the sellers or the buyers in a market happen to be especially rich, or especially poor, or especially "deserving," or especially "undeserving." For example, imagine an artificial case where 1 million very rich producers sell milk in competitive markets to 50 million very poor people. Some people would then be tempted to approve of any interference that lowered milk price. "That leads to what we call a fairer income distribution," they might say.

Without foisting his ethical judgments on others, the economist can remind us:

Interfering with the competitive supply-and-demand mechanism is an inefficient[14] way of cor-

---

[13] Or what if many monopolists entered the industry, with all keeping their price too high but with total business so divided up among them that none ends up making any exorbitant monopoly profit? Then the evil effect on the income distribution would not exist, but the resulting wasteful pattern of inefficient production in the industry and too high price could persist until doomsday. More on this when Chapter 26 treats imperfect competition along the lines of Harvard's late E. H. Chamberlin.

[14] The fact that buyers and sellers are different people who may have different incomes or worth hides the truth that the competitive equilibrium point has certain allocative efficiency properties in solving the WHAT and HOW economic problems. So consider a simplified case where I trade only with myself. I have 10 hours of leisure worth exactly $2.50 per hour to me. I can produce 1 Q unit with each hour of work or sacrificed leisure. Suppose the first Q unit is worth exactly $4 to me, and successive Q units are worth $3, $2, $1, and $0. Figure 20-10 shows *my* supply and demand for Q. Equilibrium is at E, where I consume exactly 2 of Q. I get $4 + $3 of "satisfaction" from them (as shown by light shading) and 8 times $2.50 from my 8 hours left of leisure (as shown by heavy shading), or $27 of satisfaction in all, as shown by the sum of the areas. You can show that any disturbance which makes me work 1 hour too much, or too little, kills off 50 cents of my satisfaction. Distortion of a second hour kills off $1.50 of satisfaction; each further distortion takes a heavier and heavier toll, as shown by the growing discrepancy between dd and ss. (See Figs. 22-4, 26-5, and 32-2, for more on "consumer's surplus," which can be used to demonstrate monopoly harm or price-control inefficiency.)

EFFICIENCY OF SUPPLY AND DEMAND

FIG. 20-10

recting the income distribution. Whatever distribution you want to end up with can often be more efficiently attained by using the tax system to redistribute income rather than using *ad hoc* Robin Hood interferences in a single market.

Indeed, if taxation always could be counted on to keep society's FOR WHOM problem optimally solved, then perfect competition (were it to prevail!) could be counted on to solve most WHAT and HOW problems efficiently.

Naturally, all this is a controversial area. There is no one answer, and any observer of the modern world can see that nations everywhere do interfere with the price system at many points. EXAMPLES:

Blood for transfusions is not primarily obtained by commercial bidding, but rather through much voluntary effort. (Why?) Doctors often charge rich patients more than poor ones, in part subsidizing the latter from revenues of the former. (Why this private system of taxation?) Milk and other basic foods are often subsidized. To the degree that our demands reflect merely manipulated fads, engineered by profit-seeking advertisers, the merits of "consumer sovereignty" fade away.

The next chapter will deal with the extensive agricultural aid programs which the government has been following. And later chapters will discuss the effects of monopolistic imperfections of competition after competitive demand and the dependence of competitive supply on costs have been studied.

SUMMARY

A. ELASTICITY OF DEMAND AND SUPPLY

1 A basic problem of microeconomics is the mechanism of market pricing: how it grapples with the economy's problems WHAT, HOW, FOR WHOM. The supply-and-demand curves in Chapter 4 explain what goes on in each particular competitive market.

2 Elasticity of demand depends on what happens to total revenue as price is cut. Demand is elastic, inelastic, or unitary, according to whether a reduction in price increases, decreases, or does not change *total* revenue. The numerical coefficient of elasticity of demand is defined as "the percentage increase in quantity divided by the percentage cut in price." Depending upon whether the percentage rise in Q exceeds or falls short of the percentage fall in P, we have $E > 1$ or $E_d < 1$, with $E_d = 1$ in between. (Elasticity is dimensionless, involving percentages; it is not to be confused with absolute slope, as numerical tables and graphical measurements make clear.)

3 Elasticity of supply measures percentage responsiveness of amount Q supplied by producers when market P is raised by a given percentage.

4 Marshall stressed the time element: (*a*) *momentary* equilibrium of fixed supply; (*b*) *short-run* equilibrium with output varying within fixed plants and firms; (*c*) *long-run* equilibrium of normal price, when numbers of firms and plants, and all conditions, adjust to the new level of demand.

B. APPLICATIONS AND QUALIFICATIONS OF SUPPLY AND DEMAND

5 The apparatus of supply and demand enables us to analyze the effect of shifts in either curve, or in both simultaneously. Beginners must avoid the pitfall of confusing the expression "an increase in demand" (i.e., an outward *shift* of the whole demand curve) with "an increase in quantity demanded" as a result of a reduction in price (i.e., a movement along an unchanged demand curve).

6 A tax of so many dollars per unit of a good will lead to a new equilibrium intersection; its burden will be shifted forward to consumers rather than backward to the producers to the degree that the demand is inelastic relative to the supply.

7 A thousand forces affect price; but in a free competitive market they do so only by acting through supply and demand. For example, cost of production affects competitive price only through affecting supply, not otherwise.

8 Although the government usually affects price by operating on either supply or demand, occasionally it sets maximum ceilings or minimum floors that interfere with the workings of competitive markets. Under such circumstances, supply and demand need not be equal; some producer or consumer may *wish* to sell or buy more than he is able to do at the legal price. Distortions and inefficiencies result. Unless the discrepancies are parceled out by legislation (rationing, etc.), disorder and black markets may result.

9 Haphazard, arbitrary interferences with supply and demand will often be harmful. Monopoly interference provides an obvious case, and here the evil is not so much that the distribution of income is distorted as that society has to put up unnecessarily with reduced relative output of a good that it really wants and really can afford.

Even in cases where government is interfering with supply and demand for the purpose of achieving some desired distribution of income or some other social goal, there may be hidden costs in the use of so inefficient a device—and often the same goal could be accomplished better by use of the tax system and preservation of the efficiency of market pricing.

CONCEPTS FOR REVIEW

microeconomics, macroeconomics
total revenue, $P \times Q$
elastic, inelastic, unitary elastic
elasticity of supply
Marshall's three time periods
demand versus amount demanded
shift versus movement along a curve
possible efficiencies sacrificed when
    government interferes with supply and
    demand to achieve a worthy goal
cost of production, supply, and price

incidence of a tax
    forward shifting on to consumers
    backward shifting on to producers
rationing and price fixing
    maximum-price ceilings
    minimum-wage floors
monopoly reduction of relative outputs
    versus monopoly distortion of
    income distribution
government actions to influence
    supply and demand curves

QUESTIONS FOR DISCUSSION

1. What factors might increase the demand for wheat? The supply?
2. Which do you think has the most inelastic demand: perfume, salt, penicillin, cigarettes, ice cream, chocolate ice cream, Sealtest chocolate ice cream? Why?
3. When demand is elastic (inelastic, or unitary), what will a rise in P do to total revenue? What will higher Q do in the three cases?
4. "P drops by 1 per cent, causing Q to rise by 2 per cent. Demand is therefore *elastic*, with $E_d > 1$." If you change 2 to $1/2$ in this passage, what two other changes will be required?
5. Explain Marshall's three time periods, their equilibria, the slope of $s_L s_L$

6. Examine the diagram at right, which shows demand and supply curves for wheat for different years. Plot intersection points. Fill in the column at the right showing the price and quantity of wheat for each of the four years. (Note how hard it would be to estimate demand or supply curves from a plot of intersections.)

Year	Price	Quantity
1980		
1985		
1990		
1995		

7. As an extra-credit problem for those who like simple geometry and algebra, try to justify the E_d rule given in footnote 3 (page 354) for a straight line. In the triangle at right, the dd has the equation $Q = b - (b/a)P$, where b is the Q intercept and a the P intercept, and the absolute inverted slope of dd is $-(dQ/dP) = -\triangle Q/\triangle P = b/a$. Now apply the formula $E = -(dQ/dP)(P/Q)$ to get

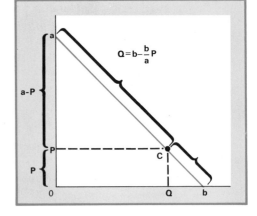

$$E_d = \frac{b}{a}\frac{P}{b-(b/a)P} = \frac{P}{a-P}$$

—the ratio of the lower vertical bracket to the upper. Can you show, by the property of similar triangles, that

$$E_d = \frac{P}{a-P} = \frac{bC}{aC}$$

equals "the length of the straight line below the point divided by its length above the point," as stated in footnote 3?[15]

---

[15] ... As another extra-credit problem, try to relate Table 20-1's so-called "arc elasticity" formula for two different points on dd to the so-called "point elasticity" formula just given. First, draw an extended straight line through the two points on dd. Second, locate their average or midpoint on the line. Third, calculate E_d as the ratio of the extended line segment below this point to that above it. You will thus end up with a geometrical interpretation of

$$E_d = -\frac{\triangle Q(P_1 + P_2)/2}{\triangle P(Q_1 + Q_2)/2}$$

Those who tackled the mathematical question 10 of Chapter 4, page 76, can calculate ... E_d from the demand function $Q = f(P)$. Define $E_d = \displaystyle\lim_{\triangle P \to Q} \frac{-\triangle Q}{\triangle P}\frac{(P_1 + P_2)/2}{(Q_1 + Q_2)/2} = \frac{dQ}{dP}\frac{P}{Q} = \frac{-P\{df(P)/dP\}}{f(P)}$

For $f(P) = b - (b/a)P$, calculate $E_d = P/(a-P)$. Show E_d to be respectively 1, 2, 1/3, k for $f(P)$ successively $c/P, c/P^2, c/P^{\frac{1}{3}}, c/P^k$. Taking logarithms (to any base) of the last expression, verify $\log Q = \log c - k \log P$ does give $E_d \equiv k$. [HINT: $(dQ/Q) \div (dP/P) = -d\log Q/d\log P \equiv -k.$]

APPENDIX: Cases on Supply and Demand[1]

Proposition 1. **(a) As a general rule an increase in demand —supply being constant—will raise price.**
(b) Probably also, but less certainly, increased demand will increase the quantity bought and sold. A decrease in demand has opposite effects.

Proposition 2. **An increase in supply, demand being constant, will almost certainly lower price and increase the quantity bought and sold. A decrease in supply has opposite effects.**

These two important propositions summarize the *qualitative* effects of shifts in supply and demand. But the exact *quantitative* degree of change in price and quantity depends upon the specific shapes of the curves in each instance. Here, then, are a number of possible cost and supply situations.

Case 1. Constant cost. Imagine a manufactured item, like pencils, whose production can be easily expanded by merely duplicating factories, machinery, and labor. To produce 100,000 pencils per day simply requires us to do the same thing as when we were manufacturing 1,000 per day, but on a hundredfold scale. In this case the supply curve *ss* in Fig. 20-11 is a horizontal line at the constant level of unit costs. A rise in demand will shift the new intersection point *E'* to the right, raising *Q* but leaving *P* the same.

What will be the effects of a sales tax of, say 5 cents per pencil, on output and price paid by the consumer? Fill in the diagram in the Fig. 20-6 manner.

Case 2. Increasing costs and diminishing returns. Suppose an industry like wine-grape growing requires a certain kind of soil and location (sunny hillsides, etc.). Such sites are limited in number. The annual output of wine can be increased to some extent by adding more labor and fertilizer to each acre of land and by bidding away more hill sites from other uses. But as we saw in Chapter 2, the law of diminishing returns will begin to operate if variable factors of production, like labor and fertilizer, are added to fixed amounts of a factor like land. Why is that? Because each new *variable addition* of labor and fertilizer has a *smaller proportion* of land to work with. By the same token, each fixed unit of land has more labor and fertilizer cooperating with it. Therefore land's productivity and earnings are higher. The result: Getting extra amounts of wine sends total costs up more than proportionately. Therefore the cost per unit of wine is rising. The supply curve travels upward from southwest to northeast because at lower market prices, less will be supplied. At higher prices, more will be supplied.

Figure 20-12 shows the rising supply curve *ss*. What will be the effect on price of an increase in demand? Effect on quantity?

[1]Many courses may prefer to study this Appendix after Chapter 23 or 24.

Case 3. Completely fixed or inelastic supply and economic rent. Some goods or productive factors are completely fixed in amount, regardless of price.

Thus there is only one *Mona Lisa* by Leonardo. Nature's original endowment of the "natural and indestructible" qualities of land can also often be taken as fixed in

FIG. 20-11

FIG. 20-12

FIG. 20-13

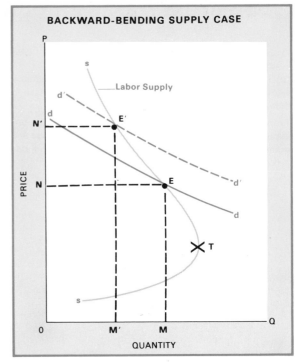

FIG. 20-14

amount. Raising the price offered for water power cannot create more than Niagara Falls. High-paid artists and businessmen who love their work would continue to work at their jobs even at low pay. Once a toll bridge is built, it must earn "what the traffic will bear" regardless of past sunk costs.

In all such cases the supply curve goes vertically up and down, at least in the relevant region. In Fig. 20-13, a higher price cannot elicit an increase in Q; nor is the higher price necessary to bring out the existing Q, for even at lower prices the same amount will still be forthcoming. Because it is price-*determined* rather than price-*determining*, the return to such a factor of production is called a "pure economic rent," or "surplus," which need not be paid to call out the required supply.

If demand now shifts upward, the whole effect is to raise price. Quantity is unchanged. And the rise in price exactly equals the upward shift in demand. (More on this in Chapter 28's section on rents and costs.)

Likewise, if a tax is placed upon the commodity, its whole effect is to reduce the price received by the supplier by exactly the amount of the tax. The tax is shifted back completely to the supplier, who absorbs it all out of his economic rent or surplus. The consumer buys exactly as much of the good or service as before and at no extra cost.

Case 4. A backward-rising supply curve. Early explorers often noted that, when you raised the wages of natives, you received *less* rather than more labor. If wages were doubled, instead of working 6 days a week for their minimum of subsistence, the natives might go fishing for 3 days. The same has been observed among so-called "civilized" people. As improved technology raises real wages people feel that they ought to take part of their higher

earnings in the form of more leisure, less work. (In Chapter 22, the discussion of the marginal utility theory, or income- and substitution-effects, will explain why a supply curve might bend backward.)

Figure 20-14 shows such a supply curve of labor. At first it rises as higher wages coax out more labor, but beyond the point T, higher wages induce more leisure and less work. An increase in demand does increase the price of labor in agreement with Proposition 1(*a*). But note how lucky we were to have added the words "but less certainly" in 1(*b*)! For the increase in demand has *decreased* the quantity of labor.

A partial verification of such a possibility is found in the fact that a decrease in demand for farm products during a depression often causes farmers to work harder in order to restore their incomes. The result: More rather than less is produced in response to a decrease in demand.

Case 5. A possible exception: Decreasing cost. Heretofore our examples have agreed with Proposition 1(*a*), that an increase in demand raises price. But what about the often observed case where an increase in demand is followed by economies of mass production and decreasing costs?

A good theory must make room for all the facts. So we must frankly admit that our first proposition may break down and have exceptions. Of course, we can save some face by pointing out that many of the important reductions in cost following an increase in demand really represent

FIG. 20-15

FIG. 20-16

permanent downward shifts in the supply curve rather than downward movements *along* a falling supply curve.

Let us illustrate this by the case where the government increases its demand for radar sets. The first few sets built must be constructed in the laboratory by experimental methods. They are tailor-made and very expensive per unit. But the know-how gained in the process makes possible the further production of sets for much less per unit. Even if demand went back again to its previous level, price would not return to its previous higher level. In traveling along the arrow *EE'* marked with a question mark in Fig. 20-15 we are not moving reversibly along the supply curve. Instead, the supply curve has shifted irreversibly downward from *ss* to *s's'*, so that even when demand is back again at *dd*, the price is now lower at *E"* than it was originally.

The case discussed really does not come under the heading of Proposition 1, but under Proposition 2 dealing with shifts in supply. The final result agrees with the latter's conclusion that an increase in supply will lower price and increase quantity. (Compare *E* and *E".*) But the present case is still an unusual one because the shift of supply has been *induced* by a shift in demand.

In economic history, there have been important cases of reduced cost over time as a result of technological progress that was partly induced by the expansion of a mass market. Goods are constantly being improved in quality and cheapened in price.

What about the case of genuine *reversible* economies of large-scale production—cases where going back to small-scale production does send costs up again? The alert modern economist will not deny its importance; but he will suspect that some monopolistic imperfection of com-

petition is present. He will point out that in a competitive industry each firm would have *already* expanded its output to where the *extra* cost of producing a unit of output has begun to turn up. This would be because each competitive producer has no fear of spoiling his own market and has every incentive to expand his production through and beyond the decreasing-cost stage.[2] (Later chapters analyze the imperfect competition that results when a few firms have decreasing cost and hence expand to capture much of the market.)

Case 6. Shifts in supply. All the above discussion, with the exception of part of Case 5, dealt with a shift in demand and no shift in supply. To analyze Proposition 2, we must now shift supply, keeping demand constant. This is done in Fig. 20-16.

If the law of downward-sloping demand is valid,[3] then increased supply must send us *down* the demand curve, decreasing price and quantity. The student may verify, by

---

[2]There remains the possibility mentioned in Chapter 24: the case of an $s_L s_L$ curve that is downward-sloping because of Marshallian *external* economies.

[3]In Chapter 22 we shall meet the legitimate exception to the law of downward-sloping demand in the case of the Irish peasants who might be forced by higher potato *P* to consume *more* of such necessities. Another exception is provided by items such as diamonds or chic hats, which are valuable, not for their intrinsic qualities so much as for their "snob appeal" and expensiveness, and which may therefore fall off in demand if their price is cut. What appears to be another exception is the case in which a short-run rise in *P* may make people expect future *P* to be still higher, thus causing them to buy more rather than less now and thereby leading to unstabilizing speculation; but this is more properly to be interpreted as a case where the whole demand curve is shifting, rather than as a northeast move up *dd*.

drawing diagrams or by comparing automobiles and wheat, the following quantitative corollaries of Proposition 2:

(a) An increased supply will decrease price most when demand is inelastic.

(b) An increased supply will increase the quantity bought and sold least when demand is inelastic.

What are common-sense reasons for these? Illustrate with elastic autos and inelastic wheat.

Case 7. A dynamic cobweb. There is a famous economic case which can be used to show that the tools of supply and demand are not restricted to handling static and unchanging situations, but can also be used fruitfully to analyze dynamic situations of change. (The next sections can be skipped by the time-pressed reader.)

Suppose that a competitive crop—let us take the conventional example of hogs for pork production—is auctioned off in the market in the usual way so as to fetch the P given by running up vertically from any given Q to the dd demand curve.

But now we want to make the supply side dynamic. Suppose farmers look at today's P and use it to determine the Q they will bring to market in the *next* period: specifically, if today's P is high, they begin to breed many new pigs, to feed and fatten them, and finally to bring them to market some months from now. The farmers do indeed have an ss supply curve, but it acts with a time lag and connects next period's Q with this period's P. (It is understood that we define a period as the time involved in producing hogs.)

If the market price were at the intersection of ss and dd in Fig. 20-17, this would represent an unchanging equilibrium in exactly the same way that it did in the non-dynamic cases. Today, tomorrow, and in the period after that, the farmers would be on their ss curve producing the amount shown by E; and the amount consumers would gladly demand at that P would just match what farmers will gladly supply. As yet, then, no difference.

But suppose that, for some reason, such as hog cholera, the crop initially drops to Q_1, which is below the equilibrium amount Q^*. We run up to the demand curve to E_1 and see that we get the higher P corresponding to the reduced crop. But that is not the end of the story. We are not at long-run equilibrium; because how much will the farmers produce tomorrow at this higher P_1? They will run over rightward to their supply curve and produce in the second period at the point marked F_2. We can see that this amount of Q is above the equilibrium Q^*. What will it sell for in the competitive market? We run down to the demand curve and see that P will have to fall to the level shown at E_2. But we are not yet in final equilibrium. At this low price, farmers will plan to cut down tomorrow's production by going leftward to their ss curve, ending up at F_3. From there we move upward to the dd curve, to find the P_3 given at the E_3 point.

And thus it goes on and on. First Q is low and P is high. But high P makes next period's Q high and next period's P low. So—like a man on a tightrope who goes too far on

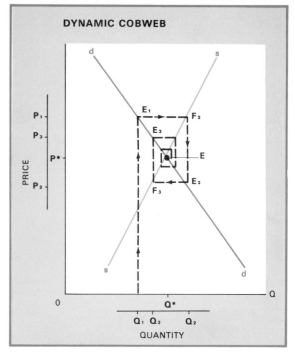

FIG. 20-17

one side, then corrects himself by going too far on the other—market price oscillates in successive periods above and below equilibrium, tracing out a spiderlike cobweb.

What is the final outcome? Figure 20-17 was drawn with the supply curve's slope at E *steeper* than the demand curve's falling slope. So, as can be seen from the diagram, the oscillations finally do dampen and die out: the cobweb winds inward to E. We are then back at equilibrium, where we can stay forever. Forever? Well, at least until the next outside disturbance comes to set off still another dying-out oscillation.

Not all equilibrium points are so dynamically stable. Figure 20-18 puts a microscope on the region around E in a number of other possible situations. Thus, in the first diagram, ss has been made *flatter* than dd, and the cobweb diverges outward in an explosive oscillation.

In the second diagram, the straight lines are of the *same slope* and we get a perfect cobweb: depending upon how severely it is disturbed, the market will oscillate endlessly around equilibrium, getting neither more nor less violent in its swing. (This is like the case of an ideal frictionless pendulum which would repeat its swings forever.)

The last diagram is designed to show that there is no need to stick with straight lines. Because its ss is flatter (more "elastic") than dd at the equilibrium point, any small disturbance will *at first* send the system into increasing oscillations. But no explosion can go on forever in real life; and the curvature of the schedules finally brings the system to the stable "box," indicated by the letters $ABCD$.

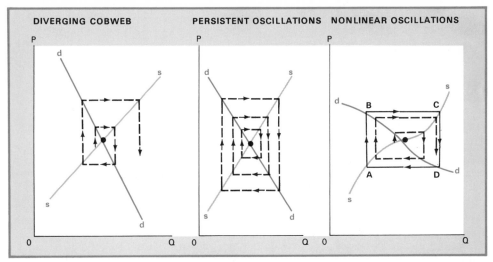

FIG. 20-18

Ultimately, then, the system oscillates repeatedly in an every-other-period box and the amplitude or degree of the oscillation will be determined by the curvatures of *dd* and *ss*. After any new disturbance, the system tends to come back to this box from within or without; and even if stationary equilibrium were restored at *E* by accident, the slightest new shock would send the market away from such an unstable equilibrium point. (The thoughtful student may ask at this point: Could prices swing forever in this every-other-period fashion without shrewd speculators beginning to notice the pattern? Would they not then tend to buy at low *P*, store, and resell at high *P*, thus

tending to wipe out the price differentials? The Appendix to the next chapter deals with dynamic speculation and suggests that just this might indeed happen.)

There was space here for only the briefest account of the cobweb model. Statistics show that a corn-hog cycle like this has been part of modern history. And our simplified model throws some light on the business-cycle phenomena dealt with in Part Two, where a free enterprise system would tend to fluctuate if not moderated by public policy and equilibrating market mechanisms. Corporations, like pig farmers, can swing from one extreme to the other, thus causing instability.

CONCEPTS FOR REVIEW

price rise from *dd* increase
probable quantity rise
constant costs, horizontal supply
Increasing costs, rising *ss*
inelastic supply, vertical *ss*, rent
backward-rising supply

decreasing costs and monopoly
increased *ss* lowering *P*
dynamic supply and demand cobweb
lagged supply
unlagged demand
every-other-period oscillation of *P*

21
SUPPLY AND DEMAND AS APPLIED TO AGRICULTURE

Though government subsidies to ease adjustment burdens and sustain incomes in the face of unfavorable prices have not, on the whole, been a major feature of government policy in Canada, nevertheless such policies may, and in some cases have, slowed down adjustment processes.... We continue to have too many farms, with many of the farmers earning low incomes.
ECONOMIC COUNCIL OF CANADA, FIRST ANNUAL REVIEW

The economist's model of perfect competition, in which a homogeneous product is produced by many different people and auctioned off in a well-organized market, does not fit most of Canadian life at all closely. Therefore, in later chapters, we shall have to supplement it by the new tools of imperfect, or monopolistic, competition.

There is, however, one great area that does provide a valuable application of the basic tools of supply and demand. Agriculture is an important problem area. It makes the news. It shifts votes. No one can possibly understand the vital policy issues in this field without first understanding the basic economic concepts of supply and demand. This chapter puts them to work.

RELATIVE DECLINE OF AGRICULTURE

Farming is still our largest single industry. But the percentage of people engaged in it has been declining steadily for the last two centuries and it is no longer true that we are a nation of farmers. Though farmers still swing much political weight, today only 5.6 percent of Canadian workers are in agriculture compared to 35 percent in the 1920s and 25 percent after World War II. One agency forecasts that the 1980 figure will be 4 percent.

Why this relative shift away from farming? People seek the higher and more stable incomes of the city, shorter hours, and what many seem to regard as the better social life in town; they flee from ancient discrimination.

Figure 21-1 shows that, over most of the 30 years since World War II—a period that is very short compared with the history of land settlement and farming in Canada— (a) farm-operator incomes have been unstable; (b) they have risen more slowly than stable industrial wages until 1973 and (c) farm-product prices have risen more slowly than the cost of living. Obviously, living on a farm has been both more precarious and less financially rewarding than most city work.

However, the alternatives are not always so attractive either. The NEW index of Chapter 10 and the urban-issues discussion of Chapter 39 show problems of modern life that many farmers are happy to avoid.

Furthermore, the instability of farm incomes sometimes brings a bonanza. The events of 1973-5 (devaluation of the dollar; crop failures in Asia; drought in Australia and Africa; loss of Peruvian fish) sent the demand for and price of Canadian foods sky-high. The index of farm prices rose 31 percent in one year, but grain and meat did even better. Farmers prospered because the cost of farm inputs and expenses rose only 18 percent. After making allowance for a number of items, and after including the increase in value of not-yet-sold inventories, net farm incomes rose *90* percent in one year! Production of foods was virtually unchanged. This is one of the periodic rewards of accepting the risks of an unstable industry. The economic system— the elasticity of food supply—moves in quickly to push such peaks down again.

DIFFERENTIAL BIRTH RATES In a way, the out-migration from the country is lucky. For, as we saw in Chapter 2, birth rates are higher in rural areas than in cities. If it were not for this migration, cities

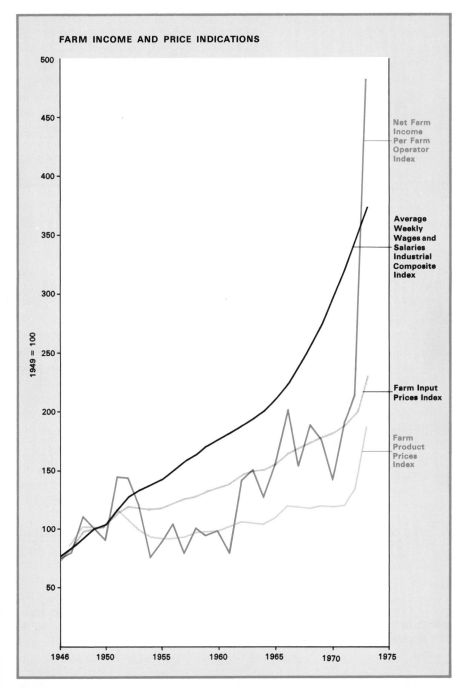

FARM INCOME AND PRICE INDICATIONS

Net Farm
Income
Per Farm
Operator
Index

Average
Weekly
Wages and
Salaries
Industrial
Composite
Index

Farm Input
Prices Index

Farm
Product
Prices
Index

1949 = 100

FIG. 21-1. Farm incomes lag behind industrial wages; and farm product prices lag behind input costs.
1970 and 1973-74 illustrate the instability of farm income. In late 1974 net farm incomes, having overtaken industrial wages, were on the way down again. (Sources: Statcan 11-003, 11-505; Department of Finance *Economic Review April 1974;* Canada Yearbook. Net farm incomes drawn from national accounts.)

might grow smaller and smaller; the rural share of total population would grow larger and larger. What does the law of diminishing returns tell us such an eventuality would mean? It would mean a great reduction in the productivity of each man-hour spent on the farm. The land would become crowded with many people, each producing little and each unable to buy many of the comforts of life with his produce.

Does this sound far-fetched? It is already a true picture of about two-thirds of the globe. In Asia especially, standards of living are pitifully poor. With three out of every four persons engaged in producing the food necessary for life, only one out of four can be producing the comforts of life. Contrast this with our near self-sufficiency, where each producer is today efficient enough to feed more than thirty other people as well. But Canada is not self-sufficient in food. Instead, we export large proportions of certain crops and import other foods from warmer climates.

TECHNOLOGY, TASTE, AND TRADE
Besides the differential in birth rates, there are two other reasons why agriculture is a problem area:

Technological progress has been greatly reducing the number of people needed to produce any given total of food and fiber. Use of the tractor, the combine, irrigation, fertilizer, experimental planting of varieties of wheat, and numerous other examples come to mind.

Coupled with the improvement in labor-saving technique is the unshakable fact that, *as we get richer, we do not want to expand our food consumption by as much as we want to expand our consumption of city products. Moreover, potential customers overseas do not want to use their scarce foreign exchange for our grains.* This has been shown by almost every statistical investigation here and abroad.

Birth rates, tastes, and technology dictate that agriculture must go on exporting people to industry, or increasing food exports abroad.

AGRICULTURE'S LONG-RUN DECLINE: GRAPHICAL ANALYSIS
THE PRODUCTION-POSSIBILITY FRONTIER This basic tool can illuminate the decline in

agriculture. Turn back to Fig. 2-3 of Chapter 2. The figure shows that tremendous technological change has shifted out the *p-p frontier*; the even greater productivity in food production—from the use of tractors, fertilizers, hybrid seeds, and insecticides—is indicated by the strong eastward shift that flattens the whole curve. What does this flattening of the curve imply for the trend of farm prices relative to industrial prices? It means that a larger amount of food can be got from the same resources relative to nonfood. So food costs and prices must, in free markets, fall relative to nonfood.

This prediction is borne out by actual food price statistics. Farm prices have, in general, declined relative to the prices of all other goods.[1] Even expanding foreign markets for meats and grains, based on higher incomes abroad, droughts, and expanding populations, cannot prevent technological progress from gradually eroding relative farm prices.

A second reason for this price trend can also be seen back in Fig. 2-3. Food is a necessity whose expenditure drops relative to higher and higher incomes. As each nation grows richer, its move to *B* from *A* is not northeastward but almost due north, to an even flatter part of the technically flattened new *p-p frontier*. No wonder food prices drop in competitive markets (unless they are rescued by new export markets).

SUPPLY AND DEMAND CURVES A single diagram is more useful in explaining the sagging trend of farm prices than libraries of orations and editorials.

In Fig. 21-2 let the point *E* represent the initial equilibrium of supply and demand at some earlier period. Now see what happens to these curves as the years go by. We know that *dd* will shift rightward as population grows and as higher real incomes make people want to consume more food at the same price; but we do know that basic foods are the kinds of necessities which do not grow in the family budget at all proportionately to increases in real income, and

---

[1] The ratio of farm to nonfarm prices measures the extent to which farmers achieve "parity" in the pricing of their produce. In the United States, policy has resulted in giving the value of the ratio in 1913 a target value of 100. Whenever farm prices fall, the policy implication is that the government should support them until the ratio rises to the 1913 level. The value of the ratio since 1949 is indicated by the relationship of the two bottom lines in Fig. 21-1.

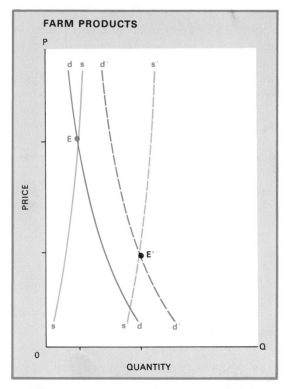

FIG. 21-2. One diagram goes far to explain the farm problem.

As the years go by, the increase in demand for farm products generated by population and income growth tends to be less than the vast increase in supply generated by technological productivity improvements. Thus free prices fall. With both schedules highly inelastic, prices fall hard; farm incomes deteriorate. And small shifts in inelastic curves generate large price fluctuations.

we realize that population no longer grows at the prodigious percentage rates of the nineteenth century. So the rightward demand shift to $d'd'$ is of modest amount.

What about supply? Though many make the mistake of thinking of farming as a backward business, statistical records show that productivity in agriculture has increased at a pace even faster than productivity in industry. So each new improvement helps to shift the ss curve a great deal to the right.

What, then, must be happening to the new equilibrium E' that would prevail in the market if the government did not intervene? Certainly a shift in supply that outstrips the shift in demand must lead to a *downward trend of market prices* (relative, of

course, to the general price level, so that effects of over-all inflation are disregarded). Naturally, this declining price trend means financial pressure and hardship on those farmers and rural workers whose efficiency has not undergone tremendous increase; and it means that there will be considerable pressure for people to leave the countryside for jobs in industry. It also means that consumers are paying lower prices for the raw-material component of their foods[2] and that the economy is reallocating its resources toward the things that are now most demanded in our growing society.

And, as we know, it means strong political pressures for government aid to agriculture.

INSTABILITY IN AGRICULTURE

Farming is an up-and-down industry. Oats, wheat, beef, pork, and other farm products are sold in highly competitive markets whose prices change yearly, daily, hourly, and by the minute. The farmer swings at the very end of our see-sawing economy. Good times bring him great percentage increases in income. Depressions cause his cash income to drop away to very little. The farmer particularly benefits from wartime demand conditions; and unlike most of the community, the farmer can ride out an inflationary period of skyrocketing prices. But since 1947 farm income has been sliding downward relative to other incomes, both in total and in per capita terms.

If we look closely at farm statistics, such as those in Fig. 21-1, we note a surprising fact.

Farm *incomes* fluctuate between boom and bust to a greater degree than do nonfarm incomes, but farm *production* is remarkably more stable than in-

[2] Even though the price the farmer gets for the food he sells will fall, the retail price need not fall so much or may even rise in the years ahead. Why? Agricultural experts claim this is not so much because railroads, packers, and supermarkets extort an undue share of the food dollar as that we consumers today want our food more and more fabricated (e.g., frozen, cut, cleaned, cooked, minutely packaged, premixed for baking, and so forth) and that greater technological progress may be taking place in producing raw food than in processing and marketing it. In the 1970s the farmer gets but one-third of the retail food dollar, as compared with about one-half in the years of high farm prices, right after World War II.

dustrial production. Stability of farm output contrasts with instability of farm prices!

Even the weather, which is a great threat to the stability of farm production in *any one* region, does not cause such sizable fluctuations in *total* farm crops over the whole nation. In the last quarter century, industrial production has fluctuated considerably more widely than has agricultural production.

The farmer's supply curves are relatively inelastic for many reasons. (1) When *P* falls, his own effort to increase output may increase, as he desperately tries to maintain family income. (2) Many of his costs go on anyway, whether he produces much or little, and he can save but little extra cost by cutting his *Q*; so he tends not to cut volume. (3) Once a farmer has planted a crop, he can do little to increase his output volume until the next crop season.

The amount of farm products demanded, in addition to growing little when income rises, is also quite inelastic in response to price changes.

What, then, is the result of (1) relatively inelastic demand coupled with (2) relatively inelastic supply when (3) both curves are quite shiftable?

To answer this, take a sheet of paper and construct price and quantity axes. Then draw on it a quite vertical supply curve intersecting a quite vertical demand curve, much as in Fig. 21-2. Now shift either curve a little bit. Do you see how great are the resulting shifts in *P*? Would anyone like having his standard of living dependent on a tiny shift of supply and demand, when inelastic curves produce a tremendous change in family income?

Figure 21-1 showed that fluctuations in the prices received by farmers are greater than the fluctuations in the prices of the things they must buy. In the Great Depression days of the early 1930s, prices received by farmers dropped about twice as far as did prices elsewhere. Even in the prosperous 1920s the farmer did badly; and, to make things worse, he then carried a heavy burden of mortgage debt left over from the war boom.

GOVERNMENT AID TO AGRICULTURE

From folk myths to cowboy films, the public seems always to have hated a landlord and loved a farmer, and perhaps this attitude has fostered the fairly

widespread public support for farm aid. Even the skeptical 1969 Task Force on Agriculture, while asserting that agriculture should be "much as any other industry," proposes a complex list of boards and programs that is consistent with our history of politically inspired government assistance to farmers.[3]

Prior to the Great Depression of the 1930s, governments gave agriculture aid in almost every form except in the marketing or pricing of farm products. Even this is not quite true: each province's department of agriculture, in company with the federal government, has long done what it could for rural voters; transportation and crop research in particular. But the economic effect of such measures on specific regions was indirect. Mostly the farmer sold his grain, or fruit, or daily products on markets that (apart from slight sheltering of sales in Canada by tariffs) were exposed to the chill winds of international competition. Apart from tariff bargaining, to make sure that foreign markets were open to Canadian foodstuffs, the government left the food export industry on its own.

GRAIN AND THE WHEAT BOARD   The first steps away from individual selling were taken by the farmers themselves, through grain pools and marketing boards. (The setting up of these organizations was partly responsible for the emergence of farmers' political parties in the 1920s.) Cooperation was a way of life as well as a method of business, and pool-movement leaders like A. J. McPhail had prestige that is rarely found in industry.

At first,[4] under the general heading of the principles of cooperation, they aspired to only two goals: to organize one central selling agency that would "even-up the bargaining power" between buyers and sellers; and to create a system of mass storage, the costs of which would be shared, to hold much of the crop off the market in bumper-crop, low-price years,

---

[3] See the comprehensive *Canadian Agriculture in the Seventies*, Report of the Federal Task Force on Agriculture (Ottawa: Information Canada, December 1969).

Much of the historical and descriptive material in this section, and in the next, are background for the understanding of supply and demand, especially as applied to Canadian agriculture. Some readers may prefer to skip forward to the important price supports section on page 381.

[4] During World War I the government had moved to market the entire prairie crop in the 1917, 1918, and 1919 crop years. But the subsequent Mackenzie King and Meighen governments declined to resume this intervention.

and to sell this "carry-over" in leaner, high-price years. But this would work only if they had unusual foresight: to be able to identify unusually large crops and unusually low prices and further, to be able to predict the crop and price in the following year. If they did not, they might carry over the stored crop into another lowprice year, incur storage costs, forgo income from the unsold stored wheat, and have to either dump the carried-over wheat onto a market where it would push down the world price further, or to carry over an even larger amount to next year. This situation actually arose. The pools decided to carry over into 1930 an amount which was actually over 50 per cent of the 1929 crop. But the next year there was an even lower grain price. Eventually the federal government stepped in, taking over the pools' central selling agency, and the pools reverted to merely running their cooperative elevators.

Note two things. Even at its strongest, the pool complex was never a wheat monopolist. One reason for this was that many farmers still sold through the companies, thus competing down the Canadian price. A more important reason was that Canadian wheat was never more than a large competitor in the world wheat market. Even if every prairie farmer had delivered his grain to the pools, such *monopsony* (single wheat-buyer) power in Canada would not have given the agency *monopoly* (single wheat-seller) power in the world market.

Note also that the government's role was very limited. It was by this time highly committed to backing the pools. The provinces had created laws that put the pools into business; had provided inspection and investigation services; and, together with Ottawa, had bailed the pools out more than once. But intervention was minor until in 1935 the federal government set up the Wheat Board, which offered to buy grain at "emergency" prices, somewhat below the price that it thought would be ruling. Thus it provided a sort of minimum price. Mostly, in the Great Depression, equilibrium prices were above this floor, and the Wheat Board had little delivered to it. Not until 1938-1939, when the Wheat Board's floor price was 80 cents and the market price was lower, was almost the whole prairie crop delivered to the Wheat Board. These stocks could not be sold until wartime shortages developed. We'll see below how such floor price mechanisms work.

Nowadays, the Wheat Board still acts as single selling agency. Most of its wheat is sold to Western world markets at prices set by an International Wheat Agreement (IWA) between the main exporting countries and almost 40 importing countries, or by direct sale to other governments such as Russia and China.

What, then, is the role of the government in setting the price received by grain growers? The subsidy to the grain grower is relatively small and indirect. The Wheat Board sells on the competitive world grain market; deducts its expenses and those of the transport, storage and milling; and, after a complex series of payments and adjustments, returns all the residue to the farmer.

Only rarely has the government controlled total planted acreage; it did so in 1941 and 1970. The 1970 scheme ("Operation LIFT") paid operators of up to 20 million acres $6 per acre for summer-fallowing—i.e., not producing anything. Furthermore, the Wheat Board, in deciding which wheat producers are allowed to deliver (sell) their wheat to the glutted elevators, heavily favors those who have increased fallow (for forage) acreage on their farms. The scheme may be the most ambitious ever seen. From a late 1960s acreage of 30 million, the area had fallen in 1972 to 19 million. However, as farmers actually withdraw their lowest-yielding acreage, and as they increase cultivation on their remaining land, production falls by a smaller percentage than acreage.

Apart from LIFT and the small pre-delivery subsidies, the Board and the governments have confined their roles to those of railway and port manager, super-broker, barker, and advisor—not principal participant.[5]

---

[5] The Wheat Board is not the only form of government intervention in the grain trade. The Board of Grain Commissioners runs some public elevators and has an important inspecting and grading role. The Prairie Farm Assistance Act takes one percent of all farmers' grain prices on the prairies and pays it out to farmers in regions of temporarily low yield. The fund was supposed to be self-liquidating, but since 1939, the federal government has had to add almost as much as the farmers have paid in. Ottawa and the provinces run Crop Insurance Acts. These so far cover less than 60,000 farmers altogether, who have preferred this approach to the one percent fund approach. Finally, since 1929, Ottawa has backed the Farm Credit Corporation. Its recent loans average over $28,000, at about 8 percent to about 5,000 borrowers a year on mortgage-type loans up to 30 years. This

MARKETING BOARDS

Although the "wheat-board radicals" had thoughts about controlling the price of wheat, they have had little success. Marketing boards for other crops on the other hand have been able to operate on Q, the amount supplied, so as to make the price higher than it would be otherwise.

Marketing boards go back a long way; but because they are mostly under provincial jurisdiction and operate on prices of produce for local consumption, they are less well known or nationally important than the grain organizations.[6]

Like the grain pools, marketing boards grew out of cooperation. Farmers who produce fruit, poultry, tobacco, vegetables (such as sugar beets, soybeans, and potatoes), honey, and some dairy products have wanted to control the marketing of their crops. They hope to cut down the distribution, storage, and selling expenses, create a larger demand, and bargain on more even terms with buyers, instead of being forced

to accept the posted price of a local produce dealer. For most of them the market is within the same region, and their farming area is the lowest-cost source for that market.

Short-circuiting the long historical and legal chronicle, imagine that you are a farmer in a fruit area. Crops are good, but your per-bushel price barely covers your costs. You know that retailers a hundred miles away are selling your fruit at twice the price you get. How can you get a larger farm price?

1. You are only one of many farmers. The final market is strictly competitive. If you advertise your fruit most of the advantage will, arithmetically, flow to other farmers and to your dealer. Clearly you have to get together with other sellers.

2. So you form a co-op. This way you can run your own advertising, buying, selling to wholesalers in the city, storage, and packing. Maybe you can do it as cheaply as your former dealer; maybe you even hire him to manage your co-op. But now there is one more buying plant, all plants including yours will have slightly less business, and the industry as a whole has excess buying and packing capacity. So overhead (fixed) costs of the whole industry will go up a bit unless the fruit business is expanding anyway.

3. How can you get a larger share of that final price? You now are a major seller and can deal on even terms with the big city wholesale buyer. He offers you $1 per bushel for your fruit. You refuse, demanding $1.25. Now comes the test. If you have succeeded in getting enough members so that your co-op controls a large fraction of the total supply, he (or a competing wholesaler) will have to pay the price.[7] But if your group is small, you'll be left with your fruit unsold.

4. The problem now is that if you get the price up to $1.25, you can do so only by holding back some from the market—by reducing your Q. This means

---

low rate involves a considerable subsidy to the borrowers, but less than 30,000 borrowers are heavily involved at any one time. There are also a small farm development or farm improvement loan plans where small loans (about $3,000) are guaranteed by Ottawa.

[6]For over forty years, the constitutional position of marketing boards has swung back and forward between Ottawa and province. Usually, either government has been willing to accept jurisdiction. But opponents of the boards have fought their controls and "fees" by claiming that they were *ultra vires* (beyond the constitutional jurisdiction of) whatever government set them up; and often these opponents have won their court cases. The status of the boards is ambiguous because agricultural jurisdiction is rather uncertainly shared by both levels of government; because the products controlled are sometimes purely local but sometimes move in interprovincial trade; and because the "fees" collected to run the boards are sometimes declared by the courts to be indirect taxes (see page 148) on produce and so beyond provincial jurisdiction. After more than forty years, the legal questions are by no means cleared up; the framers of the BNA Act failed miserably to leave a constitutional peg for these bodies.

In 1972 the federal Parliament passed the Farm Products Marketing Agencies Act and subsequently appointed a six-member National Farm Products Marketing Council. The federal legislation makes it possible to co-ordinate the operations of producer marketing boards, established under provincial marketing legislation, into a nation-wide marketing system.

A national marketing agency will be set up for a commodity only if the majority of Canadian producers of the commodity— eggs, for example—are in favor of doing so. The marketing legislation applies to all farm products which, in interprovincial and export trade, are not covered under the Canadian Wheat Board Act and the Canadian Dairy Commission Act. The Marketing Council will oversee the establishment and operation of national marketing agencies.

---

[7]Assuming you did not set the price so high that the wholesalers could import fruit cheaper than $1.25. If you are wise, you have got your MP to persuade the government to ban the import of fruit during your marketing season. Even then, the wholesaler may bring fruit from a distant region of Canada. Finally, your $1.25 may be so high that he refuses, knowing that customers will buy little fruit at retail after he has added his costs to your price. That is, he knows the final market demand is very elastic. (Try drawing a diagram, adding the wholesaler's $1.00 costs to the various wholesale prices.)

that each member gets a high price on *some* of his fruit, but the rest of it must be stored for next year, sold for low-value uses (juice, jam, animal feed), or destroyed. You can guess how the typical member will respond: he'll withdraw from the co-op, and take his fruit to the old dealer who will buy his whole crop at a price just below the $1.25 you've set. Other members will do this too and, unless you take action, the whole market will settle down, gradually, to the old $1.00 price; and your co-op will have few members.

5. How can you prevent this erosion of the monopoly price you've managed to set? Early organizers tried evangelism for voluntary cooperation. Everyone must stick by the cooperative selling agency. Growers must pledge, in writing, to deliver all their fruit to the co-op. When this failed, they turned to the government.

6. The government, usually provincial, is helpful. It has a Marketing Board Act designed to convert your group into a monopoly. The government will conduct a vote among all the producers in the area. If a specified majority agree, a board will be formed, made up mostly of farmers in the region. When set up, they have authority to control the marketing of *all* the produce in the region. They are not co-ops, and may allow the produce to flow through both co-ops and private-dealer channels. But they will at least conduct a sort of "collective bargaining" with city buyers on terms, prices, and grades of produce. If they are more ambitious, like the pioneering Okanagan apple growers, they will make vigorous attempts to control wholesale price, not only by bargaining, but by holding produce off the market in storage. And they will undertake retail advertising to broaden the market (shift the demand curve to the right).

7. You may even want to follow the Ontario tobacco growers, whose marketing board sets maximum production quotas for its members. If you can't get the farmers in your region to agree to go that far, you may at least follow some of the milk boards, who set quotas on the amount they'll accept from each member for the "fluid-milk" market. Many farmers in their regions have no quotas, and so can sell no fluid milk at all. (They can sell milk at lower prices to cheese factories, skim-milk plants, and ice-cream dairies.)

Marketing boards are more pervasive than people realize. There are about 100 of them now, controlling about one-half of the agricultural trade in Canada. Obviously, they are most successful when the producers for a certain commodity are grouped together in one region, within one province, so that they can organize themselves completely. Note that, with the exception of tobacco and some dairy boards, they do not control the amount *produced*. They attempt instead to bring about "orderly marketing" of whatever Q their members deliver. The role of the government is chiefly to set up the mechanism and declare it to be legal. Otherwise, it would be a "combination in restraint of trade", preventing individual producers from trading at whatever price, with whatever buyer, they choose.[8]

PRICE SUPPORTS

When most people speak of government aid to farming, they either confuse the grain marketing boards with some sort of government financial subsidy, or talk about price-support programs. These are very prevalent in the United States, affecting an enormous number of farmers, especially wealthy and efficient farmers. The general philosophy is clear enough. The years 1909-1914 are looked back upon as the golden age of agriculture. So over the years the U.S. government has been pressed to somehow make prices as relatively favorable as they were then.

Figure 21-1 shows how Canadian Farmers have sold their produce for prices that since 1949 have risen less rapidly than the prices farmers, and their wives, have had to pay. If one pays attention only to the ratio of these two price indexes, one can of course make a strong case that farmers are being ill-treated by the economic system. "Parity" in the treatment of farm and nonfarm prices requires that farm prices be boosted to a higher level.

But deeper analysis shows that the attempt to peg farm prices at an arbitrary high level will result in an

---

[8] Actually, few members of marketing boards make large or any profits. Why? First, boards are rarely set up until market prices have fallen well below profitable levels for most producers in the regions. Second, if a monopoly profit is made and distributed, new producers flock in until it is dissipated in new capacity. The boards with quotas (tobacco and milk) try to prevent this by restricting the amount (Q) they will accept; their most efficient members do make some profit.

avalanche of surplus farm goods, and it has done so in every country that has supported prices. (Show the gap between the $s's'$ and $d'd'$ of Fig. 21-2 at prices kept higher than E', and show how that gap will grow over time.) The dollar costs of aid become astronomical. The distortions of production become cumulatively greater and greater. Thus the government storage bins are bursting, and policy-makers' time is spent working out new schemes to store the produce in emergency granaries, or on the farm, or give it away (preferably abroad, where it will not take some of the market and shift the demand curve to the left).

Compared to wasteful U.S. price-support programs, Canadian farm price-supports are pretty modest. But the same principles are involved, and occasionally for certain products, the government has been caught in the same trap. So, although Canadian agriculture is *not* dominated by the U.S. parity system (nor by another U.K. price-escalation system), it is worth examining details of price-support programs.

We have already seen the real reason for the failure of farm prices to keep up with other prices.[9] Technical progress has simply been more rapid on the farm than in town. A recent study by L. Auer of the Economic Council of Canada has been summarized thus:[10]

"Labour productivity in Canadian agriculture has advanced over the past two decades at nearly 6 per cent per year ... Over one-third of this gain has been associated with the movement of workers out of agriculture.[11] Another third is attributable to increased capital and materials inputs, and the balance to other productivity improvements (such as new varieties of crops and new farming techniques)."

[9] The discussion refers to the ability of Canadian farms to supply more and more food at the old real costs. In addition, it must always be remembered that Canada sells on international food markets. Each foreign competing supplier is also getting increases in productivity. And, for many products, there is an increasing number of competing countries.

[10] L. Auer, *Canadian Agricultural Productivity*, Staff Study No. 24, Economic Council of Canada, December 1969 (Queen's Printer, Ottawa, 1970), p. 39. Reproduced with the permission of Information Canada.

[11] The significance of this movement is explained on page 29 of the same publication from which the above quotation was taken. The explanation given is the following: "The most significant contribution to growth in labour productivity has come through adjustments in agricultural employment. Today, compared with two decades ago, a substantially greater output is produced by

City production of manufactured goods has also shown some improvements in efficiency, but nothing like this. So why in the world should city and farm items swap in a constant "parity" ratio? If they did, the falling, relative real costs of farm products would create huge profits from increasing farm production, and the city would be swamped by extra food supplies. But, as Figure 21-1 shows, they didn't. The growing relative efficiency of farm production led to a fall in farm prices, which is what champions of farm price-support programs want to prevent.

The Agricultural Prices Support Act was passed in 1944, to help farmers adjust from the war to peace-time economies. In 1958 it was superseded by the act that established today's Agricultural Stabilization Board, or ASB.

For a list of nine commodities (three meats; three nonprairie grains; and butter, cheese, and eggs) the ASB is required to support the price. At what level? Not at the 1914 parity-ratio level, but at least at 80 per cent of the average price each has sold at over the previous ten years.

The ASB may also, on instruction, support other prices at any percentage of this ten-year base that the Cabinet decides. Over the years, fourteen commodities have appeared at one time or another on the ASB's noncompulsory, cabinet-decided list.

The ASB was given a fund of 250 million dollars to work with in 1958. In the early 1970s it was spending about 120 million dollars per year, mostly in two types of price support: government purchase of selected products, and government deficiency payments to producers of other products. These are explained below.

FORMS OF INTERVENTION IN FARM PRICING

What are the economic mechanisms by which the government can help, or seem to help, the farmer? We have seen that the marketing schemes now in effect require government permission, because they do what combinations of producers in other industries

substantially fewer farmers. As older farmers have retired and many of the younger farm people have found employment in the nonagricultural sector, some of the marginal farm land has been abandoned or has reverted to forest land and some of the better farm land has been absorbed into larger farm units. Through further mechanization, the enlarged farm units could often be operated without additional farm labour."

are forbidden to do: they join together to attempt to fix prices. We have also seen that price-support programs exist, in which the government makes a direct subsidy transfer to the growers of certain crops. Altogether, there are five types of cases:

1. Outright *gift* or relief payments, given to needy farmers who have established their need and misery.

2. Government programs that aim to increase the demand for farm products or cut their real costs of production.

3. Marketing-board programs that aim to cut the amount supplied and so raise price (i.e. to cut by the use of quotas or by limiting the acreage planted, the amount delivered to the board, or to cut the amount offered by the board to the market by getting rid of or storing part of what has been delivered to it).

4. Price supports that involve the government's buying, storing and reselling the product.

5. Price supports that require the government to make up the "deficiency" in prices, but not to buy or hold the produce. In the United States, this type of action is named after Secretaries of Agriculture Benson and Brannan.

Case 1. Gifts and relief. There is nothing complicated about outright gifts or transfer payments, which might well be adjoined to our social security system or be part of Chapter 40's negative income tax. The organized farm pressure groups do not particularly want such aids, even though in strictest economic logic they may be the most defensible of all: If our nation wants to alleviate the burden on farmers (or the poor anywhere!) and provide minimum standards, outright gifts will clarify exactly what is involved and what it costs, thereby enabling the electorate to decide rationally what it wants to accomplish.

The dislike of farm pressure groups for gift or relief programs is not surprising, for the successful farmers who tend to constitute the pressure groups number less than one-eighth of all farmers but produce more than one-third of the value of farm output! On the other end of the ladder, almost two-thirds of the farmers sell less than $10,000 worth of produce a year and produce less than one-third of the amount of all crops sold each year. Most of them are in poverty; those who are not too old work much of the year off the farm at other jobs. A large number of programs reach out to help these people. But the current belief is that the long-run solution to the rural poverty problem is not in crop support programs. (The crops of poor farmers are too small to draw much subsidy.) Rather, the solution lies in farm renewal and farmer resettlement (discussed later, see page 388).

Case 2. Demand promotion and research. After the post office and national defense departments, agriculture is the biggest employer in the federal government. In addition, each province has an agriculture department and one or more colleges of agriculture. Each of these institutions is searching for ways to make farming more profitable or more pleasant. Some of the employees are directly engaged in promoting markets, but most work in labs or directly with farmers, introducing new methods and varieties of produce. The success of the Department's science service in developing rust-resistant wheat is well-known; and similar services are provided for other crops.

Farms are still small business, and research and promotion for such firms can hardly be expected to be conducted by the farmers themselves. True, some new processes, fertilizers, and implements are developed for profit by manufacturers, and explained to the farmers. But the government does the rest. Some observers find it odd that much of government is encouraging reduced production or sales, and financing the evacuation of farms, while another branch is trying to increase productivity.

ECONOMICS OF THREE MAIN PRICE PROGRAMS
To understand the remaining three programs, our economic tools of supply and demand are absolutely necessary. Let us see how each case works.

Case 3. Sales or crop restriction. We have seen how marketing boards attempt to monopolize their local markets for vegetables or dairy products or fruit. The stronger ones, by the use of quotas, actually reduce (or prevent the increase of) production. The rest try to sell all that is delivered, but in a given year they may hold some off the market, storing it or consigning it to a low-price use (such as the milk that is delivered to factories and so does not enter the fluid-milk market).

In our diagrams, the hold-back of produce from the market is seen to be identical in effect to the restriction of production. If farmers sell (or produce) a smaller total Q, they will each receive a higher P. Because the demand for farm products is generally inelastic, limiting Q will actually *raise* the total revenues received by farmers—as the last chapter showed. Of course, consumers will be hurt by a scarcity of goods and by higher prices, just as they would be if a disaster such as a flood or a drought created a scarcity of foodstuffs. And it can be shown that many of the methods used to cut down on Q—such as holding wheat acres down to a quota, but leaving farmers free to use tremendous doses of fertilizer to expand

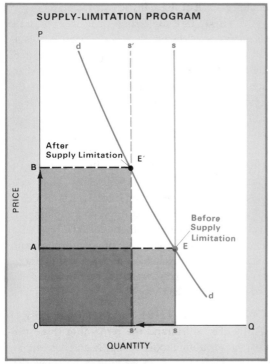

FIG. 21-3. A cut in supply raises price and total revenue
Before government intervenes, the *ss* supply curve intersects the inelastic *dd* curve at the low price shown at E. As an individual competitor, each farmer has no motive to do anything to improve the situation. But if all together can form a marketing board to put monopolistic limits on their total Q, they can benefit.

When controls cut supply from *ss* to *s's'*, P rises to E'. Because demand is inelastic, total gross farm income is thereby increased. (Recall that $P \times Q$ revenues at E and E' are measured, respectively, by the $OsEA$ and $Os'E'B$ rectangular areas. Let your eye confirm that the gain in E' height over E outweighs the rectangle's loss in width; with elastic demand, the reverse would have been true.)

production on the quota land—will lead to inefficient use of resources in producing the reduced Q.

To the extent that some of the benefits from the monopolistically contrived higher prices accrue to poverty-stricken farm families, there may be certain Robin Hood-like social gains to offset the social costs: current farm suffering may be alleviated; and some of the benefit may be used to get the young people out of low-productivity agriculture.

On the other hand, some of the desirable long-run shifts out of agriculture, and economic adjustments, may be slowed down by the sales-restricting boards and programs. Figure 21-3 tells its own story:

If a crop is sold on a market in which the demand is inelastic, reducing the amount offered on the market will bring not only a higher price, but also higher total receipts to farmers.

This is what we learn from supply-and-demand diagrams. What do such higher receipts mean to farming? Low-efficiency farms, which, at the lower price E would have had to turn to other crops or shut down altogether, are able to stay in production. If they had made the "adjustment" (of shutting down or turning to other crops), resources of labor, land, and capital would be reapplied to making or growing other things that society wants. But the higher farm receipts at E' frustrate this adjustment.

In terms of the production-possibility frontier of Fig. 2-3, a sales-reduction program means that society is pushed *inside* the producible frontier. Not only is it getting less of the restricted-sales crop, but it is also not reallocating resources to produce something else.[12] Society is deliberately shifting economic re-

---

[12] Of course, it is not uncommon in North America to restrict acreage and planting, rather than sales after production. When, in addition, farmers restrict supply because they are *paid* not to produce, they gain both ways. Under Operation LIFT, for example, revenue gained from output restriction was $6 per acre for all the acres that formerly yielded the supply between Os and Os' which have now been taken out of production.

Such schemes, whether subsidized or not, have side-effects that may be valuable: Soil conservation may be achieved if land gets a rest. They may also trigger some population exodus from rural regions. But prolonged study has shown that something different happens: the higher prices induce farmers to put the same amount, or even more, of labor or capital on the restricted acreages. Thus their *output does not fall*, though the cost of delivering a certain tonnage of crop usually goes up. They are now using more of society's resources than before, which means that there, too, society is pushed *inside* the production frontier by the acreage-restriction program. (LIFT was supposed to avoid these perils by running for only a year or so.)

sources away from places that produce the extra goods which people's dollar votes in the market place show they really want. Either those resources go into idleness, as occurs with land no longer cultivated, or they may go into secondary uses for which they are ill-fitted and which involve producing items that people do not much want.

Does the raising of farmers' receipts mean that sales restriction is bad? Not necessarily, since noneconomic ethical and political issues are also involved. But going *inside* the production frontier does mean that each bit of benefit to some farmers is bought at the price of a reduction in the output and income of *all* society. This sacrifice is more than economically and technically needed to raise farmers' receipts by a stated amount. It does suggest that society look around for *more efficient* methods.

Case 4. Price support through government purchase. This case, exemplified by our long experience with support of butter prices, is a little harder. Now the ASB guarantees the farmer a price higher than would have prevailed in the market. This "floor price" is shown by the black line *BB'* in Fig. 21-4. At so high a price, consumers will not buy all the butter supplied. Consumers will be on the demand curve at the point *C*. But farmers are supplying the full amount shown by the point *F*. If government does nothing, price must fall to *E*, which is below the support price (80 per cent of the average price in the last ten years).

So what must the ASB do? By outright purchase it must acquire the unsold portion between *C* and *F*, marked with an arrow. This will either go into cold storage, or be dumped abroad (as part of foreign aid perhaps), or (in the case of some types of perishable product) be left to rot. What, then, has been the final result?

The government has increased the price received by farmers from *E* to *F*. But unlike the sales-restriction case, the farmers can now sell as much as they want to; so the increased price is clear gravy to them, representing a clear increase in their incomes. The consumers are now paying a higher price and buying less; to them Case 4 is just as bad as Case 3.[13] Who then is footing the bill for the extra income

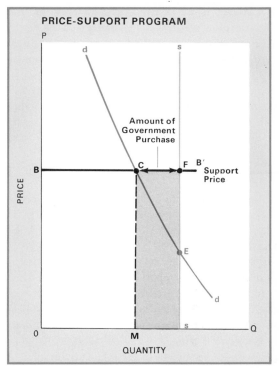

FIG. 21-4. Government purchases support price by acquiring unsold surplus.

Price is kept at the indicated floor or support price *BB'* by the government's stepping in and acquiring for storage unsellable surplus shown by *CF*. The shaded area shows the total cost to the government of raising market price from *E* to *F*. Note that domestic consumers pay the higher price and get no current benefit from the *CF* part of the crop.

now received by the farmers? Obviously the government: The Treasury is having to shell out its tax receipts equal to the part of the butter output they must buy times the full market price. (In terms of area, the Treasury's expense is shown by the shaded area *CFsM*. Can you explain why?)

---

[13] The last two sentences need to be modified. In practice, the ASB and the Dairy Commission can set quotas on the amount of output from each farm for which they will support the price (or

make deficiency payments in Case 5). And, if farmers are allowed to sell as much as they want to at the supported price, they presumably do so efficiently. If so, society is not *inside* its production-possibility curve as it was in Case 3. It is merely too far southeast on it, producing more of the supported crop than dollar votes call for.

Also, in practice, the ASB and its agencies can subsidize dairy products directly. This would be represented by a downward shift of elastic supply curve (not the inelastic supply curve used in the above three cases).

Of course, if the demand curve *dd* were in later years to shift upward so that it intersected the supply curve at F or above, then the treasury would not have to intervene to ensure the supported price. Indeed, it might in such a prosperous year exactly reverse the procedure; instead of buying part of the butter output to put it in cold storage, it might withdraw some from cold storage and sell it. The interested reader can draw a new *d'd'*, to see how stabilization works.

Case 5. "Deficiency" price supports. This is the hardest case of all.

It has been used to support the prices of beets, potatoes, and eggs. Butter and other products, however, have been supported by the programs outlined in Case 4 above.

In a "deficiency-payment" program, the farmer is again guaranteed a support price *BB'*, just as in Case 4. But Fig. 21-5 must now show the new fact that food, instead of being left in storage, is to be resold to the public for current consumption at whatever market price it will bring.

How is the farmer to receive the support price if market price proves to be below that figure? The ASB *simply writes him a cheque for the difference.* In effect, then, it is much as though the government had bought the crop at the support price—as in the support of Case 4—but had then sold it on the open market for whatever price it would bring.

Every bit produced, as shown by the *ss* supply curve, will now go to the consumer. Consumption will end up at the original point *E*. Why? Because the "law of supply and demand" tells us that, for consumers to buy the full crop, price must fall to the point where the demand curve intersects the market supply. But producers are promised the support price for their entire crop. So the price they are to receive is indicated by *F* (just as in Case 4). Who pays the difference? The government—by sending each primary producer a cheque, whose amount per ton is shown in Fig. 21-5 by the vertical arrow *EF*—pays the difference between the producer's and consumer's price *on each and every unit produced!* (In terms of area, the expense to the government is the shaded rectangular area *ABFE*.)

An important but tricky question is the following: Will the "deficiency" plan of Case 5 cost the Treasury more or less than would the plan of having the government withhold

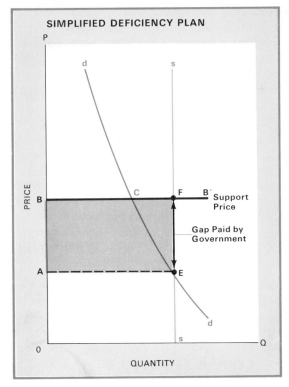

FIG. 21-5. Under "Deficiency" plan, the government pays farmers gap between actual consumer's price and producer's supported price.

Price to consumer is permitted to fall to *E*. It then makes up, by direct payments to farmers of *EF* per ton, the difference between the low market price and the desired support price. Farmers end up with total price return shown at *F*. The shaded area shows the cost to government of the direct payments involved in such a two-price system.

from the consumers part of the crop as outlined in Case 4? The answer to this complicated question turns out to depend upon our old friend the elasticity of demand and upon nothing else.

Look at the problem this way: Under either plan the *producers* are equally well off, being at *F* in both cases and receiving the same total income. Remember, too, that under either plan the producer's revenue can come from only two sources: the total revenue paid by the consumers plus the government's contribution. Hence, to answer the question, "Which plan costs the government more dollars?" we need only to answer the much simpler question, "Which plan collects the greater total revenue from consumers: the plan where the consumers pay a high price and buy little or the plan where consumers pay a low price and buy much?"

But note: this is nothing but the question we have met repeatedly in connection with the definition of elasticity. A point high upon the demand curve, such as *C*, will collect more total revenue than a point low down, such as *E*, provided the demand is *inelastic* in that interval. If demand were *elastic*, then the reverse would be true.

So now we can answer the question of relative cost as follows: The "deficiency" plan of making more food available to consumers will currently cost the Treasury more money than will a purchase-for-storage-or-destruction program provided the demand curve is *inelastic*. If it has been *elastic*, the reverse would have been true. (Of course, wasteful storage costs militate against Case 4.)

From the standpoint of political economy, a plan which brings price to the consumer more nearly down to the social cost of producing food would have much to be said for it even if it should happen to result in costing the Treasury more money. If farmers are to get the same income by one way or the other, the important thing to us consumers is not so much how we divide our payments between market purchases and taxes as that food be produced and consumed up to the point where utilities and costs are more nearly in balance.[14]

ISSUES IN FARM AID

Roughly speaking, the history of Canadian farm policy has been a movement through these three cases. But not in exact sequence: at the present time much of the farm output is still under marketing boards (Case 3), while there is an increasing tendency to help farmers by "deficiency" payments (Case 5). The prolonged butter surplus (Case 4) made housewives aware that they paid more for this fat than for the competing margarine at a time when butter stocks were glutting the cold-storage warehouses, being dumped abroad, or being processed down into low-value butter oil, for sale to industry. This made the scheme unpopular. Once the subsidy was explicit, farmers also became critical. And foreign butter pro-

ducers, sometimes observing that Canada was dumping subsidized butter in their markets, became very unfriendly.

Canada had, until February 1970, avoided acreage-limitation schemes of the type long favored in the United States. However, faced with a record wheat surplus, the government attempted to deal with it by offering western farmers some 140 million dollars to remove from production 22 million acres (which yielded most of the western wheat crop) during 1970. In effect, the farmers are paid *not* to produce. Like the sales-limitation scheme of Case 3, this scheme should tend to raise wheat prices.

In comparison, the marketing board approach is much less effective *potentially*, because most boards have not the power to reduce deliveries to them; but it is perhaps more workable, because the farmers themselves have the responsibility of setting the price and disposing of any unsold surpluses. The fact remains that, to the extent that either the acreage-limitation or the sales-limitation version of Case 3 is effective, it brings increased receipts to farmers by a hidden sales tax on food rather than by glaring subsidy items in the federal budget.

Are the gainers people whom we want to help? Many tough-minded economists would argue that much of the benefit of marketing boards, the Wheat Board, and price-support programs now goes to the most prosperous commercial farmers. Too little filters down to the really poor farmers, who have little production to support. Economists favor programs which extend to farmers in a more efficient way whatever aid it is decided they ought to have—so as to leave the rest of us with more than we now get. Such programs would involve more careful pinpointing of those who merit aid from the standpoint of need—as through a negative income tax.

In such a turnabout there would be three elements: the system of pricing farm produce; the "adjustment" of the agricultural part of society to changing demands; and the aid paid to those who could not adjust without hardship.

PRICING FARM PRODUCTS   There would be more reliance on market forces in determining food and fiber prices. As farm productivity increased or demand failed to grow fast enough, prices would be allowed to fall. Consumers generally would be able to afford more food, and especially more of the ex-

---

[14] If *ss* were drawn more realistically so as to be somewhat rightward-sloping, we should have the evil of too much *Q* being coaxed out by the too-high government subsidy; consumers would be getting too much farm *Q* at a *P* below true social costs of resources used.

pensive protein foods such as milk and meat. Commercial farmers would feel pressure on them to become more efficient, and many of the remaining farm families would find their incomes below what they could earn in industry or in the service occupations.

HELPING FARM "ADJUSTMENT" The price system would thus tend to drive people into new types of farming and off the farm altogether. This is a familiar process: farm boys have been migrating to the cities for decades. The labor force began to fall about 1930, though in the Depression it was easier to keep alive on the land than in the city. After the war, the migration began in earnest. By 1970 the farm labor force was just one-third of what it had been in 1941. Then it had made up one-quarter of the total national labor force, but this fraction has since been reduced to one-sixteenth, or about 450,000 workers. Those remaining on the land have tended to use it more intensively (putting in more machine hours and fertilizers per acre) and more extensively (doubling farm size). This is, of course, one reason why productivity has climbed so fast.

But many persons are unable to "adjust" to these new methods. They have not the youthful flexibility, nor the capital, nor the skill to become successful commercial farmers, no matter how hard they work. Neither have they the adaptability to move away into industry. This is the "adjustment" problem. Left alone, their income drops annually and rural slums develop.

Helping farmers to adjust has recently become a top-priority item on the government's agenda. Since World War I, the government has given advice on new crops and methods, has helped to pay for land clearing and improvement, and has acted as an increasingly liberal lender of farm-improvement capital. In 1961 the Diefenbaker government introduced ARDA (Agricultural Rehabilitation and Development Act), and the succeeding government expanded it, to study, promote, and subsidize better land use, and to strengthen the depopulated rural communities. Perhaps more important, other government programs are coming to grips with the retraining of farm youth and older farmers, some for continued work on the land, and many for the cities. Transport and removal expenses are sometimes of-

fered by Ottawa, and the provinces are spending 30 to 40 million dollars each year on this approach. But much remains to be done, especially for older farm families, or those without education. "Adjustment" may be for them a process of going on the relief roll.

FARM AID Noncommercial farmers who could not adjust would be left behind by a market-determined set of farm prices. In the turnabout of farm policy, they would have to be helped—not so much because they live on the farm, but for the same reason that government welfare aid is given to any families that are in poverty. Economists believe that most farm aid recipients would be over 45 or 50 years of age. In many parts of Canada, they would probably be encouraged to keep their homes and a little land, but to release most of their acreage to neighbors who could consolidate small holdings into workable farm enterprises.

The economists who stress these three elements say:

> The Canadian consumers value food so little relative to its costs and to alternative manufactured goods and services as to make farm prices low. Since only the most efficient farms can make a competitive living, resources should be encouraged to be drawn out of agriculture. Except for subsidies to alleviate and expedite the transition, government should rely on income supports and social security to help the rural poor—helping people not because they are farmers but because they suffer from poverty.[15]

Looked at properly, Canada's real farm problem is that of rural poverty. Real incomes on the farm and in small towns average far below those elsewhere: 840,000 people fell below the poverty line in 1970. Although less than 30 per cent of the population is rural, approximately 40 per cent of the impoverished live in the country. Silently, invisibly, they lead miserable lives in the Maritimes and Quebec, where most of the rural poor are concentrated.

Solutions for them will not come from the mechanisms of supply and demand. The solutions must

---

[15] Refer to page 365 for a graph of the argument that uninterfered-with pricing has a property of being "efficient," even if not necessarily "equitable."

come—as Chapter 39 shows—from transfer-payment programs, from education subsidies, from relocation and retraining, and from family-planning clinics. The mixed economy, and not *laissez-faire*, must provide the solutions.[16]

SUMMARY

1 Although the rural birth rate is higher than the urban, a persistent cityward migration means that the percentage of the population engaged in agriculture is declining. Improvements in agricultural techniques mean that supply increases greatly and that the same total of food can be produced with fewer workers; also, as incomes increase, the demand for food increases less than proportionately.

   So free-equilibrium prices tend to fall. Farm income tends to be both low and unstable; as a result, government adopted a variety of programs to support farm-product prices and maintain farm incomes.

2 Pegging prices at any ancient average ratio, despite its superficial plausibility and fairness, utterly disregards basic changes in demand and real costs of production. As time passes, such a ratio will produce prices differing sharply from "natural competitive" levels here and abroad. The results are huge surpluses, with the wrong goods being produced with growing distortions of efficiency. If we had frozen resource use at the 1800 or 1850 or 1929 rural-urban proportions, poverty would have been perpetuated.

3 Aid programs involving (1) direct gifts or (2) promotion of demand and of cost research require no deep economic analysis. But the tools of supply and demand are needed to understand these three aid programs: (3) sales by marketing boards; (4) government price support by storage programs; (5) resale to consumers at competitive market prices of food bought at a pegged price, with the government footing the bill for the "deficiency." (Hybrids of all three are frequently legislated.) The resulting programs are colossally expensive, economically inefficient, and satisfactory to no groups.

4 Because high and inflexible price support causes storage to grow astronomically and sends the government's aid costs skyward, Case 4 in practice leads to more and more of Case 3. (Farmers like 4 and accept 3 only as a necessary evil; consumers dislike 3 and 4, but like 5.)

5 The long-run solution must involve maintenance of prosperity outside agriculture, so that people can continue to move to the lines of highest productivity and so that demand for agriculture will be optimally high. But mere prosperity in industry is not enough. The 1920s and 1970s show that the city and town can prosper while the country's economic position deteriorates.

   In the long run, resources have to be helped to move out of low-efficiency rural uses and into more productive uses. That means a continuation of the trend toward fewer but more efficient farmers, and a need for short-runs aids to help and speed the adjustment to this trend and to ease its human burdens. It also means flexible pricing practices that permit efficient Canadian farms to help feed the world. And, as Chapter 40 shows, the rural exodus creates urban problems elsewhere.

---

[16] All this will remain for a long time a political issue. No one will begrudge the farmer his desire to be free from wildly fluctuating prices. In the Appendix we shall see how private speculators on an organized exchange are supposed in traditional theory to be able to iron out any *foreseeable* fluctuations. The question remains whether, gifts aside, we can expect the government to make better forecasts of the uncertain future than private speculative market can, and whether we can expect the government, through its various support programs, to be better than private markets in stabilizing prices.

CONCEPTS FOR REVIEW

inelastic farm demand and supply
farm technology and declining
  percentage of income spent
  on food
free-farm-price trends
marketing boards
deficiency payments

Q limitation, P support, direct payments
  with consumer and producer P's
  different
pros and cons of free farm prices
solutions for short-run instability
measures for long-run adjustment
rural poverty and welfare aid

QUESTIONS FOR DISCUSSION

1. Contrast long-term and cyclical patterns of agriculture and industry.
2. Describe government indirect and direct farm aids.
3. Why might limiting a farm's acreage in one crop not reduce the total of it much? How would it affect noncontrolled crops? Fertilizer demand?
4. Use the p-p frontier concept to evaluate harm from farm aid.
5. "Major premise: Society should help poor people. Minor premise (of doubtful validity as stated): Farmers are poor people. (Dubious) Conclusion: Therefore society should help farmers. Actually, if society is to subsidize individuals, it should not be done on the basis of the occupations but because they are *poor*—*i.e.*, aid on an *income basis*." Does this argument by Professor Dudley Johnson fit with the 1969 Task Force on Agriculture's recommended income boosts that are restricted to the poorest and oldest *farmers*?

Appendix: Economics of Speculation, Risk, Insurance, and Conservation

Here we apply the tools of supply and demand to analyze price relations across space and time and the important problems involved in risk, speculation, and gambling. We deal not only with the purchase and sale of actual commodities such as corn or barley, but also with the purchase and sale of something more mysterious—of bits of paper.

These bits of paper are called "commodity futures": they are contracts that brokers deal with on organized commodity exchanges like the Chicago Board of Trade or the Winnipeg Grain Exchange. You and I may buy or sell such commodity futures even though we have never seen any real barley or corn. As speculators in such futures, the last thing in the world we should want to happen would be for a truck to roll up to our door seeking delivery of real honest-to-goodness commodities.

Yet, as we shall see, even though speculators never touch the real thing, they may under certain conditions be helping to even out the consumption of the crop between harvest times and be helping to carry over the proper amount of grain and fiber between seasons.

In his autobiography, the elder statesman Bernard Baruch said that ten years after he heard Professor George B. Newcomb lecture on supply and demand at City College of New York, he had made more than a million dollars from speculation—implying that those lectures may have had something to do with it. Certainly, this Appendix is not designed to make you rich, and if you skip it, your knowledge of the rest of the book need not suffer much. But speculation is a fascinating topic and can serve as an example of important applications of supply and demand. Inevitably, it is a complicated subject which no elementary book can pretend to treat completely.

GEOGRAPHICAL PRICE PATTERNS

In a well-organized competitive market, there tends to be at any one time and place a single prevailing price. This is due to the action of professional speculators or "arbitragers" who keep their ear to the market and, as soon as they learn of any price differences, buy at the cheaper price and sell at the dearer price, thereby making a profit for themselves—at the same time tending to equalize the price.[1]

Two markets at a considerable distance from each other may have different prices. Wheat in Winnipeg may sell for a few cents more per bushel than identical wheat in Reg-

ina, because of shipping, insurance, and interest charges involved in transportation. If ever the price in Winnipeg should rise by more than the few cents of shipping costs, speculators will buy in Regina and ship to Winnipeg, thereby bringing the price up in Regina and down in Winnipeg to the normal maximum differential.

Nobody legislates these patterns. They follow from supply and demand.

SPECULATION AND PRICE CONTROL OVER TIME

In an ideal competitive market there tends to be a definite pattern of prices over time just as there is over space. But the difficulties of predicting the future make this pattern a less perfect one: we have an equilibrium that is constantly being disturbed but is always in the process of reforming itself—rather like the ocean's surface under the play of the winds.

STABILIZING SEASONAL PATTERNS Consider the simplest case of a grain, like barley, that is harvested at one period of the year. This crop must be made to last all the year if privation is to be avoided. Since no one passes a law regulating the storage of grain, how is this desirable state of affairs brought about? Through the attempts of speculators to make a profit.

A well-informed speculator who is a specialist in this grain realizes that, if all the grain is thrown on the market in the autumn, it will fetch a very low price because of the glutting of the market. On the other hand, months later, with almost no grain coming on the market, price will tend to skyrocket.

The above description tells what would tend to happen were it not for the action of speculators. Speculators realize that by (1) purchasing some of the autumn crop while it is cheap, (2) withholding it in storage; and (3) selling it later when the price has risen, they can make a profit. This they do. But in doing so, they increase the autumn demand for grain and raise its autumn price; and they increase the spring supply of grain and lower its spring price. At the same time that they are equalizing the price over the year, they are also equalizing the supply coming on the market in each month—which is as it should be.

Moreover, if there is brisk competition among speculators, none will make an excessive profit over the costs that he incurs (including of course the wages necessary to keep him in this line of activity). The speculator himself may never touch an ear of barley, nor need he know anything about storage, warehouses, or delivery. He merely buys and sells bits of paper. But the effect is exactly as described.

Now there is one and only one monthly price pattern that will result in neither profits nor losses. A little thought

[1]On the floor of the Winnipeg Grain Exchange, the important market for grain, a number of important "pit brokers," or dealers, are said to make all their profits on price changes within each day, closing out all their transactions every night and sleeping peacefully until the next day. "Pit scalpers" on the floor of the Chicago Board of Trade, and specialists at the New York Stock Exchange ～t similarly.

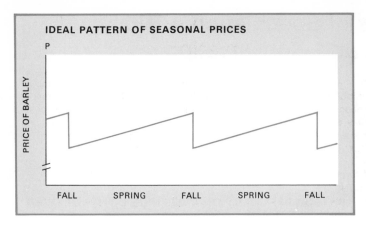

IDEAL PATTERN OF SEASONAL PRICES

PRICE OF BARLEY

P

FALL   SPRING   FALL   SPRING   FALL

FIG. 21-6. For a good to be stored, expected price rise must match storing cost.
Ideally, P is lowest at harvest time, rising gently with accumulated storage costs until the next harvest. This flexible pattern tends to even out consumption over the seasons—as compared with a harvest glut with very low autumn price and summer scarcity with sky-high price.

will show that it will not be a pattern of constant prices. Rather, the ideal price pattern will involve lowest prices in the autumn and then gradually rising prices until the peak is reached just before the new corn comes in. The price must rise from month to month to compensate for the storage and interest costs of carrying the crop in storage —in exactly the same way that the price must rise over space from one mile to the next to compensate for the cost of transportation.[2] Figure 21-6 shows the behavior of prices over an idealized yearly cycle.

STABILIZING FORESEEABLE FLUCTUATIONS Not all fluctuations in activity can be so accurately forecast as the seasonal harvesting of a crop. No one can predict with confidence next year's weather or the likelihood of a recession in the near future. But to the extent that speculators can form any accurate guesses today about the future *scarcity* of a commodity, they will tend to buy it now for *future* delivery, thereby causing (1) a withdrawal of present supply, (2) an increase of present price, (3) an increase in amount stored, (4) an increase in future supply, (5) a reduction in future price—or in all a relative stabilization of price and consumption over time.

The reader should try to visualize the opposite process by which speculators stabilize prices when they correctly foresee an exceptionally large future crop and a low future price: how they then begin to "sell short"[3] for future delivery, tending to depress current prices, raise consumption, and reduce carry-over of stocks.

[2] Do I, as a warehouse storer, need a crystal ball to tell me price will rise enough to pay me to store corn today? No. The market today will quote me a future price—for delivery of corn some months hence—and when this future price sufficiently exceeds the current spot price for physical corn, I get the signal to store corn.

[3] There is nothing mysterious about selling short. I simply put in an order to my broker in which I agree in return for a certain price *now*, to deliver *at some later date* an amount of grain. Usually, at the time of putting in the order, I do not have the grain on hand. But I legally fulfill my contract by later "covering," i.e., buying the grain and making delivery. If I later have to pay a higher price in covering than I now receive when selling short, then I take a loss. But if I have guessed right and prices do fall in the intervening period, then I "buy in" for less than I have sold and make a profit.

SPREADING OF RISKS Aside from their possible influence toward stabilizing prices, speculators have another important function. By being willing to take risks on their own shoulders, they enable others to avoid risk.

For example, a warehouse owner must carry large inventories of grain in the course of his business. If the price of grain goes up, he makes a windfall capital gain; if down, he incurs a windfall loss. But let us suppose that he is content to earn his living by storing grain and wishes to forgo all risk taking. This he can do by a process called "hedging." This complicated procedure is rather like a man who bets on the East to win the Grey Cup and then washes out this transaction, or covers it, by placing an equal bet on the West. Whichever side wins, he comes out the same, his left hand winning what his right hand loses.

To get a notion of how the complicated process of hedging works out, here is a highly simplified example. Suppose I am buying and storing barley in the late fall. I am a specialist in running a warehouse and wish to stick to my job rather than become involved in the risky business of taking speculative bets as to whether the price of barley will go up between now and the next spring when I expect to stop storing barley and to sell it. In effect, I should really like to sell it now for an agreed-upon price that will compensate me for my 9-cent-per-bushel storage expenses between now and later delivery time. If a speculative market exists, that is precisely what I can do by the device of hedging.

How do I hedge? For each 5,000 bushels of barley I buy in November to put into storage until next May, let us suppose I have to pay $1.24 a bushel to local Manitoba farmers. I look up the price quoted today, November 30, on the Winnipeg Grain Exchange for next May barley futures and see that this quotation is $1.33. I realize that this 9-cent ex-

Selling short in the stock market works out similarly, except that I am free to cover and make future delivery of the stock at any time I please. Meanwhile the man who has bought the stock receives his stock shares. How? As a result of the fact that my broker, obligingly, lends me the stock certificates to make delivery. Later, when I cover, I buy in some stock and turn over the certificates to my obliging broker.

cess over today's price will give me a fair return for my expenses of storage and that is why I am glad to store. I now hedge by *selling* a 5,000-bushel May-barley future contract. (The brokerage commission on this "short sale" transaction will be less than 1/2 cent per bushel; my broker will require that I put up less than 10 cents per bushel as "margin" to ensure that I will fulfill my contractual obligation, and he will neither know or care whether I actually have some physical barley with which I might make later delivery.)

Now I am hedged. I happen to own 5,000 bushels of physical barley in storage. I also have sold 5,000 bushels of May barley futures. What will happen if slack barley demand and a tremendous winter wheat crop cause the price of barley to fall to $1.14 by next May?

My brother, who owns a warehouse and bought barley in the fall as I did *but did not hedge*, will now lose 10 cents per bushel. Indeed, he is worse off than that, because he is also out the 9 cents that it costs him to keep his warehouse going (watchmen's pay, and so forth). So he has really lost 19 cents per bushel *in toto*.

What about me, the cagy hedger? I do lose 10 cents a bushel *on my physical barley* because of the unforeseen change in price. But when, as May arrives, I look in the paper for the Grain Exchange quotation on my May future, I am relieved to see that it has fallen from $1.33 all the way down to $1.14—at which price I buy in, or "cover," my futures. Thus, *on short sale of my futures* I have gained 19 cents, or exactly as much as I (and my brother) have lost *in toto* on the sale of physical barley. *The hedge has protected me from all price fluctuations:* my left futures pocket has gained what my right physical-barley pocket lost. The speculator who made my hedge possible took price risks off my shoulders.[4]

To the extent that speculators forecast accurately, they provide a definite social service. To the extent that they forecast badly, they tend to aggravate the variability of prices. Were it not for the detailed statistical information provided by the Department of Agriculture and private agencies, the traders of the Winnipeg Grain Exchange would find themselves at the mercy of every idle rumor, hope, and fear. For speculation is often a mass contagion, like the inexplicable dancing crazes that swept medieval villages, the Dutch tulip mania that sent the price of a single bulb higher than that of a house, the South Sea Bubble in which companies sold stock at fabulous prices for enterprises which would "later be revealed."

GAMBLING AND DIMINISHING MARGINAL UTILITY[5]

The defenders of speculation resent the charge that it represents simply another form of gambling, like betting on the horse races or buying a lottery ticket. They emphasize that an uncertain world necessarily involves risk and that *someone* must bear risks. They claim that the knowledge and the venturesomeness of the speculator are chained to a *socially useful purpose*, thereby reducing fluctuations and risks to others. (We have just seen that this is not always the case and that speculation may indeed be destabilizing; but certainly, no one can deny all validity to the above claims.)

Why is gambling considered such a bad thing? Part of the reason, perhaps the most important part lies in the field of morals, ethics, and religion; upon these the economist is not qualified to pass exact judgment. There is, however, a substantial economic case to be made against gambling.

First, it involves simply *sterile transfers of money or goods* between individuals, creating no new money or goods.[6] Although it creates no output, gambling does nevertheless absorb time and resources. When pursued beyond the limits of recreation, where the main purpose after all is to "kill" time, gambling subtracts from the national income.

The second economic disadvantage of gambling is the fact that it tends to promote *inequality and instability of incomes*. People who sit down to the gambling table with the same amount of money go away with widely different amounts. A gambler (and his family) must expect to be on the top of the world one day, and when luck changes—which we have seen to be the only predictable thing about it—he may almost starve.

LAW OF DIMINISHING MARGINAL UTILITY AND CHANCE But why is inequality of income over time and between persons considered such a bad thing? One an-

---

[4]To check your understanding, work through the case where a war sends up the price of physical barley in the May markets to, say, $1.43. Now my unhedged brother, in addition to his 9-cent return as a warehouseman, makes an additional windfall risk profit of 10 cents per bushel. What about me? On my physical barley which I bought at $1.24 and sell for $1.43, I gain; but I lose 10 cents on having to buy in my May futures at 10 cents more than I sold it for. So I end up making my 9-cent warehouse return and no more—regardless of what can happen to barley price fluctuations.

Actual hedging of millers, farmers, and storers can become more complicated. Also, it could happen that, in order to coax out speculators, the quotation in November of the May future would on the average have to sell for a little less than the $1.33 such physical barley can be expected to sell for in May; this means that the risk-bearing speculators require a premium for the insurance-like risk they are providing—a premium that, like any other cost, must be borne by producers and ultimate consumers.

[5]This discussion provides an alternative introduction to the theory of marginal utility which is picked up in orthodox fashion on page 400.

[6]Actually, in all professional gambling arrangements, the participants lose out on balance. The leakage comes from the fact that the odds are always rigged in favor of the "house," so that even an "honest" house will win in the long run. Moderate gambling among friends may be considered as a form of consumption or recreation activity whose cost to the group as a whole is zero. Oddly, some people who do not trust their ability to save do use steady purchase of "numbers" tickets as a way to cut down on current consumption and put themselves in the position of occasionally accumulating larger sums of money. In some past and present societies, the enhancement of inequality of income distribution by gambling may have made a roundabout contribution to social thrift and capital formation.

swer is to be found in the widely held belief that the gain in utility achieved by an *extra* $1,000 of income is not so great as the loss in utility of forgoing $1,000 of income. Where that is the case, a bet at fair odds involves an economic loss: the money you stand to win balances the money you may lose; but the satisfaction you stand to win is *less* than the satisfaction you stand to lose.

Similarly, if it could be assumed that individuals are all "roughly the same" and are ethically comparable, so that their utilities can be added, then the dollars gained by the rich do not create as much "social welfare" or total utility as the dollars lost by the poor. This has been used not only as a criticism of gambling, but as a positive argument in favor of "progressive" taxation aimed at lowering the inequality of the distribution of income. The issue of incentives must also enter into forming any decision on policy, since discussions elsewhere show that redistributing the national pie may lessen its total.

Just as Malthus saw the law of diminishing returns as underlying his theory of population, so is the "law of diminishing marginal utility" used by many economists to condemn professional gambling. According to this theory, as money income increases, each new dollar adds something to utility, but less and less. Similarly, each extra unit of any good that can be bought with money contributes less and less satisfaction or utility. When we get as much of a good as we wish (e.g., air), it becomes a "free good" because still further units add nothing new to our utility.[7]

WHY IDEAL STABILIZATION BY SPECULATORS IS OPTIMAL

We can now use the tools of marginal utility to show how ideal speculation would maximize total utility over time. Suppose every consumer has a utility schedule that holds for each year independently of any other year. Now suppose that in the first of two years there was a big crop—say, 3 units per person—and in the second a small crop of only 1 unit per person. If this crop deficiency could be foreseen, how should the consumption of the two-year 4-unit total be spread over the two years?

If we agree, for simplicity, to neglect all storage, interest, and insurance charges and all questions of utility

commensurability over time, we can prove *that total utility for the two years together will be maximized only if consumption is equal in each year.*

Why is uniform consumption better than any other division of the available total? Because of the law of diminishing marginal utility. Here is the reasoning:

Suppose I consume more in the first year than in the second. My last unit's marginal utility will then be low in the first year and high in the second. So if I carry some crop from the first to the second year, I shall be switching from low to high marginal utilities—and that will maximize my total utility.

But is not that exactly what the following ideal speculation pattern would accomplish?

If speculators can neglect interest, storage, and insurance charges and happen to forecast accurately next year's low crop, what will they do? They will figure it pays to carry goods over from this year's low price resulting from the high crop, hoping instead to sell at next year's scarcity price. But as each speculator subtracts from this year's supply and adds to next year's, what must finally happen? Equilibrium can be reached only when the two prices have been equalized! Then there will be no further incentive to carry over more crop.[8] (Of course, a small payment for the speculator's effort might have to be included—but we have agreed to waive all costs just to keep the example simple.)

Do not for a moment get the impression that real flesh-and-blood speculators can guess the future infallibly. They often make mistakes and often are prey to rumors and mass enthusiasms. So the process is not as ideal as here pictured. Still, to the degree that speculators can intelligently foresee the future—and those who have a terrible batting average may get eliminated fast as their capital is lost—they (and for that matter, *farsighted* government agencies, too) may help to provide a useful stabilizing function.

ECONOMICS OF CONSERVATION

These remarks on the social usefulness of speculation apply also to the market in natural resources. Commodity speculation rarely stretches into the future for more than a year, whereas decisions about whether to hold or use minerals, trees, and oil involve decades or centuries; but the theory is the same.

---

[7]The astute reader will note (1) that economics proves that those subject to diminishing marginal utility should not gamble and should insure, but that a man with *increasing* marginal utility will maximize his expected utility by gambling and by noninsuring; and (2) that any economist who uses observations on a person's reaction to situations involving probabilities as his test of how marginal utility varies for that person may end up with the following circular reasoning: those who gamble should gamble; those who insure should insure. So the case for prohibiting gambling must rest on extraneous ethical or religious grounds; or must be withdrawn; or must be based on the notion that society knows better than individuals what is truly good for them; or must be based on the notion that we are all imperfect beings who wish in the long run that we were not free to yield to short-run temptations. Some political economists feel that moderate gambling might be converted into socially useful channels.

[8]A graph can illuminate this argument. If utility could be measured in dollars, with each dollar always denoting the same marginal utility, the demand curves would look just like the marginal utility schedule of page 000. The two curves of Fig. 21-7 show what would happen if there were no carryover—with price first determined at A_1, where s_1s_1 intersects dd, and second at A_2, where the lower supply s_2s_2 intersects dd. Total utility of the shaded areas would add up only to $(4 + 3 + 2) + 4$, or $13 per head. But with optimal carryover to the second year of 1 unit by speculators, P's and Q's will be equalized at E_1 and E_2, and now the total utility of the gray areas will add up to $(4 + 3) + (4 + 3)$, or $14 per head. (Show that the gain in utility of $1 is measured by the light block, which represents the excess of the second unit's marginal utility over the third unit's marginal utility; one can show that equality of marginal utilities is optimal.)

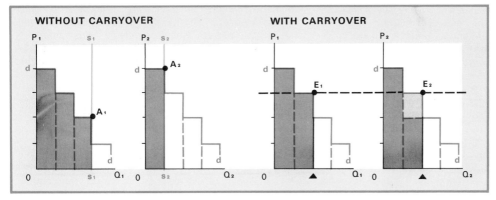

FIG. 21-7. The dark gray areas measure total utility enjoyed each year. Carrying one unit to the second year equalizes Q and also P, and increases total utility by the amount of the light gray block.

To simplify the idea of conservation, suppose many owners of potential iron mines are trying to decide whether to exploit their properties this year, or whether to hold back (either by mining slowly or simply by sitting on their undeveloped ores). The answer of the Conservation movement used to be: "Hold back. We are using up our resources too fast. None will be left for future generations. Society should restrain mineral owners from profiting today at the expense of the future."

This particular plea is rarely heard from Conservationists today, because it was based on a misunderstanding of how to make a maximum profit from holding a stock of anything, barley or ore. Leaving aside many complications (chiefly of the impact of the rate of interest, which we will encounter in Chapter 30), the Conservationists were wrong not about the ethics of considering the needs of later years, but in their belief that today's owner disregards them.

Imagine that you are an owner, and that you know what the Conservationists suggest: that other owners are profiting by selling today, and that there will be a serious scarcity in the future. How will you react? Just as the warehouseman did on page 392: hold your supply off today's market; allow today's price to rise; increase the amount of ore stored (in "reserves"); reduce the *future* scarcity of ore. Why? Because if you and the Conservationists are right about the future scarcity, mineral prices will be high then, and you can make a greater profit from your tons of ore reserves then than you can at today's prices. And other ore-property owners will also hold back (if their studies also suggest future scarcity). If all owners agree on the future scarcity, all will tend to hold back until present price rises and expected future price and scarcity fall sufficiently to (1) balance production and (2) equalize prices and profits, in the two periods.

Clearly, this is Conservation through the market. And just as clearly, it is an application of the theory of specu-

lation and price behaviour through time. And, just as in speculation, gambling is likely to enter, resulting in either too much or too little being allocated to future use. Another similarity is in the uncertainty of future supplies: huge new discoveries of your mineral may be made before the future date arrives, thus depressing the price and wiping out your expected profit. Uncertainty about the likelihood of such discoveries affects different owners differently ways: some like to take a chance, others like to make hay while the sun shines, even if it means forgoing a probable larger future profit.

Of course, Conservationists don't know any more about the future than owners in the industry. Society has to accept the future supplies based on a guess made by *someone*. In the price system, the guess is made by thousands of owners who, studying reported reserves and forecasts of consumption, stand to make the most profits from their own ores by making correct guesses.

ECONOMICS OF INSURANCE

We are now in a position to see why insurance, which appears to be just another form of gambling, actually has exactly opposite effects. For the same reasons that gambling is bad, insurance is economically advantageous. Whereas gambling creates risks, insurance helps to lessen and spread risks.

In buying fire insurance on his house, the owner seems to be betting with the insurance company that his house will burn down. If it does not—and the odds are heavily in favor of its not burning—the owner forfeits the small premium charge. If it does burn down, the company must reimburse the owner to the tune of the agreed-upon loss. (For the obvious reason of removing temptation from hard-up home owners who like fire engines and excitement, the face value of the policy tends to be something less than the money value of the property insured.)

What is true of fire insurance is equally true of life, accident, automobile, or any other kind of insurance. Actually, at the famous Lloyd's of London, which is a place for insurance brokers to come together, you can arrange to insure a ball team or vacationer against rain, dancers against infantile paralysis, *and* a hotel keeper against a damage suit from the widow of a man killed in a fight with another man who bought a drink in the hotel's cocktail lounge; and you can get numerous other bizarre policies. But by the common law, Lloyd's may refuse to bet $10,000 with me that it will not snow on Christmas, since I do not have an "insurable interest" of that amount and the bet would be unenforceable in the courts. But a ski-resort owner, who stands to lose that much if it does not snow, would have such an insurable interest and could certainly buy such a policy. Economic theory shows that the difference between these two cases is that insuring the resort owner *stabilizes* income while insuring me *destabilizes* it.

The insurance company is not gambling, because what is unpredictable and subject to chance *for the individual* is highly predictable and uniform *in the mass*. Whether John C. Smith, age twenty and in good health, will live for 30 more years is a matter of chance, but the famous *law of large numbers* guarantees that out of 100,000-odd twenty-year-olds in good health, only a definite proportion will still be alive at the end of such a period of time. The life-insurance company can easily set a premium at which it will not lose money. Certainly, therefore, the company is not gambling.

What about the buyer of insurance? Is he gambling? The reverse can be shown to be true: the man who does not insure his house is doing the gambling. He is risking the whole value of his house against the small premium saved. If his house does not burn down in any year, he has won his bet; if it does, as occasionally must happen, he loses his bet and incurs a tremendous penalty.

At this point, a sporting man will say, "So what? Of course, a man gambles when he doesn't buy insurance. But the odds on such a bet are not unfavorable. In fact, they are favorable, because we know that the insurance company is not in business for its health. It must keep records, it must support insurance salesmen, and so forth. All this costs money and must be 'loaded' onto the insurance premium, detracting from the perfect mathematical odds of the buyer and making the odds for the nonbuyer a little better."

To which a rational man will reply: "When I am among friends, I don't mind a small game of chance for relaxation even at slightly unfavorable odds. But when a big bet is involved, even if the odds are favorable, then I pass. I insure my house because I hardly miss the premium each year: but if it burned down without being covered, I'd feel the loss an awful lot. When I insure, my living standards over time and my income remain the same, come what may. When I don't insure, I may be up for a while, but I risk going way down."

Obviously, the law of diminishing marginal utility—which makes the satisfaction from wins less important

than the privation from losses—is one way of justifying the above reasoning.[9] *This law of diminishing marginal utility tells us that a steady income, equitably divided among individuals instead of arbitrarily apportioned between the lucky and unlucky people whose house did or did not burn down, is economically advantageous.* (Also, when a family chooses to buy hospital and medical insurance, it may express the belief that this will be relatively painless forced "saving against a rainy day." This self-imposed "compulsory-saving" feature is another benefit of insurance.)

Quite a few nations and several provinces have been helping pay for government and relieving the tax burden by introducing official lotteries and even off-track betting. The cynical notion here is that one might as well channel private vices to the public good. Also, there is the realistic consideration that law enforcement to rule out illegal gambling may be quite imperfect: legal gambling may be a way of checking organized crime.

WHAT CAN BE INSURED

Undoubtedly, insurance is a highly important way of spreading risks. Why, then, can we not insure ourselves against all the risks of life? The answer lies in the indisputable fact that certain definite mathematical conditions are necessary before sufficiently exact actuarial probabilities can be determined.

First, we must have a *large number of events*. Only then will a pooling of risks and a "cancellation" and "averaging of extremes" be possible. The bank at Monte Carlo knows there is safety in numbers. The lucky streak of an Arabian prince one night will be canceled by his next night's losings or by the losings of a fake Balkan countess. Once in a blue moon someone may "break the bank"; but in a few more lunar cycles the "house" will more than break even.

But large numbers are not enough. No prudent fire-insurance company would confine itself to the island of Montreal even though there are thousands of buildings there. *The uncertain events must be relatively independent.* Each throw of the dice, each chance loss by fire, should stand relatively by itself. Obviously, a disaster like the Halifax explosion in 1917, or the San Francisco earthquake, would subject all the buildings in the same locality to the same risk. The company would be making a bet on *one* event, not on thousands of independent events. Instead, it must diversify its risks. Private companies cannot, without government aid, bear the risks of nuclear-bomb insurance. Nor is it possible to buy unemployment insurance from a private company. Depressions are great

---

[9]Figure 21-7 of this Appendix can show all this. Change the titles "Without Carryover" and "With Carryover" to "Without Insurance" and "With Insurance" to see the gain in utility from insuring. Then, to prove the loss from gambling, relabel the left-hand figure "After Gambling" and the right-hand one "Before Gambling." To illustrate that equal incomes maximize the sum of utility of two ethically commensurable people relabel Fig. 21-7 again to read "Before Redistribution" and "After Redistribution."

plagues which hit all sections and all classes at one and the same time, with a probability that cannot be computed in advance with any precision. Therefore only the government, whose business it is to take losses, can assume the responsibility of providing unemployment compensation.

There still remain, and probably always will, numerous risks of personal and business life. No one can insure the success of a new beauty shop, a new mousetrap, or a hopeful opera singer. Without error there cannot be trial; and without trial there cannot be progress.

SUMMARY TO APPENDIX

1 The intelligent profit-seeking action of speculators and arbitragers tends to create certain definite *equilibrium patterns of price over space and time*. To the extent that speculators moderate price and consumption instability, they perform a socially useful purpose. To the extent that they provide a market and permit others to hedge against risk, they perform a further useful function.

But to the extent that speculators pile onto price changes and cause great fluctuations in stock and commodity prices, and in foreign exchange rates and gold prices, they do social damage.

2 Over a long period of time, property owners apply the theory of speculation to determine the amount of natural resources that will be available for the future. The Conservation movement used to argue the market took no account of future scarcities.

3 The economic principle of diminishing marginal utility is one way of showing why consumption and price stability is good, and why gambling is economically unsound and insurance is sound. There are fundamental differences among what can be insured by private rather than social agencies and what can scarcely be insured at all.

CONCEPTS FOR REVIEW

spatial P equality but for transport costs
ideal seasonal price pattern
conservation through the market
hedging, speculation, and short-sale

law of diminishing marginal utility
consumption stability versus instability
gambling versus insurance
social versus private insurance

QUESTIONS FOR DISCUSSION

1. How does ideal speculation work to stabilize seasonal prices? To spread risks?
2. "If all mineral owners were equally pessimistic about future ore discoveries, the price of ore would stay at a constant level." Why?
3. "Insurance reduces total risk; gambling increases the total. Therefore the former is good and the latter is bad." Explain.
4. "I love the thrill of gambling, of risking all on the turn of a card. What do I care for odds or economic principles?" Can economic science pass judgment on whether such a person should gamble or not?
5. Can you reverse the reasoning concerning the desirability of gambling and insurance so that it will apply to two individuals with increasing rather than decreasing marginal utility of income?
6. List some important differences between private and social insurance.
7. *Extra-credit problem* (for students of statistics): Suppose each of four cab companies faces accidents "normally distributed," with a standard deviation, $\sigma_i = \$3,000$, around a mean loss of $50,000. Let them now pool risks through mutual reinsurance. Show that this gives a total mean loss of $200,000 (or still $50,000 for each one's fair share; but now total variance is only 4 × $(3,000)^2$, or $\sigma^2 = 4\sigma_i^2 = \$36,000,000 = (6,000)^2$). So each ends up with a standard deviation of only $1,500 = \$6,000/4$—halving the risk through quadrupling the size! Can you use the same reasoning to see the following? (a) Diversifying your wealth into *four* independent stocks, each with the same mean return and same (independent!) variability, will *halve* the expected variability of your portfolio. (b) Pooling the independent peak-load demand of two utility systems will reduce the need to have twice the standby capacity.

22
THE THEORY OF DEMAND
AND UTILITY

What is a cynic? A man who knows the price of everything, and the value of nothing.
OSCAR WILDE

In a competitive market, price is determined by the schedules of supply and demand. But what principles of economics lie behind the demand schedules? What principles behind the supply schedules?

In this chapter we shall investigate briefly the economic principles of *total utility* and *marginal utility* which underlie the market demand schedule, leaving to subsequent chapters a survey of the cost concepts which underlie the competitive supply schedule and the behavior of monopolists.

SUMMING INDIVIDUAL DEMANDS TO GET MARKET DEMAND

The demand curve for a good such as tea is arrived at for the whole market by summing up the amounts of tea that will be demanded by each customer. Each consumer has a demand curve along which the quantity demanded can be plotted against the price of tea. It generally slopes downward and to the right, declining from northwest to southeast. If all consumers were exactly alike in their demands and there were 1 million consumers, then we could think of the market curve as a millionfold enlargement of each consumer's demand curve.

But people are not all exactly alike. Some have high incomes; some low. Some greatly desire tea; others prefer coffee or concerts. What must we do to the demand schedules or curves of each consumer to arrive at the total market demand *DD* curve?

All we have to do is calculate the sum total of what all the different consumers will consume at any given price; we then plot that total amount as a point on the market demand curve; or if we like, we may set the total down in a demand table like that first seen in Chapter 4.

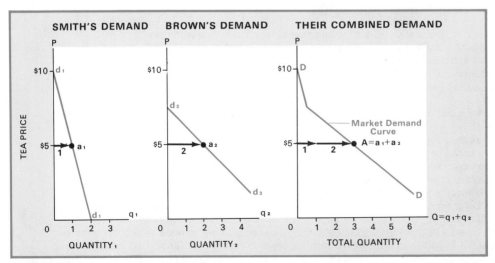

FIG. 22-1. To get market demand, we add all consumers' demand curves.
At each price, such as $5, we *horizontally* add quantities demanded by each person to get market quantity demanded.

Summary. We sum individual amounts demanded at each price to end up finally with the market demand curve. (Figure 22-1 adds demand curves "horizontally.")

DEMAND SHIFTS FROM INCOME AND OTHER CHANGES

Factors other than changes in the price of tea can change the quantity demanded of tea. We know from budget studies, from historical experience, and from thinking about our own behaviour that an increase in money income is a factor that will normally tend to increase the amount we are willing to buy of any good. Goods that are necessities tend to be less responsive to income changes, and goods that are luxuries tend to be more responsive; a very few abnormal goods, called "inferior" goods, may actually go down in quantity bought when we get enough income to be able to afford to replace them in the budget by other goods. (Hamburger, bologna, soup bones and offal, lard, and oleomargarine might be examples of inferior goods, but the species is so rare that we can generally neglect it in our discussions.)

Let us now show what all this means in terms of the demand curve. This curve is, of course, simply the graphical picture of the response of quantity bought of a good to the change in its *own* price. But quantity bought may change also as a result of changes in the *price of other goods* or as a result of a change in the consumer's *income*. The demand curve is drawn on the assumption that these other things do not change. But what if they do? Then the whole demand curve will *shift* to the right or to the left.

Figure 22-2 illustrates such changes. Given a certain income and established prices for all other goods, we can draw the consumer's demand for tea *dd*. First, assume price and quantity are at point *A*. Suppose now that his income rises. Even though the price of tea is unchanged, he will in all probability buy more tea than before; hence the demand curve will have shifted to the right, say, to *d'd'*, with *A'* indicating his new total purchase of tea. If his income should fall, then we may expect a reduction in quantity bought—there *must* be a reduction if income falls far enough. This downward shift we illustrate by *d"d"* and by *A"*.

SHIFTS IN THE DEMAND CURVE

FIG. 22-2. Demand curve shifts with change in income or in another good's price.
With higher income you'll want to buy more of a good, thus shifting *dd* to *d'd'*. (Explain why: and why lowering income will shift *dd* to *d"d"*.) Similarly, a rise in price of coffee, which is a substitute for tea, might shift tea's *dd* out to *d'd'*. (What would a cut in coffee price do? Can you explain why a great rise in price of lemon, a complementary good used with tea, might shift *dd* leftward to *d"d"*?)

Income is only one of many factors that the position of the demand curve depends upon. An increased taste or a fashion for tea would also shift the demand to the right, and a decreased taste would have the opposite effect. Advertisers seek to shift the *dd* curve. Even if each person consumed the same amount of a good, a growth in population would have the effect of increasing the total market demand for a product. If people think that a boom is about to get under way, they may increase their purchases now in order to beat the gun.[1] Still other factors operate all the time to shift demand.

---

[1] In fact, when I see in today's paper that the price of tea is going up, I may rush out to buy more: this may seem superficially to be an exception to the law of downward-sloping demand, but (as discussed on page 371, footnote 3) it can be reconciled with that law when we realize that I am buying more because of the *rising* price of tea and because I want to be able to buy less of it tomorrow when its price will have stabilized at a high level. Despite this *dynamic* effect of *changing* prices, it remains true that at a steady high price for tea, I shall consume less than at a steady low price (if other goods' prices do not change).

CROSS RELATIONS OF DEMAND: SUBSTITUTES AND COMPLEMENTS

Everyone knows that raising the price of tea will decrease the amount demanded of tea. We have seen that it will also affect the amounts demanded of other commodities. For example, a higher price for tea will lower the demand for a commodity such as lemon; i.e., it will shift the whole demand schedule of lemon downward. But it will also increase the amount demanded of coffee. Probably it will have little or no effect on the demand curve for salt.

We say, therefore, that tea and coffee are rival, or competing, products, or *substitutes*. Tea and lemon, on the other hand, are cooperating, or *complementary*, commodities, so-called *complements*. In-between pairs such as tea and salt are said to represent *independent* commodities. The reader will of course be able to classify such pairs as beef and pork, turkey and cranberry sauce, automobiles and gasoline, truck and railroad freight, oil and coal.

Besides showing effects of income changes, Fig. 22-2 also illustrates the effect of changed prices of other goods. A fall in the price of coffee may well cause our consumer to buy less tea; the demand curve shifts to, say *d"d"*. But what if the price of lemon were to fall? The change may be small or nonexistent. But if there is any change, it will be in the direction of *increased* tea purchases—a rightward shift of *dd*. Why this difference in response? Because coffee is a rival, a *substitute* product for tea; lemon is a *complementary* commodity to tea.

THE LAW OF DIMINISHING MARGINAL UTILITY[2]

Return to the law of downward-sloping demand, which is so basic that we have to investigate the economic principles operating in the background to justify and explain it. A century ago economists hit upon the fundamental notion of "marginal utility,"

and it was from this analysis that they felt able for the first time to derive the demand curve and explain its properties. There is space here only to sketch the basic notions underlying such theories, leaving refinements and developments to specialized treatises on advanced economic theory.

As a customer you will buy a good because you feel it gives you satisfaction or "utility." A first unit of a good gives you a certain amount of psychological utility. Now imagine consuming a second unit. Your total utility goes up because the second unit of the good gives you some additional utility. What about adding a third and fourth unit of the same good?

A century ago economists proclaimed an important law that sounds like the law of diminishing returns; but instead of referring to the extra output added by successive doses of a factor input (as in Table 2-2 on page 22), this is a law about the behavior of psychological utility as you add more and more of a good. It can be described by words, by a table of numbers, and by two curves.

The law of diminishing marginal utility. As you consume more of the same good, your *total* (psychological) utility increases. However, let us use the term marginal utility to refer to "the extra utility added by one extra last unit of a good." Then, with successive new units of the good, your total utility will grow at a slower and slower rate because your psychological ability to appreciate more of the good tends to become less keen. This fact, that the increments in total utility fall off, economists describe as follows:

As the amount consumed of a good increases, the *marginal utility* of the good (or the extra utility added by its last unit) tends to decrease.

Column (2) of the table with Fig. 22-3 shows that *total utility* enjoyed increases as Q grows, but at a decreasing rate. Column (3) measures *marginal utility* as the increment of total utility resulting when one last unit of the good is added; the fact that marginal utilities in the table are declining exemplifies the law of diminishing marginal utility.

Figure 22-3(a) pictures how total utility increases, but at a decreasing rate. Figure 22-3(b) depicts marginal utilities—increments of utility (not the total of utility itself). Whether we work with sizable units of

---

[2] Recall that an alternative introduction to the idea of diminishing marginal utility was provided in the Appendix to Chapter 21 p. 393.

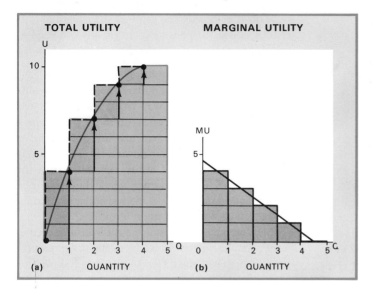

(a) TOTAL UTILITY / (b) MARGINAL UTILITY

FIG. 22-3. Curves as well as numbers can show law of diminishing marginal utility.

Although *total* utility rises with consumption, the table shows it rises at a decreasing rate. This means that marginal utility—the extra utility added by each last extra unit of the good—will be decreasing. From this psychological fact, earlier economists prepared their demonstration of the law of downward-sloping demand.

The gray blocks show the extra utility added by each new unit. The fact that total utility increases at a decreasing rate is shown on the right by the declining steps of marginal utility. If we make our units smaller and smaller, the steps in total utility are smoothed out and total utility becomes the smooth red curve. Now *smoothed marginal utility is shown in (b) by the black downward-falling smooth curve,* and marginal utility becomes indistinguishable from the slope of the smooth curve of (a).[3]

the good and measure utilities by blocks and steps, or whether we smooth the drawings by use of the brown and black curves to reflect continuously divisible units, the law of diminishing marginal utility means that the relations in Fig. 22-3(b) must slope downward and—what is exactly the same thing—that the total utility relations in Fig. 22-3(a) must look concave from below, reflecting total utility's growth becoming less and less.

The validity of the law of diminishing marginal utility seemed probable to economists of an earlier generation as they looked into their own minds for their own psychological reactions to extra consumption. These findings of *introspection* seemed strengthened when they learned about numerous laboratory experiments by psychologists of the 1850s.

Suppose you blindfold a man and ask him to hold out his hand, palm up. Now place a weight on his palm; he certainly will notice it. As you add more units of weight, he notices their addition too. But after his palm is carrying a good deal of weight, you can add just as big a weight as you did in the beginning, and yet this time he will reply that he is not conscious of any addition. In other words, the greater the *total* weight he is already carrying, the *less* will be the effect of an extra or *marginal* unit of weight.

When older economists learned that perception of sound, light, and other sensations seemed to show a similar Weber-Fechner law of decreasing marginal effect, this

DECLINING RATE OF INCREASE OF *TOTAL* UTILITY

(1) QUANTITY OF A GOOD CONSUMED	(2) TOTAL UTILITY	(3) MARGINAL UTILITY
0	0	
		4
1	4	
		3
2	7	
		2
3	9	
		1
4	10	
		0
5	10	

TABLE 22-1

[3] NOTE: It will be found that the sum of all the marginal utilities in Table 22-1's Column (3), if reckoned above some point, must equal the amount of total utility in Column (2) at that point. (Thus, 4 + 3 + 2 does give us the 9 shown in Column (2). What does 4 + 3 give?) In terms of Fig. 22-3(b), the area under the marginal utility curve, as measured by blocks or by area under the smooth curve, must add up to equality with the numerical height of the total utility curve shown in (a)—it being understood that we make our comparison at a specified quantity level. All this portrays the fact that total utility is the sum of all the marginal (or extra) utilities added from the beginning.

gave them even greater confidence in the law of diminishing marginal utility.[4]

EQUILIBRIUM CONDITION: EQUAL MARGINAL UTILITIES PER DOLLAR FOR EVERY GOOD

What is the fundamental equilibrium condition that has to be satisfied if a consumer is spending his income on the variously priced goods so as to make himself truly best off in terms of utility or well-being? Certainly he would not expect that the last egg he is buying brings him exactly the same marginal utility as the last lamb chop he is buying. For lamb chops cost much more apiece than eggs. On reflection, it would seem more reasonable that he should keep buying a good which costs twice as much per unit as another until it ends up in his equilibrium bringing him just twice as much in marginal utility.

In short, if he has arranged his consumption so that every single good is bringing him marginal utility just exactly *proportional* to its price, then it would seem that he could not better himself by departing from such an equilibrium. This same fundamental condition can now be stated: A consumer with a fixed income and facing given market prices of goods can come into his equilibrium of maximum satisfaction or utility only when he acts thus.

Law of equal marginal utilities per dollar. Each good —such as sugar—is demanded up to the point where the marginal utility per dollar (or penny)

spent on it is exactly the same as the marginal utility of a dollar (or penny) spent on any other good —such as salt.

Why must this law hold? If any one good gave more marginal utility per dollar, the consumer would gain by taking money away from other goods and spending more on that good—up to the point where the law of diminishing marginal utility brought its marginal utility per dollar down to equality. If any good gave less marginal utility per dollar than the common level, the consumer would buy less of it until the marginal utility of the last dollar spent on it had risen back to the common level.[5]

This fundamental condition of consumer equilibrium can be written in terms of the marginal utilities and prices of the different goods as follows:

$$\frac{MU \text{ Good } 1}{P_1} = \frac{MU \text{ Good } 2}{P_2} = \frac{MU \text{ Good } 3}{P_3} = \cdots$$
$$= \text{common } MU \text{ per dollar of income}$$

The logical meaning of this condition rather than the rote memorizing of a formula is, of course, what matters.

Nor need all this apply just to spending money. Suppose you have only a certain number of hours to spend on study for examinations. If you are so uncreative as to seek merely to maximize your grade average, how should you allocate your time? By spending equal hours on each course? Not necessarily. You have to shift from history to chemistry, from German to economics, until you are getting *the same marginal grade advantage from the last minute spent in each alternative use.*[6] The same marginal rule can show you how to allocate your time on a pleasant

---

[4] The modern generation, however, has found that the exact way in which one measures utility is not particularly important to explain the price-quantity demand curve. Some economists would still use introspection. Others would want to observe whether you had to give a man 2 to 1 odds to get him to wager on the toss of a fair coin the loss of a new hat against the winning of a second new hat; and they would conclude from this that the marginal utility of the second hat decreases to half the marginal utility of the first hat. Such economists thus hope to measure his marginal utility "behavioristically" rather than introspectively. Probably the majority of economists in advanced graduate theory today would feel that what counts for consumer demand theory is whether certain situations have *more* total utility than others. These economists would not care to look for any numerical measure of utility beyond such "greater or less than" comparison; they would use the "indifference curves" of the Appendix to this chapter. By any of these methods, the general properties of the market demand curve can be securely established. (NOTE: Demand theory never has any need to make interpersonal comparisons of utility that involve adding or comparing utilities of different minds.)

[5] At a few places in economics the indivisibility of units is important and cannot be glossed over. Thus, Cadillacs do not come like peas, and their indivisibility may matter. Suppose I buy one but definitely not two Cadillacs. Then the marginal utility of the first car is enough larger than the marginal utility of the same number of dollars spent elsewhere to induce me to buy this first unit. The marginal utility that the second Cadillac would bring is enough less to ensure I do *not* buy it. When indivisibility matters, our equality rule for equilibrium can be restated as an inequality rule. NOTE: As mentioned, the validity of the equilibrium condition can be made quite independent of how, or whether, we measure utility *numerically*. Only relative marginal utilities matter.

[6] This does not mean that you study to get the same 89 grade in all classes. Your average may be maximized with grades of 93, 92, 90, and 81, but with each marginal hour of study adding one-tenth of a grade point to any subject.

weekend. Our marginal equilibrium condition is not merely a law of economics; it is a law of logic itself.

THE LAW OF DOWNWARD-SLOPING DE-MAND Can we derive the consumer's demand curves with respect to price from the fundamental equation conditions written out above? Yes, we can. Imagine that the price of clothing P_1 is cut while P_2, P_3 ... and income all remain unchanged. Furthermore, in order that the marginal utility per dollar be the same for all goods, the algebraic equality is to be maintained.[7] Then a fall in P_1 requires an equi-proportionate cut of MU Good 1. But by the law of diminishing marginal utility consumers' MU for any good falls only when more of the good is consumed. Hence the fall in P_1 must lead to an increase in Q.

Similarly, faced with a rise in P_1 (all other prices, income and the fundamental equality remaining unchanged), our consumer can raise MU Good 1 only by buying less of it.

Hence our consumer always responds to a change in price by an opposite change in amount purchased. This is the contribution of the concept of diminishing marginal utility to the problem of explaining downward-sloping demand. (The Appendix contains a more rigorous derivation of this result.)

A final remark may be in order at this point. A consumer is not expected to be a wizard at numbers or graphs, nor need he be, to approximate the demand behavior of this chapter. He can even make most of his decisions unconsciously or out of habit. As long as he is fairly consistent in his tastes and actions, all he has to do to make the present analysis relevant is to avoid repeating those mistakes which he found in the past did not give him the goods and services he most wanted and to avoid making wild and unpredictable changes in his buying behavior. If enough people act in this way, our scientific theory will provide a tolerable approximation to the facts.

SUBSTITUTION- AND INCOME-EFFECTS: A DIGRESSION

The concept of marginal utility has lent credence to the fundamental law of downward-sloping demand.

A different way of looking at the same problem makes no mention of marginal utility explicitly; but it does lead rigorously to the desired result, and does provide an interesting insight into the factors that tend to make the response of quantity to price very great or very little.

SUBSTITUTION-EFFECT The first factor explaining diminishing consumption when price rises is an obvious one. If the price of tea goes up while other prices do not, then tea has become relatively dearer. It pays, therefore, to *substitute other goods for tea in order to maintain one's standard of living most cheaply.*

Thus tea becomes a relatively more costly source of stimulation than before, and less of it will be bought and more of coffee or cocoa. Similarly, a rise in price of movies relative to stage plays may cause the consumer to seek less of his amusement in the more expensive direction.

The consumer is doing here only what every businessman does when rises in the price of one productive factor cause him to adjust his production methods so as to substitute cheap factor inputs for the costly factor inputs. By this process of substitution, he is able to produce the same output at least total cost. Similarly do consumers buy satisfaction at least cost.

INCOME-EFFECT In the second place, when your money income is fixed, being forced to buy a good at a higher price is just like having a decrease in your *real* income or purchasing power, particularly if you have been buying a great deal of the raised commodity. With a lower real income you will now want to buy less tea. Thus, unless a good is an "inferior" good like bologna or oleo, the income-effect will *reinforce* the substitution-effect in making the demand curve downward-sloping.[8]

---

[7] This explanation of the law of downward-sloping demand is only roughly correct unless we confine it to changes in clothing spending so small as to leave unaffected the marginal utilities of the other goods and so the alegbraic equality MUi/Pi.

[8] Income- and substitution-effects not only explain the downward slope of demand but also explain a possible, albeit extremely rare, exception to that law. When the 1845 Irish famine greatly raised the price of potatoes, families who consumed a lot of potatoes merely because they were too poor to consume much meat might have ended up consuming *more* rather than less of the high-P potatoes. Why? Because now they had to spend so much on potatoes, the necessity of life, as to make it quite impossible to afford any meat at all and hence were forced to become even more dependent than before on potatoes. In brief, the substitution-effect was here overcome by the perverse income-effect applicable to a peculiar "inferior" good, such as the potato,

Of course, the quantitative importance of each of these effects varies with the good in question and with the consumer. Under some circumstances the resulting demand curve is very *elastic*: as where the consumer has been spending a good deal on the commodity and where ready substitutes are available—for example, a drunkard's demand for gin. But if a commodity, such as salt, involves only a small fraction of the consumer's budget, is not easily replaceable by other items, and is needed in small amounts to complement more important items, then demand will tend to be *inelastic*.

THE PARADOX OF VALUE

The preceding theories help to explain a famous question that troubled Adam Smith in *The Wealth of Nations*. He asked, How is it that water, which is so very useful that life is impossible without it, has such a low price—while diamonds, which are quite unnecessary, have such a high price?

Today even a beginning student can give a correct answer to this problem. "That's simply explained," he will write on an examination. "The supply and demand curves for water are such that they intersect at a very low price, while the supply and demand curves for diamonds are such that they intersect at a high price." (Today he could add that water is no longer all that cheap.)

This is not an incorrect answer. Adam Smith could not have given it because supply and demand curves as descriptive tools had not yet been invented, and were not to be for 75 years or more. But after he had mastered the lingo, old Adam Smith would naturally ask the question, "But *why* do supply and demand for water intersect at such a low price?"

The answer is by now easy to phrase. It consists of two parts:

Diamonds are very *scarce*, the cost of getting *extra* ones is high; and water is relatively *abundant*, with its cost low in many areas of the world. This first part would have seemed reasonable to even the classical economists of more than a century ago, who

would probably have let it go at that, and would not have known how to reconcile these facts about *cost* with the equally valid fact that the world's water is more *useful* than the world's supply of diamonds. In fact, Adam Smith never did quite resolve the paradox. He was content simply to point out that the "value in use" of a good—its total contribution to economic welfare—is not the same thing as its "value in exchange"—the total money value or revenue for which it will sell. Smith had not arrived at the point where he knew how to distinguish *marginal* utility from *total* utility!

Today, we should add to the above cost considerations a second truth:

The *total* utility of water does not determine its price or demand. Only the relative marginal utility and cost of the *last* little bit of water determine its price. Why? Because people are free to buy or not buy that last little bit. If water is priced higher than its marginal utility, then that last unit cannot be sold. Therefore the price must fall until it reaches the level of usefulness of the last little bit, no more and no less. Moreover, because every unit of water is exactly like any other unit and because there is only one price in a competitive market, *every unit must sell for what the last least useful unit sells for*. (As one student put the matter: The theory of economic value is easy to understand if you just remember that the tail wags the dog: concentrate on *marginal* and not on *total* utility.)

Paradox resolved: The more there is of a commodity, the less the relative desirability of its *last* little unit becomes, even though its *total* usefulness always grows as we get more of the commodity. So, it is obvious why a large amount of water has a low price. Or why air is actually a free good despite its vast usefulness. The many *later* units pull down the market value of *all* units.

CONSUMER'S SURPLUS

The foregoing discussion emphasizes that the accounting system which records the "total economic value" or revenue of a good (price × quantity) differs from the measurement necessary to record "total welfare." The total economic value of air is zero; its

---

which tends to *decrease* in the poor man's budget when incomes rise. This *curiosum* is attributed to Sir Robert Giffen, a Victorian economist (NOTE: In the case of ordinary inferior goods on which we spend little money, the perverse income-effects will not outweigh the substitution-effects to produce the odd Giffen case.)

contribution to welfare, very great.[9] Similarly, if we increase the quantity produced of a good, we increase the community's welfare; but if it is a good like wheat, whose demand is inelastic, we do at the same time destroy some economic value.

Thus, there is always a sort of gap between total utility and total market value. This gap is in the nature of a surplus, which the consumer gets because he "receives more than he pays for." Nor does he benefit at the expense of the seller. In a swap, one party does not lose what the other gains. Unlike energy, which cannot be created or destroyed, the well-being of all participants is increased by trade.

It is easy to see how this consumer's surplus arises. Each unit of a good that the consumer buys costs him only as much as the last unit is worth. But by our fundamental law of diminishing marginal utility, the *earlier* units are worth *more* to him than the last. Thus, he enjoys a surplus on each of these earlier units. When trade stops benefiting him and giving him a surplus, he stops buying.

As final clinching evidence that the consumer always receives a surplus, we may cite the fact that a ruthless seller could present the consumer with an ultimatum—what is called an "all-or-none" offer: "Either you pay me an extra amount of money for the whole block of the good that you are consuming, or you must go without all the units, from first to last. Take it or leave it!" The consumer would certainly be willing to pay extra rather than do alto-gether without the good of this discriminating monopolist.

How is the concept of consumer's surplus used? It is sometimes needed to help make correct social decisions. Suppose a new side road would cost the locality $100,000. Being free to all, it is expected to bring in no dollar revenues, and all the utility it gives to each user will represent his consumer's surplus. (To avoid extraneous interpersonal difficulties, let us assume there are 1,000 users all exactly alike in income and in their benefit from the road, and all equally worthy.) If each such similar man enjoys $100 (the road's *per capita* cost) or more of consumer's surplus from the road, they should all vote to build the road. If the consumer's surplus of each is less than $100, it is uneconomical for them to tax themselves for this public project.[10]

Many ingenious ways have been suggested for measuring consumer's surplus, but they are of no particular significance here.[11] The important thing is to see how lucky the citizens of modern efficient communities really are. *The privilege of being able to buy a vast array of goods at low prices cannot be over-estimated.*

This is a humbling thought. If ever a person becomes arrogantly proud of *his* economic productivity and *his* level of real earnings, let him pause and reflect. If he were transported with all his skills and energies intact to a primitive desert island, how much would his money earnings buy? Indeed, without capital machinery, without rich resources, without other labor, and above all without the technological knowledge which each generation inherits from the society's past, how much could *he* produce? It is only too clear that all of us reap the benefits of an economic world we never made. As L. T. Hobhouse said:

---

[9] Or, as Smith would say, its value in use is very great; its value in exchange, negligible.

[10] See Chapter 32 Appendix, Fig. 32-2, for a diagram illustrating this all-or-nothing social decision.

[11] In the special case where money provides a firm measuring rod of utility, consumer's surplus is easily measured and depicted. In Fig. 22-4, when the consumer buys *OM* sugar at *ON* price for each, he pays the total revenue indicated by the lighter rectangular area *OMEN*; but that much sugar gives him total utility (expressed in money) which is the whole area *OMER*; the darker triangular area *NER* left over is his consumer's surplus, and it obviously will be greater the lower the price becomes.

This geometrical concept is useful in illustrating how taxes, farm quotas, and monopolistic interferences create social inefficiency and loss.

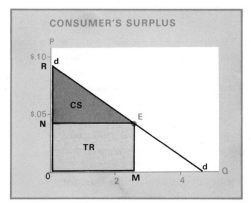

FIG. 22-4

The organizer of industry who thinks that he has "made" himself and his business has found a whole social system ready to his hand in skilled workers, machinery, a market, peace and order—a vast apparatus and a pervasive atmosphere, the joint creation of millions of men and scores of generations. Take away the whole social factor and we have not Robinson Crusoe, with his salvage from the wreck and his acquired knowledge, but the naked savage living on roots, berries, and vermin.

SUMMARY

1 The market demand curve for all consumers is derived by adding *horizontally* the separate demand curves of each consumer. A demand curve can shift for many reasons, such as the following: Normally, a rise in income will shift *dd* rightward, thus increasing demand; a rise in the price of a *substitute* good (coffee for tea, and so forth) will also create such an upward shift in demand; a rise in the price of a *complementary* good (such as lemon in its relation to tea) will represent a cross effect that shifts the *dd* curve downward and leftward. Still other factors—such as changing tastes, population, or expectations—can increase or decrease demand.

2 The concepts of total and marginal utility were introduced to explain the law of downward-sloping demand. The fact that *total utility* rises with each new marginal addition of a good but at a decreasing rate of growth can be expressed in a technical way. With equal additions to a good's quantity, its marginal utility (which is the increment of utility coming from adding a last extra unit of quantity) tends to decrease.

3 To get the most total utility, the consumer must achieve a fundamental marginal condition for demand equilibrium: A consumer has not maximized his well-being until he has succeeded in *making equal the respective marginal utilities per dollar spent on each and every good.* (BEWARE: The marginal utility of a $25-per-ounce bottle of perfume is not equal to the marginal utility of a 10-cent glass of cola; but their marginal utilities divided by price per unit—that is, their marginal utilities per last dollar, MU/P —are to be equalized in optimizing equilibrium.)

   This is a fundamental rule of logic that transcends demand theory: If you want to allocate any limited resource among competing uses, whenever the marginal advantage in one use happened to be greater than in another, you can benefit by transferring from the low-marginal-advantage use to the high—until a final equilibrium is reached at which all have become equal.

4 We can use the diminishing marginal utility concept to explain the downward-sloping demand curve.

5 Without using the marginal utility concept explicitly, we can gain new insight into the factors making for downward-sloping demand by analyzing the effect of a price rise into (a) its *substitution-effect* component and (b) its *income-effect* component. When P for a good rises, I tend to maintain the same level of well-being by *substituting* other goods for the good that has just become more costly. Reinforcing this decrease in a good's Q that arises out of substitution is the income-effect: Since I ordinarily buy less of the good in question when my family income is lower, the rise in its price—which has produced a *drop in my real income* or purchasing power—thus induces a further cut in consumption as the result of my now having a lower real income.

6 Adam Smith's paradox of value—that a commodity important for welfare may sell for less in the market than one less important—is clarified by the distinction between the concept of marginal and total utility. The scarcity of a good, as determined by its cost and

supply conditions, interacts with the market demand for the good as determined by the usefulness of its *marginal* unit (not the usefulness of the *total* stock of the good).

7 The fact that market price is determined by marginal rather than total utility is dramatized by the concept of *consumer's surplus*. Since we pay in the market the same price for each unit that the marginal unit is worth to us, we reap a consumer's surplus on all the previous units. This consumer's surplus reflects the benefit we gain from being able to buy at low prices, rather than being confronted by a ruthless monopolist who insists we pay him for the whole of our consumption just what that total is worth to us. However difficult it may be to quantify consumer's surplus, advanced treatises show it is a concept relevant for many social decisions—such as deciding when the community should incur the heavy initial expenses of a road or bridge.[12]

Without reading the Appendix, we can go from the utility background of demand to the next chapter's cost background of supply.

CONCEPTS FOR REVIEW

market versus individual demand	law of diminishing marginal utility
demand shifts from income and other changes	equating marginal utility of last dollar spent on each good, $MU_1/P_1 = MU_2/P_2$
substitute, complementary, and independent goods	value in use versus value in exchange
income-effect and substitution-effect	paradox of marginal versus total utility
	consumer's surplus

QUESTIONS FOR DISCUSSION

1. As you add horizontally the demands of more and more people, the aggregate market curve begins to look flatter and flatter on the same scale. Show that this merely reflects the fact that the same cut in price induces more new sales from many buyers than from few. (NOTE: Elasticity need not change. Guess why. HINT: E is dimensionless, unaffected by scale changes.)

2. List several goods in order of their responsiveness to higher income.

3. Which of the following goods do you think could be classified as *complementary, substitute,* and *independent* goods: beef, ketchup, lamb, applesauce, cigarettes, gum, pork, butter, paperbacks, taxis, and oleomargarine? Illustrate the resulting shift in the demand curve for one good when price of another good goes up. How would a change in income affect the demand curve for butter? The demand curve for oleomargarine?

4. Explain the difference between marginal and total utility. State the law of diminishing marginal utility. Be sure you understand what it means in terms of numbers and diagrams.

5. Why is it nonsensical to say, "In equilibrium, the marginal utilities of all goods must be exactly equal"? Reword to give a correct statement and explain.

6. If you wanted to avoid using the marginal utility concept, show that you can still justify the law of downward-sloping demand by reasoning that involves (a) substitution-effect and (b) income-effect.

7. How much would you be willing to pay rather than give up *all* movies? How much do you spend on movies? Estimate roughly your consumer's surplus.

[12] See Chapter 32 Appendix on this topic.

8. *Extra credit problem:* Your utility function for food, q_1, and clothing, q_2, is given by the logarithmic function of Weber-Fechner and Bernoulli, namely, $U = 2/3 \log q_1 + 1/3 \log q_2$. You can calculate your marginal utilities of the goods by taking the derivative of the U function with respect to each q_i: we use the rule for differentiating the natural logarithm, namely $d \log q_i/dq_i = 1/q_i$, showing that as you consume double of any good, its *marginal* utility halves (which is not to deny that its total utility does rise, but less than doubles). Hence, we get for food and clothing marginal utilities: $MU_1 = 2/3/q_1$, $MU_2 = 1/3/q_2$. To maximize U subject to the budget restriction: income (per week) $= I = P_1 q_1 + P_2 q_2 =$ expenditure on the goods, we invoke our maximizing rule of equal-MU_i-per-dollar:

$$MU_1/P_1 = MU_2/P_2 \text{ or } 2/3/P_1 q_1 = 1/3/P_2 q_2$$

This says, "Food expenditure, $P_1 q_1$, must be twice clothing expenditure; or we spend two-thirds our income on food and one-third on clothing." Hence, final demand functions are, $q^*_1 = 2/3 I/P_1$, $q^*_2 = 1/3 I/P_2$. EXAMPLE: for $I = \$12$, $P_1 = \$1$, $P_2 = \$2$, we get $q^*_1 = 8$, $q^*_2 = 2$. Can you verify all this by solving the budget equation for $q_1 = (I/P_1) - (P_2/P_1)q_2 = 12 - 2q_2$; substituting into U to get $U = 2/3 \log (12 - 2q_2) + 1/3 \log q_2 = f(q_2)$; then finding the maximum of $f(q_2)$ by differentiating it with respect to q_2 and equating to zero, namely, $f'(q_2) = 0 = -(2/3)2/(12 - 2q_2) + 1/3/q_2$, which can be solved for $q^*_2 = (1/4)(12 - 2q^*_2) = 3/(3/2) = 2$. Then $q^*_1 = 12 - 2q^*_2 = 8$. QED.

Appendix: Geometrical Analysis of Consumer Equilibrium

It is instructive to show graphically, and without using the language of numerical utility, exactly what the consumer's equilibrium position looks like.

THE INDIFFERENCE CURVE

We start out by considering a consumer who buys only two commodities, say, food and clothing, at definite quoted prices. We suppose the consumer can tell us whether (1) he prefers a given combination or batch of the two goods, say, 3 units of food and 2 of clothing, to some second combination or batch, say, 2 units of food and 3 of clothing, or (2) he is "indifferent" as between the two combinations.

Let us suppose that, actually, these two batches are equally good in the eyes of our consumer—that he is indifferent as to which of the two he receives. Let us go on to list in Fig. 22-5's table some of the other combinations of goods between which he is likewise indifferent.

Figure 22-5 shows these combinations diagrammatically. We measure units of clothing upon one axis and units of food upon the other. Each of our four combinations or batches, *A, B, C, D,* is represented by its point. But these four are by no means the only combinations that would leave our consumer just indifferent as between them. Another batch, such as 1 1/2 units of food and 4 of clothing, might be ranked as equal to any of *A, B, C,* or *D* above, and there are many others not shown.

The curved line of Fig. 22-5, linking up the four points, is an "indifference curve." *Every* point thereon represents a different combination of the two goods; and the indifference curve is so drawn that, if our consumer were given his choice of any point on it, he would not know which one to choose. All would be equally desirable to him, and he would be indifferent as to which batch he received.

It should be noted that this indifference curve is of convex curvature viewed from below. As we move downward and to the right along the curve—a movement which implies increasing the quantity of food and reducing that of clothing—the slope of the curve becomes more nearly horizontal. The curve is drawn so because this illustrates a property which seems most often to hold true in real life and which we may call the "law of substitution":

The scarcer a good, the greater its relative *substitution* value; its marginal utility rises relative to the marginal utility of the good that has become plentiful.

For example, the consumer who is at position *A* in the table with Fig. 22-5 is willing to give up 3 units of clothing in order to get a second unit of food; thus, at *A,* he would swap 3 of his 6 clothing units in exchange for 1 extra food unit. But when he has moved to *B,* he would sacrifice only

INDIFFERENCE COMBINATIONS		
	FOOD	CLOTHING
A	1	6
B	2	3
C	3	2
D	4	1½

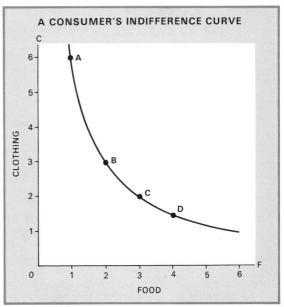

FIG. 22-5. Getting more of one good compensates for giving up something of the other. The consumer likes situation *A* exactly as well as *B, C,* or *D.*
The food-clothing combinations that yield equal satisfaction can be plotted as a smooth "indifference curve" (or so-called "equal-utility contour"). This is convex (from below) in accord with the law of substitution, which says: As you get more of a good, its "substitution ratio," or "indifference slope," diminishes.

1 of his remaining clothing supply in order to obtain a third food unit—a 1-for-1 swap. For a fourth unit of food, he would sacrifice only 1/2 unit from his dwindling supply of clothing.

If we join the points *A* and *B* of Fig. 22-5, we find that the slope of the resulting line (neglecting its negative sign) has a value of 3. Join *B* and *C,* and the slope is 1; join *C* and *D,* and the slope is 1/2. These figures—3, 1, 1/2—are simply the "swapping terms" that we noted just above.

But to move from *A* to *B* is to move a considerable distance along the curve. What about the swapping terms for smaller movements? If the consumer is at *A* and we consider a movement to the intermediate position (not shown in the table) of 1 1/2 food and 4 clothing, the swapping ratio would be 4. And it is clear that, as the movement along the curve grows smaller, the closer the swapping terms come to the actual slope of the indifference curve.[1]

So the slope of the indifference curve is the measure of the terms on which—for very small changes—the consumer would be willing to exchange a little of his supply of one good in return for a little more of the other.

And an indifference curve which is convex in the manner of Fig. 22-5 conforms to the law of substitution earlier noted. As the consumer's food goes up—and his clothing goes down—food must become relatively cheaper and cheaper in order for him to be persuaded to take a little extra food in exchange for a little sacrifice of clothing. The precise shape and slope of an indifference curve will, of course, vary from one consumer to the next; but for this introductory discussion, it seems reasonable to assume that the general convex shape of the curve in Fig. 22-5 is typical.

THE INDIFFERENCE MAP

Our previous table is one of an infinite number of possible tables. We could have started out with a still higher level of satisfaction or indifference and listed some of the different combinations that belonged to it in the mind of our consumer. One such table might have begun with 2 food and 7 clothing; another with 3 food and 7 clothing. Each table could be portrayed graphically; each has its corresponding curve. Figure 22-6 shows four such curves; the old curve of Fig. 22-5 is now labeled *U₃*. This figure is analogous to a geographical contour map. A person who walks along the path indicated by a particular height contour on such a map will find that he is neither climbing nor descending; similarly, the consumer who moves from one position to another along a single indifference curve enjoys neither increasing nor decreasing satisfaction from the change in the flow of goods he is getting. Of course, only a few of the possible indifference curves or equal-utility contours are shown in Fig. 22-6.

Note that, as we increase both goods and hence move in a northeasterly direction across this "map," we are crossing successive indifference curves; we are reaching higher and higher levels of satisfaction. Unless the consumer is satiated, he would be enjoying increasing satisfaction from receiving increased quantities of *both* goods.

[1]By the arithmetic slope of the indifference curve, we mean this: To find the slope of the curve at, say, point *B*, take a ruler and place it so that it is just tangent to the curve at *B*—it touches the curve, but does not cross it either above or below *B*. Mark the points at which the ruler's edge crosses the two axes. The slope is the ratio of the distance cut off on the vertical axis to the distance cut off on the horizontal axis; e.g., at *B*, the slope is 6/4, or 1 1/2. Intermediate texts refer to the slope of the indifference curve at any point as the "substitution ratio," or "the marginal rate of substitution," or the "*relative* marginal utility ratio" at that point.

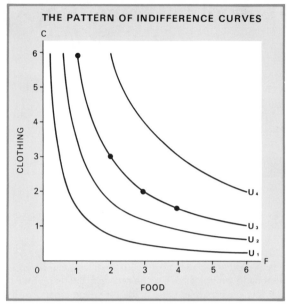

FIG. 22-6. The curves labeled, *U₁*, *U₂*, *U₃*, and *U₄* represent indifference curves, or equal-utility contours. (Why is it better to be on a farther-out indifference curve?) *U₃* is the indifference contour of Fig. 22-5.

Hence, curve *U₃* stands for a higher level of satisfaction than *U₂*; *U₄*, for a higher level of satisfaction than *U₃*; etc.

BUDGET (OR CONSUMPTION-POSSIBILITY) LINE

Now let us set the consumer's indifference map aside for a moment and give him a fixed income. He has, say, $6 per day to spend, and he is confronted with fixed prices for each food and clothing unit—$1.50 for food, $1 for clothing. It is clear that he could spend his money on any one of a variety of alternative combinations of food and clothing. At one extreme, he could buy 4 food units and no clothing; at the other, 6 clothing units and no food. The table with Fig. 22-7 illustrates some of the possible ways in which his $6 could be allocated.

Figure 22-7 shows these five possible positions on a diagram with axes similar to those of Figs. 22-5 and 22-6. Each position is indicated by a small black dot, and it will be noted that they all lie on a straight line, which is labeled *NM*. Moreover, any other attainable point, such as 3 1/3 food units and 1 clothing unit, would lie upon *NM*. The straight line *NM* sums up all the possible positions that our consumer could occupy in spending his $6 of budget income.[2]

[2]This is so because, if we designate quantities of food and clothing bought as *F* and *C*, respectively, total expenditure on food must be $1 1/2*F* and total expenditure on clothing, $1*C*. If daily income and expenditure is $6, the following equation must hold: $6 =

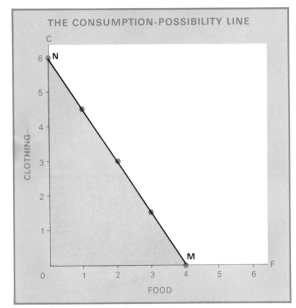

FIG. 22-7. The budget limit on expenditures can be indicated by a numerical table. The costs of these budgets (reckoned as $1.50F + $1C) all add up to $6 Income.

The budget constraint plots on a diagram as a straight-line tradeoff, whose absolute slope equals the P_F/P_C ratio. NM is the consumer's budget line. When he spends just $6 daily, with food and clothing prices $1.50 and $1, he can choose any point on this line. (Why is its slope $1.50/$1 = 3/2?)

The slope of *NM* (neglecting its sign) is 3/2, which is necessarily the ratio of food price to clothing price; and the common sense of line *NM* is clear enough. Given these prices, every time our consumer gives up 1 1/2 clothing units (thereby dropping down 1 1/2 vertical units on the diagram), he can gain 1 unit of food (i.e., move east 1 horizontal unit). Or what is the same thing, he can exchange 3 clothing units for 2 food units. We can call *NM* the consumer's "budget" (or "consumption-possibility") line.

THE EQUILIBRIUM POSITION OF TANGENCY

Now we are ready to put our two parts together. The axes of Fig. 22-7 were the same as those of Figs. 22-5 and 22-6. We can superimpose the red budget line *NM* upon the consumer's indifference map, as in Fig. 22-8. He is free to move anywhere along *NM*. Positions to the right and above *NM* are barred to him unless he has more than $6 of income to spend; and positions to the left and below *NM* are unimportant, since we assume that he will want to spend the full $6.

$1 1/2F + $1C. This is a simple linear equation, the equation of the budget line *NM*. NOTE:

Arithmetic slope of *NM* = $1 1/2 ÷ $1
                   = price of food ÷ price of clothing

Alternative Consumption Possibilities		
	FOOD	CLOTHING
M	4	0
	3	1½
	2	3
	1	4½
N	0	6

FIG. 22-8. Now we combine the budget line and indifference contours on one diagram. At *B* the consumer reaches highest indifference curve attainable with his fixed income. *B* represents tangency of budget line with highest indifference curve. (Why? If slopes were unequal, *NM* would intersect a *U* contour and he could cross over onto higher satisfaction levels.) At tangency point *B*, substitution ratio equals price ratio P_F/P_C. This means that all goods' marginal utilities are proportional to their prices, with marginal utility of the last dollar spent on every good being equalized—as demonstrated in the chapter's main text.

Where will the consumer move? Obviously, to that point which yields the greatest satisfaction; or, in other words, to the highest available indifference curve, which in this case must be at the black point *B*. At *B*, the budget line just touches—but does not cross—the indifference curve U^3. At this point of tangency—of the budget line to an indifference contour—is found the highest utility contour he can reach.[3]

Geometrically, the consumer is at equilibrium where the slope of his budget line is exactly equal to the slope of his indifference curve. And as already noted, the slope of the budget line is the price ratio of food to clothing.

[3]At any point on *NM* other than *B*, *NM* is crossing indifference curves. And as long as the consumer can keep crossing indifference curves, he can keep moving to higher ones.

We may say, then, that optimal equilibrium is attained when the consumer's *substitution* ratio (or slope of relative marginal utilities) is just equal to the ratio of food price to clothing price.[4]

CHANGES IN INCOME AND PRICE

Our understanding of the process will be furthered by considering the effects of (a) a change in money income and (b) a change in the price of one of the two goods.

INCOME CHANGE Assume, first, that the consumer's daily income is halved, the two prices remaining unchanged. We could prepare another table, similar to Fig. 22-7's table, showing the consumption possibilities that are now open to him. Plotting these points on a diagram such as Fig. 22-9, we should find that the new budget line occupies the position N'M' in Fig. 22-9. The line has made a *parallel* shift inward.[5] The consumer is now free to move only along this new budget line. Again he will move to the highest attainable indifference curve, or to the point B'. A similar tangency condition for optimal equilibrium again applies. The black curve through B'B depicts the Engel's curve of consumption changes with income.[6]

SINGLE-PRICE CHANGE Now return our consumer to his previous daily income of $6, but assume that the price of food rises from $1.50 to $3. Again we must examine the change in the budget line. This time we find that it has pivoted on the point N and is now NM'',[7] as in Fig. 22-10.

The common sense of such a shift is clear. Since the price of clothing is unchanged, the point N is just as available as it was before. But since the price of food has risen, point M, which meant 4 food units had been purchasable, is no longer attainable. With food costing $3 per unit, only 2 units can now be bought with a daily income of $6. So the new budget line must very definitely still pass through N, but it must pivot around N and pass through M'', which is below M. (The new line has a slope of 3/1. Why?)

Equilibrium is now at B''; we have a new tangency situation in that equilibrium. Higher food price has definitely reduced food consumption; higher P_F may change clothing consumption in either direction. (The dd demand curves of this chapter were derivable by plotting the P_F, Q_F data that you should be able to read off from the black curve passing through B and B''.)

---

[4]The substitution ratio, or slope of the indifference curve, can be shown to be nothing but the ratio of the marginal utility of food to the marginal utility of clothing. So our tangency condition is just another way of stating that a good's price and its marginal utility must be proportional in equilibrium—the consumer there getting the same marginal utility from his last penny spent on food as from his last penny spent on clothing (in agreement with page 402).

[5]The equation of the new broken red N'M' budget line is now $3 = $1 1/2F + $1C.

[6]Recall the important budgetary income-expenditure patterns of Fig. 11-1, page 187.

[7]The budget equation of NM'' is now $6 = $3F + $1C.

To clinch understanding, the interested reader can work out the cases of an increase in income and a fall in the price of clothing or food. (In a diagram like those of Figs. 22-9 or 22-10, he can connect all the tangency points gen-

FIG. 22-9. An income change shifts the budget line in a parallel way. Thus, halving income to $3 shifts NM to N'M', moving equilibrium to B'. (Show what doubling income to $12 would do to equilibrium. Guess where the new tangency point would approximately come.)

FIG. 22-10. A rise in the price of food makes the budget line pivot on N, rotating from NM to NM''. New tangency equilibrium is at B'', with less food and either more or less clothing. (Can you handle a change in P_C?)

erated by income changes to get the Engel's budgetary patterns of Chapter 11.)

BALANCED-PRICE CHANGES Suppose *all* prices exactly *double*. Then it is easy to see that this is exactly like a *halving* of income. Hence Fig. 22-9's halving of *NM* to get *N'M'* will handle this case. This illustrates an important property of consumer demand.

Changing all prices and income in exactly the same proportion leaves equilibrium quantities demanded quite unchanged.

This provides the germ of truth underlying the Quantity Theory of Money and Prices (of Chapter 15 and Chapter 18 Appendix).

SUMMARY TO APPENDIX

1 An "indifference curve" or "equal-utility contour" depicts the points of equally desirable consumption. The indifference contour is usually drawn convex from below, in accordance with the empirical law of diminishing relative marginal utilities (or of substitution ratios).

2 If a consumer has a fixed money income, all of which he spends, and is confronted with market prices of two goods, the budget (or consumption-possibility) line upon which he is free to move is a straight line. The steepness of the line's slope will depend on the ratio of the two market prices; how far out it lies will depend on the size of his income.

3 The consumer will move along this budget line until he reaches the highest indifference curve attainable. At this point, the budget line will touch, but not cross, an indifference curve. Hence, equilibrium is at the point of *tangency*, where the *slope of the budget line* (the ratio of the prices) exactly equals the *slope of the indifference curve* (the substitution ratio or relative-marginal-utility ratio of the two goods). This provides an additional proof that marginal utilities are made to be proportional to prices.

4 A fall in income will move the budget line parallel inward, usually causing less of both goods to be bought. A change in the price of one good alone will, other things being equal, cause the budget line to pivot so as to change its slope. In any case, whatever change has occurred, a new equilibrium point of highest satisfaction will be reached. It is at a new point of tangency, where the marginal utility per dollar has become equal in every use. By comparing the new and old equilibrium points, we trace out the usual *dd* demand curve and income pattern.

CONCEPTS FOR REVIEW

indifference curves or contours
slope or substitution ratio
budget or consumption-possibility
   line, *NM*
convexity and law of diminishing
   relative marginal utilities

optimal tangency equilibrium:
   P_F/P_C = substitution ratio
   = MU_F/MU_C
parallel and pivoted shifts of *NM*
   and new tangency equilibrium
   after income or price changes

QUESTIONS FOR DISCUSSION

1 Explain why one, and only one indifference curve will go through any point on an indifference map: i.e., why two such curves never cross.

2 If the consumer is at a point on his budget line where it *crosses* an indifference curve, explain why he cannot have reached equilibrium. How will he still want to keep moving?

3 Can *you* generate food's ordinary *dd* demand curve from Fig. 22-10? To get the demand for clothing, show that *NM* must now pivot around *M* rather than around *N*.

4 Give Robinson Crusoe (or Utopia) a production-possibility curve between food and clothing like the curve of Fig. 2-8. Give him the indifference curves like those of this Appendix. Can you depict the basic equilibrium of any economy from the resulting tangency and interpret its price aspect? (Peek ahead to page 422, footnote 9, for the answer.)

5 If the indifference contours were concave instead of being convex, show that the law of diminishing relative marginal utilities would be negated. And then note that a tangency point would be a point of minimum total satisfaction rather than a point of maximum satisfaction.

6 In Fig. 22-8, label the indifference contours with the utility numbers 1, 2, 3, 4. Show that any other four numbers would give the same demand equilibrium, provided only that they are in more-or-

less the same relationship. Infer from this that only "ordinal utility" rather than "numerically measurable" utility is needed for demand economies.

7 *Extra credit problem:* Can you explain how a consumer's-surplus diagram can illustrate the deadweight harm, or economic inefficiency, that any sales tax must entail? The figure below is much like Fig. 20-9 and Fig. 22-4. Each new unit of good bought will add more and more utility, as shown by the area under the *d* curve and as measured in terms of the unchanging units of utility from leisure forgone, reckoned at $2.50 for each of the 10 hours of the day. Now suppose the government needs to raise $5 (or 2 hours) per person for its army or roads. The most efficient tax would be for it simply to take $5 as a lump-sum tax from the man, as shown by the rectangle marked $5 at the southeast of the diagram, subtracted from his leisure. But suppose, instead, we put a sales tax of $1.00 per unit on this good he buys. With the supply curve shifted upward as

from *s* to *s'*, the new equilibrium will be shifted up from *E* to *E'*, as shown by the rectangle *sAE's'*. The government will collect exactly its needed $5 of taxes (explain!). But the consumer has cut back sharply his consumption of this good, and now the utility benefit of this good in excess of its forgone utility leisure—its "consumer's surplus"—has gone from being the triangle *sEd* to being the smaller triangle *s'E'd*. The tax rectangle *sAE's'* is an *unavoidable* loss, for the government cannot get its resources for the army without depriving us citizens of labor-leisure resources. But what about the little, barred triangle *AEE'*? That is the avoidable, or dead-weight, loss of consumer's surplus that results from using a sales tax with its distorting of equilibrium away from true social costs and human utility.

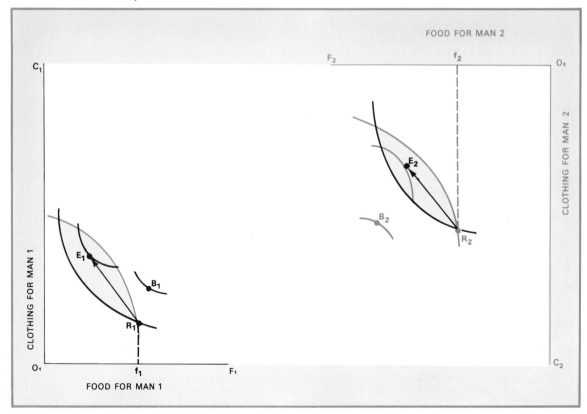

8 Geometry buffs can interpret the accompanying diagrams to show how the efficiency of rationing can be improved on. Before war, Man 2 at red B_2 is richer than *Man* 1 at black B_1. With food scarce in wartime, men are rationed to R_1 and R_2 points of food consumption. But the men have unequal substitution slopes there (as shown by light comparison curve of the other chap). Hence, shaded areas show how *both* can be made better off if the rich man can buy some of the poor man's food ration. They trade on parallel black arrows, ending at black E points (of equal slopes!) where no further mutually beneficial moves are possible. Can you show that prerationing equilibrium of pure competition at B_1 and B_2 was "efficient" in the sense that *both* could *not* be made better off? HINT: Slope at B_1 equals slope at B_2 because of common tangency to common market-price ratio. NOTE: Final efficient E situation might also have been reached by a heavy money tax on the rich with scarce goods being auctioned off to all men at common E_i price ratio. (Reference: Question 4 of Chapter 27's Appendix uses a similar geometric technique of "box diagram" useful for more advanced "welfare economics" and you might later reread the two together.)

23
COMPETITIVE SUPPLY

Cost of production would have no effect on competitive price if it could have none on supply.

JOHN STUART MILL

The last chapter looked behind the market demand curve for its base in terms of the marginal utilities of individuals. It showed how the demand curves of the different individuals in the market place can be summed to form the aggregate market demand schedule.

In this chapter we look behind the supply curve of the industry to find its base in the costs of the different competitive firms. A new concept—that of "marginal" or "extra" cost—is seen to be crucial.

We are interested in competitive supply not merely as a descriptive device. Here in this chapter, we are also interested in showing that the marginal cost concept has a crucially important role to play in allocating for any society its resources in the most efficient manner. (We leave to the following chapter a

detailed view of the different kinds of costs that are important in economics.)

SUMMING ALL FIRM SUPPLY CURVES TO GET MARKET SUPPLY

Figure 22-1 showed how we add horizontally all individual demand curves to get the aggregate market demand curve. The same horizontal addition applies to supply.

Suppose we are dealing with a competitive market for fish. How much of this commodity will be brought to market at each different level of market price? Firm A will bring so much to market at a particular price; Firm B will bring so much at this same

FIG. 23-1. To get market supply curve, we add all firms' supply curves.
At each price, such as $40, we add quantities supplied by each firm to get total market quantity supplied. This applies to any number of firms. In fact, if there were a thousand identical firms, the market supply curve could be made to look just like the supply curve of each firm by a careful thousandfold change of horizontal scale in the third diagram; if no horizontal scale change is made, aggregate supply must look flatter than each firm's.

price; Firm C will bring the amount shown on its supply curve; and so it goes. The total Q that will be brought to market at a given market P will be the sum of all the q's which firms will want to supply at that price. And similarly at any other price.

Summary. To get the aggregate SS supply curve for a good, we must add horizontally the ss supply curves of the independent producers of that good.

This is illustrated for two firms by Fig. 23-1. Recall that the firms' momentary-run supply curves are defined as the inelastic supplies in a time period so short that no variability in output is possible:

To get the *industry's* vertical momentary supply curve $S_m S_m$, add horizontally, at the same P, *all firms'* vertical momentary supply curves.

Now recall from Chapter 20 that Marshall's "intermediate" or "short-run" equilibrium is defined as that period of time in which the firm is stuck with certain fixed commitments, but in which some variable factors of production can be altered so as to produce more output along the various firms' supply curves:

Again, to get the industry's *short-run* supply curve $S_s S_s$, add horizontally at the same P the *short-run* supply curves of the fixed number of firms which exist in that short run.

Our problem is to see how a firm's supply curve is determinable from its costs.

DEFINITION OF MARGINAL COST NUMERICALLY AND GRAPHICALLY

Basic to industry supply is Marginal (or extra) Cost. Table 23-1 shows how we calculate Marginal Cost: By subtracting the $16,000 total cost of producing $q^* = 400$ units from the $16,040.05 total cost of producing $q = 401$, we find $MC = 40.05 for producing 1 more unit beyond q^*; to produce 1 less unit involves a difference, $MC = 39.95, or $16,000 — 15,960.05$. So at q^* itself we may, by disregarding or averaging over the trifling differences caused by the trifling lumpiness of units, estimate $MC = 40.

Definition: Marginal Cost at any production level q is the total cost of producing one extra unit more

TYPICAL CALCULATION OF MARGINAL COST

(1) QUANTITY PRODUCED, q	(2) TOTAL COST TC	(3) MARGINAL COST MC
390	$15,960.05	
		$39.95
400	16,000.00	
		40.05
401	16,040.05	

TABLE 23-1. Marginal or extra cost can be shown numerically by subtraction.
The difference in total dollar cost from producing an extra unit is found by subtracting adjacent items of total dollar cost in Column (2). At $q^* = 400$, $MC = 40 to a high degree of approximation.

(or less);[1] it comes from subtracting total dollar costs of adjacent outputs.

Just as we can calculate MC for $q^* = 400$, we can calculate it for any and every q. Table 23-1 put a microscope on cost behavior around 400 and 401 units. To see the big picture,[2] let us stand off and see how the Marginal Cost curve behaves at *all* levels of output.

Figure 23-2 and its table show that Marginal Cost is related to Total Cost in the same way that Fig. 23-3 related marginal utility to total utility. From Fig. 23-2(b), you will see this:

MC tends to be U-shaped: ultimately it is rising, even though there may be an initial phase in which MC is falling.

Why can you expect Marginal Cost to be ultimately a rising curve? This takes us back to the law of diminishing returns of Chapter 2. Behind the dollar costs of the firm lies the production relationship between the firm's output and the labor and other factor inputs it hires. This will be discussed in depth in Chapter 27, but here we can indicate the general logic of the situation.

[1] WARNING: MC is usually *not* the same as average cost per unit, which we get by dividing total cost by number of units produced: MC is extra cost, or incremental cost, or differential cost; or, as we have seen from the use of the word "marginal" in connection with *extra* utility, the appropriate name is indeed Marginal Cost.

[2] Figure 23-2 and the accompanying table measure q in units of hundreds; hence, $q = 300, 400, 401, 500$ in Table 23-1 would show there as $q = 3, 4, 4.01, 5$, etc.

FIG. 23-2. Marginal cost is to total cost as marginal utility is to total utility.
To find the *MC* of producing the fifth unit, we subtract $160 from $210 to get $50. At *P* = $40,
it will not pay to produce the fifth unit, but it will pay to produce the fourth unit. (Compare
this table with marginal utility Table 22-1 .)

In (a) a smooth curve has been shown through the points of *TC*. In (b) a smooth curve has
been drawn through the steps of extra cost. Ultimately *MC* is rising, but it may at first fall,
giving the curve a U-shaped contour.

CALCULATING MARGINAL COST		
(1) OUTPUT (IN HUNDREDS) *q*	(2) TOTAL COST *TC*	(3) MARGINAL COST *MC*
0	$ 55	
		$30
1	85	
		25
2	110	
		20
3	130	
		30
4	160	
		50
5	210	

TABLE 23-2

Suppose some factor is held fixed in the short run
we are considering: it could be fixed land, or, in manufacturing, it could be fixed plant capacity. Suppose
that we get our varying amounts of *q* by hiring varying amounts of some factor input such as labor. If we
can always buy labor at the same wage per unit, the
only reason why our marginal or extra cost of getting
more *q* should rise would be because the extra prod-

uct added by each successive unit of labor is going
down. Hence, if we do get diminishing returns to the
varying labor factor, we shall certainly get increasing
Marginal Cost.

Costs and productivity returns are merely opposite
sides of the same relationship.

Why does *MC* often decline *at first*, as shown in
Fig. 23-2(b)? Recall that the law of diminishing returns tends *ultimately* to hold: at the beginning, it
might be negated by a strong tendency toward
increasing returns, owing to the economies of large-
scale production associated with indivisibility of the
process and chances to introduce more elaborate division of labor as scale expands. If at first we have
strong *increasing* returns, we must at first have
declining rather than increasing Marginal Cost.[3]

---

[3] Later we shall examine the behavior of Marginal Cost in the
long run. Suppose we consider so extended a period of time that
nothing can be regarded as fixed. Old plants can wear out and be
replaced. New plants can be designed and built. Old land obligations can expire. New land contracts can be made. And so forth.
In the long run, as a small firm, we may be able to buy *all* the factors of production in balance at unchanged prices. Now what
will happen to long-run costs, particularly long-run *MC*, if the
firm has no fixed factors and can enjoy "constant returns to

We can summarize the relationship between the productivity laws of returns and the laws of Marginal Cost:

A tendency for varying factors to show diminishing returns when applied to fixed factors implies a tendency for MC to be rising. If at first there is increasing returns, there will at first be declining MC—ultimately to be followed by diminishing returns and increasing MC.

COMPETITIVE MAXIMUM PROFIT: DETERMINING THE QUANTITY TO SUPPLY

It is evident that costs are vital determinants of how much a firm will be willing to supply. It would supply nothing if market P were too low to cover its out-of-pocket expenses, and would supply much if P were very high. To decide how much to supply at each market P, the firm will want to know the *extra* or *marginal* cost to it of each extra unit of q. Thus, consider Firm A in Fig. 23-1, which is shown supplying 4 (hundred) units at a market price of $40 per unit. Why does $q = 400$ and not 401 or 3.99?

At first you might be tempted to reply: "Firm A has no choice but $q = 400$ because that is all it can sell at $40—no more, no less." What is wrong with such an answer? It overlooks the facts that this is a model of *perfect competition.*

Definition: A perfect competitor is too small and unimportant to affect the market price. Like a wheat farmer, he is a "price taker" who can sell *all* he wishes to at the ruling market price. In terms of elasticity of demand, a perfect competitor faces a (virtually) horizontal *dd* demand curve for *his* product—his elasticity of demand being infinite.[4]

scale"? (This is defined as a state where there is no reason for diminishing returns to operate, since *all* factors grow in balance, and where all economies of large-scale production have already been realized.) *Answer:* If long-run constant returns to scale holds, then doubling all inputs will exactly double their total dollar costs and will at the same time exactly double total output. Hence, there will be constant Marginal Cost, *MC* being *horizontal* rather than rising or falling. (See Chapter 24 for the longest run "planning" or envelope cost curves.)

[4] Figure 23-3 shows the contrast between the industry demand curve *DD*, relating P to the sum of firm demands $Q = q_1 + q_2 \ldots$, and the *dd* curve facing any one small competitor. If there are thousands of firms in the industry, the draftsman will have

Granted that a perfect competitor can sell any q he chooses at the going P, how does he pick his best q supply response? A perfect competitor picks the quantity he will supply by referring to his marginal cost curve, so that $P = MC$. Why?

He will do this because he is interested in maximizing the total profit he can earn. Profit is the difference between the total revenue he receives from selling his output and the total cost incurred in producing that output. He increases his total profit so long as the *extra* revenue brought in from the last unit sold is greater than the *extra* cost which that last unit entailed. Total profit reaches its peak —is maximized—when there is no longer any extra profit to be earned by selling extra output. The last little unit he produces and sells is just in balance as far as extra revenue and extra cost are concerned. What is that extra revenue? It is price per unit. What is that extra cost? It is marginal cost. Q.E.D.

Specifically, in Fig. 23-1(a), why might you choose to produce quantity $q^* = 400$ at $P = \$40$? Only one answer is correct: Because the 401*st* unit would involve you in extra (or so-called "marginal") cost of just over $40; and the 399*th* unit involved you in extra cost of just under $40; so that the 400*th* unit of q involves an *extra* or *marginal cost* just exactly equal to price P of $40. (To clinch your understanding, refer back to page 417's Table 23-1 to verify optimality of $q^* = 400$.)

DERIVING THE FIRM'S SUPPLY CURVE FROM ITS *MC* CURVE

We say that a competitive firm is at its Maximum-profit position when it is definitely producing all

to train a microscope on point A of the industry *DD* curve to show how this sloped curve will reappear as the horizontal *dd* curve to the Lilliputian eye of the firm.

FIG. 23-3

FIG. 23-4. Profit-maximizing competitor has supply curve determined by Marginal Cost.

If you can sell all you wish at P given by horizontal $d'd'$, your Maximum-profit equilibrium comes at its intersection with the MC curve at A: your maximum profit is positive; and the gray-shaded triangle shows you would lose some profit if you produced less than at A, since your extra revenue of P would exceed your extra cost, MC.

If P dropped to $d''d''$ level, you maximize profit at C: $P = MC$ there minimizes your unavoidable short-run loss. If P falls below Shutdown cost, your revenue fails to cover out-of-pocket expenses and you will shut down. If P is at Break-even cost B, your maximized profit (inclusive of normal return to your labor and capital) is just zero: new firms will not enter, and old ones will not leave.

units with MC less than P, and is not producing further units for which MC is definitely greater than P. Evidently, its Maximum-profit supply response comes when it follows the rule

Price = Marginal Cost or $P = MC$

This means that the firm's *supply curve* is given by its rising MC curve as shown in Fig. 23-4. Thus, at the indicated horizontal $d'd'$ level of $50, the firm will find its Maximum-profit supply response at the intersection point A. (To check this, note that the loss of profit from producing a little less than at A is shown by the shaded triangle, depicting the surplus of P over MC on the last little units.)

Alternatively, suppose the firm were faced by a horizontal dd at $40. Its maximum-profit supply response is shown at the intersection point B. It happens, as our original cost Table 23-1 shows, that the firm just breaks even, covering *all* its long-run costs at this point (total cost = total revenue = $16,000).

Or suppose the firm faced $d''d''$. At this price below $40, the firm cannot break even; but it does *minimize its short-term losses* (or maximize its 'algebraic' profit) there at the C intersection with the MC curve (as you can show by penciling in a shaded triangle like that at A).

Thus, we see that the firm's competitive supply curve runs along its rising MC curve.

The next section establishes the lower end of the rising supply curve.

TOTAL COST AND SHORT-RUN SHUTDOWN CONDITIONS [5]

Recall that earlier the "short run" was defined as that period of time in which certain equipment, resources, and commitments of the firms are fixed; but it is a period long enough for the firm to vary its output by hiring more or fewer variable factors of production, such as labor, raw materials, and so forth. It is certainly not a precise period of time which will be the same for all industries. Even within an industry, we can be asking questions about "short-run" periods of different duration. At one ultra-short extreme, so many decisions have already been frozen as to make the resulting Marginal Cost curve practically a vertical and inelastic line. Or at the other extreme, we can permit so much time to pass as to let more and more of the equipment have a chance to wear away or be replaced, thereby making the resulting Marginal Cost curve almost as flat as it will be in the longest run, when *no* fixities are possible except those associated permanently with the management of the firm itself.

Now consider a firm making its short-run decisions. It has a certain "fixed cost": this is defined as the total of costs that will go on anyway because of its fixed commitments that are already frozen in the short run; examples would be bond interest, rentals,

[5] This section may be skipped in a brief course.

overhead salaries, franchise taxes and so forth. The rest of its "total cost" is called "variable cost"; this is defined as the sum of all costs that vary with output; examples are cost of materials, wages for workers on the production line, and so forth. Chapter 24 will discuss all these in detail.

But now consider the firm facing lower and lower P. It always has the option of producing nothing at all. How much will it then lose? With its revenue zero and all its fixed cost going on anyway, its shutdown loss will exactly equal its fixed cost. When P falls so low as to recover *less revenue than the variable cost it incurs* to produce positive q, the firm will prefer to shut down completely: why should it produce if that means it incurs a loss greater than the fixed cost it incurs when shut down? So this rule holds:

Shutdown cost. At the critically low market price where the firm just recovers its *variable* cost by producing, it will be on the verge of shutting down. Below that point, it will produce nothing at all.

Above that P, it *will* produce along its short-run Marginal Cost curve. For, at such $MC = P$ points, the firm will be getting something toward covering its fixed cost; and either it will be getting maximized positive profits, or at least will be minimizing its losses (and in that sense maximizing its algebraic profit).

The location of the Shutdown cost was shown in Fig. 23-4. The MC curve slopes up from below that point, but there the supply curve does not run along the MC curve.

We can summarize what has now been established. Just as marginal utility lies behind the demand curve, Marginal Cost lies behind the supply curve. *The supply curve of an industry is seen to be the summed rising MC curves of the firms in that industry.*[6]

SYNTHESIS OF MARGINAL COST AND MARGINAL UTILITY

Having described market equilibrium, we are now in a position to understand *how important the MC con-*cept is in helping society to organize its production efficiently and responsively. We can now combine cost and utility, or more precisely Marginal Cost and marginal utility.

ROBINSON CRUSOE Begin with the simplest case—that of Robinson Crusoe. A single man, so the story goes, works so many hours picking strawberries. (a) Each extra berry brings him *diminished* marginal utility. (b) Each extra hour of sweaty labor brings him *increasing marginal disutility*. (c) Working with fixed land, each extra minute of work, because of the law of *diminishing returns*, brings less and less extra berries.

It must follow from these assumptions that Crusoe will work up to the critical equilibrium intersection where a declining marginal-utility-of-berries curve

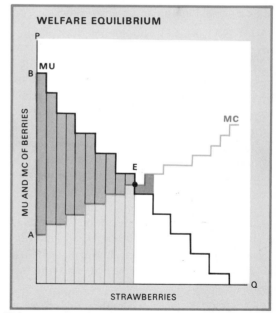

FIG. 23-5. Supply-demand intersection can help solve the Planner's welfare optimum of marginal utility and Marginal Cost.

Here Robinson Crusoe or a communal-state Planner utilizes apparatus of supply and demand to determine optimal well-being output. Black *MU* curve intersects light red *MC* curve at *E*. Cost of picking strawberries is given by light red area, measuring "utils" of forgone-leisure. Vertical slabs of light gray shaded area under *MU* give excess strawberry utils over utils of cost. Hence light gray shaded area of consumer's net surplus is maximized by producing at *E* intersection (dark gray shaded area to the right of *E* shows loss from producing too much).

---

[6] The next chapter will discuss the longest-run case in which new firms can come into the industry and old firms leave it.

(which looks like both an *MU* and a *dd* curve) intersects with a rising marginal curve of disutility involved in providing the effort needed for additional berries (which is like an *MC* and *ss* curve).

Figure 23-5 gives the Robinson Crusoe welfare equilibrium.[7] The light red *MC* curve is now rising because diminishing returns makes the *MC* of extra strawberries rise; the black curve falls because of diminishing *MU*. Welfare is maximized at *E*, where *MU* of berries is in balance with *MC* (measured, remember, in utils of forgone-leisure). The "triangular" area *AEB* represents the consumer's (net) surplus, and it is larger at *E* than anywhere else. (The shaded dark gray "triangle" beyond *E* shows the loss of well-being from producing that many berries. You can pencil in a similar "triangle" to the left of *E* reflecting what you would lose of consumer's (net) surplus if you did *not* produce the last units.)

COMMUNAL STATE Economics is a science of *society*, not of a single isolated individual. Still, we can keep our story simple if we now apply it to a communal state, where all families are treated exactly alike or where some single benevolent or malevolent dictator provides the utility and disutility magnitudes that are to be maximized.

Figure 23-5 still serves to show optimal welfare for a monistic, communal state, just as it did for the one-man Crusoe world. Now a Planner, using computers or market devices, would want to realize the same *MU* and *MC* equality shown there.

Indeed, both Crusoe and a planning board might achieve the *MU* = *MC* equilibrium by introducing a price of strawberries,*P*.[8] Then by equating *MU* = *P* and *MC* = *P*, they would succeed in achieving their welfare optimum.

MANY GOODS One last complication before considering the real world. Crusoe or a planning board would have to cope with many goods: strawberries

---

[7] To keep matters at their simplest, suppose we can ignore (b) the increasing marginal disutility of sweaty labor, by continuing the measurement of all our welfare costs to fixed "disutils" of labor time; or better, what is the same thing, we consider each hour of forgone-leisure as having a constant marginal utility so that we can arithmetically reckon both disutilities and costs in these leisure-labor utils. This important notion of "forgone-*opportunity* cost" will be discussed again in the next chapter.

[8] This price could be in units-of-utility-of-forgone-leisure. Or, if we defined labor so that $1 equals the wage of 1 unit of work and 1 unit of forgone-leisure, then strawberry *P* could be expressed in dollars.

versus tea versus cotton gloves, etc. Suppose labor is freely transferable among the different activities— tea, berries, etc. And, to keep the parable simple, suppose that *varying* labor is applied to different grades of *fixed* land, each land being completely specialized to its industry. Clearly, then, each good will have a rising *MC* curve in terms of labor (and hence leisure-utils) applied to it.

What about society's (or Crusoe's) marginal utility from berries, tea, gloves, etc.? For simplicity suppose each good *independently* has its own total utility and marginal-utility schedules like Fig. 22-3. Now comes the vital question. How should Crusoe or the Planner most efficiently allocate labor among the different industries to effect the optimal-welfare pattern of berry production, tea production, etc.?

Obviously, to maximize welfare and allocation efficiency we must in each industry[9] get a balance of

---

[9] For each new industry, we draw a new diagram like Fig. 23-5, and again maximize the area of "consumer's (net) surplus" where $P_i = MC_i$ and P_i reflects *MU* of the *i*th good as determined from consumer *dd* curves. WARNING: if coffee is not *independent* of tea, you could not draw its diagram *independently* of that of tea. Also, if the transferable factor inputs in terms of which we measure the MC_i did not satisfy our simplifying axiom of strict constancy of forgone utils, the consumer's-surplus exposition here would have to be made more complicated; advanced economics handles the problem rigorously by the more complex tools of intermediate economic treatises. Fig. 23-6 here uses the methods of the Appendix to Chapter 22 to show the same welfare optimum as did Fig. 23-5. Robinson Crusoe maximizes welfare at *E*, where MC_{tea}/MC_{gloves} (as measured by the dark red slope of his *p-p frontier*) and MU_{tea}/MU_{gloves} (as measured by the black slope of his indifference curves) are each equal to the market P_{tea}/P_{gloves} (as measured by the dark red slope of the price-line through *E*). Verify that *E* does represent the highest well-being possible for this simplified society. The same story holds if the black contours depict Planners' preference.

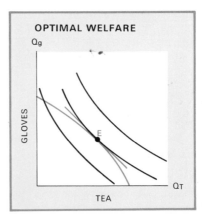

OPTIMAL WELFARE

Qg

GLOVES

E

QT

TEA

FIG. 23-6

MU and of *MC*. If tea involves twice the *MC* of strawberries, its *P* must be twice as great. These $P_i = MC_i$ equivalences are vital in any society aiming to solve WHAT and HOW efficiently.

By now, the essential point should be obvious enough. But in leaving it, please notice that a simple "labor theory of value" will not properly solve the problem. Only if you reckon the *Marginal Cost* of a good can you get its proper price in terms of labor or of anything else!And setting prices merely proportional to labor used in an industry does not properly adjust for the scarcity of nonlabor inputs.

EFFICIENT MARKET ALLOCATION OF PRODUCTION

Now forget parables. Forget Robinson Crusoe. Forget a communal state. What about the anarchy of a million small competitors? Can a perfectly competitive market really achieve the same optimal *MC* equilibrium?

QUALIFICATIONS The answer is, "Yes." Better still, "Yes, maybe." First, you must rule out monopoly: no one expects that an unbridled profiteer will achieve the social optimum. Second, you must not be considering cases where people's demand curves *deviate* from true utility. That is, don't try to apply the theory to heroin production. Or, if you believe that because of advertising and conformity consumers have let themselves demand worthless gadgets that don't deserve to have the word "utility" applied to them, don't try to apply the theory to that area. If there remains a group of goods and industries —say shoes, beef, housing, etc.—where there are many reasonably informed consumers and many mutually competing competitive producers, then you may hope to achieve efficiency[10] by market pricing along *MC* lines.

[10] If the dollar votes of different consumers represented an "equitable" allocation, so that each person's dollar represented as ethically deserving a pull on the market as any other's, there would be no need to make the following important qualification: Efficient production and pricing does not mean that the FOR WHOM problem of society is being properly solved; it only means that the WHAT and HOW problems are being solved in the best way they can be solved consistent with the *existing distribution* of dollar-voting power and of sharing in national wealth and GNP. This qualification is vital.

MARKET SYNTHESIS Now turn to Fig.23-7 to see how a competitive system does bring out a balance between utility and cost. On the left, we add horizontally the demand curves for all consumers to get the market *DD* curve in the middle. (Recall Chapter 22.) On the right, we add all the separate firms' *MC* curves to get industry *SS* curve in the middle. Note what the equilibrium price at the *E* intersection achieves: it gives people on the left what they are willing to pay for and buy of the good at the *P* reflecting efficient social *MC*. On the right, we see that the equilibrium market price does allocate production most efficiently. (That is, the light red area *SS* in the middle does represent the minimized sum of light red cost areas on the right![11])

Summary: The ideal competitive market is a device for synthesizing (1) the willingness of people to pay for goods with (2) the actual (minimized) marginal costs of those goods. Without conscious planning, the competitive market does achieve the Robinson Crusoe or Planning Board most-efficient allocation of resources to determine HOW to produce each good.

Although Fig. 23-7 shows only one good, say, wheat, it can be duplicated to show how shoe production gets organized. Remember that labor and other resources are transferable not only between different wheat farms but also between the wheat and the shoe industries. Their respective MC_i reflect these social costs; and without the $P_i = MC_i$ conditions being satisfied, economic allocation would be "inefficient" in the following strong sense: "Unless *all* $P_i = MC_i$, one can reorganize production and make *everybody* better off—the poor, the rich,[12] wheat producers, shoe producers, etc!" Who pays for such an improvement? No one. It comes from cutting out deadweight waste and inefficiency in social allocation!

[11] Because dollar-voting power may not have been distributed so as to reflect ruling ethical notions of proper welfare and equity, the area under the market *DD* curve has not been shaded: for that would involve "adding" incommensurable utilities of different persons' dollars and an illegitimate leap from consumer's surplus to consumers' surplus. Remember the last footnote's qualifications!

[12] This is the first time we meet explicitly an important concept of intermediate economics, namely "pareto-optimality". Named after Vilfredo Pareto, an equilibrium is said to be "Pareto-optimal" if (and only if) there is no possible movement from it that could make *everyone* better off.

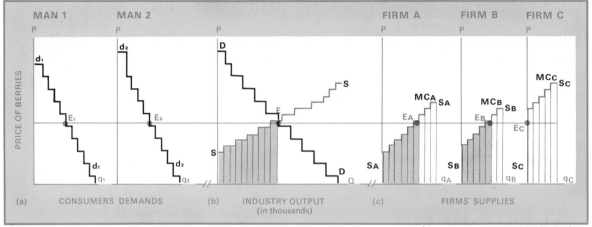

FIG. 23-7. Competitive-industry market integrates consumer demands and producer's minimized cost.

(a). Individual demands (as derived from Chapter 23's marginal utility considerations) are shown on the left. If there were 1,000 consumers like Man 1 and 1,000 like Man 2, we would add (horizontally) all their *dd* curves to get industry *DD* curve in the middle.

(b). The market brings together all consumer demands and firm supplies to reach equilibrium at *E*. The horizontal black line shows where each consumer on left and each firm on right reaches equilibrium. (Note: Light red area under *SS* represents total social cost (e.g., labor-leisure) of *Q*, and this area is at a minimum when all *MC*'s are equal).

(c). For each of these competitive firms, profits are maximized when supply curve is given by rising *MC* curve. Light red area represents firm's cost of producing. When $MC_A = P = MC_B$, we have Least-cost efficient allocation for industry!

FINAL SUMMARY OF EFFICIENCY OF MARGINAL-COST PRICING

A coldly objective scientist, who wanted to know nothing beyond how to describe and analyze competitive supply behavior and who had not the slightest interest in society's welfare, would consider the Marginal Cost concept important. But what about a person who was concerned also with human happiness and with the social efficiency of a pricing system? He would find the equating of price to Marginal Cost even more interesting. Our analysis has demonstrated the following remarkable truth:

Only when prices of goods are equal to Marginal Costs is the economy squeezing from its scarce resources and limited technical knowledge the *maximum* of outputs. Only when each source of an industry's output has had its rising *MC* equated to *any* other source's *MC*—as will be the case when each *MC* has been set equal to the common *P*—can that industry be producing its total *Q* at *minimum*

Total Cost. Only then will society be out on its production-possibility frontier and not inefficiently inside the frontier.

This equal-marginal-cost dictum is as applicable to a communist, socialist, or fascist society as it is to a capitalistic society. Unless wheat cultivation has been pushed in different parts of the Soviet Union so as to equalize Marginal Costs (including transportation), the Planners there will be failing to achieve the abundance of wheat and other goods that could be theirs with more efficient allocation of resources. (Perhaps it is not surprising to learn from reading the recent debates in their own economic journals that they are gradually becoming aware of this basic fact of logic and economics.)

Because Marginal Cost has this optimality property, it can with some care be used as a yardstick to detect inefficiency in any institutional setup. Thus, if perfectly competitive industries did not exist at all, or if they were rarer even than they are today, one would still derive great benefit from defining and studying the concept of Marginal Cost.

NONOPTIMALITY OF COMPETITIVE *LAISSEZ-FAIRE* PRICING

But we must not leave the subject of efficient pricing without a warning. We have *not* proved that *laissez-faire* with perfect competition maximizes the greatest good of the greatest number. We have *not* proved that it produces a maximum of social utility. We have *not* proved that it results in the best attainable level of social welfare. For people are not equally endowed with purchasing power: some are very poor through no fault of their own. Some are very rich, and not necessarily because of any virtue or effort that they or their ancestors have ever performed. So the weight of dollar votes, which lie behind the individual demand curves on the left side of Fig. 23-7, is not necessarily equitable or even tolerable as judged by many ethical systems (various forms of Christianity, Buddhism, "fair shares," etc.). In terms of many ethical systems, the social welfare might be improved by redistributive taxation, rather than letting the end result depend upon *laissez-faire* pricing by the property ownership that happens to prevail. All that marginal-cost pricing has been demonstrated to have in these discussions is the property of helping to lead to "efficiency"—efficiency in the sense that there is no "deadweight loss" in the system; i.e., *no possibility of making everybody better off* by moving from within to the edge or boundary of the production-possibility curve of Chapter 2. This type of falling short of full production possibilities will be referred to again in Chapter 26, footnote 10. When we depart from $P = MC$ pricing, along with inequities of distribution goes the inefficiency of deadweight loss. Marginal-cost pricing is part of the recipe for getting the good society: it is not alone a sufficient condition for having achieved it.

This completes our discussion of the relationship between Marginal Cost and industry supply, and of marginal-cost pricing in its relationship to efficient allocation of resources. The next chapter will go more deeply into the nature and variety of concepts of cost. And later chapters will examine the important cases that deviate from perfect competition —such as monopoly or oligopoly.

SUMMARY

1 In a competitive market, aggregate supply of a group of independent firms comes from adding horizontally their separate supply curves.

2 The short-run is defined as that period of time in which some of the firm's productive factors and costs are fixed and some are variable.

3 For a firm we can define Marginal Cost as its *extra* or incremental cost of producing an *extra* unit of output, and can compute the instantaneous rate of Marginal Cost at each output from a smoothed schedule or graph of costs.

4 Behind cost relations lie production relationships and schedules. Thus upward or downward slopes of costs and of productivity-returns are reverse sides of the same coin; when the law of diminishing returns ultimately holds, the MC curve ultimately rises; when there is an initial stage of increasing returns, MC initially falls; if *all* factors of production could be brought in balance at unchanged prices, and if output were then to show constant returns to scale, long-run Marginal Costs could be horizontal forever.

5 A perfectly competitive firm is defined as one which is able to sell all it wants to at the posted market price. To maximize its (algebraic) profit, it will move along its (horizontal) demand curve until it reaches its rising Marginal Cost curve. At this intersection, $MC = P$, and the firm is maximizing its profits or minimizing its losses. So the industry supply curve from a given number of firms will come from adding horizontally their relevant Marginal Cost curves.

6   Out-of-pocket costs (or avoidable, variable costs) must be taken into consideration in determining a firm's short-run "Shutdown point." Below some critical P the firm will not even be recovering in price revenues the variable cost that could be saved completely if it shut down; so rather than end up losing more than its fixed cost, it will shut down and produce nothing at lower P's.

7   Beyond its importance for describing and explaining *competitive supply*, the concept of Marginal Cost has great importance for *welfare economics*. The problem of HOW goods are to be produced is being solved most efficiently only if every source of production for a good is being utilized up to the same MC level—an optimal result that is guaranteed when $P = MC$ everywhere. The problem of WHAT goods are best to be produced and in what amounts is solved in a Robinson Crusoe or Planning world by equating marginal utilities and Marginal Costs. Just as MU lies behind *dd,* so does MC lie behind *ss*; the competitive market, despite its surface appearance of anarchy and chaos, does provide one method for achieving economic efficiency. (WARNING: By itself, competitive pricing cannot ensure that the FOR WHOM distribution of dollar voting power is ethically optimal: taxes and transfers might be needed for that, after which competitive pricing could do the rest of the job.)

CONCEPTS FOR REVIEW

summing *ss* curves to get *SS*	Shutdown cost (or point)
Marginal (or extra) Cost	Robinson Crusoe or Planner's welfare
$P = MC$, Maximum-profit condition	optimum at $MU = MC$
identity of firm *ss* supply curve and	industry efficiency of
rising MC curve	$MC_A = MC_B$
diminishing returns and rising MC	market efficiency of $P = MC$

QUESTIONS FOR DISCUSSION

1. Show that the differences between momentary, short-run, and long-run periods are a matter of degree and not of kind. In reality, there is a continuum of time periods in which there are fewer and fewer factors that are *fixed*. Give reasons why (positive) Marginal Cost might at first fall and later rise.

2. "If a good can be stored, momentary supply will not be inelastic. When P gets very low, producers will *reserve* some product, storing it for future sale at a higher P." Justify. Can you show that this makes $S_m S_m$ have a rising slope?

3. Why would you ever supply goods at a loss along a short-run MC curve?

4. "If I can get more than enough to cover my fixed costs, I will produce, forgetting my variable costs." Show that two words have been exactly reversed here.

5. Appraise this dialogue. *A*: "What does efficiency matter if the wrong people have all the money?" *B*: "Why risk making everybody worse off? Besides, use the tax system for redistribution rather than deviate from competitive pricing at $P = MC$ since the latter method of redistribution is an inefficient device." *A*. "But will the tax system be so used?"

6. *Extra-credit problem*: Utopia can generate power from two generators: the newest one has lower *MC* at first. Show that only at peak loads will the firm use the older generator, only after the new generator's *MC* rises above the beginning *MC* of the older generator. At high loads, it should charge high *P*, equal to the common *MC*'s of the two. (Hint: Add the two *MC* curves horizontally as in Fig. 23-1.)

24
ANALYSIS OF COSTS AND LONG-RUN SUPPLY

A class in economics would be a real success if the students gained from it a real understanding of the meaning of cost in all its many aspects.

J. M. CLARK

The previous chapter introduced the definition of marginal cost, a fundamental concept that was seen to lie behind the supply curve of the competitive firm. Here in this chapter we shall go deeper into a variety of different cost concepts.

To understand the Maximum-profit equilibrium of any firm—whether it be the most perfect competitor, the most complete monopolist, or anywhere in the vast terrain of imperfect competition—we need to know how marginal and total costs are related to other cost concepts (such as average, or unit, costs) and to the breakdown between fixed costs and variable costs. Then we shall be ready in Chapter 25 to see how the marginal cost of *any* firm, whether competitive or not, has to be related to a similar concept on the demand side—namely, Chapter 25's *marginal* (or extra) *revenue*—in order to arrive at the Maximum-profit equilibrium of the firm.

TOTAL COST: FIXED AND VARIABLE

Consider a typical firm that produces the output q. At this stage, we do not care whether it is a perfect- or imperfect-competitor. At any one time, it has a certain state of technical knowledge, and it is confronted with the prices of the labor and other factor inputs it must buy. Now its accountants have been able to calculate what will be *its total dollar costs for producing each different level of q.*

Table 24-1 shows the simplified Total Cost[1] for each different level of output q. Columns (1) and

[1] These data depend upon engineering technology *and* upon the market prices of labor, land, fertilizer, and other factor inputs that the firm needs to produce each output of the good in ques-

(4) are the crucial ones, showing that TC goes up as q goes up. This is natural because it takes more labor and factor inputs to produce more of a good, and these extra factors involve an extra money cost. It costs \$110 in all to produce 2 units, \$130 to produce 3 units, and so forth.

FIXED COST Columns (2) and (3) break down Total Cost into two components: total Fixed Cost, FC; and total Variable Cost, VC. Figure 24-1(a) shows the breakdown.

Even when the firm produces zero output, it must honor its short-run commitments (contractual rentals, watchmen's pay) and continue to incur its total Fixed Cost of \$55. By definition, FC is the amount of cost that goes on independently of output; so it remains constant at \$55 in Column (2). Another name for Fixed Cost is overhead cost.

VARIABLE COST Column (3) shows total Variable Cost. By definition, VC begins at zero when q is zero. It is the part of TC that grows with output; indeed, the jump in TC between any two outputs is the same as the jump in VC. Why? Because FC stays constant at \$55 throughout and cancels out in any such comparison. (By subtraction, fill in the blanks in the third column of Table 24-1 with the missing VC data.)

tion. Before its accountants and production men were able to write down the numbers in Table 24-1, they had to make efficiency decisions in *engineering*, ensuring that the physical inputs cannot be combined to give more physical output. And what is not so obvious until we have studied production theory in Part Four, the firm must also have made minimizing decisions of an *economic* kind in arriving at its lowest expense for each q produced.

Various Cost Concepts

(1) QUANTITY q	(2) FIXED COST FC	(3) VARIABLE COST VC	(4) TOTAL COST $TC = FC + VC$	(5) MARGINAL COST PER UNIT MC	(6) AVERAGE COST PER UNIT $AC = \dfrac{TC}{q}$	(7) AVERAGE FIXED COST PER UNIT $AFC = \dfrac{FC}{q}$	(8) AVERAGE VARIABLE COST PER UNIT $AVC = \dfrac{VC}{q}$
0	55	0	55		Infinity	Infinity	
				34			
				30			
1	55	30	85		85	55	30
				27			
				25			
2	55	55	110		55	27½	27½
				22			
				20			
3	55	75	130		43 1/3	18 1/3	25
				21			
				30			
4*	55	105	160	**40**	40*	13¾	26¼
				50			
5	55	155	210	60	42	11	—
				—			
6	55	225	280		46 4/6	9 1/6	37 3/6
				80			
				90			
7	55	—	370		52 6/7	7 6/7	45
				100			
				110			
8	55	—	480		60	6 7/8	53 1/8
				120			
				130			
9	55	555	610		67 7/9	6 1/9	61 6/9
				140			
				150			
10	55	705	760		76	5 5/10	70 5/10

*Minimum level of Average Cost.

TABLE 24-1.
From schedule of firm's Total Cost, all other costs can be computed. All the costs can be calculated from Column (4)'s rising TC. Columns (5) and (6) are the important ones to concentrate on: incremental Marginal Cost, calculated by subtraction of adjacent rows of TC and shown in bold red; the light numbers of smoothed MC come from Fig. 24-1(b). In Column (6) note the point of minimum cost of $40 on the U-shaped AC curve. (Realize why the light $MC = AC$ at the minimum.)

Definitions: "Total Cost" represents lowest aggregate dollar expense needed to produce each level of output q. TC rises as q rises.

"Fixed Cost" represents the total dollar expense that goes on even when a zero output is produced. It is often called "overhead cost" and usually includes contractual commitments for rental, maintenance, depreciation, overhead salaries and wages, etc. It is a sunk cost that is quite unaffected by any variation in q; in the time period for which it is sunk, the only rule is this: Disregard Fixed Cost because FC cancels completely out of every decision.

"Variable Cost" represents all items of TC except for FC—as, for example, raw materials, wages, fuel, etc. Always, by definition,

$$TC = FC + VC$$

(Note that TC and VC always show exactly the same increments ($= MC$) as q changes, because FC is a strict constant.)

Review carefully how in Figure 24-1(a) the rising TC curve is shown broken down into its constant FC and rising VC components.

MARGINAL COST REVIEW

We saw in Chapter 23 how Marginal Cost is defined as the increment of Total Cost that comes from pro-

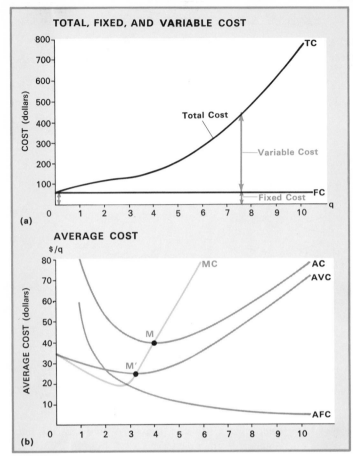

(a)

(b)

FIG. 24-1. Total cost curve gives all other curves.

(a). The total Fixed Cost curve is horizontal by definition. Adding on top of it the rising total Variable Cost gives the rising Total Cost curve.

(b). The light-red curve of Marginal Cost falls and ultimately rises, as in Chapter 23. *MC* is shown as a smooth curve after the steps of incremental cost are smoothed out; the numbers from the smooth *MC* curve are given in light red in Column (5) of Table 24-1 (and correspond to the slope of Fig. 24-1(a)'s*TC*).

By dividing *TC* by *q*, we can plot Average Cost: *AC* = *TC/q*. Similarly *AFC* comes from *FC/q*, and *AVC* comes from *VC/q*. At any point, we can add these two gray curves, *AFC* and *AVC*, and also get the *AC* curve at that point.

Note that *MC* intersects the U-shaped *AC* at *AC*'s minimum. This is no coincidence. To the left of *M*, *MC* is less than *AC* and hence is pulling *AC* down. To the right, *MC* > *AC* and hence is pulling *AC* up. At the *M* minimum point, *MC* = *AC;* hence *AC* is horizontal there, being neither raised nor lowered by the equivalent *MC*. Also *MC* cuts the *AVC* curve at its bottom.

ducing an increment of one unit of *q*. (Recall that "marginal," whether applied to utility, cost, or anything else, always means "extra," "additional," or "incremental" in economics.)

The dark red *MC* numbers in Column (5) of Table 24-1 come from subtracting the adjacent *TC* numbers in Column (4). Thus *MC* is $30 in going from 0 to 1 unit of *q* (i.e., $85—$55 = $30).

MC is seen to be $110—$85 = $25 in going from *q* = 1 to *q* = 2. *MC* is $20 for the third unit of *q*, $30 for the fourth, and thereafter rising steadily until it is shown as $150 in going from *q* = 9 *to q* = 10. (What is *MC* in going from *q* = 5 to *q* = 6? Pencil in your answer.)

Instead of getting *MC* from the *TC* column, we could as easily get the *MC* number by subtracting each *VC* number of Column (4) from the row below it. Why? Because Variable Cost always *grows* exactly like Total Cost, the only difference being that it must

—by definition—start out from 0 rather than from the constant *FC* level. (Check that 30—0 = 85—55, and 55—30 = 110—85, ...)

Figure 24-1(a) and (b) shows the behavior of Total Cost (in black) and Marginal Cost (in light red). Note that the *q* axes of the graphs are just lined up so that the eye can see the correspondence between *TC and MC*.[2]

[2] As in Fig. 23-2, we have assumed that units can be made indefinitely small, so that the smoothed-instantaneous *MC* values can be plotted and read off to give the red numbers of Table 24-1, Column (5). To help understand the smoothed-instantaneous *MC* at point *q*, see Fig. 24-2. It helps to clarify the distinction al-

This example shows MC to be U-shaped—at first falling, but ultimately rising. We saw why on page 417: At first there may be great economies in using some or all of the productive factors on a larger scale; and so MC at first falls down to a minimum positive number before again rising. If we stick to the short run where some factors of production are fixed, ultimately the old law of diminishing returns will operate to reduce the extra product that comes from adding equal physical and dollar increments of the varying factors onto the fixed factors. So the cost of getting extra product will ultimately become more expensive, and the short-run curve of Marginal Cost will ultimately be rising.

Marginal Cost has many uses. We saw in the last chapter that the rising MC curves of the firms provide us with the rising short-run ss supply curves which we sum horizontally to get the industry's short-run SS supply curve. In the next chapter we shall see that any firm—monopolistic or competitive—will find its Maximum-profit equilibrium by nicely

---

ready mentioned between MC as an increment of cost for a finite step between two points of q, and MC as a smoothed-out instantaneous rate depicting the tangential slope at which TC is rising at one given q point. The distance from a and b represents one extra unit of output. The distance from b to a' represents the resulting increase in Total Cost, which is the first and simplest definition of incremental Marginal Cost. The second definition is given by the slope of the Total Cost curve at point a—and what mathematicians call $d(TC)/dq$—or what is the same thing numerically, by the distance from b to c divided by the unit distance a to b.

In the limit, as the size of the extra units becomes small and we reexamine the ratios in the new smaller triangle, the discrepancy between the two definitions becomes relatively negligible. (That is, $ba \div bc$ approaches 1 as a' approaches a.)

RELATION BETWEEN SLOPE AND MARGINAL COST

FIG. 24-2

balancing its extra cost against its extra revenue (i.e., by finding an intersection of its Marginal Cost curve and what will be defined as its "Marginal Revenue" curve).

AVERAGE, OR UNIT, COST

But first turn to Column (6) of Table 24-1. This gives Average Cost (per unit), which is simply the Total Cost divided by the number of q units produced.

$$\text{Average Cost} = \frac{\text{Total Cost}}{\text{output}} = \frac{TC}{q} = AC$$

In Column (6), when only 1 unit is produced, Average Cost has to be the same as total Cost, or $85/1 = \$85$. But for $q = 2$, $AC = TC/2 = \$110/2 = \$55$, as shown. Note that Average Cost is, at first, falling lower and lower. (We shall see why in a moment.) But AC reaches a minimum of $40 at $q = 4$, and then slowly rises.

Figure 24 1(b) gives a careful plotting of U-shaped AC, nicely arranged below the TC it came from. We can now break down Average Cost into its two components, fixed and variable, just as earlier we had the breakdown of TC into FC and VC. By dividing each of the last two by q, we get Average Fixed Cost, $AFC = FC/q$ of Column (7); and Average Variable Cost, $AVC = VC/q$ of Column (8).

AVERAGE FIXED COST Since total Fixed Cost is a constant, dividing it by q gives in Column (7) a steadily falling Average Fixed Cost curve. The AFC curve in Fig. 24-1(b) looks like a unitary demand curve, or hyperbola that approaches both axes: it drops lower and lower, approaching the horizontal axis as the constant FC gets spread over more and more units. If we allow fractional and zero units of q, AC starts infinitely high, as the finite FC is spread over tinier and tinier units of q.

AVERAGE VARIABLE COST AVC of Column (8) and Fig. 24-1(b) at first falls and then ultimately rises. We could have predicted this U-shaped behavior of AVC from the U-shaped behavior of MC. When MC at first falls, each new q is pulling down the Average Variable Cost calculated over all the items.

THE POINTS OF MINIMUM AVERAGE COST Figure 24-1(b) is an important economic diagram. Fix it on your eye's retina. Note particularly the typical U shape of the *AC* curve.

The AC curve is always pierced at its minimum point by the rising MC curve.

This is no coincidence. And now we can explain why this has to be in the case.

Any average curve is pulled downward when *MC* is less than *AC*; if the last increment of cost is less than the average of all previous ones, it must pull the average down! But when *MC* gets as big as *AC*, *AC* no longer is pulled down; it now turns sideward or level. Then, if *MC* rises above the *AC*, it must of course pull *AC* up. So at the point where rising *MC* = *AC*, and only at that point, shall we find the point of Minimum *AC*.[3]

Summary. So long as Marginal Cost is below Average Cost, it is pulling Average Cost down; when *MC* gets to be just equal to *AC*, *AC* is neither rising nor falling and is at Minimum *AC*; after *MC* is above *AC*, it is pulling *AC* up. Hence:

At bottom of U-shaped *AC*, *MC* = *AC* = Minimum *AC*

Likewise, the *MC* curve cuts the *AVC* curve at the bottom of its *U*, pulling it down before this point because *MC* < *AVC* and pulling it up beyond that point because *MC* > *AVC*.

Now that we know how the *MC* curve intersects the *AC* and *AVC* curves where their U's bottom out, we can describe exactly how the firm's Shutdown cost and Break-even cost of Fig. 23-4 had been determined. The Break-even cost of long-run no-profit competitive equilibrium is seen here in Fig. 24-3 to be at the bottom of the U-shaped *AC* curve, in accordance with

P = MC = Minimum AC, in long-run equilibrium of zero excess-profits.

Likewise, the Shutdown cost would come at *M'*, once the horizontal *dd* of the firm had fallen to a level of

---

[3] Here is an explanation of the *MC* and *AC* relationship in terms of college grade averages. With *MC* below *AC*, Average Cost keeps being pulled down by the lowered cost of the final unit—just as one's cumulative grade average is pulled down when one's incremental average in the junior year is less than one's cumulative average up to that time. Only when one's "marginal or current" grade average crosses above or below one's cumulative grade average will the latter reverse its direction.

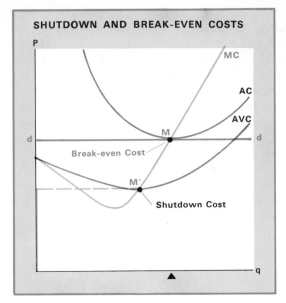

FIG. 24-3. Competitors are in long-run equilibrium where price-equals minimum average cost.

The Break-even cost is at *M* where *dd* is tangent to *AC* and *AC* is at its minimum. The short-run Shutdown cost is similarly at the bottom of the *AVC* curve, at *M'*.

P so low as to just cover minimum *AVC*. A price below this level would cause the firm to produce zero output.

LONG-RUN-PLANNING ENVELOPE CURVE[4]

We now have all the technical apparatus of the various cost concepts needed to permit us to tackle the problem of how any firm will find its Maximum-profit equilibrium. But one last technicality is needed to explain how a firm may *in the longest run* be able to have lowest costs through adapting and varying the size of its plant.

Recall that, once the firm has a fixed plant, it has a short-run U-shaped *AC* curve (call it *SAC* to emphasize its short-run nature). If the firm builds a larger plant, the new *SAC* curve must be drawn to the right. Now, suppose the firm is still in the planning stage, still quite uncommitted by any fixed obligations. It can write down *all possible* different U-shaped *SAC*

---

[4] For more on this see the extra-credit problem, question 10, at the end of this chapter.

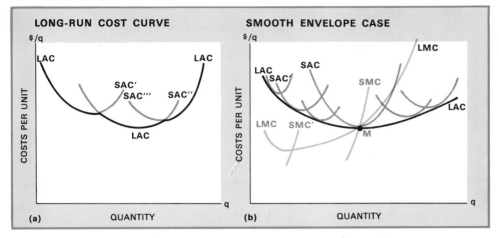

FIG. 24-4. In the longrun, a firm can choose its best plant sizes and its lower-envelope curve.
(a) *LAC* is the black "envelope" or lower frontier of the three possible choices of plant.
(b) There is now an indefinite number of choices and we get *LAC* as a smooth black envelope. In the usual manner we can derive from the black *LAC* curve its light red marginal curve, *LMC*.

curves, and then choose to select for each prescribed output the *SAC* that gives it the lowest costs. As *q* changes permanently, the firm hops to a new *SAC* curve.

Figure 24-4(a) shows how, in the longest run, the firm selects *SAC'* for low *q*: for intermediate *q*, it does better to plan to use *SAC''*; for still larger *q*, *SAC'''* leads to lowest costs. The black curve of Long-run Average Cost (*LAC*) is composed of the three *lowest* branches. Figure 24-4(b) shows the same lower limit in the case where the firm has choice of infinitely many smooth short-run *AC* curves (*SAC*, not *AVC!*): now *LAC* is the U-shaped smooth "lower-envelope" curve; and *its* well-behaved *LMC* provides the firm's long-run Marginal Cost curve, emerging from the *LAC* minimum point with a gentler slope than the short-run *SMC* curve there.

TASKS ACCOMPLISHED AND TASKS YET TO COME

The first half of this chapter is done. The important concepts of cost have been introduced: Total Cost, and its breakdown into total Fixed and total Variable Costs; Marginal Cost; all the different Average Costs (per unit), *AC*, *AFC*, and *AVC*; the interrelations be-

tween marginal and average concepts, including their intersection at the minimum point of the U-shaped average curve; finally, long-run envelope cost, *LAC*, when the number of plants and all elements can be adjusted to the level of production.

Since competitive *firms* must in the longest run realize a price equal to average cost—so that total dollar revenue equals total dollar cost, with no excess-profit—we are now equipped to carry on the analysis of longest-run competitive *industry* supply.

TOTAL COST AND LONG-RUN BREAK-EVEN CONDITIONS

Once I am stuck with certain fixed cost commitments, I will be willing to produce in the short run along my *MC* curve above the Shutdown cost—even though I am not earning enough to cover *all* my costs —as the last chapter showed. But only at some higher point on my *MC* curve will I be earning enough to cover *all* the costs that have to be met if I am to stay in business after the short run is over and I have regained my long-run freedom (1) to renew my old commitments or (2) to move to another industry.

There is, then, a critical "Break-even cost" below which *long-run P* cannot remain if I am to stay in this business. If every other firm were exactly like me, the long-run industry supply would dry up completely below this critical Break-even level which covers all costs of staying in business.

Now let us suppose further that entry into the industry is absolutely free in the long run, so that any number of firms can come into the industry and manage to produce in exactly the same way and at exactly the same costs as the firms already in my industry. Under such conditions of free "replication," it is obvious that long-run *P* cannot remain above this same critical Break-even cost at which they all cover their long-run total costs—including in these (1) all labor, materials, equipment, taxes, and other expenses; (2) all wages payable to the identical managers at the level determined competitively by the bidding in all industries for people of such talents and industriousness; and (3) the interest yield that any of them could get on the amounts of capital that they tie up in this industry instead of investing it elsewhere.

Long-run Break-even condition: This comes at a critical *P* where the identical firms just cover their full competitive costs. At lower long-run *P*, firms would leave the industry until *P* had returned to the critical equilibrium level; at higher long-run *P*, new firms would enter the industry replicating what existing firms are doing and thereby forcing market price back down to the long-run equilibrium *P* where all competitive costs are just covered.[5] Thus, as shown back in Fig. 24-3,

$$P = MC = \text{minimum competitive costs, the long-run Break-even equilibrium}$$

Figure 24-5 shows the longest-run supply curve for the industry. If this industry uses general factors, such as labor, that can be attracted from the vast ocean of other uses without affecting the level of wage rates, we get the case of constant costs as shown by the horizontal $S_L S_L$ supply curve.

[5] If investors tend to be overoptimistic and repeatedly produce an oversupply in the industry so as to create permanent losses on the average, full competitive costs might be defined compatibly with such chronic losses resulting from repeated miscalculations. And, of course, those who own exceptionally good cornland will be garnering as part of their costs juicy rent returns.

FIG. 24-5. Long-run industry supply depends on cost conditions.

With entry and exit free and any number of firms able to produce on identical, unchanged cost curves, the long-run $S_L S_L$ curve will be horizontal at each firm's Break-even level. If industry cannot attract all the factors it uses at unchanged factor-prices, the $S_L S_L'$ supply curve will have to slope upward as each firm's cost curves are all shifted upward.

By contrast, suppose the labor readily attracted from other industries must be applied to fixed factors peculiar to this industry alone—as, for example, rare vineyard land for the wine industry. Then enhanced *DD* for wine must intersect a rising $S_L S_L'$ long-run supply curve, as shown. Why rising? Recall the law of diminishing returns: varying labor, applied to fixed land, produces smaller and smaller increments of wine product; but each dose of labor costs the same in wages—and, hence, *MC* of wine rises. This longest-run rising *MC* means the supply curve must be rising.

It will be noted that in industries where $S_L S_L'$ slopes upward, owners of mines, land, know-how, and any other productive factors peculiar to this industry will earn a higher income (or what will be called "rent") from them as the industry expands.

If you do not like their earning such an extra return, you might take some of this away from them by taxes or other devices. But any special price ceilings placed on them in order to keep them from reaping such a return will definitely interfere with the equality-of-marginal-cost condition that is needed for maximal social efficiency—and such egalitarian legislation should be passed only if no better way of achieving this purpose can be found and the game is deemed worth the candle it will cost.

The relative rise in this industry's P and in its peculiar-factors' prices is a fact, but it also can be termed a desirable fact. Why? Not because the consumers who must pay more for this good are undeserving, nor because owners of the peculiarly scarce productive factors are especially deserving of higher incomes. Then why? Because any expansion of Q ought to be accomplished *efficiently* with least possible sacrifice of other Qs: the especially scarce factors have now to be severely rationed and be given more of other factors to work with; this will come about, not by a planning board's edict, but by a rise in the prices of this good and its peculiar factors, which will both signal the news of what must be done for efficiency and actually induce people to make the substitution needed if society is not to be inefficiently inside its *p-p frontier.*

If entry is really free, not only has perfect competition the nice property of ensuring that *each firm* ends up on an efficient *SAC* curve and at the minimum point on it, but in addition the Invisible Hand ensures that *industry* gets its Q from the proper number of firms as some are squeezed out or attracted in.[6]

IMPLICIT- AND OPPORTUNITY-COST ELEMENTS: A DIGRESSION

It is important to stress that the "full competitive minimum costs" which have to be just covered by normal price include more than accountants usually include in costs. Economists include a normal return to management services, as determined competitively in all industries; and a normal return to capital, as determined competitively elsewhere by industries of equal riskiness. In the above sense we may say that "normal profits" are included in costs and that "excess-profits" are competed away by entry of new firms, and "abnormal losses" are eliminated by long-run exit of firms.

IMPLICIT-COST ELEMENTS The return to a factor of production is economically important regardless of how it happens to be owned. To the economist, the returns that go to factors of production owned by the firm itself are so important as to deserve a new name: in contrast to wages that are *explicitly* paid to outside labor, we defined the concept of "implicit wages" as the return to the labor provided by the owner himself; and similarly, implicit rent and interest would be the returns to the land and capital provided by the owner himself rather than hired from outside owners.

Through miscalculation, a person may fail to receive his implicit wages in the short run; on the other hand, he may in the short run be getting more than the needed implicit return, the difference being a transient profit that has not yet been competed away. If he owns some special factors of production, like rich ore land, exceptional know-how, or fertile soil, his accounts may show a high return even in the long run; but we realize this is not so much profit as a return to that special factor of production he is lucky enough to own.[7]

OPPORTUNITY-COST ELEMENTS Related to the above discussion is an even broader notion about cost. The man in the street can clearly recognize costs that are actual cash payments; the accountant must go well beyond that. But the economist goes even further. He realizes that some of the most important costs attributable to doing one thing rather than another stem from the *forgoing opportunities* that have to be sacrificed in doing this one thing.

---

[6] If industry demand is large enough to permit numerous firms, then the optimal quantity each firm should produce is at the bottom of its U. It can be proved that the no-profit no-loss condition of ruthless competition will then achieve the most efficient number of firms to *minimize TC* for the industry's Q. For why force more expensive extra output from an existing number of firms if it can be got cheaper by replication of firms? And why not be sure that each of the identical firms produces neither too much nor too little, instead producing that Break-even q where $P = MC$ and where, likewise, P equals the lowest Average Cost per unit that will keep the firm in business in the long run? (If market demand is not large enough to keep numerous competitors viable, there will arise problems connected with the discreteness of firm sizes that will be depicted in Fig. 25-2). See question 10 for more on this.

[7] If he happens to own very fertile land and persists in cultivating it by uneconomical methods, he will be paying for his folly or stubbornness by forgoing the high return such land is capable of yielding; in dollars, the land becomes worth more to others than to him, and if he refuses to rent or sell it, he is as surely spending his sustenance to please his own tastes as he would be doing if he sold the land and spent the proceeds on wine, song, or being a country squire. A young person with high IQ and versatile talents who stays in a dull dead-end job or dying industry is similarly squandering his economic potential—but he may be happier that way.

Thus, Robinson Crusoe pays no money to anyone, but realizes that the cost of picking strawberries can be thought of as the sacrificed amount of raspberries he might otherwise have picked with the same time and effort or the sacrificed amount of forgone-leisure. This sacrifice of doing something else is called "opportunity cost." (Note that opportunity cost would still exist even if he loves to spend that hour in doing both kinds of picking and recognizes not the slightest disutility or sweat in performing that type of work.)

How does all this apply to industry supply and the firm's Break-even costs? In this way: The long-run Break-even level of costs includes, in addition to *explicit* cost outlays, those *implicit* costs that accrue to factors which might otherwise be used in alternative ways. If my labor in wheat could have been used in rye or even in some other man's wheat patch, then its value in those uses has to be met[8] or I shall not continue to supply it to my own wheat patch. For these reasons, full competitive cost intimately involves *opportunity cost*. The latter is an important concept, which covers much more territory than does the notion of implicit costs. The prices of labor and other factors that competitive farmers in an industry are forced to pay out explicitly depend importantly on the forgone opportunities for use in other industries or for leisure; and this means that all competitive costs involve opportunity costs in the background.

The terminology of economists is not uniform in this connection, but the concept of opportunity cost is important and we shall run into it again and again.

DECREASING COSTS AND THE BREAKDOWN OF PERFECT COMPETITION

Economic textbooks of years ago used to supplement the cases of horizontal supply and upward-sloping supply by a third case in which Marginal Costs of the firms were falling rather than rising and in which this was thought to create an industry long-run supply curve that sloped gently downward. Actually, if we review our argument of page 420 telling us why a maximizing firm will want to produce where $MC = P$, we see that the argument *fails completely* in the case where the firm's MC curve is a downward-sloping one. For if you move to the right of a point on a falling MC curve, you find that your additional P per unit is in excess of the now lower MC; and so in the case of decreasing Marginal Cost, the firm will expand its output more and more beyond the MC curve to gain extra profit.

Under decreasing Marginal cost, the first firm to get a head start will find its *advantage increasing the greater it grows*. As it forces other firms to contract their q's, their disadvantage will become aggravated as they are forced to travel back up their falling MC curves.

The result must be obvious:

Under persisting decreasing costs for the firms, one or a few of them will so expand their q's as to become a significant part of the market for the industry's total Q. We shall then end up with one of the following three cases:

(1) a single monopolist who dominates the industry

(2) a few large sellers who together dominate the industry and who will later be called "oligopolists"

(3) some kind of imperfection of competition that, in either a stable way or in connection with a series of intermittent price wars, represents an important departure from the economist's model of "perfect" competition where no firm has any control over industry price.

As the next section will show, when the firms in this industry all expand together, they could create what are called *external economies* (or *diseconomies*). Thus, a school for fishermen might become feasible only at high industry Q; and this training might cause a downward shift of every firm's cost curves as the industry total Q rises. The result could be an *industry* $S_L S_L$ curve that slopes *downward* owing to *external* economies without the breakdown of perfect competition. But external economies do not alter our main conclusion.

---

[8] The *best* alternative use is of course the proper one to use in reckoning opportunity cost. If alternatives exist along an infinite and smooth continuum, such opportunity cost will set a tight limit on costs to this industry. If alternatives come in steps, then the next-best alternative may give us only a lower limit on factor-price, leaving a possible area in which it has to be determined by the "rent" analysis of Part Four.

Internally decreasing cost for any firm destroys perfect competition, as Chapter 25 will discuss further.

EXTERNAL ECONOMIES AND DISECONOMIES[9]

Our discussion of decreasing costs has shown that it would be wrong to draw a curve of downward-sloping industry supply based upon costs falling *internally* within the firm. There is, however, a possible theoretical case in which the expansion of the Industry's Q somehow causes each firm's cost curves as plotted against its q to *shift downward*. Alfred Marshall deemed this a case of downward-sloping industry supply based upon what he called *external economies*.

An "external economy" is defined as a favorable effect on one or more persons that emanates from the action of a different person or firm; it shifts the cost or utility curve of each person it helps, and such an *externally* caused shift should be distinguished from any *internal* movement along the affected individual's own cost curve.

An "external *dis*economy" is defined in the same way, except that it refers to external *harm* that is done to others. The case where expansion of fishing by others in limited waters serves to shift up each boat's cost curves would be an example of an external diseconomy; another case would be one where each man's haste to drill for oil near his neighbors' boundaries lowers the amount of oil each recovered. Smoke nuisance and water pollution are two other familiar instances.

External economies have a considerable importance in connection with government activities that provide benefits to many individuals (so-called "public goods"). They are important too in connection with growth, where the building of a public road or some kind of "social overhead capital" like a hospital or dam has favorable external repercussions on many families, firms, and industries. The kinds of favorable external economies that are peculiarly associated with expansions along an industry supply curve—our main subject here—are not so easy to find. But here are a few examples.

Because fishing Q is expanding, the number of

trained fishermen that any firm might find to hire may go up. Or it may now pay the government, or some profit-seeking monopolist, to build a training school for fishermen, whereas previously such a school could not pay because of its high marginal cost at low scales of operation. A similar case would be one where specialized machinery for the fishing industry was producible by another industry only with excess capacity at decreasing marginal cost. Or if all of us in a neighborhood keep bees, I may find that I gain more wandering bees from your nearby acres when total Q of the honey industry rises; whereas when total honey Q is small, I find that some of my bees wander uselessly off to neighboring cornland and my neighboring corngrower has few bees that might in return wander back to me. Or one might conjure up the case where, when I drain my mine of water, I cannot help but make your neighboring mine somewhat drier and thereby confer an external economy on you.

It is easier to find examples of so-called "external diseconomies" resulting from larger-scale industry Q. Recall that these are defined as harmful effects upon other people that result from one man's production. Thus, expanding along a supply curve for steel will cause great belching forth of smoke. This external effect is not only a nuisance, it may actually be harmful to good health and costly in terms of needed cleaning bills. Smog in many cities comes from the external diseconomies of each man's auto and factory. The greatest external diseconomy of all results from one country's setting off nuclear bombs and filling the whole atmosphere with radioactive fallout.

One does not need the case of the nuclear bomb to know that, *wherever there are externalities a strong case can be made for supplanting complete individualism by some kind of group action*: consumers should be made to pay for the smoke damage that their purchases make inevitable, as would be the case if we supplemented *laissez-faire* by a tax or by coercive ordinances; a conservation subsidy to farmers, so that they will keep trees growing and thereby prevent disastrous floods hundreds of miles downstream, might represent rational social policy; regulations that prevent smallholders from digging oil wells frenziedly at the edge of their neighbors' property would be economically efficient. The reader can

---

[9] This section is independent of the rest of the chapter.

think of other limitations on individual freedom in the interest of all, arising from countless other externalities.[10]

No more need be said at this point about externalities. They can shift firm cost curves and thereby alter the slope of industry supply curves upward and downward. But even more important is their general role in connection with causing free pricing to be non-optimal, thereby creating a *prima facie* case for zoning laws, government controls, effluent taxes and penalties, and alert planning.

The main concepts, and their relation to supply in the short and long run, have now been introduced. In the next chapter we can pit cost against revenue to learn how any firm finds its Maximum-profit equilibrium.

SUMMARY

1   Total Cost can usefully be broken down into its Fixed and Variable Cost components. *FC* cancels out of all decisions relevant to the period for which it is truly fixed.

2   Marginal Cost is the increment of extra Total Cost resulting from one increment of extra *q*. (If our units are divisible, *MC* can be defined as the slope of the smooth *TC* curve at any *q* point, and this slope will give a close approximation to the extra cost of producing one more small *q* increment.)

3   Average (total) Cost, *AC*, is the sum of ever-declining Average Fixed Cost and of usually U-shaped Average Variable Cost. *AC* is U-shaped, being intersected at its bottom by the rising *MC* curve. Similarly, *AVC* is cut by *MC* at its bottom.[11]

4   In the long run, when all fixed commitments expire and a firm is free to plan to operate any number of plants, the long-run cost curve *LAC* (and *LTC*) must be the lower-envelope frontier of best choice of plant for each level of output. This frontier will be a smooth envelope, containing at any point a tangential short-run cost curve, if potential plant sizes are smoothly continuous. Usually the long-run curve *LAC*, and its associated marginal curve, will be U-shaped: ultimately it will rise if not all factors of production (including management) are expandable at constant prices; and at very small outputs, indivisibilities in the inputs or the methods of combining them will cause costs initially to fall.

5   An industry's long-run supply curve, $S_L S_L$, must take into account the entry of new firms and exodus of old ones. In the long run all the commitments of any firm will expire, and it will decide to stay in business only if price at least covers all its long-run costs—whether they be "explicit" out-of-pocket payments to labor, lenders, material suppliers, or landlords; or whether they be "implicit" wages (defined as the "opportunity costs" of

---

[10] The late Professor A. C. Pigou, Marshall's prize pupil at Cambridge, was the economist who most emphasized the problem of externalities. There is a clear-cut economic case for a tax (or a subsidy) whenever an external diseconomy (or economy) creates a divergence between private pecuniary Marginal Cost as seen by a firm and true social Marginal Cost.

But this truth is quite independent of the supply slope of the *industry* in question. And Marshall and Pigou erred in thinking that a tax should be put on an industry whose supply curve rises in the fashion of Fig. 24-5(b); for they failed to recognize that the supply curve may rise because some *pecuniary* factor costs are raised to the firms externally by the expansion of industry *Q* —as Allyn Young pointed out half a century ago. We may add, they also erred in thinking an industry should be subsidized if its *SS* curve slopes down, since the firms' curves may have been

shifted down externally by pecuniary reductions in its factor input prices: so long as government assures that such a factor input is sold at *its* declining *MC* price, the pecuniary external economy it creates for our industry can be safely ignored. Young correctly emphasized that external *technological* economies and diseconomies merit interference. He showed that imposing a rent on private property in land succeeds in preventing it from becoming overcrowded by rugged individualists. Similarly, in the case of overcrowded fishing waters, subdividing the sea might somewhat reduce social inefficiences; but certain government fees and rules of the road might well be devised which would do still better than would ordinary private ownership of the sea's acres.

[11] See no. 9 in the Questions for Discussion section for useful rules about *AC* and *MC* curves.

its owners' labor which could be employed elsewhere in producing or in leisure) or implicit interest and rent on the property assets owned by the firm (and whose opportunity costs are measured by what they will fetch in other equally risky uses).

6 Under conditions of free entry, where no one firm has any particular advantages of location, skill, or resources specialized to this industry, one can expect in the long run that free entry of would-be competitors will compete away any excess profits earned by existing firms in the industry. So, just as free exit means P cannot fall below the Break-even cost, free entry means it cannot persist above that point in the long-run equilibrium. Where an industry can expand by replication without pushing up the prices of any factors peculiar to it or used in peculiarly large proportions by it, the resulting long-run supply curve will be horizontal.

7 More likely, any but the smallest industry will generally use some factors of production in large enough amounts to force up their prices slightly. As a result, its long-run supply curve will be sloping upward, at least gently.[12]

8 It is not true that *downward*-sloping Marginal Cost curves of competitive firms can serve as their supply curves—for the very good reason that their profits will be at a minimum along such curves and they will rush away in either direction from such points. As a result, one or a few firms will tend to expand and the remaining firms will tend to contract. Thus lasting decreasing costs that are *internal* to firms implies the destruction of perfect competition. So it is wrong to talk of decreasing supply curves in such a case, or of competitive supply at all.

9 There is, however, the possibility that *external economies* could prevail in an industry. In such cases expansion of *industry Q* could *shift* downward the cost curves of *single firms*; and in the complicated adding of the resulting supplies of all firms, the industry supply curve could end up as downward-sloping.

The concept of external economies or diseconomies is important beyond any such Marshallian application to industry supply. By definition, such externalities involve good and bad economic effects *upon others* resulting from one's own behavior. Since one person takes into account in the search for individual gain and well-being only private money benefits and costs as seen by him, there will then be a divergence between *social* costs and *pecuniary-private* costs. This means that there is a *prima facie* case in such instances for group action, by subsidy or public control, to expand situations fraught with external economies; and a similar case to contract, by tax or fiat, activities involving external diseconomies and public policy.

CONCEPTS FOR REVIEW

Total Costs: Fixed and Variable
$TC = FC + VC$
$AC = TC/q = AFC + AVC$
Marginal Cost (incremental and
   smoothed)
long-run envelope of cost, LAC
   and LMC

Break-even point at $P = MC = $ Min AC
Shut-down point at $P = MC = $ Min AVC
horizontal and rising $S_L S_L$
implicit costs and opportunity costs
decreasing costs and breakdown of
   competition
external economies and diseconomies

---

[12] Or in extreme cases, where the labor it uses actually is supplied by families in reduced amounts when Q expansion bids up the wage, the industry $S_L S_L$ curve could even bend backward toward the northwest, as in Case 4 of the Appendix of Chapter 20.

QUESTION FOR DISCUSSION

1. Make a list of cost elements: wages, salaries, fuel, rentals, etc. Divide them into the Fixed and Variable categories. (Your division will depend on your time periods.)

2. Explain the difference between Marginal Cost and Average Cost. Why should AVC always look much like MC? Why is MC the same when computed from VC as from TC?

3. To the \$55 of Fixed Cost of Table 24-1, add \$90 of additional FC. Now calculate a whole new table, with the same VC as before but new FC = \$145. What happens to MC, AVC? To TC, AC, AFC? Can you verify that minimum AC is now at $q^* = 5$ with AC = \$60 = MC? (You can check MC and TC of your table against Chapter 25's Table 25-3.)

4. Explain why MC cuts AC and AVC at the bottom of their U's. Recall, in connection with Chapter 23, that minimum AVC can be shown to provide the short-run Shutdown cost, and minimum AC to provide the long-run Break-even cost.

5. Explain how the long-run envelope cost curve is defined as the lower frontier of all short-run curves. Illustrate with (*a*) the case of a few plant sizes, and (*b*) the case of infinitely-continuous plant sizes.

6. Relate the rising MC curve to the law of diminishing returns. Contrast the falling part of the curve with that law.

7. Interpret this dialogue. A: "How can competitive profits be zero in the long run? Who'll work for nothing?" B: "It is only *excess*-profits that are wiped out by competition. Managers get paid for their work; owners get a normal return on their capital in long-run equilibrium—no more and no less."

8. Give examples of external economies. External diseconomies. What public interferences do you suggest? What rights to sue in court? Distinguish from opportunity costs.

9. *Extra-credit problem*: With the help of the adjoining diagram, puzzle out the meaning of the following rules. *First rule*: If a Marginal Cost curve is below its associated Average Cost curve, it is pulling the AC curve down; if MC is above AC, it is pulling AC up; if MC = AC, AC must be horizontal. *Second rule*: If AC is a straight line, as in (a), (b), or

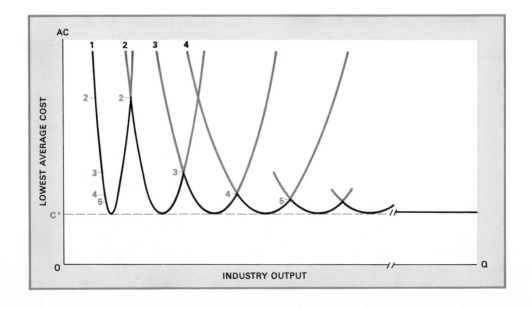

(c), *MC* will be a straight line starting from the same vertical intercept point but with twice the slope of *AC*. (NOTE: This tells us how to find the *MC* point above or below the *AC* point on *any* non-straight-line *AC* curve. At a chosen *q* in (d), merely draw the tangent straight line to *AC*; from that line's vertical intercept, draw an *MC* line with twice the slope; read off from this last line the *MC* value at your chosen *q* level. Of course, you must draw two new straight lines for every different *q* level.) Final query: Note horizontal red line in (b); label it *dd* for perfect-competitor's demand. Shade in triangle formed between *dd* and *MC* and note that you gain by increasing your *q* indefinitely!

10. *Extra-credit problem*: Can you interpret the adjoining diagram to show that society does get industry *Q* at lowest dollar and resource cost when each of many firms is at bottom of its U-shaped *AC*? First U on left comes with 1 firm. Second U comes with *Q* divided equally between 2 firms (so second U is merely the first with twice the horizontal scale; and similarly for the *n* = 3, 4, ... U's). Beyond the // break, *n* is large—say, 100 firms. Naturally, industry *Q* is procured at least cost on *black lower curve*, with lower and lower red switch points at which it just pays to add one new firm. Then to see how costs *for each typical firm* drop as *Q* and *n* grow, concentrate on the markings on the left side of the first U. With *n* = 1, the sky is the limit. For *n* = 2, the red 2 shows highest that *AC* can ever be for any firm; for *n* = 3, red 3 gives lower highest *AC*; and numbers (which are drawn at exact level corresponding to respective switch points) drop to minimum *AC* when *DD* is big enough for numerous competitive firms to survive. So beyond the // break, with many firms, the black industry curve looks smoothly horizontal.

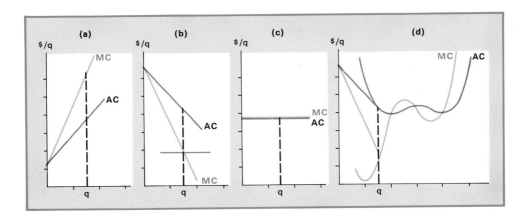

11. *Extra-credit problem*: Interpret the accompanying diagrams. Assume that labor and land are the only factors of production. *(a)* The first three depict Adam Smith's labor theory of value: each 1 hour's labor catches 1 beaver; each 2 hours' labor catches 1 deer; then long-run supply curves are constant or horizontal; then the production-possibility frontier is a straight line, with relative prices or exchange values set by embodied labor requirements of 2 to 1. *(b)* The second three diagrams depict a case where scarce Ricardian land and diminishing returns (to labor producing corn) destroys the labor theory of value and produces cornland rent. As people demand more corn, the corn industry moves on its rising *MC* or $S_c S_c$ curve. The rising corn receipts are divided between variable labor costs (the dark red area under the *MC* curve) and between competitively bid-

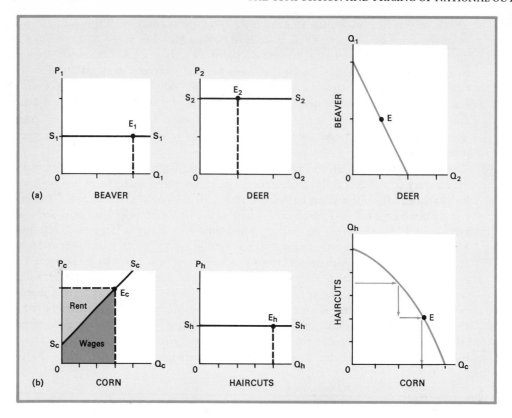

up land rent (the light red area, often called by economists "producers' rent" or "producers' surplus"). By contrast, since haircuts need labor only, $S_h S_h$ is horizontal. Why is the $p\text{-}p$ frontier for corn and haircuts concave from below?

25

MAXIMUM PROFIT EQUILIBRIUM: IMPERFECT COMPETITION

Both monopolistic and competitive forces combine in the determination of most prices.
EDWARD H. CHAMBERLIN

In the last several chapters we have studied the workings of competitive supply and demand in considerable detail. For the most part, we have been studying the case called "perfect competition."

Perfect competition means something very definite to the economist. As we saw, the economist means by it something *much stronger* than the man in the street and the businessman do when they talk of "strong rivalry and keen competition among different business firms and industries."

The special case of perfect competition is very important. But it is only one case, and economists pay it so much attention because of the light it throws on the *efficiency* of resource use. Certainly, it cannot faithfully represent many of the facts about modern industries. The real world—as we know it in North America, Europe, or Asia—contains significant *mixtures of monopoly imperfections along with elements of competition.* The real world, then, is for the most part to be classified in the realm of "imperfect competition": it is neither perfectly competitive nor perfectly "monopolistic."

The remaining chapters of Part Three, therefore, will give us the tools to analyze imperfect as well as perfect competition. They will show what modifications have to be made in any conclusions that were based on an analysis of perfect competition. We shall see that the way a pricing system succeeds in solving the basic problems of WHAT, HOW, and FOR WHOM is affected to an important degree by any elements of monopolistic imperfection that may be involved in numerous modern industries.

Part A of this chapter gives an overview of *patterns of imperfect competition and of real-world market structure.* It also presents a new important tool—the concept of Marginal Revenue. Part B portrays the equilibrium analysis of an idealized monopoly firm, to show how it *achieves maximization of profit by balancing its marginal cost and marginal revenue.* We then are ready to appraise at the end of this chapter the inefficiency inherent in imperfection of competition, and to develop in the Appendix the principles of public regulation.

A. OVERVIEW OF MARKET STRUCTURE AND THE CONCEPT OF MARGINAL REVENUE

PERFECT COMPETITION CONTRASTED WITH IMPERFECT COMPETITION

Figure 25-1(a) reminds us that, to an economist, a perfect competitor is defined as a firm that has no control over price—in the sense that it faces an essentially *horizontal dd* curve along which it can sell as much or as little output as it likes.

Remember how strict this definition of perfect competition is. Think of any commodity that comes

to mind: razor blades, toothpaste, steel, aluminum, potatoes, wheat, cigarettes, tobacco, nylon, cotton. Which fit in with this strict definition? Certainly not razor blades or toothpaste, or cigarettes.

Neither aluminum nor steel meets the definition of perfect competition. For a long time there was only one aluminum company in North America, Alcoa (Aluminum Company of America); and even today there are only Alcoa, Alcan, Reynolds, Kaiser, and one or two others. Contrast this with the case of thousands, if not millions, of cotton and wheat farmers.

FIRM DEMAND UNDER PERFECT COMPETITION

P

PRICE (dollars per unit)

d ——————————————— d

0   q

(a)   FIRM QUANTITY

FIRM DEMAND UNDER IMPERFECT COMPETITION

P

PRICE (dollars per unit)

d'
d

d'
d

0   q

(b)   FIRM QUANTITY

FIG. 25-1. Acid test for imperfect competition is downward tilt of firm's demand.

The perfect-competitor firm can sell all it wants to along its horizontal *dd* curve, never depressing market price. But the imperfect-competitor firm will find that its demand curve slopes downward as its increased *q* forces down the *P* it can get. And unless it is a sheltered monopolist, a cut in its rivals' *P*'s will appreciably shift its own *dd* leftward to *d'd'*.

What about steel? It is true that one plant's steel output may be much like another's, but it is not true that any of the well-known firms (Bethlehem in the United States, or Stelco in Canada) is so weak that it could never depress the price of steel by throwing on the market as much as it could comfortably produce.

When you go down the above list, you will find that only potatoes, tobacco, wheat, and cotton come within our strict definition of perfect competition. Nylon must compete with cotton; that is very true. But in the economist's strict sense, nylon is not a product supplied under "perfect competition," nor is each of its few producers a "perfect competitor" in the economist's sense of the term.[1]

IMPERFECT COMPETITION DEFINED

But suppose the single firm finds itself facing a demand curve which slopes appreciably downward as in Fig. 25-1(b)—which means that when it insists on

[1] Sometimes economists use various synonyms for perfect competition: they often call it "pure competition," in contrast to "impure, or imperfect, or monopolistic competition"; or they occasionally call it "atomistic competition," to convey the notion of numerous small firms which combine like a multitude of tiny atoms to make up the industry. Occasionally, too, an economist will say: "By perfect, I mean really perfect. The wheat market isn't 'perfect competition' unless everyone in it is perfectly *informed* about all the future, there being nowhere any *uncertainty*." However, that is not the sense used here for perfect competition. The price of wheat will fluctuate in a way that no one can now forsee, but as long as *no seller can appreciably influence wheat price*, we shall agree to call the wheat market *perfect*. (Naturally, once you bring government buying programs into the wheat picture, as in Chapter 21, you are bringing monopolistic imperfections into this perfect-competition setup.)

throwing more on the market, it definitely does depress price along its *dd* curve—then the firm is classified by the economist as an "imperfect competitor."

Definition: "Imperfect competition" prevails in an industry or group of industries wherever the individual sellers are imperfect competitors, facing their own *nonhorizontal dd* curves and thereby having some measure of control over price.

This does not mean that a firm has absolute monopoly power over the price it can charge; as we shall see, there are varying degrees of monopolistic imperfection in different imperfectly competitive markets.[2]

Mind you, this does not mean that the owner of an imperfectly competitive firm is of poor character, that he beats his wife, or fails to pay his bills. Nor does the fact that a firm is an imperfect competitor mean that it is not keenly seeking to outsell and out-advertise its rivals. Intense commercial rivalry and "perfect competition" are not at all the same thing; indeed, Farmer Jones, perfect competitor, will do no advertising at all. Why should he? He can sell all the wheat he can produce without depressing market price. But Imperial Tobacco, producer of Buck-

[2] The standard book on all this is E. H. Chamberlin, *Theory of Monopolistic Competition*, Eighth Edition (Harvard University Press, Cambridge, Mass., 1963), especially Chapters 1 and 4. Chamberlin prefers the term "monopolistic competition" for what is here called "imperfect competition," but may give the impression to the layman that there is something especially nasty, or illegal, in not being a perfect competitor, which is not Chamberlin's view. Also, confusion can result from the fact that "monopolistic competition" is sometimes used by Chamberlin as a name for Fig. 26-3's special large-group case of symmetric sellers of differentiated products, an ambiguous usage avoided in this book.

ingham and other cigarettes, and an imperfect competitor, will spend much of its energies in trying to outsell Exports and other brands, the snuff industry, and even the candy industry.

COST PATTERNS AND STRUCTURE OF MARKET IMPERFECTION

At the end of Chapter 24 we saw that continuing decreasing cost is incompatible with perfect competition. If every, or even *any*, firm in an industry could always bring down its Marginal and Average Cost in the long run merely by expanding its output *q*, it would soon expand to become an important fraction of the industry. In short, it would expand to become some kind of monopolist, ceasing to be a price taker and now having some measure of control over the price it gets. As soon as it has control over price, it will cease to follow the *P = MC* rule for profit maximization. Presently we shall see why. (And as soon as somebody in the system raises Price above Marginal Cost, a critic is able to find a flaw of inefficiency in the economic organization of society.)

Figure 25-2 illustrates some patterns of costs which lead to a breakdown of perfect competition. In Fig. 25-2(a) the firm is shown to have Average and Marginal Costs that fall forever. It displays "increasing returns to scale": as *q* grows, the firm finds more elaborate ways of specializing its equipment; it organizes its work gangs in larger and more efficient units; it can afford ever larger boilers and machines, which display greater net efficiency. All this without end. No matter how big is the demand for its product —no matter how far out the industry *DD* curve happens to lie—the most efficient operating size for this one firm will be greater, and peaceful competitive coexistence of thousands of price takers will be quite impossible.

Perhaps the pattern of unlimited decreasing cost is unrealistic. Perhaps *ultimately* the economies of scale will all have been achieved, and the cost curves will level out or turn up. Figure 25-2(b) illustrates such a case: the firm's longrun *MC* and *AC* curves do finally turn up. But, alas, they do not turn up soon enough to avoid the breakdown of perfect competition. For note where the industry total demand curve *DD* now lies: it does not provide a big enough market to enable *numerous* firms to coexist at the efficient level of cooperation called for by the indicated cost curve. We shall still end up in some kind of mo-

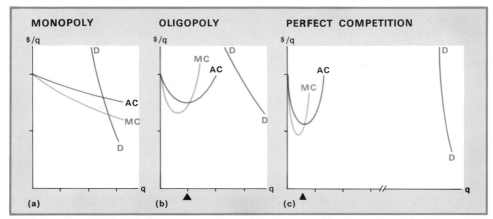

FIG. 25-2. To avoid monopoly or oligopoly, average costs must turn upward soon.
When costs fall indefinitely, as in (a), any one firm can expand to monopolize the industry. In (b) costs eventually turn up, but not soon enough relative to total industry demand *DD*. Coexistence of numerous perfect competitors is impossible; some kind of few-seller oligopoly is likely. In (c) total industry demand *DD* is so vast relative to efficient scale of any one seller as to permit viable coexistence of numerous *perfect competitors*. [What if firms contrive to differentiate their product in (c), fragmenting the market and moving *DD* far to the left, ending up in some kind of Chamberlinian imperfect competition—like (b) or (a)?]

nopoly or few-seller "oligopoly" situation. (*Oligos* means "few" in Greek.)

In Fig. 25-2(c), the outlook is more favorable for perfect competition. Why? Because the industry *DD* is so great compared with the optimum size of each firm, we can hope to replicate the large number of firms needed for truly perfect competition.

There is one encouraging feature of the modern industrial state. Large corporations find it pays them to produce many *different* products, not just the single *q* shown in these diagrams. Thus, Ford produces trucks, tractors, refrigerators, precision equipment, and not just automobiles. It is a big company—but it is not really big in the refrigerator or tractor or equipment markets. It must compete with other giants in these markets. As far as producing more refrigerators is concerned, its costs will *not* continue to fall, as in Fig. 25-2(a) or (b), until it has a dominant position. Actually, because of the *competition of numerous other conglomerate giants*, Ford's costs relative to each diverse market's demand might look more like that of Fig. 25-2(c). (The result is encouraging because it may lead to a tolerable approximation to the *P* and *MC* equivalences of efficient, perfect competition.)

As Adam Smith wrote, "Specialization is limited by the extent of the market." He meant by this that you often cannot use the most efficient known methods when serving a *small* market.[3] And this provided him with good ammunition for attacking the mercantilistic interferences by governments of his time that served to fragment the *DD* demands into many smaller *DD* demands—one for each country or county. He might have gone on to add this:

If you are *still* in the stage where efficient specialization is being limited by the extent of the market, then you are not yet in the state appropriate for perfect competition; instead, not-yet-exhausted economies of scale leave you in some area of imperfect or monopolistic competition. In such a case there is all the more reason for society to promote measures that will extend the market.

One more important point. Suppose we begin in the Fig. 25-2(c) situation where *DD* is large enough relative to the efficient size of firm operation to permit coexistence of numerous viable competitors. But suppose something arises to fragment the aggregate

DD demand into much smaller separate demands for the different firms. Then perfect competition will be dethroned. Since the new *DD* curve confronting any firm or segment of the market will be moved far to the left, we are really back in Fig. 25-2(b) or even 25-2(a).

Such a case arises when restrictive tariffs inhibit the international flow of goods and so fragment markets and encourage monopolistic situations. That even the man in the street understands this point is shown by the popular slogan "The tariff is the Mother of trusts (combines)." The aim of tariff-reduction programs, the European Common Market, and free trade in automobiles and parts is to place every *DD* curve far to the right, thereby promoting vigorous and effective competition.

DIFFERENTIATION OF PRODUCTS

What is not so obvious is that the *DD* demand curves for an industry can be *deliberately* fragmented into smaller segments by the profit-seeking activities of firms. This is what the late Edward Chamberlin called "differentiation of product."

CONTRIVED PRODUCT DIFFERENTIATION Each seller tries to make his produce a little different from that of any other sellers. He avoids the price competition of classical "perfect competition." Instead, he introduces brand quality competition, precisely because it is a profitable form of imperfect competition.

EXAMPLE: He makes penicillin a little different chemically. He seeks patent protection. He advertises, or sends so-called "detail men" to call on doctors, to make them think his penicillin is different, whether or not it significantly is; or more important, he advertises so that you will attach significance to such differences as are there.

What is the result when everybody successfully differentiates his product? The result is that the *DD* curves of Fig. 25-2(c)'s model of perfect competition are moved so far to the left as to become like those of the models of monopoly or oligopoly shown in Fig. 25-2(a) and (b). Fortunately, each firm is not able at will to differentiate its product successfully to any degree that it wishes, even though Galbraithian converts do exaggerate the unilateral power of advertisers.

---

[3] Later chapters show that Canada—a *small* market—must either import products made in specialized plants elsewhere, or make do with the products of less efficient domestic methods.

Chamberlin would agree with much that has been said here. But he would resent the implication that all product differentiation is an artificial, contrived thing whose only purpose is to increase monopoly power and bilk the consumer. Rather, he would insist that people's tastes differ: different people want different degrees of supposed or real effectiveness of penicillin; and even the same person may not want all his units of penicillin to be of the same degree or area of effectiveness. Creating a great variety of differentiated products is often, Chamberlin insists, a genuine catering to basic human wants and needs. Chamberlin does not agree that we would be better off if we all agreed to wear a few basic styles of clothes, each produced in long and efficient factory runs. He would stress that all tastes, including noble tastes for Bach and Rembrandt, are made by society rather than arising from the individual himself. The change of fashion, frivolous though it be, adds zest to life.

In effect, Chamberlin is *reemphasizing the importance of decreasing costs* in making perfect competition *unviable*. He is saying, "Once we replace a homogeneous output Q of the industry (or what is the same thing, the homogeneous output q of a typical firm) by a whole complex of somewhat different $Q_1, Q_2, \ldots$, then the demands will just not be big enough to permit you to have many different producers at the bottom of their efficient U-shaped cost curves." Chamberlin is arguing, "You think that as DD grows in Fig. 25-2(b), with population or for any other reason, society will move from the imperfect-competition model of (b) to the perfect-competition model of (c). But you are wrong. With the *bigger scale* of DD will come a bigger opportunity for making *more*, and more minute, *differentiations of product*."

NATURAL PRODUCT DIFFERENTIATION
Even if we do not agree with Chamberlin's implication that the world is perpetually destined to the realm of imperfect competition regardless of increases in scale, we must concede that he does have a valid and important point. His general *Weltanschauung*—that the economic world cannot be properly understood in terms of the simple models of perfect competition or complete monopoly, but must be interpreted in terms of a richer theory that involves phenomena not to be described as mere

blends of these polar cases—is made more convincing by the following considerations:

Products are often differentiated by natural as well as man-made causes. Space itself, and the transport costs associated with it, provide one important example.

Consider the steel industry. Steel is produced most efficiently in very large-scale plants. Yet North American demand for steel is also enormous. So you might expect numerous replicas of the steel plant of the most efficient size. This expectation is not realised, because the huge North American demand does not constitute a single market for steel. Instead, buyers in each small region are cut off by distance—transport costs—from each other and from remote plants. It would be ridiculous to think that any region (central Canada, or even New York City) could have the scores of independent integrated steel sellers needed for perfect competition. So, each region winds up with efficient large-scale U-shaped costs close to the left of its relevant DD curves.[4]

Similarly with grocery retailing. In order to reach minimum LAC, each store must expand to the size of a super-market, or even larger. But if each corner store and grocery grew to that size, there'd be dreadful overcapacity and widespread bankruptcies. At the same time wearisome consumer travel-time to the remaining large stores would favor widespread location rather than centralization. Thus small suburbs wind up with their own stores, high on their LAC curves, selling to DD curves pushed to the left by consumer refusal to invest in travel time and gasoline to shop at fewer, but less costly, supermarkets.

Thus we may conclude that:

large-scale U-curves, confronted by either man-made or natural differentiations of product that shift leftward and steepen the DD levels of demand, make the non-competitive coexistence of numerous rival firms possible. In such markets the relevance of the perfect-competition model is damaged. And $P = MC$ efficient social pricing is lost.

---

4 Import quotas or tariffs keep inefficient plants in business by strengthening the natural distance or transport fragmentation of markets. And even efficient firms, unable to penetrate larger markets across tariff frontiers, cannot reach the bottom of U-shaped cost curves and may experience higher levels of LAC than less efficient firms selling in wider, free-trade markets.

But the other extreme, monopoly power, need not reign unchecked. Because larger firms may produce many many different kinds of product, each firm in each of its markets may be forced to meet the competition of other large firms in each separate line. (If or where this happens, $P = MC$ conditions may be approximated.)

Let us now survey the principal patterns of imperfections of competition.

THREE KINDS OF IMPERFECT COMPETITION: MONOPOLY, OLIGOPOLY, AND DIFFERENTIATED PRODUCTS

MONOPOLY How imperfect can imperfect competition get? The extreme case would be that of a *single* seller with practically complete monopoly power. (He is called a "monopolist," from the Greek word *mono* for "one" and *polist* for "*seller*.") He is the only one producing in his industry, and there is no industry producing a close substitute for his good. (In Fig. 25-1(b) a change in another firm's price would shift his *dd* curve negligibly.)

Exclusive monopolies, like public utilities or telephones, are usually regulated by the government; and even they must usually take account of the potential competition of alternative products—oil for gas, or cables for telephones. This shows how relatively unimportant complete monopolies are.

OLIGOPOLY We have seen that this horrible-sounding word means "few sellers." Oligopolists are of two types.

First, an oligopolist may be one of a *few* sellers who produce an *identical* (or almost identical) product. Thus, if A's steel is much the same as B's steel, then the smallest price difference will drive the consumer from A to B or vice versa. Neither A nor B could be called a monopolist. Yet, if the number of sellers is few, each has a very appreciable effect on market price.

This first kind of oligopoly is thought to be common in a number of our basic industries where *product is fairly homogeneous* and size of enterprise

large—as in the aluminum and iron industries. Another example would be that of moving freight from coast to coast by any of the three or four alternative rail and sea routes. In the old days when rail rates were unregulated, there would be periodic price wars in which each route undercut the other in an attempt to gain more of the business: sometimes it would become cheaper to move freight from Vancouver to Montreal than to move it from Vancouver to Chicago, and occasionally it might be cheaper to move freight from Vancouver to Chicago via Montreal, with all the implied wasteful cross-haulage.

The second kind of oligopoly is typified by the case where there are *few* sellers who sell *differentiated* (rather than identical) products. The Big Three in the auto industry are examples: three producers dominate the industry, but the Fords, Chevrolets, and Plymouths that they make are *somewhat differentiated* products. In the cigarette industry, a few large sellers own the numerous brands and types (filter, king-size, and regular) that compete for and get the bulk of the business. In heavy machinery, such companies as General Electric, Massey-Ferguson, Allis-Chalmers, and others illustrate the case of an oligopoly that has few sellers and some differentiation of product.

MANY DIFFERENTIATED SELLERS This is the last in our list of imperfect competitors. Here there are many sellers, but now they do *not* produce *identical* products as in the case of perfect competition. Instead, they produce "differentiated products," i.e., products which differ somewhat in real qualities or which the buyer thinks differ in real qualities. My toothpaste is a little different from yours; and if I raise my price above yours, I may still hope to sell a good deal to those consumers conditioned by my advertising or by past use of my product.

Advertising, brand names, trademarks, patents, and custom may explain why there is product differentiation. Or it may merely be that a given barber shop or grocery store is in a locality near to certain consumers: the fact of this nearness may give it a measure of monopoly power; and yet, if its price gets too high, it will find itself losing trade to more distant competitors. (In Fig. 25-1(b) when your rivals cut their P, your *dd* curve shifts downward *appreciably*.)

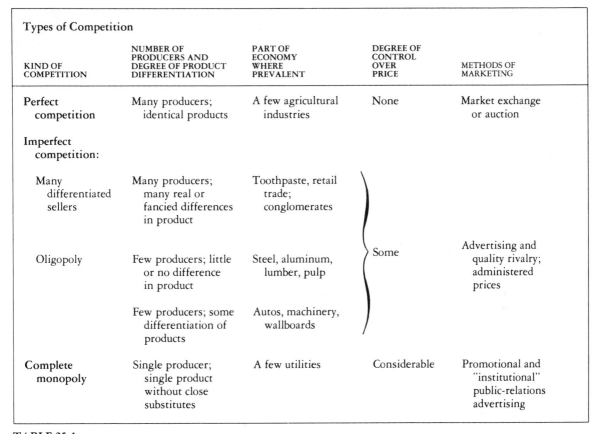

Types of Competition

KIND OF COMPETITION	NUMBER OF PRODUCERS AND DEGREE OF PRODUCT DIFFERENTIATION	PART OF ECONOMY WHERE PREVALENT	DEGREE OF CONTROL OVER PRICE	METHODS OF MARKETING
Perfect competition	Many producers; identical products	A few agricultural industries	None	Market exchange or auction
Imperfect competition:				
Many differentiated sellers	Many producers; many real or fancied differences in product	Toothpaste, retail trade; conglomerates	Some	Advertising and quality rivalry; administered prices
Oligopoly	Few producers; little or no difference in product	Steel, aluminum, lumber, pulp		
	Few producers; some differentiation of products	Autos, machinery, wallboards		
Complete monopoly	Single producer; single product without close substitutes	A few utilities	Considerable	Promotional and "institutional" public-relations advertising

TABLE 25-1.
Most industries are imperfectly competitive—a blend of monopoly and competition.

BRIEF SUMMARY OF KINDS OF COMPETITION AND MARKET STRUCTURE

Table 25-1 presents a brief picture of the various possible categories of imperfect and perfect competition. It merits close study, for we shall later examine each of its cases.

The remainder of this chapter will analyze the principles of profit maximization, concentrating mostly on the limiting case of a complete monopoly. As has been mentioned, few firms in real life enjoy anything like a complete monopoly: usually some other products will be partially substitutable for the ones you sell. If for some unnatural reason you were in a position of practically unchecked monopoly, we

can be sure that the modern mixed economy would make you subject to public regulation. The example of public regulation of such utilities as electricity, gas, and telephones comes immediately to mind; and by the end of the chapter we shall be in a position to understand the proper principle of monopoly regulation.

The tools useful to understand Maximum-profit equilibrium for the complete monopoly—namely Marginal Cost and Marginal Revenue—turn out to be the tools needed to understand Maximum-profit equilibrium in the more realistic cases of oligopoly and various forms of imperfect competition. They lay the groundwork for Chapter 26's study of the combines policy of government to prevent and control monopolies.

PRICE, QUANTITY, AND TOTAL REVENUE

What is the Maximum-profit output q that a monopolist will try to produce in any situation? What is the accompanying Maximum-profit price P that it should charge? It turns out that old and new *marginal* concepts provide the key to the common-sense trial-and-error procedure of maximizing profit. The final results will agree with common sense, after analysis discloses the good sense in common sense.

As far as costs are concerned, all the tools that we shall need have already been developed in Chapter 24's discussion of costs (*MC, AC, TC,* and so forth). Here, therefore, we can begin with the sales revenue side of things. From the firm's demand curve *dd*, we know the relation between P and the q it can sell. Table 25-2 indicates this relationship for a hypothetical firm, in Column (2). And Fig. 25-3(a) depicts, in red, the *dd* demand curve for this monopolist (who is given, for simplicity, a straight-line demand curve). Column (3) of Table 25-2 shows how to get the firm's Total Revenue by multiplying $P \times q$: thus 0 units bring in $TR = 0$; 1 unit brings in $TR = \$180 \times 1$; 2 units bring in $\$160 \times 2 = \$320$. The general rule is this: $TR = P \times q$.

Total Revenue at first rises with q, since the reduction in P needed to sell the extra q is moderate in this first *elastic* range of the demand curve. But when we get to some intermediate point on *dd*, TR reaches its maximum—at $q = 5$, $P = \$100$, and $TR = \$500$. In-

creasing q beyond this point brings you into *inelastic* demand regions, and now the percentage cut in P needed to sell 1 per cent more q is so much greater than 1 that it cuts down on TR. Figure 25-3(b) shows TR to be dome-shaped, rising from zero to a max-

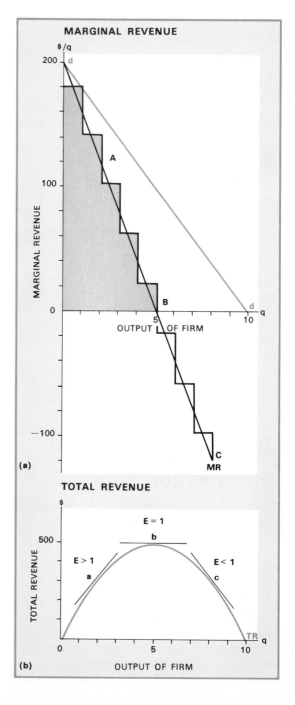

FIG. 25-3. Marginal Revenue curve comes from demand curve.

(a). The black steps show the increments of Total Revenue from each new unit of output as calculated from Table 25-2 (or from the TR of Fig. 25-3(b) below). *MR* falls below P from the beginning, actually dropping twice as fast as the straight-line *dd* curve. *MR* becomes negative when *dd* turns inelastic. Smoothing the incremental steps of *MR* gives the black *MR* curve, which in the case of straightline *dd* will always have twice as steep a slope as *dd*.

(b). Total Revenue is dome-shaped, rising from zero (where $q = 0$) to a maximum (where *dd* has unitary elasticity) and then falling back to zero (where $P = 0$). TR's slope gives instantaneous *MR*, just as its jumps give incremental *MR*.

TOTAL AND MARGINAL REVENUE

(1) QUANTITY q	(2) PRICE $P = AR = \dfrac{TR}{q}$	(3) TOTAL REVENUE $TR = P \times q$	(4) MARGINAL REVENUE MR
0	$200	$ 0	+200
			+180
1	180	180	+160
			+140
2	160	320	+120
			+100
3	140	420	+ 80
			+ 60
4	120	480	+ 40
			+ 20
5	100	500	0
			— 20
6	80	480	— 40
			— 60
7	60	420	— 80
			—100
8	40	320	—120
			—140
9	20	180	—160
			—180
10	0	0	

TABLE 25-2. Marginal Revenue numbers come from demand schedule P and q data:

From demand curve data, Total Revenue is easily computed. To get dark red Marginal Revenue, we increase q by a unit and calculate the difference in Total Revenue it brings. Note MR is at first positive, but after demand turns inelastic, MR becomes negative. Price never becomes negative, but MR lies below P because of loss owing to the necessity to lower price on previous units if the new unit of q is to get sold. (Light red data of instantaneous Marginal Revenue come from smoothered MR curve of Fig. 25-3(a).)

imum of $500 and falling back to zero when P has become vanishingly small.

Already Table 25-2 illustrates an important fallacy: "A firm out to maximize its profits will always charge what the 'traffic will bear.' That means charging the highest possible price." This statement is wrong. A profit maximizer may not be an altruist; but that does not mean he is a fool. To charge the highest possible price is to sell no q at all and to get no TR at all! Even if we reinterpret this doctrine to mean charging the highest price at which anything at all can be sold, it is obvious that selling but one unit even at a high price is not the way to

maximize your profit. Even if we neglect (for a moment) all costs, the correct interpretation of charging what the traffic will bear must mean that we find the best *compromise* between a high P and a high q if we are to get the best profit. In Table 25-2, it is at $q = 5$ that $P \times q = TR$ is at a maximum: this is the point where demand elasticity turns into demand inelasticity.

Before proceeding now to introduce the important concept of Marginal Revenue, we can note the fact that the *Price* at which each q is sold could be called *Average Revenue* to distinguish it from Total Revenue. Thus, we got $P \equiv AR$ by dividing TR by q (just as we earlier got AC by dividing TC by q). Verify that if Column (3) had been written down *before* Column (2), we could then have filled in Column (2) by division.

MARGINAL REVENUE AND PRICE

We need a test to determine whether Total Revenue is gaining or losing as we increase q. Marginal Revenue is the convenient concept for this purpose.

Definition: "Marginal Revenue" is defined as the increment of Total Revenue (plus or minus) that comes when we increase q by an increment of one unit. MR is plus when demand is still elastic, minus when demand is inelastic, and just crosses zero when demand turns from being elastic to being inelastic. (If units of q are divisible, the MR steps of Fig. 25-3(a) can be replaced by a smooth MR curve.)

The dark red numbers of Marginal Revenue are shown in Column (4) of Table 25-2; they are calculated by subtracting the TR we get by selling q units from the TR we get by selling $q + 1$ units, the difference being our extra revenue or MR. Thus, from $q = 0$ to $q = 1$, we get $MR = \$180 - 0$. From 1 to 2, MR is $\$320 - 180 = \$140$.

MR is positive until we arrive at $q = 5$, and negative from then on. That does not mean you are giving goods away at a negative price. Actually, Average Revenue, which is P, continues to be positive. It is merely that, in order to sell the sixth unit of q, you must reduce the price so much on *all* the units as to end up getting less *TR*—which is what the negative *MR* is telling you.

This warns us: Do *not* confuse Marginal Revenue with Average Revenue or Price. The table shows they are different. Review Fig. 25-3(a) and note that the plotted black steps of *MR* definitely lie below the red *dd* curve of *AR*. *MR* has already turned negative when *dd* is only partway down toward zero.

Just why is *MR* definitely less than *P* (or *AR*) for the imperfect competitor? True, I sell my last unit of *q* for *P*. But what did I have to do to coax out that last unit of sale? Clearly, I had to lower my *P*, since I didn't face a perfect competitor's horizontal *dd*. But in lowering my *P* for the last new buyer, I also had to *lower P for all the previous buyers*. So my extra revenue, my *MR*, is evidently less than *P* by this loss on previous units from the price drop. QED.

Summary: With *dd* demand sloping

$$P > MR \ (= P - \text{Loss on previous } q)$$

In Column (4) of Table 25-2, the red numbers of the smoothed *MR* are also seen to be less than Column (2)'s *P*'s.

Only under perfect competition, where the sale of extra units will never depress price at all, is the loss-in-revenue term zero. Only then will Price and Marginal Revenue be identical. Graphically, a straight-line *MR* curve always has twice the steepness of the *dd* curve. But if *dd* is horizontal, as in perfect competition, so then must *MR* be: thus, a perfect competitor's *dd* and *MR* coincide as the same horizontal line!

This completes our analysis of Marginal Revenue and equips us for the task of finding Maximum-profit equilibrium of the firm.

B. MAXIMUM-PROFIT MONOPOLY EQUILIBRIUM: DIVERGENCE OF PRICE AND MARGINAL COST

Now suppose the firm wants to maximize its Total Profit. To do this it must bring in, along with the Total Revenue information it gets from its demand side, the Total Cost information described in Chapter 24.

Definition: Total Profit equals Total Revenue minus Total Cost:

$$TP = TR - TC = P \times q - TC$$

To maximize its profit the firm must seek out the equilibrium price and quantity, *P** and *q**, that gives it the largest difference, *TR* — *TC*. Common sense tells us this Maximum-profit will occur only where the firm's Marginal (or extra) Revenue has just come into balance with its Marginal (or extra) Cost.

We may now bring all our relevant facts together in a supertable, Table 25-3. Total Profit is, of course, the column of greatest interest in this table.

What quantity *q** will maximize Total Profit, and at what price? The easiest way to solve this problem is to compute Column (5), Total Profit, which is simply the difference between Total Revenue and Total Cost. This column tells us:

The optimal quantity is 4 units, with a price of $120 per unit. After taking account of Total Cost, we see that no other situation will give us as much profit as the $230 at *q** = 4 and *P** = $120.

Another way of arriving at the same result is to compare Marginal Revenue, Column (6), and Marginal Cost, Column (7). (*MR* is computed from the *TR* column, as in Table 25-2. Recall from the last chapters that *MC* is similarly calculated from *TC*.)

As long as a step toward extra output gives us more Marginal Revenue than Marginal Cost, our profit is *increasing* and we continue to produce more output. But whenever Marginal Cost exceeds Marginal Revenue, we *contract* output. Where is equilibrium?

Maximum-profit equilibrium is where Marginal Revenue and Marginal Cost are equal.

MR = *MC*, the Maximum-profit point

This second way of finding the optimum point by comparing Marginal Cost and Marginal Revenue is neither better nor worse than the first method of simply examining Total Profits. They are essentially exactly the same method.

Summary of firm's revenue, cost, and maximum profit

(1) QUANTITY q	(2) PRICE P	(3) TOTAL REVENUE TR	(4) TOTAL COST TC	(5) TOTAL PROFIT TP	(6) MARGINAL REVENUE MR	(7) MARGINAL COST MC	
0	200	0	145	−145	+200	34	
					+180	30	$MR > MC$
1	180	180	175	+5	+160	27	
					+140	25	
2	160	320	200	+120	+120	22	
					+100	20	
3	140	420	220	+200	+80	21	
					+60	30	
4	120	480	250	+230	+40	40	**MR = MC**
					+20	50	
5	100	500	300	+200	0	60	
					−20	70	
6	80	480	370	+110	−40	80	
					−60	90	
7	60	420	460	−40	−80	100	
					−100	110	$MR < MC$
8	40	320					

TABLE 25-3. Equating Marginal Cost to Marginal Revenue gives the firm's Maximum profit output and price.

Total and Marginal Cost of production are now brought together with Total and Marginal Revenue. The Maximum-profit decision is where $MR = MC$, with $q^* = 4$, $p^* = \$120$, and maximum profit $TP = \$230 = \$120 \times 4 - \$250$. (NOTE: For convenience, the light red MR and MC numbers are put in to give the smoothed instantaneous values at each q point itself: disregarding these, we could get the same result.)

GRAPHICAL DEPICTION OF FIRM'S MAXIMUM-PROFIT POSITION

Fig. 25-4 shows these procedures. In Fig. 25-4(a), MC intersects MR at E, the Maximum-profit point, where $q^* = 4$. We run up vertically from E to the dd curve to G, where $P = \$120$. The fact that G lies *above* F, the point on the AC curve at $q^* = 4$, guarantees a positive profit. (We cannot read directly the amount of Total Profit unless we calculate the area of the shaded rectangle.)

The same story is told in Fig. 25-4(b) with total curves. Total Revenue is dome-shaped. Total Cost is ever-rising. The vertical difference between them is Total Profit, which begins negative and ends negative. In between, TP is positive, reaching its maximum of \$230 at $q^* = 4$, where the black slopes of the TR and TC are equal and parallel: if these MR and MC slopes were pointing inward in a non-parallel fashion (as at $q = 2$), we should gain a little extra

profit by contracting q. At $q^* = 4$, things are just right. This is verified by the Total Profit curve, whose black slope is horizontal at its peak: TP's slope is clearly the difference $MR - MC$, and this slope should definitely have a zero value at the maximum.[5]

Summary on *excess of P above MC*. For the firm with some monopoly power, maximizing profits by equating Marginal Revenue to Marginal Cost leads to a price that is *above* Marginal Cost. The canny seller *contrives an artificial scarcity of his product* so as not to spoil the price he can get on the earlier premarginal units.

---

[5] Those who know elementary calculus need not use the finite-step definitions of MR and MC as $\triangle TR$ and $\triangle TC$. Instead they can use the smoothed instantaneous slopes of the TR and TC functions of q: i.e., define $MR = d(TR)/dq$ and $MC = d(TC)/dq$ and note that maximizing $TR - TC$ of profit requires finding the q^* root of the equation: $d(\text{profit})/dq = 0 = d(TC)/dq - d(TR)/dq = MR - MC$. QED. (See extra-credit problem, question 7, at the end of this chapter for more on this.)

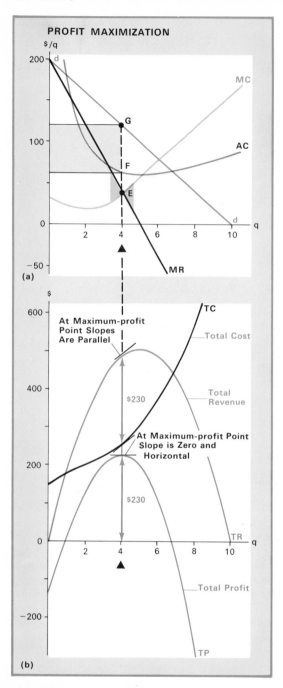

PROFIT MAXIMIZATION

(a)

(b)

FIG. 25-4. Graphs of marginal and total curves show maximum-profit equilibrium.

(a). At E, where MC intersects MR, equilibrium position of Maximum profit is found. Any move from E will lose some profit. Price is at G above E; and since P is above AC, the maximized profit is a positive profit. (Can you understand why the red shaded rectangle measures Total Profit? And why the gray triangle of shading on either side of E shows the reduction in Total Profit that would come from a departure from MR = MC — i.e., the greater loss of extra revenue in comparison with extra cost?)

(b). This tells the same story of maximizing profit as above, but uses total concepts rather than marginal concepts. Total Profit is given by vertical distance from TC up to TR. This is at a maximum where the two curves have equal and parallel slopes, MR = MC. This is necessary if red TP curve is to be at a maximum, with its black slope horizontal as MR cancels out MC.

add to your confidence in the result if you find that the general MR = MC rule is consistent, when applied to a *perfect competitor*, with Chapter 23's P = MC rule for a profit-maximizing perfect competitor. It is? Yes, indeed. Here is why:

For a small perfect competitor, Marginal Revenue works out to be exactly the same thing as Price. With no need to cut your P to sell an extra unit of q, the incremental Marginal Revenue it brings you is precisely the P received from that last unit, with no loss on previous units being subtracted.[6] Hence, MR = MC and P = MR do lead to the special rule for profit maximizing by a perfect competitor:

P = MR = MC at a perfect competitor's Maximum-profit point.

These tools to show how a rational firm will find its maximum-profit equilibrium will later apply to firms under monopoly, or anything else.

PERFECT COMPETITION A SPECIAL CASE OF IMPERFECT COMPETITION

This completes our discussion of Marginal Revenue and Marginal Cost as tools to maximize profit. It will

[6] If you redraw Fig. 25-4(a) for a perfect competitor, make *dd* horizontal and coinciding with *MR*. Then proceed to find the *MR* and *MC* intersection as usual (which gives the old *MC* supply story of Chapter 23). In the new Fig. 25-4(b), *TR* merely becomes a straight line, rising from the origin, but the slopes of *TR* and *TC* must still match at the Maximum-profit equilibrium point.

BYGONES AND MARGINS

While economic theory does not necessarily aim to make you a successful businessman, it does introduce you to some new ways of thinking. Here is one instance.

The economist always stresses the "extra," or "marginal," costs and advantages of any decision. He says:

Let bygones be bygones. Don't look backward. Don't moan about your sunk costs. Look forward. Make a hard-headed calculation of the *extra* costs you'll incur by any decision and weigh these against its *extra* advantages. Cancel out all the good things and bad things *that will go on anyway*, whether you make an affirmative or negative decision on the point under consideration.

This disregarding of bygones is extremely important, and most successful decision-makers practice it intuitively, even if they have not had a formal course in economics. Here is an application of this principle:

The Crown taxes a monopolist a flat sum for his match-monopoly franchise—say $100 per day, no matter what he does. How will this affect the new Maximum-profit P and q? If you have grasped the tools of this chapter, you will discover that a flat-sum tax will not shift either the MR or MC curve. If the monopolist successfully maximizes his profits before and after the tax and if nothing else changes and if he stays in business, *the flat-sum tax will have absolutely no effect on price or output*, but will be borne completely by the monopolist! (Can you verify that adding $100 to every TC number in Table 25-3 merely subtracts $100 from every profit in Column (5), leaving you with the same Maximum-profit $q^* = 4$ and $P^* = \$120$?)[7]

HOW IMPERFECTION OF COMPETITION AFFECTS RESOURCE ALLOCATION

In the next chapter we shall study some of the important cases of imperfect competition—oligopoly,

[7] Suppose the King put a flat-sum of $230 on Fig. 25-4's monopolist to wipe out all his profit. The new Fig. 25-5 shows the story. MR, MC, and dd are exactly as before. (Why?) But now AC has been shifted up because of the tax spread over each unit, which adds $230 of new Fixed Cost: only at the price of G, where the dd curve is *tangent* to the new AC curve, can the firm break even; everywhere else it makes a loss; maximizing profit by finding $MR = MC$ now means avoiding loss. (But see the Appendix for a demonstration that taxing away monopoly profit still leaves society with a discrepancy between Marginal Cost and Price or Marginal Utility.)

and so forth. This will involve us in important public questions that lie in the field of "combines policy." As preparation, let us see again how deviations from perfect competition affect the efficiency with which a free-price system solves the important problems of WHAT, HOW, and FOR WHOM.

Suppose that, under free pricing, firms do definitely face a sloping demand curve so that their Marginal Revenue and hence Marginal Cost is below their Price. Then, to the degree that such imperfect competitors intelligently pursue their self-interest, they will *not* be led by Adam Smith's Invisible Hand to perform the acts needed to promote the general interest.

Let us recapitulate how this divergence between Price and Marginal Cost affect the goodness or badness of the way the economy is organizing its production and distribution. We have already met this complex question, and will do so again.

EXCESS PROFIT OF MONOPOLY First, the imperfect competitor may be earning more than he would if the government somehow made him compete like a perfect competitor. If so, is that excess profit a good or a bad thing? Is he a more worthy man than most? Is he poorer than most, and more in need? (And will he use his gains to subsidize the arts, or to pay for vulgar display? Will he use any monop-

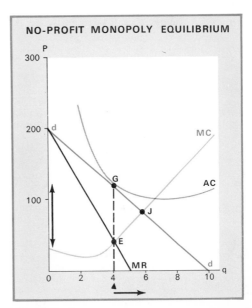

FIG. 25-5

oly profits to sponsor new industrial research? Or to sponsor research in ways to convince consumers that his product is better than those of others?)

When the man in the street thinks of the monopoly problem, he gives most weight to the above type of questions—to the way it affects the FOR WHOM problem of distribution.[8] *Yet, even if it has no harmful effect on income distribution, imperfection of competition could still represent an important economic evil.*

DEFICIENT OUTPUT OF MONOPOLY To see this, imagine that all money votes are distributed properly and that A is the only imperfect competitor in the system. Everyone else is a perfect competitor, who keeps his MC equal to his P. Price is the signal that consumers use to indicate how much they value various goods. Costs, and particularly Marginal Cost, are the indicators of how much of society's valuable resources each good's production utilizes: our scarce land, our sweaty labor, and other resources that could produce other goods. Everywhere else, competitive firms are giving people what they most want and are producing right up to the point of $P = MC$, where goods are shown to be worth what they cost. (If you are unsure of this, flip back to Fig. 23-7 to refresh your understanding.)

But take the imperfect competitor A—the one deviant. What is he doing? A is not forcing people to buy from him. But the fact that A faces a sloping demand curve shows he does have some control over P.

How is he using that power? Does he produce goods up to the point where their social cost—as measured by his MC—is equal to what the last unit of the good is worth to society—as measured by market P resulting from consumer money votes? No.

The imperfect competitor is contriving to keep things a little scarce. He is contriving to keep P above MC because in that way he sets $MR = MC$ and thereby maximizes his profit. So society does not get quite as much of A's good as it really wants in terms of what that good really costs society to produce.[9]

Do not think A is a villain. If he did not intelligently try to maximize his firm's long-run profits, he might be displaced by the stockholders or be sued. Even if A owned the company and chose to lower P to MC, he would be shunting money from his wife and kids to the public at large. While there is no law against his being such an altruist, such as Santa Claus, the betting odds are against this. And in any case such an optimal solution to the problem *by chivalry* has nothing to do with Adam Smith's Invisible Hand—which insisted that *self*-interest (not altruism) would perform, under ruthless competition, the miracle of providing for the general interest.

The clue to the Invisible Hand paradox is this: Adam Smith would have to rely on strictly defined "perfect competition" to get his result. As soon as we have imperfect competition in the real world, we have left the Garden of Eden and there arises the problem of how to minimize the evil and wastes involved in such imperfections of competition. Chapter 26 analyzes the main forms of imperfect competition and surveys the antitrust policies of modern governments. And the brief Appendix to this chapter indicates the *economic* principles that should underlie public regulation of monopoly and imperfect competition and shape antitrust philosophy and law. The monopoly firm must be made to behave socially.

---

[8] In Fig. 25-5, the monopolist was stripped of his excess profit by taxes, but the vertical arrow showing the discrepancy between P(at G) and MC (at E) shows that monopoly q is still too small and should be expanded as shown by the lower horizontal arrow.

As the next chapter shows, imperfect competition might result in no one's making a profit if there is "free entry" into the Chamberlinian industry in question. Yet P might still stay above MC, and so the result might still be tremendous wastage of resources because we have too many corners with too many gasoline stations, each with too many idle attendants (who in the end are not even well rewarded for being imperfect competitors). To be sure, more gas stations could mean shorter walks for people out of gas and more consumer convenience generally; but who is to say that the optimal amount of such differentiation-of-product convenience is being provided under any particular regime of imperfect competition? The moral is this: Imperfect Competition can introduce a new evil that was not present either under perfect competition or under perfect monopoly—namely, excessive differentiation of products, but without excess profits being achieved by anyone.

[9] As Fig. 20-9 showed, it is a social inefficiency when monopolists' outputs are too small and competitors' outputs get expanded beyond their optimal amounts. Chapter 23's Fig. 23-7 clinched the point with its comparison of competitive MC pricing with a Crusoe-Planner optimum of welfare. See this chapter's Appendix, pages 459-460 for more on this.

SUMMARY

A. OVERVIEW OF MARKET STRUCTURE AND THE CONCEPT OF MARGINAL REVENUE

1 Most market situations in the real world can be thought of as falling on a line somewhere between the limiting extremes of perfect competition and complete monopoly. Imperfect competition involves some control by each of its firms over its own price, by virtue of the fact that there are not *a very large number of rivals* who sell *exactly the same product* as it does. (Note the italicized words.) Important cases are (a) *Oligopoly*—few sellers of similar or differentiated products—and (b) *many sellers of differentiated* products.

2 Decreasing-cost tendencies are destructive of perfect competition, since one or a few corporations then kill off the numerous sellers needed for the competitive model. (However, big conglomerates, which produce many products and invade one another's markets, may each find themselves constitutional rather than absolute monarchs, unable to dominate their separate markets by exercise of unilateral, unchallenged power.)

3 From the firm's demand curve, we can easily derive its Total Revenue curve. From the schedule or curve of Total Revenue we can easily derive its Marginal Revenue—the extra revenue resulting from the sale of an extra unit of output. Ordinarily, Marginal Revenue will fall short of Price because of the *loss on all previous units* of output that will result when we are forced to drop our price in order to sell an extra unit of output.

B. MAXIMUM-PROFIT MONOPOLY EQUILIBRIUM: DIVERGENCE OF PRICE AND MARGINAL COST

4 A firm will find its Maximum-profit position where the last little unit it sells brings in extra revenue just equal to its extra cost. This same *MR = MC* result can be shown graphically by intersecting *MR* and *MC* curves, or by equality of the slopes of the Total Revenue and Total Cost curves. In any case, *Marginal Revenue = Marginal Cost* must hold at the equilibrium position of Maximum profit always.

5 Economic reasoning leads to an emphasis upon *marginal* advantages and disadvantages —to a *cancellation of bygones* and factors that go on no matter how you make a decision.

6 Imperfection of competition, by putting *P* above *MC* for some goods, acts as one extra deterrent to Adam Smith's Invisible Hand, which tried to convert mankind's selfish interest to a best solution of society's WHAT and HOW problems (but, alas, not necessarily to a best solution of the FOR WHOM problem.)

CONCEPTS FOR REVIEW

perfect versus imperfect
   competition
decreasing costs and monopolistic
   imperfection
monopoly, oligopoly, product
   differentiation (natural or
   contrived)
rivalry versus perfect competition
MR = MC condition at Maximum
   profit

MR in relation to *P* (loss on
   previous units)
MR = P, *P = MC*, for perfect-competitor
bygones versus relevant alternatives
inefficiency of *P > MC*
imperfection of competition and
   Smith's Invisible Hand

QUESTIONS FOR DISCUSSION

1. List distinguishing features of perfect and imperfect competition. How might you characterize Stelco, Eaton's, Loblaws, Algoma Steel, Bell Telephone, Farmer Jones?

2. "A corporation charges what the traffic will bear." Explain the error here and restate correctly in terms of the Marginal-Revenue and Marginal-Cost concepts.

3. What is MR's numerical value when dd has unitary elasticity and TR is constant?

4. Relate MR to P, at $q = 4$ or 5 in Tables 25-2 and 25-3. Show loss on previous units.

5. Figure 25-4(a) and (b) describes the Maximum-profit equilibrium position. Explain in detail that it really shows two different ways of describing exactly the same fact, namely, that a firm will stop when the extra cost of a further move just balances its extra revenue.

6. Here is a hard question. "If a monopolist is big enough to affect the P for the good he sells, he may also be big enough to affect the price of materials and the labor he buys. (He becomes what is called a 'monopsonist'—or 'single buyer.') In computing MC as it *looks to him*, he will debit against the last unit of q the *rise* in wage forced on all the *previous* units of labor by his need to hire more labor. Private pecuniary MC, so computed, is higher than the true MC society wants P equated to for efficiency. Interpret this if you can (but if you cannot, don't worry as Chapter 28's footnote 6, will return to this).

7. *Extra-credit problem:* Firm A has dd demand function, $P = 15 - .05q$, and hence $TR = qP = 15q - .05q^2$. Its $TC = q + .02q^2$. Verify: $MR = d(TR)/dq = 15 - .1q$, $MC = d(TC)/dq = 1 + .04q$. So $d(\text{profit})/dq = 0$ at $MR = MC$ or at $15 - .1q = 1 + .04q$ or at $q^* = 100$. Then $P^* = 15 - 5 = \$10 > MC^* = \$5$. Maximum-profit $= \$1,000 - (100 + 200) = \$700$. Can you show that a tax of $\$1$/unit will add $1q$ to TC, cutting q^* by $100/14$ units and raising P by $5/14$ units? Were A a perfect-competitor with horizontal dd at $\$5$, its Maximum-profit on $q^* = 100$ would have been $\$500 - \$300 = \$200$; and now a $\$1$/unit tax would cut competitor's q^* by more than monopolist's—namely, by $100/4 = 25$ units. [HINT: Now maximize $\{5q - (q + .02q^2)\} - 1q$].

Appendix: Monopoly Regulation and Exploitation; Game Theory

Figure 25-6 repeats a monopoly equilibrium like that of Fig. 25-4(a). The monopolist is seen to be (1) making a profit, as shown by the red-shaded rectangle near G; and (2) charging a P above MC, as shown by the EG discrepancy.

Suppose a public-utility commission is set up to regulate the monopolist. Or suppose the government Combines Investigation Branch of the Department of Consumer Affairs threatens to arrest him. If the regulators decide to make him charge a price that will wipe out his excess-profits, they will move him to H, the intersection of his dd and AC curves. Here P = AC, and price covers only normal costs.

How good is this solution? Economically speaking, it probably does represent something of an improvement. First, the owner of the monopoly is presumably no more deserving, or poorer, than the consumers. So there is no reason to let him extort monopoly profits from them. By wiping out monopolistic profit, we probably have a more "equitable distribution of income." (WARNING: Value judgments that go beyond technical economics are involved in such a conclusion.)

Second, the regulators have lowered the discrepancy between Price and Marginal Cost in making the monopolist cut his P from G to H. Why deem this an improvement? Because (equity considerations aside and assuming that dollars truly reflect social utilities and social costs) the expanded q units are worth more to people in marginal utility than their extra or Marginal Cost. (PROOF: Between G and H, dd lies above the MC curve.)

IDEALLY REGULATED PRICING

If P = MC is such a good thing, why shouldn't the regulators go all the way and make the monopolist lower P until he is at the intersection point of the dd and MC curves (at J)?

Actually, requiring P = MC is the ideal target for optimal efficiency. But with a decreasing-cost situation like this one—and we saw in Fig. 25-2, that much of monopoly, oligopoly, and other forms of imperfect competition come from decreasing-cost cases—setting P = MC while AC is still falling will involve the firm in a chronic loss. (REMEMBER: Falling AC means MC < AC; or P = MC < AC.)

How can society achieve its ideal of P = MC, where the marginal utility of output just matches its Marginal Cost at the equilibrium amount? The answer involves a permanent government subsidy to the decreasing-cost producer. Where does the subsidy come from? From the general budget (and ideally from taxes collected on a "lump-sum" basis so that people's marginal decisions are not distorted by attempts to minimize taxes).[1]

What if dd in Fig. 25-6 shifts to intersect MC at J', beyond the bottom of U-shaped AC? Then the state should insist on having P at the profitable J' point, not at the new H' Break-even point. But, as with profitable TV channels, the government should auction off licenses or tax away all their excess-profit.

HELPING ALL We can now demonstrate that if $P_1 > MC_1$ in one monopolized industry and $P_i = MC_i$ in all other per-

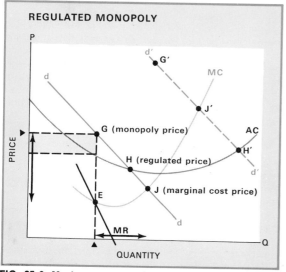

REGULATED MONOPOLY

FIG. 25-6. Maximum-profit equilibrium for the unregulated monopolist is at G, directly above the intersection of MR and long-run MC, with P above MC and with monopoly profit shown by the shaded rectangle.

Public-utility regulation of the monopoly would set its price down to the H intersection of demand with long-run average cost; this wipes out excess profit; more important, it brings price down closer to the Marginal Cost level at J, where marginal social costs and benefits are appropriately balanced.

Ideally, P should be forced all the way down to MC at J, with the chronic loss being covered by permanent government (lump-sum) subsidy.

---

[1]Some qualifications are given in advanced treatises. (1) If lump-sum taxes are not politically feasible, the evil from P>MC must be balanced against the distortion from taxation. (2) As Fig. 32-2 will show, a decision has to be made whether the money needed to subsidize the J point could not be used better elsewhere, with this q set equal to zero. (3) If the consumers of this good are especially "deserving"—or if this should be a good that society paternalistically deems even more worthwhile than the valuations that consumers themselves act on—there may be a case for even greater subsidy. (Reverse the argument if the good is opium or is something bought only by those who already have too large a share of society's income.) (4) Recall Fig. 25-5 (and see Fig. 26-3), where it is shown that a flat-sum tax could wipe out the monopolist's profit but leave you with the socially inefficient P — MC discrepancy. (5) If in many other industries P>MC, it may not be optimal to bring P all the way down to MC in this industry alone.

fectly competitive industries, then it is possible to expand the monopoly Q_1 and contract the competitive outputs in such a way as to make *any* (and hence, if we wish, *every*) consumer or worker better off.[2]

Suppose we define units of goods so that monopoly P_1 equals competitive P_2 (i.e., we could use a dollar's worth of monopolized berries and of competitive wheat as our amounts). Since only the monopolist's P exceeds MC, this means that the ratio of MC in monopoly to MC in the competitive industries is less than 1. But recall from Chapter 22 that for each consumer $MU_1/P_1 = MU_2/P_2$. Hence, for any single consumer the ratio of marginal utilities is exactly one, and is thus greater than the ratios of Marginal Costs. This means that the monopoly good is being kept so scarce that it is still yielding more MU_1 than its true MC_1 cost.

Any one sovereign consumer could command: "Transfer a small amount of labor from competitive industry 2 to monopoly industry 1. This will give you *more* than 1 unit of new Q_1 for each lost unit of old Q_2, because $MC_1 < MC_2$, (that is, the resources in one extra unit of Q_1 are less than the resources in one extra unit of Q_2). Now freeze everyone in Canada except me at their old consumption levels. Then they are certainly *as well off as before*. But when you give me more than 1 new Q_1 for 1 sacrificed old Q_2, I am certainly *now better off* since previously each good has had the *same MU* to me. Hence, any one man like me can be made better off by removing monopoly imperfections without hurting anyone else! QED."

EXPLOITATION OF LABOR: A DIGRESSION This sagacious consumer might even add: "Actually, dividing up the benefits more widely, you could have made *all* people who consume the two goods better off.

"And furthermore, any worker who now chooses to work an extra new minute picking berries in the monopolized industry will find that the true amount of new berries he picks is greater than what he could buy at the monopolist's P_1 with his last minute's wage—because the monopolist is marking up P_1 over true Marginal Cost. (NOTE: the same improvement is *not* possible under competition.)

"Hence, the monopoly imperfection is indeed inefficient in the sense that there is seen to exist a way to depart from it and improve any worker's welfare while at the same time not hurting *anyone* else (i.e., have the worker spend an extra minute picking berries and eating them)! QED again."

Summary of Digression: **Monopolistic deviation from $P = MC$, means "exploitation" of labor (and other transferable resources), in the sense that society's labor is misapplied as between goods and leisure or as between too-scarce monopolized goods in relation to too-plentiful competitive goods.**

[2]In terms of the concept mentioned in Chapter 23's footnote 12, this is being said: "It is not 'Pareto-optimal' to have $P_i > MC_i$ anywhere: everyone could be made better off by the proper move to $P_i = MC_i$". The Pareto-optimality concept does not come to grips with "interpersonal equities", but it does throw light on the problem of "efficiency".

We shall have more to say about exploitation in Parts Four and Six. But one warning is in order here. Often monopolies can afford to pay workers *even more* than competitive industries can, sharing so to speak a mite of the monopoly swag with the workers. So raising wages in monopoly industries by trade-union action is *not* the way to get rid of *this* kind of exploitation.[3] It is *all* society that is being exploited, and it is a task for combines policy to reform the situation.

ECONOMIC WARFARE AND THE THEORY OF GAMES

Oligopoly sometimes breaks out into intermittent warfare. Steinberg's, Loblaws, and Dominion cut and recut retail food prices, hoping to win a larger share of the consumer market—or even to drive the weakest out altogether. When Boeing and Douglas first brought jet planes to market, each had to wonder how high his rival would set his price, asking, "What do they think we think they will do?"

Such a situation, "where two (or more) *free wills* each choose strategies that will affect both *inter-dependently*," constitutes the essence of the philosophical problems involved in the theory of games. This theory, which sounds frivolous in its terminology borrowed from chess, bridge, and war, is fraught with significance and was largely developed by John von Neumann (1903-1957), Hungarian-born mathematical genius (and one of the three coin-ventors of the United States hydrogen bomb).

Here we can only sketch the general notions involved in game theory.[4] Figure 25-7 shows a case of perpetual price cutting. Eaton's advertises, "We will not be undersold," but other stores, for example, Woolco, advertise, "We sell for less." Suppose, in Fig. 25-7, Woolco decides to sell for 10 per cent less. The vertical black arrows show Woolco's (or Black's) price cuts; the red horizontal arrows show Eaton's (or Red's) responding strategies of matching them.

It is just as if Black and Red were playing a chess game: at Black's turn, he moves north-south; at Red's turn, he moves east-west. Here the game ends in mutual ruin, at zero price, where 90 per cent of nothing is compatible with equal (zero!) prices.

But finally Woolco gets wise and realizes that when it cuts P_1, the other P_2 will not stay constant but will follow it downward. Only if it is short-sighted does it think it can move south; actually as Red reacts to match, both move southwestward together toward lower profits for both. If there were but two sellers and no combines laws to worry about, the two might collusively raise price to the monopoly level that maximized joint profits and represented $P > MC$.

[3]See footnote 6, for union actions that can offset "exploitation of labor" by employers who have monopoly-bargaining buying power in the labor, not the Q-good, market.

[4]Aside from the classic by von Neumann and Morgenstern cited in next chapter's footnote 3, the reader might study John McDonald, *Strategy in Poker, Business and War* (Norton, New York, 1950).

FIG. 25-7

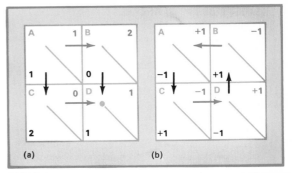

TABLE 25-5

Black knew Red would really stay in his first column, Black would gain by cutting P_1 down to C, getting the lion's share of the business there with payoff 9 >6. But, of course, Red will now prefer to match Black's $1 P_1, taking us from Cell C to D.

Here at D (whose excess-profits just happen to be minimal), the competitive solution is stable. (That is, 0 is the largest black number in the *column* Red has picked, and 0 is the largest red number in the *row* Black has picked. Verify this light-red-dot-equilibrium.)

But we must be warned. The competitive solution is not stable as against a "collusive" move from D to A. This might come about by overt agreement or by tacit agreement. (If Black were reluctant to follow suit, Red might in Hitler fashion blackmail him by threatening mutual ruin through cutting P far below any cost levels.) The only safe guarantee of competition is thus the potential pressure of really numerous sellers.

These game-theoretic considerations show the importance to oligopolists of finding some way to "agree." And they help explain, along with next chapter's "kinked" demand curve, why oligopoly prices tend to be administered in a "sticky" or rigid way. Were prices to change often, tacit agreements would be hard to identify and enforce.[5]

[5]Collusion is less worrisome in the simpler two-person games studied by von Neumann, the "constant-sum" games in which the red and black payoffs add up to the *same* constant in *every* cell, as in the accompanying Table 26-5 (*a*) and (*b*).

In (*a*), cell D is a stable solution—representing what is called a "saddlepoint," i.e., a cell which gives maximum black numbers in *its* column and *minimum* black (and hence, maximum red) numbers in its row.

But in (*b*), which can be given a penny-matching interpretation (Red turns up his coin to try to match Black's, winning in A and D and losing in B and C), you will find no such minimax or light-red-dot stable saddlepoint. (Thus, from A, Black moves to C; then Red moves to D; then Black to B; then Red back to A; and so we oscillate counter-clockwise forever!)

Von Neumann proves this remarkable theorem about (*b*); namely, each player should introduce *randomized* strategies: thus if each charges $1 or $2 with equal and independent probabilities, neither can then gain in *average* payoff by departing from this stable, minimax saddlepoint solution. Using probabilities, every constant-sum matrix has a saddle point. (Von Neumann proves many other fascinating theorems. For example, chess is as "trivial" as ticktacktoe. This means that when played "correctly," it must *always* end in the *same* one of the following: a draw, first man wins, second man wins—but what that outcome is for chess with its multiplicity of moves, no one knows, not even the electronic computer.)

TABLE 25-4

Our joint-strategy diagram can be replaced by an equivalent two-way table (or "game-payoff matrix"). In Table 25-4 Black picks his P_1 strategy by selecting a row. Red's P_2 strategy involves his choosing a column. Then in each of the four cells A, B, C, D the black number represents Black's profit-payoff at those prices and the red number gives Red's profit-payoff. Thus, in Cell A joint profits of 6 + 6 (thousand dollars) are maximized at the common monopoly price, $2 = P_1 = P_2$. But A is not "stable," in that if

PRISONER'S DILEMMA AND LOVE Game theory can throw light on one of the great needs of our age—the need for altruism. (In a more sentimental time, love might be the word.)

In the game matrix of Table 25-4, self-interest (in a word, selfishness) was channeled by the mechanism of economic competition to bring the system to cell D, which happens in this context to be the optimum state. Thus, by a happy accident so to speak, there does exist a facet of social life—the perfectly-competitive market, when that is strictly applicable and viable—where Adam Smith's Invisible Hand does contrive the maximum of well-being out of the motivation of selfishness.

But that is a lucky accident, unlikely to be realized in other social situations. The following model, or fable, called "prisoner's dilemma," illustrates this basic truth in game-theoretic language. Table 25-6 is like Table 25-4, but reinterpret it in terms of prisoner's dilemma so that Black and Red are two prisoners who have been caught in a joint crime. The Crown Prosecutor interviews each separately, saying "I have enough on both of you to send you to jail for a year. But if you *alone* will confess to the 10-year crime, I'll make a deal with you: You'll get off with a 3-month sentence, while your partner will serve 10 years. But if you *both* confess, you'll both get 5 years."

What should Black do? Confess and hope to get only a short sentence? That's better than the year from not confessing. But wait. There is an even better reason for confessing. For suppose Black doesn't confess and unknown to him, Red does confess. Black stands to get 10 years! Better than *that* is to confess and get no worse than 5 years. Red is in the same dilemma: If only he knew what Black is thinking (or what Black thinks Red thinks Black is thinking . . .).

Note that selfishness leads inevitably to long prison terms—5 years—in cell D of Table 25-6. Only by altruism —or social agreement (in this case, collusion)—can the best *common* state of the world, cell A, be realized.

To see the need for altruism—or failing that, for collective decision making—apply Table 25-6 to the air pollution problem. (Replace not-confess by not-pollute, . . . , etc. And assume that when I pollute and you do not desist from polluting, I will be somewhat worse off if I alone decide to desist.) Then the same logic as in Table 25-6 proves that nationalistic pursuit of self-interest leads to all nations breathing the same foul and polluted air that shortens life expectancies.

Thus, game theory does point up the need for brotherhood and common rules of the road.

POWER Critics of political economy claim, often with some justice, that it has not mastered the analysis of power. General Motors can harass a Ralph Nader by pri-

TABLE 25-6

vate investigations into his sex life, in the hope of quelling his criticisms. The employer in a one-plant town, like the seigneur during feudalism, may have the power to drive women into prostitution or concubinage if he withholds his job-giving powers. IT&T can use its vast finances to lobby in Washington—to get contracts, or soften antitrust prosecutions.

Von Neumann's theory of games provides some tools for analyzing power. Thus, the impotence of perfect-competitors to raise price above marginal cost is not understandable in terms of Freudian concepts. Or in terms of class-struggle terminology. It is the fact of "constant returns to scale"—*if* that fact prevails, so that what one firm can do can be easily replicated by countless others—that enables us to understand and predict this impotence.

Similarly, the power of a monopolist has to be understood in terms of his patents, or technological secrets, or the increasing-returns nature of his industry that makes giant scale mandatory and frees him from threat of effective competitors.

Beyond the simple two-person games of earlier tables, von Neumann has developed an elaborate theory of *collusions*. (*Trivial example:* Given three sadists, we can assert: Some two will gang up on the third. *More profound example:* Given universal suffrage, the majority will legislate in some degree against the minority of plutocrats—who in turn can be expected to use their financial power to try to limit this redistribution.)

CONCEPTS FOR REVIEW

$P = MC < AC$ regulation
improving all when $P_1 > MC_1$
economic warfare, P cutting
monopoly exploitation of labor
profit-payoff game matrix
row and column strategy
stable point
constant-sum game

collusion
prisoner's dilemma
randomized strategies and
   necessarily-existent stable
   saddlepoint or minimax
altruism and love
power

26

IMPERFECT COMPETITION AND COMBINES POLICY

The French colony of Canada was, during the greater part of the last century and some part of the present, under the government of an exclusive company. Under so unfavourable an administration its progress was necessarily very slow ...

ADAM SMITH (1776)

Chapter 25 gave us the tools for analyzing the actual markets of the real world. Now we seek answers to questions like the following: How do firms actually go about setting their prices? What is the role of the theoretical tools developed to analyze profit maximization? What are some of the important patterns of imperfect competition? Part A deals with these subjects.

Part B then takes up the basic problem of the relevance of economics to improving the workings of the system. What are the important issues for public combines policy raised by patterns of imperfect competition?

A. ANALYTICAL PATTERNS OF IMPERFECT COMPETITION

DO FIRMS MAXIMIZE PROFITS?

To what degree do businessmen actually try to maximize their profits? To what extent do they succeed if they do try to? It is not easy to give precise answers to these questions. Certainly, this much is true:

If a firm is absolutely reckless in calculating costs and revenues, then the Darwinian law of survival of the fittest will probably eliminate it from the economic scene. Therefore those firms which actually do manage to survive cannot be completely oblivious to the maximization of profits.

That does not necessarily mean of course, that every oligopolist or monopolist is seeking desperately to squeeze the last ounce of profit from every transaction. As soon as the firm gains considerable size and begins to enjoy some control over price, *it can afford to relax a little* in its maximizing activities.

More important, it is good business to take the long view and not concentrate on purely immediate gains. Many acts of apparent generosity can be amply explained in terms of public relations, and the maximization of *long-run* profits.

Consider a firm that is maximizing its profits in a fairly sensible manner. Does that mean that it is calculating geometrical curves of cost and revenue and from them deriving elaborate measures of marginal cost and revenue? Obviously not, as you will soon learn if you inquire about current business practices.

But even if the firm is not itself tackling the problem with conscious awareness of the particular marginal tools of the theoretical economists, *to the extent that it is truly making a pretty fair guess as to where its highest profits are realized*, it will be succeeding in making marginal revenue and marginal cost approximately equal. It does this without curves, just by feeling its way to the optimum by trial and error, and increasingly by utilizing giant computers and involving the statistical and mathematical techniques of operational research, linear programming, and probabilistic decision theory.

MARKUP PRICING

One of the reasons why business is a challenge is the fact that best guesses must be made on the basis of incomplete information. It is no small task for a large or small business to make an estimate of the shape of the demand curve for its products. Because other things do not remain equal, a company has no exact way of judging the elasticity of demand for its many products. The CNR can only guess whether a 20 percent cut in fares will bring in many more customers.

Many observers claim that modern business firms —even the largest—cannot in real life accurately determine marginal revenue and marginal cost. They cannot determine their optimum price and output with neat exactitude. Yet the day's work must somehow get done. Prices must be set on their products. Here is where it is claimed that average, or unit, cost plays an important role. The argument goes as follows:

Put yourself in the position of the president of a company producing many products. Prices are partly at your disposal. Your last year's sales are known to you, but your next period's sales can only be guessed even if you leave prices unchanged. Not knowing the extent or elasticity of demand for your products, you will be unable to determine marginal revenue. What will you do?

Probably, you call in your accountants and sales managers and ask, "What is our likely volume if we stay on our toes and keep our share of the market?" In answering, the sales force has to guess at the probable level of business activity, consumers' needs, results of market surveys, and much else.

After they have made their estimates, you turn to the cost experts and probably ask for the average cost of producing each product in question at those levels of output. There will be plenty of headaches in aiming at any sort of figure. For example, how should the administrative and plant overhead costs be allocated between different products? Or if a given process simultaneously creates joint products like meat and hides, how should the costs be allocated between them? Or if a building will last for many years, how much should be charged against current operations?

Headache or no headache, it is the practice of accountants to come out with some sort of answer as to average costs. Management must now decide by how much to mark up price over the cost figure. Depending upon its estimate of the consumers' reaction and the pricing policy of its competitors, the firm may perhaps decide on a 5, 10, 30, or 110 per cent markup.[1] Whether aware of it or not, the businessman is making some kind of implicit guess about his demand elasticity in setting his markup.

In bad times, when price competition is particularly keen, businessmen may even set prices at less than "full costs" because they realize that fixed expenses will go on whether or not production is at a low level. But price will never be set below average *variable* costs unless the item in question is being used as a "loss leader" to attract other business now and in the future, or unless the firm is willing to incur temporary losses in order to crush a rival and drive him out of business completely.

Many investigators of actual business pricing policies have testified that corporations often do follow the above-described practice of quoting administered prices on a "cost and markup" basis, hoping thereby not only to recover their "full cost outlays," but also to make a return on their investments. Their evidence therefore seems realistic, but it is not very informative. It stops tantalizingly short of telling *why* the average markup is 40 per cent in one industry and 5 per cent in another; it cannot tell why, before World War II, General Motors in the auto industry was able to earn 30 per cent on the book value of its invested capital while Ford, almost as large, could earn but 1/2 of 1 per cent. Demand and cost just have to be regarded as lurking in the background of any business case.

Careful reading of the foregoing account suggests that it is compatible with the principles outlined in Chapter 25. So long as the percentage markup is subject to the pressures implicit in *MC* and *MR* analysis, markup pricing may hinge on the same conditions (rather than being claimed as an alternative to) as profit maximization theory.

GALBRAITH'S NEW INDUSTRIAL STATE

Prior to John Kenneth Galbraith's 1958 masterwork, *The Affluent Society*, this versatile giant emphasized in his 1954 *American Capitalism* the notion of "countervailing power." Thus a mammoth corporation like General Elec-

---

[1] General Motors, one of the world's most successful enterprises, has used such markup methods for 50 years. Note that the average costs used prior to markup will for most firms *not already* include a return on the firm's own equity capital.

tric produces, among many other things, refrigerators. It is, of course, checked somewhat in its market power in selling them by the competition of Westinghouse, Philco, General Motors, and many other selling rivals (particularly in this post-Galbraithian era of proliferating "conglomerates," which merge into one large corporation unrelated activities that cut across scores of industries).

Competition by selling rivals is old-fashioned competition, which may or may not suffice to prevent monopoly. Galbraith's emphasis is on something different.

COUNTERVAILING POWER This is the check upon a giant corporation that comes from the organized competition among *the units it buys from* and among *the units to which it sells.* Countervailing power is the check on GE that comes from its being faced with a giant trade union in the market where it buys its labor; from its being faced with a government-led cartel of farmers and miners when it buys its raw materials; from its being faced by powerful groups of retailers to which it must sell, and which use their mass purchasing power to bargain down price and keep profits in check.

Essentially then, *countervailing* power adds, along with the conventional competition of rival sellers, the checks and balances of competition between giant buyers and sellers at every stage in the productive and distributive process.

To the degree that it does prevail, a world of countervailing power will improve on the performance of a mixed economy in comparison with an unlimited oligarchy of giant trusts. But it does take us a long way from the world of simple *laissez-faire,* and inevitably it relies heavily on lobbying, and influencing politicians, to influence prices or sales.

THE TECHNOSTRUCTURE In his *New Industrial State,* 1967, Galbraith views the large corporation as the strategic economic unit of our time. Having much at stake, the corporation desires *stability,* not adventure or uncertainty. Desiring growth, growth, growth, it embraces rational *planning.* Needing *experts,* it increasingly uses, and *is increasingly taken over by,* a new breed of technicians. These bureaucrats are professional managers, who possess the esoteric skills of science, engineering, and social psychology. Members of this technostructure shuttle back and forth to government and political offices. This year the wonder-boy graduate of the business school is merging seven companies; next year he is in Ottawa, helping draw up a trade agreement with Communist China, or in Washington, helping negotiate an arms treaty with the Russians.

It is Galbraith's contention that all over the world—in Vancouver or Vladivostok, in Peking or Poona—there is a *convergence* toward the same kind of society. On the other side of that bargaining table, the expert faces someone who is essentially his twin—the graduate of the top Moscow Institute, or the Inspecteur de Finance who led his class at the Ecole Polytechnique or the Ecole Normale Supérieure. In what may be Galbraith's own Walter Mitty dream of glory, the new establishments everywhere are converging to the same pattern—to a "meritocracy" based on expert skills, in short, to a "technostructure."

PLUSES AND MINUSES Critically, how are we to evaluate these new ideas? To say they are nonsense would itself be nonsense. To insist that they are not new—that Veblen had prophesied the triumph of the engineers 50 years ago, that James Burnham had stressed the role of the bureaucracy, that every tired radical of the 1930s took it for granted that consumer preferences were shaped by advertising efforts and did not well out of the spontaneous nature of man—is beside the point: those who live on in the history of thought and ideas are not those who first think of a notion, but rather those who synthesize its various meanings, who package it, and put it across.

Scholarly research is still going on to document quantitatively the merits and demerits of the Galbraithian vision. The findings seem, all over the Western world, to be converging to a balance sheet something like the following.

1. Experts are increasingly in demand. But Galbraith exaggerates the unilateral power that they can exercise. Those who control the plurality of stockholders' votes—themselves usually a minority—still call the tune. The minute the company hits upon hard times and slow growth, the whiz-kid expert is reminded of the layman's definition of the expert — "a bastard from out of town". All this applies, as well, to the Soviet or Chinese computer expert who gets too big for his breeches. Those with ultimate power listen to, but also put into their place, members of the technostructure.

2. Large corporations do certainly have the elbow room for unilateral action denied to a small farmer or conventional family enterprise. They can give money to slum clearance. They can relax in their pursuit of profit. They can pursue growth even when it is more that of cancerous than of healthy cells. They can tempt consumers to buy the goods that the corporation would like to sell.

But the large corporation is not an absolute monarch. Ford could not sell the famous Edsel; every year

Types of Competition

Kind of Competition	Number of Producers and Degree of Product Differentiation	Part of Economy Where Prevalent	Degree of Control Over Price	Methods of Marketing
Perfect competition	Many producers; identical products	A few agricultural industries	None	Market exchange or auction
Imperfect competition:				
Many differentiated sellers	Many producers; many real or fancied differences in product	Toothpaste, retail trade; conglomerates		
Oligopoly	Few producers; little or no difference in product	Steel, aluminum, lumber, pulp	Some	Advertising and quality rivalry; administered prices
	Few producers; some differentiation of products	Autos, machinery, wallboards		
Complete monopoly	Single producer; single product without close substitutes	A few utilities	Considerable	Promotional and "institutional" public-relations advertising

TABLE 26-1. This is a reminder that most industries fail to be perfectly competitive (Source: Table 25-1).

dozens of new products and names are launched, and sunk without a trace—All have had the Madison-Avenue wizardry of product and market analysts to justify them to the great corporations who try them out. The losses range from the hundreds of millions for new types of aircraft, nuclear generators and computers, to the hundreds of thousands for new brands of cigarettes and deodorant. If one minority group of management lets profits languish so that the common-stock holders do not get capital gains, another ring of capitalists will stage a successful "take-over". The new crew may not be gentlemen from Upper Canada College, but this is the mixed economy's way of cutting its losses.

Having said all this, the objective scholar must assert that economics will never be quite the same as in the days before the Galbraith trilogy.[2]

OLIGOPOLY: COMPETITION AMONG THE FEW

Table 25-1, page 449, gave a classification of different forms of market structure. It is important enough to warrant reproducing in this chapter as Table 26-1 (see above). Monopoly (one seller) is a rare case. Duopoly (two sellers) happens occasionally, particularly in geographically distinct markets where a couple of steel makers or a couple of railroads or trucking companies dominate the market.

More common still is the case of *oligopoly* (few sellers). We saw in Chapter 6, page 000, that most large-scale industries are dominated by a few giant firms. In the production of pig iron, matches, and soap, a few big firms predominate, and the same is

[2] For attacks on Galbraith, both from the left and the right, see P. A. Samuelson, *Readings in Economics* (McGraw-Hill, New York, 1973, 7th ed.). Those who study the modern corporation with the objectivity of an anthropologist studying a new culture testify that the large firm is neither absolute monarch nor slave to impersonal market forces. For every case where it pays some

management to overstress growth at the expense of profitability, there is a case where losses are cut on activities that didn't work out. Only those who knew the old-fashioned owner-entrepreneur realize how often he failed to maximize profits in the pre-Berle-Means days, and how more commercially rational are modern corporate cost-minimizers and capital budgeters.

true among the distilleries, tobacco processors, petroleum refineries, and breweries. Similar conditions prevail in other industries. In automobiles, the Big Three saturate most of the market; and so it goes in the aluminum, aircraft, meat-packing, and communications industries.

An economic theory of oligopoly has been developed to try to account for the facts of *administered* prices (which, by definition are posted prices that change infrequently), and to account for the prevalence of markup pricing. Let us consider the case of three or four dominant firms. Already we know that the pattern of costs and returns is likely to be such that the *optimal size of efficient production*—at the bottom of Chapter 25's U-shaped long-run AC curve (see page 431)—will be *very large relative to the total market demand.* That is why the three or four firms do not become thirty or forty, or three hundred, or three thousand.

Thus, it probably costs a billion dollars to produce an integrated steel plant. Canada has only four integrated producers. If steel could be produced at the scale that wheat is produced, there would be thousands of Canadian steel companies, and the industry would have to fear much more competition than it now gets from European and Japanese imports and shipments from the eastern United States.

Figure 26-1 shows the large-scale operation of a typical oligopolist. The most acute case threatening instability of oligopolistic competition is that in which the different firms produce virtually *identical* or *homogeneous* products. If Firm A's sulphuric acid undersells Firm B's by even $1 a cartank, A will get practically all the business. In this case, we oligopolists are practically sure to recognize our "mutual interdependence"[3] —namely, that we must end

FIG. 26-1. Oligopoly means few sellers of identical products or differentiated products.

After experience with disastrous price wars, each of the few rivals who dominate a given market is almost sure to recognize that price cutting begets canceling-out price cutting. So the typical oligopolist will estimate his demand curve *dd* by assuming others will be charging similar prices (and by taking into account the potential entry of new oligopolists). Since he gains little from cutting *P*, he will settle for sizeable markup of *P* over *AC* where *MC* = *MR*.

up charging about the same prices, and that any initial advantage I get in undercutting your price will be lost when you are induced to cut your price in return. That is why the *dd* demand curve shown for Corporation A in Fig. 26-1 is *not* drawn up on the assumption of "other things (including rivals' prices) being held constant"; instead A's *dd* is just exactly as inelastic as the whole industry's *DD*, since it is A's prorated one-third or one-fourth of the shared market.

Where is the Maximum-profit equilibrium for the oligopolist? It is shown in Fig. 26-1 at *E*, the intersection of his *MC* and *MR* curves, with *P* at *G* on *dd* just above *E*. If you turn back to page 454, you see that this oligopoly equilibrium *looks* much like the

---

[3] A century of theorizing by economists about what Mind A thinks Mind B will do if *he* thinks A will do such-and-such culminated in J. von Neumann and O. Morgenstern, *The Theory of Games and Economic Behavior* (Princeton University Press, Princeton, N.J., 1953, 3rd ed.). This mathematical theory, while it cannot clear up all the philosophical problems of how two omniscient minds will act against each other in an interdependent world, does offer many fine insights for political warfare as well as economics. (EXAMPLES: A teacher picks quiz questions *at random* from a book; a watchman makes his rounds at random, not in a discernible pattern. Facing you as a smart rival, I shall work hard to maximize my *most vulnerable* defence, knowing you will find out the weakest link in my chain. I bluff at poker, not simply, as some think, to win a pot with a *weak* hand, but

rather to ensure that all players do *not* drop out when I bet high on a good hand.) The Appendix to the previous chapter surveys game theory.

simple monopoly equilibrium of Fig. 25-4(a). Only the assumption about rivals' prices differs.

INFLEXIBLE, ADMINISTERED PRICING But there is an important difference under oligopoly. A monopolist might be expected to change his price every time his *dd* or *MC* curve shifts, which could be every year, every quarter, every month. We need an economic theory to explain the more inflexible price quotations administered typically by oligopolists. We deduce the needed theory of P inflexibility from the fact that rivals may behave one way when you *cut* your price—namely, *matching* your cuts and thwarting your hope for new business; and they behave another way when you *raise* your P above the customary level—namely, holding their prices constant in order to pick up some of your customers. In consequence, you have little motive to change your price in either direction. Instead you "administer" your own price in a rigid fashion, particularly since each oligopolist learns from experience that it is easier to agree—tacitly or explicitly—on a common P that is fixed rather than on one that is changing from month to month.[4]

Figure 26-2 illustrates the "kinked" or "cornered" demand curve that economists postulate to explain rigid price behavior. The equilibrium price G is shown in Fig. 26-1 and Fig. 26-2 at about that markup level over costs which the oligopolists think will be best for them in the long run.

But at G there is a kink in the effective demand and marginal revenue curves of the oligopolist. Why? Because if he cuts his P below G, his rivals will follow him, and he moves down the $d^n d^n$ curve, which corresponds to the old steep dd[5] curve in Fig. 26-1. But what if he *alone* raises his P above the tacit customary price at G? No rival will follow him, because they all hope to pick up some business at his expense. Most, but not all, of his customers are likely to leave him: hence, for *increases* in P, he is on the more elastic dd curve that reflects what he would sell

FIG. 26-2. A kinked or cornered demand curve can explain rigidity of oligopolists' administered price.

The $d^n d^n$ curve through G, which corresponds to the dd curve in Fig. 26-1, is the demand curve when all sellers move prices *together* and share total market. However, dd is the more elastic demand curve when this firm *alone* changes its price and loses sales to its rivals. Below G, as others match your price cut, $d^n d^n$ prevails. Above G, when rivals do not match your price increase dd prevails. Geometrically, the different demand curves generate different MR curves, with the FC vertical discontinuity (or "kink") resulting from the corner at G. Considerably shifting MC curves will still lead to intersection on FC, and hence unchanged oligopoly price and quantity at G.

when he *alone* changes P while all rivals *hold their prices constant* at the customary G level.

Geometrically, the corner on the demand curve implies the vertical discontinuity in the MR curve marked FC.[6] And now see that the MC level for the firm could shift considerably—anywhere between F and C—without changing the q^* intersection of MC and MR or the Maximum-profit P^* at G.

A "cornered" or "kinked" demand curve around an administered level of markup price—because P cuts are matched and P increases are not—can help

---

[4] The remainder of this section can be skipped if desired.

[5] Actually, it would be realistic for them to draw up their $d^n d^n$ curves allowing for entry of *potential* rivals who might be tempted into the industry if they collude on so high a P as to make it profitable for new firms to come in. In consequence, each firm's $d^n d^n$ might be somewhat more elastic than that for the whole industry, but still more inelastic than the dd that results from no change in rival's P induced by your change in P.

[6] The straight-line geometry of page 440 diagram can demonstrate this. The flat dGd straight line generates the flat MR line; the steeper $d^n G d^n$ line generates the steeper MR line; between these MR lines comes the vertical "kink," FC.

explain rigidity of oligopoly price compared with both perfect-competition and complete-monopoly flexible price. Also, this rigidity makes tacit agreement more easily possible.

COLLUSION, TACIT OR EXPLICIT We see why combines policy should be greatly concerned with the problem of oligopoly collusion. Even where there is some differentiation of products, if there are but two, three, or a few sellers, they may come to realize that their prices are closely *interrelated*. Each will guess, or may soon learn from experience, that when it cuts its price, its rivals tend to meet or to exceed such a price cut. Economic warfare may result for a while, until the few sellers come to realize that they are in the same boat.

Before the antitrust laws were important, such oligopolists might have formed an explicit "trust;" or a tight little cartel or combine. Meeting at celebrated dinners, such as those that Judge Gary of the United States Steel Corporation held decades ago, the sellers would collusively set some kind of monopoly price. As high as a full-monopoly price? Sometimes, if they were sure they could keep newcomers out. But in the more realistic case where the oligopolists had to take account of the fact that setting a high price would tempt new rivals into their field, they would agree on a price higher than the purely competitive one but set with some moderation for fear of attracting new entry.

Today it is illegal for combines, cartels, or "trusts" to set prices collusively and shamelessly in order to maximize their mutual profits. Thus sellers of cement have been recently heavily fined (over $400,000) for being in constant touch with one another to set prices and to arrange their bidding for contracts for ready-mix. But such explicit arrangements are only the tip of the iceberg. If a few large firms encounter the same problem, experience suggests that they may—without ever meeting, phoning, winking, or corresponding—arrive at a *tacit* mode of behavior that avoids fierce price competition. With or without a price leader, the sellers may be quoting rather similar prices—prices which come nowhere near the level of *MC*, as in the case of the perfectly competitive industry discussed in Chapter 23.

The richness of possible outcomes would exhaust a specialized book on the subject. The final equilibrium may end up much or little above the firm's marginal cost level. If fear of entry is great and if the number of existing sellers is considerable, then the $d^n d^n$ curve might be quite near to horizontal and give results not too different from perfect competition. But if sellers are few, and if they are large relative to the total demand, not very fearful of new entrants, and keenly conscious of the *mutuality* of their interest, the tacit price pattern may become a very high one relative to long-run or short-run marginal cost.

Also, oligopolists love to shift rivalry and competition into dimensions other than price: into advertising the real or fancied merits of their brands, into changing the wrapping of their product and the size of its replacement parts, into providing quick and reliable service.

FIG. 26-3. Free entry of many imperfect competitors can wipe out profit but still leave waste.

The typical seller's original profitable *d'd'* curve will be shifted downward and leftward by entry of new rivals. Entry ceases only when each seller has been forced into a long-run, no-profit tangency such as at *G*. Such rivals split up the markets without depressing price to the marginal cost level as in perfect competition. He and all his rivals end up with *P* above *MC*; and producing *q* at which long-run average cost is still falling, because it is less than the particular q^* which is at the bottom of the U-shaped curve. (Note: *MR'* is marginal to *d'd'*, and *MR* is marginal to the later *dd*.)

Some of this is undoubtedly valuable; some is definitely wasteful. What is the net balance of advantage over disadvantage? A priori reasoning alone cannot tell us; even study of the facts cannot lead to a conclusive answer independent of ethical value judgments.

But what needs emphasizing by the economist is this: Once the rules of perfect competition do not apply, there is no Invisible Hand principle which sets up a presumption that the working out of *laissez-faire* is likely to be in the direction of satisfying wants more efficiently.

MANY DIFFERENTIATED SELLERS: WASTE UNDER FREE ENTRY

Let us leave few-seller oligopoly and turn to the case of many sellers, but not of a homogeneous single product. This important case is the brainchild of the late E. H. Chamberlin.

In Fig. 26-3 a typical seller is briefly in short-run equilibrium at G'. His $d'd'$ is sloped because his product is a little different from anyone else's. However, we assume that *entry is free* for new firms to produce their own differentiated products on as favorable terms as our typical seller can produce his.

Since he and all the other initial sellers are making good profits at the initial G', new firms are tempted into the market. These new entrants cut into his demand and shift his $d'd'$ curve leftward to dd until it just touches (and does not cross above) his AC curve.

Thus, final long-run equilibrium for the typical seller ends up at the *tangency* point G—the only point at which the seller can avoid losses. Note that downward-sloping dd means that tangential AC must be falling and that final output is smaller than the q^* corresponding to the bottom of the U-shaped AC curve.[7]

Chronic excess capacity and waste. Free entry into the large group of sellers of *differentiated* products

merely divides up markets, leading to ex prices at the tangency points of downward-slo demand curves with still-falling long-run A curves. Minimum-cost scale of production is not attained. The imperfect competitors make no monopoly profits, but price does not get lowered to the bottom-of-the-U level. The consumer has to pay for chronic excess-capacity operation of too many sellers, each producing too little. These wastes are different from those of complete monopoly, and of course different from the efficiency of perfect competition.

If consumers were willing to sacrifice the differentiation of product, a lower equilibrium P would be possible as fewer firms were used more intensively to produce a more standardized output. But *laissez-faire* has no way of deciding how much extra people *ought* to pay in return for the extra variety of products they enjoy in Fig. 26-3.

---

typical perfect competitor is one of so many producers of an *identical* good that he faces a practically horizontal ("infinitely elastic") dd curve, even though the industry's very much larger DD curve can be very much more inelastic. If there is free entry and exit of well-informed firms that can replicate the cost conditions of any one firm, long-run equilibrium at E will involve no excess of profit over competitive costs (including properly computed implicit- and opportunity-cost returns). Society is getting its total output most efficiently, in recognition of the $P = MC$ condition of Chapter 23: It has neither excess capacity nor too few firms (forcing out of existing firms any output that could be obtained more cheaply by adding new firms).

PERFECT COMPETITION

FIG. 26-4

---

[7] The Chamberlin excess-capacity tangency of Fig. 26-3 should not be confused with the tangency under *perfect* competition shown here in Fig. 26-4. As discussed in earlier chapters, this

COMBINES PROBLEMS

...TES OF IMPERFECT ...ION ...LATED

Before going into the legal, historical, and institutional aspects of combines legislation, we ought to remind ourselves what the economic evils are that are associated with various monopolistic and other imperfections of competition.

MONOPOLY RESTRICTIONS It is not the profit a monopoly (or an oligopoly, for that matter) makes that constitutes its greatest evil, but rather its tendency to set too high a price in relation to social marginal-cost pricing. To see this, imagine our taxing away all the monopolist's profit by imposing on him a franchise tax of just the right size.

Clearly, the monopolist would end up with no profit. The state would get its profit, but the monopoly would not lower its P or raise its Q. Why not? Because the intersection of MR and MC would be unchanged by a lump-sum franchise tax: since such a tax is a fixed cost that varies not at all with Q, it will not affect MC; and MR depends only on the demand curve, not on costs or franchise taxes. So the consumer goes on getting too little of the product and paying too high a price. The state has now become the villainous recipient of monopoly profit and has failed to correct the misallocation of resources.[8]

The moral: It is the contrived divergence between P and MC that constitutes the true additional burden of monopoly.[9]

[8] Figure 20-10, and Chapter 25's Appendix have elaborated on this.

[9] Advanced treatises use the accompanying Fig. 26-5 to approximate the "deadweight loss" due to monopoly. At the competitive ideal I, each similar consumer enjoys Marshallian consumer's surplus given by the whole triangular area NIR. When monopoly raises P to the Maximum-profit point G, the consumer loses to the monopolist that part of his consumer's surplus represented by the profit rectangle $NEGN'$ and is left with but $N'GR$.

What happens to the little triangle EIG? It is lost to everybody and represents "deadweight loss." Thus consumers lose more than the monopolist's profit; and even if they took back the $NEGN'$ profit by lump sum taxation, they would be losing to the devil of inefficiency the "deadweight triangle" which is *of no benefit whatsoever to anybody.*

OVERENTRY AND "SICK" INDUSTRIES

Many fields are characterized by an excessive number of firms.[10] Most of these do a small volume of business and remain in the industry only until they have lost their capital. Grocery stores, taverns, funeral homes, restaurants, nightclubs, and gasoline stations are typical examples taken from retail trade. But much the same thing is true of the textile trade, the dress trade, and many others that require little initial capital.

Why don't such unprofitable concerns leave the industry? The answer is, They do. But as fast as they leave, new firms enter the industry, leaving the total number unchanged and even growing.

Why do new firms enter the industry in the face of the fact that most existing firms are incurring losses? Apparently, partly out of ignorance and partly out of misplaced hope. An old couple putting their lifetime savings of a few thousand dollars into a little retail grocery store do so in the belief that

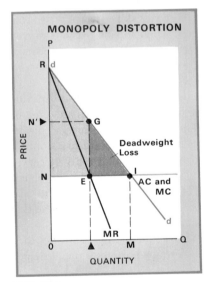

FIG. 26-5

[10] Even if, as Chamberlain insists, people may want some of the extra variety of differentiated products that the tangency solution of Fig. 26-3 makes possible, that pattern cannot be ideally efficient. For it can be shown that wherever P exceeds MC anywhere, there definitely exists a new configuration (possibly involving subsidies, as in Chapter 25's Appendix) in which *everyone* can be made better off. This point is alluded to again on page 473, footnote 11.

their venture will be different, theirs will succeed—and anyway, in the grocery business no one need starve. But alas, with no special business aptitude and with less than the minimum amount of capital necessary for efficient operation, they last in business only until their original capital has gone.

Such chronically overcrowded industries need not be what the economist has called "perfectly competitive"—although in the case of agriculture or "cotton gray goods," they may happen to be approximately so. Having too many firms in a perfectly competitive industry is an undesirable condition, involving as it does wastes of resources and losses. But at least in such a *competitive* industry the consumer partly gains, through lower prices, what the overoptimistic producers are losing.

Unfortunately, in most chronically overcrowded sick industries, market competition is quite *imperfect*. Being inefficient producers, the small concerns do not sell very cheaply. Instead of competing on a price basis, they tend to charge fairly high prices and simply to *divide* the business.

The resulting economic situation under this form of free-entry numerous-seller imperfect competition may be worse even than under complete monopoly: not only is price excessive, but in addition valuable resources are wasted because each firm has too much idle plant and manpower. The situation is triply bad: producers incur losses, resources are wasted, and the prices charged the consumer are too high; and there is the new element here that the producers incur chronic losses.

Our earlier diagram from Chamberlin, Fig. 26-3, showed how imperfect competition may result in wastage of resources, too high price, and yet no profits for the imperfect competitors. It can show too how the spirit of Marshall's long-run analysis can be applied to the sector of imperfect competition characterized by free entry.

Imagine the diagram shows such a typical imperfect competitor, say, a local barbershop that can count on some customers' being unwilling to walk a long way to get a haircut. Its original demand $d'd'$ slopes downward; and hence it has been marking up P above MC. It is maximizing positive profit and charging more than full unit costs(AC).

But now other barbers see this profit oppo[r]. They move in. There is now one barbershop every three blocks rather than for every four. Wha[t] happens to the demand curve for our typical barber? Clearly, entry of new competitors divides up the existing business and causes demand to shift downward and leftward to dd, with each barber wasting more time in frustrating idleness. Now at the new maximum-profit point, each barber makes no profit, as can be seen from the fact that the new demand curve just touches tangentially the average cost curve. Marginal cost is equated to new marginal revenue—but that serves only to avoid losses, not to produce a positive profit.

The long-run equilibrium at G, which Marshall might shudder to call "normal," very clearly shows that price is higher than the most efficient cost level which prevails at the bottom of the U-shaped average-cost curve. The barbershop has excess capacity, with empty chairs much of the time. (Of course customers have to walk only three blocks now, not four, and may have to wait less. And that is worth something. But note that they have never, in most cities, really been given the choice of a slightly longer walk and haircuts at the lower prices that efficient capacity utilization would make possible.[11])

If there is lasting overentry of overoptimistic barbers, draw in a $d''d''$ curve still lower than dd and show wasteful social losses, and turnover of disappointed entrepreneurs. You can do the same in the case of perfect competition illustrated in Fig. 26-4 (see footnote 7).

EVILS OF OLIGOPOLY Recall the already mentioned freight price wars of the past century. Customers shipping goods always pick the route that offers even a few pennies saving. Thus, each of the three or four carriers would intermittently undercut

---

[11] Repeatedly, in our discussion of pricing "efficiency," we have seen what is proved rigorously in advanced texts: price in excess of marginal costs leads to a state of "Pareto-nonoptimality", a state from which it would be possible theoretically to make *everybody* better off—barbers, bald people, long-haired people who hate long walks and waits, and everybody else. But do not leap from this to the invalid inference that variety does not matter or that enforcing $P = MC$ everywhere would (in decreasing-cost situations with differential products) lead spontaneously to the "ideal" amount of variety. Here is a case where defining an optimum is actually a difficult social task.

:dules, until finally a disastrously
is reached. At the same time, for
hippers were at the mercy of one
vould jack up the rates, thus cre-
ous, discriminatory pattern of
charg

Even without government regulations, in industries characterized by heavy overhead costs and identical products, there is often a realization that competition is ruinous. Therefore, tacitly or explicitly,
the firms try to agree on a price that maximizes the
long-run profits of all. Secret committees, keeping
one eye on the officers who enforce the Combines
Act, may impose penalties on any chiseler in the industry who makes secret price concessions. Occasionally, as new conditions or firms upset the status
quo in the industry, another price war may break out
—to last until everyone has again learned his lesson
and the morale of the industry is restored.

In appraising oligopoly we must note that the desire of corporations to earn a fair return on their *past*
investments can at times be at variance with the
well-being of the consumer. Too much plant capacity
may have been built in the industry in the past; but
that is not justification for continuing high prices
and scarce output. Competition, which the businessman regards as destructive, cut-throat, and ruinous, may actually be the only way to get the redun-
dant plant capacity into operation or to discourage its
maintenance. (Having made the mistake of building
the plants, society ought not to add the further error
of failing to use them to best advantage.) Losses
or subnormal profits is the free-enterprise way of
discouraging excess capacity, brutal as that may
sound.

The pulp, steel, and other raw material industries
are examples of this pattern of imperfect competition. How does all this work out these days in
practice? In 1958-1960 we hit a lull. Pulp production
went down to half its capacity. Some feared this
would initiate a wave of price cuts which would reduce pulp companies' earnings to the break-even
point or below. Did it work out that way? Not quite.
The industry discovered it could make more (or lose

less) money at levels far below capacity; price morale
stayed high in the industry. It was not until 1964,
when sales were up, profits were becoming large,
and many new firms were threatening to enter pulp
production, that West Coast firms began to cut prices
—partly, at least, to discourage entry.

In a perfectly competitive industry, when demand
shifts leftward, P will fall. Profits will decline
greatly. Yet competitive Q may not fall much at
all, being sold for whatever it will fetch. The consumer does benefit from what the producer loses,
and in time output will adjust to the new state of
demand.

By contrast, under oligopoly, price tends to stay
firm with output taking up the great variation.
Plants stand idle, and the product is not cheapened,
in the hope of coaxing out new quantity
demanded.

This downward inflexibility of "administered" (or
named) prices, many economists fear, adds to the
danger of creeping inflation. Why? Because if prices
and costs rarely ever fall, there is but one way for the
price index to go.

MONOPOLY AND CORPORATE VIGOR

All is not evil in any field. Some claims for
strengths and virtues in imperfect competition are
frequently made.

One argument stems from foreign trade. It is argued that in international markets for complicated
products like nuclear power or aircraft, small national firms will be shot down like flies. Successful
international competitors must build from a national
monopolistic power base. Technological efficiency
and market success abroad are not compatible with
consumer sovereignty at home.

This argument can easily be oversold. It is difficult
to see why *competitive* efficiency at home, with
$P = MC$, cannot through replication, lead to success
abroad. However, the argument is really meant to
apply to dynamic growth, not stable competitive
markets. It is implied that if one firm, or consortium,
can specialize at home and abroad, undisturbed by
price problems, it can eventually gain a commanding
lead in world exports. To comment on this aspect of

12 The Board of Transport Commissioners was established in 1904
to prevent such unstable price conditions, and to regulate rates
where competition could not be relied on to keep them down.

monopoly, we must turn to the field of research and development (R. and D.) and major innovation.

Both in domestic and in international markets, some firms get considerable control over price by virtue of their technological efficiency, new methods, patents, trademarks and advertising. Their "monopoly profits" from these controlled prices are then plowed back, into further research and into advertising, so that they are always abreast, or ahead of their rivals. Pharmaceutical firms like CIBA and industrial-chemical firms like CIL are perhaps typical. Although this may work a hardship on small firms, who claim they cannot effectively compete with the R. and D. of the giants, the real point is that *industrial research may be subject to economies of large scale.*

It is salutary to turn back to Schumpeter, whose eulogy of the dynamic innovational power of monopoly has already been cited (page 110). In another place he dismisses the textbook picture of capitalist reality which dwells too much on price, even quality, and competition. He writes:

" ... it is not that kind of competition which counts but the competition from the new commodity, the new technology, the new source of supply, the new type of organization (the largest-scale unit of control for instance) — competition which commands a decisive cost or quality advantage and which strikes not at the margins of the profits and the outputs of the existing firms but at their foundations and their very lives. This kind of competition is as much more effective than the other as a bombardment is in comparison with forcing a door, ... "[13]

Notice that little applied research expenditure today is carried on by small businesses, and that, for better or worse, most developmental outlays are, statistically, part of the promotional struggles of big businesses. Weigh this with the realisation that some applied industrial research is not for technical improvement but for aggressive war on consumers' fears and ignorance (via advertising and taste creation).

Do not forget that regardless of amounts spent, many of our best discoveries come from small business, government labs and research institutes, lone-wolf inventors and dissatisfied consumers, and from university researchers. (When Oxford's John Jewkes traced the source of the more important inventions of this century, he found that less than half came from laboratories of large corporations.) Furthermore, ask yourself if Schumpeter's economic progress, with its perennial gale of "creative destruction" of old producers by new entrepreneurs, requires thorough-going monopoly everywhere, or whether moderate departures from pure competition (such as we have today), are enough.

These are open questions today. Some experts seek the efficient use of resources of the competitive norm. They want the occasional blessings of major innovations and the continuing benefits of technological improvements to be "passed through" to consumers. P should equal MC, always. At least, profits should be plowed back into further research.

The other school asks, "In controlling, do we emasculate vigor?" Why worry about the wastes of advertising and hucksterism? We must create an atmosphere of dynamic international competition and innovation in which new ideas and new men are not stifled either by the caution of the private managerial technostructure or the public controls over industry in search of perfect competition. Thus the two schools are widely divided: must the giants, and potential giants, of the new industrial state be kept under control? Will ever-vigilant scrutiny and surveillance of price policies dampen and defuse the engines of growth and change? Or are the abuses of monopoly worse than their benefits?

This concludes our discussion of monopoly as a necessary condition for private innovation. In the remainder of this chapter we assume that citizens prefer more competitive efficiency and justice to the dangerous waters of unrestricted monopoly's "creative destruction". Certainly few scholars, or businessmen, advocate the Schumpeterian model of innovative monopoly capitalism.[14]

---

[14] Schumpeter died before the days of consumerism and environmentalists. As a liberal he would probably have approved of the former's attack on business frauds and advertising excesses. But he might have been a little sceptical of the latter's concern about pollution, wilderness destruction and NEW. Like anti-trust policies and enforced competition they would seem to him overly-cautious impediments to monopolistic innovations, that if introduced earlier, would have prevented the bursts of technological change, railway construction, mineral and forest exploitation, city-building and land settlement that he saw as the essence of economic growth.

[13] Joseph A. Schumpeter, *Capitalism, Socialism and Democracy*, 3rd edn., (Harper and Row, New York, 1942), p. 84.

WHAT TO DO ABOUT MONOPOLY IMPERFECTIONS

Is there no hope for limiting monopoly and oligopoly? Yes, there is.

For one thing, if we make sure that *barriers to entry are kept to a minimum*, the fear of potential competition and the actuality of it may help to keep the oligopoly's prices down.

For a second thing, if we *lower tariff barriers* to imported goods, we both increase the sources of potential competition and lower the maximum to which Canadian prices can be raised.

For a third thing, if *government combines policy* bears down hard on the slightest sign of collusion to keep prices firm and to control supply, the oligopolists may find it harder to equate their marginal revenue and cost at a level far above society's true marginal cost.

For a fourth thing, some economists—such as George J. Stigler of the University of Chicago—would argue that large firms should be broken up into many small pieces. He thinks the bottom of U-shaped cost curves comes early enough to make this a practical possibility that will not sacrifice any appreciable economies of large-scale production. With sellers now numerous, he hopes that competition can become much more like perfect competition than like oligopoly. (Needless to say, Stigler is against any mergers that might reduce numbers still further; and he believes that many of today's giants grew from mergers which had as their goal not *productive efficiency,* but rather *monopoly control over market price*.)

This is clearly a controversial area. Government regulation and government combines laws are the principal weapons the mixed economy uses to improve the workings of the price system. However, the courts' decisions, based on the interpretation of statutes, are of little help in making up our minds what a good policy *would* be. For example, the Supreme Court of Ontario found that a merger being carried out by Canadian Breweries Ltd. (Carling, O'Keefe, Dow, and other brands) with other breweries was acceptable because, with three large national breweries left, Canadian Breweries would still face competition. But the U.S. Supreme Court, a short time earlier, forbade Bethlehem Steel's planned merger with other firms, even though the resultant giant would have had no more than 20 per cent of the U.S. steel market. The two cases are very

similar. Both firms argued in defence of their mergers that they would become more efficient in production as they grew—that is, that the bottom of their U-shaped cost curves would be far to the right. But although this argument was contested by the prosecution in both cases, the two courts' judgments were based chiefly on whether competition remained after the mergers, not on whether increased efficiency would result and should be encouraged. Thus the courts, especially in Canada, have not really dealt with the question of whether increase in size, *per se*, is a good thing.

Fifthly, where government cannot limit monopoly, it cannot regulate it, as the next section shows.

PUBLIC-UTILITY REGULATION

To show what government can do about monopoly, let us consider in detail a monopoly under government regulation. Such "public utilities" include gas and light companies, telephone and communication services, broadcasting, satellites, airlines, railroads and public carriers, and so forth. Their importance is shown in Table 26-2. Since it seems uneconomical to have two local sets of telephone wires, an exclusive franchise is given to a single company. (Why not the same for milk delivery—another hard question.)

The government gives the utility company a complete monopoly, but then steps in to protect the con-

Percentage of GDP Subject to Pricing or Combines Laws, 1967	PER CENT OF GDP
Subject to Combines Act (mostly commodity-producing)	53
Subject to Agricultural Marketing Boards, etc.	5
Subject to Public-Utility Regulation	12
Service industries under public ownership or jurisdiction	10
Not regulated (mostly services)	20

TABLE 26-2. Most of GDP is subject to some pricing restrictions.
The Combines Act covers only about half of Canadian production, but other regulations also exist. (Source: Economic Council of Canada, *Interim Report on Competition Policy,* **Queen's Printer, Ottawa, 1969;** adapted from Table 7-1 and other Tables.)

sumer by setting maximum rates. Usually this is done by public regulating commissions, which specify the *maximum prices* that can be charged for each kind of service.

The rates selected as representing a fair return have often been in the neighborhood of from 7 to 11 per cent depending on the current state of expectations about inflation. (Recall that even if the real percentage rate remains constant, lenders will tend to add to it the expected percentage rate of price increase before agreeing to a long-term loan.) Of course, the very act of setting a rate appears to many critics to amount to a "guarantee" that removes the *motivation* of the utility, or phone, company to keep down its costs.

It is a complex problem, that of determining the *capital-value* base of the company to which this "fair rate" is to be applied. Three measures of fair capital value have been suggested at times: (1) *original cost* (minus depreciation—i.e., the sum of all past prudent investments; (2) *current reproduction or replacement cost* (minus depreciation)—or the cost of replacing the company's equipment at *present prices*, corrected for age and condition of the property; and (3) *capitalized market value* of the public utility's securities or assets.

ADVANTAGES AND DISADVANTAGES OF DIFFERENT METHODS OF REGULATION

Of these methods, the third is universally recognized to be nonsensical. As was shown in the earlier discussion of good will (Chapter 6), the market value of any income-earning property is given by capitalizing its annual return by the interest rate.[15] For a regulating authority to use capitalized market value as a base for measuring capital would be tantamount to recognizing *any level of earnings*, high or low, as fair. (For example, let the earnings be high—excessively high. The stock market will then pay a lot for them.) Once capitalized into a new base, excessively high earnings will appear as only moderate interest returns, and the same is true of excessively low earnings. The method of capitalized earnings begs the question that the authorities must answer!

Canadian regulation has therefore vacillated between *original* cost and *reproduction* cost. So long as the general price level does not change, the two are

[15] The capitalization process is more fully discussed in Chapter 30.

not very different. But over a period of decades, when prices may greatly increase, reproduction cost will involve higher earnings and rates than original costs. In periods of declining prices, the reverse discrepancy is to be observed: original-cost capital-value (or rate base, as it is often called) tends to favor investors over customers. Canadian provincial authorities have tended to prefer the more easily calculated original-cost base, and this once was also the implicit policy of the Canadian Transport Commission on railroad rates.[16] All in all, however, reproduction cost leads to a more flexible price structure, gives less weight to the dead hand of past costs, and helps keep abreast of inflation.

ECONOMIC LIMITS TO RATE-SETTING POWERS But the freedom of the authorities to set rates always has economic limitations. It is obvious that a rate set too low will drive out investors, make utilities unable to maintain their equipment and lines, and bring public service to a halt. Fear of this has, in the opinion of Canadian writers on utilities, always kept authorities erring slightly on the side of generosity in deciding on a "fair return" on capital. But there is also a "competitive" limit preventing rates from being set too high. Even in the early days, railroad transport boards found that, if rail freight rates were set too high, traffic would be diverted via U.S. lines, or highway or steamship alternatives. That is, the fair return on capital could not be granted to utilities whose demand curves were made elastic by potential substitutes. Today this "com-

[16] From the standpoint of the advanced discussions of "welfare economics," neither method is ideal as the last Appendix made clear. Some writers in this field have set up a perfectionist formula that would involve pricing of public-utility services at not more than the extra or marginal costs of services. (We have already seen many times why $P = MC$ is "efficient".) However, marginal-cost pricing is a doctrine which, as a practical matter, few economists would endorse all the way. It could lead to excessive returns to the owners if demand was large in comparison with capacity. But with decreasing-cost situations so likely in the public-utility area, it would more likely give *inadequate* returns to original investors. Although the government could then, if it wished to, *by a subsidy* secure justice for investors without interfering with the desirable output or price, this would represent such a departure from present practice as to be unlikely to come about fully.

The great public projects like the South Saskatchewan dam and the Great Slave Lake railway are from one point of view partial approaches to such a system of pricing. But their multiple national and regional purposes make it difficult to compare them with the pricing policies of more routine public utilities.

petition between natural monopolies" is even keener. A gas utility has very limited scope for asking higher prices: if it gets them, it will lose its customers to the oil companies and other energy sellers. Even hydro utilities face competition: consumers can use oil or gas for many purposes, and industrial buyers can generate their own power if the utility's rate is set too high. Similarly, road carriers cannot easily set (or have set for them) high per-mile rates, or customer firms will run their own trucks.

PUBLIC OWNERSHIP VERSUS PUBLIC REGULATION OF MONOPOLIES

Where many utilities are publicly owned, the downward pressure on rates is also maintained by a rule that Crown corporations are not to be run for a profit. But often this rule is not followed, by government liquor stores, for example. Anyway, it is no substitute for close regulation both of allowable expenses in the rate base and of rates themselves. Many provincially and federally owned utilities run at no profit because they offer expensive services that private utilities would abandon. Rural electrical service is a good example. Another is telephone service: we are told that Bell Telephone kept away from small rural systems because they were unprofitable at rates acceptable to public utilities commissions. Yet in the provinces with publicly owned telephone systems, rural services are widely provided, and are in effect subsidized by city telephone users. Thus a "no-profit" *rule* cannot guarantee that costs will be kept down, or rates and profits reasonable.

This is a sobering aspect of increased government ownership of pipelines and energy sources. The new federal and provincial corporations may indeed, by takeovers, prevent the profitable exploitation of monopolized industries. But what we need is efficiency, not no-profit. The fact that new public corporations make no profit may merely reflect bad management, or imprudent capital spending. It does not necessarily signal that monopoly wastes have been ended.

But *competition* still works to keep down rates, even in publicly owned services. Indeed, the CNR's rates over the years have been influenced chiefly by (1) parliamentary intervention to get low rates for regions like the maritimes and the prairie wheat belt, (2) the existence of competitive routes, such as the Panama Canal and inland waterways, and (3) the decisions of the Board of Transport Commissioners on the privately owned CPR's costs. And, where Canadians are frequently aware of prices in the United States, potential or demonstrable competition from new services already available in the United States may serve as well as actual competition.

The threat from competition today, however, is felt in a new way. Transportation, broadcasting and energy policies have been switched from regulation to keep customers from being exploited, to rather more explicit attempts to serve larger national goals. This is obviously true of the National Energy Board, which governs the export of energy to the United States from terms of reference that are only partly concerned with Canadian consumers, and are also concerned with Canadian taxpayers and Canada's future industrial prospects. This is also true of transportation. Utilities commissions, Parliament, and government royal commissions now seem to be struggling to free competitive private and public airlines and railways from regulation, and attempting instead to regulate their investment policy (and line-abandonment policy) so as to achieve explicit national and regional ends. The sanction from competition is only potential. New policy makers are saying, "Unless the railways or pipelines do so-and-so, the regions they serve will fail to develop as they should. This is bad in itself, and, incidentally, it will mean that there is no future traffic or business for the utilities." The McPherson Royal Commission on railroads was a good example of this planning approach to utility and railroad policy.

The reader who reflects on these examples may see a trend. Usually, and properly, natural monopolies have been regulated to prevent prices and rates being set too high. The utilities decided on much of their capital investment and expansion policy, however, the utility commissions being there chiefly to determine what a "fair return" ought to be on both old and new investments. Today the monopoly position of utilities is less strong. Each is becoming more like a firm in small-numbers, differentiated-products industry. The gap between its P and MC depends on the vigor of competition and on the ease with which new competitors can enter the market. The trend seems to be to regulate the conditions under which this competition can take place, to make sure that it doesn't involve reckless commitments for labor or equipment; at the same time, being careful not to discourage competition or to entrench utilities in monopolistic positions. This trend is vague so far; all that can be observed is that regulatory policy is no longer concerned solely with commissions that set or guarantee rates and prices.

COMBINES POLICY AND TRUSTBUSTING

The economics of Canada's particular policies to control "combinations in restraint of trade", or combines, have not been widely studied. Until the late sixties, no more than a handful of academics from all fields have been fully informed on the laws and their administration. This is quite unlike Germany, Britain, or the United States, where economists, lawyers, and historians have devoted professional careers to one or another aspect of their monopoly laws. And recent elections have suggested that ministers cannot yet build Canadian cabinet careers on trustbusting in consumer and corporate affairs.

American leadership stems chiefly from the fact that at the turn of the century trusts were becoming both the engine of further American economic development and the object of popular fear of their increased economic and political power. Small companies were merged into big; big and small companies combined collusively to limit supply and raise price. By retaliatory price-cutting, such trusts could and did brutally punish smaller firms that did not follow the trusts' price leadership. At the same time huge stock-market promotions of the securities and shares of the new mergers flourished. (While similar events were taking place in Canada, Canadian public opinion was really focused on other economic problems.)

EARLY U.S. TRUSTBUSTING Around 1889-1890, both countries took the first legal steps to go beyond the old common-law checks on combines. Canada added to its criminal Code the famous Section 411, forbidding combinations that *unduly* lessen competition in production or sale of goods. (The federal government cannot easily regulate trade and commerce by civil law-making, because most trade and property matters are under provincial jurisdiction.) Soon after, the United States passed its Sherman Antitrust Act, making it illegal to monopolize trade or to combine in restraint of trade. There is no record of these Acts being vigorously enforced at the time; indeed, it is evident that few people had a clear idea of which actions were to be regarded as illegal.

Then in the early 1900s came the era of "trustbusting." The Roosevelt and Taft administrations dusted off the Sherman Act, and through the Supreme Court challenged the merging or monopolizing activities of J.P. Morgan, E. H. Harriman, and James J. Hill on railroads; of Duke on the American Tobacco Company; and of Rockefeller on the Standard Oil Co. The last two were broken up into independent companies. These were the great capitalists and the great firms of the day.

The tide of prosecution was stemmed by the view eventually taken by the U.S. Supreme Court that the Sherman Act could be applied only to *unreasonable* agreements, mergers, or predatory actions against competitors. With this doctrine, the Court eventually decided that United States Steel, a huge merger promoted by Morgan, Carnegie, Gary and others, was not an "unreasonable" project: "bigness" was not in itself to be a crime. In 1914, the Clayton Act and the Federal Trade Commission Act were also passed. The former exempted trade unions from being prosecuted as combines, but did not succeed in defining the practices to be forbidden more precisely. The latter set up a powerful body which polices industry, chiefly to prevent misleading advertising claims and other unfair methods of competition by particular firms.

The U.S. courts' insistence that mergers had to be "unreasonable" to be illegal was of course very similar to the Canadian law's insistence that only practices that "unduly" lessened competition were illegal. Both left the onus on the courts to decide what was unreasonable or undue. And in Canada because few companies were prosecuted, no body of case-law was set up to clarify what was "undue."

In both countries the vigor of public antipathy to combines was diverted to other subjects in the 1920s. Antitrust actions languished. Under Mackenzie King, however, Canada did make a start on combines legislation by passing the Combines Investigation Act. Like King's Industrial Disputes Investigation Act, which was discussed in Chapter 7, this measure relied on investigation and *publicity*. A small staff was appointed to investigate suspected infractions of the Criminal Code section on combines, and of some sections that were inserted into the new act. The staff report was published, even if no legal prosecution was undertaken by the government. The staff was kept busy, but their reports and subsequent actions were directed mostly against small suppliers, contractors, and dealers. So inconspicuous was the Act that books published in the 1930s, criticizing what they called the trend to monopoly, sometimes failed even to mention the Combines Act!

During the Great Depression, antitrust and combines legislation had a mixed career. Left-wing politicians spoke with dislike of "monopoly power." Prime Minister R. B. Bennett launched a large "price spreads" investigation, because it was alleged that the prices paid to farmers, other suppliers, and "sweated labor" by larger industries were far below prices paid by consumers for their product. Indirectly, this was an allegation that monopoly power caused P to have a too-wide spread above MC. The commission uncovered some sensationally bad working conditions in certain industries, but little usable evidence of monopoly. In the United States, interest in trustbusting was for a while replaced by laws pointing in the other direction. The National Recovery Administration (later found unconstitutional) would have authorized Depression-weakened firms and workers to form cartels to hold up prices. And "fair-trade" acts authorized or ordered retailers to sell only at prices set by the manufacturers of branded goods. Such policies are called "resale price maintenance."

Until Franklin Roosevelt's Attorney General Thurman Arnold reversed the trend in the late thirties, the mix of laws and administration in both countries was calculated to keep prices *up* rather than down. Indeed, economist Lloyd Reynolds wrote a treatise with the suggestive title "The Control of *Competition* in Canada," not "The Control of Combines."

During World War II, both countries were too concerned with production and fair allocation of food and clothing to be worried about inefficient mergers and combines. Economist John Kenneth Galbraith has shown that it was actually convenient for harassed war production directors to be able to get together a very few heads of very large firms to plan output and price policies.[17] In peace time this would have been called collusion.

COMPETITION POLICY SINCE WORLD WAR II

IN THE UNITED STATES Under Presidents Truman and Eisenhower, the United States attacked trusts with renewed vigor but uncertain purpose. For example "bigness" itself was challenged: the A & P stores were prosecuted in the face of defence evidence that large-scale operations promoted efficiency

and lower consumer prices; DuPont was forced to relinquish its controlling ownership of GM stock and to give up its joint ownership of CIL in Canada. A little earlier, antitrust pressure had forced a complete split between Aluminum Co. of America and Aluminium Ltd. of Canada (Alcoa and Alcan). Industries such as glass, cigarettes, cement, steel and many others came under attack.

The justice department's antitrust division hired hundreds of lawyers; and in recent years, attorney generals have made their reputations as trustbusters.[18] In the 1960s, federal legal prosecutions and legislation tended to go beyond the original reasons for fearing size or collusion. Now any act or *horizontal merger* that tends to increase "market power" or to prevent increased entry, however minor, seems subject to legal restraint.

IN CANADA After a 1950 investigation of combines policy, the government changed the set-up. Till then one Commissioner had been free to choose the industries he would investigate and publicly report upon. Investigated industries felt that (although an adverse report did not mean that a court must find a firm guilty) the single Commissioner had been both prosecutor and judge.

The new (and present) procedure (now under the Department of Corporate and Consumer Affairs) provided two offices: (a) a Director of Investigation and Research, with a staff to collect evidence about certain firms' and industries' marketing practices and to put them before (b) a Restrictive Trade Practices Commission, for reviewing this evidence. When published, the Commission's report may (or may not) serve as the basis for a prosecution by the Department of Justice; the final decision, as before, is up to the courts. Until the early 1960s, the industries tackled (while much more significant than those investigated before the war) were still not the giants of Canadian industry. Rosenbluth has estimated that,

---

[17] J. K. Galbraith, *American Capitalism* (Houghton Mifflin, Boston, 1952).

[18] Few of these cases involved old-style collusion. The usual government target was a merger or sheer bigness. Sometimes pricing practices (such as the basing-point system mentioned later) came under attack. In 1961 General Electric and Westinghouse were actually found guilty of surreptitious collusion in setting prices of heavy electrical goods. The cloak-and-dagger practices sent some of their executives to jail and made their companies liable for *treble* damages to over-charged companies. Of course, "attack" does not mean "guilty." Many government prosecutions have failed.

until about 1960, less than 10 percent of the GNP was produced by industries that had even been looked at by the "combines cops". Rubber, flour-milling, and brewing were the biggest industries involved in cases.

The spirit of the combines law was not changed by the new procedures, it remains that monopolies, mergers and price-fixing in restraint of trade are prohibited if they operate to the detriment of the public—consumers or rival businessmen. In 1960 Justice Minister Fulton's amendments made the law slightly more permissive of joint ventures in research or data collecting; otherwise, discussion of combines policy remained moribund till the late sixties when, in response to a government reference, the Economic Council of Canada launched a full inquiry into federal policy reform, concerned with two subjects: consumer affairs and competition policy (the new name for combines policy).[19]

After an interval, the government made two attempts to legislate the new ideas. First, Ron Basford introduced a "Competition Bill" in 1971; but the heat of the business response and public indifference led to its withdrawal before the 1972 election. Mr. Herb Grey introduced a different bill in late 1973, but this too was abandoned before the 1974 election. Politics did not seem auspicious for competition policy enthusiasts. Neither Mr. Basford nor Mr. Grey survived in their consumer and corporate affairs cabinet portfolio. Left-wing politicians did assail the corporate rip-off, but competition was not their remedy. Conservatives, Social Credit and the right-wing were hostile. The public seemed interested only in the related consumer-protection and foreign-ownership aspects. What the future holds is unknown. It is unlikely the 1900 law and the 1950 procedure can bear the strain of 1970 practices. But only a few economists and academic lawyers seem interested. Here are the main topics in the discussion of a new statute.

STRATEGY The prevailing Canadian view is that one set of business practices should be illegal *per se*, regardless of their effect and regardless of their possible justification. All such offences should be prosecuted. Courts or other agencies should prosecute all firms using these practices. A contrary view was advanced by Stefan Stykolt, that inquiries and government procedures should be limited to those cases where "there is a good chance of applying corrective measures"—that is, given that enforcement is costly the aim should be to make the economic system more efficient, not to try to punish all transgressors.[20] A third view is that built into the Combines Act: that public inquiry and publicity are the best guarantees of private competitive behaviour.

PROCEDURE The Canadian constitutional division of powers over industry between Ottawa and the provinces has tended to maintain the role of the "combines cops" as potential prosecutors in *criminal* proceedings. Few matters are finally resolved by the Commission. It is now proposed that certain trade or market practices should be illegal offences *per se*, regardless of whether they tend to limit competition "unduly"; they could be dealt with in ordinary courts, or in a special administrative tribunal. In addition there might be a discriminatory role for such an administrative tribunal, commission or board which could make orders forbidding a certain activity which was not strictly illegal, such as mergers or price discrimination.

BUSINESS PRACTICES ILLEGAL *Per Se*

Among these, it has been proposed, would be rigging bids among tenderers or buyers at an auction, price agreements, collective boycotts, price-fixing, and collusive controlling or allocation of markets or entry to markets.

---

[19] By mid-1974, no new policy had been adopted, and the literature tended therefore to be persuasive rather than descriptive. The 1966 E.C.C. reference inspired a number of reports and discussions. Most important have been the Council's own informative report: *Interim Report on Competition Policy*, Ottawa, July 1969, and the Reuber-Roseman report cited below. Professor Milton Moore's *How Much Price Competition?* (Montreal, McGill-Queen's University Press 1970) has been an influential essay. These have been accompanied by a wider-than-usual cluster of studies, conferences and tracts, in which the names of York University's David McQueen, Queen's University's L. A. Skeoch and U.B.C.'s Gideon Rosenbluth are among the other economists most frequently encountered. For a full 1971 discussion, see *Canada's Competition Policy*, a symposium volume published by the Conference Board in Canada, Montreal 1971.

[20] For the two sides of this view, see G. Rosenbluth and H. Thorburn, *Canadian Anti-Combines Administration, 1952-1960* (Toronto, University of Toronto Press, 1963); and Stefan Stykolt, *Efficiency in the Open Economy*, (Toronto, Oxford University Press, 1969).

There are already, in the combines laws, several outright offences. Most important is *resale price maintenance*, a practice that prevents any dealer from pricing a branded good below the maintained "fair" or "suggested" price. Most retailers favored the practice because it exempted them from vigorous price competition and from cut-rate, discount, cash-and-carry, or other low-cost outlets. Instead, competition could lead only to rivalry on convenience of location, service, credit terms, or advertising. Manufacturers also favored the practice because it tended to keep prices high (in unstable oligopolistic situations) while keeping wide the number of outlets carrying their goods—a form of advertising. Both retailers and manufacturers were opposed to "loss leader selling": the practice, they said, was followed by bad retailers who sold well-known branded goods at a low price (or at a loss) in order to attract customers in to buy other things as well. Electric kettles and electric shavers were said to be often used as loss leaders.

Clearly, resale price maintenance is a practice that economists will oppose. It either reduces competition, denying to low-cost outlets the greater turnover and still lower costs they could pass on to consumers, or it forces all retailers to compete in one way: by accepting additional costs of advertising, services, etc. The Invisible Hand is not allowed to work; and more stores are kept in business than the public would patronize if goods could be sold both cheaply by no-service stores and more expensively by smaller and more convenient outlets.

In the United States, price maintenance (or "fair trade") is required or allowed in some states and forbidden in others. In the United Kingdom, it was forbidden, after a long parliamentary battle but few industries have yet been freed of maintained price. Canada has forbidden RPM since 1952. The consequences of this legislation have been studied several times, and it is concluded that although few businesses can be shown to have failed because RPM is now banned, prices are indeed somewhat more variable and flexible among competing outlets. Justice Minister Fulton's 1960 amendments have, however, weakened the legislation somewhat. It is observable that manufacturers are able to advertise "suggested" prices applicable in all outlets. And manufacturers now may refuse to sell to dealers who use their products as loss leaders or who mislead the public about them. Another way around RPM's illegality is for the manufacturer to sell "on consignment". In this way,

the manufacturer sells directly, at his own price, to the final customer; there need be no price-fixing agreement with the retailer.

DISCRETIONARY ROLE FOR COMMISSION OR TRIBUNAL

There are a number of practices which might either be illegal *per se*, or subject to inquiry, review and final order by a special administrative commission or tribunal. Among these are refusal to deal; consignment selling; exclusive or solus selling; full-line or tied selling; and restriction to a certain regional market. All these are practices by which a manufacturer or wholesaler prevents entry of a rival or a new distributor, or protects an old customer or distributor.

In the 1973 competition report, Grey proposed that the present Restrictive Trade Practices Commission (reformed and strengthened) would pass on these, using civil or administrative, not criminal procedure.

MERGERS AND AGREEMENTS

Which procedure should the government use for the big problems: firms in one industry merging to increase concentration and monopoly power? Under the present law, a firm may combine with one after another of its rivals until ... the courts find that competition has been *unduly* restricted. The Canadian courts have rarely found that, as long as *one* other firm survived, competition is at an end. The American courts have been readier to stop mergers that reduce the rest of the industry to 50 or 40 percent of the market.

In 1971, Basford suggested that the tribunal or board should have jurisdiction to review monopolies and forbid mergers, independently of the courts. This idea is now in abeyance and no new proposal about mergers has been made.

CONGLOMERATE MERGERS What to do about conglomerate mergers, when one firm takes on subsidiaries in other industries, unrelated by market or technology?

Conglomerates have no effect either on the degree of monopoly concentration or the manufacturing efficiency in a particular market. Their attractiveness is elsewhere, following paths explored years ago by CPR, Argus Corporation, and utility holding companies, and by George Weston. Now Domtar, Imperial Tobacco, Noranda, and Seagram-Distillers Limited, like the U.S. Litton Industries, Ling-Temco-Vought, and a host of imitators, each have taken over dozens of smaller firms in unrelated industries. Thus a firm might begin with toothpaste but soon acquire scores of companies by clever offers of new varieties of securities—preferred stock, convertible preferred, second convertible preferred, convertible bonds, bonds with attached (but detachable) warrant options to buy the common. One had to be an Einstein of finance to calculate the amount of dilution of ownership that would occur if all convertible securities were ultimately to be converted into common stock. Often, little conglomerates would take over giant cash-rich companies many times their own size, using in the end the cash of the company taken over to pay for the acquisition. Thirty-year-old whiz kids pyramided thousands of dollars into tens of millions almost overnight.

Each new successful acquisition increased total sales and reported per share earnings, thereby enabling the conglomerates to acquire still more companies at lower and lower cash cost. (Often the reported gain in earnings was misleading, being merely the product of imaginative accounting, which ignored potential dilution by conversion, treated once-and-for-all paper gains on security sales as if they were recurring operating earnings, juggled the accounting treatment of good will, and reported as current income items for which payment would be received only in future installments. Franchise and land companies were some of the worst offenders.)

But what, after all, does the toothpaste business have in common with meat packing? Or neon signs with campers and trailers? Or grain handling with airlines? Good modern management, coupled with adequate finance, can of course help in any line of activity. And the history of the East India and Hudson's Bay companies does remind us that in underdeveloped countries the only way to get the efficiencies associated with large-scale corporations may be through conglomerates.

By the early 1970s, the bubble had burst on many conglomerates. It was a chain-letter form of growth which had to grow even faster in order not to lead to a disillusionment and collapse. When earnings growth paused, investors turned elsewhere. Now "conglomerate" became a dirty word. Conglomerate stocks dropped. Widely-heralded takeovers and acquisitions failed. Mergers were blocked in the United States by the Nixon Justice Department. Bigness as such was held against them, on the *simpliste* theory that the unit with the "deeper pocket" can outbargain and destroy its competitors. There were threats to tax them, or take away from them the usual privilege of having bond interest tax-deductible.

Fear of "reciprocity"—the practice of one big business to buy products from its own branches or from those other companies who reciprocate with purchases from it, even at unfavorable market terms—became rampant in the U.S. Antitrust Division and in the courts. Nonetheless, Professor Stigler, in a task-force investigation for President Nixon, concluded that reciprocity is quite trivial in economic importance and that much of the hostility to conglomerates is hysterically irrational. Often those seeking take-overs represented "outsiders", self-made newly arrived chaps who had not belonged to the old corporate elite. Their crudities were thus specially resented. And yet, corporate oligarchies that had grown soft and arrogant under previous minority rule were often goaded into reform by fear of take-over or even replaced by those better able to utilize the corporation's resources.

Take-overs, like bankruptcy, represent one of Nature's methods of eliminating deadwood in the struggle for survival. A more open—and more efficiently responsible—corporate society can result. But, without public surveillance and control, the opposite could also emerge. The Darwinian jungle is not guaranteed to produce a happy ending. Influencing and corrupting governments may be the only thing conglomerates are better at—as is suggested by the IT&T scandals during the Allende Chile take-over and with the Nixon Administration.

FOREIGN TRADE, TARIFFS, AND CONCENTRATION

Many of the industries prosecuted in Canada, the United Kingdom, or the United States have broad foreign ramifications. Some of them own subsidiaries abroad, some are world-wide oligopolists in certain products, and many of them have colluded with one another to share foreign markets. (For example, Britain's Imperial Chemical Industries (ICI) and the United States' DuPont divided up the world for the sales of certain chemicals. In Canada they shared the market by setting up CIL which, jointly owned, manufactured or sold both their products.) Finally, as in most countries, Canadian exporters are not forbidden to combine for the exploitation of foreign markets. (For example, Canadian newsprint suppliers have long been accused by American publishers of combining to maintain newsprint prices in the United States. The newsprint exporters are guilty of no crime even if this is true, for Canadian law does not prohibit such joint action. Similarly, American exporters are bound to submit only to a lightened version of their domestic antitrust rules.)

Volumes have been written about such "international cartels," which have denied consumers in less-developed countries the advantages of vigorous price competition.[21]

A less-studied aspect of foreign connections is the effect of the Canadian tariff on domestic competition and efficiency. Canada is a good test case. Many Canadian manufactured products are sold behind a tariff barrier. This barrier, (say 20 per cent) when added to the foreign selling price, provides the lowest level at which foreign competitors can sell in the Canadian market. Canadian firms can successfully undercut imported goods at any lower price. The result of this protection (in many but by no means all Canadian manufacturing industries) has been that prices tend to move swiftly to the protected level, regardless of costs of production in Canadian plants. There is in effect an "administered price," dictated by the government, as described on page 474.

Canadian economists like Stefan Stykolt, Harry Eastman, and H. E. English have studied the effect of this protection on the performance of industry. In general, their conclusion is that oligopoly tends to result, as in the earlier case of administered prices. Part of the reason is that the protection given is excessive; prices are set comfortably high enough to bring profits, and then to attract new industries. Because the Canadian market is small, the new firms and the old cannot expand, and tend to work with much of their productive capacity underused. This is the same inefficiency that emerges under ordinary oligopoly: prices are inflexible and the economy finds that it has allocated too many resources to the industry.

A further explanation is that a large number of near-competitive American and European firms, finding that they cannot export to Canada, tend to set up manufacturing subsidiaries within Canada. These "miniature replicas" as English has named them, attempt to turn out the whole range of products and items made by the parent company for the larger markets abroad. This means that these plants cannot achieve full mass-production economies: their markets in Canada are too small. Thus their costs *are* higher than abroad, perhaps even up to the level of the tariff-protected price. But the resource-allocation effect remains—there are too many resources in Canada devoted to producing administered-price products.

To deal with oligopolies that are protected by tariffs in Canada, the combines authorities can recommend the removal of tariffs. Because this device eventually requires parliamentary action, not a court decision, it is used infrequently. Economists who believe that economic efficiency is endangered by the high tariff wall have urged consideration of its reduction as a leading means to competitive behaviour.

FOREIGN OWNERSHIP

To many Canadians in the seventies, the significance of the tariff lies in its encouragement of foreign ownership. [Up to twenty years ago, the most-debated effects of the tariff were, in addition to the previous section's discussion of oligopoly, as follows: (*a*) forcing Canadians to buy high-cost, homemade goods rather than low-cost imports; (*b*) creating jobs for Canadian workers; (*c*) encouraging industrialization of Canadian regions; and (*d*) diverting Canadian production away from specialization toward low-output self-sufficiency. Rarely was foreign ownership seriously discussed as a good or as an evil in itself.] See the Appendix to Chapter 35 for a more thorough discussion of foreign ownership.

Whether foreign ownership is beneficial is not the issue here. The aim is simply to point out that for foreign firms the processes of adjustment to tariff barriers may proceed either by the establishment of new plants and branches in Canada (as in the case of GM, Phillips, Datsun, or Volvo) or by the take-over of firms in the same industry which already exist in Canada. That this process must result in oligopolistic manufacturing industries is a *hypothesis* tested and so far confirmed in an increasing number of industry studies. That these oligopolies must have higher costs and prices than oligopolies abroad is a *theory* that is not necessarily the best explanation of Canadian industrial structure. But that this foreign investment has taken place mainly by take-overs of

---

[21] There are real resource-allocation effects too. If lack of competition between two chemical firms selling in a small country means that consumers must pay high prices, the result is not merely a redistribution of income from buyers to sellers in the same economy. The buying country must sell an extra amount abroad to pay for its high-price imports, or go without them, or a bit of both. These extra amounts are one measure of the real loss of a country when a monopoly uses too little capacity and competitive industries too much, within one country.

FIG. 26-6. (SOURCES: G. L. Reuber and R. Roseman, *The Takeover of Canadian Firms, 1945-1961, An Empirical Study,* Economic Council of Canada, Special Study No. 10. Queen's Printer, Ottawa, 1969, and *Report of the Director of Investigation and Research Combines Investigation Act,* Consumer and Corporate Affairs, Information Canada, Ottawa, 1973, pp. 51-2.)

Canadian firms is a belief that has recently been disproved in a study by Reuber and Roseman.[22]

Fig. 26-6 shows that, at any rate for the period 1945-1961, the number of take-overs or mergers, es-

[22] G. L. Reuber and R. Roseman, *The Take-over of Canadian Firms, 1945-1961; An Empirical Study.* Economic Council of Canada, Special Study No. 10 (Queen's Printer, Ottawa, 1969). There was a slight difference between the types of Canadian and foreign take-overs. Canadian firms tended to acquire other firms for vertical or horizontal integration, but only about 8 per cent were interested in building "conglomerates" whereas almost 12 per cent of foreign take-overs were of the conglomerate type. Foreign interest in horizontal, or market-extension, mergers was much less than Canadian interest.

pecially of *foreign* take-overs, was relatively small (relative to the 100,000 firms available). And the foreign take-overs in this whole period after World War II rarely accounted for as much as 15 percent of the total foreign ownership in any industry. *Foreign investors proceeded by investing in firms they already controlled or by establishing new firms, rather than by mergers and take-overs.*[23]

[23] As shown in Fig. 26-6, foreign take-overs declined in 1972 while total mergers and acquisitions increased. Perhaps this shows that foreign (particularly U.S.) firms were wary of the growing sentiment against foreign ownership in Canada. (This senti-

THE FUTURE OF COMPETITION POLICY

Compared with the United States, or even with the United Kingdom, Canadian public attitudes and resultant policy to prevent monopolistic inefficiency is unspectacular. Politicians ignore the subject, if they can. The legal mind is not interested in relative prices, price flexibility, or resource allocation; yet lawyers advocate, make, and administer the policies. The number of economists employed at any stage of an investigation or trial is very small; and recent economists' crusades to sell a new competition policy have been unsuccessful.

Some countries are even more lax than we are. For example, the governments of some Western European countries and of Japan seem actively to encourage mergers and cartels as a means of preventing the "wastes" of competition, encouraging exports, and exerting government controls for other purposes. Yet, except perhaps Japan, these countries (with the advent of the Common Market) have been strengthening their antitrust statutes, and groping toward what American economist J. M. Clark has called the concept of "workable competition."

What is to be done?[24] Many critics, notably Rosenbluth and Thorburn, simply urge the government to get on with what is already has power to do: to show more nerve in tackling Canadian giants. Stykolt urged gunning for big industries in cases where success would really push the economy out towards its *p-p frontier.* The 1969 Report of the Economic Council of Canada, on competition policy was in partial agreement with the positive Stykolt approach; for it urged escape from criminal law and the use of an economic tribunal:

" ... most of the practices to be referred to the tribunal are capable in some circumstances of working to the public advantage, but the distinction between likely good and bad ef-

fects may require a difficult weighing of relevant economic circumstances and probabilities and therefore a kind of expertise that only a body of mixed professional disciplines could provide. The tribunal would be armed with injunctive remedies, the power to recommend other remedies, and with a power of general inquiry."[25]

This idea is still out of political reach. Some progress has been made with outlawing a few business offences *per se.* Some new prosecutions have been made of price-fixing behaviour, under the existing law. And—not mentioned here—considerable changes have been made in legislation governing advertising and consumer protection. But the basic problem, of uncompetitive or monopolistic selling, has not been tackled in Canada. While the U.S. anti-trust legislation is neither completely logical nor successful, one has only to examine Canada, Europe, or Japan to realize how much better off the United States is because of its omnipotent threat of legal prosecution. American enterprise is kept on the defensive and would never dream of adopting the flagrant devices that are all too common in Canada.

Repeatedly, in Part Three, we have stressed the basic problem of how a pricing system solves society's questions WHAT, HOW, FOR WHOM. This frames the rational goal of competition policy.

We cannot expect competition to become everywhere "perfectly perfect," in the strict sense of the economist, but we can try to make it "workable." By public and private policies we can hope to improve the efficiency with which market prices reflect underlying needs, desires, and wants against the background of true costs of goods—costs in terms of alternative goods that could be produced and in terms of used-up scarce productive factors which involve sweat and disutility.

Part Four will be concerned with identical problems that arise in connection with the pricing of land, labor, and capital. Again, the function of such pricing in solving society's problems is the focal point of interest.

---

ment culminated in the 1973 passage of the Foreign Investment Review Act which rendered all proposed foreign take-overs subject to approval by the newly set-up Foreign Investment Review Agency.)

[24] See G. Rosenbluth and H. Thorburn, *Canadian Anti-combines Administration,* 1952-1960 (University of Toronto Press, Toronto, 1963); Stefan Stykolt, *Efficiency in the Open Economy* (Oxford University Press, Toronto, 1969); and Economic Council of Canada, *Interim Report on Competition Policy* (Queen's Printer, Ottawa, 1969).

[25] Economic Council of Canada, *Interim Report on Competition Policy* (Queen's Printer, Ottawa, 1969). Reproduced with the permission of Information Canada. For a full and influential discussion of many of the reforms initiated and proposed since 1969, see A. M. Moore, *How Much Price Competition?* McGill-Queens University Press, 1970.

SUMMARY

A. ANALYTICAL PATTERNS OF IMPERFECT COMPETITION

1 Few business firms are able to develop exact curves of cost and revenue. This does not mean that they are oblivious to profit maximization. In terms of trial and error, they may be doing a tolerably good job of keeping alive as a business entity and of achieving long-run optimum profits.

2 Under imperfect competition, a firm may have to make rough guesses in setting its price. Often it will use some kind of *markup* over an estimate of unit cost. Nonetheless, it is often market conditions that determine how much of a markup any firm can safely count on getting; so in a sense the problem is merely re-posed. Only factual investigations of each situation can tell what the result is likely to be.

3 In Galbraith's vision of the new industrial state, bureaucrats of the technostructure exercise unilateral power to mold consumer tastes. They may be checked by the "countervailing power" of their large-scale suppliers or customers; and despite Galbraith's prose, even the largest corporations are subject to checks of numerous rival conglomerates, making collusion difficult and despotic rule shortsighted.

4 Various patterns of imperfect competition lend themselves to economic analysis: (1) monopoly, (2) oligopoly, in which few sellers compete with similar or differentiated products, (3) Chamberlinian models of many sellers of differentiated products, and finally (4) the case of perfect competition itself. The kinked demand curve of oligopoly helps to explain its rigid administered pricing. The no-profit tangency equilibrium of Chamberlin's large group leaves society with the wastes of excess capacity and overdifferentiated products.

B. MODERN COMBINES PROBLEMS

5 The economic evils of such imperfections transcend the mere matter of monopolistic profits: entry may cut out excess profits *without* bringing prices down to marginal costs; overentry of imperfect competitors may waste resources without giving the consumer the benefit of lower prices; monopolistic and oligopolistic pricing above true marginal cost brings distortion of resource allocation (inefficiency and non responsiveness) even if the firms involved have their excess profits taxed away.

6 Against the evils of monopoly and oligopoly must be weighed the possible Schumpeterian *dynamic* efficiencies that they may introduce. A large firm in a pro- tected market may have the wherewithal to develop new inventions and also the assurance that it will not lose to competitors the advantages of its own research ef- forts. In strongly decreasing-cost industries, there is no hope for viable *perfect* com- petition, and substitute checks on the powers of few dominating firms have to come from either public control or tariff reduction.

7 By public regulation of utilities and by various formal and informal combines activities of the state, some of the checks and balances that are not automatically enforceable by per- fect competition can be achieved by governmental action.

8 The history of Canadian combines legislation and enforcement has been an irregular one. Inaction has been followed by vigorous action; and sometimes by various backward steps. Although the legal mind of courts and legislators has not always concentrated on

what economists consider the key pricing issue, some evolutionary progress has been made. After economists realize that perfect competition is not spontaneously attained or enforceable, the problem of defining and approaching "workable competition" becomes paramount. Here is the frontier for economic research and policy.

9   The rapid and flashy growth of conglomerates was prominent in the 1960s but by the end of the decade the bubble had burst for many of them.

10 Tariffs have often resulted in a "protected-price level" (foreign selling price of import plus tariff imposed on it) toward which some prices of Canadian manufacturers tend to move—in effect an administered price with the consequent oligopoly inefficiencies. In other cases, foreign producers have set up Canadian subsidiaries to jump the tariff. In this case, too many producers of too many products, produced on too small a scale to be efficient, exist. Again, the result is an inefficient allocation of resources.

11 Foreign ownership may also take the form of foreign take-over of existing Canadian firms, though the majority of recent foreign investment has not, as it is often alleged, been through this type of take-over.

CONCEPTS FOR REVIEW

fair return on original or reproduction
  cost or on market valuation
publicly owned utilities as measuring
  rods
Combines Investigation Act, Sherman
  Antitrust Act
conglomerates
Schumpeterian dynamic advantages
challenge of "workable
  competition"

markup pricing, administered P
Galbraithian countervailing
  power and technostructure
free entry
oligopoly, with or without tacit
  collusion
no-profit equilibrium of producers
  of differentiated products
evils of imperfect competition
utility rate regulation

QUESTIONS FOR DISCUSSION

1. Give examples of behavior by business firms suggesting that they do seek to maximize their profits. Give some apparent exceptions.

2. Suppose you ran an electric company. How could you go about maximizing profits? How would you estimate elasticity of demand? Would an economics textbook be the source for learning how to be successful in this respect?

3. What are meant by markup and administered pricing? Why is the *willingness to sell more* the sign of imperfect competition?

4. Describe the pattern of imperfect competition in the auto industry, cigarette industry, aluminum industry, mousetrap industry, women's-dress trade, retail grocery trade, barbershop trade, undertaking industry, pulp and paper industry, farm pulpwood industry.

5. "The tragedy of monopolistic competition often has nothing to do with excessive profits. Rather, there may be no profits at all, the high price being frittered away in small volume and inefficient production." Discuss.

6. U.S. decisions had the effect of breaking off the partnership of ICI and DuPont in Canadian Industries Ltd. (CIL). Now ICI owns CIL and DuPont has its own Canadian

subsidiary. Do two such competitors duplicate perfect comp￢
advantage to Canada from this breakup? Did Canada lose the
production in one big firm?

7. Canada now effectively permits export cartels. Is such collu
   cost foreign competition? To meet foreign cartel com￢
   exporters want to work together? Will their doing so affe
   Canadian customers?

8. Consider the role of the tariff and of the degree of ￢
   industry. Why do tires cost more in Canada than in the Un￢

9. Some Americans argue that "A & P is bad just because it is big." L￢
   the impact of A & P on the farmers and suppliers from whom it buys a￢
   chains and stores with whom it competes. Do not neglect the consumers to ￢
   sells.

10. "Combinations of workers in unions must be forbidden if industrial combines are
    banned." Comment.

11. "Resale price maintenance should be encouraged because it protects customers from
    dealers who give no service and don't know their products." Consider this and other
    arguments for RPM.

27
THEORY OF PRODUCTION AND
MARGINAL-PRODUCTS

Knowledge is the only instrument of production that is not subject to diminishing returns.

J. M. CLARK

In the next few chapters of Part Four we shall be primarily concerned with how factors of production get priced in the market place—with the determination of (1) *rents* of land and other resources (Chapter 28), (2) *wages* of various kinds of labor (Chapter 29), (3) *interest* rates on capital assets (Chapter 30), and (4) *profit* (Chapter 31); there follows a grand summary (Chapter 32).

Economists call this the problem of "distribution." They do not mean by this term what the man in the street means when he refers to distribution as the marketing of goods and the carrying of goods to the final consumer. Instead Part Four distribution deals with the problem of FOR WHOM goods are to be produced. It is pricing of factors of production by supply and demand that is helping determine FOR WHOM. This same factor pricing also operates to solve the problem of HOW society is to produce.

The theory of distribution is still in an unsettled state. Questions still being debated among economists are these: What is the role of *power* relations, as against *market* relations, in determining how large a share of the national income goes to labor? To property? To different classes of labor (skilled, unskilled), and of property owners (landlords, interest-receiving *rentiers*, equity shareowners)? Here in Part Four we shall give the theories of microeconomics all the rope they can use to try to corral the complex trends of factor shares in distribution. Later, in Part Six, we shall meet some alternative models of distribution.

Why are wages some three-quarters of the total national product? To understand this we must study the forces that determine market wage rates, market land rentals, market interest rates. Thus, if technological changes, (reflecting, for example, automation), lowered market wage rates relative to the returns to property, the wage share might fall. Because the number of owners of property is so much smaller than the number of owners of labor, the result would be to shift the Lorenz-curve measure of inequality toward greater income inequality. We can understand the economic forces affecting income distribution best by examining the markets where factors of production get priced. This analysis seeks to give us insight into optimality equilibria and into "exploitation."

The key to such factor pricing is sought in the economic *theory of production*. So, as a prelude to our general discussion of distribution of income, this chapter investigates the theory of production. It defines the important economic concept of "marginal-product" and relates this to the familiar law of diminishing returns. Finally, the chapter will show that the demand curves for the various factors of production—the demands for labor, land, and so forth—are to be expressed in terms of their marginal-products.

DEMAND FOR FACTORS A JOINTLY INTERDEPENDENT DEMAND

The basic peculiarity about the demand for inputs stems from this technological fact: Factors usually do not work alone. A shovel by itself is worthless to me if I wish a cellar; a man with his bare hands is equally worthless. Together the man and shovel can dig my cellar. In other words, the quantity of a good produced depends *jointly* upon all the available factor inputs.

Sir William Petty put the matter in this striking seventeenth-century way: Labor is the father and land the mother of product. One cannot say which is more important in producing a baby—a mother or a father. So, too, one cannot in most cases hope to demonstrate how much of the physical product has been *caused* by any one of the different factors *taken by itself*. The different factors *interact* with each other. Usually they reinforce each other's effectiveness, but sometimes they are substitutes for one another and they compete with, rather than complement, each other. There is an important consequence of this jointness, or interdependence among the productivities of the different factor inputs, namely: The amount of labor demanded will depend on its wage rate, but the labor demanded will depend also upon the price of machines. The same is true of the demand for machines. By raising miners' wages, John L. Lewis created good business for power tools.

Thus, the demand for each input will depend upon the prices of *all* factor inputs, not on its own price alone. *Cross* elasticities between different factors are as important as regular *"own"* elasticities.

It is this interdependence of productivities of land, labor, and capital goods that makes the problem of distribution complex. For suppose we had to distribute at one harvest time the whole aggregate of output constituting the NNP. If land by itself had produced so much, and labor by itself had produced so much, and some third factor had by itself produced the rest, distribution might seem easy indeed. Crude notions of fairness might suggest that each factor share be simply set at what each has alone produced. Ethics aside, under free supply and demand if the separate factors could produce goods by themselves, they could jolly well make sure that they got the fruits of their activity; so, with all value judgments disregarded this would be a good description of the facts.

But reread the above paragraph and underline such words as *"by itself* produced" and *"has alone* produced." They refer to an *independence* of productivities which we know is simply lacking in the real world. If land and labor *together* produce the corn harvest, just how do you unscramble the separate contributions that supply and demand will parcel out

to each?[1] A proud Canadian worker might reflect on what *he* would produce and get in India or in Canada as it was in 1900.

How is the problem resolved? It gets resolved by the process of supply and demand, operating in perfectly or imperfectly competitive markets and modified by government laws. A brief analysis of the economic theory of production provides the indispensable key.

TECHNICAL LAW RELATING OUTPUT TO INPUTS: THE "PRODUCTION FUNCTION"

The theory of production begins with specific engineering or technological information. If you have a certain amount of labor, a certain amount of land, and certain prescribed amounts of other inputs such as machines or raw materials, how much output of a particular good can you get? The answer depends upon the state of technology: if someone makes a new invention or discovers a new industrial process, the obtainable output you can get from given factor inputs will go up. *But at any time, there will be a maximum obtainable amount of product for any given amounts of factor inputs.*

This technical law relating inputs to outputs is so important that economists have given it a name. They call it the "production function."

Definition: The production function is the technical relationship telling the amount of output capable of being produced by each and every set of specified inputs (or factors of production). It is defined for a given state of technical knowledge.

Here are some examples.

An agricultural engineer lists in a thick book the various combinations of land and labour that will produce various

---

[1] Labor leaders used to say, "Without labor there is zero product. So attribute to labor *all* the product." Spokesmen for capital used the same bad logic to produce the opposite result: "Take away all capital goods, and labor scratches a bare pittance from the earth; so practically all the product should go to capital." The trouble with such foolish proposals is that, taken together, they allocate 200 or 300 per cent of the total product to the two or three factors, whereas there is only 100 per cent of the harvest to be allocated. And it makes no sense to say, "There is some truth on both sides; so let us apply the Golden Mean and, by a rule of unreason, give each of the factors the largest equal shares that will use up the available 100 per cent of the product." A real-world economy is not a courtroom where nimble legal minds illogically split hairs in order to solve society's problem of FOR WHOM.

quantities of corn. On one page of the book he lists the alternative combinations of land and labor needed to produce 100 bushels of corn; on another page, the alternative factor input combinations that will produce 200 bushels of corn; and so forth. Another example of a production function would be the chemical engineer's listing of the various ways of producing gasoline of a given octane rating.

The concept of an "average"—such as the "arithmetic mean" or "geometric mean" of two positive numbers—can help you understand the production function. Recall the *arithmetic mean* of two numbers, such as 8 and 2, is half their sum, or 5. Similarly, we define the *geometric mean* of two positive numbers as the square root of their product. For 8 and 2, we get a geometric mean of "square-root of 16," or 4. (Don't be surprised that the geometric mean is less than the arithmetic mean; it always will be if the numbers are not equal.) Now suppose 1 man on 1 acre of land produces 1 unit of corn output. Suppose statisticians tell us that the production function in this corn industry is "the unweighted geometric mean of the two inputs." Can we then predict how much 1 man will produce on 16 acres of land? Yes, the production function constitutes our needed law or formula. To get the geometric mean of 1 x 16, we take the square root of their product to get 4 of corn output as our answer.[2]

There are thousands of different production functions in the Canadian economy: at least one for each of the innumerable firms or productive units. A purpose of this chapter is to show how the firm's production function lies behind its Total Cost curve discussed in Chapter 24 and to show how this provides the basis for the firm's derived demand for land, labor, capital, fertilizer, and numerous other productive inputs that it goes out into the market to buy.

Thus, the firm is poised between two kinds of markets: (1) the commodity market in which it appears as a supplier, selling its wares along the demand curve *of its customers*; and (2) the markets for factors of production in which it itself appears as a demander, buying inputs so as to minimize its total costs of production and to produce its Maximum-profit output. It is these factor markets that put prices upon the various productive inputs of the

community, and thus determine the distribution of income (wages, rent, interest, etc.).

THE AGGREGATE PRODUCTION FUNCTION FOR THE WHOLE ECONOMY

Suppose, first, we put away our microscope and train a telescope on the aggregate magnitudes of total labor, total capital, and total product for American manufacturing. Such magnitudes must be measured with care and involve innumerable index-number problems of correct weighting; yet they are useful in giving a broad description of society. Back in the late twenties, former U.S. Senator Paul H. Douglas, then a University of Chicago professor of economics, won an important prize for his pathbreaking statistical measurement of the United States' production function. His technique was widely adapted to the measurement of production functions elsewhere: manufacturing in Canada, for example. Later M.I.T.'s Robert Solow carried these studies a significant step further by showing how technological progress has been improving the productivity of American labor and capital.[3]

What have Douglas and Solow shown? Their statistics suggest that labor is the single most important factor of production in a certain subtle sense. Both labor and capital are needed in production: take away all capital, or alternatively all labor, and you will be left with negligible total product. But they find that a 1 per cent increase in labor seems to increase output about three times as much as would a 1 per cent increase in capital. This largely corresponds with the widely known fact that wages are about three-fourths of the national product, while one-fourth (which is one-third of wages) is about the share of property incomes.[4]

[3] P. H. Douglas, *Theory of Wages* (Macmillan, New York, 1934); R. M. Solow, "Technical Change and the Aggregate Production Function," *Review of Economics and Statistics*, vol. 39, 1957, pp. 312-320. Neither study measures land's separate contribution and share. In the 1970s this would probably be only about 5 per cent for the whole economy, and much less for manufacturing alone; but early in the century it was perhaps double that. Further work by E. Denison and D. Walters will be cited in Chapter 37, where modern growth models are discussed.

[4] That is, their so-called Cobb-Douglas production function is the weighted geometric mean of footnote 2's numerical example. Consistent with the law of diminishing returns, discussed in Chapter 2 and in the next sections of this chapter, a 1 per cent

[2] We'll learn in a moment that it turns out to be more realistic to give labor 3 times the weight of other factor inputs; so the fourth root of 1 x 1 x 1 x 16 gives us the empirically more correct answer of 2 rather than 4, the augmentation of land not being so important in the case of the weighted geometric means as in the unweighted case.

EMPIRICAL FINDINGS There are numerous other findings from such studies, many of which have received important corroboration from similar undertakings in, or about, other countries. Here are a few of the most important empirical findings about the American economy:

1. The productivity of both labor and capital has been increasing throughout this century because of improved technology and skill. The average rate of improvement appears to be between 1 and 2 per cent per year.

2. The amount of capital has been growing at a faster rate than the labor supply because of thrift on the part of society as a whole and slower growth in man-hours worked. As a result, each laborer has more capital goods to work with, and his productivity wages have tended to rise even faster than the 1 to 2 per cent attributable to technological growth alone. Canadian data show a similar trend, although the capital has often been borrowed from abroad rather than being the result of local thrift.

3. The return per unit of capital might have been expected to encounter diminishing returns because each capital unit now has less labor to cooperate with it. Yet capital's return per unit has in fact remained about the same. Why? Because of the offsetting effect of *technological progress.*

Technical improvements would probably have raised profits on capital had not the diminishing returns to increasing capital per laborer been taking place as an offset. In consequence of these simultaneous offsets, the sharing of the growing social pie has remained not too far from the same three-fourths and one-fourth level—a remarkable fact in view of the growing union movement, the vast structural changes in the American economy since 1900, and the widespread notion that "automation" has downgraded the value of human brain power and skills.

Similar statistical measurements all over the globe help to put flesh on the bare bones of the economic theory of production and distribution, and serve as factual tests of the validity of economic principles—principles that Chapter 37 will use for growth theory. But now let us put the production function under a microscope.

increase in either factor *alone* increases product by *less* than 1 per cent: actually by 3/4 per cent in the case of labor and by 1/4 per cent in the case of capital.

MARGINAL-PRODUCTS DEFINED

In Chapter 2, the law of diminishing returns was defined. Figure 27-1 reproduces a table (like that shown earlier on page 000) of diminishing *extra product* for varying extra labor units added to fixed land. Back there, we were using the production-function concept without yet knowing the name.

Now we can introduce the economist's name for extra product. Recall that in economic theory the word "extra" is typically replaced by the word *"marginal."* It is natural, then, to define terms as follows:

Definition: The "marginal-product" of a productive factor is the extra product or output added by one extra unit of that factor, while other factors are being held constant. Labor's marginal-product is the extra output you get when you add one unit of labor, holding all other inputs constant. Similarly, land's marginal-product is the change in total product resulting from one additional unit of land, with all other inputs held constant—and so forth, for any factor.

Note that the marginal-product of a factor is expressed in *physical* units of product per unit of extra input. So careful economists often speak of "marginal-physical-product" rather than plain marginal-product, particularly when they want to avoid any possible confusion with a later *dollar* concept called "marginal-revenue-product."

MARGINAL-PHYSICAL-PRODUCTS AND DIMINISHING RETURNS

Column (3) of the table in Fig. 27-1 can now be identified with the term "marginal-physical-product." Note the drop from 20 to 1, in accordance with diminishing returns. The same marginal-product is pictured in the lower diagram, which shows the steady drop of labor's marginal-physical-product. This reflects the fact that the upper chart shows *total* product rising in ever-smaller steps as we hold land constant and add equal extra units of labor. The law of diminishing returns could be renamed the "law of

(1) UNITS OF LABOR	(2) TOTAL PRODUCT	(3) MARGINAL- PHYSICAL- PRODUCT
0	0	
		20
1	20	
		10
2	30	
		5
3	35	
		3
4	38	
		1
5	39	

FIG. 27-1. Diminishing returns can be stated, numerically and graphically, as diminishing marginal-product. Marginal-physical-product is calculated as difference to total product added by 1 extra unit of input (as when fourth worker adds 3 = 38 — 35 units of product). Each new worker adds diminishing marginal-product.

The upper diagram shows that total product increases by smaller and smaller steps as new input units are added.

The lower diagram shows the declining steps of extra- or marginal-product. Smoothing the steps gives the declining curve of smoothed marginal-physical-product. The area in (b) under the marginal-physical-product curve (or of the rectangles) adds up to the total product shown in (a) above. (For example, 20 + 10 + 5 = total product of 35 for three men. What gives total product for four, or five, men?)

diminishing marginal-physical-product."[5] For brevity, one often skips the word "physical" when no misunderstanding is possible and writes *MP* for *MPP*.

It is also important to note here that both the total product and the marginal-physical-product are directly related to Chapter 24's cost-of-production curves. The physical units of output are the same units (or *q*) found in Table 24-1 on page 429. But now we ask "given another unit of an input, how much output or additional output will be produced?" We will look more deeply into this relationship further on in this chapter.

What is true for one factor input is also true for another. We can interchange land and labor, now holding labor constant and varying land. We can make up a new table, showing land's marginal (physical) product in its column. And this would also presumably obey the law of diminishing returns. Why? Because now each of the extra land units would have less and less of the fixed labor factor to work with.

---

[5] This is the same principle of diminishing marginal returns that we have already encountered in the production-possibility curve, and in the ultimately rising marginal cost curve of the firm (Chapter 23).

DISTRIBUTION SOLVED BY MARGINAL-PRODUCTS

Now the riddle of the Sphinx—how to allocate among two (or more) cooperating factors the total product they *jointly* produce—can be solved by use of the marginal-product concept. John Bates Clark, a distinguished Columbia University economist, provided a simplified theory of distribution around 1890. It can be applied to competitive price-and-wage determination when there are any number of goods and factor inputs, but it is most easily grasped if we concentrate on one total harvest output—call it corn, or a basket of goods, or just Q. A production function tells how much Q is produced for each amount of man-hours, L, and number of acres of homogeneous land, A.

Although diminishing returns applies when one factor is added to the other fixed factor, perfect competition is best maintained when there are "constant returns to scale" when *all* factors are increased simultaneously in the same proportion. (Thus, when Clark doubles land *and* labor, he finds output has just doubled; when he increases L and A by any equal per cent, Q increases by that same per cent. For if Q were to grow by a greater per cent, there would be long-run decreasing costs for each firm, and the firm that grew largest first could create a monopoly.)

Now Clark reasons as follows. A first man produces great marginal-product because he has so much land to work with. Man 2 adds a large, but slightly smaller, marginal-product. But the two men are alike: they must get exactly the same wage. Which wage? The MP of Man 1? The lower MP of Man 2? The average of these? Under free competition, where landowners are free to employ as few or many L as they like, the answer is plain. Landlords will never freely hire that second man if the market wage they must pay him exceeds his marginal-product. So the dd demand curve for labor will ensure that *all* the men who get hired will receive *the lowest marginal-product of the last man*.

What happens to the excess of MP produced by the first man and all the earlier men up to the very last? That stays with the landlord. It is his residual rent. In free competitive markets, no one can take it away from him. Is he "profiteering"? Not in the usual sense of the word. Each landowner is but one of thousands: any acre of his is no better and no worse

FIG. 27-2. Marginal-product principles determine traditional factor distribution of income.

Total wage is light gray rectangle's area: the wage-rate altitude times labor-quantity base. Rent gets what is left over, as shown by the dark gray residual triangle. Total product, the sum of wage-rectangle plus rent-triangle areas, is area under demand curve of society's marginal-product (the sum of all the vertical slabs—representing marginal products—added by each new worker).

than the acres of the rest. Just as worker competes with worker for jobs, landowners compete with landowners for workers. There are no conspiracies, no employer associations, and no unions in Clark's competitive world.

Figure 27-2 shows that the marginal-product curve of labor gives the dd demand curve of all employers in terms of real wages (in corn, or market baskets of goods, or Q units). The population supply gives us ss, and the equilibrium wage comes at E. The total wage share of labor is given by $W \times L$ (for example, $W = 5$ and $L = 1$ million, total wages = 5 million); this is indicated by the light gray area of the rectangle at E.

We have determined not only the distributive share of labor, but also land rent. The indicated rent triangle simply measures all the "excesses over final marginal-product that the early workers brought and never got paid in wages." Whether fair or unfair, all the men are alike; all landlords are free competitors who can demand or not demand as they like; so it is inevitable that all workers get paid the *MP* of the last worker and, because of diminishing returns, that there be left the residual triangle of rent that goes to the landowners.

This completes the marginal-productivity theory of distribution. Note that labor wages get more than property rents in this example: the wage rectangle of *MP* is about three times as large as the residual rent triangle of property. That is realistic, but it depends on the facts of technology. If a new invention made the *dd* of *MP* decline very rapidly, land's triangle might swallow up 60 to 80 per cent of the total NNP!

If mass immigration or seven children per family increased *L* so much as to move society down the *dd* curve to a low wage, the rectangle share of labor *might* fall relative to the rent triangle of land. It might, but might not. Here is the explanation:

An increase in *L* along the *dd* curve of *MP must* always raise the *absolute* total of land's rent triangle. (Try it.) What about the absolute total of labor's rectangle? The elasticity discussion of Chapter 20 reminds us that labor's total wage rectangle will most certainly increase if *dd* has more-than-unitary elasticity. But can labor's rectangle grow *as great* in percentage as land's triangle, or even greater? Although not obvious until you experiment with drawing in *dd* curves, the answer is definite: Yes, the relative share of wage's rectangle can increase and the relative share of land's triangle decrease if the marginal-product curve slopes downward slowly enough. Senator Douglas' researches in the United States, corroborated for England and elsewhere by the late Sir Arthur Bowley, suggest that, despite changing birth rates and technology, labor's relative share remains surprisingly constant over the decades.

GENERALIZATIONS Before summarizing the marginal-productivity theory of wages, let us appreciate J. B. Clark's advance over such classical economists as David Ricardo, a follower of Adam Smith, and a leader of economic thought in the early nineteenth century. Ricardo would have soon grasped, and agreed with, Clark's Fig. 27-2; it fits in well with Ricardian rent theory. But Clark said more than that. He also proved these remarkable facts:

You can switch the roles of labor and land. Now hold labor constant. Add successive units of variable land to fixed labor. Calculate each successive acre's marginal-product. Draw a *D'D'* curve show-

ing how many acres labor-owners will demand of land at each rent rate. In the new version of Fig. 27-2 that you draw, find a new *E'* point of equilibrium. Identify land's *rectangle* of rent as determined by *its MP*. Identify labor's *residual* wage triangle. Ricardo would recognize the complete symmetry of the factors; that *all* factors can be thought of as having their distributive shares determined simultaneously by their respective interdependent marginal products.

That is not all. Instead of labor and land, suppose the only two factors were labor *L* and some versatile capital goods *K*. Suppose a smooth production function relates *Q* to *L* and *K*, with the same general properties as in Fig. 27-2. Then you can redraw Fig. 27-2 and get an identical picture of income distribution between *L* and *K*.[6]

SUMMARY Marginal productivities provide the clue to competitive pricing of factor inputs—of labor or of skilled and unskilled labor, of each grade of land, of capital goods (i.e., rentals for their use), of fertilizer, and of other inputs.

Profit-maximizing employers in competitive factor markets will have their demand curves for inputs determined by what additions to their product successive units of a factor will bring, i.e., by marginal-products. In the simplified Clark case of a single *Q* output, firms' physical *MP*'s are added horizontally—as *dd* and *ss* curves were added in Chapters 22 and 23—to get the market demand *dd* for labor or any other factor. At the level deter-

---

[6] That is still not all. Suppose we have three (or more) factors of production: *L*, *A*, and *K*. Again assume that a well-behaved production function gives *Q* output in terms of all three factor inputs. Again vary *L* alone; calculate its *MP*'s. Then vary *K* alone; calculate its *MP*'s. Vary *A* alone; calculate land's diminishing *MP*'s. Now set up *three* simultaneous, interdependent demand curves of marginal-products. Set up three supply curves for the factors. It will follow that all *Q*, and no more, will get distributed by competition among the three factors according to equality of each factor-price to its marginal-product: $P_L = MP_A$, $P_A = MP_K$, P_K = price charged for use of capital good = *MP* . All of any factor gets what its last unit produces of *MP*; the residual surplus, of early units' *MP*'s over final *MP*, provides just enough *Q* to pay the other factors their final *MP*'s .(Some qualifications of this simple Clark model will occur in the Appendix to this chapter. Note here that monopoly bidding by employers would require alterations in the Clark model, as shown in Chapter 29's footnote 7.

mined by intersection of each *dd* with its factor-supply *ss*, we get

Wage = Marginal-product of labor
Rent = Marginal-product of land
And so forth for any factor.

This distributes 100 per cent of *Q*, no more and no less, among all the factors of production.

COMPETITIVE EQUILIBRIUM A GOOD THING?

We have now completed a sketch of how the marginal-product theory "distributes" total product between two factors—land and labor—in a simplified world.

We have simply been observing how hard-boiled competition would work itself out under simple conditions. Just as the jungle has its laws without regard to right and wrong, so does the competitive market have its brute facts.

But did you notice one efficient thing that happened? Without a planning board, *society got its food produced in the most efficient way.* How did that happen? Well, efficiency certainly requires that the homogeneous land and labor be everywhere combined for food in exactly the same proportions. (PROOF: Suppose society were using much labor on half its land and little labor on the other half. The law of diminishing returns tells us that the marginal-product of the workers will be less on the dense than on the sparse half. So we can get some extra *Q* by shifting men to the sparse acres with higher *MP*. Maximum output comes when marginal-products are equal on both halves, i.e., when uniform labor and land are combined in the same proportions on both halves. QED.)

Ruthless competition with only the commercially fittest surviving did bring about the desirable equality everywhere of factor proportions and marginal-products. How did it do this? By landlords' seeking maximum rents; by workers' seeking maximum wages; by market prices being forced to lowest costs of production by inexorable competitive forces. These were the vital processes. (WARNING: A tendency toward "increasing returns to scale" would have killed off perfect competition and have brought in monopoly to spoil the whole story. Note also that if different acres were of different qualities, we would no longer use the same proportion of labor on

each; instead the desirable equality of marginal-products of transferable labor would be achieved by competition's making sure that relatively more laborers get used on the better lands—a sensible result!)

We shall see again, in Chapter 32, that competitive pricing can help solve efficiently the HOW problem of any society. We shall see that charging a rent for God-given land is necessary if such scarce land is to be rightly allocated. But notice that we have not proved that the competitive result is "fair" or "equitable": efficiency by itself does not necessarily imply justice in distribution. To this issue we now turn.

THE CONCEPT OF "EXPLOITATION"

For two centuries socialist critics of the present order, particularly Karl Marx, have asserted that labor has the right to the full product of society. What price the efficiency of marginal-product distribution if it gives a sizable fraction of the total product to property owners? This, they asserted, represents "exploitation" of labor.

It is naive to think that if a word exists, there must always then exist some obvious real phenomenon corresponding to it. Thus, if I can say the name of a unicorn, need there be in some jungle somewhere such an animal with a horned horse's head and a goat's beard? Or, if I can think of a perfect God-Being, *ergo* must He exist? Or, if the dictionary contains the word "exploitation," must there surely be some simple meaning to the concept that anyone can understand even *before* he has studied economics? To the scholar who studies economics and does research in the field, a naive approach must be replaced by an attempt to analyze and isolate the meaningful and true concept of exploitation.

The late Oskar Lange, who as an expert on both the modern mixed economy and on Marxian theory served as professor, diplomat (and Vice-President) in the United States and Poland, produced a fruitful interpretation. In his view, all that Marx wished to convey by the concept of "exploitation of labor" could be achieved without the trappings of the "labor theory of value" (which seemed to deny that scarce land and tools also contributed to competitive costs and to true social costs). Said Lange in effect, "The fact that people, who don't deserve to own the tools of production which work with labor and which are given their positive marginal-products out of the total product that might otherwise go to labor, receive a substantial fraction of the GNP, is ethically bad. The cure is to see that labor owns the tools of production and nature's gifts of land and other natural resources. Then labor, either in the form of wages or in the form of *its* share of property income, will indeed get all of the national product. Anything else is exploitation even in a prosperous capitalistic system where wages are very high (and much higher than are total incomes in egalitarian socialist societies)."

When we come to discuss land reform and increased education for labor, we shall see how laborers may come themselves to get a larger part of the property income of society. But before we leave the subject of exploitation, notice that the Lange (FOR WHOM) version of the concept does not depend upon monopoly or upon any imperfections of bargaining power between employer and employees.[7] What is involved here is a "value judgment" about the distribution of wealth ownership, not an alternative scientific finding.

MARGINAL-PRODUCT THEORY OF THE SINGLE FIRM[8]

Our main task is done. But there remains the need (1) to tie up these theories of production and distri-

[7] See Fig. 29-7, for a discussion of a quite different concept of exploitation based on employer monopoly power in the buying-of labor (so-called "monopsony"). Still a third concept of exploitation, explored on page 000 of Chapter 25's Appendix, of a factor like labor comes from what Cambridge's Joan Robinson calls "monopoly power of the firm in its product markets." As will be seen in the next sections, such a firm will be paying its factors less than the money value for which their marginal-products actually sell. Instead the factors get marginal revenue (which is less than price) times their marginal-products. Since the biggest and most monopolistic firms usually are the ones that actually pay the highest wages, such Robinsonian exploitation really means merely that monopolists are producing too little of their goods, that society at large is being exploited by this inefficiency, and that workers cannot from their wages buy for themselves the last extra product that an extra hour of work might actually produce.

[8] This section gives a bird's-eye view of least-cost theory of factor demand, which is explained at greater length in the Appendix. Brief courses and readers in a hurry may skip this section, and the appendix, without discontinuity.

bution with Maximum-profit decisions of the firm, and (2) to show that the cost curves of Part Three were implicitly based on the marginal-productivity decisions of this chapter.

MARGINAL-REVENUE PRODUCT AND MAXIMIZING PROFIT Exactly what does each last worker bring to my firm in cash dollar terms? He brings his marginal-physical-product; that we have seen. But he does not want his wage paid in *toothpaste*: the market wage is in *dollars*, not q units. And I, the employer, want to maximize dollars of profit.

Under perfect competition, the answer is easy. The marginal-physical product the worker brings me, MPP_L, can all be sold at the market price for my q output, P_q, which I as a perfect competitor cannot affect. If his MPP_L is 8 units of q and each sells for $P_q = \$5$, clearly, the dollar value of the last worker to me is $\$40$ (= $\$5 \times 8$). Generally, then, under perfect competition, each laborer is worth $P_q \times MPP_L$ to the firm. (For acres of land, this would be $P_q \times MPP_A$.)

But perfect competition is merely one limiting case of imperfect competition. It is the case of a horizontal dd schedule for my q. In the more common case of imperfect competition, dd is somewhat downward-sloping: Chapter 25 taught that the actual marginal revenue I then get from each extra physical q is *less than* market P_q (because of loss on previous units). With $MR_q < P_q$, the laborer's marginal-physical-product of 8 units will *not* be worth the market $P_q = \$5$ to me. How much, then? If $MR_q = \$3 < \$5 = P_q$, the answer is clear-cut: his final MPP_L is worth to me only $\$3 \times 8 = \$24$.

Generally, then, a firm's demand curve for a factor, such as labor, is given in dollar terms by "marginal revenue of q" times "marginal-physical-product of L." This important concept is given a name and defined as follows:

Definition: "Marginal-revenue-product" is defined as marginal-physical-product multiplied by the marginal revenue the firm gets for its extra physical goods sold.

Marginal-revenue-product of L

= $MR_q \times$ marginal-physical-product of L

Marginal-revenue-product of A

= $MR_q \times$ Marginal-physical-product of A

And so forth.

Now we can put the new concept to work.

Rule: The firm's demand curve for any factor is given by its curve of marginal-revenue-product for that factor, a curve which declines because of (1) diminishing physical returns and (2) the downward slope of the MR_q curve which generally prevails under imperfect competition.

In Maximum-profit equilibrium, every firm faced with competitive factor-prices—the money wage, the money rent rate per acre of land, and so forth—will aim to achieve

> Marginal-revenue-product of L = Price of L
> Marginal-revenue-produce of A = Price of A
> And so forth.

Maximum-profit equilibrium is attained when every factor is hired until its marginal benefit and costs are equated.[9]

MARGINAL-PRODUCTS AND LEAST-COST

Chapter 24 presented Total Cost data for each firm q. How did such minimal TC estimates get made? Marginal-productivity theory can now give the answer. Engineers told the firm it could produce $q = 9$ units with much land and little labor or with little land and much labor. Which is a more efficient choice: $A = 10$ and $L = 2$ or $A = 4$ and $L = 5$? Evidently, that must depend on the wage and rent rates the firm faces. If P_L = \$5 per hour and P_A = \$2 per acre, 10 acres and 2 hours give lower TC than do 4 acres and 5 hours. (Why? Because (\$2 × 10) + (\$5 × 2) = \$30 < (\$2 × 4) + (\$5 × 5) = \$33.)

What is the rule to follow to get lowest TC? The Least-cost position for producing each q comes from studying the marginal-physical-products of land and of labor. If an acre of land cost P_A = \$200, which is 100 times more than an hour of labor's factor-price P_L = \$2, no one in his right mind can expect Least-cost to come from achieving equal *physical*-marginal-products of land and labor. Since land costs 100 times as much, it must be made to give us 100 times the MPP of labor.

It is evident that what has to be equalized is the MPP per dollar spent on each factor if TC is to be minimized for producing $q = 9$. (Recall Chapter 22's similar equating of marginal-utilities-per-dollar.)

Least-cost rule: To get the lowest Total Cost at each point on its TC curve, a rational firm will hire factors until it has equalized the marginal-physical-product per last dollar spent on each factor of production.

$$\frac{\text{Marginal-physicial-product of } L}{\text{Price of } L}$$
$$= \frac{\text{Marginal-physical-product of } A}{\text{Price of } A}$$
$$= \dots, \text{at Least-cost}$$

An obvious corollary of the above[10] can now be stated.

Substitution rule: **If the price of one factor, like labor, rises while other factor-prices remain fixed, it will generally pay the firm to produce its same q outputs by substituting, for the factor now become dearer, more of the remaining factors. (A rise in P_L will thus reduce MPP_L/P_L and cause L to be fired and A hired until equality is restored, thus lowering the amount of needed L and increasing the demand for land acres; a fall in P_L will do the reverse. A rise in P_A alone will, by the same logic, cause labor to be substituted for now dearer land.)**

FINALE We have shown that the bird's-eye view of Clark's aggregate distribution is completely compatible with the realistic microeconomic pricing of any number of goods produced by any number of factor inputs. The triad of forces which determines competitive microeconomic distribution and value theory is seen to be (1) technology (the production function), (2) tastes and dollar-vote-power to demand various goods (the ultimate demand curves for goods, from which factor-price demands are derived), and (3) relative factor supplies (as determined by nature's abundance, inherited and acquired abilities, disutilities of different occupations).

The picture is oversimplified but important.

---

[9] Repeatedly in Part Three, we saw that departures from the conditions of perfect competition led to inefficiencies and to nonresponsiveness to people's dollar-vote desires. It is to be understood here, therefore, that such aberrations will be ruled out *only* in the special case where $P_q = MR_q$, i.e. where the demand curve for q is perfectly horizontal so that $P_L = P_q \times MPP_L'$ etc. This is actually what happened in the Clark model, where perfect competitors produced a homogeneous Q and had no "spoiling of the market problem" to bring MR_q below P_q and distort resource use.

[10] The Least-cost rule involves no mention of marginal revenue, because it applies for *all* q on the TC curve even before the firm's demand curve has been mentioned. The Appendix will relate it to the marginal-revenue-product rule of Maximum-profit where $MR = MC$.

SUMMARY

1 Distribution is concerned with the determination of different people's incomes, or with the basic question of FOR WHOM economic goods are to be produced. To understand what determines labor's and property's share in national product, and to understand forces acting on the degree of equality of income, distribution theory must study the problem of how the different factors of production—land, labor, capital, entrepreneurship, and risk-taking—get priced in the market. Thus it must study how supply and demand interact to determine all kinds of wages, rents, interest yields, and profits.

   Market supply and demand forces setting these incomes also determine the distribution of the aggregate national income, unless society intervenes. *Ethically*, however, there is no reason to prefer market-determined income distributions from redistribution brought about by society's transfers. However, a socially desirable distribution of income may not be one of maximum efficiency. These chapters simply focus on the economic, rather than the governmental, forces at work.

2 To understand why the demand curves for the factors of production are what they are, we must investigate the theory of production and cost within each firm. This is because the demand for factor inputs is a *joint demand*—joint because the factors interact in producing final product.

3 The relationship between quantities of available factor inputs—land, labor, machines, fertilizer—and quantity of output is called the *production function*. By varying one factor in successive small increments, we define its marginal-physical-product. Diminishing returns implies falling *MPP* of any factor if other factors are held fixed. But when *all* factor inputs increase *in balanced proportion*, the J. B. Clark model of competition presupposes that there will be exactly *constant* returns (i.e., constant returns *to scale*).

4 Competition of numerous free landowners and labor-owners will ensure that total product gets allocated among the factors by each having its factor-price equal to its marginal-product. That will allocate *exactly* 100 per cent of the product. Any factor, not just labor alone, can be the varying factor: because each of it gets paid only the *MP* of the *last* hired, there is enough of a residual surplus left (from the triangle of excess-of-early-over-last-*MP*'s) to pay the other factors their exact marginal-products. Hence, Clark's neoclassical theory of distribution, although simplified, is logically complete and a true picture of idealized competition.

5 Ambitious attempts to measure an aggregate production function for the whole of American manufacturing seem to provide rough corroboration for the theories of production and marginal-products. In this century, technological progress has been shifting the productivities of both labor and capital upward. At the same time capital has been growing faster than the labor supply, with the following implications: (*a*) the increase of capital per worker has shifted his productivity wages up even faster than technological change would alone; (*b*) the tendency of each unit of capital to encounter diminishing returns has just about been canceled by technological innovations; (*c*) the relative shares of labor and property incomes have remained at about three-quarters and one-quarter despite the vast institutional changes in union organization and in automation of production. (Chapter 37's growth theory will return to this.)

6 When the marginal-products of a factor in different uses are all equal to their common market wage, society's resources are being most efficiently allocated. (Any deviation from this inequality, whether under centralized planning or under monopoly

imperfections interfering with perfect competition, means that we are inside rather than out on Chapter 2's production-possibility frontier.) To socialists, like Poland's Oskar Lange, the efficiency of the marginal-product method of costing factor inputs (to enlarge the size of the social pie) was not an excuse for labor's not receiving all of the product. If owners of scarce land and scarce tools could withhold them from workers except when they command a fraction of the GNP through their competitive marginal-product prices, then to Lange that represented "exploitation" even if he had no particular use for Marx's labor theory of value (and even if other kinds of exploitation associated with monopoly power of firms in commodity of labor markets were absent or could be assumed to be ignorable).

7 If the firm is given ruling market prices of all factors and is given engineering, technical information about the effects of factor changes on final product, it can simultaneously solve the two problems (*a*) of substituting the different factors for each other so as to realize the Least-cost combination—at which he has *equalized the marginal-physical-product per dollar spent on every factor used*—and (*b*) of finally determining which of all possible outputs is his Maximum-profit position, where $MR = MC$.

8 An exactly equivalent condition of factor equilibrium is the following *equality* of marginal-*revenue*-products to factor-prices. Why must this hold in the Maximum-profit equilibrium? Because any businessman with common sense will stop hiring any factor at the point where what its marginal-physical-product will bring in to his firm in actual dollars of marginal revenue begins to fall short of the market price he must pay to hire as much or little as he wants.

9 Our analysis has shown why, when a factor-price rises, the quantity of it that is demanded will tend to fall. Higher labor price will cause other factors to be substituted for it in producing each output; and higher labor cost probably means that the Maximum-profit output will be at a lower level where MR equals a now higher MC.

What is the same, the marginal-revenue-product demand curve for the factor tilts downward because of technical diminishing returns, reinforced by spoiling of the monopolist's market. (This last fact reminds us that monopolists produce too little and hire too few factors.)

In the next few chapters we shall apply these principles to show how supply and demand operate in the factor markets to determine rents, wages, and other factor-prices. The Appendix to this chapter provides a review of the theory of production for those interested in a more geometrical approach.

CONCEPTS FOR REVIEW

FOR WHOM, HOW, factor pricing, distribution theory	marginal-product, marginal-physical-product, marginal-revenue-product, and factor-prices
joint demand	
production function	marginal-physical-product-per-last-dollar spent on each factor equalized
diminishing returns	
symmetry of land and labor	substitution rule of Least-cost
MP rectangle, residual rent triangle	$MR = MC$ and Maximum-profit q ... monopoly output and misallocated factors
relative constancy of labor and property shares	exploitation as low competitive returns and as monopoly victimization

QUESTIONS FOR DISCUSSION

1. What do economists mean by the theory of "distribution"? Is it what the census means when it discusses retailing?
2. Explain the "production function concept". Then explain the various marginal-products.
3. Explain Clark's distribution theory, varying land in a new version of Fig. 27-2.
4. Define marginal-revenue-product, distinguishing it from marginal-physical product. Give a common-sense explanation to show that Maximum-profit is not attained unless each factor-price exactly equals its marginal-revenue-product.
5. Convince a skeptic of the truth of the rule that to reach a Least-cost point you must equalize the marginal-productivity-per-dollar spent on every factor. Show this to be true even when we have not yet decided on the Maximum-profit output.
6. Suppose NNP grows in a mixed economy faster than labor supply in every decade. If, contrary to Karl Marx's predictions, wage share stays about the same fraction of NNP, show that real wages rates must rise.
7. *Extra credit problem:* Let output be Q and inputs be L(for labor) and A(for acres of land). Show that the *arithmetic mean* of L and A, namely $Q = 1/2\ L + 1/2\ A$, would not make a good production function because it does not show diminishing marginal-products. (HINT: Each equal increment of L by 1 always increases Q by the same increment of $1/2$.) But the *geometric mean* $Q = \sqrt{LA} = \sqrt{L}\ \sqrt{A}$ is a good production function with diminishing returns. (HINT: The square roots of 1, 2, 3, ... are 1, 1.41, 1.73, which do show decreasing increments of Q, namely, .41, .32,. ... Actually the Appendix's Table 27-1 satisfies this special symmetric case of the so-called "Cobb-Douglas" form, being like $Q = 141\sqrt{LA}$. The general Cobb-Douglas production function is $Q = bL^k C^{1-k}$, with all variables positive.)

Appendix: Graphical Depiction of Production Theory

The production theory of this chapter can be graphically presented. Table 27-1 is a numerical example of a simple production function relating output to two factor inputs, labor and land. It is the form of a two-way table, looking like a baseball schedule or a mileage chart of distances between cities.

Along the left-hand side are listed the varying amounts of land, going from 1 unit up through 6. Along the bottom are listed amounts of labor also happening to go from 1 through 6. Output corresponding to the specified land row and labor column is listed inside the table.

If we are interested in knowing exactly what output there will be when 5 units of land and 2 units of labor are available, we count up 5 units of land and then go over 2 units of labor. The answer is seen to be 448 units of product. Similarly, we find that 3 units of land and 6 of labor will produce 600 units of output. Thus, for any combination of labor and land, the production function tells us how much product we shall have (using, of course, the best methods of the technical engineer).

THE LAW OF DIMINISHING MARGINAL-PHYSICAL-PRODUCT

The law of diminishing returns can be nicely illustrated by Table 27-1.

First recall that we have given the name "marginal-physical-product of labor" to the extra production resulting from *one* additional unit of labor, land being held constant. At any point in Table 27-1 the marginal-physical-product of labor can be derived by subtracting the given number (representing product at that point) from the number on its right lying in the same row. Thus, when there are 2 units of land and 4 units of labor, the marginal-physical-product of an additional laborer would be 48, or 448 minus 400 in the second row.

By the "marginal-physical-product of land" we mean, of course, the extra product resulting from one additional unit of land, labor being held constant. It involves a comparison of adjacent items in a given column. Thus, when there are 2 units of land and 4 units of labor, the marginal-physical-product of land is shown in the fourth column as 490 — 400, or 90. The reader should be able to compute the marginal-physical-product of labor or land at any point inside the table.

Having defined what we mean by the marginal-physical-product of an input, we are now in a position to restate the law of diminishing returns:

As we hold a fixed input constant and increase a variable input, the marginal-physical-product of the variable input will decline—at least after a point.

PRODUCTION FUNCTION RELATING AMOUNT OF OUTPUT TO VARYING COMBINATIONS OF LABOR AND LAND INPUTS

TABLE 27-1. When you have 3 land units and 2 labor units available, the engineer tells you your maximum obtainable output is 346 units. Note the different ways to produce 346 and to produce 490.

To illustrate this, hold land constant in Table 27-1 by sticking to a given row, say that corresponding to land equal to 2 units. Now let labor increase from 1 to 2 units, from 2 to 3 units, and so forth. What happens to product at each step?

As labor goes from 1 to 2 units, product increases from 200 to 282 units, or by 82 units. But the next dose of labor adds only 64 units, or 346 — 282. Diminishing returns has set in. Still further additions of a single unit of labor give us, respectively, only 54 extra units of output, 48 units, and finally 42 units. The reader should check some other row to verify that the law of diminishing returns holds there too. He should also verify that the same law holds true when labor is held constant and land is added in a number of steps. (Examine the changes in product in any *column*.)

At this point, it is well to recall the explanation given for diminishing returns. In Chapter 2, it was attributed to the fact that the fixed factor decreases *relative* to the variable factor. Each unit of the variable factor has less and less of the fixed factor to work with, and it is only natural that extra product should begin to fall off.

If this explanation is to hold water, there should be no diminishing returns when both factors are increased in proportion. When labor increases from 1 to 2 and land *simultaneously* increases from 1 to 2, we should get the same increase in product as when both increase simultaneously from 2 to 3. This can be verified from Table 27-1.[1] In the first move we go from 141 to 282, and in the second move the product increases from 282 to 423, an equal jump of 141 units.

Also, this explanation of diminishing returns in terms of the proportions of the inputs would lead us to expect that increasing land will improve the marginal-physical-product of labor. Again this can be verified from our table: The fifth unit of labor adds 48 units of product when there are only 2 units of land; but at 3 units of land, a fifth unit of labor adds 58 units of Q.

LEAST-COST FACTOR COMBINATION FOR A GIVEN OUTPUT

The numerical production function shows that the engineer is not able to tell us definitely how any given output is to be produced. There is more than one way to skin a cat. And there is more than one way to produce any given output. Thus, the black numbers in Table 27-1 show that the output q = 346 can be produced in any one of the ways shown in Table 27-2.[2]

As far as the engineer is concerned, each of these combinations is equally good at producing an output of 346 units. But the accountant, interested in keeping profits of the firm at a maximum and costs at a minimum, knows

[1] Not all production functions met within real economic life would have these special properties of so-called "constant returns to scale." Recall from Chapter 2 the discussion of increasing returns to scale, or economies of mass production.

[2] You can make up a similar table for output equal to 490.

Equal-Output Factor Combinations

	LABOR L	LAND A	TOTAL COST WHEN $P_L = \$2$ $P_A = \$3$	TOTAL COST WHEN $P_L = \$2$ $P_A = \$1$
A	1	6	\$20	—
B	2	3	13	\$7
C	3	2	12	—
D	6	1	15	—

TABLE 27-2. Factors can be substituted for one another to produce the same output.
When $P_L = \$2$ and $P_A = \$3$, calculate total of wage cost plus land cost to verify that their combination gives lowest cost \$12 at *C*. Show that lowering P_A to \$1 causes land to be substituted for labor as you move from *C* to *B*.

that only one of these four combinations will give Least-cost. Just which one will depend, of course, on the respective prices of the two factors of production.

Let us suppose that the price of labor is \$2 and the price of land \$3. Then the sum of the labor and land costs in situation *A* will be \$20 (= 1 × \$2 + 6 × \$3). And costs at *B*, *C*, and *D* will be, respectively, \$13, \$12, \$15. At these stated factor input prices, there is no question but that *C* is the best way of producing the given output.

If either of the input prices changes, the equilibrium proportion of the inputs will always change so as to use *less* of the input that proportionately has gone up most in price. This is just like the substitution-effect of Chapter 22's discussion of consumer demand. Thus, if labor stays at \$2 per unit but land falls to \$1 per unit, the new optimal combination will be *B*, where more land is substituted for reduced labor and where total cost is only \$7. The reader

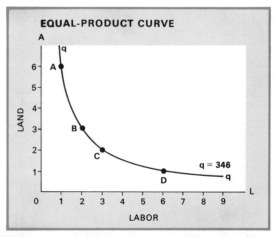

FIG. 27-3. All the points on the curve represent the different combinations of land and labor that can be used to produce the same 346 units of output.

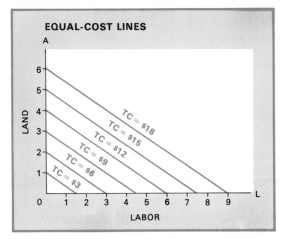

FIG. 27-4. Every point on a given line represents the same total cost. The lines are straight because of constant factor-prices, and they all have a numerical slope equal to the ratio of labor price to land price, $2/$3, and hence are parallel.

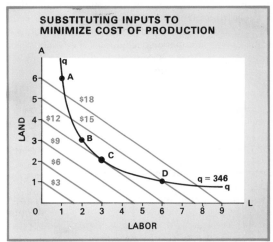

FIG. 27-5. To find Least-Cost equilibrium for fixed output of 346, we move along black curve of alternative factor combinations and strive to be on lowest parallel line of total cost. Where the equal-product curve touches (but does not cross) the lowest total-cost contour is the Least-cost optimum position. This tangency means that factor-prices and marginal-physical-products (or "substitution ratios") are proportional, with equalized marginal-physical-products-per-dollar.

should verify this by computing the new total expense of all other combinations and seeing that they are higher. (Pencil in missing costs in Table 27-2.)

Exactly the same sort of thing can be done for any other output; as soon as all input prices are known, we can experiment until we have found the Least-cost input combination. (To guarantee your understanding of the principles involved, work out the optimum production decision and cost for output equal to 490 units when price of labor is $4 and price of land is $3. See that 3 labor and 4 land units will turn out to produce Least-cost of $24 for $q = 490$.)

EQUAL-PRODUCT AND EQUAL-COST CONTOURS: GRAPH OF LEAST-COST POSITION

The common-sense numerical analysis of the way in which a firm will combine inputs to minimize costs can be made more vivid by the use of diagrams. From the production schedule we can draw a picture of the different input combinations that will produce a given output. Figure 27-3 is the exact counterpart of Table 27-2. In it the smooth curve indicates the different combinations of labor and land that yield an output of 346 units. This could be called a "production-indifference curve" by analogy with the consumer's indifference curve of the Appendix to Chapter 22. But a more expressive name would be to call it an "equal-product" curve. (You should be able to draw in on Fig. 27-3, as a dotted curve, the corresponding equal-product curve for output equal to 490. You should realize that an infinite number of such equal-product contour lines could be drawn in, just as a topographical or weather map could be covered with an indefinitely large number of equal-altitude or equal-pressure contour lines.)

Given the price of labor and land, the firm can evaluate the total cost for points A, B, C, and D or for any other point on the equal-product curve. Obviously, it will be maximizing its profits only when it has found that optimum point on the equal-product curve at which it reaches Least-cost.

Purely as a graphical trick, the firm might try to save itself much tedious arithmetical computation by evaluating once and for all the total cost of every possible factor combination of land and labor. This is done in Fig. 27-4, where the family of parallel straight lines represents all possible equal-cost curves when the price of labor is $2 and the price of land $3.

To find the total cost for any point we have simply to read off the number appended to the equal cost line going through that point. The red lines are all straight and parallel because the firm is assumed to be able to buy all it wishes of either factor input at constant prices. The lines are somewhat flatter than 45° because the price of labor P_L is somewhat less than the price of land P_A. More precisely, we can always say that the arithmetic value of the slope of each equal-cost line must equal the ratio of the price of labor to that of land[3]—in this case 2/3.

---

[3]The careful reader will notice the parallel between the geometry of this section and that of the analysis of consumer equilibrium in the Appendix to Chapter 22. Each equal-cost line indicates all the possible different quantities of labor and of land that the firm might buy for any given cost outlay. Each line is straight since its equation is $TC = \$2L + \$3A$. In the Appendix to Chapter 22, the consumer is buying goods, not factor services; otherwise his "consumption-possibility line" exactly parallels the equal-cost lines we are now discussing. We can explain, similarly, why the

It is now easy to recognize the optimum equilibrium input position of the firm at which total costs are minimized for the given output. The single black equal-product curve has superimposed upon it the family of red equal-cost lines. This is shown in Fig. 27-5. The firm will always keep moving along the black convex curve of Fig. 27-5 as long as it is able to cross over to lower cost lines. Its equilibrium will therefore not be at *A, B,* or *D.* It will be at *C, where the equal-product curve touches (but does not cross) the lowest equal-cost line.* This is, of course, *a point of tangency,* where the slope of the equal-product curve just matches the slope of an equal-cost-line and the curves are just kissing.

We already know that the slope of the equal-cost curve is P_L/P_A. But what is the slope of the equal-product curve? This slope is a kind of "substitution ratio" between the two factors, and it depends upon the *relative* marginal-physical-products of the two factors of production, namely, MPP_L/MPP_A—just as the rate of substitution between two goods along a consumer's indifference curve was earlier shown to equal the ratio of the marginal, or extra, utilities of the two goods (Appendix to Chapter 22).

LEAST-COST CONDITIONS

Thus, our Least-cost equilibrium can be defined by any of the following equivalent relations:

1. The ratio of the marginal-physical-products of any two inputs must equal the ratio of their factor-prices.

That is, substitution ratio, or
$$\frac{\text{marginal-physical-product of labor}}{\text{marginal-physical-product of land}} = \frac{\text{price of labor}}{\text{price of land}}$$

2. The marginal-physical-product-per-dollar received from the (last) dollar of expenditure must be the same for every productive factor.

That is,
$$\frac{\text{marginal-physical-product of } L}{\text{price of } L}$$
$$= \frac{\text{marginal-physical-product of } A}{\text{price of } A} = \cdots$$

Relation 2 is discussed in detail in the main body of the chapter. (It could also be derived from relation 1 by transposing terms from one numerator to the other denominator, i.e., by "interchanging means and extremes", as in going from $a/b = c/d$ to $a/c = b/d$.)

But the student should not be satisfied with any such abstract explanation. He should always remember the common-sense economic explanation which shows how a firm will redistribute its expenditure among inputs if any one factor offers a greater return for each last dollar spent

slope of an equal-cost line equals the ratio of the two prices involved.

But note this difference: The consumer was assumed to have a fixed budget; hence, he had but one consumption-possibility line. The firm is not limited to any particular level of costs; so it must consider many equal-cost lines before discovering its Least-cost equilibrium.

on it. Finally, we may state the above Least-cost relations in the following form:

3. Input prices and their marginal-physical-products must be proportional, the factor of proportionality being marginal cost.[4]

MC of output x marginal-physical-product
of labor = Price of labor
MC of output x marginal-physical-product
of land = Price of land
And so on for any number of inputs.

The Least-cost relationships 1, 2, and 3 are all equivalent. Each holds at every point along the Total Cost curve, *whatever the output.* They do *not* tell the firm where it should finally produce.

MARGINAL-REVENUE-PRODUCT CONDITON OF MAXIMUM-PROFIT

But now we add the Maximum-profit condition that $MR = MC$; and we recall the definition of "marginal-revenue-product" as equal to "marginal-physical-product times marginal revenue." Then we can combine the Least-cost relations of item 3 just above and the Maximum-profit relationship to reach our final equilibrium condition:

Marginal-revenue-product of labor = price of labor
Marginal-revenue-product of land = price of land
And so on for any number of factors:

$$MR \times MPP_i = P_i$$

Thus, our graphical analysis has arrived at the same final result as our common-sense reasoning of this chapter—which tells us that we shall stop hiring more of a factor only at the point where the marginal-revenue-product it brings just matches its market price. This is what lies behind the firm's demand curve for a productive factor.

FIXITY OF PROPORTIONS

An important qualification must sometimes be made. We have calculated the marginal-physical-product of any one input by (1) holding all the other inputs constant and then (2) increasing the input in question by 1 unit. The resulting increase in physical product was then measured, and that was identified as the factor's marginal-physical-product. But in some technological processes the factor inputs work very intimately together, so that, when you increase only one of them, holding the others constant, you get *zero extra product;* and when you decrease one factor alone, you lose *the whole product* produced by both together.

Only when you change them both *in combination* do you seem to get a nice smooth curve of marginal-physical-product.

[4] Why are these marginal-physical-products-per dollar each equal to the reciprocal of marginal cost, or to $1/MC_q$? Because extra output per dollar is nothing but the upside-down of extra dollars per unit of output, which is what we always have meant by *MC.*

SMOOTHING DISCONTINUITIES Certainly, such extreme discontinuities can sometimes happen. But perhaps they do not occur quite so often as some critics have claimed. Thus, critics often point out examples where one man is always using one shovel or where it seems to take a certain amount of gold to produce a watchband and no amount of labor can substitute for this gold. But actually, in any digging operation, extra shovels[5] must usually be kept on hand; and if shovel prices were very high and wages were low, workers on different shifts might use the same implements so that the shovel requirements could be kept to a minimum; also, we might in time change the size of the shovels or introduce bulldozers, thereby changing the proportions of the factors. Or in the above case of the gold watchband, there will almost certainly be some waste of metal in the form of shavings and dust; and if wages were low enough relative to the price of gold, it would pay us to hire more men to produce the same number of watchbands out of less gold—labor being, in effect, a substitute for the use of more gold.

Numerous other arguments and examples could be given in reply to those who stress fixity of factor proportions and discontinuities in substitutability and marginal-products. Nonetheless, in some technical processes, there may not be continuous substitutability between the various inputs, and so the calculated marginal-physical-products may become very erratic and lumpy.

FIXED-COEFFICIENTS CASE It was once thought that lack of substitutability would spoil the economic theory of production; but that is not always so.

To see the case of fixed proportions, we would have to replace the smooth black contour of Figs. 27-3 and 27-5 by a black L-shaped equal-product contour. Regardless of how high or low the positive P_L/P_A ratio is, the Least-cost point of "tangency"—where the black contour touches but does not cross the minimal red line of TC—comes always at the corner of the L. Hence, the Least-cost condition is even more easily found in the fixed-proportions case. (There now will be *no* substitution when one factor becomes dear relative to another, for the reason that no technical substitutability is possible.)

The derived demand of firms for factors is still well determined, but with the difference that there may be inelastic stretches and some discontinuities in the factor-input demand curve. In Fig. 27-2, a vertical *dd* curve would spoil the simple Clark tale of rectangle and residual triangle.

Fortunately, dropping the one-good assumption of Clark and replacing a single Q by many goods ($Q_1, Q_2, \ldots$) can sometimes restore determinacy of distribution. Let's see why.

[5]Probability variations strengthen the case for variability of proportions. Even with one machine to one operator, the fact that each machine has a probability of breaking down means that eleven machines for ten men is better—on the average!—than ten machines.

INTERCOMMODITY SUBSTITUTION AND QUALIFICATIONS

It is not hard to show what happens when we drop the simplified case of a single product. As any factor, such as unskilled labor, becomes more plentiful, its marginal-revenue-product and rental will tend to fall. Not only will more of it tend to be substituted for other factors in each line of production, but in addition, *those special goods which happen to use much of this factor in their production* will fall in price more than will other prices generally. This relative price drop will tend to cause consumers to use more of such cheapened goods, and in this way the derived demand for the factor will become even more elastic.

Thus, *in addition to intracommodity technical substitutability between factors, there is also intercommodity substitutability resulting from differential price effects.* This suggests how distribution will be determined even when the continuous-substitutability assumptions of the marginal-product theory of production break down. If factors must be used in fixed proportions, their derived demands are still perfectly well determined. These demands, together with supply relations, help determine all prices. Intercommodity substitutions now become extremely important, as do the supply conditions for the factors.[6]

[6]An example illustrates how intercommodity substitutions can determine factor-prices even in the worst case of fixed-proportions, e.g., where 1 unit of land *and* 1 unit of labor are needed to produce a unit of wine and where 1 unit of land *and* 2 units of labor are needed to produce one of bread. Assume wine sells for $10 per unit, bread for $12. Bread differs from wine by $2 in price and cost; and in terms of factor inputs, it differs by what? By 1 extra unit of labor. Hence wages must be exactly $2 per unit (= $12 — $10), and land use must be priced at $8 per unit [= $10 — $2, or $12 — (2 x $2)]. So from commodity prices we can obtain factor-prices—even in this fixed-proportions case.

You will realize that the prices of wine and bread had also to be determined by supply and demand and will depend in part upon how much income goes to hungry laborers and thirsty machine owners and upon the initial supplies of the factors. For example, imagine that we started with a supply of 200 acres of land and 300 laborers, and let us summarize the resulting general equilibrium. *If* we had started with factors in a 1:1 ratio—say, 200 of each—and *if* we required them to be fully employed, they would *all* have to go into wine production. We could not possibly produce any bread and still keep all our factors employed. Similarly, if our factor totals had been in a 1:2 proportion—say, 200 acres of land, 400 laborers—we should have to produce nothing but bread to preserve full employment.

But we start with a halfway ratio—200:300. Common sense and simple algebra tell us that we must then split our land half and half between the two industries, thereby using up the total of both factors in producing 100 wine units and 100 bread units. The prices of these supplies of goods would then be determined by the interplay of competitive supply and demand for the two goods and for the two factors, and thus we end up at the above equilibrium prices for goods and services.

[NOTE: A factor-price can be made zero by some demand and supply patterns, but this "free factor" possibility is neglected for simplicity. Neglected too is the case where one of the *q*'s produced is *zero*. (If both goods used both factors in the same ratio that they are inelastically supplied, we would indeed be in a singular case where equilibrium would be indeterminate.

Finally, note this. To understand the different aspects of the problem of distribution is to begin to understand much of the history of the classical and modern theories of distribution and of competitive pricing. But it does not tell us much about the cases of imperfect competition: (1) where there may be economies of scale that lead to a few firms' gaining semi-monopoly power, and (2) where consumers may develop a special preference for products that can be produced only by factors owned by a single firm. As Chapter 31 shows, in these cases the firms may earn "monopoly profits" or "monopoly rents" which the attempted competition of other firms may not take away from them. To "natural scarcity" is then being added artificial "contrived scarcity," brought about by someone's holding in his supply for fear of "spoiling the market."

Turn to Fig. 23-6. With fixed coefficients, the red frontier becomes two straight lines intersecting in a corner point like E. The slope of the black indifference curve—slope "tangential" at E to the red frontier will determine final goods' price ratio; and this price ratio will determine factors' price ratio.)]

SUMMARY TO APPENDIX

1 A production function lists, for each labor row and each land column, the output that is producible. Diminishing returns, to one variable factor applied to a fixed factor, can be shown by calculating the falloff of marginal-products in any row or column.

2 An equal-product contour, usually drawn to be convex (from below), depicts the alternative input combinations that produce the same level of output. The slope, or substitution ratio, along such an "isoquant" equals relative marginal-products (e.g., MPP_L/MPP_A). Contours of equal Total Cost are parallel lines with slopes equal to factor-price ratios (P_L/P_A). Least-cost equilibrium comes at tangency point, where equal-product contour touches but does not cross the lowest TC contour. There marginal-products are proportional to factor-prices, with *equalized* marginal-product-per-dollar spent on all factors (e.g., equalized MPP_i/P_i).

3 Of all points on TC curve, the Maximum-profit equilibrium comes where $MR = MC$; there each factor has marginal-revenue-product just equal to its price. (The Least-cost condition $P_i = MC \times MPP_i$ becomes at Maximum-profit $P_i = MR \times MPP_i$ as in main chapter.)

CONCEPTS FOR REVIEW

convex equal-product contours
parallel equal-TC lines
substitution slope = MPP_L/MPP_A
P_L/P_A = slope of parallel
  equal-TC lines

Least-cost tangency:
  $MPP_L/MPP_A = P_L/P_A$ or

$MPP_L/P_L = MPP_A/P_A = 1/MC$
Maximum-profit condition,
  $MR \times MPP_L = P_L, \ldots$

QUESTIONS FOR DISCUSSION

1. Show that raising labor wage while holding land rent constant will steepen the red equal-cost lines and move tangency point C in Fig. 27-5 northwest toward B with now cheaper input substituted for now dearer one. Should union leaders recognize this?

2. (The remaining questions are not easy and can be skipped by those who have no interest or training in geometry and elementary calculus.) The famous statistical equation of Senator Douglas related Q output to L labor and C capital by the formula $Q = 1.01 L^{.75}C^{.25}$. [Ignoring the 1.01 scale factor and identifying marginal-products with partial derivatives, show that labor's relative share is given by $WL/PQ = L(W/P)/Q = L(\partial Q/\partial L)/Q = L(.75L^{.75-1}C^{.25})/L^{.75}C^{.25} = .75$. Show also that capital's share is $C(\partial Q/\partial C)/Q = .25$. Instead suppose $Q = [(3L)^{-1} + C^{-1}]^{-1}$, a weighted *harmonic mean*. Verify that $MPP_c = \partial Q/\partial C = [1/3(C/L) + 1]^{-2}$, and hence the nonlabor share, $C(\partial Q/\partial C)/Q$, declines as C increases relative to L as a tedious calculation shows.]

3. Let $P = P(q)$ be the declining demand curve for a monopolist firm, with $TR = qP(q) = R(q)$. Let its total costs be given by $TC = P_L L + P_A A$. Let its production function be written as $q = q(L,A)$, with marginal-products given by $MPP_L = \partial q/\partial L$, etc. Then Maximum profit requires the max-

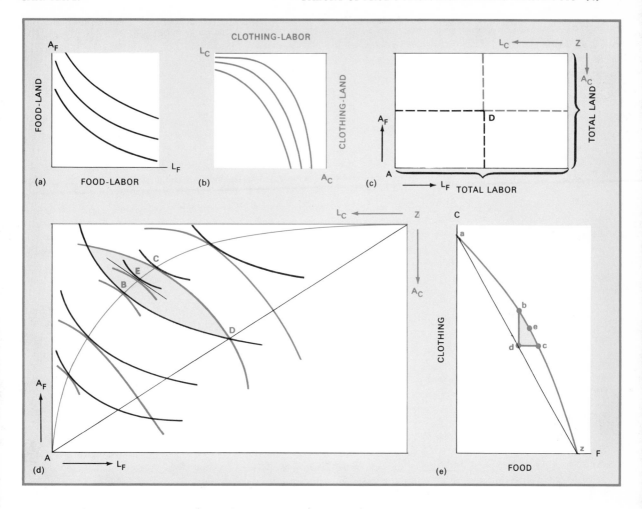

imization of $R - C = R[q(L,A)] - P_L L - P_A A$. Such a maximum requires differentiating partially with respect to each input, giving us by the chain rule for the calculus the equality of marginal-revenue-products to factor prices.

$$\partial \{R[q(L,A)] - P_L L - P_A \ A\} / \partial L =$$
$$R'[q] \times \partial q / \partial L - P_L = O_A \qquad \text{QED}$$

and do likewise for the $MR \times MPP_A$ equivalence. In the case oi perfect competition, set $P(q) \equiv P$, a constant; then $R[q] \equiv Pq$, $R'[q] \equiv P$, and you derive the equivalence of factor-price and value of its marginal-product. Do it.

4. As a test of creative free association, use the following geometry to understand an important the-orem in modern welfare economics: "Planners or markets are socially efficient, being out on and not inside society's production-possibility frontier for butter and guns (or, better, for food and clothing) only if the ratio of labor's marginal-physical-product to land's marginal-physical-product has been equated in every industry—equated to a common wage-free ratio."

   HINT: We superimpose (a) and (b) on (c) to get (d). At inefficient point like D, lack of tangency leads to shaded area of waste. At typical efficient frontier point on red AZ curve, black and red MPP ratios are equal to common wage-rent as shown by mutual tangency to fine black line through E. Be sure you relate (e)'s inside point to the nontangency point D in (d).

4

Distribution of Income: The Pricing of the Productive Factors

28
PRICING OF FACTOR INPUTS:
LAND RENTS AND OTHER RESOURCES

The price of pig,
Is something big;
Because its corn, you'll understand,
Is high-priced, too;
Because it grew
Upon the high-priced farming land.

If you'd know why
That land is high,
Consider this: its price is big
Because it pays
Thereon to raise
The costly corn, the high-priced pig.

H. J. DAVENPORT

Chapter 27 gave an overall view of the micro-economic theory of the distribution of income by means of marginal-products. In this chapter we shall develop the details by which the marginal-product demand curves for factors interact with various supply curves for the factors of production to determine their market prices. Thereby the relative income shares of the owners of the factors of production (the FOR WHOM of *laissez-faire* economics) get determined.

Also in this chapter, as a convenient preparation for the following chapters' discussions of wage, interest, and profit determination, we shall study the special case of rents to land and other natural resources that are in relatively inelastic supply.

DEMAND FOR FACTORS A DERIVED DEMAND

Begin with some obvious and elementary observations about factor demand.

Why do consumers demand a finished output like a magazine or an overcoat? They do so because of the satisfaction they hope to enjoy from its use. But why does a businessman demand a factor input such as fertilizer or sulfur or unskilled labor? Surely not for the *direct* satisfaction he hopes to get. He wants the productive factors because of the production and revenue that he hopes to secure *indirectly* from those factors.

Satisfactions are in the picture, but at one stage removed. The satisfactions that consumers get from an overcoat help to determine how much a textile company can sell the coat for and how many coats it can sell. Therefore you would be right to insist that consumer demands do *ultimately* determine the firm's demand for inputs. The firm's demand for labor is *derived indirectly* from the consumer demand for its final product.

So economists speak of the demand for productive factors as a "derived demand."

Definition: Derived demand refers to the fact that, when profit-seeking firms demand a factor of production, they do so because that factor input permits them to produce a good which consumers are willing to pay for now or in the future. The demand for the factor of production is thus derived ultimately from consumers' desires and demands for final goods.

In short, effort involved in making coats or sewing machines is of no interest to society for its own sake; we pay men and machines to sew because of the satisfaction believed to be gained from the finished product. Sometimes the derived demands go through many stages: Wool is wanted to spin yarn; yarn is wanted to weave cloth; cloth is wanted to make coats. All the previous demands are derived from the ultimate consumer demand for the satisfactions to be secured from the finished product.

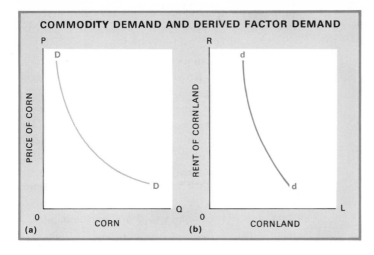

COMMODITY DEMAND AND DERIVED FACTOR DEMAND

FIG. 28-1. Demand for factors is derived from demand for goods they produce.

The red curve of derived demand for cornland in (b) comes from the light red curve of commodity demand for corn in (a). Shift the *DD* curve up, and up goes the *dd* curve. (Make the *DD* commodity curve more inelastic and vertical, and in part the same tends to happen to the *dd* factor curve.)

Figure 28-1 shows how the demand for a given input, such as fertile cornland, must be regarded as derived from the consumers' demand curve for corn. This assumes, of course, that we hold constant the prices of such cooperating inputs as fertilizer, labor, and farm machinery. Chapter 27 showed this: At each land-rent price prevailing in the market place, any small farmer must decide on the Least-cost combination of the various inputs, and he must also decide on the Maximum-profit scale of his output to throw onto the market. Therefore each farmer will want to hire more and more of cornland up to the point where its marginal-revenue-product is equal to its market rental. At that point, the last unit just brings in an amount equal to its extra cost. That is why it is the equilibrium point at which the farmer ceases to demand more or less.

Recall that we are dealing with a competitive industry in which the single farmer is too small to affect the market price of corn. In such a competitive industry, no one need worry about spoiling the market for the previous units of corn being sold; consequently, marginal revenue and price are the same thing. It follows that marginal-revenue-product will be exactly the same thing as marginal-physical-product times corn price. For such a special perfectly competitive case, economists often use the special name "value of the marginal product" instead of marginal-revenue-product.

Five principles governing elasticity of this factor demand will perhaps seem reasonable. Demand for a factor tends to be the more inelastic (1) the more inelastic is the demand for the product; (2) the less important a fraction of total cost is this indispensable factor ("It is important to

be unimportant"); (3) the less other factors can be technically substituted for this factor; (4) the more inelastic are the supplies of other factors; and (5) the more inflexible is the administered price at which the firm continues to sell its product. (Skilled electricians meet all the first four requirements: little is spent on them; they are indispensable; other labor, such as carpenters and masons, is inelastically supplied; and the demand for the new structures is quite inelastic. See Chapter 29.)

FACTOR-PRICE DETERMINATION BY SUPPLY AND DEMAND

Until now we have worked only with the demand curve for a factor, taking its market price as given to the demanders. But obviously it is *all the firms together* that determine the factor's market price that each small firm faces. Let us now see how the total demand curve of all firms for the factor, together with its total supply curve, will interact to determine the equilibrium price tending to rule in the market place.

Figure 28-2 repeats the total derived demand curve for cornland *dd*; it was arrived at by adding together the demand curves of all the firms.

Now it is one of the peculiarities of land that, unlike most things, its total supply is relatively fixed by nature and in general cannot be augmented in response to a higher price for it or diminished in response to lower land rentals. (This is not strictly true. Land can sometimes be created by drainage, and

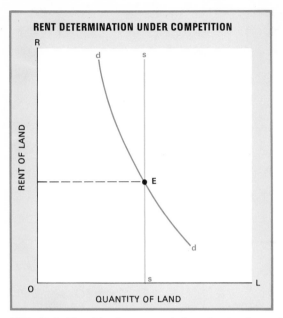

FIG. 28-2. Fixed land must work for what its demanders will bid.

Perfect inelasticity of supply characterizes the case of so-called "pure economic rent." We run up *ss* curve to factor demand curve to determine rent. (Aside from land, we can apply rent considerations to oil and mining properties, outstanding hockey players, and anything in inelastic supply.)

the fertility of existing land can be depleted by overcropping.)

Nonetheless, we can accept the complete fixity of land's supply as its characteristic feature. By tradition, we may confine our discussion to the "original and inexhaustible gift of nature" whose total supply is by definition *completely inelastic*. It was the price or return to such a factor that the classical economists of the last century called "rent."

This differs from ordinary usage in which rent or rental is the money paid for the use over a period of time of anything—of a house, truck, and so forth. (For the rest of Part Four we shall use the word "rent" to refer to the return to a factor whose supply is completely inelastic and "rental" to refer to money paid for the services, over a period of time, of any factor.)

In Figure 28-2, the supply curve for land *ss* is made to be completely inelastic because of the fixity of its supply. The demand and supply curves intersect at the equilibrium point *E*. It is toward this factor-price that the rent of land must tend. Why? Because if rent rose above the equilibrium price, the amount of land demanded by all firms would be less than the existing amount that would be supplied; some property owners would be unable to rent their land at all; therefore they would offer their land for less and thus bid down its rent. By similar reasoning, the rent could not long remain below the equilibrium intersection. If it did, you should be able to show how the bidding of unsatisfied firms would force the factor-price back up toward the equilibrium level. Only at a competitive price where total amount demanded of land exactly equals the total supply will there be equilibrium. It is in this sense that supply and demand determine any factor-price.

Note that the man who owns land does not have to be a particularly deserving citizen in order to receive this rent. A virtuous and poor landowner will be given exactly the same rent by competition as will a wealthy wastrel. It is the productivity of the acre of land that is being paid for, and not the personal merits of the landowner.

Even this productivity of the land is not something absolute. For example, what would happen if the price of corn were to fall greatly because people began to desire other goods? Then the derived demand for cornland would shift drastically downward and to the left. What will happen to the rents received by landowners? After a time, rents must sink down to a new equilibrium inter-section. The land is not less productive in a technical sense than it was before, and the landlords are neither more nor less virtuous than they were before. But factor demand-and-supply intersection has changed.

A factor of production like cornland is said to earn a "pure economic rent" (1) when its total supply is regarded as perfectly inelastic; and (2) when we can assume that the land *has no other uses*, such as in the production of sugar or rye. Adam Smith's great follower in England, David Ricardo, noted in 1815 that the case of such an inelastically supplied factor could be described as follows:

It is not really true that the price of corn is high because the price of corn land is high. Actually the reverse is more nearly the truth; the price of corn land is high because the price of corn is high!

Land's total supply being inelastic, it will always work for whatever is given to it by competition. Thus the value of the land is competely derived from the value of the product, and not vice versa.[1]

RENT AND COSTS[2]

Some economists went so far as to say: "Rent does not enter into the cost of production." As a digression let us see why.

The last section shows that there is a grain of truth in this. But still it is very dangerous terminology. If you were a farmer trying to go into the corn raising business, you would certainly find that the landlord has to be paid like anybody else. You would certainly include rent in your costs of production; and if you could not pay your rent, you would go out of business.

IMPLICIT VERSUS EXPLICIT RETURNS

Even if you were a farmer who owned your own land, it would be a mistake to think that rent does not enter into your costs of production. After you had paid all your other bills, including wages to yourself at least as great as what you could earn elsewhere in the market, there would have to be left an amount at least equal to the market rental value of your land. For what if there were not? Then you would soon find that it would be better for you *to rent out your farm on the open market* and hire out your own labor to somebody else.

Sometimes economists call rent paid by a man to himself "implicit" rather than "explicit" rent. Very clearly, implicit rent is as much a part of long-run competitive firm costs as are any other costs, and the same can be said of the implicit wages or implicit interest earned on any other factors that you could sell rather than use personlly. The reader is urged to refer to the discussion of opportunity cost and im-

plied cost in Chapter 24 (page 435), which bear on this point.

RELATIVITY OF VIEWPOINT

When some economists claim rent does not enter into society's cost of production, what are they driving at? As already noted, they are saying:

Since rent is the return to an inelastically supplied factor that would still be supplied to the community even at much lower prices, the direction of causation goes as follows: *"The prices of goods really determine land rent—rather than land rent determining the prices of goods."*

At this point we must avoid our old enemy "the fallacy of composition." What appears as a cost of production to each and every small firm using a particular kind of land may, as we have seen, be to the whole community merely a derived price-determined rent expense rather than a price-determining one. More than that, suppose the land is specialized and can be used only for the production of one industry. If a grade of land is inelastically supplied to one industry and, having no place else to go, will always work for whatever it can earn there, its return may appear to every small firm as a cost like any other. But as scientific observers of the whole industry, we still must recognize that the land return is a price-determined rent and not a price-determining cost.

Now let us move on to an alternative case. Suppose this land can be used for a variety of industries: for corn growing, rye growing, buckwheat growing, cattle grazing, and so forth. Then to each small industry (such as buckwheat growing), land's return will definitely appear as a necessary expense that the consumers of buckwheat will have to pay as cost before they can get their buckwheat. One small industry is just like any one small firm in this case: although the total of land is *inelastic* in supply for *all* uses, to any *one* small firm or industry it is in completely *elastic* supply.

To conclude: Whether rent is or is not a price-determining cost depends upon the viewpoint: that of a small firm, small industry, large and even exclusive-user industry, or whole economy. What is a price-determined rent return to a factor which is inelastic in supply to the whole community or dominant industry may, to each firm and to any small industry that is only one of many

---

[1] Land is not the only factor whose return may be considered as economic rent. For an example where most of a wage payment is a "pure rent," see page 531. And in the short run, the supply of a machine or plant may be entirely fixed; thus a hydroelectric plant takes a long time to build, still longer to wear out. The return to any factor in temporarily fixed supply is sometimes called a "quasi rent"—"quasi," because in the long run, its supply need not be fixed. Those farmers who petition for higher farm prices because of higher land and livestock prices, without knowing it, illustrate rent and quasi-rent doctrines.

[2] This theoretical digression may be skipped by brief courses.

potential users, appear as a price-determining cost.[3]

HENRY GEORGE'S SINGLE-TAX MOVEMENT: TAXATION OF LAND "SURPLUS"

In the last part of the nineteenth century, settlers from the Old World were moving out to the frontiers of North America, Australia, and Africa, and even to newly reclaimed lands in Europe. As more and more people arrived, each acre had more people to work with. In a sense, therefore, the land became more productive. In any case its competitive rent value certainly tended to rise, and consequently its purchase price. This created handsome profits for some of those who were lucky or farsighted enough to get in on the ground floor and acquire land early. As the comedian Will Rogers put it, "Land is a good investment. They ain't making no more."

Nor was this true only in agriculture. All through the West men can remember when towns first began, and how they could have "picked up a quarter-section, where Main and Railway Avenues now cross, for $5 an acre. Now it's selling for $5 a front-foot." They would have been rich if they had bought before the site values soared with the growth in urban population. *Urban sites with good locations earn rents in the same sense that fertile areas or those rich in natural resources do.* Many people began to wonder why lucky landowners should be permitted to keep these "unearned land increments."

Henry George, a printer who thought much about economics, crystallized these sentiments in the single-tax movement. This movement had a considerable following a century ago, and there are still some adherents to it in New Zealand, Denmark, and western Canada. It is not likely, however, that anyone running for public office on a single-tax platform will again come so close to being elected as George did in 1886, when he was almost elected mayor of New York City. Nor is it likely that anyone will soon come along and write so persuasive a bible for the movement as Henry George did in his *Progress and Poverty*, a book which sold millions of copies. Anyone who recommends that the *government* establish an urban-land bank to stop speculation and/or to capture the increase in land value is echoing George's platform. Britain may do it in the 1970s—she tried in 1945.

TAXING LAND'S UNEARNED SURPLUS

This is not the place to attempt any assessment of the merits and demerits of such a political movement. But one important principle of distribution and taxation can be illustrated by the valid central tenet of the movement:

Pure land rent is in the nature of a "surplus" which can be taxed heavily *without distorting production incentives or efficiency.*

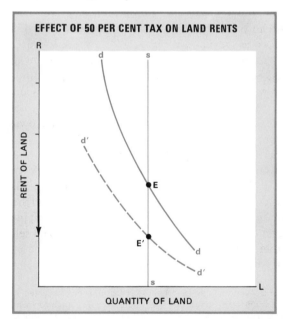

FIG. 28-3. Tax on fixed land is shifted back on landlords, skimming off pure economic rent.

A tax on fixed land leaves rentals paid by users unchanged at E but reduces rent retained by landowners to E'. (What can the landowners do but accept less return?) This provides the rationale for Henry George's single-tax movement.

[3] The Davenport verse opening this chapter hints at such a conclusion. To cover this case, economists use the technical expression "opportunity cost." (Recall Chapter 24's discussion around page 435.) To each owner of land, using it in his own business is wise only if its marginal product there will be sure to cover his "opportunity cost" or cost forgone in not selling it in the market for others to use. Similarly, a competitive industry can employ a factor only if its derived worth there measures at least up to the opportunity cost of using it elsewhere. In the terminology of Chapter 2's production-possibility frontier: The cost of guns is the forgone (or opportunity) cost of not producing butter even if every factor were in inelastic supply and earning price-determined or "residual" rents that are quite unnecessary to elicit their supply and effort.

Let us see why. Suppose that supply and demand create an equilibrium land rent, as in Fig. 28-3 at *E*. Now what would happen if we were to introduce a 50 per cent tax on all land rents? Mind you, we are not taxing buildings or improvements; for that certainly would affect the volume of construction activity. All we are supposed to be taxing is the yield of the *naturally fixed supply* of agricultural and urban land sites, assuming that this can somehow be identified.

There has been no shift in the total demand curve for land; firms are still willing to pay the same amount as before for the same amount of land. Hence, with land fixed in supply, the market price that they pay must still be at the old intersection *E*. Why? Because supply has not changed and neither has demand. Because at any higher price than before, some land would have to go without any demanders. Hence, competitive rents could not permanently be raised to land users.

Of course, what the farmer pays and what the landlord receives are now two quite different things. As far as the landlords are concerned, once the government steps in to take its cut of 50 per cent, the effect is just the same as if the *net* demand *to the owners* had shifted down from *dd* to *d'd'*. Landowners' equilibrium return *after taxes* is now only as high as *E'*, or only half as high as *E*. *The whole of the tax has been shifted backward onto the owners of the factor in inelastic supply!* The landowners will not like this. But under competition there is nothing they can do about it, since they cannot alter the total supply and the land must work for whatever it can get. Half a loaf is better than none, or even than one-fourth of a loaf.

ETHICAL ISSUES Whether or not it is a fair thing to take away part of the return of those who own land is quite another question. Perhaps many voters will feel that such owners are not less deserving than are investors who have put their money into other things; perhaps many will feel that no one should have the right to benefit from nature's windfall gifts of oil, minerals, or soil fertility.[4] But these are political questions that are not to be discussed at the present point. What is relevant is to point out

that a similar 50 per cent tax put upon a factor of production whose total supply is *not* completely inelastic would certainly produce definite effects on the factor-prices charged in a competitive market. To some extent this tax would distort the pattern of production, and it would shift part of the burden *forward* onto the users of the factor and onto consumers. Thus, if the same acre of land were to be taxed differently when used for wheat rather than for corn production, this would certainly have distorting effects on the price of wheat relative to that of corn.

Since production studies show that pure land rent typically would be barely 5 per cent of the total GNP, if Henry George were alive today and facing the need of government for more than 25 per cent of GNP, he would undoubtedly change the name of his movement from "the single tax" to "the useful tax on unearned land surplus."

SUPPLY AND DEMAND FOR ANY FACTOR

The competitive determination of land rent by supply and demand is only one instance of the general analysis applicable to *any* factor or production. How is the rental value per week of a tractor to be determined in a competitive market?

We first sum up the derived demands of all business firms for tractors. (Of course, these derived demands have behind them marginal-revenue-product considerations of the last chapter; but this behind-the-scenes relation need not concern the observer of the aggregate market demand for this factor.) Along with the *dd* curve shown in Fig. 28-4, we must also have a supply curve such as *ss*. But there is now no reason why the supply curve should be perfectly vertical. It may now be positively elastic, rising upward toward the northeast.

(EXAMPLE: The case of tractor supply, dependent on rising marginal costs of production.) Alternatively, if the factor of production were labor, it might be that people would feel they could afford to work *fewer* hours when wages rise, so that the *ss* curve might eventually bend backward and northwestward from the vertical, rather than rising forward.

---

[4] In most countries, the owner of land is not permitted to claim the full reward from lucky mineral discoveries on "his" terrain.

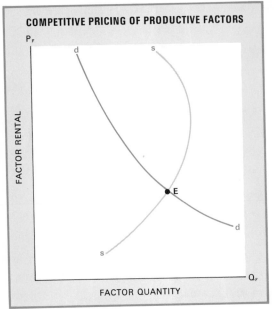

COMPETITIVE PRICING OF PRODUCTIVE FACTORS

FIG. 28-4. Factor supply and derived demand together determine factor prices and income distribution.
Land's share in national income rises when its rent is bid up. Skilled and unskilled labor shares are determined, in competitive markets, by interplay of factor supply and demand. The same would hold for any factor.

In any case, whether the supply curve is vertically inelastic, positively elastic, or negatively elastic, there will be an *ss* curve as in Fig. 28-4.

Where the derived demand curve for a factor intersects its supply curve, the final equilibrium factor-price will be set. And if the demand curve for the factor shifts upward, its market price will tend to rise; on the other hand, if the supply offered of any factor increases, so that the supply curve shifts rightward, then the factor-price will tend to fall.

In a competitive market economy, therefore, factor-prices and the distribution of income are not determined at random. There are definite forces of supply and demand operating to create high returns to scarce factors that are very useful in producing the things wanted by people with purchasing power. But any factor's earnings will tend to drop if more of it becomes available, or if other close substitutes for it are found, or if people stop wanting the goods that this factor is best suited to make. Competition gives, and competition takes.

FACTOR PRICING AND EFFICIENCY: RENT AND FACTOR-PRICES AS DEVICES TO RATION SCARCE RESOURCES

Competitive supply and demand helps determine the FOR WHOM problem of society. Whether or not we like its answer to this distribution question—and in the case of rent, Henry George certainly did not—we have to admit that it does contribute to an *efficient* solution of the HOW problem for society.

Thus, as a result of supply and demand in markets for goods and for factors, in North America where land is plentiful and labor scarce, we find extensive farming. In Europe or Asia, where people are plentiful relative to land, we find intensive agriculture.

Why? Because of government planning? No, not necessarily.

Rather it is the *signalling* of market pricing that results in efficient HOW. Land has to be auctioned off at a low price here; labor auctioned off at a high price here. So every farmer, seeking his Least-cost combination lest he go bankrupt, substitutes land for labor here. Contrariwise abroad, cheap labor gets substituted for land. (More than that: with labor scarce here, we find that fussy vegetables, which require much care, get priced relatively higher than those which lend themselves to extensive methods. So the resulting high commodity prices tend to make us *substitute the cheaper land-intensive goods* in our diet for the more expensive labor-intensive ones. Abroad the opposite commodity substitutions take place. Hence, the pricing system signals best commodity substitutions, as well as best factor substitutions!)

COMMON PROPERTY Thus, we see that charging rent has a function—even if you later tax part of it away. And we can now appreciate examples showing how troubles in the real world come from the fact that there is no way to charge the appropriate rents.

Item: The sea is free to all. So everyone fishes in it until the fish are all killed off or decimated. If society could somehow charge rents for commercial fishing licenses, we might in the long run all be better off—including fishermen! Refer to the discussion of external diseconomies in Chapter 24, and show that letting workers overrun Ontario farmland at zero rents would lower society's efficiency in using those acres.

Item: Our roads get very crowded on weekends and during rush hours. We usually cannot charge tolls or rents. If we could, we might coax shoppers and people who are on the margin of indifference to do their driving at some less crowded time.

Item: Even if policemen can inspect and make collections from parking meters at a cost which is a negligible fraction of the revenue collected by parking meters, it may be socially desirable to keep the tolls of such meters high enough to create a rational use of limited curb space.

What have these examples in common? A price is not charged for the factor land. Why? Because some acres of land are not owned by a "landlord" who could offer them at a price, but are either the *common property* of everyone, or from the point of view of law, not anyone's property. Such situations are exemplified by the common pasture land of feudal days.

Environmental problems and pollution are a modern case in point. Consider the person with a litter-disposal or waste-discharge problem. Perhaps he can deal with junkman, car wrecker or oil-products re-refiner. But if recycling or salvage is not profitable, he must look for land or water in which to dump his wastes. Some farmer may agree—at a price that reflects the competition between waste-dischargers and crops for the available acreage, to provide land for this purpose. Much cheaper, from the dischargers' point of view, is to dump the waste on common (usually Crown) land, in the river or sea, or send it in smoke up the chimney into the atmosphere.

The result is ecological and environmental damage. Economists agree that the lack of a price on land's *absorptive* or *receptive capacity* has had an inefficient outcome. They differ, however, in their policy recommendations. Some simply say that, if a price cannot be charged, other regulations must be used instead, such as today's controls imposed by governments on effluents. A second group argues that prices *ought* to be charged for the use of—that is, to ration—environmental receptive capacity; they support the idea of fees or charges on effluent flows. A third group goes farther and suggests ways in which private property rights to discharge effluents could be auctioned or leased to particular dischargers, just as land is now; they want to reduce the extent of

common property. A fourth group is neutral among these three proposals, saying that the best way out of the no-price, common-property pollution dilemma is a matter of the effectiveness and the administrative costs procedures in each particular case. (Surely they are right.)

Thus charging a rent can lead to efficient solutions to the HOW question. Increased realisation of this leads to a second level of inquiry: how much should the rent be? and, how can the resource be appropriated into property units for charging a rent or tax? But to conclude that charging rent or distributing property rights is efficient is not sufficient to justify proposed or existing institutions and property taxes. They may induce a distribution of rental income, or land ownership that may decrease or increase justice. Such conditions must be attacked or defended not from the HOW or efficiency point of view, but in terms of ethical value judgments concerning the proper FOR WHOM resolutions in society.

CONSERVATION AND LAND TENURE

Ricardo and Henry George emphasized the original, unaugmentable, and indestructible gift of Nature. Actually, much of the land we use *has* been augmented by man: it has been drained, filled, and fertilized by investment effort quite like that which builds machines and plants. Equally important, Nature's gifts *can* be destroyed. There are now deserts where green acres once flourished. There are used-up mines; deforested timber lands; eroded and depleted top-soils. Part of the rental element in the sale of Alberta oil is a return of capital for this exhaustible resource. More and more we must go to less accessible or lower-grade deposits for raw materials to feed our machines.

Not all exhaustion is undesirable; indeed it is an inevitable part of production. Mines must be emptied and forests cut to obtain metal and wood products, even when some re-cycling of materials is a technical possibility. It is even possible to argue that a rational program for mankind might involve centuries'-long using-up of the reproductive powers of farm fertility, fisheries' environments, forest sites and the like, instead of their conservation in their original state. More likely, an optimum program calls for some augmenting of these resources. In any case, the choices are always open, to every generation, to deplete, conserve, or renew.

Charging rents or royalties for these resources is a way of governing the rate of their use. Firms can compare today's and expected future rents in deciding when to exploit. Thus newly-expected future energy shortages may induce oil-land holders to raise the price they demand today, persuading energy consumers to turn to other sources or reduce consumption; and incidentally, reducing the expected future shortage. The opposite is also true: news of a break-through in nuclear fission, rendering petroleum obsolescent, can cause landlords to cut the rents charged for today's resources. Likewise, the royalties demanded by farmers and provinces for timber serve to spread out or concentrate the time-rate of cutting. In any case, the mere fact of using-up or exhausting a resource is not necessarily inefficient.

But in no-tenure, common-property systems, the self-interest of owners and tenants may well lead to the rapid using up of natural resources. No single person can reap rents by holding back. The result may be inefficient in two ways. First, the lack of a price, and the lack of property from which an owner could exclude users, will lead to using-up at a rate faster than *any* owner, tenant or user would choose. This is the fisheries, or gold-rush, case as first discussed in Chapter 21's Appendix. Second, the lack of a property or rights system that identifies landowners with a particular resource can lead to "external diseconomy" burdens on other people. These create a presumption toward public action, as outlined in the preceding section's discussion of pollution. The damage to others may be in many forms: unsightly slag heaps or open-pit mining dumps and cavities; local unemployment; soil and fisheries' damage from floods after deforestation.

With so many ways of killing off Nature and reviving her, "conservation" and "depletion" have become imprecise words. Economists are learning that it is no longer helpful to think of land as in fixed supply. Like machines and schools, it can be protected, adapted, preserved, worn-out, according to our decisions.

Efficiency calls for private or government decisions that do not treat land as free and without alternative uses. Whether this should be done by preservation policies, controlling present users, pricing use,

setting up special private property rights transferable in the marketplace, or government management as a social good, is now under debate. The choice is not between ideal perfect competition and public regimentation, but between alternative blends of imperfect *laissez-faire* and imperfect public coordination.

That is why we observe today's patchwork of land-law, public access, and restriction of private freedom to use land. One of the first tasks of government was to set up a system of private titles to land, so that it could be husbanded and transferred efficiently. Furthermore, they experimented with titles to fresh air, waste disposal, and access to wilderness. But governments also intervene in this age-old property system to limit private decisions. They make zoning restrictions and draw up regional and urban plans. They employ the right of expropriation, in which owners are made to sell their land at publicly determined prices. Parklands, owned by government, are used to create "external economies" and common consumption benefits. In Britain, Italy, France, Sweden, and elsewhere, limitations are put on the windfall capital gains that can be secured by those lucky enough to own farmland where a new city is to be located or those clever enough to speculate successfully on future developments.

CONCLUSIONS

The same general principles determining land rent also determine the prices of all inputs: capital goods, natural resources, or labor. Thus the rentals of threshing machines or of trucks are determined in essentially the same way. We might even go so far as to say that wages are the rentals paid for the use of a man's personal services for a day or a week or a year. This may seem a strange use of terms, but on second thought, one recognizes that every agreement to hire labor is really for some limited period of time. By outright purchase, you might avoid ever renting any kind of land. But in our society, labor is one of the few productive factors that cannot legally be bought outright. Labor can only be rented, and the wage rate is really a rental.

The next chapter deals with the peculiar problems of wages and labor markets. Chapter 30 will analyze the problems of capital and interest, which will be seen to be important in determining the supply of durable goods available for rental and use.

SUMMARY

1 Factor demand curves are derived from commodity demand curves. An upward shift in the latter causes a similar upward shift in the former; and inelasticity in commodity demand makes for inelasticity of derived factor demand.

2 We add up for all the firms their derived demands for a factor in order to get the aggregate demand curve. This, together with the specified supply curve of the factor, can be expected to determine an equilibrium intersection. At the equilibrium market price for the factor of production, the amounts demanded and supplied will be exactly equal—only there will factor-price have no tendency to change. Anywhere above the equilibrium price, suppliers will tend to undercut the market and to cause price to fall; anywhere below the equilibrium price, shortages will cause demanders to bid the price upward, restoring the equilibrium.

3 The unchangeable quantity of natural land is an interesting special case where the supply curve happens to be perfectly vertical and *inelastic*. In such a so-called *pure* rent case, competition will still determine an equilibrium market rental. But in this case, we are faced with a cost element that is more price-*determined* than price-*determining*; the land rent is more the result of the market prices for the finished commodities than their cause. (Yet we must not forget that, to any small firm, or to any industry too small to affect appreciably the total demand for land, rent will still seem to enter explicitly or implicitly into the cost of production just like any other expense. To such a small industry, rent reflects the opportunity cost of using land elsewhere and appears to be as much price-determining as any other cost element.)

From the standpoint of the community as a whole, the rent of an inelastically supplied factor will be reckoned in the GNP at its full dollar value, like anything else. But below the veil of money, it still remains true that this factor would be willing to work for less if it had to, and in that sense its return is in the nature of a "surplus" rather than in the nature of a reward necessary to coax out the factor supply. This provides the basis for Henry George's "single-tax" program, proposing to tax the unearned increment of land value—and without any shifting forward of the tax to the consumer or distorting effects on production.

4 Whatever some may feel about the ethical nicety of its answers to the FOR WHOM problem, proper factor pricing does under perfect competition contribute to efficient solution of society's HOW problem. Indeed, *not charging rents*, or otherwise interfering with the *pricing* of factors of production may cause inefficient overcrowding and bad choice of use in many situations.

But market efficiency is only one of society's aims. Land use is so fraught with "neighborhood and externality effects," that society interferes with market processes by zoning and other land-use controls. Pollution, depletion of exhaustible resources, distorting forms of land tenure, and destruction of the natural environment are also special problems calling for special examination. Furthermore, market efficiency may clash with ethical ideals of distributional fairness; then each society must choose its own mixture of efficiency and equity.

5 The general principles of supply and demand can also be used to explain the competitive price determination of all services other than those of land. In common everyday usage, we speak of rent or rental as the price paid for the use of any factor input, whether the factor's supply curve is inelastic or not. The rental of all inputs—including the wages that have to be paid for the use of the services of human beings and the rentals of durable machines—is determined in a competitive system by supply and demand.

CONCEPTS FOR REVIEW

derived demand
inelastic supply of God-given land,
    pure rent
society's rent as firm's cost
single tax, backward shifting of land
    tax, unearned increment
price-*determined* expense versus
    price-*determining* expense

supply-and-demand equilibrium
factor-price equilibrium
price signaling of efficient factor and
    commodity substitutions
HOW, FOR WHOM, and rents
resource exhaustibility and conservation
market versus ethical determination of
    land use and income distribution

QUESTIONS FOR DISCUSSION

1. Define the "pure rent" case. Explain the sense in which price of such a factor is "price-*determined*" rather than "price-*determining*." Show that, nonetheless, an increase in supply of the rent-earning factor will depress its return and lower prices of goods that use it much.

2. What was the Henry George single-tax movement all about? Use a diagram to show the effect of taxing "pure rent." (Apply this to a hockey players inelastic supply. Consider the expansion teams in hockey: was the supply of players really inelastic? Explain why Alfred Marshall used the term "quasi-rent" to describe the rent going to factors that were more elastically supplied in the long run than in the short run.)

3. Discuss why it might avoid confusion if you reserved the word "rent" for the strong case of inelastically supplied factors and used "rentals" for the more general case.

4. North America is now faced with problems of air and water pollution. The motorist and industry are probably the prime causes. What interferences with freedom will preventive measures require?

5. Are rents always "unearned"? Discuss the case of gains made by the CPR and others on land grants adjoining their railways.

6. *Extra credit problem:* See if you can puzzle out how economists define "producer's surplus (or rent)" in close analogy to Chapter 22's "consumer's surplus (or rent)." The accompanying diagram shows two industries, corn and wine. Each is produced by transferable labor, which must work with cornland or vineyard land, no land being transferable between industries. Each diagram is like Fig. 23-7(b). Labor-leisure is assumed to have strictly constant marginal utility in the background: each S_iS_i' curve rises because transferred varying labor encounters diminishing returns on fixed specialized land. Each D_iD' curve falls for

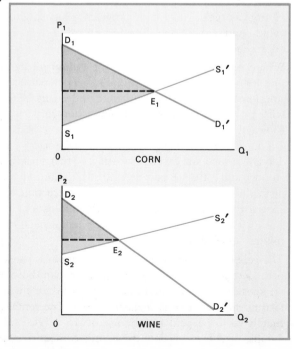

the usual declining marginal-utility reasons. Note the grey-shaded-areas of consumer's surplus, much as in Fig. 22-4. But now note that the light red-shaded areas can be thought of as representing producer's surplus or rent. Thus, the second diagram shows less-diminishing returns and hence less-rising rent to vineyard land. If vineyard land were superabundant and therefore free, the supply curve there would be horizontal and there would then be only grey consumer's surplus with no light red producer's surplus there at all.

29
COMPETITIVE WAGES AND COLLECTIVE BARGAINING

The laborer is worthy of his hire. **NEW TESTAMENT**

A man is much more than a commodity. Yet it is true that men do rent out their services for a price. This price is the wage rate, and of all prices it is by far the most important.

What is supposed to determine the general wage rate under competitive conditions? This is the first problem we shall tackle, in Section A below. Then, in Section B, we shall investigate the effect of deviations from competitive conditions. Developing further the problems introduced in Chapter 7, we shall analyze the economics of collective bargaining between trade-unions and employers.

A. THE DETERMINATION OF THE GENERAL WAGE UNDER COMPETITION

Wage rates differ enormously. The average wage is as hard to define as the average man. An auto executive may earn $500,000 a year at the same time that a clerk earns $10,000 and a farm hand $6,000. In the same factory, a skilled machinist may earn $250 a week, while an unskilled man gets $150. Experienced

FIG. 29-1. Favorable resources and technology explain high Canadian wages:
Supply and demand determine a higher competitive wage in Canada than in Europe.

women may be paid $150 a week at the same time their younger brothers are starting at $160. Part of any theory of wages must explain these differentials.

But important as these wage *differences* are, we must not overlook the general wage *level*. Wages of virtually every category of labor are higher than they used to be half a century ago. Wages are higher in North America than for similar categories in Europe; higher in Sweden than in Italy; higher in northern than in southern Italy; higher in Europe than in Asia; higher in some subsistence economies than in others. Economics aims to provide understanding of such basic facts.

REAL WAGE DETERMINATION FOR A SINGLE GRADE

Let us begin by examining the simplified case of wages paid for similar jobs to laborers who are all exactly alike in skill, effort, and every other respect. Then competition will cause their wage rates per hour to be exactly equal. No employer would pay more for the work of one man than he would pay for his identical twin, and no worker would be able to ask more for his services.

How is this single market wage determined? If we know the supply and demand curves for these laborers—as in Fig. 29-1(a)—then the competitive equilibrium wage must be at E_c the intersection point. If the wage rate were lower, spirited bidding by frustrated employers would restore the equilibrium.

We are interested in *real wages*—in what the wage will buy—and not just in the money wage. Therefore, in our illustrations, we express wages in money units whose purchasing power over goods is held constant at the level of some particular year and place, e.g., in terms of Canadian dollars of 1975 purchasing power. By definition, an index of the real wage represents an index of actual money wages deflated (or divided) by an index of the price level. (EXAMPLE: Between 1968 and 1973 money wage rates increased by 46 per cent; however since prices increased 27 per cent in that period, real wages increased by only 15 per cent (1.46/1.27 = 1.15).

Imagine that, in comparison with Europe, Canada is typical of North America as a whole. Imagine further that Fig. 29-1(a) represents the state of affairs

in North America and Fig. 29-1(b) that in Europe. Why are wages so much higher in North America than in Europe? Is it because we have unions and they do not? Or because we have passed higher minimum-wage laws than they? Experts doubt that these factors can explain the difference. In any case, such factors have been ruled out in our simplified competitive case. A true answer would be:

Supply and demand are such in North America, compared with Europe, as to lead to a higher real wage here.

But *why* are supply and demand such as to lead to high North American wages? What lies behind these schedules? Why is labor's productivity (its marginal product) so high here? Why do competing employers who ruthlessly seek to maximize their profits find themselves, in North America, bidding real wages up so high?

RESOURCES, CAPITAL, AND TECHNOLOGY

In the first place we recall that the derived demand schedules for labor slope downward. Applied to page *492*'s *aggregate* production function for all of North America, the law of diminishing returns suggests that adding more and more labor to the same North American natural resources and land area will tend to diminish labor's marginal productivity, wages, and per capita (average) productivity. Suppose you let North American population increase so as to shift the supply curve *ss* far to the right in Fig. 29-1(a). Then the wage might fall to the European level or even lower.

One important explanation of high wages throughout North America, therefore, lies in the sphere of economic geography:

Compared with the size of its working population, North America is generously supplied with land, fuels, forests, minerals, and water power.

The per capita supplies of these vital sinews of modern industrial production are less in Europe and still less in many other regions. What resources we do not possess in abundance, we have been able to trade for.

But economic geography does not tell the whole story. Two regions may be exactly alike in endowment of natural resources; but if one uses superior technological methods, its productivity and real wages may be much higher than the other's (compare Denmark and Crete; or Hong Kong and Calcutta; or Connecticut and Mississippi). In part, using superior technological methods involves better know-how, better applied science, better economic laws and customs, better management, more highly skilled and educated people, and better work methods; in part, it involves relative abundance of capital goods—of man-made machinery, fabricated materials, and industrial plants.

These explanations of higher costs may be envisaged also as explanations of each place's position on the long-run envelope curve introduced in Fig. 23-4. Consider Canada and the U.S. Canadian costs are higher and wages are lower. Why? Because small markets for each firm find Canada placed high on the left part of this curve, while the U.S. is down near point *M*. How can Canada improve its costs and labor productivity? This is obviously a question of a choice among three policies: fewer firms, more access to U.S. customers (free trade), or more Canadians (immigration). (Recent analysis by J. H. Young, S. Star and others suggests that immigration at recent rates would take decades, perhaps centuries, to reduce the gap between Canada and the U.S.). Canadian economists have been accustomed to describe all this as the high cost of running a small-scale economy. The high cost can be expressed also as a lower wage rate.

Just why North America developed a superiority in know-how and capital availability is not well understood by economic historians. Our lead is beginning to narrow, as all countries acquire the same know-how and capital investment. But the truth of this superiority is not in doubt.

IMMIGRATION AND RESTRICTIONS OF LABOR SUPPLY

This raises the question, Why don't Europeans and Asians move from their low-wage area to our higher-wage area? People *did* migrate to this country in great numbers, especially between 1880 and 1890, and between 1900 and 1930. A few came to seek religious freedom, many came as political refugees, but by far the greatest number came to better their economic condition.

In Canada and the United States, laws have been passed limiting immigration. Some Europeans are welcome, but others, and non-white people, are less so. [1] This is a first example of interference with free play of competition in the wage market. By keeping labor supply down, a restrictive immigration policy tends to keep wages high. Let us underline this basic principle:

Limitation of the supply of any grade of labor relative to all other productive factors can be expected to raise its wage rate; an increase in supply will, other things being equal, tend to depress wage rates.

The law of diminishing returns makes it easy to understand why medical associations and trade-unions have favored restrictions on immigration. The same analysis helps to explain why unions have pressed for (1) a shorter and shorter working week and more days of vacation per year; (2) restrictions on child labor, encouragement of early old-age retirement; and exclusion of women from some areas of labor; and (3) restrictions on degree of effort and speed-ups. The old labor jingle

    Whether you work by the week or the day,

    The shorter the work the better the pay.

expresses the hope that workers can travel upward on the demand curve for labor.

THEORY OF THE OPTIMUM POPULATION

At this point we must be careful not to overstate the law of aggregate diminishing marginal (and per capita) returns. Working against it, for a range at least, is a counterlaw: *the law of specialization, of increasing returns to scale, or of economies of mass production.*

One of the reasons the United States is so prosperous is that it is so *large* a free-trade area. Modern technology increasingly requires larger and larger

---

[1] In 1967, Canada adopted the point or assessment system for potential immigrants. Under this system, admission of immigrants became based upon such factors as education and training, occupational skill, and occupational demand; rather than on race or color. However, it still has the effect of discriminating against certain nationalities and racial groups.

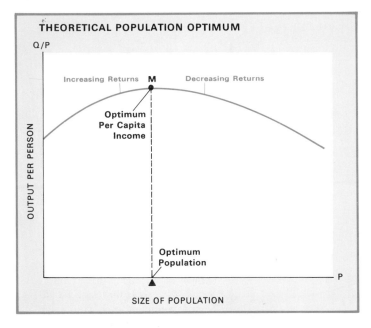

FIG. 29-2. Per capita incomes average out highest at population not too large or small.

At the point where decreasing per capita returns begins, output per person is at its very highest.[3] Unfortunately, economists are unable to estimate just where the optimum is for a modern nation. (Warning: Since total output does not get divided equally between labor and property owners, any optimum must take into account the distribution of the social pie.)

plants: unless you can produce a thousand electric refrigerators per day, you will not realize the full economies of large-scale mass production. Before the Common Market brought down trade barriers in Europe, a small country found it difficult to have an efficient domestic industry unless it could use its colonies to augment its limited domestic market.

This raises a question: Would the huge American economy be better off in the 1970s if its population were cut by one-half? If you apply the law of diminishing returns uncritically, the answer is, Yes. But in view of the counterlaw of increasing returns, the answer is in doubt.

This discussion suggests a rather interesting theory of population. Why not have the best of both situations? Why not take advantage of increasing returns per capita as well as of diminishing returns? Specifically, why not aim at letting population grow up to the exact point where increasing returns end and decreasing returns begin? This point will give the highest level of real wages or real incomes, and is called the "optimum population." Figure 29-2 illustrates how the optimum is defined at the very top of the productivity curve.[2]

THE IRON LAW OF WAGES: MALTHUS AND MARX

In Chapter 2, we encountered the Malthusian theory of population, and we shall meet it again in Part Six. According to this theory, you should draw in on Fig. 29-1(a) a *horizontal* long-run supply curve of labor. This should be drawn in at the wage level corresponding to the lowest standard of living at which people will just reproduce their numbers. A century and a half ago, economics was called "the dismal science" because many classical economists believed wages tended toward the bare minimum of subsistence. Our survey of rising living standards and growing populations showed how unrealistic for the West is the notion of a bare-minimum long-run supply curve of labor, and how misleading it would be as a basis for any long-term "laws of motion of the capitalist system."

A quite different version of the iron law of wages are provided by Karl Marx. He put great emphasis upon the "reserve army of the unemployed." In effect, employers were supposed to lead their workers to the factory windows and point to the unemployed

---

[2] Figure 29-2 plots *average* rather than *marginal* product: i.e. total NNP ÷ people

[3] This increase and then decrease in output per person was first discussed in Chapter 2. See page 22.

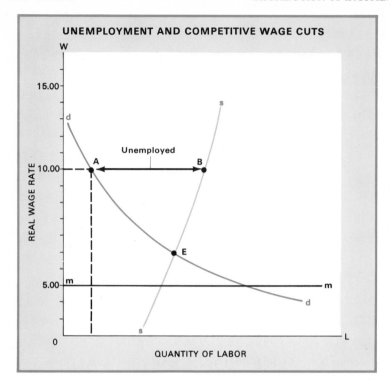

FIG. 29-3. Marxians exaggerated power of "reserve army of unemployed" to depress wages.

The "reserve army of the unemployed"—as shown by *AB*—is not able to depress real wages to the *mm* "minimum-subsistence" level. It can only depress competitive wages from *A* to *E*. If labor supply became so abundant that *ss* intersected *dd* at *mm* the wage would be at a minimum level, as in many underdeveloped regions; but institutional or legal changes can do little when marginal productivity remains abysmally low.

workers out at the factory gates, eager to work for less. This, Marx thought (or is interpreted by naïve Marxists to have thought), would depress wages to the subsistence level.

Let us try to show this on our diagrams. Figure 29-1(a) is redrawn as Fig. 29-3. Suppose that the wage is at $10.00 per hour in 1975 prices. Employment is at the level indicated by the point *A*. At this high wage, there would indeed be unemployment, as alleged. The amount of unemployment would be represented by the distance between the labor supplied and demanded *AB*. In our simple, idealized model of competition, such unemployment could certainly be expected to put downward pressure on wages.

But does the basic Marxian conclusion follow? Is there any tendency for real wage rates to fall to a *minimum subsistence level* such as *mm* in Fig. 29-3? None at all. There is absolutely no reason why in our simple model, real wage rates should ever fall below the equilibrium level at *E*. In a country well-endowed with capital and natural resources, this competitively determined equilibrium wage might be a very comfortable one indeed. Only in a less fortunate country should we expect it to be anywhere near as low as the minimum of subsistence. Thus we reach an important principle:

If competition in the labor market were really perfect, there would be no necessary tendency in an advanced country for wages to fall to any minimum-subsistence level.

Employers might prefer to pay low wages. But that would not matter. In a competitive market they are unable to set wage rates as they would *like*. As long as employers are numerous and do not act in collusion, their demands for any grade of labor will bid its wage up to equilibrium level at which the total forthcoming labor supply is absorbed. The workers may aspire to still higher wages, but under competition they do not get what they would *like* either; as long as they do not act collusively to limit the labor supply, their wishes will not serve to make wages rise above the competitive level.

LUMP-OF-LABOR FALLACY AND THE THIRTY-HOUR WEEK

It would be wrong to think that diminishing returns alone explains why unions pursue policies to restrict labor and effort. There is a related and still more powerful reason why workers fight for shorter hours. They fear unemployment; they tend to think the *total amount of work to be done is constant* in the short run. So what happens if a foreigner is put to work? Or a woman comes into the labor market? Or an old man refuses to retire? Or a fellow worker works too efficiently? Or a machine replaces a man? Or men work overtime? Each of these looms up as threat to a worker's job and livelihood.

This attitude, that there is only a fixed amount of work to be done, is sometimes called by economists the "lump-of-labor fallacy." We must give this notion its due. To a particular group of workers, with special skills and status and stuck in one region, the introduction of technological change may represent a real threat. Viewed from their personal standpoint, the lump-of-labor notion may not be so fallacious.

True enough, in a great depression, when there is mass and chronic unemployment, one can understand how workers generally may yield to lump-of-labor philosophy. But the lump-of-labor argument implies that there is only so much useful remunerative work to be done in any economic system, *and that is indeed a fallacy.*

If proper monetary, fiscal, and pricing policies are being vigorously promulgated, we need not resign ourselves to mass unemployment. Though technological unemployment can't be shrugged off lightly, its optimal solution lies in combining expansionary macroeconomic programs (fiscal and monetary policies) with retraining policies that create adequate job opportunities and new skills, rather than in restrictions on production.

There are, of course, still other arguments for or against cutting standard working hours from, say, 40 per week to 30. As our standards of living and productivity rise, it is only natural that we should feel we can afford more leisure. Historically, working hours have been progressively shortened, as we have already seen. Saturday work will no doubt become rare

as it already is in Australia and New Zealand. Probably there will be a trend toward increased vacations with pay—not so much because the vacation will improve workers' productivity as that people get enjoyment from summer and winter vacations. Taking more time off will probably be one of the ways in which we shall choose to enjoy the fruits of technological progress. No doubt, too, our grandchildren will choose to work a still shorter week; but that should reflect choice, not necessity.

Still, at this stage of history would workers really wish to purchase 10 extra hours of leisure per week if this meant forgoing a sizable fraction of real and money income—say, 20 per cent of what potentially might be earned? One wonders. As our economy approached full employment in the 1960s, agitation for the 30-hour week declined. This suggests that the unemployment rather than the leisure argument really carried most weight. Moreover, when a union leader favors a shorter week, he at the same time asks that there be no cut in take-home pay. What worker could be against a free present of more leisure? A few pages later we shall investigate the degree to which unions can squeeze higher wages out of employers. But there is little doubt that drastic shortening of hours would imply lower real earnings than a full-employment economy is capable of providing.

FOUR-DAY WEEK In the early 1970s, a number of firms began to experiment with a 4-day, 10-hours-per-day workweek. Since this still leaves the total workweek at 40 hours, it shouldn't be confused with a movement toward fewer hours at the same pay.

What are the advantages of this 4-day week? Usually it means the weekend begins on Friday or ends Monday night. It involves one less round trip of commuting. Employed wives and mothers particularly like it, since it gives them better chances to shop. For the employer, it may mean happier workers, and a gimmick to attract more recruits for employment. It also can mean less turnover time. (Two shifts instead of three may become feasible if one is 10 hours.) Better work scheduling may be possible. (A paint factory finds 4 cycles per day 4 days a week is better than 3 cycles 5 days a week. When all phone calls *within* an insurance company are banned from 8 to 9 A.M., efficiency leaps as each person catches up on schedule and planning.)

The 4-day week has disadvantages. That tenth hour can be tiresome—and inefficient. Car pools may be disrupted. Some people dislike leisure around the house.

In summary: The 4-day week is no panacea for labor relations. It will grow (and occasionally be abandoned). Perhaps its big importance is to facilitate the evolution toward a *shorter* workweek. (Only this feature, generally, appeals to the unions.)

GENERAL SUPPLY CURVE OF LABOR

Return now to the case of perfect competition. What is the supply curve of labor like? How does the wage rate affect population? How does the wage rate affect people's desire for a longer or shorter average working day? Influence the number of people *not* in the labor force (age of retirement, years of schooling, and women workers)? Will higher wages motivate people to work more effectively or make them feel they can afford to relax?

These questions show that the supply of labor involves at least four dimensions: (1) population, (2) proportion of the population actually in the labor force, (3) average number of hours worked per week or year by workers, and (4) quality and quantity of effort and skill that workers provide.

These four labor-supply dimensions all depend on sociological as well as economic forces.[4] The third, though, is of particular economic interest.

"SUBSTITUTION-EFFECT" VERSUS "INCOME-EFFECT" What effect will wage rates have on the number of hours worked per year? We have already touched on this earlier. A diagram may help

---

[4] The labor force sometimes tends to grow in deep depression: when a husband is thrown out of work, his wife and children may seek jobs. Tending to cancel this is the fact that women and other workers are, under prosperous conditions, attracted into jobs by plentiful employment opportunities. The labor force grew less from 1957 to 1967 than demographers had expected: apparently the high level of unemployment discouraged new entrants. When full employment finally reappeared, new entrants were coaxed back; U.S. experts estimate that every time aggregate demand policies create 10 new jobs, 3 additional persons will enter the labor market.

Unemployment also deters inter-regional migration in search of a job. See recent research by Vanderkamp, and particularly T. Courchene, *Migration, Income, and Employment: Canada, 1965-68*, C. D. Howe Research Insitute, [n.p.], 1974.

BACKWARD-BENDING SUPPLY CURVE

FIG. 29-4. At a high enough wage we can afford to work less:

Above the critical point *c*, raising the wage rate reduces amount of labor supplied. (Income-effect overcomes substitution-effect: at higher income, one feels he can afford more leisure even though each extra hour of leisure is costing him more than before.)

to make the issues clear. Figure 29-4 on this page shows the supply curve of total hours that a group of people will want to work at each different wage. Note how the supply curve rises at first in a northeasterly direction; then at the critical point *c*, it begins to bend back in a northwesterly direction. How can we explain why higher wages may either *increase* or *decrease* the quantity of labor supplied?

Put yourself in the shoes of a worker who has just been offered higher hourly rates and is free to choose the number of hours worked. You are torn two different ways: On the one hand, you are tempted to work some extra hours because now *each hour of work is better paid*. Each hour of leisure has become more expensive—hence you are tempted to *substitute* extra work for leisure. But working against this so-called "substitution-effect" is an opposing "income-effect."[5] With the wage rate higher, you are, in effect, *a richer man*. Being richer, you will want to

---

[5] See Chapter 21 for a discussion of "substitution-effects" and "income-effect" in connection with consumption. The income-effect of a wage increase is defined as its tendency to make you feel richer and able to afford more pleasurable leisure. Its substitution-effect is its tendency to make you want to react to the

buy more clothes, more insurance, better food, and more of other consumer goods. But most important for the present problem, *you will tend also to buy more leisure!* Now you can afford to take Saturday off, have a week's vacation in the winter or an extra week in the summer.

Which will be more powerful, the substitution-effect or the income-effect? Or will they just balance each other and cancel each other out—so that the supply curve neither rises forward nor bends backward, but rises perfectly vertically and inelastically? There is no one answer. It depends upon the individual. In Fig. 29-4, from s' to c the substitution-effect outweighed the income-effect. But from c to s'', the income-effect was the more important.[6]

RENT ELEMENTS IN WAGES OF UNIQUE INDIVIDUALS

Generally, one could expect that, after people receive a comfortable margin over what they consider to be conventionally necessary, further increases in wage will not bring forth further hours of work. This was tested by a tax lawyer who studied his professional and business friends in New York City to learn the effect on them of heavy graduated taxes. Somewhat

to his surprise, he discovered that taxes seemed to make them work harder so as to maintain their previous standards of living. Apparently, the short-run income-effect of reduced after-tax wages was more powerful than the substitution-effect. But probably most powerful were their nonmoney drives—desire for achievement and liking for their work. A Harvard Business School study gathered similar evidence, as did a study of English accountants and solicitors.

As we shall see in Chapter 31 on profits, the most harmful effects on incentives of our increasingly high tax rates seem to involve risk taking and venture capital rather than any connection with the supply of effort by gifted people. Most of the high earnings of outstanding individuals can probably be classified as "pure economic rent." Babe Ruth earned $100,000 a year playing baseball, something he liked to do anyway. Outside the field of sports it is doubtful if he could have counted on earning more than, say, $5,000 a year. Between these two limits his supply curve was almost completely *inelastic*, and so economists can term the excess of his income above the alternative wage he could have earned elsewhere *a pure rent*, logically like the rent to nature's fixed supply of land as discussed in the last chapter.

B. COMPETITIVE WAGE PATTERNS

Let us now turn from the supply of labor in general to investigate the vital problem of *differentials* between the competitive wage paid in each category

of job. The next few sections discuss why supply and demand curves for different occupations intersect at different wage levels. The resulting pattern of wages is referred to often as the "wage structure."

EQUALIZING DIFFERENCES

When you look more closely at the differences among jobs, some of the observed pay differentials are easily explained.

Jobs may differ in their unpleasantness; hence wages may have to be raised to coax people into the less attractive jobs. Such wage differentials that simply serve to *compensate for the nonmoney differences among jobs* are called "equalizing differences."

Steel erectors must be paid more than janitors be-

higher price of leisure—higher because of the higher hourly wage you now forgo to get each hour of leisure—by substituting for leisure the new goods your higher pay will buy. These two effects of a wage change oppose each other; when the income-effect wins, labor's supply curve bends back. (Recall Fig. 19-13).

[6]On the hypothesis that the substitution-effect is most powerful, we would expect that taxes on wage income would cut labor supply. The verification of the hypothesis is important for tax, wage, and welfare assistance policies. What are the findings? Chaterjee and Robinson, surveying 369 Ontario taxpayers, found no important tax effects on work effort. (See A. Chaterjee and J. Robinson, "Effects of Personal Income Tax on Work Effort: A Sample Survey," *Canadian Tax Journal*, May-June, 1969.) Fields and Stanbury found that even many heavily taxed lawyers and accountants in England seem insensitive to tax burdens. (See D. Fields and W. Stanbury, "Incentives, Disincentives and the Income Tax: Further Empirical Evidence," *Public Finance*, No. 3, 1970. See this paper also for references to an extensive literature stemming from pioneering studies by G. F. Break.)

cause people do not like the risks of balancing aloft. Workers often receive 5 per cent extra pay on the 4 p.m. to 12 p.m. "swing shift" and 10 per cent extra for the 12 midnight to 8 a.m. "graveyard shift." For hours beyond 40 per week or for holiday and weekend work, 1 1/2 times the base hourly pay is customary.

And when you observe a doctor who earns $60,000 a year, you must remember that at least a part of this is an equalizing difference needed to induce people to incur tuition costs and endure the lack of pay during training. Similarly, a man who now earns more in Ontario than he did in Nova Scotia had to be induced to cut his home ties and to pay for the move to a different province.

Consider a group of absolutely identical people. Each person's job choice may be considered as that person's choice among the *supply* curves of labor for different jobs. Each person will "offer labor" to an occupation at a price that reflects personal judgment about the attractiveness of the work. Jobs that involve dirt, strain, unwelcome responsibility, tedium, low status, frequent layoffs, danger, a short career will be the least attractive. Less labor will be offered at each wage than in pleasant or attractive occupations open to the same people. Hence the wages will be bid up to a higher level in the unattractive jobs; and workers in the pleasant occupations find their remuneration bid down by numerous applicants. Thus white-collar and clerical workers are often paid less than for blue-collar jobs.

To test whether a given difference between wage rates is an equalizing one, you must find people who are well qualified for *both* jobs. If they tell you that they would take the higher-paying job in preference to the lower, then the pay difference is *not* equalizing. It must be due to the causes outlined in the next section.

Differences in training are important here. Many jobs require years of education and on-the-job training. Some of this training may be interesting and pleasant in itself. But much of it is dull and it is costly: it absorbs time and resources that would have a high value elsewhere. The prospect of this costly training deters people from entering such occupations. This gives rise to an equalizing pay differential, large enough to coax new entrants to make the required "investment" in themselves.

NONEQUALIZING DIFFERENTIALS: DIFFERENCES IN LABOR QUALITY

If all labor were homogeneous, we have seen that every observed competitive wage differential could be explained as an equalizing difference. But turn to the real world. True, some of the observed differentials can be regarded as equalizing. Yet everyone knows that the vast majority of higher-paid jobs are also *more pleasant*, rather than less pleasant. Most wage differentials cannot therefore be of the equalizing type. What, then causes them?

Are they perhaps due to the fact that competition is imperfect? Undoubtedly, some observed differentials are of this type. Studies show that workers do not have anything like perfect knowledge of job opportunities. Trade-unions or minimum-wage laws or a monopoly by the workers in a particular occupation can also explain part of the existing nonequalizing differentials. If you removed these obstructions due to monopolistic or imperfect competition, enough people would flow into some of the higher-paid jobs to bring pay in these jobs into equality with that prevailing elsewhere. We shall analyze these interferences with competition in a moment. But never forget that many of the observed differentials in wages have little to do with the imperfections of competition; they would still persist if there were no monopoly elements.

Even in a hypothetically perfect auction market, where all the different catgories of labor were priced by supply and demand, equilibrium would necessitate tremendous differentials in wages.

This is because of the tremendous *qualitative* differentials among people—traceable to differences in environmental opportunity that go back to early life and to other individual differences—all of which lead to competitive wage differentials.

No one expects the competitive wage of a man to be the same as that of a horse. Then why expect one man to receive the same competitive wage as another man or woman? A zoologist may call us all members of the same *Homo sapiens* species, but any personnel officer who is trying to equalize the marginal-physical-product-per-dollar expended in every direction knows that people vary much in their abilities and contributions to his firm's dollar revenue.

There are more than 8 million people in our labor force. There is no single factor of production called labor; there are thousands of quite different kinds of labor. Yet, if you are hiring men to shovel railroad trains out of a blizzard, it will probably pay you to lump together as one indistinguishable factor of production all adult males of certain ages who appear to be reasonably healthy, muscular, and sober.

Thus, the labor market will always group people into certain general classifications for purposes of wage determination. But even after arbitrary (and often bigoted) groupings are made, many distinguishable categories of labor remain, with wide dispersion of pay.

"NONCOMPETING GROUPS IN THE LABOR MARKET"

A century ago, economists began to call these different categories of labor "noncompeting groups in the labor market." Instead of being a single factor of production, labor was recognized to be many different factors. Economists expected that as many different wage rates would result as there were noncompeting groups. Their instinct was sound, but there is some danger of misunderstanding their terminology.

In the first place, we must not think that in a perfectly competitive labor market the so-called "noncompeting groups" would disappear. We should still have different categories of labor—just as the near-perfect wheat market has winter wheat, spring wheat, grade 2 red wheat, etc. Second, no one can doubt that these different groups are in some sense competing with each other. Just as I decide between hiring a horse and a tractor, so must I decide between hiring a very skilled, fast-working, high-paid worker and a lower-paid, less skilled one (or more than one).

The essential point, then, is this: The different categories compete with each other; yet they are not 100 per cent identical. They are *partial rather than perfect substitutes.*

Workers can to some degree cross over from one category into another. If welders' wages were to become $100,000 a year, I might study the art and stop being a teacher. Or if I did not, others would. Therefore, even when the wages of the different categories of labor are different, quantitative wage differences

are still subject to the laws of supply and demand. "Cross elasticity" of supply becomes very important: The wage you must pay to recruit foundrymen depends on what the nearby auto plant is paying men on the assembly line.

Or take the case of skilled surgeons. In all countries, they receive high pay compared with butchers. Why? Because their work is important? Only in part on this account. For suppose that (1) every year as many babies were born with the capacity necessary for a surgeon as with the capacity necessary for a butcher, (2) we knew how to train surgeons in no time at all, and (3) a surgeon's activities and responsbilities were not regarded as less pleasant or more taxing than those of a butcher. Then do you really think that surgeons would continue to receive higher earnings than butchers? And if you think the sanctity of human life is the key explanation, how do you account for the fact that plastic surgeons are often more highly paid than heart surgeons?

GENERAL EQUILIBRIUM OF LABOR MARKET

In real life as we know it, distinctions are not absolute. There is some mobility between different jobs; differences in wages will tend gradually over a long period of time to encourage greater and greater mobility; nor is it necessary for all workers to be mobile —a few movers are enough.

But there will still remain certain permanent barriers to mobility that depend upon the irreducible differences in biological and social inheritance. Hence, wage differentials will persist even in the long run—unless offset by social policy.

Do these cases suggest that in the long run, all wage rates, and salaries, will be the same? That no wage differential could persist because mobility between jobs and markets would iron it out?

The answer is, maybe. There are certain permanent barriers to the required mobility. These may perpetuate pay differences. First, lack of information. People who don't know about better pay can't move to get it. Because information is costly, enough people may never move to remove the differential.

Second, jobs differ in the required training. The more dull, costly and special the training involved, the fewer the applicants, and the higher the pay.

Competitive Wage Determination	
SITUATION	RESULT
1. People all alike—jobs all alike.	No differentials.
2. People all alike—some jobs differ in disutility.	Equalizing wage differentials.
3. People differ, but each type of labor is in unchangeable supply ("noncompeting groups").	Wage differentials that are "pure economic rents" or "surplus."
4. People differ, but there is some mobility between groups ("partially competing groups"; "cross elasticity" important).	General equilibrium pattern of wage differentials as determined by general demand and supply (includes 1-3 as special cases).

TABLE 29-1. Competitive wage structure shows great variety of patterns.

Third, differences in biological inheritance lead to unequal entry among occupations. Deafness, tallness, IQ, dexterity may all be factors here.

Fourth, social inheritance. Background and upbringing may continue to disqualify some people from training and jobs. (This is a *supply* barrier. On the demand side, bigoted and ignorant employers may reject workers on ethnic, sex or age grounds, except at a lower wage.)

These are formidable barriers. Some of them may be removed, eventually, by social policy and general education. But some will persist even in the long run.

How big will these differentials be? Suppose we made it easy for people to get the education they are fitted for and to travel from one region to another where their skills can be better used. And suppose we provided people with the best possible information about job opportunities and about their personal potentialities. Then differentials would be much reduced. But for such differentials as remain, how exactly are they determined? The answer is provided by supply and demand.

The market will tend toward that equilibrium pattern of wage differentials at which the total demand for each category of labor exactly matches its competitive supply. Only then will there be general equilibrium with no tendency for further widening or narrowing of wage differentials. Table 29-1 sums up our conclusions.

C.   IMPERFECTIONS OF THE LABOR MARKET AND COLLECTIVE BARGAINING

Real-world labor markets are far removed from the ideal model of perfect competition. You can grade wheat into neat market categories, but you cannot do that with human beings. No auctioneer allocates workers to the highest bidders. Area studies show that workers often have only the most imperfect knowledge of nearby job opportunities and wage rates.

WAGE STICKINESS Two tests indicate that the labor market is imperfect. When there is a considerable increase in unemployment—as in sluggish 1970—do wage rates drop as they would in a competitive market? History answers, No.

You may be every bit as capable as someone who has a job, and yet there is no way that you can take his job away by underbidding him. Just imagine going to Ford or any large corporation when the next depression comes, brandishing your degrees and certificates of IQ and excellence, and offering to work for less than they are paying. Could you get a job that way?

WAGE POLICY OF FIRMS The fact that a firm of any size *must* have a wage policy is additional evidence of labor market imperfections. In a perfectly competitive market, a firm need not make decisions on its pay schedules; instead it would turn to the morning newspaper to learn what its wage policy would *have* to be. Any firm, by raising wages ever so little, could get all the extra help it wanted. If, on the other hand, it cut the wage ever so little, it would find no labor to hire at all in a perfectly competitive labor market.

But just because competition is not 100 per cent perfect does not mean that it must be zero. The world is a blend of (1) competition and (2) some degree of monopoly power over the wage to be paid. A firm that tries to set its wage too low will soon learn this. At first nothing much need happen; but eventually it will find its workers quitting a little more rapidly than would otherwise be the case. Recruitment of new people of the same quality will get harder and harder, and slackening off in the performance and productivity of those who remain on the job will become noticeable.

Availability of labor supply does, therefore, affect the wage you set under realistic conditions of imperfect competition. If you are a very small firm, you may even bargain and haggle with prospective workers so as not to pay more than you have to. But if you are any size at all, you will name a wage for each type of job, then decide how many of the applicants will be taken on; and in view of the number of applicants who respond, you may raise or lower your wage rate. You will find it a perplexing task to decide on an optimal wage policy.

EQUALITY OF BARGAINING POWER? One of the reasons given in the past for starting trade-unions was the feeling that unorganized workers, facing financially strong employers, lacked "equality of bargaining power." By union organization it was hoped that a greater equality of bargaining power could be restored. But exactly how one goes about measuring equality or inequality of bargaining power remains a difficult problem.

It is safe to say that prior to the formation of labor unions, the labor market was not a perfectly competitive one in the economist's sense of the term. And after the formation of unions it continues to differ from the perfectly competitive model. Moreover, a number of the features of labor markets usually associated with unions are also present even where there are no unions. Thus, large companies that have no union will typically introduce a standard trend-rate of pay and be slow to change it, even though the

number of workers locally unemployed might go up or down. In years of labor market slack these firms raise their wage rates as much as unionized trades do, despite the fact that competitive theory would expect them then to be cutting rates.

FOUR WAYS UNIONS SEEK TO RAISE WAGES

Leaving the oversimplified picture of perfect competition behind, we can use economic theory to analyze how unions operate. How might unions hope to raise wages in a particular industry?

There are four main methods of raising wages, all interrelated: (1) Unions can *reduce the supply* of labor. (2) They can use their collective bargaining power to *raise standard wage rates* directly. (3) They can cause the derived demand curve for labor to *shift upward.* (4) Unions can resist exploitation of laborers facing an *employer with monopoly bargaining power.* These four devices are much alike and often reinforce each other, but they also display significant differences.

1. *Restriction of labor supply.* We have already seen that a union may restrict the supply of labor in order to travel upward on the derived demand curve for labor. Immigration barriers, maximum-hour legislation, high initiation fees, long apprenticeships, refusal to admit new members into the union or to let nonunion members hold jobs—all these are obvious restrictive devices that have been used in the past. In addition, there are other, more subtle restrictions on labor supply: explicit union limits on work loads (artificial limits put on number of bricks laid or looms attended, width of paintbrush, stand-by orchestras, "bogus" type, and similar "feather-bedding" labor practices) and implicit understandings forcing a slowdown of the working pace.

2. *Raising standard wage rates.* Direct limitations on the labor supply are today no longer so necessary to unions, except to reinforce the ability of the union to secure a high standard wage rate and to maintain it. Union leaders have learned this important economic fact:

If you can persuade or force employers always to pay a high standard wage—a wage rate that is publicly known and adhered to—then the supply of

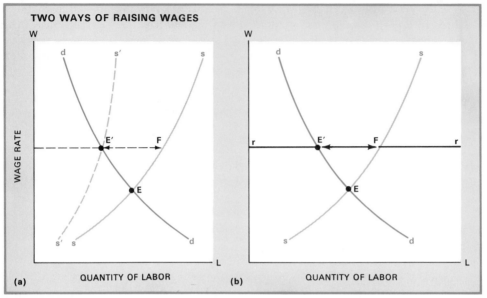

FIG. 29-5. To raise pay, unions restrict supply and enforce standard wage rates:
Raising the standard wage to *rr* in (b) has exactly the same effect on wages as reducing the effective supply from *ss* to *s's'* in (a); the workers from *E'* to *F* are excluded from employment in either case.

labor will take care of itself. At the standard rate, employers will hire the number of men they want, and any surplus job applicants will be *automatically excluded* from that labor market.

Figure 29-5(a) and (b) contrasts *direct* restriction of labor supply and *indirect* restriction via a high standard wage. In Fig. 29-5(a) the union cuts down supply from *ss* to *s's'* by insisting on long apprenticeships and high training fees. The wage consequently rises from *E* to *E'*. (Test your understanding of this: Explain the effects on doctors' earnings of a policy that reduces the relative number of medical students.)

Alternatively, in Fig. 29-5(b), the union gets all employers to agree to pay wages no lower than the minimum standard rate, as shown by the horizontal line *rr*. Note that here, too, the equilibrium is at *E'* where *rr* intersects the employer's demand curve. The workers from *E'* to *F* are as effectively excluded from jobs as if the union had directly limited entry. What now limits supply? It is the lack of job opportunities at the high standard wage rate.

3. *Shifting the derived demand curve upward.* A union may hope to increase wages by any policy that

improves the demand for labor. Thus, like the International Ladies' Garment Workers Union, it may study ways of reducing garment prices by improving productivity of labor and management, or it may help the industry advertise its products. *Or,* in order to protect its industry, the union may press the government to maintain or increase an existing tariff, or to impose a new one, hoping thereby to raise the demand curve for domestic workers. *Or* it may persuade the government to pay higher rates on public contracts and to write make-work featherbedding restrictions into building codes. *Or* it may help the employers in an industry to maintain a high monopoly price, with some of the extra profits going into higher wages.

Moreover, if collective bargaining raises wages, and *if increased wages increase the marginal productivity of labor,* then labor will have shifted its own demand curve upward. Figure 29-6 on the following page depicts the case in which an increase in the wage from *rr* to *r'r'* itself results in an upward shift in the demand curve for labor—from *dd* to *d'd'*. Note that at the new equilibrium *E'*, both wage and employment have increased.

In the old days, the standard example of this was

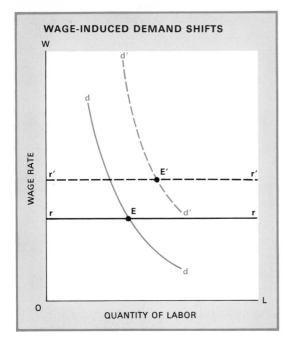

FIG. 29-6. Some union policies try to shift the labor demand curve upward.

Raising wages (from *rr* to *r'r'*), by making ill-fed workers stronger or resentful ones more energetic, in this case shifts the curve of demand productivity upward (from *dd* to *d'd'*), with employment actually increasing (from *E* to *E'*).

the case where workers were being paid so little that they were malnourished and hence inefficient; higher wages might then have made them more efficient and thus resulted in lower rather than higher production costs. Today, in this country, few workers are as physiologically undernourished. But psychological elements can be as important as physiological. Many an employer has found that too-low wages are bad business even from a hardboiled dollars-and-cents standpoint. The quality and contentment of his workers fall off so much that he is losing rather than gaining from the cheeseparing.

It can be argued that high wages have a favorable "shock effect" on the employer's efficiency in using labor. One reason advanced for the high productivity of North American industry, even back in the nineteenth century when unions were unimportant, was the fact that high farm earnings made it necessary for industry to develop good machine methods in order to be able to pay high wages and still stay in

business. Adversity, in the form of a kick in the pants from unions or from fate in general, can at times galvanize businessmen into finding improved methods. How much there is to this shock-effect argument, nobody knows. It should therefore be used with caution.

4. *Removing exploitation by monopolist of labor (the "monopsonist").* Finally, there is the case where unions arise to offset monopoly power that employers may have in a labor market that has been far from competitive. Suppose there is a company town: unless you work for the dominant firm, you are unemployed; your alternatives are few or nonexistent, and you must take what the employer offers. In this case the employer does not think of himself as too small to affect appreciably the wage he pays; he does not hire factors up to the point where their marginal-revenue-products (as defined in the chapters just preceding) are equal to the wage he pays. Instead, the employer realizes that hiring an extra worker will raise the wage he must pay to all, and hence he had better not hire that worker unless his marginal-product much *exceeds* the wage.

In this situation (which economists call "monopsony," after the Greek words for the situation in which there is a "single buyer," just as "monopoly" means the situation in which there is a "single seller"), *organizing a union can result in higher wages and without any decline in unemployment!* Once the employer realizes the union is going to see to it that he must pay the standard wage, he will again be a "wage taker" who will hire men up to where their marginal-product fully equals that standard wage.

The lessening of exploitation by union organization is more important in isolated places, like the tin mines of Bolivia or the lumber camps of Canadian history, than it is in a modern economy where people are, in fact, mobile in moving to better job opportunities. There do still, however, remain areas of agriculture where employers hire workers below the market because of the workers' lack of other opportunities or their ignorance of such opportunities as do exist.[7]

---

[7] Intermediate economics texts show that, where an employer was previously possessed of monopoly-buying-power over labor, collective bargaining can—if not pushed to excess—right the balance, leading to both increased wages *and* increased employ-

WAGE INCREASES AND REDUCTIONS IN EMPLOYMENT If raising wages means simply that you climb up the existing demand curve for labor, then employment will decrease in consequence. This is because demand curves almost always slope downward and to the right.[8] The amount of unemployment created in a particular occupation by wage increases would depend upon the elasticity of the demand curve for that particular category of labor. We saw in earlier chapters that a factor demand is a "derived demand," and we discussed in the previous chapter some of the conditions that determine how elastic or inelastic the derived demand might be.

THEORETICAL INDETERMINACY OF COLLECTIVE BARGAINING

Just as unions sometimes realize it would not be to their interest to get higher wages, managements sometimes take the view that an increase in wages would improve their long-run corporate earnings. But both these views are exceptional. Usually, at any collective bargaining conference, the workers are pressing for higher wages and fringe benefits than management wishes to pay.[9]

What will be the terms of the final agreement? Unfortunately, this is one important question that no economic theory can answer with precision. The

game-theoretic[10] result depends on psychology, politics, and countless intangible and unpredictable factors. As far as the economist is concerned, the final outcome is in principle indeterminate—as indeterminate as the haggling between two millionaires over a fine painting.

Eight main arguments will be appealed to during the bargaining:

1. If the cost of living is rising, the union economist will talk a great deal about the workers' *standard of living*; but if prices are falling, the employer brings this up.

2. If the company and industry have been prosperous, the union will stress *ability to pay*; but if the industry has had low profits, the employer will emphasize this fact.

3. If *productivity* has risen or fallen recently, this will be introduced into the negotiations by one of the interested parties.

4. If other firms in the same area are paying *going wages* higher or lower than the firm in question, this fact will be brought out.

5. Labor will extol the philosophy of high wages as a means of bolstering *purchasing power* and national prosperity; management will emphasize the higher-cost aspects of wage increases.

6. If a *national pattern* of "fourth- or nth-round" wage increases of so much per hour has already been set by a few "key bargains" in large industries such as pulp, steel, or automobiles, that will have a great weight in the deliberations.

[10] See Chapter 24's Appendix for rudiments of the theory of games.

---

ment. Before unionization, the employer monopsonist who is on his toes will set his equilibrium wage at *mm* in Fig. 29-7. This will be lower than the so-called "competitive wage" at *E*. Why will the monopsonist's equilibrium be at a point like *M*? The monopsonist will not want to travel upward from *M* to *E* because he realizes that any employment increase beyond *M* will raise the wages paid to *already hired workers* by more than the extra revenue resulting from hiring the new men. But now let the union raise the wages toward *E* by collective bargaining; the monopsonist employer now reluctantly travels up the *ss* curve, as shown by the black arrows. Note we do not travel up the marginal-revenue-product curve *dd*. Wages and employment both rise together. (QUERY: Suppose collective bargaining raises the standard wage to a level *r"r"* that lies *above E*. By drawing in the resulting arrows *above E* on *dd*, show that now unemployment will follow. What then will happen to employment? Draw in the resulting black arrows on the demand curve.)

[8] Cases have been noted where short-run demand is virtually completely inelastic.

[9] Part of the wage demand might take the form of a demand for pensions, a welfare-insurance fund, or a fund to soften automation's impact; but the same principles apply.

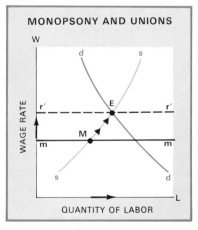

MONOPSONY AND UNIONS

(vertical axis) WAGE RATE
(horizontal axis) QUANTITY OF LABOR

FIG. 29-7

7. North American workers and employers have grown accustomed to steady money-wage increases. Almost as certainly as spring brings robins, it brings wage increases. So General Motors and many other firms build into their wage agreements a steady upward trend—the so-called "improvement factor." This may mean an average 3 to 4 per cent wage boost each year in addition to any cost-of-living escalator wage clauses.

8. The government may set forth *guideposts* for wages and prices as part of an "incomes policy," and these may be appealed to or ignored depending on the interests of the bargaining parties. As we shall see in Chapter 41, such guideposts broadly aim to have money wages increase with the *average* trend increase of *national* productivity: then if prices are lowered in industries of above-average productivity growth and raised in those of below-average, the general price level can be stable and customary wage-property shares be preserved. Or controls may supercede guideposts.

Most often, labor and management will arrive at a new yearly contract after some days of negotiation. But sometimes when they get stalled, a government conciliation officer may try to narrow down the few-cents disagreement. Then a conciliation board may be appointed to make a report to the government and to the two parties. Unfortunately, economic theory cannot tell us how such a board will arrive at its final decision. All the previously mentioned factors will be weighed, plus the all-important question, What decision is likely to be *acceptable* to both sides?

STRIKES AND COLLECTIVE BARGAINING

Both sides realize that failure to reach agreement will mean a costly strike. It may sometimes happen that management refuses to go above $7.00 an hour while labor refuses to take less than $7.10. A "work stoppage" will result. Should we call this an "employees' strike" or an "employer's lockout"? In popular speech, it will certainly be referred to as a strike. But since either party knows it can end the work stoppage by agreeing to the other party's terms, we could call it either.

Newsmen ask why workers go out on strike just because of a 10 cent disagreement; they point out that it might take two or three years for the workers to recover—at 10 cents an hour—their loss of earn-ings during the strike. But the workers look at it differently. To them the employer caused the strike by his stubbornness. They point out that the employer will lose more by the strike than refusing the extra 10 cents would save him in many years.

Actually, a strike is *not* over just the last 10 cents disagreement! The workers believe that the employer would not have been forced from $6.00 up even to $7.00 except for the threat of a strike, which hangs over the negotiation like a time bomb. To keep the bomb from going off, both sides must agree.

Threats become hollow unless occasionally carried out. Both parties must show that they are truly prepared to incur at some point the costs of a strike. Thus, suppose the employer was deprived, voluntarily or by law, of the right to refuse any wage demand if it would bring on a strike. Would this cost him only 10 cents an hour? Obviously not. There would then be no reason why the union might not hold out for a $2.00 rather than a $1.00 wage increase. Similarly, if the union could never exercise the right to strike, why should not the employer offer $5.00 rather than $7.00 per hour if he can get labor at that rate?

RESULTS FROM RECENT RESEARCH: QUALIFICATIONS

Patient research by labor economists has cast light on other aspects of the central importance of the union in the worker-market.

STRIKE PRONENESS The outline of the factors influencing the elasticity of derived demand would suggest that certain kinds of industries would grant wage increases without much quarrel, while in others they would be achieved only reluctantly, and perhaps after frequent resort to strikes. Remember that wage increases tend to follow changes in the cost of living, profits of the employer, or higher wages elsewhere. Thus the demand curve does not stay still through time. Still, other things being the same, economists have tended to look to the elasticity of demand for a region or industry's final product as one source of explanation of different tendencies to strike or to lose days of work in disputes.

On the whole, this kind of explanation does not work. True, certain industries and regions do lead others broadly in strike proneness: Canada tends to lead the United States; British Columbia to lead Canada; mining to lead dry cleaning; and men do go on strike more than women. But these are only broad tendencies. Furthermore, economists have not been able to use elasticities of supply or demand to explain them, in particular cases.

Instead, labor economists have found that *sociological* characteristics of the workers in an industry are the best explanation of why they strike more than men in other industries. One of the chief of these is "isolation": miners and workers in the woods are physically isolated from other contacts except with each other, the job, and the bosses; and city workers of certain ethnic origins or in certain occupations (like longshoremen) are also isolated from the rest of the urban labor force. Indeed, they suggest that a whole country's strike proneness may be better understood by examining the number of such "isolated" industries than by looking for special economic aspects of the country's industries or labor markets.

CAN UNIONS RAISE WAGE RATES? The advocates of organized labor claim unions have raised real wages; the critics blame unions for having done just that and for having thereby distorted the efficient use-pattern of resources. Despite this agreement that unions raise real wages, the true facts are not all clear.

This finding raises the question: how would theory suggest unionism would make a difference? One kind of answer is to assert that a unionized industry should make greater wage gains than a nonunionized industry. (This is not a very convincing claim: would a unionized obsolescent farm-wagon industry make greater wage gains than a nonunionized computer industry? Still, if the unions are widely spread over many kinds of industry, the test has some interest.) Studies of the U.S. economy since the burst of union organization in the 1930s show a poor result for unions. Low-paid, unorganized workers like domestic servants and farm workers have made the greatest percentage and the greatest absolute wage gains. In fact, the *percentage* differentials between them and organized workers have been diminishing, as simple arithmetic would show they must.

It is true that the average wage in unionized industries is about 20 per cent higher than the average wage in nonunionized industries. But that in itself

does not *prove* that unions are responsible for the difference. The industries that are unionized tend also to be those dominated by large rather than small enterprise and by firms which use workers of higher-than-average skills. Even before they were unionized, these same industries paid higher-than-average wages.

On the other hand, well-known studies present data in which it appears that since the mid-1930s, *recently*-unionized industries have gained greater wage increases than nonunionized industries, and also greater than *long*-unionized industries. This suggests that the wage impact of the union may be only in its early years, not over its whole life.

"KEY" BARGAINS Such statistics on the differential movements of union and nonunion wages cannot give the whole answer to the question whether unions have raised wages. Labor spokesmen claim that unions also help raise wages for *the unorganized workers*. Thus, a nonunion industry's policy may be to follow "key" bargains in the wage scale hammered out in unionized plants nearby. Industry raises wages in order to keep the union out, the figures will give the union no credit for its indirect influence. On the other hand, suppose the targets for union organizers are profitable, expanding, high-productivity, concentrated industries; then the union may be riding aboard a moving demand curve and be given credit for wage increases that would have occurred even in its absence. Which is cause and which is effect?[11]

PITFALLS IN THE CONCEPT OF A GENERAL DEMAND FOR LABOR A second important warning must be given. It is legitimate to draw up a demand curve of the usual general shape for one *small* labor market: as long as *all other* prices and wages are more or less unaffected, it is indeed true that a higher money wage in one sector is the same as a higher real wage there; it is true also that employment there can be expected to fall off somewhat at the higher wage.

But remember the fallacy of composition. What is true for any *small* sector of the economy need not be

---

[11] See Sylvia Ostry and Mahmood Zaidi, *Labour Economics in Canada,* 1972, for references to studies by Reuber, Wilson, Vanderkamp, Swindinski and other Canadian economists on the importance of unionism and of the bargain in "key" parts of the Canadian labor market.

true for the *whole aggregate*. If all wage rates rise, it is dangerous to suppose that commodity prices will remain constant. Thus, doubling all money wages *might* well result in a doubling of all prices. Were that the case, the real wage would not be changed at all. And hence, in a diagram such as Fig. 29-1, we should be moving neither upward nor downward on the demand curve. (Turn to Fig. 29-1 and note that the vertical axis represents real wages in dollars of *constant purchasing power*.)

Remember that wages are not simply costs: they also represent *incomes* of most of the population. Therefore the sales revenue of business enterprises is vastly affected by a substantial change in wage levels. Since the demand for labor is a demand derived from the demand for business products, it is clear that any change in general wages must shift the general demand curve for labor. Hence, it is dangerous to argue in terms of an unchanged demand curve for labor.

To illustrate this pitfall, ask the following question: in 1932 when there was widespread unemployment, would an all-round cut in money wages have *increased* employment? Or, as claimed by the trade-unionists, would such a decrease in general money wages have decreased "purchasing power" and *decreased* employment?

To the extent that a halving of wages would result in a halving of all prices, of all money incomes, and of all money spending, the answer must be obvious. Such a completely balanced deflation would neither help nor hurt the unemployment situation.[12] This serves as a warning against accepting the superficial claims of those critics of labor who argue in terms of simple *dd* curves, and of those friends of labor who argue in terms of "purchasing power."

SUMMING UP We may cautiously conclude discussion of the economic effects of unions by quoting in turn from two leading students of labor economics, Princeton's Albert E. Rees and Yale's Lloyd G. Reynolds. According to Rees,[13]

"We tend to overemphasize the role of the unions, both in ... their own industries and ... the economy as a whole ... The other two thirds may have their wages and salaries influenced by what the unions do, but I feel there are very strong independent forces on the demand side that govern their rates of pay ... Even in the ... unionized (one third) there are some very weak or almost impotent unions that have had very little to do with the wages of their members ...

"In a series of rough guesses, I would say perhaps a third of the trade unions have raised the wages of their members by 15 per cent to 20 per cent above what they might be in a nonunion situation; another third by perhaps 5 per cent to 10 per cent, and the remaining third not at all ... The high figures tend to be found, not in periods of inflation, but in periods of prosperity combined with stable prices. ... In [an inflationary] period like 1946-1948, for example, the union people may even lag behind simply because of the rigidities involved in the collective bargaining process."

And Reynolds states the following conclusions of his researches:

"Summing up these diverse consequences of collective bargaining, one can make a strong case that unionism has at any rate not worsened the wage structure. We are inclined to be more venturesome than this, and to say that its net effect has been beneficial. This conclusion will doubtless strike many economists as surprising ...

"Fears that complete unionization will bring seismic disruption of the wage structure do not seem to be well founded.... The countries with the strongest union movements appear to have a wage structure which is more orderly and defensible than the wage structure of countries where unionism has been weak."

In Part Six's Chapter 41 we shall face the important problem, as yet unsolved, of finding an "incomes" or "guidepost" policy that will make full employment compatible with reasonably stable price levels.

---

[12] Today most economic theorists believe that the favorable effects during recession of any overall general wage cut will depend upon how it affects the balance of saving and investment, or total real demand. If (a) lower wages cause prices to drop and (b) people's cash and holdings of government bonds do not drop in proportion, then the increase in people's real wealth may have expansionary effects on the real propensity to consume and on employment. But falling prices may aggravate debts and bankruptcy and, by making people pessimistic, may harm investment; consequently, most advanced treatises in economics seem to advocate expanding people's real wealth and real consumption schedule by means of expansionary bank and financial policy rather than by deflation. (Chapter 17's Appendix discusses this so-called "Pigou effect.")

[13] The Rees' quotation is from *Wage Inflation* (National Industrial Conference Board, New York, 1957), pp. 27-28; the Reynolds' quotation, from L. G. Reynolds and C. H. Taft, *The Evolution of Wage Structure* (Yale University Press, New Haven, 1956), pp. 194-195.

SUMMARY

A. WAGE DETERMINATION UNDER PERFECT COMPETITION

1 In perfectly competitive equilibrium, if all men and jobs were exactly alike, there would be no wage differentials. The equilibrium wage rate would be determined by supply and demand. To the extent that Country A has (1) more natural resources per worker than Country B and (2) better productive methods (because of capital availability and technical knowledge), to that extent the competitive wage in A is likely to be higher than in B.

2 The law of *diminishing returns* suggests that a reduction of labor relative to natural resources might be expected to raise real wages. While this principle lies behind labor's immigration policy and other restrictions, historical examples of economies of mass production do point to the operation of a countertendency of *increasing returns*. In theory, the "*optimum* population" size is at the point where the two countertendencies have reached a balance of maximum per capita income.

3 Though Malthusian overpopulation threatens many an underdeveloped country such as India, there is no tendency for population growth in Canada and developed nations to push real wages down to a minimum-subsistence level. Pressure exerted on real wages by the "reserve army of the unemployed" tends to depress real wages only to the *equilibrium* level. In the Western world, this equilibrium wage is much above the physiological *subsistence* level and rises steadily.

4 Fear of unemployment leads often to acceptance of the "lump-of-labor" fallacy. This belief that there is only a fixed amount of useful work to be done may result from experiencing technological unemployment or depression. It lies behind much of the agitation for a 30-hour week and featherbedding work rules. But the problem of unemployment calls for macroeconomic policies to furnish adequate job opportunities, not for defeatist restrictionism.

5 The supply of labor has four dimensions: population size, percentage of people gainfully employed, average number of hours worked per week and per year, and quality of effort of workers.

6 As wages rise, there are two opposite effects on the supply of labor: The "substitution-effect" tempts each worker to work longer because of the higher pay for each hour of work; the "income-effect" exerts influence in the opposite direction—in that higher wages mean that workers can now afford more leisure along with more commodities and other good things of life. At *some* critical wage, the supply curve may bend backward. The labor supply of very gifted, unique people is probably quite inelastic. Their wages are largely "pure economic rent."

B. COMPETITIVE WAGE PATTERNS

7 Once we drop the unrealistic assumptions concerning the uniformity of people and jobs, we must explain the pattern of substantial wage differences that characterize even a perfectly competitive labor market. "Equalizing wage differences" which compensate for *nonmonetary* differences in the unpleasantness, danger or training required, explain many of the differentials.

8 But differences in the *quality* of various grades of labor are probably the most important cause of wage differences. Although it cannot be claimed that labor consists of wholly

"noncompeting groups," it is nonetheless true that there are innumerable categories of partially competing groups.

9 When the relative wage of one category rises, there are substantial cross-elasticity effects on labor supply as some people switch to the improved-pay occupation. The final pattern of wages would, in a perfectly competitive labor market, be determined by the general equilibrium of the interrelated schedules of supply and demand. cf Table 29-1.

C. IMPERFECTIONS OF THE LABOR MARKET

10 Labor markets are not perfectly competitive in real life. With unions or without them, employers usually have some control over wages, but their wage policy must be conditioned by the available supply of labor.

11 Unions affect wages by (*a*) restricting labor supply, (*b*) bargaining for standard rates, (*c*) following policies designed to shift upward the derived demand schedule for labor, and (*d*) countering exploitation of labor by employers with monopoly bargaining power (i.e., by so-called "monopsonists").

12 Relative increases in wages will result in most industries in less employment there. This assumes the union is moving *along* a given demand schedule (i.e., that there are no demand shifts from higher productivity).

13 At the collective bargaining table the following are some of the determining factors around which argument is likely to center: (*a*) cost and standards of living, (*b*) ability to pay and profits, (*c*) productivity trends and improvement factors, (*d*) "going wages" paid elsewhere in the locality and in the industry, (*e*) the influence of higher wages on purchasing power and on the level of costs, (*f*) the "national pattern" as determined by "key bargains" in important industries, (*g*) continuous increases based upon improvement factors from long-term technical improvements, and (*h*) government guideposts designed to keep increases in money wages in line with *average* productivity increases of the economy. Economic theory cannot tell just what the final wage bargain will be, it being theoretically indeterminate.

14 Usually a compromise settlement will be possible. But the *threat* of strike is ever-present and conditions the whole bargaining procedure. In vital industries, however, the interest of the public transcends the individual interests and rights of the disputing parties; consequently, voluntary collective bargaining is subject to government controls whenever damaging work stoppages occur.

15 Historically, the extent to which unions have succeeded in raising wages is in doubt. Since the mid-1930s union membership has greatly increased, but in this same period wage differentials seem to have remained about the same in absolute terms. Heavily concentrated and expanding industries may have been targets for unionization, and the high wages may have been the result of factors associated with or causing unionizing rather than of unionization as such.

16 A final warning is in order: We must beware of the fallacy of composition in ascribing to the *demand curve for labor in general* the shape characteristic of the *demand curve for one small category of labor*. Wages are more than costs; they also constitute much of the income of consumers and heavily react back upon the demand for products of business. A *general* change in money wage rates can be expected to have important effects on prices. To the extent that a general wage change is balanced by an equivalent percentage change in *all* prices, little substantive effect upon unemployment may result.

CONCEPTS FOR REVIEW

general equilibrium	noncompeting groups
real versus money wages	standard rate
optimum population	monopoly-employer exploitation
subsistence wage level	elastic, inelastic derived demand
backward-bending supply curve	collective bargaining
income- versus substitution-effect	strike, lockout, work stoppage
rent element in wages	percentage and absolute differentials
wage patterns and differential	"incomes policy"
equalizing and nonequalizing wage	"key" bargains
differences	

QUESTIONS FOR DISCUSSION

1. Explain narrowing of wage differentials from competition of like people.
2. What factors of technology, economic geography, and legislation help to determine the level of real wages? Show how diminishing returns and countertendencies are linked with the theory of optimum population.
3. Define and contrast "equalizing and nonequalizing differences in wages." Which concept is exemplified by high wages that contained much "pure economic rent"? What about noncompeting groups?
4. Give a list of imperfections in the labor market. Show that not all are related to monopoly power or to trade-union organization.
5. Give three ways unions try to influence wages, as described in this chapter. Contrast the first two, and gauge their importance. Do the same for the third method.
6. "Unions can raise real and money wages in a particular industry, but the result will be less employment." Evaluate, utilizing the elasticity of demand for labor.
7. What is the public interest in voluntary collective bargaining?
8. Explain dangers involved in treating the general demand for labor like a particular group's demand. Show that wages are costs *and* sources of demand.
9. Prime Minister Trudeau tried in the 1970s to keep the government out of collective bargaining. Do you think this is possible; in a (*a*) rail strike, (*b*) steel strike, (*c*) longshoreman or teamster strike, (*d*) one-town-newspaper strike, (*e*) auto strike, (*f*) postal strike? Where would you draw the line?

30
INTEREST AND CAPITAL

How to have your cake and eat it too: lend it out at interest: **ANONYMOUS**

The preceding chapters have sketched the determination of the rents of resources and the wages of labor. Now in this chapter we turn to the third great category of productive factors, capital; and to the determination of its special price, which is called "interest."

Capital theory is one of the most difficult parts of economic theory. For this reason, an introductory treatment cannot hope to grapple with all the important issues. It seems best, therefore, to proceed as follows:

The main part of this chapter summarizes in an uncritical way the basic notions about capital and interest found in every standard treatment of the subject. Then, at the end are briefly given some of the key qualifications that ought to be made concerning the oversimplified traditional treatment. For the Appendix are reserved certain special topics of classical capital theory and its modern qualifications.

LAND, LABOR, AND CAPITAL

Our traditional account of capital theory begins with a rather arbitrary division of all productive factors into three categories:

1. *Natural resources* provided by Nature in fixed supply, which cannot be augmented or used up. The return of this inelastic factor is called (pure economic) *rent*.

2. Human *labor* resources, not produced in response to economic conditions, but taken by the economist as determined by social and biological factors. The return of this human factor is called *wages* (which includes the salaries for brain and managerial workers as well as wages for manual workers).

In the oversimplified traditional account, factors (1) and (2) are called "primary factors of production" —primary in the sense that their supplies are deter-

mined largely outside the economic system itself. To them we must now add an "intermediate" factor.

3. Capital goods, *produced by the economic system itself* to be used as productive inputs for further production of goods and services. These capital goods, which are both outputs and inputs, can be long- or short-lived. They can be rented out in the competitive market just the way acres of land or hours of labor can be rented out. Their rents—or perhaps we might use the term "rentals," to avoid confusion with pure economic rent to land in fixed supply—these rentals of capital goods are determined by the same demand conditions of marginal productivity discussed previously.

However, in the traditional capital theory, the return or yield of capital is not taken to be the *rentals* of capital goods. What, then, is it?

The yield of capital is the *interest rate per annum*, which is a pure percentage per unit time—independent of dollar or other value units. Of what is the interest rate 5 per cent per annum the yield? Obviously, it is the yield applied to the *dollar* value of capital goods.[1]

CAPITALIZATION OF ASSETS

Now we can take a brief look at the important economic process by which capital goods get priced in the market at their "capitalized value." The *interest rate* plays a key role, and when this rate drops from a high to a low level, we shall see there must result a considerable rise in the capitalized value of machines, bonds, annuities, or any other asset providing a stream of future property revenues.

---

[1] In taking a census of total capital, we should not add to the 1-million-dollar value of a firm's plant, equipment, and inventory the 1-million-dollar value that its common-stock shares may sell for in Montreal. That is, we must avoid double-counting.

To see how assets get capitalized, look at the simplest case of a piece of land or an annuity contract that is certain to pay you the *same* number of dollars each year from now until *eternity*. It turns out we can quite easily write down the formula for the present capitalized value V of any *permanent* income stream of $1 per year or $N per year. We ask, "How many dollars put out every year at the market rate of interest i per annum will give us exactly the same return of $1 per year or $N per year?" The answer is summarized in the rule

$$V = \frac{\$N}{i}$$

where V = present capital value often called
       "present discounted value")
N = permanent annual receipts
i = interest rate expressed as a decimal
          (e.g., .05, or 5/100, corresponding to 5 per
          cent)

Thus, if the interest rate will always be 5 per cent, any permanent income will sell for exactly 20 (= 1 ÷ 5/100) times its annual income.[2] (To check our formula, realize that a principal of $20 at 5 per cent will yield $1 every year; so $20 must be the perpetual stream's capitalized value.)

NET PRODUCTIVITY OF CAPITAL

Now we ask ourselves this question: Why do people ever bother to transform the primary factors of labor and land into intermediate capital goods or into capital? The answer: It is a technological fact of life that you *can get more future consumption product by using indirect or roundabout methods.*

---

[2] In the Middle Ages, they called this "20 years' purchase" and thus got around the taboo against interest. Show that 4 per cent interest means 25 years' purchase; 6 per cent, 16 2/3 years'. (See the Appendix for discussion of capitalization of nonpermanent income streams.)

  NOTE: After land has been capitalized, its rent may appear as *interest* earned on its market value. In principle, *all* the nonwage part of NNP could be reported as interest on the value of property: if selling ourselves into slavery were not illegal, even wages might be reported as interest on the capital value of men! As is noted in Parts One and Six, investing in human capital by education and training is important: much of the wage of a high-income surgeon can be regarded as interest and return of principal on his parents' or spouse's investment in his training.

To see this, imagine two islands exactly alike. Each has exactly the same primary factors of labor and land. Island A uses these primary factors directly to produce consumption product; she uses no produced capital goods at all. Island B, on the other hand, for a preliminary period sacrifices current consumption; instead she uses some of her land and labor to produce intermediate capital goods such as plows, shovels, and synthesized chemicals. After this preliminary period of net capital formation, she ends up with a varied stock of capital goods, i.e., with a sizable amount of capital. Now let us measure the amount of consumption product she can go on permanently producing with her land, labor, and constantly replaced capital goods.

Careful measurement of Island B's "roundabout" product shows it to be greater than Island A's. Why is it greater? Why does B get *more* than 100 units of future consumption goods for her initial sacrifice of 100 units of present consumption? That is a technological engineering question. To sum up, the economist traditionally takes the following answer as a basic technical fact:

There exist roundabout processes, which take time to get started, that are more productive than direct processes.

From this basic technological fact we can now draw an important economic conclusion:

After allowing for all depreciation requirements, capital has a *net productivity* (or real interest yield) that can be expressed in the form of a percentage per annum; and the only reason you do not take further advantage of this opportunity to get more product by roundabout methods is that you must cut down on present consumption if you are to speed up capital's rate of growth and *future* consumption.

DEFINITION OF NET PRODUCTIVITY OF A CAPITAL GOOD OR INVESTMENT PROJECT

We need an exact definition of the net productivity of any capital project. We first calculate the original dollar cost of the factors bought to begin each roundabout process. Then we calculate the total receipts that the roundabout methods give. We know very well that the receipts total must add up to more than the original cost total, else there is no net productivity. Having satisfied ourselves that there is indeed a positive net productivity, we need a way of measuring it quantitatively so as to make diverse projects comparable—projects involving apples and oranges, projects involving 50-year bridges and 5-month beer. Our final solution is to look for a measure that is a *percentage per annum.*

We end up defining the net productivity of a capital project thus:

A capital or investment project's net productivity is that annual percentage yield which you could earn by tying up your money in it. What is the same thing, the project's net productivity is that market rate of interest at which it would just pay to undertake it.

EXAMPLE: I buy grape juice for $10, and a year later sell it as wine for $11. If there are no other expenses and no risk or effort to me, my interest yield (or "net productivity") is 10 per cent per annum—equal to $1/$10.[3]

As a community transfers part of its resources away from current consumption and toward capital accumulation, projects with lower and lower net productivity will be undertaken. Thus, this 50-year bridge with a net productivity of, say, 10 per cent will not be worth building if the market rate of interest is 11 per cent. But when the market interest drops to 10 per cent or below, you will build the bridge.

The law of diminishing returns is invoked as more and more capital goods of all types become available to work with the limited supply of natural resources and land and with the more slowly growing number of workers. It implies that society and the private investors will run out of new projects with net productivities as high as the previous ones. And unless off-

set by technological innovations, this law of diminishing returns would work itself out in interest rates and investment yields falling through time as the community successfully saves. For without such a fall in interest, the low-yielding long-lived projects would not get undertaken.

A BIRD'S-EYE VIEW OF INTEREST DETERMINATION

We can now define the rate of interest and summarize the forces traditionally supposed to determine its competitive level.

Definition: The market rate of interest is that percentage return per year which has to be paid on any safe loan of money, which has to be yielded by any safe bond or other type of security, and which has to be earned on the value of any capital asset (such as a machine, a hotel building, a patent right) in any competitive market where there are no risks or where all risk factors have already been taken care of by special premium payments to protect against any risks.

Thus, in an ideal capital market, the riskless rate of interest might be set by supply and demand at 6 per cent, just as the rent of fertile land is set at $20 an acre per year and the wage of skilled labor is set at $250 per 40-hour week.

That does not mean that I shall make a small loan at so low a rate to an applicant whom I do not know and who has lost three jobs in six months' time: I may have to charge him as much as 20 per cent per annum to compensate me for having to investigate him, dun him for collection, and cover the risk premium from default and costly litigation. Nor shall I buy risky mining stock that yields only 6 per cent. At any time there is a whole spread of interest rates for ventures of different riskiness, and this whole spread will move up or down when the pure, riskless rate of interest changes.

What are the changes in supply or demand that could move the pure interest rate up or down? Certainly, if scientists and engineers create new opportunities for capital investment, which have their *net productivities* greatly increased from the previous equilibrium, this will tend to bid up the market rate of interest. On the other hand, if people become *less impatient* to consume now rather than in the future,

---

[3] Here are two more examples. I plant a pine tree at labor cost of $50 plus 25 years' land rental cost—paid in advance—of $50, or $100 in all. At the end of 25 years the grown tree sells for $430. The net productivity of this capital project is then 330 per cent per quarter-century, which, interest tables tell us, is equivalent to a net productivity of 6 per cent per year. Or I buy a $10,000 truck. For 10 years it earns annual rentals of $5,000, but I pay $3,000 annually for fuel, driver, and maintenance. Its scrap value is zero. What is its net productivity or yield? The same as that of an annuity of $2,000 per year payable for 10 years and bought for $10,000. Compound interest tables for annuities show this truck's yield to be 15 per cent per year.

their successful attempt to save—to shift resources from consumption-goods production to formation of capital goods—will bid down the interest rate, as more and more capital accumulation leads to diminishing returns and creates the need to take up capital projects with lower and lower net productivities.

As Yale's great expert Irving Fisher put the matter a half century ago:

Supply-and-demand determination of the interest rate means that its level is determined by interaction between (1) people's *impatience* to consume now rather than accumulate more capital goods for future consumption (perhaps in old-age retirement or for that proverbial rainy day); and (2) *investment opportunities* that exist to receive higher or lower net productivities from such capital accumulated.

The market rate of interest has two functions: it *rations out*, into the uses with highest net productivities, society's *existing scarce supply of capital goods*; and in the long run, it may (or may not[4]) induce people to *sacrifice current consumption and add to the stock of capital.*

GRAPHICAL DETERMINATION OF INTEREST

Supply and demand diagrams can amplify this survey of interest determination. But in the field of capital theory, they become rather complicated. At this point we can greatly simplify the exposition of the traditional theory if we agree to concentrate on the case where all physical capital goods are exactly alike

---

[4] There is evidence that some people save *less* rather than more at higher interest rates; that many people save about the *same* amount regardless of the level of the interest rate; and that some people are induced to consume less only by the promise of higher interest returns. As we saw in the discussion of substitution- versus income-effects, in Chapters 22 and 29, economic principles alone cannot give us a decisive prediction as to whether or when a supply curve will become backward-bending. The bulk of the evidence suggests that the level of interest tends to cancel out of consumption and saving decisions, even though a rise in the rate paid by a trust company may bring it increased business because people will tend to transfer their assets from chartered banks or mutual funds (without their having altered consumption one bit). Some classical economists sought to justify interest as the reward for the pain of abstinence and waiting, just as they justified wages as the reward for sweat and psychic disutility. This gave rise to jests among Continental socialists concerning Baron Rothschild's painful sacrifices!

and highly versatile. (Of course, in the real world, they are not all alike; and therefore advanced treatises have to go through a rather lengthy discussion to show how the diversity of capital goods is to be handled.[5])

Figure 30-1 on the following page illustrates how the interest rate is determined in traditional capital theory. Curve *dd* shows the demand curve for the stock of capital. Remember how the demand for labor was formed from the marginal productivity curve for labor. Similarly, the demand for capital is a "derived demand"—derived ultimately from the value of the extra consumption goods that extra capital makes possible. The demand for capital is made up of its *net productivity curve* (reckoned as a yearly per cent, as we've seen).

DIMINISHING RETURNS We see the law of diminishing returns applying to capital as well as to other factors; that is shown by the *dd* curve's sloping downward; e.g., at levels where capital is very scarce, there are some very profitable roundabout projects that yield 12 or more per cent per annum. Gradually, through thrift, capital formation takes place and the community finds it has exploited all the 12 per cent projects; with total labor and land fixed, diminishing returns to the varying capital have set in. The community must then invest in 11 and 10 per cent projects as it moves down *dd*.

In Fig. 30-1, capital formation has taken place in the past, bequeathing the existing supply of the stock of capital as given by the vertical supply curve *ss*. The equilibrium rate of interest must in the short run take place at the intersection of the *dd* demand curve and the *ss* short-run supply curve. Here's why. Below the equilibrium interest rate, there would exist too many investment projects; above the equilibrium rate, there would be too few; and the community's stock of capital is just big enough to take care of the projects yielding at least the shown equilibrium interest rate of 8 per cent.

SHORT-RUN EQUILIBRIUM Why is the equilibrium at *E* only a short-run, moving equilibrium? Because 8 per cent is a rather high rate; and even though capital is currently scarce enough to keep us at *E*, people are shown as wanting to go on saving part of their income there. This means the commu-

---

[5] See the Appendix's Fig. 30-3, for some further discussion of this problem and of the Fisher analysis.

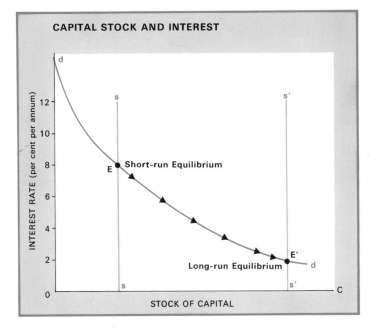

FIG. 30-1. Traditional theory determines interest rate by intersecting
supply and demand.

Existing *stock* (supply) of capital intersects net productivity schedule to
determine a moving equilibrium rate.
Continued capital formation shifts *ss*
sideward and leads to the indicated
fall in interest rate along *dd*. Long-
run equilibrium interest rate is at *E'*,
where net saving ceases.

nity will have capital formation continuously taking place; so, as time passes, the community will be moving southeast on the *dd* curve as shown by the black arrows.

Specifically, (1) we move rightward because the accumulating amount of positive investment and capital formation means that the capital stock, and therefore the short-run supply curve, is being pushed more and more rightward. (In each new short run, the curve will again be vertical but farther to the right.) Now why does the interest rate move downward? (2) It moves downward because the law of diminishing returns tells us—other things such as labor, land, and knowledge of technology remaining unchanged!—that the net productivity of the increased stock of capital goods falls to ever lower percentages.[6]

---

[6] The process of accumulating capital goods faster than labor grows is important, and will be called "deepening of capital" in Chapter 37 (in contrast to mere duplication of capital goods to match a growing labor force, which is called "widening of capital"). The steady-state equilibrium shown at *E'* could, if population were growing at, say, 2 per cent per year, be a moving equilibrium in which capital is being accumulated *in balance* with labor, with no "deepening" but only "widening." See page 557, Appendix, footnote 2.

LONG-TERM STEADY-STATE EQUILIBRIUM

The equilibrium at *E* was in the nature of a short-run equilibrium; short-run in the sense that people were still saving at the interest rate shown there. Capital was still growing, as is indicated by the black arrows; we were still moving down the *dd* curve. The interest rate at *E* was just big enough to keep us growing at the rate we were growing. But the interest rate at *E* is not yet low enough to choke off all desire to save, not yet low enough to make the community's average propensity to consume equal to 100 percent.

It is at *E'* that *long-run equilibrium* is finally achieved. Again, the existing stock of capital is being auctioned off in the market for the highest short-run interest rate it can fetch. (You run vertically up the *s's'* supply curve and read off the *E'* interest rate.) But now interest is so low that the net saving is zero; now capital stops growing, and the supply curve no longer shifts rightward. The arrows converge on *E'*: at higher interest, capital would grow through positive saving and investment; at lower interest, it would decline through positive disinvestment and dissaving. So *E'* represents the stable long-run equilibrium that could prevail in the absence of technical change.

ANCIENT MISCONCEPTIONS ABOUT INTEREST

Before proceeding to criticize and qualify its over-simplifications, we can use the traditional theory of capital and interest to clear up some ancient debates.

FAIRNESS AND INEVITABILITY OF INTEREST Pointing out that money is "barren," Aristotle said it was unfair to charge positive interest for loans. Many sophisticated medieval Schoolmen followed him in this view that interest represents unjustified usury. Indeed, throughout the Middle Ages, interest was forbidden by canon law; and many were the dodges to get around these restrictions.

How do we answer this view? First, we could point out what has been shown in earlier chapters—that holding a cash balance often does serve a useful function for which people will gladly pay up to a point. But let us meet the issue head on. Let us make the realistic assumption that when I borrow money from you, my purpose is not to hold onto the cash: instead I use the borrowed cash to buy capital goods; and, as we have seen, these intermediate capital goods are so scarce as to create a net product over and above their replacement cost. Therefore, if I did not pay you interest, I should really be cheating you out of the return that you could get by putting your own money directly into such productive investment projects!

CONSUMPTION LOANS The Biblical utterances against interest and usury clearly refer to loans made for consumption rather than investment purposes. Suppose I, a poor man, borrow from you, a rich man, so that I can eat more today or pay a hospital bill. (a) Is it fair that I should have to pay you interest? (b) How do such consumption loans affect the short-run and long-run equilibrium interest rates?

The answer to the second question will help answer the first. Consumption lending is today less important than productive-investment lending; therefore productive investment primarily determines the behavior of interest rates.[7]

Now we can treat the fairness question. Are we assuming that there is effective competition in the money market for consumption loans so that no one —rich or poor—can take unfair *monopoly* advantage of anyone else by preventing him from borrowing at the cheapest available terms? If we explicitly assume effective competition *and* that people will not rashly sacrifice their future well-being just to consume more now, then it is hard to see why there is anything more unfair about *loan* transactions between rich and poor than there would be in *other* competitive transactions between rich and poor, e.g., when a rich butcher sells a poor consumer a pound of meat. Of course, the poor man would rather pay nothing for the meat than have to pay a positive price. But being a scarce good, the meat commands a positive price and one that changes with supply and demand. If the existing distribution of income seems unfair to the populace, the field of taxation would seem to offer the best remedies—not random interference with competitive loan or other market transactions.

IS A ZERO INTEREST RATE POSSIBLE? In a world of perfect certainty, it is hard to see how people could ever save enough to bring the net productivity of capital all the way down to a zero interest rate. As long as there is a single hilly railroad track left, it would pay at a zero rate of interest to make it level. Why? Because over enough years, *any* saving in fuel would pay for the cost. As long as any increase in time-consuming processes could be counted on to produce any extra product and dollars of revenue, the yield of capital could not be zero. Also, as long as any land or other asset exists with a *sure perpetual net income*—and as long as people are willing to give only a *finite* amount of money today in exchange for a perpetual flow of income spread over the whole future—then we can hardly conceive of the rate of interest as falling to zero.[8]

---

[7] Nonetheless, to the extent that there is a desire to borrow now for present consumption purposes, we can take this into account in Fig. 30-1. If some people want to dissave, their consumption borrowing will make the community less thrifty as a whole than it would otherwise be. So we find the *ss* curve of the stock of capital shifting more slowly rightward; and we thereby progress more slowly downward on the *dd* curve from E toward E', with interest not falling so fast nor so far.

[8] Under realistic conditions of uncertainty, we must qualify the above. Before you have recovered the costs of leveling the roadbed of the railway, airplanes might make railways obsolete—or earthquakes might undo your work. In 1932 people expected and experienced zero or negative returns from most capital projects. That is why investment ceased. Even today, if the profit rate (pure interest rate plus premium to cover risk) got forced down to a low enough level business as a whole might be unwilling to undertake an investment level equal to desired full-employment saving. Fiscal budgetary deficits would then be indicated. See Appendix, page 558 for more floors to returns.

A zero rate of interest is a little like an "absolute zero of temperature" in physics. We can imagine getting close to it, but we can hardly imagine actually reaching the limiting state of a zero equilibrium rate of interest. Thus, interest is a basic phenomenon that would not disappear even in the most ideal economic world.

INTEREST UNDER SOCIALISM? Our economic analysis suggests that thinking is superficial if it concludes that interest is solely a monetary phenomenon of predatory capitalism. Students of planning in a centralized socialistic society have discovered that even such a society must introduce a concept like the interest rate into its plans. Every known society has, since Eden, had some limits on its supply of capital goods. Every society, therefore, has the important task of screening out investment projects, giving first priority to those that are most immediately productive of the things that society wants. Even in Utopia, you simply cannot do everything at once.

How, then, does the screening out among possible projects take place, so that definite priorities can be given? Clearly, there is no alternative but to choose (1) how much of present resources are to be used, and (2) how much of future useful products will be created. To reduce all the alternative patterns into a final single figure is not easy; but something like our earlier calculation of net productivities must be made. Unless you are satisfied to toss a coin or proceed by guess in your collectivist's society, *you have to introduce first those investment projects with the higher net productivity.* After much investment has gone into these in the past and diminishing returns has brought down the yield, you can go on to lower-net-productivity projects.

At some point, therefore, something like the interest rate necessarily comes into being. Recent studies show that the social engineers of the Soviet Union are anxious not to be denounced as capitalistic apologists, yet they need some form of interest rate (or "discount factor," or "pay-off period") for making efficient investment calculations. As a result, about a dozen different accounting methods are in vogue there for introducing a very thinly disguised interest-rate concept into Soviet planning procedures. But, of course no person need receive interest *income* from them.

SUMMARY OF INTEREST DETERMINATION

We have now seen what determines interest rates over time. If Robinson Crusoe (or a Communist dictator or the average citizen in a free economy) cuts down on current consumption, then capital formation can be higher and capital goods can grow faster in number. The more capital goods there are, the lower their net productivities will tend to be. Why? Because of our old friend the law of diminishing returns: with population and natural resources unchanged, when you add more and more physical capital goods—or, what is closely related, when you make production more and more roundabout and time-consuming—you will add to total product, but generally at a decreasing rate.

When you have built the bridges, dams, factories, and production lines that yield a net productivity of 20 per cent, you have then to go on to investment projects with 19 per cent and still lower net productivities. The market rate of interest that can be earned on investments will thus fall, and this will be the signal for investors to undertake projects which were previously unprofitable at the earlier higher rates of interest.[9]

Two kinds of thrift are involved. First, people must resist the temptation to eat up some of the capital that was amassed in the past; they must "abstain" from consuming more than their current incomes, that is, continue to replace capital and abstain from making net saving become negative. Second, if there is to be positive capital formation, the community must usually be willing to undergo "waiting"—waiting in the sense of giving up consumption goods now in return for more such goods in the future.

All in all, consumption-saving decisions plus the technical net productivity of capital goods are needed to explain behavior of interest rates over time.[10]

---

[9] What is the same thing, a lowering of the interest rate at which we calculate present discounted values (as indicated on page 558) will raise more and more investment projects above their initial cost—and they will be undertaken to society's advantage.

[10] As we shall see, the government—through its monetary and fiscal policies that favor or retard the rate of capital formation and ensure against the paradox of aborted thrift—is also an important determinant of investment and interest rates. So two economies in which *private* individuals and corporations show the same thrift propensities may develop very differently over a decade or century, depending upon the policies being followed by government.

SOME MAJOR QUALIFICATIONS

Now the main task of this chapter has been completed. But any traditional account of capital theory is in need of some important qualifications. This chapter concludes with only brief mention of the more important ones. The Appendix provides further discussion.

TECHNOLOGICAL DISTURBANCE   In real life we cannot hold other things constant while the economy proceeds to accumulate capital and travel down the road of diminishing returns. In particular, new inventions and discoveries are constantly being made. Such technological changes will often raise the net productivity and the interest rates to be earned on the community's present capital stock and its future extensions. So, instead of there being a movement down an unchanged schedule, inventions may cause an upward shift of the net-productivity-of-capital schedule.[11] (All this is not a fanciful possibility. Historical studies suggest that, for Europe and North America generally, the tendency toward falling interest rates via diminishing returns has been just about canceled out by technological progress: though real wage rates have been rising, the real interest return on capital has not been generally falling in this century, as would have been expected from the primitive classical analysis of capital accumulation of Fig. 30-1.)

If technical change came to an end, the rate of interest might again march down toward zero or to the point where no saving took place. But, actually, new inventions are constantly coming along to give interest rates an upward lift. Some economists (such as Schumpeter) have likened the process to a plucked violin string: other things being equal, the string will gradually come to rest as competitive capital formation undermines net yields; but before this can happen, some outside event or invention comes along to pluck it once more and to set it again into motion. (See Chapter 37 and its Appendix for more on this.)

UNCERTAINTY AND EXPECTATIONS   Our exposition of the traditional capital theory has assumed perfect foresight. This is a serious oversimplification. In real life no one has a crystal ball to read the future: all evaluations of capital and all investment decisions, resting as they do on estimates of future earnings, must necessarily be guesses—accurate guesses based on much thought and information in some cases, wild guesses in other cases, but in every case uncertain guesses. Each day we wake up to learn that our expectations were not quite accurate and have to be revalued; each night we go to bed realizing that the next morning will have some surprises for us.

The next chapter will show how significant uncertainty is for profit theory. Here, in connection with interest and capital theory, we must note an important effect of uncertainty:

Investors' optimism about future yields and risks can change markedly in a very short time; hence all relations will be very *shiftable*. They will shift with changes in opinion and rumour; with changes in population trends; with changes in technology and innovation; etc.[12]

SHIFTS IN SCHEDULES WITH INCOME   Even without disturbing outside factors, there is a serious drawback to traditional schedules. Changes in the level of *real income* profoundly *shift* classical saving and investment schedules at each rate of interest. (Only recall our long statistical and theoretical discussions of Part Two dealing with the propensity to consume and save at different levels of income. Also recall discussions of investment induced by increases in the level of income relative to fixed capacities of capital—or what is closely related, the "acceleration principle" of Chapter 13.)

Shifts of the basic schedules—as e.g., of *dd* in Fig. 30-1—represent serious weaknesses in the traditional theory. Many classical economists of a century ago were unaware of this problem because they had the comfortable view that chronic unemployment was impossible and income would not fluctuate. They did not always know why they believed full employment was inevitable. But they did believe that

---

[11] Some inventions may be "capital saving" and twist the net productivity relationship downward, often tending to lower interest. (See Chapter 37.) Note that inventions may also destroy some capital by making it obsolete; and changes in consumer tastes can have similar disturbing effects.

[12] To illustrate this subjective volatility, Keynes once characterized the 1929 crash as "a sudden collapse in the (net productivity or) marginal efficiency of capital"—a true, but surface, explanation.

"supply always creates its own demand and general overproduction is an impossibility."[13]

REAL VERSUS MONEY INTEREST RATE In Brazil interest rates often exceed 40 per cent a year. During the 1923 German inflation, they often were 1 million per cent per month! Canadians who bought government savings bonds a decade ago, with a nominal yield of 4 1/2 per cent, can actually buy less today with $100 than they could ten years ago with the $75 the bonds cost—entailing a "real interest return" of less than zero per cent.

These examples stress the need to define the "real interest rate" as the "money interest rate" minus "the percentage price rise." (Recall Chapter 15's discussion of the *real* rate of return, on page 247.) Thus, if the money rate is 8 per cent for Canadians and the annual price rise is 5 per cent, then the true real rate of interest is 8 — 5 = 3 per cent. So to speak, 100 market baskets of goods lent today give you next year only 103 (not 108!) market baskets in return.

As people come to anticipate a steady rate of inflation, they build into their interest-rate supply and demand schedules an allowance for the inflation. They begin to prefer common stocks, shunning low-interest bonds. Thus in the 1970s, interest rates of 8 and 10 per cent became common. High rates? Yes, in money terms. But the calculated *real* interest rate held steady for 1965 to 1972 at the rather moderate level of 3 per cent before it fell in 1973.

PUBLIC AND PRIVATE POLICY IN DETERMINING CAPITAL FORMATION

Concretely, how does the modern *macro*analysis fit in with the valid elements of the traditional microeconomic theory? Here is its basic contribution:

---

[13] For example, some believed in a miraculous law of conservation of market purchasing power: what was not spent in one direction they said *had* to be spent in another. A more defensible version of the theory claims that, if only wages and prices were never sticky, then flexible decreases in all prices and wages would ultimately so increase the real purchasing power of the coin and currency in each man's pocket as to reduce his thriftiness enough to restore full employment. The modern version of this hyper-deflation theory we have associated with A. C. Pigou, who did not recommend it for policy purposes. (See Appendix to Chapter 18 on Say's Law and Pigou effects.)

Fiscal and monetary policies interact with private thrift to determine how fast society builds up its capital.

Consider, for example, a successful pattern of full-employment equilibrium without inflation. Recall that this requires the saving and investment curves of the theory of income determination in Chapters 12 and 13 to be intersecting at full employment, with no inflationary gap and no deflationary gap. Two instances are shown in Fig. 30-2.

The community's propensity-to-save-out-of-income curve will crucially depend upon budgetary fiscal policy. To see this, suppose tax rates are very high, so that revenues collected at full employment are very high relative to expenditure, the budget being overbalanced. Suppose, too, that the taxes fall most heavily on the relatively thriftless lower-income groups. Then the community's propensity-to-consume schedule will be a low one at every level of national income, including the full-employment level. The amount not consumed (equal to net personal saving *plus the government surplus*) will then be very great at every level and—what interests us here—*SS* will be great at the full-employment level of income shown in Fig. 30-2(a).

Would such a depressed consumption level cause unemployment? Not if macroeconomic management is working.[14] Aggressive easing of monetary policy (open-market purchases, reduced secondary-reserve requirements, lowered Bank Rate, and possibly aggressive selective credit programs) will push the community's investment schedule upward. Result: Tight fiscal policy plus very expansionary monetary policy have given us a full-employment income characterized by very high capital formation and relatively low consumption (see in Fig. 30-2(a)).

We can work out the opposite mix of tight monetary and easy fiscal policies appropriate for a community that seeks a high-consumption low-investment full-employment income, as in Fig. 30-2(b). Looked at together, the two diagrams (a) and (b) show the alternative annual rates of capital formation in two societies, each charactierized by the same degree of private thrift (as measured by family budget studies at each level of disposable income), but with alternative public policies. Note the re-

[14] See pages 309-310.

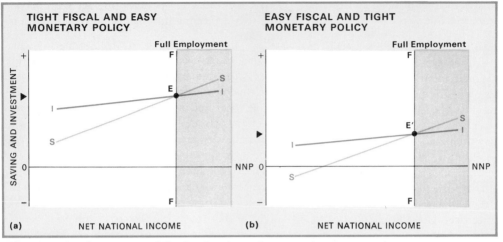

FIG. 30-2. Mix of monetary and fiscal policy determines rate of capital growth.
(a) By tight fiscal and easy monetary policies, the first economy is causing full-employment saving and investment to reach equilibrium at E, with rapid rate of capital formation. (b) The second economy uses easy fiscal policy (low taxes and deficits) matched by tight monetary policy to create a low-saving-and-investment (high-consumption) full-employment equilibrium. Note that E' is much lower than E in investment.

sulting differences in capital formation, and remember that diminishing returns would be operating to bring down interest more rapidly in the high-investment society unless offset by special technological progress there.

A SOBERING PUBLIC RESPONSIBILITY We conclude, then, with two reminders. Macroeconomic management can banish the paradoxical possibility of thrift becoming abortive and can in this sense validate the classical notions concerning capital formation and productivity. On the other hand, modern societies necessarily are engaging in monetary and fiscal policies—and it is these public policies that to an important degree do shape the resulting sharing of high-employment output (NNP) between consumption and investment.

This power over the community's rate of capital formation should constitute a sobering responsibility for the voters in any modern democracy.[15]

SUMMARY

1 We can apply *primary* factors of production, land and labor, in indirect ways by introducing *intermediate* productive factors called *capital goods*. It is taken as a technological fact that this "roundaboutness" yields a *net productivity* over and above all

[15] Joan Robinson and Piero Sraffa of Cambridge University have pointed out that there may be no unambiguous way to define the degree of roundaboutness of the production process. They have also cogently pointed out that although labor and land might be characterized under simplifying conditions by "the quantity of labor, and the quantity of land," it is not possible under realistic conditions to reduce a heterogeneous array of different kinds of capital goods—hammers, raw leather, engines of type 99a and of 13d—into a meaningful, quantitative magnitude called "homogeneous capital." Hence, it is false to think that one can speak of the marginal productivity of capital in the same concrete terms that one can hope under suitable conditions to speak of the marginal productivity of labor or of clay land of defined grade. These considerations lead critics to introduce macroeconomic as well as microeconomic elements into a model of income distribution, and also to invoke institutional elements of power—militant trade-union bargaining, etc.—into their models. See the appendixes to this chapter and to Chapters 37 and 41 for some qualifications that this entails for the traditional theory of interest expounded in this main chapter.

replacement costs, expressible as an annual interest percentage and subject to the usual law of diminishing returns. (Read again the exact definition of net productivity.)

2 To get the capitalized value of an asset, the interest rate is needed. It is also the device society uses to select investment projects that are most urgent and economical. When interest is high, only projects with highest net productivities can qualify. Gradually, after much past capital formation has invoked the law of diminishing returns, the interest rates will be falling. This provides the signal for introducing capital projects with lower net productivities.

3 Thrift, in the sense of *abstaining* from consuming past capital accumulations and *waiting* for future consumption goods rather than consuming now, interacts with the technical net productivity of capital goods to determine the developing pattern of interest rates and capital formation. Even outside a collectivist world, government monetary and fiscal policies play an important role in this process.

4 Even a planned state which is not run for private profit or gain would have to use some device like an interest rate as a sieve to determine which of the many possible investment projects represent the best use of the resources available today after present consumption needs have been determined. "Come the revolution"—come *laissez-faire*—Nature's law of diminishing returns (of "future consumption goods" in return for "sacrificed present consumption goods") is likely still to be in business.

5 Consumption loans, while they are of minor importance today, do have some influence on the rate at which the community accumulates capital rather than consumes. Like the subjective factors of thrift, abstinence, waiting, foresight, impatience, and so forth, (a) personal borrowings do interact with (b) the technological fact of opportunity to invest in long-lived projects with a net yield.

   Critics of interest had in mind the occurrence of consumption loan transactions in highly imperfectly competitive markets where the poor might be regarded as being at the mercy of the rich lender's bargaining power. Today no one would be in favor of usurious overcharges that take advantage of the poor man's inadequate access to competitive loan markets or his desperate neglect of his own future; but economists and philosophers recognize that the net productivity of capital is the technological fact most basic to modern-day interest: when you lend me money, you are giving up the opportunity to invest in land, machines, bonds, and stocks—forgone opportunities of which interest is some kind of measure.

6 Important qualifications of the oversimplified traditional capital theory include the following: Lack of perfect foresight means that the capital net productivity is very *shiftable* as expectations, technology, and income levels change. Also, a classical theory that ignores deviations from full-employment income does need modification. Finally, to get the real rate of interest, one must subtract from the money rate the anticipated percentage rate of price inflation.

7 A great variety of compensating monetary and fiscal policies can succeed in maintaining reasonably full employment. Stable employment being assumed, Fig. 30-2 gives the needed qualification to the traditional theory; and it reveals that public policy has great responsibility for determining whether the composition of the full-employment national income will be heavily weighted toward investment or toward consumption; this means that the central bank and the legislature between them shape the environment within which private thriftiness provides one part of total social thriftiness.

CONCEPTS FOR REVIEW

net productivity of capital

indirect, roundabout methods and
   diminishing returns

interest rate per annum

capitalization by $V = \$N/i$

choosing among investment projects

zero interest under any ism

abstinence and waiting

uncertainty and technological change

real versus money interest rate

austere fiscal policy and easy monetary
   policy, or opposite

public responsibility for rate of capital
   formation

QUESTIONS FOR DISCUSSION

1. Give some examples of efficient roundabout processes. Of "produced" or "intermediate" outputs that serve in their turn as inputs.

2. Contrast three "prices" of capital: (*a*) rental of a capital good, (*b*) market price of the capital good, and (*c*) interest yield on the value of the good.

3. Irving Fisher wrote a book with the title *The Theory of Interest*. He gave it the subtitle *As Determined by Impatience to Spend and Opportunities to Invest*. Explain what these mean. Defend the following: "Fisher should have added 'and as affected by government monetary and fiscal policies.' "

4. "The interest rate was simply a bourgeois device for exploitation." Discuss.

5. Protestant, Catholic, and Jewish organizations today issue mortgages to build local places to worship, and they invest any surplus funds in bonds, or possibly, as in the case of the Church of England, in equity stocks. How might they ethically distinguish this from "taking usury"?

6. How do innovations and expectations affect traditional interest theory?

7. Interpret macroeconomic management in a modern mixed economy. Contrast full employment *cum* "tight money" and "easy fiscal policy" with its opposite.

8. Explain the rule for calculating present discounted value of a perpetual income stream. At 5 per cent, what is the worth of a perpetuity paying $100 per year? Paying $200 per year? Paying $N per year? At 6 or 8 per cent, what is the worth of a perpetuity paying $100 per year? What does doubling of the interest rate do to the capitalized value of a perpetuity—say a perpetual bond?

Appendix: Theoretical Aspects of Interest, Money, and Policy

Here, very briefly, can be mentioned some elaborations and qualifications of this chapter's discussion.

PRODUCTIVITY OR IMPATIENCE?

Some people like to find a single cause for everything, and such people ask: "Is interest caused by the productivity of capital? Or by the fact that savers must be paid for the unpleasant task of 'abstinence' or 'waiting'? Which is more important: opportunity to invest or impatience to spend?"

Our previous argument shows this is a false antithesis. *Both* factors operate to determine the time path of interest: the impatience to spend, or the tendency to prefer the present to the future, limits the growth rate and attained size of capital; and the productivity factor tells us what is the interest or net productivity that can be earned as we have various amounts of diverse capital goods. Just as both blades of a scissors are needed to cut—so that you cannot say that one blade rather than the other is doing the actual work—similarly, both factors, impatience *and* productivity, interact to determine the behavior of interest rates.[1]

DETERMINATION OF THE INTEREST RATE

Can our account of interest determination avoid the use of Fig. 30-1's simplifying concept of a stock of homogeneous capital? Yes, in a number of ways, some of which are too complex to explain in an introductory work. Thus, we may work with a variety of different physical capital goods and processes, being careful never to add their heterogeneous units together, noting that the sum of their capitalized market values does depend (in a virtuously, and not vi-

ciously, circular way) on the market interest rate, and never forgetting that it is machines and not hunks of dollars which enter into physical production functions. If the realistic problem of uncertainty about the future and the risks thereby implied could be ignored, advanced treatises can show rigorously how an equilibrium interest-rate pattern can be defined in such a heterogeneous model.

This is clearly not the place for such refinements. But it is desirable to mention that a theory of equilibrium interest rates can be given which avoids the homogeneous-capital assumptions of Fig. 30-1.

The key to a simple approach comes from Fisher's diagram, Fig. 30-3, in footnote 1, which states the following fundamental proposition about the theory of interest:

Society can exchange present consumption goods for future consumption goods at a trade-off rate depicted by the rate of interest.

LONG-RUN EQUILIBRIUM How long could this accumulation process of sacrificing current consumption go on? Just as Fig. 30-1 suggested, it can go on until the interest rate is zero, or until people want to do no net saving. At the zero rate of interest, if we could ever quite reach this point on the horizon, the plateau of consumption would be as high as is technically possible with the given labor, land, and primary resources. It would be a kind of "golden age."[2]

[2]Advanced books show that this golden rule must be modified if primary resources such as labor are *all* growing at 3 or 5 per cent

---

[1]Those who have mastered the indifference-curve graphs of the Appendix to Chapter 22 can use Fig. 30-3 to see that positive interest is caused by two factors: (1) a vertical bias of the *AB* production-possibility frontier between present and future consumption goods, and (2) a general vertical bias of the typical consumer's indifference contours between present and future consumption goods. Hence, the tangency-equilibrium at *E* has a slope steeper than 1.0, corresponding to positive interest. The experienced reader will recognize that these can be related to Bohm-Bawerk's three famous causes for interest. His third cause, technological superiority of roundabout processes, and his first cause, the expectation by the typical consumer that his future dollars will have lower marginal utility because his income will be higher in the future (as a result of technological progress or of the productivity of roundaboutness), relate to factor (1). Bohm's second cause—systematic time preference by consumers for present rather than future goods, for rational reasons of life's uncertainties and brevity or for irrational reasons—relates to (2). [Suppose we were to rule out factor (1) by making *AB* "symmetrical around the 45° line" and rule out factor (2) by making the indifference curves "symmetrical around the 45° line." Having thus ruled out net productivity and time preference, we should find that the equilibrium interest rate must then be zero. Leaving either bias in, or both, leads to positive interest.]

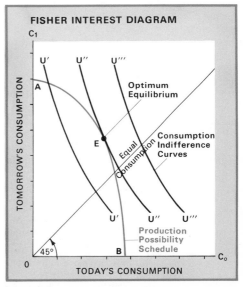

FIG. 30-3.

In real life three or more things keep us from reaching the golden age:

1. People may be so impatient that at some interest rate like 3 per cent, they won't want to do net saving.

2. Inventions will come along and offset diminishing returns by shifting upward Fig. 30-1's *dd*.

3. There is always riskiness in a dynamic society: long before the pure interest rate reaches zero, the profit-rate-inclusive-of-premium-for-risk may have hit a floor below which investment lags. We must examine this important matter.

AN UNCERTAINTY FLOOR TO RISKY RETURN?

It may be that under conditions of perfect certainty, persistent thrift can lead to no floor for interest except that of zero. But what about the real world where a measure of uncertainty must always be feared for any actual investment project? Can it not be the case that investors will dislike the task of taking risks on their shoulders? That they will insist on a rate of return on such investments which includes a certain definite positive percentage premium? Thus, even if the rate of interest to be earned on perfectly safe holdings were forced down to zero, might not people still insist on a 5 per cent after-tax return on a risky investment in a machine or in the purchase of land that produces an uncertain yearly rental?

This floor at 5 per cent, or at some positive level above zero, might be a realistic problem to contend with. And if it were to materialize, some serious problems for full-employment policy might one day arrive. Here is why: Suppose that Bank of Canada expansionary policies lowered the rate of interest on very safe short-term government bonds toward zero; this could be expected to bring the rates of return on risky enterprises down from, say, 12 per cent to 8 per cent. And since at the lower rate many new investment projects would now pay, an upswing in investment spending might result that, through the mechanism of the familiar multiplier process, would lift output, income, and employment.

But suppose all this were not enough to reestablish full employment. Then the Bank of Canada could do more of the same. *But by no amount of expansionary moves could it reduce the safe interest rate below the floor of zero.* And it might well be the case that a zero floor on safe holdings could pull the rates on risky investment down only to their floor of 5 per cent—and no further. Then it would be quite

conceivable that the sticky 5 per cent floor would bar further reduction in rates needed to coax out a pace of current job-giving investment big enough to restore full employment.

Therefore it is conceivable that an impasse, a kind of Day of Judgment for our mixed system with its inflexible wage and price levels, might arrive when conventional measures to stimulate investment could not restore full employment and let our optimistic "managed money" work itself out smoothly and fully.[3] Fortunately, deficit budgetary policies can come to the rescue!

While this pessimistic possibility may not now be at hand, a prudent society has to keep it in mind. And if that unhappy day should ever approach, more extensive remedial programs (such as investments, tax credits and insurance of loan risks or new institutions to provide venture capital) could be imaginatively explored.

MARKET CAPITALIZATION OF ASSETS EQUALS PRESENT DISCOUNTED VALUE

Here we can go beyond page 546's simple case of perpetual annuities to the general case. Under conditions of absolute certainty, anyone can borrow or lend as much as he wishes at the single competitive market rate of interest. Every asset must be yielding that same market rate of interest. This equality of yield results from the way competitors bid up or down the market price of any asset—whether it be a bond, stock, patent, going business, corner lot, or any earning stream of net rentals whatsoever.

What exactly is the formula for the capitalized market value of *any* asset?

Under absolute certainty, every asset will be capitalized *by the price bids of buyers and sellers* in the market place

---

per year. Then the golden age of maximal per capita consumption comes when the interest rate has been brought down also to 3 or 5 per cent: then the young earners in society, who are saving for their old age, are just enough more numerous than the retired earners, who are eating up what they had earlier saved; and then there is just enough net saving and investing to keep all capital goods growing in full proportion to the growth in primary labor. Then we have an equilibrium, a nice moving equilibrium with balanced growth (and "widening of capital"). (If land will not grow at all, Malthus reminds us that this Eden must, in the absence of inventions, ultimately end with stationary population.)

[3]Without risk the problem of placing my assets is easy. I put all my wealth in Bank A if it offers me 5 3/4 per cent while Bank B offers only 5 per cent. I put all my wealth in building stores or tools if they offer more than Bank A's 5 3/4 per cent. So long as I know I can get any safe positive interest return, I hoard no money, keeping only minimal balances for transaction purposes. Without any risks, so long as interest yields remain positive, we should never run out of investment opportunities and into unemployment problems on this account.

With risk, if I obey the law of diminishing marginal utility of Chapter 22, the Appendix of Chapter 21 showed that I shall avoid gambling and want insurance (since a gain in my wealth will be worth less to me than an equivalent *dollar* loss). Now I refuse to put all my eggs in one basket: I put some money in both banks in case one should fail; I prefer $5,000 in Canadian Pacific and $5,000 in Chemcell to $10,000 in either one alone; I buy many independent stocks for my portfolio; I particularly buy both ice and coal stocks so as to be hedged against the worst that can happen. For safety's sake I always hold some idle cash even though it pays no interest. When the pure interest rate is below 2 per cent, I would just as soon hoard cash equal to a large fraction of my wealth or just as soon hold less. This is why Part Two's problem of great unemployment can persist: when a low investment schedule intersects the saving schedule at a point of low-employment GNP, and with profit and interest rates already at their bottom, there is relatively little that conventional banking policy can do in such unlucky times. Then we thank Providence for fiscal policy!

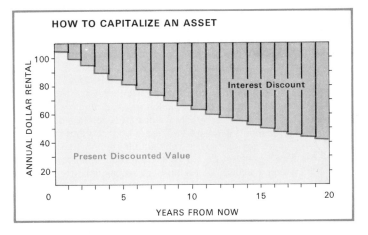

HOW TO CAPITALIZE AN ASSET

(Chart: ANNUAL DOLLAR RENTAL (vertical axis, 20 to 100) vs YEARS FROM NOW (horizontal axis, 0 to 20). Labeled areas: "Interest Discount" (upper) and "Present Discounted Value" (lower).)

FIG. 30-4. The present value of a machine giving net annual rentals of $100 for 20 years (with interest rate prescribed at 6 per cent) is shown by the lower area. The upper area shows what has been discounted away. (Why does raising the interest rate depress the market price of an asset such as a machine or a bond? Note that the higher interest rate enlarges the discount area subtracted.)

at the *present discounted value* of all its future net receipts. These dollar receipts cannot simply be added up regardless of the date when they are received. The farther off in the future a given dollar receipt is, the less it is worth today. Why?

Because the positive market rate of interest means that all future payments must be *discounted*. A building far off looks tiny because of spatial perspective. The interest rate produces a similar shrinking of time perspective. Even if I knew you would pay $1 to my heirs 999 years from now, I should be foolish to advance you more than a cent today. To see why, let us review the arithmetic of this discounting process.

At 6 per cent interest I can set aside about 94 cents today, and it will grow to $1 within the year. Hence, the *present discounted value* of $1 payable a year from now is today only 94 cents (or to be exact 100/1.06 = 94 36/106 cents). The present discounted value of $1 payable in 2 years' time is only about 89 cents, or $1/($1.06)^4. Similarly, any tables of compound interest will show how to compute present discounted values.[4]

Computation of PDV: To arrive at any asset's present discounted value, let each dollar stand on its own feet: evaluate the present worth of each part of the stream of future receipts, giving due allowance for the discounting required by its payment date. Then simply *add together* all these separate present discounted values. Thus we have arrived at the asset's capitalized market value, or what is called its "present discounted value." (See the Appendix Summary for the general formula.)

[4]The general rule for present discounted values is the following: To figure out the value today of $1 payable t years from now, ask yourself how much must be invested today at compound interest to grow into $1 at the end of t years. Now we know that at 6 per cent compound interest any principal grows in t years proportionally to $(1 + 0.06)^t$. Hence, we need only invert this expression to arrive at the final answer. Therefore the *present discounted value* of $1 payable t years from now is only $1/(1 + 0.06)^t$. What if the interest rate were 8 per cent per annum? Replace 0.016 by 0.08. What if the interest rate were i per cent?

Figure 30-4 shows this graphically for a machine that earns steady net annual rentals of $100 over a 20-year period and has no scrap value at the end. Its present value is not $2,000, but only $1,147. Note how much the later dollar earnings are scaled down or discounted because of our time perspective. The total area remaining *after* discounting (the light-red area) represents the total of the machine's *present discounted value*—its capitalized market value.[5]

[5]Can you now verify our $V = \$N/i$ perpetuity formula? In high school algebra we learn to sum a convergent geometric progression
$$1 + K + K^2 + \ldots = \frac{1}{1 - K}$$
for K any fraction less than 1. If you set $K = \dfrac{1}{1 + i}$ you can with a little work verify our capitalization formula for a permanent income stream: write out *all* the discounted terms.
$$\frac{\$N}{1 + i} + \frac{\$N}{(1 + i)^2} + \cdots$$
$$= -\$N + \$N \left\{ 1 + \frac{1}{1 + i} + \left(\frac{1}{1 + i}\right)^2 + \cdots \right\}$$
$$= -\$N + \$N \quad \frac{1}{1 - \dfrac{1}{1 + i}} \quad = \frac{\$N}{i} \quad [QED]$$

But note that common-sense economics gives us an equally convincing proof: At interest i, $\$N/i$ is the only sum *whose earnings will exactly match the $N per year of income.*

(A FINE POINT: Sometimes you cannot be sure just which of two machines is the more "durable" one that will be brought into use at a lower interest rate. Suppose Machine A yields $100 of output one period from now and $132 of output three periods from now. Let Machine B yield $230 units of output two periods from now, and let it cost the same as A. Which is more durable? More capital-intensive? We can't say. At very low rates of interest, present discounted value or *PDV* of A exceeds *PDV* of B, since 100 + 132 > 230. At very high rates of interest, *PDV* of A exceeds *PDV* of B, since the second and third periods' outputs are discounted away to almost nothing. But at intermediate interest rates, between 10 and 20 per cent per period, calculation shows *PDV* of B exceeds *PDV* of A, and B will be chosen. This "reswitching" phenomenon spoils any simple diminishing-returns story, as advanced treatises show.)

ACTING TO MAXIMIZE PRESENT DISCOUNTED VALUE Our formula tells us how to write down in our balance sheets the value of any asset once we know how that asset will be used. But note that an asset's future receipts usually depend on our business decisions: Shall we use a truck 8 or 9 years? Shall we overhaul it once a month or once a year? Shall we replace it with a cheap nondurable truck or an expensive durable one?

There is one golden rule for giving correct answers to all investment decisions:

Calculate the present discounted value resulting from each possible decision. Then always act so as to achieve the maximum present discounted value. That way you will have more wealth, to spend whenever and however you like.[6]

RESWITCHING AND ALL THAT[7]

Traditional capital theory, scholars now recognize, is overly simple. They know that an increase in the money supply will not be neutral in its real-life effect on interest rates. They know that the level of unemployment, and the macroeconomic policies of government,[8] can affect the rate of interest.

But there are more subtle difficulties with the simple notion of (a) a homogeneous stock of measurable capital, and (b) the law of diminishing returns as applied to capital's "set productivity" or "degree of roundaboutness." Briefly, we can indicate some of the important modern critiques.

The classical parable has been challenged in its overly simple claim that people (1) give up current consumption goods ("waiting and abstinence"); (2) transmute them into a greater quantity of some homogeneous stuff called "capital"; (3) then collect the marginal productivity of such capital in the form of interest, in exact analogy to the fact that wage rates and rents are the marginal productivity of labor and land; and (4) experience declining interest rates as more capital accumulates, for the alleged reason that capital is subject to the law of diminishing returns just like any other factor input.

Nonsense, Joan Robinson has pointed out again and again. Throw out the notion that the rich man earns his interest by the sweat of his abstinence in much the same way that the worker earns his wage by the sweat of his brow. There is no abstract quantity of capital to put in an aggregate production function like $Q = 1.01\ L^{.75}K^{.25}$. If abstract K does not exist, how can its marginal product $\partial Q/\partial K$ exist? Or how can we hold "it" constant to compute neoclassical marginal products of labor, $\partial Q/\partial L$?

To dramatize the oversimplicity of the neoclassical parable, critics belonging to this "Anglo-Italian" school—P. Sraffa, L. Pasinetti, N. Kaldor, and Joan Robinson being prominent members—point out cogently that there is no technological way of validating in the most general case the primitive notion that "lower interest rates involve *more-roundabout* methods of production." An example involving so-called "reswitching" illustrates the point.

WELL-BEHAVED PARABLE Suppose there are two ways of making 1 unit of sulphuric acid (or standardized wine). Method A requires 7 units of labor 2 periods *before* the final output is produced. Method B requires 5 labor units 3 periods before final output.

"Obviously," says the neoclassical parabolist, "B is more roundabout than A. And actually, only when the interest rate falls below 40 per cent will B be more profitable to use than A. [EXPLANATION: 7/5 = 1.40.] But that is as it should be, since society can't move to the longer pipelines of B until some rich man (or the state) is prepared to sacrifice some present goods for future ones. Also, when many do accomplish this thrift and accumulation of (or 'deepening' of) capital, the lowering of interest rate they accomplish [and the new higher GNP for society!] raises real wages of workers, as we can verify by some elaborate calculations of how final product's cost is now broken down between wages and interest."

These are tall claims. But they are deflated when we alter the numerical example.

RESWITCHING EXAMPLE Suppose, instead of Method B, the only alternative to A were the following Method C. In Method C, you produce 1 unit of product with 2 labor units 3 periods earlier and 6 labor units 1 period earlier. Now the critic has his turn.

Which is more roundabout and time-intensive, A or C? As Piero Sraffa pointed out in his classic 1960 book *The Production of Commodities by Means of Commodities* (Cambridge University Press, Cambridge, England), there is no technological way to say which is the more time-intensive.

What can we say? Suppose the interest rate were zero (or very small). Since 7 < 6 + 2, Method A must be cheaper at very low interest rates. Again, at very high interest rates—say 200 per cent per period—compounding 2 labor units for 3 periods will be much, much worse than 7 for 2 periods. So again, at very high interest rates, Method A will be selected over C by ruthless competition.

But, with the help of compound interest tables (or the quadratic equation of Question 4, page 562), we can ascertain that Method C will be cheaper than A at all interest rates between 100 per cent per period and 50 per cent! In brief, at low i we encounter reswitching back to the

---

[6]This rule shows that business decisions in an ideal capital market would be independent of the decider's *personal* consumption-saving time preference. Why? Because it is always better to be able to sell out now for a larger money sum than for a small sum, no matter in what time pattern you decide to spend on consumption. In imperfect markets, personal time preference may matter.

[7]This section may be skipped. Footnote 5's fine point provided an example of reswitching for a durable machine.

[8]See the Hicks-Hansen diagrams in Chapter 18's Appendix. We can be, and stay, at full employment by having contractionary fiscal policy shift the *IS* curve rightward while expansionary central bank policy shifts the *LM* curve rightward. (Can you show how to get a high-consumption, low-investment, full employment by reversing this prescription?)

methods used at high *i*. What now of the notion that Baron Rothschild's abstinence is needed to accumulate capital in order to bring down the interest rate and raise workers' real wages!

In this simple model, use of power by unions or the state, to lower the interest rate from 101 to 0.001 per cent will shift the distribution of income from little going to workers to *almost all* going to them.

EVALUTION The science of political economy has not yet the empirical knowledge to decide whether the real world is nearer to the idealized polar cases represented by (*a*) the neoclassical parable, or (*b*) the simple reswitching paradigm. The opinions of the authors should not be foisted on the beginning reader. But they are owed to him.

When we consider what great amounts of plant, equipment, and inventories could do for developing countries like India, Brazil, or South Korea, for planned economies like Russia, China, or North Korea, for advanced economies like Japan, Italy, the United States or Canada, the authors are led to think that *great gains in the size of the social pie to be divided up in the future can be hoped for from capital accumulation at the expense of present-day consumption*. But this does not mean that private property, unequally distributed, is the only twentieth-century mechanism to bring this about.

In conclusion, the economic concepts that all can agree on, regardless of reswitching, are twofold.

1. Any tradeoff between present and future goods is subject to diminishing returns in the manner of Chapter 2's guns-and-butter concave frontier.

2. The lower is the interest rate (or profit rate—they are the same thing in absence of uncertainty), the higher will be the real wage [in accordance with Fig. 37-2(b)'s factor-price frontier, to come later].

SUMMARY TO APPENDIX

1 Technical opportunities to invest (to swap present consumption for future consumption goods) interact with people's subjective time preferences (about how much to consume or to add to the accumulated stocks of past capital formation) to determine the interest rate. As in all markets, *both* supply and demand factors interact.

2 Avoiding the highly useful device of homogeneous stock of physical capital, we can still have a complete interest theory along Fisher lines. The interest rate equals terms of trade at which we can get next year's consumption goods for today's—106 chocolates next year for 100 today means a real 6 per cent interest rate per annum.

3 The formula for capitalizing the asset value of a perpetual constant income can be extended when receipts are neither constant nor perpetual. Each dollar payable *t* years from now is worth only its "present discounted value" of $1/(1 + i)^t$. So for any net receipt stream $(N_1, N_2, \ldots, N_t, \ldots)$,

$$PDV = \frac{N_1}{(1 + i)} + \frac{N_2}{(1 + i)^2} + \cdots + \frac{N_t}{(1 + i)^t} + \cdots$$

4 Under conditions involving no uncertainty and no technical innovations, if the community insisted on accumulating more and more capital, diminishing returns might finally force capital's net productivity and the interest rate indefinitely down toward zero. Under real-life conditions of great uncertainty, there is the possibility that the floor on risky returns would be considerably higher than the floor of zero return on risk-free loans. So we cannot rule out the pessimistic possibility of a future Day of Judgment, where the authorities would have to supplement the orthodox methods by which the central bank eases interest rates if they are to succeed in coaxing out the volume of job-creating investment needed to keep employment high or full. But that day seems remote.

5 Reswitching examples alert us to the fact that, in the general case, there is no technological criterion of "roundaboutness or time-intensity of capital and the productive process" that can be applied independently of observed lowering of the market rate of interest. In general, one cannot assert that of two societies alike in know-how, A, with a lower interest rate, must have a higher steady-state plateau of real consumption than B, with a higher interest rate. However, the real wage in A must in *all* examples (not involving extraneous joint products) be higher when the interest rate is lower; and, always, as you give up more and more chocolates today, the increments of chocolates tomorrow diminish.

CONCEPTS FOR REVIEW

abstinence, impatience, waiting
opportunity to invest
present discounted value
interest rate and planning

tradeoff between today's and
    tomorrow's consumption
uncertainty
reswitching versus parables

QUESTIONS FOR DISCUSSION

1 After the H-bomb was developed, my time preference for present over future consumption increased. After having learned that my uncle will bequeath me a fortune a decade from now, the same happened. Was this rational? Thinking of a lobster dinner tonight, I offer you $9 on Monday for $8 now. Is this irrational?

2 Two communities have the same technological production functions. Why might they show different interest-rate patterns in history?

3 Give reasons why lower interest rates might increase investment demand.

4 *Extra credit problem:* If a doubling of i halves the *PDV* of a perpetuity, can you show that the truck in Fig. 30-4 will *less* than halve in capitalized value? (HINT: The perpetuity has a rectangle that goes on forever, with its red area getting less and less. The truck lacks this infinite tail off to the right. Now the early year receipts get hardly changed in value at all, since, say, .96 is not much changed when it becomes .92. So the average change in all the truck's red area is less than that for the perpetuity.) By similar reasoning establish the rule: Interest changes have their biggest effects on *long*-term bonds; their least effects on *short*-term bonds—whose principal will be repaid soon and is therefore hardly affected by any discounting. Also, can you verify the reswitching example's demonstration that only below 50 per cent and above 100 per cent interest will Method A displace Method C? [HINT: $7(1 + i)^2 = 2(1 + i)^3 + 6(1 + i)$ has roots $= i = 0.50$ and 1.00.]

31
PROFITS AND INCENTIVES

The world will always be governed by self-interest. We should not try to stop this, we should try to make the self-interest of cads a little more coincident with that of decent people.

SAMUEL BUTLER

In addition to wages, interest, and rent, economists often talk about a fourth category of income: profit. Wages are the return to labor; interest is the return to capital; rent is the return to land. What is profit the return to?

The answer that economists give is a complex one. This chapter will show that the word "profits" has many different meanings in everyday usage. From these different possible meanings, the economist, after careful analysis, ends up relating the concept of profit to dynamic innovation and uncertainty-bearing, and to the problems of monopoly, incentives and exploitation.

We shall first discuss the main notions of profit. The usual profit figures bandied about will not check with any of these, as we shall see. Then, along with analyzing the notion of competitive profit as a return to risk bearing and other traditional notions, we shall discuss criticisms of profit as the fruit of monopoly and exploitation.

REPORTED PROFIT STATISTICS

When a statistician from the United Nations or Statistics Canada gives newspaper reporters a figure involving profits, what does he usually include?

Certainly he includes *corporation earnings*—whether they are paid out as dividends or retained as undistributed profits. (In some reports he includes, and in some he excludes, corporate profit taxes, and sometimes he "adjusts" corporate profits for changes in evaluation of inventories due to price-level changes. So you must be careful in using published statistics.) He may also give another figure that has the flavor of profits about it; namely, *income of unincorporated enterprises* (farmers, the self-employed,

doctors and other professionals, partnerships, and so forth).

We understand how he arrived at such a statistical figure of profits for a corporation or an unincorporated enterprise. From the sales revenue of the firm, he subtracted its costs: cost of materials, wage payments to employees, bond interest, depreciation, expense, land rents, and the rest. What is left goes into the figures as profit.

Polls of public opinion show that people generally exaggerate the size of profits. The majority will answer, "Over 25 per cent," when asked how large corporate profits bulk in the national income; not a few answer, "Over half." The prosaic truth, when we examine official income and tax statistics, is otherwise: Corporate profits after taxes, in the mixed economies of the 1970s, are significantly below 10 per cent of total GNP! (In 1972, a year of fair expansion for Canada, corporate profits after taxes were under 9 per cent; before taxes, less than 15 per cent.) Since (because of double counting of bread sales as well as wheat, flour, and dough sales) total sales are a multiple of GNP, profits as a percentage of the corporate sales dollar are only a few per cent; and it is this very low number to which apologists for profits tend to appeal in their campaigns to improve people's attitudes toward profits.

FIRST VIEW: PROFIT AS "IMPLICIT" FACTOR RETURNS

To the economist, such statistical profits are a hodgepodge of different elements. Obviously, part at least of reported profits is merely the return to the owners of the firm for the factors supplied *by them*. Thus, part may be the return to the personal work provided by the owners of the firm—by the farmer and his family, by the doctor, by the partners, or by corporate executives who also happen to be principal stockholders. Part may be the rent return on self-owned natural resources. Part may be the equivalent of interest on the owner's capital. (Recall Chapter 24's discussion of implicit costs and opportunity costs.)

This shows us the first fact about profit:

Much of what is ordinarily called profit is really nothing but interest, rents, and wages under a different name. *Implicit* interest, *implicit* rent, and *implicit* wages are the names economists give to this part of profit, i.e., to the earnings of *self-used* factors.

SECOND VIEW: PROFIT AS THE REWARD TO ENTERPRISE AND INNOVATION

Suppose we lived in a dreamworld of perfect competition, where we could read the future perfectly from the palms of our hands and where no innovations were permitted to disturb the settled routine of things. Then, the economist says, there would really be no profits at all!

Here is what he means.

The statistician might still be reporting some profit figures to the press; but we know that, under these ideal equilibrium conditions, the *implicit returns* to the labor and property supplied by owners *would exactly swallow up all the profits reported.* Why? Because owners would hire out their factors on the market if they did not get equal rewards from using them in their own businesses. And because people who previously were hiring out their labor and property services would soon go into business for themselves if they knew they could earn more in that way.

Perfectly free entry of numerous competitors would, in a static world of perfect knowledge, bring price down to cost and squeeze out all profits above and beyond competitive wages, interest, and rent.[1]

We do not live in such a dreamworld. We never shall. In real life somebody must act as boss to decide

how a business shall be run. Competition is never "perfectly perfect." Somebody must peer into the future to guess whether there will be a demand for shoelaces or what will be the price of wheat. And in the world as we know it, there is a chance for a man with a brand-new idea to invent a revolutionary machine or a softer soft drink—to promote a new product or find a way to lower costs on an old one.

Let us call the man who does any of these things an *entrepreneur* or *innovator.* Although it is hard to draw the line, let us distinguish him from the bureaucratic executive or manager who simply keeps an established business running. Many economists—such as the late Joseph Schumpeter, Austrian-born economist who taught at Harvard—do not think of the wages of management as profit: they think of management as wages—implicit or explicit, and high as they may be in the competitive market for gifted managers. But they think of *profit as the return to innovators or entrepreneurs.*

Today it is easier for us to understand this distinction than it used to be half a century ago. We are all acquainted with huge corporations run by managers who own less than 1 per cent of the common stock. Although these executives run the business, they are paid wages much like anybody else. Management of this type is a skill not different in kind from other skills, such as being able to keep books or supervise production. People who possess this skill are bid for in the marketplace, and like any other factor, they move into those jobs where they will receive the highest wages.

The innovator is different. Though he may not always succeed, he is trying to carry out new activities. He is the man with vision, originality, and daring. He may not be the scientist who invents the new process, but he is the one who successfully introduces it. Maxwell developed the scientific theory of radio waves, Hertz discovered them experimentally, but Marconi and Sarnoff made them commercially profitable. On the other hand, De Forest, who discovered the triode tube, also sought to put his inventions to commercial use; yet he went broke a number of times and on each occasion disappointed the hopes of investors who had put money into his enterprises. Many try; a few succeed.[2]

---

[1] If people like running their own business, they may gladly take lower implicit wages. If, by contrast, people dislike having to boss other people and if it is tiring to take responsibility for management decisions, then management wages may have to be higher.

[2] Incidentally, the problem of innovation provides a partial defense of patents. Society deliberately gives a man a monopoly;

The dollars earned by the successful innovators are defined by some economists—like Schumpeter—as profit. Usually, these profit earnings are temporary and are soon competed out of existence by rivals and imitators. But as one source of innovational profits is disappearing, another is being born. So these profits will continue to exist.

THIRD VIEW: RISK, UNCERTAINTY, AND PROFIT

If the future were perfectly certain, there would be no opportunity for a bright young man to come along with a revolutionary innovation; everything would already be known. This shows that innovators' profits are closely tied up with risk and uncertainty. Frank Knight, a famous University of Chicago economist of the last 50 years, had an important theory that *all true profit is linked with uncertainty.*[3] Innovators' profits, discussed in the preceding section, represent but one important category of uncertainty-induced profit.

A factual examination of the great fortunes of the past shows a strong element of luck in many of them. Oil discoveries, fortunate patents, marketing and speculative successes are examples of the chance elements in a profit-and-loss system.

In examining any profit figures, we must always keep uncertainty and risk in mind. We saw in earlier chapters that some low-grade risky bonds may appear to be yielding 12 per cent at the same time that high-grade safe bonds yield only 8 per cent. But if the chances are that 1 out of 20 low-grade bond issues will default on their principal in the coming year, then you are fooling yourself if you think that these bonds are a better buy. Actually, the extra 4 per cent may just cover the risk of default.

While people who buy lottery tickets face uncertainty, the promoter of the lottery faces no risk. He knows *he* will come out ahead. Similarly, a large insurance company may rely on mathematical laws of probability to reduce its relative riskiness. Why? Because the different risks tend to be canceled by each other if the numbers are large enough. To the extent that we can eliminate uncertainty by pooling and spreading risks, the problem of profits fails to arise. It arises only for the irreducible minimum of riskiness that remains.

In some years, the total losses may be greater than the total profits. Then risk bearers as a whole have paid out to labor, to capitalists, and to landowners more than those factors would have earned if the future had been certain. In another year, the algebraic total of Knight-defined profits may turn out to be positive—so that the factors of production have then received less than they would have if the future were certain. A big question is this:

Are risk bearers on the whole overly optimistic? As a class, do they lose money and subsidize the other factors of production? Or are risk bearers as a class overly "pessimistic"—as claimed in most economics textbooks—so that profits represent a net positive payment for the service of risk bearing? Many economists think that businessmen on the whole act as if they dislike mere riskiness, and hence they must on the average be paid a positive premium or profit for shouldering risks.

FOURTH VIEW: PROFIT AS A PREMIUM FOR RISK BEARING

All this means that, for risky industries, long-run costs of production must be high enough to include, along with wage and interest costs, *a positive profit premium* to compensate for aversion to risk and coax out the supply of risk bearing.

EXAMPLE: Wheat involves harvest risks due to weather. Production of synthetic rubber does not. Suppose both involve the same wage costs per unit; suppose both involve the same capital outlay per unit. Suppose capital in rubber pays a sure return of 10 per cent, but in wheat there are even odds that on each dollar invested you double your money or lose half of it. Your average return is then $1/2(2.00) + 1/2(.50) = 1.25$, or 25 per cent per year. The 15 per cent premium, over and above the safe 10 per cent interest return, is competitively needed profit; and at the intersection of the long-run *dd* and *ss* schedules of the wheat industry, such profit will be included as a cost that must be covered.

---

this contrivance permits him artificially to keep something *partially* scarce. But society hopes the offered bribe of temporary monopoly will encourage the invention and the disclosure of things that would otherwise be 100 per cent scarce.

[3] Frank H. Knight, *Risk, Uncertainty and Profit* (London School of Economics and Political Science, Series of Reprints of Scarce Tracts, No. 16, 1933).

We summarize the notion of profit as the reward of risk bearing thus:

If people generally act like risk averters, feeling that the marginal utility of the dollars they gain is less than that of the dollars they lose, they will prefer smaller steady incomes to erratic incomes even when those average out to a higher figure. Therefore, *economic activities that involve much uncertainty and risk*, which will fall on the people (who engage in them, *will be forced by competitive entry and exit of risk takers to pay*, over the long run, a *positive profit premium to compensate for aversion to risk*. The yield on capital invested in such industries will involve, in addition to pure interest corresponding to safe investments, an extra element corresponding to positive profit.[4]

Here, actually, we have the economist's traditional view of profit—as a fourth component of competitive price to be added to wages, interest, and rent to compensate for risk bearing.

Competitive price = wage + interest + rent + profit risk-premium

FIFTH VIEW: PROFIT AS A "MONOPOLY RETURN"

Most people are critical if not downright suspicious of profit, regarding it (like oil in gears) as at best a necessary evil. The critic of profits does not have in mind implicit wage earnings, or canceling-out risk-premia in competitive markets. His image of the profiteer is more likely that of a fat man with a penchant for sly arithmetic who somehow exploits the rest of the community. Presumably what critics have in mind is a fifth, quite different meaning of profit: *profit as the earnings of monopoly.*[5]

"NATURAL SCARCITIES" When we examine the ownership of productive factors, we see that no two factors are quite alike. Your abilities as a worker and those of your neighbor are somewhat different. If we define your precise pattern of abilities as a sep-

arate factor of production, then we must admit that you do own and control an appreciable fraction of the total of that unique factor of production—100 per cent, in fact. Or you may be the sole owner of the patent to a particular process, or own the only site where the river narrows down to its most suitable place for a bridge. Or there may be no acre of Ontario land quite like yours.

Let us see how this ties in with imperfect competition. Your neighbors are a little different from you, certainly. But probably they are enough like you that the hourly wage rate for your services would not be appreciably higher even if you *withheld* some from the market. You really do not possess any appreciable monopoly power because the demand for the factor you own is, for practical purposes, infinitely elastic.

The same is true of your acre of good Ontario cornland. If you let half of it stand idle, the price of corn would not be affected; and the derived price for each acre of your land would be unchanged, even though you and your family know that there is really no other farmstead quite like it.

And note this: If the land is sufficiently fertile, you will, of course, be making a fine living off your farm. Perhaps you may even be in the top 2 per cent of the income distribution. Even though competition is perfect, this rent return to the land you own *cannot* be competed away by rival farmers. Because the Good Lord made only a limited amount of fertile Ontario farmland, it will earn a rent for its owner—regardless of how he originally acquired title to the land. *Competitively determined rents are the results of a natural scarcity.* They yield a "surplus" but not a pure profit.[6]

"CONTRIVED SCARCITIES" It is quite a different matter if the demand for one of your factors of production is negatively inclined rather than infinitely elastic. (Let us review what this means: It means that when you raise your price, you still can sell *some* of your factor; this is the sense in which

---

[4] Other productive factors, such as labor in risky occupations, may also have profit premiums as bait necessary to keep them in the trade (e.g. fishermen on shares, miners on piece rates).

[5] Brief courses may wish to skip the rest of this chapter.

[6] If there is great inequality in the distribution of ownership of factors of production, then even under the most perfect competition (where pure profit is zero) there can still result a very rich, possibly idle, minority of plutocrats surrounded by masses of lower-income people. Recall Chapter 27's discussion of exploitation.

you have some monopoly control over price.) If you are the sole owner of an important patent, it will pay you to charge a price so as to limit its use. If audiences swoon to your singing as to nobody else's, then you will have to remember that the more you sing, the lower will be the price the customers will pay for your singing. If you own the best site for a bridge, then you must be careful not to sell anyone else the lot next to it; otherwise, he will be able to offer the bridge builders a site nearly as good as yours, and this will limit the dollars you can derive from yours. Thus, part of the rent you earn on Nature's bridge site has a monopoly element in it by virtue of your withholding its use for fear of spoiling your dollar market.

What does all this add up to? It means that, *as soon as there is an appreciable deviation from perfect competition, it will pay you to take account of the fact that you will spoil the market the more you offer of your factor.*

Any profit-maximizing firm takes account of the loss on all previous units resulting when it sells an extra unit of product, and it is its marginal revenue—lower than price because of the loss on previous units—which a prudent firm concentrates on. Again with you as the owner of a factor: you are interested in the *marginal*, or *extra*, *revenue* that the factor brings you. You will not withhold all the factor from the market—that would bring you in *no* revenue at all. Nor will you provide so much of the factor that it becomes a free good and brings in no revenue. As a quasi-monopolist, or imperfect competitor, what will you do to maximize your return? You will withhold just as much of that service as will bring its marginal revenue down to zero and give you maximum return.[7]

Our principle is this: *Under imperfect competition, it pays people to limit the supply of their factors somewhat.* By definition, natural scarcities

are such that nothing can be done about them. But under imperfect competition, we encounter in addition so-called "contrived scarcities."

Hence, the fifth view of profits as a monopoly return is often reformulated in the economics textbooks to read as follows:

Part of what is called profit is the return to a contrived or artificial scarcity.

This return takes the form of rent, wages, or interest, depending upon the nature of the factor in question and on the contractual relations set up to handle the particular situation. (For example, an investor may buy the bridge-site land at the full capitalized value of its monopoly earning power. To him, the return will seem to be interest.) So monopoly profits are inextricably tied up with wages, interest, and rent.

Wherever contrived scarcities exist, they distort the optimum pattern of resource use. They may also create high earnings for the people involved. But high earnings do not always follow. Thus, under imperfect or monopolistic competition, there may be many taxicabs or grocery stores. Each owner may have a sloping demand curve and may be setting a price in excess of marginal cost. Yet there may be so many imperfect competitors that none of them is earning more than he could get in a perfectly competitive industry. Wiping out the imperfections and illegally contrived scarcities may improve the pattern of production, but still might not have much effect on relative distribution of income. (See Chamberlin's Fig. 26-3.)

Progressive redistributive taxing of personal and business income, in order to achieve less inequality in the Lorenz curve of income distribution, may itself have some adverse effects on efficiency of resource allocation. High marginal tax rates could diminish risk taking and effort. Or, because of tax loopholes, there might actually result too much venturesomeness.[8]

---

[7] Of course, there may be some discomfort to you in rendering the service, or you may have the opportunity of selling the service in some other market—as in the case where you could use your bridge site to grow corn. In these cases, you will obviously equate marginal revenue to some defined positive marginal *cost* rather than to zero. Toronto's Burton Keirstead has considered a theory of profit in which monopoly control over price reduces the risk of loss from innovation. Thus he combines three of the views discussed above. B. S. Keirstead, *Capital, Interest and Profits* (Oxford, Blackwell, 1959).

[8] A 1953 Harvard Business School study suggests that the rich men it examined were able to keep their tax rates down to 50 per cent on the average, and that taxes pushed some toward venturesome investment. "Appreciation-minded investors ... may have been so stimulated by the tax structure to seek out investments offering unusually large capital gains potentialities, such as promising new ventures, as actually to increase the flow of capital to such situations." J. K. Butters, L. E. Thompson, and L. L. Bollinger, *Effects of Taxation: Investment by Individuals* (Harvard Business School, Boston, 1953).

SIXTH VIEW: PROFIT AS MARXIAN SURPLUS VALUE

A final view held for profit is that of Karl Marx. Everything in the national income that does not go to the worker—i.e., all return to property, whether it be in the guise of interest or profit—constitutes surplus value.

As will be seen in Chapter 41, Marxians wish to analyze the deviation of capitalist pricing from the "labor theory of value." In that labor theory of value, all goods would sell at their socially necessary labor costs: food which required 2 hours of direct labor to produce would sell for half that of housing which required 4 hours, and one-third that of clothing which required 6 hours of combined direct and indirect labor. Under the strict labor theory of value, all the GNP would go to labor and none to property. (In Proudhon's colorful phrase: "All property is theft!")

But, pointed out Marx, under capitalism the labor is employed by capitalists. These exploiters pay labor less than the product it produces. In the simplest case of Marx, capitalists mark up each commodity by a constant rate over the wages paid—by the "rate of surplus value."

EXAMPLE: Though food costs 2 hours to produce, the worker works 6 hours to buy it. Then the rate of surplus value is 200 per cent: $(6—2)/2 = 2.00$. In effect, of the 12-hour day each man toils, he works 4 hours for himself, 8 hours for the exploiting capitalists.

Chapter 27 mentioned that something over three-fourths of the national income goes to wages and salaries, and one-fourth to various property owners in interest, rents, profits, etc. Because Marxians would regard many high executive salaries as having in them elements of profit or surplus value, more than one-fourth of the NNP would be regarded as surplus value. Critics ask:

Are any profits necessary? The world's stock of land and capital goods exists; but why should anyone get an income from owning it? Why shouldn't the state get the income (whether reckoned as marginal-products or by whatever rational planning allocation and costing) and distribute it to the workers (i.e., to everybody) in transfer payments or public goods?

Defenders of profits and property incomes reply:

If you don't keep rewinding the clock of entrepreneurial venturing, the nationalized clock will slow down. Resources don't, in a dynamic world, organize themselves; the inherited stock of capital goods will obsolesce, left to anarchism or bureaucratic planning. The checks and balances of competition, plus democratically voted income distribution by progressive taxation of incomes and wealth and by welfare transfer payments, will outperform the good intentions of government ownership and control of production.

The next chapter and its appendix on socialist pricing will return to this fundamental debate. Value judgments, and not merely scientific appraisals of empirical experiences, must obviously play a crucial role in such discussions.

This survey of the variegated notions on profit reveals an important generalization. *Much of the hostility toward profit is really hostility toward the extremes of inequality in the distribution of money income that comes from unequal factor ownership;* this is distinguishable from hostility toward profit created by imperfections of competition. Chapter 40 will return to the challenge of inequality.

SUMMARY

1 In traditional microeconomic theory, just as competitive price must cover *(a) wage* cost of labor, *(b) rent* cost of land, and *(c) interest* cost of capital, it must also cover *(d) profit*-risk-premium cost of inducing people who are averse to variability of returns (plus and minus around mean values) to bear risk.

2 In popular parlance, profit as reported in national-income statistics is a highly miscellaneous category: it is the total of lumped-together corporate earnings and income of unincorporated enterprise. Economically we must distinguish half a dozen different profit concepts.

3 The special category of *high temporary earnings resulting from innovation* is often termed profit by many economists. Routine management earns wages, they say, but profit may accrue to genuine entrepreneurship.

4 *Uncertainty* is the all-pervading fact of life. It makes innovation possible and also creates positive and negative divergences between what factors expect to earn and what they actually end up earning. Knight and other economists define profit and loss as the *unforeseeable discrepancies created by uncertainty*.

5 Profit as an undeserved return to property and as the evil fruit of monopoly is a concept with many facets. (*a*) Even if perfect competition prevailed in all goods and factor markets, many critics would deplore the deviation from the labor theory of value represented by any return to landowners, machine owners, or highly paid executives. (*b*) Or the critic may distinguish between competitive rents to "natural scarcities" and monopolists' returns from "contrived scarcities." (*c*) Profit is sometimes regarded as a taxable surplus; or, in Marxian terminology, surplus value is the ethically unwarranted markup over labor costs that causes the worker to toil part of the day for his own wage subsistence and the rest of the day for his capitalist exploiter.

   The next chapter will review microeconomic pricing and distribution of income, showing how, under dynamic conditions, the problem of knowledge and information is tied up with the problem of incentives and efficiency criteria.

CONCEPTS FOR REVIEW

profit as premium for risk bearing	contrived versus natural scarcity
reported statistics of profits	rent and surplus, incentive
implicit versus explicit factor	payments
returns	Marxian surplus value
wages of management	ethical questions and value
innovation, uncertainty	judgments
imperfections of competition,	hostility to profit as hostility to
monopoly	income inequality

QUESTIONS FOR DISCUSSION

1 Contrast, for a safe industry (salt) and a risky industry (apple growing), the breakdown of P into four symbolic components: $P = w + r + i + x$. What is x?

2 "It is misleading to talk about 'a profit system.' Ours is a *profit-and-loss* system. Profits are the carrots held out as an incentive to efficiency, and losses are the kicks that penalize using inefficient methods or devoting resources to uses not desired by spending consumers. This metaphor of carrots and kicks is ancient, but apt." Evaluate.

3 Give cases of innovation; of risk taking. How will taxes affect them? What is meant by perfect competition? by imperfect competition? Can you specify a monopoly profit ("contrived" as against "natural") that all will think bad?

4 Discuss ethical and incentive aspects of taxing so-called "profits" or higher incomes.

5 Define "implicit" factor earnings. Contrast with other profit concepts.

6 We each work 12 hours a day: 8 hours for our own subsistence, 4 hours for the capitalist boss. Verify the rate of surplus value as 50 per cent. (HINT: 4/8 = .50.)

32
EPILOGUE TO MICROECONOMIC PRICING

Truth can never be told so as to be understood and not be believed. **WILLIAM BLAKE**

Parts Three and Four are now completed. Let us review the broad principles of *value* and *distribution*.

SURVEY OF THE INTERDEPENDENT PRICING PROCESS

We have seen:

1. How competitive supply and demand operate in a *single* market, in both the short and long run.

2. How the relative marginal utility (or indifference) preferences of men lie behind their respective demand curves.

3. How total, marginal, and average costs all lie behind the competitive supply curves.

4. How the technical production function relating output to factor inputs lies behind the cost curves, which have been minimized by the firm's demanding inputs until their *marginal-physical-products are proportional to factor-prices*.

5. How these marginal-physical-products and *marginal-revenue-products*, summed for all firms, provide the "derived demands for the factors."

6. How these derived demands for land, labor, or capital goods interact with their market supplies to determine factor-prices such as rent, wages, rentals, and so forth.

7. How primary resources like labor and land are used to make produced capital goods, which are in turn used in roundabout ways to increase society's final output; that this "net productivity of capital" is reflected in the rate of interest, which, in the absence of technical change, is generally subject to diminishing returns in some analogy to the way labor and land are subject to that law; and that competitive markets evaluate all assets at their "present dis-

counted values," using interest yields to screen out best investments.

8. Finally, how, along with elements of wage, rent, and interest costs, competitive prices have in them an element of profit as the systematic premium needed to coax risk-averting people to invest their shiftable funds into industries with great variability of returns around their predictable mean level of returns.[1]

SIMULTANEOUS MUTUAL DETERMINATION

Notice that, in the listing of eight steps above, each follows from the preceding one—from step 1 to step 2 and then step 3, until finally we come to step 8. In the textbook chapters they follow in almost the same order.

But in real life, which comes first? Is there any order and sequence, with prices being determined in single markets on Monday, consumers evaluating preferences on Tuesday, businessmen reckoning costs on Wednesday and marginal-products on Thursday? Obviously not. All these processes are going on at one and the same time.

That is not all. These different processes do not go on independently side by side, each in its own little

---

[1] Pursuit of profit and avoidance of loss is supposed to furnish the motive force behind the whole competitive process. Paradoxically, under static conditions free of uncertainty and innovational change, competitive profits—other than implicit factor returns and wages of management—would tend to zero; but dynamic innovational change creates and recreates Schumpeterian profits that are constantly being eroded by imitation under monopolistic competition. Also irreducible Knightian *uncertainty* constantly throws up a divergence—plus and minus—between equilibrium returns and actual returns of all the factors. Chapter 31 discussed all this.

groove, careful not to get in the way of the other. All the processes of supply and demand, of cost and preference, of factor productivity and demand—all these are really different aspects of one vast simultaneous *interdependent* process.

Thus, the supply curve for wheat given in the first chapter of Part Three is itself the resultant of the cost calculations given at the end of Part Three, of the production considerations given early in Part Four, and of the wage and rent and interest determinations given late in Part Four. Actually, you can take any one of the eight steps in the outline and draw arrows connecting it causally *with every other step*.

Figure 32-1 gives a summary picture of the interdependent system which economists call "general equilibrium." Recall the circular-flow diagram on national income (Fig. 10-1), showing plumbing pipes carrying dollars clockwise from business to families and from families to business. That gave what economists call the "aggregative," or "macroeconomic," picture of the nation's grand economic totals.

Now turn to Fig. 32-1. It also gives the circular flow of dollars. But this time we take a microscopic approach—what economists call the "micro-economic" picture. Now we do not talk about the grand total of factor incomes; instead we show derived demand by business for skilled labor, unskilled labor, good vineyard land, and for every other factor of production. Nor do we speak of total consumption: we specify; we show the consumer's demand for coffee, tea, shoes, and for each and every commodity or service.

Note that in the lower loop we have for each factor *both* a supply and a demand. (QUERY: Which of these schedules comes from business? Which from consumers?) And in the upper loop, you see *both* a business supply and consumer demand for each good. (Where?)

Thus, we can give an optimistic answer to the logical purist who poses the embarrassing question: "Your economic system isn't determinate until you have found conditions to determine a price *and* a quantity for *each* output and for *each* factor input. Do you have enough simultaneous conditions (or equations) to make your interdependent equilibrium system determinate?"

Fortunately, we can answer: "We do have for each output or input *both a supply and a demand condition.* So we can hope that the system will, by trial and error in the market place, finally settle down—if left undisturbed!—to a determinate competitive equilibrium. [2] And we can add: "The final competitive equilibrium is an 'efficient' one. Because prices equal marginal costs, output is being maximized, factor inputs minimized; and because prices reflect relative marginal utilities for each consumer, people who like apples are not being given oranges, etc. From so efficient a final point, you can no longer make everyone better off. You can help Joe only by hurting Tom."

Figure 32-1 here is the final development of Figure 3-1 where we first asked how a price system goes about solving WHAT, HOW, and FOR WHOM. Only after mastering the tools of Parts Three and Four can we present this culmination of our original inquiry.

IMPERFECTIONS OF COMPETITION

This survey proceeded on the basis of some heroically abstract assumptions: no monopolies, no imperfections, no dynamic innovations or unforeseen disturbances, no governmental distortions, and so forth. Figure 32-1, therefore, is like the no-friction model of the physicist; it is not a picture of the real world as we know it when we step outside the library and rub elbows with real, live, breathing people on the street.

Yet, even though every engineer knows he must meet friction, he does find the frictionless model a valuable tool in throwing light on complicated reality. So it is with our ideal competitive model. In the long run, many imperfections turn out to be transient. *The competitive model, therefore, may suggest in its oversimple way some interesting hypotheses that turn out to have a measure of long-run validity!*

---

[2] Léon Walras, a French economist of three-quarters of a century ago, is usually credited with the discovery of general equilibrium. But W. S. Jevons of England, C. Menger of Austria, Alfred Marshall of England, J. B. Clark of the United States, Vilfredo Pareto of Italy, and Knut Wicksell of Sweden all made significant contributions; and even in Adam Smith you can hunt out the germ of the idea of general equilibrium. By use of topology and set theory, the system has now been analyzed with rigor, thanks to J. von Neumann, A. Wald, K. J. Arrow, G. Debreu, and others.

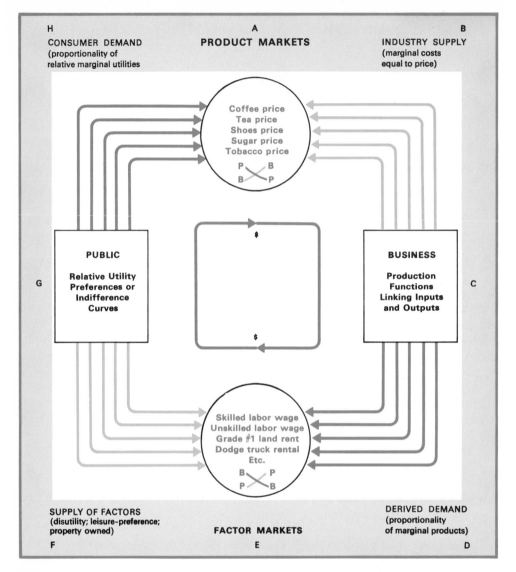

FIG. 32-1. What, How, and For Whom is determined by general equilibrium pricing.
The clockwise money flow is broken up to show consumer demand meeting industry
supply at *A* to determine equilibrium price and quantity of each good. Similarly, derived
factor demands of business meet public's supply of factors at *E* to determine equilibrium
factor-prices and amounts. (Interpret what is going on behind *B, D, F,* and *H*—and inside
C and *G*—and compare this with the What, How, and For Whom of Fig. 3-1.)

EXAMPLE: An invention cuts cost of aluminum; the competitive model says price will fall and pressure will be put on use and price of steel. The sophisticated student of imperfect competition says the real world is not perfectly competitive, so no hard-and-fast conclusion can be drawn. Still, bet with him that the above result will happen *in the long run*—and probably you will win his money. A sure thing? No, but often a good bet.

Even if we agree that the perfect-competition model does give some approximate descriptions of reality, we cannot be satisfied with such crude approximations. Forty years ago an economics textbook would have had to confine itself to the case of perfect competition, and let it go at that. Thanks to the pioneering work in the theory of imperfect and monopolistic competition over the last generation, economists now have the tools (marginal revenue, etc.) to analyze oligopoly, monopoly, differentiation of products of numerous sellers, collective bargaining, and various intermediate cases. (Recall Chapter 26 and Table 25-1.)

We have seen that prices are often inflexibly administered, changing rarely and being subject only to minor hidden discounts, which is in contrast with the minute-to-minute volatility and year-to-year gyrations of competitive prices. We have seen that two union men may work in the same city or block at different wage rates for comparable work; that interference by a union with wage setting may correct a previous monopoly condition of unequal bargaining, or may increase the departure from the model of perfect competition. We have seen Chamberlinian cases where free entry may squeeze out profits while still leaving price above minimum average costs. We shall see, in Chapter 39, that prejudice under *laissez-faire* may lead to unequal employment opportunity and to both social inefficiency and inequity. We have emphasized repeatedly, and shall have reason to emphasize again, that "externalities" distort the system from its efficiency and optimality conditions. (Polluting products do not bear their full social costs. Knowing we cannot appropriate to ourselves all the returns from our inventing, we spend too little under *laissez-faire* on research and development.)

There is no need, therefore, to warn against overemphasis on the elegant model of perfect competition as an exact description of economic reality.

A WORD ON "WELFARE ECONOMICS"

Even if perfect competition were a poorer descriptive tool than it is, students of economics would still want to study it intensively and master its principles. This is so for a reason unconnected with mere description. The competitive model is extremely important in providing a bench mark for appraising the *efficiency* of an economic system. Russians, Chinese, Indians, as well as Swiss need to study its analytical principles.

For the most part in any science, scholars discuss what *is* and what will be under this or that situation. The task of positive description should be kept as free as is humanly possible from the taint of wishful thinking and ethical concern about what ought to be. Why? Because scientists are cold-blooded robots? No, because experience shows again and again that a more accurate job of positive description will be achieved if one *tries* to be objective. (Experience also shows that, try as we may, we humans never succeed in separating completely the objective and subjective aspects of a discipline. Indeed, the very choice of what scientists choose to measure, and the perspective from which they observe and measure it, and the reactions the observer produces in that which is observed—all these factors make the distinction between *is* and *ought*, between objective and subjective issues, at bottom a matter of degree rather than of kind. Recall, for example, Chapter 1's bird-antelope paradox and be warned that Part Six will be much concerned with policy and value judgments.)

The citizenry, unlike the specialist, is in the end perhaps most interested in problems of "norms," of what *ought* to be done, of policy rather than mere description. That citizenry is best served by the scientists who can give it the most accurate description of what is relevant, and of what the consequences of different policy actions will be.

Very briefly then, in this epilogue, let us devote again a few lines to implications for economic welfare that have been developed in Parts Three and Four.

EFFICIENCY OPTIMALITY First, we have seen repeatedly that a regime of perfectly competitive pricing would have certain efficiency properties if conditions were really present for the maintenance of perfect competition. Adam Smith, in his talk about an Invisible Hand, which leads the selfish actions of individuals toward so harmonious a final result, did have some point. Smith never could state or prove exactly what that point was, but modern economics can state this property of ideal competitive pricing:

Under perfectly perfect competition, where all prices end up equal to all marginal costs, where all factor-prices end up equal to values of marginal-products and all total costs are minimized, where the genuine desires and well-being of individuals are all represented by their marginal utilities as expressed in their dollar voting—*then* the resulting equilibrium has the efficiency property that "you can't make any one man better off without hurting some other man."

What does this mean exactly? It means that a planner could not come along with a slide rule and find a solution different from the *laissez-faire* one, which could improve the welfare of *everyone*.[3]

ARBITRARY DISTRIBUTION OF DOLLAR VOTES

What does it not mean? It does not mean that actual *laissez-faire*, with the imperfections of competition that will go with it, leads to efficiency, or necessarily even to a close approximation of efficiency.

And inefficiency aside, it does *not* mean that *the people who are deemed by various religious or ethical observers to be most worthy, most deserving, or most needy will necessarily get their ethically best share of goods and services. Laissez-faire* perfect competition *could* lead to starving cripples; to malnourished children who grow up to produce malnourished children; to perpetuation of Lorenz curves of great inequality of incomes and wealth for generations or forever. Or, if the initial distribution of dollar-wealth votes, genetic abilities, early conditioning, and training happened to be appropriate, perfect competition might lead to a rather egalitarian society characterized by uniformity greater than might please many an aristocratic ethical tradition. Or more likely, lead to inequality deemed too glaring.

In short, Adam Smith, in the famous passage quoted on page 43, had no right to assert that an Invisible Hand channels individuals selfishly seeking their own interest into promoting the "public interest"—as these last two words might be defined by a variety of prominent ethical and religious notions of what constitutes the welfare of a nation. Smith has

proved nothing of this kind, nor has any economist or philosopher since his time.

REDEFINING THE INVISIBLE HAND DOCTRINE

If Smith were alive today, he would agree with all this; and one ventures the guess, from his biography, that he would probably reword his doctrine pretty much along the following lines.

1. Only if abilities and *dollar-wealth votes were originally distributed in "an ethically optimal" manner*—and kept so distributed by nondistorting, nonmarket interventions—could even perfectly competitive pricing be counted on (*a*) to produce an efficient configuration of production out on society's production-possibility frontier (and not inside it), and (*b*) to give people what they really deem is best for them, in accordance with their dollar votes that now reflect equally significant social utility. But if *laissez-faire* were abandoned in favor of an ethically proper distribution of wealth and opportunity, the perfect-competition equilibrium could be used as an instrument to attain optimally efficient and equitable organization of society.

2. Admittedly, *the demands of people in the market place sometimes do not reflect their true well-being* as these would be interpreted by even the most tolerant and individualistic of ethical observers. (EXAMPLE: A dope addict's craving for heroin even at the expense of his food or his children's food; a child's desire for a seventh lollipop; a diabetic's craving for sweets; a spendthrift's mortgaging his house for an advertised sports car.) As a pragmatist, were Smith alive today, he would say, "People are entitled to make their own mistakes in many matters, but it is arrogant to think that anyone who is not a minor or a lunatic is in every respect a sovereign will; as people conscious that we were born not perfect and as inhabitants of a post-Freudian world, *we* shall sparingly and for good cause want (with due process) democratically to place restrictions on our *own* behavior. So again, *laissez-faire* perfect competition would not inevitably be the ideal."

Then, after emphasizing the need for tolerance and the virtues of freedom, Smith might strike a more technical note.

3. Where there are monopolistic imperfections that produce deviations from ideal competitive marginal-cost pricing—and in situations of strong in-

---

[3] If *A* is the competitive equilibrium, there is no point *B* the planner could devise which could be approved over *A* by a *unanimous vote*. Some would be hurt in going to *B*, some might gain; but the gainers could never find it worthwhile to give big enough bribes to win the losers over to approving the move to *B*. Graduate treatises call this a case of "Pareto optimality," named after Pareto's work at the turn of the century as elucidated in our time by Abram Bergson of Harvard.

creasing returns and decreasing costs, such deviations are practically inevitable—of course there is a *prima facie* case that *laissez-faire* pricing is not efficient. Public scrutiny, to see whether democratic controls would make the situation better or worse, has to be presumed in such quasi-monopoly situations.

4. Finally, Smith would add that wherever there are "external economies and diseconomies" (such as were analyzed at the end of Chapter 24 and in the discussion of public versus private goods in Chapter 8), there is a *prima facie* case for study to see whether zoning laws, taxes or subsidies, and government expenditure and regulation should be initiated in some degree. Where the checks and balances of perfect competition are not operative, the Darwinian struggle for existence is not led by an Invisible Hand to any kind of optimum. The creative role of government in economic life is vast in an interdependent, crowded world.

CONCLUSION

The reader is warned that all the above issues of welfare economics can be given varying interpretations and can lead to controversy or debate. Such debates cannot be resolved within the realm of positive science alone. Conservatives may legitimately interpret the above principles in terms of their version of the good society. Middle-of-the-roaders may do the same for theirs. And radicals may call for small or large reforms of the present structure of a mixed economy by giving their interpretation of these principles. That means the reader may do so, too. Economic science arms one for the great debate; it does not preclude that debate or prejudice its conclusions.

The following Appendix gives in greater depth a view of the efficiency aspect of the system of interdependent economic pricing under capitalism or socialism.

Appendix: Review of Commodity and Factor Pricing: General Equilibrium and the Parable of Ideal Welfare Pricing

PARABLE OF UTOPIAN PRICING

Economists used to be twitted that their books always harped on Robinson Crusoe. True enough: we do find that the economic decisions of a single man furnish a dramatic way of simplifying our basic principles. But these days we have an even more dramatic device for illustrating the fundamental facts of economic life: we use the example of a fully collectivized society. This retains the same simplicity of ultimate decision making, but at the same time it involves the social interactions between people that the Crusoe model lacks. The contrast between such a model and our realistic everyday world is, of course, enormous. And therein lies its value. By examining the logic of such a model, we get new insight into the nature of our own pricing system.

Let us, therefore, examine how our economic analysis of pricing can be applied to a completely artificial planned society of the kind never seen in Russia or anywhere else. Call it Utopia, call it Hades, it exists. In analyzing the problem of pricing in a planned socialist state, we kill two birds with one stone:

1. We get one of the best possible reviews of the overall working of a perfect *capitalistic* price system.

2. We get an introduction to problems of "welfare economics", the study of what is considered right and wrong about any economic system. This depends, of course, upon ethical points of view, themselves necessarily beyond science. But the economist may help to throw light on how successfully an economic system realizes any suggested ethical *goals*.[1]

A DILEMMA FOR CENTRALIZED PLANNING

The earlier chapters of this book have shown how a system of market prices operates so as to solve the basic economic problems of WHAT, HOW, and FOR WHOM. To drive home what all this really means, try a mental experiment. Suppose you were given the job of making the blueprints for a completely planned economic system. How might you begin?

First, let us suppose you are interested in giving people what *they* want, not in telling them what they *ought* to want. Obviously, you cannot give them everything they want: land, labor, capital goods, and technological knowledge are limited in amount. So you must make compromises and choices.

You may say: This is merely a complicated mathematical problem, calling for the use of lots of high-powered electronic high-speed calculating machines. But remember that we shall have to deal with the millions of items that are to be found in department stores, with thousands of grades of productive factors, and with numerous individuals and families. The number of unknowns of the mathematical problem will be in the millions, and the number of steps to its solution in the billions of billions. No known set of calculating machines or computers can tackle such a problem.

You are stumped. And discouraged. Perhaps you will lower your sights and stop being a perfectionist. Instead of giving people exactly what they think they want, you may decide that there will be only a few types of, say, shoe styles and sizes, so that the calculation problem will be simplified. Or you may start to give people goods that *you* find it convenient to give them.

One thing is clear: If centralized planning means that one centralized person must have in his mind all the myriad intricacies of detail, then it is an impossible job to do with any efficiency.[2] So you will naturally begin to experiment with various devices to *decentralize* the job. And quite probably you will end up by introducing a *pricing* system in many ways like that of capitalism. How might such a system work?

PRICING IN A UTOPIAN STATE: CONSUMPTION-GOODS PRICES

In your new society, the consumer will still have *freedom of choice* and will not have dictated to him the relative amounts of different commodities which he is to "enjoy." As in the capitalist system, each person will receive a sum of money or abstract purchasing power to spend among different commodities as he wishes. Thus, vegetarians will not have to eat meat, and those who prefer meat will be able to satisfy their preference.

How will relative prices between salmon and ham or any other consumers' goods be set by the socialist state? Generally speaking, prices will be set with the same double purpose as in a capitalist society: (1) just high enough to

---

[1]For example, he may be personally opposed to an equal distribution of income, but that does not prevent him from measuring the degree of success in reaching this common ethical goal or of the costs involved.

[2]Perhaps Lenin had his tongue in cheek when, just prior to the October Revolution of 1917, he wrote: "The bookkeeping and control necessary for this (production and distribution) have been simplified by capitalism to the utmost, till they become the extraordinary simple operations of watching, recording, and issuing receipts, within the reach of anybody who can read and write and knows the first four rules of arithmetic". This is as ironic as his later characterization of Communism as "democracy plus electricity", a witty half-truth like the aphorism attributed to him: "Liberty is precious—so precious that it must be rationed".

ration out the existing supplies of consumers' goods, so none are left over and none are short; and also (2) just high enough to cover the socially necessary extra costs of producing the goods in question. In technical terms, relative Ps are to be set equal to relative "marginal utilities" and "marginal costs."

THE DISTRIBUTION OF INCOME

So far the process has worked much like the capitalistic system. Almost by definition, however, socialism means a society in which most land and capital goods or non-human resources of all kinds are owned collectively by society and not individually by people. In our society, a man who owns 50 parcels of Toronto land, each of which produces $60,000 of net rents per year, will receive an income of 3 million dollars per year—which may be 500 times what a night watchman is able to earn, and 150 times what the average skilled engineer can earn. In a society where most property is owned collectively and not distributed with great inequality among different individuals, an important source of inequality of income would be absent.

Many people profess to hold the ethical and philosophical belief that different individuals' wants and needs are very much alike, and that the present market mechanism works inadequately because the rich are given so many more votes in the control of production than the poor—which makes the market demand for goods a faulty indicator of their true social worth.

Such people with a relatively egalitarian philosophy will welcome a great reduction in the spread of incomes between the lowest 90 per cent of all families and the highest 10 per cent. They may argue that taking away $1,000 from a man with an income of $100,000 and giving it to a man with an income of $5,000 will add to social well-being (by taking dollars from a place deemed low in marginal social utility to a place deemed higher). After the distribution of income between families has been determined correctly, according to society's fundamental (a-scientific) value judgments, then and only then will it be true that the dollars coming on the market will be valid indicators of the value of goods and services; and only then will they be serving to direct production into the proper channels and goods into the right hands.

Hence, *lump-sum taxes will be used in Utopia to give ethically proper income distribution*. So goes the argument.

SOCIAL DIVIDENDS How is what is considered the proper ethical distribution of income to be achieved— aside from the negative act of wiping out unduly high property owning and the appropriate lump-sum taxing of individuals?

Perfectionists have two answers: (1) in part, by letting people get some of their income in the form of wages; but (2) in part by having these wages supplemented by receipt of a lump-sum *social dividend payment* or negative income tax. This cash payment in an egalitarian society might involve differences to compensate for different

numbers of children, age, health, and abilities acquired or inherited.

It is an ethical rather than a scientific question as to just how large, relatively, each person's final income ought to be. As a science, economics can concern itself only with the best means of attaining given ends; it cannot prescribe the ends themselves.

Indeed, if someone decided that he preferred a feudal-fascistic kind of society, in which all people with little black mustaches were to be given especially high incomes, a pathological economist could set up the pricing rules for him to follow to achieve his strange design best. He would be told to determine his social dividend payments to achieve the required optimal distribution of income, after which each dollar coming on the market could be regarded as correctly representing (that eccentric's) true social values.

The social dividend differs from a wage because it is to be given to every individual *regardless of his own efforts*. That is why it is called a "lump-sum" dividend or transfer.[3] (Any bonus based upon productivity or effort is to be treated as a wage.)

We have not yet seen how wages are to be determined, but before doing so, let us first turn to another important problem.

PRICING OF NONHUMAN PRODUCTIVE RESOURCES AND INTERMEDIATE GOODS

What should be the role of land and other non-human productive resources as an element of cost in such a utopia?

Some people would say that such nonhuman resources should not enter into cost at all; that only human sweat and skill are the true source of all value; and that any extra charges, based upon the cost of land or machinery, represent a capitalistic surplus which the owners of property are able to squeeze out of the exploited laboring masses, by virtue of the private monopoly of ownership of the means of production. We have seen that this view is the traditional "labor theory of value," of Karl Marx and John Locke. (Learned scholars disagree about just what Marx meant by the "labor theory of value," and debate whether he intended it to apply to a socialist economy in the short or long run.)

We need not enter into this dispute. However, it is important to note that, in its simple form, *the labor theory of value will lead to incorrect and inefficient use of both labor and nonlabor resources in even the most perfect socialist society*.

So long as any economic resource is limited in quantity —i.e., *scarce* rather than free—the socialist planners must give it a price and charge a rent for its use. This price need not, as in the case of the millionaire under the capitalistic system, determine any individual's income. It can be a purely bookkeeping or accounting price (or so-called

---

[3]If the state is providing public goods for the people which require the use of more resources than the state owns, most of the social dividends may have to be *negative*—lump-sum taxes, rather than transfers.

"shadow price") set up by the planners, rather than a market price. But there must be a price put upon the use of every such resource.

Why? First, we must price nonhuman resources to ensure that society is deciding HOW goods shall be produced in the best way, so that we really end up on the true production-possibility frontier of society and not somewhere inside it.[4] It would be absurd to get rid of the capitalistic system with its alleged wastes due to unemployment, and then, by stupid planning, end up far inside society's true production potentialities.

Related to the above point is the second need for all resources to be given a value if correct prices are to be charged to consumers for those final goods *that use up a great deal of scarce resources*. In other words, for society to find itself in the best of all possible positions out on the production-possibility frontier, we must price such consumption goods as food and clothing so as to reflect their true relative (extra or marginal) costs of using up *all* scarce resources. Otherwise, the free choice exerted by consumers on their dollar spending will not truly maximize their own and society's preferences, with *utilities and costs properly balanced at the margin*.

THE EXAMPLE OF LAND RENT

The foregoing two reasons may be hard to grasp. However, let us try to make the necessity for nonlabor pricing clear by considering a single land example. Suppose there are twins in a farming utopia. What if one were to produce wheat on an acre of good land, and the other were to produce less wheat by the same year's work on an acre of bad land. If they are identical twins, working equally hard, we would certainly have to agree that their wage rates ought to be the same.

Now, if wages were to be treated as the only cost, in accord with the labor theory of value, then the same price could not be charged for the two different outputs of wheat, even though the kernels of wheat were identical. The good-land wheat would have involved low labor costs and will have to sell for less than the poor-land wheat.

This, of course, is absurd. A well-wishing social planner might try to get around the dilemma by charging the same price for both, losing money on the poor-land wheat and gaining on the other. Or what is almost the same thing, he might say, "To keep the costs of the two wheats the same, let us pay the twin on bad land lower wages than his brother; but then let us make the richer brother share his wages with the poorer."

Such a solution is not absurd, but it falls short of achieving the desired best results: maximum production and equal pay for equal human effort. In particular, *it fails to shift more labor onto the more productive land*.

The only correct procedure is to put an accounting price or rent tag on each land, with the good land having the higher tag. The prices of both kinds of wheat will be

equal, because the land cost ("Ricardian rent") of the good-land wheat will be just enough higher than that of the poor-land wheat to make up the difference.

Most important of all, the socialist production manager must try to minimize the combined labor and land cost of producing each kind of wheat. If he does so according to the marginal-product principles discussed in Part Four, he will accomplish something important, undreamed of by the simple believer in the labor theory of value.

He will find it pays to work the good land more intensively, perhaps with the time of 1 1/2 men until the extra product there has been lowered by the law of diminishing returns so as to be just equal to the extra product on the poor land. Only by putting a price upon inert sweatless land are we using it, and sweating breathing labor, most productively! The price or rent of land rises so as to ration its limited supply among the *best* uses.

Note, too, that the most finicky humanitarian will have nothing to complain of in our solution. By transferring labor from one acre to the other until labor's marginal productivity has been made equal, we get the largest possible total production of wheat.[5]

The two brothers are paid the same wages because they have worked equally hard. But their wages are not high enough to buy all the wheat, since part of the cost of the wheat has come from (bookkeeping) land-rent charges. However, the people through their government own the land equally. The land's return does not go to any property owner but is available to be distributed as a lump-sum social dividend to both brothers and to others according to their ethical deserts.

By putting a proper accounting price or rent on land, society has more consumption than otherwise possible!

If we turn now to the production of more than one consumer's good, it will be obvious that their cost prices must be made to reflect the amount of socially limited land and machinery which they each use up. Field crops such as wheat require little labor and much land compared with a garden crop such as tomatoes. If we price each good on the basis of labor costs alone, wheat will sell for too little, and too much land will be forced out of tomato production. All people will be worse off than they need be.

MARGINAL-COST PRICING

One last point concerning the final determination of a product's cost and price. After the costs of all necessary factors of production have been added together to arrive at total cost, the planning authorities must set their prices at the marginal cost of production. Or more accurately,

---

[4]See Question 4 of Chapter 27's Appendix for proof.

[5]As earlier discussions of marginal productivity have shown, *total product will be at a maximum only when labor has been transferred from the land where its marginal-product is low to the good land where its marginal-product is high*. Every such transfer must necessarily yield us extra product, until finally no further increases in output can result when the marginal-products have been equalized in the two uses.

the socialist managers of a plant must behave like a perfect competitor: they must *disregard* any influence that their own production might have on market price and must continue to produce extra units up to the point where the last little unit costs just as much as its selling price.

For many industries, such as railroads, where unit costs are constantly falling, setting marginal costs equal to price will imply that *full* average costs are not covered. In a noncapitalistic society the difference would be made up by an (accounting) lump-sum grant from the state; for if a railroad system is worth building, it is worth being utilized well.[6]

RULES FOR RESOURCE PRICING

Correct social planning requires that all scarce resources, whether human labor or not, be given accounting prices at least. The final costs of consumers' goods should include the sum total of *all* extra costs necessary to produce each good, or in short, should equal *marginal cost*. The demand for consumers' goods is really an indirect demand for all productive resources, a demand which can be kept in proper check only by putting appropriate valuations on productive resources.

Otherwise, society's valuable nonhuman—and human! —resources will be incorrectly allocated and the market pricing of finished goods will not lead to maximum consumers' satisfaction. It is to be emphasized that the accounting prices of land and other nonhuman resources need not, in a socialist state, be part of the incomes of anyone. In the language of the visionary critic of private enterprise: no one is "exploited" by having a property owner skim off part of the final product. Instead, the contribution of capital and land to production is given to people in the form of government goods and the algebraic *social dividend*.

ROLE OF THE INTEREST RATE IN UTOPIA

We have seen that the interest rate has an important function in a capitalistic, socialistic, or any other kind of economic system. Capital goods have a "net productivity." As long as resources can be invested for the present or the future, it will be necessary to make important decisions with respect to capital. Shall we apply present land and labor to the production of a corn crop this year or to apples 15 years from now? Shall we have grape juice today or wine 10 years hence? Shall we replace a wornout loom with a new expensive one which yields its services over a period of 20 years or buy a cheap one that will last only 14 years? Every one of these questions can be answered only by using an interest rate to relate future and present economic values. Without such an interest rate, the existing stock of fixed and circulating capital cannot be devoted to its best uses; and whatever amount of national income society has decided to invest in capital formation cannot be embodied in the best form without such an interest rate.

The interest rate acts as a sieve or rationing device: all projects that can yield 10 per cent over time are undertaken before any projects that yield only 8 per cent.

It should be added that many economic writers on socialism do not think that the rate of interest should also determine—as it does in our economy, to some degree—the rate at which capital growth is to take place at the expense of current consumption. The decision as to how much should be saved would be determined by the state "in the light of national and social needs," and not by the "haphazard" notions of individuals with respect to the future. But the level of social saving and capital growth once having been determined, the interest rate must be used to

---

[6]The long-run question as to whether to build a railroad in the first place may involve an "all-or-none decision," which cannot be made step by step. In such a case, there must still be a balancing of the extra (or marginal) advantage and extra cost to society of the enterprise. But for such a big step, price is no longer a good indicator of total welfare, since—as we saw in Chapter 22—there is always an element of consumer's surplus in the total amount of goods a person consumes over what he has paid for them.

Figure 32-2 pictures a case where *dd*, which we assume reflects true marginal utilities to society, everywhere lies below decreasing long-run *AC*. So pricing at long-run *MC* can never recover full long-run social costs. Yet, with the *a* area a little larger than the *b* area, the total-utility area under *dd* is greater than the total-cost area under *LMC*. So society should produce at *E*, giving a lump-sum subsidy to cover the inevitable loss or somehow getting people to pay more for their earlier units that yielded great consumer surplus. (EXAMPLES: A railroad line to a country region; a monorail for urban commuters.) If *dd* shifted down enough to make *a* < *b*, the whole project should never be undertaken in the first place, or should not ultimately be replaced. Even if *dd* shifted up a bit, so that part of it lay above *LAC* and price *could* cover all costs, *P* still should be kept down to *LMC* for efficient pricing. (All this needs qualifications if dollars do not represent true and constant marginal utility and true social costs, as in a world of many monopolies and in making big decisions.) Also, taxing to finance the subsidy may involve some distortions; so we may have to settle for a second-best solution with *P* between *LMC* and *LAC*.

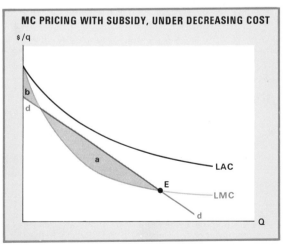

MC PRICING WITH SUBSIDY, UNDER DECREASING COST

FIG. 32-2.

allocate scarce "capital supplies" optimally and to determine the priority of alternative projects.[7]

WAGE RATES AND INCENTIVE PRICING

We must now return to the problem of how the utopian planners would set wage rates, and then we are done. If the amounts of labor of all kinds and of all skills were perfectly fixed, there would be no reason why labor should not be given accounting prices just like any other productive factor. Workers would receive no wages at all. They would then receive all the national income in the form of an enlarged *social dividend*.

However, if heterogeneous people are to be free to choose their own occupations and given the choice of working a little harder and longer in return for extra consumption goods, then it will be necessary to set up a system of *actual market wages* at which people can sell their services.

Wages may differ depending upon how the irksomeness and unpleasantness of the job affects voluntary labor supplied; and unlike now, the pleasanter jobs may then be the lower-paid, and the ditchdiggers or garbage collectors may have to be higher-paid to attract people into these jobs. Occupations that require much training and skill will receive high pay, but much of that pay may be spent by the state in providing the education necessary to acquire those skills. Piece rates might be used, and a worker with a 20 per cent higher productivity will be receiving higher (pre-tax and pre-social-dividend) wages. Workers will in every case be offered wages equal to their marginal, or extra, productivity.

Therefore, it is not necessarily true that all incomes will be a dead level in the utopian society. They will differ somewhat as a result of two distinct factors: (1) society's appraisal of the "needs and worth" of different individuals —as reflected primarily in the size of the individuals' lump-sum *social dividends*, and (2) the need for wages to differ to provide incentives and to compensate people for extra disutility and effort. Incomes need not differ, however, because of inequality in the ownership and inheritance of property and genetic talents. Wage rents (like Babe Ruth's) and rents to state-financial training could be heavily lump-sum-taxed, exactly like Henry George's surplus land rents.

SUMMARY OF UTOPIAN PRICING

1. A utopian system could make use of four different kinds of pricing: (*a*) consumer-goods prices, (*b*) wage and incentive rates, (*c*) accounting prices of intermediate goods or produced factor inputs, and (*d*) final lump-sum dividends (when positive, subsidies; when negative, taxes). The first three prices would be determined by supply and demand. Any consumption good would be pro-

duced up to the point where the full marginal cost of production (necessary to keep all resources from other uses and from leisure) is just equal to the price.[8]

2. The final distribution of income would be made to correspond to what society regards as the ideal distribution pattern by means of payment of a lump-sum social dividend to people, depending upon "need, wants, and deservingness," but not—like a wage—on effort or performance. In Utopia, it might be felt that a much more nearly equal distribution of income will be necessary before the dollar votes of consumers can be expected to reflect true social preferences. However, this is an a-scientific, ethical question; and we could use the same economic principles to make blueprints for an *in*-egalitarian utopia.

3. None of these processes except the last requires detailed *comprehensive planning by a central agency*. Mathematicians would not have to be called in to solve thousands and thousands of simultaneous equations. Instead, the *decentralized planners* would proceed by successive approximation, by trial and error—setting provisional market and accounting prices and cutting them or raising them, depending upon whether available supplies are piling up or running short.

It would be naive to think that any actual society would succeed in reaching the ideal equilibrium positions described above. Errors of foresight would inevitably be made. Existing vested interests, anxious to preserve their security in a dynamic world of change, would resist and sabotage such change in the same qualitative fashion as they have done in historical societies. Even when politicians and the electorate do not pay much attention to the incentive mechanisms outlined in the preceding pages, the importance of this discussion is that it teaches us how to appraise the mechanical efficiency of pricing in a *non*socialist society.

BRIEF HISTORY OF WELFARE PRICING

A brief history of welfare pricing doctrines may be of interest. From Smith's time at least, men saw beauty in the *laissez-faire* mechanism and inferred that it must have teleological significance in giving efficiency. But they were often uncritical, and often they overlooked the assumption that dollar votes were to be distributed in the ethically desired way; and they could not prove what they believed. Around 1900 Pareto showed that an ideal socialism would have to solve the same equations as competitive capitalism. Around 1920, Ludwig Von Mises, perhaps unaware of Pareto's proof, set forth the challenging view that rational economic organization was *logically*

---

[7]There is no logical reason why individuals who are willing to forgo present for future consumption should not be permitted to do such voluntary extra saving and receive an interest return equal to the net productivity of capital.

[8]The decentralized managers of industries could generally achieve this result by seeking to maximize their net algebraic profits, measured by accounting points or actual dollars, but with *all* prices taken as given parameters. (NOTE: Under cost conditions suitable for viable *laissez-faire*, this type of behavior is actually policed by competition; but where bureaucrats "play the game of competition," there may be a hard administrative problem to make sure they do act as price-takers.)

impossible in the absence of free markets. Fred Taylor of Michigan, A. P. Lerner of England and California, and Oscar Lange of Poland answered Mises with the view that socialism could conceptually solve the problems of economic organization by a decentralized process of bureaucratic trial and error—"playing the game of competition" and "deliberately planning not to plan".

F. A. Hayek has argued that this answer overlooks the problem of giving *each man the initiative* to better the existing allocation of resources and that only with actual free enterprise do you efficiently utilize the dispersed information which each of us may possess. He points out that it is naive to think that production and cost functions are known. They and shifting demand functions must be learned and be improved on. Who can police the Lerner-Lange decentralized bureaucrats to motivate them to play this competition game? And who can audit that they truly do, if their self-interest in the form of profits or higher incomes is not involved? (The Appendix to Chapter 3 discusses the trends in the communist countries of Eastern Europe (Yugoslavia, the Soviet Union, etc.) toward more reliance on market pricing and profitability calculations.)

WELFARE ECONOMICS

On the basis of the above principles of pricing, we are in a position to see what friendly and unfriendly critics think is wrong in our system, or not necessarily right from various ethical viewpoints. Critics list the following possible deviations from the social optimum:

1. The existing distribution of property, income, education, and economic opportunity is the result of past history and does not necessarily represent an optimum condition according to the ethical philosophies of Christianity, Buddhism, paganism, or other ideologies. Defenders of the capitalist system counter with the claim that such deviations from the optimum distribution can be corrected by appropriate tax policies, if that is desired.

(There are, though, some costs to be incurred in our capitalistic system from such policies because of taxation effects upon incentives, risk-taking, effort, and productivity.)

2. The widespread presence of monopoly elements in our system and the limited appearance of perfect competition mean that production is rarely being pushed to the optimum point of equality of marginal cost to price; because the elasticity of demand is not infinite to imperfect competitors, production is pushed only to the point of equality of marginal cost to marginal revenue. Because of the fear of "spoiling the market," monopoly price is then too high and monopoly output continues to be too low relative to competitive outputs.

This is related to a further Chamberlinian evil under imperfect competition when entry of new firms into an industry is very easy. There may then tend to be an inefficient division of production among too many firms; the *P* charged is too high, but through wasteful use of resources, no one need be making any profits.

3. Remember also the failure of *laissez-faire* pricing to deal properly with "externalities". (For example, the fact that individual firms, in making their decisions *do not* take into account some possible effects of their production decisions on *other* firms or industries. In digging his oil well, Pat does not mind that he may be robbing Mike's oil pool; and the same with Mike—with the result that less oil is obtained in the end, and with more cost.) Because of such "external diseconomies or economies", apparent "private marginal costs" do not reflect true "social marginal costs"; and certain lines of activity deserve to be contracted and others to be expanded.[9]

4. Finally, of course, as shown in Part Two, under a *laissez-faire* system, there may be great wastes due to cyclical unemployment. Consumers, labor, farmers, and business, together with public fiscal and monetary policy, must be mobilized in a never-ending war against this scourge.

SUMMARY TO APPENDIX

1 In a pure, unmixed, competitive society, the economic problems of WHAT shall be produced, HOW, and FOR WHOM are solved in an interdependent manner by the impersonal workings of profit-and-loss markets. Each variable depends upon every other, but all tend to be simultaneously determined at their general equilibrium values by a process of successive approximations and readjustments.

2 Unless a utopian economy were uninterested in efficiency and economizing, or in freedom of choice of goods and jobs, it would have to institute a system of pricing. However, some prices would be purely accounting or bookkeeping figures; in addition, the final determination of the distribution of income would involve an outright social dividend or tax, in various lump-sum

---

[9]Compare A. C. Pigou, *Economics of Welfare* (Macmillan, New York, 1932).

The paradox that really perfect competition would discourage people from inventing (since they would know their profits would disappear) can be understood in terms of external economies: my

pecuniary reward from an invention may be much less than its social value after it has been widely imitated. Governmental activities are needed when "public goods" involve external benefits to more than one person at the same time, as shown in Chapter 8. See, too, Chapter 24's discussion of external economies.

amounts to people as determined by explicit a-scientific ethical decision of government and society designed to make dollar votes properly reflective of society's value judgments.

3 From the standpoint of welfare economics, it is seen that any capitalistic system may depart from what is considered a social optimum in three main ways: through improper distribution of income, monopoly and externalities, and unemployment.

CONCEPTS FOR REVIEW

interdependence, general equilibrium	incentive wages and job choice
determinate final equilibrium	accounting prices versus actual prices
efficient final equilibrium	monopoly restrictions
labor theory of value versus proper pricing of nonhuman resources	"external" divergences between social and private cost-benefits
interest rate in capitalism and socialism	information and incentives
social dividend: lump-sum tax or transfer incomes	welfare economics, ethical distribution questions, value judgments

QUESTIONS FOR DISCUSSION

1. Summarize how a pricing system works to solve the three fundamental economic problems. Illustrate their interdependence.
2. Discuss the four kinds of prices in a planned, utopian state.
3. What do you deem to be imperfections in our economic order? Virtues? What defects would plague a collectivist society?
4. "It is a vicious circle, to talk about simultaneous equations determining equilibrium. Suppose that I say, 'My age, X, is twice yours, Y. Your age, Y, is twenty-five years less than mine.' What a swindle: To know X, I must first know Y; but to know Y, I must first know X!" Show that the logical circle is a virtuous one, not a vicious one. The only solution to $Y = 2X$ and $X = Y - 25$ is obviously $X^* = 25$ and $Y^* = 50$. So it is with supply and demand determining wheat's P and Q. And so it is with general equilibrium.
5. *Extra-credit problem* on general equilibrium and welfare pricing: Half the people own no land; half own all the land; all work the same 10-hour day. Everybody spends half his income, whether large or small, on food, and half on clothing. Clothing is produced by labor only; food is produced by a production function involving labor and land, being a constant-share, unweighted geometric mean (or Cobb-Douglas) function—so that half the returns of food go to land and half to labor. Can you verify the following general-equilibrium solution?

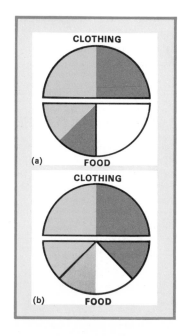

The proletariat, or workingclass taken all together, will get only three-eighths of the national income: half of the half GNP that goes to clothing they get for their labor in clothing; but land subtracts off half of the half GNP that goes to food, and of the remaining share for labor, the proletariat get half for *their* labor, i.e., $(1/2)(1/2) + (1/2)(1/2)(1/2) = 3/8$, as can be verified from the medium-red area of the accompanying social pie. Now suppose it is deemed ethically just that all people should share alike. By redistributive taxation of all land rent à la Henry George, or by nationalization of land and lump-sum dividends of its equilibrium rent to all, the final distribution of income will be made equal for both classes, as shown by the second social pie's equal light- and dark-shaded areas.

5

International Trade and Finance

33
THE BALANCE OF INTERNATIONAL PAYMENTS AND FOREIGN EXCHANGE

MISS PRISM: Cecily, you will read your political economy in my absence. The chapter on the Fall of the Rupee you may omit. It is somewhat too sensational. Even these metallic problems have their melodramatic side.

OSCAR WILDE, The Importance of Being Ernest

In the earlier chapters of this book, with the exception of Chapter 14, we took international trade more or less for granted. Here, in Part V, we concentrate on the interesting *international* economic problems arising as soon as an economy engages in foreign trade.

This chapter and its Appendix deal with the *monetary* mechanisms involved in international trade. Then the next two chapters concentrate on the basic *real* factors which underlie international trade and which are often obscured by the monetary veil that covers all international transactions. These basic real factors are involved in any rational appraisal of the problems raised by tariffs and other barriers to the international division of labor. In Chapter 36 all these principles are put to work to help us understand the contemporary international economic scene.

International trade is important for the following basic reason:

Foreign trade offers a "consumption-possibility frontier" that can give us more of all goods than can our own domestic production-possibility frontier!

EXAMPLE: Each of us ends up consuming more than he

could produce alone. The world is out on—and not inside —its true production-possibility frontier. That is the essence of foreign trade. So simple. And yet apparently so hard for members of parliament and voters to grasp and remember.

Our task in Part Five is to study the mechanics of international trade and finance: foreign exchange rates; balance of international payments; foreign aid and loans; tariff duties and quotas; the so-called "principle of comparative advantage", which tells what kind of trade will take place, and why it ought to; and finally, the international economic problems of the 1970s, such as pegged versus flexible exchange rates, the European Common Market and common currency, the World Bank, the International Monetary Fund (IMF), long-term international adjustment and liquidity problems, "free-tier gold" versus "official gold", Special Drawing Rights (so-called "paper gold"), "gliding bands" of exchange rates, problems of international capital flows, foreign investment and ownership, and so forth.

These are anything but abstract economic problems. They are the news that is being reported on the front page of tomorrow's newspapers. And they make the difference between fruitful international exchange and chaos.

A. MECHANISMS OF FOREIGN EXCHANGE AND TRADE

FOREIGN EXCHANGE RATES

First, how does trade take place? If I buy maple sugar from Quebec or pig iron from Hamilton, I naturally want to pay in dollars. Also, the farmer and steel

producer expect to be paid in dollars, for the reason that their expenses and their living costs are all settled in dollars. Within a country, economic transactions seem simple.

If, however, I wish to buy a British racing car directly, matters are more complicated. I must ultimately pay in British money, or what is called "pounds sterling," rather than in dollars. Similarly, a man in Britain must somehow get dollars to a Canadian producer if he wants our merchandise. Many Canadians have never seen a British pound note. Certainly they would accept pounds only if they could be sure of converting them into Canadian dollars.

Clearly, therefore, exports and imports of goods between nations with different units of money introduce a new economic factor: the *foreign exchange rate*, giving the price of a foreigner's unit of money in terms of our own.

Thus the price of a British pound was about $2.30 (Canadian) in 1974. There is also a foreign exchange rate between our money and the currencies of each and every other country: about 20 cents for the French franc; about 40 cents for the Deutschemark; and so forth.[1] In mid 1974 the price of a U.S. dollar hovered around $0.97.

Given the foreign exchange rate, it is now simple for me to buy my British car. Suppose its quoted price is £2,000. All I have to do is look in the newspaper for the foreign exchange rate for pounds. If this is $2.30 per pound, I simply go to a bank or post office with $4,600 and ask that the money be used to pay the British car exporter. Pay him what? Pounds, of course, the only kind of money he needs.

Whether I use the post office or a bank or a broker is of no particular importance. In fact, it is all the same if the British exporter sends me a bill requesting payment in dollars or if he deals with me through a Canadian dealer. In any case, he ultimately wants pounds, not dollars, and will soon trade the $4,600 for £2,000. (Needless to say, we are neglecting all commission charges and the cost of money orders.)

You should be able to show what a British importer of Canadian copper has to do if he wants to buy, say, a $23,000 shipment from a Canadian exporter. Here pounds must be converted into dollars.

Why, when the foreign exchange rate is $2.30 per pound, will this cost him £10,000?

EXCHANGE RATE MECHANISMS. The businessman or tourist need not, as an individual, know more than the above in order to do his international business. But the true economics of these actions cannot be grasped until we can explain *why* the exchange rate is at the level it is; and what economic principles underlie foreign exchange movements. We will find the whole economy is usually involved, not merely the foreign-trade sectors.

There are at least four different, and important, cases to study:

1. The working of some kind of pure or modified *gold standard*.

2. The mechanism of *flexible* or *floating* exchange rates.

3. Government *controls* and flexible rates by pegging rates or otherwise.

4. The present-day hybrid regime, with its blend of (a) stable exchange rates; and (b) floating rates with a wide band; and (c) a hoped-for reform— "crawling pegs" or gliding bands.

THE CLASSICAL GOLD STANDARD

This first case has been historically important. In severely modified form it still shapes today's system. We have already seen aspects of it in Chapter 17's section on foreign exchange and gold, which it would be useful to review in connection with this chapter.

Suppose people everywhere insisted on being paid in bars of pure *gold metal*: weight alone would count, and its shape—whether round like a ball or coin, or irregular like a sliver, or cylindrical like a broom handle—would not matter so long as there were a guarantee of its purity and weight. Then buying a bicycle in Britain would require payment in gold at a price expressed in ounces of gold; and buying pig iron in Hamilton would involve the same kind of payment. By definition, there would be no foreign-exchange-rate problem.

Since slivers and blobs of gold are inconvenient to carry and to assay for purity and for weight, it became customary for the state—in earlier days the prince—to stamp out in *coin* form a specified num-

---

[1] There are also foreign exchange rates between the Deutschemark and the French franc. But these rates between other countries need not interest us much, particularly since, in a free competitive market, the mark-franc rate can be simply calculated from the mark-dollar and franc-dollar rate, because sharp-eyed international arbitragers see to it that relative "cross rates" do not get out of line: thus a mark must sell for a little less than 2.0 (= $.40/$.20) francs. Of course, these examples have to be modified whenever official exchange rates alter.

ber of ounces of gold, carrying the seal of the state to guarantee purity and weight.

With gold coins as the exchange medium, would not foreign trade still be like domestic trade? Yes, essentially. But with some minor differences: If we used ounces and France used grams to measure weight, you would merely have to have a table of units' conversion. And the same problem would arise if Queen Victoria chose to make her coins about 1/4 ounce of gold (the "sovereign") and U.S. President McKinley chose to make his 1/20 ounce of gold (the dollar). In that case, the pound sovereign, being five times as heavy as the dollar, would naturally have an exchange rate of $5 (American or Canadian) to £1.

Now that is essentially how the pre-1914 gold standard actually worked. Of course, local pride tended to keep the Americans and the British using their own coins. But anyone was free to melt down U.S. coins and get them converted into British coins (at nominal costs). So, except for the trifling costs of melting down, shipping across the ocean, and re-coining, *all countries on the gold standard had essentially stable exchange rates whose par values, or parities, were determined by the gold content of their local money unit.*

Minor qualifications: "gold points." Gold being quite inconvenient to carry around for spending purposes, inevitably governments issued paper certificates which were pledged to be redeemable in gold metal. People had the right to turn in gold for certificates and certificates for gold, and they often exercised that right. Also, in those days ocean transport was slow and costly: so there were "gold points" around the true mint parities within which the pound and (U.S.) dollar exchange rates could fluctuate. Thus, if it costs 2 cents to ship 1/4 ounce of gold either way across the Atlantic Ocean (inclusive of insurance and interest costs), could the exchange rate depart a little from $5? Yes. In New York, the quoted price of a pound could rise to as much as $5.02 before it would pay to get gold bars and ship them to London to be exchanged for pounds; a price higher than $5.02 could not prevail because enough gold would be flowing to keep the price no higher than the upper gold point. It should be evident that the pound could fall below the mint parity of $5 by 2 cents to $4.98. When the exchange rate got down to this lower gold point, it would be cheaper for gold to be shipped from Britain to the United States. All this actually happened (except that $5 is substituted here for the correct pre-1914 parity of $4.87 (U.S.) to simplify the arithmetic, and the shipping costs are given only approximately). Before 1914, the for-

eign exchange rate of the pound and the U.S. dollar stayed essentially constant, varying but a trifle from these weight-determined mint parities when the gold points were touched and gold had to flow in the indicated direction.

THE HUME GOLD-FLOW EQUILIBRATING MECHANISM
Now that the mechanics of the problem are understood, we probe deeper to answer this question:

Under the gold standard, what kept the United States from buying more goods from Britain than Britain bought from her—which, after all, would have required Americans to keep shipping gold in final payment? How do gold flows get stopped and trade *equilibrated*?

This is a good question, and the mercantilist writers (who preceded Adam Smith and his friend the noted philosopher David Hume) gave a plausible but superficial answer. The mercantilists had said:

"A country will lose its gold unless the Prince introduces tariffs and quotas to cut down on imports of goods; and unless he gives subsidies to encourage exports; and unless he forbids skilled workmen to take their knowledge abroad and makes sure that all shipping takes place in our own boats, however dear they may be." As an afterthought, almost too obvious to require mention, they said: "Of course, losing gold is a terrible thing for a nation. Don't ask why. Everyone knows it to be one of the worst tragedies that can happen to a nation."

David Hume in 1752, and economists ever since, **have given the refutation** to this mercantilist reasoning. First Hume noted that it could not be true that everyone would all the time be losing gold under free trade. Where would it go—into the sea? And he demonstrated that it is no tragedy at all if a country goes permanently from having 10 million ounces of gold to having 5 million, or even 1 million. *If* having half the amount of gold means merely that *all* prices are exactly halved, no one in the country is the least bit better or worse off. So, losing half or nine-tenths of a nation's gold is nothing to worry about, Hume pointed out, if it merely ends up with an equivalently reduced price level.

Here it is well to recall the crude quantity theory of money and prices discussed in Chapter 15. David Hume, along with John Locke and earlier writers, was one of the first to enunciate and hold to this theory concerning the proportionality of all prices to the stock of money (in this case M being gold).[2]

Now comes the second and important part of Hume's classical refutation of mercantilism and defense of free trade. He asserted that there was a four-pronged mechanism that tended always to keep in equilibrium the international balance of payments of countries on the gold standard. Briefly, the Hume mechanism is this.

Whenever one country imports too much and begins to lose gold, its loss of gold *reduces its price and cost level,* thereby (1) *decreasing its imports* of foreign goods that have become relatively expensive, and (2) *increasing exports* of its now cheapened home-produced goods.

The other country, which had been having a so-called "favorable balance of trade," in which it was sending more goods abroad than it was importing and merely receiving barren gold in exchange, now has (via the quantity theory) its price and cost levels of goods *raised.* This is a further reason (3) for its now-expensive *exports to go down* in physical amount and (4) for its citizens to import *more* of the now-cheap goods of the first country. Thus the excessive trade flow will be reversed.

The result of this four-pronged gold-flow price-level mechanism is (normally) to improve the balance of payments of the country that was losing gold and worsen that of the country with the favorable balance of trade—until *equilibrium* in international trade is restored at relative prices that keep imports and exports in balance with no net gold flow. In theory the *equilibrium* is stable and self-correcting without tariffs or other state interference.

FLEXIBLE OR FLOATING EXCHANGE RATES

Having seen how an idealized gold standard works, we turn now to the case where supply and demand are left free to determine the foreign exchange rate. In the absence of any tie to gold, the pound might have had an average price of $4.00 or $5.00 in the

1940s, and in this decade, an average price of about $2.50 (Canadian). Who knows, perhaps next decade it could be at $4.50, or $3, or $1.50, once floating exchange rates become the rule.

The forces of supply and demand will determine the answer. As we have seen, Canadians need pounds to buy British goods, and the British need Canadian dollars to buy our products. Suppose that Canadians want to buy so many British goods at an existing $2.50 level, but that the British want few Canadian goods. Then we may be demanding more pounds as needed foreign exchange than they will be wanting to supply us with. If there is no longer a gold standard, one cannot get gold and ship it over so as to keep the foreign exchange rate within narrow gold points around the $2.50 parity. Instead, *our urgent demand for pounds will bid up the foreign exchange rate*—the price of a British pound in Canadian dollars. How far? Just far enough so that, at the new higher price of, say, $3.10 for the pound, our total demand for foreign exchange (in this case pounds) will be brought down into equality with the now larger amount of foreign exchange the British willingly supply.

Two main steps are involved: (1) With the higher price of pounds in Canadian dollars, it will cost more to import British bicycles and the number of them we demand will fall off in the usual fashion. (2) With our dollar now cheaper, our goods will cost less to the British and they will want to demand more of our export goods. (If we look at these two effects, from both their viewpoint and our own, we have something like the four-pronged action of Hume. But with certain important differences. Our *whole* domestic wage and cost level need not change, and neither need theirs. The change in the foreign exchange rate can *itself* bring about enhanced *relative* dearness and cheapness of export- and import-price levels.)

The familiar curves of supply and demand developed in Chapter 4 and Part Three are used in Fig. 33-1 to show equilibrium determination of flexible exchange rates. Canada's *dd* curve comes from our desire for foreign exchange to buy import goods, to make tourist visits, to hire shipping and insurance services, to finance our troops abroad and our foreign-aid grants, to pay the dividends and interest we owe to foreign owners of our securities and property;

---

[2] He admitted that the equilibrium predicted by the quantity theory would not take place instantaneously; indeed, he was one of the first to recognize that a period of rising M and rising prices, when it was first happening and was not foreseen, would give profits to businessmen by causing their prices to rise more than their costs; he thought this would be good for full employment and capital formation in the short run.

FIG. 33-1. Floating exchange rates are forced flexibly up or down by supply and demand for goods or capital movements.

Behind our *dd* is our desire to import British goods, buy British securities, visit the Bard's grave, and so forth. Behind their *ss* supply of pounds to be traded for Canadian dollars is their desire for our export goods and other items and their need to send us earnings on our past capital movements. If the rate were *E*, there would be an excess of foreign currency that they would want to supply us over what we should want to demand. Such an excess of supply would bid the rate back down to *E*, where the market of foreign currency for dollars is just cleared.

(If we doubled our domestic money supply and all prices, *purchasing-power-parity* doctrine says curves should shift up to twice the scale resulting in exact doubling of *E*'s price, a hundred percent appreciation of the pound relative to the depreciated dollar.)

and also to finance long-term investment abroad by Canadian firms or stock buyers, and short-term investment in foreign near-term bonds or savings accounts.

What is behind the British demand for dollars—which shows up as the *ss* supply curve of the pound-foreign-exchange they offer us? The exactly similar items in *their* balance of payments: desire to import our export goods, need to pay us dividends, etc.

At the *dd* and *ss* intersection, the flexible foreign exchange rate will be established, having then no tendency to rise or fall from this equilibrium level.

PURCHASING-POWER PARITY THEORY. A classical economist like Hume would understand all this very well. In fact, he (and Ricardo around 1817 and Sweden's Gustav Cassel around 1917) would seek as a clue to the equilibrium level of a flexible exchange rate, the relative behaviour of its price level.

Purchasing-power parity. Let Canada and Britain be at equilibrium, say, at $2.50 per £1. Now let Canada double *all* her prices by domestically inflating her *M*; and let Britain keep her *M* limited enough to produce a steady price level. Then, other things being equal (such as employment remaining full and there being no inventions, crop failures, tariffs, or change in tastes), the new *dd* and *ss* intersection will come at twice the old $2.50 rate, namely, at $5.00 per £1.

Hume's reasoning would be classically simple. With all wages and prices here *exactly doubled* (and *M* doubled here to finance them), we can *buy exactly the same* physical imports and *sell exactly the same* physical exports at the new exchange rate which has doubled like everything else. (It is just as if every Canadian old dollar is now called two Canadian dollars.)[3]

Now we can examine under a floating-exchange-rate mechanism what happens when a country imports too much, and compare the result with the Hume gold-equilibrating mechanism. If we buy more from British sellers' catalogues, (or invest more money in North Sea oil wells), such changes will obviously shift our *dd* upward and rightward. If we have more domestic inflation than they, our export-good prices will rise; such changes will shift their *ss* leftward and upward. With what resulting intersection? With a new higher equilibrium level of the exchange rate.

Note the result for our trade with Britain: the new

---

[3] Cassel and other writers developed the doctrine of purchasing-power parity to predict how much World War I currencies would depreciate when internal inflation sent their price levels up by 100 per cent or more. His long-run predictions worked out better than his short-run predictions, but neither had perfect accuracy. In the real world, unlike the classical model, other things did not stay equal.

higher cost of pounds will coax out more Canadian exports. And it will choke off some British imports. These changes will go on just enough to have an *equilibrating* effect like Hume's. (The final result will be the same, but the route to equilibrium is different in that, with flexible rates the impact is chiefly on the exporting and importing sectors, not the gold mechanism's impact on our whole economy.)

FIXED OR PEGGED EXCHANGE RATES

Most governments have been unhappy to allow the forces of supply and demand to determine the international value of their currency. At one time or another they have attempted to "fix" or "peg" the rate. When they do this, the fluctuations that come from changes in imports or capital movements are prevented, or at least controlled and regulated.

One apparent mechanism goes back to the gold standard. Countries declared that their currency would exchange for a certain number of ounces of gold, always. This was the mechanism by which gold was said to be worth, for thirty years, 35 dollars per ounce. Subsequently, all other countries declared either a gold, or a U.S.-dollar value for their currencies. This gold-exchange standard appears to be just a variant of the earlier gold standard.

But actually these decreed exchange ratios, based on gold amounts, are merely targets or standards—they are not mechanisms, as the old gold standard provided. For now we must ask how the countries' governments are to *hold* the rate at the particular level chosen.

In the days since World War I, two answers have been given. The United States, and for certain periods, other countries, stuck with gold. If their currency was wanted by other countries, they sold it for gold. If the reverse was true, they bought it back from other countries by parting with their stock, or reserves, of gold. Thus just as though gold were a commodity, they maintained its price in terms of U.S. dollars—*or the price of U.S. dollars in terms of gold*. This technique of fixing the exchange rate demands a willingness to acquire and hold very large amounts of gold. It is an expensive system, rejected by countries that did not wish to make the sacrifice involved in importing gold for reserves instead of other goods for consumption.

Thus most countries, while decreasing a gold value for their currency, have dealt only in small amounts of gold. They have maintained the value of their currency instead by, in effect, shifting the supply and demand curves of Figure 33-1 up or down, till they intersect at the desired pegged rate.

You can apply the supply and demand diagrams of Chapter 21 to this case, and work out the techniques that have been used, or could be. New twists are invented all the time.

Briefly, the government maintains a stock of foreign currencies (or gold), which it uses for buying its own currency from foreigners to keep its own rate from *depreciating*, or falling in price. Its buying thus makes the supply of say, Canadian dollars, smaller, and tends to raise the intersection E in Figure 1. Thus it can force its currency to *appreciate*. If its currency is appreciating beyond the target limit it has set, it can instead offer to buy foreign currencies, thus increasing the supply of its own currency held by foreigners and increasing its reserves of foreign exchange. How it would obtain and keep enough in its Exchange Fund account, and what it would do if its supply of domestic currency depleted, was discussed in Chapter 17. Just as important, what would it do if its efforts to prevent depreciation were halted by the depletion of its reserves of foreign exchange? Since World War II, the world has seen these restrictions:

(a) *Borrowing*. Countries have replenished their stock of foreign currencies by borrowing them from international organizations like the International Monetary Fund (IMF) or from particular foreign countries. This allows them to keep on buying their own currency and preventing a depreciation, until supply and demand conditions change again, or until the reserves run out again. (Obviously, before they borrow gold or foreign exchange from other countries, they will confiscate all the gold or foreign exchange their own citizens happen to be holding. This is one frequent aspect of emergency exchange control.)

(b) *Devaluation*. Countries have "devalued" the fixed value of their currencies. That is, a country using a currency (such as the Canadian dollar) has reduced the amount of some other currency, or of gold, that could be officially purchased with one dollar. This step is exactly equivalent to increasing the dollar price of gold, or of one unit of American or European, or Japanese currency. Britain, for example, devalued its currency steadily after World War II by reducing from $5.00 to about $2.50 the amount of U.S. currency that could be bought with one pound sterling. More dramatic were Nixon's 1971-1973 devaluations of the U.S. dollar which raised the official price of an ounce of gold from $38.00 to $42.22.[4]

Such steps usually mean that the *depreciation* of the currency that would have come slowly if the rate of exchange had been allowed to float on a flexible market, instead comes all at once, in a devaluation from one fixed or pegged rate to another.

(c) *Exchange controls.* Many countries have shifted *ss* leftward by restricting foreign travel and imports, controlling business freedom to invest in foreign enterprise, and cutting down on foreign contributions to defense, aid, etc. They do this by restrictions, quotas, and permits. They may also force those who want to acquire foreign currency (supply domestic currency) to buy it at specially high rates. Likewise they may shift *dd* by subsidizing exports, promoting tourist visits, making foreign investment attractive by tax gimmicks, etc.

To compare these three responses to an unwelcome depreciation, we may say that *devaluation* amounts to accepting whatever supply and demand dictate; *borrowing* reserves is a way of postponing devaluation, that may, with luck, make devaluation unnecessary if demand or supply changes; and *controls* are workable for years at a time, as prolonged episodes in Canada, the U.K., France, Italy, India and Israel have at various times illustrated.

OVERVALUATION.

When a country's imports (and capital outflows) exceed its exports (and capital inflows), we will say in the next Part that it has a balance-of-payments deficit.

We can diagnose a chronic balance-of-payments deficit being caused by an exchange rate that has been pegged too high. Its costs are not competitive, and $M > X$, because it has *overvalued* its currency.

---

[4] If a country has a chronic deficit, and devalues, the rise in its gold price also implies its currency's devaluation in terms of all other currencies on gold parities. To revalue gold was what experts advised for the U.S. in the late '60s. But if the other countries also devalued, no change in exchange rates trade flows or U.S. deficits would result. The only change would be that the world would have more gold, measured in the units of *any* currency. This may be defined as an increase in international liquidity, and has been claimed as a worth-while goal in itself.

Consider the country it is trading with. That country must be running a chronic surplus. Its currency is said to be *undervalued*.

How to cure the disequilibrium? Economists say: "Devalue the overvalued currency, or let it depreciate on a flexible exchange market. What is exactly the same thing—repeat, *exactly*—revalue the undervalued currency, or let it appreciate by floating upward. That should help to restore equilibrium".

Politically, countries are happier to devalue than to revalue upward. Thus in Germany and Japan, two nations with stubborn payments surpluses from 1960 to 1973, vested interests grew up in their swollen export industries. The payment surplus was their export boom; they hated to see it go. (We'll see more on this in Chapter 36.)

CANADIAN EXPERIENCE.

Canada is almost the only country that has extensive experience with a floating exchange rate since the end of World War II. In 1951, despairing of finding a "pegged" rate that would be appropriate for the fluctuating foreign demands for Canadian exchange, the authorities turned the dollar loose on the world markets to find its own level. Within a year these foreign demands had increased, and the price of the Canadian dollar rose from about $.95 to $1.03 (U.S.). Thereafter the Canadian dollar fluctuated, but remained at a "premium" until 1961-1962, when it was again pegged.

Being *flexible* should not be confused with the effect of the appreciation of the Canadian dollar. Even if our dollar had not been free to fluctuate, even if our exchange rate had been fixed, it might well have "pegged" at a premium during the 1951-62 period. For if foreigners were willing to buy our goods at $1.05 (U.S.), they would have taken many more at $1.00 and our total exports would have been much greater. Economists today argue about whether that would have been a good thing, for it is true that both larger exports and smaller imports would have been a help during Canada's late-fifties' unemployment. But our foreign-payments accounts would have been in substantial surplus; all that we need note here is that the flexible rate, in floating to an appreciation, helped to keep this surplus down.

Between 1962 and 1970, as the final panel on Fig. 33-2 shows, the Canadian dollar was again "pegged", being held within narrow limits around $.92 1/2 (U.S.). Then in May 1970 Finance Minister Benson announced that the strong upward pressure (*dd*) was too great. Instead of a re-valuation, the government decided to free the Canadian dollar to find its own level, propelled less by rising exports than by new capital inflows. Fig.33-2 shows that, as in 1951, our dollar rose rapidly in U.S. terms, reaching a high in 1972.

"Pegging" the rate officially is of course the same as unofficially intervening on an allegedly floating exchange market and preventing the rate from moving far. The Exchange Fund account was used extensively in 1970 and 1971, its holdings of U.S. dollars almost doubling—to 5 billion dollars. This activity is known as a "dirty-float"—the dollar was not free to find its own level.

But such intervention—described in Chapter 17—was not active in 1973 and 1974.

THE EVOLUTION OF THE EXCHANGE RATE MECHANISM

Now that we have seen the workings of pure gold, flexible and fixed exchange rate mechanisms, we can chronicle briefly the evolution from gold to the hybrid system of the middle seventies. The story is taken up again in Chapter 36, where we examine future modifications which we hope are on the way.

MONTHLY EXCHANGE RATE FOR U.S. DOLLAR IN CANADIAN CENTS, 1947-1974

FIG. 33-2. The Canadian dollar has responded to capital movements, speculation.
The freeing of the Canadian dollar from a pegged rate at the end of May, 1970, was a reversion to the system of the 1950s. The 1949-1950 rates were a response to Korean War transactions and speculation; the 1960-1961 rise was caused by capital inflows and government intervention.

LIVING UNDER THE GOLD STANDARD.

There is nothing sacred about gold. Silver, platinum, lead, or for that matter paper napkins would do, provided they had convenience for exchange, could not be falsified, and were enough limited in supply to keep the price level from soaring. Actually, the old gold standard was in its heyday only for a brief half-century prior to 1914. Before the nineteenth century, Britain had been more on a silver than on a gold standard, and had stumbled onto the gold standard as a result of market revaluations of the two precious metals without anyone's realizing it. Her great prestige caused France, the United States, and the rising empires of Germany and Japan to adopt the gold standard later.

Even in its brief heyday, several crises caused the gold standard to be "suspended"—to break down periodically (as, for example when the American Civil War forced the United States off gold for more than a decade). Only Britain's firm £4 1/4 to the ounce of gold kept the gold-standard idea alive. Moreover, the price level was at the mercy of the happenstance of gold discoveries. If world physical production was increasing in the years 1875 to 1895 at the rate of 5 per cent per year, the gold supply would—according to the quantity theory of money—have to increase by 5 per cent per year to keep prices stable. But mines, because of the ending of the Californian and Australian gold rushes, were not producing this much gold then; and as a result prices were sagging all over the world in the last third of the nineteenth century.

This "great depression" gave rise to much social unrest. In an ideal world of perfect price and wage flexibility, where the quantity theory worked smoothly both down and up, falling prices should not have mattered much. But as Hume himself insisted, prices and wages tend to be sticky downward; and falling price levels tend to lead to labor unrest, strikes, and unemployment, and radical movements generally. Precisely that happened in the United States and other countries during the period from 1875 to 1895.

The most important radical movement formed in the United States during this time was the Populists. It drew for its membership principally on debt-ridden farmers who were suffering from a persistent drop in farm prices, and on western silver miners who faced falling silver prices after the United States

went on the single gold standard in 1873. Since a gold shortage seemed to be squeezing all prices downward, there was a clamor on the part of these people for the use of silver to supplement gold. This culminated in the historic speech by William Jennings Bryan at the 1896 Democratic Convention, in which he spoke in favor of 'bimetallism' and warned against crucifying mankind on a cross of gold.

FRACTIONAL RESERVES IN BANKING.

With Germany and Japan going on the gold standard, the deflationary pressure on prices would have been even worse had it not been for growing methods of economizing on gold. Modern banks, which hold only fractional reserves, began to develop: the demand-deposit M they created meant that not quite so much gold was needed to keep up with growing total output. Moreover, most of the countries on the gold standard did *not* keep 100 per cent gold reserves to back up the token coins and paper currency they issued. Thus, if the typical country held only one-fourth gold against its paper money, only a quarter as much gold would have to be mined to support the same world price level.

This process of domestic banking evolution to economize on the use of gold is important. For, as we shall see, it foreshadows the modern international development of economizing on and displacing gold by creating so-called "paper gold," i.e., SDRs which are Special Drawing Rights in the International Monetary Fund (IMF). "Bimetallism", mentioned in the previous section, was also proposed as a means of economizing on the use of gold.

Bimetallism would mean that the nation's treasury would exchange its currency for *either* gold or silver, at some agreed-upon ratio. For example, the U.S. Treasury would exchange U.S. dollars for 16 ounces of silver *or* 1 ounce of gold. Unless all countries agreed upon the same 16/1 ratio, there would be a one-way movement of each metal to the place where it was most valued; and the place where gold was most valued would be on gold standard, while the place where silver was most valued would be on the silver standard. As a result, with every change in the relative supplies and demands for the two metals, there would be an ensuing fluctuation in the foreign exchange rates between the two countries. (The percentage size of the fluctuation could be only two-sixteenths if their respective bimetallic parities were 16/1 and 18/1. Even if all countries went on the same 16/1 ratio, any tendency for relative (marginal) mining costs to differ from this ratio would result in all of one metal being sold to all the treasuries of the world. For example, if the official parity is 16/1 and the ratio in the market is 20/1 (indicating that 20 ounces of silver is as cheap to produce as 1 ounce of gold), then, by a form of what is known as Gresham's Law—"bad money drives out good"—all silver would be sold to the government for gold coins. Gold coins would remain in circulation, and every ounce of silver would disappear at once. The world would buy and sell with gold—it would be on a gold standard.

Canada has never had official bimetallism, but in the early days, before she had her own coinage, she made official the coins of both the United States and Great Britain. In order for people to know how much to pay in taxes in either kind of coinage, she established an official parity ratio between the sterling and U.S. coins and notes. Because of the fractions involved, the rounded-off value of a British shilling was placed at 25 cents in gold instead of at the 24 cents ruling in London or New York. Shillings were thus overrated in Canada and appeared in large numbers, tending to drive out other coinage used in Canada.

Today no one favors two kinds of money.

THE GOLD-EXCHANGE STANDARD.

Another development helped economize on gold. Many countries, particularly small ones (like the Philippines), kept their money exchangeable at fixed rates with respect to gold. But they held little or no gold. Instead, they would hold the money of some big countries (like Great Britain and the United States) which were on the gold standard. So long as the small country could stay on such a "gold-exchange standard," the effect would be much like the pure gold standard, but with great economizing on gold.

Fortunately for those who favored the gold standard, the deflationary pressures eased some when gold was discovered in the Klondike and South Africa in the mid-1890s and when the cyanide process greatly increased the output of gold mines. Together with the increasing leverage attained by having smaller and smaller fractional-reserve ratios and more and more gold-exchange standards, the increase in mining enabled the world to keep on the gold standard and stave off deflation up until the 1929 crash. Some experts actually attribute that slump to an increasing shortage of world liquidity.

THE DOLLAR AS KEY CURRENCY.

During the Great Depression of the 1930s, political unrest and fear of Hitler's aggression caused an avalanche of gold to flow into the United States. After World War II people said with some exaggeration that *the world was in fact on a dollar standard*. The American dollar was the "key currency" in terms of which international trade and finance were carried on. Private and governmental reserves were kept largely in the form of U.S. dollar balances (i.e., in cash, bank deposits, and liquid short-term dollar securities). Whereas before 1914 the pound had been king, by 1945 the U.S. dollar, linked to gold, was *the* key currency.

The link to gold was maintained by the post-war Bretton Woods agreement, which set up the International Monetary Fund, World Bank, and a code of conduct accepted by the world's central banks and governments. Target exchange rates, called parities, were defined in the Charter in terms of ounces of gold—but also in terms of dollars. And in the following decades both the Fund and individual governments worked as though the dollar, not gold, was the world standard.

Bretton Woods, as Chapter 36 will show, called for a blend of fixed rates with longer-run flexibility. And this system prevailed until the early 1970s. Fixed exchange rates, within narrow bands similar to gold points, held between most pairs of countries for many years at a stretch. When the cost or burden of maintaining a particular stable rate became unbearable, in the pressure of world supply and demand pressures for change (augmented by speculative gambling that the fixed rate would be changed), a country would make (with Fund consent) a once-for-all devaluation or revaluation to a new parity level.

The link to gold was snapped in 1971 and 1973. Under Nixon the U.S. finally agreed that the dollar was overvalued in terms of gold—and all other currencies. First the dollar price of gold was adjusted. Then gold convertibility was abandoned completely. No longer would America even pay lip service to its Bretton Woods undertaking to make U.S. dollars convertible on demand into gold—or on demand into yen, marks, sterling or any other international currency at the IMF's official exchange-rate parities.

Until then, apart from Canada's experiments in floating rates in the 1950s, the nations had, by fixing their rates, maintained the semblance of a gold-based world system. But the system easily relapsed toward flexibility, for the governments only had to stop defending the particular parities, and supply and demand took over to float rates toward equilibrium prices in terms of each other.

POST-BRETTON WOODS: MANAGED FLOATING?

We shall study in Chapter 36 the search for a new international system, probably without gold. At the present time—1974—the world is in transition, or in uneasy limbo. The system in use is neither fish, nor fowl, nor good red herring. We are not on the pre-1914 automatic gold standard with its special-flow self-correcting mechanism. We have not gravitated to the opposite extreme of *laissez-faire* exchange-rate markets where currency prices depreciate and appreciate to whatever structure of levels they are bid to restore balance-of-payments equilibrium.

1971 SMITHSONIAN PARITIES VERSUS FLOATING RATES. In early 1971, holders of U.S. dollars began to show a clear preference for marks, yen and even sterling. The old IMF parities were so clearly wrong that first Germany, then other European countries, Canada, and as mentioned above, the U.S. abandoned their attempts to fix rates and, from August to December, allowed all rates to freely float.

In December at the Smithsonian Institution in Washington, D.C., the main IMF members met and set new fixed parities. The U.S. dollar was devalued about 10 percent in terms of an average of European and Japanese money   (New arrangements about holding and trading gold were also made, but gold is no longer important.) And "fixed" rates were now to be flexible within a 2 1/4 percent band on each side of the fixed parity. This meant that rates could fluctuate in a five-percent band and still be considered "fixed."

But by June 1972 these parities had been exceeded and or abandoned by several countries, and the U.S. dollar was devalued again in terms of gold in January 1973. Since March 1973 "generalised floating" has again been the rule.

The Snake in the Tunnel. In the midst of this world-wide breaking-out from gold or dollar parities, the members of the European Common Market attempted to work toward monetary union. For political reasons, they wished to end fluctuating rates between their members and even to move to a single currency. They were aided by the Smithsonian parities, which obliged each European currency to remain within a five-percent band. Thus the various currencies in Europe already moved together in a "tunnel". The next

step was to link the franc, mark and other moneys into a tighter band of European parities, moving up and down within this tunnel. This was the snake. But by 1973, the Smithsonian tunnel had vanished and in 1974 France and Germany were no longer linked. Only Scandinavia and Germany retained the vestige of a "snake"; and perhaps the ancestor of the future gliding-band system advocated below.

SDRs: PAPER GOLD. The total value of international trade has been growing in recent decades at about 8 per cent per year on the average. Gold from mining has been growing at less than 2 per cent per year. Obviously, the healthy growth of trade could come to a halt, in a crisis brought on by a shortage of international liquidity—*if* we were to stick with metallic gold as our primary reserve source.

Sensibly, the IMF and the leading 123 nations of the world have decided to do internationally what most nations have done domestically: to replace metallic gold by new kinds of currency and moneys.

Special Drawing Rights (SDRs or "paper gold") are created annually and given to each country according to its economic importance and size. A country can use its SDRs like any other reserve. When it has adverse trade balances, it can settle them by giving SDRs to the surplus country it owes.

So long as nations sensibly limit the growth of new SDRs, and parcel them out equitably (perhaps giving less developed nations favorable treatment as a form of aid), eventually the world will be able to play down the ancient role of metallic gold as part of the monetary system.

GLIDING BANDS. The automatic gold standard is gone. So are the IMF fixed parities. The world does not yet accept permanently floating exchange regimes feasible for the key nations. Where does that leave us?

The next stage of evolution must be toward a hybrid system of "crawling pegs" or "gliding bands".

In a nutshell, "gliding bands" means that exchange parities (and the widened bands around them in which exchange rates can move) can float up or down to a maximum of, say, 1 or 2 per cent per year. Thus, in a decade, we can contrive parity changes of 10 to 20 per cent—and can do so without tempting speculators to engage in destabilizing bull or bear raids.

Such slow, steady changes ought to go a long way toward adjusting to the dynamic differences among nations in their trends of (a) productivity growth, and (b) internal cost-push inflations. Figure 33-3 shows how the gliding band or crawling peg might work. Assume that Britain's costs rise faster than Canada's—as shown by the upper red curves. Then pegging the pound-dollar parity at $2.30 per pound would eventually lead to disastrous British deficits and Canadian surpluses. Even if, as here, we exaggerate the width of the permitted band from the 2 1/4 percent of 1975 to 8.7 percent on either side of parity, that cannot stave off disaster. Equilibrium parity must be permitted to go in time below $2.10.

Crawling peg—or better as a name, gliding bands—to the rescue! The dashed gray line of parity is permitted to move annually by 1 or 2 percent. It slowly works its way downward. Why downward? Because Britain's chronic payments deficit triggers depreciation of the pound. This limits and cures her deficit. But note—gliding bands work in either direction. By the period's end, Britain's costs and prices grow less rapidly than Canada's costs and prices. So the parity and bands glide upward—as they then should.

Chapter 36 will return to the problem of new monetary mechanisms. Gliding bands are not perfect. They are only a halfway house, and in the 1970s the world has not yet reached agreement on them. But they point the direction toward progress.

We have been surveying international trade mechanisms with a telescope in the first part of this chapter. In the remaining sections, we must train a microscope on the balance of payments of a country.

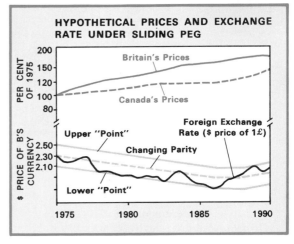

FIG. 33-3. Gradual, limited exchange-rate flexibility is provided by "gliding-band" (or "crawling-peg") reform.

Widened gray bands around dashed gray parity are shown here (in exaggerated degree). But line of parity crawls downward as Europe's prices soar relative to ours and gives her chronic balance-of-payments deficits. As whole band glides flexibly down by at most 1 to 2 per cent per year, in a decade's time equilibrating accommodation can be made to gradual drifts in relative rates of technical change and cost-price inflation. (NOTE: The band glides upward at end of period, as America begins to run an overvalued dollar and to experience greater inflation.)

B. BALANCE OF INTERNATIONAL TRADE AND CAPITAL MOVEMENTS

THE BALANCE OF INTERNATIONAL PAYMENTS

Instead of referring to $E - M$ we now investigate exactly what is meant by a country's "balance of payments". This is a statement that takes into account the values of all goods, gifts, foreign aid, capital loans (IOUs), and gold and international reserves coming in and going out, and the interconnections among all these items that lie behind Fig. 33-1's curves.

The balance of international payments sum-marizes these important relations. If you understand it, you have a fairly good grasp of foreign trade.

Statistics Canada keeps records and makes estimates of all international transactions in a year. For example, from customs statistics it learns about merchandise imports and tourist spending. It must also record or guess at amounts of money lent abroad, gold movements, interest and dividends received or sent abroad, money sent home by emigrants, and so forth. They are all fitted into the "balance of international payments" for each year—simply a double-entry listing of all items, drawn up by economists in such a way that it must always show a formal over-all net balance.[5]

The Canadian balance has been prepared for many years; it was one of the first national statements to be officially presented. It is usually in two parts:

I. Current Account
    Merchandise (or the "balance of trade")
    Nonmerchandise (or "invisible" items)
       Travel
       Interest and dividend payments
       Freight and shipping outlays
       Inheritances and migrants'
       remittances home
       Other current transactions (including
       many by government and also
       the sale of insurance services)

II. Capital movements
    In long-term forms
       Government
       Private
    In short-term forms
       Government
       Private
       Other short-term (a residual,
          balancing item)

III. In addition, there is usually a final item that shows the change in the government's holdings of foreign exchange and gold, and in its net IMF position.

THE CURRENT-ACCOUNT BALANCE. The totality of items in Part I is usually referred to as the "balance on current account." This important magnitude summarizes the difference between our total exports of goods *and services* and our total imports of them.

In a moment, we shall see how any surplus or deficit balance on current account is "financed"—or, more precisely, is offset—by capital movements under Section II and Section III. But before doing this, we shall describe briefly Section I's major current items.

[5] Articles brought in by smuggling and some innocent items elude the record keepers; so it is necessary to introduce a miscellaneous category of omitted items, such as GNP's "residual error of estimate".

Centuries ago, when *merchandise* items predominated, writers concentrated on this narrow category alone. If merchandise exports were greater in value than merchandise imports, they spoke of a "favorable balance of trade"; if imports exceeded exports, they spoke of an "unfavorable balance of trade." This is not a good choice of terms, for we shall see that a so-called "unfavorable" balance of trade may be a very good thing for a country.

In addition to such so-called "visible" merchandise items, we must not forget the important role played these days by the "invisibles." These consist of such nonmerchandise items as travel and tourist spending, shipping and insurance services, interest earnings from abroad, and the gifts that immigrants send back home. On reflection, one realizes that an invisible item such as a Canadian's buying a drink in Paris has the same effect on the final balance of payments as does his importing French wine to be drunk in Canada. And when we provide shipping insurance service, that acts like an export.

PAYMENTS (DEBITS) AND RECEIPTS (CREDITS). A good way to decide how any item should be treated is to ask the following question: Is the item like one of our merchandise exports, providing us with more foreign currencies? Such an export-type receipt is called a "credit item" and adds to our supply of foreign money. Or is the item like one of our merchandise imports, causing us to use up our stock of foreign currency? Such an import-type payment is called a "debit item" and adds to our demand for foreign money.

To show how this rule works, ask the following question: How shall we treat interest and dividend income on investments received by Canadians from abroad? Clearly, they are receipt items like exports, in that they provide us with foreign currencies. The reader can reverse the argument to show that the interest and dividends which we mail out to foreigners must be treated like payment items—like imports, they use up our foreign currencies.

At this point a close look at Table 33-1 will be helpful. It presents official data on the Canadian balance of international payments for 1973. Note its division into sections: current and capital items. In addition, there is a short third section: changes in reserves. Each row is numbered for easy reference.

Then, after each item has been listed by name in Column (a), we list in Column (b) the receipts (or "credits") we have earned from selling export-like items for foreign currencies. Next, in Column (c), are listed the payments (or "debits") that use up our holdings of foreign currencies when we buy import-like items. The second main section of the table is discussed later.

THE 1973 CURRENT ACCOUNT. In the first section, it is shown that our merchandise exports in 1973 gave us receipts of 25.4 billion dollars, but our merchandise imports cost us payments of 23.2 billion dollars. Thus the difference (or "balance") between the two trade items was in that year 2.11 billion dollars. It shows in the last Column (d). (A minus sign means that our "credits", or receipts, were smaller than our "debits", or payments; otherwise the balance is positive.) When this balance was positive, it used to be called "favorable"; even today our merchandise-trade export-surplus is called, misleadingly, a "favorable balance of trade". And when the balance is negative, it is called an "unfavorable balance of trade".

This term is deceptive because it suggests that only *visible* or merchandise trade is important, ne-glecting the next few items that also bring in current receipts or cause current payments, though they are "invisibles". The reader can interpret each line of these current items. Gold for export was negligible in 1973 but is itemized here to separate this semi-monetary item from ordinary merchandise, which is what it really is. The rest are routine. Foreigners travel in Canada, pay interest and dividends to Canadian owners of shares and bonds, pay rates for freight transported on Canadian carriers, send money "back home" to Canadians, buy insurance from Canadian companies, and in other minor ways make available to Canadians foreign money just as they would if they were buying Canadian goods. And Canadians make payments abroad on the same items.

The table shows that total current payments by Canadians are *larger* than their total current receipts. Thus the balance of *trade* (merchandise), though positive, is more than offset by the other items in the *balance on current account*, making it, in the older phraseology, "unfavorable."

(Government's foreign transactions are not well shown in the Canadian official balance on current account. Mutual aid payments to NATO countries are not shown at all. "Official contributions" are amounts paid by Canada as its

CANADIAN BALANCE OF INTERNATIONAL PAYMENTS, 1973

Section 1: Current Account

No.	Items (a)	Current Receipts (b)	Current Payments (c)	Balance on Current Account (d)
1	**Merchandise** (adjusted)	$ 25.4	$ −23.2	$ 2.1
	Nonmerchandise:			
2	Gold production available for export	—	—	—
3	Travel	1.4	−1.7	−0.3
4	Interest and dividends	0.6	−1.9	−1.3
5	Freight and shipping	1.4	−1.5	−0.1
6	Transfers: migrants and personal payments etc.	1.0	−0.4	0.6
7	Official contributions	—	−0.6	−0.6
8	Other current transactions	1.4	−2.7	−1.3
9	Sub-total nonmerchandise trade	5.8	−8.8	−3.0
10	**Current account balance**	$ 31.3	$ 31.7	$ −0.4
11	With the United States			−1.2
12	With Great Britain			0.6
13	With all other countries			0.3

Canadian Balance of International Payments, 1973 (in billions of dollars) (Continued)

Section II: Capital Account

No.	Items (a)	Capital Movements (b)
	Capital Movements in Long-term Forms:	
	Direct Investment	
14	Direct investment in Canada	$ 0.7
15	Direct investment abroad	−0.6
	Canadian Stocks	
16	Trade, new issues and retirements	—
	Canadian Bonds	
17	Trade in outstanding bonds	—
	New issues minus retirements	—
18	Government of Canada	−0.1
19	Provincial and Municipal	+0.7
20	Corporate	—
21	Other long-term capital	—
22	**Sub-total Capital Movements in Long-term Forms**	$ 0.7
	Capital Movements in Short-term Forms:	
23	Resident holdings of foreign bank balances	$ −0.5
24	Nonresident holdings of Canadian assets	0.3
25	Other short-term capital movements (*residual* item)	$ −0.6
26	**Sub-total Capital Movements in Short-term Forms**	$ −0.8
27	**Total Capital Movements**	$ −0.1

Canadian Balance of International Payments, 1973 (Continued)
Section III: Change in Holdings of Foreign Exchange and Gold

No.	Items	Capital Movements
28	Total current and capital account balances (Items 10 and 27)	$ −0.5
29	Change (reduction) in official gold and foreign currency holdings	0.5
30	Change in SDR position	0.0
31	Over-all net balance of international payments	0.0

TABLE 33-1
(Source: Statcan and Bank of Canada.)

membership fees and quotas for the U.N., International Monetary Fund, etc., as shown in Chapter 36. Such payments as supplies for Canadian ships abroad are included among "merchandise imports." Obviously some official gifts *in kind* to foreign countries cannot be shown because they do not lead to Canadian receipts of foreign currencies, nor do we make payments abroad. For example, if we give locomotives to an underprivileged country, the payment is made at home, to our locomotive producers. There is no international financial transaction.)

In arriving at the "balance on current account" we have completed our survey of the *first* section of the table. We see that the balance is equal to —0.4 billion dollars. Although every item has contributed to the final balance, it is clear that trade (exports) has had a positive influence, and interest and dividends (foreign earnings on funds lent to our industry and governments) a strong negative, or "unfavorable" influence.

As a matter of fact, we have run a negative balance on current account for most years since World War II, as may be seen in Fig. 33-4. How can we do this? Indeed, because there must be some countries that typically run positive balances, how does *any* country offset its unbalanced current account? The answer is shown, for Canada, in Sections II and III of the table:

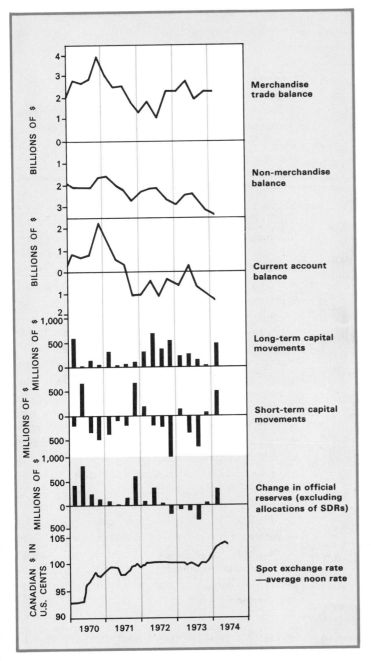

FIG. 33-4. Changes in Canada's balance of payments items change net reserves and net exchange rate. (Some items are seasonally adjusted, some not.)
(Source: *Bank of Canada Review,* **May** 1974.)

either we borrow from abroad or we reduce our gold and reserve-asset holdings. The other countries, with positive current-account balances, must do the opposite: lend abroad or add to their holdings of gold and reserve assets. *For it is a tautology that what you get you must either pay for or owe for.* So, if Canada doesn't pay for all she imports with her exports, she must owe someone for the rest. In owing, she is *defined* to have borrowed. This fact of double-entry bookkeeping means that the whole table of the balance of international payments must show a final definitional balance. (Statistical errors and omissions, as in the case of GNP residual error of estimate discussed in Chapter 10, must of course be reckoned with if the double-entry bookkeeper is not given all the accurate facts; but this should not affect the *logic* of the perfect balance.)

CAPITAL ACCOUNT. Let us look at Section II of the table. It shows the long-term and short-term loans Canadian companies and persons make or receive from private foreign citizens. (E.g., Ford of Canada may receive funds from its parent in the United States; a Montreal trust company may make a loan in Latin America; you may make a deposit in a London bank or buy shares in a Texas oil company.) It also shows *government* capital transactions (foreigners may buy Canadian government bonds; Quebec may borrow in New York; Canada may repay Britons for bonds issued years ago; the United States makes a payment to Canada as part of the Columbia River Treaty).

It is easy to decide which capital transactions are payments by Canada and which are receipts, if you follow this rule: Always think of Canada as exporting and importing *capital securities*—or, for short, exporting and importing IOUs. Then you can treat these flows like any other exports or imports. When we lend abroad, is it a positive or negative item? Though our capital goes abroad, we are *importing* IOUs. Thus the sign is negative and the item is a payment, or a debit.

To avoid confusion, try another example. When we "import" capital heavily, as the table shows we do, we actually *export* securities and IOUs. Thus the borrowing is given a plus sign, just as if we were exporting newsprint. When we have a negative current account balance, we are importing more than we export. To offset this import balance we export IOUs, giving us a positive capital account balance. The positive cancels the negative.

Item 22 shows a total of 0.7 billion dollars. This is positive: we were exporting long-term IOUs, or borrowing from abroad, chiefly by selling new issues of Canadian public and private securities to foreign lenders. This, too, has been typical of our post-World War II history—Canada has had more long-term investment opprtunities than Canadian lenders could handle. But another big item is "direct investment in Canada," (Item 14) which is the measure of the amounts foreign companies have contributed directly to their subsidiaries and associates (like Esso in Im-

perial Oil, General Electric in Canadian General Electric, and so on). At the same time, Canadians have been investing directly and in foreign securities abroad, but the totals are smaller. Over time, long-term investment inflows have been positive, as Fig. 33-4 illustrates.

The next group of items deals with short-term transactions. These are available in detail, and show mostly how we have drawn on or added to our holdings of bank deposits and other liquid assets abroad, and how foreigners have acted similarly. In the year 1973 a myriad of such individual, provincial, and municipal changes resulted in Canadians moving their wealth into foreign bank accounts to the extent of 0.5 billion dollars, with a minus sign. This was, however, partially offset by foreigners tending to move their money to Canada to buy Canadian assets such as short-term bills: Item 24. Thus these two measured short-term amounts produced a net out-flow of —0.2 billion (= —0.5 + 0.3 billion).

On most capital accounts, Item 25 is very large. This is because "other short-term capital movements" is the *residual* or balancing-figure which forces Sections I, II, and III into equality. In the case of Canada in 1973, we know that after taking account of all statistics showing current-account items, and all long- and short-term capital-movement and gold items, Canadians *must* have lent the rest of the world 0.6 billion dollars. It would do so chiefly by IOUs and accounts payable by foreign merchants and importers. The reader should note that, although this is not the last item in the table, it is in fact that free or flexible item that the government statisticians add to or subtract from to make sure that the two Sections of the table are in balance. (One result is that the item also includes amounts large enough to balance errors and omissions made in compiling other items in the table.)

OFFICIAL HOLDINGS BALANCE. After this residual item, the final items just tidy up the totals and provide a little more statistical information. Item 27 shows the total of all capital movements in long-term and short-term forms: a modest net capital outflow of only 0.1 billions.

Taking the year as a whole, the Canadian economy had, on capital account, in long-term borrowings and short-term loans, withdrawn more from abroad than it had provided. How was this managed? Obviously, since every other source of payment has been mentioned, Canada must have dug into its official pocket —that is, into reserves—to pay off the remainder. Indeed, there was in 1973 more to be financed than the capital outflow. In addition, Canada had on current account, a payments outflow balance of $0.4 (negative). So, adding the current-account and capital-account outflows together, she had to come up with $-0.5 billion.

This is the main point of the third Section of the table. The amount of current and capital outflow are totalled in item 28. Then the decline in reserves is shown as item 29 (this is positive, as though it were a monetary *export* of gold and foreign currencies), exactly enough to finance the total current and capital outflows. Item 30, Canada's gain or loss of "paper gold" or SDRs, happened to be zero in 1973. Thus the change in official holdings of monetary reserves both reflects and measures the change, and finances it, so that the final over-all balance of all three Sections is equal to zero. It is in fact a much-used indicator of the *over-all balance*, both in one year and over a run of years, of Canada's international payments. It is also referred to as the "official-settlements", "official-holdings", or "official-reserves" balance. These names stress that the items chosen for emphasis are changes in amounts that Canadian authorities owe (or are owed by) foreign central banks in their roles as those who must take responsibility for their countries' networks of private and public transactions in ways that do not affect their exchange rates. (See below).

"The basic balance": There are other ways of adding to or deleting items in the final balance that have been proposed as useful single indicators of the outcome of a year's trade and payment. Some economists have advocated the "basic balance" (basic deficit or surplus), and it was stressed in earlier editions of this book. This is the total of the independent or autonomous traders' and investors' net demands for Canadian dollars. It is calculated by adding the current account balance—$—0.4 billions to *long-run* investment in Canada of $+0.7 billions, giving a basic surplus of $+0.3 billions. The difference between this surplus and the official-settlements balance mentioned earlier is the $—0.8 billion short-term outflow. The basic concept differs from the official-settlements balance not only in amount (as it must) but also in sign. But, taking one year with another, we are likely to get the same message whichever concept we choose to measure and publish.

FIXED AND FLOATING EXCHANGE RATES

A reading of the balance of payments helps in understanding the difference between a floating and a fixed exchange rate. The decrease in official Canadian holdings of reserves (Item 29, Table 33-1) is a manifestation of a decrease in foreign demand for Canadian currency; or, to put it another way, it is a manifestation of an increase in Canadians' demand for foreign currency at the existing exchange rate. This can be shown on Fig. 33-1. E, the existing exchange rate, has already been set by the forces of supply and demand for the Canadian dollar, or, what is the same thing, for foreign currency, here the Pound Sterling. Now, with the rate remaining *temporarily* fixed, move the supply curve of pounds to the left. The British, perhaps, are buying less Canadian raw materials.

What happens? The new supply curve cuts our demand curve for pounds at a higher level than E, indicating that, with a freely floating exchange rate, the price of pounds in Canadian dollars would tend to rise (and that the price of Canadian dollars in pounds would tend to fall).

Imagine that this change had been permitted in 1973. Then Canadian exports would have been cheaper so that more would be bought. Foreigners might also have been encouraged to buy Canadian securities or to make more direct investments in Canada.[6] At the same time, Canadians would have found that imports were dearer and therefore would have bought less foreign-made goods. Thus, in 1973, a floating exchange rate would have tended to wipe out the capital-account deficit, though it would have taken more than one year to make itself felt. A more serious factor for Canadian growth is that it would not have acted very effectively on the balance of capital movements in long-term forms, but rather would have pushed the current-account balance toward a smaller deficit, tending automatically to offset any independent flow of capital. Actual experience in

---

[6] Actually this deterrent would not be very powerful unless potential foreign investors feared a later depreciation of the Canadian dollar (i.e. a reversal of the initial increased price of the Canadian dollar), which would make investments less valuable when measured in foreign money. The reader should try to explain to himself why anticipation of later appreciation is a strong spur to buying securities or equities in a foreign currency.

1973 showed that, while the floating exchange rate did tend to prevent a large current-account surplus, it had little effect on what were continuing capital *in*flows stemming from a variety of causes unrelated to the current account or the exchange rate.

What we should remember from the preceding discussion of a hypothetical floating exchange rate is that the surplus *tends* to be wiped out by a consequent fall in the price of foreign currency. Similarly, a deficit tends to be wiped out by a rise in that price.

STAGES OF A COUNTRY'S BALANCE OF PAYMENTS

Historically, the United States has gone through four stages often said to be typical of the growth of a young agricultural nation into a well-developed industrialized one. A review of this history may be useful to consolidate understanding.[7]

1. *Young and growing debtor nation.* From the Revolutionary War era until just after the Civil War, the United States imported on current account more than she exported. Britain and Europe lent her the difference in order to build up her capital structure. The United States was a typical young and growing debtor nation.

2. *Mature debtor nation.* From about 1873 to 1914, the U.S. balance of trade appears to have become favorable. But growth of the dividends and interest that she had to pay abroad on past borrowing kept the balance on current account more or less in balance. Capital movements were also nearly in balance, new lending just about canceling borrowing.

3. *New creditor nation.* In World War I, the United States expanded her exports tremendously. At first, private U.S. citizens made loans to the warring Allied powers. After she got into the war, the government lent money to Britain and France for war equipment and postwar relief needs. The United States emerged from the war a creditor nation. But her psychological frame of mind had not adjusted itself to her new creditor position. She passed high tariff laws in the 1920s and in 1930. Because she refused to import, foreigners found it difficult to get the dollars to pay interest and dividends, much less repay principal.

So long as the United States remained in this third stage of being a new creditor country—so long, that is, as she kept making *new* private foreign loans all through the

1920s—everything momentarily appeared all right on the surface. Americans could continue to sell more than they were buying, by putting most of it "on the cuff." The rest of the world met this export surplus by sending gold and IOUs. As long as Wall Street bankers could interest Main Street investors in foreign bonds, everything seemed rosy. But by 1929 and later, when Americans would no longer lend abroad, the crash finally came. International trade broke down. Debts were defaulted. The United States, as much as the rest of the world, was to blame.

4. *Mature creditor nation.* Britain reached this stage some years ago, and as in all such cases, her imports exceeded exports. Before we feel sorry for her because of her so-called "unfavorable" balance of trade, let us note what this really means.

Her citizens were living better because they were able to import much cheap food and in return did not have to part with much in the way of valuable export goods. The British were paying for their import surplus by the interest and dividend receipts they were receiving from past foreign lending.

Fine for the British. But what about the rest of the world? Where they not worse off for having to send exports to Britain in excess of imports? Not necessarily. Normally, the capital goods that Britain had previously lent them permitted them to add to their domestic production —to add *more* than had to be paid out to Britain in interest and dividends. Both parties were better off. Nineteenth-century foreign lending was twice blessed: it blessed him who gave and him who received. Of course, international trade and finance did not always operate quite so smoothly. Some investments proved unwise. Political problems of colonies and nationalism complicated the situation. And the whole process went awry and broke down after World War I.

America is now moving into the mature stage, where her earnings from abroad must finance her net imports from abroad and also her aid and security programs. Past capital movements are responsible for these vital investment earnings.

At one time this system of "stages" of a country's balance of payments was widely used by economists and was interlocked with a classification of stages of the country's internal economic development (primary production, secondary manufacturing, services, and the production of luxuries, etc.). However, economists are no longer so keen about it. It does seem to fit the U.S. and British facts. But it no longer seems to offer useful predictions about other countries. For example, it suggests that Canada should soon move into Stage 3. Does this look likely? Will the British

---

[7] This section may be skipped if desired, as the approach described is no longer found serviceable.

soon move back to Stage 1, 2, or 3? Or will they trim their imports to their receipts and stay in Stage 4?

INTERNATIONAL CAPITAL MOVEMENTS AND FOREIGN OWNERSHIP

Turn now to the nature of capital movements. If political problems of nationalism and domestic problems of unemployment did not enter the picture, then the fundamentals of international lending would be easy to understand. We could easily cut through the fog of money and finance and concentrate on the real aspects in terms of goods and resources.

How does capital grow within a country? By our diverting labor, land, machinery, and other resources away from the production of current consumption goods. Instead, we plant trees, drain rivers, or build new machinery and buildings. All these add to our future income and consumption.

We are postponing present consumption for future consumption—for an even *greater* amount of future consumption. Where does the increase in future consumption come from? As Chapter 30 showed, *capital goods have a "net" productivity*. This constitutes the real aspect of the interest rate.

Different parts of the world have different amounts of resources: labor, minerals, climate, know-how. Were it not for ignorance or political boundaries, no one would push investment in North America down to the point of 5 per cent returns *if elsewhere there still existed 10 per cent opportunities*. Some capital would certainly be invested abroad. This would give foreign labor higher wages, because now the foreign worker has more and better tools to work with. It would increase foreign production. By how much? Not only by enough to pay for the constant replacement of used-up capital goods but, in addition, by enough to pay North Americans an interest or dividend return on their investment. This interest return would take the form of goods and services which North Americans receive from abroad and which add to their standard of living. An all-wise scientist would probably approve of the process.[8] It would make sense to him because capital is

going into the regions where its productivity is highest.

When would North Americans be repaid their principal? So long as they are earning a good return, there is no reason why they should ever wish to have it repaid. However, the once-backward country may finally become rather prosperous. It may wish to pull in its belt as far as consumption is concerned and to use its savings to buy out North American ownership in its factories, farms, and mines. But suppose that North Americans are rich, with plenty of savings and with so much capital at home that their rate of interest is low. They might not particularly wish to sell out or be repaid. They might raise the selling price of their farm and factory holdings abroad. In other words, they might be content with a smaller percentage interest return. Thus, there is no necessary reason why a country should ever be paid off for its past lending, unless it has become relatively poorer.

ECONOMIC NATIONALISM. When nationalism rears its head, matters change. Within one country, interest and dividends may stream from country to city and from West to Center, until doomsday. People do grumble about absentee owners, as Quebec grumbles about English-Canadian control and as Westerners attribute all misfortune to Toronto. But each province has courts and police to see that property rights are respected, and even the most radical Quebec nationalist has hesitated to suggest that his compatriots seize the T. Eaton Stores in Quebec.

Not so between nations. When a country is capital-poor it is anxious to borrow for schools, hydro systems, factories, and mines. After it becomes richer and more self-aware, it becomes unhappy to have to pay interest and dividends abroad. It smarts under the realization that much of its domestic trade is directed, at some levels, by foreigners. It gives little weight to the memory that its jobs were created and its prosperity sustained in part by past borrowing. More than an economic burden is involved: politically, countries do not like the principle of absentee ownership by foreigners. Such countries have taken a

---

[8] A qualification is in order. Sometimes a multinational corporation gets ownership of mines or oil wells even though it has brought in few funds net from abroad. Governments may have permanently given away the nation's resources. Sometimes the politicians are over-eager for economic development. Sometimes they are corrupt.

variety of courses. Canada has been unsure, sometimes discouraging foreign take-overs and investments, but usually passive politically and welcoming individually. Thirty years ago Mexico set a precedent by confiscating foreign-owned oil properties. Between these extremes are other ways of getting rid of foreign liabilities and control: buying off at fair or unfair prices, failing to make promised payments, interfering with business operations till harassment and losses lead to sale, etc. These measures have recently been explored by the newly-rich oil countries of Arabia. Chapter 35's Appendix discusses foreign ownership.

Economics and politics mix in ways too complicated to resolve. Some say "Trade follows the flag." Others say the flag follows trade. Some say the pursuit of economic gain is the primary motive behind the imperialistic search for colonies. Others claim that national power (offensive and defensive) is an end in itself; that economic well-being is sacrificed to this end; and that economic resources are sought for their contribution to military strength (offensive and defensive) rather than for their contribution to economic well-being.

According to this view, without wars and nationalism, anyone could invest and trade anywhere, and sensible people should prefer to live in small countries unhindered by costly military establishments and colonial administration. At the opposite extreme is the view that victory in battle, rather than comfortable living, is the only worthy end in life; that the foreigner is of no importance compared with the fatherland; that he can be stripped of his goods and land, and be made to work for the conquerors. The world of the last few centuries lies somewhere between these extreme cases.

SUMMARY

A. MECHANISMS OF FOREIGN EXCHANGE AND TRADE

1 Buying or selling abroad presupposes a foreign exchange rate between home and foreign currencies. Two countries on a gold standard have a stable foreign exchange rate set by the stable, parity prices at which they each buy and sell gold—whether gold bars, coins, or gold-exchange standards, or any other variants are used.

2 Classical economists (such as David Hume) relied on gold movements to alter relative price levels, (a) raising exports and (b) curbing imports of the deficit country, and (c) cutting exports and (d) raising imports of the surplus country.

3 Once stable exchange rates under a gold standard were abandoned, flexible foreign rates would get set by interaction of supply and demand schedules for foreign exchange. The adjustment now involves changes in export and import prices and not necessarily absolute price levels.

4 Gold coin and bullion evolved into gold-exchange standards internationally and fractional-reserve banking domestically. In time the dollar displaced the pound as a key currency. And by the 1970s, the modified-gold-standard regime of Bretton Woods finally broke down.

5 The post-Bretton Woods system involves (a) widened currency bands, (b) the two-tier gold system, (c) beginning of "paper gold" (SDRs of the IMF) to permit growth of international liquidity and gradual playing down of metallic gold in the monetary system. Gliding bands (or crawling pegs) are on the agenda just ahead, so that both deficit countries and surplus countries can make small parity adjustments and thereby avert the cumulative breakdowns and crises of pegged exchange rates.

B. BALANCE OF INTERNATIONAL TRADE AND CAPITAL MOVEMENTS

6 The balance of international payments refers to all transactions that use up foreign exchange or make foreign exchange available to us. It relates the total of our exports of goods and services to our imports. Our exports of goods, services, gold, or IOUs are receipt items, or "credits," making foreign currencies available to us. Our imports of those items are payments, or "debits," using up foreign currencies.

7 Our net balance on current account comes from adjusting our merchandise trade balance for "invisible" service items. It and long- and short-term capital movements constitute the "over-all balance" which has to be offset by changes in holdings of foreign exchange and gold and by changes in our net IMF position.

8 As a nation passes from the "young debtor" to the "mature creditor" stage, its payments go through a characteristic sequence of stages, ending up living off earnings from past foreign investments.

9 No problem in international finance is more important than that of understanding the real and the monetary aspects of capital movements in their effect upon the industrial development of nations and nationalistic rivalries.

10 Foreign borrowing often implies foreign ownership and loss of national self-determination.

CONCEPTS FOR REVIEW

gold standard versus floating
   exchange rate
currency depreciation and
   appreciation vs. devaluation
fixed rates and IMF parities
gold-exchange and dollar standard
gliding bands (crawling pegs)
debits and credits

balance of payments
balance of trade

"favorable" balance
invisibles, government items
IOUs, capital movements
"gold points"
Canada's over-all balance,
   basic balance
gold and reserves movements
net foreign investment and foreign
   ownership
historical capital movements,
   in politics and economics

QUESTIONS FOR DISCUSSION

1. Contrast free and stable foreign exchange rates. Explain each.
2. Explain "widened bands" with, or without, gliding or crawling bands.
3. What is the meaning and sense to the purchasing-power-parity doctrine?
4. Draw up a list of items that belong on the credit or receipt side of the balance of international payments and another list of items that belong on the debit or payment side. What is meant by a "favorable balance of trade"? By the balance on current account? By an over-all balance? Why the term "invisible items"? What is the difference between short- and long-term capital movements?
5. If a young, developing country tends to be in debt to the rest of the world, what will be the signs of its balances on (*a*) merchandise, (*b*) current payments, and (*c*) long-term

capital in its balance of payments statement? Contrast these balances with those of a "mature creditor," such as Great Britain in 1913, living on the fruits of her property and loans overseas.

6. "Foreign lending causes war. Foreign giving postpones war. Free foreign trading prevents war." Comment.

7. Will freely-fluctuating rates *always* equilibrate trade flows? Assume that all payments are for trade (no capital movements), and that the Canadian dollar has depreciated in terms of yen. This will raise Canadian exports and cut Canadian imports. But the *payments* total for the exports may fall if the Japanese demand for them is less than unity; the *dd* curve for Canadian dollars in Fig. 33-1 will slope the wrong way if $E_J > 1$. Similarly, the slope of the *ss* curve depends on the E_C for imports of Japanese goods into Canada. Can you see how Alfred Marshall, and later Abba Lerner were led to their rule that $(E_J + E_C) > 1$ in order for equilibrium in payments to exist between Canada and Japan? (This is sometimes, on very narrow assumptions, cited as a condition for introducing flexible rates.)

34
INTERNATIONAL TRADE AND THE THEORY OF COMPARATIVE ADVANTAGE

The benefit of international trade—a more efficient employment of the productive forces of the world.

JOHN STUART MILL

Again and again we have seen how specialization increases productivity and standards of living. Now we must show exactly how this works out·in the field of international trade, going behind the façade of international finance.

Why did North America specialize a century ago in the production of goods from the farm and forest, exchanging these for the manufactured output of Europe? Why is it able today to export highly complex mass-produced goods —and why does it also import highly complex goods? Why is the agriculture of Australia so different from that of Austria? How great would be the costs of complete self-sufficiency to a modern country? How do all countries benefit from trade?

The key to the correct answers to such questions, and many more, is provided by the theory of comparative advantage or "comparative cost." Developed more than a century ago by David Ricardo, John Stuart Mill, and other English followers of Adam Smith, the theory of comparative advantage is a closely reasoned doctrine which, when *properly* stated, is unassailable. With it we can identify gross fallacies in the political propaganda for protective tariffs aimed at limiting imports. With it, we can identify the germs of truth that sometimes appear in the heated claims for tariff protection.

DIVERSITY OF CONDITIONS BETWEEN NATIONAL REGIONS

For simplicity, begin by imagining two regions. Say, Europe and North America, or the tropics and the temperate zones. Each is endowed with certain quantities of natural resources, capital goods, kinds of la-

bor, and technical knowledge or know-how. The first link in the comparative-cost chain of reasoning is the *diversity in conditions of production between different countries.* Specifically, this means that the production possibilities of the different countries are very different. Although people could try to produce something of every commodity in each and any region, it is obvious that they would not succeed; or if they did succeed, it would be only at a terrific cost. Smith pointed out that, with hothouse procedures and forcing methods, wine grapes could perhaps be grown in Scotland; but the cost in terms of economic resources would be exorbitant, and the resulting product would be scarcely fit to drink.

Even if by chance two countries can both produce the same commodities, they generally find that it pays for each to concentrate its production especially on some goods—and trade them for other goods.

If we consider trade between, say, the temperate zones and the tropics, the foregoing proposition will seem true. Of course, resources near the equator are more productive in the growing of bananas, and northern resources are better designed for wheat growing. Everyone can readily see that in this case specialization and trade will increase the amount of world production of goods, and also each country's ability to consume both goods.

It is not so immediately obvious, but it is no less true, that

International trade is mutually profitable even when one of the two countries can produce *every commodity* more cheaply (in terms of labor hours or all resources) than the other country. Can Canada with $5 an hour wages benefit from trade with Japan where wages are $2 an hour? Yes, asserts the theory of comparative advantage.

One country may be *absolutely more efficient* in the production of *every* good than is the other country; and this means the other country has an *absolute* disadvantage in the production of every good. But so long as there are differences in the *relative* efficiences of producing the different goods in the two countries, we can always be sure that even the poor country has a *comparative* advantage in the production of those commodities in which it is *relatively* most efficient; this same poor country will have a *comparative* disadvantage in those other commodities in which its inefficiency is more than average. Similarly, the rich, efficient country will find that it should specialize in those fields of production where it has a comparative advantage, planning to import those commodities in which it has a comparative disadvantage.

A traditional example used to illustrate this paradox of comparative advantage is the case of the best lawyer in town who is also the best typist in town. Will she not specialize in law and leave typing to a secretary? How can she afford to give up precious time from the legal field, where her comparative advantage is very great, to perform typing activities in which she is efficient but in which she lacks *comparative* advantage? Or look at it from the secretary's point of view. She is less efficient than the lawyer in both activities; but her relative disadvantage compared with the lawyer's is least in typing. Relatively speaking, the secretary has a comparative advantage in typing.

So with countries. Suppose North America produces food with one-third the labor that Europe does, and produces clothing with one-half the labor. Then we shall see that North America has a comparative advantage in food and a comparative disadvantage in clothing—this, despite the fact that North America is absolutely most efficient in everything. By the same token, Europe has a comparative advantage in clothing.

The key to the concept is the word "comparative"— which implies that *each and every* country has both definite "advantage" in some goods and definite "disadvantage" in other goods.

"NORTH AMERICA" AND "EUROPE": A SIMPLE CASE

Let us illustrate these fundamental principles of international trade by a simplified example. Consider North America and Europe of a century ago, and concentrate on only two commodities, food and clothing. In both Canada and the United States, land and natural resources were then very plentiful relative to labor and capital; but in Great Britain, France, the Low Countries, and Germany, people and capital were plentiful relative to land.

This contrast is best seen if we look at the *intensive* agriculture of a country such as Belgium. There, in order to get the greatest possible output, small plots of land have to be cultivated assiduously by many people using much fertilizer. Compare this with the extensive agriculture of early North America: one family cultivated many acres, and national product was maximized by each man's "spreading himself thin" over the virtually free land. A Belgian farmer would have thought this wasteful. But in view of the relatively high cost of North American labor or capital and the low cost of land, it was prudent.

Of course, if surplus population could have all migrated from Belgium to North America, the law of diminishing returns would have caused real wages in North America to fall toward equality with rising wages in Belgium; and high land rents in Belgium would have fallen toward equality with rising rents in North America.[1]

But suppose that immigrants from abroad are to be kept out of North America in order to keep labor scarce and wages high. From this same selfish point of view, should Canada and the United States also impose a protective tariff designed to keep out imports from abroad? Or should they not? To answer this important social question we must measure carefully the amounts of food and clothing that will be produced and consumed in each country (a) if there is no international trade and (b) if trade, according to comparative advantage, is permitted to follow its own course.

THE LAW OF COMPARATIVE ADVANTAGE

David Ricardo, stockbroker and self-made millionaire, expert on the theory of land rent and of currency, came up in 1817 with the beautiful proof that

---

[1] Actually, this would have tended at the same time to increase *total world production*. Why? Because the transfer of workers from their poor Belgian farms to rich North American farms would increase their productivity and total world output.

international specialization pays for a nation. This is the famous theory of comparative advantage, or, as it is sometimes called, the "theory of comparative cost."

For simplicity Ricardo worked with only two countries; we shall call them *America* and *Europe*, and make the unimportant assumption that they are both about the same size. For simplicity he worked with only two goods; we shall call them food and clothing. For simplicity Ricardo chose to measure all costs in terms of hours of labor; we shall do the same, recognizing that more advanced treatises and the Appendix to this chapter can give some of the needed qualifications when our simple assumptions are relaxed. The germ of truth in the principle of comparative advantage will still remain.

UNCOMMON SENSE Using common sense, people will probably agree that trade between America and Europe is likely to be mutually profitable in a first simple case where European labor has greater productivity in one good and American labor has greater productivity in another.

In this case, to produce a unit of food in America requires a smaller number of labor hours than is needed in Europe to produce it, while to produce a unit of clothing takes a smaller number of labor hours in Europe than in America. The man in the street needs no Ricardo to tell him that in such a case America will probably specialize in food production, exporting some food for Europe's clothing exports.

But Ricardo showed much more than this. He showed that even in a more difficult second case— where American labor (or resources generally) is more productive than Europe's *in both* food *and* clothing—trade is still likely to be mutually advantageous.

Table 34-1 illustrates this principle of comparative advantage. In America a unit of food costs 1 hour of labor and a unit of clothing costs 2 hours of labor. In Europe the cost is 3 hours of labor for food and 4 hours of labor for clothing. By forming the proper two ratios of these four crucial numbers, Ricardo can prove conclusively that America and Europe will *both* benefit if America specializes in food and exports it for the clothing exports that Europe specializes in.

Before examining this, listen to the European in the street as he says:

AMERICAN AND EUROPEAN LABOR REQUIREMENTS FOR PRODUCTION		
PRODUCT	IN AMERICA	IN EUROPE
1 unit food	1 labor hr.	3 labor hr.
1 unit clothing	2 labor hr.	4 labor hr.

TABLE 34-1 Comparative advantage depends only on *relative* industry efficiencies and inefficiences.

America has lower labor costs in both food and clothing: our labor productivity is between two and three times Europe's (twice in clothing, thrice in food). Yet it pays both of us to trade: America to export food, in which we have greatest comparative advantage (greatest *relative* efficiency), and to import clothing in which we have comparative disadvantage (least relative efficiency). Our comparative disadvantage is Europe's comparative advantage: she has relatively "least inefficiency" in clothing exports; most "least efficiency" in food, which she'll import. All depends on four labor-cost numbers: particularly on the ratios 1/2 and 3/4: Our 1/2 being less than her 3/4, we export food.

Mon Dieu! Trade could never be profitable for us with the American colossus. Her efficiency will enable her to undersell us in every line—food and clothing. She is twice as productive as we are in clothing, and three times as productive in food. We need import tariffs and quotas to protect the honest European worker.

Now listen to what is being said in America by the man in the street and the legislators who have not grasped the law of comparative advantage:

Since Europe is less prosperous (and less productive) than America, the European wage level most assuredly will be far below that enjoyed by Americans. If we subject the American workers to the unbridled competition of the European, who subsists on less per day than we do, the real wage of the American worker must fall drastically. A protective tariff against cheap imports is desperately needed to maintain the American standard of living.

What Ricardo shows is that both arguments are wrong.

In free-trade equilibrium, Europe's real wage rate will be somewhere between one-half and one-third of America's—not low enough for her to undersell us in all goods; and also not high enough for us to undersell her in all goods. But these final free-trade real wage rates will be higher in each region than they were in pretrade self-sufficiency—because workers everywhere get the imported goods for fewer hours of labor.

It follows as a corollary that prohibitive tariffs on either or both sides will reduce real wages in both places. (And we may add this in our day: There are better tools than protective tariffs to make sure that there are plenty of job opportunities in both places—namely, the tools of proper fiscal and central-bank monetary policies, and appropriate flexible exchange-rate policies.) Let's now prove all this.

BEFORE TRADE. We start with a prohibitive tariff that has killed off all international trade. Table 34-1 shows that the real wage of the American worker for an hour's work as 1 unit of food or 1/2 unit of clothing. The European worker is even less well off and gets for an hour's labor before trade only 1/3 unit of food or 1/4 unit of clothing.

Evidently, under domestic competition alone in each isolated continent, the price ratios of food and clothing will be different in the two places because of the difference in relative labor cost ratios. In America clothing will be 2 times as dear as food because it takes twice as much labor. In Europe clothing will be only 4/3 times as dear as food.

AFTER TRADE Now we repeal the protective tariff and make trade free. The relative prices of clothing and food must now come to a common level, just as the water in two connecting pipes must come to a common intermediate level you remove the barrier between them. Why?

Competitive merchants buy where things are cheap and sell where they are dear. With clothing relatively more expensive in America, merchants will soon ship clothing from Europe to America and ship food from America to the European markets, where it has been relatively dear. The American clothing industry will feel the keen price competition of imports, and if the values in Table 34-1 do not change, it will lose *all* its workers to its rival American food industry. The opposite will happen in Europe: workers will leave the food industry for the clothing industry, in which Europe has a comparative advantage.[2]

America as a whole has benefited. Like any merchant who will buy electric power from another firm if he cannot produce it as cheaply himself, America has taken advantage of the fact that clothing does cost her less by barter than by domestic production. The same goes for Europe's benefit from specializing in clothing and getting her food more cheaply by barter than by domestic production.

Example of benefit. Each unit of American labor still gets the 1 unit of food it produces there. But now 1 unit of American food trades for *more* than 1/2 unit of clothing. How much more? Certainly not more than the 3/4 ratio set by Europe's costs. The common ratio after trade will be somewhere between 1/2 and 3/4. American labor gains in clothing by any degree that it exceeds 1/2. Similarly, European labor gains in bartering clothing for food by any degree that the ratio falls short of 3/4. (See footnote 2 and the Appendix for elaborations.)

Granted that Ricardo has proved that both countries have benefited from trade in accordance with comparative advantage, what about the workingman in each place? Table 34-1 can show that his real wages have improved in both places. Now the American worker's day of labor will buy him the same food as before, but he gets *more* imported clothing for a day of labor and can now afford to consume more of *both* goods. Likewise, the European worker can get more of the cheapened food for a day of his labor, and inasmuch as he gets the same real wage in clothing, his budget is also better off. It is the expanded *world* production of both goods, which specialization and trade created, that makes it possible for *everyone* to be better off.[3]

---

[2] A 1970 Cornell student, Henry Morgenstern, wrote the authors the following rule. Write down the relative labor costs from each country's column: 1/2 and 3/4, here. Find the country with the *smallest* fraction: 1/2 here. Its numerator tells us the good it will export: in this case, food is America's export. (Likewise, the denominator of the largest fraction, of 3/4, tells us that Europe exports clothing.)

[3] To see this graphically, look at Fig. 34-1(a), which shows America's red domestic production-possibility frontier, with its slope depicting a 1/2 clothing-to-food price ratio.

Europe's black domestic production-possibility frontier has its 3/4 slope. (Since Europe's population happens to be about equal to that of America, why is the black curve this much "smaller" than the red? Because America has double or more the productivity of Europe.) Ricardo says, "It is the difference in slopes that makes profitable trade possible." How profitable? The limits (as explained in the Appendix) are shown by the light gray areas between (*a*) each country's domestic curve and (*b*) a line drawn parallel to the other country's curve passed through each point of specialization. Thus the intermediate fine black arrows, with

The principle of comparative advantage restated: Whether or not one of two regions is absolutely more efficient in the production of every good than is the other, if each specializes in the products in which it has a *comparative advantage* (greatest *relative* efficiency), trade will be mutually profitable to both regions. Real wages of productive factors will rise in both places.

An ill-designed prohibitive tariff, far from helping the protected factor of production, will instead reduce its real wage by making imports expensive and by making the whole world less productive through eliminating the efficiency inherent in the best pattern of specialization and division of labor.

OTHER CAUSES OF INTERNATIONAL TRADE

DECREASING COSTS   If economies of mass production are overwhelmingly important, costs may decrease as output expands. This would strengthen the case for international exchange of goods. In fact, decreasing costs are a second great factor—in addition to differences in comparative costs—explaining

slopes intermediate between *A*'s 1/2 and *B*'s 3/4, are one possible outcome: at post trade equilibrium with food selling for two-thirds clothing (i.e., at 2/3), *A* gains by producing food alone and exporting it for clothing: *E* gains by producing clothing and exporting it in exchange for food.

why specialization and trade are profitable. For, as was discussed in Chapters 3 and 25, large-scale specialization is most fruitful when there is a widely expanded market.

In fact, even if there were no differences in comparative costs between two countries, it might pay for them to toss a coin to decide who was to produce each of two goods subject to increasing returns or decreasing costs. Complete specialization would increase world production of both goods. This may be illustrated by our example in Chapter 3 of the identical Indian twins who, despite their similarity, still find it advantageous to specialize to reap the efficiencies of "mass" production. As we'll see in Chapter 36, the expanded European Common Market hopes to reap the advantages of such an extended division of labor.

These decreasing costs may rise not only from mass production inside an industry but also from the adaptation of the community to providing special skills, markets, transportation networks, and supplies. Such "external economies" were explored in Chapter 24. Mass production and external economies explain many puzzles in economic history, and are a technical way of expressing the idea: "It was a historical accident that the city of Nottingham in England started to make lace, but once it got started no other region could meet its quality and low costs." The most recent example of an economic *policy* depending on the appearance of decreasing costs is the Canadian-American automobile-tariff agree-

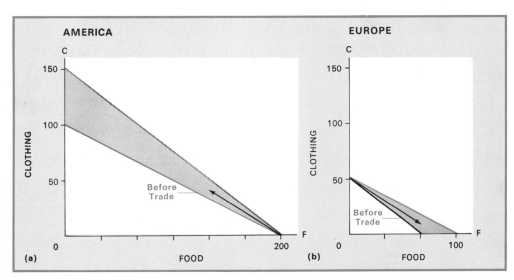

FIG. 34-1.

ment. Canadian negotiators felt that the previous higher cost of automobile production was due to the lack of a Canadian home market for real mass production. Thus, when the U.S. market was opened to certain Canadian factories, Canada, too, experienced economies of mass production and decreasing costs over time.

Another very practical aspect of decreasing cost is the possibility that it may lead to the breakdown of perfect competition. Consider a Canadian manufacturing firm which produces small amounts at high costs. If it can begin to expand its sales, its costs will decrease, and it will undercut its competitors. If the process continues, it may even become a monopolist, its greater size enabling it to take over the whole domestic market. By excluding foreign competitors, a protective tariff would serve only to consolidate the position of the monopolist, whereas free trade may enlarge the market sufficiently to promote competition. This is recognized in the old slogan, "The tariff is the mother of trusts." Freer international trade is often an effective and efficient way of *breaking up* monopoly positions and has been recognized as such in our Combines Act.[4]

DIFFERENCES IN TASTES OR DEMAND

Here is a third possible cause for trade. Even if costs were identical in the two countries and were increasing, trade might take place as the result of differences in *tastes*.

Thus, it might pay both Norway and Sweden to produce fish from the sea and meat from the land in about the same amounts. But if the Swedes have a relatively great fondness for meat and the Norwegians for fish, then a mutually profitable export of meat from Norway and fish from Sweden would take place. Both parties gain from this trade. The sum total of human happiness is increased, just as it is when Jack Spratt trades fat meat for his wife's lean. Both get some "consumer's surplus" from the swap.[5]

We have now gone beyond the financial facade of international trade to the real fundamentals. Now we can handle the remaining two chapters of Part Five.

FOREIGN-TRADE SUPPLY-AND-DEMAND CHARTS[6]

The foregoing theory of comparative advantage stripped international trade down to its barter essentials. It said nothing about dollars, pounds, or foreign exchange rates. How does the matter appear to the perfect competitors in one small food industry in America? Why does competitive P settle down so that America exports this item of wheat but not that item of cloth? How do the supply and demand curves look in the competitive market for a small clothing item exported by Europe—say, linen cloth? Or for an American export item like wheat?

Figure 34-2 first takes up the case of an American export good, wheat, in the simplest case where Europe's unit of money—call it a pound—is always worth exactly $3. Figure 34-2(a) shows the American demand and supply curves $d_a d_a$ and $s_a s_a$ for wheat expressed in dollars (which, by a 1/3 scale change, can also be read in pounds). Figure 34-2(b) shows the European supply and demand for wheat as $d_e d_e$ and $s_e s_e$ (in pounds, with vertical scales nicely aligned so as to be read in dollars or pounds).

Suppose trade in wheat were prohibited by quotas, tariffs, or sky-high transport costs. Where would pre-trade equilibrium be in each nation? Under such an assumption of no trade, equilibrium would be at the separate intersection points A_a and A_e: Wheat's price (per bushel) in America would be $2, or £2/3; its price in Europe would be $6, or £2. Both markets are cleared; exports and imports are, of course, zero.

Now open up trade in wheat. If there are zero transport costs, quotas, and tariffs, both markets must have the same price. Why? Because sharp-eyed arbitragers could buy where wheat was cheap and send it for sale to where it was dear. With what re-

---

[4] Still, one must admit that violently decreasing-cost situations might under free trade lead to bigger monopolies, and that decreasing-cost situations may have in them some of the valid elements of the "infant-industry" argument to be met in the next chapter.

[5] Even two individuals with identical amounts of two goods and the same tastes may in rare instances trade. Two sailors, each with a fifth of whisky and a fifth of gin, might toss a coin to decide who is to have two fifths of gin and who two fifths of

whisky. You can reason out why the same might be true of herring and chocolate, but not of corned beef and cabbage. This fourth cause of trade is primarily of curiosity value.

[6] The next two sections are quite independent of the rest of this chapter, except for points 5 and 6 in the Summary. The next chapters do not require them or this chapter's Appendix.

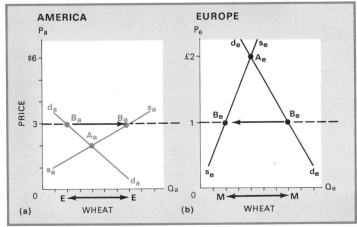

FIG. 34-2. Supply and demand schedules determine dollar and pound prices of American exports.

With zero trade, American wheat price is at A_a below European price at A_e. With free trade, goods flow from low- to high-price place, finally equalizing P's at that level where the export arrow just matches the import arrow.

sult? Evidently, P_e would fall and P_a rise until equality was achieved. The amount of the price changes would depend on the slopes of each country's dd and ss curves.

The condition for the new free-trade equilibrium is that the new common price should coax out an import demand abroad just equal to the export supply from home.

Free-trade equilibrium is at the $3 and £1 level, where America's export arrow EE or B_aB_a just matches (and opposes in direction) Europe's import arrow MM or B_eB_e. No other equilibrium can persist. (Exactly £1 is, of course, a coincidence.)

Figure 34-3 shows exactly the same phenomenon for the case of Europe's clothing export, linen. Who decides that linen will be Europe's export and wheat America's? The levels of the no-trade equilibria in-

tersections predetermine the decision: goods flow uphill toward higher prices under free competition! (Because A_e is below A_a, Europe exports linen.)

The reader could draw a new figure where the no-trade P's happen to start out equal and where free trade leads to zero trade. This is a rare razor's-edge case of coincidental levels. However, in real life, there are always transport costs that impede trade. Thus, although bricks may seem to be cheaper in America, if the difference between the no-trade equilibrium intersections is less than the substantial *costs of shipping* heavy and bulky bricks, each country will produce its own bricks and there will be neither exports nor imports. Goods try to flow uphill toward higher prices, but transport-cost or tariff impediments can inhibit their flow —resulting in some goods being purely "domestic goods" in both countries.

This supply-and-demand analysis is a simple extension of that given in Chapter 4 (or Part Three). It

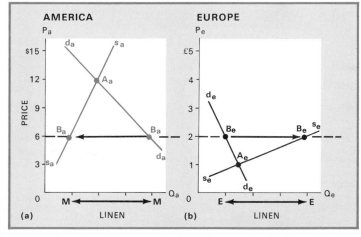

FIG. 34-3. Supply and demand schedules determine dollar and pound prices of American exports.

Lower European P at zero trade means linen will be imported from Europe when trade is permitted. Common P is where imports and exports match. (Quotas, tariffs, or transport costs will make P's unequal.)

is useful. But note that we should have to go to Ricardo's deeper analysis of comparative advantage to explain *why* the wheat prices will be such as to give America a money-cost advantage in exporting this food item. That same analysis of basic comparative advantage is needed to explain why the clothing item, linen, will have *dd* and *ss* intersections causing Europe to export it.[7]

EFFECTS OF TARIFFS AND QUOTAS

PROHIBITIVE TARIFF Figure 34-3 can be used to illustrate the effect of an American tariff (or "customs tax") on the import of linen. If America taxes linen imports by more than the difference in price ($9 ≡ £3 = $12 − $3) shown between the no-trade A_a and A_e intersections, how much linen will get sent there? Absolutely none: the tariff of more than $9 will be a prohibitive one, shutting out all imports. Why? Because an importer who tries to buy linen at the European A_e price of $3 (or £1) or more can sell it for only $12 (or £4). But the tariff the importer has to pay would come to *more* than that difference! Hence, such a tariff kills off *all* the advantage of specialization and trade.

A smaller tariff will kill off some (but not all) linen imports, in that sense partially "protecting" America's domestic linen industry.

SOCIAL COST OF TARIFFS What happens to the American linen industry? The tariff gives it a higher price than it would have under free trade. The typical effect, then, of any tariff that "protects" against imports is to raise the price to the domestic consumer.[8]

But does not the American government collect in tariff revenue about what the consumers now pay in extra prices? Our special example of a prohibitive tariff points up the negative answer that generally applies. Here consumers pay more in price but the government collects nothing! This needs emphasis, and shows how foolish it is to try to measure a tariff's height and capacity for doing harm by the tax revenue it brings in.

Also, any tariff that limits imports makes American consumers pay a higher P for all the domestically supplied output, and *none* of this shows up in government revenue.

The higher P lowers the satisfaction and well-being of consumers. Whom does it benefit? The suppliers of this particular industry do benefit. If linen were a monopoly industry, the monopolist would benefit and could afford to lobby for tariffs. Some of the benefit would trickle down to his employees and to owners of resources especially fitted for linen production. Even if, as in Fig. 34-3(a), there is perfect competition rather than monopoly, the productive factors specialized for the protected industry will stand to get some benefit (higher P for linen, more jobs, high wage rates, higher economic rents on factors inelastically supplied to that industry).[9]

When the spouse of one of these specialized employees complained about the high cost of linen and of living generally, resulting from a high-tariff government, the employee could reply: "Stop complaining. *We* get more than *we* give as a result of the tariff. It's *the rest of the community* that experiences the net harm from the cessation of linen imports".

In wheat and other nonprotected industries, employees and consumers can both legitimately complain about this linen tariff. Indeed, let us consider (a) the harm done to consumers, (b) the revenue collected by government, and (c) the benefit received by suppliers. What is the net effect, on the supposition that both rich and poor, worthy and unworthy, are equally involved on all sides of the argument? The

---

[7] Economists explain: these supply and demand curves of Marshall depict only "partial equilibrium". They have to be anchored on "general equilibrium" analysis, of which Ricardian comparative advantage is a simple but vital case.

[8] The price rise need not be as great as the tariff itself; it will be that great only if, to continue our example, the European industry is so large compared with America's use of the product that one or both of their *ss* and *dd* schedules can be regarded as virtually horizontal, America's imports being too small to affect their prices appreciably.

[9] Indeed, if $s_a s_a$ were completely vertical, all the money newly extorted from the consumer would be transferred to the producers in extra rent: this would presumably be a switch from not particularly unworthy consumers to not particularly worthy producers. But with $s_a s_a$ having some positive elasticity, the higher P will coax out extra domestic Q; this will represent a definite social inefficiency, to the degree that resources are drawn from fields where America has a comparative advantage into protected industries where she has a comparative disadvantage. In the extreme case of a horizontal $s_a s_a$, where factors are indifferent between this and other industries, *all* the tariff's benefits to producers are frittered away in inefficient resource allocation and not even do those in the industry derive a selfish benefit at the expense of the hard-hit consumers.

Appendix shows that the harm of a prohibitive tariff outweighs its gain, in this sense:

A system of prohibitive tariffs puts a society inefficiently *inside* the consumption-possibility-frontier that would be available if the efficiencies of international exchange and division of labor were utilized. This is absolutely true of the world as a whole, and absolutely true for a country that cuts off all imports and becomes self-sufficient.[10]

QUOTAS The effect of a prohibitive tariff could be achieved by imposing a zero quota on all imports. The prices would find their A_d and A_e levels in both markets as before. Consumers in America will be hurt; and in the sense described above, they will be hurt more than producers are helped.

Suppose the quota is set, not at zero, but, say, at half the level of free-trade imports. The reader can verify that, in the special case of Fig. 34-3's straight-line curves, the American P will rise half the distance between the free-trade B_d price and the no-trade A_d price. (In Europe P will fall halfway.) Only at these new respective P's of $\$9$ and £1 1/2 will the arrow of Europe's physical linen exports match America's arrow of physical linen imports. (Verify.)

The quota has produced a price difference between America and Europe. As just said, that equilibrium difference is defined as just large enough to make exports and imports match. (Note: A tariff on each unit import of linen, which was exactly equal to this price difference, could have achieved the same equilibrium.[11]

[10] It is also true with rare (and unimportant) exceptions for a country that levies prohibitive tariffs on a subset of its goods. The exceptions apply to a country large enough to affect appreciably the relative prices of the goods it imports. By levying sufficiently small, shrewdly gauged tariffs, it might exploit its monopoly power to "make the foreigner pay" for its tariff. (This is an esoteric point, which could be illustrated by means of utility-disutility areas under the schedules in Fig. 34-3(a). But readers of Chapter 25's discussion of marginal revenue (and the loss taken on all earlier units when an extra unit of q is sold by a monopolist) can understand the point thus: The last little unit of import under free trade brings America zero marginal benefit; that is why it is the last unit. If America imposes a tiny tariff to keep it out, she does force a reduction in the P she pays on *all* previous units imported. So America could benefit a little from such a move (unless the $s_e s_e$ and/or $d_e d_e$ curves were horizontal). However, Europe could do the same to America's wheat, and when all play this game there is some presumption that world inefficiency will make all (or most) worse off.)

[11] This gives the clue to how to compute the equilibrium prices for any tariff rate between the prohibitive and zero levels. In Fig. 34-

There is thus no essential difference between tariffs and quotas. Except this: A nonprohibitive tariff at least gives revenue to the government, in part offsetting the net harm done to the importing country by the restriction on imports. A quota, on the other hand, puts the profit from the contrived price difference into the pocket of the importer lucky enough to get a quota license. He can afford to wine and dine the officials who give out import licenses; or if they are not already his kinfolk or political cronies, he can afford to bribe them.

This is why economists generally regard tariffs as a lesser evil than quotas. "At the least," they advise, "if you must introduce inefficient restrictive quotas, be sure that the government auctions off the scarce import-quota licenses so that the Treasury gains the swag and so that bureaucracy is not put under the strain of corruption and exercise of arbitrary power and caprice."

The harmful effects of a nonprohibitive tariff or quota are seen to be of the same type as, but of lesser quantitative degree than, those of prohibitive tariffs or quotas. Generally, there is net harm done to the citizenry as it is forced to curb its consumption of the goods it desires most and to channel resources from lines of true comparative advantage to economically inefficient uses. Generally, real wages and average living standards are hurt by tariffs and quotas.

TRANSPORTATION COSTS The economic costs of moving bulky and perishable goods also lessen the extent of profitable regional specialization.

The effects are like those produced by the passage of artificially restrictive tariff legislation. In the case of transportation costs, the evil is unavoidable, whereas protective tariffs or artificial barriers to interregional trade within a nation are squarely the responsibility of man.

This ends two sections of digression on particular markets' price equilibrium under trade and tariffs. We return again to basic comparative advantage.

3, shift the whole exporting country's diagram upward by the amount of the tariff (so that its vertical-scale prices now differ from the importing country's vertical scale by the amount of the duty). Then move a horizontal ruler up and down until you have located exactly equal export and import gaps between the respective schedules.

QUALIFICATIONS AND CONCLUSIONS

Of course, comparative advantage holds for *any* two countries and goods, not just for America and Europe and food and clothing. (Ricardo used England and Portugal and cloth and wine in his examples.) The following Appendix shows how the principle of comparative advantage can be generalized to handle any number of countries or regions. Instead of using simple labor-cost examples, we could easily measure costs in terms of "doses" of labor, land, and capital goods of fixed proportions. We can also allow for changing factor proportions and diminishing returns. For all this and more, see the Appendix.

Perhaps a more serious defect of comparative advantage is its static assumptions. The theory is stated in terms of barter and relative price ratios. It disregards all stickiness of prices and wages, all transitional inflationary and overvaluation gaps, and all balance-of-payments problems. It supposes that when workers go out of one industry they always go into another more efficient industry—never into chronic unemployment. It ignores sticky money wage rates set at too high a level to employ all workers at home.[12]

No wonder this abstract theory sold at a discount during the Great Depression. Recently its prestige has been coming back. To the extent that we can in the future avoid inflexible exchange rates and wage rates and can count on successful macroeconomic management, which mobilizes modern theories of monetary and fiscal policy to banish slumps and inflations—to that extent will the old classical theory of comparative advantage retain its vital social relevance.

If theories could win beauty contests, comparative advantage would certainly rate high in that it is an elegantly logical structure. It is a highly simplified theory; an oversimplified one, as far as our rushing out to make immediate applications to real life is concerned. Yet, for all its oversimplification, the theory of comparative advantage provides a most important glimpse of truth. Political economy has found few more pregnant principles. A nation that neglects comparative advantage may pay a heavy price in terms of living standards and potential growth.

SUMMARY

1 As soon as there are diversities of productivities within a country, specialization and exchange become profitable. The same holds for nations: international exchange is an efficient way for us (in effect) to transform one good into another, more efficient than having to rely solely on domestic production.

2 Without much study of economics, people see that trade is mutually beneficial between the tropics and the temperate zones—or between two countries where one is more efficient in producing one good and the other is more efficient in producing the other good. But it takes the important Ricardian principle of *comparative* advantage to see that trade is no less mutually beneficial between two countries (or as in the case cited of the lawyer and stenographer, between any two units) even when one of the countries happens to be *absolutely* more efficient in every industry than is the other.

As long as there is a difference in *relative* efficiency, every country must enjoy both a comparative advantage and a comparative *dis*advantage in some goods. There will then be powerful benefits to be derived from *specializing* in those goods in which there is a comparative advantage, *trading* them for the goods in which the other country has a comparative advantage.

[12] See the Appendix to the previous chapter for a demonstration that overvaluation of a country's currency can undercut these basic classical principles.

3 The law of comparative advantage not only predicts the geographical pattern of specialization and direction of trade; it also demonstrates that *both* countries are made better off and that the real wages (or returns to the factors of production taken as a whole) are improved by trade and the resulting *enlarged* totals of world production. Quotas and prohibitive tariffs that re-create *autarky* (i.e., national economic self-sufficiency, not to be confused with political *autarchy*) will hurt real wage and total factor returns—not help them.

4 Decreasing costs (economies of scale) are an important cause of specialization and regional trade. Differences in tastes can also cause trade.

5 Completely free trade will equalize prices in supply-demand markets for one small good causing the good to be exported from the country with lowest zero-trade prices. The equilibrium uniform P is at the level which equates physical exports to physical imports.

6 A tariff or quota, by lowering imports, will cause a rise in domestic P and a fall in foreign P. (So long as some imports continue, the P's will differ by the amount of the tariff.) The harm done to the domestic economy, from higher P and decreased home consumption, and from wastage of resources on goods lacking comparative advantage, will generally exceed the benefit to producers. Transport costs also cut down on trade and well-being.

7 The important law of comparative advantage must be qualified to take into account certain interferences with it. Thus, if exchange-rate parities and money wage rates are rigid in both countries or if fiscal and monetary policies are poorly run in both countries, then the blessing of cheap imports that international specialization gives might be turned into the curse of unemployment. With proper public policies, modern nations can achieve a managed macroeconomics which need not sacrifice the great benefits from trade, but rather can re-create the environment in which the principle of comparative advantage will apply.

CONCEPTS FOR REVIEW

personal and regional diversity
   and specialization
absolute versus comparative
   efficiencies
comparative advantage and
   disadvantage
taste differences in trade

barter versus domestic production
international price equilibrium
quota and tariff equilibrium
prohibitive quotas or tariffs,
   and lower real wages
sticky money-wage or
   exchange rates

QUESTIONS FOR DISCUSSION

1. "Buying a good cheaper abroad than we can produce it at home is to our advantage." Is this consistent with comparative advantage? Show that it indeed is.

2. Are real wage levels, like water in connecting pipes, brought to the same level by completely free international trade? Why not? Are international prices? Why?

3. What happens if two countries are exactly alike in productivity and efficiency? Explain. Justify the slogan "Vive la différence!"

4. Holland's Jan Tinbergen, using modern linear programming to analyze geographical capital-labor supplies and industrial intensities, estimates the following 1970 pattern of true comparative advantage for the world. (a) The United States would produce planes,

chemicals, drugs, pumps, vacuums, cast iron, telecommunication equipment, soaps, and ceramic products. (b) Western Europe would concentrate on autos, textile machineries, alcoholic beverages, batteries, washing machines, animal and vegetable oils. (c) Japan would be the shipbuilder for the world. (d) The less developed countries would produce textiles, shoes and glass. (e) The Soviet Union, to Tinbergen's surprise, would produce computers. Which of these allocations seem most reasonable? Which seem least reasonable?

5. What if (1,2;3,4) in Table 34-1 became (1,2;1 1/2,3)? Can you show that all trade is killed off? And that this certainly would be a worse position for America? (Footnote readers: redraw Fig. 34-1 with equal p-p slopes.) Show that if it now becomes (1,2; 1 1/2,4,) Europe will export food.

6. Can a country once have a comparative advantage, say, in electric generating equipment, and then lose it? What then *will* happen? Should it?

7. Why might a new continent have a comparative advantage in food?

8. "If some goods continue to be imported after a new tariff the sum of the rise in domestic P and the fall in foreign P must equal the new tariff." Can you show why?

Appendix: Comparative Advantage Amplified and Qualified

Our discussion of comparative advantage has until now followed Ricardo and measured all costs in terms of labor. Modern economists know that the theory is still valid even if you do not want to assume a labor theory of value. The production-possibility, or transformation, frontier that we used in Chapter 2 to discuss guns and butter, or Agriculture (food) and Manufactures (clothing), is the tool that enables us to dispense with labor units: users of the production-possibility frontier choose to measure the cost of clothing in terms of the food we must sacrifice to get more clothing. (This is sometimes called "opportunity cost.")

The first part of this Appendix follows through in detail the America-Europe food-clothing case showing the irrelevance of absolute labor costs.

AMERICA WITHOUT TRADE

In Chapter 2, we saw that every economy has a production-possibility (or transformation) schedule indicating how much of one commodity, food, can be produced if all resources are diverted to it; also how much of the other commodity, clothing, can be produced if all resources are diverted to its production; and how either good can be transformed into the other.

For simplicity, let us suppose food can always be transformed into units of clothing in America at the *constant ratio* of 10:3. For each 10 units of food sacrificed, we can always get 3 units of clothing. We further assume that, when all resources are diverted to food production, America will have altogether 100 (million) units of food.[1]

Then, clearly America can, if she chooses, have 90 units of food and 3 units of clothing, 80 and 6, . . . , or finally 0 of the food and 30 of clothing.

We may put this in the form of a schedule, as shown in Fig. 34-4's table. It may be plotted in Fig. 34-4, just as was done in Chapter 2, Fig. 2-2. The solid line *AD* is America's production-possibility frontier. Their new production-possibility frontier is a straight line, whereas the earlier one was rounded, being concave when looked at from below. The straight-line production-possibility schedule has been introduced in order to keep the argument simple—to relieve the student from having to remember many different cost ratios. As will be seen later, this will not seriously affect the validity of the argument. The few qualifications needed are made later.

So far we have been talking only about production.

However, if America is isolated from all trade, what she produces is also what she consumes. Let us suppose, therefore, that the emphasized quantities for *C* in Fig. 34-4's table represent the amounts produced and consumed by America in the absence of trade; or in numerical terms, America then produces and consumes 30 units of food and 21 units of clothing.

Why was this particular combination decided upon rather than one of the other possibilities? We know from earlier chapters that in a competitive system nobody "decides" upon this, but that the price mechanism, operating through supply and demand for goods and services, determines WHAT shall be produced, HOW, and FOR WHOM. Well, the indicated quantities are the WHAT. Very little need be said here about the HOW, except for the obvious remark that agricultural food production will require more land relative to labor than will more highly fabricated clothing output. As to the FOR WHOM, we need only remark parenthetically that scarcity of labor in America will mean rather high wages for workers, while superabundance of land here will mean low rents (per acre) for landlords.

TECHNICAL PROGRESS Let's now introduce Europe into the picture. Before doing so, it will pave the way for the later argument to interject a question. What would happen if some American (like Eli Whitney, inventor of the cotton gin, for example) should make a clever invention, allowing each 10 units of food to be transformed into 6 rather than 3 units of clothing. Would America be potentially better off?

The answer is, obviously, Yes. The production-possibility curve has shifted outward and upward and is now shown by the broken line *AD'* in Fig. 34-4. (Show that America could now go from *C* northeast to a new point *C'* and have *more of both* food and clothing.)

EUROPE WITHOUT TRADE

We can now do for Europe exactly what was done above for America, but with an important difference. Europe's plentiful endowment of labor relative to land would give her a different cost or transformation ratio between food and clothing.

Figure 34-5 and its table define Europe's straight line *p-p* frontier. Europe is given a comparative advantage in clothing rather than in food. For her, each 10 units of foods may be transformable into, say, 8 units of clothing. She gets 5 more than was true of America because of her comparative advantage in clothing. However, in terms of food, America gets 10/3, or 3.33 units, for each unit of clothing sacrificed, while Europe's comparative disadvantage in food production gives her only 10/8, or 1.25 units

---

[1]Note that labor is never mentioned in the following discussion. But if you wanted to relate this discussion to Ricardo's labor treatment, you could merely change the numbers in Table 34-1 from (1,2: 3,4) to (3,10: 8,10), or more generally to (3a, 10a; 8b, 10b), where a and b are arbitrary positive numbers depending only on units and absolute efficiencies.

Production-Possibility Schedule of America (10/3 Constant-Cost Ratio)

AMERICA

POSSIBILITIES	FOOD, MILLIONS OF UNITS	CLOTHING, MILLIONS OR UNITS
A	100	0
B	50	15
C	30	21
D	0	30

TABLE 34-2.

FIG. 34-4. The constant-cost line *AD* shows America's domestic production-possibilities frontier. The new frontier *AD'* indicates an increased ability to produce clothing and means that America can move northeast from *AD*, enjoying more of both goods.

of food, for each sacrificed unit of clothing. *The important thing to concentrate upon is the difference in the two cost ratios: 10/3 for America and 10/8 for Europe.*

We shall still keep the two continents isolated from each other. What is Europe's exact production-possibility schedule? Let us suppose that Europe's population is so large and her land area such that before trade she was producing and consuming 50 units of food and 80 units of clothing. This fact, plus the constant-ratio 10/8, tells us all we have to know in order to draw up Europe's complete production-possibility schedule as in the table of Fig. 34-5, and in its *ad frontier*.

THE OPENING UP OF TRADE

Now, for the first time, let us admit the possibility of trade between the two regions. Food can be bartered for clothing at some *terms of trade*, i.e., at some *price ratio*.[2] To dramatize the process, let us suppose that in mid-ocean there stands an impersonal auctioneer whose business it is to balance supply and demand—offers of clothing and offers of food. He does this by calling out to both countries an exchange rate or price ratio between food and clothing. Until supplies and demands are balanced, he keeps the bidding going. When he finally hits on the equilibrium price level *at which supply and demand balance*, he raps his gavel three times and says, "Going, going, *gone!*"

Probably, he will suspect in advance that Europe is going to specialize in clothing production, in which she has a comparative advantage, and that she will wish to export part of her clothing production in exchange for food imports. But he has no idea what the final exchange ratio, or terms of trade, between food and clothing will be—whether it will be 10/3, 10/8, 10/5, 10/6, or anything else. For that matter, if the auctioneer is very new at the game,

[2]Terms of trade (or an exchange ratio) of, say, 10 food for 6 clothing means that clothing is more expensive than food, with the price ratio (clothing price)/(food price) = 1 2/3 = 10/6.

or very stupid, he may think that the final equilibrium exchange level, or terms of trade, will be 10/1 or 10/12.

LIMITS TO FINAL EQUILIBRIUM. Actually, neither of these last two can be the final exchange ratio. He would soon learn this from bitter experience. For let him tell America and Europe that they can get all the clothing they want in exchange for food at the rate of only 1 unit of clothing for every 10 units of food. What will America do? By producing at home, she can get 3 units of clothing for each 10 of food. Clearly, she will not be persuaded into trading food for clothing on those terms; she would rather remain self-sufficient.

That is only half the story. Why should not America go to the other extreme and export clothing in exchange for food imports? Each 1 unit of clothing gets her 10 units of food from the auctioneer. What will 1 unit of clothing get at home in domestic food production? Obviously, from Figure 34-4 and its accompanying table, only 10/3, or 3.33, units of food. At 10/1, therefore, America should certainly shift all her resources to clothing production; she should export some of her surplus clothing in return for food imports.

Now, what about Europe? At home she gets only 10/8, or 1.25, units of food for each unit of clothing. At 10/1, she too will want to trade clothing for food. We see, therefore, what a green hand the auctioneer was. By calling out 10/1, he brings a flood supply of clothing on his head and only demands for food. Since he has no supplies of either good up his sleeve he must now change his tactics. He must raise the price of food relative to the price of clothing. He had better try the ratio 10/2, or perhaps even 10/9. You are

Production-Possibility Schedule of Europe (10/8 Constant Cost Ratio)

EUROPE

POSSIBILITIES	FOOD, MILLIONS OF UNITS	CLOTHING, MILLIONS OF UNITS
a	150	0
b	100	40
c	50	80
d	0	120

TABLE 34-3.

now in a position to reason why neither of them will do: why 10/2 will still induce a tidal wave of clothing and, on the other hand, why 10/9 represents the opposite error, in which there is a tornado of food.

Clearly, *the final exchange ratio cannot be outside the original two-country limits of 10/3 and 10/8!* Anywhere between is a possibility—with America following her comparative advantage and specializing in food, and Europe following her comparative advantage and specializing in clothing.

EXACT DETERMINATION OF THE FINAL PRICE RATIO

Just where between the domestic cost ratios will the terms of trade settle down? Some of Ricardo's immediate followers were foolish enough to say, "Split the difference between the two countries' cost ratios, and pick 10/5½ as the equilibrium ratio."[3]

Actually, as John Stuart Mill, the third great classical economist (after Smith and Ricardo), showed a little later, *the exact final level of the terms of trade between the two cost ratios will depend upon the strength of world supply and demand for each of the two commodities.* If people have an intense desire for food relative to available supplies of food and clothing, the price ratio will settle near the upper limit of 10/8; if clothing is much demanded by both countries, the final price ratio will settle near 10/3.[4]

---

[3]Or would they have said halfway between 10/3 and 10/8, giving us 110/48, which corresponds to 10/4 4/11? Both answers are silly. Back in Fig. 34-1, footnote 3 in Chapter 34, there is no sense to saying that the final terms-of-trade parallel arrows are at *half* the shaded angle. They can be anywhere in the shaded area, depending on supply and demand.

[4]Also, if America were very small relative to Europe, so that its supplies made hardly a "dent" on the market, then the price ratio might even stay at Europe's 10/8. America would then be specializing in food and importing clothing, but all America's food exports would amount to so little that Europe would still have to produce some food for herself. This is possible only at a price of 10/8. America would in this case get all the gains from international trade. It pays to have a large (different!) neighbor.

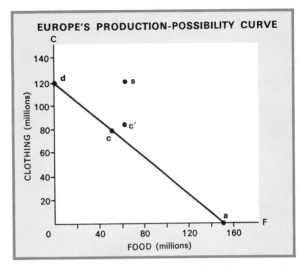

FIG. 34-5. Before international trade, Europe is on her domestic production-possibility curve at C, consuming just what she produces. (Disregard the points C' and S until later in the chapter.)

Mill did what our auctioneer would have to do. He drew up a schedule showing supply and demand at *each possible price ratio:*[5] how much food America would wish to export and how much food Europe would want to import; and at the same time, how much clothing Europe would

---

[5]The indifference curves in the Appendix to Chapter 22 can be used to summarize each country's tastes for food and clothing. Together with the *p-p* curves, these could derive the reciprocal demand curves of Mill, shown in Fig. 34-6. Unlike ordinary *dd* and *ss* curves, C is trading against F, not against money; hence, relative prices P_C/P_F, rather than money P_C, are plotted. (If tastes and incomes vary within each country, aggregate indifference curves would be replaced by more elaborate analysis.)

FIG. 34-6.

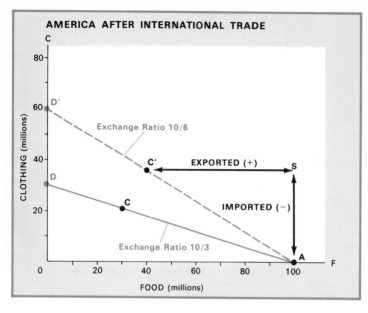

FIG. 34-7. The line *AD* represents America's domestic production-possibility curve; the line *AD'*, her new consumption-possibility curve when she is able to trade freely at the price ratio 10/6 and in consequence has decided to specialize completely in the production of food (at *A*). The black arrows from *S* to *C'* and *A* to *S* show the amounts exported (+) and imported (–) by America. As a result of free trade, she finally ends up at *C'* with more of both goods than before at *C*.

be willing to export at each price ratio in comparison with the amount of clothing America expected to import.

At one, and (usually) only one, intermediate price ratio, exports and imports will balance. At this equilibrium price, exports and imports will "mesh" (or match), quantitatively as well as qualitatively; the auctioneer and Mill will heave a sigh of relief, and trade will continue indefinitely until tastes or technology have changed.

For our numerical problem it has been assumed that the equilibrium terms-of-trade ratio is 10/6, a little "nearer" to Europe's pre-trade ratio than to America's.

America concentrates her production completely on food. In Fig. 34-7, America has her production at *A*. But since she can now trade freely at 10/6, America is no longer limited to her old production-possibility curve. By trading, she can now move on the broken line *AD'* just exactly as if a fruitful invention had been made. Is America made potentially better off by trade? Indeed she is. Just where she will stop on this broken line, which we may call her new *consumption*-possibility curve, depends upon the workings of her internal price system. We assume that this causes her to stop at the point *C'*, where 40 units of food and 36 units of clothing are consumed. The black arrows show America's exports (+) and imports (–).

All this is summarized in America's rows in Table 34-4 page 623. This table should be studied carefully. To understand it is to understand the comparative advantage.

As a result of specialization and trade, America has become better off; she has more clothing and more food to consume. The same is true of Europe. What is the black magic by which something seems to have been got for nothing? In Table 34-4 the rows marked World, which re-

present the sum of the American and European rows, give the answer. *World production of both goods has been stepped up by specialization and trade.*

Actually, the sixth row gives the data the auctioneer would be most interested in. He is assured that equilibrium has been reached by two facts shown there: (1) World consumption of each product is identical with world production—no more, no less; and (2) the amounts that each country exports are just balanced by the amounts that the other country wishes to import. Thus the price ratio 10/6 is the right one.[6]

This completes our explanation of comparative advantage. You might test your full understanding by filling in on Fig. 34-5 for Europe everything that has already been filled in for America on Fig. 34-7.

Europe's new consumption-possibility line, made possible by trade, pivots around the point *d* on the vertical axis and goes through *c'*. Draw new arrows from *d* to *s* representing the amounts exported (+) and imported (—) as was done on Fig. 34-7. Note that Europe's arrows match America's but are opposite in sign and direction. (Why is this quantitative meshing of exports and imports

---

[6]To find this equilibrium, the auctioneer could have made up a whole book of such tables, each page corresponding to a different price ratio. Only one page is the right one, however, because at all other prices the algebraic total of exports and imports would not cancel out. Thus, at 10/7, America's desire for clothing imports would surpass Europe's willingness to export clothing. The world as a whole would be trying to consume more clothing than had been produced. Since the auctioneer has no inventories to draw upon, he would have to turn the pages toward a higher price for clothing and a lower price for food. On the right page the price ratio would be an equilibrium one: exports would balance imports, at the *E* intersection of Fig. 34-6.

SUMMARY SHOWING SPECIALIZATION AND GAIN FROM TRADE ACCORDING TO COMPARATIVE ADVANTAGE

AREA COMPARED	EXCHANGE RATIO OF FOOD FOR CLOTHING PC/PF	FOOD PRODUC- TION	FOOD CONSUMP- TION	FOOD EXPORTS (+) OR IMPORTS (−)	CLOTHING PRODUC- TION	CLOTHING CONSUMP- TION	CLOTHING EXPORTS (+) OR IMPORTS (−)
Situation before trade							
America	10/3	30	30	0	21	21	0
Europe	10/8	50	50	0	80	80	0
World	none	80	80	0	101	101	0
Situation after trade							
America	10/6	100	40	+60	0	36	−36
Europe	10/6	0	60	−60	120	84	+36
World	10/6	100	100	0	120	120	0
Gains from trade							
America	—	—	+10	—	—	+15	—
Europe	—	—	+10	—	—	+ 4	—
World	—	+20	+20	—	+19	+19	—

TABLE 34-4
International trade makes possible larger world production and consumption of all goods. How these net gains are shared between countries depends on competitive supply and demand. (Small regions may benefit most.)

necessary at equilibrium?) The eager reader could add to the example labor measurements and wage data. Finally, note that comparative advantage, not absolute labor advantage, is the all-important condition.

MANY COMMODITIES

Very briefly, we must now show what happens when we remove some of the oversimplifications in the foregoing discussion. The conclusions are not essentially changed, and even the changes in details are usually not too difficult.

First note that until now we've simplified the story by considering only two commodities, food and clothing. Obviously, food stands for many different items (beef, milk, etc.), and similarly does clothing. Moreover, the advantages of exchange are equally great when we consider the thousands of commodities that can and do enter all phases of international trade.

As is shown in advanced treatises,[7] when there are many commodities producible in two countries at constant costs, they can be arranged in order according to their comparative advantage or cost. For example, the commodities automobiles, flax, perfumes, watches, wheat, and woolens might be arranged in the illustrated comparative-advantage sequence in Fig. 34-8. This means that wheat costs are lowest relative to all other commodities in America; Europe has its greatest comparative

[7]For example, G. Haberler, *Theory of International Trade* (Macmillan, New York, 1937). Haberler also pioneered the use of *p-p frontiers* in trade theory.

advantage in perfumes; its advantage in watches is not quite so great; and so forth.[8]

This ordered array of goods might have arisen from the numerical data of Table 34-5, which are presented only for the curiosity of more advanced readers and which are not essential for the above discussion. As before, it is not necessary to measure costs in terms of money or labor, but only in terms of the relative commodities into which any good can be "transformed." Suppose that we choose to measure the costs of every good in both countries in terms of woolens—selected arbitrarily because it comes last alphabetically. Then our data might be arranged alphabetically as in Table 34-5. This means that in America one must give up the production of 1,000 units of woolens to get 1 automobile, while in Europe the cost of 1 automobile is the sacrifice of 3,000 units of wool production. Therefore the comparative cost of automobiles relative to woolens is in Europe three times that in

(1) GOODS	(2) AMERICAN COST RATIO, IN TERMS OF WOOLENS	(3) EUROPEAN COST RATIO, IN TERMS OF WOOLENS	(4) COMPARATIVE EUROPEAN COSTS, IN TERMS OF AMERICAN COSTS (4)=(3)÷(2)
Automobiles	1,000	3,000	3.0
Flax	0.8	1.6	2.0
Perfumes	5.0	3.0	0.6
Watches	50	75	1.5
Wheat	0.2	0.8	4.0
Woolens	1.0	1.0	1.0

TABLE 34-5.

FIG. 34-8.

From the beginning we can be virtually sure of one thing. The introduction of trade will cause America to produce wheat, and Europe perfume. But where will the dividing line fall? Between automobiles and flax? Or will America produce flax and Europe confine herself to watches, woolens, and perfumes? Or will the dividing line fall on one of the commodities rather than between them, so that, say, flax might be produced in both places at once?

You will not be surprised to find that the answer depends upon the comparative strength of international demand for the different goods. If we think of the commodities as beads arranged on a string according to their comparative advantage, the total demand-and-supply situation will determine where the dividing line between American and European production will fall. And an increased demand for automobiles and wheat, for example, may tend to turn the terms of trade in the direction of America and make her so prosperous that it will no longer pay her to continue to produce her own flax.

MANY COUNTRIES

So much for the complications introduced by many commodities. What about many countries? Europe and America are not the whole world, and even they include many separate so-called "sovereign nations."

Introducing many countries need not change our analysis. As far as any one country is concerned, all the other

America, and so forth for the other goods. Now what can we infer? Very obviously, Europe's relative cost advantage is greatest in perfumes and least in wheat; in between, the commodities are arranged as shown in Fig. 34-8's beads. The fact that the figures in the last column are predominantly greater than 1 in no way reflects on the efficiency of Europe; it merely results from the accidental fact that we chose woolens as our common denominator in which to express costs. Had we selected wheat or watches the opposite would have been the case, and yet none of our results would be any different—except for a "scale factor" (such as converts inches to feet or yards).

TECHNICAL NOTE: Anyone who feels he must bring in labor productivities can write the respective American requirements in labor days as $A, B, C \ldots$, and Europe's as $a, b, c, \ldots$ The whole analysis can then be worked out in terms of comparative ratios of the form $A/B, C/B. \ldots$, and $a/b, c/b, \ldots$; to explain trade patterns it is never necessary to compare absolute advantages between countries $A/a, B/b, \ldots$ Of course, if he wants to compare money and real wages, these absolute advantages are necessary: by extending the analysis of Table 34-1, it can be shown that the ratio of European to American real wage must fall between the least and greatest of $A/a, B/b, \ldots$; just *where* between depends on the working out of reciprocal demands. Likewise, the terms of trade between any two goods, e.g. $price_a /price_b$ must lie between a/b and A/B.

nations with whom she trades can be lumped together into one group as "the rest of the world." The advantages of trade have no special relationship to state boundaries. The principles already developed apply between groups of countries and, indeed, between regions within the same country. In fact, but for historical accident, they would be more applicable to trade between the prairies and Ontario than to trade between the United States and Canada.

From the standpoint of pure economic welfare, the slogan "Buy Canadian" is as foolish as "Buy Ontario" would be, or "Buy Toronto," or "Buy Don Mills, Ontario." Part of our high per capita income and much of our economic activity come from the fortunate fact that there are no restrictive customs duties between our provinces.[9]

TRIANGULAR AND MULTILATERAL TRADE. There is, however, one new aspect introduced by the existence of many countries. Consider merchandise trade, ignoring "invisible items" for the minute. Canada has long found it very profitable to trade indirectly with the United Kingdom. She has traditionally sold Britain raw materials, agricultural products, and some finished commodities. But Britain does not sell her manufactured goods to Canada; instead she exports manufactured goods, such as clothing, to the United States. Thus we have a very advantageous "North Atlantic triangle" of merchandise trade. Since the Great Depression this triangle has rounded out into a "world loop" of trade, with many spirals and diagonals. Part of it would look like this: Canada sells raw materials and wheat to Great Britain; she sells manufactured goods, such as clothing, to the countries of Africa and Southeast Asia; they sell rubber and other raw materials to the United States; the United States sells machines and other manufactured goods to Canada. Figure 34-9 shows the trade and the arrows show the direction of export surpluses.

What would happen if all countries tried to sign bilateral trade agreements, so that Canada could not and would not buy from the United States unless they bought an equal amount from us? And so forth, with every two nations? Clearly, trade would be cut down severely. Imports would balance exports, but at the level of whichever is the lower. Each trading region would end up worse off.

INCREASING COSTS

Returning again to two countries and two commodities, we must now drop the assumption that costs are constant.

[9]Nevertheless Canada, with a population that is one-tenth of that of the United States, is plagued by the problems of a relatively small market.

FIG. 34-9.

The *p-p frontiers* of Figures 34-4, 34-5, and 34-7 should better have been bowed, as they were in Chapter 2. It is no longer possible to specify a single cost figure for each country.

On the whole, America is better endowed for food production than Europe; still, after a great amount of American food is produced, the cost of *extra* food will begin to exceed that of Europe. Even after American competition has drastically lowered the price of food relative to clothing, a little of the best land in Europe will be able to hold its own in food production. In the same way, the first little bit of American clothing production which can be achieved at low costs will continue even after international trade has reached an equilibrium level. However, any attempt to expand American clothing production further would entail higher extra costs and competitive losses.

We may summarize the modifications in international trade made necessary by increasing costs as follows:

As a result of international trade, each country will tend to specialize, as before, in the commodity in which it has the greatest comparative advantage; and it will export some of that commodity in exchange for the other country's surplus exports. But because of increasing relative costs, specialization need not be complete: something of both commodities may still be produced in either country, because even the less favored commodity may have low enough costs to compete when its production is small.[10]

[10]For the geometrically minded, Fig. 34-10 may be helpful. It shows America's condition before and after trade when increasing costs prevail. The production-possibility curve is now bowed out. Before international trade, America is consuming and producing at *C*. The domestic price ratio is 10/3, just equal to the ratio of extra costs of getting (at *C*) a little more clothing for a little sacrificed food. This is shown by the slope of the *AD* curve at the pre-trade *C*.

After trade, when the common price ratio is 10/6, American production shifts to *B*, toward less clothing but not away from clothing altogether. The new production point *B* will be reached as a result of competition, because the slope of the curve there— i.e., the ratio of costs of extra clothing for extra food—is 10/6, or just equal to the common international price ratio. Only at *B* will the value of America's GNP (evaluated at the 10/6 price ratio) be at a maximum.

The straight line represents the new consumption-possibility curve America can achieve as a result of trade. It is straight and not bent because the auctioneer offers to trade freely, giving

DETERIORATING TERMS OF TRADE Now that comparative advantage has been covered, we can tie in the last chapter's discussion of overvaluation. Combining that discussion with the present one, here is an aspect of overvaluation that could be discovered only by analytical economics. Again, let A be America, using dollars, and E Europe, now using pounds.

Suppose that the productivity miracle in E involves a significant increase in her ability to produce the goods that A was previously exporting or producing for home consumption. Again A has an overvalued currency, just as in the previous case of across-the-board unbiased productivity advance in E. Again A has unemployment stagnation. Again equilibrium can be restored by depreciation of A's \$1 relative to E's £1. But with this important difference:

Under unbiased technical change abroad, the new equilibrium terms of trade of A could be presumed to be about what they had been before. However, with technological change abroad biased toward improvements designed to narrow the gap between productivity *in those goods where A was enjoying comparative advantage*, there is a strong presumption that the new equilibrium will involve a permanent deterioration of A's terms of trade.

A is actually (somewhat) impoverished by the technical advance abroad, or at least slowed down in her rate of material progress by this event. How can she be hurt if her productivity has not deteriorated? Because worsened terms of trade cause A to lose some of the "consumer sat-

America at the 10/6 ratio as much or little clothing for food as she wishes. The final levels of consumption, determined by supply and demand, are shown at *C'*. As before, the directional arrows indicate exports or imports.

There are still gains from trade; but because of diminishing returns and increasing costs, there is not so much specialization as before and not quite such large gains. Note that at the equilibrium point, where no further trade is possible, relative (extra, or "marginal") production costs in the two countries are equal, each to the common price ratio 10/6.

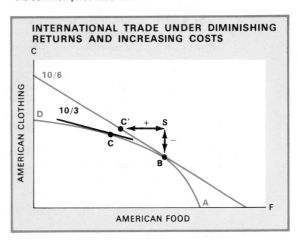

FIG. 34-10.

isfaction" she enjoyed when she was gaining from international trade.

The universe was not made such that what helps one *must* help all; often what helps one thereby hurts another. In this case A, who is already quite rich, may find solace that E is becoming less poor and not regret too much the slight sacrifice implied for A. Chapter 36 shows that the foregoing analysis had relevance to the world of the early seventies. It all did happen that way.

INTERNATIONAL GOODS MOVEMENTS AS A SUBSTITUTE FOR FACTOR MOVEMENTS

Having acknowledged the law of increasing costs described in Chapter 2 and elsewhere and gone beyond the straight lines of the overly simple labor-only model, we now examine implications of the related law of diminishing returns within each country.

After international trade takes place, resources in Europe flow from food to clothing production. Because clothing requires relatively much labor and little land, the pressure of population on the limited land of Europe is relieved. Land is no longer relatively so dear; rents fall compared with wages. In America the reverse happens after trade: concentration upon food production, in which labor is economized and land heavily utilized, tends to raise rents relative to wages.

In each case the free international movement of goods has effects which are partly like those following from free international movement of factors of production. Just as the movement of labor from Europe to America would relieve the scarcity of labor in America and of land in Europe, so the movement of clothing from Europe to America and of food from America to Europe tends to make the superabundant factor in each country less abundant and the scarce factor less scarce.

The person who has most clearly emphasized how commodity trade partially relieves the scarcity in all countries of the less abundant factors of production is the Swedish economist and statesman Ohlin (pronounced O'Leen).[11] He has made the following important addition to the classical doctrine of comparative cost:

Free movements of labor and capital between countries will tend to equalize wages and factor-prices.

However, even without any movements of productive factors across national boundaries, a tendency toward partial (but not necessarily complete) equalization of factor-prices will often result from the free movements of goods in international trade.

It is clear, therefore, that although international trade increases national product in Europe, it may at the same time so reduce the share of particular groups that they are made worse off. Thus, the large British landowners who a century ago constituted the backbone of the Conservative party may have been selfish in opposing the famous repeal of the English corn-law tariffs in 1846, but they were not necessarily unintelligent in making their unsuccessful last-ditch fight to retain protective tariffs on imported grains.

SUMMARY TO APPENDIX

1 If nature endows two regions unequally with factors of production, the *relative* cost of transforming one commodity into another domestically will probably be different for the two areas. (For example, a land-rich area will have a comparative advantage in food and other land-intensive goods; a labor-rich area's comparative advantage will be in labor-intensive goods.)

2 Under free trade, goods will exchange for each other at a price ratio somewhere *intermediate* between the original domestic cost ratios of the two countries (depending on reciprocal supply and demand).

3 Each country will specialize in the commodity in which it has a comparative advantage and export its surplus of that product for imports from abroad.

4 Each country is made better off by trade and specialization: America can get by trade more units of clothing than when she domestically transforms food into clothing; Europe does better when she trades clothing for food, doing better than when she domestically transforms clothing into food.

5 When there are more than two goods, the same principles of comparative advantage apply. The same is true when there are more than two countries trading, or when we have many factors of production other than labor.

6 Trade is *indirect* production. It is efficient production. Efficient production is always better than inefficient production. (Note that advantages of trade have nothing to do with *relative wage rates.*

[11]Bertil Ohlin, *Interregional and International Trade* (Harvard University Press, Cambridge, Mass., 1933). Ohlin acknowledges inspiration from the earlier eminent Swedish economic historian, Eli Heckscher.

Under free trade, a country's wage tends to be pulled up to the higher levels of productivity of its export industry, not down to the low-efficiency level of its import industry.)

7 Free migration of productive factors, can, without trade, equalize factor-prices. But even without migration of any factors, free movement of goods in trade can work to reduce or sometimes eliminate the differences in factor-prices that result from different geographical factor proportions.

CONCEPTS FOR REVIEW

straight-line and concave
  p-p frontiers
specialization point
terms of trade
pre- and post-trade equilibria

world loop of trade
matching trade arrows
many-good ordered array of
  comparative advantages
factor-price equalization by trade

QUESTIONS FOR DISCUSSION

1. Two countries have the same-sloped *p-p frontiers* that are straight lines. Why will there still have to be self-sufficiency even if one greatly exceeds the other in labor productivity all around?

2. Show that I benefit if your *p-p frontier* is as different from mine as possible.

3. Why would you expect land-rich Canada to export wheat to labor-rich China?

4. *Extra-credit problem:* Add to Table 34-5 the information that woolens happen to cost 1 hour's labor in each country. Begin with $3 to £1. With wages in America $6 an hour and £1 in Europe, show that the cost-price of flax will be the same in both countries. Which goods will *A* produce cheapest? Which goods will *B*? Now let American wage rise relative to that in Europe, (or let the dollar appreciate relative to the pound). Show that American exports will suffer and that American imports will rise.

35
THE ECONOMICS OF
TARIFF PROTECTION AND
FREE TRADE

To the chamber of deputies: we are subjected to the intolerable competition of a foreign rival, who enjoys such superior facilities for the production of light that he can inundate our national market at reduced price. This rival is no other than the sun. Our petition is to pass a law shutting up all windows, openings and fissures through which the light of the sun is used to penetrate our dwellings, to the prejudice of the profitable manufacture we have been enabled to bestow on the country. Signed: Candle Makers. F. BASTIAT

Chapter 34 showed that free trade generally yields greater consumption for all nations. Why then, are there impediments to trade, such as tariffs? This chapter analyses the economics of the tariff, and the appendix goes on to discuss the related issue of foreign ownership.

It would be absurd to try to decide whether God exists or not by counting on one hand all the arguments in the affirmative and on the other hand all the arguments in the negative, and then to award the decision to the side with the greater *number* of points. It is as absurd to evaluate the case for tariff protection by a mere count of unequally important pros and cons.

Indeed, as was shown in the previous chapter, there is essentially only one argument for free or freer trade, but it is an exceedingly powerful one, namely:

Free trade promotes a mutually profitable regional division of labor, greatly enhances the potential real national product of all nations, and makes possible higher standards of living all over the globe.

Recall that putting on a tariff duty (i.e., tax) discourages imports and raises prices to the domestic consumer. By killing off the fruitful international division of labor, it "protects" the relatively inefficient domestic producer. Import quotas do the same.

The arguments for high-tariff protection against the competition of foreign imports take many different forms. They may be divided into three categories:

1. Those that are definitely economically false, some so obviously and palpably as hardly to merit serious discussion, but some whose falsity can be detected only by subtle economic reasoning.

2. A few arguments for protection that are without validity in a perfectly competitive "classical" static full-employment world, but that do contain some kernels of truth for a sizeable nation which monopolizes some crop, or for a nation undergoing economic development and subject to underemployment and balance of payment problems (an overvalued currency).

3. Finally, certain noneconomic arguments that may make it desirable national policy to sacrifice economic welfare in order to subsidize particular activities admittedly not economically efficient.

NONECONOMIC GOALS

Let us begin with the last category of arguments, for it is most simply disposed of. If you ever are on a debating team and are given the assignment to defend free trade, you will strengthen your case at the beginning by conceding that economic welfare is not the sole goal of life. Political considerations are also important. Thus, it may be necessary to become partially self-sufficient in certain lines of activity, even at great cost, because of fear of future wars.

An example is petroleum production. If mineralogical know-how and capacity are considered necessary for national sovereignty and if the right amount of capacity is not able to survive under free trade, the economist cannot assert that national policy should be against protection of this industry. But he can suggest that a *subsidy* to domestic production might be preferable to a tariff: This would bring the domestic price down to the international price instead of raising the price to the consumer up to the domestic cost; also the subsidy would show clearly what the costs of national sovereignty are and would better enable the public to decide whether the game is worth the candle.

SECURITY AND WAYS OF LIFE

The problem of whether to support our shipyards and merchant marine is similarly perplexing, when by doing so we both inspire retaliation by other countries and sacrifice the benefits to be gained from their comparative-advantage efficiencies. The economist can claim no special competence to advise on this problem. He can point out that selfish economic interests often conceal their true motives under a guise of nationalism and try to justify uneconomic projects in terms of national defense. He can ask suspiciously, "Was the increase in subsidies to Canadian shipyards justified by our defense needs for such capacity? Or was this merely a case of political pressure?" Finally the economist can also point out that mutually profitable international trade may help to promote international understanding and unity, and that political interferences with trade have in the past provided some of the frictions that led to war.

In conclusion, it is well to point out other noneconomic goals that may deserve consideration. Society may feel that there is some special sanctity about farm life, something worth preserving in the way of life of the "stout agricultural yeoman or happy peasant." (It is to be doubted that people who rhapsodize in this fashion typically come from farms.) Or some may agree with various foreign generals who think that rural living is worth fostering because the country has a higher birth rate than the cities.

Economist Harry Johnson has pointed out that many countries have a "preference for industrialization" and are willing (in international tariff-bargaining sessions) to disregard their comparative advantage in raw-material production in order to keep a wall of tariff protection around their emerging manufacturing industries. Johnson argues that it is not for economists to say that this preference is irrational or that the new countries could get their man-

ufactured goods cheaper if they imported them: a national aim is a national aim, even if it is "noneconomic."

In all such cases, subsidies rather than tariffs seem called for. A tariff is simply a rather indirect and clumsy form of subsidy that draws attention away from the problem.

Do not be left with the impression that the noneconomic arguments are generally favorable to tariffs. Any Member of Parliament who has gone on a foreign junket knows the serious harm done to Canada's reputation abroad by her capricious and discriminating barriers against the products of certain countries. And nothing is so detrimental to Canadian popularity abroad as our reputation for being a high-tariff country. Foreigners are convinced that as soon as they threaten domestic producers, we will clamp down with quotas and tariffs even though the consumer must pay higher prices at home. So it is to our political interest to resist many of the pressures that make for restrictions on international trade.

GROSSLY FALLACIOUS ARGUMENTS FOR TARIFF

KEEPING MONEY IN THE COUNTRY

To Abraham Lincoln has been attributed the remark, "I don't know much about the tariff. But I do know that when I buy a coat from England, I have the coat and England has the money. But when I buy a coat in America, I have the coat and America has the money."

There is no evidence that he ever actually said this; but it does represent an age-old fallacy typical of the so-called "mercantilistic" writers of the seventeenth and eighteenth centuries who preceded Adam Smith. They considered a country lucky which *gave away* more goods than it received, because such a "favorable" (!) balance of trade meant that gold would flow into the country in question to pay for its export surplus.

In this day and age it should be unnecessary to labor the point that, while an increased amount of money in the hands of one person will make *him* better off, doubling the money in the hands of everybody in a full-employment economy will only serve to raise prices. Unless the single individual is a demented miser like King Midas, the money makes him better off, not for its own sake, but for what it will buy or bid away from other individuals. For society as a whole, once full employment is reached, new money cannot hope to buy any new goods.[1]

A TARIFF FOR HIGHER MONEY WAGES

Today it is agreed that extreme protection can raise prices and attract gold or international reserves into one country, if all other countries do not retaliate with tariffs. The tariff may even increase *money* wages; but it will tend to increase the cost of living by more than the increase in money wages, so that *real* wages will fall as labor becomes less productive. It is simply not the case that our general living standards can be raised by protecting every domestic industry threatened by cheaper imports.[2]

One could go on endlessly giving examples of protectionist fallacies that every thoughtful person can explode in a minute by subjecting them to analysis. This does not mean that such crude fallacies can be dismissed as unimportant. Actually, they are most important of all in shaping legislation, the other, fancier arguments simply being used as window dressing.

TARIFFS FOR SPECIAL GROUPS AND REGIONS.

The single most important source of support for a protective tariff is the people who think they are protected. They include not only businessmen, but—more important politically—organized labor, civic governments, provincial governments, regional planners, and all persons who wish to preserve the local or regional economic base. These are the power base of the so-called "interest groups" who prevent Parliament from allowing the erosion of the protective tariff.

Sometimes this motivation is embodied in the powerful pressure groups that flock to Ottawa to back a tariff application or fight a tariff reduction. They explicitly acknowledge that a tariff on their products will help *them*, whatever its effect on total production and consumption. In the nineteenth century, Ottawa was very receptive to tariff suggestions. Today its resistance has stiffened somewhat, and lobbies are maintained in the capital to drum up enthusiasm for the good old cloth, chemical or buttonhook industry. But these lobbyists are only the spokesmen. Millions of voters also believe they have a vested interest in our high-tariff policy.

Economically the case for freer trade may be strong, but politically the case for protection tends to exert undue pressure. Why? Because *freer trade helps everybody a little,* while *protection helps a few people a lot.* Does it matter politically that the bad points of protection outweigh the good? Not if those few who benefit from protection (or who are kept by protection from suffering harm) are politically active in pressing for their cause. It is much harder to organize the masses of consumers and producers to agitate for the even larger gains that they get from an efficient pattern of national specialization and trade. If political votes were in exact proportion to *total* economic benefit, every country would selfishly legislate most of its tariffs out of existence.

SOME LESS OBVIOUS FALLACIES

A TARIFF FOR REVENUE

First, there is the claim that the tariff should be used to raise government tax revenue. Actually, a customs duty on imports is only one form of regressive sales tax, and a rather bad one. A customs duty or tariff is especially bad because it draws economic resources away from their best uses. If the people who advance the revenue argument were really sincere, they would advocate an excise tax that would *also* fall on domestic production. (Canada has a few "excise duties" that do apply to both imported and home-produced goods, but they are supplemented by additional customs duties on imports.) Such a combined excise-and-tariff provides no protection at all.

For emerging countries with ill-developed tax-collection machinery it is often argued that a customs duty is the only available source of revenue. Most of the Commonwealth countries made their start by depending on customs and even today Canada gets about 7 per cent of all public revenue from tariffs (10 per cent of federal revenue). This argument is obviously most relevant when a country has just one port of entry, where all the trade can be observed and taxed. But it has little to do with an argument for tariff protection, for a prohibitively high tariff that kept

---

[1] Of course, the gold might be spent abroad. But this perfectly sensible way of improving welfare by importing was precisely what the mercantilist "bullionists" were arguing against.

[2] See Chapter 34's discussion of comparative advantage and effects of a tariff.

out all imports would collect no revenue at all! (In 1890, the U.S. Congress found itself with a surplus of tax revenue over expenditure. It met the problem of excessive tariff revenues, not by lowering tariff rates, but by *raising them high* enough to reduce the total of revenue collected.)

COMPETITION FROM CHEAP FOREIGN LABOR

A second argument has always carried immense weight in every industrialized country. In Canada it has been put forward both by industry and by trade unions. According to its usual version, "If we let in goods produced by cheap pauper foreign labor —by Chinese coolies who live on a few cents' worth of rice per day or by low-paid Japanese textile workers—then the higher standard of living of Canadian workers cannot be maintained." So stated, the argument cannot stand up.

We have seen that trade is mutually profitable even if one country can produce every good more cheaply in terms of resources than the other. The important thing is comparative advantage, not absolute advantage. In the last analysis, trade boils down to two-sided barter. One country cannot indefinitely undersell the other in every line of merchandise.

Earlier we showed that full employment at home need not depend in the long run on foreign trade. If, then, everyone in this country remains fully employed at his most suitable occupation, is it not to *our selfish advantage* for the workers of other countries to be willing to work for very little?

To put the matter another way: The comparative-cost doctrine shows that we benefit most by trading with countries of the Far East or the tropics which are *very different* from ours, rather than with countries such as England or Germany which have an industrial economy like our own![3] Against the pauper-labor argument, there is the clinching fact that the analysis of comparative advantage showed that absolute wage levels had nothing to do with the long-run increase in national income that resulted from trade.

So much from a theoretical point of view. If we turn to the real world, we find the arguments to be

---

[3] This argument must be qualified and amplified. Backward countries, so poor that they have little real purchasing power with which to import, at best can export little to us. Most trade today is between industrialized countries. As a backward country advances industrially, it buys more from industrial countries, not less; but perhaps not proportionately more, and perhaps there is *less consumer's surplus from trade* accruing to both parties.

even more incorrect. Canadian workers beg for tariffs, saying, "protect us from the 'unfair competition' of high-paid efficient American workers who have skill and machinery far better than our own." The rest of the world lives in fear of competition from American mass-production industries. The English protectionist claims that the American worker in Bridgeport, Connecticut, who is paid $6.00 per hour is more than three times as efficient as the English worker who gets paid $2.00 an hour. This is perhaps an overstatement, but it is close to the important truth.

High North American real wages come from high efficiency, not from tariff protection. Such high wages do not handicap us in competing with foreign workers.

A TARIFF TO RAISE WAGE SHARE

Thus far we have had nothing but adverse criticism for the "cheap pauper foreign labor" tariff argument. To be objective—and without objectivity there can be no science—we must admit that it may have the following iota of possible truth. The Ohlin proposition in the Appendix to the preceding chapter suggested that free trade in goods may serve as a partial substitute for the movement of factors of production from countries where they are plentiful to countries where they are scarce. Thus North American importing of Europe's labor-intensive commodities, such as clothing, is a partial substitute for the immigration of European labor to North America. This implies that relative labor scarcity on this continent could be alleviated by our international specialization in labor-economizing products and that real wages here might actually *fall* under conditions of free trade. Real national product would go up, but the relative and absolute share of labor might go down.

Although admitting this as a possibility, most economists believe its grain of truth for a typical country is outweighed by more realistic considerations. No doubt immobile laborers such as textile or furniture workers might be hurt by removing a tariff or quota. But since labor is such an important and flexible factor of production, it seems likely that other laborers would gain from expanded trade more than those hurt would lose. Labor as a whole would presumably in the long run share in the increased GNP from trade.

Some Canadian economists have made serious investigations of the applicability of the Ohlin idea to Canada's tariff. Admitting that the tariff diverts Canadian capital and labor to low-productivity industries (compared to the comparatively advantageous export industries), they argue that Ontario and Quebec wage rates are higher than they would be if Canada specialized in low-labor industries such as pulp, mining, and wheat, and imported automobiles, furniture, and cloth.

Although admitting this as a theoretical possibility, most economists deny that it is actually true. Its validity depends upon the facts in each case. It is true that the pulp industry uses (creates a demand for) fewer workers than the protected automobile industry, per dollar of product. But it also demands *more* labor than the protected chemical, oil-refining, or smelting industries. Without finer measurement, no tariff policy conclusion can be reached. It seems likely that with labor such an important, flexible, and mobile factor of production, the losses from free trade suffered by some workers would be more than offset by the gains of others and of the same workers in new jobs.

In the mid-1950s, a new element was added to the debate. Pointing to Canada's easy-immigration policy, economists like Toronto's John Dales argued that tariffs do not raise wages but simply create more jobs that attract more immigrants. Thus the tariff maintains the cost of living above its international level,[4] but immigration prevents the Ohlin real-wage effect from emerging. The result is more industry and population than would exist if there were free trade: not higher per capita real incomes or real wages.[5]

The topic is still under discussion among economists, especially in Canada and Australia. The consensus so far is that while Ohlin may be correct that protection of labor-using industries may raise the percentage of the GNP going to wages, this rise may be cancelled out by the fall in the GNP per capita, in which labor shares.

A TARIFF FOR RETALIATION Some people admit that a world of free trade would be preferable

[4] In 1956, John H. Young estimated for the Royal Commission on Canada's Economic Prospects that Canadians paid about 3 1/2 to 4 per cent more for their gross private expenditure than they need have if they had bought goods at world price levels. This amounted to about 1 billion dollars at that time. (*Canadian Commercial Policy*, Ottawa, 1957.)

[5] John H. Dales' argument in *The Protective Tariff in Canada's Development*. It involves an extension of similar hypotheses by Queen's University Principal W. A. Mackintosh in the 1930s and by Manitoba's Clarence Barber in the *Canadian Journal of Economics and Political Science* in 1955.

to a world of tariffs; but they say that so long as other countries are so foolish or so wicked as to pass restrictive tariff legislation, there is nothing that we can do but follow suit in self-defense.

Actually, however, a tariff is much like an increase in transportation costs. If other countries were foolish enough to let their roads go to ruin, would it pay us to chop holes in ours? The answer is, No. Analogously, if other countries hurt us and themselves by passing tariffs, we should not add to our own hurt by passing a tariff.

To make sure that you grasp the point that our tariff harms us as well as the foreigner, you should realize that there are four gains when a trade-agreements program succeeds in getting another country and ourselves to lower tariffs reciprocally. The other country's tariff reduction bestows gains (a) on us and (b) on them. Our tariff reduction adds two more gains: (c) for ourselves and (d) for them.

Therefore the only possible sense in the argument that we should retaliate when a foreign country raises tariffs is that our threat of retaliation may deter them from raising tariffs, and our promise to reduce tariffs may persuade them to reduce theirs. This would justify our passing an occasional tariff as a bluff, but if our bluffs do not work, we should give them up.

Most realistic students of political science infer from historical studies that retaliatory tariffs usually lead other nations to raise theirs still higher and are rarely an effective bargaining weapon for multilateral tariff reduction. And even in the smaller forum of Canadian-U.S. tariff bargaining, it is difficult to show that the occasional spiteful "retaliatory" tariffs had much to do with the subsequent hauling down of tariff barriers. On the other hand, many economists argue that the "Reciprocity" plea, the offer to cut tariffs in return for desired cuts by the other country, has usually met sympathetic (though not always effective) responses.

THE "SCIENTIFIC" TARIFF This is one of the most insidious arguments for a tariff; insidious because it often sounds plausible and moderate but, if taken literally, would mean the end to all trade! According to its usual form, tariffs should be passed to "equalize the cost of production at home and abroad." Chapter 34 showed all the advantage from trade to rest on *differences* in cost or advantage. If tariffs were passed raising the costs of imports to that of the highest home producer, no goods would come in at all.[6]

There is nothing scientific about such a tariff. It is a grave reflection on the economic literacy of the Canadian people that this least defensible of all protectionist arguments is still sometimes pleaded. We are fortunate that it has not been taken as seriously by Canadian governments as it has by the U.S. Congress, which even wrote it into law upon occasion.

KEEPING AN INDUSTRY INTACT, AND DECLINING REGIONS
According to this view, a country should keep tariffs high enough to prevent an industry from having to go out of business entirely, though low enough to allow "some" imports in. It is therefore like some of the "noneconomic" arguments in favor of tariffs—those to do with keeping defense industries going as a matter of military preparedness. (The U.S. Congress for example has decided that when imports become so large that the survival of a home industry is in danger, it will be declared to be at the "peril point," and tariffs may be increased, or quotas tightened, to protect it from further decline.)

This argument sounds moderate. If home industries have many firms, some with high costs and some with lower costs, the tariff that keeps the industry intact may in fact only have to be high enough to protect one or two uneconomic plants; no more. The economist dislikes it, not for the relatively small cost that it may impose on consumers, but because its basic philosophy runs completely counter to the economic theory of comparative advantage. Our nation gains from trade by *specializing*, i.e., by giving up certain activities and moving their resources into other industries in which we have a greater comparative advantage. The industries in which we have strong comparative disadvantage should never have come into existence. And suppose an industry formerly had a comparative advantage but has lost it —because other industries have had greater technological improvements, because the domestic factors it uses have become more expensive through becoming more valuable elsewhere, because factors for that industry have become relatively cheaper abroad, or for any other reason. Then this industry *ought* to be killed off by the competition of our more productive industries. It ought to reach and pass the peril point.

This sounds ruthless indeed. No industry willingly dies; no region gladly undergoes conversion to new factor uses. In truth, any field that is imperiled is probably already a sick industry with a past history of suffering. So the already weak industry and region feels it is being singled out to carry the burden of getting the country into a more productive configuration.

The best plan, then, is to adopt policies that will aid the factors of production to be used efficiently (instead of being forced on consumers who would rather buy imports). In some regions this is easy enough. For several years Canada has had "designated areas," which, like Britain's development areas, consist of euphemistically named depressed regions. The government's policy is to attract new industries to these areas, so that they will fill the employment positions once occupied by the dying industries. To do this, it gives income-tax rebates, accelerated-depreciation tax allowances, or outright subsidies. For example, at the beginning of 1971, the federal government promised $30,000 for each new job created by industry in certain designated areas.

However, these rehabilitation or redevelopment programs have their drawbacks. Many communities and regions that formerly sold to the Canadian market (or were exporting regions) are ill-adapted to the location of new industries. Even if government subsidies tempt new factories, the fact remains that out-of-the-way locations will have permanently high costs. Thus subsidies may have to be perpetual (even if hidden in perpetual tax remissions or enforced low freight rates that are covered by high freight rates on other lines of the railways); or local workers may have to agree to perpetually low wages; or the new industries will soon become sick in their turn.

Official opinion now is beginning to accept the view that the best thing that can be done for some of these regions is to help them to close down, giving the vested factors time to move. On the one hand, if tariffs are to be removed immediately, government programs may be set up to retrain workers, lend or

---

[6] With nonconstant costs the scientific-tariff formula is indeterminate. A zero tariff may equalize foreign costs with those of our few most efficient producers; an almost prohibitive tariff equalize with our high-cost producers. Where can one scientifically draw the line?

give them a moving allowance, help them to find new houses and jobs in active regions, and pay them well for their old properties.[7] On the other hand, the tariff reduction can take place gradually, in step with retraining and other policies designed to speed the transition and spread the burden more widely. (Canada has so far considered only the automobile tariff in this way; but the U.S. 1962 Trade Act specifically links general tariff reductions with location and mobility concessions.)

Much of what is said in the last two paragraphs applies to any declining industry or region, regardless of whether import competition is the source of the decline. Fortunately, full employment and rapid over-all growth help in the task of transferring factors to new industries and products. Although jobs and earnings falter in the buggy industry, the buoyant automobile industry clamors for skilled workers. Thus it is clear that policies that encourage strong export industries and high domestic demand (through the skillful use of monetary and fiscal weapons) will tend to clear up much of the depressed-region or sick-industry problem automatically. Having adopted such policies, the nation can with good conscience strive for the increase in real income made possible by specialization—and re-specialization—according to the principles of comparative advantage. Striving to "keep industries intact" is a negation of this goal.

THE "FOREIGNER WILL PAY," OR TERMS-OF-TRADE-ARGUMENTS[8]

After dealing with fallacious tariff arguments, we find it refreshing to come now to a possibly valid one

—which hopes tariffs will shift the terms of trade against the foreigner. Indeed, it is about the only argument that would be valid even under static competitive conditions, and it goes back 150 years to John Stuart Mill. Paradoxically, valid arguments for protection seem mostly to have come from free traders, not from protectionists!

If the United States puts a tariff on rubber, Mill would argue, that will raise the price in the States over its price abroad. But with U.S. demand now curtailed, and as the United States is an important demander of rubber, the price abroad will be bid down. So part of the tariff really falls on the foreigner. (Show that a smaller country, like Canada, could not use this argument, since it cannot budge world prices.)

In summary, a judicious tariff might improve an important country's terms of trade (defined as the ratio of her export to her import prices).

But here is a warning. *Prohibitive* tariffs, which suit the protectionist who really is against all trade, could never be justified by this terms-of-trade argument. Why? Because killing off *all* trade would kill off all the advantage you get from shifting the terms of trade in your favor. Mill and modern economists therefore insist that the "optimal tariff" is one just large enough to improve your terms of trade and just small enough to keep your physical exchange of imports and exports at the level most favorable to your own country.

Most economists think that all this would imply rather small tariff rates for most countries. And they hasten to point out that when all nations pursue such terms-of-trade tariff policies, the world pattern of production and exchange becomes less efficient. So most (if not all) nations tend to end up worse off under such beggar-my-neighbor policies.

ARGUMENTS FOR PROTECTION UNDER DYNAMIC CONDITIONS

At last we are arriving at a point in the protection versus free-trade debate where those in favor of tariffs can begin to score some weighty points. Three important arguments fall in this category: (a) that a tariff may help to reduce unemployment, (b) that tariffs may create diversified industries more im-

---

[7] A few years ago, economists who urged mobility-creating programs were told that they were politically impossible; local politicians would always oppose measures that reduced their local electorate, even if each member of the departing labor force was benefited. This resistance still exists. But the federal Manpower, Industry, and Forestry departments now have in hand programs that make up a package of the kind mentioned in the text; and provincial governments are cooperating.

[8] The argument is exactly like that of a domestic monopolist who raises his price above marginal cost but does not raise it sky-high, instead stopping where $MR = MC$. It was anticipated in Chapter 33, Chapter 34 (footnote 9), and Chapter 34's Appendix. Advanced texts sometimes call this optimal tariff a "scientific" tariff. But don't confuse this with the cost-equalizing tariffs.

mune to risk, and (c) that temporary tariff protection for an "infant industry" with growth potentialities may be desirable.

TARIFFS AND UNEMPLOYMENT Historically, one of the strongest arguments for protection has been the desire to make or preserve jobs. Earlier we discussed the favorable multiplier effects of exports and foreign investment on jobs and domestic spending, and also the unfavorable "leakage" effects of imports. So beggar-my-neighbor high-tariff policy might increase employment in the short run before other nations retaliated.

But can we accept such measures as a valid part of our national full-employment program? Is not freer trade much like a scientific discovery of new machinery and methods? Both represent increases in our *potentially producible* level of real national output; but either *might* in the short run tend to lower our actual *attained* level of output and employment. And yet, there is no need, in either the short or the long run, to tolerate a gap between actual and potentially producible product, for that represents an unnecessary frittering away of the gains from progress.

How, then, do we meet the arguments relating unemployment to too low tariffs? We refute these arguments just as we refute arguments concerning "technological unemployment." We point out the existence of domestic monetary, foreign-exchange-rate, and fiscal policies that can successfully *and efficiently* solve the problem of economic slump. (Recall Part Two's macroeconomics.) If workers displaced by imports can find other jobs in a buoyant labor market, this protection plea loses its force.

Once again, we realize how vitally important it is to insist on rational macroeconomic management that employs the tools of monetary and fiscal analysis to create the favorable environment for stability and growth which is vitally necessary if the classical principles of economics are to be relevant and valid.

A further point needs emphasis. Today we include in a rational program the requirement that the foreign exchange rate not be a disequilibrium one. If the dollar parity represents "overvaluation," unemployment may result (as was shown in Chapter 33's Appendix). Of course, a tariff might work a little to offset such an overvaluation. But it is much more efficient—and equitable too—to lower the exchange rate rather than to rely on quotas, tariffs, and exchange controls.[9]

DIVERSIFICATION TO REDUCE TERMS-OF-TRADE RISK Comparative advantage might tell a country to specialize completely on one good or a few goods. So she is to put all her eggs in one basket. But then what will happen if the prices of those goods drop? Or if her export prices oscillate? She will find such variations in her terms of trade very destabilizing to her real income; and she may be left with an industry which has become permanently unprofitable.

To avoid the perils of "monoculture," Latin American economists advise the introduction of tariffs. Just as an investor in securities will diversify to reduce risk rather than keeping all his eggs in one basket, so a country is to use tariffs to induce diversification.

This argument certainly deserves careful examination. Note though that it assumes private citizens are neglecting to take account of the riskiness in future prices of the industries they put their money and labor skills into. This argument has to assume that the government is better informed than private investors, or at least that the government is more far-seeing than private investors in taking account of the future perils of price drops and price gyrations. If the future risks are genuine and are foreseen by private investors, those investors will not be misled by temporarily high profits into investing in these few industries; in truth, such industries will not then have a genuine long-run comparative advantage, and there will be no effective tendency to specialize in them.[10]

At this point a related argument for tariffs should be mentioned. Dr. Raúl Prebisch, long adviser to the U.N.'s Economic Commission for Latin America, argued that the *long-run terms of trade are always shifting against agricultural products*. So nations that

---

[9] If money wage rates are generally too high, the dollar may be "overvalued". Chapter 36 shows this could call for a new exchange-rate parity.

[10] Suppose private employers do foresee the risk, but think they can fire workers when export prices drop, thereby throwing the burden of the unemployed on the state. Then we face a genuine so-called "external diseconomy," which might justify government intervention in the form of tariffs, quotas, or other programs. Also, recall the limited conditions under which the "foreigner will pay" argument has terms-of-trade validity.

specialize in them are betting on the wrong horse. He argued that their governments should instead impose tariffs aimed at building up manufacturing industries whose future terms of trade would be more favorable. Against this argument is the following: If past and future reductions in food prices are matched by even greater drops in real food costs, because agriculture undergoes great technological improvements, then long-run comparative advantage might still validly tell a nation to specialize in food to improve its real income or, in other cases, to minimize its losses. (See Chapter 36.)

This argument is really a debate about what the *future* comparative advantage of the countries in question will be. To the degree that governments are smarter than private investors in discerning trends threatening to the terms of trade, a valid case can be made for their interfering with free-market forces. But if government is wrong in its comparative-advantage forecasts, the loss in real income to the nation can become very considerable, and the nation may find its rate of development slowed down.

TARIFFS FOR "INFANT INDUSTRIES"

Alexander Hamilton, in his famous "Report on Manufactures," raised this argument. It is also associated with the name of a nineteenth-century German economist, Friedrich List, and it has received the cautious blessing of John Stuart Mill, Alfred Marshall, the late Professor Frank W. Taussig, and some orthodox economists.

According to this doctrine, there are activities in which a country would really have a comparative advantage, *if only it could get them started*. If confronted with foreign competition, such infant industries are not able to weather the initial period of experimentation and financial stress; but given a breathing space, they can be expected to develop economies of mass production and the technological efficiency typical of many modern processes. Although protection will at first raise prices to the consumer, once the industry grows up it will be so efficient that cost and price will actually have fallen. If the benefit to consumers at that late date would be enough to more than make up for the higher prices during the period of protection, a tariff is justified.

There is certainly something to this, at least as a possibility. Historical studies have turned up some genuine cases of infant industries that grew up to

stand on their own feet; but history reveals even more cases of the contrary—of perpetual infants!

Unfortunately for the practical importance of this argument, infant industries cannot swing many votes. It is not they who tend to receive protection from tariffs, but rather the old and powerful vested interests who have never shed their diapers for these many years.

THE "YOUNG-ECONOMY" ARGUMENT The infant-industry argument probably had more validity for Canada as it was in 1867-1897 than it has today.[11] Rather than lobbying for tariffs to protect it in its "infancy," any industry that now foresees eventual tariff-free low-cost mass production can more easily borrow from a receptive capital market to get the breathing space, working capital, and experience it needs. And the argument has more validity for present-day underdeveloped nations than for those which have already experienced the transition from an agricultural to an industrial way of life. In a sense, such nations are still asleep; they cannot be said to be truly in equilibrium. All over the world, farmers seem to earn less than industrial workers. Consequently, there is everywhere a relative growth of industry and a decline of agriculture. Populations migrate cityward, but this movement is not rapid enough to achieve an equilibrium of earnings and productivity. A strong case can be made for using moderate protection to accelerate these economically desirable long-run trends. Such a defense of protection might better be called a "young-economy" rather than an infant-industry argument.

One final word: Please note that the infant-industry or young-economy arguments are not contradictory to the principle of comparative advantage. On the contrary, their validity rests upon the presumption of an induced, dynamic shift of the production-possibility frontier outward and in the direction of a *new* comparative advantage in the lines needing *temporary* protection.

---

[11] John H. Young, in his book on *Canadian Commercial Policy*, has reminded us that earlier Canadian politicians were usually in the habit of praising the tendency of a high-tariff policy to make a country self-sufficient; or as John A. Macdonald put it, "a union in interest, a union in trade, and a union in feeling." Although it was also hoped that the tariffs proposed in 1879 would help in "blasting a way into the markets of the world" (see Fig. 35-1), the Canadian "National Policy" associated with the Macdonald governments in fact rarely made use of any version of the infant-industry argument.

CONCLUSION

While this chapter has usually spoken of tariffs, almost everything said would apply equally well to any other impediments to trade. Thus, quotas have all the bad effects of tariffs, and often quotas are even more restrictive.

Finally, we should mention the so-called "invisible tariff." In many countries—and Canada is no exception—the complicated administration of the customs can be as bad as the monetary duty that has to be paid. If an importer's shipments are unduly delayed or if a foreigner's exports to us are refused admittance for complicated reasons of health or of failure to comply with arbitrary regulations, then such red tape can be as harmful to trade as outright tariffs or quotas. Work toward simplification of customs administration still has a long way to go.

This completes our discussion of the tariff controversy. No fair-minded reader who takes the trouble to think the matter through can fail to see how shallow are most of the economic arguments for tariff protection. The only serious exception is the infant-industry or young-economy argument.

It is not surprising, therefore, that economists—who are supposed to agree on almost nothing—have been overwhelmingly in favor of steps to lower trade barriers. It has even been suggested that this enthusiasm alone is responsible for the disregard of their recommendations by Canadian statesmen, the "great Canadian noneconomists" as one writer has ruefully called them. In Canada, decisions have been particularly hard, for "noneconomic objectives" aimed at building a Canadian nation at almost any cost have been thought to run counter to free-trade principles. Economists are not agreed that the objectives are contradictory. (Is it a condition of nationhood that all Canadians drink Canadian apple juice? Is the United States less a nation now that it imports European transformers and Japanese transistors?) However, their stronger pleas have been unattractive to the politicians.

Thus the "National Policy" to protect Canadian manufacturing prevailed over the "Reciprocity" program to negotiate reciprocal tariff reductions, all the way to zero tariffs, with the United States and other countries. Sir Wilfrid Laurier tried Reciprocity with the United States on the electorate in 1911, and lost his majority to Sir Robert Borden. And in the 1920s

and 1930s, tariff reduction moved backward as much as forward. But in the late 1930s Canada negotiated a reciprocal trade agreement with the United States; in the 1940s she eventually joined the General Agreement on Tariffs and Trade (GATT); and major Canadian political parties have from time to time proposed, very tentatively, free trade with the European Common Market, with the Commonwealth countries and the Common Market, with the United States and, recently, with the "North Atlantic" countries.

Meanwhile, progress is being made. First, we had free trade with the United States in farm equipment. Second, the more controversial automobile agreement has opened the U.S. market to some Canadian exports.[12]

In the 1960s, Canada participated in the "Kennedy Round" of tariff reductions at the GATT (General Agreement on Tariffs and Trade), which were touched off by the Kennedy Trade Expansion Act of 1962. The U.S. administration was authorized to reduce existing U.S. tariffs by 50 per cent in reciprocal negotiations. From 1963 to 1967, almost 50 countries participated in the subsequent bargaining, and it is said that tariff cuts were made on a total of 45 billion dollars of trade.

The European Common Market, Britain, Japan, and the United States all made substantial reductions, thus assisting the entry of the products of Canada and other exporters into these markets. Most participants bargained about "linear" or equal percentage-point reduction on all tariffs. But Canada had little to gain from tariff reduction by countries that imported our raw materials on which tariffs were already low, and so instead she offered certain specific tariff reductions in return for specific concessions by our customers. This approach opened up some markets to Canadian exporters (and to their rivals in other exporting nations). On manufactured

---

[12] The automobile agreement is too involved to be explained here. Roughly speaking, it encourages Canadian manufacturers to make parts for export by mass production, by allowing them to import for sale in Canada a high value of fully manufactured American cars or parts, duty-free. With some misgivings, the United States has agreed to remit duties on the imports of such Canadian-made parts. The chief popular criticism has been that although Canadian car manufacturers now pay less duty on imports, they have not been forced to cut their prices. The industry explains that it needs the extra earnings to cover the extra investment in facilities.

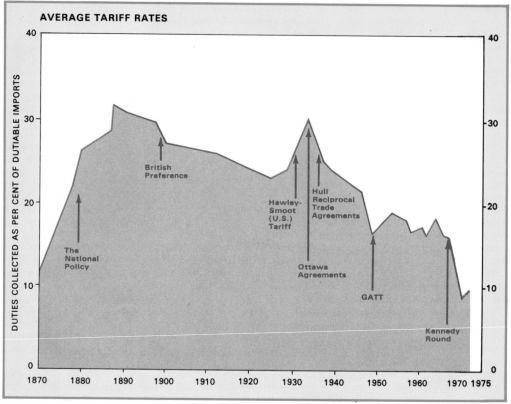

FIG. 35-1. Tariffs reflect national policy and international attitudes.
After waves of tariff protection under the National Policy in the 1890s and in the Great Depression of the 1930s, Canada, like other Western nations, has now reduced the general level of her tariff rates. (Sources: John Young, *Canadian Commercial Policy: Canada Year Book.*)

goods, Canada reduced percentage rates modestly by between 2 1/2 to 5 per cent.[13]

Figure 35-1 indicates that, measured by the burden on dutiable imports, Canada has some way to go to achieve the standing of a low-tariff nation. But concessions and participation in the Kennedy Round all suggested that, perhaps in spite of the arguments given by economists, Canada was slowly moving in the general direction of tariff reduction.

A topic which has captured a lot more public interest than the tariff is foreign ownership. The Appendix to this chapter addresses this important issue.

SUMMARY

1 The case for freer trade rests upon the increased productivity that international specialization, according to the law of comparative advantage, makes possible. Higher world production is made possible, and all countries can have higher standards of living. Trade between countries with different standards of living is especially profitable.

---

[13] Canada completed those tariff cuts in 1969, ahead of schedule. By 1972, all participant nations had completed most scheduled reductions with European and U.S. tariffs at a lower percentage rate than those of Canada.

2 Most arguments for tariff protection are simply rationalizations for special benefits to particular pressure groups and do not stand up under analysis.

3 An exception to the law of comparative advantage is provided by the need to favor certain uneconomical lines of activity for reasons of national defense. Perhaps outright government subsidies would be better in such cases.

4 The only other exception of any practical importance in a full-employment economy[14] is provided by the case of infant industries or young economies that need temporary protection in order to realize their true long-run comparative advantages. To the degree that public planning for development can discern long-run trends better than the free market can, trade interventions to spur industrialization might turn out to be beneficial.

   In a Canadian context, reducing tariffs often raises the fear of increased foreign control over the Canadian economy. The appendix to this chapter analyses the foreign ownership question.

CONCEPTS FOR REVIEW

tariff protection, quota
grossly fallacious arguments
higher home market and wage
national-defense arguments
subsidy versus tariff or quota
scientific cost-equalizing

terms-of-trade shifts
unemployment and tariffs
infant industry and young
  economy
GATT and Kennedy Rounds
legal or voluntary quotas

QUESTIONS FOR DISCUSSION

1. What do you think is the single most favorable argument for a tariff or quota?

2. List fallacious tariff arguments. Weigh pros and cons. (Apply to, say, steel.)

3. Comment critically on the infant-industry and young-economy arguments. What is their relation to comparative advantage?

4. Mention some noneconomic considerations relevant to tariffs.

5. Relate the declining-region and "scientific tariff" arguments to comparative-advantage theory.

6. Suppose labor productivity grows mightily abroad, and Canadian goods start to be undersold in every line. Suppose that a mixed economy like ours has sticky wage rates. Suppose devaluation of the dollar is not feasible. Show that new tariffs might be a stopgap measure.

7. *Extra-credit problem:* To understand the fact that the foreigner can be made to pay part of a tariff, go back to linen imports in Fig. 34-3(b): Suppose a new tariff lowers the black arrows of imports shown there. Can you see that the new equilibrium position must involve lower price of linen there? So America is helped by the tariff to buy a bit more cheaply.

---

[14] The "foreigner will pay" argument is more interesting theoretically than in practice. Note that as suggested in Chapter 33 a country that has an over-valued currency will hear many such exaggerated pleas for blockages to international trade.

Appendix: Foreign Ownership of Canadian Industry and the Multinational Corporation

Foreign ownership is one economic issue about which the Canadian public has an opinion. Unlike tariff, inflation, or unemployment policy, whether to control foreign ownership is not a difficult subject to the average citizen. It is seen, with some accuracy, as one aspect of national independence. Furthermore, even the most vehement opponent of foreign ownership knows that to do something about it would have costs—of slackening growth and employment. This appendix provides some facts and some analysis.[1]

The state of the discussion today is something like this. Many Canadians are employed by foreign-owned firms, especially in the manufacturing, mining and oil and gas industries. They, their unions and their governments deplore talk that might lead to their own jobs being threatened. Many other people are opposed to a large foreign presence in the Canadian economy, especially an American presence. Between these two parties the issue is often indistinct, but it can be sharpened as follows:

"Would the benefits to Canadians of reducing foreign ownership exceed the costs?"

We shall see that the causes of foreign ownership are part of a phenomenal rise in international *direct investment* everywhere. Its impact on Canadians depends on region and industry. Its disadvantages are often beyond the scope of economic analysis, but will be sketched below. Governments are moving to reduce the speed of foreign ownership, but slowly.

COSTS. Comparing the gains and costs of foreign ownership is difficult because the political decision must give weight both to some people who resent and fear foreign control and the multinational corporation, and to people who do not mind it (and even some who would like to see more of it).

To the former, the costs of foreign ownership are direct and high. To them the mere fact that Americans, Japanese and others have *power* over large fractions of our mining, energy, communications and manufacturing sectors is all that matters. They support policies that will reduce this power—regardless of cost. They are less interested in how this power has been used, as revealed, for example by the "performance" of foreign controlled firms, in providing secure jobs, paying interest and taxes, expanding the country's exports, or providing customers with a high quality of goods. Their dislike of this power being in the hands of non-Canadians is a value judgement that must be respected, just as feelings about other aspects of national—or provincial—self determination and autonomy are respected.

The relationship of all this to political ideas has several dimensions. First, the left wing in Canadian politics tends to be more opposed to foreign control than the right wing, although it should be added that many Canadian businessmen at all levels agree with the mildly nationalistic platform of the Conservative party and the editorial opinions of, say, the *Financial Post* in favour of greater protection of Canadian enterprise, financial markets, trade unions and research policies from foreign control (or competition!).

Second, the opposition to foreign control and ownership is directed more against the U.S. than Japanese or European investors in Canada. This echoes both anti-American-imperialist ideas in many countries, and anti-Viet-Nam partisanship.

Third, the opposition to American industrial power in Canada reflects a fear that foreign dollars control Canadian politicians, voters, or both. This can arise from diverse sources: contributions to candidate or party election funds, running candidates, or simply consisting of well-informed, well-organized, persistent sources of pressure, or advice. Thus it has been said that the presence of foreign ownership in the B.C. pulp industry, the Alberta oil industry, the Manitoba mining industry, several Ontario and Quebec manufacturing industries (textiles, automobiles, publishing) and raw materials industries in maritime provinces have led these provinces' governments to promote favourable legislation. Such claims obviously need careful verification: "compared to what?" Compared to their policies if the ownership had been Canadian but outside the province? to their policies if there had been no industry? or if the ownership had been local? Which is the proper comparison?

A corollary to this third point is that in regions where industry is dominated by foreign firms, the governmental process may suffer from the absence of alternative spokesmen for business points of view who are visible, Canadian and politically responsive.

These political ideas play an extremely important part in the Canadian debate about foreign industrial power, and lie behind many value judgements about the desirability of Canadian economic independence policies. But this is not the book to analyze them or predict their influence. Instead the following paragraphs present a brief guide to the reader who wishes to go beyond the assertions about power and politics mentioned above, and is looking to economics for answers to such questions as why there is foreign ownership and how it changes what might otherwise be.

THEORY OF FOREIGN INVESTMENT

Readers are so accustomed to foreign ownership that they neglect to ask themselves where it fits in the theory of international economic relations discussed in this book. Close scrutiny would tell them that it does not fit well. The reason is that international capital mobility, the flow which feeds increased foreign ownership, is generally post-

[1] It should be read in conjunction with this book's discussion of the multinational firm (Chapter 6 and Chapter 26's discussion of mergers). The relation of direct investment and foreign ownership to the balance of payments was discussed in Chapter 33. In addition to the references discussed elsewhere, note particularly Gilles Paquet, ed., *The Multinational Firm and the Nation State*, Toronto: Collier-Macmillan, 1972.

poned for later discussion in more advanced courses. Introductory discussions of international trade, such as Chapter 34's, are based on the law of comparative advantage; and this in turn rests on the assumption that factor supplies of land, labor and capital in each country are *fixed*.

This assumption has been relaxed only in the chapters on the balance of payments (Chapters 33, 36) and on international population migration (Chapter 2). To picture further what is going on when factors are mobile, consider a country's production-possibility curve. Capital inflows cause this curve to shift outward, as with the "growth" curves of Figure 2-5. (So would population immigration.) Unless labor and capital arrive in the same proportions, the slope and curvature of the production-possibility curve will alter as it shifts outward, bringing about relatively increasing returns to the factor that increases least and decreasing returns to the factor that increases most. If labor and capital are fully mobile, each will move to the nations where wages or capital returns are relatively highest, mobility stopping only when production-possibility curves are essentially similar everywhere. If the world's total supplies of labor and capital are not fixed, but are growing, then both factors will tend to flow from the countries where they are being produced and accumulated, to countries where they are more scarce. In brief, wealthy savers in high-income countries will tend to move their capital, in long-term form, to countries where capital formation is slower and the return therefore higher.

DIRECT INVESTMENT. Already, in Chapter 33, we have seen the forms this foreign investment can take: inter-governmental (including aid); private portfolio lending (importing common and preferred shares); and direct investment. Both portfolio and direct investment lead to ownership and control of firms in foreign countries, through gradual acquisition of majority shareholdings, takeovers and mergers, or through starting new firms or branches of those at home. As Chapter 33's cycle of indebtedness showed, capital movements used to take place through portfolio investment: European lenders buying the bonds of foreign governments and private railways. Today this still goes on, but *direct investment* is the new force to be reckoned with. As recently as 1946, foreign portfolio wealth in Canada was 50 percent greater than directly-owned capital, but just twenty years later, with foreign capital quintupled, foreign portfolio wealth was 33 percent *less* than direct.

THE RESULTS

The vast increases in foreign capital inflows have had the results that might be expected. The pattern has been repeated in many countries, but the impact of foreign direct investment is nowhere as striking as Canada.

CAPITAL GROWTH. It is possible that as much as one-third of today's industrial capacity is based on foreign direct investment. That is, it can be argued that, in the absence of this inflow, Canadian industry's equipment would be only two-thirds its present size, or that one-third of today's Canadian industrial labor force would have to migrate elsewhere (or would never have migrated to Canada). This is a maximum estimate, for it is obvious that in the absence of direct investment, Canada could have borrowed at least some of this capital abroad in portfolio form. Both data and assumptions are vague in this area, but to fix ideas, we may assume that if the real capital goods owned by foreigners were to go up in flames, thus reducing both the capital goods with which Canadians worked, and the output of industry, the present average level of consumption of all Canadians might be restored after no more than two years' growth, allowing for capital from new Canadian saving, depreciation allowances, portfolio borrowing abroad; the possibility of using less capital per worker; and the reduced need to pay dividends, minus the increased flow of interest payments, abroad.[2] The calculation is not meant to be taken too seriously as a forecast, but it does illustrate both that Canadian industrial growth (and employer and local income) *does* depend, as every Chamber of Commerce knows, on foreign-owned firms' growth but that it would be possible for Canadian growth, after a serious setback, to resume its previous path.[3]

FOREIGN DOMINANCE BY DOMESTIC INDUSTRIES. Direct investment in Canada is undertaken, mostly, by firms (not individuals). They have a three-way choice: export to Canada, lend to new or existing Canadian firms, or invest directly. Why do so many choose direct investment?

The exporting route has usually been exhausted before they turn to foreign investment. Usually Canada has erected a tariff barrier, a tax obstacle or imposed an import quota, that makes selling from abroad into the Canadian market unsuccessful. Perhaps there is also a transportation barrier, so that the Canadian market must be served from plants near customers.

To understand the remaining choice between portfolio and direct investment, it must be realized that large foreign firms are not so much looking for places to invest

---

[2]This guess germinated from an interesting calculation by John Helliwell and Jillian Broadbent, based on a model by Philip Neher, reported in "National Economic Issues: The View from the West Coast" an issue of *B.C. Studies*, Spring 1972. These UBC economists dealt with all foreign capital, not with direct capital only.

[3]A salutary exercise for the reader is to attempt to analyze how, if foreign investors were shut out, Canada would adjust. Because the marginal efficiency of investment may reflect a greater demand for investment funds than Canadian savers will supply at any GNP below the full-employment/inflation barrier, interest rates in Canada would rise and credit conditions would tighten. Some of the needed inflow of machinery would be financed by exports, especially those made by labor-intensive means. For a full discussion, see the Neher article cited in the previous footnote.

money, as places to employ their accumulated experience in product-development, marketing, financing, shipping, packaging, advertizing and so forth. Thus, although they may sometimes be tempted to buy into an existing Canadian firm, or just to help it with finances, they will more usually choose to start a new firm or subsidiary. This process often starts in Canada or Europe, but it spreads to other countries, and the firm eventually becomes a *multinational enterprise*.

The following table shows that foreign direct investment has been most important in a limited list of domestic industries. Usually they manufacture differentiated products and are tariff-protected and oligopolistic. At the bottom of the table are a set of industries that are owned and controlled in Canada.

Obviously, not all manufacturing industries are foreign controlled. Among these are furniture (19 per cent); food (32 per cent); textiles (40 per cent); and printing and publishing (21 per cent).

FOREIGN DOMINANCE OF RAW-MATERIAL INDUSTRIES.
For many American, Japanese and European firms, the export option does not apply. They are probably in the business of importing raw materials and refining them. Thus they have two motives: (a) to exploit their experience and know-how, as with firms selling domestic products (e.g. Canadian mining companies that operate in the U.S., Ireland and Australia); and (b) to reduce the risks of oligopolistic competition in the procurement of basic supplies by *vertical integration* among mines, mills, smelters and factories (aluminum, iron and oil companies are obvious examples).

The result is that for Canada in 1967-8 the same sources as in the previous table inform us that 75 percent of assets

in petroleum/natural gas industries were foreign owned; 65 percent in mining and smelting and perhaps 35 percent in lumber and pulp and paper. Imperial Oil and Shell, Kaiser and U.S. Steel, Canadian International and Scott paper are obvious examples.

CHARGES AGAINST FOREIGN OWNERSHIP

Listing these six reasons which, alone or in concert, may explain why most of Canada's automobile, appliance, forest-products, mining, food-products, publishing, hotel, and even oil companies are owned and/or controlled by foreign firms does *not* establish that anything is wrong. By now, the debate on the merits and evils of foreign investment, ownership, and control, which has grown from a few murmurs in the early 1950s, sprawls over a very large literature. Not only left-wing philosophers like the NDP's Waffle group, but also middle-of-the-roaders like Walter Gordon and Lester Pearson and more right-wing groups like trade unions and the western branch of the Conservative Party, have complained about the "takeover" of Canadian industry and resources, the "sellout" or "give-away" of Canadian resources. Even to summarize their arguments is difficult. If you are disturbed about this question, read some of the pieces in footnote 4 below before you jump to a conclusion.[4]

The empirical and theoretical objections to foreign ownership are mostly based on the claim that local subsidiaries, having the welfare and profitability of the parent firm as objectives, cannot be expected to serve equally well the aims of the "host" country (e.g. Canada). The dispute about this claim of foreign subsidiaries is on two levels: theory and performance. At one level, there is argument about the acceptability or attractiveness of the *hypothesis* that firms owned abroad behave differently, or

---

Foreign Control of Canadian Industries, Judged by Percentage of Capital Book Value Owned, 1967 and 1968.

Manufacturing	percent
Machinery	72
Tobacco	84
Transport equipment (incl. autos)	87
Rubber producers	93
Petroleum products	99
Chemicals	82
All manufacturing	58
Construction	15
Transportation	9
Communications	1
Public Utilities	3
Wholesale Trade	28
Retail Trade	21
Finance	13

TABLE 35-1
These are industries that sell to Canadian consumers.
(**Source:** *Foreign Direct Investment in Canada,* (**The Gray Report**), Ottawa 1972, Tables 5 and 6.

---

[4]In many respects, U.K. and Australian writers on the economics of the foreign ownership question are well ahead of their Canadian counterparts. The most recent of Professor A. E. Safarian's works is his contribution to the Officer and Smith volume on *Issues in Canadian Economics*, Toronto, McGraw-Hill Ryerson, 1974 and the readable *The Performance of Foreign-Owned Subsidiaries in Canada* (Montreal, Canadian-American Committee, 1969), containing some useful references to other countries. Three more "official" studies are Irving Brecher and S. S. Reisman, *Canada-United States Economic Relations*, Royal Commission on Canada's Economic Prospects, 1957; *Foreign Ownership and the Structure of Canadian Industry* (Report of the Task Force on the Structure of Canadian Industry—the "Watkins Report"), 1968; and Herb Grey's *Foreign Direct Investment in Canada*, Ottawa, Information Canada, 1972. Recently a number of symposium papers dealing with many countries, including the home countries of the investors, has appeared: C.P.Kindleberger, Ed. *International Corporation: A Symposium* (Cambridge, Massachusetts: M.I.T. Press, 1970). See also Sperry Lea and Simon Webley, *National Corporations in Developed Countries: A Review of Recent Research and Policy Thinking*, British-North American Committee, 1973.
In Chapter 6's section on foreign ownership we have already suggested a number of studies by authors opposed to foreign direct investment. Eric Kierans has promised readers a book on foreign investment (and ownership) of the mining industry.

badly, just because of that foreign ownership. Such arguments, however, may be inconclusive because, as is generally admitted, forces other than foreign control influence the performance not only of these firms but also of their foreign parents and their Canadian-owned/controlled rivals with both of whom they're implicitly compared. (*NOTE: ownership and control are not identical. See below.*)

EXPORTS It is often said that foreign-owned firms restrict their Canadian subsidiaries by keeping export markets in third countries for the parent company. Thus Imperial Chemical Industries and DuPont were never enthusiastic about Canadian Industries Limited hunting for markets in Latin America. On the other hand, the Commonwealth preference—which meant lower tariffs on "British" goods—gave Canadian branches markets in other Commonwealth countries that were closed to their parent firms. That is, individual examples abound, pointing both ways.

Safarian's statistical evidence here is interesting but inconclusive. In Canada and Great Britain subsidiaries of foreign manufacturers tend to export *more* than domestic manufacturers as a whole, partly because they are concentrated in "export" industries. Such evidence does not reveal whether their exports are less than if their parent firms' hypothetical restraints on their exports were removed.

IMPORTS "Foreign-owned firms tend to import parts and components more than native firms, especially if the subsidiary is a miniature version of a multiproduct foreign parent." This assertion accords with our observation of branches in Canada of such large manufacturers as Phillips, BMC, Westinghouse, Hershey, Reckitt-Colman, and Mitsubishi. But note too that it conflicts with the widely accepted view that the Canadian tariff, in excluding imports, leads to the establishment of foreign subsidiaries. Which tendency is the more important?

Probably, both are significant. Foreign ownership is one important response to the tariff, making goods sold in Canada less expensive to consumers than if they were priced at foreign costs plus tariff. Consequently, only those brands and products which it does not pay to manufacture in Canada, even under shelter of the tariff, are imported. It is true, then, that foreign-owned subsidiaries tend to import more, both of components or parts to be assembled here, and of finished products. This tendency, however, can be seen chiefly as a preference of foreign exporters for selling directly through their own marketing and distributing outlets, usually connected with their subsidiary manufacturing plants, if any, rather than through Canadian importing agents or independent manufacturers in Canada who might wish to expand their lines. This preference for marketing through subsidiaries is strongest when the parent firm deals in one of Chapter 24's "differentiated" products, for then it becomes profitable to key distribution to advertising of the parent firm. Undifferentiated, unbranded, or standard trade items, on the other hand, might as well be sold through agents, jobbers, and wholesalers.

Thus it is possible that foreign-owned subsidiaries as a group are simultaneously avoiding the tariff on some goods by manufacturing them and importing others. That subsidiaries rather than Canadian-owned firms do the importing is of no great importance. Rather, the question to be investigated (for the benefit of those who dislike importing and exporting and the resulting division of labor) is whether, in the absence of foreign ownership, imports would be less. There is no evidence that they would[5]

The "problem" of imports, indeed, is an object lesson for those who question the need for economic *analysis* of foreign ownership and investment. Those who promote tariff policies leading to Canadian self-sufficiency have been beguiled into using the evidence about imports as evidence of the harmfulness of foreign ownership, thus implicitly supporting the most feasible alternative to importing: the setting-up of foreign manufacturing in Canada. Whatever one's aims, honest partisans must thoroughly analyse so-called problems to avoid blindly citing both desired policies and their undesired side effects as "evils."

EXTRATERRITORIALITY This word has been re-defined to describe a particularly direct type of foreign influence: the obedience of a subsidiary to the same laws (on exports, blockades, sanctions, etc.) apply to the parent. For example, recall that MLW-Worthington wanted to export locomotives to Cuba and was prevented from doing so by the fear that if it violated U.S. law, its American directors could be prosecuted. Because such a law has been in effect outside the United States, it is said to be operating "extraterritorially." (In this case, the sale eventually went ahead.)

Extraterritoriality is easy to understand. No foreign government wants its national corporations to escape national policy by establishing a nonconforming subsidiary elsewhere. Thus Canadians would not wish Massey-Ferguson to escape Canada's sanctions policy toward Rhodesia simply by operating through a subsidiary in Lisbon; nor would the United States wish her firms' subsidiaries either to trade with nations with whom she was

---

[5]Bruce Wilkinson and Kari Levitt both suggest that subsidiaries show a bias toward importing because their parent firms do not charge them the full price, something that anti-dumping laws prevent between exporter and independent importer. But if this practice exists, it seems rather merely to create an "unfair" advantage for integrated importers over independent importers. Their evidence does not indicate that this bias leads to imports being greater: only that imports tend to become concentrated in foreign-owned subsidiaries, at some gain to the consumer at the cost of the foreign exporter.

For a new survey of this and the other topics discussed in the Appendix, see Kari Levitt, *Silent Surrender*, (Toronto: Macmillan of Canada, 1970).

J. C. McManus, in a contribution to Gilles Paquet, ed., *The Multinational Firm and the Nation State*, Toronto, Collier-Macmillan Canada Ltd., pp. 66-93, denies the role of the tariffs.

more or less at war or to evade her comparatively strict antitrust, tax, and foreign-currency-conservation policies. Indeed Tax Treaties between pairs of countries contain many sections which in effect keep taxpayers under national laws even if they flee abroad.

But treaties are reciprocal whereas extraterritoriality is the naked application of foreign laws to domestic action, and therefore particularly offensive to those jealous of national independence. Even those politicians least concerned about nationalism are alert to prevent extraterritorial application of U.S. policies.

RESEARCH AND DEVELOPMENT Concerned with our country's technical development, many scientific and engineering observers fear that foreign ownership will prevent both basic and applied (technical) research in Canadian industry. Instead, they say, multi-national concerns tend (quite rationally) to centralize their research in large laboratories, or universities, nearer their home base.

This process, of course, is essential to the very transfer, of technical information and skills outward from the parent company to its subsidiaries in other countries, that has persuaded many writers (like Harry Johnson) that international direct investment is a swift vehicle for the worldwide transmission of new ideas, processes, and consumer desires for goods and services. Thus the fruits of scientific and technological advance achieved abroad are received at the price of stunting scientific and, especially, technological establishments at home and their educational offshoots in universities. "So be it," say many consumers who enjoy the power to buy foreign goods, even if their buying decisions remove the justification for more research and development in Canada. "Let science flourish," respond Canadians who deplore the branch-plantism that has deprived us of the harvesting of our plans for the *Arrow* airplane, a Canadian-made communications satellite, or astronomical telescope, and that will soon witness the capture of all electronics activity by American, European, or Asian firms. So desperate have been Canadian scientists that many have espoused a more vigorous Canadian defense effort simply because of its scientific spin-off!

It is certainly true that Canada, Australia, France, and Great Britain are all low private spenders on R & D, while having high proportions of foreign ownership of industry. Perhaps as a response, Britain seems in the past decade to have turned major responsibility for technology over to government laboratories. France's Jean-Jacques Sevan-Schreiber in his *Le Défi Americain,* has urged his countrymen to use the European Common Market to set up firms with science establishments to rival these in the United States.

Safarian's research findings on Canadian R & D is consistent with the view that, even in research-oriented industries, much of the R & D is centralized in the parent's head office. However, he does not find that Canadian subsidiaries perform less research than their resident-owned counterparts—if anything, they seem to do more. It is ob-

viously vain to expect that General Motors, General Electric, or Bell will ever perform 10 per cent of their basic or development research in Canada, even if Canadian scientific and taxation policies do make it attractive for them to expand their present efforts. Whether it is in our interest to get them to do much more awaits the economic study of science policy promised by Ottawa.

EMPLOYMENT In less-developed countries, the chief aim of "nationalistic" policies is to hire, train, and promote local citizens, and the chief objection to foreign corporations, is their slowness to meet these aims.[6] This reminds us that, from a social point of view, the chief efficiency aim of producers should be to make the best use of society's resources—instead of importing foreign resources (workers). But a difference of opinion may arise about how best to utilize local resources. The profit-maximizing corporation and the economic planner may agree that foreign talent is needed to complement local workers and to bring out the best in them. On the other hand, if such an outlook should be adopted as a policy, broader and less nationalistic than the aim described above, not only may it make an enclave or bridgehead of foreign professionals unpopular in the short run by frustrating nationalistic sentiment, but also it may in the long run inhibit on-the-job training of potential local recruits. Such recruits of course will support "nationalistic policies" that open jobs to them. Indeed, Toronto's Albert Breton, in a well-known technical article on the economics of nationalism, has gone so far as to claim that nationalistic movements (such as Quebec's vis-a-vis Canada, or Canada's vis-a-vis the United States) are simply a means whereby a middle-income bourgeoisie (managers, professionals, authors, actors, professors) creates and protects a market for its own services. While this skepticism is extreme, its plausibility does illustrate that foreign control, even if it operates to make the best use of existing labor resources, may create diminished employment opportunities chiefly for members of an elite. The outspoken elite, identifying its own welfare with national interests, is not always supported by blue-collar workers on matters of foreign ownership and control.

Studies of American-owned firms in Canada, Australia, and Great Britain all suggest that, while these firms may have substantial autonomy or discretion, around one-third of their high-ranking executives and members of their boards are Americans; many of those who are on the boards of subsidiaries located in Canada do not live here.

RENT FROM NATURAL RESOURCES. The data above show that foreign ownership of firms in oil, gas and min-

[6]Not always, however. In India and Pakistan foreign corporations are criticized because they hire the best local graduates, at high salaries (thus diverting them from lower-paid government work or teaching). Even in Canada, the practice of large foreign corporations in promoting Canadian executives up to leadership in the parent is much criticized as a "brain drain"; and so is the opposite practice of not promoting Canadians.

ing can justly be summarised as "take-over". What concerns many critics, from McGill's Eric Kierans to Waffle spokesmen is not take-over, but sell-out: the question whether these exhaustible, limited resources (mostly still owned by the Crown) have been leased or licensed to firms (mostly foreign-owned) at fees, charges or royalties that fail to capture the "rent".

Foreign ownership is relevant here. If Canadian firms have managed to make unreasonably large profits because the Crown has not been a high-rental landlord, there is still a likelihood that, because the dividends are not remitted abroad, the wealth as built up in Canada will accrue to the benefit of certain Canadians. But if it is remitted abroad, the rent might, from the point of view of Canada, never have existed. It is by definition an amount in excess of the sum needed to attract exploration and development; therefore, the employment and so forth created would have existed without such large profits.

Hardly anyone explicitly favours sell-outs or giveaways. Only political, administrative and measurement problems keep them going. Should foreign owners pay a higher percent of their pure rents than Canadian firms? How is pure rent to be distinguished from net revenues which are needed to attract industry to mining and exploration? How are investors to be given the security they need to justify investment? How are the provinces to be persuaded, and supported, to take strong action? Should the rents they collect be shared with other provinces, or kept locally?

Most provinces owning their own *lands and forests* have at one time or another invoked nationalistic restrictions on the right to purchase or lease these lands. Most recently they have tended to restrict ownership of lakeshore cottage property, revealing a belief that Canadians, perhaps because they have lower incomes, cannot or will not outbid Americans, and some have limited the sale of Crown lands to Canadian residents. However, the latter regulation does not stop Canadian land speculators from buying property and selling it to those who can afford the highest prices. Thus the willingness, of individuals and governments, to sell a "public good" (see page 144 for this technical expression) when the price is high enough results in the subdivision of that good for private use and hence in its availability for purchase by foreigners. Other nationalistic restrictions on land or forest acquisition are usually designed to protect local processing mills, smelters, or refineries against the export of raw ore or wood.

The issue of the export of *water* is currently newsworthy and is undoubtedly an instance of the absence of even "accounting prices" (Ch. 32's Appendix, page 578) or other efficient or equitable devices to ration water use in either Canada or the United States. Consequently water for drinking, for receiving industrial effluents, or for irrigation is sought, held, and often wasted by rhetorical, legalistic, diplomatic, and political processes. Some enemies of water export believe that sales at *any* price will eventually place Canada at a competitive disadvantage to

U.S. industry. Analytically, they are wrong: some price exists whereby both seller and buyer are better off trading *some* of a commodity than they would be if no transaction takes place. Their distrust may simply reflect the real difficulty of ensuring "armslength" or impersonal pricing of raw materials and water at the border: very often buyers and sellers work in a "market" in which there are no competitors, and in which both are representing a common owner or political agreement. Most economists—not all—agree that it is worthwhile striving to achieve a rational price at which the buyer is willing to buy and the seller to sell (though the level decided on may result only in small sales), rather than taking the position that sales to the United States are by definition undesirable. Writers today argue that the need is to make sure not only that rent is recovered but also that today's rent is as high as that which might be earned if resources were left undisturbed to the best future date: this has been called the "user cost" of present exploitation. Such postponement, as the section on conservation (page 394) has explained, will make the resource available when it is most needed. It is additionally claimed that it is impossible to arrest or reverse energy flows once they are begun, so that sovereignty over even the future disposal of these resources is actually lost forever. Some energy flows (of hydro power and of coal) *have* been altered or reversed. But the point is a matter of fact—if the seller reserves the right to cut off sales at a future date, will political realities preclude this action? If so, and if reversal will be sought, then sales now are more expensive in terms of *future* utility than the price obtained makes them appear to be.

POLICY ALTERNATIVES

It is clear that, except for the implementation of an extreme policy, foreign ownership and control are not one issue, but many. The extreme policy would be that further economic congress with the United States is increasingly undesirable. In that case the issue would merely be to decide on a program of increasingly severe restrictions on foreign investment and ownership, and possibly on migration, imports, and exports. (Recall Chapter 22's discussion of the relation between imports and exports and fiscal policy in an open economy such as Canada's.) The cost, in broad terms, would be the sum of the loss of the present specialization and division of labor that trade allows, the choice of occupation and location that labor mobility permits, and the reduction of capital and know-how that investment brings. Against these costs must be ranged the benefits of independence. This would be welcome *in itself* to many Canadians. It might also bring incentives to inventiveness, originality, and risk-taking that would make Canada in self-sufficiency a richer country than pessimistic economists usually predict. Undoubtedly, however, there would be less capital per person for some time, less employment, more emigration, and lower incomes.

In the absence of this all-enveloping, monolithic program, however, handling each of the "problems" listed in the sections above requires a complex of restrictions and requirements that threaten to assume mercantilistic, if not Byzantine, proportions. As the listing suggests, free foreign ownership or use of natural resources is already somewhat restricted, and many steps are being taken for both extending these policies to other fields of foreign entry (teaching in universities, banking, shipowning, publishing, or broadcasting) and intensifying the existing restrictions (e.g., uranium mines may not now be sold to U.S. interests).

Because the impact of each special policy instrument is likely to be relatively small (and evadable) it is not appropriate to devote much space to them here. Among the first steps was the fortifying of a statistical base for action in CALURA, the Corporations and Labor Unions Reporting Act of 1967. Next, Canadian control or participation was made a requirement in various sectors of industries under direct national control: banking, insurance, airlines, radio, TV, magazine publishing (via the income tax), and mining (via mineral and oil leasing regulations in the northern territories). All this was based on (1) outspoken remarks in the *Report* of the Walter Gordon Royal Commission on Canada's Economic Prospects, 1958; (2) influence of Gordon when the Pearson government was formed in 1963; (3) *Report* of the Watkins Task Force on Foreign Ownership (1968); (4) *Report* of the Wahn (parliamentary) Committee in 1970; and the staff work within the government leading to the *Gray Report* in 1972.

In 1971 the Government breathed life into an old idea: the Canada Development Corporation. It has wide terms of reference, and could become, as was once announced, an instrument to "buy back Canada". Since it got down to business, its one great step in this direction has been to capture control of the U.S.-based Texasgulf Inc., with assets over a half-billion dollars and large operations in Canada—and in four other continents.

Many of the steps above have been followed, and in some cases anticipated, by provincial governments. Quebec, Ontario, Manitoba and B.C. have set up agencies not unlike the CDC; part of their job is to reduce the need to depend on foreign capital in certain industries, especially mining. Ontario has taken various *ad hoc* steps to aid particular industries, especially publishing. Several of the provinces are introducing new provincial lands' policies that may reduce the freedom of foreigners to buy or hold commercial or vacation property.

At the national level, the most recent step has been the setting up of the Foreign Investment Review Act. It will come into force in several phases. In the first phase, in 1974, any foreign firm or group planning to take over a Canadian firm must notify the Department of Industry, and get permission. Final ruling will be by the Cabinet. The Trudeau government announced also in 1974 that it planned soon to proclaim the second phase of the Act's provision, limiting the establishment of new businesses by foreigners. But this will obviously be a difficult part of the legislation to administer. An agency has been set up to handle the administration of both phases, but by 1975, very little has yet occurred or been announced.

It is obvious that all these policies may degenerate into tariff-like protectionism. Badly-located or poorly-managed Canadian firms may be rescued from American takeovers and from bankruptcy on nationalistic grounds, when social goals might be better served by their disappearing.

The purpose of this discussion has not been to settle the extent to which nationalistic policies should interfere with unrestricted movement of people, capital, know-how and goods across the border, but to indicate that partial policy instruments have been proposed and are being established. Many leave discretion to administrators. How vigorously these will be enforced remains to be seen.

THE RANGE OF POSSIBLE POLICIES. 1. Foreign ownership which reduces sovereignty over resources, factors, and trade within Canada is undesirable, and therefore should be stopped. Such statements simply beg all the difficult questions about amount and quality of intervention and are undebatable in economist's terms.

2. Foreign ownership reduces the choices open to Canadians; narrows future development of the country into too few channels; and creates some of the more unattractive aspects of the "branch economy," with an uncommitted managerial elite, etc. Such statements, too, verge on being simply undebatable statements of tastes or preferences. However, they can be confronted with the cost of remedying these effects as measured by reduced incomes, wages, or choices of goods and services. Hence a choice between the economic isolation and self-sufficiency advocated by extreme nationalists and integration with the world economy can in principle be made, or the degree of independence which is desirable determined.

3. A third position concentrates on resources and energy. Foreign control of resources is undesirable if the resource is exhaustible because the rent may never accrue to Canada. Trade in natural resources is in principle acceptable, but is actually undesirable because Canadians cannot trust themselves and their customers, to strike a bargain that is sufficiently advantageous to present-day and future Canada. This position can be dealt with by advocating that institutions be set up to attempt to solve the pricing problems and to set all-or-nothing conditions of sale.

4. Foreign investment is highly desirable because it is the chief channel by which know-how is internationally transmitted.

5. Integration into the world economy is desirable because it promises the high personal incomes by which groups of people can afford to establish any given set of national institutions. Only rich people, it is argued, can afford the luxuries of nationalism. (Nonsense, goes the reply, this argument is circular: if rich people do choose nationalism, you say they are then bound to become

poorer. If so, why not opt for nationalistic policies immediately?)

6. Restrictions on freedom to invest, trade, or move factors or goods are illiberal and therefore undesirable. Furthermore, any nationalism at all simply impedes the arrival of a better world. Like the first statement, this sixth one is largely undebatable in economic terms, merely stating a preference for individualism and a certain version of *laissez-faire*.[7]

SUMMARY TO APPENDIX

This listing of causes, problems, political positions and suggested policies does not point to any single policy for Canada. The following points have emerged.

1 Foreign ownership is a side-issue of international direct investment.

2 The opposition to multinational firms and foreign ownership is based largely on a fear of economic and political *power* being wielded in Canada by foreigners. Such fears are just as important as market preferences, and must be given due weight. But it must be noted that the most outspoken opponents of foreign ownership do not necessarily represent a majority who are sufficiently unhappy about foreign power that they are prepared to bear the costs of reduced employment, investment, and know-how, etc.

3 Much of this appendix has consisted of a survey of these costs—the loss of whatever advantages of growth, technology and jobs foreign ownership brings.

4 The interconnection of the ownership and tariff issues has brought out that these advantages might be different, and smaller, if it were not for tariff protection of foreign-controlled industries.

5 The question is not resolved by examining the behaviour or performance of foreign-owned firms. Few differences from the performance of Canadian-owned businesses have been revealed.

6 Care must be taken that ownership policies do not merely become a new form of protection for Canadian firms due to fail because of weak management, outmoded technology, or wrong location.

7 The range of possible policies indicates many compromises are available.

---

[7] An important Malthusian argument about nationalism is nowadays forgotten, even in the midst of concern about the environment. Some people argue that neither the world community in general nor the UN in particular can arrest world population growth soon enough to prevent serious overloading of the world's ability to produce food and energy. Accordingly they urge that individual large nations, as a temporary measure, take on the responsibility for world survival by keeping their populations down, preventing immigration, and endowing birth-control measures abroad. But an important counter-argument asserts that the earth's ecology, and its population are each one and indivisible; no single nation can stem the tide of too many people. When the world is seen as a group of nations each with its own behavior and net rate of increase, according to Charles G. Darwin, " ... the limitation of population is an unstable process, which cannot persist." He argues that, even if, over most of the world, there is severe population pressure and famine, the hope of civilization will be in a single universal culture, transcending nations. For the best investigation of this point of view, see Sir Charles Galton Darwin, *The Next Million Years* (New York: Dolphin Paperbacks, 1952).

36
CURRENT INTERNATIONAL ECONOMIC PROBLEMS

Before I built a wall I'd ask to know what I was walling in or walling out, and to whom I was like to give offence.

ROBERT FROST

We must now turn to the main international economic problems in the years ahead. How can we understand the important facts? Which economic policies must we avoid? Which policies must we follow?

Economists have achieved more unanimous agreement about the principles of international trade than about any other aspect of their subject. Yet the gulf between the plain man's beliefs about international finance and those of the experts is wider than elsewhere in economics, though that gulf has seemed to be narrowing slightly in recent decades.

Section A provides a survey of the main historical and contemporary trends in foreign trade. Section B analyzes the breakdown in the international system—pegged exchange rates, the United States' chronic gold drain and the world shortage of international liquidity. Against this background, Section C surveys the basic reforms in international finance that are now pending.

A. MODERN TRENDS AND INSTITUTIONS OF INTERNATIONAL FINANCE

TRENDS, 1914-1945

EXPORTS AND JOBS The first decade of the century was Canada's. Immigration and investment were very high, and exports of wheat, forest products, and minerals mounted. As in the 1950s, this had all been accompanied by an immense inward capital movement from Europe and the United States. But by 1913 Canada was entering a period of stagnation, which the early years of World War I did little to change. The smallness and weakness of the new economy was revealed when European capital ceased to flow in, and export markets were closed by the blockade. During the early years of the war, Canada borrowed heavily abroad—but later she reached full employment and borrowed at home.

In the United States, as the belligerents increased their imports from industrial America, the foreign-trade multiplier, explained in Part II, went to work to send her soaring out of her prewar depression to great prosperity. Gold and gilt-edge certificates

flowed in. Then, when the United States entered the war in 1917 the demand for shot and shell took over, producing by a domestic multiplier all the trappings of a boom: high prices, plenty of jobs, and an expanding GNP.

Both economies wound up the war decade with a sharp recession, and a serious inflation.

After 1921, the North American economy prospered. Canada entered another investment boom, this time depending very heavily on U.S. long-term capital inflows. Canadian exports and imports both increased and international indebtedness in all forms became large. The United States steadily raised tariff levels, which were alleged to "protect the American workers' standard of living."

The United States became in truth a "young creditor" nation. Many wise and foolish, charitable and hard-nosed loans were made, not just to Canada, but to all the world. This lending contributed to the general U.S. prosperity, as the funds borrowed were eventually spent on U.S. goods. Such added *exports E*, like *I* and *G*, increased GNP and employment.

GREAT DEPRESSION AND BEGGAR-MY-NEIGHBOR POLICIES

At the end of 1929, the stock market crashed. International lenders to European and Latin-American borrowers found their securities were worthless, and their attempts to recall their short-term funds made the monetary strain worse. Prices of primary products, like wheat, sagged. As aggregate demand fell, the political pressures for protection strengthened. Tariffs were raised, quotas imposed. The central European countries, alarmed by the flight of "hot" short-term capital, imposed foreign-exchange controls. Heavily involved in these exchange flights, Britain was forced off the gold standard in 1931, which led to a further fall in the export prices of the primary-producing countries.

In 1930, the United States raised the level of its tariffs to an all-time high with the introduction of the Smoot-Hawley tariff. Canada retaliated with tariff increases in 1930-1931 (see Fig. 35-1), and by 1932 she had raised her duties by an average of 50 per cent. H.L.Mencken, who never failed to call attention to the comedy of American life, rubbed his hands to see the farmers—who were net exporters and not importers of goods—being given import tariffs on their export products in return for their political support for tariffs on manufactured imports. Canada would have amused him just as much, though Canadian protection was unimportant abroad compared to the actions of the United States. Now the creditor of all the world, the United States was *trying to collect debts from abroad* and, at the same time, *shutting out the import goods that could alone have provided the payment for those debts.*

The fallacy of composition was at work. Every country believed that, if *it* could develop a favorable balance of trade, its employment would increase at the expense of its neighbors; in effect, it would be succeeding in exporting some of its unemployment. But for everybody to run a favorable trade balance simultaneously is a self-contradiction—as impossible as for everybody to be taller than anybody else.

Of course, the attempt to be taller—to generate a favorable surplus of exports over imports—could be predicted to cut down on the fruitful division of

labor. And precisely that happened. As much as domestic and total world production declined, the volume of international trade declined still more. The situation reached the height of absurdity when countries traded with each other only on a *bilateral* basis: A bought from B only as much as B bought from A; under Hitler's economic adviser, Schacht, Latin American countries sent staples to Germany in return for aspirin, which piled up in warehouses.

Today, even schoolchildren ask why people did not insist on deliberate programs of fiscal and monetary expansion. It is only too easy to remake history *after* the fact. But—and this is what concerns us here—one reason a single nation could not introduce expansion at home was the rational fear that if she increased her GNP while others kept theirs depressed, her imports would grow in the face of languishing exports. Thus, she would lose gold and, under the gold standard, she would either have to contract again or be forced into devaluation or bankruptcy.

As it happened, by 1931 England, Scandinavia, and the pound-sterling Commonwealth countries were forced off the gold standard. With the pound depreciated, these countries could afford to push their *internal* expansion; and if you look at the records, you see that Sweden and Britain were already recovering from the Depression when the United States, Germany, and France were experiencing the worst of it. Undoubtedly, some of the depreciating countries gained at the expense of those that stayed orthodoxly on gold. But the most authoritative studies suggest that the gain to the depreciating countries came *primarily from the freedom depreciation gave them to expand domestically.*

Was old-fashioned virtue rewarded? Not in the 1930s.. Belgium clung precariously to the old gold mint parities, even after Roosevelt deliberately devalued the United States dollar and Canada followed part way. Political unrest and depression were Belgium's reward—until 1936, when she gave up the struggle and, instead of being smitten by thunderbolts for her apostasy, she immediately registered relief in her production and unemployment statistics. France, having been the wayward inflationist in the 1920s, practically tore herself apart politically by clinging to the old gold parity into the late 1930s.

The Canadian depression was almost as deep as the American, and its recovery almost as slow, even though it cut itself off from gold earlier. It was not until World War II that full employment was approached. Toronto's A. E.

Safarian has suggested three reasons for Canada's incomplete recovery.

1. The market for most Canadian exports was the United States. The failure of the United States to recover by 1937-1939 meant that the Canadian industrial capacity installed in the 1920s could not be used.

2. Trade restrictions, crop failures, and heavy overhead costs prevented the smooth adaptation of the Canadian economy to rising aggregate demand.

3. Depressed investment schedules, resulting from previous excessive private investment and pessimistic expectations of future markets, led to stagnant investment activity.[1]

In the down-swing, government policy was confined to raising the tariff. In the subsequent up-swing, high taxes and low government spending characterized domestic policy. Men felt that salvation could only come from an improvement in the international economic situation.

WAR The Depression, which hit Germany and the United States especially hard, contributed to Hitler's rise to power. His preparations for war "solved" Germany's mass-unemployment problem and proved the potency of Keynes-like fiscal and monetary policies. When World War II came, the vast deficits in each country, financed with a new supply of money, brought about vast increases in the G of $C + I + G$ and had the predictable effect of, first, expanding production enough to get rid of unemployment, and second, swelling total demand so much as to create inflationary gaps and outright inflation. Exchange control, and rationing, were imposed everywhere.

Countries tried to use taxation instead of increasing M to finance armaments and exports. Full employment ruled in all belligerent countries, for the first time since 1931. Most goods were allocated internationally by controls, not by the market mechanism.

POSTWAR ADJUSTMENT AND THE "DOLLAR SHORTAGE"

When World War II was over, the scarcity of resources remained. The United States towered above its allies and former enemies in productive capacity.

Most countries tried to produce and consume more than their war-modified or war-shattered economies would permit.

Even Canada, which tried to maintain its exports to Europe on a loan or grants basis while importing consumer and capital goods from the United States, was forced to ration U.S. dollars and control imports. In Europe, the need to rebuild, develop, and make up for wartime scarcities led to pressure to import what was required as soon as possible; so dollars were carefully allocated to the most urgent needs. When American sources of supply were surveyed, it was found that the U.S. dollar was a seriously "undervalued currency" in the following sense.

Undervalued dollar and dollar shortage defined: The total world demand for American dollars to buy needed imports from the United States was much greater than the total that private citizens in the United States would want to supply (to pay for trips to Paris and Rome, for goods and imports, direct investments, etc.). In a free-exchange-rate world, the price of the U.S. dollar would have been bid sky-high; much of the rationing and control could have been abandoned.

Under the conditions of 1945-1950, in the absence of vast U.S. aid programs and other countries' tight regulation of imports and capital movements, when applied to the U.S. dollar the dd and ss schedules of Chapter 33, Fig. 33-1, would have shown a tremendous "dollar gap" at existing foreign exchange rates; this could have been met only by dropping to an equilibrium intersection where the U.S. dollar was much, much dearer in terms of foreign currencies—perhaps at $2 per £1 rather than $4, which was then prevailing, and likewise for the mark, franc, and yen.

The previous paragraph defines the technical meaning of the term that used to be heard so widely then, namely, the "dollar shortage", or "dollar gap".

How was the gap handled? Not by immediate postwar devaluation (although later in 1949 Britain did drop the pound from $4 to $2.80). Instead, the so-called dollar gap was handled primarily by comprehensive exchange and imports controls on the part of the nations with "overvalued currencies" and, as we shall see, by vast U.S. aid and loan programs.

[1] A. E. Safarian, *The Canadian Economy in the Great Depression*, Canadian Studies in Economics No. 11 (Toronto, 1959), pp. 142-143.

AID PROGRAMS

After the United Nations Relief and Rehabilitation Administration (UNRRA) had helped meet the immediate postwar aid needs, the United States introduced her dramatic Marshall Plan for European recovery. Subsequently, the United States shifted her grants to the North Atlantic Treaty Organization (NATO) and other military alliances. (Thus, the "Truman Doctrine" brought financial aid to Greece when that country was threatened by communism. Even Yugoslavia received aid.) The details of postwar aid are worth recalling. The gap was not filled by government loans nor by private capital movements. It was filled by a program of official gifts ("aid") on a scale previously unknown in peacetime. Why?

One U.S. motive, still sometimes operative, was fear of communism. Full stomachs may not save a democracy, it was argued, but empty ones can seal its doom. Putting modern guns into the hands of friends was intended both to help their defense and to save the lives of U.S. soldiers. Secondly, because other advanced nations—such as Britain, Germany, and the Soviet Union gave foreign aid, an element of emulation and competition also entered U.S. motivations.

Third, close and sceptical study of the Marshall Plan and other foreign-aid programs shows that the United States in the postwar period had "do-good" motivations. Call this altruism if you wish, or call it long-run expediency: the United States' future existence depends upon a stable international order not overly hostile to Western economic and social ideas.

Fourth, it is possible that some U.S. leaders embraced aid expenditures to prevent a great depression at home. This would be a Marxist interpretation of their motives. But the facts do not support this hypothesis: aid programs fuelled inflation and aggravated domestic scarcities, and there was an outcry *against* aid.

These staggering U.S. expenditures were the most costly, but not the only elements in postwar aid. Other countries, notably Canada, joined in aid to the war-torn European economies, and these helped narrow the dollar gap.

Soon the program joined many donors to recipients in all five continents. After a while the Marshall flows to France and Germany were phased out,

to be replaced by relief and development-aid to the developing countries. These have taken three forms:

TECHNICAL AID AND ASSISTANCE. Known as "Point Four" for it place in President Truman's 1949 inaugural speech, it soon became perhaps the most effective permanent source of change in backward economies, used by all donors.

BILATERAL FINANCIAL AID. As the western economies became stronger, they renewed their prewar financial aid to their old colonies, and then to other developing regions. Much of this, from France and the U.K. for example, was both large and quite independent of that from the U.S. Other wealthy countries joined in, and eventually the 16 advanced-economy members of OECD were giving in various forms over 20 billions per year (in 1972) in discriminating bilateral aid projects to selected regions.

MULTILATERAL AID. A third route is multilateral, or collective, aid. One set of such channels is set up under the U.N.: FAO; ILO; WHO; UNICEF; and the U.N. Development Fund are good examples, although most of them have been forced to specialise in providing technical know-how rather than funds. The best-known route for multilateral development assistance has been the "World Bank" (the International Bank for Reconstruction and Development, or IBRD) and its satellite, the International Development Agency.

Such multilateral agencies have the advantage that their aid is non-political and non-military. Amounts handed over to each project are based, in the case of the U.N. on need and productivity, and in the case of the world bank on somewhat the same profitability principles as would guide a private bank: security and repayment. Indeed the World Bank may be thought of as a private bank, owned by most of the western U.N. members, borrowing in wealthy markets and skillfully lending for promising long-term projects in less-developed economies. (More on this in Chapter 38.) The weakness of multilateral aid agencies, especially of those in the U.N. stems from their neutrality and freedom from political ends. Few donor countries want to turn large sums over to agencies so that the eventual gift (or loan) is essentially anonymous, or unidentified as to particular source either by the giver or the receiver. This characteristic makes it difficult for politicians to sell larger gifts to their voters (just as individuals may be glad to make some unentangling contribution to their Community Welfare drive, but having no connection with or responsibility to any particular recipient, are unwilling to consider an increase in their usual donation). And, to the extent that aid projects have side purposes (military; population-control; peace-keeping; drug-traffic regulation) the non-political aspect is not an advantage. Consider Canada's own preference for aid to francophone, and to former British colonial, economies.

THE INTERNATIONAL MONETARY FUND

The IMF, like the World Bank, grew out of the 1944 international conferences held in Bretton Woods, New Hampshire. It hopes to secure the advantages of the gold standard without its disadvantages; e.g., exchange rates were at first envisaged to be relatively stable, but with international cooperation to replace the previous automatic mechanism. Also, countries are to be spared the need for making adjustments that involve *deflating themselves into drastic unemployment*. It hopes to lessen need for import controls.

Ordinarily, a country will go along paying for its imports by means of its exports or long-term borrowing. Suppose a country, say, Britain, is in need of short-term credit from the Fund. How does the Fund enable such a debtor country to get hold of dollars, for instance? It does this by extending "purchasing rights." It simply permits the British to buy with British currency some of the Fund's own holdings of U.S. dollars. After the British balance of payments has improved, Britain is expected to buy back with gold (or with U.S. dollars or, as we'll see, with the new SDR's or "paper gold") the pounds she has sold to the Fund.

The Fund tries to set up rules and procedures to keep a country from going too deeply into debt, year after year. After a country has been piling up debts for a considerable period, certain financial penalties are applied. More important, the Fund's directors consult with the country and make recommendations for remedying the disequilibrium. However, they do not advise a country to create a depression in order to cut its national income down to such a low level that its imports will finally fall within its means. Instead, the country itself is permitted to depreciate (or appreciate) its currency by up to 10 per cent. This tends to restore equilibrium in its trade by expanding its exports and contracting imports.

If this is still not enough to correct the so-called "overvaluation" of the debtor country's currency, the Fund authorities may, after proper consultation, permit still further devaluation of the debtor country's exchange rate. But note this: All changes in rates are to take place in an orderly way. Most of the time, there is to be international stability. There is also provision for long-run flexibility when needed, which is better by far than waiting for a great smash.

By the 1960s the IMF realized (what Keynes and others had urged at Bretton Woods) that it must shift onto the *surplus* countries some obligation to help restore basic equilibrium. Thus, Germany may be encouraged to revalue the mark (as she did in 1961, 1969, and 1971). Such countries may be encouraged to lower import barriers and export subsidies; to lend abroad and increase their foreign aid; to reflate their domestic economies if stagnation exists. In 1971 at the Smithsonian Conference in Washington, widespread appreciation of currencies relative to the dollar was, as we saw in Chapter 33, finally agreed on; and likewise, again in February 1973.

THE EUROPEAN COMMON MARKET AND FREE-TRADE BLOCS

The previous chapters analyzed the economic gains from freer trade. One way of reducing trade impediments is for several countries to form a customs union. Within such a union, tariffs and quotas might be reduced or banished; but they might still persist with respect to external trade.

THE EUROPEAN ECONOMIC COMMUNITY (EEC) One of the most exciting international developments of the century has been the formation of the European Economic Community, popularly known as the European Common Market. With vigorous U.S. encouragement, Belgium, France, Italy, Luxembourg, the Netherlands, and Western Germany signed the Treaty of Rome (March 1957) and other instruments to create the European Economic Community, which came into effect on January 1, 1958. The experience of the EEC is a valuable reminder of the merits of free trade. Building on the law of comparative advantage, the liberalization of internal trade[2] has been a major factor in the remarkable growth the EEC has achieved since 1958, particularly in comparison with the stagnation experienced by the U.K. (Finally, on January 1, 1974, the U.K., Ireland and Denmark joined the EEC.[3])

The EEC is not content simply with internal free trade. It is striving to become one market instead of nine, with free movement, not just of goods, but also of labour and capital, and with common macroeconomic policies as well.[4] Progress has been made, but much remains to be done; and there is fear the mid-1970s will be a difficult time for EEC as it tries to assimilate its three new members and grapples with the severe problems posed by the energy crisis of 1973. Specifically, since the EEC imports over 60% of its energy requirements, the increased price of oil is expected to reduce the growth of GNP by 1½ points in 1974. And this is not to mention the problems of inflation and international monetary instability which plague the rest of the mixed economies as well. If it does stay together, and grows, the EEC may well become the largest market in the world.

BLOC-BUILDING. The excluded countries (Austria, Denmark, Norway, Portugal, Sweden and the U.K.) anxious about the loss of markets for their exports, formed EFTA (European Free Trade Area).

Though disparate in size and development, they nevertheless did expand inter-member movement of goods in what was virtually free trade of non-farm products. However, the EFTA is not to be compared with the EEC in scope. Denmark and the U.K., as already mentioned, subsequently joined the EEC; and switched their attention from simple tariff-reduction within the EFTA to the mammoth trade, migration, developmental and agricultural macroeconomic policies of the EEC.

Americans, Britons, and Canadians have also discussed other means of achieving wider free trade. The Common Market looked as though it might shut out other exporters and so even *reduce* world trade. The General Agreement on Tariffs and Trade (GATT) could move no faster toward lower tariffs than the slowest negotiator.

Among the suggestions for new arrangements was not only the make-shift EFTA, but, more ambitiously, a North Atlantic Free Trade Area (NAFTA). In 1963, 1965, and 1967 there were advanced schemes whereby Canada, the United States, perhaps Great Britain, and also perhaps other developed countries, would virtually eliminate their trade barriers to one another over a fairly long transitional and adjustment period.[5]

Other blocs have been proposed, or exist, especially in Latin America. The increasingly unrestricted trade among the Soviet-system countries is another form of trade bloc.

Some economists have worried whether this confining of lowered tariff barriers to membership of an exclusive bloc is truly a movement toward an efficient world specialization and trade pattern. They ask, "Won't there be a danger that the lower-than-average tariffs between the countries inside the

---

[2] At its inception the EEC sharply reduced internal tariffs; by the end of 1968 all internal non-agricultural tariffs had been removed. In 1973 all quantitative restrictions on trade (quotas and tariffs) were forbidden, subject to a few exceptions, and 1978 is the ambitious deadline for the removal of all known impediments to internal trade, quantitative or otherwise.

[3] Whether this expanded membership will be stable is, in mid-1975, open to question. Britain's Prime Minister Wilson committed himself to re-open negotiations, and many Britons from all parties, are hostile to the EEC's limitation on national freedom to make and change domestic policies. France too has pulled back from German leadership and British "interference" in agricultural and industrial goals of the old EEC six.

[4] As the "snake within the tunnel" section of Chapter 33 showed, the EEC has also had ambitions about one "Eurocurrency"

[5] Would free north-south trade mean the end of industry in Canada? Actually, no. An outstanding series of studies of the impact of this program on Canadian industry has been made.[6] It has indicated that, with the type of transitional provisions made familiar by the smaller-scale Automobile Agreement, revamped Canadian industries could sell in the larger North American market competitively with U.S. industry (and, for that matter, with Japanese and European industry). But in the 1970s, the wave of nationalism in Canada, the U.S. withdrawal from foreign entanglements, and the British entry to the EEC may have caused interested policy-makers to shelve this idea, until, as with GATT, the nations can again establish a common cause.

[6] See the trade-liberalization studies by English, Wonnacott, Johnson, Singer, Bond, and others in the slim paperback series *Canada in the Atlantic Economy* (Toronto: University of Toronto Press, 1968-1970).

union will distort the 'normal' pattern of trade (and each country's specialization in certain products) even more than it is already being distorted by separate nations' tariffs? Won't the differences between the 'ins' and the 'outs' be magnified and represent a distortion as serious as the pre-bloc situation?"

Others have replied: "Two wrongs don't make a right. If you can't get rid of trade impediments everywhere, at least get rid of them where you can. Then maybe a few great customs unions can ultimately merge into a worldwide free-trade area."

No definite answer will cover every case. Perhaps most economists would venture the guess that the lowering of tariffs in Europe did create much new production and trade among the new partners. Its effects on the division of labor would be beneficial to them, and they would ultimately be beneficial to other countries, if trade is later opened up to them. Readers can try for themselves another version of this problem by asking, "If Canada and the United States reach free trade, so that appliances and machinery are produced indifferently, and more economically in both countries, do their consequent improved efficiency and improved real incomes fully balance the loss of the chance for such specialization suffered by excluded Japanese or German exporters?"

FREER MULTILATERAL TRADE: GATT

During the 1930s, as remarked above, tariff levels had gone sky-high. Under the Ottawa agreements, the British countries seriously thought of Commonwealth self-sufficiency. Germany, Italy, France, and the USSR were keen to export but stubbornly reduced their imports. But readers should note that since World War II (in fact, since the round of bilateral treaties for reciprocal tariff reduction between the United States and other countries negotiated by Cordell Hull after 1935—see Fig. 35-1) most countries have been steadily whittling down their protective barriers. Economists properly stress that the barriers are still high; but they should not exaggerate the situation.

All stand to gain if fruitful multilateral trade can be restored. As mentioned in Chapter 35, the General Agreement on Tariffs and Trade (GATT) is a most important development toward international cooperation.

The so-called "Kennedy Round" was the sixth round of tariff reduction under the auspices of GATT, earlier efforts having taken place in 1947, 1949, 1951, 1956, and 1961. Agreement was made difficult by the wish of certain members of the Common Market, most notably France, to increase farm tariffs. The next round should go forward in 1975/6.

B. BREAKDOWN OF THE INTERNATIONAL MONETARY SYSTEM

Now that we have surveyed the events and institutions of international finance and trade, we can face up to the burning issues that confront the world in rebuilding the collapsed Bretton Woods system.

FROM DOLLAR SHORTAGE TO DOLLAR GLUT

The Marshall Plan and other aid programs soon began to have very favorable effects on the less-than-most-affluent countries—Japan, Germany, the Netherlands, France, and Italy. Primarily on their own, by a process no one had predicted, they began a miraculous sprint of productivity growth in the 1950s. This miracle persists.

This growth in the *competitiveness* of foreign economies, plus the expensiveness of United States' *cold-war programs* (the Korean conflict, the Vietnam war, the NATO alliance, etc.), plus U.S. *civilian foreign-aid programs* plus the burgeoning outflow of *direct foreign investment by U.S. corporations* facing juicy profit opportunities abroad—all these factors led to a gradual cessation of the dollar shortage and an actual swing toward a shortage of foreign currencies. The "dollar shortage" of the 1950s turned into the "dollar glut" (i.e., draining of gold from the

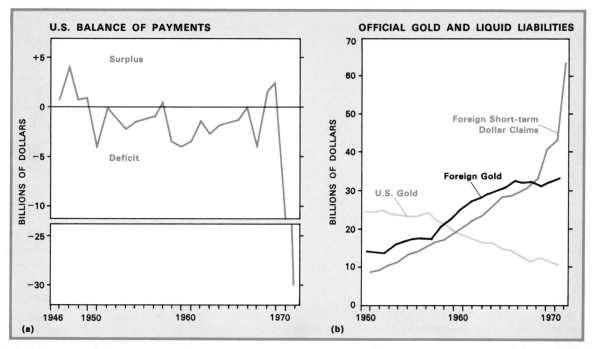

FIG. 36-1. Chronic overvaluation of dollar caused hemorrhage of gold and reserves, soaring balance-of-payments deficit.

By the late 1950s the "dollar shortage" was over. The dollar shifted from currency undervaluation to increasing overvaluation, culminating in the 1971 debacle and in the further 1973 devaluation. Note growth of United States dollar liabilities abroad.

(Source: U.S. Department of Commerce, U.S. Official Settlements Balance.)

United States with chronic U.S. balance-of-payments deficits) of the 1960s and the early 1970s. Relatively high costs in the United States led inevitably to "overvaluation" of the dollar.

At first the drain on the U.S. gold supply went unnoticed. But after 1958, everybody could see that a new trend was in the making.

Figure 36-1(a) shows that in 1959 the United States' balance-of-payments deficit was as large as her surplus had been in 1947. Note that in 1970-71 the deficit exploded, requiring breaking of the diagram's scale. This deficit was financed in part by a dramatic gold outflow: between 1949 and 1973 the United States' gold stock fell from its peak of 24 billion dollars to about 10 billion dollars. But to an even greater extent it was financed by foreigners accepting U.S. short-term IOUs. Figure 36-1(b) shows how liquid claims on the United States have grown to vastly exceed her gold holdings. No wonder the U.S. dollar had to be devalued in 1971 and again in 1973!

For the 25 years from 1933 to 1958, thanks in part to Hitler and the political uncertainties that sent gold to the United States for safekeeping, U.S. economic policy was *emancipated completely* from any concern for her international balance of payments. Now, she too has a balance of payments deficit, and has been forced to consider fiscal, monetary, and balance-of-payments problems together. Since 1960, every U.S. official decision about domestic policy, foreign aid or about military action had been constrained by the threat of an adverse effect on the balance of payments.

With the gold drain, the U.S. rejoined the human race. As Chapters 17 to 19 and their appendices showed, for most countries the problems of internal and external balance are not separable. Canada, U.K., France, Germany, Japan, even China and the U.S.S.R. must trim their domestic sails to suit the international weather. In particular, recall that monetary policy attracts changes in capital movements; and that successful changes in $C + I + G$ may be burdened by changes in imports; all bringing unwanted changes in exchange rates, balance of payments, or even price levels. The U.S. devaluation and cutting-off from gold in 1971 and 1973 eased her international constraint, but it could not liberate her.

REASONS FOR CHRONIC U.S. INTERNATIONAL DEFICIT, 1955-1973

Many reasons are given for the United States' chronic international deficit. Most have an element of truth in them, but we shall see that the crucial cause for the 1955-1973 period is probably to be found in the vast improvement of technical productivity in other countries in recent years. Below are the causes commonly named for the deficit:

1. *Too much U.S. inflation.* If a country has more rapid wage increases than its neighbor, and if these are not matched by compensating differentials in worker productivity gains, then it is indeed likely to find itself running into a deficit.

If we turn from conjecture to fact, an examination of any of the usual over-all index numbers of money prices and wages will show that up to 1965 there had not been more inflation in the United States than in other countries, such as the European nations and Japan. There is this grain of truth, however, in the overpricing allegation. If one leaves over-all indices and turns to certain important *sectoral* price indices, it will indeed be found that American prices long rose relative to those of other countries. No wonder that Japanese steel invades the U.S. Pacific Coast and that foreign producers of such U.S. staples as *barbed wire*, *cars*, and *TV sets* have almost insolently captured traditional U.S. home markets.

2. *Excessive aid and military programs.* Until Vietnam, U.S. governmental foreign-aid and military programs had not grown much in relative size; rather, it was more the case that, with the growth in private long-term investment, the United States' surplus on current *private* account was no longer large enough to let her aid programs be as extensive as they had been previously.[7] After 1965, Vietnam

did become an important aggravator of her payments deficit.

3. *Lack of trust in the U.S. dollar.* From 1933 to 1955, the U.S. dollar was considered everywhere to be a holding even better than gold. It was *the* key international reserve currency. But what happens when people and governments begin to believe that the United States is in international disequilibrium? And when they become apprehensive that the dollar *might* depreciate relative to gold? It is natural enough that, under these circumstances, some governments and private persons should, before the 1968 two-tier gold system made official gold unavailable for private persons, want to take out gold from the United States rather than continue to hold dollar currency or dollar IOUs. This so called "shift in international liquidity preference" can help explain some of the chronic gold drain from the United States that led to the London gold panic of 1968.[8]

4. *Discriminations abroad against U.S. goods.* While the dollar was in short supply abroad, it was understandable that barriers against U.S. exports should have been common in other countries.

5. *The rapid growth of productivity abroad.* From the long-run viewpoint, the fundamental cause of the change in the United States' international position would seem to be the remarkable speeding up of productivity increase in Western Europe and Japan. The production technology gap, particularly in the goods which the United States customarily exports and specializes in, has been narrowing. Even with the real wages abroad rising more rapidly, foreigners can

---

[7] If you plot (a) the United States' declining share of world exports against (b) the post-World War II rise in the ratio of her export prices to those abroad, the result does look a little like a down-

ward-sloping dd curve, with the rise in relative P explaining the loss of relative Q.

Even experts often don't realize how high the United States' surplus on current private account must be if she is to stay in healthy equilibrium with free long-term investment and to carry on aid and military operations abroad. Equilibrium might then require the expansion of U.S. exports of goods and services, in comparison with her imports, by enough to create a current private surplus of as much as 8 to 10 billion dollars! Would such a sizable surplus harm her trading partners? Some fear so. Others, concerned by financial disequilibrium and equilibrium of comparative advantage, urge that this be achieved. The United States is already supplying the rest of the world with the means to finance her enlarged surplus; hence they cannot be harmed. The private surplus must be large enough, however large that is, to fit in with over-all international equilibrium.

[8] It is not yet clear whether the freezing of the U.S. dollar from gold—and the implied lack of U.S. responsibility for gold's future price—has succeeded in restoring trust in the dollar.

produce for themselves more cheaply than the United States has been producing for them; hence they can outsell her increasingly. Auto, steel, and TV imports typify the changing patterns of comparative advantage. Only in the highest-technology items—aircraft, computers, automatic machine tools—does the U.S. maintain its export shares.

6. *High investment abroad by U.S. firms.* The miraculous productivity spurt abroad created tremendous profit opportunities for U.S. corporations. In the last decade, instead of wishing to invest in underdeveloped countries, they hastened to build branch factories in Canada, Europe, and, when possible, Japan.

By 1965 the outflow of direct investments by U.S. firms had become so large that the government introduced a *voluntary* capital control program applied to bank loans and corporate retained earnings and bond issues.

In 1968 these voluntary restrictions became ineffective, and were replaced by mandatory controls and quotas. Other measures also were developed. One was an *interest-equalization tax.* This encouraged Americans borrowing at domestic rates but, by placing a tax of 10 per cent or more on foreign loans, denied access to the U.S. finance market to non-American borrowers. Another was an income tax device (subsidy) to U.S. corporations that replaced their direct investments in producing abroad with exports from U.S. plants.

HOW THE U.S. DEFICIT GREW AND THE U.S. DOLLAR FELL.

Of course, the U.S. deficit did not become chronic instantaneously. It took some time for the 1945-55 dollar shortage (payments surplus) to melt into a dollar glut. With the wisdom of hindsight we can distinguish the following phases.

The decade of the sixties began with the U.S. dollar *overvalued.* Not just the export-sector, but all U.S. prices and costs tended to be higher than those in the miracle economies of Germany and Japan. Thus she began to experience increasingly tough competition in foreign markets, capital outflows, and unemployment at home. This was a condition that could only be remedied by a fall in wages and prices, relative to those in the surplus countries. Surprisingly, this remedy was achieved for a while. Full employment in Europe and Japan caused wages and costs there to rise faster than in the U.S., and the U.S. dollar looked less overvalued, at least until the Vietnam War.

Then U.S. wages and prices, too, began to escalate as quickly as in Germany and Japan. The dollar weakened steadily thereafter. Deficit trade balances, combined with official and private capital movements, sprayed dollars over the world, to buy cheaper or better goods of Germany and Japan.

The dollar being the official reserve key currency of the Bretton Woods set-up guaranteed that it would always be accepted by foreigners, even when it was being used to increase U.S. firms' ownership of foreign industry. But nemesis came in the form of the demand for gold. Foreign sellers were increasingly unwilling to hold dollars and returned them to the U.S. for conversion to gold (or marks or yen). The resultant outflow of gold, and the U.S. "benign neglect" of the problem, led to speculators engineering a flight from the dollar. Their "hot money" went abroad in millions. (Or, better, their "cool money" went abroad, since the chief speculators were treasurers of multinational corporations who thought of their actions as "protecting and hedging" exchange risks.)

This threw the ball into the courts of foreign central banks. Either they had to swallow all the dollars thrust at them (turn back to Chapter 17 for the inflationary consequences of this) or they would have to revalue their currencies (or let them float in appreciation relative to the dollar). Revaluation and appreciation, giving U.S. exporters easier entry into markets previously lost to dollar goods, were politically unpopular. Anyway, said the surplus countries, it's up to the U.S., not us, to change the exchange rates.

By 1971 inflation at home, a bad merchandise deficit on current account and short-term capital flight conspired to justify the first U.S. dollar devaluation since 1933. This was built into a new scale of IMF national-currency parities, under the "Smithsonian" agreement. But months later this scale had been rejected everywhere, and most currencies had been allowed to float.

By early 1973 the U.S. dollar had fallen to $42.22 per ounce of gold, and even farther in terms of yen, marks and Canadian dollars. The U.S. dollar was now valued, like all other currencies, by supply and demand of traders, investors, and governments. No longer need the U.S. look for measures that would fit the dollar for the $35.00 per ounce value wished on it in 1963 and 1944. (Few of these ideas were very promising anyway except as short-run expedients: sell-more and buy-less campaigns; getting America's friends and allies to shoulder part of her aid and military bills; insisting that U.S. aid be spent on American goods; cutting tourist duty-free allowances; and interest-equalization taxes and so forth. Apart from some sort of devaluation, the only real long-run cures for overvaluation had been accelerated U.S. technical progress and/or accelerated inflation in Germany and Japan, to lower the ratio of real costs in the deficit U.S. to real costs in her surplus rivals' economies.)

But these remedies were hard to come by. Little wonder that Nixon twice devalued the dollar.

This devaluation and the floating of most of the world's currencies had immense importance. The dollar was still the "key currency" only in the sense that nothing had taken its place. Gold had become "just a commodity". The fixed parities for national currencies, established at Bretton Woods and revised by the Smithsonian agreement, had neither gold nor dollar as a base.

The time had come to search for another system.

C. STRUCTURAL REFORM OF INTERNATIONAL FINANCE

Was the gold drain from the United States merely symptomatic of a more wide-spread malaise? Growing world production requires growing money supplies; but can gold mining keep up with this need? Growing international trade, and freer trade in a world more susceptible to political and economic irregularities, require larger liquid reserves for countries to hold as protection against swings in their balance of payments—particularly in mixed economies that will not let the rules of the gold standard dictate internal inflation or depression to achieve Hume's classical equilibrium. Will world gold supplies be adequate or even useful for this need, particularly in an environment where key currencies like the pound and dollar no longer command the respect that enabled them once to serve as a substitute for gold reserves?

Many economists, remembering the sobering experience of 1929, strongly believe that the whole world is in need of some basic *structural* reforms to provide needed elasticity in international reserves.

By the early 1970s, what was already evident to experts became unmistakably clear to government officials and financial interests generally—namely, that the pre-1971 international U.S.-dollar-and-gold standard was in serious trouble, and was probably not viable without fundamental reform. Four basic problems characterize the Bretton Woods system: (1) pegged parities; (2) dollar disequilibrium; (3) growing shortage of reserves; (4) direct investment and "foreign ownership".

ACHIEVING FLEXIBILITY OF EXCHANGE RATES.

A quarter of a century after Bretton Woods, experience has shown the system set up there to be flawed at the core by its reliance on exchange-rate parities that were to be *constant*. Economic theorists know that modern mixed economies are prone to drift apart through the years in their trends of price levels, wage costs, and productivities.

Hence, suppose the U.S. dollar and the German mark have exchange rates in equilibrium in 1949. Why should those rates still be suitable 20 years later? German productivity might outstrip the United States in an unpredictable way—and that is what happened. The United States might get involved in military programs necessitating vast offshore expenditures—and that too happened. Inventions may affect different regions differently in terms of their international competitiveness. Cost-push inflation may proceed at different rates in different countries. Consumer tastes may change, causing what was an equilibrium parity to become a currency overvaluation or undervaluation. In a world where *everything changes*, where no price remains constant, why continue trying to build an international edifice on a foundation of pegged exchange rates?[9]

[9] The architects of Bretton Woods did provide for *occasional* discontinuous exchange-rate adjustments by international agreement with the IMF. But what they did not sufficiently realize was the fact that such adjustments would be made only *after* the dis-

CORRECTING DOLLAR DISEQUILIBRIUM

Compounding this basic flaw of inflexibility of exchange rates has been the fact that the United States dollar itself—the linchpin of the system—became progressively out of equilibrium in the score of years following 1953.

"The dollar is even better than gold". Such a statement might have been true in the two decades following 1933, when there had been the dollar shortage and when U.S. currency was undervalued. But as we have seen, two decades of chronic United States balance of payments deficits evaporated the attractiveness of U.S. dollars as a key international asset.

LONG-RUN GOLD AND LIQUIDITY SHORTAGE

This brings us to the third basic flaw in the international system. The long-run supply of gold cannot possibly keep up with the liquidity needs of growing international trade. Year in, year out, the volume of international trade increases annually at a 7 or 8 per cent rate. But dwindling world gold production from the mines of South Africa and Russia can increase at barely 2 per cent per year. And much of this new gold, hoarding quite aside, is preempted for normal *industrial* use. Hence any international system *dependent inflexibly* on gold for its reserve base is doomed to ultimate liquidity shortage and emphysema.

As mentioned earlier, the replacement of gold coin by other forms of currency and the development of fractional-reserve banking systems served to economize domestically on gold in the last 75 years. Even then the system was being afflicted with sagging price levels until luck in the form of Alaskan and African gold rushes intervened. By 1929 luck had given out, and again by 1968 the gold-exchange and dollar-standard devices for stretching out the use of gold had reached dangerous limits.

As long ago as 1955, Yale's Robert Triffin correctly prophesied the need for fundamental institutional reform to increase international liquidity.[10] Since the U.S. gold outflows provided a gold infusion to the Common Market countries and the rest of the world generally, the problem of U.S. dollar disequilibrium served inadvertently to cover up and divert attention for a time from the long-run insufficiency of gold. (Refer back to Fig. 36-1.)

DIRECT INVESTMENT AND "FOREIGN OWNERSHIP"

To these three technical problems and the politics of their solutions, we must add the problem of direct investment. At one time both long- and short-run capital movements took the form of IOUs and debts from portfolio lenders, with which borrowers could acquire foreign consumer and capital goods.

In this century, increased productivity, tariff barriers, and transport costs have led to equity purchases and *direct* investment by manufacturers and services of the main lending countries. The portfolio lenders and money market lend to the U.S. firm or investor, not abroad. The structural problems mentioned above led to (1) increased direct investment to avoid the instabilities of trade in goods and (2) U.S. borrowing in host countries (France, Canada, Australia) to finance foreign acquisitions, instead of borrowing at home (thus leading to complaints about those countries paying for the acquisition of control over their economies by firms in the United States, Japan, or Germany). Sometimes they borrowed "Eurodollars", actually supplied to European money markets by other U.S. lenders. In any case, the multinational, technical, foreign owner tended to supply know-how and ambition rather than goods or finances. Obviously, foreign ownership is not *basically* due to the absence of flexibility in the structure of international finance. But it is clear that the overvaluation of the U.S. dollar should be seen as a result not only of U.S. payments weakness, but also of an unusual period of acquisition of direct control of foreign enterprises. See the Appendix to Chapter 35 for

---

equilibrium state had become apparent to all, and that this recognition would provide a field day for speculators who could sell the weak currency short, knowing that there was no risk of its moving against them and a great chance that it would move in their favor. Moreover, the speculators acting in concert could hope to precipitate the crisis which would make them their profit.

[10] Indeed Lord Keynes at Bretton Woods in 1945 had already proposed a gold substitute—a new currency unit for international reserves called "Bancor". In addition to the Triffin Plan there have been a Bernstein Plan, a Stamp Plan, a Posthuma Plan, a "Link-Aid" Plan (giving poor nations new reserves); and similar plans for creating new reserve units, credits, or versions of "paper gold".

more on foreign ownership.

Unrealistic and inflexible dollar values tended to spawn U.S. investment abroad and some withdrawal from trade.

THE TWO-TIER GOLD SYSTEM

By 1968, time had run out on the precarious gold-and-dollar standard. When the rush for gold by hoarders became a stampede which would have stripped Fort Knox of all its gold within a matter of weeks, the ten leading nations of the world met during March, 1968, in Washington and Stockholm. They suspended all gold payments from official central banks to the free market. Henceforth there was to be a two-tier system.

THE OFFICIAL TIER   In the official tier, gold payments are made only between governments, and always at the official IMF parities. Thus, within the Club of Ten, if Germany has an export surplus with the United States that is to be partially paid for in gold, each $42.22 million payment will involve the United States sending Germany (or, more likely, merely earmarking in the vaults of the New York Federal Reserve Bank) a million ounces of official gold or paper gold equivalent.

Essentially, all the gold in the official reserves as of March, 1968, was frozen forever into reserves. None can ever go outside the Club of Ten and the hundred other nations that belong to the IMF.[11] No government in the Club is to buy gold from any government that ever deals with the free market in gold.

FREE-MARKET TIER.   Outside the IMF club, gold became completely demonetized. Gold mines opened and produced under the stimulus of auction prices in London or Zurich. Jewellers and dentists pay the $150 or so for their industrial supplies. Speculators can hope to make capital gains if they buy before prices rise, otherwise they may lose their shirts if the gold prices tumble. *No central bank or financial authority protects or manages price* in this tier.

EVALUATION AND PROSPECTS.   How has the two-tier system worked? Surprisingly well, but like every market where there are two prices for one

---

[11] At first General de Gaulle tried to block the new system. But the events of 1968 (student riots and the general strike) so depleted France's gold reserves as to make her return to the fold.

good, leakages and strains have appeared.

In 1973 one aspect of the 1968 agreement was changed. Monetary authorities are free now to sell gold to *private* buyers at a price higher than the official $42.22. But the central banks are still prevented, both by Bretton Woods and by the 1968 rules, from making official transactions or settlements between countries at any price than the official one.

1974 saw the first revision of this. Italy, in desperate need of reserves, arranged to *borrow* reserves from other central banks against the security of her large gold stocks valued at second-tier, free-market, prices. There was some grumbling but no real effort to prevent this deal.

These both may be minor breaches of the 1968 two-tier system. No small central bank appears to be buying gold at the official price from other central banks, and feeding it surreptitiously to the free market turning a neat $100 per ounce profit. For the first time the international financial system seems to be indifferent to the whims and fads of gold hoarders and industrial gold users.

The two-tier system however cannot go on forever, unless the free price drops. It is bound to give way to speculative pressure. In any case it is only a milestone on the way to structural reform. Although it took 100 years to persuade the nations that international liquidity was too important to be entrusted to the gold mining industry and market, the acceptance of that message hardly counts as a constructive step. Now the central banks are left with their official gold reserves in ever smaller ratio to the expanding total value of world trade. This will throttle such trade unless other reforms, such as "paper-gold" SDRs and other reforms are adopted.

THE QUEST FOR REFORM

With gold out of the way, or relegated to commodity status, we may explore the main "reforms" currently being debated. What should be the main elements of a new system? None of the proposals is completely new, having already a limited, *ad hoc* usefulness in today's expedient "system".

The most important proposals are: (1) using gold as a reserve asset, with its *official* price massively increased; (2) abandoning gold or any one currency standard, depending on a system of freely floating currency price or flexible exchange rates; (3) reliance on newly-created paper gold, or SDRs as a reserve asset; (4) adoption of gliding bands or crawling pegs instead of an inflexible fixed-rate system or a flexible floating system.

INCREASING THE PRICE OF GOLD

This first proposal would, today, involve returning to the use of gold as an essential reserve asset. Then increase its *official* price to $70, $140 or $210 per ounce. Similarly, increase gold's price in terms of *all* other currencies. This massive "devaluation" of all currencies, being in balance, will result in no change of the relative prices of currencies or exchange rates. But, at the stroke of a pen, any shortage of international liquidity will have disappeared.

This proposal was associated with de Gaulle and his economic adviser Jacques Rueff, with Oxford's Sir Roy Harrod and with the Bank for International Settlements at Basel. What are we to think of it today? Naturally the gold-mining industry would love it, not only in virtuous Canada but also in less meritorious South Africa and the USSR. So do the gold hoarders, speculators and others who bid the second-tier price up to $220 and more, lusting after a once-for-all capital gain.

Self-interest aside, what are the plan's merits and demerits? For Rueff, an archconservative, the price of gold is to be raised once and for all, *and then mankind is to go back onto a rigid gold standard*. Gold is to serve as a *discipline* for governments. The moment a nation inflates, it will lose gold and be forced back into deflation. If capitalists disapprove of their government, they can hoard gold coins and take their money abroad, creating a run on the currency and bringing down the ruling government. (This happened repeatedly in the history of France and other countries during the capitalist era.)

For Sir Roy Harrod, a Keynesian expansionist, doubling or tripling the price of gold is favored for reasons diametrically *opposed* to those of Rueff. With one stroke of the pen, governments everywhere will be given their freedom to pursue *expansionary* policies for another quarter of a century. After that time, another stroke of the pen. ...

Most experts regard gold as an anachronism. How absurd to waste resources digging gold out of the bowels of the earth, only to inter it back again in the central banks' vaults! And why adopt a plan that gives a windfall profit to gold interests? But the even more important objection to reliance on a rise in the price of gold is this:

Modern mixed economies will not go through the agony of deflating themselves, running the risk of mass unemployment and stagnation, merely to obey the rules of the automatic gold-standard game. And if the gold-standard game is *not* played according to its rules, small disequilibria will not be prevented from accumulating into major disequilibria with ultimate crisis and breakdown.

Even though the world will not revert to the automatic gold standard, it is a fact that official gold does still exist and is an important part of official international reserves. Hence the new IMF reforms are able, as we shall see, to *build around* gold and *supplement* it with new reserve assets.

FREELY FLEXIBLE EXCHANGE RATES

This second "reform" is at the other extreme from that of restoring the automatic gold standard. In effect, it is proposed to make permanent what was the actual system of 1973-4:

1. Turn all exchange rates completely over to the free market. Avoid all intervention.

2. Forget about the balance of payments. *Let supply and demand intersect to produce whatever pattern of exchange rates will clear the market.*

3. Rely on the development of a speculative market in foreign exchange to offer importers and exporters the opportunity—at a price, of course, but, under vigorous competition, not necessarily a very high price—to "hedge" their international merchandise and capital transactions.[12]

[12] To ensure against the risk that the foreign exchange rate for marks will rise 10 per cent between now and the time my import of German dyestuffs arrives, I turn today to the forward market and buy marks 90 days ahead. Who sells them to me? Possibly a Canadian exporter who wants to play safe and know exactly how many dollars he's going to get for the computer he is shipping today to Germany, and for which he will be paid marks in 90 days. But even if export and import transactions in both directions don't balance out, some speculators with sporting blood will sell marks forward hoping to be able to buy them cheaper later. If speculators are overoptimistic, they may end up providing this

For the mechanics of how freely floating exchange rates work, the reader can refer back to Chapter 33. The main point to emphasize is that now a country can be free to do anything it wishes domestically, letting the exchange rate move to adjust in consequence. Thus, if the United States wilfully inflates its domestic prices to double or quadruple previous levels, there is nothing to stop it. (But, of course, as Chapter 33's discussion of purchasing-power parity shows, the foreign exchange rate for the U.S. dollar—in terms of the mark or the currency of any other country which has kept its prices stable—will automatically *depreciate* to about a half or a quarter of its previous level, going from, say, 4 marks to a dollar down to 2 marks to a dollar, or even 1 mark to a dollar.

It is precisely this *autonomy* of domestic policy under floating exchange rates which opponents criticize. They fear that healthy hedging possibilities and fruitful international trade will be possible only if exchange rates *do not move chronically in one direction*—i.e., only if a nation does not chronically induce or countenance inflation. "But," these critics point out, "if, after all, the country is going to have to *desist* from chronic inflation, there has been no true escape from the disciplines of the gold standard in the end; and one might as well have the advantages from the beginning that come with the traditional *fixed* exchange rates."

They go on to argue, "Within the 10 provinces, we do not have floating exchange rates. That would hurt

hedging service even at a loss to themselves; or if risk-taking is so irksome as to require a positive premium for hedging, that cost will be added onto the price of international goods and, to a degree, will lessen the volume of and gains from trade. The analysis of hedging and speculation in a market for wheat, as described in the Appendix of Chapter 21, cannot be confidently applied to foreign exchange markets. Speculation in foreign exchange is more in danger of being destabilizing, since there is no natural par of supply and demand set by crop conditions and basic human demands for wheat. Instead, when our dollar is weak, all the speculators will pounce on it and make it weaker; they will force Canada into depreciation and into internal inflation, and thereby the new proper level for our dollar will be permanently lower, rewarding the speculators for their bear raid. Some critics go on to argue that if Canadian authorities resist such raids by keeping a tight rein on the domestic money supply, price level, and GNP level, they are as much restrained by the balance of payments as under a stable exchange standard: so why give up advantages of fixed exchange rates if you are going to have, in any case, their disadvantages? The answer of course is that a "tight rein" is a matter of degree. The restraint of a fixed rate is more chafing than that of a flexible rate.

the intranational volume of trade and division of labor. So why give up stability of exchange rates internationally?"

How do the advocates of flexible exchange rates reply? First, they stress that within a country like Canada there is one central government, one central bank and money system, and one labor market in the sense that workers can migrate from a region of serious unemployment to one with high employment. All these features are lacking internationally.

Second, advocates say that flexible exchange rates were never intended as a panacea. What they can do is make the effects of unavoidable creeping inflation and price rigidities in the *mixed economy a little more tolerable*. Advocates of flexible exchange rates still insist that the economy will function best only if chronic inflationary and deflationary gaps are avoided by proper macroeconomic policy.

EXPERIENCE AND EVALUATION

CANADA. The characteristics of the flexible-rate "system" cannot be gauged by the Canadian use of it in 1951-62 and since 1970. For the rest of the world's rates were fixed, so Canada was only a partial, not a general, illustration.

This experience did however, cast some light on the problem of speculative action to bring about instability. There is little doubt that the rate was "attacked" from time to time, in the hope of initiating a run and reaping windfall profits. Some of these attacks were fought off by Canadian authorities, using the Exchange Fund Account to keep an orderly market in the Canadian dollar. Since short-term capital flows are volatile, there were indeed speculative gains to be made. But the main difference was that the rate "wasn't going anywhere". The authorities had no parity to maintain; they accepted any push or pull that revealed itself; and so provided no fixed target rate from which speculators could attempt to topple the Canadian dollar exchange rate.

THE WORLD. What happened when the world decided on floating rates in early 1973?

First there were months of panicky "dirty floats" or "managed flexibility". Not content to allow the market to set relative currency prices, the nations intervened constantly to maintain the Smithsonian parities, the tunnel, the snake, or at least day-to-day stability. These interventions provided the fixity that speculators love to break down.

The theory would predict that large capital flows would move exchange rates, and that floating exchange rates would soon remove a target from its vulnerable level, so that capital flows and speculative currency movements would be clamped and would reverse themselves. These predictions were sustained. In spite of rigid capital controls in a few countries, the movements of trade and capital were accommodated by free exchange rates, and speculators were forced to look for the longer-term gains that would come from eventual depreciation (or appreciation) of a particular currency.

Thus into mid-1974, exchange rates reflected rather than determined currency movements; and these in turn reflected interest-rate differences, inflation rates, tax rates, and political events. Speculation for capital gains certainly existed, but probably less than would prevail under the vulnerable Bretton Woods pseudo-fixed parities.

Thus world experience to the mid-1970s confirms earlier Canadian experience: fears about speculation being destabilizing (that is, justifying the hopes of bulls or bears by being pushed farther and farther in one direction) are not serious enough to worry about. Both fixed and flexible rates can be attacked by speculators. Canada's experience was that, so long as the government is prepared to accept the market's judgment of the value of the Canadian dollar, the flexible rate will not fluctuate unduly. It is the determination of a government to fix its rate at a certain level that attracts speculative bets that it will fail to do so; and sometimes the speculators win their bets.

SDRs (PAPER GOLD) AND CONVERTIBILITY

The third reform being developed is a plan for (a) augmenting or even replacing official gold as international reserve asset, by (b) the creation of a new reserve asset—the Special Drawing Rights. In 1969 the IMF members amended the original Bretton Woods agreement, to allow them to issue SDRs annually.

The SDR is a fiduciary, paper, or fiat asset, but it originally had a physical definition of its value: 0.888671 grams of gold. Hence its nickname, "paper gold". Each year the members vote to decide how many SDRs to create; the exact amount is proposed by the Director General of the IMF. The *allocation* of the new SDRs among members is still a matter for discussion. So far they have been shared out strictly in proportion to members' (voting and capital) quotas in the Fund; thus the U.S. gets 25 per cent, Canada 3 per cent and so on. But there is a view that there ought to be a "link" between their allocation and the needs of the poorer members of the IMF. Under the "link" approach, the developing nations would get a higher proportion of newly-issued SDRs than their present quotas warrant. Many of the developed, industrial, nations oppose this means of giving aid, as simply confusing the basic, monetary, purpose of the SDR.

Like the two-tier gold system, the invention of the SDR appears to be another milestone in the basic reform of the international monetary mechanism. At long last, multilateral agreement, not gold mining economics, determines the amount of international reserves.

But many questions remain. Why use the SDR rather than restoring the dollar as a "key" currency? Why should past investment in gold, by rich and poor countries, be forgotten? Isn't the rate of creation of SDRs likely to be as reckless as the flow of dollars was?

One question at least has been resolved—the fixed gold valuation of an SDR. In 1970 the 0.888671 grams of one SDR were worth one U.S. dollar. By 1974 SDRs were worth U.S. $1.20 (i.e. a little more than $1.15 in Canadian funds). After July 1974 they were valued at the *total* of a basket of sixteen IMF currencies: 7.1 Canadian cents, 40 U.S. cents, 44 French centimes, 4.5 British pence, and so forth. When these floating currencies depreciate against the U.S. dollar, the dollar value of the SDR goes down, and vice versa.

The IMF hopes that this freedom from gold or any one currency will keep the SDR "stable" in world purchasing power and thus usable not only as an international reserve asset free from volatile exchange risks but also, in its own right, an international standard of value.

THE GLIDING BAND, OR CRAWLING PEG WITH WIDENED BANDS

The fourth proposal is the crawling peg. The new SDR system will work better if it is freed from its convertibility into gold at a fixed rate, and given some degree of flexibility. Yet the world's bankers do not yet wish to leap to full-floating flexibility.

Crawling pegs, or gliding bands, constitute a possible scheme for monetary reform. A compromise between the Bretton Woods fixed-ratio system and indefinite floating, it stands some chance of acceptance by both gold and anti-gold experts. Its main outlines are repeated here from its introduction in Chapter 33.

1. Within any one year the exchange-rate *parity* is to be permitted to move some maximum stipulated amount, say, 1 or 2 per cent.

2. This slowly crawling parity level is to be surrounded by a *widened band*, within which supply and demand is free to set the actual exchange rate.

Even if foreseen, such a crawl in parity is not great enough to tempt an avalanche of speculation. But it produces enough flexibility to permit an 11 or 22 percent adjustment of exchange rates over a decade! And that should be sufficient to compensate for the normal drifting apart of wage and price levels due to technological change, changing tastes, and different degrees of national wage-push inflation.

For the economics of the crawling peg, the reader can refer back to Chapter 33, particularly to Fig. 33-3. Part of that figure is reproduced here as Fig. 36-2. In this example, the dollar-pound parity begins at $2.30 in 1974. But now the exchange rate is no longer held within the $2.28 to $2.32 band formerly set by the old-fashioned "gold points" or IMF system. Now the exchange rate can vary between $2.10 and $2.50 per pound. And next year, with parity moved[13] to, say $2.25 by Britain's deficit, the range would be $2.05 to $2.45.

The attitude to completely floating rates in 1973 and 1974 has by no means been unfavourable. Prac-

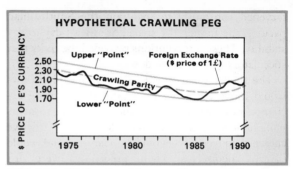

FIG. 36-2. Gliding band (or crawling peg) offers floating and fixed exchange rates.
Instead of fixed parity at $2.30 per £, under this plan the parity can crawl downward or upward by 1 or 2 per cent per year, achieving in a decade's time the 11 or 12 per cent needed to adjust for drifting apart of cost levels. Also, at any one time, the band between upper and lower "points" within which supply and demand can freely operate, is considerably widened.
(Source: Figure 33-3.)

tical men and bankers have quickly learned to adjust and hedge; and tourists and governments have also learned to accommodate their international financial planning. This experience has increased the desire for easy exchange-rate flexibility as a central feature of the future mechanism, to avoid the bitter episodes of major revolutions of the Bretton Woods fixed parities. Thus the gliding band proposal seems a helpful compromise, acceptable both to those who wish to avoid open-market fluctuations and those who wish to achieve smooth flexibility.

OTHER PROPOSALS

How to get from here to there? Ten years ago we had dollar convertibility, fixed exchange rates and gold reserves. Today we have none of these. The previous sections have reviewed the proposed directions for reform. Some of these are already in limited use, especially general managed floating. How are the nations to move forward to a non-gold, semi-flexible system?

It is clear that this transitional problem is as serious as the question about the most desirable reforms. Today we lack the Bretton Woods 1944 opportunity when the world's moneys were under war-time control and world trade was minimal. The new system must be introduced piecemeal into today's open, flex-

---

[13] There are a variety of details proposed for the crawling peg. Thus, some would have the change be gradual within the year; some would permit the change to be determined by the governments involved; some would make the movement of the crawling peg to be determined by an automatic formula in terms of certain averages of previous months' deficits (and surpluses!).

ible-exchange markets, not imposed as a single monetary package.

The elements of the new system, and the transition, were first discussed in 1972, by the IMF's Committee of Twenty (finance ministers). This committee's work was therefore begun when the final abandonment of fixed exchange rates had yet to come, and when the era of "managed floating", the international stresses and strains of the Arab oil crisis had hardly begun.

THE OIL CRISIS

In the wake of the 1973 Middle East war, the members of OPEC, in October 1973, launched on (a) cutbacks, embargoes and boycotts of particular petroleum customers; and (b) a series of abrupt rises in oil prices. Over the twelve months of 1973, petroleum shipped to consuming countries *trebled* in price.

It is still too soon to summarize the impact on foreign payments of this astounding change. Note the following.

(a) Oil customers were in the midst of a business upturn, with demand increasing cyclically as well as secularly.

(b) U.S. gas and oil were, unlike the first Suez crisis, not available for export.

(c) The group of countries that were the largest importers of petroleum was a different set than that which, in 1973, had balance of payments surpluses. Indeed, with the exception of the U.S. and Canada, oil and gas reserves seemed to be found mostly in countries with deficits.

The results were first evident in employment and in merchandise-trade deficits. Japan, Italy, the U.K., and Holland were very badly hit. Some of these are shown in Figure 36-3, where currency prices are shown as a percentage of their 1970 (pre-Smithsonian) parity. It can be seen that the currencies whose values were recovering at the end of 1973 were (apart from Switzerland) those with some energy-resource self-sufficiency. The yen, like the lira, the deutsche mark, and the pound, fell sharply. (Later, the deutsche mark appreciated again.)

What of the Arabs and their wealth? The exchange-rate disturbances may have shaken out in two years, as the petroleum market stabilizes and as new supplies become available. In the mid-1970s the real strain on the world financial system was the one-way

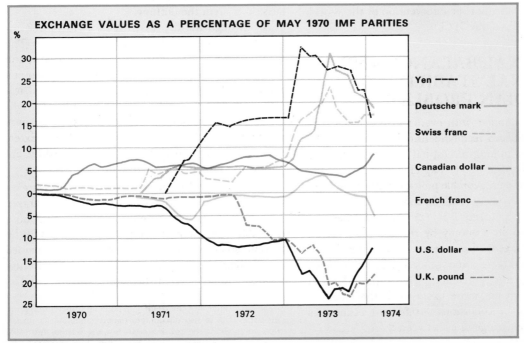

FIG. 36-3. Effective changes in exchange rates during the petroleum crisis.
(**Source:** *Bank of Canada Review,* February 1974, p. 10.)

flow of payments to OPEC members. Reminiscent of the dollar shortage period discussed in Part A of this chapter, the world's problem is how to handle oil revenues and profits so as to (a) obtain the goods and services wanted by OPEC members for current consumption; (b) invest in industrial capacity in OPEC economies for economic growth and development; (c) until the labor force is ready for (b), invest in bank accounts, and interest-bearing assets abroad; (d) purchase enterprises and businesses abroad for long-term profit; and (e) accomplish the above goals while "recycling" funds to the energy-deficit countries: Japan, U.K., Italy, India and a score or so of developing countries. At the present time, the OPEC countries find it very difficult to increase their imports. Hence their customers are in deficit and they are in surplus. Some of the latter, even with high exports and full employment, are in desperate straits on their balance of payments, willing to borrow from OPEC members or anyone. One of the interesting questions of the 1970s will be whether London, Zurich and New York, the chief financial centres where OPEC members can invest their new-found surpluses, will succeed in distributing these flows through the money markets to the customers worst affected. Or must there be intervention by the World Bank, the IMF, or the OECD?

EXTERNAL BALANCE AND INTERNAL STABILITY: THE CANADIAN PROBLEM

The reader familiar with events in Canada in the past few years can readily identify Canada's concern over changes in long-run capital flows and point to the following causes: (1) Capital may be "pushed" from abroad by unfavorable political conditions, high savings rates, and especially by low yields and lack of investment opportunities. (2) Capital may be "pulled" into an economy by resource discoveries, new markets, general prosperity, tariff protection of particular industries, and generally, by high yields and investment opportunities. Thus capital flows in long-run form are more likely to be the result of comparisons of conditions *inside* two economies than of the exchange rates between them.[14]

This conclusion indicates one aspect of a very old problem: how is a country to achieve both internal full employment (often called "internal balance") and external payments balance? For generations the authorities of England and the United States gave external balance a higher priority. Thus, if capital inflows were too great for external balance, they would attempt to lower investment yields at home, even if this policy would produce internal stagnation or unemployment. The reader will note this attitude was similar to the gold-standard approach to the balance of trade: when imports are too great the outflow of gold would be corrected by effects causing internal deflation and unemployment.

Nowadays countries are less prepared to give external balance such a high priority. For example, in the early 1960s, the Kennedy administration's easy-credit-conditions policy, which helped to return the country to full employment, also caused an outflow of long-run capital seeking higher yields on loans elsewhere. As we have seen, the United States decided that internal prosperity was more important than seeking an instant stop to the capital outflow; so instead of raising interest rates at home she imposed the interest equalization tax and tried by moral suasion to stem the outflow.

All through the depressed years 1958-1962, Canada maintained relatively tight credit conditions. The external result was a fairly high capital inflow, and an exchange rate that placed the Canadian dollar at a premium, discouraged exports, and encouraged imports. The internal result of such comparatively tight credit conditions was that business expansion was discouraged and unemployment was high. Externally, Canada's financial position looked healthy, but output and growth were arrested.

In the early 1970s, substantial upward pressure on Canada's exchange rate resulted from large and rapid inflows of short-term capital combined with a more favorable movement (reduction in the deficit) in the current account. Canadian interest rates remained above their counterparts in the U.S., which augmented and accelerated the capital inflow. The Ex-

[14] Of course, investment opportunities inside Canada may be the result of its exchange rate. A high rate may discourage imports and

so attract capital into the country to build up import-competing industries. But it also discourages exports and so dries up the flow of funds to the raw-material-shipping sectors. Advanced texts stress that whether an exchange rate shift increases or decreases long-run capital inflows depends on whether the export or the import industries are the more capital-intensive.

change Fund Account, in attempting to maintain the $0.92 pegged rate, was forced to purchase the foreign exchange. This in itself would have *expanded* the domestic money supply. The monetary authorities, faced with this situation, used open-market operations to counteract this expansion of the money supply and limit its growth. This policy put more upward pressure on domestic interest rates and so stimulated *further* short-term capital inflows. The Government's solution eventually was to alter the exchange rate. This was done in June, 1970, by allowing it to be determined by the demand and supply forces in the market, i.e., by allowing it to "float."

Earlier, in the inflation-policy discussions of 1968-1969, many economists deplored attempts to use monetary policy. Why? The exchange rate was then fixed. So tighter credit conditions, raising interest rates, *attracted* foreign capital thus providing alternative lenders, or as mentioned above, forcing the government to expand the domestic money supply (to replenish the Exchange Fund Account).

These examples of the apparent incompatibility of internal and external balance have recently been intensively studied by economists. They have asked: what combinations of internal and external policies can produce certain outcomes, such as full employment, a stable price level, and foreign balance?

The nature of the analysis is too advanced to explore here. But an example will show how the reasoning runs.

Assume capital is perfectly mobile, running into a country when interest rates rise, and out when they fall. Many questions can be asked, but consider this one: will monetary or fiscal policy be a more effective stabilizer when exchange rates are flexible?[15]

If the country uses monetary policy to counter a domestic slump, credit conditions will ease and interest rates fall. Capital will then tend to leave the country. This will cause the flexible exchange rate to fall. In turn, this will cause exports to rise and imports to fall. Thus, with mobile capital and flexible rates, both domestic investment *and* exports will rise when monetary policy is used. Both will have a multiplied effect on the home economy.

In contrast, if the country uses fiscal policy, say deficit spending financed by government borrowing, interest rates will tend to rise—they will not fall, anyway. Thus capital will tend to enter the country. Exchange rates will tend to rise, and the balance on current account will show a

[15] See Chapter 33's discussion of flexible exchange rates.

fall in exports and a rise in imports. These effects will cancel out the employment-creating effect of the fiscal policy.

Thus, with mobile capital and flexible exchange rates, monetary policy is more effective than fiscal policy for fighting stagnation and unemployment. This is why, during the early period of flexible exchange rates, economists urged Mr. Coyne to get easier credit conditions for Canada, rather than urging the government to undertake fiscal policy.[16]

Every country is faced with these choices among levels of internal and external balance. It is usually impossible to be in ideal equilibrium in both. In the '60s and the '70s for example, Germany suffered an excessive gold and capital inflow while coping with potential internal inflation and serious labor shortage. In Britain, meanwhile, persistently her internal price level got out of hand, and her current account floundered into increasing deficit—finally, to deal with the last problem, she revalued then floated the pound sterling. Canada like the United States, had full employment and rising prices, but Canada had a heavy capital inflow and the United States a chronic drain of gold and capital.

INFLATION. These older problems of the '60s and '70s were dealt with by various combinations of monetary and fiscal policy on the one hand, and exchange revaluations and international gold and dollar movements on the other. Today's problem has become one of inflation.

Previously, the countries attempted to prevent *unemployment* while keeping the exchange rate fixed. More recently they have attempted to avoid inflation, or stagflation. The academic economists' recipe has been unchanged. Use demand management's repertoire of monetary and fiscal policies to bring about domestic full employment without inflation. Throw in incomes-policies as required. Cool by insulating from foreign price-level increases. How? By using a flexible or floating exchange rate.

[16] Note that the analysis depends heavily on capital being perfectly mobile in response to credit conditions (interest rates). When capital movements are motivated by other things, the analysis has to be modified. The entire set of possibilities has been clearly worked out in a set of articles by R. A. Mundell. See for example his "Capital Mobility and Stabilization Policy Under Fixed and Flexible Exchange Rates," *Canadian Journal of Economics and Political Science* (November, 1963), pp. 475-9. Similar points have been made by Harry Johnson in his book *The Canadian Quandary* (Toronto: McGraw-Hill, 1965).

With flexible rates, rising foreign price levels for all goods and services, translated into import and export prices, are transformed into falling prices of foreign currencies. Increasing demand for the Canadian dollar, to buy cheaper Canadian goods, and diminishing supplies of this dollar (because foreign goods are rising in price), provide the dynamic explanation of the change. This is what *purchasing power parity* would predict also.

In the 1970-4 period, this indeed happened as between pairs of countries: those with the greatest rate of inflation (like the U.K.) suffered the greatest depreciation of their currency.

But are economists right that the flexible exchange recipe will prevent the transmission of inflation across frontiers? The time is too early yet to bring in a verdict, for lags and expectations are very important in pricing. Canadians tend to copy U.S. wage increases and price increases, and to keep the U.S. wage-price pattern and its change intact in trade and capital flows. If the flexible rate is to insulate Canadian prices, it will probably take several years before a pronounced difference is observable.

In the meantime, the government and the central bank must be watched. The bank's policy may well be to keep interest rates in Canada the same as in the U.S., rather than allow capital movements that push the exchange rates apart. (If a Canadian anti-inflation policy requires higher interest rates, there will tend to be a short-run capital inflow and an appreciation of the Canadian dollar.) This may be what the doctor ordered, but it will be unpopular with interest groups depending on exports. Anyway, it is difficult to explain high interest rates to business and home-building voters observing lower U.S. rates.

The government may also have a fit of nerves. To protect exporters, and to appease consumers of expensive imported goods, it may shrink allowing the Canadian dollar to appreciate. Instead, it may choose a "dirty float"—fixing the dollar by accumulating foreign exchange and "printing" more Canadian money.

The government's problem is indeed politically unattractive. To insulate ourselves from U.S. and foreign prices, we must adjust, in the sense used in Chapter 33's discussion of the gold standard and flexible rates. We must allow our currency to appreciate steadily, and indefinitely, to fill the increasing gap between foreign price index and ours. This process will be making life more difficult for our exporters, and for our import-competing industries. They will argue that there are worse things than having an inflation at the U.S. rate, and urge the government to let interest rates fall and the exchange rates to remain fixed.

Furthermore, as between Canada and the United States, there are experts, like the Economic Council of Canada's André Raynauld, who say that the two countries' policies, and moneys cannot move far apart.

If Raynauld is right, the Mundell thesis about optimal currency areas does not apply to the Canadian-American situation. The best we can do is to accommodate by micro-controls to macro policies which are essentially the same in the two countries. Canadian economists, both theorists and measurers, are investigating again the lessons of the earlier flexible-rate decade. Can we determine independently our own combinations of monetary, fiscal policies in demand management, and our own combination of unemployment and inflation? "More research is necessary."

SUMMARY

A. MODERN TRENDS AND INTERNATIONAL FINANCE INSTITUTIONS OF

1 Expanded exports—as in World Wars I and II—will have multiplier expansionary effects on a country. If previously it had unemployment and excess capacity, the result will be more jobs and output. If previously it had inflationary pressures, the result will be an intensification of them. The beggar-my-neighbor policies of the depressed thirties, by which each nation vainly tries to export its unemployment abroad, are self-defeating.

2　The World Bank, the International Monetary Fund, aid programs, Point Four assistance, the reciprocal-trade program for tariff reduction, the European Common Market—all these have been and are important factors in the postwar bid for more rational world trade.

3　The first decade after World War II was the period of dollar shortage. The United States dollar was undervalued in the sense that the other countries of the world, disrupted by war and with high cost structures, were avid to buy from her more than she wanted to buy from them. The sizable devaluations abroad in 1949, plus aid programs, America's cold-war spending, and finally, the miraculous spurt of productivity in the Common Market and Japan—all brought dollar shortage to an end.

B. BREAKDOWN OF THE INTERNATIONAL MONETARY SYSTEM

4　In the last decade a basic disequilibrium in America's balance of payments became evident: the United States' surplus on private current account simply was not large enough to offset (a) her substantial government defense and aid programs, and (b) the large volume of long-term foreign investment by United States firms seeking the high profits offered abroad in miracle-growth countries such as Canada.

5　No single factor can account for the reversal of dollar shortage. Certainly a basic cause seems to be the more rapid rate of growth in productivity in Western Europe and Japan than in North America rather than any upswing in U.S. generosity or—until Vietnam! —domestic inflation. This "basic imbalance" in the annual international flows places important constraints on domestic growth and stabilization policies.

6　No single remedy for a chronic U.S. payment disequilibrium could be prescribed. Steps to improve the situation would include sharing by others of aid and military burdens, lessening of discriminations, programs designed to improve the United States' productivity and selling efficency, better control over the cost-push pressures, and resort to protectionism and controls on foreign investment and trade. Finally, the U.S. had recourse to devaluation of her seemingly overvalued currency. The era of benign neglect only put off the day of reckoning. In the 1970s, the U.S. abandoned its role in the Bretton Woods system of gold convertibility to the U.S. dollar to which fixed rates were related.

7　The search for a new system, not based on U.S. dollar deficit reserves, commenced.

C. STRUCTURAL REFORM OF INTERNATIONAL FINANCE

8　The gold drain of the United States long covered up (a) the basic weakness in a world of change (and in which mixed economies will not submit to deflation and inflation) of a dollar-and-gold standard system based on *fixed* exchange rates; (b) the growing disequilibrium of the (overvalued) U.S. dollar over 15 years, a fact of especial importance in view of the dollar's role as key currency; and (c) long-run liquidity shortage of reserves in a world where foreign trade grows at 7 or 8 per cent per year while gold from mines grows at barely 2 per cent.

9　The major structural reforms involve (a) a massive increase in gold price; (b) freely floating, flexible exchange rates set completely by supply and demand; and (c) some version of the gliding band (or "crawling peg") providing limited flexibility of parity in any year, but necessary long-run flexibility. (Usually *widened* bands are proposed as part of the crawling peg.)

10　The two-tier system of gold, plus creating paper gold in the form of Special Drawing

Rights by the IMF, provide transition reforms. Coupled with initial parity realignments and a crawling peg, they can provide the world with a more rational and viable system. Both gold and the dollar can be phased out as sole resources, and some kind of ultimate dollar convertibility can be achieved.

CONCEPTS FOR REVIEW

exports, foreign investment, and
   the multiplier
World Bank and IMF
   aid programs
Common Market, customs union
GATT, the Kennedy Round
internal and external balance
dollar shortage to dollar glut
   and chronic deficits
financial discipline

productivity growth abroad
floating versus stable exchange
   rates
overvaluation, undervaluation
devaluation and gold's price
gliding band, or crawling peg
   widened bands
international liquidity plans
paper gold (SDRs)
two-tier system

QUESTIONS FOR DISCUSSION

1. Describe analytically post-World War II changes in the position of the U.S. dollar.
2. Contrast and compare the World Bank and the Monetary Fund.
3. Draw up a list of what you consider our most important international economic problems.
4. What effects can Canada expect from the European Common Market?
5. "Not a single industry should be sacrificed in the name of the GATT program for realizing freer multilateral trade". Do you agree?
6. Try using world production-possibility to illustrate the role of our post-World War II aid to the rest of the world. Was this merely "generosity"? Did generosity play any important role?
7. Contrast "dollar shortage" and "dollar glut". Diagnose and prescribe needed reforms.
8. Apply to an overvalued pound the reasonings used earlier for the U.S. dollar.
9. Why would you expect an interest-rate equalization tax on all foreign long-term securities to help U.S. capital accounts and international deficit? How might explicit taxing of foreign investment help the United States to reattain equilibrium?
10. Give pros and cons of flexible exchange rates, changing gold price, two-tier system.
11. What do you understand the term "paper gold" to mean?
12. Can you sit down and write out in a couple of paragraphs just what is meant by "gliding bands, or crawling pegs"?

6

Current Economic Problems

37
THE THEORY OF GROWTH

... when you can measure what you are speaking about, and express it in numbers, you know something about it; when you cannot measure it, when you cannot express it in numbers, your knowledge is of a meager and unsatisfactory kind; it may be the beginning of knowledge, but you have scarcely, in your thoughts, advanced to the stage of science ...   LORD KELVIN

In the final section of this book, we can mobilize the tools of economic analysis to show their relevance to the burning issues of our age. To theories of economic growth (Chapter 37). To the processes by which the less developed countries can better their economic well-being (Chapter 38).

As old problems get partially solved, new problems are forced into the social agenda. Chapter 39 analyzes the problems of cities and the polluted environment. Chapter 40 faces up to the age-old curses of poverty and discrimination. Chapter 41 discusses new currents in economics and ideology: the old and the new left; *laissez-faire,* or libertarianism; mainstream liberalism and its critics; the young and mature Karl Marx.

The key word in many economic discussions these days is "growth". Why did Germany and Japan grow faster than the other Western countries in the 1950s? Is the USSR growing as rapidly as it claims? Is it possible for it to grow as fast as a mixed enterprise system like ours? In overcrowded countries like India and Egypt, can the desperate effort to improve technology and to mechanize production overtake exploding population?

All the tools of economic analysis developed in this book are needed to shed light on such difficult and important social problems. This chapter will apply the *principles* of economic theory to the process of growth and development, in preparation for the next chapters' applications.[1]

STAGES OF HISTORY

Napoleon agreed with Voltaire that history is but "a fable agreed upon." It was long the fashion to regard economic development as a timetable. Dr. Spock can guess that a baby at so many weeks will begin to see things, and he can make predictions about when it will walk and talk. Often he may err, but *it is remarkable how predictable the stages of biological growth prove to be.* Scholars used to think economic history could be treated in the same way.

Friedrich List, in his 1841 *National System of Political Economy*, was one of the first to divide economic history into stages. Especially in Germany, this became a popular notion a century ago. A new group of scholars, called the Historical School, came near to saying: "Throw away fancy theories. Grub in the facts. Collect them. Sort and sift them. Let them tell their own story."

The first step for any scientist is indeed to maintain a respect for the facts. But alas, it is not the last. *The facts never tell their own story.* Truth, like beauty, is oft in the eye of the beholder. No two writers ever seem to be told the same fables of development by the accumulated almanacs of facts. Some, and they included Karl Marx (1818-1883), saw in history a one-way evolution.

PRIMITIVE CULTURE First, there were marauding hunters and self-sufficient tribal families cultivating crops. (Supposedly, they still survive in some isolated jungles.)

FEUDALISM. Gradually, as elbow room began to be scarce, the primitive economy was succeeded by classical autarky, which evolved into feudalism. In the Middle Ages, a settled chain of command, based largely on land relationships, governed all economic and social life, from nobility down to serf.

CAPITALISM Whether or not one thought the Middle Ages idyllic, feudalism in its turn was brought to an end when the periods of the Renais-

---

[1] For a short course, skip this chapter. Or skip the theoretical "Detailed Economic Analysis of Smith-Malthus" later in this chapter.

sance and Reformation ushered in the commercial and industrial revolutions. Peasants were alienated from the soil and forced into the cities as a proletariat. Rivers were dammed to harness water, and the invention of the steam engine enabled the energy of wood and coal to replace the energy of beast and man. The Calvinist ethic helped to create business-minded entrepreneurs.

As if in a play, the curtain came down on feudalism, and mankind was supposedly ushered onto the stage of bourgeois, middle-class capitalism. (Of course, isolated countries like Japan were not expected to move from feudalism to capitalism in exactly the same time periods; but when their time came, the process could be expected to be qualitatively similar even if more compressed in duration.)

Self-satisfied historians of the Victorian age, like Macaulay or Herbert Spencer, looked upon the evolution of society as an ascent of man toward higher forms. But now that the more or less perfect state of Victorian capitalism had been reached, they thought evolution could have its final day of rest. All that remained was further progress toward removing tariffs and the few other governmental fiats still interfering with the *laissez-faire* market place. Spencer could contemplate with mathematical certainty the withering away of the state and the supremacy of free markets. Invention by science, better education of the masses, and individual intiative could be expected to produce steady gains in living standards in this best of all possible worlds. (In our time, Frederich Hayek in Freiburg and Milton Friedman in Chicago look back to the Victorian Whig society as a golden age, to be reattained by democratic dismantling of the welfare state.)

SOCIALISM AND COMMUNISM
Having eaten of the fruit of the tree of evolution, why should men think that the play of history has to be written in only three acts? In a country like Germany, which had never been imbued with the tradition of individual and business freedom, philosophers thought that capitalism, too, was but a passing stage, to be succeeded in its turn by state fascism or communism, just as it had succeeded dying feudalism. Marx and Engels wrote in *The Communist Manifesto*:

"The modern bourgeois society has sprouted from the ruins of feudal society ... The modern laborer ... becomes a pauper ... What the bourgeoisie therefore produces ... are its own grave diggers. Its fall and the victory of the proletariat are equally inevitable."

Events rarely agree with fable.[2] Thus, the revolutions in France and Germany that Engels and Marx expected failed to materialize in the weeks, months, and years after their excited letters about them were written. And real wages, instead of falling or remaining constant in the decades since Marx's 1867 *Das Kapital*, turned out on statistical examination to have been rising dramatically under industrial capitalism. Even the rate of profit stubbornly refused to follow the rate of decline predicted for it and instead wanders without any strong trend.

The single most surprising development of our age has been the unpredicted vigor of the modern mixed economy. The miracles of sustained growth in production and living standards have taken place in the second level countries—Japan, Germany, Italy, France, Scandinavia, Western Europe generally—rather than in the most advanced countries like the United States and Canada or in the less developed countries of Latin America, Africa, and Asia, whose slower rates of growth imply a widening relative gap.

Social prophets of our day such as Schumpeter and Toynbee, to say nothing of Veblen or Spengler years ago, thought of the mixed economy as "capitalism in an oxygen tent". But the growth experience of the third quarter of the twentieth century revealed that a market economy enriched by some government planning and macroeconomic controls could perform favorably in comparison with past epochs of both capitalist and communist development. We are thus warned to place limited confidence in the allegedly scientific proofs that one stage in history must inevitably be succeeded by a particular next stage.

This sketch of the development of a mixed economy is all too brief, but it represents a fair summary of economic history as presented by Western historians. Because it is completely rejected by Communist

---

[2] M. I. Rostovtzeff, *Social and Economic History of the Roman Empire* (Oxford University Press, New York, 1926), showed that an elaborate system of international markets and trade in non-luxury goods existed long before the Middle Ages. Compound interest appears on Babylonian cuneiform tablets, and some nations are repeating in the 1970s the worst errors of historic mercantilism. Neither progress nor perpetual oscillation correctly portrays the richness of economic history.

writers, Voltaire and Napoleon were wrong: apparently "history is a fable *not* agreed upon."

Let us now turn to various economic models which can help us to understand history rather than to compress it into neat explanations that pretend to predict the future with certainty. Our task is to understand the actual development of wages and profits, of labor and capital, and of national product.

THE "MAGNIFICENT DYNAMICS" OF SMITH AND MALTHUS

In *The Wealth of Nations* (1776), Adam Smith wrote a handbook of economic development. He preached the great efficiency that comes from specialization, division of labor, and exchange. He stressed the need to remove the blundering hand of mercantilistic governments; to cultivate attitudes of honesty, zeal, and thriftiness; to *unleash the competitive profit motive, which would—as if led by an Invisible Hand—achieve the maximum well-being of all.*

LABOR THEORY OF VALUE IN A GOLDEN AGE   Smith had also a theory of dynamic development. He and Malthus began with a hypothetical golden age—"that original state of things, which precedes both the appropriation of land and the accumulation of stock"—when labor alone counted, when land was freely available to all, and before the use of capital had begun. What determined pricing and distribution in this simple and timeless state? Answer: The undiluted labor theory of value.

To see this, consider Smith's famous case of deer and beaver. Suppose 2 hours of hunting yields 1 deer; or 4 hours yields 1 beaver. Then the price ratio between deer and beaver will be set by comparative labor time alone: the price of 1 beaver will equal 2 deer. Why 2 deer per beaver? Because the price ratio can be computed in necessary labor time as 4 hours (of sweaty work)/2 hours (of sweaty work).

The determination of price by labor cost alone would apply no matter how many goods there were; and it would be enforced in any primitive market by having hunters shift from one good to the other if ever that other good's price got out of line and offered a profit advantage. It is still true that supply and demand is operating in this golden age; but the situation is so simple that we do not need elaborate *dd* and *ss* curves. The long-run *ss* curves for the different goods are simple horizontal lines at the stated labor costs; so long as there is enough demand to have the goods produced at all, labor costs will be the determining factor.

NOTE: Demand is still there in the background; thus, if it would cost 10 hours to hunt a skunk, and yet nobody received any utility from skunks, skunks would not be hunted and would not be bought and sold at a price of 10 hours, or of 5 deer.

POPULATION GROWTH   Now consider Smith-Malthus dynamics. Life is pleasant in the golden age. Babies are born, and the population doubles about every 25 years. Since there is plenty of land, people move west and spill over onto more acres. National output exactly doubles as population doubles. Price ratios of deer and beaver remain exactly as before. What about real wages? Real wages still get all the national income, there being as yet no subtractions for land rent or interest on capital. What is the real wage per hour? So long as land can expand proportionally to the expansion of labor, the law of diminishing returns cannot come into operation. The wage rate per hour remains at one-half deer or at one-fourth beaver, as determined by labor productivity.

That would be the end of the story, unless some clever inventor found a new way of doing in 1 hour what used to take 2 hours. This would raise the national product per capita. Such a balanced improvement would leave the price ratio of beaver to deer unchanged; but it would double the real wage rate. In the rude dawn of the undiluted labor theory of value, investment can only raise wages and the pace of balanced expansion.[3]

---

[3] The graphical production-possibility frontier of Chapter 2 can show all this. For a society with 100 hours of labor, the *p-p frontier* must now be drawn as a straight line going from the intercept on the vertical axis of the 50 deer producible with that much labor to the intercept on the horizontal axis of 25 beaver. The absolute slope of this *p-p frontier* would give the 2/1 price ratio prevailing at any point where both goods were being produced and consumed. (The marginal-utility and indifference-curve analysis of Chapter 22 and its Appendix is still needed to tell *where* society ends up on the *p-p frontier*.) Now a new doubling of labor productivity in all industries would move the *p-p frontier* out in a parallel position so as to depict an exact doubling of national product. The interested reader can show that an invention which tripled the productivity of beaver hunting, while only doubling that of deer hunting, would flatten the shifted-out curve, changing the price ratio from 2/1 (equals 4 hours per bea-

SCARCE LAND AND DIMINISHING RE-TURNS Even had golden ages ever existed, they could not have lasted once all land became fully populated. As we saw in Chapter 2, Malthus pointed to this flaw in the happily expanding economy. Once the frontier of virgin land disappears, new laborers begin to crowd onto existing cultivated soils. For the first time, private property in land springs up; now land is scarce, and a rent is charged to ration it.

Growth does take place in this classical world of Smith-Malthus following on the golden age. Population grows, and so does national product. But product cannot grow proportionately to labor. Why? *Because with new laborers added to fixed land, each worker now has less land to work with.* Naturally, therefore the law of diminishing returns (of Chapters 2 and 27) comes into operation. The increasing labor-land and decreasing output-land ratios mean a declining contribution of each last (or marginal) worker to product, and hence declining real wage rates.

As David Ricardo pointed out:

A conflict of interests arises between classes. More babies mean lower per capita incomes and lower wage rates; lower wage rates mean higher rent rates per acre of land. Landlords gain as labor loses. This is why Carlyle criticized economics as the "dismal science."

To understand the brute fact of economic inequality, we have to jettison the simple labor theory of value and study the effects of scarcity in the productive factors that labor needs access to.

PARADISE LOST AND REGAINED How bad can things get? Gloomy Malthus thought, at least in his first edition of 1798, that the end of economic de-velopment could be only an equilibrium down at *the minimum level of subsistence.* Above this subsistence wage, population would continue to grow; below it, population would die off; only at this level could there be lasting equilibrium (Recall Chapter 2's discussion of Malthus.)

Biological fecundity was a fact of nature; diminishing returns was a fact of nature. Only sentimentalists could refuse to face the sad facts of life prevailing once man had left the golden Garden of Eden. It is for precisely these reasons that Adam Smith had earlier said: Lucky is a nation that is growing rapidly, for it has not yet made its sad rendezvous with its destined equilibrium at the minimum of subsistence. Sad is that nation which has reached the stationary equilibrium of the subsistence level, where deaths just cancel out births.

What did Malthus (and Smith) forget, or at least underestimate? Malthus failed to realize how technical innovation could intervene—not to *repeal* the law of diminishing returns, but to *more than offset* it. He stood at the brink of a new century and failed to anticipate that the succeeding two centuries would show the greatest scientific gains history has ever recorded—a chastening fact, well to keep in mind as one listens to the voice of the modern computer as it sings out the same Malthusian dirge.

DETAILED ECONOMIC ANALYSIS OF SMITH-MALTHUS

To understand the world's population problem for the next centuries—and the problems of India, Indonesia, and China in the next two decades—we must master the above classical model, which may have more *future* relevance than it has had for us since Malthus' time. As a bonus, the same graphical tools will apply when we investigate the role of capital formation as a factor of growth for Germany, Japan, Canada, the United States, and the less developed countries of the world.

Table 37-1 and Fig. 37-1 show succinctly how the tendency of population to grow when the wage is above the level of minimum of subsistence will (1) end the golden age of abundant and free land, and (2) lead to an economic growth path that approaches a stationary equilibrium at the minimum of subsistence. (Begin with the table).

ver ÷ 2 hours per deer) to 4/3 (equals 4/3 hours per beaver ÷ 1 hour per deer). Now the real wage rate has risen, but unequally when computed in terms of the different goods: the real wage has tripled in terms of beaver, but only doubled in terms of deer; lovers of fur coats have gained more than lovers of venison. (Note: Suppose laborers are not homogeneous. If men are *everywhere* twice as productive as women, Marx and Ricardo would redefine socially necessary labor units, treating 1 man as 2 basic labor units, etc. But if men are *unequally* superior to women in different jobs—being twice as productive in beaver, thrice as productive in deer, and half as productive in potatoes—the crude labor theory of value breaks down: now we must know the demand condition of non-Marxian economics to determine equilibrium prices.) Cf. Chapter 41 for more on Marx.

Relation of Output to Labor and Land						
	(1) ACRES OF LAND	(2) MAN-DAYS OF LABOR	(3) OUTPUT OF FOOD	(4) WAGE IN FOOD PER DAY	(5) LABOR'S SHARE OF NNP$_r$ %	(6) RENT IN FOOD PER ACRE
A	1,000	500	4,000	8	100	0
		501	4,008			
A'	1,000	1,000	8,000	8	100	0
		1,001	8,008			
B	1,000	3,000	20,000	5	75	5
		3,001	20,005			
E	1,000	6,000	33,600	4.2	75	8.4
		6,001	33,604.2			
Z	1,000	8,000	39,000	0	0	39
		8,001	39,000			

TABLE 37-1. Diminishing returns from population growth ends classical development.
Higher labor-land density reduces output per man, lowers the marginal-product wage;
hence land rent per ever-scarcer acre becomes increasingly positive.

Table 37-1 shows the decline in wage rate when the fixity of land keeps output from growing as fast as labor. Column (1) shows unchanged land. Column (2) shows growing labor. Column (3) shows the resulting growth in output, (Q or GNP) which, because of the fixity of land, is *less* than proportional to labor growth. All the remaining information can be computed from these production-function data alone.

To get the declining wage rate of Column (4), we have to repeat Chapter 27's calculation of what the *last* worker *adds* to total product. (Recall that this is termed the marginal-physical-product of each of the identical workers.) Let us add one worker to 1,000 existing workers at A'. Note that output rises from Q = 8,000 to Q = 8,008 units. This gives extra product per extra worker of 8; so the marginal-product and real wage rate must then be 8 units of output per worker. Check that the extra product and wage falls to 5.0 at B, to 4.2 at E, and finally to zero at Z, where land is so overcrowded as to be unable to produce any extra output regardless of added labor.

To get the relative share of labor in the net national product, we multiply the wage rate of each worker by the number of workers. Then we divide this total wage bill, wL, by total GNP, Q. Note that labor's share in Column (5) soon falls from 100 per cent of GNP to 75 per cent, and ultimately down to 0 per cent. Who gets the remaining share? By our assumption that there is no capital to clutter up the labor-and-land model, all other returns must go for

land rent. With total acres unchanged, we simply divide up land's calculated share of total output by the fixed number of acres. Obviously, the rent per acre must therefore *rise* in Column (6) as the wage rate *falls* in Column (4), just as David Ricardo warned.

GRAPH OF MALTHUSIAN DEVELOPMENT

Figure 37-1 depicts all this. In Fig. 37-1(a), we see the wage rate declining as the law of diminishing returns pushes labor's marginal productivity downward. What keeps the wage from falling down to zero on this *dd* demand curve for labor? Actually, it stops falling where *dd* intersects the *ss* horizontal supply curve set by the minimum wage at which people can subsist and just barely reproduce their numbers. The Malthusian equilibrium at E is a gloomy one, anything but golden.

Gloomy or not, it does represent a *stable* equilibrium. Test it. Let a plague temporarily reduce numbers, moving us to the left at E. Real wages then become high (as they actually did after the Great Plague of 1665), standing at a point on the *dd* curve above E. But the system cannot stay there. With wages high enough to cause population to grow, we again move gradually back toward the equilibrium at E, as shown by the converging arrows. (Note that a temporary growth of population beyond E, as from a temporary run of good harvests, will mean a wage

(a)

(b)

FIG. 37-1. Population grows until Malthusian state of minimum subsistence is reached.

Population growth moves us from the golden age of A, A', and a down the diminishing-returns marginal-product curve dd, to the Malthusian equilibrium at intersection with ss supply curve of subsistence wage. The fall in real wage rate from a to b to e implies rising rent rates along the "factor-price frontier" ff. Because inventions shift dd and ff upward and rightward, historically the real wage rose from B to B' to B'' levels, with rent rising from b to b' to b''.

rate so much below subsistence as to kill people off until the arrow moves us up dd back to E.)

Figure 37-1(b) shows that the rent rate per acre rises as the wage rate per hour falls. On what may be called "the factor-price frontier" (shown as ff), landlords are seen to be better off at the high-rent Malthusian subsistence equilibrium e than they were in the earlier golden age at a. No wonder some landlords greeted with joy the introduction of the white potato, which enabled people to live on cheaper calories, and hence in effect lowered the old ss subsistence curve and raised equilibrium rents. And no wonder some few landlords regarded the spreading of birth-control information as a threat to their own standards of living. One man's slavery is another man's comfort.

The Ricardians actually exaggerated the conflict of class interest. While population growth might imply higher rent per acre, they were wrong to think it had to imply a larger *percentage share* of GNP going to land. Note in Column (5) of Table 37-1 that labor keeps getting 75 per cent of the total, although the wage rate drops from B to E and the rent rises from b to e.[4]

[4] Very little is known about what fraction of GNP is pure land rent. One reason is that statisticians are unable to disentangle rent from profit and interest in the accounts of the major land-using companies, or from any other incomes in the accounts of many farmers. Nor are we certain whether we would expect the fraction to rise or fall over time with economic growth, once we

END OF THE LABOR THEORY OF VALUE

The simple labor theory of value, which said that the price ratios of goods can be predicted from labor costs alone, independently of the utilities which bring out a demand for the goods, thus had to be dropped to account for the facts of land scarcity. Costs of production now include rent as well as wage payments. Two goods, like food and clothing, may now have equal labor costs per unit, but if food requires more land cost per unit than does clothing, they will no longer sell on a one-to-one basis.

Worse than that, from the standpoint of an advocate hankering for a labor theory of value, suppose

know that real wages are also rising in accordance with the development of new inventions and the rise in population. It is obvious that when the Canadian prairies were opened to settlement, rent incomes must have gone up—but did they rise as fast as the labor incomes of the new settlers? Colin Clark's estimates for various countries suggest that all were able to substitute capital and labor for scarce land; and important new estimates by Edward Denison imply that while land accounted for 9 per cent of American product in the 1900s, it accounts for only 3 per cent today. However, high scarcity rents of valuable lands, mines, and forests still exist, and still create incentives for man to "invent his way" to supplying final products from raw materials drawn from cheaper and more plentiful sources. Thus Canadian oilfields and forests yield nylon and rayon in place of the scarce mulberry-leaf and silkworm needed to grow silk in Japan. See Colin Clark, *The Conditions of Economic Progress*, 3rd ed., (Macmillan, London, 1957) and for E. Denison, see *Canadian Growth Revisited, 1950-1967*, Ottawa, 1970.

that people in a capitalistic or socialistic state shift their demand toward producing more food and less clothing. This must make the price of food *rise* relative to that of clothing. Why? Because food requires more land per worker than does clothing. Hence, the fixed land becomes more scarce when people want more of the product that is "land-intensive," thus bidding up rent at the expense of wages.

Under neither socialism nor capitalism can we succeed in predicting commodity prices from labor requirements alone, taking no account of the pattern of tastes and demand and its effects on scarcity of nonlabor factors.[5]

What about labor's *right* to all the product? Labor is the only input that is human and can sweat, laugh, cry, and pray. True. Yet, even though dirt cannot sweat or cry, it does contribute toward the growing of potatoes, and needs to be economized in the good society.

One who wants to make a logical case for labor's being "exploited" need not handicap himself by a simple labor theory of value. If his philosophy or that of the state he lives in dictates it, he may challenge the *title* to land of those who call themselves landlords and *their special right* to rents. He may claim that only the peasants have a valid title to the land and to rent, or that only the state has. Who receives rents is an ethical or legal problem. But whatever its solution, rational use of land does require that a rent cost be charged the consumers who buy its products and the factors that are best fitted to work with it. (Recall the Appendix to Chapter 32 on efficient socialist pricing.)

Chapter 41 will do greater justice to the Marxian economic concepts.

---

[5] Footnote 3 pointed out that, in the golden age of free land, society's production-possibility schedule was a straight line with slope determined by labor productivities alone. Now with land scarce and more important in food than in clothing production, the production-possibility schedule is bowed out for the reasons explained in Chapter 2's discussion of the law of increasing (relative) cost. (Cf. also Appendix to Chapter 27, question 4.) The slope of the production-possibility frontier which determines the competitive price ratio now depends on where people's demand leaves us. (It can be shown that Ricardians erred in thinking they could "get rid of land as a complicating factor" by going out to "the external margin" of poor, no-rent land upon which production was so low that all its costs would have to go to labor alone. Actually that margin shifts when demand shifts.)

TECHNICAL ADVANCE AND CLASSICAL GROWTH THEORY

As mentioned, real wages have risen historically, not fallen. Population has not stabilized. Land rents per acre have risen surprisingly little and, relative to other factor-prices, have actually declined. It is evident that life has not consisted of a movement down an unchanged factor-price frontier or marginal-product curve. Inventions of science, of engineering, and of managerial practice have *shifted* the curves of Fig. 37-1 rightward and upward. The black lines of progress—*BB'B''* and *bb'b''*—show the actual course of history; the reader may draw on his copy of Fig. 37-1 the shifted *dd* and factor-price frontiers that correspond to B' or B'' and to b' or bb''. Such shifts have more than won the race with diminishing returns, making the Malthusian equilibrium-point of subsistence unrealistic in Western economies so far.

Not all inventions are even-handedly favorable to labor and to land. Thus, inventions which help to drain swamps or to grow more food on the same acres of land might help wages more than they help rents. Some economists would call these "land-saving inventions." In contrast, any inventions that tended to raise rents more than wages, thereby tending to increase landlords' share of GNP, might be called "labor-saving inventions."[6] In between would be the case of inventions that raised both factor returns by the same percentage, leaving relative shares of NNP unchanged: these might be called "neutral inventions." In the history of the West, inventions have appeared to be land-saving on balance; but few inventions have been so land-saving as actually to lower rents *absolutely* along with lowering them relative to wages.

The ghost of Carlyle should be relieved to know that economics, after all, has not been a dismal science. It has been the impatient science of growth.

STAPLES, REGIONS, AND ECONOMIC GROWTH

So far we have stressed the classical preoccupation with scarce land. But classical economists based their

---

[6] The "green revolution" of new wheat and rice cultivation in recent years seems to have been more labor-saving: the Asian peasants have not done so well as the owners who have access to irrigation and fertilizer.

theories chiefly on one-use land of varying qualities on which either it paid to grow "corn" (wheat) or it paid to abandon it. This was true even of classical authorities like Lord Durham's advisor and confidant, Gibbon Wakefield, who was much involved in land settlement schemes in the British colonies, or the earlier Colonel Torrens, an English monetary expert who did much to devise the land-registry system now used in the Western provinces and Australia. They neglected the fact that some land may earn a high rent under one use, but be valueless under another; Canadian forests, for example, were valueless when early arrivals sought only fish, rose in value under the fur trade, were declared a nuisance and avoided by those seeking their fortune in agriculture, only to come back into their own again in the lumber and pulp eras of recent history.

It was the particular contribution of Toronto's later economic historian Harold A. Innis to point out that the course of Canadian economic development depended on these successive demands for the harvest of Canadian resources. Each of them in turn dominated the growth and expansion of the economy, shaping the transportation network and pattern of settlement. Further, their successive importance as "staples," as Innis called them, depended on technological change and tastes, usually in markets remote from Canada. The fur trade, for example, depended partly on the existence in Europe of a felting process for using beaver fur in hats; the forest-products industry got its greatest boost from the growth of American literacy and the consequent demand for newsprint; waterpower development soared with the exploding world demand for aluminum, and so on.

EXPANSION VERSUS GROWTH Recently a controversy has arisen about whether the undoubted successive emergence of "staples" had much to do with economic growth. Without going into the details of the criticisms of Innis and his followers (which, like all such arguments, is a dispute about what Innis "really meant"), it is now recognized that an important distinction must be made. The periods dominated by the production and export of a single staple all brought about "expansions" in the economy. They moved the marginal-product curve dd of Fig. 37-1 upward, when dd is interpreted as applying to the use of labor in a particular region. The workers in that region, if fixed in number, would now get a higher real wage. But if they were not fixed in number, the rise in real wages would draw in workers from other regions, *and immigrants from other countries* who previously earned less than the new real wage. Thus the region would "expand" as it produced the new staple. To the extent that the new workers came from abroad, the staple would cause the whole economy to "expand"; especially when it is remembered that the expansion would both require other workers to feed and clothe the new arrivals and motivate investment (with its multiplier effects) in new canals, railways, and schools.

The critics point out that such expansion is not the same as economic growth, because neither real wages nor NNP per person may be any higher after the staple is under full production than they were originally. All that may result is that the total population and work force will be larger. Professors Gordon and Chambers, for example, say that the wheat boom between 1901 and 1911 scarcely lifted the Canadian NNP per head but merely expanded the economy sideways across the continent. (Of course, the average immigrant was better off than he had been in Scotland or the Ukraine.)

On the other hand, all economists agree that, if the Canadian population remains mobile and immigration is small, the successive appearance of staples can set the stage for steady growth. As the value of the products of the various regions rises, Canadians move to wherever their marginal productivity is highest. The final effect is that the typical worker is "re-equipped" with more productive land; this is similar to re-equipping a worker, in a given location, with newly invented tools. Whether or not the appearance of a new staple product in the economy will lift the average output depends, therefore, on whether existing workers take the new jobs, thus raising their incomes, or whether new workers come in from abroad. In turn, this depends on whether Canadians are more mobile than potential immigrants. To the extent that a new staple product raises productivity, the staple approach to economic history in countries of numerous regions can be interpreted as a special kind of theory of economic growth. It is, however, very close analytically to more general theories that depend on giving a fixed number of workers an increased amount of capital to work with, such as the models next discussed.[7]

RICARDO-MARX-SOLOW[8] MODELS OF CAPITAL ACCUMULATION

In the remainder of this chapter, we shall survey the more important model of capital and labor, pushing land and regional differences to the side as being less important for much of the developed part of the world. We can now use exactly the same tools in a simplified two-factor model.

Basic assumption of capital-labor model: One factor grows relative to another. Now population will be regarded primarily as a noneconomic variable, being stationary (or growing slowly for sociological reasons). Accumulation will make capital the varying factor. In an oversimplified model where output is produced by a relatively fixed and a relatively varying factor, the law of diminishing returns sets in. The return of the augmented factor falls; the return of the relatively scarce labor factor rises. In the absence of technical change, a stationary state of equilibrium will be approached.

NOTIONS OF CAPITAL It is now capital,[9] written as K, that is the factor growing relative to labor, L. Capital goods consist of a great variety of things: machines of various kinds; plants and houses; tools; raw materials and goods in process (seed grain, growing wheat plants, harvested wheat, flour, dough, warm loaves, wrapped and delivered bread); and canned and frozen edibles.

Society can sum the market values of these physical goods to get total wealth or total capital value; but it cannot command a million dollars of electric generators to transmute

themselves into a million dollars of oil-refining equipment. It is true, however, that as generators wear out, the resources which could have gone to replacing them can be shifted to turn out extra refining equipment; the financial counterpart of this physical alchemy is to have investors in the generator industry take the money funds accruing on account of depreciation there and transfer them to finance extra investment in the equipment industry. Result: although the total balance sheet of money capital may show a practically unchanged total, and although the national-income statistician shows only a cancellation of one kind of disinvestment against another kind of investment, still society has managed to change the physical composition of its capital without undergoing any change in current consumption of goods.

To give the idealized or stylized story of development all the rope it needs, we shall oversimplify as all statisticians and economic historians do: we shall work with an index number of real capital goods, K, supposing that its return is the rate of interest or profit.

EFFECTS OF CAPITAL DEEPENING What happens to per capita output when capital grows relative to labor—that is, when capital "deepens"? Recall what happened to output per acre when labor grew relative to land. Output there grew less than proportionally to growth in the varying factor (labor), and so its factor price (the wage) had to *fall*. A similar law of diminishing returns comes into operation in an over-simplified model whenever one factor (such as capital) grows faster than another factor (such as labor) with all technical change absent:

1. Output will not grow in proportion to the growth in the capital stock.

2. The return to capital, the interest rate per annum—or what is the same thing if we rule out risk and technical change, the profit rate—will fall as capital deepens.

3. What happens to the wage rate now that each man works with more capital goods and with the more intricate capital goods the economy can now afford in the environment of a lower interest and profit rate? Just as the rent earned by relatively scarce land rose in Fig. 37-1, here the competitive wage return to relatively scarce labor will rise, as men become worth more to capitalists and meet with spirited bidding up of their market wage rates. (NOTE: Competition, not altruism, is at work.)

4. Higher wage rates and lower interest rates do

---

[7] The important difference is that new resources for new staples may be "free," not requiring much or any previous investment, whereas new capital goods invariably require previous saving and investment. For a recent short, and interesting survey see Robin Neill, *A New Theory of Value—The Canadian Economics of H. A. Innis*, Toronto, University of Toronto Press, 1972.

[8] In the mid-1950s, Robert Solow at MIT gave new life to the one-sector Ramsey-Clark neoclassical model of growth. T Swan of Canberra and J. E. Meade of Cambridge analyzed at the same time similar adaptations of the classical Ricardo-Marx models.

[9] Chapter 30 and Appendix discussed capital theory and intractable problems of measuring it.

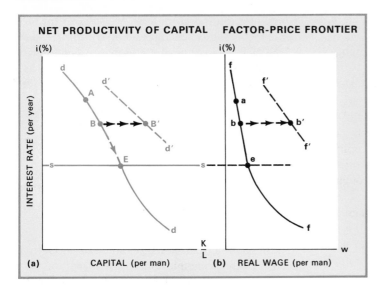

NET PRODUCTIVITY OF CAPITAL   FACTOR-PRICE FRONTIER

(a) CAPITAL (per man)   (b) REAL WAGE (per man)

FIG. 37-2. Accumulation of capital raises output and wage, tends to depress interest rate:

Adding more and a greater variety of capital goods to fixed labor will, in the absence of technical change, add less and less to total product, causing interest rate earned to fall along *dd* from *B* to *E*, which is the Ricardian equilibrium point at which saving will cease. Along *ff*, fall in interest rate from *b* to *e* must raise the real wage earnable from labor's higher productivity.

Historically, technical innovation has shifted *dd* and *ff* rightward just about fast enough to offset diminishing returns and to keep the interest and profit rate almost unchanged, as shown by horizontal arrows from *B* to *B'* and *b* to *b'*.

not necessarily imply a higher percentage *share* for labor at the expense of the percentage share of capitalists. Why not? Because the increase in capital relative to labor might offset (or even more than offset) the decline in the interest rate and the rise in the real wage.[10]

5. Finally, since output (per capita or total) grew less than in proportion to the increase in capital (per capita or total), the capital-output ratio would rise in the absence of technical change (e.g., from capital value being 3 times annual GNP up to 3 1/2 times).

Here is a final summary:

> Deepening of Capital (unchanged technology)
> Capital/labor up: interest or profit rate
> down: wage rate up: capital/output up

DEEPENING OF CAPITAL IN DIAGRAM FORM

Figure 37-2(a) and (b) needs no numerical table. It is like Fig. 37-1(a) and (b); but now capital is the relatively growing factor. Capital's amount per capita is given on the horizontal axis of (a), and its interest or profit return goes on the vertical axes. And now

[10] Example: Let capital double from 1 million dollars to 2 million dollars, while labor stays at 30 men; let interest drop from 5 to 4 per cent, and the wage rise from $5,000 per year to $8,000. Total wage's return then continues to be 3 times that of capital's, each having risen by 60 per cent from their initial respective values of $150,000 and $50,000 per year.

labor is the relatively fixed factor, and its wage goes on the horizontal axis of (b) just the way land rent did in Fig. 37-1(b).

In the absence of technical change, capital accumulation takes us down the *dd* curve from *A* to *B* and perhaps ultimately to the Ricardian equilibrium point *E* at which people feel it no longer pays them to save any per cent of their incomes for enhanced future consumption. On the factor-price frontier *ff* in Fig. 37-2(b), society can successively be at *a*; or at *b* with the higher wage rate and lower interest rate that are implied by an augmented capital stock (more machines available of *every* kind per man); or at *e* with a still higher capital-output and capital-labor ratio. The earlier literary summary of the effects of capital deepening is verified by these graphs.

TECHNICAL PROGRESS AND WAGES

Now let us reintroduce improving technology. This will shift the *dd* and *ff* curves outward, for example, to *d'd'* and *f'f'*. Instead of moving from *B* down to *E*, society may find that diminishing returns are offset; and the economy might in actual historical fact move from *B* to *B'*, negating or concealing the Ricardo-

Marx law of the declining rate of profit. Note in Fig. 37-2(b) that the real wage rate must definitely rise, with or without technical improvements, so long as the profit rate stays the same or falls.[11]

An alternative theory would ascribe the rise of wages under capitalism to (1) trade-union pressure, (2) government regulation of monopoly, and (3) interventions of a welfare and regulatory kind by democratic governments reacting to militant political pressures from the masses. This cannot be rejected as without substance, for we have seen throughout this book that government actions do have consequences for both good and evil. But the magnitude and pattern of the rise in real wages in this last century have been such as to cast doubt on labor union or political action as an important part of the explanation. Thus, real wages rose strongly in North America after World War I; yet unions were not strong, government intervention in production or income redistribution was minor, and monopoly was certainly not suppressed. Neither can it be said that *changes* in the importance of land and its rent were striking in either Canada or the United States. Similarly, Japan and West Germany have shown sharp growth in labor productivity, and this at times when government seemed pro-business rather than pro-labor.

With the advance of technology and the piling up of a larger stock of capital goods, it would take a veritable miracle (or tens of millions of immigrants) to keep real wages of men from being bid ever higher with each passing decade. Who fails to see that fails to understand economic history as it actually happened. Economic theories that do not fit these facts have had to be junked and replaced by others that do.

THE APPROXIMATE FACTS OF MODERN DEVELOPMENT

Let us summarize our theoretical researches.

So far, we have studied the crucial role of limited land and growing labor in economic progress. Then we passed from the land-labor world of Smith-Malthus, one that studied the role in economic growth of capital accumulation relative to

labor. Last, but far from least, we stressed the factor of technological change and innovation. A look at the facts will show why present-day economists think that scientific and engineering progress has been quantitatively the single most important factor for growth in the advanced countries.

Thanks to two generations of economists and statisticians, we can formulate certain general uniformities of economic development. In Canada, data have emerged from national-accounts investigations for the prewar Rowell-Sirois Royal Commission; from postwar studies by Firestone, Buckley, and Urquhart—all then connected with the Department of Trade and Commerce; from the (Gordon) Royal Commission on Canada's Economic Prospects; from studies by the Economic Council of Canada; and from steady search and consolidation in the Dominion Bureau of Statistics.[12] These sources have more or less kept pace with pioneering efforts by Simon Kuznets and colleagues working at New York's National Bureau of Economics Research; and with Colin Clark and Alec Cairncross, and many others in the United Kingdom. Few of these have been content only to gather statistics: *what* data is needed, and *how* they are to be defined can be decided only by the researcher's question. However, much of the earlier material used here has been taken from its original application and fitted into the model developed by MIT's Robert Solow.[13] The ratio chart of Fig. 37-3 shows the strong trends of Canadian economic development. Similar trends have been found for the United States and for the advanced economies overseas. Figure 37-3 is crucially important. Linger over it.

The chart shows the growth since 1926 of labor, capital, and hence of output. Population has more than doubled in over 45 years of steady growth. (Taking into account shortening of the working week and changes in age distribution and in labor-force participation, the growth in total number of manhours has been more modest.) While labor has about doubled, the stock of physical capital has in-

---

[11] Indeed, we shall see later in the chapter that, unless an invention is so "labor-saving" as to raise the profit rate enormously, it must definitely boost the real wage rate.

[12] Most Canadian material, with sources, is now available in M. C. Urquhart and K. A. H. Buckley, *Historical Statistics of Canada*, (Macmillan, Toronto, 1965).

[13] R. M. Solow, "Technical Change and the Aggregate Production Function," *Review of Economics and Statistics*, vol. 39, 1957, pp. 312-320.

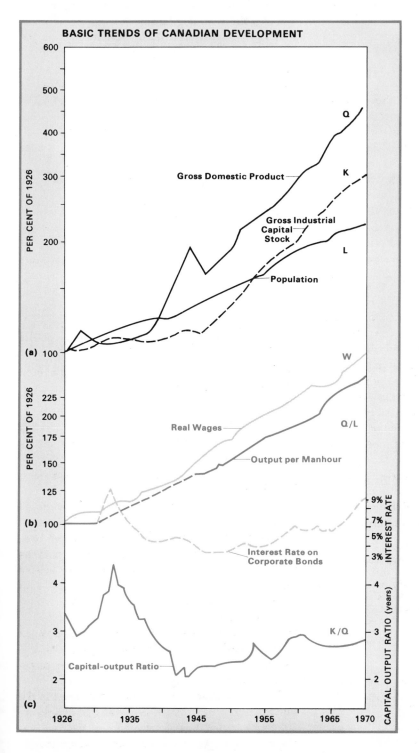

BASIC TRENDS OF CANADIAN DEVELOPMENT

Gross Domestic Product — Q

Gross Industrial Capital Stock — K

Population — L

Real Wages — W

Output per Manhour — Q/L

Interest Rate on Corporate Bonds

Capital-output Ratio — K/Q

FIG. 37-3. Economic growth has displayed striking long-run regularities.

(a) Capital stock has grown faster than labor supply. Total output has nonetheless shown natural rate of growth in full pace with output.

(b) Real wage rate has grown steadily, if anything over-matching growth in average labor productivity per man-hour. No pauperization or immiserization of the working class shows up in broad wage statistics.

(c) Without technical invention and innovation, deepening of capital relative to labor would depress interest rate and raise capital-output ratio. But, in fact, technical change seems to have just about offset diminishing returns to capital accumulation. (Hence, statical curves of Fig 37-2 must have been shifting rightward. REMARK: If higher money interest rates were corrected for price inflation, trendless oscillation of interest and profit rates would be even more apparent—in defiance of any alleged Law of Declining Rate of Profit.)

(Source: Hood and Scott, *Output, Labour and Capital in the Canadian Economy;* Statistics Canada; Economic Council of Canada, Staff Studies and *Annual Reviews.* See also J. E. La Tourette's article in the *Canadian Journal of Economics,* May 1970.)

creased to three times its 1926 size. Thus the substantial increase in capital per worker, the K/L ratio, does represent a significant amount of "capital deepening."

What about the growth in output? Has output grown less than in proportion to capital, as in the model that ignored technical change? No. The fact that the Q curve lies not between the two factor curves, but above the capital curve, shows that there must have been technical change in actual history. The close proximity of the output and capital curves shows that the capital-output ratio has not risen as in the simple deepening model; instead, as the K/Q curve in Fig. 37-3 shows, the capital-output ratio has remained remarkably constant, between 2.4 and 3.0 years since 1950 (i.e., a balance-sheet calculation of current value of all capital goods would show it to be equal to between 2.4 and 3.0 years of total product).[14]

RISING WAGES AND TRENDLESS PROFIT
The real wage has indeed risen steadily, in accordance with what one would expect from the growth in capital tools cooperating with labor, and from favorable technological trends. The interest rate—or, if we could get complete statistics, the rate of profit actually earned on more risky investments—does *not* show the decline that would be predicted from simple deepening of capital and diminishing returns. Interest rates and profit rates fluctuate much in the business cycle and war, but display no strong trend upward or downward for the whole period. Either by coincidence, or as the result of some economic mechanism that needs study, technological change has just about offset the effect of diminishing returns.[15]

[14] This chart shows a tendency for the capital-output ratio to decline in the last part of the period. Much of such a decline in K/Q results from measuring the numerator so as to deflate out of it the relative rise that has taken place in capital-goods prices compared with other prices. It would be desirable for the present purpose to present a chart in which the components of K/Q are each measured in current dollars, or in current dollars deflated by a *common* price index, but Canadian data of this type are not available.

[15] Resist the temptation to think diminishing returns is not operating: if, instead of being hidden, it were actually not operating, the interest rate would have had to *rise* strongly as a result of technical change alone. (If we corrected interest rates for price changes—e.g., subtracting 1973's high percentage price rise from 1973's bond yields, as was done in earlier chapters—we would find the "real rate of interest or profit" to have been even steadier.)

As could be expected from the deepening of capital and from technological advance, output per man-hour (Q/L) has risen steadily. Moreover—and this too represents a remarkable coincidence or the results of some economic mechanism needing study—the percentage growth in wage rates per hour has almost exactly matched the percentage growth in product per man-hour. This does not mean that labor has captured *all* the fruits of productivity advance. It means, rather, that labor must have kept about the *same share* of total product throughout the period, with property also earning approximately the same relative share throughout the period. (A closer look at the chart suggests that there *might* have been in the first half of the century a slow upward creep in the share of labor in GNP, with property's share dropping accordingly; but part of this might be the return to capital invested in human education and training.)

SIX BASIC TRENDS OF ECONOMIC DEVELOPMENT

These basic facts of economic history in the advanced nations can be summarized approximately by the following trends:

Trend 1 Population has grown, but at a much more modest rate than has the capital stock, reflecting a "deepening of capital."

Trend 2 There has been a strong upward trend in real wage rates.

Trend 3 According to what is often called Bowley's Law, the share of wages and salaries relative to the total return to property has shown considerable constancy in the long run (but perhaps with slight signs of an edging upward of labor's share).

Trend 4 Instead of observing a fall in the rate of interest or profit, we actually observe their oscillation in the business cycle but no steady upward or downward trend in this century (particularly if we deflate interest and profit rates of their price-change components, and deal with *real* rates).

Trend 5 Instead of observing a steady rise in the capital-output ratio as the deepening of capital invokes the law of diminishing returns, we find that the capital-output ratio has been approximately constant in this century.

Trend 6 The ratio of saving to output has oscillated in the business cycle—reaching about the same level at various high-employment phases of the cycle. Or taking into account the approximate constancy of the capital-output ratio, we can convert this approximate constancy of the ratio of investment to income into the following: national product has generally had a trend rate of growth at a roughly constant percentage rate per year.[16]

ANALYZING THE LAWS OF MOTION OF THE MIXED ECONOMY

While these are only approximate truths and not like the unrepeatable laws of physics, they portray fundamental facts about economic growth. How to explain them?

Trends 2 and 1—higher wage rates when capital deepens—fit nicely together with classical and neoclassical theories of production and distribution. Trend 3—Bowley's Law that the wage share is approximately constant—is an interesting coincidence that would be consistent with a *statical* neoclassical model only if it possessed a special kind of production function relating Q to L and K (what in Chapter 27 is called the "Cobb-Douglas function," for which relative factor shares are constant).

Trends 4 and 5, however, warn us that neoclassical theory cannot hold in *static* form! A steady profit rate and a steady capital-output ratio are incompatible with the more basic law of diminishing returns under deepening of capital. We are forced, therefore, to introduce *technical innovations* into our statical neoclassical analysis to explain these dynamic facts. And a good thing it is that we are told to introduce technical change, since we have much independent evidence of the importance of science and engineering in the modern era.

In terms of the analysis illustrated in Fig. 37-2, we are forced to introduce an outward shift in the *dd* and *ff* curves there to account for all five trends. Thus, the eastward move in Fig. 37-2(a) from B on *dd* to B' on *d'd'*, which cor-responds to the eastward move in Fig. 37-2(b) from *b* to *b'*, will be consistent with trends 1 to 6. The tendency toward diminishing returns has just been offset by the technical shift, with interest remaining at the same horizontal level and the wage rate rising just as much as output per head. The capital-output ratio, which cannot easily be read in Fig. 37-2, must stay constant if the interest return on capital is to constitute the same relative share as before.[17]

Professor Solow, utilizing his own methods of analysis and corroborating the independent findings of numerous scholars at the U.S. National Bureau of Economic Research and elsewhere, has come up with the following remarkable conclusion for the United States:

Less than half of the U.S. increase in productivity per capita and in real wages can be accounted for by the increase in capital itself. Considerably more than half of the increase in productivity seems to be attributable to technical change—to scientific and engineering advance, to industrial improvements, and to "know-how" of management methods and educational training of labor.

To a modified extent this finding also applies to Canada. But it needs careful interpretation.

First, although it is customary to measure and speak of the enhanced productivity of labor, there is no necessary implication that all of it (or most of it, or little of it) came from greater effort on the part of workers, or from more intensive conditions of sweat and strain; nor that it came from more effort and education, or from more initiative and incentives of the human labor force; nor, for that matter, from more energetic and clever executive management. The facts do not point to any simple interpretation.

Second, it is artificial to separate capital formation and technology completely. New techniques do tend to be *embodied* in new kinds of equipment. It is possible to imagine a stationary state—like the optimistic one of John Stuart Mill—in which there is no net saving and investment, but in which there is considerable technical progress as the depreciation charges of worn-out equipment finance their replacement by technically better equipment. Still, no one will deny that innovations can be introduced

---

[16] Example: Although Fig. 37-3 shows K/Q about 2.7, hereafter it is assigned a convenient value of 3 1/3. Then Fig. 37-3's per cent per annum growth of capital is possible only if net capital formation is 10 per cent (equals 3% x 31/3) of output, as footnote 15 and the Appendix make clear.

[17] As the Appendix shows, trends 3, 4, and 5 cannot be independent, since arithmetically the constancy of any two of the three magnitudes (iK/Q, i, K/Q) implies the constancy of the third.

faster in a society which is performing *net* investment in addition to the gross investment corresponding to replacement. We all do learn from actually doing, and the society which gets to try out more new things will run that much ahead of the one which does little or no net saving.

ARE INVENTIONS LABOR-SAVING OR CAPITAL-SAVING?

Any invention that wins its way under competition must raise the real wage rate or the interest rate or both.[18]

However, some inventions will by their nature have a tendency to increase the relative share of labor; others to increase the relative share of capital and property generally; and others to affect both factors in about the same degree. This suggests the convenience of the following definition:

Definition: An invention is called "labor-saving," "capital-saving," or "neutral," depending upon whether it tends to lower the relative share of labor, lower the relative share of property, or leave relative shares unchanged.

An extreme example of a labor-saving invention would be one that enabled unmanned machines to turn out robots that could do any of the manual and intellectual tasks of human labor. This would no doubt reduce the competitive wage drastically and could conceivably drop labor's share of NNP from its present level of about 75 to 80 per cent to below 50 per cent. An example of a capital-saving invention would be the case of a cheap computer that enabled firms to get along with much less inventory; or the invention of Kleenex tissue to replace durable handkerchiefs; or the invention of easily launched Telstar wave-reflecting satellites that made ocean cables un-

necessary.[19] It is easy to specify innumerable examples of capital-saving or labor-saving innovations and of neutral innovations in between.

The steady rise in wage rates is thought by many economists to *induce* employers to come up with labor-saving inventions. This tendency is often offered to help explain the failure of the profit-and-interest rate to fall as capital is accumulated. Marx more than a century ago had used such an explanation to account for the success of capitalists in resisting a rise in wages and in creating an industrial reserve army of the unemployed. Sir John Hicks of Oxford has in our own day advanced similar arguments of an inherent bias toward labor-saving innovation, and William Fellner of Yale has marshalled some evidence in favor of this thesis.

Whatever the ultimate merits of such arguments, we must recognize that *any* invention which lowers cost of production can benefit the first competitor who introduces it. Furthermore, since the relative share of wages in total costs has been approximately constant for a century, any employer who is planning his research expenditures over the coming years will reasonably take this into account and will do well to spend now the same number of pennies on experimentation designed to save a dollar of future cost, whatever its source.[20]

---

[18] In terms of Fig. 37-2's factor price frontier, ff must be shifted outward and upward or the invention will not succeed in the competitive market. As we'll see in Chapter 41, Karl Marx misunderstood this. He promulgated the "law of the declining rate of profit or interest rate " alongside the "law of the immiserization of the working class [falling real wage rate]". Unless one invokes diminishing returns to land in the Malthus fashion—and Marx, who hated Malthus as an apologist for the rich and as a "plagiarist," paid insufficient attention to such phenomena—one has to give up at least one of the Marxian "laws" in a competitive model.

[19] A capital-saving invention tends to tilt Fig. 37-2(a)'s productivity curve more toward the vertical and toward greater inelasticity, thereby tending to reduce the fruits of sacrificing current consumption and accumulating capital. A neutral technical change would be one that shifts Fig. 37-2's curves generally outward and upward. Advanced treatises deal with various distinct definitions of what is meant by labor-saving; the discussion here is left general so as not to be inconsistent with either the definition associated with J. R. Hicks or R. F. Harrod.

[20] A theory of induced technical change can explain and unify all the six basic trends of economic development as follows: (1) Suppose any increase in capital relative to labor will raise labor's relative share. (2) Suppose that effort devoted to making each laborer the new equivalent of more than one laborer will go up when labor cost increases as the share of total costs. (3) Finally, assume that a constant fraction of income is always saved and invested and that labor population grows at a constant slow rate. Then it will follow that the system will ultimately grow in "golden-age balance": (*a*) Capital and output will grow at the same high rate with a constant K/Q ratio; (*b*) labor population will grow at a slower rate, but because of induced technological invention "labor in effective or efficiency units" will grow at precisely the same rate as capital and output; (*c*) now with Q, K, and "effective" L growing in balance, there will be no diminishing returns to capital and hence a constant interest rate and constant relative labor share; (*d*) finally, the real wage will grow because each worker is having his

We have seen that economic analysis can shed much light on the laws of motion of the mixed economy. Admittedly, growth theory is still at the frontier of economics, and the experts are by no means in agreement on the mechanisms of explaining past and future paths of economic development. Some alternative theories are presented in the Appendix to this chapter. However, we are now armed to tackle in the next chapters the problems of growth in less developed economies and in advanced economies.

SUMMARY

1 Many writers have tried to read into economic history a linear progression through inevitable stages, such as primitive economy, feudalism, capitalism, and some form of communism. The actual facts have not agreeably stuck to such timetables; in particular, the mixed economies that dominate the Western world came into being without the permission of social prophets.

2 The classical models of Smith and Malthus describe economic development in terms of fixed land and growing population. A simple labor theory of value prevails so long as land is superabundant; and output develops steadily with population in this golden age where labor gets all the national product.

3 In the absence of technical change, increasing population ultimately exhausts the supply of free land. The resulting increase in population density invokes the law of diminishing returns: Fixity of land keeps output from growing proportionately to increased labor; with less and less of land to work with, each new man adds less and less extra product; the decline in labor's marginal-product means a decline in the competitively earned real wage. As each acre of land gets more and more labor to work with, its marginal-product and competitively earned rent go up. A fundamental factor-price frontier depicts how the rent rate must rise as the wage rate falls; but no one can predict what will happen to the *relative* shares of land and labor in national product.

4 The Malthusian equilibrium comes when the wage has fallen to the subsistence level, below which the supply of labor will not reproduce itself. However, in realistic fact, technical change has kept economic development going by continually shifting the productivity curve of labor upward.

5 With land and resources and technology changing, either expansion or growth may follow from new staples becoming profitable in new regions. The Innis model, predicting growth, depends on the extent of factor mobility.

6 The Ricardo-Marx-Solow model stresses the deepening of capital, i.e., the process of accumulating capital goods of varied types faster than the growth in population and labor hours. In the absence of technical change, an increase in capital per capita will not be matched by a proportional increase in output per capita because of diminishing returns. Hence, capital deepening lowers the interest rate (which is the same as the "profit rate" if risk is ignored), raises the real wage along the factor-price frontier, and raises the capital-output ratio.

7 Historically, trends 1 and 2 as described—a rise in K/L and in w—are consistent with the *statical* model. Trend 3's approximate constancy of relative shares of labor and property—as measured by wL/Q and iK/Q, where $Q = wL + iK$—is not mandatory in the statical model, but is consistent with a special technical case of it (Cobb-Douglas). How-

effectiveness raised by the induced technical change. QED: Rigorous proof of this was presented by several authors in the mid- 1960s without any reliance on Cobb-Douglas functions, as the Appendix will make clear.

ever, trends 4 and 5—the failure of the interest and profit rate to fall and of the capital-output ratio to rise—show clearly that technical change must be brought into the analysis. (It is as if technical change acts to augment labor in efficiency units just enough to match capital's growth: in efficiency units there emerges no diminishing returns, no rising capital/output ratio, no falling rate of profit!) Trend 6—approximate constancy of the investment/income ratio—taken together with the constancy of the capital-output ratio arithmetically implies a constant percentage growth of output per decade.

8 The facts suggest the hypothesis that capital accumulation is second to technical change in explaining rising productivity. But innovation and investment interact, as new techniques get embodied in new equipment and people learn by trying new investments. Increasing productivity can be expressed conveniently in terms of labor productivity—i.e., Q/L—but this does not necessarily imply anything about the reasons for the rise.

9 Inventions are defined as labor-saving, capital-saving, or neutral, depending upon whether they reduce labor's relative share of national product, reduce property's relative share, or leave shares unchanged. Experience with rising wage rates makes firms expect the trend to continue; whether or not they try for, and succeed in making, labor-saving inventions, firms will want to cut down on any cost items (labor, natural resources, capital costs).

Either by coincidence or by cancellation of offsetting trends, or as the result of economic mechanisms needing study,[21] the pace of invention has turned out to be just about enough to offset the effect of diminishing returns to capital on the interest and profit rate; and innovations have not turned out to be so labor-saving or capital-saving as to change much the relative shares of labor and property.

CONCEPTS FOR REVIEW

stages of history	relative factor shares
Smithian golden age	capital deepening, K/L rise
labor theory of value	capital-output ratio, K/Q
land scarcity and value	interest rate and profit rate
Malthusian subsistence wage	technical progress
factor-price frontier ff	labor-saving
marginal-product dd	neutral
diminishing returns	capital-saving
staples and factor mobility	Q growth from inventions, from more K

QUESTIONS FOR DISCUSSION

1. Does the mixed economy fit any of the timetables of history? Was it forseeable?
2. "If the democratic state subsidizes science and invention, controls the business cycle, augments full-employment thrift by a budget surplus, and introduces sensible planning, we can expect growth that would astound the classical economists". Evaluate critically.
3. Draw the parallels between the models of Figs. 37-1 and 37-2: rising labor-output ratio and rising capital-output ratio; falling wage and falling interest rate; the two factor-price frontiers; technical shifts of dd and ff in both cases; land-saving or labor-saving and neutral innovations in both cases; relative factor shares; etc.

[21] Such as that of footnote 19.

4. "Saving helps capitalists today, workers tomorrow". Assess this filter-down view.

5. "Without technical change and unemployment, persistent capital accumulation would ultimately mean euthanasia (death) of the capitalists". Use Fig. 37-2 to explain this.

6. Since labor's share shows a slight uptrend and the capital-output ratio a slight downtrend, since the interest and profit rates fluctuate considerably, and since the ratio of private net investment to GNP shows fluctuation and in recent years signs of a downtrend—in view of these facts, would you be greatly surprised if the basic trends outlined in this chapter were to show future changes?

7. Give examples of labor-saving and capital-saving inventions.

8. "Had America saved less but spent more on experimentation, she'd be richer". Comment. Does Canada gain most from U.S. dollars or U.S. know-how?

Appendix: Modern Discussions of Development Theory

Economics, not being a settled subject, is itself still undergoing development. While the broad facts of historical development discussed in the chapter are not in dispute, different interpretations of them are given by different authors. Some of the ideas associated with the names of the late Joseph A. Schumpeter, Sir Roy Harrod of Oxford, W. W. Leontief of Harvard, Professors Joan Robinson and Nicholas Kaldor of Cambridge University, and various current American economists are sketched briefly in this Appendix.

While an elementary textbook cannot pretend to resolve advanced topics, today one would consider an introduction to physics old-fashioned if it did not somewhere give the reader a glance at fundamental issues on the frontiers of knowledge: atomic theory, elementary particles, generalized relativity, etc.

Similarly many beginning students of economics will want to have a glimpse of the issues at the frontier of current economic analysis. Without mastering every intricacy of this Appendix, the interested reader can capture the flavor of developing economic thought from it. In particular, many readers who are not concerned with the rest of the theories discussed in this Appendix may still want to turn to its final discussion of the fascinating and useful subject of Leontief input-output analysis of interindustry flows.

SCHUMPETERIAN INNOVATION

Joseph Schumpeter (1883-1950) of Vienna and Harvard was author of two economic classics:[1] *The Theory of Economic Development* (English ed., Harvard University Press, Cambridge, 1934) and the posthumous *History of Economic Analysis* (Oxford University Press, Fair Lawn, N.J., 1954).

Schumpeter emphasized the role of the innovator—i.e., the inventor, the developer, the promoter, the man who initiates and recognizes technical improvements and who succeeds in getting them introduced. Like Carlyle's faith in the role of the great man in history, Schumpeter's theory regards the innovator as the dynamic actor of capitalism, who rules profitably for a day only to have his profits nibbled away by imitating competitors.

Figure 37 2(a) well represents Schumpeter's notion of what would happen if all innovations ceased. Competition and capital accumulation would quickly push society down the curve diminishing-returns *dd*; indeed Schumpeter thought that the long-run *ss* horizontal line at which the supply of new saving will disappear would be at a zero rate of interest and profit, being properly drawn in Fig. 37-2(a) down on the horizontal axis itself. (His much-attacked theory of a zero rate of interest in the innovationless stationary state can be replaced by a positive-interest-rate floor without much altering his theory of cyclical development.)

But now Schumpeter plays his trump card. Innovation is periodically shifting the *dd* curve upward and outward. The violin string is plucked by innovation; without innovation it dies down to stationariness, but then along comes a new innovation to pluck it back into dynamic motion again. So it is with the profit rate in economic life.

The profits due to innovation, we have seen, will be competed away by imitators, with labor and consumers benefiting from price reductions. The innovation-induced rise in interest rates will soon coax out saving and capital formation, until the accumulation of the augmented capital stock leads to diminishing returns, a "profit squeeze," and minimal interest. But then along comes a new burst of innovations—railroads, electricity, automation—to pluck the system back into dynamic motion, and we are off on a new repetition of the process.

Ignoring Schumpeter's specific theories of the business cycle, we see that his theory of development is completely consistent with the first two trends of economic history: rising real wage rates, and capital increase outstripping population increase. Although his general theory does not specifically call for constant relative shares, a trendless profit rate, a constant capital-output ratio, a trendless average propensity-to-consume-and-save, still all or any of these could be quite consistent with Schumpeter's general schema.

UNEMPLOYMENT IN THE STATIONARY STATE?

Ricardo, Alfred Marshall, and Schumpeter had one thing in common with Lord Keynes of *The General Theory of Employment, Interest, and Money*. They all thought that profit rates would be pushed to minimal levels in the absence of technical change. But Ricardo and company all thought that when this day of judgment came, the economy would be voluntarily consuming 100 per cent of its full-employment income; although positive investment

---

[1]As can be seen by readers of his stimulating *Capitalism, Socialism, and Democracy* (Harper, New York, 1942), Schumpeter was more than an economist. Believing the economic system to be itself essentially stable, Schumpeter advanced sociological and political reasons for his predicted decay of capitalism: he held that the very efficiency of capitalism will be its ruin, as intellectuals and the masses come to despise the market ideology and contrive to introduce hampering government interferences in the name of welfare. Unlike Marx, who thought capitalism would die of its own cancers, Schumpeter thought it would eventually commit suicide for psychosomatic reasons. The tremendous resurgence of *mixed economies* in the 25 years since Schumpeter cheerfully gave his gloomy prediction is, apparently, a deviation from *his* timetable of history, but the disaffection of affluent college activists may be a testimonial to his prophetic insight.

would cease, people would then be spending enough on consumption to maintain full employment. (In terms of the diagrams of Part Two, in the Ricardian stationary state the $C + I + G$ curve would be intersecting the 45° line at the FF full-employment level with $C + I + G$ actually equal there to $C + zero + G$, because net investment ceases in the stationary state. For the remainder of this chapter we shall interpret I as net investment rather than as gross investment; likewise for net saving.)

Keynes, on the other hand, feared that such minimal rates of interest and of profit on risky ventures might create a stationary state of stagnation with chronic unemployment:

People might still *want to save* at full employment, but no *matching real investment* would be forthcoming when the promised profit rate is too low to coax out risk-taking; and when the interest to be earned on short-term, gilt-edge government bonds has become so low as to make people indifferent between hoarding much or little safe, idle money,[2] central bank policy cannot do much to prevent stagnation.

This notion of a troublesome stationary state did not die with the 1930s. Prominent followers of Keynes at Cambridge University, such as Professors Joan Robinson and Lord Kahn have grave doubts concerning the possibility of a successful deepening of capital accompanied by full employment in a mixed economy. At the least they would stress that it will never happen by itself in a country that confines itself to orthodox fiscal and monetary policies. At the most they would harbor grave doubts that "managed capitalism" could, or would, pursue the unorthodox policies of monetary and fiscal expansion implied by a successful synthesis of neoclassical and post-Keynesian analysis.

Readers who go on to advanced economics can be referred to writings of these Cambridge authors.[3] Here, briefly, will be presented some of the points that need to be considered in doing justice to both sides of the argument as it bears on long-term economic development: no attempt will be made to identify ideas and writers meticulously.

UNCHANGEABLE CAPITAL-OUTPUT RATIO?

The land-output and labor-output ratios were not constants in the first Smith-Malthus model of development. And the capital-output ratio in the Ricardo-Marx-Solow

model of Fig. 37-2 was likewise not supposed to be a technical constant. In the absence of technical change, successful capital formation by society would enable output to grow; and the resulting phenomenon of diminishing returns would imply a *smoothly growing* capital-output ratio as capital deepening was taking place. On this view, dynamic technical change has seemed historically to provide about the extra productivity needed to offset statical diminishing returns, keeping the measured capital-output ratio constant.

Many modern economists—Professors Robert Eisner of Northwestern, Alvin Hansen of Harvard, Luigi Pasinetti of Cambridge, Dr. Gerhard Colm of the National Planning Association, and others—are of the view that the capital-output ratio is very nearly a technical *constant*, and that any attempt to accumulate capital beyond the rate required by the annual growth in output will soon be unsuccessful. Profits or rents from equipment will fall off badly after any surge of capital investment like those of 1955-1957 and 1964-1972. Excess capacity will follow, and the resulting profit squeeze will kill off private investment, as it did in the sluggish years following 1957. Therefore, they argue, any long-term theory must utilize an *invariable* capital-output ratio like that shown in the historical data of Fig. 37-3.

HARROD-DOMAR GROWTH MODELS
These concepts can be illuminated by some interesting models of balanced compound-interest (or "exponential") growth developed by Sir Roy Harrod in England and Professor E. Domar in America.[4] This theory has two aspects: the long-term "natural rate of growth" and the so-called "warranted rate of growth."

THE *natural* **RATE OF GROWTH** The historical data of Fig. 37-3 can help explain Harrod's arithmetic; and, in turn, a simple Harrod-Domar model can give an oversimplified "explanation" of those historical trends.

Suppose hours of labor L grow steadily at about 1 per cent per year.[5] And for extreme simplicity, assume that technical change is in effect making every man's efficiency as a laborer grow at another 2 per cent per year. Either because of more scientific methods of production or better education, it is as if 98 men can this year do what it took 100 to do last year; and this is repeated indefinitely. To coin a phrase, while *actual L* in its human man-hour units is growing at but 1 per cent per year, the number of "efficiency units of labor" L^* is growing at 3 per cent per

---

[2]This floor on the profit and interest rate could help account for the historical constancy of the profit rate named in trend 4 (Chap. 37), particularly if someone could supply reasons for a profit ceiling. With the profit rate allegedly running between two channels, its constancy would be removed from the realm of coincidence. (Recall also the discussion of Say's Law in the Appendix to Chapter 18. The "liquidity trap" or "depression pole," when elevated by riskiness, might provide such a profit floor.)

[3]J. Robinson, *Economic Philosophy*, Chap. 5 (Macmillan, London, 1962); *Accumulation of Capital* (Macmillan, London, 1956); N. Kaldor, *Essays on Value and Distribution*; *On Economic Stability and Growth*; *On Economic Policy* (Duckworth, London, 1960).

[4]R. F. Harrod, *Towards A Dynamic Economics* (Macmillan, London, 1948); E. D. Domar, *Essays in the Theory of Economic Growth* (Oxford University Press, Fair Lawn, N.J., 1957). The discussion of interacting accelerator-multiplier models in Chapter 14 is here applied to the trend of economic development rather than to the business-cycle deviations from that trend.

[5]Expansion of an industrial sector through the utilization of an unlimited supply of rural labor is associated with the name of W. Arthur Lewis. Such diverse economists as the conservative Gustav Cassel of Sweden and the nonconservative Karl Marx had put forth similar Ricardian notions.

year because of the annual 2 per cent efficiency improvement. This leads to the concept of the natural rate of growth.

Definition: The *natural rate of growth* of a simplified Harrod system is the percentage growth per year of its labor supply expressed in "efficiency units" (which means natural labor units as augmented by the presumed increase in technical effectiveness of each man-hour); as a condition of *balanced* growth, output and capital must also be growing at this same natural rate per year.

With GNP (or Q) and with L^* growing steadily at this natural rate of 3 per cent per year, the stock of capital K must also grow at the same natural rate of 3 per cent per year so as to keep in balanced pace. How much investment is required each year to keep K growing at this natural rate of 3 per cent? Or, in other words, how much must people be steadily saving and investing out of their annual full-employment product to keep growth nicely balanced?

Evidently the needed saving-income ratio must depend on the numerical value of the capital-output ratio K/Q times the natural growth rate.[6]

We are now in a position to write down the arithmetic formula relating three historical things: the Harrod natural rate of growth of 0.03 per year, or in the general case g per year; the historical capital-output ratio of, say, 3 1/3 (to keep arithmetic simple, not 2.7 as in Fig. 37-3), or in the general case K/Q; the required saving GNP ratio of 0.09, or in the general case s. We get:

$$s = g \times \frac{K}{Q} \text{ or } 0.10 = 0.03 \times 3\ 1/3$$

This relationship determines the amount of voluntary saving *and* investment that is needed if the Harrod natural growth is to be an *equilibrium* state.[7]

EXPLAINING THE TRENDS Can this simplified Harrod-Domar model of balanced natural rate of growth account for all six of the basic trends listed in Chapter 37? Yes, as footnote 19 hinted. Let us check them off.

The model certainly gives a deepening of capital relative to man-hours of actual L, since K grows at 3 per cent and L only at 1 per cent. (However, in this simplified model, an

---

[6]Thus, suppose Q is 900 billion dollars per year, and that the capital stock is about 3 1/3 times as great, being 3,000 billion dollars. Then to add 3 per cent to K this year we must have net investment of 90 billion dollars (equals 0.03 x 3,000 billion dollars), which means that people must be saving and investing exactly 10 per cent (equals 3% x 3 1/3) of their incomes. [Check your understanding by showing that a 4 per cent natural growth rate would in this case require a 13 1/3 per cent (equals 4% x 3 1/3) saving ratio out of income; and that a 3 per cent natural growth rate with a K/Q ratio of only 2 would require only a 6 per cent saving-income ratio.]

[7]This is really the $I = S$ schedule equality of Part Two. For in the case of the natural growth rate, $g = I/K$ or $I = gK$; hence, $I/Q = S/Q = s = g(K/Q)$, the Harrod condition.

---

observer who concentrates on L^*, labor in efficiency units, will see a constant K/L^* with no "deepening" going on but merely an apparent "widening of capital" to keep K and L^* balanced.)

Trend 2 is verified also. The wage rate rises—actually at 2 per cent per year. Why? Because each actual man (L, not L^*) collects the marginal product of the increasing efficiency units *in him*, and these units work with their full quota of capital goods.

Trend 3 is verified and is no longer a coincidence. Because technical change was so nicely neutral as to make each man take on "the strength of ten," the balanced growth in K and L^* means we are *dividing shares between the factors in precisely the same way as before*. (Recall that an observer of L^* alone merely sees balanced widening of capital, not deepening; note that no Cobb-Douglas assumption therefore needs to be made.)

Trend 4's constancy of the interest rate is now precisely verified, being neither an approximation nor a coincidence. Each unit of K, being matched exactly by the same amount of L^* as before, experiences no diminishing returns and has imputed to it the same competitive interest rate. (If degree of risk is the same, constancy of the interest rate means constancy of the somewhat higher profit rate.)

Trend 5 is of course verified, since the Harrod natural rate of balanced growth assumes from the beginning an unchanged K/Q ratio. In terms of the Ricardo-Marx-Solow model, even if the capital-output ratio *could* smoothly change, it will not have to be in a situation where widening of K to match L^* means no diminishing returns and entails Q growing in full proportion to K.

Trend 6's constancy of the saving-income ratio is verified from the basic Harrod formula for the natural rate of balanced growth at the same compound interest rate per year: s = constant g x constant K/Q.

INTERDEPENDENCE OF TRENDS As mentioned in footnote 15, Chap. 37, the six trends are not all logically independent. We could have saved time by checking any two of the three trends 3, 4, and 5, knowing that their correctness would arithmetically guarantee the correctness of the remaining trend. Here is why. If property always gets the same fraction of output, say one-fourth, and if the profit rate stays constant, then the process of capitalization of an income stream discussed in Chapter 30 shows that the value of the capital stock must be a determinate multiple of output. [I.e., K's fractional share of Q divided by the interest rate is equal to the capital-output ratio: $i(K/Q) \div i = K/Q$. Thus, if capital gets one-fourth of 900-billion-dollar Q, and this property return of 225 billion is capitalized by dividing it through by $i = 0.07\ 1/2 = 3/40$, then the value of capital is seen to be determinate at 3,000 billion dollars, or 3 1/3 (as in footnote 14's example in the main chapter) times the value of output.]

HARROD'S WARRANTED RATE OF GROWTH The natural rate of growth is designed to cope with long-term problems of economic development. A few words can be said about a related tool designed more to explain cyclical instability than trend.[8]

What if society's actual saving fraction differs from that needed to keep the natural growth rate in nice balance? That is, suppose actual desired S/Q at full employment is greater, or less, than s given by $g(K/Q)$. Too high a schedule of saving, we saw in Part Two, will tend to lead to unemployment. Too low a saving schedule, related to the investment schedule, was seen to produce an inflationary gap and a tendency toward price inflation.

Very well. No longer is the natural growth rate g the one that the system will realize. Growth in balance has now become rather irrelevant. Still Harrod can ask this rather odd question:

Starting from enough unemployed resources so that the natural growth rate of labor and other resources provides no bottleneck or ceiling—starting from there, what rate of growth of output, W, if it could be achieved and maintained, would (through "the acceleration principle" of Chapter 13) lead to a large enough volume of investment to justify (via the multiplier analysis of Chapter 13) a continuance of its own growth rate W? The answering W is defined as the "warranted rate of growth."

In short, to get W, reinterpret the old Harrod relation $s = g(K/Q)$ and work it backward to solve for the growth rate of Q rather than for the needed saving ratio s. Follow these steps: (1) Replace s by the actual saving ratio S/Q people insist on having, namely s_a (2) Replace the g specified by labor force and technological growth by the unknown warranted rate of growth W. (3) Provided that the capital-output ratio K/Q is a hard constant, let it stand. (4) Solve for W by removing K/Q to the denominator under S/Q.

We go from the natural rate to the warranted rate thus: $s_a = W(K/Q)$ replaces $s = g(K/Q)$, and

$$\frac{W = s_a}{K/Q}$$

An example will help. With $g = 0.03$ and $K/Q = 3\ 1/3$, Harrod needs $s = 0.10$ for his natural-growth process. But suppose people want to save $S/Q = 0.13\ 1/3 - 0.10$. This overthrift would lead to unemployment. But suppose somehow Harrod could start an expansion of W per cent per year in Q, which can always get the labor it needs from the ranks of the unemployed. Then how fast must it expand to generate enough I/Q to match $S/Q = 0.13\ 1/3$? If every dollar of expanded Q always requires K to expand by 3 1/3 dollars, our answer is $W = 0.13\ 1/3 / 3\ 1/3 = 0.04$. Any Q growth higher than 0.04 per year will generate $I/Q > 0.13\ 1/3$, just as any Q growth less than $W = 0.04$ will generate $I/Q < 0.13\ 1/3$.

The warranted rate is an odd concept. It does not tell what will happen in fact but only that it would have certain self-warranting properties if it came to happen by design

or by luck. Such a growth rate of output, W, if it could somehow be established and maintained, warrants a level of investment just big enough to match the voluntary saving that its own income growth entails.

CYCLES AND INSTABILITIES Two observations should be made about cyclical instabilities involved in the warranted rate of growth.

1. Once all the unemployed are back at work, the natural rate of growth g must set a ceiling against which, alas, the faster warranted rate of growth must eventually collide. Thus W of 4 or 5 percent per year and g of only 3 percent per year ultimately means the Harrod expansion will very soon hit full employment. As was seen in the Appendix to Chapter 14 on business cycles, some writers[9] have constructed a theory of a collapse into recession based upon a bouncing back of the system from its collision with the natural-rate employment ceiling.

2. The warranted rate of growth, even if originally established, will not persist after being disturbed. In the Harrod model it is definitely unstable. To see this, note that if the actual growth rate temporarily exceeds $W = 4$ per cent, this new income will be generating in desired investment *more* than the 13 1/3 ($= 4\% \times 3\ 1/3$) per cent ratio of desired saving—thereby accelerating its own growth still faster above W. (Show that a *less* than 4 per cent initial growth rate will similarly create a deficiency of intended investment relative to the 13 1/3 per cent intended saving, thereby *decelerating* its own growth still further below W.)

Just as an unmanned bicycle, which is unstable if disturbed from the vertical, can be converted into a stable system by a steadying and compensating human hand, so can a Harrod-Domar growth path, that would be unstable under *laissez-faire*, be made stable by compensating monetary and fiscal policies in a mixed economy.

NEOCLASSICAL DYNAMICS

The Ricardo-Marx-Solow model of smooth substitutability of labor for capital (i.e., of labor for a great variety of alternatively producible capital goods) has less need to work with Harrod-Domar concepts than those models which regard the capital-output ratio as a hard constant. However, it is useful to interpret the Harrod-Domar concepts for a neoclassical model like Fig. 37-2.

By a simple "neoclassical growth model" is meant one in which the state uses monetary and fiscal policies to make sure that thriftiness does not lead to unemployment and abortive thrift: by making equity and loan funds available at lower interest and profit rates (and possibly by unorthodox credit policies that provide guarantees against risks and uncertainties) such a managed system can con-

---

[8]These next two sections can be skipped.

[9]J. R. Hicks, *A Contribution to the Theory of the Trade Cycle* (Oxford University Press, Fair Lawn, N.J., 1950), gives a convenient summary of such nonlinear-cycle theories based on interacting accelerator-multiplier principles.

trive deepening of capital as described earlier.[10] Alternatively, this neoclassical model can be interpreted as picturing the technology of an efficiently run collectivist society that never faces macroeconomic problems of unemployment or of inflation due to lack of proper effective demand.

In such a society, where whatever is withheld from consumption goes into capital formation, *any* rate of growth is essentially a "warranted rate of growth." This is because there is (1) no dichotomy saving-investment problem, and (2) no hard constant for the capital-output ratio.

Here is an idealized example. Add a new supply of L to a system that has a certain K and has previously been producing a certain Q. This new L can be put to work with the given K *as rapidly* as we like. There will result a growth rate of Q that can be *as high* as the growth in L can produce. People can consume and can invest out of the new output *as much or little* as they like. Depending on *whatever amount* of capital formation they decide on, there will result a gradual accumulation of K with the K/L ratio being able to move in *any* way without causing trouble.

All the above is in sharp contrast to a model with fixed capital-output ratio, which calls for a specific W growth rate of Q. Contrast the Harrod case with the italicized words in the above paragraph!

THREE SOURCES OF GROWTH Neoclassical output growth can be decomposed into three separate sources: growth in labor or L, growth in capital or K, and technical innovation itself. Momentarily ignoring technical change, note that a 1 per cent per year growth rate in L together with a 1 per cent per growth rate in K is assumed to cause output to grow also at a 1 per cent per year rate. (Resist the temptation to add 1 per cent to 1 per cent and come out with 2 per cent; L and K cooperate in production, each needing the other.)

Suppose L grows at 1 per cent per year and K at 5 per cent. It is tempting, but wrong, to guess that Q will then grow at 3 per cent, the simple average of 1 and 5. Why wrong? Because the two factors do not contribute equal shares to product: about three-fourths of all product goes to labor as wages and only one-fourth of Q goes to property as its interest-profit share. This means L's growth rate

should get 3 times the weight of K's; hence, the correct answer is that Q will grow at 2 per cent per year (= 3/4 of 1% + 1/4 of 5%).

Hence, output growth per year follows the law

$$\% \ Q \text{ growth} = \begin{array}{l} 3/4 \ (\% \ L \text{ growth}) \\ +1/4 \ (\% \ K \text{ growth}) \\ +\text{T.C.} \end{array}$$

where T.C. means technical changes that raise productivity by shifting the *dd* curve of Fig. 37-2; and where 3/4 and 1/4 would of course be replaced by new fractions if the relative shares of the factors had changed.

If we seek to explain *per capita* growth, matters are simpler still, since this enables us to get rid of L as a separate growth source. Now, using the fact that capital gets one-fourth share of output, we have simply

$$\% \ \frac{Q}{L} \text{growth} = \frac{1}{4} \left(\% \ \frac{K}{L} \text{growth} \right) + \text{t.c.}$$

This relation shows clearly how deepening of capital would raise the capital-output ratio if there were no technical improvements being made: output per capita grows only one-fourth as fast as capital per capita, reflecting one aspect of diminishing returns.

This relation now explains the meaning of Solow's conclusion—that more than half of the increased output recorded in historical statistics seems to be attributable to scientific advance rather than to thrift and capital formation. This means that the second term in the above relation—t.c. for per capita technical change—appears on statistical measurement to have been definitely bigger than the first term representing the investment contribution. When Solow tries to allow for the fact that new techniques get embodied in new capital goods, the relative importance of the first term rises; but apparently it still remains below 50 per cent. (While the primacy of technical change seems corroborated by German or Japanese statistics, the importance of the capital factor does seem greater in Britain, Canada, and Russia.)

ALTERNATIVE THEORIES

REPUDIATION OF AGGREGATE PRODUCTION FUNCTIONS Professors Joan Robinson and Nicholas Kaldor of Cambridge University are skeptical that "capital" can be usefully measured as an aggregate, which together with labor produces aggregate output. This is certainly a healthy skepticism. They are more skeptical that the marginal productivities calculated from such an alleged production function can be used to explain wage and profit rates and the relative shares in GNP of labor and property. They go even further and doubt that economists can work with a detailed breakdown of numerous heterogeneous capital goods—machines of type A, B, C, ... —to get quantitative results at all like the neoclassical case, in an

[10]This means that the variety of possible heterogeneous capital-goods processes is so great that any reduction of interest rate—even be it as little as from $i = 0.08$ to $i = 0.079$—will ultimately make it profitable to use some new pattern of known processes. For example, at 0.079 the machine tools may be made a little more durable. In consequence, the factor-price frontier of Fig. 37-2(b) will look fairly smooth to the naked eye, even though a microscope will show that it contains little line segments that meet in corners. When we introduce realistic uncertainties into the model, one is first tempted to think that minute changes in interest rate will have negligible effects. Actually, however, replacing certainty by probabilities smooths the small steps in a demand function into a continuous curve: a small change in i, long maintained, pushes some investment projects on the borderline of doubt into actual operation. See J. E. Meade, *A Neoclassical Growth Model* (Oxford University Press, Fair Lawn, N.J., 1961), for alternative interpretations in terms of a flexible aggregate of capital.

actual realistic mixed economy of uncertainty and uneven growth.[11]

DISSENTING VOICES Robinson and Kaldor by no means agree on what is to replace the aggregative analysis. Both incline, but in different degree, toward a macroeconomic theory of income distribution with the following property:

"Here is an economy with high-property share and high growth. How wrong to think that it is the thrift of the rich (or anyone) which *causes* that fast growth. The causation tends to run the other way: fast growth produces high profits, rather than vice versa."[12]

This seems to say something more than does the familiar assertion that when a country like Japan or Western Germany experiences a miracle of productivity growth, people find it easiest to be thrifty out of the increase in income and to be slow in renegotiating real wage rates commensurate with the recent rises in marginal productivities. It is beyond controversy that such induced thrift does further speed up capital formation and (in neoclassical fashion) speeds up growth still further, but that is another story.[13] (Chapter 41 will explore further some ideological consequences of these doctrinal controversies.)

LIFETIME SAVING AND THE WEALTH-INCOME RATIO Professor Franco Modigliani of MIT has put for-

---

[11]Their works cited earlier can be contrasted by the advanced student in economics with the general neoclassical viewpoint exposited in an advanced work like R. Dorfman, P. A. Samuelson, R. M. Solow, *Linear Programming and Economic Analysis* (McGraw-Hill, New York, 1958). The latter makes the same supposition as was done here—that there are a great variety of alternative machines and processes known (or knowable) at any one time. If the interest rate changes even a little, say from 0.08 to 0.079 (as mentioned earlier), it will usually (but not inevitably!) pay to turn to a new blueprint that involves a slightly more durable machine. Hence, the *ff* curve of Fig. 37-2(b) will look almost smooth to the naked eye, even though a microscope reveals it to consist of many short line segments that meet in corners. The simplified *K* fable thus does give some useful insight into a more realistic model, be it the U.S.S.R., the United States, India, or China.

[12]In long-run balanced growth, Robinson and Kaldor identify i as g/s_p, where saving out of wages is negligible and s_p is the average propensity of *property income* to be saved. This comes from matching the bracketed terms in the following identities:

$$I = (I/K)K = [g]\,K = I = S = [s_p i]\,K$$

With the interest or profit rate known, if you believe in a constant capital-output ratio, K/Q, you can calculate property share in income as $i(K/Q)$. In effect, they say, "The share of property must somehow get spontaneously determined at just high enough a level to make the warranted rate W come into equality with the given natural rate g." But they do not supply convincing reasons why it would do so.

[13]Kaldor also has a short-run theory of distribution: when I drops exogenously in the short run, Kaldor denies that this produces multiplier drops in Q and employment (as in Chapters 12 and 13); instead this depresses business demands, causing business to cut prices (relative to wages) until total profit, iK, has dropped enough to equate $s_p(iK)$ with lowered I. Prof. Robinson disagrees with this new version of Say's Law and inevitable full employment, and most statistical analyses of profits in the mixed economy do too.

---

ward an alternative theory that is quite at variance with those just above. Modigliani does not consider the constancy of the capital-output ratio a mere coincidence. He tries to explain it, not in terms of technological production or by induced innovation as in Chapter 37's footnote 19, but in terms of people's psychological decisions about wealth, consuming, saving, and dissaving. He puts the greatest stress on lifetime patterns of saving for old-age retirement.

Here is an example. An adult works for about 40 years and lives in retirement for 20. To keep his consumption standards somewhat equal all his life, he consumes less than his income during the working years; he gradually builds up his wealth to a maximum just before retirement; then he gradually uses up capital and pension rights by his retirement consumption; at death he leaves little wealth. (What keeps the saving rate from cancelling out to zero as the old dissave what the young save? In the life-cycle model, the positive natural rate of growth (a) of populations, and (b) of per capita real income as a result of technical improvements in productivity.)

When population is growing at an even percentage rate, the age distribution remains constant over time. This steady increase in population, combined with confidently expected rising real income, causes the average level of wealth of the people as a whole to remain constant in ratio to total income. Except for the public-debt and land part of wealth, Modigliani has supplied a reason for K/Q to be constant!

A test of Modigliani's theory, as against that of someone like Kaldor who thinks that businessmen will somehow be led to make innovation and investment decisions in order to keep the K/Q ratio from changing much, would be to perform the hypothetical experiment of juggling the public debt up or down and seeing whether the K/Q ratio does change enough to keep the wealth-income ratio fairly constant. This experiment is not be recommended, but it does remind us of the assertion of Chapter 19 that a public debt can make the present generation want to do more consuming and less saving for its old age.

COMPENSATING FISCAL POLICY

Suppose it were true that monetary policy—because of balance-of-payments constraints, Eisner-like capital-output fixity, or other impotency—could make no effective change in private investment spending I. Then compensating fiscal policy would lead to results quite different from those given by *laissez-faire* models of the simple Harrod and Kaldor type.

Whenever full-employment s was out of line with I/Q, the government would run a budgetary surplus or deficit just big enough to alter the effective s for society until it equaled I/Q. The effective "warranted rate of growth" could thereby be kept equal to any prescribed natural rate of full-employment growth.

Thus, in a year like 1969 when I/Q tended to exceed full-employment s, the rational thing for the government to do was to create a large budgetary surplus: to raise tax rates and lower people's disposable incomes and personal saving, to cut down on government use of resources and on transfers, or to do both. This surplus is, in effect, government saving: call it s_G and combine it with the private saving ratio s_{pr} to get s = average (s_G, s_{pr}) as big as is needed to equal I/Q without demand-pull inflation.

During the sluggish years of the early 1960s, the opposite fiscal policies would be designed to compensate: With $I/Q < s_{pr}$, a budget deficit creates government dissaving (or negative saving); then at full employment $I/Q = s$, the average of s_{pr} and the government dissaving ratio.

In summary, *laissez-faire* Harrodian discrepancies can lose their terror and relevance in a mixed economy.

THE EXPANDING UNIVERSE: A DIGRESSION

The late John von Neumann, a brilliant mathematician who helped build the hydrogen bomb and who founded the theory of games, described an economic model in which everything could be produced out of everything. If land and/or labor are no longer scarce limiting factors, then the law of diminishing returns no longer applies. All the fruits of production, above and beyond the costs of subsistence for horses, rabbits, looms, and comfortably living men, are plowed back into the system for growth of more horses, rabbits, looms, men.

In this system, which is like Smith's golden age except that it definitely involves capital goods, there is a maximal rate of balanced growth. And it turns out that such a growth rate—call it g because of its resemblance to the Harrod natural rate of growth—is exactly equal to the interest rate i.

Because development theory, for countries like India and the United States, is preoccupied with the concept of "balanced growth," the Neumann model is of considerable interest. It is particularly relevant to the case where an industrial sector in a poor country finds it can get an unlimited supply of laborers from the rural sector at the same wage cost in terms of subsistence; needing little land, the industrial sector can "take off" and grow at a constant Neumann-percentage rate per year, provided it can produce the capital goods needed to match the new labor or can be helped by imports from foreign lenders, aiders, or exporters.

If there is technical change, the system can advance at a rate even faster than the Neumann rate, indeed, if the system can, so to speak, manufacture new inventions that make labor grow in efficiency at a steady percentage rate, it will then appear to an observer to be capable of even faster Neumann growth.

A simplest example of an expanding system would be the case of rabbits (or men) who produce 1.05 rabbits of output for each rabbit of input. The interest rate and the growth rate will obviously then be 5 per cent per period. Other examples are not so simple.

LEONTIEF'S INTERINDUSTRY INPUT-OUTPUT

The important interindustry tableau of Wassily Leontief is a modern-day realization of the eighteenth-century dream of a physiocratic economist, François Quesnay, who first envisaged the *Tableau Economique* or circular flow of economic life. A score of nations have computed input-output tables as an amplification of their national-income data and as a possible aid in development planning.[14]

Using agriculture and manufacturing as sample industries. Table 37-2 gives an oversimplified illustration of the table comprising several hundred industries that the government and Leontief have prepared for the U.S. economy. Here is its general idea. Each industry is listed twice: in a *row* as an *output*; in a *column* as a needed *input*. In addition, the final consumption of households is treated as an extra column and their *labor* (or other primary factors of production supplied by households) as an extra row. These household figures are the numbers that enter into national income or net national product and are on the shaded part of the table. (Actually Leontief also includes government, foreign trade, investment, and other detail.)

The *gross* value of agricultural output is shown by the black $1,200 (billion) twice; at its row's right as the sum of all the places where farm output went—$800 as input to manufacturing plus $400 directly consumed by households as food—and at its column's bottom as the sum of the $400 cost it paid for manufacturing inputs (chemical fertilizers, etc.) and the $800 cost it paid for labor input (and other household factors).

Give a similar interpretation of the $1,600 *gross* total for manufacturing.

The table also shows our old friend national income, or NNP (which will also be GNP if our example is simple enough to ignore depreciation). With no government or investment in the picture, NNP equals the sum of the third (shaded) column's final products; or alternatively NNP equals the sum of all factor-cost or values added shown in the shaded third row's wages. (NNP definitely doesn't include the intermediate purchases of one sector from another; the total in black of $2,800 unquestionably involves double counting. Verify: NNP = $1600.

This input-output table is more than a record of past history. How does Leontief or a planner hope to use it? *He*

[14]For additional discussion of theory and applications see Wassily Leontief, *The Structure of the American Economy*, 1919-1929 (Harvard University Press, Cambridge, Mass., 1941) 2d ed.: 1919-1939, Oxford University Press, Fair Lawn, N.J., 1951); or his *Input-Output Economics* (Oxford University Press, Fair Lawn, N.J., 1966). As part of the price that Leontief has to pay to make Walras's general equilibrium empirically measurable, he is forced to make the technical assumption that all factor proportions—to each other and to total output—are technologically *fixed* or constant. (Back in Chapter 27's Appendix, page 506, we found reason to doubt that such an engineering assumption can be strictly realistic; but Leontief's clever statistical use of fixed coefficients deserves notice. Canada's own Statcan tables have been extensively applied by Matuszewski, Pitts, Sawyer, Rosenbluth, Wonnacott, and others.

Example of Interindustry money flows during hypothetical cold-war period (in billions of dollars)	Agriculture	Manufacturing	Household Final Consumptions	Gross Totals
Agriculture		800	400	1,200
Manufacturing	400		1,200	1,600
Household labor and other factors	800	800	_____	_____
Gross totals	1,600	1,600		2,800

TABLE 37-2. The input-output tableau of Leontief X-rays the economy's structure. Each industry appears twice, in a row and column: its row lists allocation of its total gross output as inputs for other industries and for final consumption; its column shows inputs needed to produce it.

The black numbers show *gross* outputs, inclusive of amounts needed as intermediate inputs. To compute NNP without double counting, we add only the factor payments (or "value added") of the shaded row; or alternatively, only the final-consumption flows of the shaded column. (Fill in the proper NNP in the indicated blank, and check it two ways.)

New Peacetime Input-Output Flows (in billions of dollars)	Agriculture	Manufacturing	Household Final Consumptions	Gross Totals
Agriculture		640	800	1,440
Manufacturing	480		800	1,280
Household labor and other factors	960	640	1,600	_____
Gross totals	1,440	1,280		2,720

TABLE 37-3 input-out tableau helps us plan:
End of cold war causes shift from guns to butter: agricultural final consumption goes up by $400 billion; manufacturing down by same amount. Using fixed input-output coefficients from Table 37-2, Leontief calculates needed change in gross outputs shown here and, also resulting needed labor shifts and intermediate input changes. Same techniques help in development planning.

hopes to use it to forecast the effects of changing consumption requirements.

Thus, suppose Table 37-2 refers to a current cold-war situation where manufacturing employment and output have been swollen by military needs. (For dramatic effect we may think of peacetime goods or "butter" as coming largely from the agricultural sector and military goods or "guns" as coming largely from the manufacturing sector.)

Now suppose "peace breaks out." What will have to be planned for the new deployment of labor and other inputs if full employment is still to be maintained? Suppose we now want to double agriculture's final consumption, from the old red $400 to new $800, at the same time cutting the military manufacturing sector back from old red $1200 to new $800. On the basis of his assumption of fixed input-output coefficients, Leontief can solve linear equations for the new peacetime state and show that it *must* then be in

the configuration given in Table 37-3. [15] Ten per cent of the workers, calculation shows, must be shifted from war work to peace work. Similarly Leontief's tableau scheme can help plan for any development change in final-consumption goods.

[15]All details aside, his key assumption is that 400/1200 = 1/3 of agriculture receipts will always be spent on manufacturing input, with the remaining 800/1200 = 2/3 always spent on labor input. Similarly, 800/1600 = 1/2 is the fraction that manufacturing will always spend on its needed agricultural input, the remainder 1/2 being spent on needed labor input.

Table 37-2 is repeated here in abbreviated form to show how one derives the red fixed input-output coefficients

$$\begin{array}{cc} 0 & 800 \\ \underline{400} & \underline{0} \\ \underline{800} & \underline{800} \\ 1,200 & 1,600 \end{array} \longrightarrow \begin{array}{cc} 0 & \frac{1}{2} \\ \frac{1}{3} & 0 \\ \frac{2}{3} & \frac{1}{2} \\ 1 & 1 \end{array}$$

needed for the transition to Table 37-3 or to any other situation

REMARK: To avoid simultaneous equations, Leontief can use a "multiplier" method. Each manufacture requires 1/2 of agriculture as input, and each of these in turn requires 1/3 of manufacture as its input; so *indirectly* each manufacture requires 1/2 x 1/3 = 1/6 of extra manufactures to produce itself. So [1 + 1/6 + (1/6)² + ...] adds up to 1.2, which is the needed expansion of new *gross* manufacture for each 1.0 expansion of *consumption* manufacture. Similarly Leontief can calculate a multiplier for agriculture, showing how each billion-dollar change in its final consumption requires its *own* gross output to go up (coincidentally!) by 1.2 billion dollars. To compute what the shift of 400 billion dollars from guns to butter entails, Leontief must know how much gross agriculture and how much labor is needed to accommodate the 1.2 of manu-

facture that its own consumption expansion generated. The answer is not hard: The second column's bold black manufacturing input requirements give the answers—1/2 of 1.2, or .6 in both cases. The reader should now be able to verify that when 1 new agriculture consumption entails 1.2 of its *own* gross output, the amounts needed for manufacturing and labor are 1/3(1.2) = .4 and 2/3(1.2) = .8. Given the knowledge of this paragraph's "own multipliers" and "cross multipliers"—the so-called "inverse matrix"— we perceive how Leontief is able to apply them to the +400 consumption shift to agriculture and—400 shift from manufacturing to get the changes needed to convert wartime Table 37-2 to peacetime Table 37-3. (Those who have been trained in algebra may wish to supplement this terse account by the final extra-credit problem.)

SUMMARY TO APPENDIX

1 Schumpeter's stress on innovation, followed by competitive erosion of profit, is an important process of economic development.

2 If the capital-output ratio is an inflexible constant, neoclassical deepening of capital cannot be engineered by expansionist monetary policy.

3 The Harrod-Domar concept of the "natural rate of growth" g is determined by population growth and technical change. If K and Q are to grow at this balanced rate, the required fraction of income that has to be voluntarily saved is given by the Harrod condition, $s = g(K/Q)$. The warranted rate of growth W will be higher than the natural rate g if the actual desired saving ratio S/Q exceeds the s needed by Harrod's condition. In the resulting balanced growth, we must have $W = s_a$ (K/Q). Such a warranted rate would not be stably restored if departed from. And when $W > g$, a GNP expansion would ultimately run into a ceiling set by g. Fortunately, fiscal deficits or surpluses could be used to remove any discrepancy between W and g.

4 Where a neoclassical deepening of capital makes the K/Q ratio an accommodating variable, the Harrod conditions lose their terrors. Whatever people's thrift dictates for their private full-employment s, a combination of monetary and fiscal policies can hope to induce the needed offsetting investment. Such fiscal and monetary policies can speed up capital formation and the technical changes embodied in, and stemming from, such new equipment. They can help the system grow faster than the natural growth of working population. They can stabilize the achievable rate of progress so that the system will be warranted in doing what comes naturally. But, even in a flexible neoclassical technology, *laissez-faire* will not—in the absence of appropriate public monetary and fiscal policies—be led by an Invisible Hand to these ideal conditions.

5 The neoclassical model can parcel out the sources of Q growth into growth from more L, from more K, and from technical change. The last factor interacts with L through education and training and with K through embodiment in new machines. The histories of today's advanced nations suggest that technical change may have been the primary source of Q growth.

6 Robinson and Kaldor agree in their suspicion of aggregates of so-called capital and in their doubts about smooth deepening of capital under capitalism; both look to factors of dynamic growth for determination of profit shares. (Chapter 41 returns to this.)

7 It is intellectually unsatisfying to explain some constancy trends by appeal to "coincidence" or to fortuitous canceling out of diverse tendencies of diminishing returns and technical change. So one can applaud the attempts to find mechanisms (induced invention, lifetime saving, etc.) that bring the constancies about. However if, like the present writers, you would not be much surprised to see K/Q fall in the future or drift in any direction, the wage share generally rise, or the

envisaged by the planner. Now, if we call *gross outputs* of the two sectors X_A and X_M and their *final-consumption* amounts C_A and C_M, Leontief must finally allocate the total Xs thus:

$$X_A = C_A + 1/2X_M \qquad X_M = C_M + 1/3X_A$$

For the peacetime tableau of Table 37-3, this means

$$X_A = 800 + 1/2X_M \qquad X_M = 800 + 1/3X_A$$

These can be solved simultaneously by simple algebra to give $X_A = 1,400$, $X_M = 1,280$, from which all of Table 37-3 can be filled in using the red fractions. Thus, we get the industries' labor requirements:

$$L_A = 2/3X_A = 960 \qquad L_M = 1/2X_M = 640$$

rate of profit sag or soar, you must beware of "over-explanations." If a thing may actually be a coincidence, you are not saying much by calling it that. But to explain away a coincidence which truly is a coincidence is worse than a banality; it is a scientific sin.

8 Leontief's tableau of interindustry flows gives a useful picture of the relations lying behind aggregate NNP data. By posting fixed input-output coefficients, a planner can use the Leontief technique to program a shift from war pattern of consumption to peace, or any other development target goal.

CONCEPTS FOR REVIEW

innovation and deepening of capital	% Q growth = % L growth + ...
fixed versus variable K/Q ratio	% Q/L growth = % K/L growth + t.c.
natural versus warranted growth	von Neumann model with $i = g$
$s = g\dfrac{K}{Q}$ and $W = \dfrac{s_a}{K/Q}$	input-output tableau

QUESTIONS FOR DISCUSSION

1. Add acres of land, A, to the neoclassical discussion along with L, K, and T.C.
2. Contrast unemployment notions of Keynes and Eisner-Hansen with those of Schumpeter and Ricardo.
3. Why is g important for long trends? W for business cycles? Reread Chapter 14's acceleration principle.
4. Explain to yourself the basic idea of the two-way Leontief tableau. Consider how it might be used to study the appearance of new markets (if tariff-free trade patterns emerge); disarmament; industrialization of northern Canada; and transmission of foreign inflation through imports.
5. *Extra-credit problem* (very challenging): If you know matrix notation, you might be able to figure out the following summary of the Leontief input-output system, where C is the column vector of final consumptions, X the column vector of gross outputs, a_{ij} the coefficients of production, (L_j) the row vector of labor by industry, and P the row vector of prices.

$$\begin{bmatrix} 0 & 800 & \vdots & 400 \\ 400 & 0 & \vdots & 1{,}200 \\ \hdotsfor{4} \\ 800 & 800 & \vdots & 0 \\ 1{,}200 & 1{,}600 & \vdots & 1{,}600 \end{bmatrix} = \begin{bmatrix} X_{11} & X_{12} & \vdots & C_1 \\ X_{21} & X_{22} & \vdots & C_2 \\ \hdotsfor{4} \\ L_1 & L_2 & \vdots & 0 \\ X_1 & X_2 & \vdots & \sum_i C_i \end{bmatrix} ; \begin{bmatrix} a_{11} & a_{12} \\ a_{21} & a_{22} \\ \hdotsfor{2} \\ a_{01} & a_{02} \end{bmatrix} = \begin{bmatrix} 0 & \tfrac{1}{2} \\ \tfrac{1}{3} & 0 \\ \tfrac{2}{3} & \tfrac{1}{2} \end{bmatrix} = \begin{bmatrix} X_{11}/X_1 & X_{12}/X_2 \\ X_{21}/X_1 & X_{22}/X_2 \\ L_1/X_1 & L_2/X_2 \end{bmatrix}$$

In matrix notation $\begin{bmatrix} a \\ \cdots \\ a_0 \end{bmatrix} = \begin{bmatrix} a_{ij} \\ \cdots \\ a_{0j} \end{bmatrix} = \begin{bmatrix} X_{ij}/X_j \\ \cdots \\ L_j/X_j \end{bmatrix}$, and the allocation of outputs satisfies

$$X = \Big[X_i\Big] = \Big[\sum_j X_{ij} + C_i\Big] = \Big[\sum_j a_{ij}X_j + C_i\Big] = aX + C \quad ; \quad [I - a]X = C$$

$$X = [I - a]^{-1}C = AC = \begin{bmatrix} 1.2 & .6 \\ .4 & 1.2 \end{bmatrix}\begin{bmatrix} C_1 \\ C_2 \end{bmatrix}$$

$$L = \sum_j L_j = \sum_j a_{0j}X_j = a_0X = a_0[I - a]^{-1}C = a_0AC = A_0C = \sum_j A_{0j}C_j$$

Because $X_{ij} \geq 0$ and $C_i > 0$, $I - a$ will be a nonsingular matrix and its inverse $[I - a]^{-1} = A$ will have no negative elements (actually, they'll all be positive if each C takes some of every X and L for its production, as will be the elements of the row vector A representing total labor requirements direct and indirect). If labor's wage is 1, and competitive prices are given by unit cost of production, the sum of wage plus material-input costs—then $P = 1 . a_0 + Pa = a_0[I — a]—^1 = A_0$, the row vector of total labor requirements (direct labor plus indirect). In this case where output flows are measured in dollars, one can check the correctness of the operations by verifying that $A_0 = [1,1]$. If there is a positive interest or profit rate, r, we'd instead have $A_0 = a_0(1 + r)[I — a(1 + r)]^{-1}$

38
PROBLEMS OF ECONOMIC
GROWTH AND DEVELOPMENT

I believe in materialism. I believe in all the proceeds of a healthy materialism,—good cooking, dry houses, dry feet, sewers, drain pipes, hot water, baths, electric lights, automobiles, good roads, bright streets, long vacations away from the village pump, new ideas, fast horses, swift conversation, theatres, operas, orchestras, bands,—I believe in them all for everybody. The man who dies without knowing these things may be as exquisite as a saint, and as a rich as a poet; but it is in spite of, not because of, his deprivation.

FRANCIS HACKETT, IRELAND

I almost envy China that she is still in the pre-automobile stage of walking, cycling, and breathing fresh air.

DR. PAUL DUDLEY WHITE

All the economic principles we have learned can now be brought to bear on perhaps one of the most challenging problems of the next quarter century—the problem of underdeveloped economies. There are nearly 4 billion people in the world, and at this moment half of them are hungry—literally hungry. Only someone who has been pursuing beauty or health on a temporary diet of less than 1,500 calories per day will know how food can fill one's dreams and pervade every waking thought.

For conscience's sake, we are impelled to help. Besides, history teaches us that people do not always starve quietly.

DEFINING UNDERDEVELOPMENT

Writers used to speak of "backward" nations, which naturally irritated the people of those lands. To avoid offense the United Nations sometimes used the roundabout expression "developing" nations. Today most people adopt the expression "less developed" countries (LDCs). What is meant by the term? Alternative definitions are given. Most seem to involve the following:

An underdeveloped nation is simply one with real per capita income that is low relative to the present-day per capita incomes of such nations as

Canada, the United States, Great Britain, and Western Europe generally. Usually, an underdeveloped nation is one regarded as being capable of substantial improvement in its income level.

Of course, every country is underdeveloped in the sense that it is not yet perfect and hence is capable of being improved. Even the so-called "advanced" countries were once underdeveloped by our definition and had to go through the process of development. Table 38-1 gives a picture of the relative stages of development of different countries.

Less than one-seventh of the world's population live in the highly developed group A with about $2,000 per capita (in 1974 Canadian dollars); just over one-fifth live in the intermediate group B; about two-thirds live in the underdeveloped group C.

About one-third of the world's population lives in Communist societies. The Soviet Union, Czechoslovakia, and East Germany now fall in the highly developed A group, though only barely. As for the rest of the communist countries, how are their people divided among the groups? Recalling the vast population of China, we are not surprised to find two-thirds of the Iron Curtain peoples falling in the lowest group C. Little wonder, then, that economic development is a lively subject everywhere, in the East as well as in the West.

COUNTRIES GROUPED BY LEVEL OF ECONOMIC DEVELOPMENT

A. Highly developed	B. Intermediate (cont.)	C. Less Developed (cont.)
Australia	Romania	*Americas:*
Belgium	Saudi Arabia	Bolivia
Canada	Singapore	Brazil
Czechoslovakia	South Africa	British
Denmark	Spain	West Indies
Finland	Uruguay	Colombia
France	Venezuela	Dominican
Germany	Yugoslavia	Republic
(Democratic Republic)		Ecuador
Germany	**C. Less Developed**	El Salvador
(Federal Republic)	*Africa:*	Guatemala
Israel	Algeria	Guyana
Italy	Angola	Haiti
Japan	Cameroon	Honduras
Kuwait	Chad	Nicaragua
Luxembourg	Congo	Paraguay
Netherlands	Dahomey	Peru
New Zealand	Ethiopia	
Norway	Ghana	*Asia:*
Puerto Rico	Guinea	Afghanistan
Sweden	Ivory Coast	Burma
Switzerland	Kenya	Cambodia
U.S.S.R.	Liberia	Ceylon
United Kingdom	Madagascar	China
United States	Malawi	Fiji
	Mali	India
B. Intermediate	Mauritius	Indonesia
Argentina	Morocco	Iran
Austria	Mozambique	Iraq
Bulgaria	Niger	Jordan
Chile	Nigeria	Korea (North)
Costa Rica	Rwanda	Korea (South)
Cuba	Senegal	Malaysia
Cyprus	Sierra Leone	Nepal
Greece	Southern Rhodesia	Pakistan
Hong Kong	Sudan	Philippines
Hungary	Tanzania	Syria
Ireland	Togo	Taiwan
Jamaica	Tunisia	Thailand
Lebanon	Uganda	Turkey
Libya	United Arab	Vietnam (North)
Malta	Republic (Egypt)	Vietnam (South)
Mexico	Upper Volta	Yemen
Panama	Zaire	
Poland	Zambia	*Europe:*
Portugal		Albania

TABLE 38-1. (Sources: United Nations Statistical Office; and Center for International Studies, MIT, updated by authors.)

CHARACTERISTICS OF UNDERDEVELOPED ECONOMIES

To bring out the contrasts between advanced and underdeveloped economies, imagine that you are a typical twenty-one-year-old in one of the underdeveloped countries, be it Haiti, India, or Nigeria.

You are poor: even after making generous allowance for the goods that you both produce and consume, your annual income averages barely $100 per head, as against over $5,000 per head of your fellow man in North America; perhaps you can find cold comfort in the thought that only 1 in 8 of the human race averages more than $1,500 per year. For each of your people who can read, there are three like you

FIG. 38-1. Differentials of nations' living standards are great.

The poorest half of the nations receive only 8 percent of the total world income. The tenth of the world who live in advanced communist countries enjoy about 18 percent of the total but the 25 percent of the world who live in communist less developed countries receive only 5 percent of the world income, averaging only two-thirds the low per capita incomes of the other LDCs.

Contrast the inequality shown here with the Lorenz curve for India, and with that of Lorenz charts of Chapter 5 depicting inequality inside Canada and the United States, Sweden, or Ceylon.

(Sources: World Bank; U.S. Department of State.)

who are illiterate. Your life expectancy is a little more than two-thirds that of the average man in advanced North America; already one or two of your brothers and sisters have died before reaching adulthood; and though your mother has had fewer children than your grandmother did, more of your brothers and sisters have lived to maturity, thanks to imported medical techniques—and you must compete with them for subsistence.

Most of your countrymen work on rural farms; few can be spared from food production for factories or service trades. You work with but one-fiftieth the horsepower of your prosperous North American fellow man. You know little of science, but much of folklore. Your methods and tools are primitive. Nei-

ther the discipline of markets nor the deliberations of planning commissions mean much to you. As a citizen in the poorer parts of Asia, Africa, or Latin America, you and your fellows together constitute 60 per cent of the world population, but you must divide among you only 12 per cent of world income. You brood over the fact that North America, with 7 percent of the people, enjoys more than 30 percent of world income; and that the other advanced noncommunist countries, with 12 percent of the people consume another 31 percent of world income.

Figure 38-1 shows how unequal is the geographical distribution of real incomes.[1] Contrast this Lorenz curve of inequality among nations with Figs. 5-2, 5-3, and 9-2, which show less glaring inequality within a country, whether LDC or advanced.

URGENCY OF THE PROBLEM

There have always been differences between rich and poor. Why worry especially about the underdeveloped countries? Here are some reasons:

WIDENING DIFFERENTIALS In contrast to the narrowing of income differentials within the advanced nations, the divergence between advanced and underdeveloped countries is probably now widening rather than narrowing. North America and Western Europe have almost doubled their production per head since 1940. Many authorities believe that living standards in India, Indonesia, and certain other underdeveloped countries have not improved nearly that much since then and may even have deteriorated in some regions.

Much of any widening gap between the richest and the less developed countries is due to the rapid real growth rates of the former; for, it is not the case that poor countries have generally been growing less rapidly than in their past, or for that matter, less rapidly than countries now rich did when they first began to develop. Figure 38-2 puts the trends of divergence into quantitative perspective.

---

[1] Nobel-prize winners Tinbergen and Kuznets have devoted themselves to the problem of measuring the international distribution of income. Tinbergen recently concluded that the best-to-do ten percent of nations (measured by their population) showed a real income 32 times that of the worst-off ten percent. For regions within one country (states, provinces, *départements*) the figure corresponding to 32 is *two*! Tinbergen argues that this terrific gap is widening. (Source: private paper, 1974.)

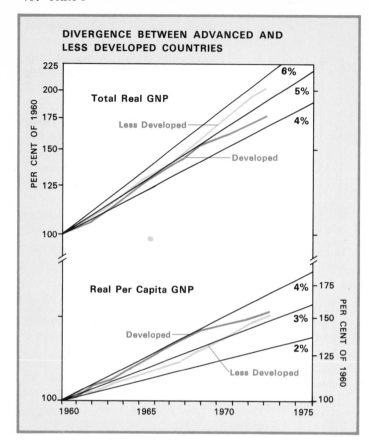

DIVERGENCE BETWEEN ADVANCED AND LESS DEVELOPED COUNTRIES

FIG. 38-2. Rich and poor economies both grow, but gap between them remains.

Much of the growth of the LDCs, as shown in the upper panel with black left-hand ratio scale, is frittered away in burgeoning population growth. As a result, per capita income of LDCs (who need it most) cannot quite keep up with growth of post-Keynesian mixed economies. (Source: Agency for International Development data on noncommunist economies, updated.)

IDEOLOGICAL STRUGGLE In the modern ideological war between the free and the communist worlds, both sides regard the underdeveloped regions as being torn between following the pattern of the mixed economy or following the pattern of socialism. Revolutionaries naturally agitate in the "Third World", never failing to point out the poverty there, never failing to contrast it with our wealth, never failing to remind the people there of real and fancied evils of "colonialism." Cuba is an example. Africa, Latin America, and Asia are cases in point.

Experience does not bear out the easy generalization, "Fill the stomachs of people, and they will refrain from going communistic." Men in utter misery often seem incapable of revolting; and the great revolutions of the past (such as the French and Russian) have often taken place *at a time when some economic progress had already been achieved.*

Nonetheless, to turn our backs on the problem of development is to court future disaster. Harvard's distinguished economic historian Alexander Gerschenkron has drawn the following important lesson from history:[2]

"The Soviet government can be properly described as a product of the country's economic backwardness. Had serfdom been abolished by Catherine the Great or ... in 1825, the peasant discontent, the driving force and the earnest of success of the Russian Revolution, would never have assumed disastrous proportions, while the economic development of the country would have proceeded in a much more gradual fashion. ... The delayed industrial revolution was responsible for a political revolution in the course of which the power fell in the hands of a dictatorial government to which in the long run the vast majority of the population was opposed. ... The paramount lesson of the twentieth century is that the problems of backward nations

[2] Alexander Gerschenkron, *Economic Backwardness in Historical Perspective,* (The Belknap Press, Harvard University Press, Cambridge, Mass., 1962), pp. 28-30.

are not exclusively their own. They are just as much problems of the advanced countries. It is not only Russia but the whole world that pays the price for the failure to emancipate the Russian peasants and to embark upon industrialization policies at an early time. Advanced countries cannot afford to ignore economic backwardness."

To reinforce this, tick off the advanced countries in Table 38-1. You cannot find a single one that had a successful proletarian revolution when its economy was strong.

GREAT EXPECTATIONS AND "DEMONSTRATION EFFECTS" Within the underdeveloped countries, people are today acutely aware of their poverty and its contrasts with rich lands. They do not like it. What is more, they insist on doing something about it.

This was not always so: a century ago the Emperor of China sent a message to the Queen of England saying that his country neither needed nor desired economic improvement. Look at today's frantic efforts in China and mark the contrast. In the ancient formula

$$\text{Happiness} = \frac{\text{material consumption}}{\text{desire}}$$

It is easy for affluent Western observers to advocate Thoreau's counsel to hold down the denominator.

So nearly perfect are modern instruments of communication that people everywhere know about—and often envy—the comforts of modern Western life. No longer do they shrug their shoulders and accept their relative poverty as the divine will of Allah. Most important, this increased awareness comes at a time when the role of government is highly developed.

Today, when people want something done, they are likely to turn to government and to insist that programs be adopted toward the desired goal. They want to foreshorten history and get now what developed lands got late.

They want better health; land reform, the breaking up of landowners' holdings; better methods of land cultivation; industrialization; political rights as individuals. It is easy to see that men want these things for natural individualistic reasons. But economic welfare is not the only reason why men desire development. Modern peoples desire development

also for reasons of *nationalism*: people want their country to be powerful, to be respected, and—let us face it—to be feared. Thus, the British and Dutch may have brought sanitation to their former colonies; they may have thereby increased people's life spans and material well-being. But they at the same time set up exclusive clubs whose front doors were barred to the native citizenry. "Freedom from contempt" is one Asian's way of describing his goal.

SUPERFICIAL THEORIES OF DEVELOPMENT

GEOGRAPHY A look at Table 38-1 shows that nearly all the advanced countries are in the temperate zones. Hence, so the argument used to go, it is all a matter of *climate*.

This sweeping explanation will not fit the facts. The first civilizations were in regions of the Mediterranean and Near East (or, if you will, in the Mayan regions of Central America). Greece was in her glory when Germans and Saxons were cowering over fireplaces in their caves.

Certainly, climate is an important factor, but it is not all-important. It does help not to have tropical heat and erosion from jungle floods. It does help not to have arctic snows. But one of the consequences of modern technology is that fevers can be checked by DDT. The bitter Oxford, Ottawa, or Oslo cold can be offset by heating; and the humid heat of Texas need no longer inhibit the pace of body and mind.

The geographical distribution of *natural resources* —topsoil, rainfall, dammable water for irrigation and power, oil and ore deposits—all these are important. But in a world where trade is increasingly possible, grave deficiencies in this area can be at least partially offset, as the examples of Denmark, Japan, and Israel have shown.

RACE Throw a stone in the advanced countries and the skin you bruise is likely to be white. Ergo, the tale ran, prosperity is merely a matter of race.

No one has yet been able to find a causal link between a tendency toward albinism and productivity; the pioneers of Egyptian, Greek, Indian, and Roman cultures were generally not blond or tall. The most remarkable phenomenon of economic development in this last century and in this last decade has undoubtedly been the Japanese. Anthropologists cannot completely agree in classifying *Homo sapiens* into the Mongolian, Caucasian, and other categories.

A glance at history—at the Ethiopian and Berber cultures, at ancient China, primitive northwestern Europe, and flowering Near Eastern cultures—reveals that many factors have been dominant, and that the factor of race itself cannot be isolated as a discernible determinant of economic development. The Chinese at home were always said to lack entrepreneurship. Yet their descendants in Malaya and Southeast Asia, with the same genes in their cells, are accused of being too successful at the art of entrepreneurship.

CUSTOM AND CULTURE Victorian England or Coolidge's America came as close as any culture ever has to being a business culture. In the 1920s a biography of Jesus in terms of accounting virtues could be a best-seller. Hence, some have leaped to the theory that people must behave like the *Homo economicus* of the classical textbooks if a nation is to prosper. (The Japanese have an apter expression: In reference to their industrial miracle of the last decades, they accuse themselves of being "economic animals".)

This is a caricature. It provides a truth, and hides a more important truth:

Material progress does depend on replacement of a belief in magic and superstition by discernment of and belief in the cause-and-effect relations of engineering and science. If a nation's traditions abhor manual work or work in general, if its people emphasize the hereafter as against this world, if they despise material prosperity, if they discourage ordinary honesty in contractual dealings with strangers; if their way of life puts a great premium on current consumption rather than provision for the future; if their government officials are corrupt and inefficient—all such cultural traits are not particularly conducive to economic development.

But putting stress on these noneconomic factors does not solve the problem of *explanation*. It poses new problems. Why did the brains that might have gone into business in many countries go into science, or the church, or the army? Why did the anthropologists who stressed the unchangeable inertia of

custom in Mexico go wrong in their predictions that penetration of the money psychology would be slow there?

We must not throw away seminal explanations merely because they turn out to be superficial and even wrong. But we must not overlook their superficialities and errors. Max Weber's celebrated emphasis on the "Protestant ethic" as both cause and effect of capitalistic development is a case in point. It did fit some facts: many of the advanced nations are Protestant. John Calvin and *some* Protestant theologians did break away from the Catholic Church's ancient edicts against interest. John D. Rockefeller, Sr., was both an avaricious profit maximizer and an ardent Baptist, who referred to his gains as "God's Gold." Yet the "buts" that have to be applied to the Weber thesis are many and serious.

Northern Italy and Catholic Rhineland showed early development. You can find in eighteenth-century Japanese writings perfect passages of Weberian Protestantism. The Jews, Chinese, and Basques have in many places played the role of the alienated stranger who pioneers in economic entrepreneurship. And if Weber seriously regards Benjamin Franklin—who undoubtedly was a prototype of the scientist, innovator, and business go-getter—as an otherworldly Protestant, biographers of that cynical deist tell us the name has almost lost its meaning. Modern statistical research on the Protestant and Catholic neighborhoods in German cities, on which Weber originally rested part of his case, has found that correct statistical tabulation even belies Weber's own findings.

Whether or not Weber in some subtle sense was right, think how badly a crude belief in his theory would have served for prediction 20 years ago: The economies that have shown the greatest miracles of growth since 1950 have been Japan, Catholic France and Italy, largely Catholic West Germany, and atheistical Russia. Such predominantly Protestant countries as Canada, Britain, and the United States have done poorly in comparison.

All this proves nothing, because there is almost nothing to prove.[3]

RECENT CONCEPTS TO DESCRIBE DEVELOPMENT

For decades now, economists have been intensely interested in economic development. While they have developed no unified theory that differs from the

[3] The reader intrigued by all this will enjoy both Max Weber's *Protestant Ethic and the Spirit of Capitalism*, (London, Unwin, 1965) and R. H. Tawney, *Religion and the Rise of Capitalism*, (Harmondsworth, Middlesex, Penguin Books, 1961), both in paperback.

basic growth models introduced in Chapter 37, they have added some special features to these models.

The following brief account represents a montage of the most important notions developed in the recent literature. It will pave the way for a systematic causal analysis in terms of the economic determinants of production: land and natural resources; labor (in quantity of man-hours and in quality of skills, training, and effort); capital formation (material and human); and finally, technological knowledge and innovation. The chapter ends with a brief discussion of modern development planning.

PRECONDITIONS FOR GROWTH Human history is long and economic development is exceptional, being primarily the outcome of the last few centuries of Western history. During most of history, life was nasty, brutish, and short. A cruel Malthusian equilibrium prevailed in which deaths kept in balance with births.

In a few lucky places, warfare diminished. Superior production methods were applied to ample resources. A surplus over subsistence became possible. And usually wealth was so unequally divided among the aristocratic landowners and the bulk of the populace that the rich were able to abstain from consumption and to funnel savings into capital formation. Economic development could now take place.

THE TAKE-OFF The more historians study the facts, the more gradual and evolutionary seems the process of growth. But revolution is always better drama and journalism than evolution. So various economists like to use words such as "the take-off," "the spurt," and the "big push" to describe the period of accelerating growth. Thus, W. W. Rostow[4] develops stages of growth different from those of Marx and other writers described in the previous chapter. One of his stages is called the *take-off*, the obvious analogy being with an airplane, which can fly only after attaining a certain critical speed.

There is no purpose here in joining the search to find out when each country had or will have its take-off: England in the eighteenth century, Japan in the

late nineteenth, the Congo in the 1990s. Nor shall we divide a country's development in stages the way Shakespeare divides a man's life into various ages. Instead, we abandon strict chronology to stress the important economic *principle* that the take-off serves to dramatize.

INCREASING RETURNS, SOCIAL OVER-HEAD CAPITAL, AND EXTERNALITIES Chapter 37's models of growth proceeded for the most part in terms of the conventional economic principle of diminishing returns—referring to statical variations in labor applied to relatively fixed land, or to variations in the stock of capital goods applied to less rapidly expanding labor supply. That conventional model of production assumed that doubling all the factors together would, typically, exactly double total product—a principle referred to as "constant returns to scale" and serving as a background to the law of diminishing returns to a varying factor.

In dynamic economic development, the phenomenon of "*increasing* returns" is to be expected. Smith's *Wealth of Nations* was in its day a manual of economic development. What Smith stressed was the advantage of *large-scale division of labor*. It is a case of the whole being bigger than the sum of its parts: if all factors together can be increased in size, product will grow *more* than proportionally. Each primitive region cannot develop the scale to achieve efficiency. A pile of enriched uranium suddenly goes active when it achieves a certain size. Similarly, the phenomenon of increasing returns can make it possible for dramatic spurts and accelerations to occur in economic development. (As we saw in Part Three, important areas of increasing returns cannot be left to the free play of competitive market forces; there is a case here for coordination to prevent monopoly and to channel it into optimal patterns.)

Professor Paul Rosenstein-Rodan introduced, three decades ago, an important related phenomenon. He spoke of the crucial importance of "social overhead capital." To develop, a private economy must have public roads, a railroad, irrigation projects and dams, public health spraying against malarial mosquitoes, etc. All these involve bulky *indivisibilities* of the increasing-returns type. No small firm or family can profitably undertake them; nor can pioneering private enterprise hope to make a

[4] W. W. Rostow, *The Stages of Economic Growth: A Non-Communist Manifesto* (Cambridge University Press, New York, 1960). See Paul A. Samuelson, *Readings in Economics* (McGraw-Hill, New York, 1973, 7th ed.), for a strong critique of the Rostow thesis by Harvard's Simon Kuznets.

profit from them before the markets have been developed. They spread their benefits *socially*. Hence, it is argued, public, as well as private, responsibility is intrinsically involved in economic development from the beginning.

Another way of putting this, as in Chapter 8, page 144, is thus:

Often there are strong *"external* economies" involved in development. A county agent adviser can simultaneously benefit all the farmers in his region. A railroad can benefit all industry. A multiple-purpose dam has similar externalities. It should be obvious that one can find examples of externalities that do not involve increasing returns, and examples of increasing returns that are unrelated to social overhead capital or externalities. But it should be evident that there is often a strong interrelationship between these three notions.

BALANCED GROWTH AND INDUSTRIALIZATION

In the development literature, there has often been a fascination with *balanced* growth. One would not want the skull to grow more rapidly than the head's skin. It is similarly argued that growth in a shoe factory should be accompanied by growth in a stocking factory and in a brewery, if what people want at a higher standard of living is shoes, socks, and beer.

For the world as a whole, the budgetary laws of Engel will impose some limited balance on consumption growth. Food will grow, but it will lag behind luxury items. Indeed, despite the emphasis on balanced growth, Colin Clark and other writers have long noted an apparent tendency for development to proceed in three stages: *agricultural* dominance first; then *manufacturing* dominance; and finally, as we all become affluent, a shift toward *services*. Supply and demand created these patterns in the old days of relatively free enterprise.

Is balanced growth inevitable or desirable for one region undergoing development? History suggests a negative answer:

Canada, as we saw in Chapter 37, grew through *specialized* "staples": fish, furs, timber, and wheat. The United States first developed by *specializing* in agricultural exports. Belgium early developed by

specializing in glass and woolen production. The whole theory of comparative advantage, presented in Chapters 34 and 35, suggested that growth within a region does *not* best take place in balance.

This does remind us of an important issue discussed in Chapter 35 as to whether there is not an "infant-industry" and "young-economy" argument that can validly be used to criticize extreme specialization of a country along a few vulnerable lines of comparative advantage. If coffee demand and supply are volatile, and if *future* comparative advantage may lie in certain nonagricultural industries, a country like Brazil may be well advised to interfere with the market tendency to specialize in coffee production. But diversification and truly balanced growth are by no means the same thing.

INDUSTRIALIZATION VERSUS AGRICULTURE New Zealand, Denmark, Holland, western Ontario, and Argentina are all regions where productivity in agriculture does not compare too unfavorably with productivity in industry. They are the exceptions. In most parts of the world, incomes in urban cities are almost double those in rural agriculture. And in the affluent nations, large parts of total resources are devoted to urban manufacture. Hence, many nations jump to the conclusion that industrialization is a *cause* rather than an *effect* of affluence.

One must be wary of making such an inference. As the saying goes, "Rich men smoke expensive cigars; but going out to buy an expensive cigar will not make you rich." Vanity seems to make each country want (1) an airline and (2) a steel mill. Analysis of present and future comparative advantage suggests that for most nations these are ornamental luxuries.

It simply is not true that the greatest productivity advances of the last century have been in industry rather than agriculture. (Recall Chapter 20's discussion of agriculture.) If Bangladesh's five-year plan could increase the productivity of farming by 20 per cent, that would do more to release resources for production of comforts than would exclusive reliance on promoting industry.

The points made here are obvious. Yet they are often overlooked in political debate. But before leaving the subject, we should point to the germ of truth in the argument for pushing industrialization in order to speed development.

City and factory life tend to break up the cake of rural custom. People in close contact mutually stimulate each other. Hence, technical change is probably stimulated in the long run by subsidy to industrialization. Fortunately, there is often much "disguised unemployment" in rural areas, in the sense that some members of each family could move to the city, or turn during off-harvest times to local industrial occupations without causing much loss of farm product.

CAPITAL NEEDS AND EFFICIENT RESOURCE ALLOCATION

To break out of a vicious circle of poverty and underdevelopment, capital formation is needed. But starving peasants cannot be expected to take much thought of the future. In past ages, inequality of land ownership probably helped solve the problem of social thrift, but in a ruthless way. Collectivist economies like China, North Korea, and Russia have shown that, by command, they can impose the same ruthless abstention from current consumption.

Why cannot free economies do the same? Why cannot they use the fiscal measures discussed throughout this book to curb consumption and stimulate investment? An important reason lies in the realm of political science. Some of the developed countries are able to impose progressive income taxes and find that the taxes do get paid. In most of the world, this is probably not possible. As well, tax administration is primitive and inefficient. People will not cooperate. The problem is made worse where poverty is so great that public officials become corrupt.

As a substitution for taxation and coercion, many writers (such as California's Professor Harvey Leibenstein) recommend that projects be favored which will produce incomes *for corporations and groups that can be counted on to do heavy investment*. They argue that this emphasis should be given even in some cases where there is an actual loss in current efficiency, not to mention the tendency to create a corporate oligarchy in a poor society.

PLANNING, WITH OR WITHOUT RESOURCE PRICING After 1930 Soviet Russia established a first, second, and third Five-Year Plan.

Most nations today, including those neutral between East and West, have similar development plans. These set up quantitative goals. Alternative goals are scrutinized for their realism and compatibility. Compromises are made, and finally a compromise set of aggregate targets is worked out.

These targets may be specified in general terms or in quite detailed terms. Thus, India will take into account her growth in labor force and food supply; her growth in capital resources from internal sources; the amount of capital she can import from America or the Soviet Union. She will canvass her need for dams and electric power; for steel mills and machinery; etc. In the end a system of priorities will have to be worked out lest the demands on the system become so great as to produce galloping inflation, or as to produce so much expenditure on imports that the country will run out of foreign exchange and have to either devalue or ration severely by austere import licensing.

Much of this planning will be in concrete physical terms. But much more has to be expressed in terms of rupees of *value*. More importantly, the planners will often find that the values quoted in the market place do not correspond to true national scarcities. Thus, in India people would starve if they were paid a zero wage; yet for many purposes labor is superabundant and ought to be regarded as almost a free factor of production. On the other hand, capital goods are truly scarce; charging fifty times as much for use of a tractor as use of a man may come nowhere near to doing justice to the tractor's scarcity and superior productivity. Hence, some sophisticated planners will actually apply corrected "shadow prices," or "accounting prices" to labor, capital, and imported goods for the purpose of getting a more rational valuation and allocation of scarce resources. That way, growth can be maximized.

CAPITAL-OUTPUT RATIOS AND SCREENING OF INVESTMENT PROJECTS Poor countries are long on labor, short on capital. They are advised, therefore, to economize on the use of heavily durable and intensely roundabout capital projects. Often they are advised to concentrate as much as they can on activities that have a low "capital-output ratio."

This advice is good. But it would be more accurate if expressed in terms of the investment concepts developed in Part Four. Each project should have calculated for it a percentage rate of return per annum: then a hydroelectric project that yields 20 per cent per annum ought to get done before a short-lived steam project that yields only 5 per cent per year—even if, to the superficial eye, the capital-output ratio of the steam plant seems smaller.[5]

We have described the general problem of underdevelopment, and surveyed the concepts used in this field. Now we can turn to the constructive task of analyzing the four economic fundamentals: (1) population, (2) natural resources, (3) capital formation, and (4) technology.

POPULATION PROBLEMS

Mere growth in numbers does not necessarily mean development. Indeed, as writers since Malthus have warned, unbridled increase in numbers is likely to invoke the law of diminishing returns and to work against increases in per capita living standards. This can create problems. Thus we find many underdeveloped countries repeating the pattern of the eighteenth- and nineteenth-century economies: improved medical technology (e.g., sanitation and, in our day, cheap insecticides) first reduces the death rate; and with birth rates remaining high, population grows rapidly.

El Salvador, Java, and many other examples underline the twin lessons:

First, much of the increase in output made possible by technological advance may be spent on duplication of numbers. And second, modern science, conquering disease faster than it operates on food supply, may in the future keep people from dying from germs—only to threaten them with death from famine as they vie for insufficient food.[6]

The grave question being asked by demographers is this:

Will birth rates fall in developing countries as they did in older countries? And before living standards do?

The Pill, loop, sterilization, rhythm techniques, and other birth-control devices do begin to cut down on the birth rate in poor countries once people come to want smaller families. When most of your offspring died in childhood, you needed many children to carry on your name and preserve your immortality. Once medical science lowers the death rate, people everywhere become more interested in preventing births of fourth and fifth children per family —eventually, perhaps, even third children.

IMPROVING HUMAN RESOURCES Since labor is an important factor of production, there is much constructive programming to be done in this area. When planners draw up blueprints for hastening economic development, they write down the following specific manpower programs:

1. Control disease and increase health and nutrition programs—both to make people happier and to make them more productive workers. Accordingly, do not look on hospitals and sewerage projects as luxuries but as vitally needed social overhead capital.

2. Educated people make more productive workers. Therefore budget for schools and other programs to reduce illiteracy. Beyond reading and writing, train people in new techniques of agriculture and industry. Send your best minds abroad to bring back knowledge of engineering and business. (But beware lest they all get drained off to the advanced nations!)

DISGUISED UNEMPLOYMENT One important condition for promoting development is the better utilization of manpower. In poor countries, particularly rural ones, often a large part of the manpower pool does almost nothing because there is nothing for it to do. Such people may not be counted in the census of unemployment, but they can scarcely be called employed; they live with their kinfolk, and when a boom or a development plan comes along, sweeping them into productive city jobs, there is almost no reduction in the product back on the farm. The same phenomenon of disguised unemployment is met in advanced countries, both in the subsistence farming regions and in the city streets, where men

---

[5] When experts shift from the capital-output ratio to the "marginal capital-output ratio" they can come out with the economists' correct yield procedures. Also, if capital will be less scarce 20 years from now—so that the correct interest rate society ought to use for its projects is 30 per cent this decade and 18 per cent next decade—a proper planning calculation will take this into account.

[6] Indians in northern Canada face this type of situation each winter.

eke out a bare existence doing door-to-door selling or begging whenever productive jobs are unavailable.

For a satisfctory solution to this under-employment and unemployment problem, governments sometimes find it desirable, along with man-power programs, to pursue expansionary fiscal and monetary policies—even though these methods raise problems of inflation and of deficit in the balance of international payments.

NATURAL RESOURCES

Presumably, most large poor countries were once rich in fertile land. But this endowment has been de-pleted, leaving large populations to divide inade-quate resources. The romantic notion of overlooked geographical areas rich in resources has largely been exploded by geographers. Generally, people have *already* settled in the most productive regions.

True, geologists are still seeking and finding new hidden resources; and there are authenticated cases where control of malaria by DDT has reclaimed from the jungle hundreds of square miles of fertile Asian land. Balanced against these cheerful consid-erations is the fact that many underdeveloped coun-tries are rapidly depleting their mines, their topsoil, and their irreplaceable natural resources.

Moreover, as was noted, many of the present-day resources of tropical countries are becoming obsolete in competition with scientific creation of *synthetic* substitutes from cheap substances found in abun-dance within the advanced countries. Thus nylon harmed the silk industry and impoverished millions; if synethic rubber were to replace natural rubber completely, Eastern Asia would find itself even harder hit.

Economic geographers are agreed that further de-velopment now largely comes from discovery and better use of existing resources. Gone are the oppor-tunities of a Columbus; and half-closing is the open door beckoning the poor of the older regions, beg-ging them to migrate to the fertile prairies of North and South America or to the empty regions of Aus-tralia and New Zealand.

Of course, the quip still holds: "There's nothing wrong with any poor country that discovery of oil can't cure." The fact that primitive Kuwait falls, in Table 38-1, in the most prosperous category illus-trates the point. Venezuela, Iraq, Saudi Arabia, Libya, Iran, and Kuwait are cases where oil could help fi-nance development.

LAND REFORM Even without creating or finding new land, nations can make better use of the land they do have. The medieval village was divided into strips of land one could hardly turn around on, and each man might have to live off the produce of two or three such strips, frequently distant from each other. The same is still true in many parts of the world. It took from the thirteenth to the eighteenth century for the painful, and bitterly resented, *enclosure* movement in England to break up the common lands and to gather together into efficient larger-scale plots the land of the country. In the pro-cess many peasants were dispossessed and wound up as landless farmhands or city slum dwellers. A fortu-nate few migrated to the Americas or Australia. The changing status of Russian peasants, later to become tied to the land as serfs, then freed, eventually emerging as today's collective-farmers provides an analogous case, including the eventual move to mis-erable housing in industrial cities. The planners of China's collectivization program are attempting to create rural communes where both farming and light industry are carried on; it is hoped in this way to get the bulk of the 800 million people out of the fields, but not out of the countryside. The displacement of small farmers in Quebec, the western plains and prairies, and the cotton-growing South (all illu-minated by our great novelists) is part of the same process. In many parts of the world, this same pain-ful consolidating of too-small holdings is yet to be carried out.

At the other extreme, we see in many under-developed countries feudal landholding of huge es-tates too large for efficiency.[7] The tenant farmer has no incentive to improve the property, knowing that he can be dispossessed at any time and having learned from bitter experience that little of the fruit of his initiative will ever accrue to him. The landlord in turn has no incentive to improve the property, never knowing whether an irresponsible tenant will dissipate the costly resources placed at his disposal.

These two situations may co-exist. They are so-cially explosive, and agitation for land reform sig-nifies a ground swell of public sentiment not long to

---

[7] We saw in Chapter 28, how inefficient systems of land tenancy can put society inside its production-possibility frontier.

be denied. More than one agricultural economist has linked productivity with land reform.

Successful reform that puts land into the hands of owners who can count on reaping the fruits of their own enterprise has, many times, literally "turned sand into gold".

The problems of natural-resource development merge with the problem of improved technology and with the problem of improved capital-goods capacity for utilizing and especially discovering natural resources.

CAPITAL FORMATION

The fingers and brains of men in the underdeveloped countries are much like the fingers and brains of their more prosperous brethren; but men in the advanced nations work with a plentiful supply of capital goods built up over the years. To pile up net capital formation requires, as we have earlier seen, a sacrifice of current consumption. But there's the rub; underdeveloped countries are already so poor as to be near the minimum of subsistence; they claim that they cannot—in fact, they generally do not—save a very large share of their current national incomes.

Thus, in the advanced nations, from 10 to 20 per cent of income may go into capital formation; but in the underdeveloped nations, the rate of saving and investment may be less than 5 per cent.[8] Merely to provide for rapidly growing population, the primitive tools and housing now enjoyed can use up most of this saving. What is left, then for development?

Until we learned how to prevent mass unemployment, many economists worried about *oversaving* in *advanced* countries. But for *underdeveloped* countries the problem is often the classical one of *undersaving*: more precisely, the problem is underinvestment in productive instruments capable of increasing the nation's rate of economic progress.

QUALITATIVE DISTORTION OF INVESTMENT
There is a further problem. Not only are saving and investment *quantitatively* low in these

countries; equally serious is the fact that the *qualitative composition of investment* is often bad from the standpoint of national development. Thus, too much of the limited saving of India goes into hoarding of gold and jewelry, imported legally or illegally into the country and using up its scarce foreign exchange.

Many underdeveloped countries, like Brazil or Chile, suffer from chronic inflation; hence, there is a natural tendency for people to invest in real estate and in hoarding of inventory. When you can make 20 per cent on your money by hoarding goods, why seek an additional and problematical few per cent from manufacturing? Thus, no less than 55 per cent of Brazil's 1947 investment was in the form of construction. Observers are also struck with the fact that, in many of the poorest regions of the world, *luxury* apartment dwellings seem to mushroom, while industry languishes.

Still another qualitative dissipation of the limited saving in an underdeveloped country comes from the frequent tendency of the wealthy to pile up their savings *abroad*, legally and illegally, thereby making them unavailable for internal development.

CAPITAL FROM ABROAD
If there are so many obstacles to domestic-financed capital formation, why not rely more heavily on foreign sources? After all, did not England in the nineteenth century invest heavily in the United States, Canada, Australia, and Latin America? Did not France before 1914 invest heavily in Czarist Russia and Egypt? And did not Germany invest heavily in Eastern Europe? Does not economic theory tell us that a rich country which has used up all its own high-interest investment projects can benefit itself and at the same time benefit a poor country if only it will shift investment to the high-interest projects not yet exploited abroad?

Actually, prior to 1914 economic development did proceed in this natural fashion. Britain in her heyday saved about 15 per cent of her national income and invested fully half this amount![9] For many reasons, we moderns cannot expect such great amounts of foreign investment. After all, was the pre-World War I pattern so natural, or was it perhaps the special result of fortuitous historical coincidences?

---

[8] In countries going through civil disorders—like Uganda or Chile —net saving could be negative. When the colonial shackles are first thrown off, a decline in income often ensues.

[9] What would be a modern comparison? Canada does not lend abroad, but is a net capital importer; the U.S. would have to lend *ten times* more abroad than she did in 1971, every year.

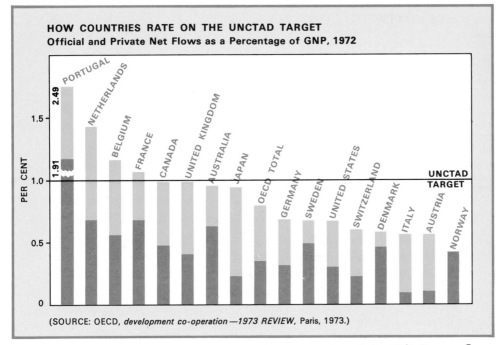

FIG. 38-3(a). The UNCTAD target is about the same as that of the 1969 Pearson Commission on economic aid. Canada does a little better than the average OECD nation on both official aid and private investment and lending.

(b). This shows that *private* lending is on the increase to all developing countries. Source: OECD, *Development Co-operation, 1973 Review* (**Paris**)

Thus, loans from Europe to the New World typically went together with migration of European peoples to those same new lands: Englishmen went along with their money, so to speak, to the American colonies, Canada, Australia, and other dominions; and notice that the same pattern of laws and customs prevailed in the capital-importing countries as in the capital-investing country.

Remember, too, that this antebellum world was an unbelievably cosmopolitan one. You could travel everywhere with no passport. You could migrate freely from country to country. You could expect low tariffs and no trade quotas. You knew the international gold standard would let you transfer capital from place to place at your slightest whim. You knew your property was safe abroad from government confiscation: Back in those days few dreamed of questioning the sanctity of private property, and those nationalistic countries which did raise such questions could be easily intimidated by dispatching battleships for off-coast maneuvers. Finally, you could buy up—literally!—dictatorial governments in many backward countries and bribe them into giving you extremely favorable mining and other concessions.

HOW MORE THAN 100 LDCs RECEIVED FOREIGN CAPITAL

Stocks (received between 1950 and 1970)		Flows Net Capital formation in 1970	
$ billions		per cent	
Direct foreign private investment	39	Direct foreign private investment	8
Private foreign debt	30	Private foreign debt	10
Public foreign debt	27	Official foreign loans and aid	20
Official grants and aid	64		
Total foreign capital 1950 - 1970	$160	Sub-Total foreign Capital	38
		Domestic saving	62
		Total capital formation	100

TABLE 38-2. Private foreign lending to LDCs is not negligible. Direct investment by multinationals may be the next phase. (Source: derived from estimates in G. Reuber and associates, *Private Foreign Investment in Development,* Oxford, 1973, pp. 5 & 255.)

If this sounds like an investor's paradise, be reminded that the historical facts were not really quite so rosy. Foreign investments often did go bankrupt, there being insufficient commercial demand for the railroads built across the plains of the New World. Also, the people in the countries importing capital do not, from their historical utterances, seem to have been too happy over this investor's paradise.

Still, the system did work. And it often did confer *mutual benefits* on both the advanced and backward areas. After dividends went abroad, a net increment of product due to the imported capital was left at home in the form of higher real wages.

Now all this is ancient history. This antebellum world is gone. Never was nationalism stronger than today. Never have borrower and lender been so in agreement: the underdeveloped countries are agreed not to sell to foreigners long-term rights in the development of their countries, no matter how advantageous the price; the developed countries are agreed it would be rash to buy bonds and stocks from backward countries in the old pattern.[10]

This does not mean we must rule out substantial foreign capital investment programs. Fig. 38-3 shows that private foreign investment in LDCs is increasing faster than official aid. For a while after World War II the European and American oil industries were the only direct private investors. There was a little more indirect (portfolio) lending, but official aid grew most rapidly.

In the last ten years the pattern has been complex. International and multinational firms—both resource-extracting and manufacturing—have multiplied their direct investment; foreign governments and firms have borrowed in international money markets and official aid has also expanded. The situation in 1970 is illustrated by Table 38-2.

The private investments were heavily concentrated in countries that contain less than 10 per cent of the world population living in developing countries. These include many of the oil-producing states, and states that are in the "Intermediate" rather than the "Less" developed countries in Table 38-1. In India, Pakistan and Indonesia foreign private investment has been large, but is negligible when measured per capita.

Foreign direct investment in the LDCs has been shown in a study by Western Ontario's Grant Reuber, and associates at the OECD, to involve many of the issues of foreign investment in Canada. The host countries generally welcome this long-term capital,

[10] If any Canadian doubts this, he has only to recall that most Canadians now vote for policies that deter and harass U.S. investment in Canada. Consistently, they do not support platforms that propose government aid to investment in underdeveloped countries.

and offer the American or European firms seeking new affiliates special tax concessions, tariff protection and subsidies. These concessions may distort the home economy more than they benefit it. Furthermore, some multinationals, unsympathetic to local aspirations, have been slow to hire local employees, but have been quick to reinvest local capital or retained earnings. However, the Reuber study suggests that foreign resource and manufacturing firms have on the whole been active in training and diffusing know-how; have experimented broadly with joint local ownership; and have also been more active than other firms in exporting.

Along with import of capital from abroad that comes from private investors interested in a profit return, there is also the possibility of foreign-aid programs from the advanced countries and development loans from the World Bank and various United Nations agencies. (Chapter 36 on international trade discussed these channels.) For the 1970s the goal has been set up that each prosperous nation devote 1 per cent of its GNP to this important purpose. But almost none have lived up to this noble target.

FOREIGN AID FROM OFFICIAL SOURCES

As outlined in Chapter 36, a large part of foreign investment flows through the International Bank for Reconstruction and Development. An increasing proportion of the IBRD's profits now go to the International Development Association (IDA) set up by the Bank to make "soft" loans to nations for education, roads, hospitals, etc. They also go into the International Finance Corporation to make loans to foreign development banks to finance private investment projects.

These are only two of what is now a long list of granting and lending agencies which receive contributions or loans, chiefly from the Western nations. Chief among these are United Nations' offshoots: the Special Fund, Children's Funds (UNICEF), relief and refugee organizations, and programs of technical assistance (UNTA); and regional agencies such as the Inter-American Development Bank and the Asian Development Bank.

Taken together, including the IBRD, these multilateral agencies now pay out well over a billion dollars a year, about one-tenth of which comes from re-

CANADIAN FINANCIAL FLOWS TO LDCs 1972	
Official Bilateral Flows	Millions of Dollars
Grants	194
Loans and Export Credits	258
Sub-Total	452
Official Multilateral Flows	
Grants to U.N. Agencies	37
Other multilateral contributions	117
Sub-Total	154
Sub-Total Official Flows	606
Private loans and investments	355
Grants by Private Voluntary Agencies	54
Total Flow of Financial Resources	1,015

TABLE 38-3.
Private lending and investment are about as important as official development grants. (Source: OECD, *Development Co-operation, 1973 Review* (Paris)).

payments on loans. Their great advantage is that they do not usually tie the recipients to purchases from particular countries, though they do usually specify the projects or items to be bought.

Table 38-3 shows how Canada's official aid to developing countries was made up. Terms and categories are discussed below.

Technical assistance. Since 1949, when President Truman enunciated his "Point Four" program, technical assistance has increased to become about 12 per cent of all Western aid. There is a limit to the capacity of the Western world to supply capital goods and food. What it has done is to spread know-how by moving advisers, teachers, and volunteers overseas, and accepting students and trainees to learn, observe, and discuss. Today the OECD countries have about 110,000 experts and volunteers in less developed countries and about 80,000 student and trainee visitors. Other developed countries, in Eastern Europe, make an equivalent effort.

Terminology: (a) Commodity grants. This is a relatively recent form of aid—most gifts have gone to Asian nations. Very similar to this type of aid, which is usually tied to the agricultural exports of the donors, is financial noncapital aid chiefly from the former imperial countries (the United Kingdom, France, Holland, etc.) to former colonies. *(b) Capital projects.* The donor countries can give assistance either by loans or by grants. For all OECD countries, loans are the chief form of aid. *(c) Export credits and development loans.* The important aspect of loans is their "grant" or "subsidy" content. To what extent is the interest and maturity of loans for exports or capital projects more generous than what is available in the donor country's commercial money market? OECD has calculated that in 1968 about 50 per cent of loans could be regarded as grants. Canada's loans are unusually "soft" or generous, so that about 65 per cent of loans have a "grant element." *(d) Multilateral contributions.* About 18 per cent of all countries' official contributions take the form of subscriptions and grants to international (multilateral) agencies (see below). *(e) Amortization receipts.* Because loans play such a large part in developed countries' aid, it is to be expected that they will receive repayments. Such amortization has reduced Canada's aid cost by 10 per cent in recent years. Like bilateral aid and loans in general, most Canadian funds are *tied* both to Canadian exports and to specific projects or items approved by Canada.

TECHNOLOGICAL CHANGE AND INNOVATIONS

In addition to the funadmental factors of population, natural resources, and capital formation, there is the vitally important fourth factor of technology. Here we can strike a cautiously optimistic note. Here the underdeveloped countries have one possible advantage. They can hope to benefit *by copying the more advanced technology of the developed nations.*

IMITATING TECHNOLOGY The new lands do not have to develop still unborn Newtons to discover the law of gravity: they can read about it in any book. They do not have to go through the slow meandering climb of the Industrial Revolution: they can find in every machinery catalogue wonders undreamed of by the great inventors of the past.

Japan, Germany, and Russia clearly illustrate all this in their historical developments. Japan joined the industrial race late: at the end of the nineteenth century she sent her students abroad and began to copy Western technology. Her government took an active and creative role in stimulating the pace of development, building railroads and utilities, and taxing heavily the newly created increments of land value resulting from the improvements in agriculture. A few energetic, wealthy families were permitted to develop vast industrial empires, while at the same time the general population was made to work, and work hard, in order to earn its living. Without relying on net foreign capital imports, Japan in a few decades had moved into the front rank; both militarily and industrially.

Only after the Revolution of 1848 did Germany really accelerate her industrialization. Through government aid to her universities, German scientists soon became pre-eminent in mathematics, physics, chemistry, and engineering. Sixty years ago, most British and American professors of these subjects—and of history, economics and philology, too—went to Germany for their postgraduate degrees. German prowess in organic chemistry, optics, glass manufacture, and electrical equipment was unsurpassed until the two world wars set her back. Russia, too, illustrates the possibility of fast development through technological imitation of Western techniques and practices.

Finally, the case of the United States itself provides an optimistic example to the rest of the world. Until Hitler made her a present in the 1930s of many of the best Continental scientists of all faiths, she could not honestly boast of having quite reached the very front rank in the field of pure science. Yet for a century American applied technology had admittedly been outstanding. Examine one by one the key inventions involving the automobile. Where did they originate? Mostly in Europe. Nevertheless, Henry Ford and General Motors long outproduced the rest of the world. "Yankee ingenuity" is a phrase that *explains* nothing; but it does refer to a real phenomenon[11] (and one now subject to erosion).

INTERPLAY OF TECHNOLOGY AND CAPITAL It is all very well to speak of underdeveloped countries copying advanced technology. But have we not overlooked something important? Is not advanced technology embodied in the form of complex capital goods? And have we not already seen that those countries are short of capital? So how can we expect them to copy superior technology?

Certainly there is much truth in these suggestions. Technological change and capital investment do go hand in hand; often they are inseparable. All the same, we are right to treat them as analytically distinct—albeit related—processes. Here is one of many examples to show why:

Farming is inefficient in many backward countries. You see peasants breaking up the soil by the same primitive meth-

---

[11] Indeed, Thomas Chandler Haliburton's *Sam Slick*, a Yankee clock salesman in the Maritime provinces, typified New England ingenuity in production and marketing almost three-quarters of a century before the rest of the world became aware of it.

ods their ancestors were using back in the time of David and Solomon. Perhaps an ingenious light plow—something simple that would cost no more than a dollar and would pay for itself in the first month—can be found that will both lessen the total amount of capital needed and greatly increase output. This shows how technological innovation can often be capital-*saving* rather than capital-*using*.

Moreover, even in the poorest countries, some gross capital formation is always going on as things are wearing out and are being replaced. Why replace them with the same thing? Why let much of the economy's capital go into mere *duplicative projects?* Surely, it is much better to embody the newly available investment funds in the form of more efficient technological implements. Thus we see how the interrelated factors of capital formation and technology can be mutually reinforcing.

ENTREPRENEURSHIP AND INNOVATIONS

Does it sound like an easy task for an underdeveloped economy? All that it must do to telescope into a few years the score of years it took us to develop is this: Go abroad and copy more efficient methods; bring them back and put them into effect at home; then sit back and wait for the extra product to roll in.

Of course, it does not work quite this way. People in the underdeveloped countries know this from bitter experience. Yet the same illusion keeps cropping up among the people in the so-called "advanced" countries. Too often we think we can send a few technical experts on a short junket to a poor country; after surveying the field for a month or so, they can write up their recommendations for improvement, and then the neatly typed report they leave behind can be "implemented." In this way development will be solved.

Occasionally, in connection with particular technological processes, experts have indeed been able to work wonders in this facile way; thus, an American expert on tanning was sent out to Libya to advise on some of its difficulties, and in a short time he did diagnose the chemical troubles and come up with an effective cure.

Technologists soon discover, however, that this sort of quick miracle is exactly what cannot be accomplished in connection with the *development of a whole economy*. Indeed, the typical pattern is one of complete disillusionment: after spending several months surveying an underdeveloped country, the expert is thoroughly impressed with the thousands of cultural and economic barriers to progress, so much so that he comes back with a hopeless feeling of defeat. This thoroughly pessimistic conclusion is probably just as wrong in its way as was the opposite optimistic illusion.

Experience shows development is truly a hard and slow process—but not an impossible one. To hasten its evolution, spontaneous entrepreneurship and innovation must develop among the peoples directly involved. Remember, many cultures begin with a contempt for dirty, hard work—a contempt they often inherit from the colonial elite who used to rule over them. Often, too, they have a contempt for business—for money-grubbing and production. Gradually, they must develop for themselves, *within their own mixed cultural pattern*, a creative group of producers alert to trying out new ways, alert to consumer wants, responsive to pecuniary risk-taking and rewards.

Why place the emphasis on creative innovation? Because it is by no means a cut-and-dried task to adapt advanced foreign technology to an underdeveloped country's own use. Remember, the advanced technology was itself developed to meet the special conditions of the advanced countries. What are these conditions? High money wage rates; laborers scarce in number but replete with industrial skills; plentiful capital inherited from the past; mass production; and so forth. These conditions do not prevail in underdeveloped lands.

Time and time again, experience has shown us how easy it is to obtain a foreign loan to put up a model factory in Turkey or a fish-freezing plant in Malaya. Often it is imported piece by piece from abroad and embodies the latest wrinkles of Western technology. Yet, with what result? With high production and sales exceeding costs, so as to yield a comfortable profit which can be plowed back into further industrialization? Only too rarely. Often such grandiose imported projects turn out to be extremely unprofitable. The factory that is an optimal investment for New York may in Ankara be a fiasco, and the Canadian fish plant may never actually get into operation.

This task of creative innovation is not one for undiluted rugged individualism. The government can do much to set up extension services in every agricultural province for consulting with farmers on the best seeds, methods of cultivation, and implements. By sponsoring vocational schools and training courses in machine methods—and in bookkeeping, too—the government itself can innovate creatively.[12] Somewhere between complete *laissez-faire* and total-itarianism a developing nation must work out its own destiny.

FIVE-YEAR PLANS: HOW TO GET FROM HERE TO THERE

The advanced nations did not develop by means of a formal plan. Historically, England and the United States grew primarily in a spontaneous and unself-conscious fashion. Much the same is true of the nations late to become industrialized, such as Japan at the end of the nineteenth century. But Japan did concentrate on popular education in the late 1800s, and Canada did stake all on tariffs and the C.P.R. later. More explicitly, the Soviet Union introduced successive five-year plans from the 1920s onward.

Today all over the underdeveloped world, planning is a fashionable word. No country is too small or backward to have its five- or ten-year plan. Sometimes these are merely fancily worded documents that have little relationship to actual reality and performance. But sometimes they are carefully executed analyses which spell out in considerable detail programs for macroeconomic and microeconomic development. Here are some of the elements involved in a good plan.

1. The plan is based upon the *initial resources* of the country, presupposing a careful inventory of present and future availability of manpower and domestic resources.

2. The plan sets up feasible *targets* or *goals* for the terminal date.

3. The plan sets out the *feasible policies* that will permit achievement of the terminal goals from the initial resources, taking into account the intermediate economic resources that can be imported from abroad (through loans or gifts) and that can be produced at home out of the initial resources through the mechanism of investment or capital formation.

DEGREE OF PLANNING At the least, a plan will involve careful computation of the macro-aggregates of gross national product: balance of saving and investment; allocation of resources between public and private sectors, between one region or another, between city and countryside. A good plan will not be so ambitious as to lead to inefficient galloping inflation, or so unambitious as to lead to stagnation and underemployment. Along with macroeconomic fiscal and monetary policies, it will take care that the resulting import demand does not exceed the available supply of foreign exchange, whether this is accomplished by the pricing system or by some method of central rationing. An ideal plan will provide for social overhead capital projects and be alert to the problems of externalities and indivisibilities.

Some plans will involve no more than "indicative planning" at the microeconomic levels, merely keeping diverse industries acquainted with what is going to happen to the aggregates and to their own share of the total, but leaving to their pursuit of profit the resulting response. Other plans will involve detailed allocation of inputs among different output uses, taking care to check the balance between inputs and outputs. They may or may not use the input-output techniques of general equilibrium developed by Harvard's W. W. Leontief, which gives a detailed view of inter-industry flows as in Chapter 37's appendix. The plan may or may not use the modern techniques of linear and nonlinear programming, in a form suitable for the giant electronic computer.

Often the plan will make mistakes. A crop failure due to bad weather may throw it out of kilter. Over-ambitious targets may produce foreign exchange shortages and rampant inflation. Sometimes the subsequent five-year plan will learn from the mistakes of its predecessors. Sometimes a situation goes from bad to worse.

A cynic can find in the annals of the 1950s and 1960s countless examples of governmental and private bungling. But an optimist, looking at "miracles" of development in Thailand, Taiwan, Korea, Puerto Rico, Brazil, Mexico, Israel and El Salvador, can face the future with some confidence in the ability of nations to accelerate their own economic development.[13]

---

[12] In helping underdeveloped areas to set up extension courses and adult education services, and in promoting cooperation, Antigonish's St. Francis Xavier University may be making Canada's most important contribution to rural development.

[13] Readers who wish to read further in this subject should know that there are many useful anthologies and monographs. One is G. Ranis, *The United States and the Developing Economies 2nd Edn.*, Norton, 1973, which despite its title is not about the U.S.

SUMMARY

1 Most of the world consists of less developed countries: countries with low per capita incomes relative to the most advanced economies; countries capable of improvement but now lagging behind the growth rates of the advanced nations. The increasing political self-consciousness of such countries, plus the eagerness of the communist ideology to help them "skip the capitalistic stage of development," reinforces our own self-interest in finding new sources of mutually advantageous aid and trade—not new objects for imperialistic make-work programs. All this, and altruism too, makes the development problem of major interest.

2 Geography and climate, race and custom, religion and business attitudes—each conditions economic development, but none does so in a simple and invariable way.

3 The phenomena of increasing returns, externalities, and social overhead capital provide some substance to notions of take-offs, spurts, and big pushes. They suggest a scope for supplementation of competitive market forces. But they do not lead at all necessarily to any simple concept of "balanced growth."

4 The key to development lies in four fundamental factors: population, natural resources, capital formation, and technology. Population causes sociological problems of explosive growth in numbers as death rates fall before birth rates fall; the Malthusian devil of diminishing returns stalks less developed realms. On the constructive economic agenda, improving the population's health, education, and technical training has high priority. The pool of "disguised unemployment" in country and city provides an important manpower source for extra product; the "brain drain" of talented men to developed countries provides an important threat to human capital of the LDCs.

5 Even in densely populated areas, discovery and better utilization of natural resources can help offset the law of diminishing returns. Land reform raises tremendous problems of transition. The process of capital formation—investing in soil conservation, irrigation, drainage, and so forth—interacts with the natural-resource category, just as it does with population, through investing in people.

6 Rates of productive capital formation in underdeveloped countries are low because of (*a*) poverty, (*b*) lack of a bourgeois ethic stressing frugality and acquisitiveness, (*c*) qualitative distortion of saving outlets toward unproductive hoarding of precious objects and idle inventory and toward luxurious real estate or money markets abroad, (*d*) emulation of consumption standards of advanced nations, and (*e*) nationalistic barriers to importing capital on terms acceptable to investors in the advanced countries and multinational corporations, (*f*) lack of substantial volumes of foreign aid from developed regions.

7 *Technological change* interacts with, and is embodied in, new capital goods. Nevertheless, it is a distinct process, and one which offers much hope to underdeveloped nations inasmuch as they can copy from advanced nations. The experience of Japan, Russia, Germany, and the United States shows that the process of adapting, to one's own fruitful uses, the methods developed elsewhere is not easy. It takes a degree of

but about the LDCs. Readable diagnoses of underdevelopment have been written by Gunnar Myrdal, *Asian Drama; an enquiry into the poverty of nations*, New York, Twentieth Century Fund, 1968; Barbara Ward, *The Rich Nations and the Poor Nations*, Toronto, C.B.C., 1961; John Strachey, *The End of Empire*, New York, Praeger, 1964 and J. K. Galbraith, *Economics of Development*. For a discussion of aid in the 1970s, see the Pearson Report, *Partners in Development*, New York, Praeger, 1969. A surprisingly complete source on aid and problems is *Development Co-operation*, a report and review book published every November by the Development Assistance Committee (DAC) of the OECD (handled by Information Canada bookstores.)

      entrepreneurship and innovation. One of development's most pressing tasks is to hasten internal growth of the scarce entrepreneurial and commerical spirit.

8 Five-year plans, involving feasible *targets* out of *initial conditions* by suitable macroeconomic—microeconomic *intermediate programs*, occur widely.

CONCEPTS FOR REVIEW

characteristics of LDCs

"take-off", "spurt", etc.

increasing returns, externalities,
    social overhead capital

capital-output ratio

balanced growth, diversification

disguised unemployment

planning, accounting "shadow
    prices"

capital and technology

population and natural resources

medical improvements without
    food

inequality, poverty, emulation,
    foreign lending and aid—as
    affecting capital formation

entrepreneurship and innovation

inflation and development

tenancy and land reform

public and private responsibility

five year plans: initial
    states, goals, programs

QUESTIONS FOR DISCUSSION

1. Would you expect everyone to agree with the praise of material well-being expressed in the quotation at this chapter's beginning? With Dr. White's quotation?

2. Bertrand Russell was one of the greatest contemporary philosophers, logicians, and writers, yet the following words of his are agreed by all competent historians to be absolutely wrong in asserting that the Industrial Revolution *worsened* living standards: "The industrial revolution caused unspeakable misery both in England and in America. I do not think any student of economic history can doubt that the average happiness in England in the early nineteenth century was lower than it had been a hundred years earlier; and this was due almost entirely to scientific technique." Actually, real per capita incomes increased. Without good 1720-1820 GNP statistics, how can he know?

3. Formulate your views on geography, race, culture, and development.

4. Why should Canada accept the Pearson Commission's recommendations to give 1 per cent of her GNP to developing nations? If your share of GNP is now about $6,000, would you prefer to keep the marginal $60, give it to those in poverty in Canada, or send it abroad? Is 1 per cent enough?

5. Delineate factors important in development; fit each into the outline involving the four main factors: population, ...

6. Is it fair for the advanced countries, in the interest of conserving bird life, to deprive poor countries of the DDT that prevents early death from malaria?

7. How would you advise the Shah of Persia to invest his oil billions? Lend abroad? To LDCs? To Canada? Invest in gas stations and refineries in Europe? Build steel works in Persia? Why?

8. Compare the Safarian work on foreign-owned corporations in Canada (footnote 4, Appendix to Chapter 35) with the Reuber report on foreign corporations (some of them Canadian) investing directly in LDCs. What are the pros and cons of foreign private investment?

39
ECONOMIC PROBLEMS OF CITIES
AND THE POLLUTED ENVIRONMENT

Ill fares the land, to hastening ills a prey, Where wealth accumulates, and men decay.
OLIVER GOLDSMITH, *The Deserted Village*

Most readers of these pages will be urbanized. If we adopt as a minimum definition of urban population at least 20,000 persons residing in one dense built-up area, almost 66 per cent of today's Canadians would qualify, as compared to little more than 6.6 per cent in 1851; 40 per cent are now living in "metropolitan areas" of at least 100,000. Fig. 39-1 tells some of the story.

Surprisingly, by international standards Canada has always been highly urbanized. Even in 1825, with over 5 per cent of their people in Quebec and Montreal, the Canadian colonies exceeded the world-wide

FIG. 39-1. By 1980, 80 per cent of Canadians will be urbanized.
Degree of urbanization is the percentage of total population living in urban centres of 1,000 persons and over. [Sources: Dominion Bureau of Statistics and L. O. Stone, *Urban Development in Canada* (Ottawa, Information Canada, 1968); and estimates by Economics Council of Canada: Fourth and Sixth *Annual Reviews*. Reproduced with the permission of Information Canada.]

urban population proportion (those living in cities of 20,000 or over). The subsequent growth of Toronto, Halifax, Saint John, Hamilton, Kitchener-Waterloo, London, Ottawa, Windsor, Winnipeg, Calgary, Edmonton, Vancouver, and Victoria has also contributed to a clustering of total provincial population, including rural populations in or near urban areas. Only Saskatchewan, Alberta, and the Atlantic Provinces have kept some uniformity of population change between rural and urban areas.

Who does live in the cities? Mostly people born there or in other Canadian urban centers. But more than one-third of city *growth* is direct immigration (especially of young women) from the rural areas, and (mostly of young men) from overseas. As migrants are usually already grown up, the cities are much less "youthful" in their age composition than the rural fringes. Thus farm populations may now become less fertile, while the residential districts of the metropolitan areas will be characterized by high birthrates and demands for schools and skating rinks. The centers of the cities, however, will be populated by the retired, older couples, unskilled newcomers, and those in real poverty.

The inward movement is most pronounced in the Prairies, and least significant in the Maritimes; but evident everywhere. Furthermore, an increasing number of people are collecting in the suburbs, or even in deep rural areas; but not on the farm. Anywhere statistics indicate a nonurban population increase, investigation discloses an isolated suburb, a mining-forestry complex, or a tourist-recreation center. The "green revolution" is steadily reducing the number of farmers, exposing everyone to a productive and efficient, but congested and polluted, man-made urban environment.

Canada's urbanization is negligible compared to the developing countries. The rate of urbanization is very high everywhere. When most readers of this book were born in the 1950s about 25 percent of the world's population was "urban". Today the figure is about 35 percent. Furthermore, the rate of urbanization is, in developed countries like Canada, only about one-third of the speed of city-peopling in the less developed countries.[1]

[1] Source: *Growth of the World's Urban and Rural Population, 1920-2000*, U.N., New York, 1969, (Number ST/SOA Series A/44).

WHAT ARE THE "PROBLEMS OF URBANIZATION?"

For the most part, they are the problems of population growth in general. For example, if Canadian natural increase and migration kept the same percentage of people on the farm and in the forests as at 1900, and allowed the towns and cities to grow only at the overall demographic rate, these towns and cities would still suffer urban growing pains. Additionally, a number of rural and foreign people *equal to the entire Canadian turn-of-the-century population* have migrated into the main cities. In a short chapter such as this, we can note only three of the many types of personal and policy problems that this massive reconcentration, superimposed on the general economic and population expansion of the nation, has produced. The first is the problem of the city center and the slum. The second is the problem of the urban-rural fringe and of land development generally. And the third is the related problem of widespread environmental pollution. [For all three aspects of urbanization, see the comprehensive *Urban Canada: Problems and Prospects*, a report prepared by Norman Harvey Lithwick for the federal Cabinet (Central Mortgage and Housing Corporation, Ottawa, December 1970).]

Older urban development in Europe and North America typically took place slowly enough for the center to restyle itself as a location for such central activities as marketing, financial services, government, retailing, entertainment, and communications. Repeatedly, older buildings were razed and street patterns adapted to new requirements; landlords and burghers combined to see that central activities did not drift elsewhere. Thus the businesses of the City of London, Wall Street, and downtown Montreal are conducted within a stone's throw of where they were carried on many generations ago.

But landlords and great corporations have recently been less successful in fixing activities at the city center.

Traffic difficulties have pulled many retailers and services outward to neighborhood centers and plazas. Old business buildings, difficult to modernize, have been relegated to low-grade uses; financial and trading activity has moved to large structures in different neighborhoods; and older areas have been razed and left as parking or vacant lots. In turn this has

WHITE NEIGHBORHOOD   **GHETTO NEIGHBORHOOD**

FIG. 39-2. Discrimination raises rents to blacks.

Demand curves are drawn to be the same per capita. (That is, tastes and incomes are the same). Without discrimination, rents would be at the common level E' and e' with the same allocation of living space per capita. (In fact the markets could be combined in the absence of segregation, with everyone living at random.) But suppose under segregation blacks are given only half their per capita share of space. Then their dd intersects their allotted ss at high e rentals. Whites' DD intersects their unfairly swollen SS at low-level E. The black arrow on the left measures the gap due to discrimination. (Though slumlords gain, landlords as a class actually lose!) If blacks are poorer than whites, the gap will be smaller. Why?

speeded the accompanying migration from central houses and apartments to dwellings in the suburbs. Thus the stage has been set for modern North American cities: some partly empty at the core, others in the process of reoccupation by newcomers in search only of cheap, central accommodation. These slums and ghettos adjoin the surviving commercial district and supplant the former blocks of town-houses and middle-class apartments that clustered nearby.

ECONOMICS OF GHETTO HOUSING   The environmental disadvantages of slum living, can have a cumulative impact in handicapping the economic status of those in poverty, especially immigrants and non-white people. They do not choose to live in smog and congestion in preference to smart apartments or suburban greenlands. But race and language often restrict their choice. At one time racial clauses in real-estate convenants and local laws were used to keep neighborhoods unmixed with newer ethnic strains. After courts and votes had weakened such excluding devices, discrimination by landlords, clubs, and real-estate agencies pretty much continued the same tendencies. In addition, foreign-language immigrants aggravated their isolation from English- and French-speaking majorities by choosing to live near other new arrivals, thus supporting their familiar institutions, churches, restaurants, and specialty stores while permitting the family elders to continue speaking their native language. This separateness also led to discrimination and bigotry against them.

In the beginning bigotry was shameless. Later it became somewhat shame-faced. More and more peo-

ple began to say: "*I* am not bigoted. But *others* are. And it is a well-known fact that property values go to pieces when (blacks, Pakistanis, Chinese, Italians, Jews, etc.) get a toehold in a neighborhood."

This then threatens to become what sociologist Robert K. Merton calls a "self-fulfilling prophecy." If people believe in it and act on it, even if originally it were false, it may become true.

However, let us turn to the economic facts about race and real estate. Take the extreme case of blacks and whites. If you tabulate bills of sale in two similar communities, but where one has had blacks move into it and the other has not, what would such a controlled experiment show? That is, of course, the relevant question, because it is obvious that many slum neighborhoods which are in economic decay will have falling prices anyway even if there are no racial intermixtures; and it is also well known that the black community tends to be confined to those decaying neighborhoods that poor people can just afford.

A careful study of *matched* city neighborhoods, carried out under the auspices of University of California [2] researchers and covering such diverse

[2] L. Laurenti, *Property Value and Race: Studies in Seven Cities*, (University of California Press for Commission on Race and Housing, Berkeley and Los Angeles, 1960).

cities as Oakland and Detroit, Chicago and Portland, revealed that it was a complete myth of the real-estate fraternity that desegregation of a neighborhood harms real-estate values. "Block busting," so-called, in fact if anything raised property values (as the block buster who spreads false rumors knows very well).

And why not, when you come to think about it? Precisely because the black buyer and renter is discriminated against, his demand bids up the prices of those properties which may be available to him. Figure 39-2 illustrates the economics of housing discrimination in a fashion anticipatory of Fig. 40-3's demonstration of the economics of job discrimination. When the real-estate market is split into two parts, and if the blacks are allotted less than their per capita supply, the auction market bids up the rentals that can be exacted from them, limited only by their incomes. After the barriers have been eliminated, rentals for similar accommodations become equalized—resulting in both a more equitable and a more efficient equilibrium.

ECONOMICS OF URBAN BLIGHT

Discussion of housing segregation brings us to the general problem of urban decay. This topic heavily overlaps the economics of races and minorities, since in regions with racial mixtures, the inner city is increasingly becoming the sole province of blacks, Chinese, North American Indians, and recent immigrant groups. Metropolitan areas continue to grow, but it is the suburban areas around the old city limits which show the most rapid growth. Half a century ago, urban sociologists such as Robert Park of the University of Chicago delineated *circular* patterns of city development. At the center is the downtown shopping district, the locale for luxury hotels, banks, and office buildings. Surrounding this nucleus is the tenderloin district of decay, where vice and vagrancy abound. Still farther out come workingmen's flats and homes; and then finally you arrive at middle-class country. Farthest out of all are the estates, polo fields, and hunting acres of the very rich.

The circles, however, fan out dynamically. As middle-class residents move farther out, their old neighborhoods change. Mansions are broken up into

rooming houses, and apartments that once housed 4 people come to house 10 or more. A new tenderloin ghetto is born.

It is a mistake to think that this is an invariable pattern. A mountain or waterfront can modify the circular form, and also restrain the outward migration of the middle class. Or the ubiquity of the auto may destroy any real notion of a *center* to the city—which becomes, and perhaps should become nothing but a concrete switchboard for the rerouting of expressway traffic. As in Manhattan and London, so in Toronto and Vancouver, slum neighborhoods are repeatedly reclaimed by the gold-coast clientele through the force of dynamic competition. But still a general circular pattern can be discerned both here and abroad.

"TRICKLING DOWN"   Experts tell us that it is *not* the case that slum and ghetto dwellers are worse housed as a whole than in the past. A count of the number of persons per bathroom, the number of hot-water versus cold-water flats, of outdoor privies versus indoor toilets, reveals that, whatever middle-class visitors may think of the inner city, conditions there are actually better now, on the average, than they used to be. This improvement has not come about as the result of generosity or public programs so much as of the exodus of previous residents to the suburbs. At one time the poor lived on the fringes and walked to work; the rich lived at the center. Later the development of radial street railways brought the poor class to the core, near their jobs. Now the poor are diffused throughout the older inner city and aging suburbs, limited in their choices by the costliness of new buildings, transport availability, and social resistance to their arrival. Houses and streets "trickle down" from middle class to poorer occupants, who are the *temporary* beneficiaries of the previous residents' migration to modern or remote houses, perhaps as a result of the growth of commercial activity in the city that attracted the immigrants and the poor.

THE URBAN-RENEWAL BULLDOZER

Ironically, the efforts by government to redevelop the inner city have in some measure served to help the middle class and hurt the poor. When old buildings are torn down and new developments put in their place, to the eye there has been an aesthetic improvement and an increase in space per person. But for whose benefit? For those tenants who lived in crowded quarters before? Only too rarely. Often the occupants are hard put to find quarters anywhere near as good as those which had trickled down to them. And the new tenants who come in are young, professional and white-collar couples who are childless and (most often) white and English-speaking. If a black family can pay $400 a month it is free to live there. If....

What can be done about this? Leave the slums to stew in their own juice, waiting for the Invisible Hand of perfect competition to rescue them? Deny governments the power to take land and buildings by expropriation? Some urbanists have suggested just this.

A more realistic approach, however, is to shape urban redevelopment along lines that will take account of the following concepts:

1. Rebuilding any neighborhood requires responsibility assumed *in advance* for those who will become the victims of the new program. This involves rehousing of those displaced, either within the new development, or through location in good housing elsewhere.

2. Residential *social capital*—utilities, transit, churches, water and sewers, recreation, trees, shopping centers, medical clinics, schools, and *social bonds and groupings*—are in just as much need of conservation or careful replacement as the private shelter of both new arrivals and the displaced.

3. Massive uniform low-income apartments can themselves become "urban blight" even before their paint and mortar dry. These developments do not confirm the ancient canard" you can get people out of the slums, but you can't get the slums out of the people." But it is a sad fact of modern life that the frustration of such asphalt jungles can produce unhappiness and danger in urban open spaces after dark. More fragmented and meticulous (and more expensive) planning remedies much of this. Urban philosophers, however, have advocated two different approaches:

(a) Public purchase of land (one version of an urban "land bank"), later sold at reduced cost to smaller private builders charged with constructing houses and apartments without further subsidy. This would help produce varied but substantial buildings and neighborhoods. Some American and European renewal has proceeded along these lines.

(b) Rent subsidies to people, so that they can fix up their own houses or take over and improve existing structures. These have in many cases added more to the total of human happiness than have architectural cakeboxes on a grand scale.

THE PROCESS OF URBANIZATION

Before further examining the disadvantages and advantages of urbanization, we should ask why cities grow. It is relatively easy to describe the pains and problems of urban growth, but very difficult to make rigorous generalizations about the process that many living persons have witnessed: the agglomeration of people and enterprises into an urban unit with an apparent *inherent* ability to grow, almost biologically, without infusions or transfers from other urban places.

We cannot pause long to speculate on the very conception of cities. Geographers have been doing empirical work on the functions cities perform, the distances between them, and their size, for many years.

The task of the urban economist is not to classify or describe, however, but to search for the properties of cities that can be analyzed with tools that also serve to analyze other economic problems. One way of doing this is to assume an "ungeographic" region: a uniform plain uninterrupted by mountains or rivers. Will there be cities now?

Yes, say common-sense observers. For agglomeration into cities will reduce transportation costs from what they would be if people distributed themselves evenly over the plain. Hence transportation costs explain the appearance and growth of cities.

No, say twentieth-century urban economists. It is true that people will seek to minimize transport costs on goods to be traded and delivered. But *why* must goods be exchanged? Why does not every unit —every family, say—produce enough for its own consumption? We know the answer from earlier discussions of returns to scale in production functions. If every good was produced under conditions of constant returns to scale, every production unit could be divided, or multiplied, until every family owned or had nearby mini-fields and mini-factories to produce everything they needed. If people tended to bunch together they would simply bid up the price of the uniform land per acre. Better to spread themselves out evenly.

If there were diminishing returns to scale in producing goods, there would be even more reason to stay apart; the smaller the factories and farms, the more could be produced altogether.

On this approach, the explanation of cities must lie in the existence of *increasing returns to scale*, industrial and social activities from specialization, acquisition of skills, mass production, and the use of Rosenstein-Rodan's increasing-returns items of social capital (see Chapter 38 and earlier references to *external economies*.) Now, says the economist, a city must emerge and transportation modes and costs will explain its shape.

Note that this explanation predicts that everyone will tend to live in *one city*! We are now forced to explain the limitations on urban growth.

First, however, we digress to examine the growth process.

HOW CITIES GROW

Here is a synthesis of many studies of urban growth. Given a population on which to draw, it is observed that cities' development tends to be self-sustaining because the grouping of industries creates both new demands and external economies in supply; such as

(1) specialized skills and knowledge that reduce labor costs for later-arriving firms;

(2) markets for specialized supplying firms and industries, that also reduce costs for everyone;

(3) by-products for other local exporters;

(4) markets for locally based business services;

(5) through increased employment, rising population and consumer expenditures, expanded retail and wholesale sectors;

(6) local manufacturing to replace outside consumer-goods suppliers, and

(7) suppliers to *these* manufacturers and

(8) users of *their* by-products, etc. ...

The reader will recognize here yet another application of the "staple" model of expansion and economic growth. The demand for other industries, skills, and products are referred to as "linkages." The typical mass of consumer fa-

cilities and services appended to any new export feature is referred to as its regional, or urban, multiplier.

EXPORT BASE MULTIPLIER   This multiplier is, *algebraically*, very similar to our import-leakage multiplier of Chapter 14. Based on the growth of (the first three items in the above list of growth processes) new exporters, their direct suppliers, and by-product processors as the "export base," it summarizes the *local* respending of new incomes paid by the export-base industries, thus creating new incomes and new local industries and employment (items 4 to 8 in the above list). The multiplier that relates the income-dollar (or employment) growth of the export base to the income-dollar (or employment) growth of the whole city or region thus depends on the extent to which the city or region relies on "imported" goods and services rather than producing them locally. Obviously, in the short run, this multiplier merely summarizes spending in existing plants and stores. Its form is

$$\text{Change in urban income} = \frac{1}{\text{MPS} + \text{MPM}} \times \text{Change in export income,}$$

where MPS and MPM, the local propensities to save and import, are defined as in Chapter 14. Regional studies have shown that MPS + MPM may amount to about 0.55, so that the change in urban income for a million-dollar rise in local export incomes would be about 1.81; probably less than 2 for any North American city.

In the long run, however, the export-base multiplier is more than a simple employment-change number. It now relates the growth of *new* products and plants to the appearance of *new* local services and jobs to serve it, and serve its employees, and *their* employees.

Will the long-run multiplier be larger or smaller than the short-run? New marketing and transport services should improve the supply of imports, and expanded tastes and incomes should sharpen demand. Hence the import leakage MPM may increase and weaken the multiplier. This would explain why many cities no longer rely on local farmers, clothing industries, furniture factories, engineering works, or shipyards to the extent that abandoned farms and plants suggest they once did. More and more, the growing city goes to specialized regions for its goods.

But statistical studies show the opposite. It is true that expanding cities import proportionately more; the very diversity of their swollen requirements guarantees that. But there is an impressive countervailing force, a concentration process, in which the rate of growth is greater in already-large cities than in smaller ones. The larger the city, the greater its *percentage* rate of growth. The export base spawns more industries and firms. The input-output[3] matrix calls on a larger percentage of the capacity of a single plant (thus drawing a new branch or firm to this new city). Furthermore, the urban area tends to have a higher-than-average-for-cities specialization not only in such fabricating industries, but also in services to business management (accounting, computing services, personnel testing, actuarial services, engineering partnerships), financial and insurance head offices, and wholesale trade,[4] while smaller and slower growing centers like St. John's, Halifax, Saint John, Hamilton, Quebec, Sudbury, and Victoria tend to specialize in provincial-government activity, one or two local export industries, and health and welfare services. Thus size and growth beget growth and size, and the multiplier in the long run becomes merely a summary of the particular urbanizing forces in each region that have selected a community as its central place. With growth and size come diversity-complexity, culture and congestion.

TWO RESTRAINTS ON URBAN GROWTH

Will urban expansion continue indefinitely? Why not? The *attractions* are great: more people, more markets, more specialization, more culture, more scope for individuality (within rigid limits), more services—all these should induce national and regional natural and migratory population growth to concentrate in larger, and fewer, cities.

There are, of course, restraining factors as well. Two of them, land fixity and congestion, can control urban growth, retarding or permitting it.

FIXITY OF LAND.   In the first place, it is obvious that land is not uniform and uninterrupted. In any one location, there is a limited amount of land of any given fertility or having such qualities as access to rivers or lakes, drainage, elevation, gradient, etc. Thus as seen in Chapters 2 and 3, the economy runs into fixity of land, and *diminishing returns* to urban scale to offset the increasing returns to agglomeration mentioned above.

To understand the result, we may picture the process. Consider such limited sites as Manhattan, Venice, Vancouver, Bruges or San Francisco. As the city grows, residents will compare their gains of lower costs with costs in other cities. These will include land rents, building and maintenance costs, and taxes. If other places have disadvantages, but lower rents—owing to greater relative availability of land for development—people and industry will gradually migrate thence, until the "equalizing differences" (Chapter 29) between the rents make up for the disadvantages of the other locations. (Thus, rents were high in Venice, but protection against invaders was good too—the high rent level was an equalizing difference. As rents rose, it paid to drain more land, build more bridges, and build houses vertically. Similarly, residents of Manhattan, San Francisco, Vancouver, and the Thousand Islands attempt to mitigate space shortage and high rents by building vertically, reclaiming hillsides and swamps, or simply using less space per person.)

The upshot of this is that, like any other economic constraint, land scarcity sets economic men searching for substitutes: new cities, new urban designs, smaller homes and plants, etc. One "substitute" is migration elsewhere, *thus restraining urban growth in one place.*[5]

---

[3] For the use of Leontief's Input-Output in forecasting the effects of a primary (export or government) change on related industries see Chapter 37's Appendix. See also "Urban Growth and Regional Contagion" in N. H. Lithwick and Gilles Paquet, *Urban Studies: A Canadian Perspective* (Methuen, Toronto, 1968).

[4] The numbers are mustered in L. O. Stone, *Urban Development in Canada* (Queen's Printer, Ottawa, 1967), Chapter 9. Geographers, sociologists and statisticians have detected national, or international, regularity in city sizes. Group cities in *logarithmic* categories of 3.3 (e.g. with boundaries of 10,000, 33,000, 100,000, 333 thousand, 1 million, 33 million, etc ...); then the number in each category will be about *twice* the number in the next-largest category. Thus, there are in Canada three metropolitan areas with over 1 million, and twice as many with a population between 333,000 and 1 million.

[5] This is a good place to review the question of land speculation first touched on in Chapter 21's Appendix. Urban development devours rural land, turning green pastures and rolling forests into suburbs, plazas, and industrial parks. As this juggernaut rolls

CONGESTION AND THE VALUE OF TIME

Congestion, like pollution, is another form of external diseconomy, diminishing return, or increasing social cost.

Is it a result of technological change? Perhaps. The transport networks and the streets of most cities were laid out before the automobile. Urban growth (to the extent that it was planned or foreseen) was expected to stretch as far as rapid transit could bring people to work. The streets would be full of pedestrians, trams and taxis.

When the automobile appeared, workers could ride from greater distances, thus justifying remoter suburbs. Although the cost in gasoline, roads and depreciation was higher than other transportation modes, an automobile offered two characteristics: *privacy* and *speed*, that were highly valued.

The speed arose not only from the faster vehicle but also from the possibility of integrated—door-to-door trips (instead of transfers and walks). In turn, the *value* of such speed arises from the rising *cost of time*. In periods of low real wages or unemployment, travelers do not resent much (may even enjoy) the long trip to work. They may even think of it as part of their leisure. But with higher real wages, when each minute is better paid, the cost of extra minutes on trams or buses increases. This may be more important than the cost of the ticket. Thus the traveller is attracted to the idea of *substituting* one mode of transport, with a lower time cost, for another.

Readers will recognize this "substitution effect"

on, far-sighted men and gamblers and fools *speculate* on a land-price rise. This has three well-known effects:

(a) it raises the assessed value of all nearby farm land, and thus the property tax burden, until farmers themselves go in for speculating or suburban land development;

(b) it creates a class of people, especially professional real-estate promoters, who have a vested interest in future development, and so tends to validate their gamble—makes it self-realizing; and

(c) it draws speculators to manipulate a price rise in an uninformed and non-competitive market, making price rises earlier or sharper than they would otherwise be.

On the other hand, speculators can perform a social function, holding land off the market until its price rise reveals that, in a competitive situation, demand has become acute; inappropriate developments are thus prevented. Indeed, faced with this resolute behavior by speculators, many municipal authorities have sought a public "land bank" to enable them to perform—for other, but not necessarily better, objectives—essentially the same role.

from Chapter 29's discussion of the supply curve of labor. The "income effect" is also important. With higher wages, you are a richer man. Every minute saved you can afford to spend on more equipment for leisure: tennis rackets, fine foods, books and—automobiles. Thus both the income effect and the substitution effect of higher real wages point toward the replacement of transit by cars.

So far so good. But will the automobile produce congestion? Directly, yes. The streets are more choked with individual cars, instead of being less choked with trams and pedestrians.

Density. But the indirect effect of the automobile on density may be an even more important cause of congestion. As the city takes in more and more acres, the number of workers arriving daily at offices and plants rises. The demand for industrial sites increases, raising their price (that is, rent). This competition for land causes gardens and vacant lots to disappear and developers to threaten parks and open space. As a substitute for acreage, architects and engineers use height and density of central land development. The rent, or land-value, curve shifts upward.

Thus an increasing number of persons must, in automobiles, find their way into the built-up area, park, and walk to jobs or shops. This is the indirect congestion effect of the automobile. The advantage of the automobile is now reduced, over rapid transit. Every driver imposes a cash cost on himself, and an external cost on others.

RENT CURVES

No simple representation of these complex interactions is possible. But, remembering that rent or land value at each location is a result of the demand of everyone to shop, live or work at that location, "rent curves" can summarize the successive steps towards agglomeration, suburbanization and congestion.

Each curve shows the maximum amount a typical urban land user or resident would be willing to pay for an acre of land, depending on that acre's distance from the city centre. Because of transportation costs the curves slope down with distance; nothing will be offered, over farm prices, for land that is so far from the centre that transport costs wipe out the profit of production or the benefit of residing there.

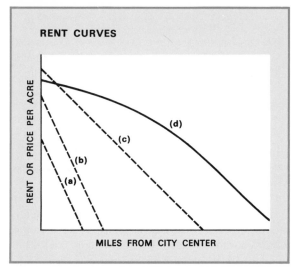

FIG. 39-3. The Automobile raises land values but congestion distorts the land-use pattern.
(a) and *(b)* show growth before the automobile; *(d)* shows the eventual flatter gradient with growth after the automobile has caused congestion.

The figure shows four curves, to illustrate the sequence of our model of urban growth. Curve *(a)* is the rent curve for a small town before the automobile. A few miles from the town hall, land values have fallen to agricultural values. Curve *(b)* shows a similar town after growth from the increasing returns of larger-scale production and urban living. Note that the gradient of the rent curve is about the same, reflecting the same costs per mile; but because the centre is more valuable the rent curve reaches farther into the countryside.

Curve *(c)* reflects both the coming of the automobile commuter and technical progress in industry. Rents shoot up at the city centre, and some persons drive great distances, in some comfort, to stores and jobs downtown.

The effect of congestion is suggested by Curve *(d)*. With further urban growth, the automobile changes the rent curve gradient. Transport and personal time-costs of reaching the city centre are now so great that business demands sites in the suburbs and in the country. The value of sites in the centre falls, and undeveloped land in the periphery soars in price.

This model raises the question whether the automobile gradient is bound to remain. That is the sub-

ject of research in the 'seventies. Can new forms of transit supplant the automobile, cut down the congestion, and still attract passengers? Our previous analysis suggests that the value of residents' time is now so high that speed is very important. Passengers have better things to do than sit in trains or buses for long. But with given street patterns, buses can give speed only if they are clear of private automobiles. How can cars, parked or commuting, be kept off the streets?

In Chapter 28 it was already suggested that charges, tolls or rents be levied to ration highway and street capacity. This pricing system can select better those with urgent reasons to use downtown streets, than can regulation or closure. But it tends to favour the rich over the poor (income and substitution effects again!) and it is costly and unpopular to administer. In any case, the remedy of the 1960s: expressways and street-widening, is on its way out.[6] The choice is now seen to be between decentralization, with satellite centres and new towns (at one end of curve *(d)*) and publicly-enforced centralization using both faster transit and reduced automobile access by pricing or outright exclusion.

POLICY RESTRICTIONS ON URBAN GROWTH

In this section we deal with those policies that government can use to shape urban development.

POPULATION POLICY. Of course cities can only grow if people come from somewhere; and three sources suggest themselves. (a) Other cities. We have already seen that economies of agglomeration may attract residents from smaller cities, unless diseconomies intervene. (b) Immigration into the economy from abroad. Most immigrants come from cities in Europe or Asia and move to Canadian cities automatically. (c) Immigration from the countryside. This has been the chief source of urban growth, if only because rural birth rates often lagged behind increasing returns to farm techniques. Even today, many young women (and men) come to town, and retired farmers also settle in the city. This source of urban growth is still significant, but there aren't so

[6] For some strong opinions about expressways, see *The Bad Trip* by economists David and Nadine Nowlan (New Press, Toronto, 1970).

many people left to migrate, and they're not having so many babies.

Thus the first policy instrument for senior governments trying to control or moderate urban growth is rural policy. While Russia and eastern Europe are still trying to get people off the farm and into urban industry, the U.K., Sweden and China are trying to keep people in agriculture, or to put industry into the fields. Canada is trying to raise rural incomes, and, given Canadian rural opportunities, is bound to encourage further migration to the cities.

However, rural growth leads to the flourishing of regional distribution and production centres: Moncton and Penticton are examples. These, if they are still villages, are unlikely ever to rival metropolitan Montreal, or even Saint John. But as "growth points", "nodes", or "pôles de croissance",[7] they may focus regional growth onto a single regional hamlet or collection point, lead to its dominance over its rivals, and so, as a part of rural revival, lead to urbanization (even with a *smaller* overall regional population, following earlier emigration). In any case, rural redevelopment will not necessarily restrain urban growth.

COST OF URBAN SERVICES. Each city is a unit of government—a "municipality." As Chapter 8 made clear, it raises revenues to provide

  (a) utility-like services (schools, sewage and garbage disposal)
  (b) true "public goods" like police protection and public-health controls and outlays, and
  (c) welfare transfers.

The divisions between three categories are not watertight; the provision of most government services includes characteristics of private (voluntary-purchase) goods, social (automatically-for-all) goods, and welfare assistance in cash or in kind. Primary education, public housing, public transit, public parks, community centers, for example, embody all three characteristics.

The larger the city, the more of these services the

municipality must provide. It finances them, to a very large extent, from property taxes of various kinds. It also has recourse to very large conditional and unconditional provincial (and federal) grants, and it can and does borrow heavily for public projects to be repaid over the projects' life out of tax revenues.

Does this municipal-service-and-property-tax mechanism inhibit urban growth? Does urban growth strain the system seriously? This question has many related questions and problems, too numerous even to list, involving actual research into the impact of various combinations of taxes, school finance, highway-and-street questions, federal-provincial-local finances, hospitals, relief systems, police coordination, pollution problems, and other standard items of local newspaper coverage. Table 39-1, on the following page, gives a recent forecast of the expected deficit.

We cannot even survey the political side of these questions. De Tocqueville rightly described local government as the "cornerstone of democracy," but it is not evident that local bureaucracies, municipal voters, or the forms, levels, or subdivisions of local participation are adequate for their tasks. Exhausted aldermen, venal councillors, super-governments, ignorant time-servers, frustrated planners, ward bosses, we know them all. But are they inevitable? Are they necessary? Are there better ways? Instead of analyzing *these* questions, we turn instead to some evidence on our economic question concerning the three kinds of municipal service.

We might expect the provision of municipal services to be a decreasing-cost industry, utilizing large capital-intensive plants to serve an increasing number of "customers", just as with railways or power companies. Recent evidence has suggested that unlimited "increasing returns to scale" *do* accrue in expanding waterworks and sewage systems. But costs of schools, police services, parks, and municipal government costs, as revealed by statistics, do not fall forever, or rise forever, with metropolitan size. There is some evidence that costs are lowest at about 100,000 population. But this evidence is so difficult to interpret as to be almost valueless, because (a) it is not clear that the *standards* of actual coverage or "courtesy" or service are the same in small and large cities, (b) in small towns, standards of public service may be poor because private alternatives are cheaply

---

[7] Some regional specialists advocate a "growth point" approach to backward rural areas. This view, sometimes a matter of description rather than of deliberate policy, has been argued by T. W. Schultz (for a recent application see his "Some Economic Aspects of the Northland", p. 353 of Officer and Smith, eds., *Canadian Economic Problems and Policies* (McGraw-Hill, Toronto, 1970). The planning version owes much to France's François Perroux.

	1969	1970	1971
Revenue from own taxes	3.9	4.3	4.6
Expenditures	7.3	8.6	9.8
Deficit (including new borrowing and senior government grants)	3.4	4.3	5.2

TABLE 39-1. Over just three years, 1969 to 1971, the annual deficit of Canadian municipalities (including school expenditures) grew by 50 per cent. This was a foretaste of the financial squeeze on the municipalities in the 1970's. (Source: Statistics Canada).

available, and (c) the studies treat fragmented many-municipality metropolises (like Montreal) sometimes as one city, sometimes as many cities. The surprising conclusion is that, while we know that some well-known large cities have bad standards of snow removal, police protection, garbage and litter collection, road repair, schools, health, welfare, water pressure, or whatever, we have *not* developed an acceptable way of comparing either the standards *or* the costs of these services over a cross-section of city sizes. It follows that we do not really know whether the cost of municipal services restrains city growth. Such statistical confusion, however may suggest that it does not.[8]

INTER-CITY RELATIONS Even if a whole metropolitan area is able to expand at constant per-capita costs, the *distribution* of these costs is important to decisions about ideal size. Obviously, city-dwellers would like large provincial grants and low local taxes, and suburbanites would prefer separate towns and villages, leaving the central city with its high density and low income to cover its own costs. Such fragmentation, however fair or unfair, leads to predictable results: high property taxes and low standards of many services in the slums and industrial districts, coupled with lower taxes, suburban sprawl, and expensive education and police services, in the surrounding towns and villages. Such contrasts have chiefly political consequences—but one economic result is the migration of certain industries and trading establishments into the suburbs—for purely fiscal (not real) reasons.

[8] Planners are very concerned with ideal city size, fragmentation, and decentralization. But they seem to give circulation, social intercourse, and economic activity as their criteria, not the cost of public services or of governments.

The division of costs between property taxes and provincial grants is also chiefly of political, not economic, importance, especially if the real costs of services do not rise with urban expansion. However, in many cities an additional consideration is that the costs of *poverty*, not just in assistance but also in police, schools, housing, health and other services, get loaded onto property taxes until they become a positive disincentive to the use of taxable urban property. From this angle, city services do restrain urban *growth*. And this effect is important, for it means that highly taxable property may flee from organized municipalities, while the unemployed poor—and some workers—congregate in the cities. The company towns of the Canadian shield exemplify this behavior.

Many orthodox economists suggest service charges and user fees (prices) in place of taxes. These would both ration the use and finance the expansion of scarce municipal services. But, by the same token, they have three drawbacks: (a) expensive collection, (b) heavy impact on poor people, and (c) inapplicability to *pure* public goods like justice or smoothly flowing traffic. But in a few cases transfers or assistance to the poor, plus service charges, may deal with some financial and congestion problems of the expanding city.

In summary, we may ask whether the costs of urban growth can actually deter urbanization. We know they cannot, because they are not experienced by those who cause them, but *externally*, by the public at large, who cannot escape them. If cities are to be held to optimum size, political action is necessary.

THE POLLUTED ENVIRONMENT

One merely sees in the city in exaggerated degree a problem common to all modern life, namely contamination of the general environment. Smog is a sign in the skies of what is impending for industrial areas everywhere. Really clear days in Montreal or Hamilton, as in New York, Paris, or Tokyo, are almost completely a thing of the past.

Mark Twain said, "Man is the only species that feels shame—or has reason to." Certainly man is the only animal who has managed to pollute the atmosphere itself. Sulfur dioxide and particulates pollute the air of every industrial region. The climate of the world changes as a result of what industry and consumer opulence have done to the concentration of carbon dioxide in the air, far exceeding the smoke and fumes of the first Industrial Revolution. Some scientists now believe that the *irreversible* accumulation of lead—chiefly from automobile exhaust—in the air we breathe will soon become a problem everywhere in the world. Strontium 90 and radioactive trace elements have been the consequence of atomic testing; and the threat of the ultimate-doomsday cobalt bomb which will end all human life forever is more than an old-wives' bogey tale. Even noise pollutes the environment, both urban and rural.

Concern about water pollution, more local and visible, began sooner. Dissolved chemicals, from DDT to toxic mercury, have recently overshadowed the earlier bacteriological threats to health. And heat, oil

spills, enriching phosphorus and disintegrating organic matter, distort or destroy normal ecological patterns, turning receiving waters into revolting, useless sumps. Table 39-2 shows that several Canadian cities still dump the bulk of their sewage untreated, while others dispose of most of their sewage through primary- or secondary-treatment plants.

EXTERNAL DISECONOMIES Here is the most general case of what we have met earlier under the heading of "external diseconomy." The most pessimistic diagnosis of all is that ultimately the automobile is the prime cause of not only congestion and urban land sprawl, but also smog. Factories can be made to have high chimneys and to burn sulfur-free fuels. Strip-mining of coal, which despoils the scenery, can be forbidden unless the topography is restored. Electric power production, which threatens thermal contamination of rivers, can be controlled by zoning ordinances and costly cooling towers. But to

Sewage Treatment in Selected Urban Areas, 1969

Metropolitan Area	Wastewater Flow (million gallons per day)	Percentage of waste water flow subject to:		
		No Treatment	Primary	Secondary
St. John's	12.7	100.0		
Halifax-Dartmouth	9.9	99.0	1.0	
Saint John	5.4	99.8		0.2
Quebec	42.0	100.0		
Montreal	290.2	91.6	2.6	5.8
Ottawa	40.0		100.0	
Toronto	194.0			100.0
Hamilton	60.0		100.0	
Sudbury	11.0			100.0
London	28.0			100.0
Windsor	4.0	85.0		15.0
Winnipeg	46.3	4.0		96.0
Regina	12.0			100.0
Saskatoon	10.0	93.0		7.0
Edmonton	37.5		46.5	53.5
Calgary	38.8		100.0	
Vancouver	100.0	59.0	41.0	
Victoria	18.0	98.9		1.1

TABLE 39-2. Many metropolitan areas simply dump raw sewage: Primary treatment removes 30-50 per cent of nonsuspended solids: secondary—or lagoon—treatment removes about 80-85 per cent of total solids and reduces the biological oxygen demand by about the same proportion. These are the largest urban centers. Smaller and poorer cities, outside Ontario, tend to dump *all* their sewage. Treatment plants are to be completed soon in many communities. [Source: Economic Council of Canada, Sixth *Annual Review* (September, 1969), Table 3-7, page 44. Reproduced by permission of Information Canada.]

deprive each commuter of his natural right of driving to work each day in a box full of air is apparently more than any modern electorate will stand.

If the consumer will not willingly pay for the extra devices needed to limit air pollution, how can one expect the auto manufacturers to solve the problem? That is like expecting the cigarette companies to commit suicide voluntarily.

Is reliance on spontaneous business efforts futile in the solution of a problem like this? Experience gives a pessimistic answer. There has been one case, though, that offers a glimmer of hope. Detergents poured into our sewage systems were found to be "non-degradable" and to continue as foam to contaminate the waters and water table into which rivers flow. Conservationists gave a great outcry. And, in this story with a happy ending, the trade association of the industry did under some official pressure sponsor chemical research that came up with a solution to that problem. By industry self-regulation, every firm in this relatively concentrated industry has adopted the new formulas, and we have heard nothing of the foam problem for many years.

Would that the same vigor had been applied to the search for detergents that do not enrich plant growth in lakes and cause them to die for lack of oxygen. Or would that the contamination of wildlife by DDT, of which the late Rachel Carson wrote so eloquently, might as nicely disappear. Or that the perfect, profitable, electric battery, or more plausibly a steam engine, could be developed to eliminate the smog effects of the internal-combustion engine.

GOVERNMENT LAWS, TAXES AND PLANNING

Since no one profit-maker has the power, or, more important, the incentive, to solve problems involving "externalities," here is a clear case for some kind of public intervention. Thus the threat of California to ban all internal-combustion engines by 1975 may be an example of the action needed to galvanize Detroit into action. Or a heavy tax on fuming fuels, vehicles, or factories might be in order. Furthermore, the consumer has an important role to play. He must not curse his utility for burning fuel oil with a heavy sulfur content, and then complain if there is added onto his utilities bill an extra charge to cover the removal of sulfur or to finance the purchase of more expensive, sweeter fuels.

Regulations. Examples of the need for controls are endless.

Lake Erie is dying, done in by the sewage, phosphate detergents, and fertilizers that have been allowed to pour into it. Not only must the cost of producing in the regions bordering on the lake be increased by the amount needed to remove industrial and other wastes, but in addition, each farmer cannot be allowed to use the chemical fertilizers *he* deems best nor each housewife the laundry soap *she* prefers—since the residue of them flows into Lake Erie.

Nor can farmers and firms elsewhere be allowed to dig all the artesian wells they please, since the water table underlying much of the country can become dangerously low from unrestrained use. Like the fisherman harvesting the fish stock, and the oil industry competitively pumping the petroleum field, they have no *incentive* to consider their externalities which raise the costs, or reduce the enjoyment, of others. Table 39-2 shows the progress made so far by municipalities forced by provinces (and bribed by Ottawa and the provinces) to treat their sewage. Regulations also attempt to control DDT, phosphates in detergent, mercury outflows, fishing catches, oil well spacing, defoliants, compulsory septic tanks, and exhaust-pipe mufflers. Others, similar in effect, are also in use—oil pumping pro-rating, some fisheries' quotas, and sprinkling regulations.

Effluent fees. Economists would like to improve on these shot-gun methods by introducing elements of the price system. For example a high "effluent fee" or tax on pollution discharges gives industries a choice: pollute and pay, or pay not to pollute.[9] Those wastes most expensive to purify will be discharged; those that are cheapest to eliminate will be purified out. The fee must then be set high enough that the total discharged is small enough to be acceptable. This system, used in Germany and contemplated under the 1970 Canada Water Act, achieves purification of a lake or river to any desired standard at the lowest social cost.[10]

Property rights. A system long advocated for fisheries' rationalization has been recently suggested by Toronto economist John Dales[11] for water pollution: property rights. A simplified version, for a small lake, would be based on a single contaminant. The lake's total absorptive capacity, of $1,000x$ pounds, would be divided into, say, 1,000 property rights of x pounds each. These would be given or sold, or auctioned, to the 1,000 lakeshore municipalities, firms, ho-

---

[9] The British Columbia compulsory buy-back of beer containers gives no choice, so is more like a regulation than a fee.

[10] In addition to effluent fees, there can be effluent *subsidies.* Towns and firms are bribed to clear up their discharges. This system has the obvious drawback of all subsidies: people gain by lying about the amount of their performance.

[11] Dales' *Pollution, Property and Prices* (University of Toronto Press, Toronto, 1969), is highly recommended.

tels, and homes. Those who had less than x pounds to discharge could sell some or all their rights, at a price, to those who had more to discharge. The price of a right would rise until everyone had cut down their effluents to that level where it was just cheaper to purify x pounds than to buy another right. And total discharge would be held down to $1,000x$ pounds. This system would share the efficiency advantages of effluent taxes but would not require the extra knowledge that tax-collectors must have to set the right rate. Given a decision about the total acceptable discharge and the number of rights, the price of the rights is set by demand, based on the alternative costs of purification in each home and firm.

Ideally, these fees or prices would wind up equal to the marginal costs of purifying wastes and to the marginal utilities (expressed in dollar voting) of extra lake purity. This is Chapter 24's welfare condition for optimum pricing.

PROFITS AND POLLUTION Many conservationists and ecologists dislike these economists' techniques for rationing the environment's absorptive capacities. Some of them shrill that *any* pollution is immoral, and should not be validated by fees or rights. This is, of course, either an assertion of fact about "absorptive capacity" or an ethical dogma. It is capable of rational argument by scientists and concerned philosophers, but not on economic grounds.

Another more interesting objection is that pricing the right to pollute is the wrong *economic* technique for dealing with the abuse of the environment. Polluters are imposing external diseconomies on other people, and enriching themselves by avoiding their total real (or social) costs of production. This diagnosis indicates that treatment should simply take the form of forcing the polluters to treat their wastes, paying for the facilities out of "profits." This proposal is not about the morality of pollution, but about *distribution*, or FOR WHOM the economic system and the environment are managed.

The proposal is not absurd. But for those who dislike profits and the unequal distribution of the GNP, it offers a too-easy solution to both injustice and pollution problems. Without full argument either way, note the following considerations:

1. Most pollution usually comes from old plants and poor municipalities. New profitable plants and towns waste less. Non-profit farmers, co-ops (and Soviet collective factories) are the worst offenders. Pollution and profit are not correlated as closely as would be convenient.

2. "Profitable" polluters are innovators or oligopolists. They will probably raise their selling prices to their customers if forced to treat their wastes. If they do not, it will be because their rivals have no similar treatment-cost liability—i.e. pollution continues elsewhere.

3. Treatment would be socially cheaper (i.e., it would use less labor and capital) if everyone were faced with an effluent tax or price than it would be if the burden were forced on to profits alone.

4. In general, *any* system that raises costs may drive the polluter to more tolerant regions. (Is this a good thing?)

5. It may be easier politically to get profitable firms to commence treatment first before towns have to raise their taxes or dig deeper into their pockets to build sewage plants.

ZERO POPULATION GROWTH? ZERO ECONOMIC GROWTH?

Our over 140 billion dollar GNE is, we have seen in discussion of NEW (Net Economic Welfare, as defined in Fig. 1-1 and Fig. 10-4) in part, an illusion. When we finally pay our way in terms of conservation and in preserving the environment, perhaps we shall have left for ordinary consumption only nine-tenths as much. Nor is it a question of *affording* these expensive private and government programs to lessen pollution. In a real sense we cannot afford *not* to have them.

And, as in all cases of public interest, there will be conflicts of interest. Shall Ontario be allowed to get gas from Lake Erie wells if drilling threatens wildlife there? Shall developers be allowed to develop a skiing facility and ski village deep in the woods if that means disturbing the water table and spoiling the serenity of nature? Or to take a smaller example that points up the dilemma: Shall small towns be permitted to remain islands of rural peace if, as a result, the teeming masses of the cities have their recreational activities limited and are forced to huddle on the hot pavements and crowd a few adjacent beaches?

Modern economics teaches us that the curse of overpopulation is not simply that of Malthusian food shortage due to diminishing returns. Growth of population makes the ideal of a stable economy in a har-

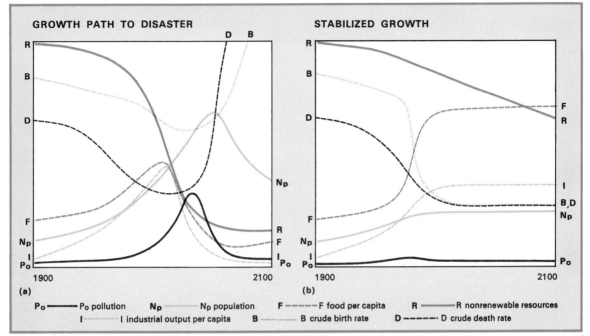

FIG. 39-4. Where, between the poles of complacency and hysteria, do these computer printouts fall?

(a) High birth rates (BB in gray) lead inexorably to red RR curve of declining resources, and to worsening pollution (P_O P_O in black). RESULT: Imminent decline in available food per capita (FF in light red); and decline in industrial output (II in screened very light red).

(b) Disaster is averted on right by immediate ZPG and ZEG (Zero Population and Economic Growth). Shift is to recycling and to services that don't use up resources. If people of the poor countries by the billions are to share equitably in stabilized world output, U.S. standard of living must halve and halve again! What mixture of pseudoscience and common sense do studies like this one by the Club of Rome represent? [Source: Meadows et al., *The Limits to Growth* (1972). Scale in original purposely left vague to indicate lack of precision of forecast.]

monious ecological environment impossible to attain.

Public opinion in the advanced world is rapidly shifting away from worship of mere growth as such. ZPG (Zero Population Growth) and even ZEG (Zero Economic Growth) are increasingly popular movements. Rachel Carson, Paul Ehrlich, Barry Commoner, and other scientists have warned that civilized life must be put on a self-sustaining, closed-system basis, lest ecological disaster overtake humanity.

Jay Forrester's *World Dynamics* (1971), and the kindred analysis in the MIT Club of Rome study, by Dennis Meadows and co-authors, *The Limits to Growth* (1972), have excited much attention—most of it favorable with the lay public, much of it critical with the economics profession. Figure 39-3 illustrates two typical computer printouts illustrative of the Forrester-Meadows methodology and recommendations.

Here we have Malthus all over again: but now the simple geometric and arithmetic progressions have become respectively exponential differential equations of biological growth running head on against assumed-to-be constant limits on total resources. "The computer that cried wolf," is how Carl Kaysen, Director of the Institute of Advanced Studies in Princeton, put it. Less objective critics, using the lingo of the programmers, have dismissed it as a case of GIGO ("garbage in, garbage out"—inadequate premises leading to misleading deductions). To dismiss such investigations without fair and constructive analysis of their content is to miss the point of their undoubted appeal to the modern mind.

In Fig. 39-4(a) on the left, we see the alleged increase in pollution, exhaustion of natural resources, and inevitable decline in future per capita real incomes. This exactly parallels Malthus's first 1798 edition in which he argued that contemporary trends could not be avoided. Then, in Fig. 39-4(b) on the right, we see, as in later editions of Malthus, how mankind can avoid its fate once it undertakes drastic measures: abolishes all population growth immediately; abolishes all net capital formation and production growth; concentrates on food and services and recycling of resources.

Sometimes to sell you must oversell. An antidote to complacency can be provided by hysteria. Few who have looked into the equations and sources of the Forrester-Meadows Club of Rome works can agree that these have realistically captured the likely pattern of the future. Not only have they conceptual flaws and factual inaccuracies, but in addition, they ignore almost completely what scarcity will do to changing relative prices, and what these differential price changes will do to encourage substitutions and to relieve the shortages. Yet they do point to some impending problems.

CONFLICTS OF INTEREST To those who happen to live in lucky regions like North America and Western Europe, freezing real incomes at their present levels would be intolerable. Nor is it convincing to claim that Americans and Europeans will give up half or more of their present real incomes so that poor people elsewhere can be raised to a tolerable minimum of life. No one believes that this will happen of its own accord.

Indeed, at international conferences, the less developed nations regard pollution concern as the luxury of the well-to-do. As has already been mentioned, they still want to develop the industry that will pollute.

A dramatic example is the complaint by Sweden that the Russians are prone to pollute the Baltic. Although it would be naïve to think that socialism cures pollution, it is no less absurd to think that it promotes pollution. It is because Russia has a lower per capita income than Sweden that she does not feel she can afford the same programs that the latter can. To prove that the system of government socialism is not the important thing, mention should be made that the Swedes complain with reason about Finland, also a poorer country.

Robert Heilbroner has put the matter dramatically.[12]

In our Spaceship Earth...sustained life requires that a meticulous balance be maintained between the life-support capability of the vehicle and the demands made by the inhabitants of the craft....We are well past that capacity, provided that the level of resource intake and waste output represented by the average North American or European is taken as a standard to be achieved by all humanity. To put it bluntly, *if we take as the price of a first-class ticket the resource requirements of those passengers who travel in the Northern Hemisphere of the Spaceship, we have now reached a point at which the steerage is condemned to live forever ... at a second-class level;* or at which a considerable change in living habits must be imposed on first-class if the ship is ever to be converted to a one-class cruise.

One leaves contemplation of these problems of poverty, urban blight, and ecological balance with a renewed feeling that the tasks of economics and of science and technology are far from solved. What is needed is use of these invaluable tools for the humane goals of the present age and not for the thoughtless replication of overaffluent life styles. Great good fortune, too, it is that in the age after Keynes we do have at least the macroeconomic tools that enable the mixed economy to afford less growth in conventional GNP, without having that slowdown lead to inequitable chronic unemployment.

---

[12] R. L. Heilbroner, "Ecological Armageddon", *The New York Review of Books*, April 23, 1970. See also his book, *Inquiry into the Human Prospect.* New York: W. W. Norton & Co., 1974.

  But recall that costs and benefits must be brought into optimal balance: to make Lake Erie clear enough for swimming may well be an uneconomic operation from humanity's viewpoint. Likewise, keeping peregrine falcons from becoming extinct at the cost of millions of deaths in Asia from post-DDT revivals of malaria could be an unspeakable tragedy.

SUMMARY

1 "Urbanization" problems are often just general problems, connected with city growth only because our whole economy is urbanized.

2 The city center dies in many expanding cities. Slum housing leads to educational deprivation and isolation. The tools of supply and demand show that extreme segregation of racial minorities, however, leads to *higher* rents and real estate values, in contradiction to the common myths.

3 Blight in the urban environment is strongly correlated with the adjustment problems of immigrant and racial minorities. Urban redevelopment measures, unless carefully planned, can harm those who are already the worst victims of city blight.

4 The process of urbanization achieves *external economies* for new industrial arrivals and expanding markets for service industries. The *export base multiplier* forecasts the growth of service population as a result of stable export-industry growth.

5 Urban growth is restrained, or influenced by, general population growth, rural development opportunities, congestion, land shortage, barriers to increases in housing, and the increasing costs, if any, of local government services. The evidence is not clear that there are serious *economic* barriers to urban growth.

6 Finally, urban blight is merely a dramatic case of the more general blight of the environment produced by the modern technological economy and growth of population. Smog and air pollution can change the climate; water pollution by sewage, industrial wastes, fertilizers, and detergents, and even by the heat thrown off from nuclear and non-nuclear power plants, makes wasteland of our earthly inheritance. These "economic externalities and diseconomies" cannot be expected to be set aright by market competition and the pursuit of profit. They call for government zoning ordinances, fiats and prohibitions, planning and coordination, subsidies, and penalties of taxation. We are not so affluent as our statistics of GNE would indicate, and much remains on the future social agenda.

7 Zero Population and Zero Economic Growth are understandable reactions to life on crowded Spaceship Earth. Smog and air pollution that can change even the climate, water pollution from sewage, industrial wastes, fertilizers, and detergents, and even from the heat thrown off by nuclear and nonnuclear power plants—these have made a wasteland of our earthly inheritance. Such "economic externalities and diseconomies" cannot be expected to be set aright by market competition and the pursuit of profit. They call for government zoning ordinances, fiats and prohibitions, planning and coordination, subsidies and penalties of taxation. Calculations of NEW show that we are not so affluent as our statistics of GNP would indicate, and much remains on the future social agenda.

8. Many economists advocate a fee to be charged for each unit of pollution discharged. Discuss the idea that a subsidy per unit *not* discharged would cause the same abatement. (*Hint:* to a polluter, a subsidy not collected, on discharges not abated, is the same as a tax—it has an opportunity cost.) Nevertheless, subsidies are not popular economic policy—Why?

CONCEPTS FOR REVIEW

"trickling down"

rent differentials in divided
   markets

external economies of urban growth

export-base multiplier

restraints on urban growth

circles of urban decay

external diseconomies of congestion
   disturbed ecology, and environmental
   pollution

ZPG and ZEG

Club of Rome

QUESTIONS FOR DISCUSSION

1. N. H. Lithwick's central chapter concludes (page 64): "The roots of the urban problem lie in the very process of urbanization itself." Is this gobbledygook? (HINT: "Urbanization" is a word that means *becoming* urban. Read the chapter. Reflect.)

2. Describe the overlap between segregated housing and economic opportunity. Between race and urban problems. Between urban blight and general environmental blight.

3. Look up "external economies" and "external diseconomies" in the Index and trace the pervasive influence in modern economics of this vital concept.

4. Can high mortgage rates actually *prevent* urban growth? How?

5. Compare civic services in a big city and a small town. Which cost most per capita? Which are best?

6. Design and discuss an effluent-fee system for a lake near you.

7. Can the price mechanism deal with pollution? Highway congestion? Could it, if incomes were divided equally?

40
ECONOMIC INEQUALITY: POVERTY, DISCRIMINATION AND REDISTRIBUTION

"...what a community requires, as the word itself suggests, is common culture.... But a common culture cannot be created merely by desiring it. It rests upon economic foundations. It is incompatible with the existence of too violent a contrast between classes, for such a contrast has as its result, not a common culture, but servility or resentment, on the one hand, and patronage or arrogance, on the other. It involves, in short, a large measure of economic equality."
R. H. TWANEY, *Equality,* London, 1931.

Man does not live by GNP alone. Better a smaller social pie divided *equitably* among the populace, many ethical observers will say, than a larger one devoted to the vulgar objects of material display. Why seek what William James called the Bitch-Goddess of success, if the price of that striving is despoliation of man's environment and in the end the non-attainment of happiness and serenity?

The issues raised in this chapter go beyond the technicalities of narrow economic analysis. Yet they are issues that have come to the forefront of debate all over the world: not only in the affluent society of North America and Europe, but also in the Soviet Union and other societies for whom affluence is just ahead.

ANALYSIS IN THE SERVICE OF CONTROVERSY

All the present issues involve value judgments and strong differences in tastes and convictions. But there is much that economic analysis can contribute to the elucidation of the issues. Thus, until you know the costs of alleviating inequality, how can you *rationally* determine how far to carry your campaign in that direction, away from abating pollution, repaving roads, or modernizing hospitals? And even if you believe that the end justifies the means, can you be sure, without economic analysis, that the means you advocate may not produce exactly the *opposite* effect?

Will a very high minimum wage add to the well-being of the poorer workers? Or will the poor be the prime victims of this well-intentioned measure?

Will putting a low interest ceiling on small loans to consumers—say, 8 per cent per annum, which to many will not seem very low—help the needy and unlucky? Or will it play right into the hands of the lobbyists for the loan sharks?

Many a social revolution—in the Middle East, in Latin America, in Africa—has aimed to help the workers and peasants, but during the transition has resulted in a lower standard of life for all the population.

The problems of social reform are not easy. If they were, many reforms which gain a consensus among men of good will would have been made long ago. On the other hand, economic analysis can reveal how specious are many of the arguments for maintenance of the status quo. Despite what your grandfather's economic textbook used to say, a rich country can afford a large measure of redistributive taxation. The Roman Empire did not really fall, or even decline, because of unbalanced budgets, bungling bureaucratic planning, or free handouts and circuses.

In short, careful economic analysis is the indispensable handmaiden of those who wish to preserve and enhance the inherited order, no less than those who seek widespread social reforms.

SINCE EDEN

Chapter 5 has already summarized the important facts about poverty and income inequality. Under *laissez-faire,* income and wealth get distributed far from equally. A mixed economy can módify somewhat the inequality of distribution of a *laissez-faire* regime. But the Lorenz curves of Figs. 5-3 and 9-1 show how considerable are the variations in economic well-being that still remain.

Chapter 5 also demonstrated how, in a growing economy, everyone may become more affluent. The numbers below any fixed standard of living shrink. But affluence also causes the whole nation *to raise the standard of what it deems the minimum* needed for a decent life. We shall, therefore, always regret the poverty of the lowest 20 per cent, which we shall always have with us.

Recognizing the impossibility of abolishing poverty when it is defined as the bottom of the income pyramid actually sharpens our understanding of more attainable goals. Thus we seek to avoid another period like the 1920s, when rising NNP distracted attention from a probable worsening of income inequality. Ironically, it was probably in the war decade of the 1940s that we succeeded not only in raising average output but also narrowing dispersion around that average.

Some ask, "Why worry about our disparities of income when poverty here is nothing in comparison with that abroad? A family on relief lives infinitely better than a peasant in India. Hunger still exists here in rural and northern pockets; but it represents largely malnutrition and *isolated* hunger, not the widespread famine that has characterized all history and still characterizes large parts of the globe."

The answer usually given by humanitarians would run something like the following:

"An affluent society can afford to provide a decent minimum for all its members. The fact that India is too poor to ensure good food and housing for most of her people may be an argument for a larger measure of our foreign aid; but it is not a valid reason for our countenancing at home the glaring disparities that the market provides in solving the basic problems of WHAT, HOW, and FOR WHOM."

INEVITABLE LAWS OF THE DISMAL SCIENCE?

We've already met the view of Pareto, that "Essentially nothing can be done about inequality. The basic forces determining inequality are apparently too strong and persistent to be affected by state intervention."

In this matter Pareto's "discovery" seemed in the tradition of most of the classical economists. The Reverend Malthus, Stockbroker Ricardo, and their popularizing disciples had all taught that economics was the dismal science of unalterable distribution of income. The wages of labor, the rent of land, the profit of capital were determined by Economic Law alone, not by Political Power. If labor unions or reform political parties tried to use the state to modify these facts of life, they would be ineffective in the end. All that they would accomplish in the attempt would be *to contrive a smaller social pie,* which would probably still get distributed in about the same way. Vexation and violence in trying to alter this would merely produce economic chaos and class warfare.

THE WELFARE STATE

Ricardo and Marx certainly failed to convince many that redistribution must be in vain. As every schoolboy knows, Bismarck in Germany and Gladstone and Disraeli in Britain began a century of increasing state intervention into the working of the price mechanism. This policy was accelerated by the Great Depression, emerging as the modern welfare state.

VOTING CLASS-INTERESTS   In retrospect there is nothing mysterious about this political process of using the state to change the distribution of income, and of wealth. Political thinkers everywhere believed in—and feared—the class struggle before Marx was born. In Europe, not only Tories but even Whigs like the historian Macaulay warned against the universal suffrage.

Give votes to all and you must expect the instinct of self-interest—that same self-interest which Adam Smith counted on to work individualistically in the economic sphere—to lead to state interference with the inequality of incomes and property.

This debate had divided the French revolutionary philosophers and the founding fathers of the American constitution. Some argued that the rights of property would be infringed if votes were given to all; under universal suffrage the poor would legislate against the established wealthy. Their point was accepted in the U.S. and the suffrage was severely limited in the new republic's first fifty years. Such a reaction led Victorian revolutionaries to prophesy that the privileged classes could *never* yield the right to vote to the proletariat. Yet in country after coun-

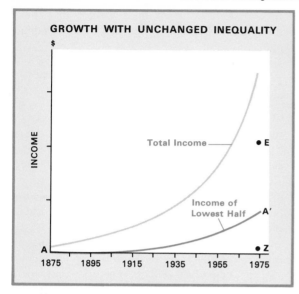

FIG. 40-1. All classes seem to have shared in this last century's progress.

Among advanced economies, real wage has shown a steadily rising trend. As capitalism gave way to the welfare state and a mixed economy, the degree of inequality has narrowed—if only slightly.

try, conscience and agitation led to widening of suffrage. Parties win or lose particular elections, but the apparatus of the welfare state continues to grow: in conservative Alberta and radical Manitoba; in Protestant Norway and Catholic Italy; in remote New Zealand, or "home" in England.

A CENTURY'S PROGRESS   Figure 40-1 provides a simplified summary of the laws of motion of economic and political development of the last century. The point *A* on the low curve shows that the lowest half of the population got much less than half of the total social product in 1875. By 1975 the total of GNP had grown mightily. If Pareto were right about the inevitability of the same relative share of product, the new division would be at *A'*. Real wages would have risen mightily—along with real incomes from property. But if the cruder forms of Marxism had been right, the system would have deteriorated to *Z*, with the poor reaching complete immiserization (and with bloody revolution unavoidable).

Actually we have no accurate statistics of Lorenz curves for a century ago. What economic historians, such as Colin Clark and Simon Kuznets, do know is that *there is some slight reduction of Lorenz-curve*

inequality in modern as compared with less-developed nations, and in welfare states such as Sweden or Israel as compared with free enterprise societies such as Switzerland. So their best guess is to suppose a country like the United States or Britain or Japan is now at a point just above *A'*. The welfare state, through redistributive taxation and through educational opportunity designed to less inequality of advantage, has moved the system somewhat toward greater equality. But note that the system is still a long way from the point *E* where both halves of the population get the same share of the total social product.

Is this limited equalization a good or a bad thing? Apologists for the system say, "It is great; look at the doughnut and how it has grown." Critics of the system say: "It is not nearly enough; look at the hole in the doughnut."

In the 1970s there *is* available an agreed-upon record of facts about real wage trends in the last century. Real wages have risen steadily and strongly in the last century. These laws of motion of capitalism are, as Chapter 37's analysis of technical change delineates, in line with what we should expect from the dynamic forces of supply and demand. Auto workers get real wages ten times what their great grandfathers got because their present-day productivity enables that wage to be paid. Even in the economic academies of Eastern Europe, it is now agreed that the mixed economies of Western Europe and North America are likely in 1999 to have real wages more than double those prevailing in the 1970s.

But these days, good is not good enough. Why be satisfied with inequalities? So declare critics of the existing order in increasing numbers.

EQUITY VERSUS EFFICIENCY

Even without the gift of prophecy, one can bet that the welfare state will long be with us. Conservative politicians have consolidated rather than liquidated the economic reforms of their predecessors when progressive, welfarist or socialist governments in North America, Norway, Australia, or Britain were replaced by more conservative parties. The question naturally arises, therefore, Why not go all or much of the way toward equality of incomes? Why wait until 1999 to do what can be done *today* by a determined electorate?

FIG. 40-2. Redistributing social pie of GNP may reduce its total.

The point **A** marks the outcome of *laissez-faire*, prior to redistributive taxation. The coloured point *E* marks same GNP with complete equality. Often, though, the attempt to redistribute income will create disincentives and resulting deadweight inefficiency. So, instead of being able to move from *A* to *E*, feasibility says we in fact will be moving along *ABZ*. The challenge is to develop tax and other programs that will minimize deadweight-loss gap between *AE* and *ABZ*.

DEADWEIGHT BURDENS Figure 40-2 illustrates the opportunities and difficulties. How can one go from the present point *A* to the equality point *E*? If we make income taxes more steeply progressive, decisions to invest in risky ventures and to work hard at one's profession will be profoundly affected. If we freeze prices and rents or put floors under wages, we alter production and employment. Conservatives no doubt exaggerate the problems of such "distortion," but only romantics deny their reality.

Schematically, the black *ABZ* curve bends inward as a result of the deadweight cost, or burden, that is inevitably associated with strong state interference with the workings of the market mechanism.[1] Indeed, experience has shown that in some cases the distortions due to interference can become so great that the attempt to help one social class at the ex-

pense of another can end hurting them all. (Thus, before the 1948 decision by Ludwig Erhard to end rationing and stifling price controls, the West German economy lingered at *B* or inside *A* southwest of the *p-p frontier* at the expense of just about every income class.)

ARGUMENT AND COUNTERARGUMENT Intentionally Fig. 40-2 presents a gloomy realistic picture of some of the difficulties. How might one react? First, some may say that the effort is still worth the cost, that greater equality is more important than greater affluence and is worth its cost. (And still others may demur, or reduce their aspirations.)

Second, one can mobilize the tools of economics to minimize the costs and distortions. Let the reader pencil in a new curve to lie between the black *ABZ* and colored *AE*: By skillful design of the programs against poverty and inequality, their deadweight burden can definitely be lessened and society may move on such a new and better curve. Thus,[2] the subsidy of low-income housing may be a more efficient long-run solution to our urban problems than freezing rents by direct controls. Some say that subsidizing low-income *people* (not houses) would bring us closest to *AE*.

CAUSES OF INEQUALITY

To alleviate inequality one must first diagnose its principal causes. Here are some of the important factors involved.

DIFFERENCES IN PROPERTY WEALTH The greatest disparities in income stem from differences in *wealth*. The Tudor monarchs became politically and economically independent when they appropriated the wealth of the monasteries. Windfall gains have helped too: Lord Durham came from a coal family; the Rhodes scholarships are based on dia-

---

[1] Experience and analysis show that even once-and-for-all confiscation can result in subsequent slower growth, unless the new order provides for efficient operation, maintenance and growth of the capital which has changed ownership. *Capital will not automatically maintain itself, or be replaced, or be augmented along the most efficient lines without public or private entrepreneurship.*

[2] Chapter 39 deals further with urban problems. See also Chapter 22's theoretical demonstration of the dead-weight loss from price-fixing-plus-rationing (Question 6 in the Appendix). Canadian housing specialist Lawrence Smith has shrewdly commented that inferior housing and slum conditions are serious, but that they would " ... probably be better attacked within the context of an integrated poverty program." Bad housing is a symptom, not a cause. See Lawrence Smith, "The Housing Market, the Housing Problem, and Government Policy," in Officer and Smith, eds., *Canadian Economic Problems and Policies*, (McGraw-Hill, Toronto, 1970).

monds and gold; the Hearst and Beaverbrook press empires were both based on resource *coups*. The special personal abilities of these men and of the Gettys and Rockefellers are dwarfed by the power stemming from their property.

Many of these differences in wealth were associated with plain luck *in discovery of natural resources*. Some were due in part to astuteness of exploration and perseverance in productive innovation. The *Wall Street Journal* and the London *Financial Times* are replete with stories of wealth in one generation due to innovational skill or luck. Since there are loopholes in the law favoring capital gains, it is not true that today's mixed economy prevents anyone from becoming a multimillionaire.

DIFFERENCES IN PERSONAL ABILITY

Some of these may be *inherited*: within every family there are evident differences in physical and mental abilities, and between families one expects from the Mendelian theory of genetics that there will be some dispersion. Students tend to think of intelligence or IQ as the important variable; but when it comes to making money, such traits as energy, ambition, canniness, and flair can be just as important. (As Mark Twain said: "You don't have to be smart to make money. But you *do* have to know how to make money!")

While differences in inherited ability play some role, the common man is inclined to overestimate them. The trained biologist and social psychologist point out that we all inherit from our environment as well as from our parents' genes. By the age of one, the affluent child of a serene and attentive mother already has a leg up in the race for economic status and success. By the time he is a six-year-old going to first grade in the suburbs, he already has an increased lead over the slum or rural six-year-old. And for the next 12 to 20 years, the scales are increasingly tipped toward those who already have.

DIFFERENCE IN AGE AND HEALTH

Even if people were all born alike and subject to pretty much the same environment, some would suffer the vicissitudes of bad health. Cardiac disaster can strike anywhere. Neurosis and psychosis are not ailments that one can choose to have or not have. Alcohol and drugs take their toll in every stratum of society. And no one stays young and vigorous forever. Under

laissez-faire it has always been the aged who have been most subject to economic want.[3]

DIFFERENCES IN EDUCATION AND TRAINING

An important factor working for reduced inequality in the last centuries has been the provision of public education. Here is the acid that has corroded the ancient order of privilege, in which there was an infinite gulf between the educated upper classes and the illiterate masses.

The provision of schooling for all the population has begun to emancipate women from the ancient domination of male chauvinists. (Indeed, Nora of Ibsen's *A Doll's House* could not have declared her independence if no careers were open to women.)

Modern economists have analyzed the problem of putting capital *into* people through education and training, in much the same way that one puts money capital into plant or equipment. To finish high school or medical school requires an investment that in the past those born poor simply could not afford. At the turn of this century only the affluent gentry went to Oxbridge and Yale; and attending even the more modest private and state-supported schools such as London, Toronto, and Michigan was reserved for a privileged few.

In a "meritocracy," opportunities to pursue advanced education and training are largely divorced from parental affluence. By fellowships and living allowances from the state and by partially repayable loans, those with the ability to benefit from education are granted the opportunity. Nor is this confined to professional training and advanced education: GNP is as much enhanced when high school dropouts are trained to program a computer or run a modern filing machine as when similar dollars are spent on a lawyer or a doctor. On-the-job training in welding, steam-fitting, plumbing, and other vocational pursuits involves great social payoff and also contributes toward the good society.

When higher education was scarce, the graduates

---

[3] In Montreal, Bi and Bi investigators found that *salaried men* of all ethnic origins did not reach the average for all men until age 30. Their highest income was attained about age 45, but they remained above average till age 65. Lowest incomes were for those under 19. A year of age increased earnings about $100 at age 45; maybe $200 in 1975. But it decreased earnings at age 65. The pattern of *incomes* is about the same, except that single persons, widows, and others suffer low incomes again at a younger age than salaried men.

of Eton, Upper Canada, and Groton, going on through Oxford, law school and the army staff school, reaped higher earnings than those who fought their way up. In part this was due to superior training and stringent selection standards. But much reflected differences in opportunity. Members of the elite were simply called to the boardroom, the professorships, and the Cabinet, though displaying no particular superiority over those from poorer schools.[4] As immigration, international competition, and more objective standards have become influential in staffing and promotion, we may expect to see more whose native tongue was not English, whose eyes are not blue, moving into high positions.

Although public expenditure on education has been an important historical influence making for a more open society, it is, alas, not the case that all such expenditures work toward reducing inequality. For there is a great deal of evidence that much public expenditure on higher education goes to *subsidize the middle classes* rather than the urban and rural poor. Calculations made for California, where college attendance is more widespread than anywhere else in the world, show that the families of students at state universities (and at community colleges, too) have incomes well above the median of the population at large. The same relative scarcity of working-class families in public or state universities is found in Canada, in Britain, on the Continent, and in the developing world.

What can be done to prevent this outright subsidy to further inequality? First, more college students from the underprivileged classes can be actively recruited by revising entrance standards to seek promise, not grades. Second, funds can be diverted from higher education into vocational schooling. Third, if access to college education adds to earnings in later life—and statistics show this is indeed so—many argue that college students should be made to pay for the full costs of their extra education. I.e., fees should be tripled or quadrupled to cover more of tuition's true costs, and more repayable loans should replace scholarships (except in the case of the very poor). Does this seem inequitable? Adherents of equality reply that it is the present system, which taxes the poor as well as the rich to pay for universities, which is inequitable. And certainly when we consider the high earnings of physicians, there is seen to be some merit in the argument.

A strategy was recently outlined by the Economic Council of Canada. If society is to benefit from the potential abilities of family members, rather than support them in poverty, "the adults in the family must be enabled to participate in the labor force currently *and to prepare their children to do so in the future.* Thus *the concept of a minimum standard of living must be based on a definition of the family not merely as a consuming unit, but also as a producing [i.e. investing unit]* ... A substantial portion of the total investment in human capital is undertaken by family ... initiatives. Public policies are needed to encourage this private investment process, and help protect it against the ravages of poverty."[5]

DISCRIMINATION AND NON-COMPETING GROUPS

Often however, equalization of education, training and even wealth does not produce equality of opportunity. Employers seem to disregard these productive aspects of workers and to show preference for male, white, young, English-speaking employees. Often this is, from their corporate point of view, a rational preference: employees, unions, and supervisors may make life easier if women, Indians, French Canadians, immigrants, and other "minorities" are excluded from the plant or office. Furthermore, of course, an ability to communicate easily with other workers, and to cooperate is an important part of what each worker contributes to an organization.

Notwithstanding these "real" disadvantages that women, non-whites or non-English-speakers (in English-speaking regions) have in comparison with typical English-speaking white male workers, it is widely admitted that Chapter 29's economic concept of "noncompeting groups" applies to them with a vengeance. Most well-paying jobs are simply not available. For example,

"Even when Indians have the necessary educational or skill qualifications for employment, they face widespread discrimination from potential fellow workers as well as from employers. Many firms follow a definite policy (informally or unofficially, where such policies are illegal in terms of provincial legislation) of refusing to hire Indians at all, or in token numbers at best. Such discrimination is not against Indians as Indians, in most cases; it has developed as a result of unfortunate experiences with or observations

---

[4] The outstanding book on all this is John Porter, *The Vertical Mosaic* (Toronto: University of Toronto Press, 1965).

[5] Economic Council of Canada, Sixth *Annual Review* (Queen's Printer, Ottawa, September 1969), p. 117. Reproduced by permission of Information Canada.

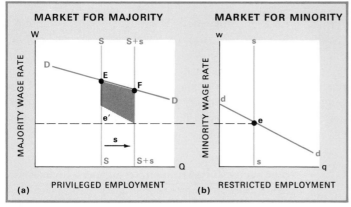

FIG. 40-3. Exclusion exploits minority and lowers GNP
Suppose a minority is excluded from good employment in (a) and must work in inferior employment in (b). Then majority *DD* and *SS* intersect at high-wage *E*; and minority *dd* and *ss* intersect in (b) at low-wage *e*. If all forms of discrimination and segregation were ended, all would go to highest-wage jobs, and members of the minority would go to (a), as shown by black arrow of shifted supply there. New equilibrium with equal wages for all would come at *F*, where *SS* + *ss* intersects demand.

The great gain in minority wages would not be at the expense of an equal fall in majority wages (which would fall, but only a little, because of the gentle action of diminishing returns). Ending discrimination necessarily increases total of product; so gainers (including now-better-off capitalists belonging to the majority!) always get more than losers lose. The gray area under *EF* measures the gain in total GNP (because the area's lower boundary is drawn at the level of the productivity in (b) above and to the left of *e*).

of them as workers which tend to build up an unfavourable stereotype."[6]

Under these circumstances, Jamieson notes, Indians react defensively and aggressively, thus confirming white opinions. In this vicious circle, the supply of Indian or any "minority" labor offered is, in effect, simply auctioned off along the demand schedules for low-skilled hours.

Figure 40-3 shows how the economics of discriminatory exclusion works, here or abroad, against men or women. Supply and demand for some favored employments are shown in Fig. 40-3(a). The supply of white, male, English-speaking, "majority" hours is shown by *SS*. The demand curve for their labor, derived from their productive worth at the margin to the employers producing the important goods in industries from which the "minority" is excluded, is shown as *DD*. Equilibrium is at the high wage shown at *E*. Meantime, what is happening to casual labor or

[6] S. M. Jamieson, "Economic Development", in Canada Department of Indian Affairs and Northern Development, Indian Affairs Branch, *A Survey of the Contemporary Indians of Canada*, ed. H. B. Hawthorn, Vol. I (Ottawa, 1966). Reproduced by permission of Information Canada.

in the enforced ghetto is shown in Fig. 40-3(b). Working with inferior tools and being permitted to produce only certain limited goods that are not particularly desired by society, the demand curve for occupations open to the minority is shown as *dd*. Their supply *ss* intersects *dd* at the low equilibrium *e*, where *their* market is just cleared. Note the discrepancy between the two equilibria.

Exclusion has discriminated against the earning power of the minority workers. They are much worse off than the favored workers. Such is the remorseless verdict of supply and demand if discrimination can be enforced by custom, law, or union collusion.

What would be the ideal situation in terms of both human equity and economic efficiency? If we let the *ss* supply of Fig. 40-3(b) be added to the *SS* supply of Fig. 40-3(a), we would have the new *S* + *s* curve of nondiscriminatory supply. Now, at little expense to majority wages, we would see a near doubling of minority wages. Where would the extra wage income come from? It would *not* come primarily from an exaction by the minority on the majority (even though justice might merit such a reparation if there were no other way to achieve equity). For these workers receive pretty much the same wage as before, their only diminution coming from the weak operation of the law of diminishing returns, as shown by the slight drop along DD. The extra income for the minority comes *from the extra* GNP that their higher productivity in their new employment brings as compared with their previous lower productivity enforced by discrimination. Instead of sweeping Milady's kitchen floor with an old broom, so to speak, now the black draws good pay working a modern computer-billing machine. Instead of existing on seasonal fur-trapping (and welfare) the Indian can work in the smelter or on the railway—or teaching French in the high school. That is the implication of Fig. 40-3 *after* discrimination has vanished and the educational disadvantages that went with it have disappeared.[7]

The day of racial nondiscrimination has not remotely arrived. Promotion is slow or rare for Indians, black immigrants, and orientals. Majority WASPs protest when minority workers are put over them as supervisors or foremen, or put alongside them on the bench or assembly line. Slowly, however, laws against discrimination, requiring equal pay for equal work, along with public education and militant protest are loosening up the pattern of segregation. The civil service started it, and industry and schools have followed, sometimes willingly, and sometimes in "tokenism" to advertise that the new vice-president, bank teller, or associate professor comes from a minority.

Of course, there is some improvement in employment status for some minorities. Most Indian families remain on welfare, but a few are in jobs closed to them a decade ago. Oriental and West-Indian workers have also broken through into many occupations with higher pay. Progress? Yes, slow progress. But note that much of the improvement came from the swing of the business cycle from the recessionary stagnation of the late 1950s to brisker growth. Fur-

---

[7] For emphasis, Fig. 40-3 is drawn with dd shown as below DD from the beginning, implying that after discrimination is removed all inferior work disappears. It would be more realistic to redraw dd so that it rises upward on the left toward the vertical W axis. Then new equilibrium comes at intersection of vertically-added SS and ss with vertically added DD and dd at an equilibrium just above F (but at a common wage lower than E). For an alternative diagrammatic approach, see Fig. 40-4.

ther progress from this factor can hardly be expected once unemployment is brought down to minimum levels. To the contrary, every extra percentage of unemployment increases the likelihood that discrimination and exclusion will reappear, preserving jobs against non-whites and women. In particular, the non-discriminatory absorption of new immigrants and adjustment of Indians becomes almost impossible when the groups are conscious rivals for scarce jobs.

The successful attainment of high employment has done more than any other single program to banish economic want and mitigate economic inequality. Differences in unemployment experienced have always been the single greatest cause of *economic variance within the working classes themselves.*

FRENCH-CANADIAN SEGREGATION

The above analysis of discrimination does not apply easily to the Province of Quebec. It is true that, near Montreal, some French-speaking workers are under disabilities similar to those suffered by non-English speakers elsewhere in Canada; this can only be treated as a variety of discrimination. But the phenomenon is better described as *segregation*: French employees work mostly for French employers. It results in part from discrimination against French workers by English-speaking employers, and leads to a parallel structure of trade and industry, duplicating some of the English-speaking structure. Of course, segregation may also arise from language barriers, educational differences, and cultural preferences, and not from discrimination.

It is not clear that segregation *in itself* is to be deplored, any more than the specialization that takes place as between French- and German-speakers in the European common market. What is a matter for worry is the outcome: higher rates of unemployment, lower-level occupations, smaller firms, and lower incomes in Quebec than in Ontario and western Canada (even after fully allowing for differences in education and rural-urban location). Racial or linguistic discrimination seems to be at least partly responsible, in the slowness of "foreign" (non-Quebec) corporations to hire or promote French-speakers and the unwillingness of English-speaking workers to cooperate in the plant with French-speakers.

The study and explanation of Quebec industry's lower incomes has been undertaken by Raynauld and others for the Bi and Bi Commission. It is clear that much of what they found can be removed if Quebec's headlong rush for higher levels of education is successful, and if Ottawa's language campaign creates a larger nucleus of bilingual workers. These two policies together may clean up much of the discrepancy, not only in Quebec but also wherever else French-speaking workers reside.

The residual "segregation" differences may be more lasting. What elements explain why Denmark has permanently lower income per capita than Sweden? Capital, natural resources, and geographic immobility of goods or factors. The same immobilities —the same reluctance of marginal units of capital to enter Quebec or of marginal members of the labor force to emigrate—may be the hard core that will maintain income differentials for a long period.[8]

ECONOMIC DISADVANTAGES OF WOMEN

No discussion of discrimination would be complete without analysis of the inferior position given to women. We saw in Chapter 5's discussion of inequality of income distribution that full-time women's earnings turn out to average less than 60 per cent of men's earnings.

Thus, female college graduates of the past enjoyed earning opportunities, over a lifetime, fully as unfavorable as male high school graduates. Although white males, for the most part, receive increases in annual earnings as they grow older, the census shows that women in their late twenties earn as much on the average as women of older ages.

How can it be that there are relatively more honors graduates among the Radcliffe fraction of Harvard students than among the males—and yet, when the twenty-fifth reunion of the class compiles frequency distributions of full-time earnings, the men *begin* where the women *leave off* in the salary scale? Little wonder, then, that school teaching and library jobs are considered to be high-

paying for a woman and quite low-paying for a similarly qualified man. If you examine the organization charts of large corporations, banks, insurance companies, how is it that there are so many male mediocrities among the vice-presidents, and so few women with rank above that of assistant vice-president (and then usually for female personnel administration)?

There is no need to belabor these facts, which are all too well known by everyone. Even after you exclude from comparison those women who genuinely want to be mothers and wives in the home, and confine your attention to those women who have made a career their principal lifetime goal, there remain differences in economic position that no psychologist has yet been able to relate to objective differences.

CLICHÉS Of course, in any society where discrimination has long prevailed, there will be no shortage of myths to explain and justify the differentials. Here are examples.

Women are built by nature to tend babies in the home. They are emotional. They have monthly ups and downs. They cannot carry heavy weights. They lack self-confidence. Men will not work under a woman. Man-to-man talk will be inhibited by the presence of women. Even women prefer a male physician to a female one. Women lack imagination and real creativity. If you mix men and women on the job, they will carry on to the detriment of efficiency and good morals. By the time you have trained a woman, she'll get married and leave you; or have a baby; or alternatively, you won't be able ever to get rid of a woman once you've hired her. If a woman does turn out to be a superlative economic performer, she's not feminine, she's harsh and aggressive, with a chip on her shoulder against men and the world (and she's killing her chances of getting married). Women workers, seeking pin money, take bread from the mouths of family breadwinners.

VICIOUS CIRCLES This list of clichés could be multiplied. And, as every social psychologist knows, discrimination feeds on itself and induces certain self-fulfilling prophecies. If long downtrodden, members of every minority group will begin to show self-hates and doubts that mirror those of the dominant society around them. As the Bird Royal Commission put it,[9] women generally work in a few occupations labelled "female", earn less money than

---

[8] In the Appendix to Chapter 34 it was explained that commodity trade between regions can compensate for factor immobility. Thus goods moving between Quebec and elsewhere could under certain circumstances in the "Ohlin theorem" equalize wages, even if French-Canadians never move. But the conditions required are difficult to satisfy.

[9] Royal Commission on the Status of Women, *Report*, Ottawa, Information Canada, 1970, page 53. This report's Chapter 2 presents a thorough study of the *economic* status, and power, of women in Canada.

men and rarely reach the top. This has been the situation for so long that society takes it for granted. In fact, its very familiarity probably does as much to maintain the *status quo* as any of the arguments offered in its defence. Seeing women in lower-paying jobs and men in senior ones leads management to think in these terms when jobs are open, and so the system perpetuates itself.

CHANGING OCCUPATIONAL AND INDUSTRIAL PATTERNS BY SEX

In turning to economic analysis, historical perspective is useful. From the dawn of recorded history, we find that women have played an important role in producing the GNP. Among human societies, as among animal species, there have been many alternative patterns of specialization with respect to hunting, foraging, herding, planting, and sowing. Only in the art of warfare have men shown any unique talent—and that claim could be disputed. Indeed, in many societies that anthropologists have studied, it has been women who have produced virtually all of the GNP, men filling at best the role of an attractive nuisance. Particularly in self-sufficient agriculture, whether of Old World peasantry or New World frontier, it has been quite impossible to differentiate between the cooperative roles of men and women in producing the GNP. Patterns of dominance, as between patriarchal and matriarchal systems, have shown no close relation to economic organization and performance.

By the nineteenth century, and with Victorian England serving as a paradigm, there grew up the caricature of the lady incapable of performing economic functions outside the home. As Thorstein Veblen wryly observed in his *Theory of the Leisure Class*, status in an affluent society was proved by the uselessness of your chattels except for display. A fair skin, never sullied by exposure to the sun, played much the same role as did the binding of feet of Chinese girl-babies: your wife, your slave, your concubine, manifestly could do no useful work—what a rich gentleman you must then be.

NEW TRENDS   As the Industrial Revolution developed, as methods of birth control released years of

a woman's life from the bearing and nurturing of infants, there was a decaying of the Victorian pattern (which in any case had only prevailed among the bourgeoisie and gentry, who always relied on lower-class women to serve as wet nurses, cooks, maids, mill hands, and prostitutes). One of the strongest trends recorded in the statistics is the increased participation by women in the labor force for pay—the words "for pay" being there to remind you that unpaid work in the home is one of the hardest kinds of work.

Many women are gainfully employed all their lives, from school to old-age retirement. Many work for some years after schooling, then drop out a few years for marriage and child bearing, returning to the job market once their youngest child passes beyond infancy. What is recent is the increasing proportion of mothers who return to work even while their children are still babies.[10]

America, which thinks of itself as advanced, is actually a laggard in the emancipation of women. India, Ceylon, and Israel have women heads of government. In Russia, most physicians by far are women. Travelers to Japan, Russia, and China are surprised to see women doing heavy work on the roads. Not only do women live longer than men, they also seem more capable of sustained acts of responsible effort than the so-called stronger sex.

ECONOMIC ANALYSIS OF SEX DISCRIMINATION: A TECHNICAL EXPLORATION

Figure 40-4 can illustrate both the fact and the tragedy of sex discrimination. We assume equal numbers of men and women, as shown by the black bracket for men being equal in length to the red bracket for women. We assume three identical industries, whose *dd* curves for labor could be filled as well by men or

---

[10] No wonder there is a demand for day-care centers. Unfortunately, such a demand has not been easy to meet. If a child is to be given the individual, professional, and loving care that middle-class mothers have insisted on in the past, no obvious pattern of organization has been found that will bring the cost per mother down to a great deal less than the working mother can earn at work. Experts who turn their attention to the analysis of corporations, cooperatives, trade-unions, and factories, should begin to focus on this quantitatively important economic problem.

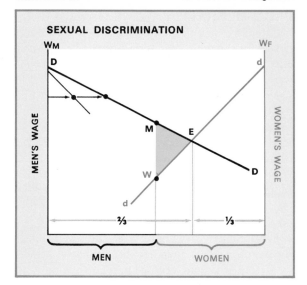

FIG. 40-4. Discrimination hurts women's wage, raises male wage, but definitely lowers total economic product. Male half of population monopolizes two of three industries, enjoys generous black *DD* demand. Female half is confined to one of three industries, with rapidly falling red *dd* (measured right to left!). Supply of men is auctioned for high wage at black *M*. Women get discriminatory low wage at red *W*. If discrimination ceases, men and women work equally in every industry. Equilibrium comes at *E* with equal wage rates for both sexes and every industry having same fraction of work force. Shaded area *MEW* measures gain in GNP from eliminating irrational discrimination.

women workers, their abilities being identical for the jobs.

But now suppose that, for reasons solely of irrational prejudice and bigotry, two industries are reserved for men. Women are crowded into the third industry. The black line *ME* shows the *DD* curve of marginal-product for the choice male industries. The red line *EW* shows demand of the "ghetto" female industry (measured right to left). NOTE: *EW* has a slope that falls off twice as rapidly as *ME*'s slope. Why? Because men can spread over *two* industries and thus slow down the workings of the law of diminishing returns. (*ME* came from adding horizontally two *EW* lines.)

Where is the bigotry equilibrium? Because we assume equal numbers of men and women, at *W* for females, where they get only 40 per cent of the wage that the males get at *M*!

Where should it be if irrational bigotry were removed? At *E*, where one-third of the women work in each industry along with one-third of the men, each getting and deserving equal pay.

Who is exploited? Women, of course. Who is the exploiter? In a sense, men—who are climbing, so to speak, on the shoulders of the downtrodden women.[11] But that is not the whole story.

Total GNP (or Net Economic Welfare) is down. The shaded triangular area, *MEW*, is a measure of the loss in total output or social satisfaction from irrational discrimination. Mankind as a whole loses. That is, the males fail to get as much economic benefit from exploitation as the females lose.

The moral of this diagram must be obvious.

QUALIFICATIONS AND CHALLENGES

One should not leave this subject with the notion that all differentials between racial, ethnic, or sexual groups are based upon discrimination. If that were so, the outlook for equality would be a more cheery one. No mere banishing of prejudice and bigotry will be able to provide miraculous uniformity of opportunity and incomes.

Many in minority groups do have poorer education. Economists know that investment in human capital is necessary if higher incomes are to be earned. Therefore, so long as employers can rationally count on women not to stay as long in their employment, they will withhold the on-job training that could be conducive to higher lifetime earnings and status.

We cannot take it for granted that all people want to be equally zealous in seeking higher earnings. Some prefer to follow the drumbeat of the counter-

---

[11] Also, in this straight-line case, employers as a whole are getting lower profits: ghetto employers happen to gain from discrimination less than employers in the two other industries lose. The present diagram is analytically a variant of that used to analyze discrimination in Fig. 40-3. It can be used to illuminate other kinds of discrimination—against Jews, Catholics, homosexuals, Chinese, Basques, Indians, etc. (The reader is warned that some of the conclusions of the straight-line case—e.g., that discrimination hurts total landlord rents—need not hold in general. But the basic conclusion, that those discriminated against lose more than the rest of the community gains, does hold: A triangle, like *MEW*, of deadweight economics loss always occurs.) Most important—but, alas, far from obvious—is the fact that society as a whole is losing.

culture, seeking richness of inner experience in preference to that of the marketplace.

But to the degree that there remains a gap between men's ethical professions and their actual practice, economic analysis demonstrates that great gains can be expected from removal of irrational discriminations.

REDISTRIBUTION

If an observer were to follow a social welfare worker on her rounds in any typical week in the 1970s, he would find that every one of the health and personality problems encountered is exacerbated by the absence of money.

An alcoholic can be desperately unhappy. But if he is of independent means, his children need not go hungry on that account and his dependence upon a steady job is vitally lessened. In a lower-middle-class family, the onset of mental illness of a mother is a financial disaster in a way that is not true at the top of the income pyramid. Were it not for state-supported mental institutions, the vast bulk of the populace simply could not cope with the problem.

What inherited property has always provided for the privileged few, the modern welfare state in limited measure provides for the bulk of the populace. As we shall see, through *direct* public services and through *transfer*-payment programs, the modern mixed economy is in effect a gigantic *system of mutual insurance* against the worst economic disasters of life. "There but for the grace of God go I," each one of us thinks when he sees disaster strike some neighbor. And realizing we are all in the same boat, we troop to the polls at election time and vote upon ourselves the costs of the mutual-benefit programs that we call social insurance, health insurance, and welfare. And, as we are about to discuss, some kind of income-maintenance plan, in the form of a negative income tax or the like, has moved to the top of the agenda for modern debate.

DIRECT PROGRAMS FOR POVERTY AND INEQUALITY

Governments have always had some responsibility for the poor. Thus Elizabethan poor farms and Victorian orphanages have formed the targets of great novels of the past.

PRIVATE CHARITY   Years ago private charity had to play a significant if inadequate role: hand-me-downs for the poor, church missions and soup kitchens, handouts for beggars, and free medical clinics were part of the conscience money that the lucky paid to the unlucky.[12] Moreover, in an earlier time, the extended family system meant that each working generation took care of its parents in retirement: the institution of the baby-sitter was almost unknown because there was always a resident maiden aunt or grandmother. After you had settled in Toronto or Montreal, your cousins from Ireland, Poland, or Gaspé could move in with you. Privacy is only a modern and middle-class privilege.

Private charity was never adequate (even though the situation would often have been frightful without it). Today, it is quite eclipsed in relative importance by the welfare functions of the state, of which the following are only a sample. The total expense is nearly 9 billion dollars per year, 5 billion dollars flowing out of Ottawa.

HOSPITALS AND ASYLUMS   Help *in kind* was the primary form that public assistance originally took. Not very long ago it was said, "Only the very rich and the very poor can afford adequate medical care." But that was of course an exaggeration except as applied to those who happened to be near a teaching hospital located in a slum, and who were not deterred by a demeaning means test from providing their bodies for medical experimentation and demonstration. As mentioned, poor farms and mental institutions are among the oldest of public agencies.

FOOD COUPONS   In Canada, some cities and provinces give welfare recipients tickets or coupons that can be redeemed for particular kinds of services or merchandise. Families that qualify by virtue of their low incomes receive stamps that permit them to get allotments of food at fractional or even zero cost.

An argument continues in the modern welfare state. One school says, "Give people money and let them buy health services and the foods they need."

---

[12] See George Orwell, *Down and Out in Paris and London* (Penguin Books, London) and James H. Gray, *The Winter Years* (Macmillan Co. of Canada, Toronto, 1967) for moving and fascinating accounts of life among the derelicts of the 1930s.

The other school says, "If you give money for milk to the poor, they will spend it on beer. Your dollar goes farther in alleviating the rickets of malnourishment and the ravages of disease if you provide the services in kind. The dollar that a man earns may be *his* to spend, but the dollar that society makes available to him to meet particular deficiencies is a dollar that society has the right *paternalistically* to channel directly to its targets."

Neither side wins the argument. Whether in Sweden or Canada, whether at the national or local level of government, both forms of aid coexist.

WELFARE ASSISTANCE In every country and city there exists some apparatus for help to the destitute. These programs involve some element of direct aid at the same time that they often involve some element of transfer of abstract purchasing power. Thus a welfare mother with three young children may be receiving a check of $450 per month. Some of this she may be free to spend as she wishes; but some part of it will be under the close supervision of the welfare worker assigned to her case, who lays down guidelines of how much can go for clothing, house furnishings, and so forth.

Because the minimum standards insisted upon by modern society have risen significantly, the cost of welfare programs has burgeoned in recent decades. Consequently there is great unease among the taxpaying citizenry over such programs. A Gallup-like poll in 1971 would show that about half the public think that welfare assistance is shot through with gross abuses. Anecdotes are told of mothers who buy color television sets with funds that ought to go for the baby. Illegitimate births among mothers on relief are not greeted with the same tolerance as are similar events among debutantes.

Among informed professionals in the area of welfare and social psychology, there is a similar feeling of disquiet with the present apparatus of welfare assistance. It is indeed costly. And often inefficient. It puts a heavy psychological tax upon the recipients, and in some cases helps to create a caste of poor who must be taken care of in the same way their parents were. A more rigorous standard of sexual and other conduct is often demanded of those on relief than the critics themselves can, with all their advantages, live up to. The father of a family on relief may find that the noblest thing he can do to enhance the well-

being of his loved ones is to leave home and disappear. Only then can his wife and children continue to get the aid they desperately need. (And lest he should return at night, the social-service caseworker is often supposed to initiate the odious practice of surprise bed checks.)

WELFARE PAYMENTS AND ECONOMIC DISINCENTIVES If a relief father were to be offered a job that paid him several hundred dollars, taking that job might in some provinces or American states cost him several thousand dollars in the form of lost relief payments. Even a steady job at the minimum wage might represent a net loss to him in terms of what is left over after *deductions* from his relief allotments.

Economically, the traditional system of welfare payments geared to need and earnings involves massive hidden costs in terms of *disincentive* effects. Literally billions of dollars of lost gross national product result from the disincentive structure of existing relief systems.

THE NEGATIVE INCOME TAX

Contemplating the great economic inefficiency of existing programs to mitigate inequality and poverty, economists of many persuasions have agreed on the need for a basic reform of the modern welfare state. The first gun was fired by Lady Juliet Rhys-Williams in Britain, in 1945. Later, both democratic advisor James Tobin of Yale and Republican brain-truster Milton Friedman published similar proposals for the United States. The basic idea is to cut through the complexity and incentive-killing morass of welfarism by using the efficient apparatus of the *income-tax* structure to attune each person's income to his needs.

This is an idea whose time has almost come. True, the Munro 1970 White Paper on income security and the Lalonde Working Paper on Social Security in Canada (1973) and the Manitoba Research Proposal on Negative Income Tax are between them unlikely to achieve a negative income tax plan much before the end of the 1970's. The same can be said for President Nixon's broad "family-assistance" bill, which was given a frigid welcome by Congress. Nevertheless, since 1967 Canada has utilized the modest Guaranteed Income Supplement for pensioners, based on income-tax computations. Almost everything is good about the negative income tax —except its negative-sounding name. A better one might be the "incencentive-guaranteed-income" plan.

HOW IT WORKS The basic notion of the broadest version is very simple. (Complexity comes only when narrower versions must be fitted into existing patterns of welfare assistance and taxation.) When I make $12,000 a year, I pay positive income taxes (as seen back in Chapter 9). When I earn an extra thousand dollars, I do pay extra taxes, but only in fractional amounts so that I am strongly motivated to earn more in order to have more.

Now consider a family below some defined poverty level—say, $5,000, in a typical year in the mid 1970s, for a couple with two children. Below that level they are deemed to have no capacity to pay any taxes; and indeed under current philosophies of equity and ability to pay, our democracy feels that they should receive government aids. In short, these aids constitute a tax in reverse—a *negative* income tax.

But here is where incentives come in. It is a common mistake to think that only the unemployed are poor, or that only fatherless families are poor. Statistics show that much of poverty is among the *working* poor—people who simply cannot earn in the marketplace what is today considered a minimum-needed income. They, and their children, are deemed to merit government help.

Yet how can these aids be given them so as not to deter their efforts and incentives? Here is where the negative income tax provides a great improvement over those welfare programs which deprive people of all assistance the moment they get even a poor job. (And, of course, those on assistance know this very well and are thus deterred from trying to improve their position.) Just as the positive income tax is geared between $10,000 and $11,000 to leave people with an incentive to better themselves, the formula for the negative income tax is gauged to leave the poor with more income after they have used their own efforts to raise their private earnings by a thousand dollars, or even by a dollar. Even when their total tax is negative, their marginal tax rate is always a positive fraction less than unity. Table 40-1 will show this.

POSSIBLE FORMULA FOR NEGATIVE INCOME TAX

PRIVATE EARNINGS	ALGEBRAIC TAX (+ if tax; − if aid received)	AFTER-TAX INCOME
$ 0	−$2,500	$2,500
1,000	− 2,000	3,000
2,000	− 1,500	3,500
3,000	− 1,000	4,000
4,000	− 500	4,500
5,000	0	5,000
6,000	+ 500	5,500

TABLE 40-1. Negative income tax sets minimum-income standards, preserving incentives and administrative efficiency.

Above an exemption level, determined by some agreed-on definition of the poverty line, people naturally expect to pay positive taxes that rise with their incomes. It is therefore logical that below the poverty line, they should receive transfer income—in effect, negative taxes. Note in the third column that incentives are maintained: it always pays in keep-home spendable income to make the effort to increase one's earnings.

POSSIBLE FORMULA Table 40-1 illustrates how a typical negative income tax might work. What is shown there for a family with two children could be easily modified in the case of more or fewer family members. And of course, as the country grows richer and can afford to be more generous, the formula could be changed to begin at a higher level and to define a poverty level that is higher both in dollar terms and perhaps in terms of constant-dollar purchasing power.

The paramount advantages of the N.I.T. are the following:

1. It can replace much of present welfare assistance that destroys incentives for persons to work themselves off relief.

2. It is less demeaning to the poor, in treating taxpayers and welfare recipients exactly alike, under the same objective test.

3. It assigns administration simply to the tax-collecting departments in Ottawa or the provinces.

4. If desired, it simplifies a nation-wide drive to obtain one minimum level of well-being across our diverse regions. (It need not, however, be so centralized.)

That these advantages are valuable is obvious. But the negative income tax has its critics too. Some say it will be costly, a swollen monstrosity like health and hospital insurance. Of course, the cost must be compared with that of whatever the N.I.T. replaces.[13] Some feel that it will not be even-handed, too lavish perhaps in rural areas and stingy in the city. Some resistance stems from a puritan approach: "Let them work for their living. They're not entitled to a guaranteed income on a silver platter".

But these are only grumbles about dollars and taxes, not about *alternative* ways of meeting the social cost of poverty and of removing the social injustice of inequality. More basic questions are these:

1. Will the N.I.T. have a less deterrent effect on work incentives than other systems of transfers?[14]

2. Should it really replace welfare programs, with their potentiality for sensitive understanding of *individual* problems?

3. Is the N.I.T. an indivisible package? Cannot the present welfare system be augmented and modified by introducing such features of the N.I.T. as the removal of the disincentive to employment?[15]

THREE OTHER GUARANTEES FOR THE JOBLESS

The guaranteed income is the most general plan so far devised, putting the same secure floor under everyone regardless of job need. It is at the opposite extreme from the social-assistance approach, with its complex system of special payments, each determined by the particular category into which the recipients' problems fall. *Between* these two extremes are three other policies that reflect the public's special concern for those of the disadvantaged and unemployed who are young enough and strong enough to work, if work can be found.

GUARANTEED JOBS. Many people feel that the main duty of the state is to make it possible for *everyone* to work. They go farther than demanding the full use of fiscal and monetary policies to prevent unemployment and claim that the government itself should become the "employer of last resort." (Good examples of this approach working during times of *seasonal* unemployment were provided by the "winter-work" schemes of the 1960s, and by the Department of Manpower's 1971 and 1972 summer-job plans for high-school and college students. A guaranteed-employment scheme is a permanent, or recession-long, variant.)

INCOME SUPPLEMENTS. The N.I.T. is not new. It has often been proposed that those who are employed, but have incomes below the minimum taxable level, ought to receive wage or income supplements. UBC's Jonathon Kesselman has reviewed the possibilities of negative taxes—that is, subsidies —on work rather than on income, and mixed formulae. (Administratively this can be done directly, or through an income-tax credit.) The Marc Lalonde White Paper is the latest official discussion of this approach. The basic reason for its attractiveness is that an increasing number of people near the poverty line have jobs, but are not able to provide a minimum decency level of consumption for their dependents. They are helped now in many ways, by free public services, day care, and so forth. Wouldn't an income supplement be more equalizing *among* these people?[16]

UNEMPLOYMENT INSURANCE. Originally based on private schemes like fire insurance, unemployment insurance became more widespread in the 1920s and the 1930s and eventually became public (governmental), compulsory, and national in scope. The latest (1971) revisions suggest that, apart from premium-like contributions, it has now lost all the usual trappings of insurance, and is primarily a pure transfer scheme to maintain worker morale and spending power during widespread cyclical unemployment. From the macroeconomic point of view, its near-automatic pay-out upon cessation of private income, and its close connection with central-

[13] This has been done. See articles in the *Canadian Tax Journal* by Hindle (March-April 1971); Smith (May-June 1965); and Christopher Green (1973).

[14] This too is under study. In New Jersey and Manitoba, trial N.I.T. schemes are examining both administration and recipient behaviour compared with conventional welfare schemes.

[15] For more on the negative income tax, see the reading by James Tobin in P. A. Samuelson, *Readings in Economics,* (McGraw-Hill, New York, 7th ed.).

[16] See C. Green "Implementing Income Supplements", *Canadian Tax Journal* (September-October 1973), a discussion of Marc Lalonde, *Working Paper on Social Security in Canada,* Ottawa, Department of Health and Welfare (April 1973). For a more technical study, see J. Kesselman, "Labour Supply Effects...." *Journal of Human Resources* (Summer, 1969).

government financing and funding, makes it a powerful employment weapon. From the point of view of a person who becomes unemployed and who may face poverty as a result, assistance begins much more quickly than a guaranteed *annual* income would. The only pity is that it works best for those who are economically strongest—the previously well-employed, and neglects those who, because of their age or their health, are outside the labor force.

CASEWORK AND WELFARE PROGRAMS

Economists are vehement that most "case" poverty (physical or mental disability that bars people from the general economic advance) stems from the same causes as insular or regional poverty and unemployment: birth to low-income parents in low-income regions. Because poverty is both the cause and the result, the argument goes, the indicated treatment is to cut through the vicious circle and guarantee a decent minimum income.

The casework tradition of social work, which is interwound with *ad hoc* welfare payments for particular disabilities, sees the problem otherwise. Social workers will still have to advise and support broken families, neglected children, sufferers from addiction, dependents of those in jail, the feeble-minded, and so forth. In the best 19th century liberal tradition, they must help those who, even with funds, would not be fully able to cope with modern society. Obviously, any guaranteed income will help these casework "clients" as much as or more than it will help the "normal" poor. But the guaranteed income program will not render social workers unemployed, nor relieve the taxpayer of the need to help those who are physically or mentally weak.

To be fair, the attacks on social work and welfarism are not necessary to any guaranteed income proposal. Its unique attraction is that it allows people in poverty to continue to receive aid without the disincentives that now confine them in workless, aimless, endless idleness.

THE QUALITY OF LIFE

This chapter has discussed the problems of inequality and of poverty. The quantity of gross national product cannot be appraised independently of its distribution. But even if inequality could be considerably reduced and poverty largely alleviated, there still remain important and vexing questions about the quality of life.

In the nineteenth century, moralists like Thomas Carlyle and John Ruskin declaimed against the acquisitive society. The poet Wordsworth expressed a common sentiment in the lines
Give all thou canst; high Heaven rejects the lore
Of nicely-calculated less or more.
And as a society becomes more comfortably situated, the more it can afford to indulge this distaste for a purely pecuniary motivation based on self-interest.

WHEN SCARCITY ENDS In truth, we do not face squarely the philosophical issue if we make an era of greater altruism wait on the disappearance of scarcity. Marxians early had the notion of the ultimate "withering away of the state," after a transitory period of state capitalism and dictatorship of the proletariat. But such pie in the sky cannot appease the legitimate desire in the here and now of a Soviet citizen for greater political freedom. Similarly, there is no great virtue in paying lip service to unselfishness *after* there is superabundance. The test of sincerity of belief in a cause is how much you will sacrifice for it.

Galbraith was premature in proclaiming the end of scarcity at mid-century. But actually John Maynard Keynes had anticipated Galbraith by almost 30 years. In 1930 Keynes made the following prophecy with respect to the future.[17]

... suppose that a hundred years hence we are all of us ... eight times better off ... than we are today. ... Assuming no important wars and no important increase in population, the *economic problem* may be solved. ... This means that the economic problem is not—if we look into the future—*the permanent problem of the human race.*

Why, you may ask, is this so startling? It is startling because—if instead of looking into the future, we look into the past—we find that the economic problem, the struggle for subsistence, always has been hitherto the primary, most pressing problem of the human race—not only of the human race, but of the whole of the biological kingdom from the beginnings of life in its most primitive forms.

Thus we have been expressly evolved by nature—with all our impulses and deepest instincts—for the purpose of

[17] J. M. Keynes, "Economic Possibilities for Our Grandchildren," reprinted in his *Essays in Persuasion* (Macmillan, London, 1933) and also in P. A. Samuelson, *Readings, op. cit.*

solving the economic problem. If the economic problem is solved, mankind will be deprived of its traditional purpose. ... I think with dread of the readjustment of the habits and instincts of the ordinary man, bred into him for countless generations, which he may be asked to discard within a few decades.

To use the language of today—must we not expect a general "nervous breakdown"? ... Thus for the first time since his creation man will be faced with his real, his permanent problem—how to use his freedom from pressing economic cares, how to occupy the leisure, which science and compound interest will have won for him, to live wisely and agreeably and well. ...

There are changes in other spheres too which we must expect to come. When the accumulation of wealth is no longer of high social importance, there will be great changes in the code of morals. We shall be able to rid ourselves of many of the pseudo-moral principles which have hag-ridden us for two hundred years, by which we have exalted some of the most distasteful of human qualities into the position of the highest virtues. ... The love of money as a possession—as distinquished from the love of money as a means to the enjoyments and realities of life—will be recognized for what it is, a somewhat disgusting morbidity, one of those semi-criminal, semi-pathological propensities which one hands over with a shudder to the specialists in mental disease.

But beware! the time for all this is not yet. For at least another hundred years we must pretend to ourselves and to every one that fair is foul and foul is fair; for foul is useful and fair is not. Avarice and usury and precaution must be our gods for a little longer still.

... in making preparations for our destiny ... let us not overestimate the importance of the economic problem. ... It should be a matter for specialists—like dentistry. If economists could manage to get themselves thought of as humble, competent people, on a level with dentists, that would be spendid!

This is indeed a passage of profound and prophetic insight. For one thing, despite the Great Depression, which had for a time set Keynes' time schedule behind, we are now right on target. In the 40 years since Keynes wrote, real output per head has grown at almost precisely the 2 per cent per annum rate that Keynes had prophesied.

For another thing, has not Keynes perhaps given a clue to the nature of the generation gap that is so prominent a feature of our time? In college youth,

among offspring of affluence particularly, we can perhaps see the change in moral code that Keynes predicted would be the outcome of affluence. In view of modern psychiatric opinion that many of the young in the advanced nations are plagued by the problem of "existential vacuum," one of whose symptoms is a disquieting search for meaning and purpose in life, there is an almost uncanny clinical precision in Keynes' diagnosis that hitherto economic necessity has shaped man's very biological nature and provided him with that purpose. For what is more purposeful than filling your belly when it is empty? Tigers in the jungle do not, Hamlet-like, debate the meaning of meaning.

ONE FOOT IN AFFLUENCE

But we are not yet arrived at Utopia. In the meantime, in the here and now, what is it that economists must economize? This was the title of a provocative address given by the late Sir Dennis Robertson of Trinity College, Cambridge, on the occasion of the two-hundredth anniversary of the founding of Columbia University. What economists economize, said Robertson, is "love," for that is the scarcest commodity in the universe. We must make what love we have go a long way. We must not waste this precious resource on petty problems *which the mechanisms of the marketplace can handle*.[18]

If the time is not yet when we can dispense with the economic system, still the time is long past when we can permit it to be master rather than good servant. We do still need the efficiency of our large corporations. But that is no reason for permitting business and industry to be the arbiters of our national policy. We must be ungrateful recipients, and indeed bite the hand that helps to feed us. This is the privilege that the abundance of science and the Industrial Revolution have given us—to reverse the roles in the Emersonian plaint that

Things are in the saddle
And ride mankind.

---

[18] And yet, as was discussed in the Appendix to Chapter 24 dealing with game theory and with the problem of prisoners' dilemma, it is only in *special* social situations, where the checks and balances of competition happen to be available, that we can dispense with love and altruism if the good society is to be achieved.

SUMMARY

1 Where economic inequality serves no economic purpose, ethical observers criticize its existence. And even where it does serve a function, such observers are willing to pay a considerable price in terms of inefficiency for alleviating it. Now that a measure of affluence, above and beyond the minimum of subsistence, is available, the citizenry insists upon certain minimum living standards for all.

2 The view, associated with Pareto, that inequality is a universal constant which cannot be much affected by policy, is not consonant with historical experience. In the advanced countries, Lorenz curves of inequality show less disparity of living standards than they do in the underdeveloped regions. Coupling Smithian self-interest with universal suffrage has led, as the founding fathers predicted, to the modern welfare state with its multifarious social security programs of *mutual reinsurance*.

3 The major causes of inequality involve differences in (*a*) property ownership, (*b*) personal ability (attributable to both environment and heredity), (*c*) education, training, and opportunity, (*d*) discrimination, and (*e*) age and health. Decaying, but still with us in some degree, is the belief that it is the fault of the poor themselves if they are poor; and that private charity should be relied on to handle the cases of greatest distress.

4 For centuries public policy has provided asylums and hospitals, poor farms and old-people's homes, and various forms of *ad hoc* relief in times of famine and depression. But only in modern times has the positive role of government become dominant. Cradle-to-grave social security and medical care are common among the mixed economies abroad. Only since the 1930s have social insurance and federally financed relief and welfare programs developed here. And only since the 1960s has there been a determined battle at the national level against poverty. Some form of the negative income tax—i.e., minimum-guaranteed-income-cum-incentives—seems the next item on the social agenda.

5 As the problem of mere survival gradually recedes into the background (at least in the West), the problem of the quality of economic life begins to take precedence over the problem of mere quantity. How we shall use our new leisure and how we shall develop new codes of conduct are some problems the future will pose.

6 Discrimination by sex can be analyzed by the same economic tools as discrimination by race, nationality, or political belief. Liberation of women, aside from being desirable and equitable for its own sake, provides also an enhancement of economic well-being through more efficient use of economic resources.

CONCEPTS FOR REVIEW

Pareto's laws	guaranteed jobs
Lorenz measures of inequality	end of scarcity
negative income tax	self-interest and altruism
discrimination and segregation	
exploitation	

QUESTIONS FOR DISCUSSION

1. From 1945 to 1975 inequality of incomes in Canada or the United States has not changed much. Is this an indictment of the system in your view? Or a symptom of the difficulty of a program for changing matters quickly in this sphere?

2. Do colleges and universities perpetuate inequality?

3. Why not jobs for all? What are next steps for reform in your view (free higher education for all, negative income tax, revolutionary change, or ...)?

4. Can you draw a graph of the tax structure both in the positive and the negative range of taxes? Is it the case that the more you earn the more you keep?

5. Was Keynes borrowing trouble in his worrying about the future? Can't people be happy without working?

6. Consider the Tawney quotation at the head of this chapter. Is Canada a community in Tawney's sense? Should incomes (including oil royalties) be siphoned out of the rich provinces and into the poor provinces? Why not into Bangladesh?

7. *Extra-credit problem:* Redraw Fig. 40-3 according to instructions of footnote 6. Better still, move (*b*) as follows: Line up *w* vertical axis to fall on (*a*)'s $S + s$ line, and flip-flop (*b*) s horizontal axis so that it runs westward rather than eastward. As before, identify E and e (with e just below E). But contrast them with nondiscrimination intersection of DD and dd at F just southeast of E and northeast of e. Shade the little triangle formed by e, E, and F. Can you deduce that it measures gain in national product from eliminating discrimination?

41
WINDS OF CHANGE:
EVOLUTION OF ECONOMIC DOCTRINES

Up to now the philosophers have only interpreted the world in various ways
The point, though, is to change it!

KARL MARX, *Thesis on Feuerbach (1845)*

Political economy is about the economic system, not about economists. To fail to realize this is to make the mistake Edward Gibbon was accused of when writing the *Decline and Fall of the Roman Empire:* namely, that sometimes Gibbon was unable to distinguish between himself and the Roman Empire.

At the end of a long book, though, we may perhaps indulge ourselves with a brief excursion into the history and present status of economics as a scholarly discipline and as a chapter in the intellectual history of mankind. We can do this with a better conscience in light of the fact that such a survey of the ivory tower will enable us to understand better the real economic events outside its windows. For, as we saw in the opening chapter, there is an irreducible subjectivity inherent in every objective science. How we are able to perceive the economic system must depend crucially on the quality of the spectacles through which we look at it. Once a student of economics knows how the theories he now fervently believes in grew out of the past, he may be better prepared for the modifications that they will assuredly undergo in the future.[1]

PREHISTORY OF ECONOMICS

Like a baby, political economy was taking shape even before it was born. The family tree of economics, shown on the back flyleaf can, with pardonable exaggeration, declare political economy to be but two cen-

turies old; *The Wealth of Nations* (1776) of Adam Smith (1723-1790) can be taken as providing its birthday.

But from its earliest beginnings, political economy was concerned with policy. Thus, both Testaments of the Bible warn against interest or usury, as do Aristotle and St. Thomas Aquinas. The predecessors of Adam Smith, the Mercantilists, were advisers to the prince, in their orientation not unlike the modern Council of Economic Advisers or the economists of the Bank of England. When the Mercantilists favored protective tariffs, it was in the sincere belief, however misguided, that these would add to the nation's prosperity.

The expression "the greatest good for the greatest number" appears and reappears long before Jeremy Bentham (1748-1832) subjected every institution in England to ruthless scrutiny in terms of its social utility; the expression was already in Machiavelli and other early writers. Adam Smith's contemporaries on the continent, the Physiocrats, who believed in a circular flow of economic life based on the primacy of land, were men of the Enlightenment, *philosophes* hopeful to reform the *ancien régime* of prerevolutionary France.

People babbled prose long before there were English teachers. The first contributors to economic analysis were certainly not professional economists. Copernicus, the astronomer, enunciated the Quantity Theory of Money and Prices—just as did John Locke, the philosopher. (Locke also formulated the labor theory of value.) David Hume (1711-1776) earned his living as a philosopher and historian; only in passing did he make his great contribution to the understanding of the automatic regulation of the gold standard by the corrective flow of specie, with re-

---

[1] Good introductions to the history of political economy are Robert L. Heilbroner, *The Worldly Philosophers* (Simon and Schuster Inc., New York, 1953), or Eric Roll, *A History of Economic Thought* (Prentice-Hall, Englewood Cliffs, N.J., 1972). The standard advanced reference is the posthumous classic, Joseph A. Schumpeter, *History of Economic Analysis* (Oxford University Press, New York, 1957).

sulting effects on price levels that served to correct the imbalance of trade. (Hume also formulated the theory of land rent and recognized inflation's stimulus to business activity.) John Law, one of the first to try to bring on prosperity by priming the pump of money creation, was a Scottish adventurer moved to France—as much rogue and confidence man as scholar. Richard Cantillon was an international merchant, one of the many early writers who was not without a commercial interest in the doctrines he was espousing.

CLASSICAL ECONOMICS: SMITH THE PROPHET OF *LAISSEZ-FAIRE*

Not only were the earliest economists interested in policy; they were even too crudely eager to interfere. It is Adam Smith's greatest contribution that he recognized in the social world of economics what Isaac Newton (1642-1727) had recognized in the physical world of the heavens: a self-regulating *natural order.* Smith's message said:

You think you are helping the economic system by your well-meaning laws and interferences. You are not. Let be. The oil of self-interest will keep the gears working in almost miraculous fashion. No one need plan. No sovereign need rule. The market will answer all things.

Adam Smith was far from being a cold geometer. He was not merely stating the syllogism of the Invisible Hand in the fashion of a high school teacher stating the Pythagorean theorem, when he enunciated his famous words:

... every individual ... neither intends to promote the public interest ... he intends only his own gain, and he is in this, as in many other cases, led by an invisible hand to promote an end which was no part of his intention. (*The Wealth of Nations,* Book IV, Chap. II).

Smith never did *prove* the truth of this. Indeed, as late as the time when the present writer was an undergraduate, no one yet knew how to prove—or even state properly!—the kernel of truth in Smith's doctrine of the Invisible Hand. *What Smith did do in his great book was to enumerate empirically countless cases of follies by government.* He raided all ancient and contemporary history for telling illustrations of

the harms from well-meaning governmental regulations.

His book is a masterpiece. It has magisterial style. It is a veritable handbook that could as well be entitled: *How to Make the GNP Grow.* And withal, it lays the foundations for the general equilibrium of supply and demand.

SPIRIT OF THE BOURGEOIS AGE But, of course, its many excellences cannot explain why *The Wealth of Nations* had so dramatic an impact on the century to follow. In a real sense, the rising bourgeois class needed a spokesman for their interests. Smith provided them with the ideology that served their purpose. Equally important, his ideology of *laissez faire* fed their self-esteem and moral needs. By minding his shop, the merchant of Manchester could know he was both doing God's will and helping the King's realm.

None of this is to imply that Smith was a flunky to the establishment. Actually, he had a healthy distrust of businessmen (saying, for example, "People of the same trade seldom meet together, even for merriment and diversion, but the conversation ends in a conspiracy against the public, or in some contrivance to raise prices"). Smith was definitely for the common man. But he was convinced, as so many economists have been since, that the road to hell is paved with good intentions. The attempt by government to keep masters from conspiring in monopolies would probably, he thought, make a bad situation worse rather than better. Smith's very eclecticism and pragmatism added to the persuasiveness of his *Weltanschauung.*

CLASSICAL ECONOMICS: AUTUMN FOR MALTHUS AND RICARDO

In the half-century after *The Wealth of Nations,* the law of diminishing returns was discovered. Ironically, just as the Industrial Revolution was suspending for the Western world the dire workings of that dismal law, the Reverend T. R. Malthus (1766-1834) enunciated the theory that growth of population is bound always to reduce mankind to the margin of bare subsistence.

The key figure of the age, however, is not so much Malthus as David Ricardo (1772-1823). To few writers is there given the luck of a Robert Frost, who appeals both to the lowbrow and the high. David Ricardo is one of those lucky few. The classical, neoclassical, and post-Keynesian scholars all trace their ancestry through his family line. And so too do the writers of Marxian socialism. We shall see that Karl Marx had little use for the vulgar bourgeois economists of the classical school. Ricardo, however, is a charmed exception, the master from whom Marx thought truth could be developed.

David Ricardo never went to college. Born to an affluent family of Spanish-Dutch Jews who had migrated to England, he was cut off by his father with £800 for having married outside his faith. Within 12 years, he retired from being a stockbroker with a nest egg in the millions. Leading the life of a country gentleman, he chanced to read Adam Smith. Fascinated, Ricardo believed that there were basic errors in Smith's analysis and also gaps in his macroeconomic writings. But for the insistent advice of James Mill, father of the precocious John Stuart Mill (1806-1873), Ricardo would have been no more than a pamphlet writer and Member of Parliament for a rotten borough. But the elder Mill browbeat Ricardo into writing his *Principles of Political Economy and Taxation* (1817), and Ricardo's fame was made.[2]

Such is the subtlety of Ricardo's logic and the obscurity of his style that he stands in some danger of being overrated, both in comparison with Smith and Keynes, and with such contemporaries as Malthus, J. S. Mill, and such later writers as Jevons, Walras, Marshall, and Wicksell. George J. Stigler, who is if anything partial to Ricardian economics, has justly observed that Ricardo's logic "was severe in its simplifications rather than superlative in its rigor."

The vices as well as the virtues of classical economics stand out in Ricardo. He maintained an overly simple, and empty, version of Say's Law, according to which supply always creates its own demand and no problem of over- or under-saving is ever conceivable. He stated results valid for the long run as if they were valid for the short. He vacillated in blowing hot and cold over the labor theory of value. His example encouraged lesser economists to try to make economics a nonempirical, purely deductive science. Many will agree with Jevons and Keynes that David Ricardo shunted economics onto the wrong track.

2 One of the great feats of scholarship of our times is the many-volume edition by Piero Sraffa, for the Royal Economic Society, of *The Works and Correspondence of David Ricardo* (Cambridge (University Press, Cambridge, England, 1953).

STAGNANT WAGE PREDICTIONS AND CLASS OPPOSITIONS From 1820 to 1870, full half a century, Ricardo kept economists and statesmen hypnotized. Like Malthus, he bet on the wrong horse of diminishing returns, just when the Industrial Revolution was bypassing and offsetting that law. In the century that was to come, when the landowner was in fact withering away in importance (recall Part Four's quoted findings of Denison that land rent has dropped to less than 5 per cent of modern GNP!), Ricardo's vision was that rents would rise and unaugmentable land form the bottleneck to economic growth.

This autumn view of the economy—inevitably on its way to a rendezvous with poverty for most people—was what the man in the street and the men of the world took from Ricardo. Equally important:

To Ricardo the most important thing in economics was the *laws of distribution* of the national product among the great classes of society: wages for workers, profits for capitalists, and rents for landowners. With a total social pie limited in its growth, what went to one social class had to be taken away from another.

No wonder the capitalists liked Ricardo. They could glean texts from him to prove that trade-unions and reforms can accomplish little for the masses. No wonder the socialists liked Ricardo. They found in him the demonstration that capitalism would have to be destroyed if workers were to get their right to the whole product. Ironically, that same self-interest that Smith and Ricardo presupposed was, in the twentieth century, to lead the proletariat, as if by "an Invisible Hand," to the ballot box—to wrest for themselves through government action a larger share of the GNP.

DECADENCE Thomas Kuhn, in his history of the physical sciences, *The Structure of Scientific Revolutions* (University of Chicago Press, Chicago, 1962, 1970), analyzes how science progresses discontinuously. An old school dies. A new school is born. It has new models and theories—new "paradigms," in Kuhn's terminology. The new school explains a wide range of facts to its satisfaction.

But schools, like people, are subject to hardening of the arteries. Students learn the embalmed truth from their teachers and sacred textbooks. The travail in which the new ideas were born is lost to view. The imperfections in the orthodox doctrines are glossed over as unimportant, if indeed they even continue to be noticed.

Decadence if not senility had set in. Thus, John Stuart Mill, himself important in areas other than technical economics (and underrated within that area of economics), could write in his middle-of-the-nineteenth-century classic *Principles* book: "Happily, there is nothing in the laws of Value which remains for the present and any future writer to clear up. . . . "

The time had come for new blood. For, as Kuhn reminds us, a discipline that does not stay young, alive and open will find itself elbowed out by fresh models (paradigms) that attempt to deal with new preoccupations. Just as western culture did not evolve merely to give a permanent role to the Canada Council, neither is political economy a three-act drama culminating in the glorious climax of today's battle against stagflation.

NEOCLASSICAL ECONOMICS

Just a century ago the tree of economics bifurcated. One branch led through neo-classical economics and Keynesian economics to the present-day era of post-Keynesianism. The other branch stemmed from Marx's *Das Kapital* (1867, 1885, 1894) and from his rediscovered earlier writings in economics.

Classical writers had emphasized cost, to the neglect of utility and demand. It was as if they had been working with horizontal *ss* curves and neglecting all *dd* curves. Around 1870, three men simultaneously and independently laid the foundations for a more symmetric, general-equilibrium analysis that could synthesize both utility and disutility elements: W. Stanley Jevons (1835-1882) in England; Carl Menger (1840-1921) in Austria; and Leon Walras (1834-1910), a Frenchman unable to get a professorial chair except in Lausanne, Switzerland.

UTILITY, MARGINALISM, GENERAL EQUILIBRIUM
The neoclassical revolution was important not merely because it discovered how to analyze demand and utility preferences. In addition, it generalized the marginal notions present in primitive form in Ricardo's theory of rent. Finally, particularly in the deep mathematical analysis of Leon Walras, the analysis of general equilibrium was achieved.

The late Joseph Schumpeter (1883-1950) used to say that of all great economists, surely Walras was the greatest, since it was he who discovered general equilibrium. It was Lagrange, "the Shakespeare of mathematics," who said: "Of all scientists Newton was surely the greatest. For it was he who discovered the system of the world. And, alas, there is but one system of the world to be discovered." Schumpeter apparently felt that Walras was also lucky as well as great, since there is only one system of general economic equilibrium to be discovered.

POLICY CONCERNS
As political economy became more "scientific," it never lost its interest in policy. Most of the great economists tell us in their autobiographies that they became economists in order to do good. Still, it is true that after a man has been a professor of economics for a lifetime, he tends to become more cautious in his belief that this measure or that will end up fulfilling its promise to improve the common lot. With age comes a preoccupation with "feasibility." It is perhaps this, more than the tendency to become reactionary as one gains honors and comfortable position, that explains the cooling off of the socialistic ardors of the English Alfred Marshall (1842-1924) or the American John Bates Clark (1847-1938).

An even more interesting case is that of the great Scandinavian economist, Knut Wicksell (1851-1926). Wicksell failed to win an academic chair until he was almost fifty. He was a premature counterculture bohemian who would not in principle agree to the sacrament of marriage with his wife. In the end, even though he thought it meant he would not get the chair his family finances so desperately needed, Wicksell could not bring himself to address the King of Sweden formally as "Your Majesty." Fortunately, "Dear Sir" got him the job.

Wicksell believed in birth control, heresy in the 1870s. He disbelieved, publicly, in the Virgin Birth and wrote a book from jail after a blasphemy conviction. When the Czar's army stood on the Swedish borders, Wicksell advised his countrymen to dismantle their army. Though he never hesitated to speak out in behalf of unpopular causes, Wicksell's recommendations to reform society were essentially an anticipation of the Swedish welfare state, with its income redistribution and transfer benefits. His was a calculated rejection of traditional socialism as an unpromising path to the better society.

MONOPOLISTIC-COMPETITION PARADIGM
What is today called microeconomics was in-

creasingly developed by the neoclassical writers. Be-latedly, by the early 1930s, the turn-of-the-century burgeoning of monopolies and imperfect competition became absorbed within the paradigm of neoclassical economics.[3] Particularly in America, and to a degree in Germany, empirical studies of patterns of competition and industrial organization flourished. Labor markets and union activity were studied intensively.

MATHEMATICAL ECONOMICS AND ECONOMETRICS Jevons, Walras, and Vilfredo Pareto (1848-1923) had already introduced mathematics into economics. But after 1930, this activity underwent a rebirth.[4]

Econometric measurement, involving the tools of modern probability and statistics and special techniques appropriate to a nonexperimental domain like economics, represents a prominent feature of our times. Also, quantitative measurement came to give economic history a new focus. National-income growth was studied by such masters as Simon Kuznets, Colin Clark, and Edward Denison. Historians studying the economics of slavery and of the revolution in railroad transportation utilized the most sophisticated tools in the armory of the economic analyst.

THE KEYNESIAN REVOLUTION

By World War II, political economy was making great strides in describing and analyzing the economic world of both less developed and developed

---

[3] E. H. Chamberlin, *The Theory of Monopolistic Competition* (Harvard University Press, Cambridge, Mass., 1933, 1962), and Joan Robinson, *The Economics of Imperfect Competition* (Macmillan, London, 1933), are the standard references. But both writers built on earlier work of Cournot (1838), Sraffa (1926), and many other contemporary writers.

[4] Writers from many countries led the wave: Ragnar Frisch, Trygve Haavelmo, and Leif Johansen from Norway; Jan Tinbergen and Henri Theil from Holland; J. R. Hicks and R. G. D. Allen from England; M. Allais and E. Malinvaud from France; migrants to America such as J. von Neumann, T. Koopmans, J. Marschak, and G. Debreu; American-trained economists such as Harold Hotelling, Paul A. Samuelson, K. J. Arrow, R. M. Solow, and J. Tobin. The present list could be doubled and redoubled in length, going back to the 1838 classic of A. A. Cournot and including the turn-of-the-century writers F. Y. Edgeworth, Philip Wicksteed, L. von Bortkiewicz, G. Cassel, and others.

regions. One thing, however, had long been lacking. Although Wesley Mitchell, Alvin Hansen, and many Continental writers, such as Arthur Spiethoff, had gone far in describing the business cycle, neoclassical economics was handicapped in that it lacked a developed macroeconomics to match its almost over-developed microeconomics.

Finally, with the Great Depression came the breakthrough of the *General Theory of Employment, Interest and Money* (Macmillan, London, 1936) by John Maynard Keynes. Economics could never be the same again. The simple-minded belief in Say's Law was banished. Even the neoclassical theories of money and the price level, which had already been developed by Marshall, Wicksell, and Yale's Irving Fisher (1867-1947), were capable of being given a more fruitful restatement in terms of the Keynesian concepts. Ironically, even the theory of full employment was capable of being demonstrated more validly in terms of the Keynesian innovations —as the pre-Keynesian, A. C. Pigou (1877-1959), handsomely conceded.

A Thomas Kuhn who applied himself to the study of economic thought would realize that it takes a generation for new ideas to become part of the conventional wisdom. Once again it was a case where, funeral by funeral, science progressed.

MAINSTREAM ECONOMICS

The whole of this book has been devoted to modern post-Keynesian political economy—the mainstream economics that prevails in America and Scandinavia, in England and Holland; and that is coming to prevail increasingly in Japan, France, Germany, Italy, and most of the Western world. The fruits of post-Keynesian economics have been the better working of the mixed economy. The era since World War II has witnessed a world growth in output and living standards unmatched in recorded history.

The purpose here, however, is not to glorify past achievements. As Chapter 40 demonstrated, the millennium has not remotely arrived for the mixed economy. We still do not know how to find that perfect incomes policy which will spare us the need to choose between the alternatives of full employment and price stability.

What we need to do at this point is to render justice to the *critiques* of conventional political economy that have prevailed in the past, that prevail now, and that will undoubtedly prevail increasingly in the future. For, as Kuhn reminds us, a discipline that does not stay young, alive, and open will find itself elbowed out by the competition of fresh paradigms and preoccupations. Just as civilization did not evolve merely in order to reach the permanent state of the post-New Deal political system, neither is political economy a drama in a finite number of acts that culminates in the new economics of Kennedy's Camelot or Scandinavia's bureaucracies.

ROMANTIC AND NATIONALISTIC REJECTIONS OF CLASSICAL ECONOMICS

America, young in the nineteenth century and vigorously growing, could not accept the autumnal scenario of Ricardian economics. One had only to look around to see economic progress, both in scale and standards of life. Henry C. Carey (1793-1879) rejected diminishing returns. Accepting a naïve labor theory of value, he deduced that technological change would set into motion the law of *increasing* real wage. Later, social Darwinism was to prevail in America, according to which ruthless *laissez faire* competition would lead to rugged growth and not to Malthusian subsistence.

Goethe's Germany, still a backwater of Europe and lagging behind cosmopolitan France and England, could also not accept the gloomy timetable of classical economics. Wagnerian-like notions of race and folk combined with Hegelian notions of historical stages to form a repudiation of classical economics and the Newtonian synthesis of the Enlightenment. Friedrich List (1789-1846), though founder of the nationalist school of German economic romanticism, spent his formative years in America. It was there that he developed his notions of protective tariffs to speed economic development and ensure organic diversity, even though his *National System of Political Economy* (1841) was later published in Germany.

GERMAN HISTORICAL SCHOOL   The Hegelian *Zeitgeist* culminated, as we shall see, in Marxian economics on the one hand. But on the other hand, it led to the German Historical School composed of scholars who professed to be rejecting all economic theory in favor of letting the multi-

various facts tell their own organic story. By the latter part of the nineteenth century, this school was associated with the *Kathedersozialisten* ("socialists of the chair") who believed in the star of the Prussian state and its fruitful interferences with the market.

We shall see that the Historical School had a strong influence on American critics of classical and neoclassical economics. But with the collapse of the German Empire in World War I and the exhaustion of its own creative energies in scholarly innovation, the Historical School simply ran out of steam.

INSTITUTIONAL ECONOMICS AND VEBLEN

Many Americans received advanced training in Germany, and brought some of the ideas of the Historical School to North America, under the new name of "Institutionalism" (c. 1890-1935). In retrospect, the chief contributions of the leaders Richard T. Ely (1854-1943) and John R. Commons may have been in their rejection of *laissez-faire* rather than in their constructive work. Their research involved abandoning much of the theorizing of Ricardo, Marshall and Mill[5] and a more uncritical and descriptive approach to business, agriculture, trade unions and, especially, governments at all levels.

VEBLEN   Thorstein Veblen (1875-1929), sometimes called the American Marx and certainly our greatest iconoclast prior to John Kenneth Galbraith, sided with the Institutionalists in rejecting neoclassical economics. Titles of Veblen's books give some flavor of the thought of this bohemian son of

---

[5] Thus the Americans, like the English, were comparatively uninfluenced by the "Austrian" school of Menger, E. Böhm-Bawerk (1851-1914), and F. von Wieser (1851-1926) which was much more deductive, conservative and neoclassical. They arrived at many of the conclusions of Walras and Wicksell, using less mathematical techniques. They also concentrated on various forms of capital theory, in this being much influenced by the Canadian immigrant John Rae and in their turn influencing Irving Fisher at Yale. Later Austrians included Schumpeter, Ludwig von Mises, Gottfried Haberler, Fritz Machlup and 1974 Nobel laureate Friederich Hayek.

[6] Canadian economist Harold Innis studied at Chicago and was much impressed by the institutionalists. However his own works on staples, the intrusion of the price mechanism, innovation and communications were quite original in their striving for a comprehensive approach to growth and change, and did not reject economic theory so much as certain European theories of the stages of growth.

Norwegian homesteaders on the Wisconsin and Minnesota frontier: *The Theory of the Leisure Class* (1899), *The Theory of Business Enterprise* (1904), *The Instinct of Workmanship* (1914), *Imperial Germany and the Industrial Revolution* (1915), *The Higher Learning in America* (1918), *The Engineers and the Price System* (1921), *Absentee Ownership* (1923).

Although Veblen and the Institutionalists had some followers in American academic life—as, for example, Wesley Clair Mitchell, the founder of the National Bureau of Economic Research and theory-eschewing taxonomist of business cycles—30 years ago Institutionalism withered away as an effective counterforce in economics. Who can explain it when a movement turns sterile? Perhaps it was the case that mainstream American economics had always been more pragmatic and empirical than Austrian or English or French economics; it was therefore able, so to speak, to absorb and take over with superior analytical and econometric tools the descriptive tasks and policy formulations of the Institutionalists.

This completes our historical sketch of classical, neoclassical, and Keynesian economics. And of the unsuccessful revolts against it by romantic, nationalistic, historical, and institutionalist schools of thought. For the rest of this chapter, the time has come to survey briefly the vigorous and still lively schools that are critical of mainstream economics of the post-Keynes age. Because any literate person should have some glimmering of acquaintanceship with the economics and thought of Karl Marx, the ideological hero of a billion people over the globe, most of the technical analysis of his economics has been placed in a self-contained appendix.

CONSERVATIVE COUNTERATTACKS AGAINST MAINSTREAM ECONOMICS

What is recognizable as a modern economic consensus is now increasingly under attack from several directions.[7] First there is simply the rejection by the conservative interests. Although in terms of

realpolitik it may be the most potent and long-lasting of the oppositions, this historic rejection lacks intellectual interest. Either you feel it or you don't, and there is not much intellectual arguing that can be done.

CHICAGO LIBERTARIANISM Roughly speaking, working our way from right to left, we have the second assault against the new economics from within the profession of economics by Libertarians—the apostles of *laissez faire.* Many of them have been Austrians, or associated with the London School of Economics, the University of Virginia or, particularly, the economics and law schools of the University of Chicago. Names like Frank Knight (1885-1972), Henry C. Simons, Friedrich Hayek, and Milton Friedman are associated with this general school.[8] Their function is valuable in reminding us what it is that market pricing accomplishes, and what we in our mixed economy sacrifice when we disregard the predictable results, through market processes or our regulations and interventions.

Thus market-oriented economists, inspired by Friedman, have warned against interfering in rental and exchange-rate markets, correctly predicting much of the long-run harm that rent controls and fixed exchange rates can bring. People of all political persuasions, before they speak, write or vote on economic policies, should read Friedman's *Capitalism and Freedom.*[9] It is punctilious, logical, persuasive. On the

---

[7] The next few sections have been adapted from P. A. Samuelson, "Liberalism at Bay," Gerhard Colm Memorial Lecture, New School for Social Research, *Social Research* (Spring 1972), pp. 16-31.

[8] Among the lay public, under the banner of Ayn Rand and avowed self-interest, there is a new radical right that is allied with the academic movement of the Chicago School. It is curious, and upon reflection perhaps not surprising, that there is a tendency for the radical left and the radical right to join in their attack on the conventional economics. This is not merely a matter of tactics, like that involved in the Weimar Republic just before Hitler's successful rise to power. Rather, it is a fact that radical libertarianism is a form of anarchism not all that different from the anti-bureaucratic anarchism of the New Left. A lengthier survey than this would tie up the Austrian School with the new Libertarian movement of Knight, Hayek, and Lionel Robbins.

[9] The University of Chicago Press, Chicago, 1962, hardcover and paperback. See also M. Friedman, *An Economist's Protest* (Thomas Horton & Co., Glen Ridge, N.J., 1972) a collection of his *Newsweek* columns. Reference was made in Chap. 17 to his monetarist position in opposition to post-Keynesian macroeconomics, an issue within the economics family, so to speak.

basis of its approach and ad hoc information, Friedman and his followers have at one time or another felt impelled to argue against almost every conceivable recent government intervention: social security; the draft; flood relief; wage and price controls; the "conscience" of big business; anti-usury laws; and so on. Most of them have the characteristic that, in Friedman's view however desirable the intended aim, the working of the market system will prevent the specific suggested legislation from achieving its goal; or will allow it only by bringing about some unintended bad result elsewhere. A large number of economists have in the past fifteen years been reminded of Friedman's home truths. If he had not written as he did, it would have been necessary to find some other way to remind the profession that good intentions alone are not adequate to guarantee good policy.

GALBRAITHIAN CRITIQUE

A third challenge to the new economics comes from John Kenneth Galbraith. By now even high school students are familiar with his works *The Affluent Society* (1957) and *The New Industrial State* (1967).[10]

Ten years ago in a presidential address to the brethren within the economists' guild, Paul Samuelson said that the noneconomists take Galbraith too seriously, but that we in the profession do not take him seriously enough. It is premature to evaluate what it is about Galbraith that differs from the new economics *and* is also likely to be deemed valid in the future. But this much can be said.

SCHOLAR AS ARTIST Many academics consider it a crime, a misdemeanor if not a felony, to write too

well: to do so, they complain, is to puff up the importance of one's ideas beyond their genuine worth. Hence, Galbraith is automatically suspect: anyone who sells so well must automatically be shallow!

Then too, as with Marx, learned men say Galbraith's ideas are not original. *The Affluent Society* is derivative even in title from R. H. Tawney's *The Acquisitive Society*; the "technostructure" is merely another name for the bureaucrats of James Burnham's managerial revolution; the manipulation of consumers' tastes by advertising is warmed-over Ruskin; emphasis on the public sector's needs is Alvin Hansen popularized; corporate autonomy is merely Berle-Means 40 years later; the glorification of bigness in corporations is Schumpeterian; the military-industrial complex stems from Eisenhower's valedictory warning.

This is to miss the point. In technology, it is not the inventor who is the innovator. And, in the history of ideas, the thinker who creates a new synthesis and speaks in telling fashion to a new age is the man who counts.

ICONOCLAST Galbraith in a sense has no disciples. There are few testable, researchable propositions in his writings that could serve for the purpose of Ph.D. theses or articles in learned journals. How can a jury prove his attitudes and insights right or wrong?

But Galbraith does provide a ware that is in great effective demand: a critique in viewpoint against the prevailing orthodoxy in economics—against the "conventional wisdom," in his phrase, the "received learning," in Veblen's. His criticism cannot itself kill. But it acts like a virus, softening the way for more deadly critiques on the part of the New Left and its professional radical economists.[11]

---

[10] Galbraith, an Ontario Scot, began his career as an agricultural economist. After achieving early fame as an impudent price controller at the wartime OPA, he became editor, philosopher, political speechwriter, politician, braintruster, novelist, art connoisseur, ambassador (to India for John F. Kennedy), memoirist, jet setter, and skier. He has been an important adviser to Adlai Stevenson, John F. Kennedy, and George McGovern. In addition to the cited books, a third work, *American Capitalism, The Concept of Countervailing Power* (Houghton Mifflin, Boston, 1956), signaled his emancipation from a successful professorial career in mainstream economics. The flavor of his catholic interests is indicated by other titles: *A Theory of Price Control; Economics and the Art of Controversy; The Great Crash, 1929; Economic Development; The Scotch; Ambassador's Journal.*

[11] For controversy between Galbraith, Robert Solow, and other economists, see P. A. Samuelson, *Readings in Economics* (McGraw-Hill, New York, 1973), 7th ed. Robert Fitch, a spokesman for radical economics, points out there that it is a superficial error to think Galbraith is radical rather than reactionary, that Galbraith is naïve in his view that a Henry Ford II (or, for that matter, a GM board) can be dictated to by computer-expert technocrats. The jury has not sustained Galbraith's view that modern corporations, run by their technostructure, are absolute monarchs that make their own markets. But, in light of Chap. 19's demonstration that the mixed economy has not found an incomes policy to conquer cost-push inflation, Galbraith's advocacy of permanent peacetime price-wage controls is intermittently influential. A topic left for advanced texts is the Galbraith-Baumol-Marris hypothesis that "maximum growth," not "maximum profit," provides the clue to corporate behavior.

RADICAL ECONOMICS, THE NEW LEFT AND MODERN MARXISM

It is certainly premature to give a textbook evaluation of Galbraith's lasting impact. In this section and the rest of the chapter we turn progressively farther leftward, until in the Appendix we discuss rigorously the Marxian theoretic approach to value and growth.

First it is necessary to recognize the confusing connections between political groups advocating "socialism" and "communism" and those economists who work on socialist or Marxist economics. There is no *necessary* link between the two. In some fields of economic history, growth economics, sociology, social legislation and politics it is nowadays impossible to avoid Marxian contributions; consequently, it is not surprising that we find economists from all political backgrounds making critiques of Marxist systems from a neoclassical point of view, and of neoclassical systems from a Marxist point of view.

Second, readers do not need reminding that important social events in the 1960s, in our own society and in the third world, were undertaken and explained in Marxist terms. Student leaders trained in the social sciences, like revolutionaries and labor leaders, had read their Marx, Mao, Lenin, Marcuse and their anarchist, nihilist and socialist peers. But much of what was being said, however cogent and persuasive, was not based upon a systematic economic view, but rather upon a "radical" or "new-left" critique, destructive rather than constructive, of what was occupying the minds and hours of nonradical economists. Skilled and respected economists (converted to a radical point of view) seemed to be using their status and prestige to urge a change of direction. Their critiques, directed at both current academic research and government policies, were based more on anger, impatience and fear than on new analytical approaches of robust logic.

Thus they reproached their colleagues for basing their studies on the underlying assumption that property (and perhaps even social class) will remain sacrosanct. They attacked their apparent acceptance of U.S. "economic imperialism". They rejected the half-hearted approach of economists to urban, sex, race and poverty issues. This produced the angry retort, of economists working in such fields, that less preaching and more research on verifiable propositions would be more persuasive.

To economists outside the U.S. this unseemly name-calling has some obvious characteristics. First, it stems from a political division that has obvious economic ramifications but has not been subjected by either side to tough-minded economic analysis. Vietnam and Watergate for example resound through some of the writing, but do not fundamentally receive economic analysis. The same is true of slightly more "economic" subjects like intervention or withdrawal of U.S. commercial and military forces from the third world: catchwords rather than researched positions dominate. Second, it is obvious that the U.S. left feels the lack of trained Marxist economists. Although many critiques are based on Marxist categories, used alike by economists and sociologists, since the days of the McCarthy purges there has been only a corporals' guard of professionals (like P. Sweezy and P. Baran) to sustain the rigor of debate.

In this the U.S. is in the 1970s much worse off than Europe. The tradition of scholarly analysis and revision of Marx's system, applied to current policy and to economic history, has been continuous in the U.K. since before respected analysts like Cambridge's Maurice Dobb, and British and European specialists like R. Meed, Oscar Lange, M. Kalecki and others have maintained a steady stream of theoretical and empirical publications. In this they have been joined by a small group of Marxist social and economic historians who have re-interpreted standard historical periods and episodes using the social-class and income categories derived from Marx. There is as well a fairly steady contact with economists working within Eastern Europe.

Thus, as Sweden's Assar Lindbeck has pointed out, a true Marxist from Europe, whether from the west or the east, is struck by both the freshness and the lack of depth of the American New Left.[12] The New Left strikes out at both the bureaucracy and the market system, thus pointing nowhere except to utopian self-sufficiency independent of *any* economic system or policy. The traditional Marxist scholar on the

[12] See A. Lindbeck, *The Political Economy of The New Left—An Outsider's View* (New York: Harper & Row, 1971). For a response, see replies by Paul Sweezy, Stephen Hymer, and others in *Quarterly Journal of Economics* (November, 1972), pp. 632-683. Cf., too, P. A. Samuelson, *Readings, op. cit.*

other hand, continues his or her study of actual and hypothetical socialist and capitalist economies, hoping to capture the essence both of different systems and different ways of analysis. No utopia waits his results.

In Cambridge England in particular, such neo-Keynesian economists as Joan Robinson, Nicholas Kaldor and Piero Sraffa have, in turning from the Keynesian short run to the long-run growth of an economy, employed neo-Marxian, capital-theoretic approaches. One of these is that value and capital derive their meaning not from market exchange of goods and factor services, but from systems of distributing the social income. A host of writers is taking up the resulting dispute with the growth economists of Cambridge, Mass., and strong points have been scored by both sides. (See Chapter 40 and its appendix.) Few of these writers are much concerned with the original Marxist questions, but many of them are adopting tools that he suggested.

The difference between the Old Left and the New Left should not be exaggerated. In the Pantheon of their saints and heroes, beginning with Marx, Engels, and Lenin, the name of Stalin has been replaced by Mao. And along with names like Gramsci, Baran, Sweezy, and Mandel, the new names of Marcuse, Fromm, and Paul Goodman have been added. But it is still the tradition of Marx that counts—not merely the mature Marx, but the young Marx too.

Our chapter concludes with a general overview of Karl Marx, leaving to the Appendix his technical economics.[13]

BIOGRAPHY OF KARL MARX

Karl Marx (1818-1883) was born the year after Ric-

---

[13] One important school critical of mainstream economics must not be ignored. Joan Robinson, Nicholas Kaldor, Piero Sraffa, and Luigi Pasinetti—the so-called Italo-Cantabridgian school (which, in fact, has able supporters all over the world, including India)—have rejected marginal-productivity doctrines of distribution (a) as mere apologetics for the status quo of capitalist society, and (b) as foundering on the analytical and empirical inadequacies of production functions that assume continuous variability of input combinations and illegitimately employ abstract aggregates of capital whose net productivity is alleged to be the interest rate. The chapter's appendix will turn to this scientific critique. Reference was already made in Chap. 27 to Kaldor's alternative macroeconomic model of distribution, and in Chapters 30 and 36 to the phenomenon of "reswitching" that is incompatible with the *simpliste* parables of thrift and its productivity fruits.

ardo published his *Principles*. Just as Newton was born the year Galileo died, Marx died the year Keynes and Schumpeter were born. On the surface, Marx lived an uneventful life of study, much of it in London exile at the library of the British Museum. But his influence lives on in Moscow and Peking; in Outer Mongolia and Cambridge, Massachusetts; in Havana and Peoria.

EARLY LIFE Descended from a long line of rabbis, Marx's father became a Lutheran in order to pursue his career as a lawyer in the years of post-Napoleonic reaction. Karl was always an outsider, even in the Prussian Rhineland where Catholics heavily outnumbered the few bourgeois Protestants. After the usual bright boy's triumphs in school, Marx went on to university study at Bonn and Berlin—first at law, until the charms of philosophy killed all career interests. Hegel's philosophy was then mesmerizing Germany. After an initial resistance, Marx succumbed to Hegelianism, but with his own replacing of mind over matter by matter over mind, and his replacing of the absolute Prussian monarchy as the culmination of history by the ultimate state of communism.

When a professorial career was closed to Marx because of his alien nature and radical ideas, he turned to journalism. Each radical paper he edited succumbed to bankruptcy or the Prussian censor. Exile to Paris and Brussels, and ultimately to London, followed. His aristocratic childhood sweetheart, Jenny von Westphalen, stood by him through thick and thin. That the life of a penniless radical scholar did not involve more of the thin was due solely to the friendship of Friedrich Engels, his lifelong collaborator and financial angel.

ENGELS AND MARX Throughout all the annals of science and revolution there cannot be a more remarkable friendship than that of Marx and Engels. Together they wrote the *Communist Manifesto* (1848) and much else. After Marx died with two of his three volumes of *Das Kapital* unfinished, Engels edited the uncompleted notes and manuscripts, even though he was himself by then old and going blind.

Engels was an important intellect in his own right, and we must not take him at his own modest evaluation when he wrote: "Marx was a genius ... the rest of us were talented at best." But this modesty vis à vis Marx undoubtedly made possible a lifetime friendship with that most truculent and difficult of men.

PERSONALITY INESSENTIALS It is the ideas and writings of Marx that constitute his importance in the history of thought and political development of the modern world. Next to these ideas, facts of his personality—such as that he was often deemed imperious, quarreling with Proudhon, Lassalle, Bakunin, and other stalwarts in the revolutionary movement—are as naught. It is enough that Isaiah Berlin could say, at the beginning of his readable little biography, *Karl Marx* (Oxford University Press, London, 1939, 1948): "No thinker in the nineteenth century has had so direct, deliberate, and powerful an influence on mankind as Karl Marx." That is all that counts. And that is what warrants our rendering him unsparing justice.

MARX'S SCHEMATA

Engels aptly characterized Karl Marx's system as a combination of German Hegelian philosophy, French socialism, and English political economy. It is with the latter that we must be concerned here—his belief *to have deduced scientifically the inescapable transition from capitalism to socialism.* But this is not to deny that economics may in the end be deemed by posterity to be the least-lasting part of Marx's thought.

PROPHECIES Each generation must recreate its predecessors. It used to be thought that Marx's great achievement was the more-than-a-million-word *Das Kapital*, which *scientifically* foretold the laws of motion of capitalism unto its inevitable death.

The law of the falling rate of profit. The law of immiserization and pauperization of the working class. The ever-growing inequality under capitalism, and gradual emergence of class consciousness on the part of the downtrodden proletariat. The necessity toward larger and larger scales of production, culminating in the demise of competition and formation of monopoly capitalism. Intensifying business cycles and crises as the masses suffer from under-consumption and lack of purchasing power, until the final cataclysmic depression sounds the death knell of the system. The desperate attempts to stave off the day of doom by imperialistic ventures in colonial exploitation, dynastic wars, and foreign investment.

Finally, the ultimate unavoidable day when, like overripe fruit ready to fall off the tree, capitalism has become so

trustified in one big combine that the workers can take over in a sudden, necessarily violent revolution.

Such is the vulgar view of what Marxism was all about. When you read biographies on members of the Old Left, to say nothing of the New, you will discover that not one in ten believers ever got past the first few chapters of Volume I. They read just enough to be able to take on faith that Spinoza-like proofs of the decline of capitalism have assured the scientific certainty of socialism.

CRISIS IN MARXISM

In 1900, a third of a century after the 1867 publication of *Capital*, even the most fervent Marxist had to face up to the fact that the absolute real wage was rising in the western world, not falling. And following Keynes' 1936 *General Theory*, the swelling of the reserve army of the unemployed and worsening of the business cycle became patently contradicted. What to do? Here were some of the patterns followed.

1. Ignore the facts. Deny them. At least gloss over them.[14]

2. Like Eduard Bernstein, revise your Marxism into a Fabian-like evolutionary socialism of the Ber-

---

[14] There are few admirers of Marx who have the unflinching candor of Joan Robinson, whose *Essay on Marxism* (Macmillan, London, 1942, 1964) provides perhaps the best short introduction to the economics of the mature Marx. A less unflinching introduction that might be read at the same time as an antidote is Paul Sweezy's *The Theory of Capitalist Development* (Oxford University Press, New York, 1943). On the false forecast of immiserization of labor, Professor Robinson says, "This error, like Jesus's belief that the world was shortly coming to an end, is so central to the whole doctrine that it is hard to see how it could have been put afloat without it. ... 'You have nothing to lose but the prospect of a suburban home and a motor car' would not have been much of a slogan for a revolutionary movement." As Paul Samuelson said on the Centennial of *Capital*, "With friends like this, one has hardly need for an enemy." Jokes aside, it is quite mistaken to charge Marx with opportunism in this. Rightly or wrongly, Marx believed that he had *deduced by cogent and innovative economic reasoning* what he was forecasting as the laws of motion of capitalism. This chapter's Appendix gives a brief overview of Marx's economic innovations. Only after one has fairly studied Marx's syllogisms can it be realized that the miscarriage of his prediction was not merely a case of bad luck (who expects prediction over a century to be immune from bad luck?). The internal logic of Marx's economics was flawed at the core: *There is no way to infer from the new concepts of surplus value* whether the reserve army of the unemployed would equal 1 or 50 per cent of the British or American labor forces of 1867 or 1967, and whether the capitalistic real wage would be changing at an average annual rate of —5 per cent, +3 per cent, 0 per cent or anything else.

nard Shaw and Webbs type. Pin your faith in trade-unions, and in winning Parliament over gradually so that prolabor legislation can be assured.

3. Like Lenin, admit that a privileged stratum of workers can themselves become bourgeois and share in the exploiter's swag. But affirm that these renegades to the proletariat are simply living off the exploitation of colonies outside the metropolitan centers of Europe and North America. And affirm that the prosperity is bound to falter in the future.

4. Reexamine and reformulate the arguments in Marx. Discover that he may not really have meant to predict falling real wages under capitalism. And elevate your requirements for tolerable economic performance of the mixed economy.

THE NEW LEFT AND THE YOUNG MARX

Today the focus has understandably shifted away from *Capital* as the capstone and culmination of Marx's writing. Instead there is a new interest in, to use a common phrase, *Marx before he was a Marxist* —the Young Marx of 1844 and the years before the *Communist Manifesto.* Further, the discovery of his 1857 notes for a monumental work that was to contain *Capital* in only one corner, the so-called *Gründrisse,* suggests to the modern age that it was wrong to think of Karl Marx as having outgrown his Hegelian garments.

ALIENATION   Thus consider the important notion of *alienation* that appeals so resonantly to our own age. Long before Marx's sojourn in the British Museum mastering Ricardo and the theories of surplus value, his Hegelian critiques had alerted him to the fact that the worker under advanced capitalism becomes an alienated cog in the machine. And, as we reread *Capital* carefully from this view, we see that Marx never abandoned the concept of alienation.

Herbert Marcuse, Erich Fromm, or Charles Reich feel no need to deny that wages are higher in 1973 America than in 1773 or 1873; and higher than in India, or Leningrad, or Peking, or Havana. The worker may not be pauperized in the sense of lacking TVs, autos, or even penicillin. But, it is argued, his spirit is pauperized as he tends the monotonous assembly line and submits to the discipline of the foreman and the regular working week. Advertising de-

bases his tastes. The press brainwashes him into voting for wasteful military expenditures that kill his neighbors overseas, and for programs that corrupt his government in the interests of the giant corporations. So clever is the system of repression that, in Marcuse's words, it represses the worker *by tolerance!*

EGALITARIAN ASPIRATIONS   In cold economic terms, grant that real wages rise.

But, ask critics, do they rise by as much as real GNP rises, so that the relative share of property is kept from being a larger fraction?

Or if, after counting in business-expense accounts and lightly taxed capital gains, it should still be the case that labor's share in the growing GNP of the mixed economy is *not* a declining fraction, nonetheless critics ask how there can be an ethical warrant for the evident continuation of unequal wealth and opportunity. "Nothing short of 100 per cent for labor of that which is rightfully labor's in a good society"—this is stipulated as the irreducible ultimate goal. Only after a rational planned society is introduced, it is argued, can the wastes of cost-push inflation and stagnation be solved. And the evils of wasteful advertising be purged.

Moreover when we turn to the Third World, socialists claim that only under communism can development take place quickly. Forced saving by the state can do what voluntary saving by the impoverished peoples can never do spontaneously. To fail to understand these aspirations is to miss the point of "the system's" critics.

THE CLASS STRUGGLE AND DYNAMICS OF SOCIAL LIFE

The appendix can be read by those who want to savor the flavor of traditional, mature Marxian economics. Before leaving Karl Marx, let us note that he was always more than a political economist. He was as much a philosopher, historian, sociologist, and revolutionist. And make no mistake. He was a learned man. To denigrate Marx, scholars sometimes point out that not all his ideas were completely original with him.[15] Of course not. Ideas never are virgin-

---

[15] As Berlin observes, "What is original is not any one component element, but the central hypothesis by which each is connected with the other." Little matter then that Spinoza and Feuerbach earlier had historical materialism; Saint-Simon and Guizot, the class struggle; Sismondi, economic crises; Moses Hess and Ba-

ally new. As Whitehead said, every great idea was originated by someone who was not the first to discover it. How Marx synthesized, shaped, and promoted his ideas is what matters. And how they were received!

CLASS INTERESTS AND IDEOLOGY The economic interpretation of history by Marx and Engels must surely rank among man's greatest achievements. To think that our ideology shapes our behavior is to stop short of being interesting. What shapes our ideology? The businessman votes conservative. The union leader votes for minimum-wage and unemployment-compensation legislation. The superstructure of opinion is not shaped by hairsplitting logical analysis. The superstructure of beliefs, laws, and ideologies is reflective of the material conditions of life and the material interests of the class.

Here we have Adam Smith's self-interest generalized away from the mundane dollar voting of the marketplace to the ballot voting of the elections and the bullet voting of the barricades. Once our eyes have been opened, can we be really surprised at the threat of a military-industrial complex? And how can we fail to realize that universal suffrage in one decade must assuredly lead to redistributive taxation in the following half-century?

The calculus of power and the calculus of dollars are not so different after all. The von Neumann game-theoretic concepts of coalition and rivalry are seen to be as applicable to the class struggle and its codes of theology as to the analysis of oligopolists selling steel in rival markets.

In conclusion, the reader of Marx can never fall into the fallacy of Whig history—fancying that the capitalism of Macaulay's time is the culmination of all evolution, or that the welfare state of the 1970s is here to stay unchanged, or even that the ultimate triumph of the victorious proletariat and peasantry will bring an end to the history of the class struggle.[16]

"This too will pass away." That is Karl Marx's ultimate thesis.

SUMMARY

1 Political economy as a discipline begins with the classical economists: Adam Smith, the critic of government interferences with beneficent and orderly *laissez faire;* Malthus and Ricardo, the gloomy prophets of diminishing returns and the struggle over distribution of the limited social income among the wage workers, landowners, and profit-seeking capitalists.

2 Flagging classicism gave way a century ago to neoclassical economics: general-equilibrium analysis of utility as well as disutility; marginalism extended beyond Ricardian rent analysis to all factors of production; econometric measurement involving increasingly sophisticated tools of mathematics and statistics; the monopolistic and imperfect-competition revolution to displace perfect competition's theoretical monopoly.

3 The Keynesian revolution added to the developing microeconomics of neoclassical economics an overdue, elaborated macroeconomics that eventually synthesized fiscal and monetary analysis, cyclical trends in unemployment and inflation. (But recall the unsolved problem of an incomes policy to cure stagflation in the mixed economy.)

4 Romantic, nationalistic, and antitheoretical rejections of mainstream economics inevitably arose: in Germany, List and the Historical School; in America, the World War I era of Institutionalist Economics and Thorstein Veblen.

---

beuf, the rise of the proletariat; Fourier and such post-Ricardians as Bray, Thompson, and Hodgkinson, the notions of exploitation and surplus value.

[16] Only a supersophisticated Marxist could have coined the wry joke that went the rounds in Poland and Czechoslovakia a decade ago: "Under capitalism, it's a case of man exploiting man. Under socialism, it's a case of vice versa."

5 The most important counterweight to mainstream economics has come from the right and the left: from conservative self-interest and the reasoned libertarianism of the Austrian and Chicago schools (Hayek, Knight, Friedman); from Galbraithian iconoclasm concerning autonomous corporations and technostructure in the affluent industrial state; from the Old and the New Left, and the new school of radical economists.

6 Globally, the Marxian offshoot from Ricardian classicism has played a pivotal role in intellectual and political history. Scientific socialism predicts with Hegelian certainty the laws of motion of capitalism: exploitation and pauperization, class struggle and class-conditioned ideology, imperialism, cyclical crises, proletarian victory. Gradual attrition of mature *Das Kapital* Marxism has shifted the limelight to earlier works, particularly those of the Young Marx, the left-Hegelian exponent of alienation.

CONCEPTS FOR REVIEW

pre-Smith amateurs: philosophers,
    merchants, Mercantilists,
    Physiocrats
Adam Smith's Invisible Hand
Ricardian diminishing returns,
    class oppositions
neoclassical economics
the Keynesian revolution

Historical School and
    Institutionalists, Veblen
Chicago School Libertarianism
Galbraith's world: autonomous
    firms and technostructure
New Left and radical economics
Marxian laws of motion and
    general *Weltanschauung*

QUESTIONS FOR DISCUSSION

1 Now that you've studied economics, how have your economic views changed?

2 Pencil in, on the back flyleaf's family tree of political economy, the romantics, Historical School, and Institutionalists. Also the living schools now putting mainstream economics into question.

3 Which parts of a modern economics textbook would be received badly in Moscow, Havana, or Peking? In Santiago or Delhi? Which would be well received?

4 If many of Marxians' most confident predictions failed to materialize, does that discredit them? Is Kuhnian science just another name for each generation's peculiar prejudices?

Appendix: Rudiments of Marxian Economics

In his mature three-volume work, *Capital* (1867-1885, 1894)[1] Marx tried (a) to lay bare the nature of exploitation of labor by capitalists, and (b) to reveal the laws of motion of developing and dying capitalism. The notions that he considered to be crucial centered in his concept of "surplus value."

Space permits us here to go only to what Marx, Engels, and Lenin thought was the heartland of Marx's theoretical contribution to economics—his belief that he had demonstrated by his new tool of surplus value the exploitation of labor by capital. As Marx put it:

Now suppose that the average amount of the daily necessaries of a laboring man *require six hours of average labor* for their production. But our man is a wages laborer. He must, therefore, sell his laboring power to a capitalist [who will], therefore, make him work, say, daily *twelve* hours ... he will therefore, have to work *six other hours*, which I shall call hours of surplus labor which surplus labor will realize itself in a *surplus value*. ... [2]

If valid, this would seem to be a grave indictment of capitalism. Engels, recognizing that here is the essence of Marx's economic innovation, went on to observe in 1891, "with every new ... invention, this surplus of its [labor's] daily product over its daily cost increases." So important did Marxists consider this surplus value of Marx to be, that Lenin, on the eve of World War I, summed up the economic component of Marxism in similar words:

The worker spends one part of the day covering the cost of maintaining himself and his family (wages), while the other part of the day he works without remuneration, creating for the capitalist *surplus value*, the source of profit, the source of wealth of the capitalist class.

Marx sought to find in labor a common denominator in which to express values. The modern view is that it is enough, in explaining relative values or relative prices of two goods—say, deer and beavers, in Adam Smith's famous example—to assert, "Supply (as determined by the difficulties of production) interacts with demand (as determined by tastes and wealth) to determine the exchange of price ratios that we observe in the market."

But remember that Marx was a nineteenth-century German philosopher: he thought there was a need for an *absolute* measure of value by which to make commensurable the incommensurabilities of deer and beaver.

"Socially necessary labor," he argued, provided the solution to the absolute standard.[3] David Ricardo, and

Adam Smith even earlier, thus provided the springboard for Marx's development of "classical economics," as shown in the family-tree chart on the back flyleaf of this book.

As Smith put the labor theory of value in a dawn-of-history Eden:

In that early and rude state of society which precedes both the accumulation of stock [i.e., the need for capital goods] and the appropriation of land, ... the quantity of labor necessary for acquiring different objects seems to be the only circumstance which can afford any rule for exchanging them one for another. If ... it usually costs twice the labor to kill a beaver which it does to kill a deer, one beaver should naturally exchange for or be worth two deer.[4]

UNDILUTED LABOR THEORY OF VALUE Replace hunting by more realistic examples of coal and corn. Let it take 4 hours of a 12-hour day to produce 1 coal. Let it take 4 hours to produce 1 corn. Then the "socially necessary" labor costs are 4 and 4 respectively.

And, if there are to be any exchanges at all, competition will set the exchange ratio at "1 coal equals 1 corn":

$$\text{Labor Value}_{corn}/\text{Labor Value}_{coal} = 4\ hr/4\ hr = 1$$

DIRECT AND INDIRECT LABOR Now complicate the story a bit. Let coal be produced by 4 direct labor as before. But now suppose each 1 of corn requires 1 of coal as raw material, along with 4 of direct labor.

How will total labor costs now be reckoned? Clearly,

$$\text{Labor Value}_{corn}/\text{Labor Value}_{coal} = (4\ hr + 4\ hr)/4\ hr$$
$$= 8/4 = 2$$

We now have 4 hours direct (or "live") labor in a unit of coal or corn. But in corn we additionally have 4 hours of indirect (or "dead") labor—namely, the 4 hours needed at the earlier stage to produce the coal raw material needed to produce corn.

In a regime of undiluted labor values, all goods have competitive values equal to their socially necessary labor contents (direct plus indirect).[5]

VARIABLE CAPITAL AND CONSTANT CAPITAL Marx gave new names to live and dead labor. The direct labor

[1] There are many convenient editions, particularly of Vol. 1, the only one completed before Marx's death in 1883.

[2] K. Marx, *Wages, Prices and Profit* (1865), Sec. VIII, as reproduced in K. Marx and F. Engels, *Selected Works* (International Publishers, New York, 1968). The Engels and Lenin quotes are from the same work.

[3] Joan Robinson of Cambridge, a brilliant critic of capitalism and an admirer of Marx, has said: "... no point of substance in Marx's

arguments depends upon the labour theory of value." See *An Essay on Marxian Economics* (Macmillan, London, 1942, 1964), p. 22.

[4] A. Smith, *The Wealth of Nations* (1776), Book I, Chap. VI.

[5] Marx, for simplicity, assumed all labor was homogeneous. Or, if, say, women are twice as productive as men in both departments or industries, he'd reckon each woman-hour as 2 lowest-common-denominator man-hours. There is no harm in this simplification, provided we realize it won't work in cases where women are three times as productive as men in welding, twice as productive in mining, and three-fourths as productive in distilling. Then general-equilibrium methods are mandatory. Like Marx, we at first ignore land.

costs—outlays for payrolls advanced to workers to spend now before the goods they work on are complete—he called "variable capital" and wrote as v: v_{coal} and v_{corn}, or v_1, v_2, and v_i, ... for the 1, 2, ..., i, ... industries or departments.

Marx gave the name "constant capital" to dead labor—i.e., to outlays for raw materials produced by labor in *earlier* stages and that are now needed for live labor to work with in this stage. He writes constant capital as c: c_1, c_2, ..., c_i, ... [6]

Here is how Marx writes undiluted labor values for coal and corn:

Labor Value$_1$ = $c_1 + v_1$ = 0 hr + 4 hr = 4 hr
Labor Value$_2$ = $c_2 + v_2$ = 4 hr (coal) + 4 hr = 8 hr

NOTE: There is no exploitation in the Eden of the undiluted labor theory of value. Labor gets *all* the product. There is no profit, no interest, no rent, no markup over competitive labor costs, no surplus, no surplus value.

Marx writes any markup or "surplus" tacked on to $c + v$ as s. For example s_1 for coal, s_2 for corn ..., s_i for industry i. Hence in our rude Eden, we have $s_1 = 0$, $s_2 = 0$, ... $s_i = 0$, and

$$c_i + v_i + s_i = c_i + v_i + 0 \text{ everywhere}$$

Each laborer, if he works 12 hours a day, works only for himself, none for an exploiting capitalist. (Thus, the minimum of subsistence he enjoys in real wages may be a very comfortable minimum indeed: he can consume 1 1/2 of corn every day, working 6 direct hours for it in the corn industry, and 6 indirect hours for it in the coal industry. Perhaps without this comfortable daily ration of 1 1/2 corn, workers will not have enough children to reproduce the labor supply.)

SURPLUS VALUE AND EXPLOITATION

Now leave Eden. Workers need corn for survival and reproduction. But they can't wait for the harvest to get the subsistence they need now if they are to perform work. And they can't produce corn unless some capitalist provides them with the coal needed (along with their direct labor) to produce the corn-industry output.

In short, a small group of thrifty or lucky capitalists, who happen to own "capital" (coal raw materials, and last season's corn to advance as food), can now garner a surplus—a profit, an interest rate, or as Marx would prefer to say, a surplus value.

MARKUP ON LIVE LABOR ONLY Here Marx rejects the bourgeois economics of Smith and Ricardo. In Volume I, Marx posits that the *surplus* or *markup, s*, is on *direct labor only*. (Remember man is measure of all things, not fetishistic commodities!)

POSTULATE: In a Marxian regime of "values," each s_i is marked up the same percentage on each variable capital,

[6]More complicated examples would involve use of machines—e.g., plows—as well as raw materials to produce corn. Then c_2 would also include the used-up amount of plows in producing corn.

v_i—not on each total capital ($c_i + v_i$). This uniform ratio of s_i to v_i is called the "rate of surplus value." We write it as r, which is the common value of all industry r's: r_1, r_2, ..., r_i ... It is simply

$$r = r_1 = r_2 = \ldots = r_i = \ldots$$
$$s_1 = rv_1, \ s_2 = rv_2, \ldots s_i = rv_i \ldots$$

An example will help. Suppose the rate of surplus value is 200%: $r = 2.00$. We each work 4 hours a day for ourselves, 8 hours for the capitalists. Now our Values Tableau begins with coal's row:

$$c_1 + v_1 + s_1 = c_1 + v_1 + rv_1$$
$$= 0 + 4 + 2.00(4)$$
$$= 12 \text{ for each coal's "value"}$$

How do we complete the corn row in the Values Tableau? Clearly, we must add the coal raw-material cost to corn's direct labor and the latter's marked-up surplus to get

$$c_2 + v_2 + s_2 = c_2 + v_2 + rv_2$$
$$= 12(1) + 4 + 2.00(4)$$
$$= 24 \text{ for each corn's value}$$

NOTE: We still do have corn double coal's value

$$\text{Value}_{corn} / \text{Value}_{coal} = 24/12 = 2$$

But now both the numerator of 24 and the denominator of 12 have ended up tripled because of the 200% surplus-value markup.[7]

Before, with $r = 0$ and no surplus value, 12 hours bought a worker 1½ of corn. Now he gets only one-third as much— namely (12 hr of the day)/(24 hr cost of corn) = ½ corn subsistence per day.

MINIMUM-OF-SUBSISTENCE EXPLOITATIVE

WAGE Evidently the higher the rate of surplus value, r, that the capitalist can exact, the lower the worker's real wage. What sets the limit on surplus value?

According to simplest Marx, just as corn and coal have their cost of reproduction, so too does labor power: Labor power will get only its cost of (re)production, not the total of what it can produce.

The minimum real wage at which labor can be recruited from the reserve army of the unemployed, and be kept reproducing itself—that minimum-subsistence level will determine the exploitative rate of surplus value r.

Our previous example applies. Suppose it takes 1/2 corn per day to keep a worker alive and reproducing himself. We should be able to deduce that the rate of surplus value is 200%, $r = 2.00$, and each worker works 8 hours a day for the exploiting capitalist and only 4 hours a day for his own subsistence.

[7]This takes place uniformly at every stage of production. Each industry's direct-labor "value-added" is marked up by the same percentage: so, by the careful value-added reckoning like that for Table 10-2's loaf of bread, we realize all final goods—coal or corn or ... —must be increased equally in value relative to an hour's wage. In consequence of the 200 per cent of markup, real wages have been exploited down to one-third their Eden level!

Recall that this gives rise to Volume I's Tableau

$c_1 + v_1 + rv_1 = 0 + 4 + 2.00(4) = 12$
$c_2 + v_2 + rv_2 = 1(12) + 4 + 2.00(4) = 24$

The laborer must pay 24 hours to buy 1 corn. He has, of course, only 12 hours in the day. Hence, we verify he gets his needed minimum-subsistence ration of

$$1/2 \text{ corn} = \frac{12 \text{ hr of the day}}{24 \text{ hr for corn}} = 1/2 \text{ corn} \quad \text{QED}$$

CONTRADICTION? Marx knew bourgeois economists would object to his making rates of surplus value the same in all industries. They could be expected to say:

"Why should the coal and corn industries, just because they have equal outlays on labor, be satisfied with the same total profit? The corn profits are too low, when they are related (as they should be) to the much larger $(c_2 + v_2)$ outlay. The coal profits are relatively too high when they are related to the no-larger $c_1 + v_1 = 0 + v_1$.

"Competition will in fact equalize the profit rates, $s_i/(c_i + v_i)$ in all industries, not s_i/v_i alone. We should put equal rates of profit, P

$$P = s_1/(c_1 + v_1) = s_2/(c_2 + v_2)$$

in the place of equal rates of surplus value."

How would Marx reply? In effect he would say:

"I agree that equal rates of surplus value imply unequal rates of profit: the more labor-intensive industries will be getting higher rates of profit." (What is the same thing, "equal rates of profit" imply "unequal rates of surplus value.")[8]

Marx might continue: "Wait until my Volume III is published, when I shall reveal to you how to replace my 'Values' Tableau based on equal rates of surplus value by a 'Prices' Tableau based on equal rates of profit."

EQUAL-PROFIT-RATE REGIME We can now write down for our coal-corn example the Volume III bourgeois alternative. Since P is earned on $c + v$, the base that is larger than v alone, the profit rate must be smaller than the 200% level for surplus value.

Our example will work out to the same subsistence-exploitative wage of 1/2 corn per 12-hour day, if we make the lucky guess of a 100% profit rate, $P = 1.00$. Now the price of coal can be written down in terms of $C_1 + V_1$ (where, be it noticed, we are better advised to use capital letters for the bourgeois "prices" regime to keep it separate from the Volume I "values" regime with its $c_1 + v_1$ small letters.) The Prices Tableau begins with

$$(C_1 + V_1) + S_1 = (C_1 + V_1) + P(C_1 + V_1)$$
$$= (0 + 4) + 1.00(0 + 4) = 8$$

for the *price* of coal.

---

[8]Marx points out one case in which there would be no contradiction between equal rates of profit and equal rates of surplus value. If the "organic compositions of capital" were the same in all industries, as measured by *equal* indirect-labor-intensities, c/v_i, then both methods will agree. Much of Marx would go through smoothly, if we would agree to this harmless simplification.

Now for the price of corn in the Prices Tableau:

$$(C_2 + V_2) + S_2 = (C_2 + V_2) + P(C_2 + V_2)$$
$$= [1(8) + 4] + 1.00(8 + 4) = 24$$

for the *price* of corn. (NOTE: Again workers are getting their subsistence of only 1/2 corn per day, derived from (12 hr per day)/(24 hr cost of corn) = 1/2.)

"EXPLAINING" EXPLOITATION Which formulation is better? "Values" or "Prices"? Bourgeois economists have answered, "Prices." Marxians would not agree.

But a month in any good library will convince any scholar that Marxians have not all agreed on *why* surplus-value concepts are better. And remember that Marx died before he had completed Volumes II and III for publication. So Engels, old and handicapped by vision problems and political demands on his time, had to edit these unfinished manuscripts for publication.

Since this is an appendix that attempts to present Marx's concepts sympathetically, leaving to advanced books pro-and-con evaluations, let us simply provide one line of defense and exposition.

1. Surplus value provides a *simpler* way to explain exploitation to beginners. It focuses on human labor as being directly exploited. (And, note, its *algebra* is much simpler for nineteenth-century readers—since solving for $P = 1.0$ can be shown to be equivalent to solving for the root of a quadratic polynomial.)

2. Marxians claim that the *microeconomic* parceling out of surpluses as between industries, around a determined average level, may indeed be compelled by ruthless competition to follow the pre-*Capital* bourgeois rules of equal profit (equal P as against equal industrial r's of surplus value). But that *average level* of profit exploitation, and how it grows under capitalism, Marxians believe can be most simply determined *macroeconomically* by the concept of surplus-value markups on exploited direct labor.

What to think? If we agree with the first point, that surplus value is an easier approximation to explain, then perhaps we need not worry if the second point of defense turns out to be deemed unnecessary by a jury a hundred years from now made up of Marxians and non-Marxians alike.[9]

LABOR-SAVING INVENTION AND THE RESERVE ARMY OF THE UNEMPLOYED

Enough of the flavor of Marx's $c + v + s$ concepts has been

---

[9]The 8 and 8 of surpluses in the coal-corn Values Tableau, Marx himself would have related in Vol. III, Book III, Chap. IX, to the total $(c + v)$ of $(0 + 4)$ plus $(12 + 4)$ to get an average profit rate of 16/20 instead of the correct $P = 1.00$. But he realized that his proposed solution to the "transformation (from 'values' to 'prices') problem" was not quite right, since in a prices regime he should be using for corn's coal its C_2 and not its c_2 taken over from the values regime. However, many Marxians (Sweezy, Dobb, Winternitz, Johansen) and non-Marxians (Bortkiewicz, Seton-Morishima, Samuelson, . . .) have shown how his transformation pro-

sketched. Let us mention some of the key trends that Marxians contemplate as the laws of motion of capitalism.

1. Capitalists have an urge to accumulate, the way a cancer cell has an urge to grow. In self-defense, as monopolies require an ever-larger scale of production to survive, capitalists are forced to accumulate. "Accumulate! Accumulate! Accumulate! That is [the Law of] Moses and the Prophets," observed Marx.

2. Accumulation tends to erode the rate of profit (and threatens to raise real wages). Therefore, labor-saving invention of machinery will be introduced to keep profits up and prevent wages from rising unduly.

RESULT: Recruits to the "reserve army of the unemployed," depressed wages, and misery.

3. These are not very cheerful laws of motion of capitalism. Therefore, after a stage of increased monopoly and intensified business cycles, the working class finally engineers a more-or-less violent revolution. "The expropriators are expropriated!"

4. As the twentieth century developed, Marxian writers like Rosa Luxemburg and V. I. Lenin added the view that mature capitalist countries will engage in *imperialistic exploitation* of colonial peoples. Capitalism's prosperity will depend on exploiting oil, bauxite, iron ore, uranium, and other natural resources. To keep up purchasing power at home and avoid mass unemployment, and to stave off falling rates of profit from accumulation at home, mature capitalist nations will indulge in much foreign investment and cold-war expenditures. So it is argued.

MODERN REALITY Enough has been said already in connection with Fig. 37-3, on what the actual trends in Canada have been: strongly rising real wage trends; constant or gently rising wage share in GNP; profit rates of no clear long-run tendency; compound-interest growth in population; and still-higher growth rate in real GNP and matching capital stock. These are what Kaldor calls the "stylized facts" that have to be explained. And they are definitely at variance with Marx's predicted trends under capitalism.

Also, in the age after Keynes, there is no need to belabor the fact that fiscal policy (deficits, if necessary) and central-bank money creation rob the Luxemburg-Lenin thesis of imperialism-to-stave-off-unemployment of whatever merit it may well have had in the era of William Howard Taft and King Edward VII.

LOGICAL NON SEQUITURS As mentioned in footnote 14 of the main part of this chapter, Karl Marx was not merely unlucky in his predicted factual laws of motion of capitalist development. The purported laws—as, e.g., the law of the declining rate of profit and the immiserization of the workers—are not cogently derivable from Marx's own conceptual schema. The level of the rate of surplus value, r, and the implied real wage (in this case, 1/2 corn per day)

—as well as their changes through time, are simply not deducible from within the Marx system.

Unlike Malthus, Marx does not put much stock in a physiological minimum-subsistence wage. He is reduced to appealing to the *deus ex machina* of a "reserve army of the unemployed" (for which he supplies *no theory* of determinate size and calculable incidence on the real wage level); and to the *deus ex machina* of whatever degree of labor-saving technical invention he needs to paint a sufficiently gloomy scenario of capitalistic development. Or, to put the same point in a different way, a Karl Marx brought back to life in J. B. Clark's era could have as easily assumed the case for immiserization by *merely postulating sufficient labor-saving technical change* in a Clark-Solow production function of aggregative type. Or, if brought to life in the post-1960 Sraffian era, Marx, eschewing surplus-value concepts, could have simply postulated low wages and high profits, again with no need or benefit from equalized-rate-of-surplus-value concepts.

REJECTION OF MARGINAL-PRODUCTIVITY DISTRIBUTION THEORY

To question the fruitfulness in 1973 of 1867 Marxian concepts is not at all thereby to prove that everything is for the best in a bourgeois world where wages, rents, and interest are agreed to be determined by global marginal-productivity theory. Notice must be taken of Joan Robinson's critique of mainstream economics' theory of distribution.

Our coal-corn example can illustrate the point she and Sraffa have stressed.

"Each different profit or interest rate will give rise to a different real wage. So long as labor and coal *cannot* be smoothly substituted for each other along equal-corn-product contours like those in Fig. 27-3, economists lack an effective equation to determine the steady-state profit rate and the corn real wage. (How much more they lack a defensible theory of distribution in non-steady states!)" This, critics say.

ALTERNATIVE THEORIES Professor Robinson, along with Kalecki and Kaldor, has suggested possible alternatives to marginal productivity. Thus, suppose labor grows at a compound rate of g per period. And suppose that σ_s is the fraction of profit income saved, with all of wages being consumed. Then in long-run balanced-growth equilibrium, we must have the following equation for the profit rate:

$$P = g/\sigma_s$$

For example, 20% = 4%/.2.

Once P is known, the corn real wage can be worked out from the profit-wage factor-price trade-off.[10]

---

cedure can be given the small needed correction, as done here. Paul Samuelson has reviewed this matter in the *Journal of Economic Literature* for 1971.

[10]To strengthen the case against the notion that thrift *always* increases some capital-output ratio and lowers the interest or profit rate, as in the simplest neoclassical parables, we may notice Chapter 30's possibility of "reswitching." Suppose that we can produce 1 coal by 4 labor invested for 1 year (two 6-month periods). This agrees with our Tableau's technology. But suppose

WAGE DETERMINATION BY POWER? Since the publication of Keynes' *General Theory* (1936), economists have realized that for workers to insist upon getting higher money wages need not mean their getting any higher real wages. Those who reject neoclassical marginal-productivity theories in favor of one or another macro theory of distribution (e.g., that of Kaldor-Kalecki) may still claim—as Böhm-Bawerk did by inference in a famous essay of 60 years ago entitled *Economic Law or Power?*—that capitalism will successfully resist any quick lowering of the share in GNP of profits.

Further research is needed if the alleged inadequacies of Marxian, neoclassical, and macroeconomic versions of distribution are not to leave economists with a vacuum where a theory of economic distribution should be. The actual real world will not know or care whether economists have "explained" distribution. But they should care.

STEADY AND EXPANDED REPRODUCTION

Whatever the ultimate failure of mature Marxian analysis to explain the dynamics of the real wage under competitive capitalism, economists of all schools can agree that Karl Marx did make one stellar contribution to what today we call von Neumann-Leontief input-output growth models.

STEADY REPRODUCTION Our coal-corn example can serve nicely. But to be the more faithful to Marx's text, we add a third department or industry that produces a purely luxury good—say, valet services, with 1 labor hour needed for each unit of good 3.

Since this is to be a model of the steady state, we assume that capitalists save nothing, $\sigma_s = 0$, spending all their profits on luxury valet services. Workers spend all their wages on their minimum-subsistence corn. Since there is no net capital formation, all the coal produced is fed back into the system as raw material.

The stage is set. Here are the physical facts.

One-third of labor will work to produce workers' subsistence. So let our economy be forever endowed with, say, 100 labor days, or 1,200 labor hours. Then half the 400 hours that serve the workers goes for live labor in the corn industry, the other half going as dead labor to the coal industry to produce the 50 of coal needed for the 50 of corn subsistence. The other 800 hours is at the exploiting capitalists' disposal and goes to the third luxury department to produce 800 valet services.

we can alternatively produce 1 coal by the combination of 24/7 labor invested for 6 months (one 6-month period) and 8/7 labor invested for 18 months (three 6-month periods). Then, at very high profit rates and very low profit rates, above 100% per 6-month period and below 50% per 6-month period, competition will switch from, and then switch back to, the 4 labor method. But in between it will pick the "24/7 and 8/7" method. How can the neoclassical parable explain the fact that reducing the interest rate first lowers the system's consumable GNP before restoring it to where it began? Clearly the usual neoclassical parable is oversimple.

Stationary equilibrium is maintained forever: The workers get their subsistence; the capitalists are doing zero net saving; exploitation proceeds to the end of time at a steady rate.

How would the "Values" and "Prices" Tableaux look? We can begin with either. That is, we can work with a 100% bourgeois profit rate, $P = 1.00$, and "prices" of coal, corn, valet service that are (8, 24, 2). Or we can work with a 200% rate of surplus value, and have "values" per unit of the three respective goods at (12, 24, 3).

Toss a coin, heads rather than tails wins, so the Values Tableau is to come first—on the left as (a) in next page's Table 41-1. (NOTE: Marx's notation reads "$400v_1$" as "400 of v_1," not as the mathematician's "400 times v_1." And likewise in all the Tableaux.)

The color coding makes it obvious that the black sum of wages does equal the black total of consumption corn. The red sum of surpluses does equal the red total of luxury goods. The pink sum of constant capitals does equal the pink total of coal raw material produced.

Now essentially the same physical story, but of course with changed pricing and valuations of the components, is shown by the bourgeois model—as (b) on the right of Table 41-1.

What is to be stressed is that the same physical totals are involved in the alternative models: the same valet services, the same subsistence corn, the same technological coal. The black numbers agree because our convention is to use labor hours as our units in both cases; also, because in either model it takes 1/2 of corn as subsistence to live each 12-hour day; and only when 1 corn costs 24 in both Tableaux, will we correctly depict the rock-bottom exploitative wage.

EXPANDED REPRODUCTION Now go to the other extreme for exaggerated emphasis. Let capitalists save *all* their incomes, instead of none of their incomes as in the state of steady reproduction. Provided the system's labor grows at 100% per period (to match the von Neumann-like 100% profit rate), Marx can show that balanced-growth equilibrium could prevail forever.[11]

Here are the new physical facts.

As before, at the beginning when, say, each 100 man-days (or 1,200 hours) are available, we must still have at hand 1/2 corn per man or 50 in all for minimum subsistence of the 100 men.

But since the system will next period be of twice the present size in *all* respects, we must be "planning" to produce now *twice* 50 corn for next period's subsistence. ("Planning" is in quotes because market forces might be the operative mechanism rather than bureaucracy or a computer.)

To produce this next harvest of 100 corn, we must now allocate 400 of our as-yet-only 1,200 hours to corn indus-

[11]*Capital*, Vol. II, Book II, Part III; Vol. III, Part VII, Chap. XLIX. The reader will note how much Leontief's input-output analysis of Chapter 37's Appendix, Table 37-2, was anticipated by Marx a century ago.

TABLEAUX OF STEADY REPRODUCTION ($\sigma_s = 0$)

VALUES ($r = 2.00$)	PRICES ($P = 1.00$)
$0c_1 + 200v_1 + 2.00(200)s_1 = \quad 600 = 12(50)$	$0C_1 + 200V_1 + 1.00(\quad 0 + 200)S_1 = \quad 400 = 8(50)$
$12(50)c_2 + 200v_2 + 2.00(200)s_2 = \mathbf{1{,}200} = 24(50)$	$8(50)C_2 + 200V_2 + 1.00(400 + 200)S_2 = \mathbf{1{,}200} = 24(50)$
$0c_3 + 800v_3 + 2.00(800)s_3 = \mathbf{2{,}400} = 3(800)$	$0C_3 + 800V_3 + 1.00(\quad 0 + 800)S_3 = \mathbf{1{,}600} = 2(800)$
(a)	(b)

TABLE 41-1

TABLEAUX OF EXPANDED REPRODUCTION ($\sigma_s = 1$)

PRICES ($P = 1.00$)	VALUES ($r = 2.00$)
$0C_1 + 800V_1 + 1.00(\quad 0 + 800)S_1 = 1{,}600 = 8(200)$	$0c_1 + 800v_1 + 2.00(800)s_1 = \qquad 12(200)$
$8\left(\dfrac{200}{2}\right)C_2 + 400V_2 + 1.00(800 + 400)S_2 = \mathbf{2{,}400} = 24(100)$	$12\left(\dfrac{200}{2}\right)c_3 + 400v_2 + 2.00(400)s_2 = \mathbf{2{,}400} = 24(100)$
$0C_1 + \quad 0V_3 + 1.00(\quad 0 + \quad 0)S_3 = \qquad 0 = 2(0)$	$0c_1 + \quad 0v_3 + 2.00(\quad 0)s_3 = \qquad 0 = 3(0)$
(a)	(b)

TABLE 41-2

try 2. Also, we must now allocate to corn production the needed 100 of coal raw material.

How much valet services are produced? None, if capitalists literally save all. The whole of their supluses are invested in the growth of coal and corn inventories.

Exactly how much coal is scheduled for production now? To meet next period's doubled raw-material requirement, we must now allocate 800 hours to industry 1 to produce 200 coal.

Toss a coin once again. This time the Prices Tableau is to come first—as Table 41-2(a).

Now the color coding is no longer quite so simple. Black corn end-of-period consumption-output measured as 2,400 on the right is *twice* the total of black wages on the left. Why? Because the system is *doubling* every period! Similarly, pink coal-output on the right must be double the total of pink coal-inputs on the left; that is why 200/2 always appears at the beginning of row 2.[12]

In leaving these Tableaux of reproduction, we may mention that Marxians can use them to disprove the contention of Rodbertus and Luxemburg that a limited-consumption system *must* ultimately run short of purchasing power. Marx sensed early what Harrod proved in our day: If a model grows fast enough, it can perform a self-war-

ranted natural growth *à la* the accelerator-multiplier model. (But, of course, it is not guaranteed without macroeconomic policy to stay on such a growth path.)

SECULARIZING MARXIAN ECONOMICS

"Religion is the opiate of the people." This well-known aphorism of Karl Marx was inverted by Raymond Aron to become, "Marxism is the opiate of the intellectuals." With less wit, one can make the serious point: In economics, too often, "Marxism is the opiate of the Marxists."

Opiate in what sense? If you look up Marx's original quotation, you will probably be surprised to see that he meant there—not that religion is the elixir fobbed off by the ruling classes to dull the resentments and pains of the proletariat but that religion is an opiate in the sense of a comfort to wretched people.

Marx's Hegelian view of an inevitable revolution, soon to come, has similarly served as a comfort to Marxians, as well as serving as an analgesic to make the pain of hope long deferred more bearable.

Unfortunately, there is still a third connotation of the word "opiate"—namely, something that dulls the power to reason. And as one reviews the analyses made by Marxists in Eastern Europe, Asia, and the West, one has to recognize that until recently the use of Marxian categories did all too often addle the wits of those hoping to understand the realistic laws of motion of Western systems.

EPICYCLES If a religion—nay, if any Kuhnian system of paradigms—is to be adhered to in an epoch of change, it must develop certain flexibility to accommodate itself to transparent contradiction.

---

[12]The sum of the red surpluses no longer equals the (zero!) total of luxury production. It could be shown that, with $\sigma_s = 1$, the total of surpluses equals net capital formation: the 200/0 increment of coal and the 100/0 increment of corn from this period to the next. The reader is invited to double all the numbers in Table 41-2, and contemplate next period's Tableaux. He will then verify that the total of the red surpluses in the first period does equal the jump between the periods in the coal and corn totals. Likewise for all the doubling and redoubling Tableaux in the future.

"To save the appearances," Ptolemaic astronomy could always add a new epicycle to allow for newly observed aberrations. Classical Marxism has survived by adaptation to the changing environment. Some well-known instances of dialectical reformulation may be mentioned.

1. The proletarian revolution is Hegelianly inevitable. But, the point is, one can hurry it along by political action.

2. The revolution is to take place first in the most advanced countries that have already gone through their bourgeois revolution and stage of decaying capitalism. But, Czarist Russia may be able to skip a revolution and the bourgeois stage. (Edmund Wilson even argued that Stalin's bureaucrats were, so to speak, Russia's bourgeoisie!)

3. The industrial proletariat is the revolutionary proletariat. But, in 1917 Russia, 1960 Cuba, and Mao's 1973 China, the peasantry may constitute the true proletariat.

4. The revolution must necessarily be violent. But, as Marx and Engels came to think late in life as they observed Victorian England, it could possibly be nonviolent, rather evolutionary, and (shades of Samuel Gompers) trade-union and political action might better the workers' lot under late capitalism.

5. Immiserization and pauperization of the working classes are corollaries of the ineluctable laws of motion of capitalism. But, when one examines closely the texts of Karl Marx, it may be that all that is meant is that (a) workers' relative share of GNP goes down; or that (b) this share fails to rise as fast as their legitimate expectations; or even merely that (c) workers under modern capitalism will feel increasingly "alienated."

One could go on, not in any sense of superior outside criticism, but because every one of these issues has played a central role *inside* the circle of discussion by the best-informed Marxists of each generation. And make no mistake. It is better to add an epicycle to explain the planet Uranus, than, ostrich-like, to deny its existence! Nonetheless, any scientific cake that you are able at the same time to have and to eat is not worth having or eating.

In conclusion, Marxism may be too valuable to leave to the Marxists. It provides a critical prism through which mainstream economists can—to their own benefit—pass their analyses for audit.

CONCEPTS FOR REVIEW

direct (live) and indirect (dead) labor

variable capital, v_i; constant capital, c_i

rates of surplus value: s_1/v_1, s_2/v_2

rates of profit, $S_1/(C_1 + V_1)$, $S_2/(C_2 + V_2)$

"Values": $c_i + v_i + s_i = c_i + v_i + rv_i$

"Prices": $(C_i + V_i) + S_i = (C_i + V_i) + P(C_i + V_i)$

exploitative subsistence wage

alleged laws of motion of wage and profit

critique of marginal productivity, reswitching, macroeconomic alternatives, power vs. law

steady reproduction Tableaux

expanded reproduction Tableaux

INDEX